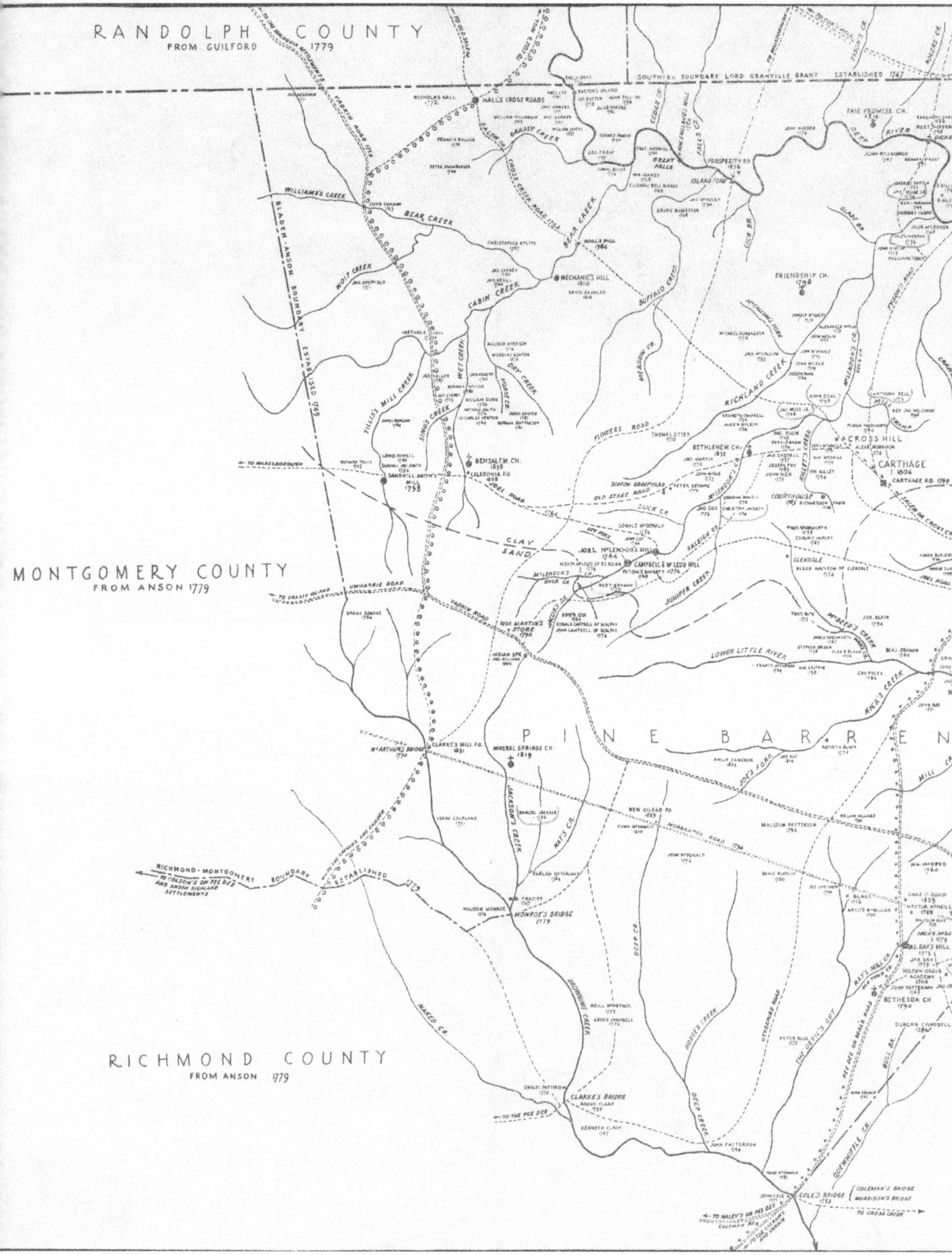

RANDOLPH COUNTY
FROM GUILFORD 1779
SOUTHERN BOUNDARY LORD GRANVILLE GRANT ESTABLISHED 1747
MONTGOMERY COUNTY
FROM ANSON 1779
RICHMOND COUNTY
FROM ANSON 1779
BLADEN - ANSON BOUNDARY ESTABLISHED 1749
RICHMOND - MONTGOMERY BOUNDARY ESTABLISHED 1779
PINE BARREN
HALLS CROSS ROADS
MECHANIC'S HILL 1810
FRIENDSHIP CH. 1790
FAIR PROMISE CH. 1814
PROSPERITY P.O. 1836
GREAT FALLS
ISLAND FORD
DEEP RIVER
BEAR CREEK
WILLIAMS CREEK
WOLF CREEK
CABIN CREEK
DRY CREEK
WET CREEK
SINGS CREEK
TILLIS'S MILL CREEK
RICHLAND CREEK
BUFFALO CREEK
MEADOW CR.
GRASSY CREEK
FLOWERS ROAD
BETHLEHEM CH. 1832
CROSS HILL
CARTHAGE 1804
COURTHOUSE
BENSALEM CH.
CALEDONIA P.O.
SANDHILL SMITH'S MILL 1758
JOEL ROAD
CLAY SAND
SUCK CR.
OLD STAGE ROAD
JOEL McLENDON'S MILL 1764
CAMPBELL & McLEOD MILL 1776
JUNIPER CREEK
GLENDALE
YADKIN ROAD
UWHARRIE ROAD
WM. MARTIN'S STORE 1790
JACOBS BR.
McDEED'S CREEK
LOWER LITTLE RIVER
NICK'S CREEK
McARTHUR'S BRIDGE 1790
CLARKS'S MILL P.O. 1831
MINERAL SPRINGS CH. 1819
JACKSON'S CREEK
JOE'S FORK
NEW GILEAD P.O. 1823
MORGANTON ROAD 1794
MONROE'S BRIDGE 1779
DROWNING CREEK
DEEP CR.
HORSES CREEK
THE DEVIL'S GUT
NAKED CR.
JAS. RAY'S MILL
BETHESDA CH 1790
CLARKE'S BRIDGE
COLE'S BRIDGE 1793
COLEMAN'S BRIDGE
MORRISON'S BRIDGE
TO CROSS CREEK
TO THE PEE DEE
TO WADESBOROUGH

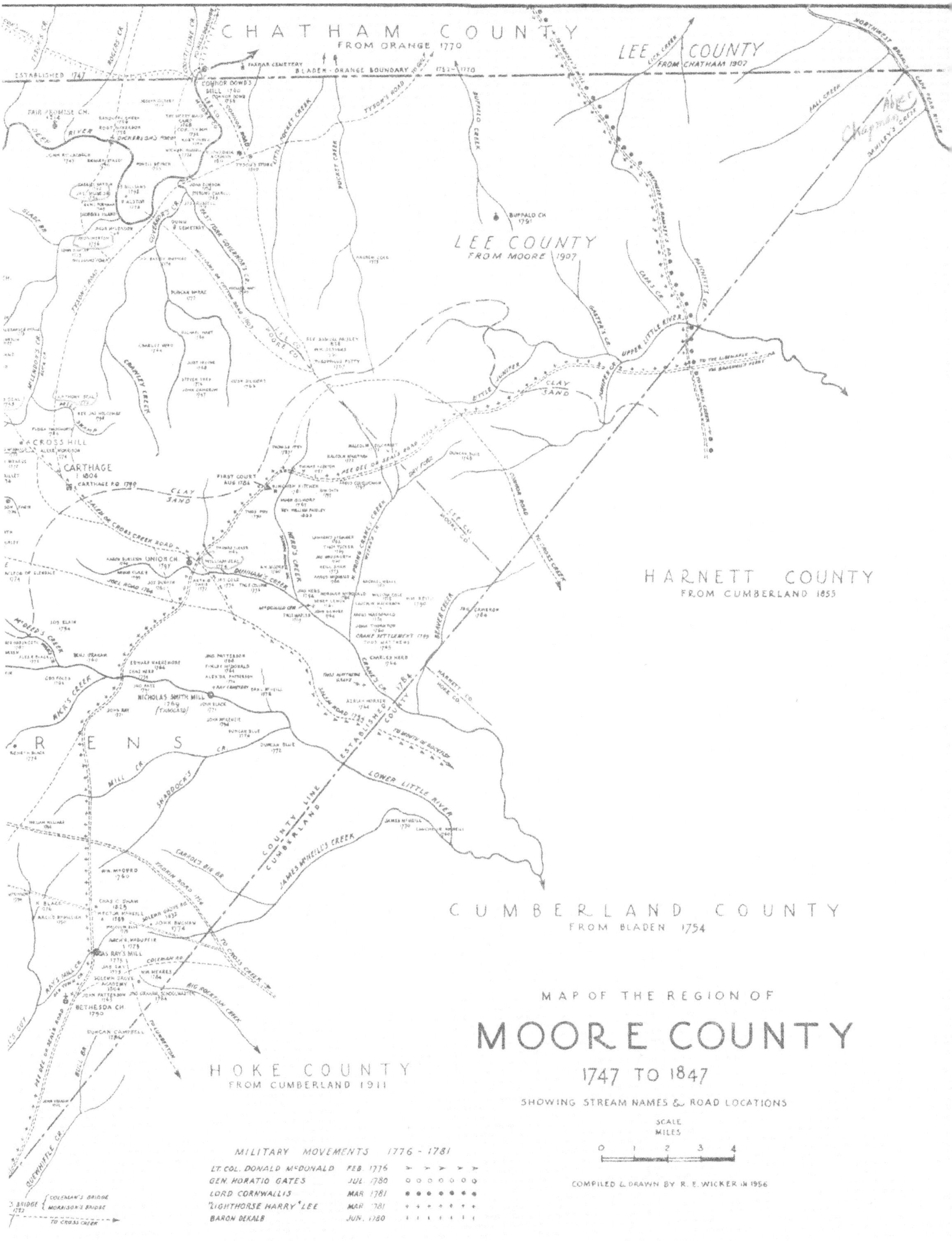
MAP OF THE REGION OF
MOORE COUNTY
1747 TO 1847
SHOWING STREAM NAMES & ROAD LOCATIONS
SCALE
MILES
0 1 2 3 4
COMPILED & DRAWN BY R. E. WICKER IN 1956
CHATHAM COUNTY
FROM ORANGE 1770
LEE COUNTY
FROM CHATHAM 1907
LEE COUNTY
FROM MOORE 1907
HARNETT COUNTY
FROM CUMBERLAND 1855
CUMBERLAND COUNTY
FROM BLADEN 1754
HOKE COUNTY
FROM CUMBERLAND 1911
ESTABLISHED 1747
BLADEN - ORANGE BOUNDARY 1752 - 1770
FAIR PROMISE CH. 1814
CARTHAGE 1806
CARTHAGE P.O. 1790
CROSS HILL
UNION CH. 1797
NICHOLAS SMITH MILL 1769
BETHESDA CH. 1790
BUFFALO CH 1791
FIRST COURT AUG 1784
UPPER LITTLE RIVER
LOWER LITTLE RIVER
DEEP RIVER
CUMBERLAND COUNTY LINE ESTABLISHED 1784
MILITARY MOVEMENTS 1776 - 1781
LT. COL. DONALD McDONALD FEB. 1776
GEN. HORATIO GATES JUL. 1780
LORD CORNWALLIS MAR. 1781
"LIGHTHORSE HARRY" LEE MAR. 1781
BARON DEKALB JUN. 1780

The Families of Moore County, NC:

1790-1850 Census and 1777-1823 Tax Records

Researched and
Compiled by

Morgan Jackson
www.MooreCountyWallaces.com

Front & Back Covers:
1833 Map of North Carolina, NC by Robert H.B. Brazier and John MacRae
Courtesy of the North Carolina Maps Digital Collection at UNC-Chapel Hill
Call Number MC.150.1833mb
http://dc.lib.unc.edu/cdm/singleitem/collection/ncmaps/id/181/rec/1

Inside Front & Back Covers:
1747-1847 Map of Old Moore County by Rassie E. Wicker
Courtesy of the North Carolina Maps Digital Collection at UNC-Chapel Hill
Call Number MC.068.1956w
http://dc.lib.unc.edu/cdm/ref/collection/ncmaps/id/3432

ISBN 978-0-578-70455-5

Published by Morgan Jackson
Raleigh, North Carolina
www.MooreCountyWallaces.com
morganjackson_1997@yahoo.com
919-624-7281

Printed by IngramSpark
www.IngramSpark.com

As always…

For my grandfather Mallie Wallace. You sparked a lifelong love of family and a burning desire to find out more about who we are and where we came from. You are missed every single day.

To my mother, Pat Wallace Jackson. Thank you for the many years of unconditional support, advice and love. And for supporting and nourishing the spark that Pop created. And for being my lifelong Editor!

And to my family…Shawn, thank you for everything, for it all. Nothing in our life happens without you. Emsley and Colt, I hope that my lifelong study of where we came from will help you keep your feet firmly on the ground and your eyes aimed at the sky.

Table of Contents

Introduction

The idea for this volume actually began many years ago...

Moore County, NC has long been a challenging place to do genealogical research due to the immense loss of records in the 1889 Moore County courthouse fire. My longtime friend, mentor and master genealogist James Vann Comer often talked about his desire to abstract the early census years of Moore County, NC along with the surviving Court of Pleas and Quarter Sessions into a master volume that would connect the threads of multiple records and provide researchers with a comprehensive view of key early records.

The focus of my research over the years has largely been on the families of northern Moore County and the prior two volumes I've published have abstracted miscellaneous and hard to find records relating to these families including land grants, deeds, church records, obituaries, school records, wills, estates, tax lists, military service and pension records, family bibles, newspaper accounts, marriage, death and court records. I excluded census records from these previous works as they would have made these volumes too massive to maneuver and these records are readily available and accessible online.

With this volume, I channeled James Vann Comer's original thought and added my own twist. Instead of abstracting the various census records, every actual Moore County Census record from 1790 to 1850 is reproduced in its entirety. While these records are available online, the volume brings the first sixty years of census records of Moore County under one cover and is fully indexed for ease of research. The surviving tax lists from 1777-1818/1823 are also included as an added bonus.

A full name index includes over 8,000 individuals. Due to the large number of misspellings of surnames in these early records, where possible, I have utilized the most popular spelling in the index rather than listing each individual spelling. For instance, Seawell, Sowell, Sewell and other variations are all located under the popular spelling - Seawell. Individuals listed as John T. Smith and John (T.) Smith may be completely different people. Generally, the letter or word inside the ( ) denotes a differentiating factor rather than a middle initial.

I am forever indebted to *Ancestry.com* and *Familysearch.org* as well as the NC Archives in Raleigh for making these records available and accessible to research. A special thanks to the archivists at the NC Archives for their dedication to preservation and their courteous assistance. And to the staff and volunteers of the Moore County Historical Association in Southern Pines and the Moore County Library in Carthage for all they do to preserve our local history. I have strived to be as accurate as possible, but readily admit that there are likely errors and omissions. Please contact me at

morganjackson_1997@yahoo.com and I will gladly make any corrections to future editions, print and online.

Along with the *Families of Northern Moore County: Abstracts of Miscellaneous and Rare Records Volumes I 1746-1830* and *Volume II 1831-1929* this book was inspired by and I hope continues to add to the volumes of genealogical research that came before. No discussion of Moore County, NC history and genealogy can be complete without paying tribute to *Miscellaneous Ancient Records of Moore County, NC* by Rassie E. Wicker; *A Guide to Moore County Cemeteries* by Anthony E. "Tony" Parker; *Moore County 1747-1847* by Blackwell Robinson, *Moore County 1847-1947* by Manly Wade Wellman and James Vann Comer's *Moore County Bible Projects Vol. I-III*, *Old Moore County Vital Statistics*, *Central North Carolina Vital Statistics* and his *Central North Carolina Collection Volume I and II*.

Morgan Jackson – June 15, 2020
www.MooreCountyWallaces.com

Cumberland County Tax/Military Districts 1777-1787

1777	1778	1779	1780	1783	1787
Campbellton		missing	Campbellton (Oveler)	Fayetteville (Livingston's)	Fayetteville Moore's
Capt Robert Cobb's	Capt Cobb's	Cobb's	Cobb's	Robertson's	Capt Robeson's (Buckhorn)
Capt John Cox's	Capt Cox's	Cox's	Cox's	John Cox's	Moore Co
Capt Thomas Dobbins	Capt Dobbins	John Dobbins	Danl Buie's	Gaster's	part of Moore Barbecue
Capt Alex Avera's	Capt Avera's	Avera's	Avera's	Turner's	Turner's Avera's Neills Crk
Capt W. Seal's	Capt William Seal's	Hunnicutt's	Seal's	Cox's	Moore Co
Capt Murray's	Capt Murray's	missing	Matthews'	Smith's	Arch[d] Smith's Carvers Creek
Capt Jacob Duckworth's	Capt Duckworth's	Duckworth's	Duckworth's	Hunnicutt's	Moore Co
Capt Hugh Gilmore's	missing	Herd's	Heard's	Thos. Gilmore's	Moore Co
Capt Armstrong's	Capt Armstrong's	missing	Hadley's	McKethan's	McKethan's Flea Hill
Capt Campbell's	Capt Campbell's	Campbell's	Crawford's	Crawford's	Moore Co
Capt Stephens'	Capt Stephens'	McCranie's	McCranie's	McCraney's	Neill Smith's McCraney's 71st & Quewhiffle
					Capt Holmes Locks Creek

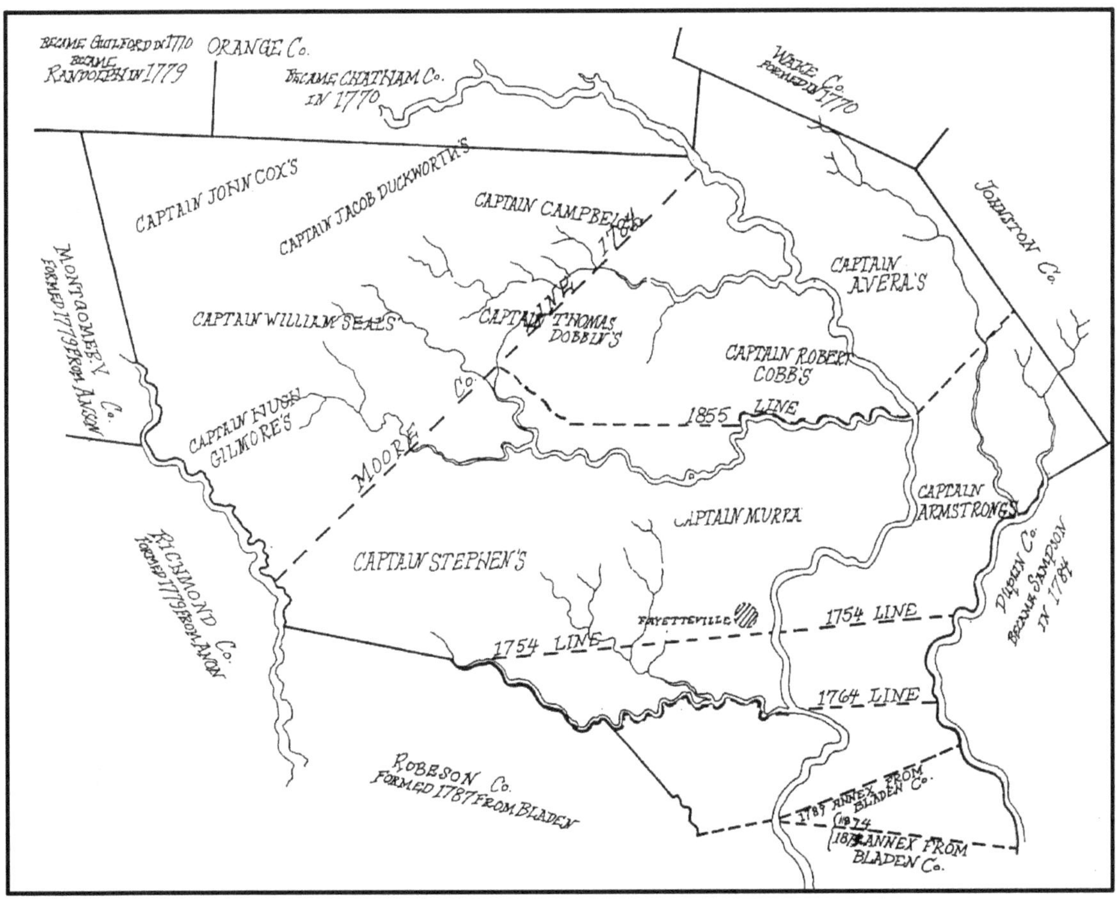

Created by Cumberland County Genealogical Society
Published in *Cumberland Chronicles* Vol. XVII, No.1, March 2002

Only the Military Districts that included present-day Moore County

Taxable property in Captain John Cox district the year 1777

No. 1	John Gardner — £	100
2	Christopher Gow	300
3	George Caringer	350
4	Orin Carpenter	500
5	Richard Dunn — £17[illegible]	176
6	William Williamson	150
7	John Keys	176
8	Richard Dunngaune	100
9	Thomas Keys	160
10	William Manus	150
11	Bartholomew Dunn	176
12	William Lee	176
13	William Manus	160
14	Isaac Dunn	100
15	Alexr. Aurly	100
16	Sefe Heter	100
17	John Hodges	100
18	Arthur Manus	100
19	Henry Jackson	100
20	Alexr. Furgerson	124
21	William Dunn	100
22	Robert Cox	150
23	Stephen Richardson	136
24	William Jackson	192
25	Francis Tidwell	150
26	James Jeffry	300
27	James Jeffry Jr.	100
28	James Morgan	146
29	Neill Watkins	136
30	William Morgan	160
31	John Morgan	130
32	John Shufell	400
		6498

Taxable Property in Captain Cox district — 1777

No	Name	£
	Brought over	6498
33	Peter Shamberger	174
34	Richard Bird	120
35	George Cagle	120
36	Jacob Statust	150
37	John Cagle	310
38	Robert Grimes	245
39	Parsons Baront	176
40	William Smith	336
41	Nathan Smith	166
42	Andrew Bates	288
43	Henry Cagle	150
44	William Barot	100
45	Daniel Campbell	200
46	John Cox	603
47	Nicholas Newton	546
48	John Williamson not valued	
49		£ 10182 ..
50		

Taxable property in Captain White's district 1777

No.	Name	£	s d
No. 1	Captain William Seale	£482	17 2
2	Christianna Jackson	620	
3	Hugh McSwain	194	
4	John Pate	160	
5	Thomas Pate	150	
6	Obed Sowel	200	
7	Daniel Shaw	110	
8	Malcom Shaw	110	
9	Francis McClendon	150	
10	James Gilmore	100	
11	Harden Howel	100	
12	John McCraw	100	
13	Roger McIntosh	100	
14	James Hill	100	
15	Ezekiel Hawson	100	
16	Richd. Fagens	100	
17	Aaron Fagans	100	
18	John Hadwell	100	
19	James Hadwell Jun.r	100	
20	Jonathan Hadwell	100	
21	Danl. Mass	100	
22	Ezekiel Smith	100	
23	Henry Dean	100	
24	Alexr. McCrea	100	
25	Norman Morrison	100	
26	Rand. Beaton	100	
27	Angus Martin	100	
28	Peter Beaton	100	
29	Angus McIver	100	
30	John Bohannan	100	
31	Neil Paterson	100	
	Carried Over	4376	17 2

Captn Seal district 1779

No		£	s	d
	Brought over	4376	17	2
32	Lochan McLain	100		
33	Norman McQuin	100		
34	John McCran	100		
35	angus Campbell	100		
36	Hugh McKoy	100		
37	Kenneth Stewart	100		
38	Danl Stewart	100		
39	Hugh McKinsey	100		
40	Neil McLain	100		
41	Alexr Stewart	100		
42	John McSwain	100		
43	John McLeod	100		
44	Angus McKay	100		
45	John McKinnon	100		
46	Daniel McLead	100		
47	David McHannan	100		
48	John McCraw	100		
49	Roger McIntosh	100		
50	Adam Morrison	100		
51	Sandy McKay	100		
52	Danl McKay	100		
53	Sandy McDaniel	100		
54	Neill McLeod	100		
55	William McLeod	100		
56	Sandy McLeod	100		
57	John Shaw	100		
58	Mrs McLeod of Glendell. husband wt Kings troops			
59	Mrs morrison, husband prisoner of war			
60	Edward Cox	453	4	
61	John Howel	524	10	
62	James McDonald	1917	15	
63	Widow McDonald	100		
64	Widow McDonald	100		
65	Danl McSwain	100		
66	Radoh Slawson	100		
	10272.6.2	£ 10272	6	

Taxable Property in Jacob Duckworth district 1777

No.	Name	£	s	d
No. 1	Ruth Rogers	266	5	—
2	Susannah Hancock	488	16	7
3	George Brewer	100		
4	John Hancock	263	15	—
5	Joel Philips	100		
6	William Potter	100		
7	Gabriel Harden Jun.	100		
8	John Philips	219	3	—
9	John Dunlop	225		
10	Gabriel Hardin Sen.	575		
11	John Hardin	675		
12	Shadrach Taylor	100		
13	Jesse Collens	100		
14	Adam Kelling	165	12	—
15	Randolph Cheek	836	12	7
16	Drury Richardson	237		
17	William Richardson	220	2	
18	Abraham Richardson	160	17	
	Carried Over	5053	3	2

Captain Duckworth's district 1777

		£	s	d
	Brought Over	5053	3	2
19	Joseph Dorr	100		
20	Benjamin Elkins	100		
21	Wilson Brown	100		
22	Anthony Steal	132	7	
23	Danl Thornton	861		
24	John Wyatt	161	10	
25	James Thornton	100		
26	William Dye Senr	100		
27	John Everton	5680	6	
28	John Hooton	100		
29	John Hunnicutt Junr	104	16	
30	Thomas Seale	100		
41	Conner Dowd	7447	14	2
42	James Muse	2435		
43	Anthony Seale	100		
44	Partin Hugood	100		
45	Isaac Hill	444	5	
46	David Lawson	135		
47	John Busbey	312	10	
48	William Hancock	100		
49	Sterling Carrol	100		
50	John Floyd	683	6	2
51	Hartwell Hunnicutt	201	5	
52	Robert Cheek	1200		
53	James Collins	100		
54	Joseph Duckworth	400		
55	Elijah Beatis	1500		
56	John Golston	100		
57	Nathan Brewer	100		
58	Benja Shealds	100		
59	John Blacket	100		
60	William Dye	100		
61	David Mellon	100		
	£	27552	2	[illegible]

Carried Over

Captain Duckworth district 1777

No.	Name	£	s	d
	Brought Over	£27 552	2	6
62	William Pain	100		
63	Isaac Pennington	500		
64	Edward Moore	150		
65	William Dunn	200		
66	Joseph Dunn	1100		
67	Richard Upton	100		
68	Benja. Atkinson	100		
69	James Hardin	100		
70	Nathan Mazus	100		
71	Hezeth McKinsey	100		
72	Thos. Atkinson	100		
73	Murdeth McCrea	100		
74	Alexr. McCrea	100		
75	Christopher McCrea	100		
76	Danl. McCrea	100		
77	Joseph Gilbert	600		
78	Thomas Tyson	300		
79	Benja. Tyson	300		
80	Cornelius Tyson	1000		
81	Jas. Whittle	100		
82	John Womble	100		
83	Danl. Gold	100		
84	Danl. Muse	100		
85	Mark Osborn	100		
86	Peter Graves	100		
87	Philipe Alston	6936	10	
88	John Carrol	700		
89	Jacob Duckworth	370		
90	Willis Dickerson	536		
91		£41 944	12	6

Taxable Property in Captain Hugh Gilmores district 1777

No.	Name	£	s	d
No 1	Thomas Matthews	£1251	2	—
2	Peter Smith	601	18	6
3	Samuel Gilmore	100	—	
4	John Gilmore	113	12	
5	John Mitch	128	12	8
6	William Gowens	290	5	
7	Neil Kelley	100	—	
8	Charles H. Gilmore	100	—	
9	Malcom Gilchrist	278	—	
10	John James	107	—	
11	Alexr. McIntosh	100	—	
12	Norman McDanald	100	—	
13	Danl. McLeod	100	—	
14	Neil McFarlin	100	—	
15	John Wadsworth	396	18	
16	Randolph McDonald	100	—	
17	Thomas Cole	100	—	
18	James Maples	100	—	
19	Robert Smith	446	14	—
20	Saml. Johnson	151	4	—
21	Colen Campbell	100	—	
22	Neil McKethen	100	—	
23	Danl. McGathea	100	—	
24	John Dawidson	100	—	
25	Isabelle Gilmore	100	—	
26	Thomas Gilmore	100	—	
27	Sarah Maples	194	2	—
28	John Gilmore	100	—	
29	James Newman	100	—	
30	Collins Hardison	100	—	
31	Husband Petty	100	—	
32	Jacob Jackson	100	—	
33	Hartwell Lankster	100		
34	Jacob Hardison	100		
		7254.	8.	2

Captain Gilmores district 1777

Nos					
Nos	Brought Over	7	254	6/8	2
35	George Gilmore		100		
36	James Gilmore		100	—	
37	William Wodworth		100		—
38	William Basten Whitfield		155	17	—
39	Arthur Davis		160	12	—
40	Abram Cole		100	—	
41	Thomas Collins Junr		100	—	—
42	Jeremiah Collins		100	—	—
43	John Gilmore		100		
44	Humphrey Gilmore		102	19	7
45	Thomas Pagerton		100	4	—
46	Thomas Smith		100	—	
47	Randolph Hunnecut		100	—	
48	William Smith		100	—	
49	John Irven		100	—	
50	Elisha Jackson		100	—	
51	William Bennorman		100	—	
52	William Ford		100	—	
53	William Collins		100	—	
54	Matthew Davis		100	—	
55	Hugh Gilmore		206	5	4
56	Benjamin Grimes		409	—	—
57	Duncan Campbell		153	15	—
58	Neill Shaw		1179	15	—
59	Duncan Buie Junr		100	—	
60	Thomas Collins Senr		704	8	
61	Duncan Buie Senr		1829	15	6
62	John Kinney		245	16	—
63	Stephen Herd		478	13	4
64	Theophilus Petty		504	5	6
65					
		£ 15	189	14	5

Only the Military Districts that included present-day Moore County

Taxable Property in Captn Gilmore's District 1778

No.	Name	£	s	d
1	Thomas Collens Senr	1080		
2	William Bennerman	100		
3	Husband Petty	100		
4	William Gowdin	510	11	
5	Humphrey Gilmore	140		
6	Ralph Davis	240	8	8
7	Thomas Collens Jr	100		
8	Thomas Tagerton	165	2	
9	Colins Hardison	100		
10	Charles H. Gilmore	145	21	
11	Thomas Maples	317	15	
12	Wm Cole	355	4	
13	George Gilmore	100		
14	Abraham Cole	100		
15	James Maples	100		
16	John Cole	322	2	
17	John Gilmore Senr	100		
18	Robert Smith	671	1	
19	Hugh Gilmore	370	2	
20	Hugh McDonald	200		
21	Thomas Eliot	272	12	6
22	Gilbert McCran	252		
23	Thomas Gilmore	100		
24	Cain Morrison	115		
25	John Petty	100		
26	Andrew Cole	240	8	
27	John Gilmore Jr	250	8	
28	James Gilmore	150	1	
29	Elisha Jackson	171	8	
30	Duncan McCran	181	16	
31	Keneth Murkinson	100		
32	Malcom McKethon	228	10	
		£7489	10	2

Capt. Gilmores district 1778

	Brought Over	£ 7	489	10	2
No 33	Jacob Hardison		137	10	
34	Thomas Sturper		100		
35	Jeremiah Collins		100		
36	Angus Love		155		
37	John McDonald		140		
38	Arthur Davis		350		
39	Matthew Davis		100		
40	Jesse Pitman		100		
41	Joseph Pitman		100		
42	William Baxter ~~Whitford~~ Whitford		242	2	
43	William Whitford		100	0	
44	Norman McDonald		148	12	
45	Neil McFarlin		100		
46	Norman Camron		100		
47	Alexr McKennis		100		
48	Daniel McClain		100		
49	Saml Johnson		315		
50	Daniel Johnson		100		
51	Alen McDonald		100		
52	Duncan Buie Senr	3	720	8	
53	Duncan Buie Junr		100		
54	Murdoch McIntosh		100		
55	Duncan McIntosh		100		
56	John Wadsworth		565		
57	Peter Smith		892	14	
58	Izabelle Gilmon		120	4	
59	John McCamler		100		
60	Duncan Campbell		136	10	
61	Malcom Gilcrist		433	10	10
62	Archd Buie		958	5	11
63	John Pitman		100		
64	Thomas Matthews	3	087		
	Benjamin Graham		665		
	Carried Over	£ 21	196	8	11

Captain Gilmores district 1778

No.	Name		£	s	d
	Brought Over		£21196	8	11
No. 66	Duncan Campbell Senr.		250	..	..
67	John Mitchel		245	3	—
68	Neil Mc Kelley		220	8	—
69	Danl. McGathea		101	—	—
70	Widow McMullen		300	10	—
71	Neil McKethon		100	—	—
72	Thomas Davis		100	—	—
73	Joseph Maples		100	—	—
74	Sarah Maples	£336.	336		
75	Josiah Williamson		992	—	—
76	Alexr. McDonald		100	—	—
77	John James		205	—	—
78	Neil Shaw		2533	2	6
79	Thomas Cole		100		
80	Pemmons Stephens		100		
81	Finley McDonald		400	—	
82	Joel Medlin		400		
83	Pool Creek John McDonald	155.	620		
84	Roger McIntosh	100.	400		
85	Danl. Finlingson	100.	400		
86	Colin Campbell	100.	400		
87	John Camron	2520	£10080		
88	Danl. McNeill	1615	£6460		
89					
			£46219	2	5

Taxable property in Captain Cox destrict 1778

No.	Name		£
1	William Keys		£350
2	Richard Dunn		450
3	John Keyes		300
4	Richard Dunn Jr.		200
5	James Jeffery Senr.		250
6	James Jeffery Junr.		780
7	Jesse Ritter		230
8	Isaac Dunn		100
9	John Hodges		100
10	William Manus		250
11	John Manes		100
12	William Smith		100
13	Alexr. Furgerson		100
14	Nathan Smith		400
15	William Barrot		160
16	James Stevens		100
17	William Dunn		100
18	William Jackson		400
19	Elizabeth Tullis		150
20	Andrew Wales		500
21	Robert Graham		300
22	Patience Barrot		200
23	George Morgan		100
24	George Wrazeel		160
25	Charles Lowel		100
26	~~Medford~~ Jeptha Medford		100
27	William Morgan		200
28	John Cagle	£800	3200
29	Henry Cagle	400	1200
30	Jacob Stutts	400	1200
31	Alexr. Otrey	100	400
32	Barthsolamy Dunn	250	1000
33	William Smith Senr.	500	2000
34	Francis Tredwell	250	1000
35	William Smith Junr.	100	400
36	Avent Smith	200	800
			£17530

(Written vertically beside entries 28–36: Did not give in their lists)

Captain Cox istrict 1778

Brought Over £ 17,530 " "

No.		
37	John Smith	100
38	Tom Smith	100
39	James Morgan	300
40	Wil Wadkins	150
41	John Field	100
42	Sampson Williams	100
43	Lenord Cagle	250
44	Saml Tedwell	100
45	William Shuffle Sr	100
46	James Lyells	150
47	John Shuffle Junr	100
48	John Shuffle Senr	800
49	Adam Comer	150
50	Peter Shumburger	300
51	William Hunsucker	100
52	George Cagle	300
53	Danl. Manos	100
54	William Williamson	300
55	Christopher Carringer	100
56	George Caringer	400
57	Symon Hart	100
58	Henry Jackson	100
59	Solomon Barrot	100
60	John Carpenter	100
61	Thomas Godfrey	100
62	Stephen Richardson	200
63	Norman McLeod	100
64	Norman McClain	100
65	Angus Stewart	100
66	John Punelson	100
67	Neil Matthewson	100
68	John McLead	300
69	Angus Campbell	100
		23,180 " "

Cont

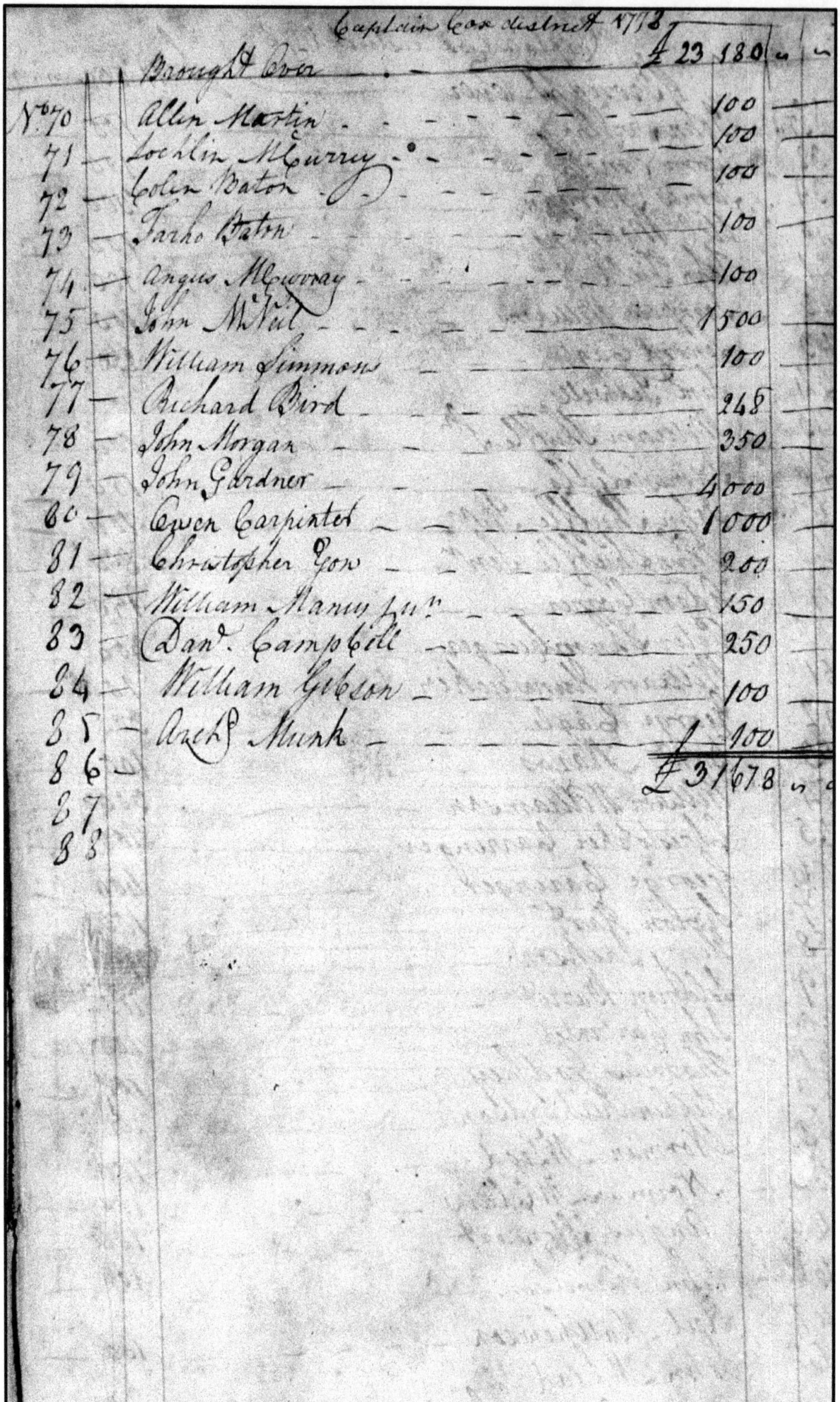

Captain Cox district 1778

	Brought Over	£23 180
No. 70	Allin Martin	100
71	Lochlin McCurry	100
72	Colin Baton	100
73	Farho Baton	100
74	Angus McMurray	100
75	John McNeil	1500
76	William Simmons	100
77	Richard Bird	248
78	John Morgan	350
79	John Gardner	4000
80	Owen Carpinter	1000
81	Christopher Gow	200
82	William Maney Jun.r	150
83	Dan.l Campbell	250
84	William Gibson	100
85	Arch.d Munk	100
86		
87		
88		
		£31678

Taxable Property in Captain Duckworths district 1778

No.	Name	£	s	d
No 1	Susanna Hancock	£ 612	15	—
2	Margeret Burns	100		—
3	Elizabeth Philips	100		—
4	William Richardson	145		—
5	John Goldson	100		—
6	John Hancock	302	12	4
7	David Lawson	100		—
8	Peter Graves	100		—
9	John Irvan	100		—
10	George Brewer	100		—
11	Joel Philips	100		—
12	Abraham Richardson	116		—
13	John Floyd Junr	100		—
14	Danl Thornton	825	15	—
15	John Busby	344		—
16	William Hancock	100		—
17	Joseph Furr	100		—
18	John Philips	341	4	—
19	Sterling Carrel	193	5	
20	Anthony Seals	100		—
21	David Melton	172	13	—
22	Edward Moore	411	4	6
23	Reuben Shields	100		—
24	Robert Moore	100		—
25	Jas Hardin	100		—
26	John Wooten	100		—
27	Aaron Teagon £145 —	145		—
28	Richd Cavemess	100		—
29	Jas Muse	2812	15	—
30	John Dunlop	378	8	—
31	Jas Gilmore	100		—
32	Ruth Rodgers	318		—
33	Anthony Street	175	2	
	Continued forward	£ 9099	8	10

Captain Duckworth district 1778

No.	Name	£	s	d
	Brought Over £	9099	8	10
No 34	Philip Alston	8363	16	—
35	Mark Cyborn	100	—	—
36	John Overton	7454	11	—
37	John Weightat	231	4	
38	Murdock McCraw	242	—	
39	Nathan Bryan	100		
40	John Lloyd Senr	897	14	—
41	Elijah Beales	1867	—	
42	Wilson Brown	100		—
43	Isaac Hill	715	5	—
44	Drewry Richardson	464	8	—
45	Heartwell Hunnicutt	353	6	—
46	William Dye	100		
47	John Gordon	2193	4	—
48	Xpher Haynes	100		—
49	Alexander McCraw	100		
50	Danl McCraw	100		
51	Adam Heller	111	4	—
52	Partain Haygood	129	8	
53	George Haygood	260		
54	William Pain	131	18	8
55	Linsey Bell	100		
56	Conner Dowd	10850	17	9
57	John Burguyne	1589	12	10
58	James Collins	373	"	"
59	John Hunnicutt Junr pole tax 4 fold	400		
60	Cornelius Tyson	6000		
61	Joseph Duckworth	2000		
62	Hardyman Rooks	400		
63	Joseph Dunn	6000		
64	William Dunn	800		
65	Richard Alston	400		
	£	62727	18	1

Captain Duckworths district 1778

No.	Name	£	s	d
	Brought over	£ 69227	18	1
No. 66	John Corrol	4000		
67	John Blanshard	400		
68	Gabriel Hardin	2800		
69	William Hardin	400		
70	Randolph Cheek	2400		
71	Robert Cheek	6000		
72	Benjamin Tyson	1200		
73	Thomas Tyson	1400		
74	Joseph Gilbert	2000		
75	Keneth McKinsey	400		
76	Benjamin Shields	400		
77	Thomas Atherson	400		
78	Benja. Atherson	400		
79	Frederick Smith	400		
80	Isaac Pennington	1600		
81	John White	400		
82	Jesse Collins	400		
83	Levy Askins	400		
84	William Moore	400		
85	William Davis	400		
86	John Woomble	400		
87	Danl. Gould	520		
88	Danl. Muse	400		
89	D Jacob Duckworth	370		
90	Thos. Seale	100		
91	Willis Dickerson	536		
		£ 90753	18	1

Taxable property in Captain William Seale district 1778

No. 1	Captain William Seale	825		
2	Joel McClendon	704		
3	Thomas Pate	374		
4	John Pate	320		
5	Isaac Sowel £640.	640		
6	Daniel Shaw	200		
7	John Morrison	130		
8	Murdoch McQueen	177		
9	John McDonald	125		
10	Sandeas McDonald	140		
11	Angus McCaskell	100		
12	Neel Patterson	140		
13	John McKoy	130		
14	Frances McClendon	250		
15	Richardson Fason	400		
16	Mary McDonald	402		
17	Christianea Jackson	1240		
18	Peter Baton	100		
19	Archd. McMullin	155		
20	John McDuffie	150		
21	Jason Wadsworth	400		
22	James Wadsworth	200		
23	James Cadwell	1425	19	11
24	James Hill	100		
25	John Black	500		
26	John Ray	200		
27	Danl. McIlwain	150		
28	Malchon Shaw	200		
29	Hugh McIlwain	300		
30	John Stewart	150		
31	John Martin	800		
32	Duncan McKoy	150		
33	Laughlin McClain	100		
34	Daniel Campbell	100		
	Carried Over £	11477	19	11

Capt. Seale district 1778

No.	Name	£		
	Brought Over	11477	19	11
135	Duncan Patterson	100		
36	John McLeod	100		
37	William White	100		
38	Hugh McKinsey	100		
39	Alexr. Patterson	150		
40	Captn. McDonalds Widow	500		
41	Hardin Howel	100		
42	James Cadwell	100		
43	Obed Sowell	300		
44	Ezekiel Slawson	100		
45	Peter Black	100		
46	Keneth Campbell	100		
47	Peter Shaw	100		
48	Norman McQueen	100		
49	John McCrain (MC)	150		
50	Angus Campbell	100		
51	Danl. Stewart	100		
52	Neil McClain	100		
53	Penelope Morrison	600		
54	— McLeod of John McLindons place	300		
55	Alexr. McCran	100		
56	John McCainnon	100		
57	Angus Beaton	300		
58	Angus McKever	100		
59	David Bohannan	100		
60	Rodham Morrison	100		
61	John Bohannan	100		
62	Keneth McDonald	100		
63	Danl. McRay	100		
64	Mrs McLeod. R.C.	200		
65	Murdock Baton	100		
		16277	19	11

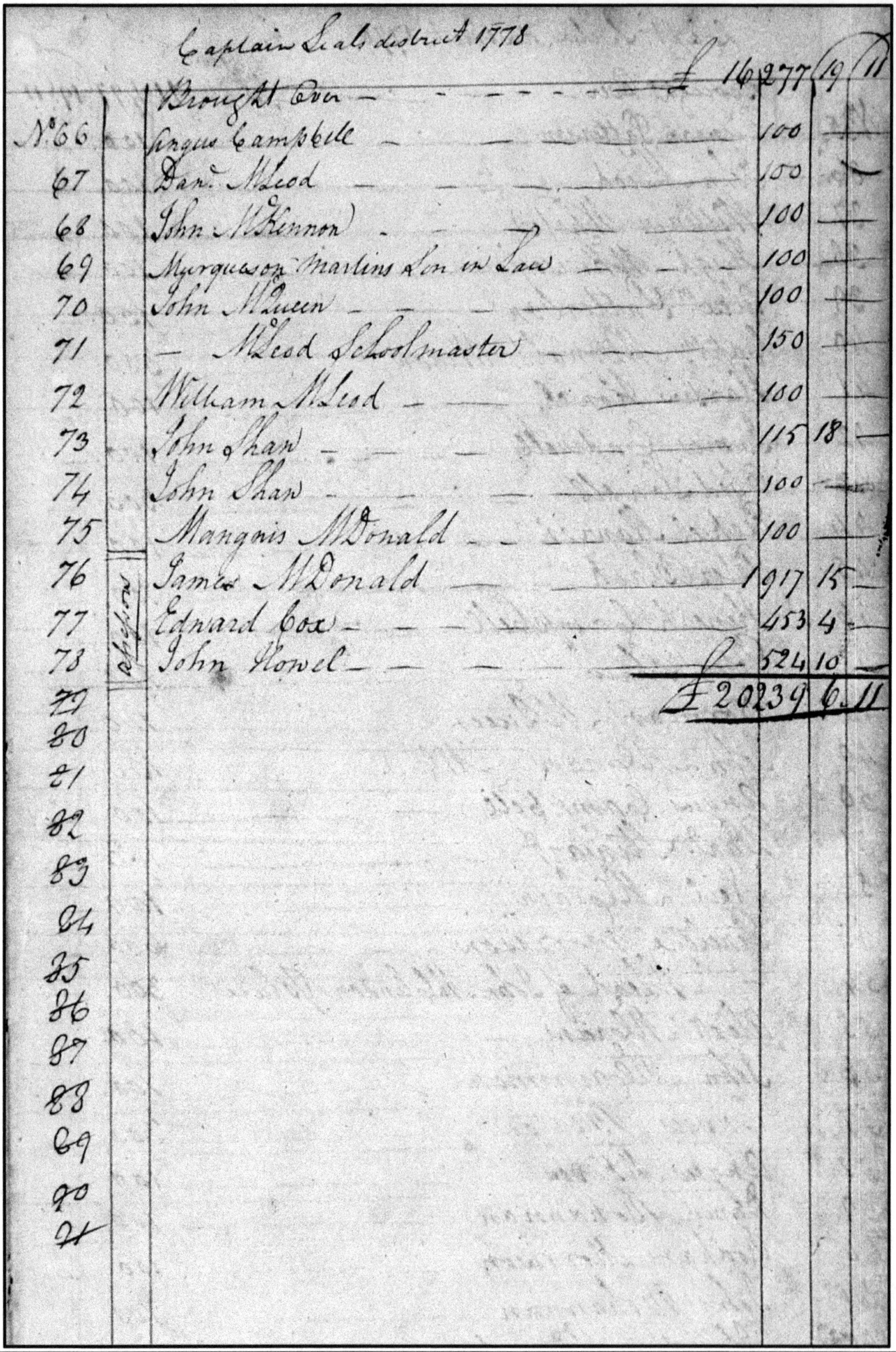

Captain Seals district 1778

No.		Name	£	s	d
			£ 16277	19	11
		Brought Over			
No. 66		Angus Campbell	100		
67		Dan. McLeod	100		
68		John McKinnon	100		
69		Murgueson Martins Son in Law	100		
70		John McQueen	100		
71		— McLeod Schoolmaster	150		
72		William McLeod	100		
73		John Shaw	115	18	
74		John Shaw	100		
75		Mangus McDonald	100		
76	[illegible]	James McDonald	1917	15	
77		Edward Cox	453	4	
78		John Howel	£ 524	10	
			£ 20239	6	11
79					
80					
81					
82					
83					
84					
85					
86					
87					
88					
89					
90					
91					

Including only the Military Districts that included present day Moore County

99 Capt Coxes District for the year 1779

Willm Menos	1000
John Garner	16000
Stuffle yon	3000
Owen Carpenter	4000
John Williamson	4810
George Carriner	5010
Betholimy Dunn	1560
Frances Pidwell – 1500	1500
Willm Williamson	1000
Richard Burd	2050
John Cagle	2600
Alexander Otry	500
William Kees	1600
John Kees	1510
Nicolus Newton	2010
David Richardson	1410
Rebacah Copelan	8050
Ansel Melton	1760
Robart Patterson	2000
Willm Richardson	100
Willm Dunn	620
John Coxt	2500
Patience Barret	844
Willm Smith	200
Andrew Bates	1500
Richard Dunn Jr	750
Richard Dunn	700
Isaac Dunn	640

£1000
16000
3000
4000
4210
5010
1560
1500
£36280
1000
2050
2600
500
1600
1510
2010
£47550
1410
8050
1760
2000
100
£60870
620
2500
844
200
1500
750
700
640
69424

Capt Coxes District for 1779
100

Isakiah Dunn	400
Angush Stewart	400
Daniel McLeod	800
Norman Morrison	800
Jeffry Medford	720
Nevel Watkins	940
John Field	650
James Morgan	2000
George Braswell	440
Willm Morgan	2200
John Morgan	3000
Adam Comer	2050
James Ledlow	1600
Nathan Smith	1440
Willm Smith	1800
Everit Smith	3200
James Smith	900
John Smith	800
Lenard Kogle	3100
George Kogle	1900
Henry Kogle	2400
Jacob Stute	2000
Willm Smith Jr	2300
Willm Barrinton	400
Daniel McDanold	200
Daniel Campbell	800
John Buchanan	450
Kenith McDonold	440
Daniel McLeod	420

£69 4 2 4
400
400
300
800
720
940
650
2000
£76 13 4
440
2200
3000
2050
1600
1440
1800
£78 6 6 4
3200
900
800
3100
1900
2400
2000
£92 9 6 4
2300
400
200
800
450
440
420
£97 9 7 4

Capt Coxes Distrit for — — 1779

101

Robert Cox —	900	£9974
	1000	900
John Carpenter		1000
	400	400
Thos Grimes		400
	400	
Soloman Barrit		300
	300	920
Simon Hart		100
Hardy Davis	930	620
	100	
Arthur Leadbeter		300
	620	
Henry Jackson		400
	900	1300
John Jenkins		
	300	1200
John Shuffle Jr.		
	400	£10582 4
John McLoed Jr.		
	1300	
Willm Jackson		
	1200	
John Jackson		

Total amount £10582 4

Capt Duckworths District for 1779

102

Joseph Furr --	260	
Randulph Hunicut	220	
Willis Dickeson ----	1610	
Anthony ~~Thomas~~ Street -----	300	
John Phillips ---	1020	
Rubin Sheals --	987	
Willm Poe	400	
Gabril Harden ---	2000	
Benjamin Sheals	220	
Willm Hancock ---	400	5217
Juanah Hancock ----	1500	
John Blanchet ----	420	
John Carril ----	3800	
John Hunicut Jr ---	800	6920
Elizabeth Dye ------	200	
Thos Busby - -	2010	
Isaac Busby ----	400	
John Overton ---	15000	
Elijah Bettis £24610	7000	24610
Edward Moore - -	1200	
Dempsy Henton 6730 -	6780	
James Henton ---	3807	
Isaac Hill ----	3200	
Phillip Alston --	25600	30537
Adam Killen	500	
Cones Dowd	21750	
Willm Poplin -	400	
David Melton - -	450	23340
John Blanchet ----	240	90624

103 Capt Duckworth District 1779

Hartwell Huncuit	450	£99624
Joseph Robertson	3200	
John Dunlap	1200	
Jones Elkins	250	5100
Joseph Duckworth	6010	£95724
James Moore	200	
Phillip Cheek	800	
Demsey Phillips	800	
William Harden	250	
Lewis Laughan	200	
George Brewer	200	
Richard Cheek	780	9240
Isaac Penington	2960	
Joseph Horses	200	
Willm Harden Sr	1700	
Elijah Hooton	210	
Levy Askins	200	£ 5270
		£110234
Not given in		
Cornelius Tison	1700	6800
Benjamin Tison	570	2280
Joseph Gilbart	1100	4400
Robert Cheek	800	3200
Willm Pain	270	1080
Benjamin Atkinson	200	800
Jesse Upton	780	3120
Willm Dunn	240	960
Total Amt		£134874

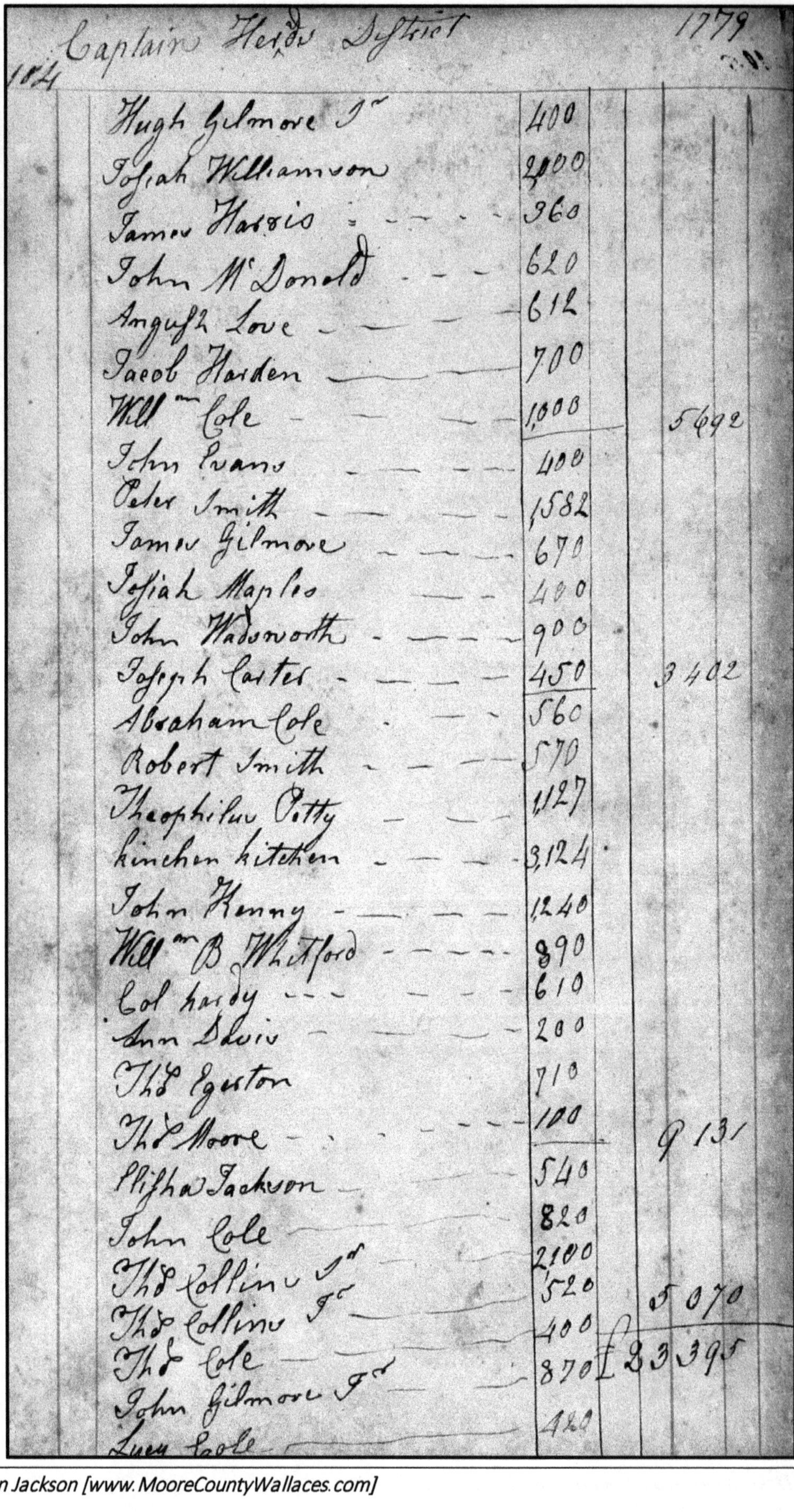

104 Captain Herds District 1779

Hugh Gilmore Jr	400	
Josiah Williamson	2000	
James Harris	360	
John McDonald	620	
Angush Love	612	
Jacob Harden	700	
Willm Cole	1,000	5692
John Evans	400	
Peter Smith	1582	
James Gilmore	670	
Josiah Maples	400	
John Wadsworth	900	
Joseph Carter	450	3402
Abraham Cole	560	
Robert Smith	570	
Theophilus Petty	1127	
kinchen kitchen	3,124	
John Kenny	1240	
Willm B Whitford	890	
Col hardy	610	
Ann Davis	200	
Thos Egerton	710	
Thos Moore	100	9131
Elisha Jackson	540	
John Cole	820	
Thos Collins Sr	2100	
Thos Collins Jr	520	5070
Thos Cole	400	£23395
John Gilmore Jr	870	
Lucy Coole	420	

Capt Heards Destrict 1779

105

Charles Gilmore	420		£23395
Sarrah Maples	415		
James Maples	260		
John Mc Intosh	400		
Duncan Campbell	790		
Alexanr Mc Intosh	750		
Duncan Mc Intosh	620		3655
Murdock Mc Intosh	250		
Kain Morrison	210		
John Mc Coly	220		
Christophe Mc Coy	810		
John Mikeson	600		
Stephan Heard	1320		3410
Matthis Davis	640		
Thos Gilmore	710		
Samuel Gilmore	400		
Thos Matthews	6,500		
John James	610		
John Gilmore Sr	300		9160
Total Amt	£		39620
			64391
			10401[illegible]
Not taken the Oath			
Malcom Mc Keithan	960 (~~1000~~)	1080	
John Camron	4000	12000	13080
Duncan Boy	12130	36390	36390 / 4947
Archibald Bouy	2630	7890	1492 / 6459
Norman Mc Donold	630	1890	
Daniel Johnston	100	300	
Daniel Mc Lain	310	930	
Hugh Mc Donold	920	2760	
Alen Mc Donold	350	1050	
		14920	

106 Capt. Heard's District 1779

Not taken the Oath

Samuel Johnston	1200	3600
Alexandr McKinnie	300	900
John Mitchel	783	2349
Neil Kelley	610	1830
Ralf Davis	820	2460
Malcom Kilchrest	2200	6600
Thos Maples	2020	6060
John McKeithan	1200	3600
Joel Medlen	100	300
Benjaman Grimes	500	1500
Neil McKethan	400	1200
Margit Mogahy	200	600
Neill Shaw	6020	18060

that Did Not give in

Daniel McNeill	12000	48000
Collin Campbell	400	1600
Duncan Blue	900	3600
Duncan Campbell	650	2600
Kinney Mirkeson	400	1600
Finley Mirkeson	350	1400
Daniel Filly	710	2840
Joel Medlin	100	400
Neil McKethan Long	400	1600

27

Only the Military Districts that included present-day Moore County

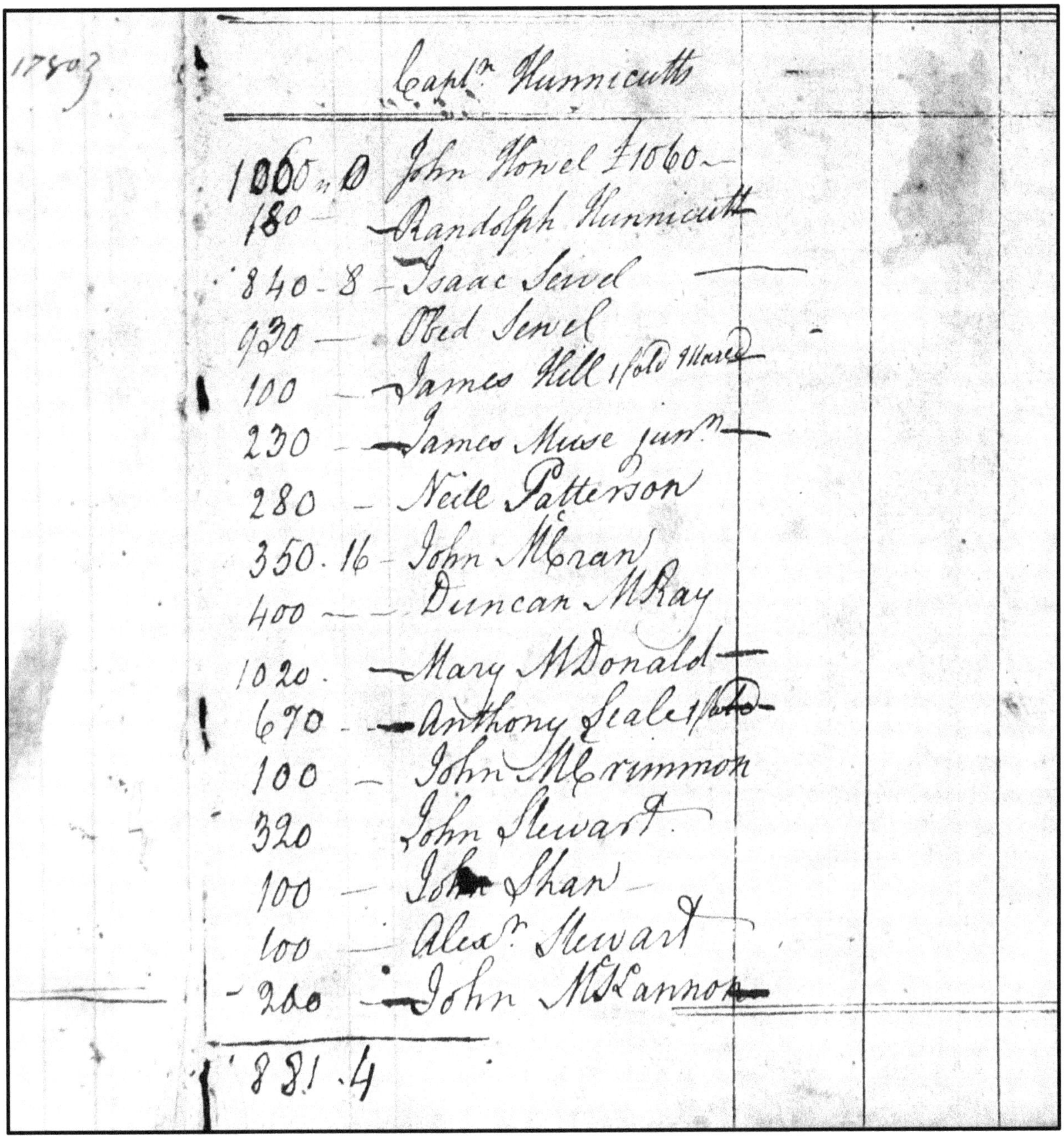

1780

Captn Hunnicutts

1060 .. 0	John Howel £1060
180	Randolph Hunnicutt
840 - 8	Isaac Sewel
930	Obed Sewel
100	James Hill 1 poll 4 Mares
230	James Muse junr
280	Neill Patterson
350 . 16	John McCran
400	Duncan McRay
1020	Mary McDonald
670	Anthony Seale 1 Poll
100	John McCrimmon
320	John Stewart
100	John Shaw
100	Alexr Stewart
200	John McLannon
881 . 4	

22

Captain Hunnicutts

		Brought Over
200	—	Angus McEver
322	—	Sarah Bahannan
510	—	Richard Fagan
532	10	Danl. Shaw
477	10	Murdoch McQueen
400	—	Malcom Shaw
310	—	Peter Shaw
100	—	Archd. Morrison
440	—	John McDonald
223	—	Neil McLannan
100	—	Angus Campbell
730	—	Neill McSwain
347	—	John Morrison
500	—	John Shaw (dancefall)
220	10	Angus McDonald
120	—	Alexr. McLeod
360	—	John McCraw
135	—	Aaron Fagins
180		Archd. Shaw
100	—	Jonathan Cadwell
100	—	Alexr. McEver
450	—	Alexr. McLeod
100	—	Angus McDonald
460	-	Angus Beaton
223	—	Danl. McQueen
330	—	Norman McLeod (S.M)
430	—	Francis McClendon
320	8	Peter Beaton
200	—	Angus McCaskell
8820,	18	

(23)

Captain Hunnicutt

	Brought over
170	Keneth McKinsie
430	John Mafsie
100	John McLeod
100	Hugh McKinsie
320	William White
1660	James Cadwell
1240	Jason Wadwoth
1088	John Pate
120	John Wadswoth Jr
683	Jas. Wadswoth
371.4	Duncan Patterson Sr.
390	Duncan Patterson
300	Danl. McIwain
100	Peter Black
830.16	John Ray 1
430	Archd. McMullin
1420	Jane McDonald
213.13	Alexr. McDonald
1497.10	Wm. Seale
3450	Christian Jackson
1624	Edward Cox
1870	John Black
300	Mrs. McLeod
600	Mr. Martin
660	Mrs. Morrison
5007.10	Jas. McDonald
6510	Jas. Muse Sr.
31487.7	

Total amount of taxable propert, for the Publick &
to this page £1001366.17.4 L. Collection due £12516.14.7 1/4
11938.3.2 1/2
Collection in Mr. Cochrans district &
amounting to £955052.16.3 | 24454.17.9 3/4

W. Rand, ?C

£6881 .. 4 .. –
8820 .. 18 .. –
31487 .. 7 –
47189 .. 9 .. – Total Amount

1780 26 Capt. heard's District

	£	s	d	£	s	d
John Jamey						
150 acers Land	225					
1 horse 4 heade Cattle money 5£	108			333		
James harries						
100 acers Land 2 heade Cattle	180					
money 25£ 12 sh	25	12		205	12	
John McDonald						
100 acers Land	180					
10 heade Cattle 1 horse	172					
money 11£16	11	16		363	16	
Anguish Love						
100 acers Land	180					
1 horse 8 heade Cattle	160			340		
Jacobe hardy						
100 acers Land	180					
2 horses 4 Cattle	188			368		
william Colell						
200 acers Land	270					
3 horses 20 Cattle	235			505		
John Evens single man	400			400		
Peter Smith						
600 acers Land	450					
6 horses 15 head Cattle	285					
money 160 £	160			895		
James Gilmore						
100 acers Land	225					
money 40 £ 1 horse	122			347		
Josiah mapels Pole T	400					
1 horse 2 Cattle	100			500		
John wadsworth						
300 acers Land	270					
3 horses 5 Cattle	185			455		
~~James Gilmore~~						
~~100 acers 1 horse~~ Void						
~~money 40 £~~						

27 Captain Heard's District — 1780

	£	S	D £ S D
Joseph Carter			
100 acres Land	180		
1 hors 8 Cattle money 10 £	110		290
Abrham Cole			
150 acres Land	270		
1 horse 4 Cattle money 00	122		392
Robert Smith			
250 acres Land	225		
3 horses 10 Cattle money 16£	256		481
theophalus petty			
350 acres Land	325		
4 horses 10 Cattle	290		
money 32 £	32		647
Hinchin Hithin			
400 acres Land	360		
4 horses money 1 £ 9 S	226	9	
3 negros	2100		2686:9
John Gilmore Sr.			
100 acres Land 6 Cattle	135		
money 72 £ 3 S	72	3	207:3
Josiah ~~[illegible]~~ willimson			
300 acres Land	360		
12 horses 10 Cattle	730		
money 18 £	18		1108
John Pinney			
100 acres Land	180		
3 horses 8 Cattle	330		
1, money & money at Pintr 172£	172		
1 Lot in Campbl	50		732
Andrews Cole			
2 horses 9 Cattle	220		
money 12 £	12		232

28 Captain Hardy District 1780

	£	s	d	£	s
william Goin					
200 acers Land	360				
2 horses 2 Cattle money 52£	190			550	
Coll hardy					
100 acers Land	180				
2 horses 2 Cattle	140			320	
Ann Davis					
1 hors 4 Cattle	120			120	
thomas Egelton					
100 acers Land	225				
1 hors 7 Cattle money 20£	160			385	
thomas more	400			400	
Elaishaw Jackson					
100 acers Land	180				
2 horses 1 Cow	120			300	
John Coal					
150 acers Land	300				
2 horses 8 Cattle money 24£	212			512	
thomas Collens Senr					
2 horses money 18£	108				
4 negros	1950			2058	
thomas Coal Jur poal tax	400				
~~100 acers Land~~					
1 horse 4 Cattle				400	
thomas Collens Jr					
100 acers Land	270				
1 horse 4 Cattle	120			390	
John Gilmore Jur					
100 acers Land	225				
2 horses 8 Cattle	188				
money 127£ 14s	127	14		540	14

29 Capt Heard District 1780

	£	s	D	£	s
Lucie Cole					
100 acers Land	135				
2 horses 5 Cattle money 4£4	160	4		295	4
Charles Gilmore 100 Acers Land	180				
4 Cattle money 1£12	41	12		221	12
Serah mapeles					
100 acers Land	180				
3 horses 10 Cattle	235			415	
James mapels	135				
100 acers Land money 10£ 8s	10	8		145	8
John mcIntosh					
1 horse 5 Cattle money 22£	153			153	
Duncan Campbell					
100 Land	225				
2 horses 6 Cattle	168			393	
Alexander mcIntosh	270				
+150 acers Land	152				
1 horse 8 Cattle				422	
Duncan mcIntosh					
150 acers Land	270				
302 1 horse 3 Cattle	93			363	
Murdoch mcIntosh					
1 hors 6 Cattle money 8£	132	8		132	8
Hein morrison					
1 hors 3 cattle	102			102	
John mcCallay					
1 horse 5 Cattle money 5£	118			118	
Cristofar mcCraw					
250 acers Land	227				
2 horses 12 Cattle money 10£	238			465	
Samuel Gillmore					
2 horses money 300£	435			435	

Capt Heard District 1780

	£	s	£	s
John murkison				
100 acers Land	225			
1 horse 4 Cattle	108		328	
Stephen heard				
350 Land	360			
5 horses 11 Cattle money 61£	399		759	
mathes Davies				
150 acers Land	180			
1 horse 10 Cattle £1=5 s	164	5	344	5
thomas Gilmore				
120 acers Land	180			
2 horses 8 Cattle money 7£	195		375	
william Bowhitfurd				
300 acers Land	360			
2 horses 3 Cattle	138		498	
thomas matthews				
1129 acers Land	1800			
negros - 6 -	2650			
4 horses 19 Cattle	550			
money 14 £	14		5014	
Persons to 3 fold				
Malcom McKeithan				
50 Acres Land	90			
1 horse 17 Cattle Money 11£4	91	4	543	1/2
	181	4		
John Camron				
300 Acres Land	225			
6 Negroes	2500			
12 horse 40 head Cattle	940			
Money 100 £	100			
	3765		11295	
Norman McDonald				
100 Acres Land	180			
1 horse 12 Cattle Money 20£	212		1176	
	392			

31 Capt Heards District 3 Fold 1780

		£	S	D	£	S	D
	Duncan Buie						
	950 Acres Land -- --	2250					
	12 Negroes of Tax Age ---	6150					
	5 horses - 48 head cattle --	1020					
	Money 393£ 16-9 -- --	393	16	9	£		
		9813	16	9	29441	10	3
Duncan	~~[illegible]~~ Buie Jun Pole Tax	400					
	~~150 Acres Land~~				1200		
	Daniel Johnston - Pole	100					
					300		
	Daniel McLain						
	2 horses 4 cattle —	148					
					444		
	Hugh McDonold						
	100 Acres Land	225					
	2 horses 13 Cattle Money 16£	254					
		479			1437		
	Alen McDonold						
	1 horse 10 Cattle ---	182					
					546		
	Samuel Johnston						
	100 Acres Land	180					
	4 horses 25 Cattle	430					
		610			1830		
	Alexr McKinnis						
	2 horses 4 Cattle —	150					
					450		
	John Mitchel						
	100 Acres Land --	180					
	2 horses 13 Cattle	238					
		418			1254		
	Neill Kelley						
	100 Acres land	100					
	3 horses 11 Cattle Money 20£	265					
		365			1095		
	Ralph Davis						
	150 Acres land	225					
	2 horses 12 cattle money 8£	256					
		481			1443		
	Thomas Maples						
	200 Acres Land	270					
	6 horses 3 Cattle	300					
		765					
	Money 65 1 Negro 700	1335			4005		

Capt Hardi District — 4 fold — 1780

02

	£	P S	£ S
Malcom Gilchrist			
300 Acres Land	360		
2 Negroes	850		
5 horses 9 Cattle Money 4£	320		
	1530		4590
Not Given in			
Duncan Campbell	500		2000
Collen Campbell	400		1600
Neill Shaw	5900		23600
Daniel Mc Neill	11000		44000
Duncan Blue	800		3200
Ben Grahams	400		1600
Jessey medlin Couper	400		1600
margrat Mc Gachey	200		800
Finney murkison	400		1600
Daniel Finley	500		2000
Catrin Mc Donald	1200		4800
John Mc Kithen	1000		4000
Neill Mc Kithen Short	400		1600
Neill Mc Kithen Long	200		800
Joel medlin	100		400

33 Capt. Seals District

Mary McDonald			
150 Acres Land	225		
2 horses 5 Cattle	95		320
Isaac Powel			
300 Acres Land	360		
2 horses 7 head Cattle	160		520
Jason Wadworth			
450 Acres Land	225		
9 horses 12 Cattle Money 15£	450		675
Neill Peterson			
50 Acres Land	90		
2 horses 10 Cattle Money 8£	198		288
John McRae			
50 Acres Land	90		
2 horses 4 Cattle Money 4£ 16s	116	16	206 16
Alexander Ferguson	100		100
Duncan McRae			
100 Acres Land	90		
2 horses 4 Cattle	130		220
Edward Cox			
500 Acres Land £	450		
8 horses 16 Cattle Money 20	540		990
James Cadwell			
350 Acres Land	450		
2 horses 11 Cattle Money 135£	335		785
James Muse Jr. Jam. Muse			
250 Acres Land	270		
3 horses 4 Cattle	175		
Money 2£	2		447

34 Capt Seale District

	£	S	D	£	S
Jonathan Cadwell					
65 Acres Land	108				
1 horse 5 Cattle Money £	97				
				205	
John Wadsworth					
3 horses 2 Cattle	155				
				155	
Archd Morrison Single Man	400				
				400	
Ann McLoed					
150 Acres Land	135				
3 horses 5 cattle	185				
				320	
Angush Campbell M man	400				
				400	
Alexr McLoed S man	400				
				400	
John Howell					
400 Acres Land	450				
3 horses 6 Cattle Money 12 £	246	4			
				696	4
Jonies Hill					
50 Acres Land	135				
1 horse 5 Cattle Money 22 £	102	8			
				237	8
Kenneth Morrison					
6oo Acres Land	450				
2 horses 16 Cattle Money 30 £	280				
				730	
Richardson Fagin					
200 Acres Land	135				
1 horse 3 Cattle Money 60 £	162				
				297	
John Tate					
200 Acres Land	100				
4 horses 7 Cattle	250				
				350	
Antony Seal					
200 Acres Land	270				
2 horses 4 Cattle	175				
Money 5 £	5			440	

35 Capt Seals District — 1780

		£	£
	Charity Muse		
	1700 Acres Land	1350	
	6 Negroes	2500	
	6 horses 16 Cattle	520	
			4370
	Charles Seal		
	100 Acres Land	180	
	1 horse 2 Cattle	92	
			272
	James Wadsworth		
	150 Acres Land	180	
	5 horses 15 Cattle Money 20£	215	
			395
Francis	~~James~~ McLendon		
	5 horses 8 Cattle	305	
			305
	Wm Seal		
	230 Acres Land	225	
	4 horses 12 Cattle	300	
	Money & Money at Int £ s 54 - 11	54 11	
			579 11
	~~John McRae~~		
	Thᵒ Seals — Thᵒ Seal		
	1 horses 5 Cattle	118	
			118
	Aaron Fagins		
	3 horses 5 Cattle	135	
			135
	Murdock McRae		
	+ 180 Acres Land	225	
	4 horses 11 Cattle	290	
	Money 10£	10	
			525

1780 Capt Seal District Not Taken the Oath & Told

	£ s d	£ s £
Daniel McIrvine		
100 Acres Land	225	
1 horses & Cattle	150	
	375	1125
John McKennan S man	400	1200
Daniel Shaw		
180 Acres Land	270	
2 horses & Cattle	180	
	450	1350
Malcom Shaw		
100 Acres Land	180	
3 horses 10 Cattle	235	
	415	1245
John Morrison		
150 Acres Land	225	
2 horse 8 Cattle	170	
	395	1185
John McDonold		
150 Acres Land	270	
2 horses 4 Cattle	148	
	418	1254
Morduch McQuean		
4 horses 5 Cattle	400	1200
Angush McDonold M man	100	300
Angush McEaver M man	100	300
Daniel Morrison M man	100	300
Hector McKenan S man	400	1200
John Shaw Single		
1 horses 6 Cattle	400	1200
Norman Morrison S man	400	1200
Duncan Paterson		
100 Acres Land	225	
1 horses 9 Cattle	190	
	415	1245

37 Capt Seals District 3 Fols — 1780

	£	S	D	£	S	D
Kenneth McKinzie 2 horses 4 cattle	175			525		
Hugh McIrvine 125 Acres Land — 1 horse 10 cattle	225 172 397			1191		
Angush Beaten 200 Acres Land — 2 horse 9 cattle — —	270 200 470			1410		
John McRae Ritch Land Creek 150 Acres Land . — — 2 horse 5 cattle	360 158 518			1554		
Neill McKenan 50 Acres Land — — — — 1 horse 4 cattle	135 112 247			741		
Angush McCaskill 100 Acres Land — — 1 horse 4 cattle	180 112 292			876		
Alexr McLaver — — 1 horse 2 cattle	130			520		
Daniel McRae 98 Acres Land 2 horses 10 cattle	225 208 433			1299		

38 1780

Parsons not Given in Capt Seals District

	Farquer McRay	400			1600
	Gilbart McRay	400			1600
	hardy howell	1000			4000
	Caller McLeod	400			1600
	obediah Sowell	350			1400
	John Stuard	225			900
Given in	Archd McMillan	420			420
	John McDuffie	200			800
	Ezeikel Smith	300			1200
	John Black	1550			6200
	~~James [illegible]~~	0000			
	Alexander Stuard	220			880
	pillip McRay	400			1600
	Ezekiel Slosen	400			1600
	Cristain ~~[illegible]~~ Jackson	3400			13600
	Daniel McQuean	360			1440
	Wm McLeod	400			1600

39 Capt Cox's District 1780

William Menis Jur				
200 acers Land - - - -	450			
11 Cattle money 3 £ 4 s	113	4		
			563	4
John Gardner				
580 acers Land - - -	3600			
10 horses 36 Cattle	1260			
20 negros - - - - -	10050			
money 38 £ - -	38			
			14948	
Owen Carpenter				
350 acers Land - - - -	1350			
17 horses 29 Cattle	1190			
1 negro money 50 £ - -	200			
			2740	
Siffle yow				
500 acers Land - - - -	1350			
5 horses 10 Cattle	370			
			1720	
John willimson				
500 acers Land	1800			
4 horses 15 Cattle money 12 £	362			
			2162	
George Carrner				
800 acers Land - - - -	2250			
7 horses 15 Cattle - - -	600			
money 4 £	4			
			2854	
Betholimy Dunn				
200 acers Land	450			
7 horses 9 Cattle - -	405			
money 5 £ 4	5	4		
			860	4
Francies ~~Hea~~ Tidwell - -				
200 acers Land - - -	450			
3 horses 7 Cattle	205			
money 1 £ 12 s	1	12		
			656	12

10

Capt Cox's District

william willimson		
100 acers Land	270	
3 horses 11 Cattle	235	
money 20£	20	
		525
Richard Burd		
150 acers Land	270	
5 horses 7 Cattle	790	
money 64£	64	
		1124
Petter Shamburgar		
100 acers Land	270	
7 horses 11 Cattle	470	
money 84£	84	
		824
John Cagle		
260 acers Land	900	
5 horses 15 Cattle	510	
money 24£	24	
		1434
Alexander otrey		
3 horses 15 Cattle	285	
		285
william Shees		
200 acers Land	450	
3 horses 10 Cattle	370	
		820
John Shees		
200 acers Land	450	
5 horses 9 Cattle	360	
		810
Niclos newton		
248 acers Land	900	
5 horses 14 Cattle	410	
1 negrow money 36£	756	2066

41 Capt Cox's District 1780

	£	s	d	£	s	d
David Richerson						
400 acres Land	450					
3 horses & Cattle money 7£	267			717		
Rebecah Coplain						
204 acres Land	180					
3 horses 6 Cattle	195			£		
money 33£ 11 S 7 d	33	11	7	408	11	7
Ansell melton						
200 acres Land	720					
2 horses & Cattle	260					
money 8£	8			988		
Robart paterson						
300 acres Land	720					
3 horses 10 Cattle	280			1000		
William Richeson						
4 cattle money 50£	100			100		
William Dunn						
50 acres Land	180					
1 hors 4 Cattle	100					
money 40£	40			320		
John Cox						
350 acres Land	450					
5 horses 11 Cattle	380					
2 negros	1400					
money 20£	20			2250		
Patience Barret						
160 acres Land	270					
1 hors 3 cattle m	120					
money 50£	50			440		

1780
42

Parsons to pay 3 fold — Cox District

	£	s	£	D
Alexander Kenady				
1 hors 4 Cattle	100		300	
John Sheffel poal Tax	100		300	
William Barret				
300 acers Land	720			
3 horses 80 £	215			
	935		2805	
Lachlon McCurrey				
1 hors 10 Cattle	143		429	
Ferguard Beaton				
100 acers Land	90			
4 horses 5 Cattle	230			
	320		960	
Lachlon McKennan				
150 acers Land	135			
1 hors 7 Cattle	115			
	250		750	
Angush Fletcher				
1 horse 11 Cattle	170			
money 3 £	3			
	173		519	
Daniel McSwean				
80 acers Land	90			
1 horses 1 Cow 12s	50	12		
	140	12	421	16
Angush McCurrey				
100 acers Land	90			
2 horses 7 Cattle	140			
	230		690	
Robert Graims				
200 acers Land	225			
5 horses & Cattle	305			
money 4 £	4			
	534		1602	

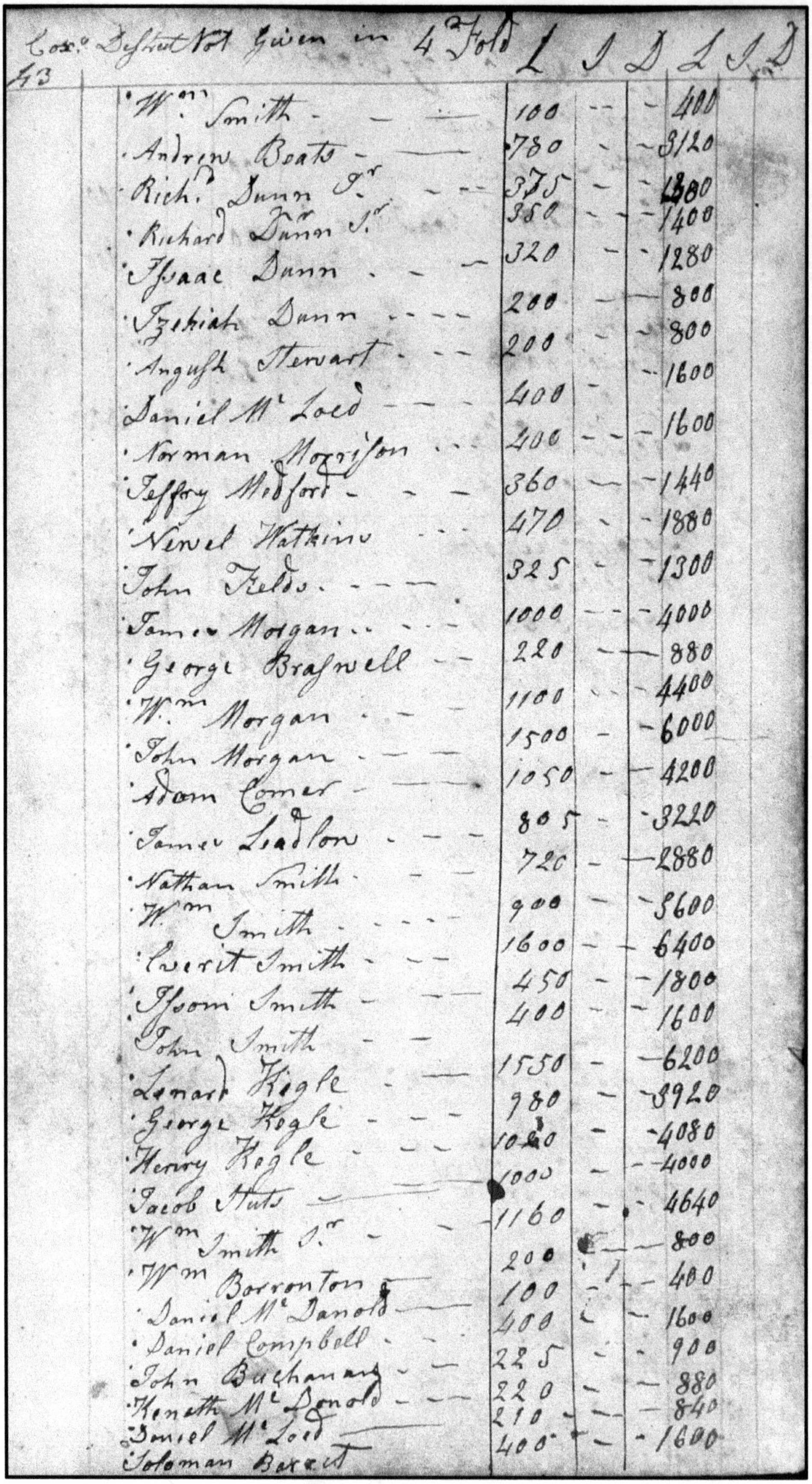

Cox.e District Not Given in 4 Fold	L	S	D	L	S	D
43						
Wm Smith	100			400		
Andrew Boats	780			3120		
Richd Dunn Sr	375			[illegible]		
Richard Dunn Jr	350			1400		
Issac Dunn	320			1280		
Izekiah Dunn	200			800		
Angush Stewart	200			800		
Daniel McLoed	400			1600		
Norman Morrison	400			1600		
Jeffry Medford	360			1440		
Newel Watkins	470			1880		
John Fields	325			1300		
James Morgan	1000			4000		
George Braswell	220			880		
Wm Morgan	1100			4400		
John Morgan	1500			6000		
Adam Comer	1050			4200		
James Leadlow	805			3220		
Nathan Smith	720			2880		
Wm Smith	900			3600		
Everit Smith	1600			6400		
Issom Smith	450			1800		
John Smith	400			1600		
Lenard Kegle	1550			6200		
George Kegle	980			3920		
Henry Kegle	1020			4080		
Jacob Stuts	1000			4000		
Wm Smith Sr	1160			4640		
Wm Borronton	200			800		
Daniel McDanold	100			400		
Daniel Campbell	400			1600		
John Buchanan	225			900		
Keneth McDonold	220			880		
Daniel McLoed	210			840		
Soloman Barrett	400			1600		

Cox District Not Given in 4 Fold

44

	£	S	D	1780 £
Simon Hart	150			6.00
hardy Davis	485			1940
Arthur Leadbetter	100			400
Henry Jackson	310			1240
John Jinkins	100			400
John Shuffle Jr	150			600
John McLeod single man	400			1600
Wm Jackson	650			2600
John Jackson	600			2400
Robert Cox	450			1800
John Carpenter	500			2000
Thos Grimes	400			1600

Capt Duckworth's District 1780

Joseph Tarr				
1 horse 6 Cattle Money £5 8	155	8	155	8
Randulph Honicut				
1 horse 7 Cattle Money £5	138		138	
Willis Dickason				
250 Acres Land	1125			
3 horses 23 head cattle	410			
Money 8£	8			
			1543	
Anthony Street				
3 horse 8 Cattle	260		260	
John Phillips				
2 horse 10 Cattle Money £ ~~40~~ 115	230			
100 Acres Land	360		590	
Rubin Sheals				
100 Acres Land	225			
2 horses 9 Cattle Money £64	269		494	
Gabriel Harden				
200 Acres Land £	900			
1 horse 8 Cattle Money 28	121		1021	
Benjamin Sheals				
2 horses 5 Cattle	120		120	
Wm Hancock 1 Man £				
2 horses 2 Cattle Money 60	400		400	
Susannah Hancock				
200 Acres Land £	630			
1 horse 9 cattle 46 Money	199		829	
John Blanchity				
200 Acres Land	90			
1 horse 4 Cattle	100			
Money 53 £2	53	2	243	2

46 | Capt Duckworth's District — 1780

Capt Duckworth's District	£	s	d	£	s
John Carril					
310 Acres Land	1350				
4 horses 17 Cattle Money £ s 28-1-4	468	1	4		
2 Negroes	850				
				2668	1 4
John Hunicute Jr					
200 Acres Land £	225				
2 horses 3 Cattle Money 120	285				
				510	
Elizabeth Dye					
1 horse & Cattle	100				
				100	
Thos Busby Admr					
750 Acres Land	900				
1 horse 6 Cattle	113				
				1013	
Isaac Busby Single man	200				
John Overton					
2050 Acres Land £	4500				
10 horses 40 Cattle Money 442	1472				
20 Negroes	9000				
				£ 14972	
Elijah Bettis					
1250 Acres Land	1350				
8 Negroes £	3900				
3 horses 9 Cattle Money 130	400				
				5650	
Edward Moore					
200 Acres Land £	360				
2 horses 7 Cattle Money 133	338				
				698	
Dempsey Hinton 5 horses 9 Cattle	450				
600 Acres Land	1225				
	2950				
5 Negroes Money	100				
				4725	
James Hinton					
500 Acres Land	990				
2 Negroes	1400				
1 horse 6 Cattle £ s	150				
Money 20-8	20	8		2560-8	

47 Capt Duckworths District £ S D £ S D 1780

Isaac Hill		
200 Acres Land	540	
2 Negroes	850	
5 horses 16 Cattle Money £20	560	
		1950
Phillip Alston		
2500 Acres Land	9000	
20 Negroes	11400	
9 horses 30 Cattle M	1380	
Money 2200£	2200	
		£ 23980
Adom Killen		
300 Acres Land £	225	
1 horse 2 Cattle Money 2£	68	
		293
Conner Dowde		
3559 Acres Land	10000	
3 Lots in uper & Lower Campbleton } 1 Lot in Chatham County }	360	
12 Negroes	4450	
6 head horses 31 head Cattle	760	
Money at Intt	989 9 7	
Stock in Trade 13030	13030	
Cash in hand	1300	
		30889:9:7
Wm Pooe single man		
1 horse Mony 2£ 14	400	
		400
Wm Poplin		
2 horse Money 5 £	140	
		140
David Melton		
100 Acres Land	90	
4 horses 13 Cattle	165	
		255
Joseph Robison		
1000 acres Land Cumbd C	1350	
100 Do Chat. Cont.	450	
1 negro	700	
5 horses	270	£ S
money & Stock in Trade	1870	4640 00

Capt Duckworths District 4 Fold Tax 1780

John Blanchet	120		480
Hartwell Hunicut	250		1000
Joseph Robertson	1700		6800
John Dunlap	600		2400
Cornelius Tison	900		3600
Jones Elkins	120		480
Joseph Duckworth	315		1260
James Moore	100		400
Benjamin Tison	310		1240
Joseph Gilbart	555		2220
Robert Cheek	450		1800
Phillip Cheek	400		1600
Densey Phillips	400		1600
Willm Harden	120		480
Lewis Laughan	100		400
George Brewer	100		400
Richard Cheek	400		1600
Willm Pain	130		520
Benjamin Atkinson	100		400
Jossey Upton	400		1600
Wm Dunn	120		480
Isaac Penington	1600		6400
Joseph Horser	100		400
Willm Harden Sr	1000		4000
Elijah Hooton	100		400
Levi Atkins	100		400

Only the Military Districts that included present-day Moore County

Capt. Thos. Gilmore's district

Name	£
John Cole	£70
John McDuffa	50
Alexr. Mentiosh	100
Wm. Going	30
Roger McIntosh	30
Wm. Baston Whitford	100
Peter Remold	20
Elijah Jackson	20
Wm. Goffey	10
Thos. Cole	20
Jas. Dickerson	20
Kenith Murchason	40
John McDonald	30
Normane McDonald	40
Mary McCray	40
Elijor Jackson	20
Thomas Egilton	110
Duncan	50
Alexr. Cole	50
John Raglan	10
Richd. Raglan	10
Christn. Smith	
Hartwell Johnston	
Thos. Collins	30
John Rimme	70
Abraham Cole	40
Thos. Gilmore	100
Thos. Collins junr.	50
John McCray	100
John Cameron, taylor	
Murdoch McCray	10
Wm. Boneman	60
Robert Smith	100
John Caroman	200
Saml. Johnston	100
Neill McKethan	100
John Mishal	50
Solomon Jones	20
Jason Wadsworth	£60
Jacob Harde	100
John Wadsworth	100
Ralph Daves	100
Angus McDugald	50
James Maples	100
Malcom Kethen	5
Martin Dye	40
Stephens Ting	20
Collin Hardy	100
Neill McKethan	150
Isaac Hone	10
John McKennon	10
Angus Mun	20
Allen Doland	20
Danl. McNeill	250
John Patterson	40
Affey McDonald	20
David Sumer	10
Benjamin Graham	100
Kenith McKethan	40
Gelson Greas	20
Charles Seal	20
Thos. Maples	140
Duncan Boice	20
Wm. Seal	120
Jesse Cooper	
Christn. McNeill	20
Wm. Cochram	10
Elizabeth Dye	10
Burrell Maples	50
Collin Campbell	50
Thos. Williams	70
Wm. Poplin	60
Danl. McLain	
Arm McGahey	100
	3795

Capt. John Cox's district.

John Garner	£210
Owin Carpinter	300
Hardy Daves	130
John Williamson	240
Eppha Medford	35
Adam Cornman	70
Wm. Williamson	90
John Morgan	90
Richd. Bird	70
George Courmer	175
Christn. Yow	160
Peter Shimberger	100
Robert Bird	50
Wm. Menes	
Alexr. Kenady	45
John Reyes	70
Wm. Menes senr.	45
Danl. Menes	
Jas. Tidwell	70
John Manes	25
Drury Richardson	70
George Cagle	90
Js. Sidlow	[illegible]
Lenard Cagle	120
Saml. Tidwell	30
Simon Hart	70
Henry Cagle	100
Js. Cockmon	10
Seth Menes	5
John Cagle	140
Jacob Stuts	120
C. Smith	90
Wm. Elmore	
Michl. Hill	70
Richd. Dunn	260
N. Newton	190
Alexr. Autry	60
Wm. Ashley	110
Jesse Riter	40

John Lane	£70
Zebuliah Coplin	20
Nathan Smith	150
Wm. Morgan	70
B. Dunn	70
Wm. Dunn	60
Susana Smith	40
Isom Smith	40
Alexr. McIver	60
B. Dunn Senr.	40
Arnold Milton	70
Danl. McKinsey	20
Isaac Dunn	10
John Fields	70
Stephen Richardson	130
John McCalley	50
Danl. McDonald	25
Alexr. Martin	40
Danl. McSwain	10
John McQuin	10
Kenth. McLoad	
Lenard Furr	10
Murdoch Beaton	30
Henry Jackson	70
Neill Mathewson	50
Wm. Moore	30
Normand Morrison	50
Wm. Smith	50
Allen Morrison	40
John Finelson	100
Thomas Reyes	120
Danl. Mathewson	10
Hezekia Dunn	15
Angus Campbell	30
David Richardson	10
John Shuffle Jur.	60
John Shuffle	120
Danl. McLoad	10
M. McLoad	30
John Buchannan	20
Kenth. McDaniel	30
Reubin Freeman	15
Peter Hart	40
Robt. Staples	20

Joseph English	£
Normand McLain	20
Danl. McLoad	410
Hector McLain	50
Malcom Morrison	50
Norman McLoad	20
Wm. Smith	20
John McDaniel	30
Solomon Barlet	410
Thos. Jinkins	410
Robert Graham	120
John Cox	450
Patience Barnett	400
Thos. Graham	30
Angus Campbell	20
Wm. Barret	100

6570

Capt. Gaster's district.

W. Kennady	99
D. McDonald	33
A. McDonald	56
D. McRae	13
J. Clark	441
D. Patterson	50
W. Johnston	114
J. Patterson	23
J. Walker	05
H. Gaster Senr	566
H. Gaster. Jur.	54
E. Walker	3
J. Walker S. M.	10
D. McLain	140
do for orphan of D. McLain	65
Small S. M.	
D. McKellar	17
N. Leitch	69
A. Campbell S. M.	+
J. Campbell	10
A. McRae	11
J. Ray	05
A. Buie Jur.	17
J. Brooks	37
J. Hapley	40
D. Munn	30
D. Grimes	36
J. McDonald	54
D. Buie blksmith	90
G. Clark	406
N. McNeill Shoemaker	216
H. Morris	63
J. Morris	09
J. Clark muddy creek	225
J & H. Smith	100
A. Clark	492
J. Chivis	30

J. Baker	£170.
J. McLain. Ind. branch	65.
Hugh Ray	106
M. Grimes	20.
D. Shaw	33
W. Clark	67.
J. McLain	40.
J. Clark. Sailor	56
J. Wats	134.
A. McLoad	52
A. McGregory	15
N. Paterson	31.
A. Smith	52.
D. Paterson	64.
D. Smith	20.
D. Campbell	164.
W. McLoad	64.
G. Buie	420.
D. Clark	16.
D. McColskey	100.
J. Buie. Senr	169
D. Buie	202
A. Buie	195
A. Buie. piper	272
J. Buie	77.
D. Clark	45
D. Buie	91.
J. Dobbins	06
J. Riddle	61
D. Buie. taylor	95.
J. McLain. boatman	47.
D. McDugald	35.
M. Buie Juniper	53
D. McCraney	53
J. Arrington	06
J. Durimple	96.
G. Anderson	66
J. Page	13.
A. McBride	2.
J. Marshburn	50
M. Marshburn	
J. Piles	50.
D. Grimes. S. M.	200.
D. King	50.
D. McLain. S. M.	200

Listed for not giving in their tax list

John Manes	£50
J. Miles	30.
J. Kennady S. M.	200.
S. Walker S. M.	200.
A Campbell S. M.	200.
M. McLain	200.
M. McLain	50.
N. Lammon	50.
A Smith S. M.	200.
L. Campbell	100.
A Cameron S. M.	200.
H. McNeill	150
A. Munn	75.
C. McKay	200.
A Stewart	75.
D. Murchason	75.

two [illegible] for not giving in their tax list carried out

10[illegible]5.

Capt. William Cox's district.

C. Cox	£196.
A. McIver	30.
P. Baton	15.
S. Cox	35.
J Warner	132.
R. Fagon	102
J. Fry	167.
A. Mares	20.
J. Cadwell	27.
J. Hill	14.
J. Muse	113.
A. McDonald	42.
A. McDonald	12.
N. McLoad	66.
D. McIntosh	13.
D. Jones	112.
J. McQuin	24.
J. Jackson	150.
J Wadsworth	105.

C. Jackson	£370.	
J Pate	90.	
J Cadwell	136.	
A Fagon	50	
J. Cadwell		
J. Cadwell jur	30.	
N. McSwain	35.	
Joel Medlin	73.	
M. Davis	230.	
K. Murchason	110.	
Alexr. McIver	13.	
A. McLachel	16.	2636

Capt. John Hunnicut's district

J. Overton	2060.
J. Phillips	130.
G. Hardin	125.
Wm. Hardin	207.
J. Fun	23.
J. James	120.
J. Petty	179.
J. Dunlop	107.
J. Blanchit	103.
A. Keating	103.
A Street	124.
J. Thornton	100.
J. Duckworth	224.
J. Hunnicut jur.	133.
E. Bitts	720.
W. Dickeson	225.
D. McKinsey	22.
R. Rogers	66.
J. Norris	15.
M. Busby	24.
H. Hunnicut	100.
R. Dickeson	30.
J. Blanchit. jur	22.
W Dunn	130.
R. Davis	20.
B. Shields	100.
McDoud	600.
W. Hardin	10.

T. Tyson	£222
C. Muse	650
L. Smith	1210
L. Askins	3
R. Clark	300
H. Hardin	15
S. Hancock	207
P. Alston	2905
R. Hunnicutt	100
	£10512

152

within the Division allotted to Guilford Dudley.

Names of heads of Families.	Free white males of sixteen years & upwards including heads of Families	Free white males under sixteen years.	Free white females including heads of Families	All other Free persons.	Slaves
Moore County.					
John Campbell	1	1	2		
Thomas Mathews	7	2	3		7
Archd. McBride	1		4		
Mary Watts			4		
William Teague	1	2	4		
John Melton Glascock	1	2	2		
James Caddell	4		2		
Nathan Fry	1		2		
John Kenney	2	2	4		
Patty Glascock	3	1	6		5
Cornelius Tison	2		2		
Benjamin Tison	1	1	3		
Mary Doud		3	5		3
Aron Tison	3	3	4		
James Sutton	1		3		
Needham Temples	2	1	1		
Hubbard Petty	1	5	6		
John Petty	1	1	6		
Milley McDaniel	3		4		
Jabas Clark	1	1	2		
William Barret	1	2	3		1
John Quimby	1				
Thomas Overton	1				14
Joseph Brown	1	1	2		
Lucy Jones			3		
Richardson Fagan	1	4	4		1
Jason Wadsworth	3	1	2		
Elijah Bettis	2	3	5		3
Thomas Grimes	3		3		
Robert Grimes	2	1	1		
Jonathan Caddell	1		4		1
Alexr. McIntosh	1	1	2		
Margaret Monro		1	4		
Mary McRae		2	2		
John McKenzie	1	2	1		
Kenneth Murchison	1	4	4		
James Hill	3		5		
William Richeson	1	2	1		
Alexr. McIntosh	1	1	3		
Drury Richeson	1	1	3		
Duncan McIntosh	1	1	2		
Nathl. Melton	1	3	1		
Mary McLennan	2	2	1		
Abner Chapman	2	2	4		17
John McIntosh	1	3	2		
Daniel McIntosh	1	1	2		
John Sinclair	1	4	4		
Ralph Davis	2		1		
Richard Bean	1	2	5		
Amount carried over	78	69	143		52

Schedule of the whole number of persons within the Division allotted to Guilford Dudley.

153

Names of Heads of Families.

Moore County

Amount brought over	73	69	143		52
William Humphry	1	1	1		
Stephen Morris	1		1		
Jesse Muse	1	3	1		
Charity Muse		1	5		2
John Bullock	5		2		
Edward Upton	1		1		
John Upton	1	2	4		
Francis Bullock	1		3		
William Seale	1	3	4		
William Dun	1	2	1		1
John Shepherd	2	1	3		3
John Carrol	2	4	3		
William Copeland	1		1		
Elijah Bean	1		1		
John Harrington	1	4	2		
John Hews	1				
Gilbert Buie	1				2
Frederick Morris	2		1		
Elijah Bettis	3	3	4		2
Grizzel Carmichael		3	3		
Robert Cheek	3		3		
William Caddell	1		2		
John Baker	1	2	4		3
Thomas Eggleton	3	2	4		
Philip Johnston	1	1	4		4
Duncan McIntosh	1	1	2		
Duncan Murchison	1	1	3		
Duncan Campbell	1	2	3		
Absalom Ottery	1	5	2		
Alexr McDonald	1				
Mary Ottery	1	3	5		
James Ottery	1	1	3		
Benja Fry	1	4	2		
Quincy Pilman	1	4	7		
William Cox	1	3	1		
John Winkenorth	1	4	3		
Miller Oliver	2	1	2		
Archd Hack	2	1	2		1
William Mears	1		2		4
William Danelly	1		1		
Daniel McIntosh	1		4		
Hugh Watson	1	3	1		
Robert Watson	2	3	2		
Vincent Davis	1		2		
William McAuley	1	4	1		
William Cook	2	4	5		
Everat Smith	2	3	3		
Leany Tidwell			2		
David Cagle	1		2		
Leonard Cagle	1	7	3		
Robert Beall	2	2	1		
William Givings				10	
Amount Carried Forwd	140	157	265	10	74

154

Names of Heads of Families.

Moore County

Amount brought Forward	140	157	265	10	74
Christopher Yow	2	5	4		
Samuel Tidwell	1		3		
Duncan Campbell	1	2	3		
James Melton	1		2		
William McKenzie	1	1	3		
Peter Garner	1	3	2		
Daniel Love	1	2	6		
Murdock McIntosh	1	1	2		
Rory McIver	5		2		
Mathew Campbell	2		6		
John McIver	1	1	7		
Henry Cagle	3	4	4		
Joseph Cockman	1	1	3		
Edward Moore Jr	1		2		
Christian Cagle	1	1	1		
Duncan Patterson	1	3	1		
William Manus	4	3	9		
James Ballard	2	2	4		
Thomas Smotherman	2	4	1		
Hugh McDonald	2	4	3		
John McLaine	1		2		
George Underwood	1	4	5		
Peter Blew	1	3	4		2
Murdock Murchison	1				
Daniel Grimes	2	1	1		
Duncan McIver	3	1	2		
Duncan Blew	1	2	3		1
Maurice Morrison	1	1	2		
John Overton Sr	1		1		23
Joseph Fry	2	2	6		
Jesse Ritter	2	2	5		
John Cagle	2	2	3		
Jacob Stutts	1		1		
Archd Ray	1		1		
Hector McNiel	3	1	3		10
William Williamson	1	4	4		1
James Manus	1				
James Ray	2	2	4		
Barbara Murchison	1	2	2		
Nancy McSwaine		1	3		
Zachariah Smith	2	5	1		
Jacob Stutts	3	1	2		
Murdock McRae	1	2	3		
Thomas Hannon Jr	1		2		
William Davis	2	3	4		6
Thomas Smith	2	1	2		
Everat Wallace	1		2		
John McDaniel	1		2		
John Blew	1	1	1		
Amount Carried Over	216	235	404	10	117

Schedule of the whole number of persons within the Division allotted to Guilford Dudley

155

Names of heads of Families. Moore County					
Amount brought over	216	235	404	10	147
John McNiel	1	2	3		
Neil McLaine	1		5		
Daniel Patterson	1		3		2
John Baker	2	1	2		
Alexr McLeod	2	1	5		
John McDonald	4		2		
Roger Cagle	1	1	2		
George Cagle	1		2		
Thomas Collins Jr	2	3	4		
Thomas Thompson	1	5	2		
William Read	1	2	4		
John McIntosh	1		1		
Daniel Manus	1	3	2		
John Williamson	1	2	3		
Darius Ramage	1		1		
John Bethune	1	2	8		
Jesse Bean	1		3		
Angus McCaskill	3	1	2		
Willis Oliver	1	4	2		
Peter Hamburger	2	3	6		1
William Teague	2	4	5		
Jesse Griffin	1		2		1
Robert Davis	2		4		1
Richard Cheek	1	2	3		
Norman McLeod	1	3	2		
George Fry	1	2	8		
Daniel Roberson	1	6	4		
John Records	1		2		9
Samuel Parsons	1		1		6
James Brady	1	3	5		
Leonard Furrow	1	4	5		
Willis Dickinson	2	2	5		
Hezekiah Dun	1	4	3		
Richard Dun	1	2	3		
Thomas Keys	2	7	3		
Theophilus Eddins	1		3		
Daniel Munro	3		1		6
John Patterson	3		2		5
Kenneth Murchison	1	3	4		
Robert Patterson	1	3	4		
Christo Bethune	1		1		
Keziah Thomas			1		
Nancy Tolman		1	2		
Alexr Campbell	2	3	5		
John Caddell	1	2	1		
William Morgan	1		4		
Robert Dickinson	1	5	4		
Amount Carried Forwd	279	321	553	10	148

156

Names of heads of Families. Moore County					
Amount brought Forwd	279	321	553	10	148
Nathan Smith	1		1		
Ambrose Brown	1		2		
John McDuffee	3	1	3		
Flora McDonald	1	2	3		
Thomas Ritter	1	1	2		
James Muse	1	4	2		
John Hargrove	1		6		
Thomas Hannon Sr	1	1	3		
Duncan Murray	1	1	3		
David Richeson	1		5		
John Morgan	2	4	4		
William Smith	1	1	4		
John Ritter	1	1	2		
Mathew Coggin	1	2	5		
John Keys	3	2	5		
John McDonald	1	3	2		
William McDonald	1		4		
William Newton	1	1	2		
Daniel Monk	1	2	2		
George Carrender	3	3	4		1
Elijah Ottery	1	3	2		
Angus McIver	1	2	1		
Malcolm McCremon	1	3	4		
Norman McCremon	1	1	2		
Joseph Allen	1	3	1		
John McNiel	1	2	3		
Benjamin Cooper	2	3	2		
Anthony Street	1	3	3		1
William King	1	2	1		
John Sewell	1	2	2		
Alexr McIver	2	2	2		
Archd Wadsworth	1				
William Hews	2	1	3		
Stephen King	2	1	4		
Murdock McKenzie	1	1	3		
Thomas Fry	1	2	5		
Edmund Hodges	1	2	4		
John McLeod	1		2		
Duncan Johnston	1	4	3		
James Collins	1	2	3		2
Burwell Maples	1	1	3		
Stephen Collins	1		2		
William Smith	1	1	4		
John Hair	1	3	3		
Henry Cox	1	1	2		
Peter Hair	1		4		
Amount Carried Over	336	395	685	10	152

Schedule of the whole number of persons within the Division allotted to Guilford Dudley

157

Names of heads of Families — Moore County					
Amount brought over	336	395	685	10	152
John Worthy	1	1	2		
James Riddle	1	3	6		1
Nelson Jackson	1				
Moses Cox	1	1	2		
Christian Jackson	1		1		2
Nancy Jackson		3	2		3
Margaret Jackson			4		
Thomas Gilmour	1	1	2		
John McAuley Sr	2		2		
Johnathan Wicker	1	1	1		
David Kennedy	1	2	1		
Alexr Kennedy	2	6	3		
Michael Bryant	1		2		
Benjamin Wicker	1	1	4		
Stephen Richeson	1	2	3		
William Copher	1	4	4		
Edmund Hurley	3	3	3		
Thomas Cole	1	2	2		
Jesse Brown	1		4		
John Johnston	1	2	3		
Martin Martin	2	1	1		
Bartholomew Dun Jr	1	1	2		
William Dun	1	3	6		
James Campbell	1	1	1		
Thomas Dun	1	1	3		
George Williams	1	4	2		
John Buchannan	2	2	2		
Bartholomew Dun Sr	1		2		
Ambrose Manees	1	4	3		
George Cagle	1	2	2		
Hector McNeel	1	1	4		
Edward Cox	1		3		
William Morgan	1	1	7		
Mary Sewell		3	3		
Nicholas Nall	2	1	3		8
Hardy Davis	1	3	4		
Thomas Davis	1	2	1		
John Garner	1	1	2		13
Lewis Garner	1	1	3		2
Bradley Garner	1	1	2		1
Samuel Dun	1		3		
Donald McQueen	1	1	4		
Murdock McKenzie	1	2	3		
Sarah McDonald	1		1		
John Spiva	1	3	4		
Murdock McAuley	1	3	2		
Hector McLaine	1	1	3		
John Cole	2	3	3		
Richard Upton	3		5		
Amount Carried Forwd	393	473	820	10	182

158

Names of heads of Families — Moore County					
Amount brought Forwd	393	473	820	10	182
Donald McDonald	1	2	4		
John Shuffil Jr	1	5	1		
John Shuffil Sr	3	1	4		
James Moore	1		1		1
Allen Martin	1	1	1		
Kenneth McDonald	1	3	5		
James Merrett	2	4	6		
Anna McLeod	2	1	1		
Peter McIntosh	1	1	3		
George Grimes	1	1	1		
John Smith	1	2	2		
William Smith	1	1	1		
Owen Carpenter	3	3	4		
Charles Campbell	1	1	3		
William Martin	1	2	3		
Murdock Martin	1	1	4		1
Kennith Morrison	1				
Jacob Harwick	1	2	2		
Angus Campbell	1	1	4		
Angus Campbell	1	2	3		
Kitchen Kitchen	1	2	7		
George Cox	1				
William Seale Jr	1	3	3		
Benjamin Sheals	2	5	3		
John Evans	1	2	3		
Joel Medlin	3	3	1		
Rebecca Medlin		1	1		
Joseph Magee	1	3	5		7
Archd Smith	4	3	6		
John Carrol esqr	3	3	5		2
Duncan Patterson	2	3	4		
James Mathews	2		1		
Benja Ragsdell	1	4	2		
Wm Ragsdell	4		2		
Hartwell Lancaster	1	4	2		
Richard Ragsdell	1	5	2		
Andrew Cole	1	2	6		
Archd Buie	1	2			
Lewis Price	1	2	2		
Burwell Phillips	1				
Mark Phillips	1	2	2		
Irwin Moore	1		1		
Lewis Phillips	1	2	1		
John Phillips	2	1	4		
Abraham Hood	1	1	2		
Amount Carried over	457	560	930	10	193

Schedule of the whole number of persons within the Division allotted to Guilford Dudley

159

Names of heads of Families.					
Moore County					
Amount brought over	457	560	938	10	193
Richard Maulding	1		1		
Neil Hews	1	3	3		
Cornelius Doud	1		3		3
John Medlen	1	2	2		
Mathews Davies	3	4	3		
Priscilla Tyney		1	1		
James Davies	1	1	2		
James Alston	1				3
Neil McLeod	3	1	1		
James Monk	1	1	2		
James Jackson	1	1	1		
Jesse Miles	1		2		
Patrick Doud	1				1
Archd. Dalrymple	1	1	3		
Henry Gaster Sr	2	1	1		14
Henry Gaster Jr	1	6	2		
John Dalrymple	4		3		5
Arthur Davies	1		2		
Charles Seale	1	3	3		
Richard Street	1	2	6		15
John Rogers	2		3		
Theophilus Petty	1				
James Maples	1	3	3		
Jacob Edwards	1	2	3		
William Hancock	1		4		
John Cameron (Taylor)	1	1	1		
John Merrett	1				
Randal Cheek	3		5		1
Joseph Magee Jr	1		2		
Josiah Holliman	1	3	1		
John Black	4	2	3		
Thomas Tison	2	4	4		
Norman McDonald	4				1
Mary McDonald			1		
Rueben Sheals	1	3	7		
Thomas Muse	1		1		
Thomas Atkinson	1				
Thomas Collins Sr	1		2		1
William Watson	1	3			
Daniel Cole	1	1	3		
David Moore	1	1	1		
Robert Blanchet	1	2	1		
Adam Comer	2	4	5		
Elizabeth Murchison			1		
Amount Carried Forwd.	517	616	1030	10	23

160

Names of heads of Families.					
Moore County					
Amount brought Forward	517	616	1030	10	237
Presley Loving	1	2	4		
William Gardner	2	2	5		
Peter Gardner	1	2	4		
Alexr. McBride	1	1	6		
Samuel Mashburn	1	2	4		
Charles Campbell	2		2		
John Love	2	2	5		
John Shepherd Sr	2		1		
William Goings	1	4	5		
Charles Campbell esqr	2	1	3		
David Wicker	2	1	3		4
Archd. Baker	4	1	5		
John Morgan	2	4	4		
Stephen Oates	1	2	2		
John Carraway	3	2	2		
Duncan McCallum	1	1	2		
Katy McDonald			2		
John Buchan	1	4	3		1
John Stutts	1	1	1		
Joseph Dun Sr	1	1	1		6
Joseph Dun Jr	1	1	4		1
Mary McRae		2	2		
Joshua Edwards	1	3	3		
Margaret McKenzie	1		1		
Allen McDonald	2	3	2		
Duncan Buie	2	5	3		
Thomas Maples	1	2	1		1
Moses Wilson	2		2		
William Williamson	2	2	4		1
John Williamson Sr	1	2	3		
Stephen Smith	1	1	2		
David Smith	1		4		
William Berryman	2	2	6		
Patience Barret		1	4		
John Cameron Sr	2	3	6		6
James Purnal	1				
John Wadsworth	1				
Daniel Buie	6		4		6
David Wicker	3	1	5		5
Thomas Thomas	1	5	2		
Alexr. Sloan	1	2	3		
Frederick Morris	2	1	1		
Henry Morris Sr	1	3	3		
Peter Morris	1	2	1		
Henry Morris Jr	1		1		
Amount Carried Over	585	690	1061	10	268

Schedule of the whole number of Persons within the Division allotted to Guilford Dudley.

161

Names of heads of Families — Moore County					
Amount bought Over	585	690	1061	10	268
Mathew Morris	1	1	1		
Duncan McRae	1	1	2		
John McFee	1	5	3		
John Cameron	1	6	1		
Asbel Monk	1				
Malcolm Monro	1	2	1		2
Neil McLeod	3	1	3		
Lewis Temple	1		1		
Daniel McLaine	1	1	4	1	
Josiah Maples	2	2	3		
John Overton (Bigg?)	1	2	2		2
Marmaduke Maples	1	2	1		
Duncan Buie	1	2	2		5
James Hayes	1	1	2		
John Carrol	3	3	5		3
Ignatius Hall	1	1	2		2
Joshua Mills	1	1	2		
Charles McLeod	1				
Murdock Campbell	2				
Abraham Cole	1	2	4		
Daniel Patterson	1		2		2
Joseph Greenhill	1	1	2		10
James Gallemore	1	1	5		
Norman Morrison	1	2	4		
Alexr Morrison	2		2		
Malcolm Morrison	2	1	3		
Alexr Monro	1	2	3		
Hector McLaine	1		2		
Ansel Melton	2	1	4		
Norman McLeod	1		2		
Murdock McLeod	1		2		
Daniel McLeod	2		1		
Nancy McLeod		3	4		
Norman McLaine	1	1	3		
Daniel Campbell	3		7		
Murdock McAuley	1		1		
Kenneth McLeod	1		1		
Jesse Ducksworth	1		5		1
Francis Myrick	1	2	2		
Daniel McDaniel	3	1	2		
James Harding	1	3	4		
Gabriel Harding	1	2			2
Kenneth Clark	5		3		6
Findley McDonald	1	4	3		
Simon Ruebottom	1		2		
Thomas Ruebottom	2		6		
Jacob Cagle	1	3	3		
Malcolm Gilchrist	3		4		
Amount Carried Forward	653	750	1182	11	[illegible]

162

Names of heads of Families — Moore County					
Amount brought Forwd	653	750	1182	11	305
Malcolm McLeod	2	1	3		
Benjamin Elkings	1	7	1		
James Elkings	1	1	5		
William Teauge (Black)	1	3	4		
John Phillips	1	1	4		
Lanier Brewer	2	4	4		
Robert Davis	2		4		1
Stephen Morris	1		1		
James Thornton	1	1	1		
William Teauge (Preacher)	2	4	4		
Amos Overton	1	3	4		
Ruth Rogers	2		2		
Elizabeth Hancock	1	3	1		
Joseph Magee	1	1	4		5
Hezekiah Johnston	1	3	3		
Duncan McRae	1	1	2		
Alexr McInnis	2	5	2		
Donald McRae	1		2		
Duncan Buie (Red)	2		6		
Frances Boyd			2		
Thomas Carlisle	1	1	1		
William B. Whitford	1	1	3		
Horah Carlisle	1	1	1		
Robert Carlisle	1	2	4		
Angus McAuley	1	2	4		
Norman McKinnen	1	1	2		
John McKinnen	1	4	2		
Murdock McInnis	1				
Neil Monro	1		2		
John Blanchet Sr	1	1	2		
Ambrose Brewer	2	3	4		
Rebecca Jones		3	2		
Moses Oliver	1				
Edward Moore Sr	1		1		
John Overton (Little)	2		3		1
Robert Carlisle	1	1	6		
Hugh Killer	3	2	4		
John Coupland	2		2		
John Hayes	2	2	2		
David Davidson	1	2	1		
John Morgan Sr	1		2		
Donald Mattheson	1	3	3		
Lewis Sewell Jr	2	3	5		
Lewis Sewell Sr	1	1	3		
Nicholas Newton	2	1	7		1
Fanny Runnals		1	2		
Sarah Runnals		3	3		
Elijah Jackson	1	4	5		
Amount Carried over	712	830	1317	11	313

Schedule of the whole number of persons within the Division allotted to Guilford Dudley.

163

Names of heads of Families — Moore County					
Amount brought over	712	830	1317	11	313
Elizabeth Jackson	1	1	3		
Niel Mattheson	2	2	3		
Mark Herrett	1				
William Paine	1	1	2		
Joseph Furr	1	4	3		
Benjamin Graham	5	4	2		
Benjamin Stephens Sr.	2		5		
John Stephens Jr.	1	1	2		
Dugal McFarland	1	1	2		
Matthew Kitchen	2	1	3		
Margery Buchannan		1	1		
Reuben Freeman	1	2	3		
John Hillyard	2	2	2		
Niel McLaine Sr.	1		5		
Cornelius Hewings	1	2	5		
Gabriel Harding Jr.	1		3		
James Bowzer		1	1	1	
John Dunlap	1	4	6		
Thomas H. Perkins	2		2		24
Benjamin Gilbert	1		2		
Sibra Gilbert		3	3		
Samuel Womble	2	2	1		
Littleton Houghston	1	1	1		
Arch'd Buie	3	1	4		8
Susannah Fields		1	2		
John Mears	1		1		
William Brooks	1	5	4		1
Henry Street	1				
Angus McDugal	1		1		
Malcolm Buie (Juniper)	1	1	5		
Ann Dey	2	2	4		
Duncan Buie (Taylor)	1	6	3		
Robert Honeycut	1	1	2		
Joseph Duckworth	1	1	4		1
Mary McIntosh			1		
Sarah Newman		1	1		
Ann Wicker			1		
Henrietta Collins			4		1
Samuel Darke	3	2	3		
John McNiel	3	2	5		11
John Cox	1	3	7		
Jasper Billings	1	1	1		
Soloman Barrett	1	1	1		
Joshua Denby	1	2	3		
John Patterson	3		2		1
Arch'd Patterson	1		2		
Amount Carried Forw'd	769	893	1438	12	36[illegible]

164

Names of heads of Families — Moore County					
Amount brought Forward	769	893	1438	12	366
Donald Patterson	1				
Duncan Johnston	3	2	4		
John Patterson	1	1	1		
Arch'd Patterson	2		2		
Norman McDuffee	2	3	1		
Donald McLaine	1	1	5		
John McLaine	1		3		
John McArthur	1				2
Flora McMillen		1	2		
Duncan Patterson	1	3	2		
Katy Clark	1	1	2		
Hugh McDonald	1				
Jesse Cooper	1	3	2		
Bartley McFarland	1				
Dickson Temple	1				
Thomas Wood	1	2	3		
Benjamin Stephens	1	1	3		
John Blanchet Jr.	2	1	3		
John Nelson	1	1	2		
William Harding (Buck)	1	2	4		
Drury Brewer	1	3	3		
William Harding	1	4	4		
Sarah Davis			1		3
John Goldston	1		2		
Philip Cheek	1				
John Stinson	2	1	3		
James Smith	1				
Duncan McDugal	1	1	3		
Malcolm Baker	1				
Daniel McIver (BSmith)	1		1		
John McLaine (Gaster)	1	2	4		
Nimrod Brewer	1				
Robert Bird	1	2	3		
William Reed	1	3	4		
John McDugal	2	2	3		
Mary Baker			1		
John Campbell	1				
Malcolm Sellars	2		2		
Aron Oliver	2		1		
Daniel Campbell	1	2	4		
Daniel McKenzie	1	2	1		
Daniel Ragsdell	1				
John Watson	1				
Mead Jordan	1	1	2		
William Smith	1	2	3		
Benjamin Yarborough	1	1	1		
Amount Carried Over	821	941	1523	12	371

Schedule of the whole number of persons

165

Names of heads of Families. Moore County.	Free white males of sixteen years and upwards including heads of families	Free white males under sixteen years	Free white females including heads of families	All other free persons	Slaves
Amount brought over	821	941	1523	12	371
John Craig	1				
Laurence Strauther	1		2		
Moses Keys	1				
John McAuley	1		1		
John Stutts	1		1		
Agnes McDuffee		1	2		
Isaac Dun	1	2	4		
Malcolm McLeod	3	1	3		
Robert Lax	1	2	2		
Christian Morrison		1	3		
Archd Gillies	1				
Kenneth McLeod	1	1	2		
Betsy McKenzie		2	2		
Augustine Lunsford	1				
Donald McDonald	1		1		
Silvanus Jones	1	3	5		
Duncan McIntosh	1		2		
Alexr McLeod	3	1	2		
George Brazel	1	3	3		
Thomas Bulling	1	1	2		
John Minyard	1	2	3		
John Hunsucker	1	3	3		
John Morris	2				
Edward Moore Sr	2	1	2		
William Cagle	1	1	2		
	849	966	1570	12	371
Add to William B. Whitford		2			
639 Heads of families	849	968	1570	12	371

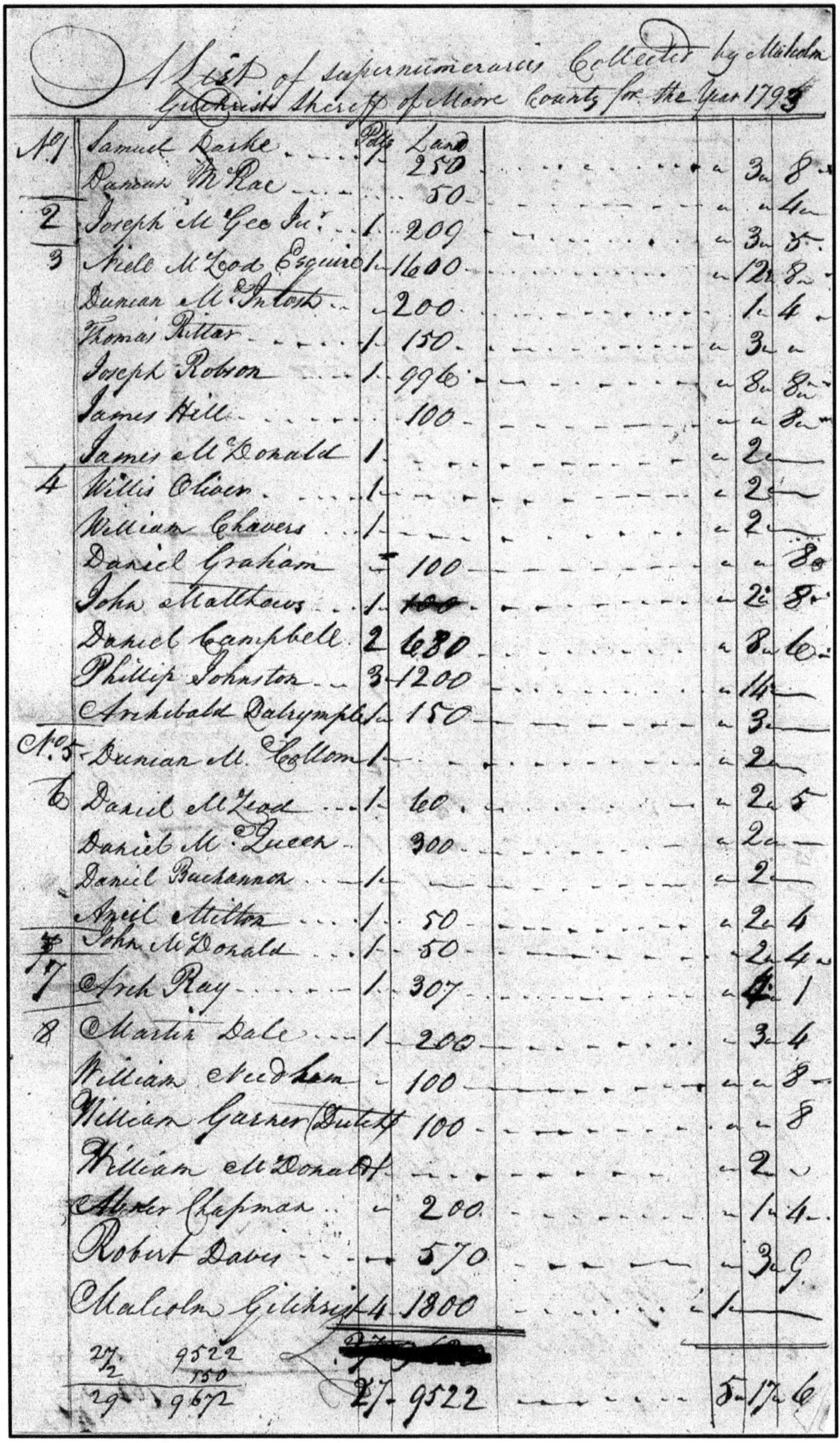

A List of supernumeraries Collected by Malcolm Gilchrist Sheriff of Moore County for the Year 1793

No.	Name	Pol[l]s	Land	£	s	d
No 1	Samuel Darke	1	250		3	8
	Duncan McRae		50			4
2	Joseph McGee Jr.	1	209		3	5
3	Neill McLeod Esquire	1	1600		12	8
	Duncan McIntosh		200		1	4
	Thomas Ritter	1	150		3	
	Joseph Robson	1	996		8	8
	James Hill		100			8
	James McDonald	1			2	
4	Willis Oliver	1			2	
	William Chavers	1			2	
	Daniel Graham		100			8
	John Matthews	1	~~100~~		2	8
	Daniel Campbell	2	680		8	6
	Phillip Johnston	3	1200		14	
	Archibald Dalrymple	1	150		3	
No 5	Duncan McCollom	1			2	
6	Daniel McLeod	1	60		2	5
	Daniel McQueen		300		2	
	Daniel Buchannon	1			2	
	Aneil Milton	1	50		2	4
~~7~~	John McDonald	1	50		2	4
7	Arch Ray	1	307		4	1
8	Martin Dale	1	200		3	4
	William Needham		100			8
	William Garner (Dutch)		100			8
	William McDonald	1			2	
	Alexr Chapman		200		1	4
	Robert Davis		570		3	9
	Malcolm Gilchrist	4	1800	1		
	27 / 2 — 29	9522 / 150 — 9672				
	£	27	9522	5	17	6

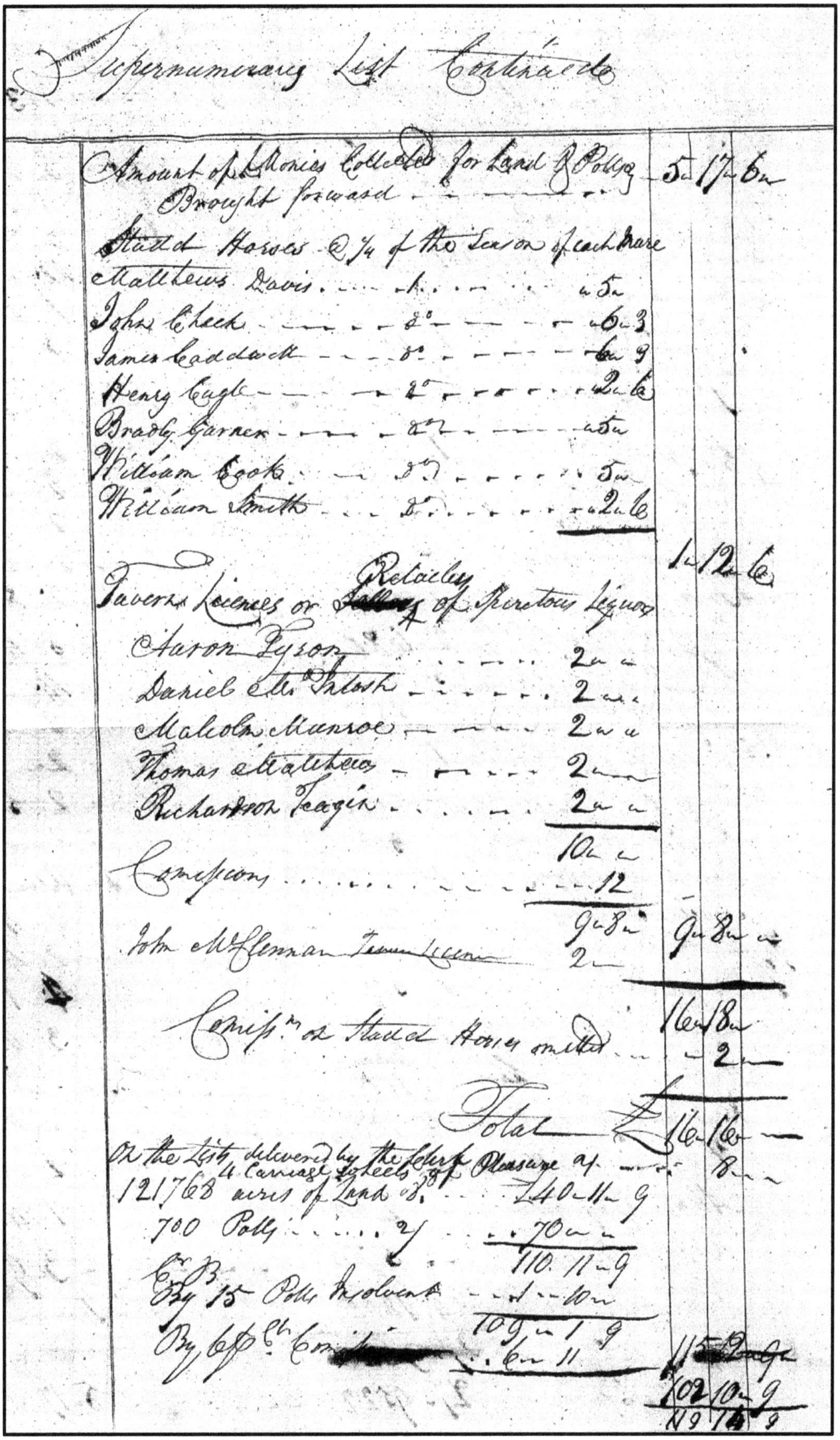

Supernumerary List Continued

Amount of Monies Collected for Land & Polls Brought forward		5	17 6
Stud Horses @ ¼ of the Season of each Mare			
Matthews Davis ... 1	5		
John Cheek ... do	6 3		
James Caddack ... do	6 9		
Henry Cagle ... do	2 6		
Bradly Garner ... do	5		
William Cook ... do	5		
William Smith ... do	2 6		
		1	12 6
Tavern Licences or Retailer of Spiritous Liquor			
Aaron Tyson	2		
Daniel McIntosh	2		
Malcolm Munroe	2		
Thomas Matthews	2		
Richardson Feagin	2		
	10		
Commissions	12		
	9 8		
John McLennan Tavern Licence	2	9	8
		16	18
Comiss.n on Stud Horses omitted			2
Total		£16	16
On the List delivered by the Clerk 4 Carriage Wheels of Pleasure at			8
121768 acres of Land @	£40 11 9		
700 Polls ... 2/	70		
	110 11 9		
Cr B			
By 15 Polls Insolvent	1 10		
	109 1 9		
By 6 p Ct Comis	6 11	115 [illegible]	
		102	10 9
		N9	14 9

On settling the following Insolvents were allowed the Sheriff for 1793

	Persons Names	Poll		
1	Marmaduke Maples	1		2 —
	Burrell Maples	1	—	2 —
2	Theophilus Eddins	1	—	2 —
	William Parrin	1	—	2 —
	Sion ~~[illegible]~~ Tarleton	1	—	2 —
	Harrison Cooper	1	—	2 —
3	James Muse	1	—	2 —
4	John Elkins	1	—	2 —
	David Holms	1	—	2 —
5	Aaron Oliver Jnr	1	—	2 —
6	James McCall	1	—	2 —
	Ambrose Brown	1	—	2 —
	William Keys	1	—	2 —
	John Thomas	1	—	2 —
8	William Newton	1	—	2 —
	Amt. of Insolvents	£1	—	10 —

these undernamed persons must Be added to the Supernumerary otherwise was ~~[illegible]~~ omitted By mistake

			s	d
ambros Brewer	100 Land and 1 pole		2	8
Jessie upton	50	1	2	4

North Carolina
Wake County } August 8th 1794

I Malcomb Gilchrist Esqr
Sheriff of the County of Moore for the year 1793
do on this 8th day of August 1793 make oath
and declare that the Lists by me now given in is
to the best of my knowledge & belief complete
perfect & entire & contains the full amount of all
monies by me or for me received or which ought
to have been received of the Public Taxes for
of the County afores^d for the year 1793 & that I have
truly & faithfully governed myself by the Act of Assembly
entitled an act to amend the Revenue Laws of the State
passed December 1791: without favor affection or
partiality to the best of my knowledge & belief

So help me God.

Malcolm Gilchrist Sheriff

Sworn to & subscribed before
me this 8th Day of Aug 1794
J. Craven Comptr

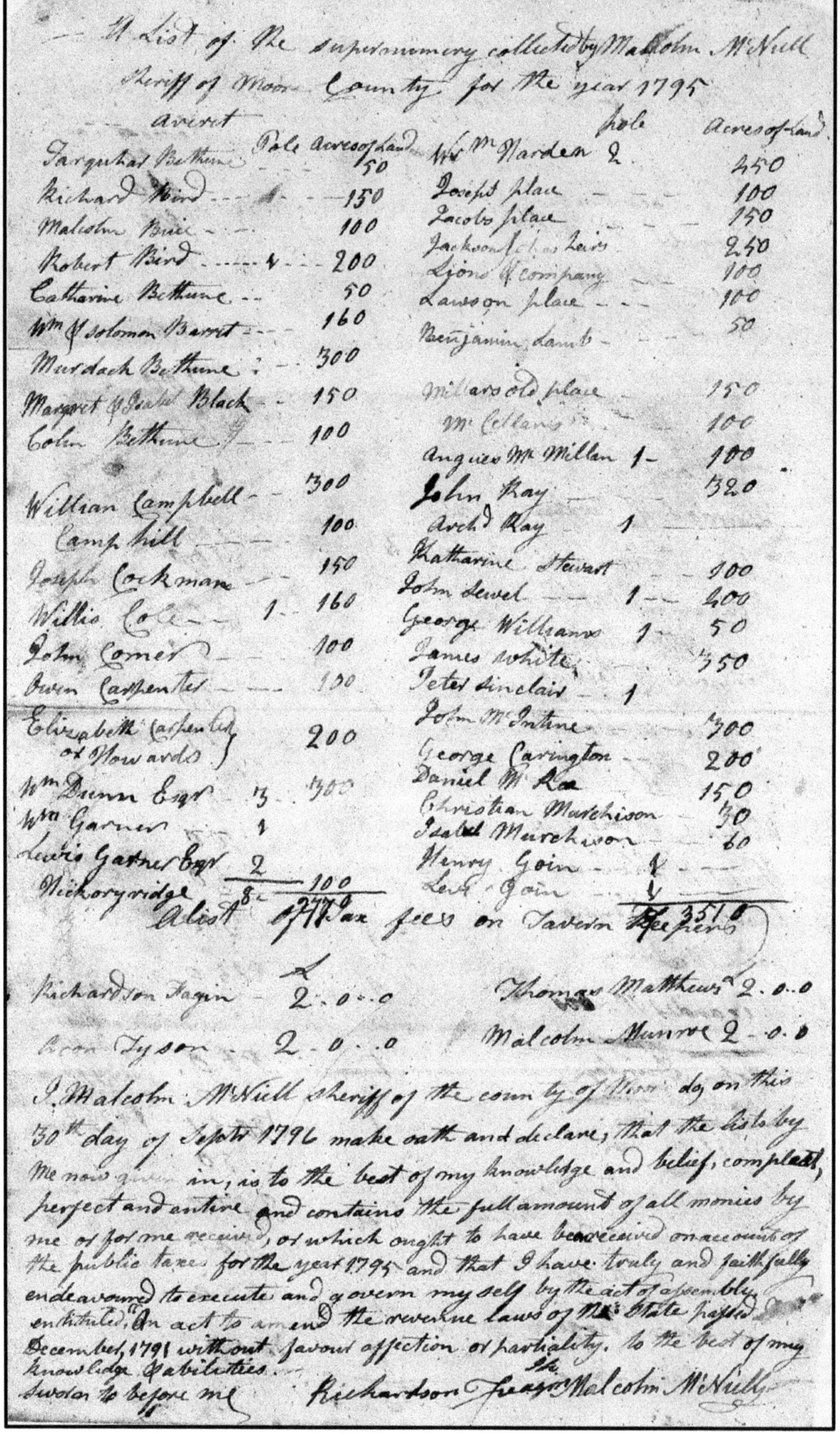

A List of the supernumery collected by Malcolm McNeill Sheriff of Moore County for the year 1795

Arrest	Pole	Acres of land		Pole	Acres of land
Farquhar Bethune		50	Wm McNarden	2	250
Richard Bird	1	150	Joseph place		100
Malcolm Buie		100	Jacobs place		150
Robert Bird	1	200	Jackson Johns heirs		250
Catharine Bethune		50	Lyons & company		100
Wm & Solomon Barrot		160	Lawson place		100
Murdach Bethune		300	Benjamin Lamb		50
Margaret & Isabel Black		150	Millars old place		150
Colin Bethune		100	McLellans		100
			Angus McMillan	1	100
William Campbell		300	John Kay		320
Camp hill		100	Archd Kay	1	
Joseph Cockman		150	Katharine Stewart		100
Willis Cole	1	160	John Sewel	1	200
John Comer		100	George Williams	1	50
Owen Carpenter		100	James White		350
			Peter Sinclair	1	
Elizabeth Carpenter or Howards		200	John McIntire		300
			George Carington		200
Wm Dunn Esqr	3	300	Daniel McRea		150
			Christian Murchison		30
Wm Garner	1		Isabel Murchison		60
Lewis Garner Esqr	2		Henry Goin	1	
Hickoryridge		100	Lewis Goin	1	
	8	2770			3510

A list of tax fees on Tavern Keepers

	£		£
Richardson Fagin	2..0..0	Thomas Matthews	2..0..0
Aaron Tyson	2..0..0	Malcolm Munroe	2..0..0

I, Malcolm McNeill sheriff of the county of Moore do on this 30th day of Septr 1796 make oath and declare, that the lists by me now given in, is to the best of my knowledge and belief, compleat, perfect and entire and contains the full amount of all monies by me or for me received, or which ought to have been received on account of the public taxes for the year 1795 and that I have truly and faithfully endeavoured to execute and govern my self by the act of assembly entituled "An act to amend the revenue laws of this State passed December, 1795 without favour affection or partiality, to the best of my knowledge & abilities.

Sworn to before me Richardson Feagin JP Malcolm McNeill

A List of the supernumery Collected By Malcolm McNiell sheriff of Moore County for the year 1795

	Polls	Acres of Land
John McCollum	1	100
Archibald Baker		100
Alexander McMillan		100
James Melton	1	100
Donald McRae		100
Nancy McLeod		100
Mary McDuffie		200
Wm Moore		250
Murdoch McSwain		150
John Martin	1	100
Benjamin Melton		100
McSwain		250
Kenneth McKenzie		50
Angus McDonald	1	50
Mary & Niel McLain		79
William McKenzie		150
Hector McKinnon		100
Charles McKinnon		50
John McAulay	1	300
Alexander McLeod	1	150
~~Thomas Moore~~		
John Dunlap	1	560
~~Archd McLaughlin~~	1	50
Jesse Upton		
Niel McLeod	1	3051
Jenny Peterson		50
Thomas Marden Perkins	24	2500
John Rutherford		400
Shadrach Rogers	1	250
Joseph Robeson	1	1015
	35	10465

Acres Land
10465
3510
13975
2779
16754
35 Polls
17
52 Polls

A List of the supernumery returned from Moore County for the year 1797

	Pole	Acres		Poles	
Bryant Boroughs	3	350	Isaac Dunn		100
John Quimby		100	Captn McKee		100
Solomon Barret	4	265	Samuel Dunn	2	600
Jesse Bean	1	200	Zachariah Davis		600
Jacob Cagle	1	150	Hardy Davis	1	825
Joab Cheek		230	Samuel Elkins	1	
George Caringer Junr	4		Effy McDonald		250
Grisey Carmichael		240	Jesse Henly		150
Colin Campbel		100	Drury Joiner	1	300
Daniel Caddle	1	300	Richardson Fagin	3	1025
Benjn Caddle	1	200	John McLain	1	200
Wm McAulay	1	384	Wm Moore		250
Wm Mainess	1	150	John McDonald	1	200
Barbara Murchison		100	Robert Moore	1	
Hector McNeill	1	150	Thos H Perkins	17	2500
James Riddle		100	Wm Richardson	1	325
John Ritter	1	350	Joseph Robeson	1	800
Niell Smith	1		Christopher Stutts		500
Nancy Williamson		147	Jeremiah Wilson		100
James Collins	1	200	Willis Oliver Junr	1	100
Samuel Hughs		150	Wm Harden	2	450
Marcum Glascock	4		Niell McLeod	1	150 9525
Niell McLeod & others	16	30246 / 34112		34	

95000 acres sold as the property of of Allen Morison & Co the 17th of Septr 1798 for the tax amount of sale after deducting the expence of advertising three pounds five shilling & six pence
120000 sold for the tax 17th Septr 1798 formerly the property of David Allison the present proprietor unknown amount of sale after deducting the expence of advertising two pounds seventeen shillings & six pence halfpenny

Malcolm McNeill Sheriff

Stud Horses

Niell McLeod one at twenty shillings the season

List of Tax fees

	L	S	D		L	S	D
Donald Paterson	2	0	0	Richardson Fagin	2	0	0
Marten Hall	2	0	0	Malcolm Munroe	2	0	0
Malcolm McNeill	2	0	0	Nicholas Hall	2	0	0
Aaron Tyson	2	0	0	John Hillyard	2	0	0
Murdoch Bethune	2	0	0	John Johnson	2	0	0

I Malcolm McNeill Sheriff of the County of Moore do on this twenty ninth day of Septr 1798 make oath and declare, that the lists by me now given in is to the best of my knowledge & belief, complete, perfect & entire & contains the full amount of all monies by me or for me received, or which ought to have been received for the year 1797 & that I have truly & faithfully endeavour to execute & govern my self by the act of assembly, entitled, "an act to amend the revenue laws of this State passed December 1791 without favor affection or partiality, to the best of my knowledge and abilities.

So Help Me God

Malcolm McNeill

Sworn to before us

Arch. Ray J. P.

John Blue J. P.

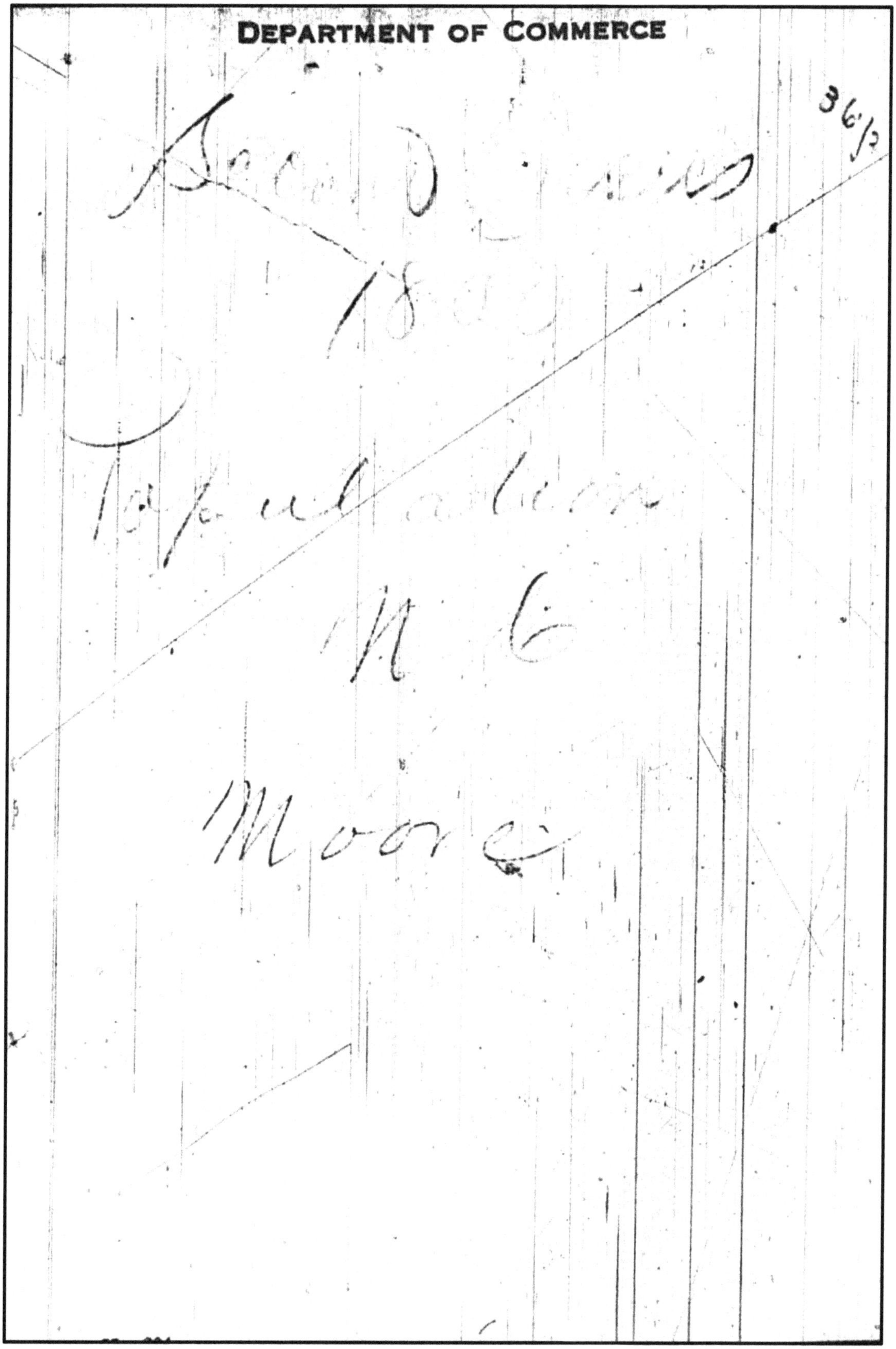
DEPARTMENT OF COMMERCE

36½

[illegible]

1800

Population

N C

Moore

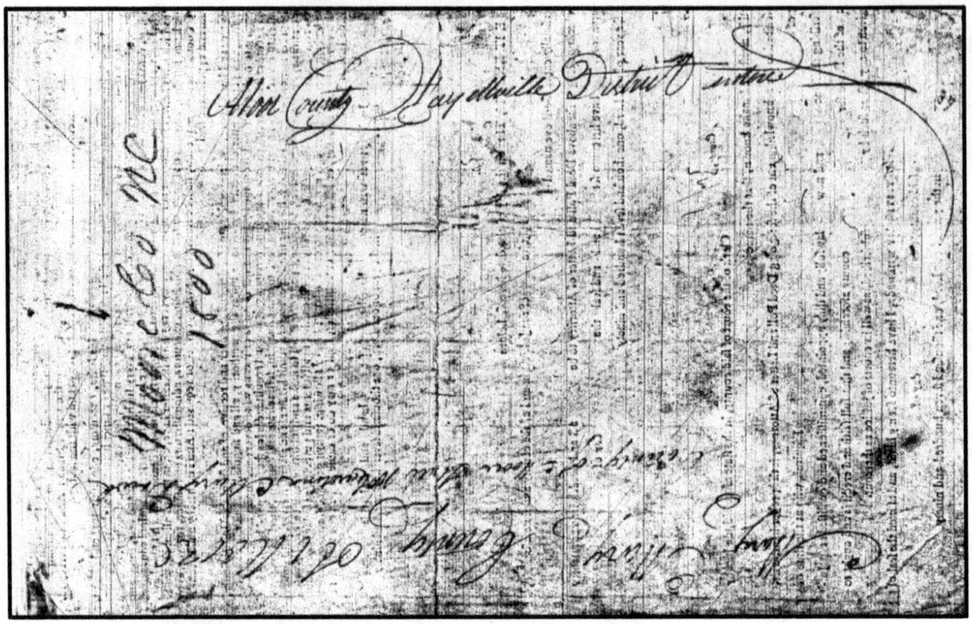
Moore County Fayetteville District

Moore Co NC
1800

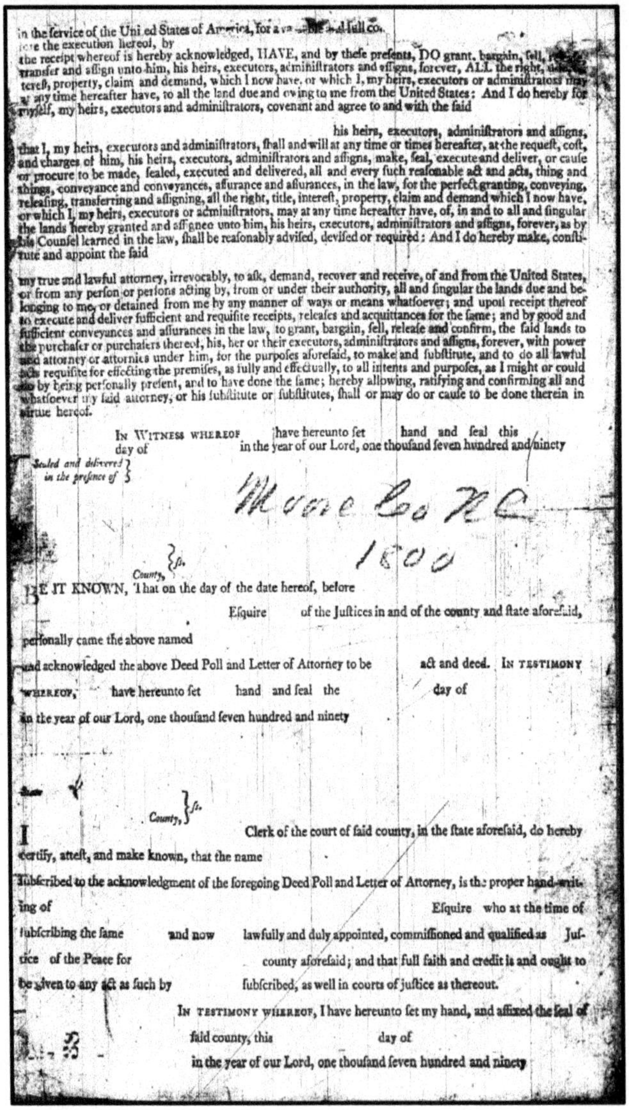
in the ſervice of the Uni ed States of America, for a va[illegible] full co[illegible]
[illegible]e the execution hereof, by
the receipt whereof is hereby acknowledged, HAVE, and by theſe preſents, DO grant, bargain, ſell, [illegible] transfer and aſſign unto him, his heirs, executors, adminiſtrators and aſſigns, forever, ALL the right, [illegible] tereſt, property, claim and demand, which I now have, or which I, my heirs, executors or adminiſtrators may at any time hereafter have, to all the land due and owing to me from the United States: And I do hereby for myſelf, my heirs, executors and adminiſtrators, covenant and agree to and with the ſaid

his heirs, executors, adminiſtrators and aſſigns, that I, my heirs, executors and adminiſtrators, ſhall and will at any time or times hereafter, at the requeſt, coſt, and charges of him, his heirs, executors, adminiſtrators and aſſigns, make, ſeal, execute and deliver, or cauſe or procure to be made, ſealed, executed and delivered, all and every ſuch reaſonable act and acts, thing and things, conveyance and conveyances, aſſurance and aſſurances, in the law, for the perfect granting, conveying, releaſing, transferring and aſſigning, all the right, title, intereſt, property, claim and demand which I now have, or which I, my heirs, executors or adminiſtrators, may at any time hereafter have, of, in and to all and ſingular the lands hereby granted and aſſigned unto him, his heirs, executors, adminiſtrators and aſſigns, forever, as by his Counſel learned in the law, ſhall be reaſonably adviſed, deviſed or required: And I do hereby make, conſtitute and appoint the ſaid

my true and lawful attorney, irrevocably, to aſk, demand, recover and receive, of and from the United States, or from any perſon or perſons acting by, from or under their authority, all and ſingular the lands due and belonging to me, or detained from me by any manner of ways or means whatſoever; and upon receipt thereof to execute and deliver ſufficient and requiſite receipts, releaſes and acquittances for the ſame; and by good and ſufficient conveyances and aſſurances in the law, to grant, bargain, ſell, releaſe and confirm, the ſaid lands to the purchaſer or purchaſers thereof, his, her or their executors, adminiſtrators and aſſigns, forever, with power and attorney or attornies under him, for the purpoſes aforeſaid, to make and ſubſtitute, and to do all lawful acts requiſite for effecting the premiſes, as fully and effectually, to all intents and purpoſes, as I might or could do by being perſonally preſent, and to have done the ſame; hereby allowing, ratifying and confirming all and whatſoever my ſaid attorney, or his ſubſtitute or ſubſtitutes, ſhall or may do or cauſe to be done therein in virtue hereof.

IN WITNESS WHEREOF have hereunto ſet hand and ſeal this day of in the year of our Lord, one thouſand ſeven hundred and ninety

Sealed and delivered in the preſence of

Moore Co NC
1800

County, ſs.

BE IT KNOWN, That on the day of the date hereof, before Eſquire of the Juſtices in and of the county and ſtate aforeſaid, perſonally came the above named and acknowledged the above Deed Poll and Letter of Attorney to be act and deed. IN TESTIMONY WHEREOF, have hereunto ſet hand and ſeal the day of in the year of our Lord, one thouſand ſeven hundred and ninety

County, ſs.

I Clerk of the court of ſaid county, in the ſtate aforeſaid, do hereby certify, atteſt, and make known, that the name ſubſcribed to the acknowledgment of the foregoing Deed Poll and Letter of Attorney, is the proper hand-writing of Eſquire who at the time of ſubſcribing the ſame and now lawfully and duly appointed, commiſſioned and qualified as Juſtice of the Peace for county aforeſaid; and that full faith and credit is and ought to be given to any act as ſuch by ſubſcribed, as well in courts of juſtice as thereout.

IN TESTIMONY WHEREOF, I have hereunto ſet my hand, and affixed the ſeal of ſaid county, this day of in the year of our Lord, one thouſand ſeven hundred and ninety

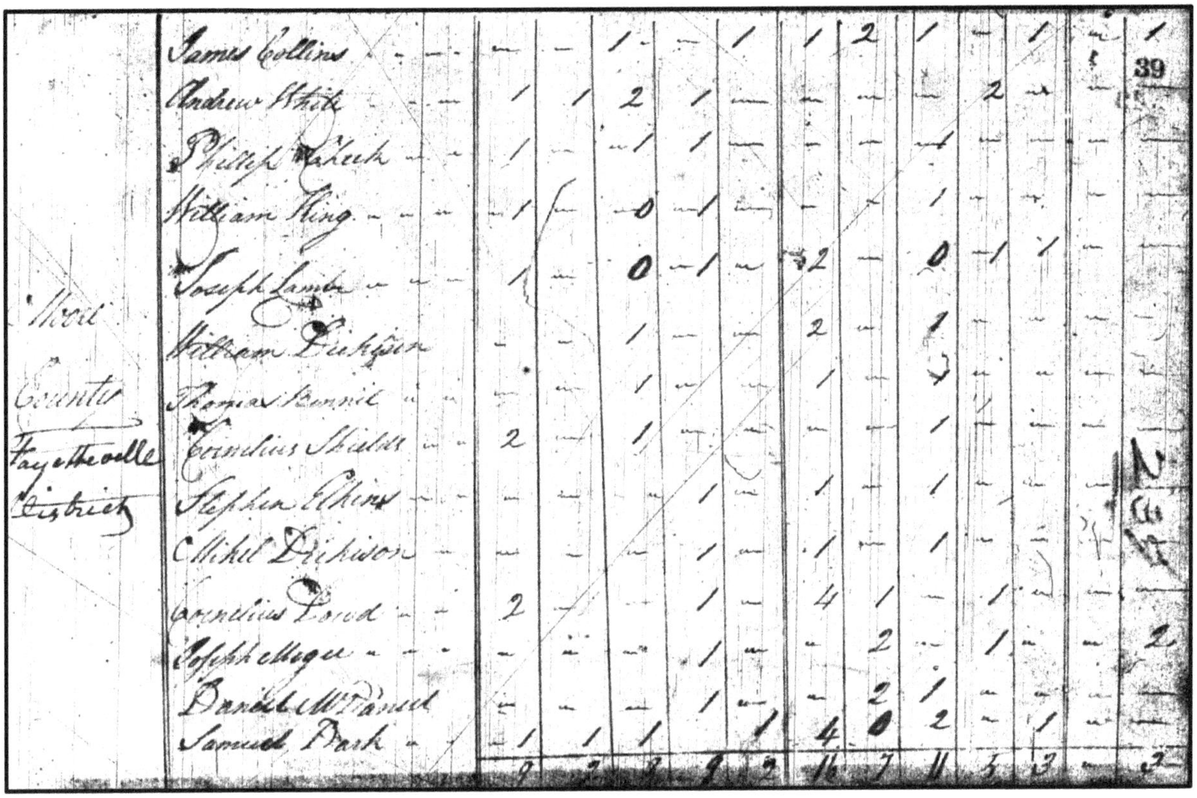

Moore County Fayetteville District

													39
Moore County Fayetteville District	James Collins	–	–	1	–	1	1	2	1	–	1	–	1
	Andrew White	1	1	2	1	–	–	–	–	2	–	–	–
	Phillip McLeod	1	–	1	1	–	–	–	1	–	–	–	–
	William King	1	–	0	1	–	–	–	1	–	–	–	–
	Joseph Lamb	1	–	0	1	–	2	–	2	1	1	–	–
	William Dickson	–	–	1	–	–	2	–	1	–	–	–	–
	Thomas Bunnil	–	–	1	–	–	1	–	1	–	–	–	–
	Cornelius Shields	2	–	1	–	–	–	–	1	–	–	–	–
	Stephen Elkins	–	–	–	1	–	1	–	1	–	–	–	–
	Mikel Dickison	–	–	–	1	–	1	–	1	–	–	–	–
	Cornelius Lloyd	2	–	–	1	–	4	1	–	1	–	–	–
	Joseph Mague	–	–	–	1	–	–	2	–	1	–	–	2
	Daniel McDaniel	–	–	–	1	–	–	2	1	–	–	–	–
	Samuel Park	1	1	1	–	1	4	0	2	–	1	–	–
		9	2	8	9	2	16	7	11	5	3	–	2

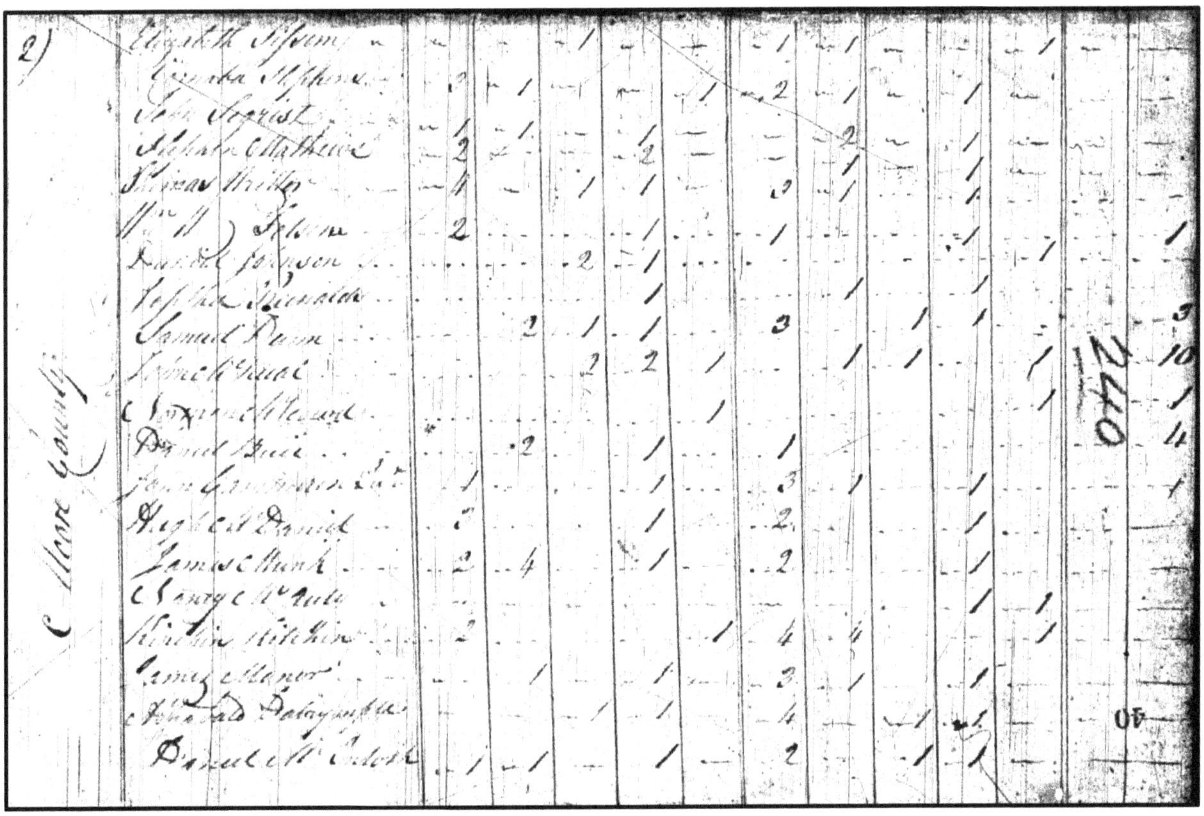

2)	Elizabeth Tyson	–	–	1	–	–	1	1	–	1	–	–	
	Lavinia Stephens	3	1	–	–	1	2	1	1	–	–	–	
	John Seagrist	1	1	–	1	–	–	1	1	–	–	–	
	Stephen Mathews	2	–	–	2	–	–	2	–	1	–	–	
	Thomas Waller	4	–	1	1	–	3	1	–	1	–	–	
	Wm H. Tyson	2	–	–	1	–	1	–	1	–	–	–	1
	Daniel Johnson	–	–	2	1	–	–	1	–	1	1	–	
	Joseph McDonald	–	–	–	1	–	–	1	–	1	–	–	
Moore County	Samuel Dunn	–	2	1	1	–	3	–	1	1	–	–	3
	Daniel McNeal	–	–	2	2	1	–	1	1	–	1	–	10
	[illegible] McLeod	–	–	–	–	1	–	–	–	–	1	–	1
	Daniel Buie	–	2	–	1	–	1	–	–	–	–	–	4
	John Sanders	1	–	–	1	–	3	1	–	1	–	–	1
	Hugh McDaniel	3	–	–	1	–	2	–	–	1	–	–	
	James Munk	2	4	–	1	–	2	–	–	1	–	–	
	George McNatt	–	–	–	–	–	–	–	–	1	1	–	
	Kinchin Hitchin	2	–	–	–	1	4	4	–	1	1	–	
	James Manor	–	1	–	1	–	3	1	–	1	–	–	
	Archibald Dalrymple	–	–	1	1	–	4	–	1	1	–	–	40
	Daniel McIntosh	1	1	–	1	–	2	–	1	1	–	–	

Moore County

Nancy Campbell	1		2	2					1	1		41
Malcolm Munroe	2	2		1		4		1	1			
Moses Carraway	2			1		1			1			
Francis Bullock	1		1	1		2	2		1			
Archabald McDugal	1				1	1			1			5
Ignatious Wadsworth			1			2		1				
Daniel Caddle	4			1			1		1			
Isaack Smith				1		1		1				
Adam White		1	2		1	3			1			5
John McIver		1	1							1		1
John Stewart	4			1		1	1		1			15
George Cox	3			1		1		1				1
Alexander McLeod		1		1						1		1
Morris Morrison	3			1			1		1			2
William Cox	1	2		1		4			1			6
Ezekel Sidebottom	1			1		1			1			
Archabald Black	3	1		1			1	1				
William King	3	1		1		1			1			1
Anne Merrit	1	2	2	1			1	2		1		
	51	28	17	33	6	31	21	11	26	14	—	[illegible]

Moore County

Willis Cole	3	2	[illegible]	1	[illegible]	1	[illegible]	[illegible]	[illegible]	[illegible]	[illegible]	
Benjamin Shields		1	2		1		1			1		
Alexander Carrell				1		1			1			
Edmond Wade			1	1					1			15
Richard Seal				1	1		1	1		1		22
James Dowd	1			1		1		1				
John Overton		2		1		2						1
John Carrell Sr.			3		1			1	1	1		3
Robert Dickison		2	1		1		1			1		
William Richardson	2	2		1		2			1			
James Stuart	2	1		1		1			1			1
Elisha Bettis				1								1
Samuel Womble	3	1		1		2			1			
George Brewer	2			1		1			1			
Edward E[illegible]	3			1		2	1		1			
Hannon Brewer	2			1		2	0		1			
William Brewer	2			1					1			
James Handerik			1	1		2		1		1		42

Moore County

Jeab Chark	2	—	—	1	—	1	—	1	—	—	43	1
Lewis Phillips	4	2	—	1	—	1	—	—	1	—	—	—
Patients Phillips	—	—	1	2	—	—	—	—	—	1	—	—
Elizabeth Hancock	1	—	—	—	—	—	1	—	—	1	—	—
Robert King	2	—	—	1	—	2	2	—	1	1	—	—
Walter Ashmore	—	—	—	1	—	—	—	—	—	—	—	—
Lewis Tempely	2	—	—	1	—	1	—	1	—	—	—	—
John Carrell Jun	—	—	—	1	—	2	—	—	1	—	—	1
Mark Phillips	1	2	—	1	—	1	1	—	1	—	—	—
Thomas Muse	2	—	—	1	—	2	—	—	1	—	—	—
Kindred Muse	1	—	1	—	—	1	—	1	1	1	244	—
Malcolm Gilchrist	2	2	—	—	1	1	—	2	—	1	—	—
Peter Carrell	—	—	1	1	—	2	—	1	—	—	—	5
Milly Dickson	—	—	2	—	1	2	1	—	—	1	—	1
Rev. Williams	—	—	—	1	—	—	—	—	—	—	—	1
James Fry	1	—	—	1	—	—	—	—	1	—	48	—
John Crichton	2	1	—	—	1	2	2	3	—	1	—	—
	40	18	13	26?	7	3?	11	10?	17	1?	—	11?

4)

Moore County

John Wagner	3	2	1	—	1	1	2	1	1	—	—	3
Thomas Tyson	2	2	3	—	1	2	—	1	1	—	—	3
Joseph Duckworth	—	2	—	—	1	1	1	—	—	1	—	8
Nathan Thomas	1	1	2	—	1	3	1	2	1	—	—	—
Duncan McIntosh	1	—	—	1	—	—	—	1	—	1	—	—
Thomas Gilmore	—	1	—	—	1	—	—	1	1	—	—	—
James Jackson	3	1	1	1	—	1	—	—	1	—	244	—
James Hobson	2	1	—	1	—	3	—	—	1	—	—	—
Patrick McLennan	—	—	1	2	—	1	—	—	—	1	—	4
George Jackson	3	—	—	1	—	—	—	1	—	—	—	11
Evan Lawler	—	1	—	1	—	2	—	—	1	—	—	—
Thomas Mallet	—	1	1	—	1	—	—	—	—	1	—	1
Malcolm McKinnon	1	1	1	—	1	1	1	—	—	1	—	—
Daniel Gillis	1	—	—	—	1	2	1	—	1	—	—	—
James Kelley	—	—	—	—	1	—	—	1	—	1	—	—
Thomas Collins	2	—	—	—	1	3	1	1	1	—	—	—
Elijah Jackson	—	1	1	—	1	3	2	1	1	—	—	44
James Collins	—	—	—	1	—	1	—	1	—	—	—	—

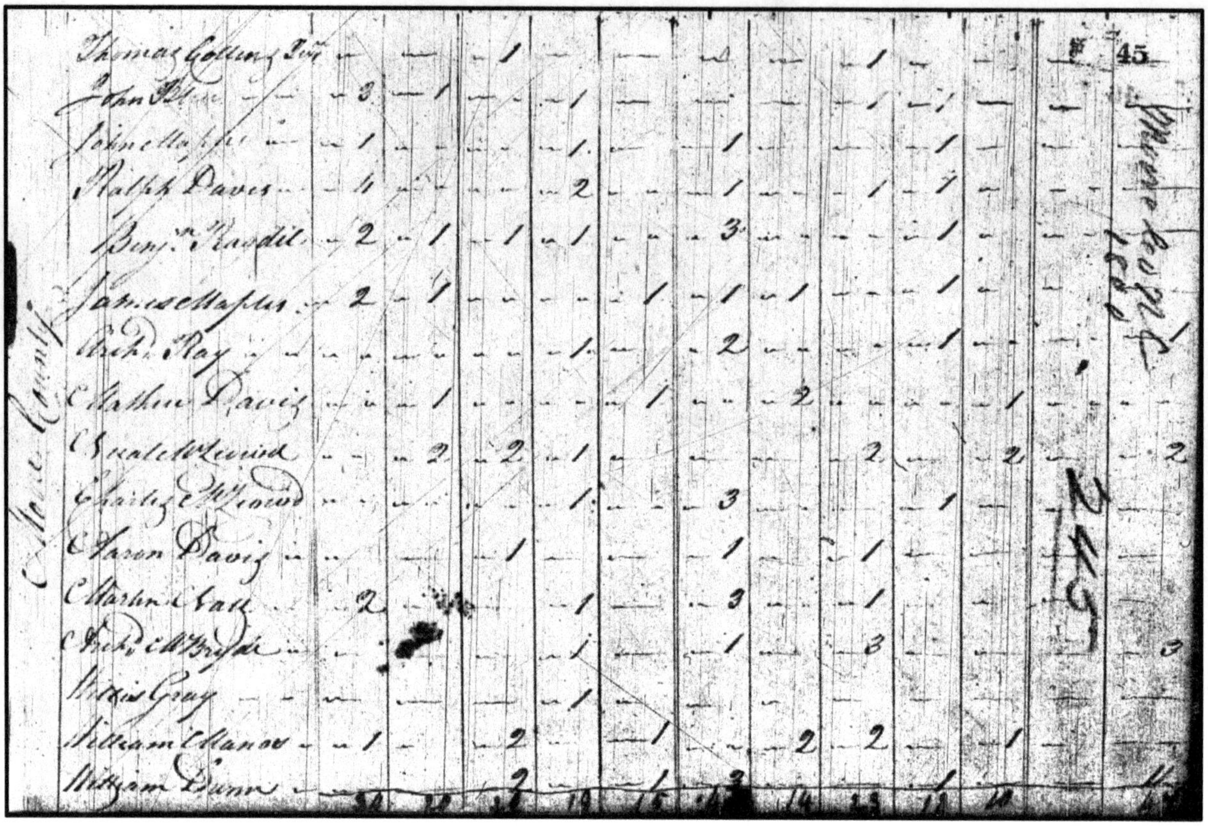

45

Moore County

Thomas Collins Jur
John Blue
John Maples
Ralph Davis
Benjn Raudle
James Maples
Archd Ray
Nathan Davis
Bealel McLeod
Charles McLeod
Aaron Davis
Martin Cass
Archd McBride
Willis Gray
William Manor
William Dunn

Moore Co NC 1800

245

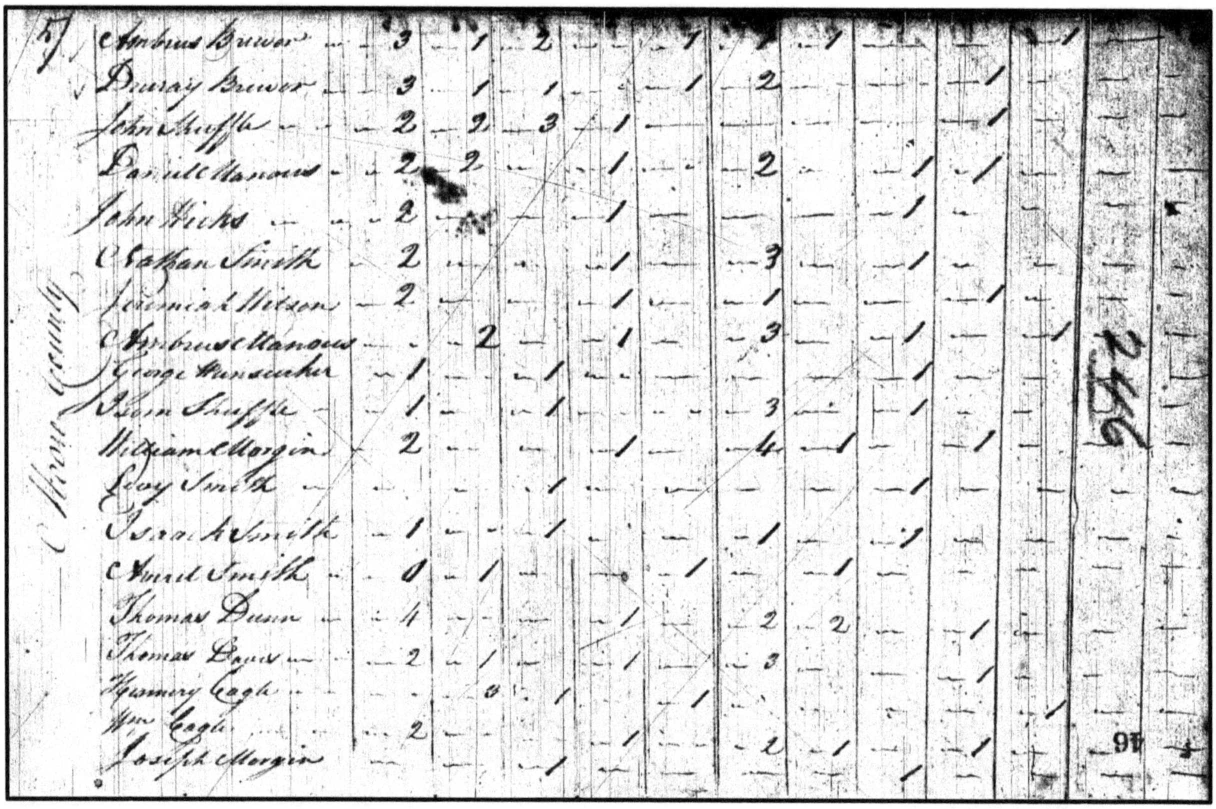

Moore County

Ambrus Brewer
Durray Brewer
John Shuffle
Daniel Manows
John Hicks
Nathan Smith
Jeremiah Wilson
Ambruse Manows
George Hunsucker
Benn Shuffle
William Morgin
Eday Smith
Isaac Smith
Anuel Smith
Thomas Dunn
Thomas Dunn
Hymery Cagle
Wm Cagle
Joseph Morgin

246

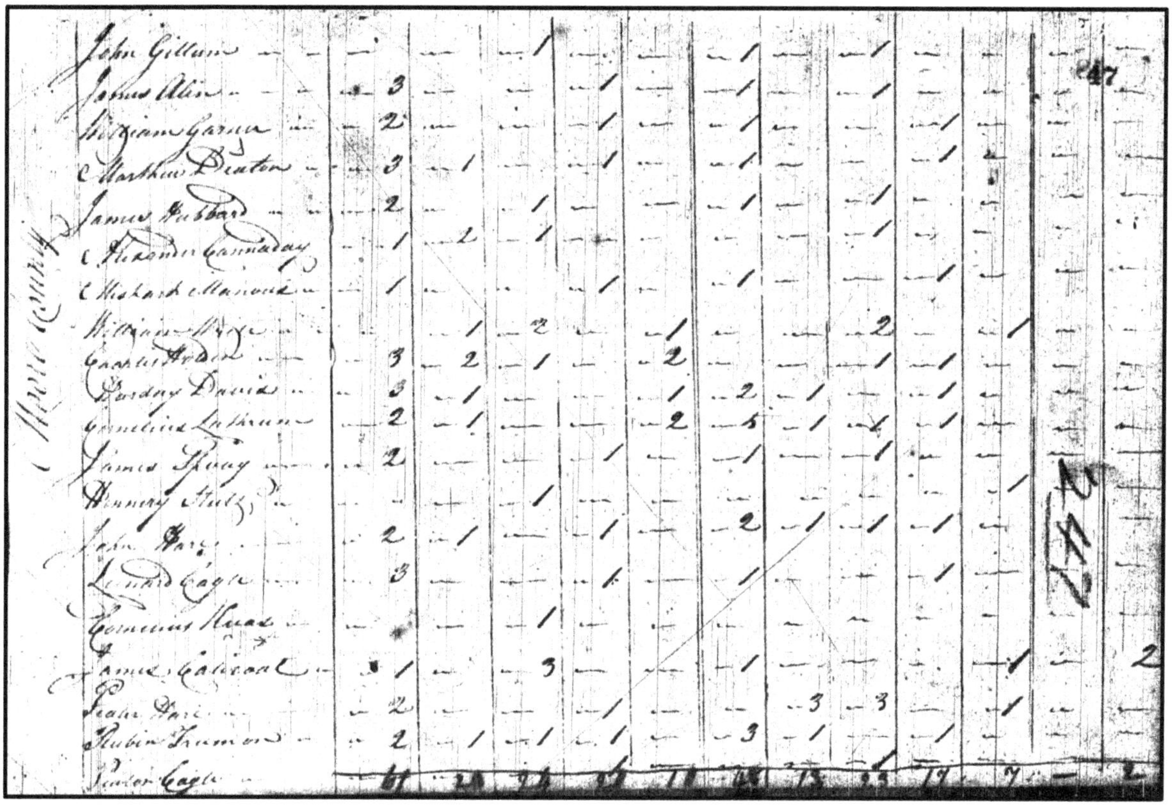

Moore County

John Gillum			1			1		1				
Joshua Allen	3			1		1		1				
William Garner	2			1		1			1			
Matthew Deaton	3	1		1		1			1			
James Hubbard	2		1			1		1				
Alexander Cannaday	1	2	1					1				
Mishack Manous	1			1		1			1			
William Wize		1	2		1			2		1		
Charles Arden	3	2	1		2			1	1			
Barclay Davis	3	1			1	2	1		1			
Cornelius Latham	2	1			2	5	1	1	1			
James Spivey	2			1		1		1				
Henry Stutz			1							1		
John Ware	2	1		1		2	1	1	1			
Leonard Cagle	3			1		1			1			
Edmund Head			1									
James Caldwell	1		3			1				1		2
Isaac Ware	2			1			3	3		1		
Reuben Freeman	2	1	1	1		3	1					
Tudor Cagle	61	29	24	17	18	23	13	23	19	7		2

47

247

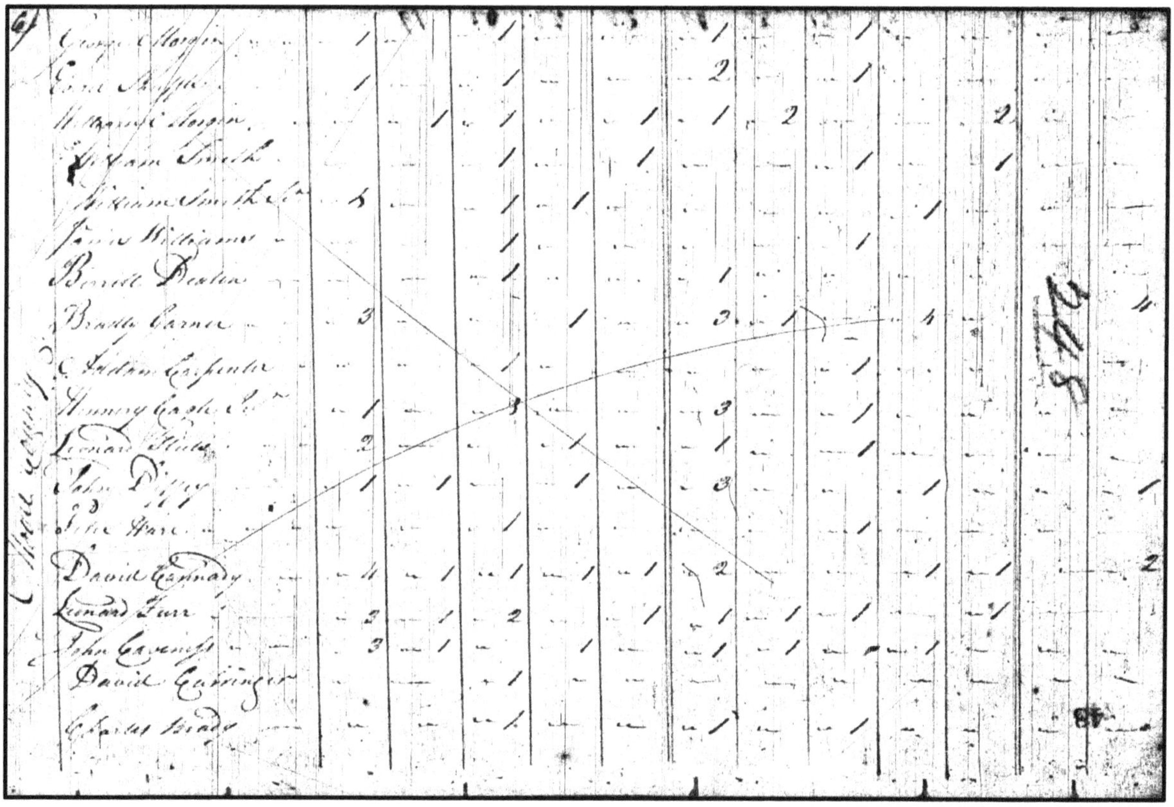

6

Moore County

George Morgan	1					1		1				
Enos Boyd	1		1			2		1				
William Morgan		1	1		1	1	2			2		
William Smith			1		1			1		1		
William Smith Sr	5		1	1				1				
James Williams			1					1				
Bennet Deaton			1			1		1				
Bradley Garner	3			1		3	1		4			4
Adam Carpenter								1				
Henry Cagle Sr	1		3			3		1				
Leonard Stutz	2			1		1		1				
John Dizey	1	1		1		3			1			1
John Ware			1					1				
David Cannaday	4	1	1	1	1	2		1	1			2
Leonard Furr	2	1	2		1		1	1		1		
John Cavenaugh	3	1		1		1	1			1		
David Carringer			1									
Charles Brady			1			1						

248

48

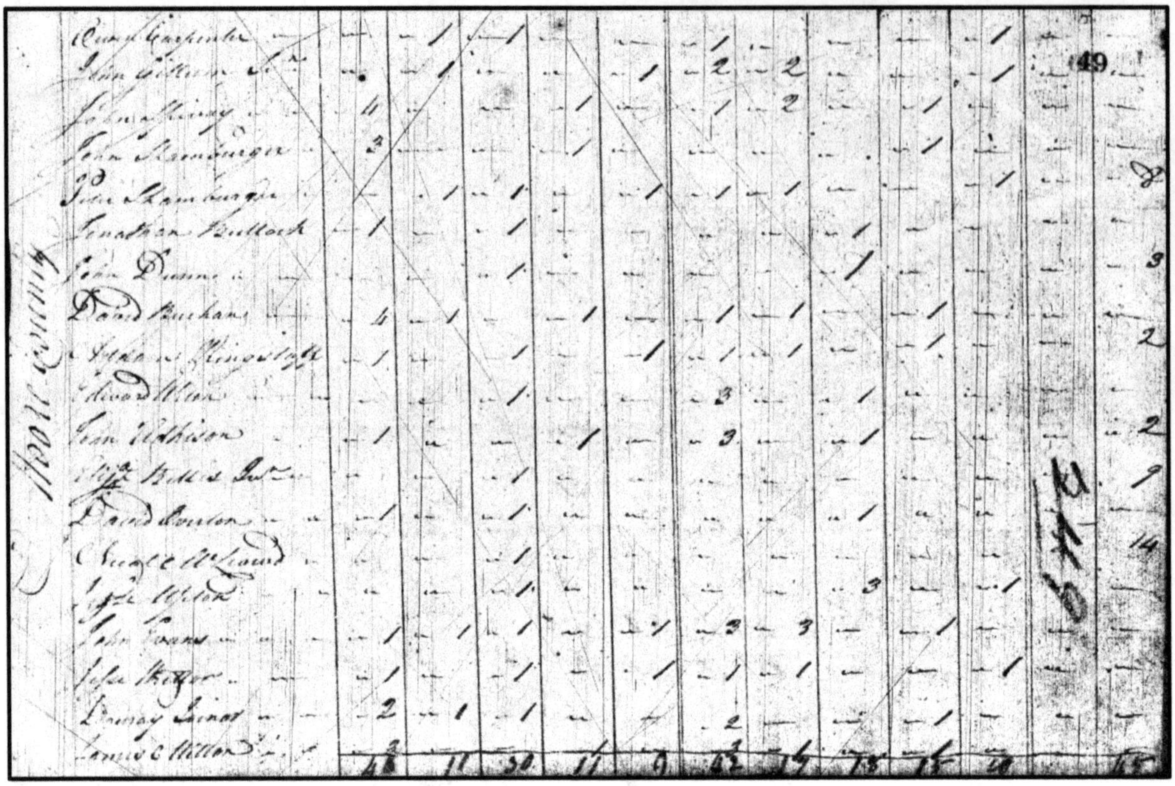

Quincy Carpenter		1	1			1				1		
John Gilliam Sr.		1			1	2	2			1		49
John Maring	4			1		1	2		1			
John Shamburger	3			1					1			
Do. John Shamburger		1	1		1	1	1			1		8
Jonathan Bullock	1		1					1				
John Dunn			1					1				3
David Buchan	4	1		1		1	1		1			
Adam Kingsloth	1		1		1	1	1		1			2
Edward Wilson			1			3		1				
John Atkinson	1			1		3		1				2
Mrs. Bills Sen.			1									9
David Overton	1		1					1				
Nugle McLeand			1									14
Jesse Wilson			1					3		1		
John Evans	1	1	1		1	3	3		1			
Jesse Keiffer	1		1		1	1	1			1		
Dempsy Linar	2	1	1			2			1			
James McMillan	2					2						

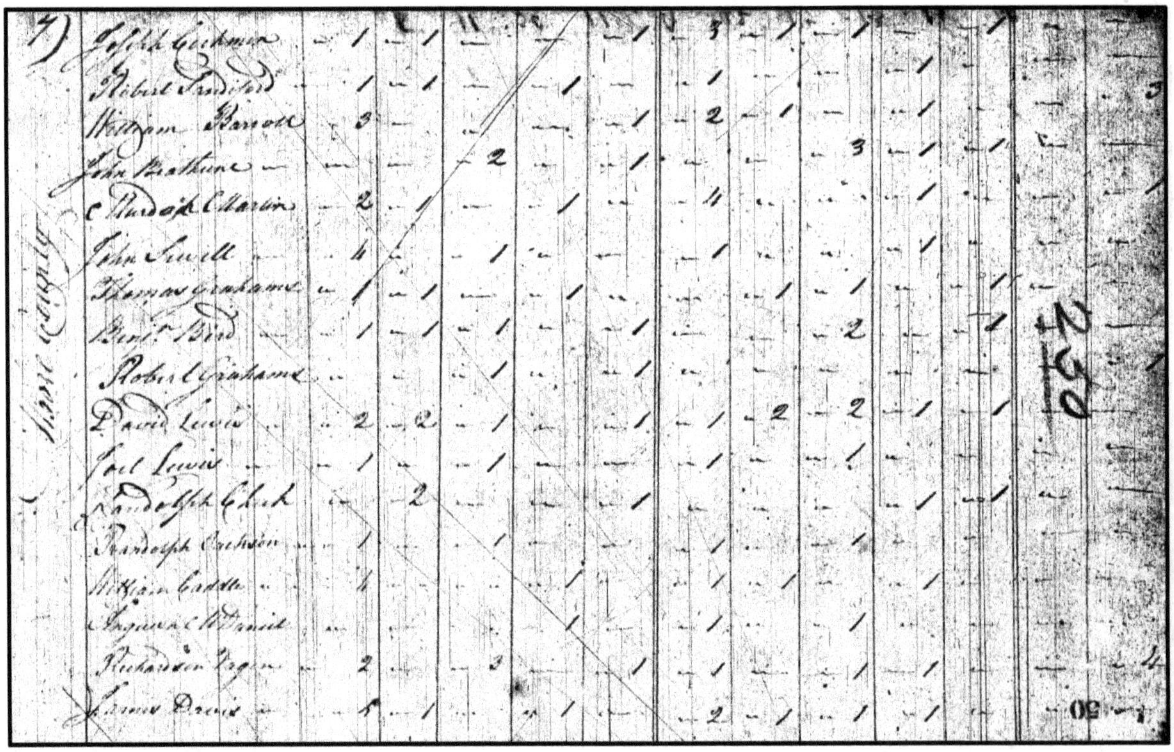

Joseph Cockman	1	1			1	3	1	1		1		
Robert Dunford	1	1		1		1			1			3
William Barrett	3				1	2	1		1			
John Bethune			2		1			3	1	1		
Murdoch Martin	2	1		1		4			1			
John Sewell	4		1			1			1			
Thomas Grahame	1	1		1			1	1		1		
Benj. Bird	1	1	1		1			2		1		
Robert Grahame			1		1							1
David Lewis	2	2	1		1	1	2	2	1	1		
Joel Lewis	1		1			1		1				
Randolph Clark		2			1				1	1		
Randolph Jackson	1		1			1		1				
William Caddle	4			1		1	1		1			
Angus McDaniel				1		1		1				
Richardson Hagan	2		3		1	1		1	1			4
James Davis	5	1		1		2	1	1	1			

Moore County — 51 — 251

John Cheek	2			1		3		2				
Daniel McLeod	1			1		1		1				
William Brannaman	1				1		3			1		
Arch'd McMillan			1									
Ralph Davis					1					1		
Brown Davis	1			1		3			1	1		
Aneas Currey	3			1	0	1			1			
William Hears					1					1		
Brown Baragher	3			1		2			1			
Arch'd McMillan	2	4	1		1			3		1		
James Campbell	1	1			1	2	2	1	1			
Shadrick Rogers	1	2			1					1		
Edmond Love	4	1			1	1	1	1	1			
Malcolm McMillan	1	2		1		3				1		
Arch'd McDaniel	1		1			2	1		1			
Aneas Currey		1	2			2	1	1		1		
Caitlin Currey				1	1				1	1		
[illegible] Cummins	4			2				1				
William Foy	1	1	1			1			1			
Anne Cordle					1			1		1		
	55	92	17	15	18	40	15	13	20	15		10

(8) Moore County — 252 — 52

John Donnelly	3			1			1		1			
Rich'd Ragsdale		2	3		1	2		1		1		
Jesse Beck				1		2	2		1			
Dan Ragsdale	2			1		1			1			
Duncan Campbell			2		1		1	1	1			
Jason Hadsworth				1		3			1			
Rich'd Parkison	2	3	1	1		2	2	1				
Daniel Jackson							1	2		1		
Aneas Colquhoun				1					1			
Samuel Stewart					1			1	1			
Isaac Hadsworth	1				1			1	2			1
James Foy	2		1		1	1	1	1		1		
John Bue		2			1	2	1	2		1		
Hugh Black					1				1			
John Hilyard	3	1		1		1	1		1			
John McNeal	1		1						1			
Hector McNeal		1			1			1				1
Malcom McNeal	2			1		3			1	1		

Moore County

53

Jacob Smith	1			1		2			1			5
Daniell McInnish		1	1		1		1		1			
Peter Blue	3	3			1			1	1			2
Isabella Blue									1	1		
Asa McLean	2	1				1	2	1	1			
Daniel McKinnon	2	1		1		2			1			
James McCallum	1			1		1			1			
Benjamin McKinnon			1		1				1	1		
Dunkin Paterson			2	2	1			2		1		
Farlan McFarlan	1		1	1		2		1	1			3
Daniell Munroe	2			1		1			1			8
John McLeod	2			1					1	1		2
Allen McDaniel	2	1	2		1	3	1		1			
John McKinzie			1							1		
Malcolm Black			3	2		1		1		1		
Finlay McDaniel		1	2		1			2		1		
Dunkin McCallum			1		1			1		1		
John McKinnon			1		1			1	1	1		
	32	19	23	11	16	30	14	[illegible]	24	16		45

253

9 Daniel Clark	2			1		2			1			3
Malcolm Clark			2					1		1		
Daniell McMillin			1					1		1		
Hugh Black	1			1		1			1			
John Munroe	2	3		1		1			1			
Dunkin Patersone		2		1		4			1			
Arch Paterson			1		1					1		2
John McNeill	2	1	1		1	3	1			1		
John Buchan	3	2	2		1	1	1		1			2
Anguish McMillin	1			1		1			1			
John Campbell	1	1		1		1			1			
Daniel McDaniel	0		2	1	1	1		1		1		
John Morrison	1		1	1		1			1			1
John Ray	3		4		1			1	1			
Dunkin Blue			2		1			1	1	1		2
Arch Ray				1		2			1			1
Dunkin Ray	2			1		1			1			
Dunkin Campbell	2			1		2			1	7	54	1
Dunkin McKenzie	2			1	1	2			1			1

Moore County

Moore Co. NC 1800

254

238 Moore County NC 1800 55

Malcolm Black	–	–	1	–	–	–	–	–	–	1	–	1
Hugh McDaniel	2	–	1	–	1	–	1	–	–	1	–	1
John Ray	–	–	2	1	–	–	–	3	–	1	–	–
John Patison	–	–	1	1	–	–	–	2	–	1	–	8
Archd Gillis	–	–	1	–	1	–	1	–	–	1	–	–
Daniel Gillis	2	–	1	–	–	–	1	–	–	–	–	–
John Paterson	1	–	1	–	–	3	1	–	–	–	–	–
Dunkin Brown	1	–	–	1	–	–	–	–	1	–	–	–
John Johnson	–	–	1	–	–	–	–	1	–	–	–	–
Archd Johnson	3	1	–	–	1	1	2	2	1	–	–	–
Archd Ray	3	1	–	–	–	–	1	–	1	–	–	1
Archd Peterson	–	–	–	–	1	–	–	–	–	1	–	–
Dugal McMillin	–	–	1	–	–	–	–	–	–	1	–	–
Daniel Graham	3	–	–	1	–	3	1	–	1	–	–	–
Archd McMillin	1	–	–	–	1	2	2	–	–	1	–	1
Dugal McFarlin	4	1	–	1	–	1	1	–	1	–	–	–
John Inger	2	–	–	1	–	–	–	1	–	–	–	–
[illegible]	3	2	2	1	–	–	–	1	1	–	–	–
Eva Hannon	[illegible]											

10 237 Moore County

Christian McIntosh	–	–	2	–	–	–	–	–	–	–	–	–
David Sears	–	2	–	1	–	3	–	–	1	–	–	–
John Fagon	–	–	1	–	–	–	–	–	–	1	–	–
Joseph Rouse	3	1	–	1	–	2	–	–	1	–	–	–
Thomas Hannon	2	–	–	1	–	1	1	–	1	–	–	–
John Hager	1	–	–	1	–	1	–	–	1	–	–	–
William Lewis	–	–	1	–	–	–	–	–	–	1	–	–
Daniel Dowdy	2	–	1	–	1	–	2	1	–	1	–	–
Benja Caddle	2	–	1	–	–	2	–	1	–	–	–	–
James Dowdy	1	–	1	–	–	–	–	1	–	–	–	–
Nancy McSwane	–	–	1	–	–	–	–	–	–	1	–	–
Jonathan Caddle	2	–	–	1	–	2	1	1	1	–	–	–
Thomas Hannon Sr	–	–	–	–	1	–	–	1	1	–	–	–
Hector McNeal	4	–	1	–	1	2	2	–	1	–	–	–
Kenneth Murkison	2	1	1	–	1	1	1	1	1	–	–	–
John Martin	–	–	1	–	–	–	–	–	–	1	–	–
Birrell Mahler	2	–	2	1	–	3	–	–	–	1	–	–
George Callen	1	1	–	–	1	1	–	1	–	1	–	–
Joseph Robson	–	–	–	–	1	–	–	–	1	–	–	–
Willoughby Rogers	2	1	–	1	–	1	–	–	1	–	–	–

Moore County — 236

Carlton Jackson	–	2	1	–	–	1	–	–	–	1	–	1
Edward Cox	–	–	–	–	1	–	–	1	–	–	–	57
Anguish McCaskill	–	–	1	1	1	–	1	1	–	1	–	–
John McCaskill	–	–	1	1	–	1	–	1	–	–	–	–
[illegible]	[illegible]	0	–	–	0	0	0	–	–	0	–	–
John McDaniel	1	1	1	1	–	2	–	1	1	1	–	–
Catharine Beaton	–	–	–	–	–	1	–	2	–	1	–	–
William Harden	1	1	–	–	1	3	–	1	1	–	–	3
Everit Wallis	4	–	–	1	–	1	1	–	1	–	–	–
Phillip White	4	–	–	1	–	2	2	–	1	–	–	–
Elijah Bettis Sr.	1	1	–	–	1	–	–	2	–	1	–	30
Archd. McLain	2	1	–	–	1	2	2	–	1	–	–	–
John Sitton	–	–	1	–	1	3	1	2	–	1	–	–
John Richardson	–	–	1	–	–	2	–	1	–	–	–	–
Samuel Martindale	–	1	1	–	1	1	2	1	–	1	–	–
Joseph Fry	3	1	–	–	1	2	1	–	1	–	–	–
Stephen Oats	2	1	1	–	1	2	2	–	–	1	–	–
Norman McLeod	–	1	–	–	1	–	–	–	–	1	–	1
Lovay McKinnady	1	1	1	–	–	1	1	–	–	1	–	6
Neal Muse	1	2	–	1	–	1	–	1	–	1	–	–
Alex. McIver	[illegible]	[illegible]	[illegible]	[illegible]	[illegible]	[illegible]	[illegible]	[illegible]	[illegible]	[illegible]	[illegible]	[illegible]

Moore County — 235

Thomas Martindale	1	–	1	–	–	–	–	1	–	–	–	–
Charles Campbell	3	1	–	1	–	1	–	–	1	1	–	1
Thomas Fry	1	1	1	–	1	1	2	–	1	1/5	–	1
George Grahams	3	1	–	1	–	1	–	–	1	–	–	–
Stephen Richardson	3	–	1	–	1	1	1	–	1	–	–	–
Nathaniel Melton	2	2	–	1	–	1	–	–	1	–	–	–
John Martin	3	–	–	1	–	1	–	–	1	–	–	–
John Wadsworth	4	1	–	1	–	1	2	–	1	1	–	–
James Melton	3	–	–	1	–	3	1	–	1	–	–	–
John Berrayman	1	–	1	1	–	2	1	–	1	–	–	–
Christopher Bethune	2	–	–	1	–	2	–	–	1	–	–	–
John McKinnion	–	1	2	1	1	–	–	–	–	1	–	–
Daniel McNeal	2	2	2	–	1	1	–	–	–	1	–	8
Norman Mathews	–	–	1	1	1	1	1	–	–	1	–	1
Martin Martin	3	–	–	1	–	1	–	–	1	–	–	–
Peter McEachern	–	–	–	1	–	1	–	–	1	–	–	2
Jesse Muse	1	3	–	1	–	3	–	–	1	–	–	–
Jarrot Tucker	3	–	–	1	–	–	–	–	1	–	89	1
George Carringer	–	–	–	1	1	1	–	–	–	–	–	–

Moore County 234

Joseph Cochman	1	1	—	—	1	3	1	1	—	1	—	—
Lewis Garnor	2	1	—	1	—	3	1	—	1	—	059	4
John Garnor	—	—	—	—	1	—	1	—	—	1	—	13
Nathan Fry	2	—	—	1	—	2	—	—	1	—	—	—
Nicholas Nall	2	—	—	—	1	3	—	—	1	—	—	14
Mark Merritt	2	—	—	1	—	—	—	1	—	—	—	—
William Jackson	—	—	—	1	—	3	—	—	1	—	—	—
Abraham Cole	1	—	1	—	—	2	—	1	—	—	—	—
Archd. Reed	3	—	—	1	—	—	—	—	1	—	—	2
Walter McBath	1	—	—	1	—	3	—	—	1	—	—	2
Robert Wilkison	—	—	1	—	—	—	—	1	—	—	—	—
Archd. Clark	1	—	—	1	—	2	—	—	1	—	—	1
Samuel Persons	4	—	—	1	—	1	—	—	1	—	—	11
Alexander Morrison	—	—	—	1	—	—	—	—	—	2	—	—
Levy Dalon	1	—	—	1	—	2	—	2	—	—	—	—
Murdock McAuly	3	—	—	1	—	1	—	1	—	1	—	—
Daniel McLeod	—	—	—	1	—	—	—	—	2	—	—	—
Norman Morrison	2	—	1	1	—	2	1	—	1	—	—	—
William Tagon	1	—	1	1	—	2	—	—	1	—	—	—
James Birched	2	—	—	1	—	3	—	—	1	—	—	—
John Merritt	—	—	—	1	—	—	—	—	—	—	—	—
Aaron Tyson	2	2	4	2	—	2	1	—	1	—	4	2
David Wadin	66	16	17	35	4	56	13	[illegible]	[illegible]	10	41	[illegible]

Moore County 235

12 Benjamin Tyson	—	1	2	—	1	2	1	2	2	—	—	—
Thomas Thompson	2	—	—	1	—	2	—	—	1	—	—	—
Daniel McIntosh	2	—	1	1	—	2	—	—	1	—	—	—
Abner Ragsdill	1	—	—	1	—	2	—	1	—	—	—	—
John Cameron	—	—	2	—	1	2	1	2	—	1	—	4
Hartwell Lanchester	3	2	1	—	1	2	1	—	1	—	—	—
John McIntosh	5	—	1	1	—	—	—	—	1	—	—	—
John Gilchrist	—	—	—	1	—	—	—	—	—	—	5	—
Henry Goin	—	—	—	—	—	—	—	—	—	—	9	—
William Goin	—	—	—	—	—	—	—	—	—	—	1	—
Alexander McIntosh	3	1	1	1	—	2	1	—	2	—	—	—
Randol Jackson	1	—	1	—	—	1	—	1	—	—	—	—
Andrew Jackson	—	1	1	—	—	1	—	1	—	—	—	—
~~[illegible]~~	—	—	—	0	—	—	0	—	0	—	—	—
Daniel McNicoll	—	1	2	—	1	—	—	—	—	1	—	—
John Boyd	—	—	1	—	—	—	—	1	—	—	—	—
Hartwell Lanchester	—	—	1	—	—	1	—	1	—	—	—	—
Josephy Pane	—	—	1	—	—	—	1	—	—	1	—	—
John Cole Sr.	—	—	1	—	—	—	—	1	—	—	—	—
Andrew Cole	—	—	1	—	1	1	1	—	—	1	—	—
Daniel McIver	1	—	—	1	—	2	—	1	—	—	—	—
John McGilvery	2	1	1	—	—	—	1	1	—	1	09	1

Herbert Cole	1		1		1			1	1	1		
John Cole Sr		1			1				1			3
John Rothy		1		1		2	1		1		61	
John Cole	2			1		2						1
James Riddle			2		1			1		1		
Daniel Murkison	1		1					1				
Nathan Lun	1		1			1		1				
John Kinney			1		1	1	1	1	1			
Stephen Collins				1								
Molley Teal	1					2	1	1		1		
Daniel Robson	3	2	2		1	3		1		1		
Daniel Stuart	3		1		1		1		1			
Joseph Johnson	1	1	1			1		2		1		
David Jones			1					1				
David Jones Sr		1			1					1		
Amous Hill				1		1		1				
Christian Murkison					1			2				
John Murkison			2	1						1		
Neal McLeod	1			1		1		1				1
Alexd McLeod			1	1	1					1		
John Sinclair		1	2		1			2		1		
Archd Curry	[illegible]	[illegible]	[illegible]	[illegible]	[illegible]	[illegible]	[illegible]	[illegible]	[illegible]	[illegible]	[illegible]	[illegible]

John Mathews	2	1			1	3	2		1			
Rory McIver			1	1	1			1		1		2
Robert Boles				1		3		1				
Robert Boles Sr			1		1		1			1		
Lucy Jain											5	
Angus McDuffie			2	1				2				
Alice Nicholson		1	2		1	1	1	1		1		
William Cole		2	1		1	1	1		1			
John McFadien	1	1		1		1	1		1			
William Elliott											2	
John Elliot											2	
Samey Scot											2	
John Ragsdil	1			1				1				
John Baker		1		1		4	1		1			
Alexander McLain	2			1		1			1			
Dunkin Murkison	2			1		2	1		1			
James McKinzie	1			1		1			2			
Alexd McIntosh			1		1			1		1		
Thomas Cole	2	2		1		2			1	1		
Dunkin McAllum	3	1	1		1	1	1	2				
Hector McGrigor	1		1		1	3	2		1		62	

230 Moore County

63

Patrick Dowd	1	–	1	1	–	1	1	–	1	–	–	–
Lazarus Birkhead	2	1	–	1	–	1	–	1	–	–	–	–
John Dunlap	2	2	1	–	1	3	1	3	–	1	–	–
Patsey Hancock	2	–	–	–	–	3	2	–	2	–	–	–
Phillip Johnson	–	1	–	–	1	5	1	–	1	–	1	6
John Torrington	3	–	–	1	–	1	–	–	1	–	–	13
John Shephard	–	–	–	1	–	3	–	–	1	–	2	11
John Sloan	–	–	–	1	–	2	–	–	–	–	–	–
Catharine Watson	3	2	–	–	–	–	–	–	1	–	–	–
Robert Watson	–	–	3	–	1	1	–	–	1	–	–	–
William Watson	–	–	–	–	1	–	–	2	–	1	–	–
Joseph Thomas	2	–	–	1	–	2	–	1	–	–	–	–
Niel Rogers	2	–	–	1	–	3	–	–	1	–	–	–
Jonathan Wicker	2	–	–	1	–	3	–	–	1	–	–	–
Matthew Wicker	–	–	1	–	–	1	–	1	–	–	–	–
John Kelly	2	–	–	1	–	1	–	–	1	–	–	–
Mary Kelly	1	2	–	1	–	–	1	–	–	1	–	–
Hugh Kelly	–	–	–	1	–	1	–	–	1	–	–	–
	[illegible]	17	16	21	12	54	17	18	22	7	14	31

229 Moore County

Mary Coffin	–	–	–	–	–	–	–	–	–	–	–	–
Grissa Carmichel	–	–	3	–	–	–	–	1	1	–	–	–
Peter McIntosh	–	2	–	–	1	1	–	1	1	–	–	–
John Watson	3	1	–	1	–	1	–	–	1	–	–	–
John McLain	–	–	–	–	1	2	–	–	–	–	–	–
John Baker	–	2	–	1	–	2	1	1	1	–	–	1
John Gunter Sr.	–	–	2	–	1	–	1	1	–	1	–	11
John Gunter Jr.	1	–	–	–	–	2	–	–	2	–	–	2
~~[illegible]~~	0	–	–	0	–	0	–	0	–	–	–	–
William Hughes	1	–	–	1	–	1	–	–	1	–	–	–
William Buie	1	–	–	–	–	1	–	1	–	–	–	–
Gilbert Buie Sr.	2	–	1	–	–	–	–	1	–	–	–	–
Daniel Buie	–	–	–	1	–	–	–	2	–	–	–	1
Duncan McDugle	3	–	–	1	–	2	–	–	1	–	3	–
John McDugle	3	–	–	1	–	1	–	–	1	–	–	–
Pleasant Wicker	3	1	–	1	–	1	–	–	1	–	–	–
Benjamin Wicker	2	1	–	–	1	2	1	–	1	–	–	–
Peter Morris	3	2	–	1	–	–	–	–	1	–	–	–
John Morris Sr.	–	–	–	1	–	4	–	1	–	–	–	–
Fredrick Morris	–	–	–	–	1	–	–	–	–	–	–	–
Henry Morris	–	1	–	–	1	–	1	–	–	1	–	–

64

Moore County 228

													65
	John Morris Senr	1	–	1	–	–	–	–	1	–	–	–	–
	Lewis Price	–	3	–	1	–	4	–	–	1	–	–	–
	Stephen Morris	–	–	–	1	–	2	–	–	1	–	–	–
	Archd Smith	2	2	2	1	1	–	1	2	–	1	–	–
	John McFarlan	3	–	–	1	–	–	1	2	–	1	–	–
	Malcom McFarlin	–	–	–	1	–	–	–	–	–	1	–	–
	Laughlin McLain	2	–	–	1	–	1	–	–	1	–	–	–
	Malcom Buie	–	1	–	1	–	3	1	–	1	–	–	–
	Neil McFadyan	–	–	1	1	–	–	–	1	1	–	–	–
	Henry Gaster	–	1	–	1	1	–	–	1	–	–	–	19
	Sion Harrington	1	1	2	1	–	1	–	1	1	–	–	1
	Robert Carlisle	–	1	–	1	1	1	1	3	–	1	–	–
	John Dalrymple	–	–	1	1	1	–	–	3	–	1	–	4
	James Dalrymple	–	–	0	1	–	2	1	–	1	–	–	1
	Allen McDugal	–	–	1	–	–	–	–	–	–	–	–	–
	Samuel Washburn	1	–	1	1	–	1	2	–	1	–	–	–
	William Buie	–	–	1	–	–	–	–	–	–	–	–	1
	Alexd McBryde	–	–	1	–	1	2	1	2	–	1	–	1
	Alexd McIver	2	2	–	2	–	2	–	–	1	–	5	–
	Dunkin McDuffee	–	–	–	1	–	2	–	1	–	–	–	–
		34	21	13	29	11	21	11	26	19	11		41

Moore County 227

15	Dunkin McIver	–	1	–	1	1	–	–	1	–	1	–	–
	Alexd McIvan	–	–	1	1	1	–	–	–	–	2	–	1
	Daniel McIver	3	–	–	1	–	1	–	–	1	–	–	–
	Randol Stewart	1	–	–	1	–	–	–	–	1	–	–	–
	Neill McLeod	1	–	–	1	–	1	–	1	–	–	–	–
	Archd Curry	1	1	–	1	–	1	1	1	1	–	–	–
	Daniel Shaw	–	1	1	1	–	–	–	1	2	–	–	–
	[illegible]	0	0	–	0	–	0	0	–	0	–	–	–
	Malcom Baker	2	–	–	1	–	2	–	1	–	–	–	–
	Dunkin Buie	3	3	3	–	1	1	–	2	1	–	–	–
	Gilbert Buie Senr	–	–	–	2	–	1	–	1	–	–	–	2
	Anguish Buie	–	–	1	–	–	–	–	–	–	–	–	3
	John Ward	–	–	–	1	–	2	–	–	1	–	–	–
	William Manly	3	2	1	1	–	1	–	–	–	1	–	–
	Seth Jackson	–	–	–	–	1	–	–	1	–	1	–	–
	William Reed	1	–	1	–	–	2	–	–	1	–	–	5
	Anguish Shaw	–	–	2	–	–	–	–	2	–	–	–	–
	John Shepphard Senr	–	–	–	–	1	–	–	1	–	–	–	–

99

Benjn Pike	1	—	—	1	—	1	—	1	—	—	—	—
Alexd Hunt	2	—	1	1	—	2	1	—	1	—	—	— 67
William Smith	1	1	1	—	1	—	1	—	—	1	—	—
Willis Oliver Senr	1	1	1	—	1	1	—	1	—	1	—	—
Willis Oliver Junr	3	2	—	1	—	—	—	1	—	—	—	—
George Underwood	3	2	1	—	1	1	—	1	1	—	—	—
Charnal Gunter	1	1	—	1	—	—	—	1	—	—	—	—
John Love	3	1	1	—	1	2	1	1	1	—	—	—
Dunkin Love	—	—	—	1	—	1	—	1	—	—	—	—
John Mathews Junr	1	—	—	1	—	2	—	—	1	—	—	—
Absalom Cox	3	1	—	1	—	1	1	—	1	—	—	—
Henry Cox	1	1	—	1	—	3	1	—	1	—	—	—
William Griffis	—	—	—	1	—	—	—	1	—	—	—	—
Anguish McLeod	—	—	—	1	—	1	—	—	1	—	—	—
Joshua Dumby	—	1	—	—	1	—	—	—	1	—	—	—
James Ballard	—	1	1	—	1	—	—	—	—	1	—	—
	35	20	16	22	11	27	6	19	13	9		12

Brittan Hammock	1	2	2	1	—	4	—	1	—	—	—	—
John Shephard Junr	2	—	—	1	—	2	—	—	1	—	—	—
Diney Hathcock	2	1	—	1	—	1	—	—	1	—	—	—
Robert Irwin	2	—	—	1	—	—	—	1	—	—	—	—
John Irwin	1	—	—	1	—	—	—	1	—	—	—	—
John Spears	2	1	1	1	—	2	2	—	1	—	—	—
John Parram	—	1	1	1	—	1	—	—	1	—	—	—
Benjn Bishop	4	—	—	—	1	—	—	—	1	—	—	—
John Huckaby	1	—	1	1	1	1	—	1	—	1	—	1
Edy Ward	1	—	—	—	—	—	2	—	1	—	—	—
Richard Stephens	—	1	3	1	1	1	1	—	1	1	—	—
Elisha Yarborow	1	—	—	1	—	3	1	—	1	—	—	2
Lewis Parrom	2	1	—	—	—	1	1	—	1	—	—	—
Lucy Stephens	—	1	1	—	—	1	2	—	1	—	—	—
Joseph Sullivant	1	—	—	1	—	1	—	—	1	—	—	—
John Godfrey	1	—	—	1	—	1	—	—	1	—	69	—

224 Moore County

69

Leroy Parrish	1	—	1	—	—	—	1	1	—	—	—	—
Reuben McCall	2	1	1	—	1	3	1	2	1	—	—	—
Murdoch Bethune	1	1	—	—	1	2	1	—	1	—	—	—
Mary McNeill	2	—	1	—	0	1	0	1	—	1	—	1
John McNeill	2	—	1	—	—	—	—	1	—	—	—	—
Lewis Sewell	6	2	1	—	1	3	1	—	—	1	—	—
Bartholomew Dunn	2	1	—	1	1	1	—	1	—	—	—	—
John McNeely	—	—	1	1	1	—	—	2	—	—	—	3
Sharwood Parrish	—	—	—	—	1	—	—	—	—	1	—	—
Jesse Lankford	1	—	—	1	—	—	—	1	—	—	—	—
Anson Melton	—	—	—	—	1	—	1	—	—	1	—	—
John Richardson	—	—	1	—	—	2	—	1	—	—	—	—
Thomas Kear	—	3	1	—	1	—	—	2	—	1	—	—
William Kear	3	—	—	1	—	—	—	1	—	—	—	—
John Kear	—	—	1	—	0	—	—	1	—	—	—	—
Nancy McLeod	2	—	2	—	—	—	3	—	—	1	—	—
Christian Stutz	2	—	1	—	—	2	—	—	1	—	—	—
Daniel McDaniel	—	—	2	1	—	—	—	2	—	1	—	—
David Richardson	—	—	—	—	—	2	2	1	—	—	—	—
	44	14	20	18	11	32	17	22	14	9		16

17 223 Moore County

John Tolmon	—	—	1	—	—	1	—	1	—	1	—	—
Bikee Sewell	—	—	—	—	—	—	—	1	—	—	—	—
George Cagle	3	1	—	1	—	2	—	—	1	—	—	—
Catharine Cagle	1	1	—	—	—	2	—	—	—	1	—	—
Jeremiah Williams	1	—	1	—	—	—	—	1	—	—	—	—
Bartholomew Dunn	—	—	—	—	1	—	—	—	—	1	—	—
Charles Sewell	—	3	—	—	1	2	—	—	—	2	—	—
Lewis Sewell Senr	—	—	—	1	—	1	—	1	—	—	—	—
Royal Pritt	1	—	—	1	—	1	—	1	—	—	—	—
Benjn Pritt	3	—	—	1	—	1	—	—	1	—	—	—
William Dunn	1	1	—	—	1	3	3	1	1	—	—	—
John Dunn	2	—	1	—	—	1	—	—	1	—	—	—
James Morgan	2	—	—	—	—	1	—	—	1	—	—	—
John Smith	1	1	—	1	—	3	1	—	1	—	—	—
Nathan Morgan	2	—	—	1	—	1	—	—	1	—	—	—
Patsey Coats	—	1	—	—	—	—	1	—	—	1	—	—
James Whitley	2	—	—	1	—	1	—	—	1	—	—	—
William Chadian	1	—	1	—	1	—	—	—	1	—	—	—

71

Moore County — 222

Allen McLain			1	1				1	3			
Hector McLain					1							
Daniel McLeod	2	2		1		3		1	1			
William Smith			1									
James Hines	2			1		1		1				
Richard Hollon	2	1			1	2	1	1		1		1
Joseph Bell	3	2			1	1			1			
Margret Hope	2								1			
Joseph Allen		2	1	1		4	1		1			
Thomas Parrish	2			1		1			1			
Murdoch McLeod	2			1		2			1			
Daniel McLeod					1					1		
Jesse Brown	3	1	1	1		1	2		1			
Murdoch McAuly	1	1	1		1	1		1		1		
Neal McLeod	1			1					1			
Norman McKinnian	4	1			1	1			1			
John Buie	2			1				2	1			
Daring Ramage					1					1		
	16	19	11	16	11	38	10	15	18	11		1

Moore County — 221

18 Malcom Morison		1			1		2			1		1
~~[illegible]~~	0			0					0			
James McDaniel	2			1					1			
Anguish Campbell	2	1			1	3	1	1	1			
Hector McLain					1	4	2	1	1			
Margret Campbell			1				2	1		1		
Thomas Hood	3	1			1	1	1			1		
Mary Sewell			1					1		1		
Ailsey Sewell			1									
James Smith	2			1		1		1				
Jeremiah Dean	2			1		1	1	1	1			
~~Daniel McDaniel~~			2	0						0		
Neal Peterson			1							1		
Stephen Davis	1		2			2		1				
~~[illegible]~~		0		0		0		0				
Norman McKinnian	4	1			1	1			1			

72

Moore County 20

Robert Teastor	X	—	1	X	—	1	—	X	—	—	—	—	73
Sarah Teastor	X	—	—	X	—	X	—	X	1	—	—	—	
Samuel Elkins	X	—	1	X	—	1	—	1	X	1	—	—	
James Elkin	—	—	1	—	1	—	1	2	1	1	—	—	
Jesse Pate	—	X	—	—	X	3	X	—	X	1	—	1	
Robert Cheek	—	X	3	—	1	—	—	X	—	X	—	—	
Daniel McWadsworth	—	—	—	X	—	X 3	—	1	X	—	—	2	
Elizabeth Brown	3	1	X	X	—	3	X	1	X	1	—	—	
William Williamson	2	—	1	X	1	3	—	1	X	—	—	4	
James Williamson	1	—	1	—	—	2	—	1	—	—	1	2	
Jacob Stutts	4	X	—	X	—	—	—	—	1	—	—	—	
Adam White	0	X	—	X	X	1	—	—	X	—	—	—	
James Cheek	—	—	—	X	X	1	1	3	X	X	—	—	
Samuel Perry	X	3	2	0	1	—	—	X	1	—	—	—	
Jephtha Medford	1	1	X	—	X	X	—	X	1	X	—	—	
Hemerick Hill	4	—	—	X	—	—	—	1	—	X	1	—	
John Moore	—	1	—	—	1	—	—	1	—	—	—	—	
Drury Richardson	—	—	—	—	—	—	—	—	—	X	—	—	
	31	10	13	10	12	24	11	20	13	11	1	8	

19

Moore County NC 21

William Williamson	—	—	1	—	—	—	—	1	—	1	—	—
Benja. Graham	—	1	3	3	1	—	—	1	—	X	—	—
Daniel McDonald	—	—	—	3	1	1	—	1	—	—	—	3
Dond. McQueen	—	—	1	—	—	—	—	4	X	1	—	—
Edward Richardson	1	—	1	—	—	—	—	1	X	—	—	—
Malcom Morrison	—	—	—	1	1	—	—	2	—	1	—	1
James Matthews	3	1	—	—	1	2	1	—	—	1	—	—
Richard Cheek	3	1	—	1	—	2	2	—	1	—	—	—
Frederick Autery	2	—	—	1	—	1	—	—	1	—	—	—
Elijah Autery	3	2	1	1	—	3	1	—	1	—	—	—
William Rhodes	—	2	—	1	—	1	—	—	1	—	—	8
Alexr. Autery	—	1	2	—	—	—	—	1	2	1	—	—
James Autery	2	1	—	—	1	3	1	—	1	—	—	—
Normand McLeod	1	—	—	1	—	2	—	—	1	—	—	—
Thos. Wadsworth	1	—	—	1	—	1	—	1	—	—	—	—
Archd. Wadsworth	1	—	—	1	—	3	—	1	—	—	62	1

218 Moore County

												75
Hugh Medlin	1	0	1	0	x	2	—	—	1	—	—	—
John Medlin	2	1	—	1	—	3	—	—	1	—	—	—
Joel Medlin	2	1	3	—	1	1	—	—	1	1	—	—
Kenneth McDonald	—	—	1	—	1	1	—	1	—	1	—	—
Christopher Yow	2	2	1	—	1	2	—	—	—	—	—	—
John Cameron Tay.	1	1	—	—	1	3	—	—	1	—	—	—
Daniel Love	—	1	1	—	1	1	2	—	—	1	—	—
Robert Bird	2	1	1	—	1	2	1	—	—	1	—	—
Andrew Yow	—	—	1	—	—	—	—	1	—	—	—	—
Robert Graham	1	—	—	1	—	2	—	—	1	—	—	—
Michael Bryant	4	—	—	1	—	1	1	—	1	1	—	—
Thos. Matthews Senr.	—	—	1	—	1	—	—	1	—	1	—	6
James Matthews	2	—	—	1	—	2	—	—	1	—	—	—
John Lewis	1	—	1	1	—	3	—	—	1	—	—	—
Ezekiah Johnston	1	1	1	—	1	2	—	—	—	1	—	—
Zachariah Smith	—	—	2	—	1	—	—	—	—	1	—	—
David Cagle	3	1	1	—	1	2				1		
Benjn. Lewis												
	39	10	15	19	15	44	0	17	16	14		18

20 — 217 Moore County

Frederick Tyler	—	1	—	—	1	5	1	—	—	1	5
John C. McKenzie	—	—	1	—	—	—	—	—	—	1	—
Francis C. Merick	3	1	—	1	—	2	—	—	1	1	5
James Hardin	1	1	1	—	1	3	—	1	—	1	—
C... McClanon	1	—	1	—	1	3	—	1	—	—	—
Patsey Graham	1	—	1	—	—	1	—	1	1	—	—
Benjn. Elkins	5	3	1	—	1	1	1	2	—	1	2
William Wilson	—	1	1	—	1	3	1	—	—	1	—
John Upton	1	—	1	—	—	—	—	1	—	1	—
Robert Davis	2	—	—	—	—	—	—	1	—	1	—
James Brady	2	1	1	—	1	1	1	1	1	1	1
George Russel	—	2	2	—	1	3	1	2	1	1	—
John Russel	1	—	1	—	1	—	—	—	—	x	—
Matthias Teag	2	1	1	—	1	3	—	1	—	—	—
John Barker	—	1	1	—	1	1	1	1	—	—	—
John Barker Jr.	—	1	1	—	1	2	1	1	1	1	—
Lucy Lawler	3	—	—	1	1	—	1	—	1	—	—
John Lawler	1	1	1	1	1	2	—	—	—	—	92

77

Patsey Pennington	–	–	–	–	–	1	–	–	1	–		
Nathan Vick	2	1	–	–	1	4	1	2	–	1		
Benjn Gilbert	1	–	1	–	–	4	–	1	–	–		
William Martin	–	1	1	1	–	–	–	–	–	–	–	1
John Cameron	1	2	3	–	1	1	–	–	–	1	–	5
Jasper Billing	3	1	–	1	–	–	–	–	1	–		
~~[illegible] McFee~~	1	–	1	–	–	–	–	1	1	1	–	
Josiah Holleman	1	2	–	1	–	2	1	–	1	–	–	–
Goddin Holleman	–	–	–	1	–	–	–	1	–	–	–	
Lucy Jones	2	–	–	–	–	–	1	–	1	1	–	
Abidnego Macala	–	1	–	1	–	2	–	–	1	–	–	
Averit Mritton	1	–	–	1	–	–	–	1	–	–	–	
Thomas Tyner	1	–	1	–	–	–	–	–	–	1	–	
Benjn Stephens	1	–	1	–	1	–	–	1	1	1	–	
John Stephens	2	–	–	1	–	1	–	–	1	–	–	
	40	20	22	11	12	37	12	18	11	17		16

The number of persons within my division consisting of Moor County appears in A schedule hereunto annexed Subscribed by me this 18th day of April 1801

Conn. Dowd Assistant to the Marshal of N. Carolina

Total of each description	834	341	392	381	218	747	264	372	353	230	31	608

Total 4.767

79

State of North Carolina }
Moore County }

Personally appeared before me a justice of the peace for said County Jesse Carroll and Thomas Dickenson and made oath on the Holy Evangelist of Almighty God that they compared the foregoing schedule with a true copy thereof taken by Cornelius Dowd assistant to the Marshal of North Carolina in said County — that they saw the said copy set up at the store house of Aaron Tyson Esq which is one of the most public places in the said County — that said Copy has remained there fifteen or sixteen days and that it still remains there posted up there — and farther these deponents say not —

Sworn to & subscribed before me this 18th day } Jesse Carroll
of April Anno Domini 1801 } Thos Dickinson

Test Thomas Tyson J.P.

I Thomas Tyson do farther Certify that the above subscribing deponents are men whom I have been personally acquainted with from their infancy — that they are men of fair character and whose veracity may be depended on

18th April 1801 Thomas Tyson J.P.

State of North Carolina } This day John Martin personally
Moore County } appeared before me Peter McEachern one of the Justices of the peace for said County & being duly sworn on the Holy Evangelist of Almighty God deposeth & saith that he saw Cornelius Dowd Assistant to the Marshal of the State aforesaid set up (as he believes) a Copy of the foregoing Schedule in the Court house of said County and that he has good reason to believe that the same remained there during the time & term of Twenty days or thereabouts and that it still remains there —

Sworn to & Subscribed before me
this 20th day of April 1801 } John Martin

Test Peter McEachern

I Hereby Certify that the above subscribing deponent is a man of true Veracity and may be depended upon

Peter McEachern

08

Moore Co NC

81

112

I John McLennon Sheriff of Moore County do hereby certify that I have seen the schedule of the number of inhabitants in Moore County taken by Cornelius Dowd that I am well acquainted in said County and have the lists of the taxables in said County now in my possession, that from these circumstances and others which come within my knowledge I am firmly of opinion that said schedule has been made out with care and accuracy

John McLennan Shff

I Archibald McBryde Clerk of Moore County do certify that I have seen the schedule of the number of inhabitants in Moore County taken by Cornelius Dowd several times since it was posted up at the store house of Aaron Tyson & Co that I have examined it several times — that from my general acquaintance in the county and copying the lists of Taxables in said County for many years and other circumstances I fully believe that the business has been done with great care and accuracy

Arch McBryde Clk

211

Moore Co N.C.

1800

Charge the man with postage $3.75

and tell him he is a fool

88

in the ſervice of the United States of America, for a valuable and full conſideration to me in hand paid at or before the execution hereof, by
the receipt whereof is hereby acknowledged, HAVE, and by theſe preſents, DO grant, bargain, ſell, releaſe, transfer and aſſign unto him, his heirs, executors, adminiſtrators and aſſigns, forever, ALL the right, title, intereſt, property, claim and demand, which I now have, or which I, my heirs, executors or adminiſtrators may at any time hereafter have, to all the land due and owing to me from the United States: And I do hereby for myſelf, my heirs, executors and adminiſtrators, covenant and agree to and with the ſaid

his heirs, executors, adminiſtrators and aſſigns, that I, my heirs, executors and adminiſtrators, ſhall and will at any time or times hereafter, at the requeſt, coſt, and charges of him, his heirs, executors, adminiſtrators and aſſigns, make, ſeal, execute and deliver, or cauſe or procure to be made, ſealed, executed and delivered, all and every ſuch reaſonable act and acts, thing and things, conveyance and conveyances, aſſurance and aſſurances, in the law, for the perfect granting, conveying, releaſing, transferring and aſſigning, all the right, title, intereſt, property, claim and demand which I now have, or which I, my heirs, executors or adminiſtrators, may at any time hereafter have, of, in and to all and ſingular the lands hereby granted and aſſigned unto him, his heirs, executors, adminiſtrators and aſſigns, forever, as by his Counſel learned in the law, ſhall be reaſonably adviſed, deviſed or required: And I do hereby make, conſtitute and appoint the ſaid Moore Co NC

my true and lawful attorney, irrevocably, to aſk, demand, recover and receive, of and from the United States, or from any perſon or perſons acting by, from or under their authority, all and ſingular the lands due and belonging to me, or detained from me by any manner of ways or means whatſoever; and upon receipt thereof to execute and deliver ſufficient and requiſite receipts, releaſes and acquittances for the ſame; and by good and ſufficient conveyances and aſſurances in the law, to grant, bargain, ſell, releaſe and confirm, the ſaid lands to the purchaſer or purchaſers thereof, his, her or their executors, adminiſtrators and aſſigns, forever, with power and attorney or attornies under him, for the purpoſes aforeſaid, to make and ſubſtitute, and to do all lawful and requiſite for effecting the premiſes, as fully and effectually to all intents and purpoſes, as I might or could do by being perſonally preſent, and to have done the ſame; hereby allowing, ratifying and confirming all and whatſoever my ſaid attorney, or his ſubſtitute or ſubſtitutes, ſhall or may do or cauſe to be done therein in virtue hereof. 1800

IN WITNESS WHEREOF have hereunto ſet hand and ſeal this day of in the year of our Lord, one thouſand ſeven hundred and ninety

Sealed and delivered in the preſence of

North Carolina

450
7
3150
2000
5150

450
7
3192
228
3420

State of

County, } ſs.

BE IT KNOWN, That on the day of the date hereof, before 1800

Eſquire of the Juſtices in and of the county and ſtate aforeſaid,

perſonally came the above named

and acknowledged the above Deed Poll and Letter of Attorney to be act and deed. IN TESTIMONY WHEREOF, have hereunto ſet hand and ſeal the day of

in the year of our Lord, one thouſand ſeven hundred and ninety

County, } ſs.

I Clerk of the court of ſaid county, in the ſtate aforeſaid, do hereby certify, atteſt, and make known, that the name

ſubſcribed to the acknowledgment of the foregoing Deed Poll and Letter of Attorney, is the proper hand-writing of Eſquire who at the time of ſubſcribing the ſame and now lawfully and duly appointed, commiſſioned and qualified as Juſtice of the Peace for county aforeſaid; and that full faith and credit is and ought to be given to any act as ſuch by ſubſcribed, as well in courts of juſtice as thereout.

IN TESTIMONY WHEREOF, I have hereunto ſet my hand, and affixed the ſeal of ſaid county, this day of

in the year of our Lord, one thouſand ſeven hundred and ninety

A List of Persons who have failled to give in their Taxable property in Moore County 1807

	Polls	Land	Retailers	Stud Horses	Cotton Machines
Niell McLeod Surveyor	3	3700	-	-	-
James Adkins	-	900	-	-	-
The Estate of Wm. Armstrong	-	200	-	-	-
Murdoch Bethune	-	-	1	-	-
Wm. McAuley	-	-	1	-	-
Angus McQueen	[illegible]	150	-	-	-
Josiah Tyson	-	-	1	-	-
Reuben Shields	-	-	1	-	-
Rodrick Murchison	1	-	-	-	-
John Murchison	1	-	-	-	-
John Carrell Jun	2	300	-	-	-
Samuel Dunn	2	-	-	-	-
Richard Ragsdale	1	-	-	-	-
	10.	5250	4		

A List of Persons names who have failed to give in ~~for the year~~ their Taxable property for the year 1808 in Moore County

Name	Poles	Lands	Retailers	Stud Horses	Stores
Murdoch Bethune	-	-	1	-	-
Neill McLeod Merchant	9	1794	1	20	1
Wm McAulay	1	650	1	-	-
John McNeill Cumberland County	-	200	-	-	-
Griffin Carmical	-	100	-	-	-
Alexr Carmicall	1	-	-	-	-
Wm Badget	1	-	-	-	-
John McLeod	1	-	1	-	-
John Medlin	-	-	-	20	-
John Rogers	1	-	-	-	-
Lot Rogers	1	-	-	-	-
Wm Sears	1	-	-	-	-
John Murchison	1	-	-	-	-
Rodrick Murchison	1	-	-	-	-
John McDonald	1	-	-	-	-
James Dowel	1	-	-	-	-
Benjamin Atkinson	1	-	-	-	-
Adam Comer	-	360	-	-	-
Ambrose Brewer	-	-	-	15	-
Edward Beason 1806 & 1807 & 1808	-	650	-	-	-
Jonathan Caddell	-	200	-	-	-
Thos Greane	1	175	-	-	-
Robert Dickinson	-	250	-	-	-
Richard Ragsdale	1	-	-	-	-
Benjamin Bishop	-	100	-	-	-
Sampson Smith	1	-	-	-	-
	24	4479	4	3	1

A list of Persons Names who failled give in Their Taxable property for the year 1808 in Moore County

Name	Polls	Land	Retailing	Stud Horse
	24	4479		
Gilbert Buie	2	300	-	-
Thomas Tyson	-	2700	-	-
John Boyd	1	-	-	-
	27	7479		

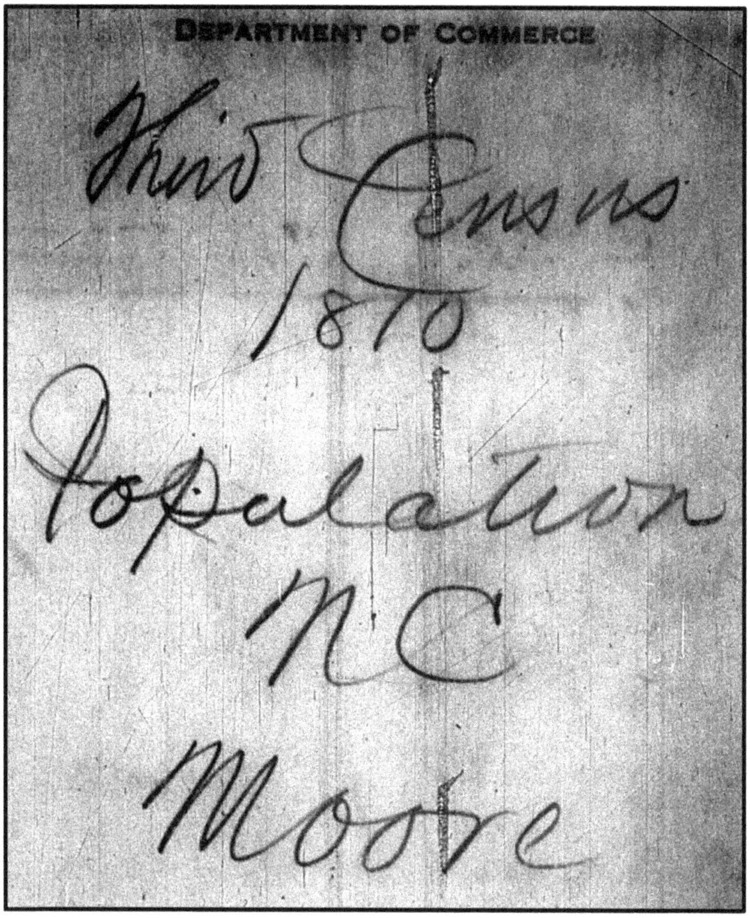
DEPARTMENT OF COMMERCE

Third Census
1810
Population
NC
Moore

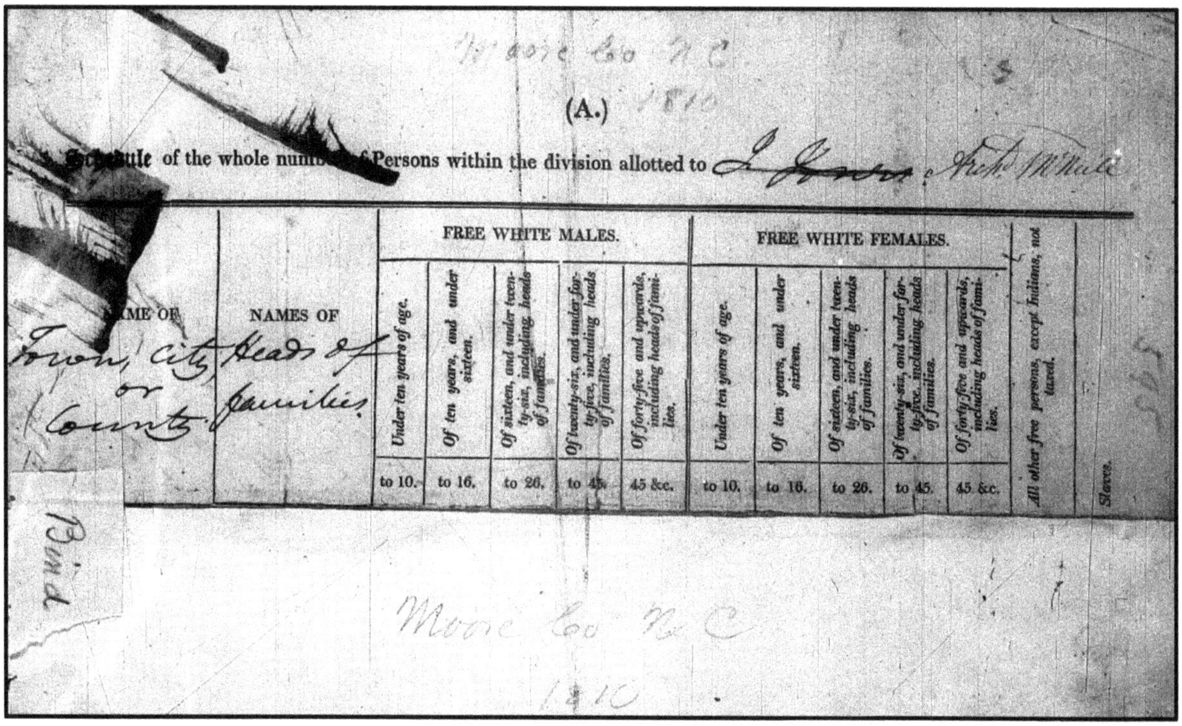
Moore Co NC
1810

(A.)

Schedule of the whole number of Persons within the division allotted to ~~J. Jones~~ Arch. McNeill

NAME OF Town, city or County	NAMES OF Heads of families	FREE WHITE MALES.					FREE WHITE FEMALES.					All other free persons, except Indians, not taxed.	Slaves.
		Under ten years of age.	Of ten years, and under sixteen.	Of sixteen, and under twenty-six, including heads of families.	Of twenty-six, and under forty-five, including heads of families.	Of forty-five and upwards, including heads of families.	Under ten years of age.	Of ten years, and under sixteen.	Of sixteen, and under twenty-six, including heads of families.	Of twenty-six, and under forty-five, including heads of families.	Of forty-five and upwards, including heads of families.		
		to 10.	to 16.	to 26.	to 45.	45 &c.	to 10.	to 16.	to 26.	to 45.	45 &c.		

Bind

Moore Co NC
1810

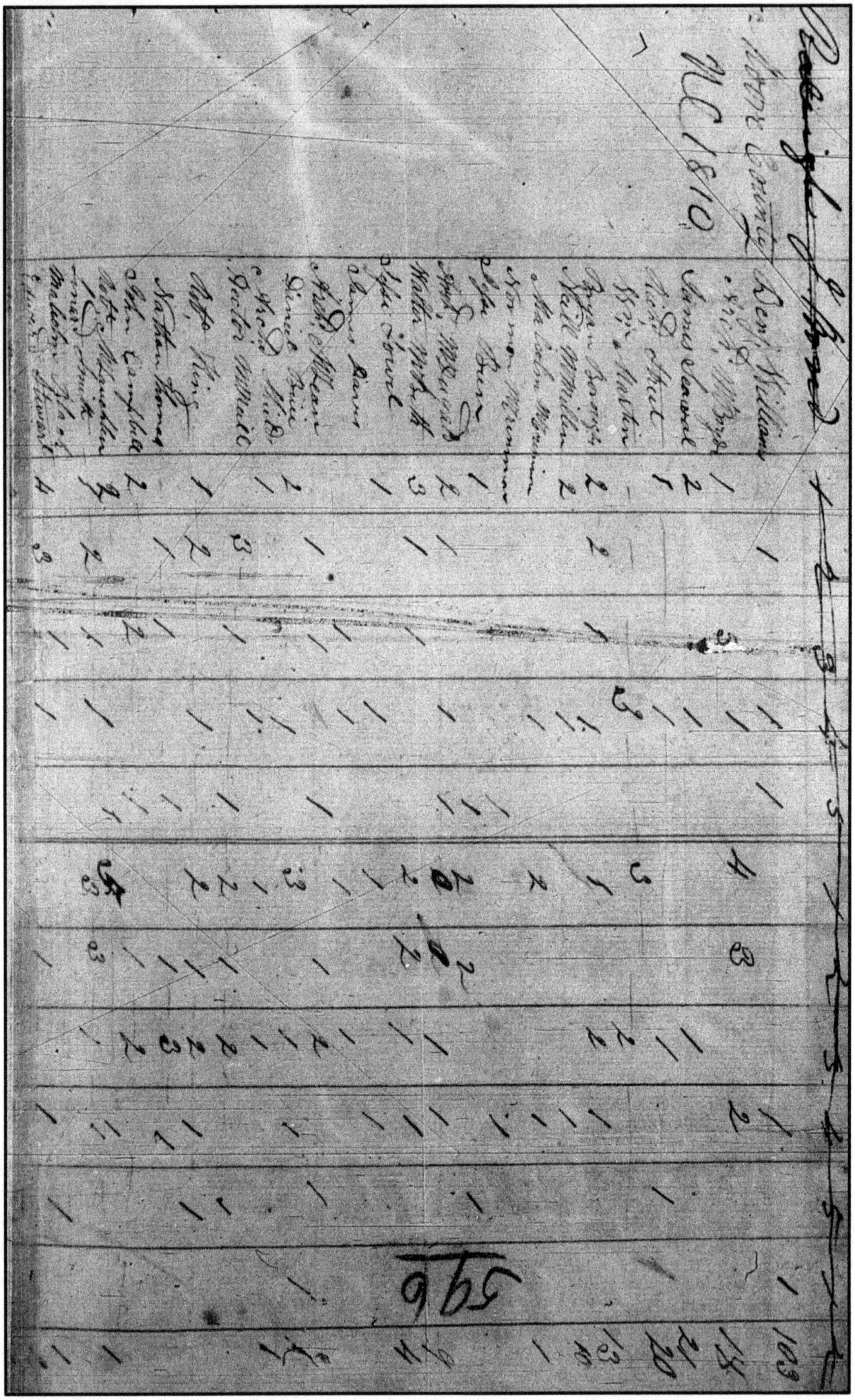

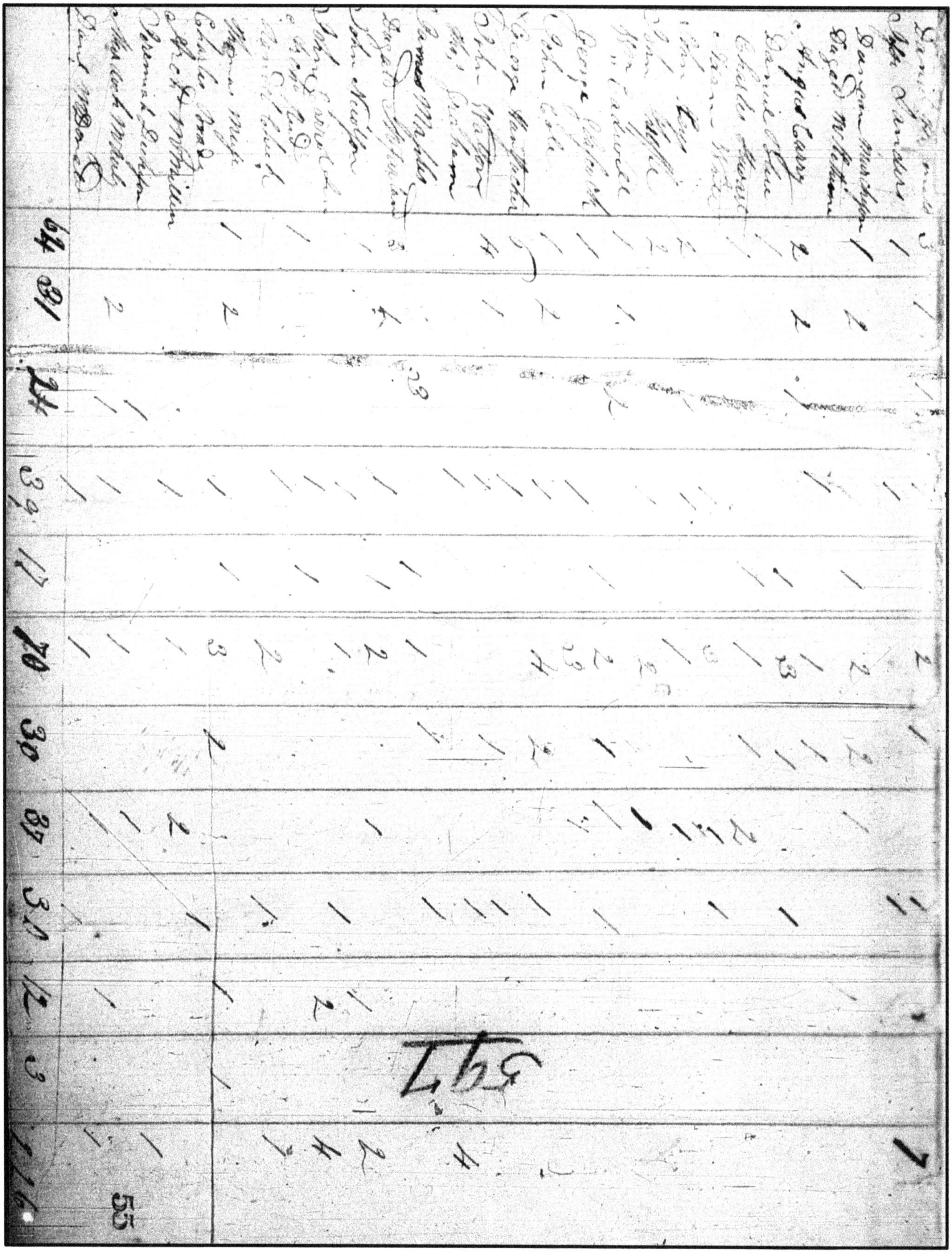

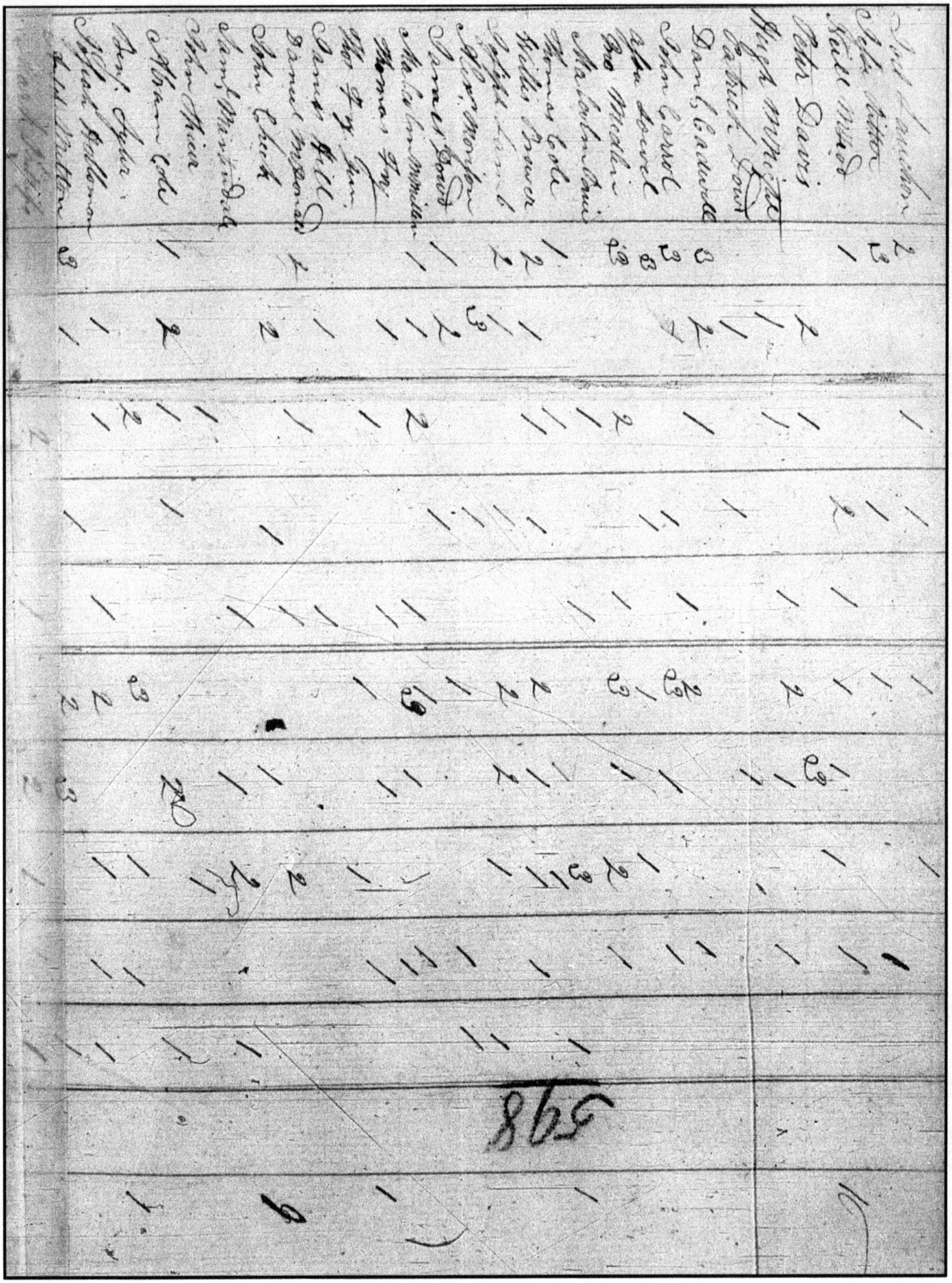

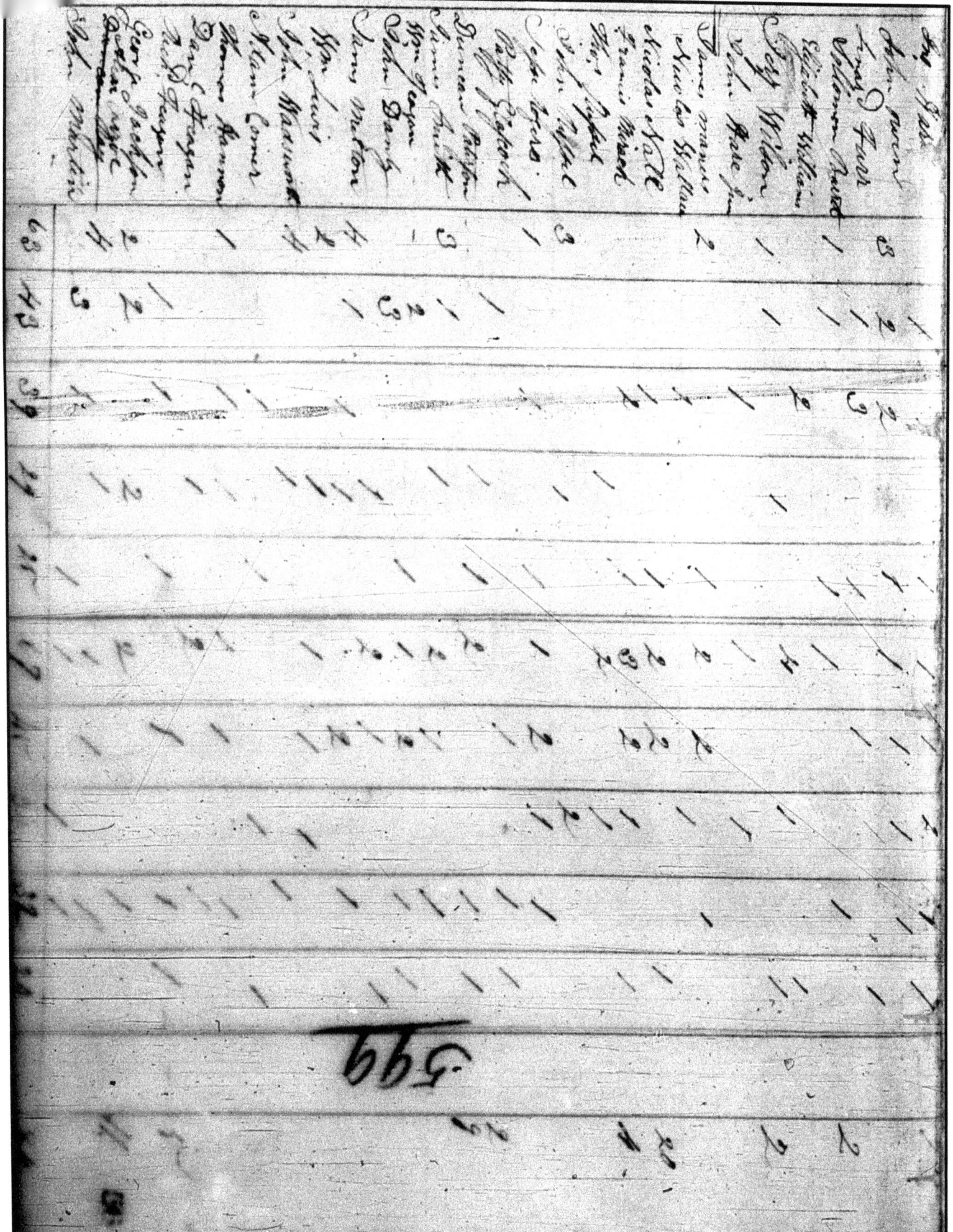

Jno. Hare
John Owen
Lenard Farr
Sollomon Barrett
Elizabeth Williams
Terry Wilson
John Hare Jun
James Maness
Nicolas Wallace
Nicolas Nall
Francis Mirach
Thos. Russell
John Russell
Jesse Rogers
Patty Glascock
Duncan Patterson
James Smith
Wm. Feagan
John Danly
James Melton
Wm. Lewis
John Wadsworth
Adam Comer
Thomas Hannon
Danl. Feagan
Richd. Feagan
George Jackson
Allen Rowe
~~Duncan May~~
John Martin

63 43 39 24 25 17

599

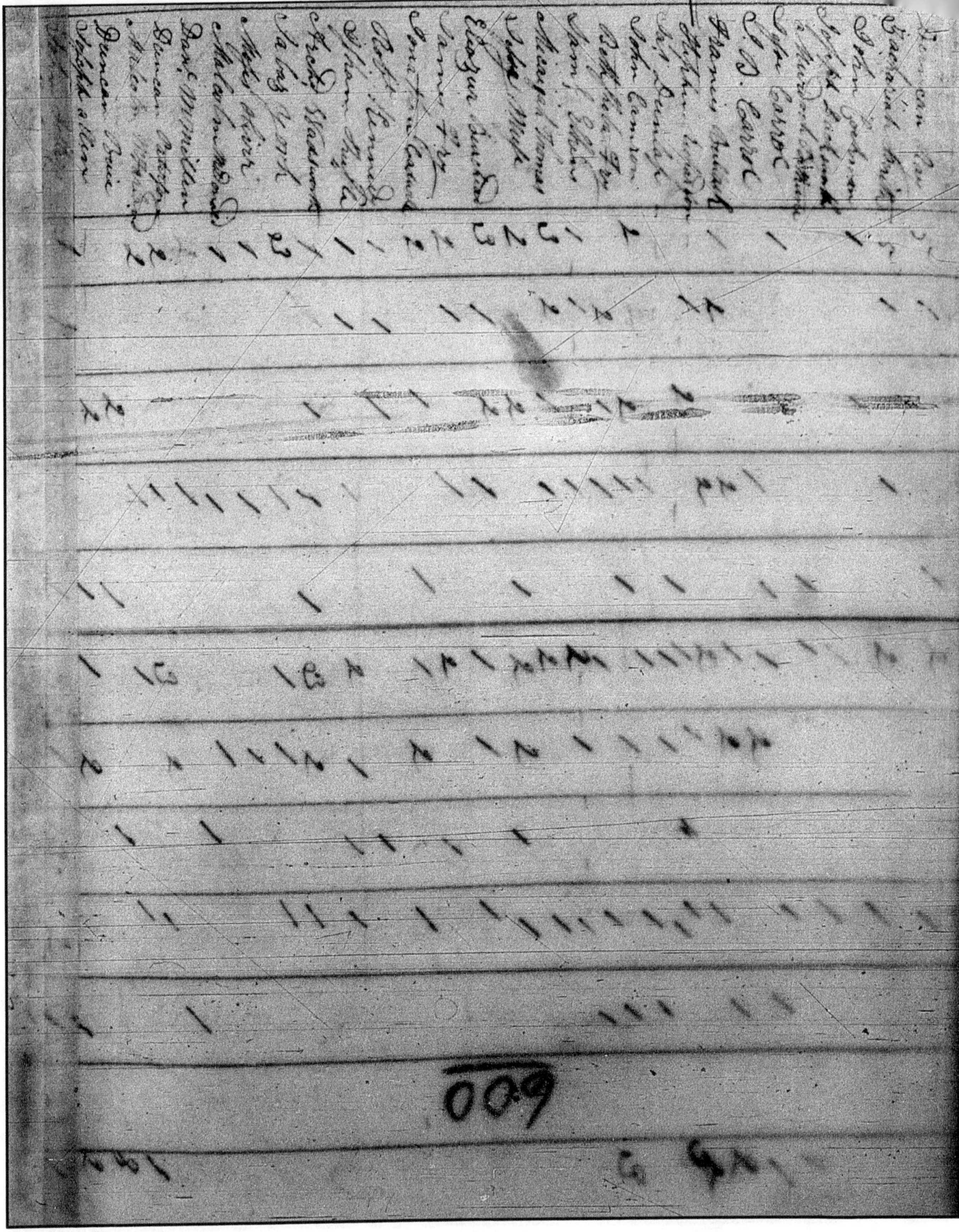

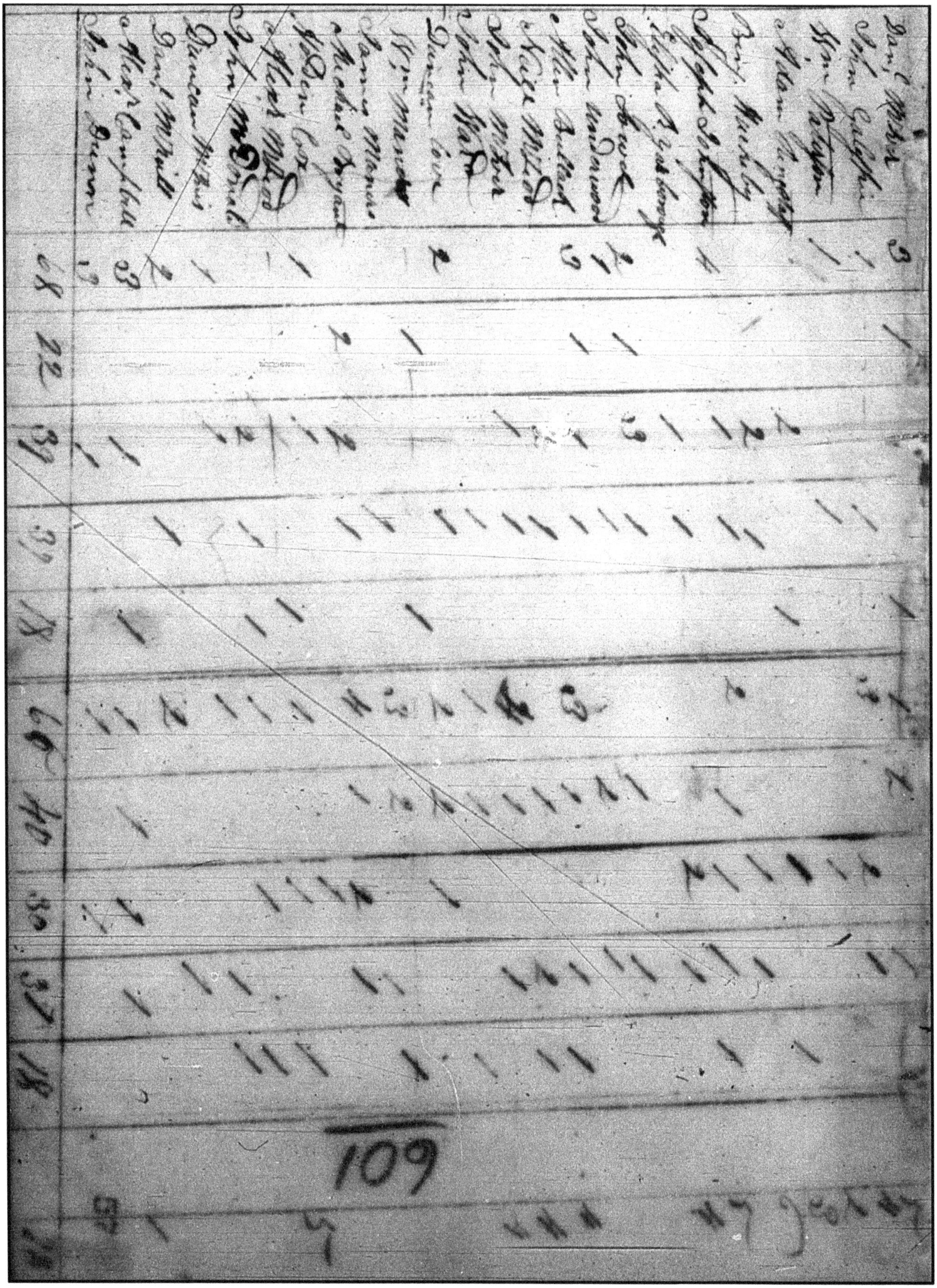

Danl. McIver
John Galaspie
Wm. Paterson
Adam Nungstag
Benj. Huckeby
Joseph Johnston
Elisha R. Yarborough
John Sewel
John Underwood
Allen Bullach
Neill McLeod
John McIver
John Ward
Duncan Love
Wm. Manes
James Manes
Michael Bryant
Holden Cox
Alexr. McLeod
John McDonald
Duncan McInnis
Danl. McNeill
Alexr. Campbell
John Dunn

68 22 39 37 18 66 40 30 37 18 … 109

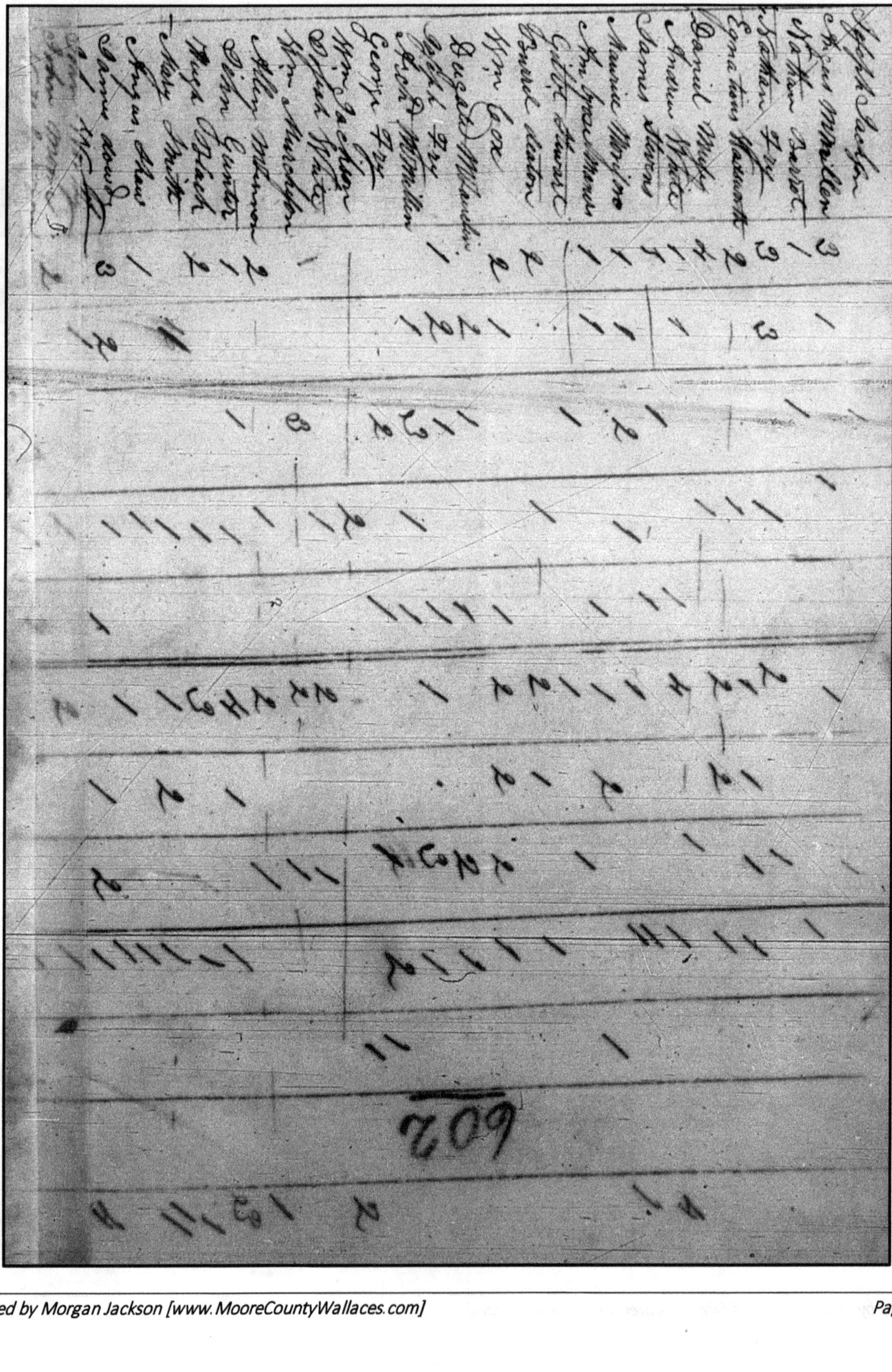
Joseph Jackson
Angus McMillen
Nathan Barrot
Nathan Fry
Egnatious Wadsworth
Daniel Mufey
Andrew White
James Stevens
Maurice Morison
Ambrose Menes
Gilbt Stewart
Burrel Deaton
Wm Cox
Dugald McLauclin
Joseph Fry
Archd McMillen
George Fry
Wm Jackson
Josiah White
Wm Murchison
Allen McKinnon
John Gunter
Hugh Black
Mary Smith
Angus Shaw
James Dowdy
John [illegible]
John [illegible]

602

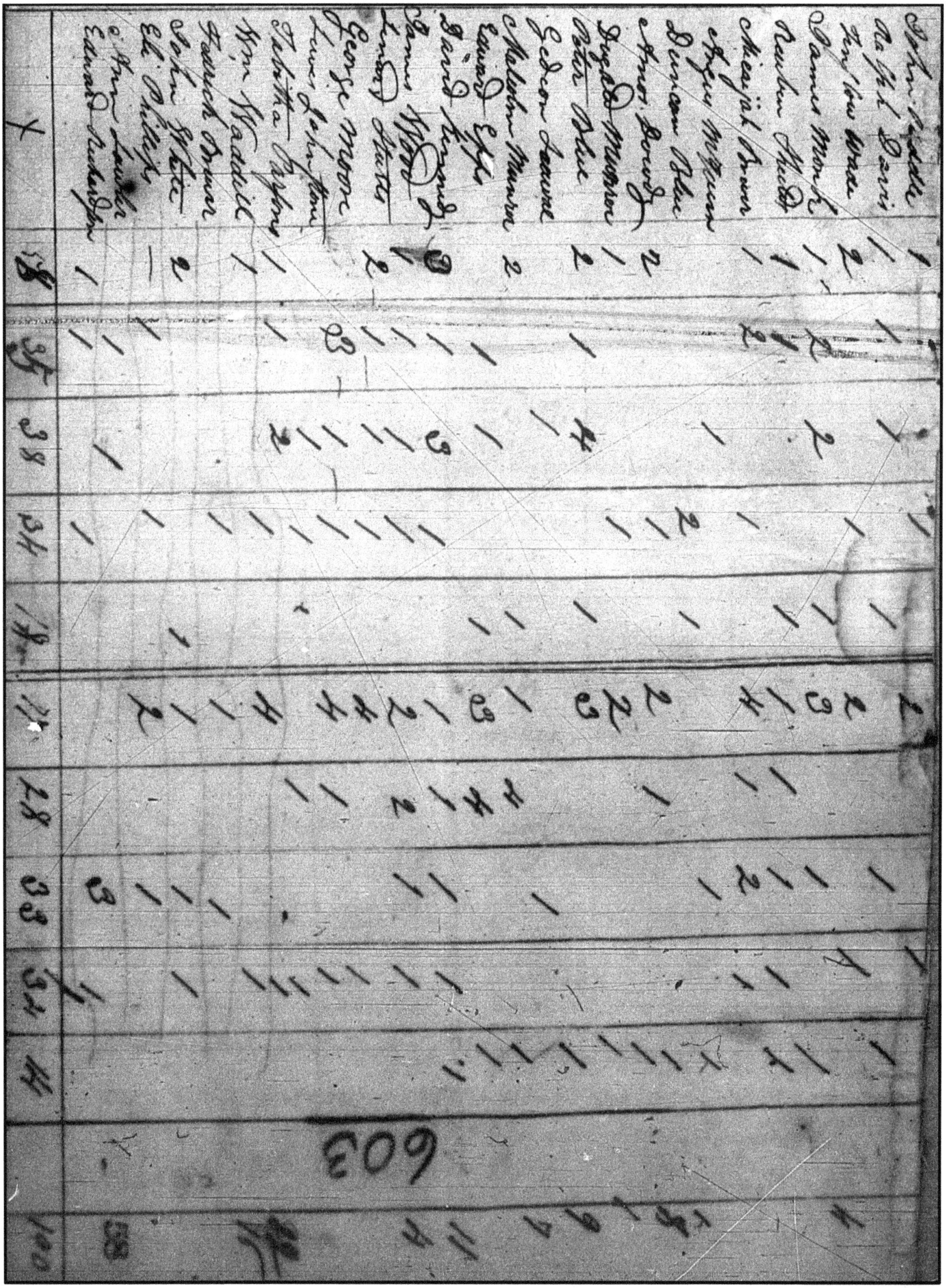

John Liddle	1			1		2			1			
Ralph Davis	1	1	1		1			1		1		
Tinslow Wade	2			1		2			1			4
James Monk	1	2	2		1	3		1		1		
Reuben Shields	1	1			1	1	1	1	1	1		
Micajah Brewer	1	2		1		4	1	2	1			
Angus McQueen			1					1		1		
Duncan Blue				2	1					1		18
Amos Dowdy	2			1		2	1			1		
Dugald Munroe	1			1		2				1		1
Peter Blue	2	1	4		1	3				1		9
Gedeon Laawre			1					1		1		7
Malcolm Munroe	2				1	1	4			1		
Edward Epps		1	1		1	3	4			1		
David Kennedy	3	1	3	1		1	1	1	1	1		11
James Wood	1	1	1	1		2	2	1	1			4
Lenard Stutts	2	1	1	1		4			1			
George Moore		3	1	1		4	1		1			
Lewis Johnstone			1	1			1		1			
Tabitha Parsons	1	1	2	1		4			1			[illegible]
Wm Waddell	1			1					1			
Fedrick Brewer				1		1		1				
John White	2				1	1		1	1			
Eli Phillips	—	1		1		2		1				
Ann Lawler		1	1					3				58
Edward Richardson	1	1		1					1			
X	58	35	38	34	18	[illegible]	28	33	34	14		100

603

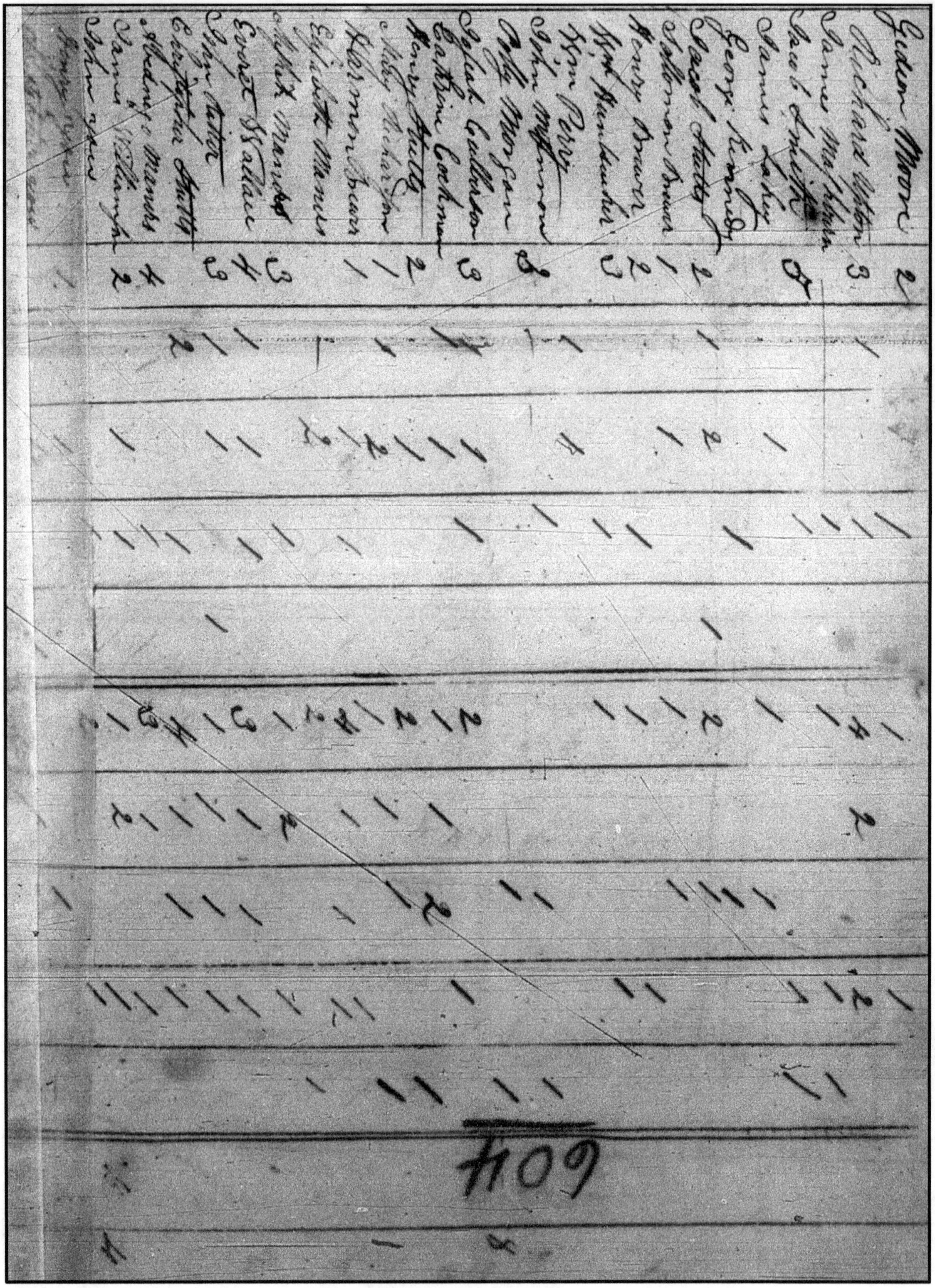

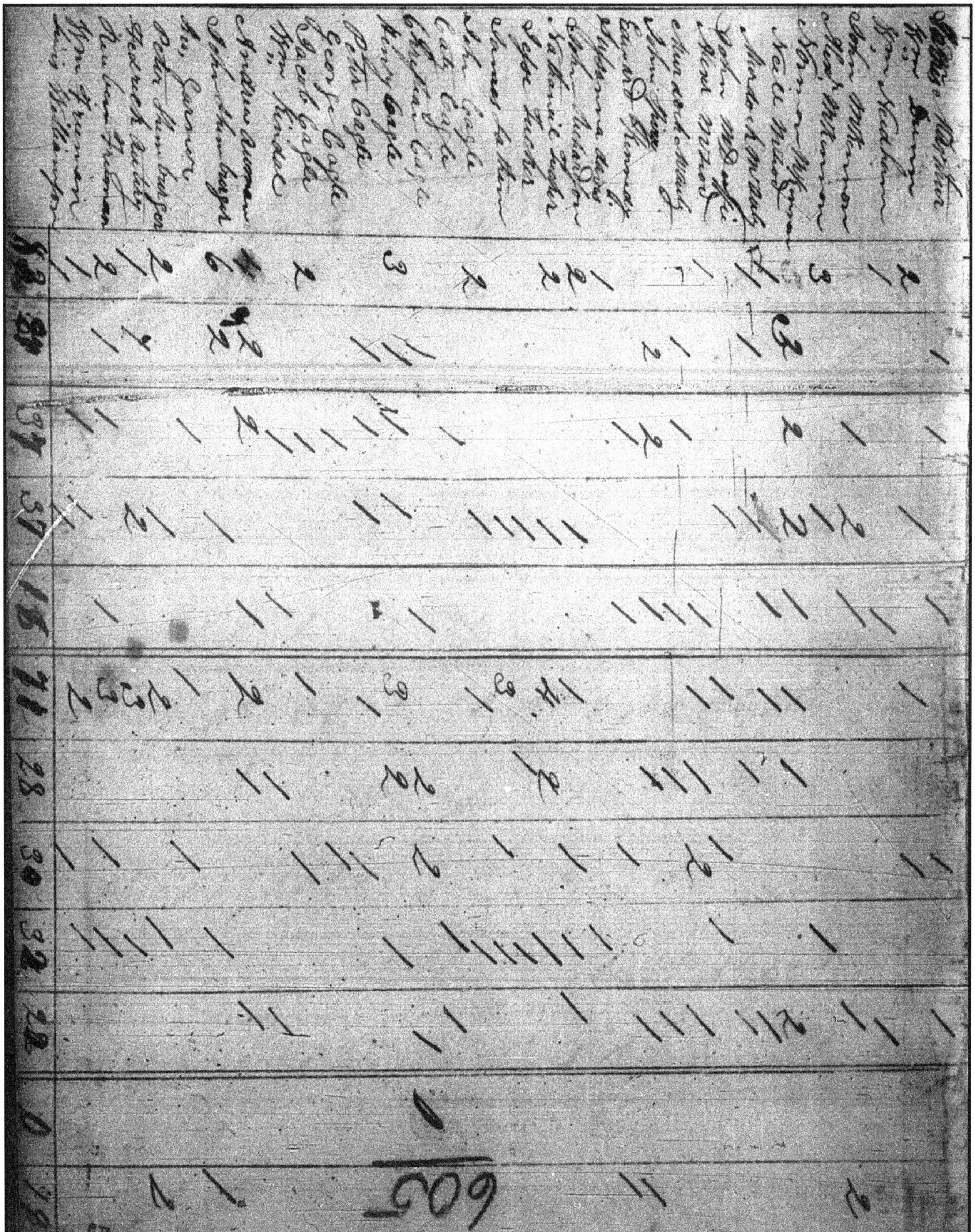
James McArthur
Wm Dunn
Wm Needham
John McKinnon
Alexr McKinnon
Norman McKinnon
Neill McLeod
Murdoch McAuly
John McDuffie
Alexr McLeod
Murdoch McAuly
John Spivey
Edward Kennedy
Sussanna davis
John Richardson
Nathaniel Tucker
Jesse Tucker
James Gathen
John Cagle
Caty Cagle
Christian Cagle
Henry Cagle
Peter Cagle
George Cagle
Jacob Cagle
Wm Kindal
Andrew Auman
John Shamburger
Wm Garner
Peter Shamburger
Fedrick Autery
Reuben Freeman
Wm Freeman
Lois Williamson
605
59

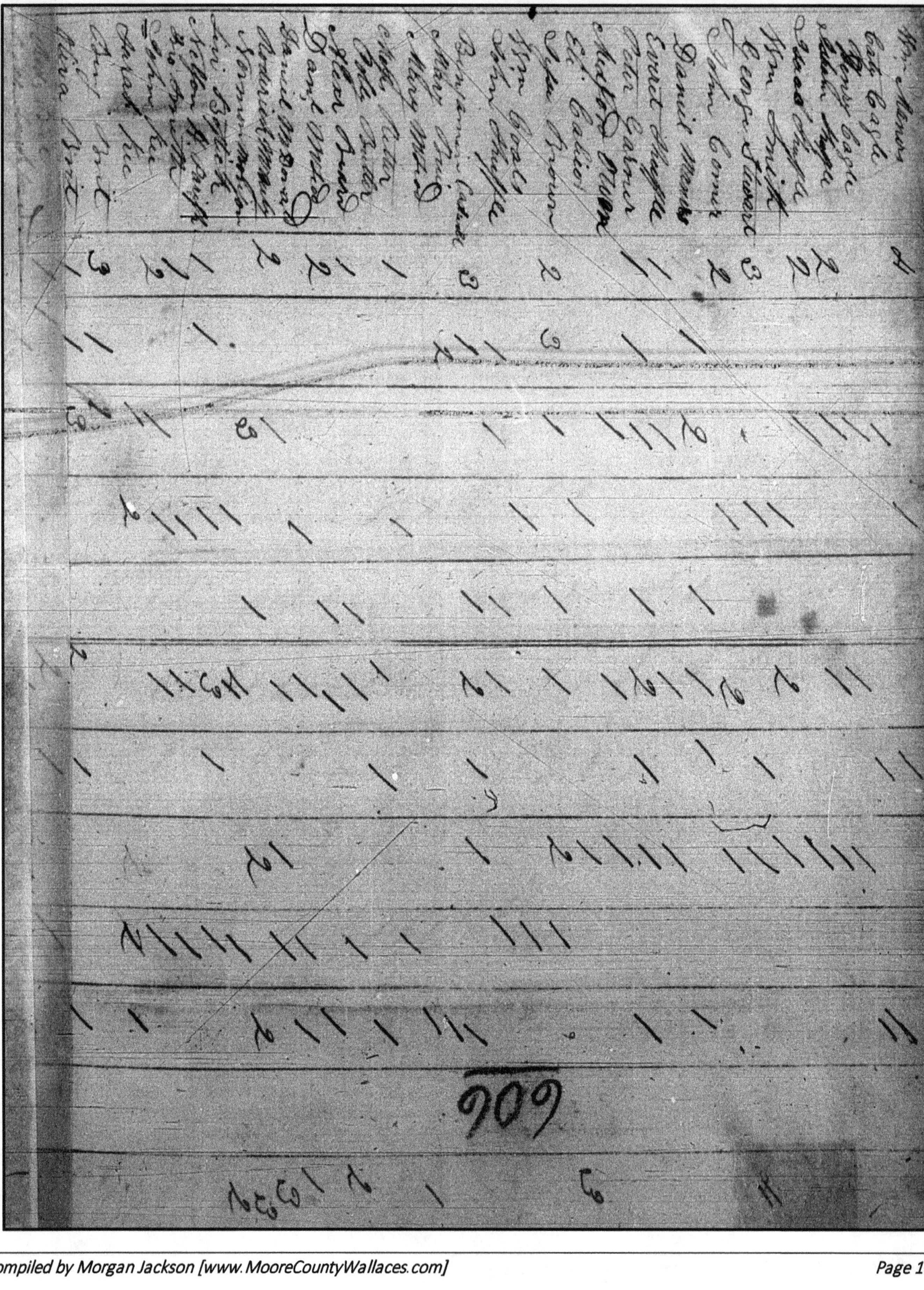
Wm Manors
Caty Cagle
Henry Cagle
Isham Shuffle
Isaac Shuffle
Wm Smith
George Stewart
John Corner
Daniel Manors
Everet Shuffle
Peter Garner
Medford Olvam
Eli Calicot
Jesse Brown
Wm Coals
John Shuffle
Benjamin Cadwell
Mary Brin
Mary McLeod
Moses Ritter
Polly Butler
Alexr Beard
Danl McLeod
Daniel McDonald
Roderick McAuly
Norman McLeod
Levi Bostick
Nelson H. Parish
Geo Smith
John Kee
Sarah Kee
Benj Brit
Oliva Brit
606

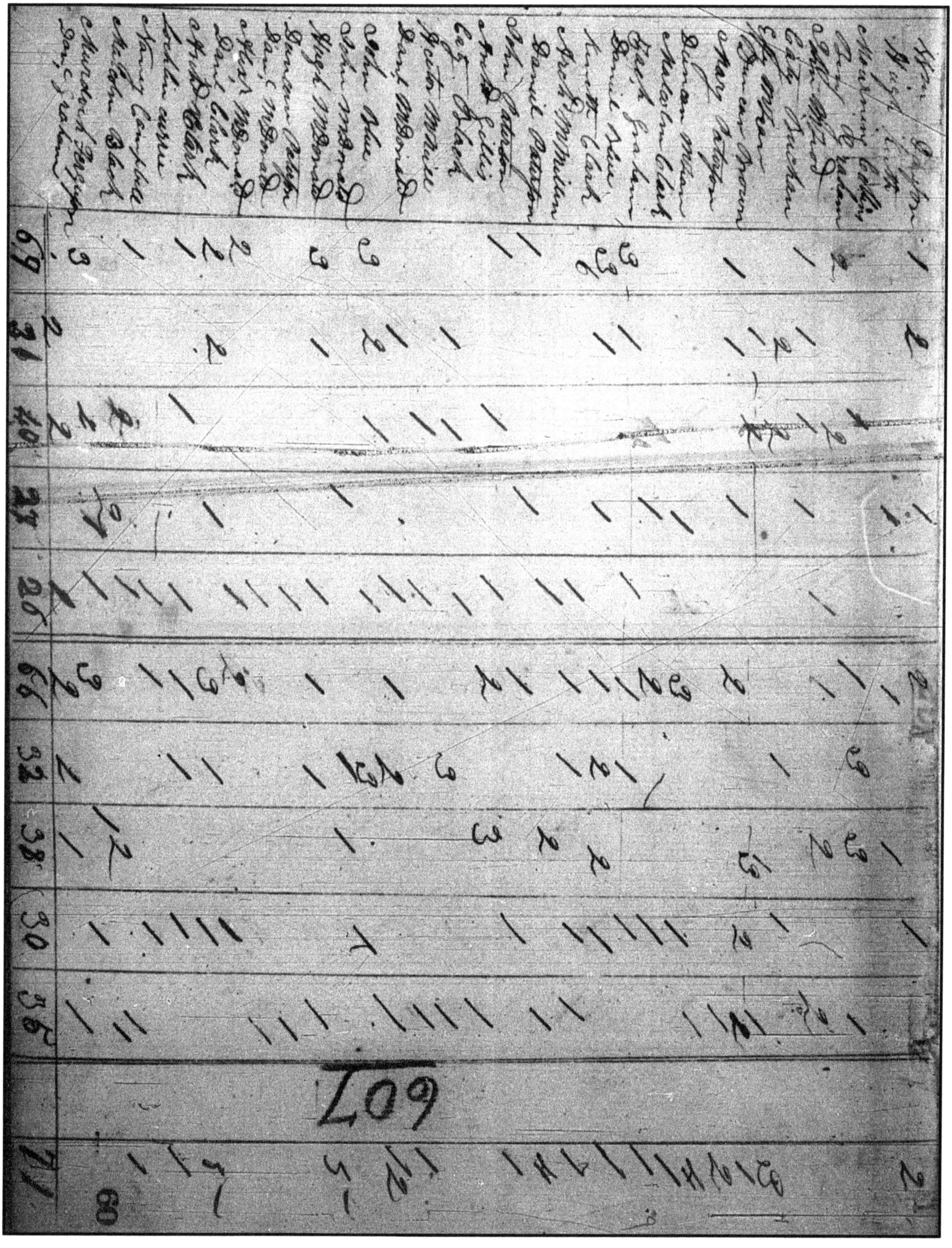
Wm Dayton
Hugh Leith
Mourning Collins
Benj Graham
John McLeod
Caty Buchan
Effy McLean
Duncan Brown
Mary Paterson
Duncan McLean
Malcolm Clark
Zach Graham
Daniel Blue
Kenneth Clark
Archd McMillan
Daniel Paterson
John Paterson
Archd Gillis
Caty Black
Hector McNeill
Danl McDonald
John Blue
John McDonald
Hugh McDonald
Duncan Paterson
Danl McDonald
Alexr McDonald
Danl Clark
Archd Clark
Lochlin Currie
Nancy Campbell
Malcolm Black
Murdoch Ferguson
Danl Graham

69	31	40	2?	26	66	32	38	30	35	607	71

60

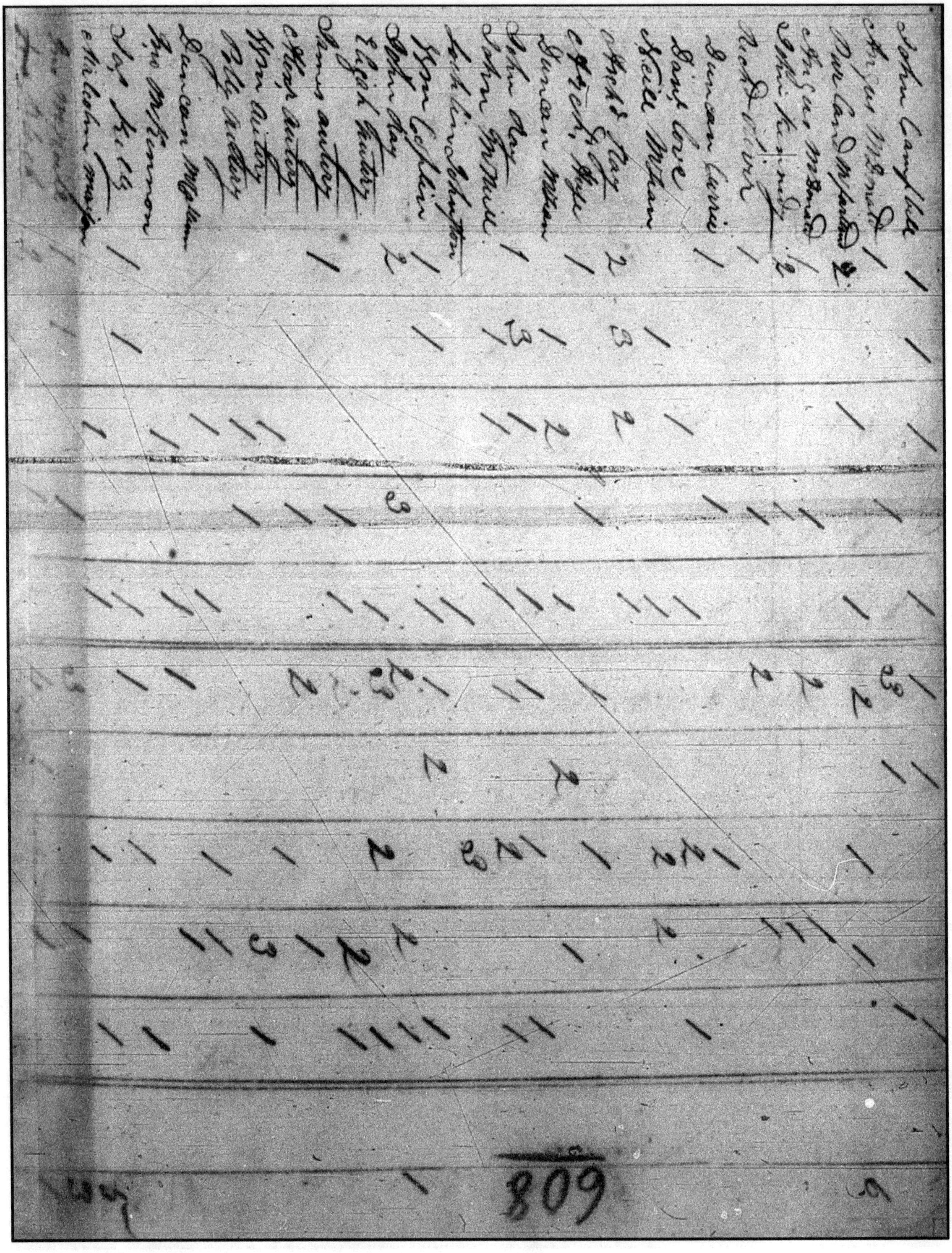
John Campbell
Angus McDonald
Durland McFarland
Angus McDonald
John Kennedy
Richd Oliver
Duncan Currie
Danl Love
Neill McLean
Archd Ray
Archd Hyde
Duncan McLean
John Ray
John McNeill
Lochlin Johnston
Wm Coplin
John Ray
Elijah Autery
James Autery
Alexr Autery
Wm Autery
Polly Autery
Duncan McCallum
Jno McKinnon
Jas Kelly
Malcolm Mason
Jno McN[illegible]
[illegible] Black

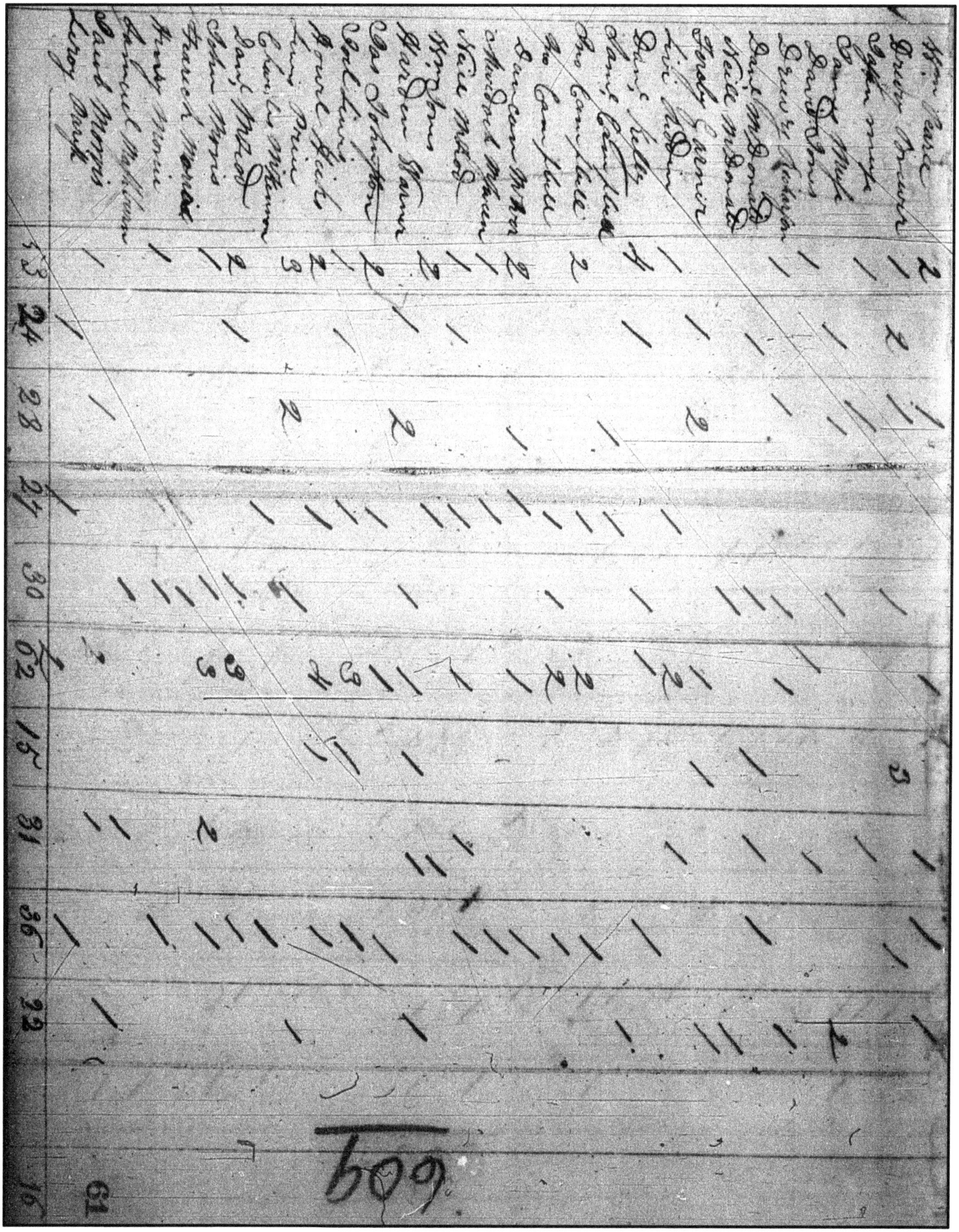

Wm Pearce	2		1			1		1	1	1		
Drewry Brewer	1	2	1		1		3		1	1		
Jaffen Muse	1		1					1				
James Muse		1	1		1					2		
David Jones	1				1	1		1				
Drewry Richardson	1		1		1	1				1		
Danl McDonald		1			1		1	1	1			
Neill McDonald					1					1		
Forby Garner		1	2			1	1			1		
Lin Redden	1			1		2		1				
Danl Kelly	4	1			1	1			1	1		
Saml Campbell			1	1					1			
Jno Campbell	2			1		2			1			
Jno Campbell				1	1	2			1			
Duncan McIver	2		1	1		1			1			
Murdock McQueen	1			1					1			
Neill McLeod	1	1		1		1		1	1			
Wm Jones	2			1				1				
Harden Warner		1	2	1	1	1	1	1		1		
Jas Johnston	2			1		1			1			
Joel Lewis	1	1		1		3	1		1			
Lowel Hicks	2			1		4	1		1			
Lewis Price	3		2		1					1		
Charles McKennon				1					1			
Danl McLeod	2	1			1	3			1			
John Morris	1				1	3		2	1			
Francis Morris					1							
Henry Morris	1				1				1			
Samuel Mathburn					1			1				
Jacob Morris	1		1			1		1		1		
Leroy Parish		1		1		1			1			
	53	24	28	27	30	62	15	31	36	22		16

609

61

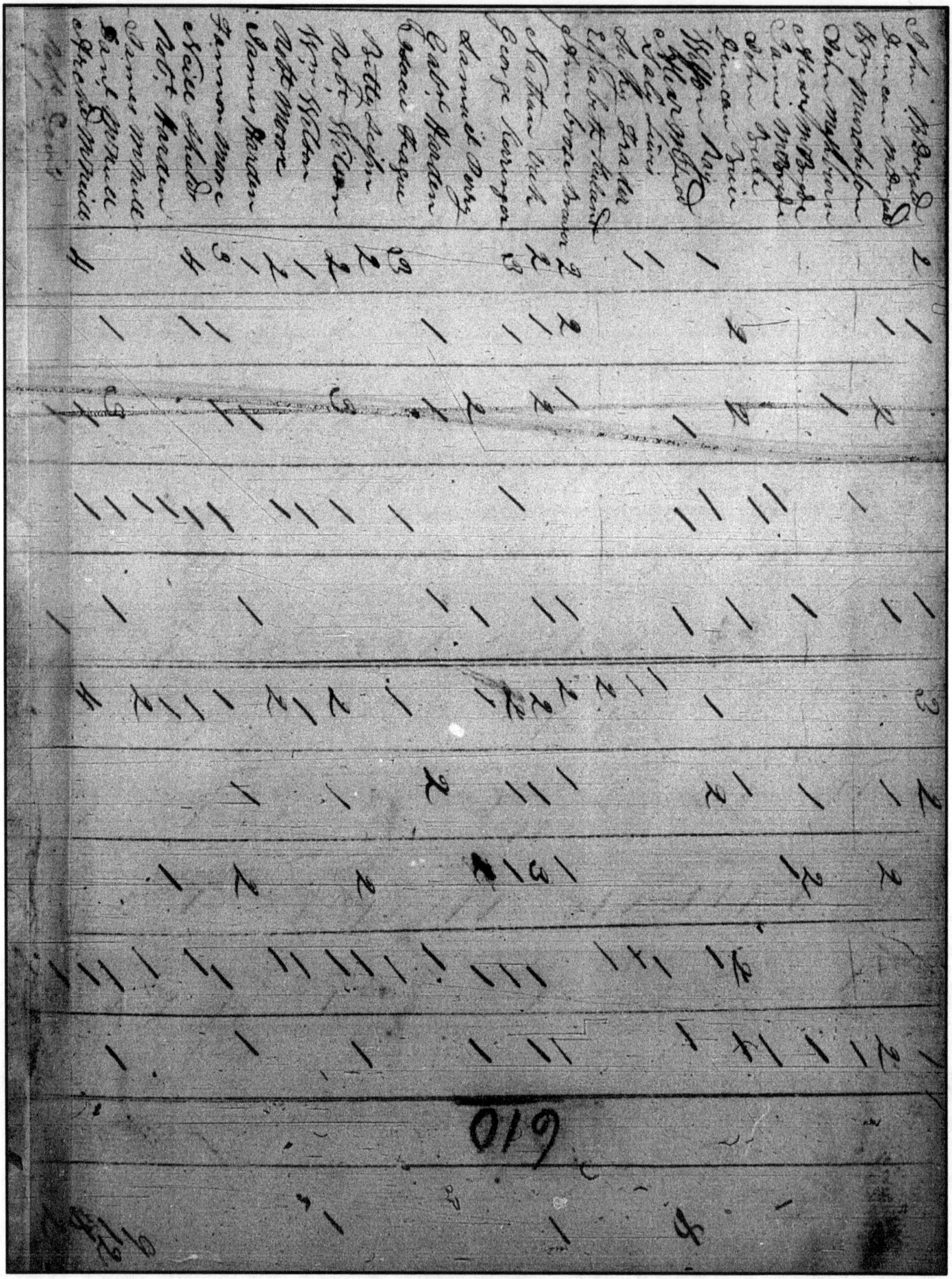
John McDougald
Duncan McDougald
Wm Murchison
John Mashburn
Alexr McBryde
James McBryde
John Buie
Duncan Buie
Willson Ray
Alexr McLeod
Saly Lewis
Luky Frazer
Elizabeth Huland
Ambrose Brewer
Nathan Vick
George Kerringer
Samuel Perry
Gabl Harden
Isaac Teague
Betty Seism
Robt Wilson
Wm Wilson
Robt Moore
James Harden
Fannon Moore
Neill Shields
Robt Harden
James McNeill
Danl McNeill
Archd McNeill
610

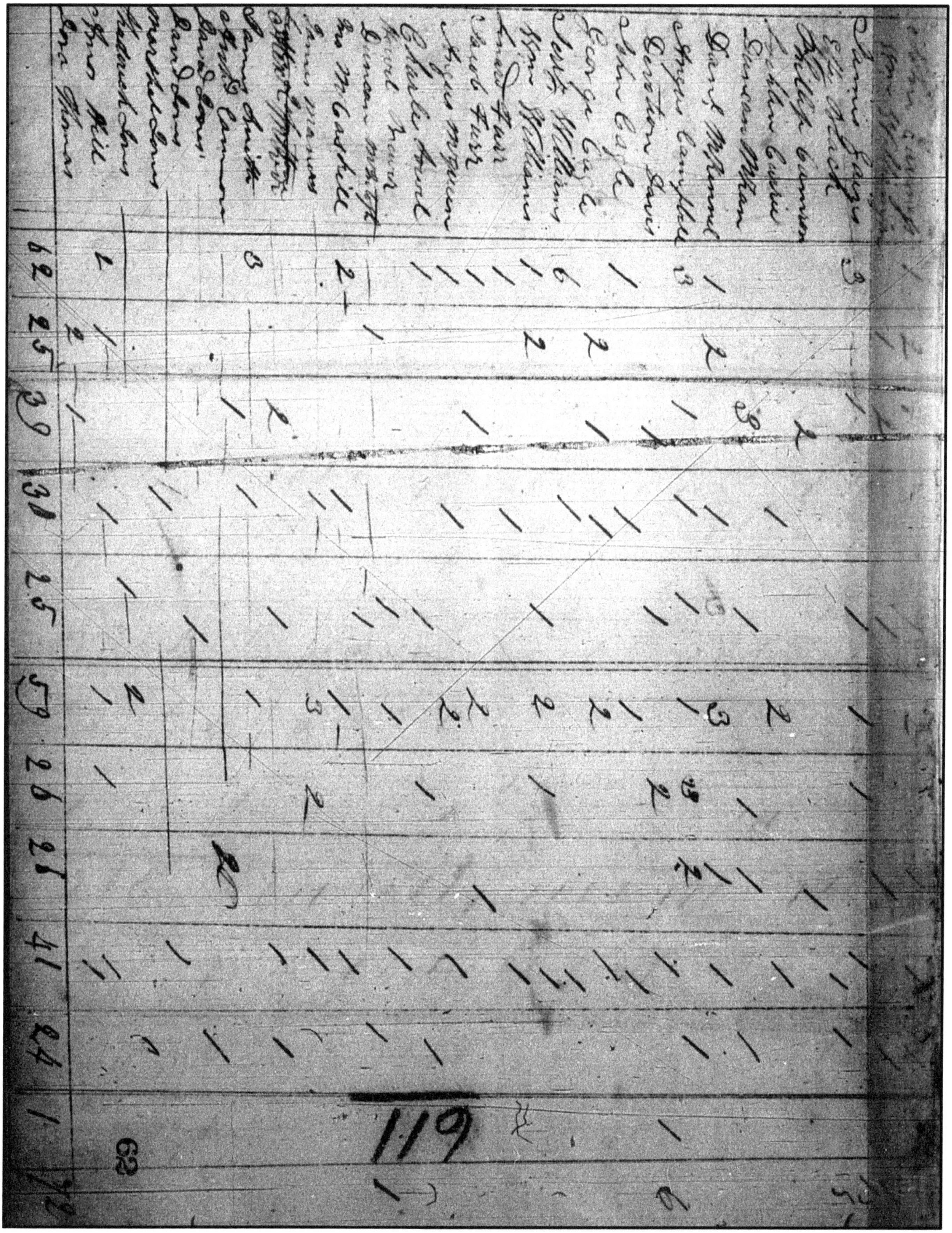

Name	M 0-10	M 10-16	M 16-26	M 26-45	M 45+	F 0-10	F 10-16	F 16-26	F 26-45	F 45+	Other Free	Slaves
[illegible]												
[illegible]												
James Gayes	3		1		1	1	1		1	1		5
Effy Black								1	1			
Phillip Cameron			2									
Lachlan Currie				1		2		1	1			
Duncan McKan			3		1		1	1		1		
Danl McKinnel	1	2		1		3		1	1	1		
Angus Campbell	3		1	1	1	1	3	2	1		1	6
Devotion Davis			1		1		2		1			
John Cagle	1			1		1			1			
George Cagle		2	1	1		2			1			
Jesse Williams	6			1					1			
Wm Williams	1	2			1	2	1		1			
Leonard Furr	1			1								
Jacob Furr	1		1			2		1				
Angus McQueen	1			1		2			1			
Charles Hurd	1				1		1		1	1		
Howel Brower					1	1			1			1
Duncan McIntosh		1			1					1		
Jno McCaskill	2			1		1			1			
James Manus				1		3	2		1			
~~Alexr McIver~~			2		1				1	1		
James Smith	3			1		1						
Andw Cameron			1					2		1		
David Jones					1							
David Jones									1			
Marshal Jones				1						1		
Shadrick Jones					1	2						
Amos Hill	2	1		1		1	1		1			
Ira Thomas		2	1									
	62	25	39	31	25	59	26	26	41	24	1	72

119

62

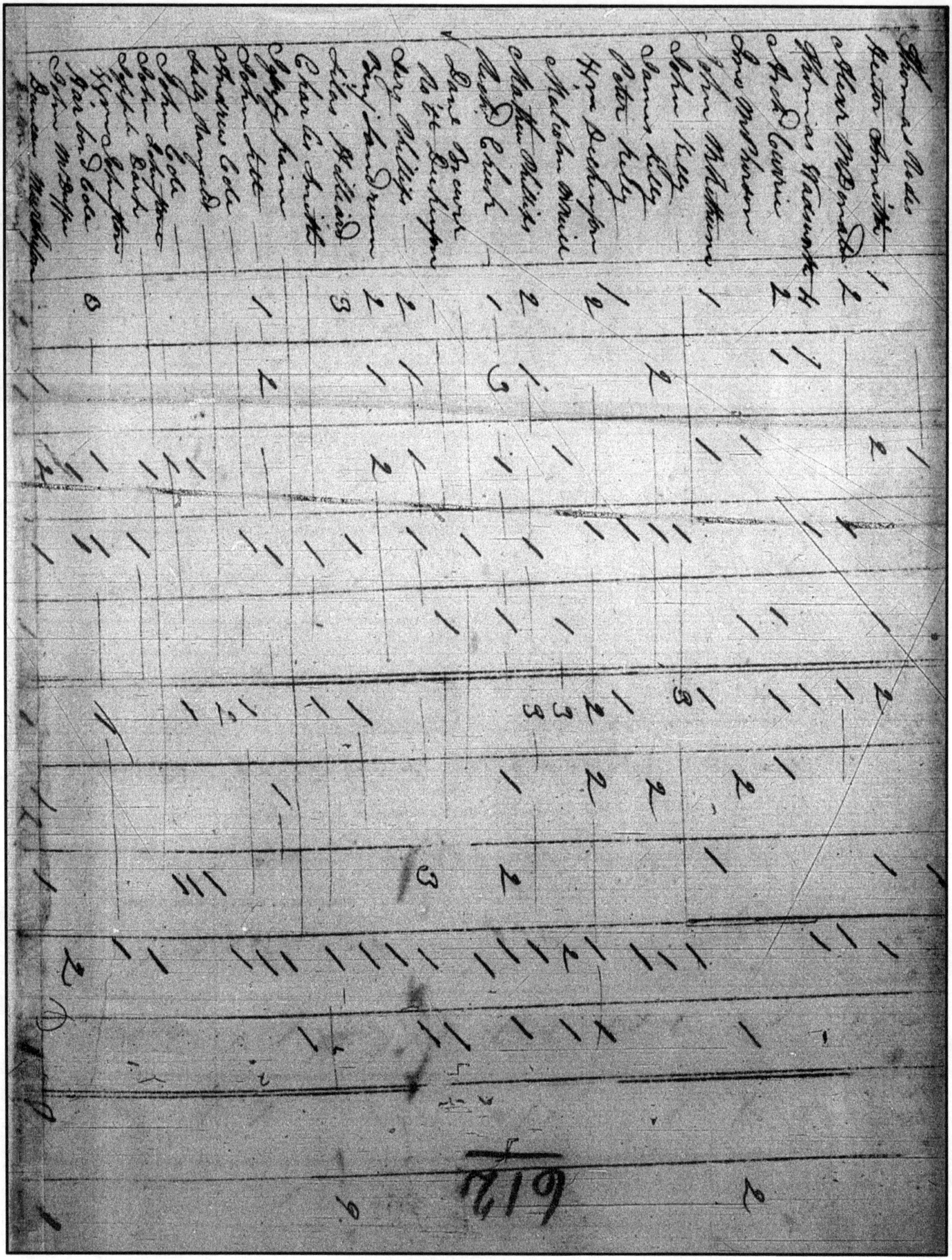

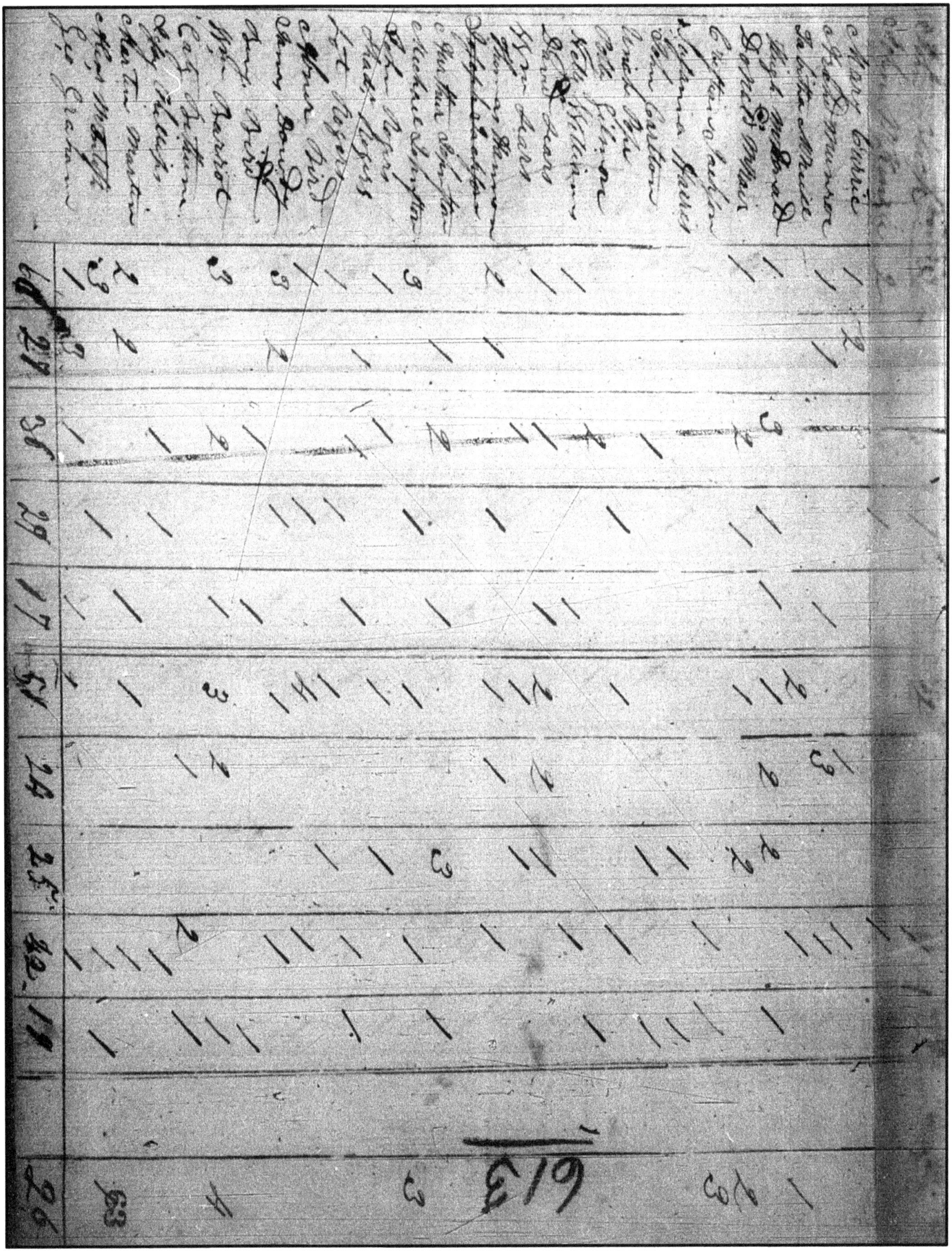

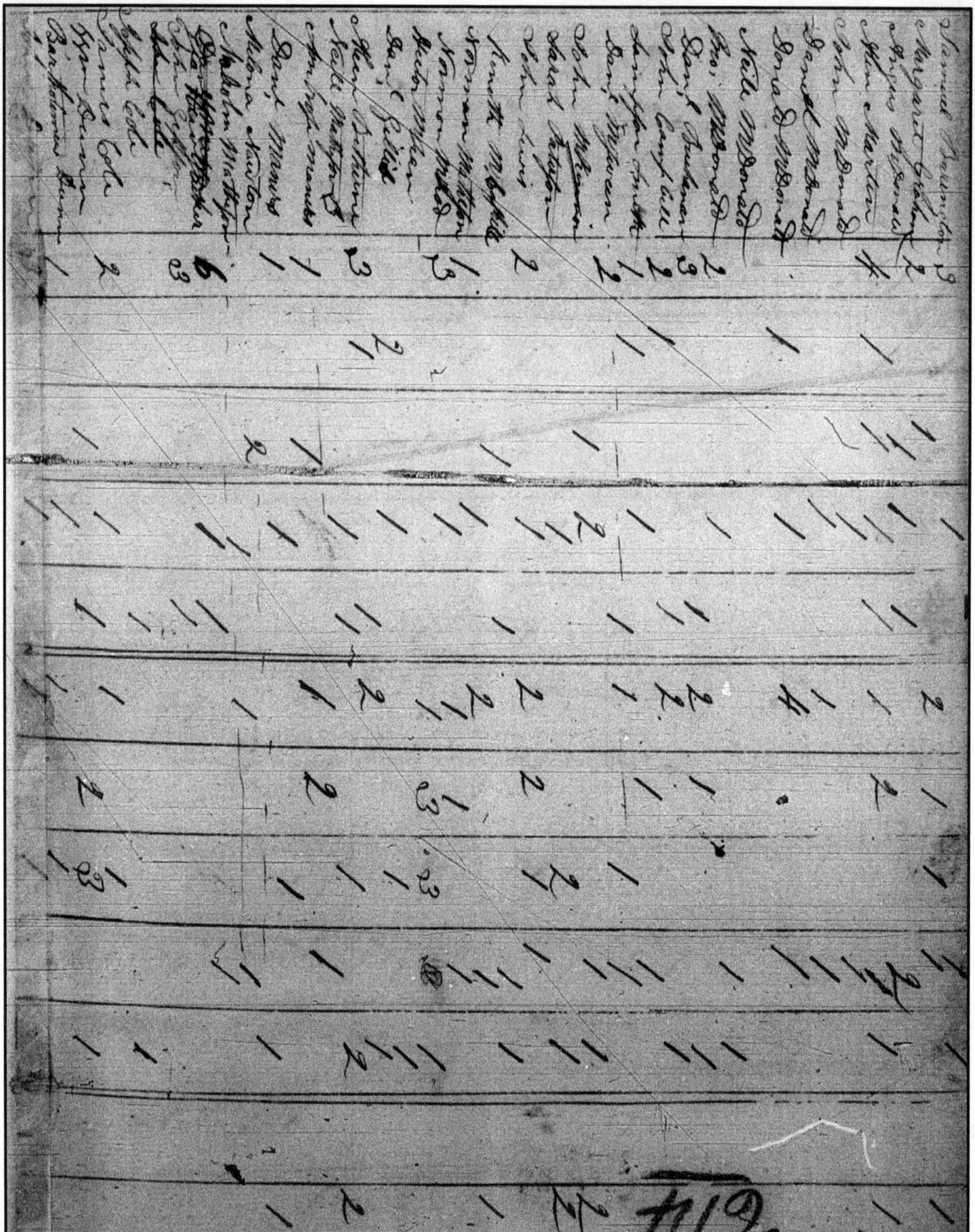

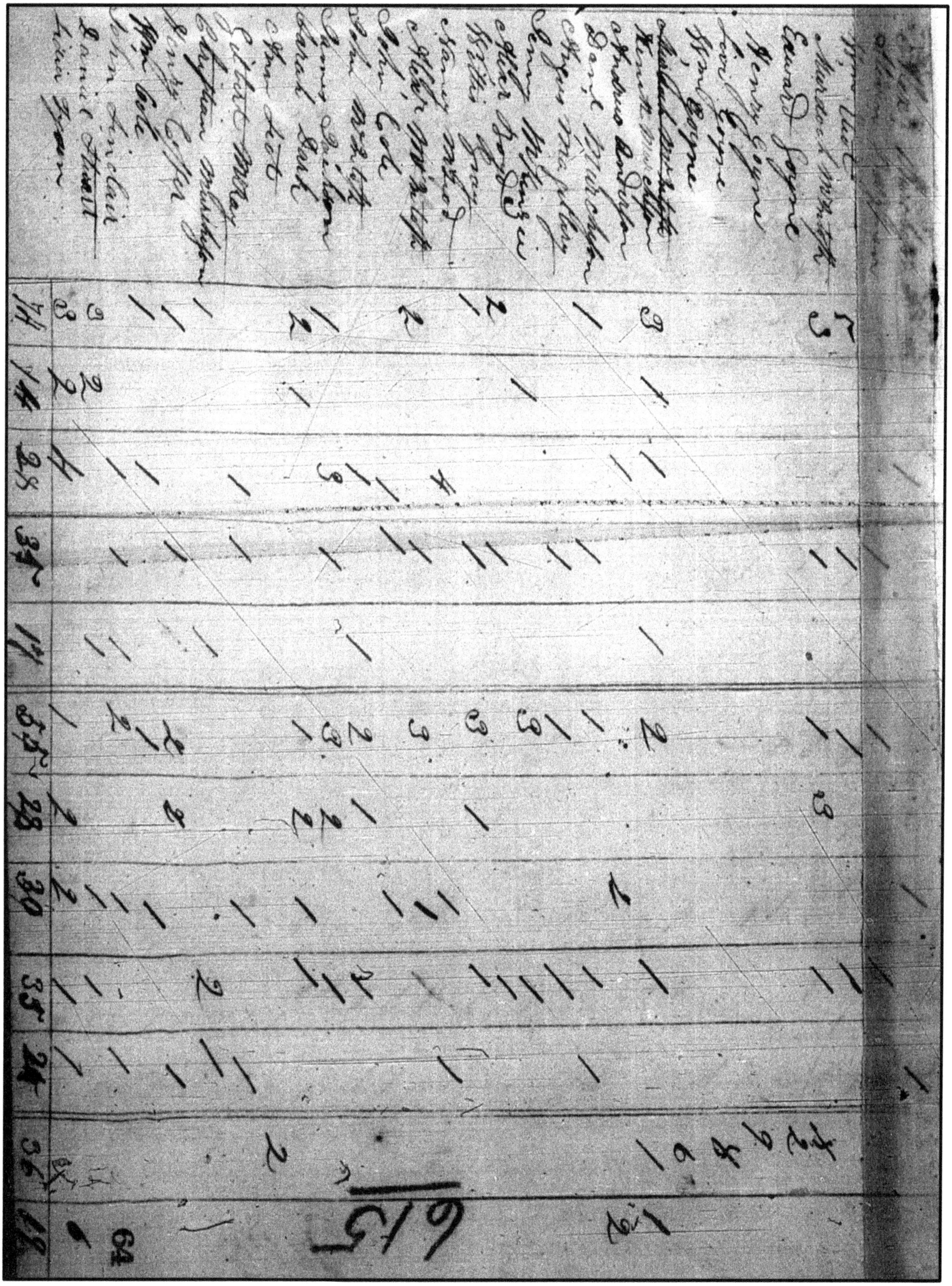

Alex'r [illegible]			1					1		1		
[illegible]				1		1			1			
Wm Elliot	5			1		1			1			
Murdoch McIntosh	3			1		1	3		1		8	
Edward Goyne											2	
Henry Goyne											9	
Levi Goyne											8	
Wm Goyne											6	
~~Murdoch McIntosh~~												
Kenneth Murchison	3	1	1		1	2			1		1	1
Andrew Anderson			1					2				2
Dan'l Murchison	1			1		1			1	1		
Angus McGillary				1		1			1			
Jenny McKenzie		1				3			1			
Alex'r Boyd	2			1					1			
Willis Gray	1			1		3	1		1			
Nancy McLeod			4	1				1		1		
Alex'r McIntosh	2			1		3		1				
John Cole			1	1				1				
John McIntosh			1		1	2	1		1			
James Jackson	1		3	1		3	2		1			
Sarah Dark	2	1				1	2	1	1			
Ann Scot											2	
Gilbert McKay			1	1				1		1		
Christian Murchison	1				1				2	1		
Henry Coffer	1			1		2	2			1		
Wm Cole	1		1			1		1				
John Sinclair			1	1	1	2		1		1		
Daniel Stuart	3	2			1			1	1			
Lidia Tyson	3	2	4			1	2	2	1	1		
	74	14	28	34	17	55	28	30	35	24	36	18

615

64

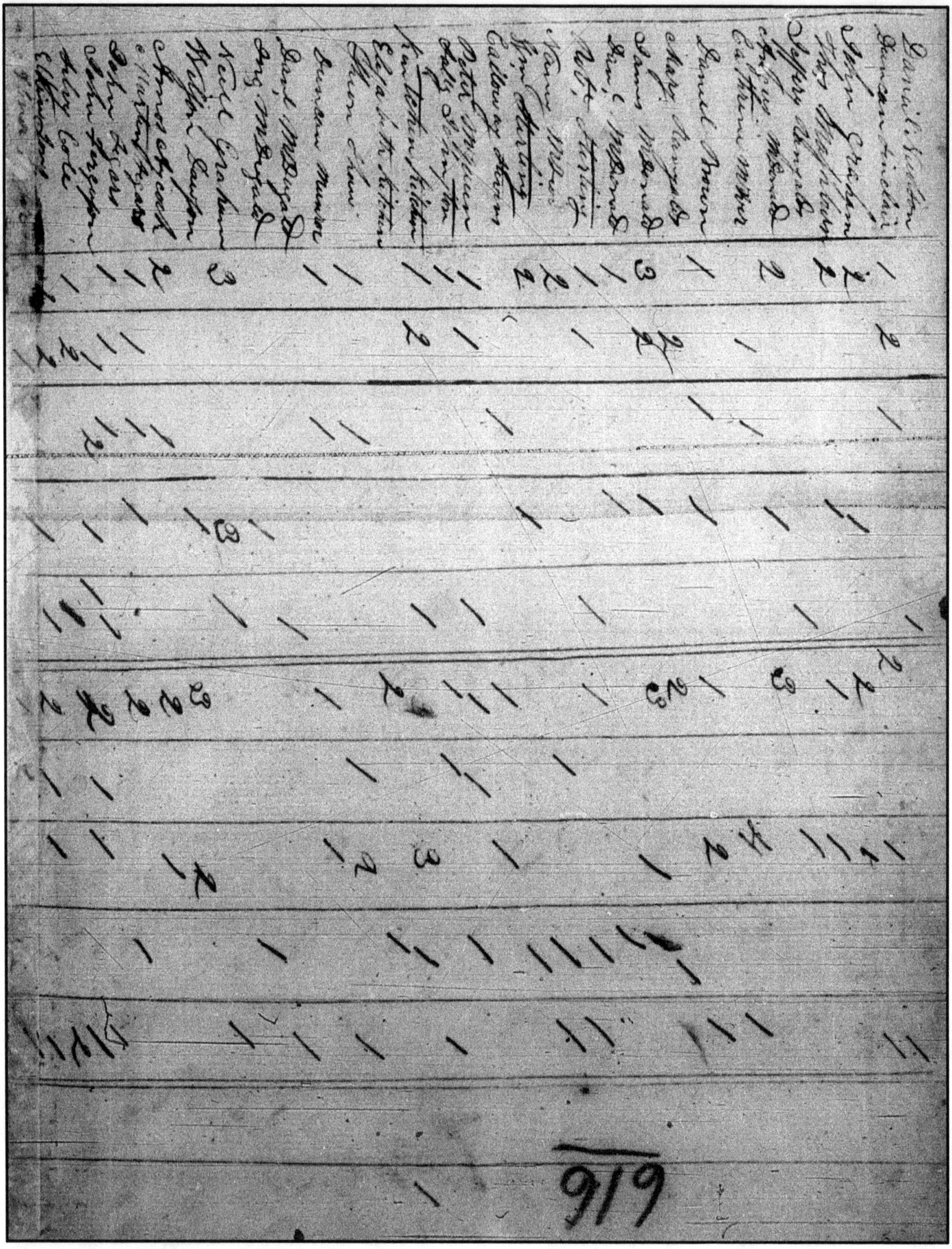
Danial Nealson
Duncan Sinclair
John Graham
Thos Mashburn
Jeffery Rangals
Angus McDonald
Cathrine McKee
Daniel Brown
Mary Rangals
James McDonald
Danl McDonald
Robt Sterling
Nancy McKee
Wm Sterling
Calloway Stevens
Peter McQueen
Sally Johnston
Kentchen Kitchen
Elizabeth Kitchen
Sheon Shaw
Duncan Munroe
Danl McDugald
Ang McDugald
Neill Graham
Willson Dawson
Amos Aycock
Martin Hegars
John Hegars
John Ferguson
Isley Cole
Elkin Long
616

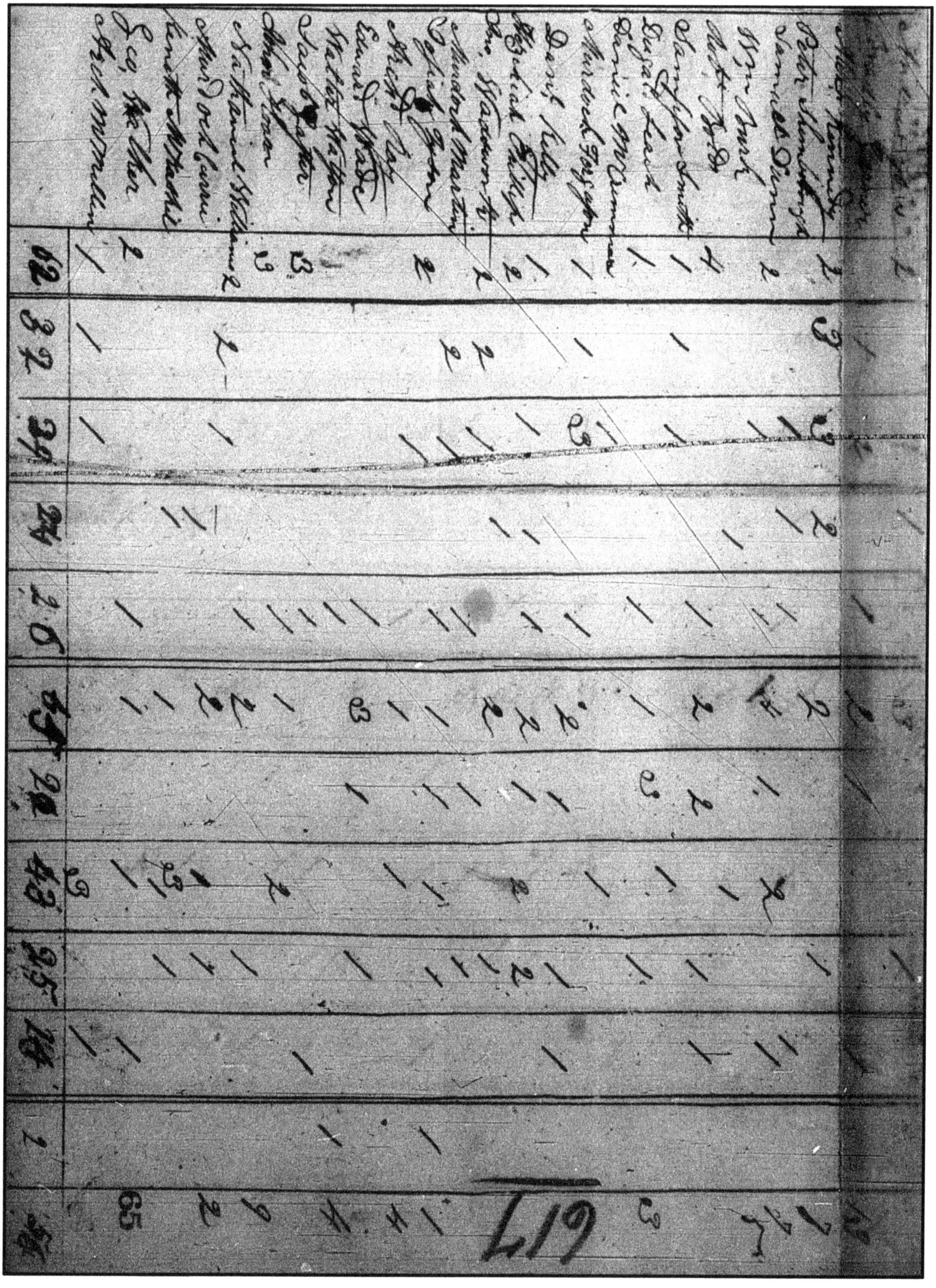
Alex. Kennedy
Peter Shemburgh
Samuel Dunn
Wm Burk
Robt. Boid
Sampson Smith
Dugal Leach
Daniel McCrimmon
Murdock Forgason
Danl. Kelly
Hezekiah Phillips
Jno. Wadsworth
Murdock Martin
Josiah Tyson
Archd Ray
Edward Wade
Walter Watson
Jacob Yaster
Thos. Hoan
Nathaniel Williams
Murdoch Currie
Kenneth McKethil
Geo. Walker
Arch. McMillen
62
32
39
24
26
65
20
43
25
14
2
56
617
65

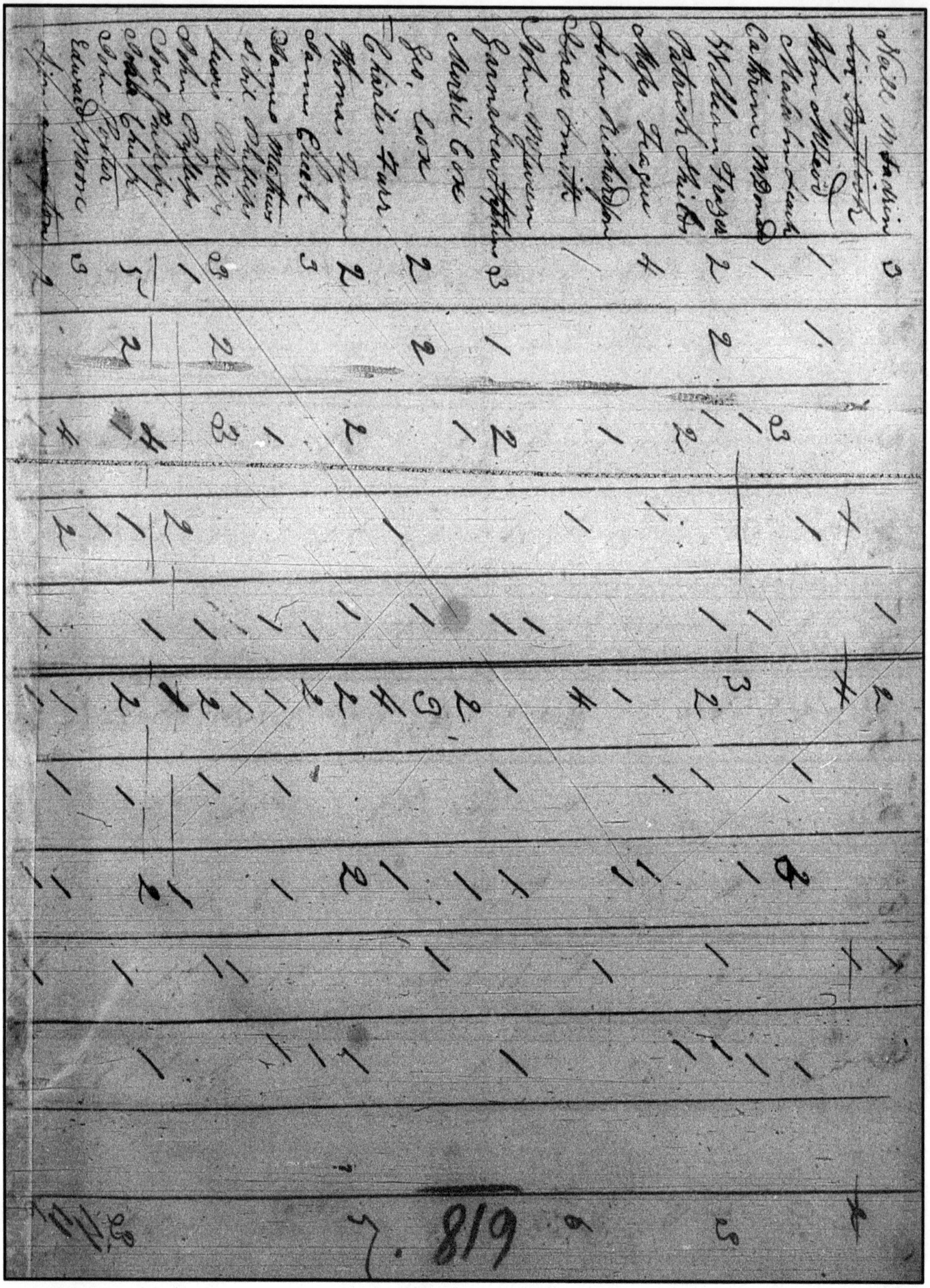

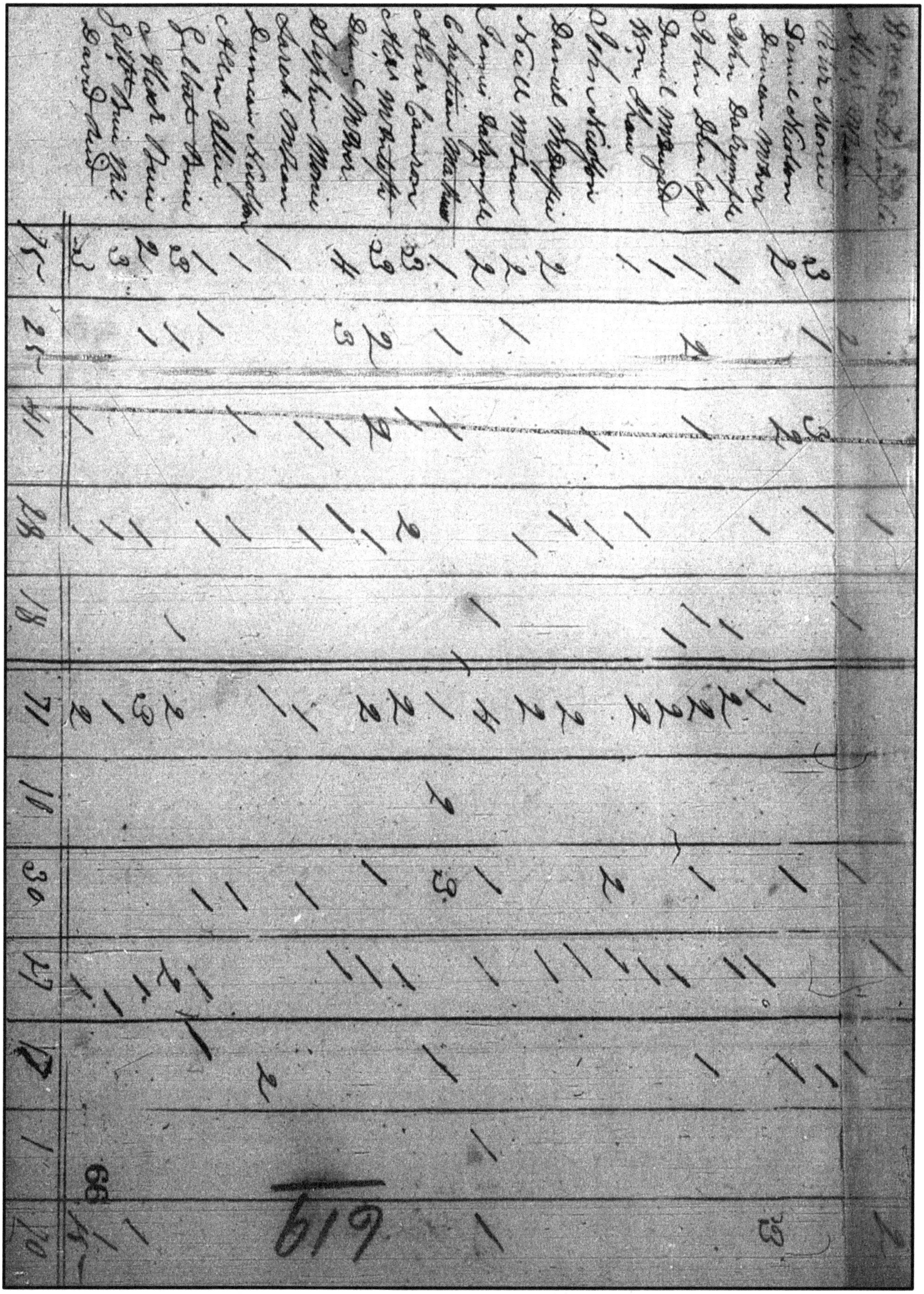

[illegible] Dalrymple				1					1			1
Alexr McLean		2			1			1		1		
Peter Morrie	3	1	3	1						1		
Daniel Nicolson	2		2			1		1		1		
Duncan McIver				1		1			1			3
John Dalrymple	1				1	2			1			
John Dunlap	1	2	1		1	2		1		1		
Daniel McDugald	1				1	2			1			
Wm Shaw	1			1		2			1			
John Nicolson			1	1				2	1			
Daniel McDuffie	2			1		2			1			
Neill McLean	2	1		1		2			1			
James Dalrymple	2				1	4		1	1		1	1
Christian Mathews	1	1	1			1	2	3		1		
Alexr Camron	3		1	2		2			1			
Alexr McIntosh	3	2	2	1		2		1	1			
Danl McIver	4	3	1	1					1			
Stephen Morrie			1	1		1		1				
Sarah McLean	1					1				2		
Duncan Nicolson	1		1	1				1				
Allen Allen	1	1		1				1	1	1		
Gilbert Buie	3	1			1	2			2			
Alexr Buie	2	1		1		3			1			1
Gilbt Buie Mil	3			1		1			1			1
David Reid	3		1	1		2			1			1
	75	25	41	28	18	71	11	30	27	17	1	70

66

619

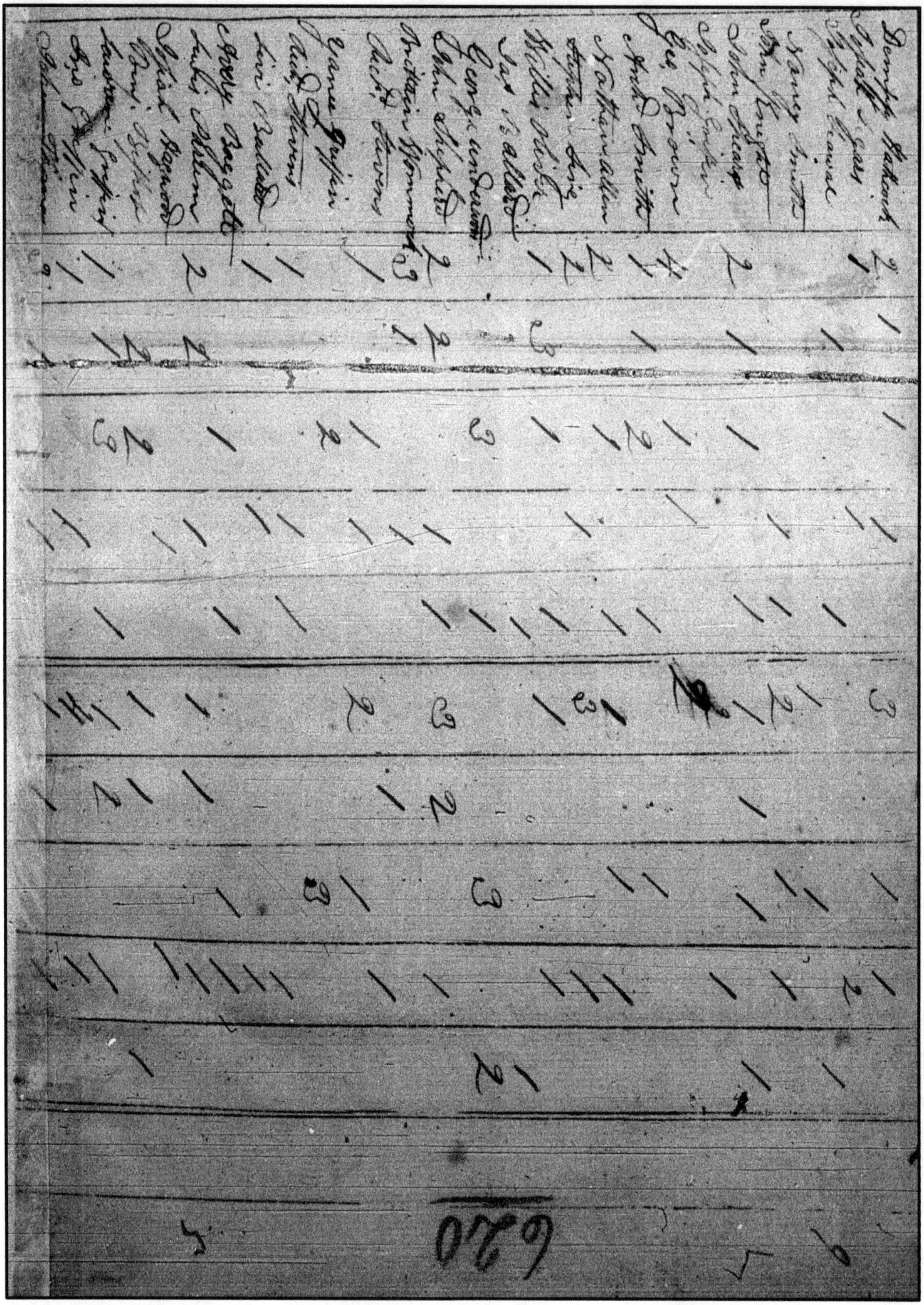

Dempsy Hathcock	2	1	1	1		3		1	1			
Josiah Segars	1			1					2			
Joseph Cawal		1			1			1		1		9
Nancy Smith						1		1	1			
John Knight				1	1	2			1			
John Shearer	2	1	1		1	1	1	1	1	1		5
Joseph Griffin									1			
Geo. Brown	4		1	1		2						
Archd Smith	1	1	2		1			1				
Nathan Allen	2		1		1	1		1	1			
Stephen Sevy	2			1		3			1			
Willis Olive	1	3	1		1	1			1	1		
Jas. Ballard					1							
George Underwood			3		1			3		2		
John Shepherd	2	2		1	1	3	2		1			
Brittain Wommock	3	1		1			1		1			
Richd Stevens	1		1	1		2		1				
Yancy Griffin			2					3				
Richd Stevens	1			1	1				1			
Levi Ballard	1			1					1			
Avery Baggett			1		1			1	1			
Lewis Parham	2	2		1		1	1		1			5
Josiah Haywood				1					1			
Benj. Bishop		2	2			1	1		1	1		
Lawrence Griffin	1	1	3		1	1	2		1			
Jno Griffin	1			1		4			1			
John Thomas	2	1		1		1	1		1			

620

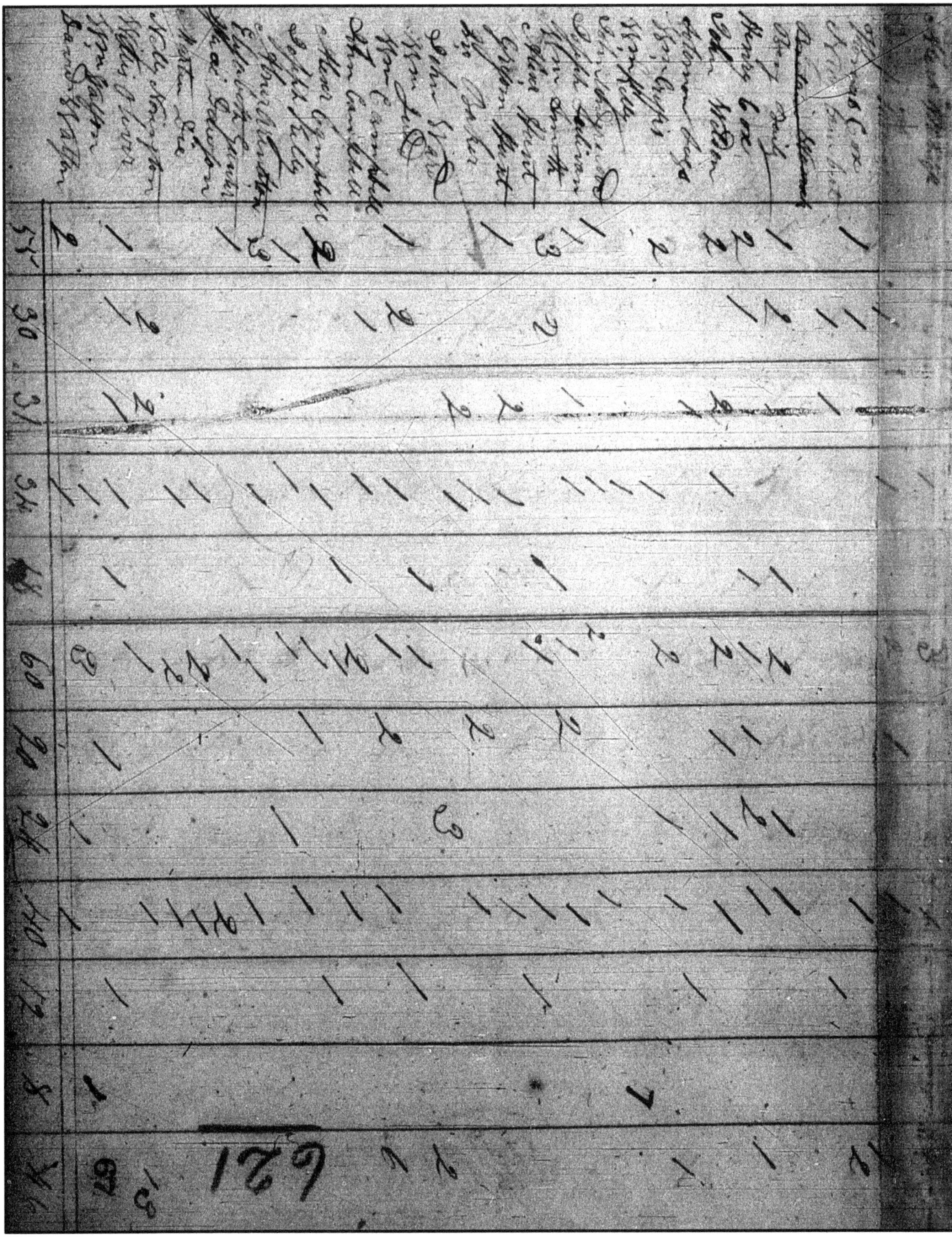

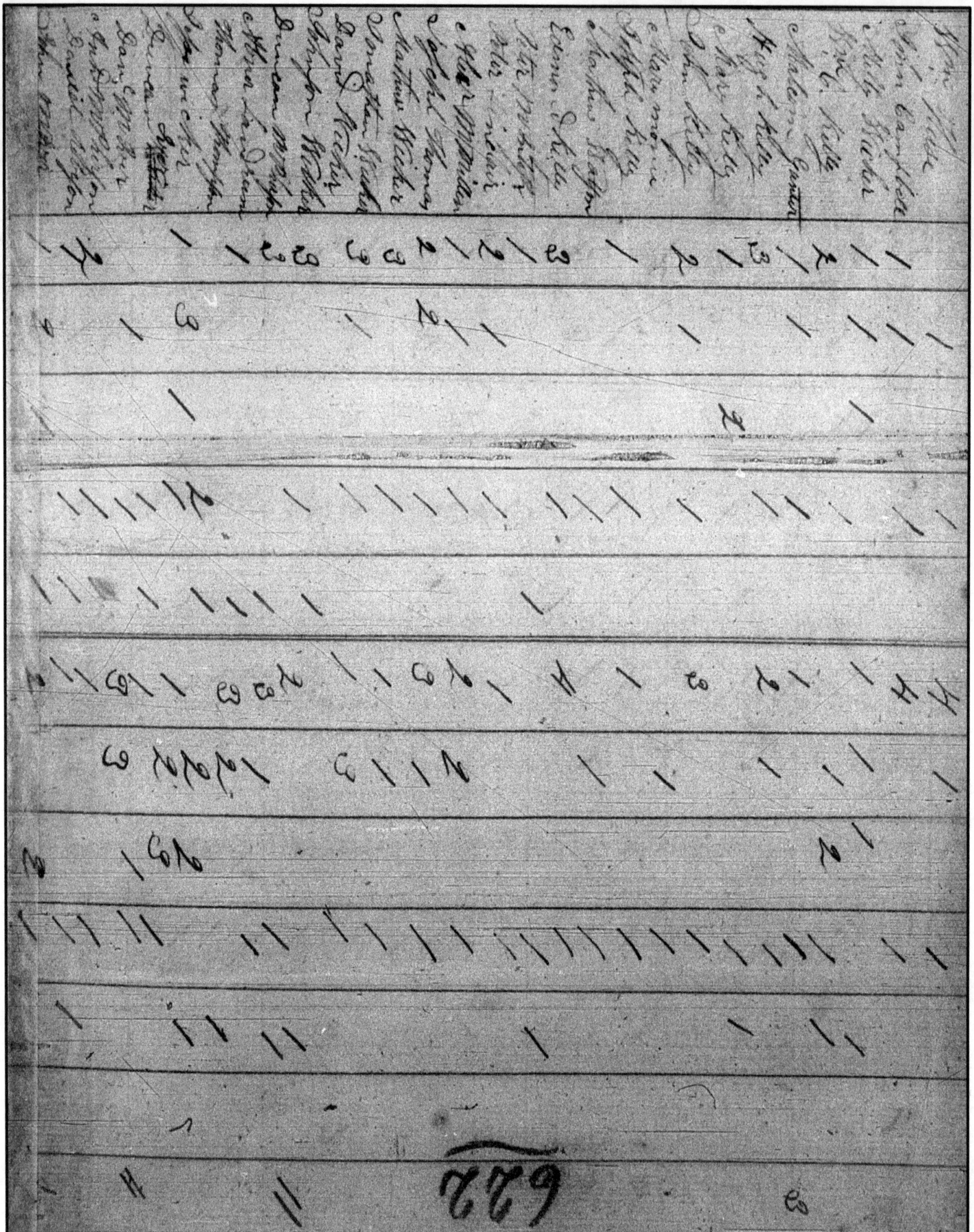

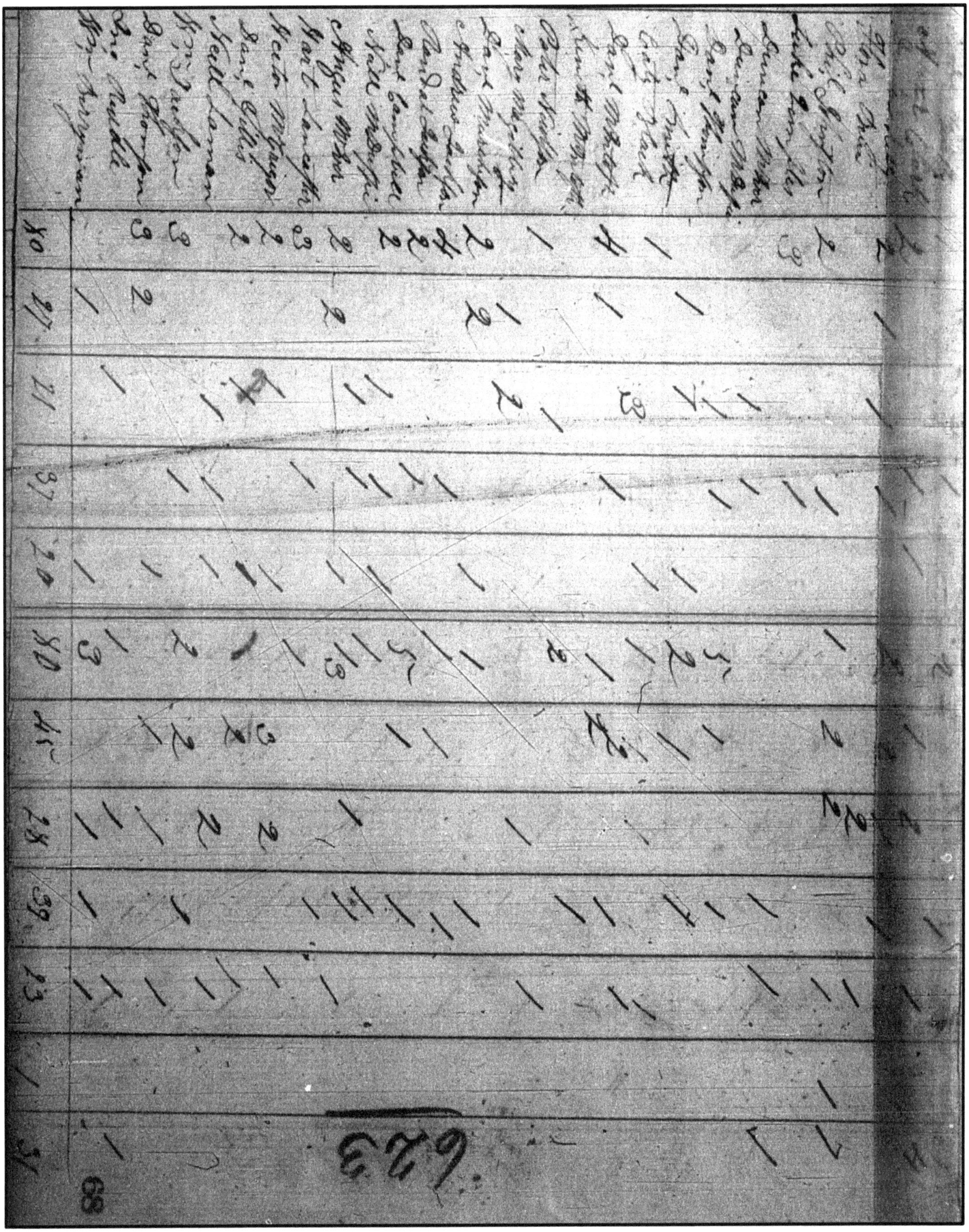

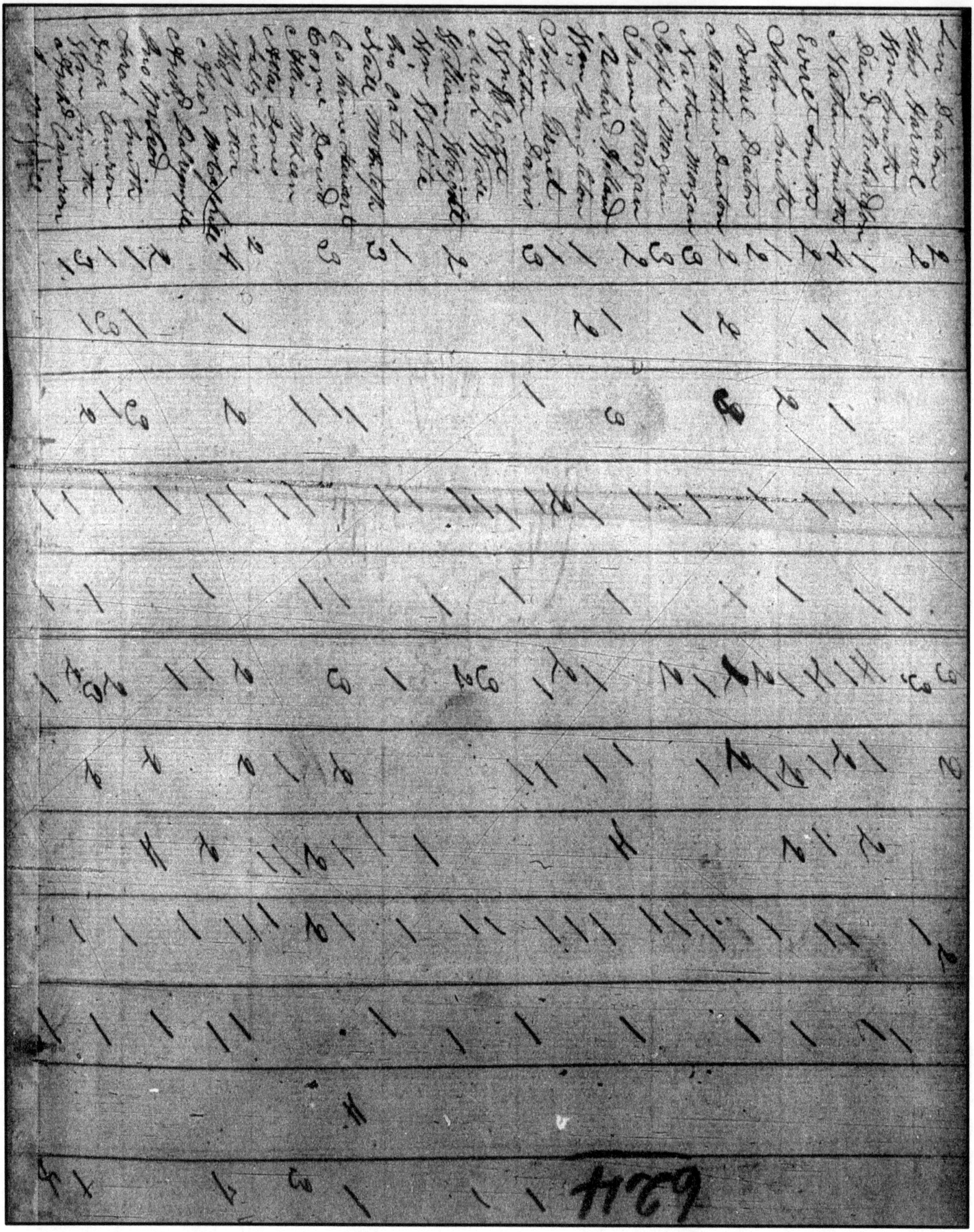

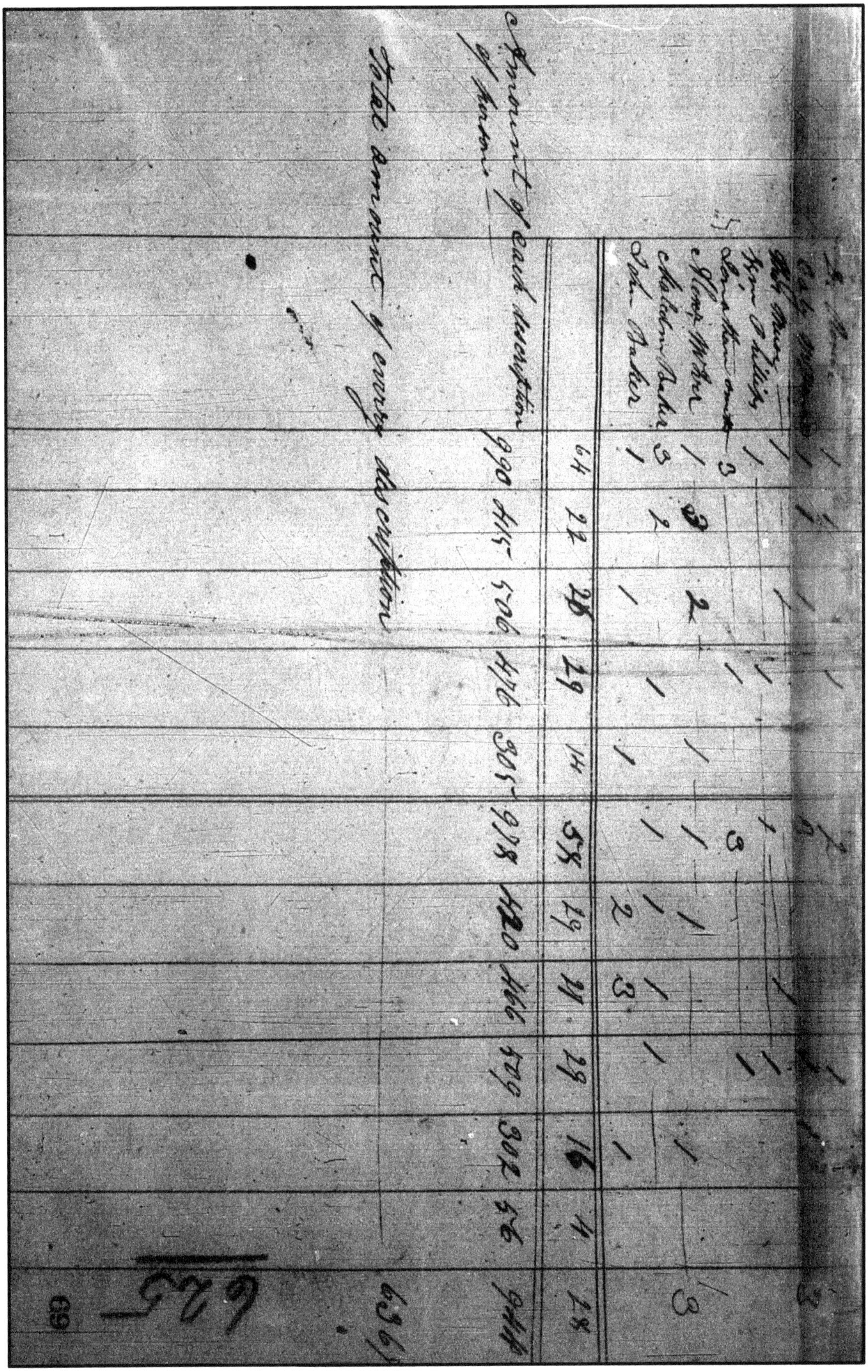

J. Moore	1	1		1		2			1			
Caty McD[illegible]	1	1	1			2			1	1		3
Wm Murr[illegible]	1		1			1		1	1			
Wm Phillips	1			1		1			1			
Jonathan Smith	3			1		3			1			
Alonzo McIver	1	3	2		1	1	1			1		3
Malcolm Baker	3	2		1		1	1	1	1			
John Baker	1		1		1		2	3		1		
	64	22	26	29	14	58	29	21	29	16	4	28
Amount of each description of persons	990	415	506	476	305	978	420	466	509	302	56	944

Total amount of every description 6361

625

69

Tax List
Moore County
1815

Names	Land	Dolls	Cents
John L Ward	6472	1295	
Arch^d Wadsworth	570	595	
Arch^d Reed	313½	733	
Arch^d Curry	300	450	
Angus Curry	150	100	
Arch^d McMillin	150	25	
Arch^d McDugald	600	1000	
Arch^d McMillin	450	200	
Arch^d Graham	350	200	
Alex^r Curry	420	300	
Bright Robarts	350	1000	
Benjn Siler	200	200	
Dickson Cole	100	150	
Daniel Kelly	450	375	
Daniel Bric	700	1000	
Duncan McMillin	150	160	
Daniel Graham	203	100	
Daniel McDugald	180	100	
David Graham	250	255	
Duncan Smith	82	32	
Daniel McDonald	1700	1300	
Duncan Monroe	100	100	
Elizabeth Kitchen	149½	200	
Zach^h Graham	354	354	
Fredrick Siler	995	1345	
George Walker	200	100	
Hugh Kelly	170	170	
Hugh McDonald	250	250	
Hugh Keith	200	200	
John Maples	150	75	
John Johnson	200	50	
James Kelly	150	100	
Jacob Mathews	470	1600	
John Worthy	876	930	
Do	50	50	
James Worthy	150	300	
James Maples	120	240	
John Bails	700	700	
	13,600½	16404	

Names	Land	Dolls	Cents
James Monk	150	80	
James Curry	320	50	
John McLeod	554	762	
John Sellars	348	348	
Jacob Gaster	250	325	
Do Do	50	100	
Barbary Dye	184	180	
James Turner	100	100	
John McDugald	100	100	
Kinchin Kitchen	450	700	
Lockart Fry	144	140	
Do Do	50	50	
Do Do	30	35	
Malcom McNill	300	200	
Murdoch Ferguson	260	174	
Malcom McNill	350	200	
Murdoch Ferguson	250	70	
Do Do	300	300	
John Maples	136½	75	
Do Do	50	75	
Martin McPherson	569	500	
Niell Cameron	320	700	
Niell McLeod	500	700	
Peter Sinclair	300	400	
Do Do	250	200	
Robt Starling	475	270	
Samson Smith	220	200	
Randolph Johnson	186	186	
Rodrick Murchison	358	350	
Do Do	100	50	
Randol Jackson	124	200	
Speas Ham	755	736	
John Boyd	75	75	
Wm Horser	25	25	
Thomas Fry	72	150	
Thomas Rhoads	482½	400	
Thomas Davis	440	440	
Thomas Fry Junr	74	100	
Thomas Maples	573½	1000	
Walter McBeth	640	640	
Wm Frazure	130	80	
	11,065½	11,486	

Name	Land	Dolls	Cents	Name	Land	Dolls	Cents
Wm Smith	745	400		Daniel McRae	100	60	
Willis Dickinson	321	640		George Russell	130	190	
Wm Dickinson	145	250		Do Do	60	60	
Wm Dawson	783	850		George Frazier	110	200	
Do Do	254	700		William Russell	180	250	
Thomas Gilmore	96	20		Daniel McNeill	340	340	
Elisha R. Yarborough	168½	300		Do Do	50	50	
James Smith	345	200		" "	200	150	
Morris Morrison	200	250		" "	360	25	
Do Do	650	650		" "	577	575	
Samuel Johnston	228	200		Benjn Gilbert	650	1200	
Peter Smith	250	150		Richd Street	200	600	
Robt. McLauchlin	250	250		Do Do	400	100	
Neill Peterson	175	250			22	5	
Silvey Cole	150	100		" "	32	15	
Randol Martin	350	350		" "			
Neill Shaw	241	125		Saml Martindale	330	350	
Charles Stewart	252	280		Alexr McLeod	200	200	
Catharine Stewart	100	50		Alexr Carrell	375	400	
Daniel Campbell	1610	1000		Jesse Upton	100	50	
Peter Kelly	450	355		John Kelly	300	100	
Temperance Riddle	249	300		Duncan McLeod	400	200	
Do Do	100	50		Lewis Phillips	150	450	
Daniel Cameron	59½	388		Eliza Williams	2293	5000	
John Cameron	50	50		Do Do	1220	2500	
Duncan Cameron	20	12	50		100	150	
Catharine Cameron	300	600		" "	237	230	
John Stewart	670	400		" "	100	150	
Peter McKellar	250	250		" "			
Duncan Buie	1456	1775	25	John Handcock	250	500	
Do Do	100	25		Robt. Boals	344	300	
" "	640	160		Hugh McKnight	400	400	
"	150	37	50	James England	350	700	
Malcom Gilchrist	300	125		Barnaba Sears	50	50	
Malcom Johnson	479	194	75	Murdoch McKinzie	206	2600	
Amos Hill	50	50		Do Do	384½	200	
Robert Smith	37	10			436½	230	
Daniel Cameron	200	200		" "	420	550	
John Cameron	2492	2000		"	270	400	
Thomas Gilmore	200	220		M. McKinzie & Co.	150	50	
Peter Monroe	250	200		Do Do	350	250	
				"	50	50	
				Eli Lawlor			
				Heirs of J. Barker	100	100	
				Heirs of J. Brewer	100	100	
	15951	16118	00		13077	20070	

Names	Land	Dolls	Cents
Aaron Tyson & Co.	350		
Do. Do	100		
" "	125		
" "	150		
" "	200		
" "	150	the whole	
" "	200	is at	
" "	300	1240	
Saml. Perry	650	650	
Bryan Boroughs	662		
James Brady	100	150	
Wm. Tyson	334½	165	25
Do. Do	300	300	
Ditto & Co.			
Wm. Martin	1080	2400	
Do. Do	100	100	
" "	500	50	
" "	50	50	
Heirs of Jno. McAulay	800	200	
Daniel Gillis			
Saml. Murley &	280	1350	
Richd. Street's Estate	300	150	
" "	600	100	
" "	200	50	
" "	200	200	
Cornelius Tyson	550	550	
Do Do	436	3000	
" "	313	100	
" "	160	75	
" "	200	100	
" "	315	90	
Aaron Tyson's Estate	172		
Do Do	160		
"	183		
"	100		
"	78	the whole	
" "	659	at	
"	32	6500	
Cornelius Tyson & Co	300		
Do Do	19		
" "	22½	whole at	
" "	53	250	
	11,774	18,125	25

Names	Land	Dolls
Robt. Davis	1300	1500
Ambrous Brewer	178	280
Do. Do	100	100
"	148	150
Archd. Shields	230	900
Do. Do	70	30
James Davis	400	750
Do. Do	300	70
James Cheek	200	200
George Stewart	200	200
Patty Phillips	160	500
Randol Cheek	60	100
Cornelius Shields	1156	1500
Do Do	166	250
Edwd. Beason	355	355
Joseph Holloman	965	600
Isaac Roberts	1650	1250
Owen Roberts	287	600
Brinkley Phillips	20	150
Wm. England	412	700
Do. Do	100	50
Hugh McIver	100	100
Joel Pope	150	150
John Seat	50	50
George Jackson	1300	1000
Do Do	400	600
" "	200	100
Francis Myrick	300	300
Kenneth McCaskill		12,000
Jonathan Caddell	100	150
Benjn. Pope	35	20
Joab Cheek	604	1200
Mathew Phillips	150	200
John Phillips	100	125
Benjn. Tyson	600	1400
Do. Do	440	200
John Murchison	400	1500
Saml. Campbell	323	300
John Campbell	185	270
Do. Do	170	230
"	230	40
John Ritter	660	800
Joseph Pierce	180	140
Abednego Mauness	250	250
Jacob Stutts	400	400
	15,738	31,760

Names	Land	Dolls	Cents
John Tyson	400		
Do Do	500	the whole at	
"	50	2350	
Tinsley Wade	420	500	
Wm Persons	325	500	
Angus McBean	525	500	
Isaac Teague Junr	50	75	
Isaac Teague Senr	30	50	
Leonard Smith	200	300	
John Danelly	450	600	
Richd Upton	133	133	
Sally & Isaac Wells	355	355	
William Phillips	50	75	
Abner Lawlor	50	75	
Jacob Cubertson	120	150	
Rodrick Murchison	257	250	
Do Do	100	20	
Gideon Seawell	1000	2000	
Charles Smith	250	800	
Allen Jones	400	2000	
Joseph Seawell	200	300	
Joseph Johnston	526	600	
Robt. Wilson	600	1100	
Micajah Brewer	313	250	
Harmon Brewer	50	50	
John Upton	220	220	
Jesse Upton	400	-	
Drury Richardson	375	250	
John Cheek	450	-	
Do Do	330	the	
"	615	whole at	
"	235	2050	
Adam White	740	1000	
James Shields	200	100	
Jesse Ritter	155	250	
Wm Dowd	552	1000	
Corn. Dowd	1000	1000	
Do Do	445	500	
"	400	400	
	13471	19803	

Names	Land	Dolls	Cents
Henry Eagle	150	150	
Do Do	100	100	
"	25	25	
"	100	100	
"	50	50	
"	25	25	
"	100	60	
Lewis Lawhon	100	100	
Samuel Elkins	75	200	
Joel Lawhon	420	730	
Neill McIntosh	519	650	
Thomas Ritter	550	800	
Joseph Rouse	50	100	
John Lawhon	100	90	
Jesse Rodgers	223½	250	
Do Do	250	50	
Daniel Muse	100	150	
Charaty McDaniel	93	50	
John McDonald	200	400	
John Dunlap	1300	1300	
Isaac Smith	37	100	
Tobias Fry	100	150	
Julious Glascock	125	325	
Dugald McLauchlin	350	312	50
Joseph Fry Senr	610	400	
John Martin	440	300	
Do Do	300	750	
"	385	30	
"	100	50	
Lewin Birkhead	100	75	
Eleazer Birkhead	303	650	
Henry Craven	250	700	
Do Do	101	80	
John Spear	100	100	
Lockart Fry	100	70	
Do Do	50	100	
Rebecca Hannon	100	35	
William Caddell Sr	150	300	
Daniel Patterson	330	228	
James Fry Sr	200	300	
James Muse Jr	94	180	
Hardin Womer	344	516	
Do Do	100	150	
George Fry Sr	200	230	
Amous Dowdy	150	50	
Do Do	100	75	
	9849½	11636	50

Names	Land	Dolls	Cents
Saml. Jackson	776	600	
Do Do	374	374	
" "	300	150	
" "	100	25	
Kinneth Murchison	240	480	
William Lewis	400	300	
Holden Cox	100	200	
Hugh Black	200	200	
James Dowdy	228¾	132	
Alexd. McCaskell	100	100	
Murdoch Curry	200	200	
William Fry	100	40	
Do Do	100	30	
Malcom McCrummen	100	100	
Do Do	50	12	50
Mark Phillips	125	250	
John Phillips	100	100	
Hiram Hill	150	300	
Nehemiah Birckhead	25	50	
Jesse F. Muse	125	125	
David Sears	150	150	
Michel Johnson	250	175	
Archd. Black	700	700	
Daniel Caddell	340	680	
John McKinzee	393¾	400	
John McIvor	325	600	
Thomas Muse Jr.	100	200	
Patrick Dowd	150	500	
Richardson Feagin	897	1600	
Do Do	200	100	
Daniel Feagin	50	120	
Jesse Bean	160	320	
John McDonald Jr.	50	50	
Nathan Fry	389	194	50
James B. Muse	260	500	
George Glascocks Heirs	150	250	
Neil Black	100	200	
John Medlin Jr.	300	100	
	8.858½	10.608	

Names	Land	Dolls	Cents
Jesse Sanders	100	150	
Do Do	100	150	
" "	60	60	
Elizabeth Sesson	100	80	
John Tyson	400	400	
Do Do	400	600	
" "	50	50	
James Johnston	200	55	
William Griffith	75	100	
Daniel Blue	250	250	
Murdoch McIvor	400	250	
Dugald McMillin	50	12	50
Thomas Graham	600	600	
Do Do	100	100	
Isaac Gowell	94	50	
Do Do	1	50	
Jesse Gowell	550	550	
Asa Gowell	520	920	
Do Do	149	650	
Adam Comer	460	500	
Margaret McQueen	200	400	
Alexd. Medlin	212	106	
Charles Furr	270	200	
Laughlen Curry	300	250	
Eli Phillips	289	250	
Neill McKethen	490	500	
Do Do	100	50	
" "	1000	950	
Samson D. Smith	200	300	
Benjn. Phillips	100	200	
John Ritter	50	40	
James Smith	460	300	
Ann White	950	950	
Jesse Muse Esq.	625	1350	
Thomas P. Muse	150	350	
William Barrett	815	1600	
Do Do	280	500	
" "	138	40	
" "	100	20	
John McIver	637½	637	50
Do Do	550	550	
" "	33	33	
" "	250	250	
" "	50	25	
" "	100	50	
" "	100	50	
" "	150	150	
	13.258¼	15679	

Names	Land	Dolls	Cents
Samuel How	160	160	
Armstrongs Heirs	200	100	
John McKay	600	600	
James Atkins	700	700	
Malcom McGilvery	225	400	
Kenneth McIver	519	300	
Duncan McIver	765	300	
Angus Chisholm	96	50	
Isaac Williams	100	80	
Danl. Murchison	109	100	
John McIver	592	400	
Duncan McPherson	50	50	
Allen McLeod	200	100	
Angus McGilvery	200	100	
Daniel Robeson	86	50	
Daniel McIver	773	700	
Angus McIver	105	52	50
Abraham Cole	475	450	
John McIver	119	100	
Daniel McIver	920	500	
Archd. Cameron	150	300	
Daniel McDuffie	370	200	
Daniel Cameron	258	127	
Hugh Cameron	250	375	
Duncan Murchison	370	170	
John Sinclair	537	250	
John Campbell	150	150	
Evander McIver	275	125	
Gilbert McRae	150	200	
Donald McDonald	164	150	
Archd. McDonald	200	150	
George McRae	100	150	
Murdoch McMillan	375	1500	
Nancy Murchison	150	75	
Angus McDonald	152	152	
Duncan McCollum	242	240	
Miles McGinnes	110	50	
Alexd. Clark	1000	1000	
	11997	10.656	50

Names	Land	Dolls	Cents
Gilbert Clark	100	50	
Duncan McDuffie	150	120	
Daniel McIver Esqr.	480	500	
Duncan Kelly	266	400	
Neill McNeill	160	160	
Robert Watson	589	600	
Daniel Stewart	600	400	
Daniel Thompson	160	600	
Neill McLeod	119	40	
Alexd. McIntosh	180	90	
Kenneth McKinzie	200	100	
Thos. Cole Sr.	300	400	
Daniel Campbell	455	500	
Do Do	75	50	
Kenneth McIntosh	267	275	
Alexd. Nicholson	100	50	
Stephen Berryman	260	125	
Thos. Cole Jr.	225	434	
Alexd. McIntosh	1000	1000	
Margaret Monroe	194	300	
Rebecah Johnston	100	75	
Catharine Johnston	20	50	
Archd. McPherson	212	112	
John Cole	673	650	
Catharine Black	150	100	
Kenneth McKinzie	100	50	
Murdoch McKinzie	48	30	
Joseph Tyson	175	1000	
Do Do	530	750	
Daniel Murchison	1662	1500	
Do Do	300	300	
Dugald Stewart	72	50	
John McIntosh	138	69	
D. McIntoshs Heirs	575	300	
William Coffer	57	40	
Daniel Lemmon	125	100	
Andrew Anderson	200	120	
John McDonald	61	50	
Charles McKinnon	200	200	
Kenneth Murchison	830	800	
Duncan McCall	100	100	
	12.208	12660	

Names	Lands	Dolls	Cents
Alexr. Murchison	312	250	
Archd. McBryde	669	Both at	
Do Do	260	1200	
Hugh McDonald	143	120	
John Lummon	125	100	
Niell McDuffie	173	150	
Daniel Thompson	550	350	
Murdoch McIntosh	625	625	
Robert McIver	250	400	
Daniel Murchison	1009	300	
Thos. Thompson	800	800	
Alexd. McLain	100	100	
Duncan Thompson	200	100	
Rebeccah Cole	200	150	
Daniel Nicholson	425	212	50
John McIntosh	165	150	
John Nicholson	100	150	
Henry Coffer	158	125	
Jeptha Reonalds	110	100	
Angus McCall	100	100	
David Walker Esqr	225	400	
Johnston Walker	393	225	
Isaac Walker	115	57	50
Aaron Tyler	114	40	
Andrew Brown	200	200	
Allen Thomas	116	225	
Alexd Hunt	400	100	
Alexd Campbell	87½	120	
Angus Shaw	186	140	
Alexd Buie	500	500	
Archd Douglas	124	217	
Saml Baley	187	370	
Abel Douglas	474	950	
Archd McGilvery	315	300	
Abner Harrington	100	100	
Alexd Carmicle	100	200	
	10118½	9626	

Names	Lands	Dolls	Cents
Alexd McBryde	500	200	
Creasy Stephens	200	150	
William Hughs	337½	200	
Joseph Kelley	70	100	
William Knight	91	100	
Duncan McIver	300	400	
Daniel McLeod	1616	500	
John Shephard	350	350	
Gilbert Buie Capt.	317	500	
William Dalrymple	913½	800	
Jinnet Dalrymple	63½	125	
John Dalrymple	634	550	
Archd Dalrymple	1037	800	
Daniel Nicholson	25[illegible]	170	
Christian Mathews	250	100	
Dugald Mathews	200	60	
John Campbell	206½	200	
Edmond Kelly	75	37	50
Duncan McIver	833	780	
John Watson	900	900	
William Weldon	150	175	
Daniel McIver	694	600	
Daniel Shaw Senr	150	109	
John Walker Senr	439½	500	
John Underwood	84	150	
William Reid	340	600	
John Baker	488	200	
Malcum Baker	345	200	
Peter Sinclair	144½	140	
Peter McIntosh	250	250	
Fredrick Thomas	450	600	
Martin Thomas	333⅓	500	
John Kelly	436½	400	
John Thomas	118	225	
William Smith	450	300	
Grisom Hunt	100	75	
Peter Sexton	300	450	
Duncan Cameron	125	62	50
	15542¼	12559	

Names	Land	Dolls	Cents
Robert Wommock	100	250	
William A. [illegible]			
Benj.n Muckle	100	100	
David Watson	270	200	
Peter Morris	200	200	
William Murchison	150	90	
Daniel McDugald	370	400	
Britton Wommock	863½	1267	
Benj.n Huckabay	220	110	
Joseph Thomas	119	250	
William Shaw Capt.	370	307	50
Hugh Kelly	50	100	
Geo. Harrington	380	600	
John Buie (Tay son)	50	20	
James McBryde	200	225	50
William Buie Esq.	907	453	50
Arch.d Buie	150	30	
Malcom Shaw	300	225	
Sarah McLain	100	100	
Allen Ellis	100	50	
Mathew Morris	350	310	
Catharine Conley	50	60	
Malcom Buie	600	300	
Duncan McDugald	100	120	
Burrell Baley	93⅓	63	
Benjamin Bailey	200	200	
John Morris	875	750	
Dugald Cameron	125	50	
James Mangum	161	320	
Rich.d Huckabay	320	550	
Benj.n Thomas	450	700	
Lewis Parham	257	700	
Rich.d Oliver	540	60	
Nathaniel Allen	200	100	
Malcom McNeill's Heirs	1390	150	
Malcom Gunter	250	250	
John Sloan	185	220	
Malcom McFarland	415	400	
Neill McNeill's Heirs	150	150	
	11,711⅓	10492	50

Names	Land	Dolls	Cents
James Dalrymple	535	500	
Hector McNeill C.C.	450	600	
Neill McNeill's Heirs	113	60	
Neill McNeill	100	50	
John McNeill	150	150	
John Shephard	1070	1000	
John McFarland	375	400	
John Gunter	300	2000	
Daniel McNair	475	225	
Martin Dye	100	100	
John Welden Esq.	361	350	
Joseph Bookers Heirs	180	180	
Henry Cox	400	500	
William Rollins	150	100	
Thomas Cox	200	300	
John Ward	200	250	
Jonathan Hanley	150	200	
John Holder	100	75	
William Hunt	200	300	
Dempsey Hunt	200	250	
Moses Oliver	450	100	
Benton Drake	100	50	
William Fuller	40	40	
Micajah Baggett	105	80	
William Crawford	280	400	
Charles Crawford	312	350	
Henry Morris	183	120	
Jacob Morris	50	50	
Mary Morris	183	120	
John McDugald	520	220	
Neill McFadyen	850	600	
Jonathan Walker	300	240	
John Godfrey	100	75	
Milley Webb	230	200	
Duncan Buie (Tay)	350	150	
James Mashborn	120	50	
Dempsey Hathcock	234	200	
Booker Parrish	22	25	
William Watson	1500	1500	
	11,938	12,160	

Names	Land	Dolls	Cents
William McCauley	900	900	
Niell McKay	450	600	
John McMillen Heirs	300	300	
Charles Blalock	150	180	
Luke Woodill	100	100	
William Campbell	895	750	
John Blackmon	150	200	
Phil Johnson	952½	960	
Larkin Johnson	100	50	
Elander Worthington	300	900	
Hugh McLain	1844	4000	
Alexd McIvers Heirs	387½	300	
Duncan McIver	75½	64	
Kenneth McIver	75½	64	
Catharine McIver	75½	64	
David Reed	1013	2000	
Robt Grahams Heirs	300	250	
Do Do	100	100	
Allen Morrison	190	30	
Do Do	200	20	
" "	290	30	
" "	160	25	
" "	200	30	
" "	130	25	
" "	420	120	
" "	109	30	
" "	10	60	
" "	205	200	
James McArthur	50	50	
John Morrison	100	100	
Alexd Autrey	208	416	
Ann McLeod	200	150	
Do Do	400	150	
Jeremiah Williams	110	150	
Mathew Denton	313	450	
Do Do	100	25	
" "	200	200	
" "	100	80	
	11963½	14123	

Names	Land	Dolls	Cents
John Gibson	93	100	
Charles Leavell	172	100	
George Hundsucker	148	148	
Do Do	60	62	
Jacob Furr	137	137	
Do Do	313	313	
John Dunn	135	136	
Daniel Chisholm	150	107	
Henry Stutts	200	300	
Do Do	100	50	
"	150	200	
Jacob Smith	300	75	
Ezekiel Autrey	100	140	
John Lewis	230	200	
Henry Campbell	125	100	
Malcom Morrison	274	200	
Allen Bethune	200	100	
Daniel McKinzie	60	40	
Angus Campbell	157	117	75
Do Do	150	75	
Kenneth Clark	100	100	
Do Do	500	122	50
Leonard Furr	235	175	[illegible]
Do Do	50	37	50
James Autrey	132	66	
Murdoch McKinzie	150	112	50
Do Do	200	50	
John Smith	100	100	
Norman McLeod	200	100	
Mary Buie	200	200	
Britton Britt	50	60	
Do Do	130	65	
Kenneth McCaskill	60	100	
Daniel McDonald	100	100	
Alexd Ray	120	100	
William Copeland	204	204	
Abigail Harden	50	50	
Isham Smith	70	70	
John McNeill	200	200	
Do Do	100	100	
" "	362	362	
" "	300	300	
James Manes	150		
John Melton	160	80	
Christopher Stutts	150	400	
	7327	5956	16

Names	Lands	Dolls	Cents
Hector McNeill	164	164	
Murdoch Mathewson	310	232	50
Angus McLain	200	125	
Evert Wallis	100	100	
Jesse Phillips	136	136	
Angus McDonald	133	100	
Alexd. McKinzie	150	150	
John Kennedy	100	100	
George Cagle	114	50	
Do Do	100	150	
" "	60	120	
" "	50	25	
" "	30	30	
Normond Mathewson	100	50	
Do. Do	100	75	
" "	100	25	
" "	50	10	
" "	250	200	
John Kinnon	250	367	50
Do Do	50	50	
" "	50	50	
" "	150	82	50
Normond McKinnon	10	25	
Angus McKinnon	60	50	
Rodrick McAulay	200	250	
Do Do	100	50	
John Campbell Senr	50	25	
Do. Do	100	50	
" "	100	50	
Hector McLain	100	100	
Do. Do	50	25	
" "	100	100	
Alexd. McLeod	100	100	
Do Do	200	150	
John Patterson	450	500	
John Kees	55	82	50
Neill McLeod	150	75	
Normond Morrison	300	300	
Do. Do	150	150	
Daniel Buchan	365	273	75
John Cockmon	100	100	
James Hains	50	50	
Stephen Richardson	400	600	
James Wood	450	725	
Lewis Garners Heirs	425	425	
	6812	6648	75

Names	Lands	Dolls	Cents
James Milton	350	300	
Kenneth McCaskill	365	212	
Donald McDonald	160	160	
Murdoch McAulay	200	100	
Do. Do	65	50	
" "	50	50	
David Richardson	75	75	
James Dunlap	100	150	
Do Do	350	450	
Thomas Harwell	100	100	
Do Do	50	25	
Levy Deaton	200	400	
Do Do	60	100	
"	90	110	
John McDuffee	160	50	
Normond McKinnon	228	228	
John McCrummon	70	20	
Joseph Cole	250	200	
William Smith Senr	50	150	
Do Do	225	250	
Ann McLeod	100	60	
Nathan Morgan	169	250	
Daniel McCrummon	100	150	
Do Do	300	300	
" "	70	50	
Alexd. McIntosh	146	220	
Do - Do	200	150	
" "	150	50	
" "	50	25	
Margaret Jackson	300	100	
Hector McLain	100	100	
William Dunn	100	200	
Do. Do	64	64	
Murdoch McAulay	60	60	
Do Do	150	150	
Daniel McDonald	200	150	
Do Do	100	25	
Mary McLeod	175	175	
Rody Britt	225	150	
Elijah Autray	250	200	
Kenneth McCaskill	50	50	
Do Do	50	50	
Alexd. Morrison	100	200	
Do Do	72	50	
William Jones	100	100	
Do Do	125	125	
Benjn. Caddell	100	100	
Do Do	200	50	
" "	100	50	
	7184	6584	

Names	Land	Dolls	Cents
Daniel Gillis	100	125	
Do Do	100	25	
Bartholomew Dunn	128	128	
William Gilmore	100	60	
William Feagin	400	300	
Simon Lewis	100	50	
Birrell Deaton	100		
~~[illegible]~~			
Shadrick Maness	50	70	
George Kennedy	32	80	
Angus Morrison	145	45	
John Smith Senr	125	170	
Samuel Kees	230	300	
Catharine Cockman	150	150	
Solomon Barrett	300	300	
William McLeod	150	150	
Anthony Aiton	150	150	
Malcom Matthewson	60	150	
Do Do	50	100	
" "	41	50	
John McDonald (M.S.)	133	100	
John McDonald	50	50	
Do Do	85	42	50
" "	150	75	
Murdoch Martin	200	670	
Do Do	200	200	
" "	30	1	10
George Graham	150	150	
Do Do	150	150	
" "	100	100	
	80	80	
Allen Martin	320	200	
John Campbell	50	25	
Do Do	150	30	
" "	50	25	
Neill McMillen	50	12	50
Do Do	30	15	
" "	336	40	
	20	10	
Daniel McNeill	50	50	
Do Do	30	15	
" "	40	35	
John McKinnon	50	25	
Do Do	50	25	
Duncan McNeill	100	50	
Do Do	50	50	
	5215	4629	10

Names	Land	Dolls	Cents
John Campbell	50	25	
Laughlin Curry	220	110	
Do Do	150	37	50
" "	50	12	50
" "	20	10	
" "	100	25	
Hugh McDonald	50	50	
Do Do	50	25	
" "	50	12	50
" "	50	12	50
" "	50	12	50
" "	210	100	
Daniel McDonald	100	25	
Do Do	50	12	50
" "	50	12	50
" "	50	12	50
" "	40	10	
John McNeill Strong	50	50	
Do Do	64	10	
	286	30	
Daniel McDonald	88	88	
Do Do	50	25	
Effy Black	50	25	
Do Do	50	12	50
" "	10	2	50
Duncan McInnish	50	25	
Do Do	50	25	
	50	50	
John Patterson	30	15	
Do Do	100	20	
" "	100	50	
" "	50	50	
" "	50	25	
" "	50	25	
	100	50	
Duncan McLain	50	25	
Rodrick McCrummen	100	50	
John McInnish	100	50	
Laughlin McKinnon	50	50	
Do Do	25	12	
Phillip McDonald	100	50	
Do Do	93	23	25
" "	50	12	50
" "	8	2	
"	42	42	
	20	10	
Donald McDonald	50	50	
Do Do	50	25	
	242	6	50
Malcom McDonald	100	100	
Do Do	50	25	
	97	24	50
Angus McDugald	50	25	
Do Do	100	50	
	3777½	1715	75

Names	Land	Dolls	Cents
Malcom Black	100	25	
Do Do	100	100	
" "	100	100	
" "	100	100	
" "	150	75	
" "	100	100	
" "	100	50	
" "	100	25	
" "	100	25	
" "	200	65	
" "	60	15	
" "	50	12	50
" "	50	12	50
James Ray	100	300	
Do Do	133	33	25
" "	100	100	
" "	200	50	
" "	200	50	
Angus McDugald	50	25	
Do Do	100	50	
John McKinnon	100	25	
John Paterson	200	100	
Do Do	100	6	
" "	170	54	
" "	100	75	
" "	64	25	
John McCollum	75	35	
Duncan McCollum	25	12	50
Do Do	50	25	
" "	100	50	
Daniel McMillen	30	50	
	200	50	
	25	6	25
John Black	30	7	50
	50	50	
Do Do	30	50	
Archd McDonald	200	100	
Do Do	50	20	
John McLeod	50	100	
Do Do	50	25	
" "	30	15	
" "	20	10	
" "	50	20	
" "	50	25	
" "	33½	15	
Alexd Campbell	57	28	50
Do Do	30	25	
" "	50	50	
" "	50	12	50
" "	100	100	
" "	15	3	75
" "	15	3	75
	4452	2488	"

Names	Land	Dolls	Cents
Archd Black	100	100	
Do Do	64	16	
Malcom Black	100	100	
Do Do	50	25	
" "	50	25	
" "	50	12	50
" "	25	6	50
" "	10	5	
" "	30	7	50
" "	50	50	
" "	50	25	
Daniel Blue Sr	50	37	50
Do Do	50	37	50
" "	30	7	50
" "	200	50	
Angus Blue	50	50	
Alexd Campbell	100	100	
Do Do	200	200	
" "	200	100	
" "	50	12	50
Duncan Black	100	25	
Duncan Ray Jr	50	40	50
Do Do	50	40	
" "	25	6	25
John McNeill Esqr	100	100	
Do Do	50	100	
" "	100	100	
" "	61	35	
" "	50	25	
" "	50	12	50
" "	25	6	50
" "	50	12	50
" "	50	12	50
" "	14	3	50
" "	37	9	50
" "	100	25	
" "	30	7	50
" "	64	16	
" "	25	6	25
" "	50	25	
" "	50	12	50
" "	50	12	50
" "	21	5	25
" "	15	3	75
" "	30	7	50
" "	30	7	50
" "	100	25	
" "	50	12	50
" "	480	120	
" "	50	12	50
" "	43	11	25
" "	264	66	
" "	89	22	25
" "	21	5	25
" "	18	4	50
" "	75	18	75
" "	25	6	25
" "	228	82	
	4231	2011	25

Names	Land	Dolls	Cents
John McLeod	60	120	
Do Do	120	120	
"	25	20	
"	50	25	
"	50	12	
"	50	12	
"	50	12	
"	33	20	
"	38	8	
Dugald Black	100	50	
Do Do	50	25	
"	50	50	
"	100	25	
"	40	10	
"	200	50	
"	100	30	
"	100	25	
"	100	25	
"	100	25	
Malcum McMillen Heirs	100	100	
Do Do	100	27	50
"	50	12	50
"	22	5	50
"	43	10	73
"	22	5	50
"	5	1	25
"	15	3	75
"	10	2	50
"	64	16	
"	64	16	
"	64	16	
"	10	2	50
"	50	12	50
"	50	12	50
"	870	217	50
"	25	6	25
"	25	6	25
"	50	25	
"	47	23	25
"	25	6	25
"	793	143	25
Christian McMillen	100	100	
Do Do	50	50	
"	100	50	
"	60	15	
"	50	12	50
"	50	12	50
"	100	25	
"	50	12	50
John Ray Senr	100	100	
"	75	75	
"	50	10	
"	100	20	
"	20	5	
"	50	12	50
Donald McDonald	60	60	
Duncan Curry	50	50	
	4985	1946	48

Names	Land	Dolls	Cents
Duncan Ray Senr	150	75	
Do Do	50	25	
"	50	25	
"	30	7	
"	50	12	
Malcom Black	50	50	
Do Do	20	5	
"	50	12	50
"	50	12	50
Peter Blue Senr	50	12	50
Do Do	10	5	
"	10	2	50
"	50	12	50
"	100	25	
"	45	11	25
"	50	12	50
"	50	12	50
"	50	25	
"	50	25	
"	100	50	
"	10	5	
"	33⅓	13	
Daniel Patterson	200	150	
Do Do	100	25	
"	50	12	50
"	50	25	
"	50	25	
"	50	12	50
Daniel Graham	100	100	
Do Do	100	50	
"	50	25	
"	50	12	50
Arch. Clark	100	150	
Do Do	50	50	
"	100	50	
"	150	75	
Alexr McFarland	60	3	50
Do Do	137½	50	
"	100	100	
"	50	12	50
"	25	8	
"	74	74	
"	50	12	50
Niven Clark	150	75	
Do Do	50	12	50
"	30	15	
"	50	5	25
"	30	7	50
Phillip Cameron	50	25	
Do Do	34	17	
"	50	25	
"	20	10	
Donald McDonald	50	12	50
Do Do	90	22	50
	3399	1685	93

Names	Land	Dolls	Cents
Daniel Love	50	125	
Do Do	50	125	
" "	20	5	
" "	149	25	
" "	49	10	
" "	45	10	
Donald McDonald	50	12	50
Do Do	90	22	50
Daniel McLain	100	25	
Do Do	30	7	50
John McDonald	60	15	
Do Do	60	15	
" "	12	3	
Malcom Munroe	100	100	
Do Do	80	80	
" "	25	12	50
" "	26	32	50
Daniel Clark	200	150	
Do Do	100	70	
" "	40	20	
" "	50	12	50
" "	60	30	
" "	30	12	50
" "	50	37	50
" "	50	12	50
Antony Graham	100	25	
Do Do	75	17½	
" "	50	12	50
" "	50	12	50
Benjn Graham	100	30	
Do Do	60	100	
" "	40	10	
" "	50	12	50
" "	100	25	
Archd Monroe	70	70	
Do Do	36	9	
" "	128	32	
Duncan Brown	30	7	50
Do Do	30	15	
" "	25	12	50
" "	25	12	50
Malcom Blue	100	25	
Malcom Smith	500	500	
Do Do	100	25	
Elkin Jones	100	50	
Patrick Blue Sr	300	75	
Do Do	106	26	50
" "	100	25	
" "	100	10	
Lauchlen McNeill	150	75	
	4121	2185	"

Names	Land	Dolls	Cents
Duncan Paterson	100	100	
Do D	50	12	50
" "	50	12	50
" "	30	12	50
" "	50	12	50
" "	94	12	25
" "	25	6	25
" "	50	12	50
" "	400	120	25
" "	300	150	
" "	50	25	
" "	100	30	
" "	300	150	
" "	100	50	
" "	100	50	
Archd Ray	87	87	
Do Do	116	116	
" "	60	30	
" "	110	50	
" "	580	145	
" "	56⅔	28	
" "	100	23	
" "	1000	180	
" "	350	80	
" "	400	80	
John Blue	100	100	
Do Do	50	50	
" "	20	20	
" "	100	25	
" "	18	4	50
" "	50	25	
" "	50	12	50
" "	26	14	
" "	20	20	
" "	80	20	
" "	64	10	
" "	50	6	
" "	18⅔	18	
" "	25	25	
" "	25	25	
" "	50	12	50
" "	12	6	
" "	50	12	50
" "	30	7	50
Rubin Trueman	100	100	
Do Do	100	100	
" "	89	200	
	50	50	
William N. Munis	133	133	
James Garner	472	47	50
Do Do	117	237	
William Trueman	100	50	
Do Do	50	80	
"			
	6303⅔	3008	25

Names	Land	Dolls	Cents
Peter Hare Sr	87¾	300	
Do Do	60	140	
" "	50	90	
" "	50	50	
" "	100	50	
" "	85	25	
" "	50	10	
" "	100	25	
" "	50	10	
John Hare Sr	140	420	
Do Do	117	234	
" "	100	250	
" "	50	100	
" "	50	50	
" "	65	32	50
" "	100	50	
John Cagle	185	200	
George Cagle	70	100	
Do Do	100	50	
John Spivay	400	400	
Do Do	100	100	
" "	100	100	
" "	100	50	
Joseph Allin	102	102	
	150	150	
	45	22	50
	50	25	
	50	25	
	9	9	
	68	68	
	50	25	
	45	22	50
	50	25	
	150	37	50
Mark Allin	275	275	
Do Do	25	25	
Allin Williamson	100	50	
Everet Sheffield	172	250	
Isham Sheffield	60	20	
Do Do	41	100	
John Caviness	200	350	
William Williamson	2952	886	50
	150	75	
	70	72	
	84	42	
	100	50	
	309½	154	50
	100	25	
	200	200	
	100	100	
Andrew Gow	100	100	
Do Do	100	100	
" "	92	92	
Christopher Gows Heirs	100	100	
	8398¾	6415	"

Names	Land	Dolls	Cents
Bradly Garner	350	350	
Do Do	110	82	50
" "	90	45	
" "	300	300	
" "	88	88	
" "	100	75	
" "	15	11	25
" "	700	175	
Joseph Morgan	200	300	
Do Do	15	7	50
" "	30	15	
" "	7	7	
Jesse Brown	575	400	
Do Do	50	25	
" "	50	25	
Peter Shamburger Sr	200	150	
Do Do	100	75	
" "	300	75	
" "	75	37	50
" "	75	37	50
John Kennedy	100	300	
Bailey Williamson	300	150	
Do Do	200	225	
William Lindel Jr	60	20	
Martin Cagle	200	300	
Nathaniel Tucker	150	350	
William Shamburger	100	50	
Nathan Smith	100	100	
Do Do	50	25	
" "	25	12	50
" "	50	50	
" "	50	50	
" "	10	10	
Daniel Maness Sr	100	50	
Do Do	120	35	
" "	100	50	
" "	4½	4	50
Isham Sheffield	100	750	
Do Do	100	95	
" "	50	50	
Milford Owens	150	150	
Edmond Hollen	100	50	
Do Do	150	50	
John Maness	100	100	
Meshack Maness	100	100	
Alexr Kennedy	660	1100	
Charles Brady	100	100	
Benjn Persons	50	100	
Edward Kennedy	50	500	
Do Do	300	150	
	7159½	7358	25

Names	Lands	Dolls	Cents
Francis Bullock	200	800	
Do Do	150	200	
" "	100	100	
" "	200	200	
" "	800	100	
" "	240	200	
" "	100	10	
" "	400	200	
" "	200	75	
Jacob Cagle	150	150	
Richd Holland	90	180	
Do Do	50	75	
" "	280	160	
" "	94	49	
" "	189	200	
John Sheffield Junr	40	175	
Do Do	150	123	
" "	27	50	
" "	26	26	
" "	87	20	
" "	3	6	
Henry Yow	200	350	
Joseph Smothermon	100	50	
Peter Shamburger W.	100	385	
Do Do	100	330	
" "	100	130	
" "	50	75	
" "	10	3	
Angus Leatch	200	220	
Alexd Leatch	124	200	
Malcom Leatch	336	320	
Peter Cagle	280	250	
Peter Gardner	94	100	
Do Do	500	250	
" "	385	96	25
David Kennedy	200	900	
Do Do	240	240	
" "	50	50	
" "	50	50	
" "	25	50	
" "	160	160	
" "	50	100	
" "	3	1000	
" "	200	100	
" "	200	100	
Cornelius Latham	150	250	
Do Do	100	50	
" "	200	100	
	77042	9008	25

Names	Land	Dolls	Cents
Nicolas Nall	300	3000	
Do Do	250	250	
" "	100	100	
" "	100	100	
" "	90	90	
" "	150	300	
Peter Davis	300	900	
Do Do	100	300	
" "	100	200	
" "	50	25	
" "	19½	10	
" "	50	25	
" "	100	100	
" "	100	50	
James Gains	699	2398	
Do Do	100	40	
John Shamburger Wr	200	750	
Do Do	230	120	
" "	60	135	
" "	100	50	
" "	100	50	
" "	68	17	
" "	300	75	
" "	20	5	
" "	300	75	
" "	200	50	
" "	250	200	
" "	225	200	
" "	150	38	
Fredrick Autrey	200	550	
Do Do	92	92	
" "	89	89	
" "	60	50	
Jeremiah Wilson	100	300	
Do Do	155	105	
" "	83	25	
" "	50	40	
" "	50	40	
George Moore	110	200	
Do Do	25	100	
" "	200	180	
Hiram Kennedy	348	348	
" "	300	100	
William Williamson	100	125	
Wm. Hundsucker	112	112	
Thomas Persons	50	100	
Do Do	69	69	
" "	410	831	
John Dunlap Jr	83	100	
	100	25	
Do Do	80	20	
" "			
	76972	13244	

Names	Lands	Dolls	Cents	Names	Lands
Jeremiah Williams -	150	150			
Do Do	150	250			
William Right Jur.	165	330			
" "	50	70			
William Brown	100	100			
William Waddill	480	1200			
William Duffee	200	200			
" "	100	8			
James Morgan	100	200			
Do Do	50	50			
" "	50	50			
" "	70	100			
" "	50	25			
" "	100	150			
Robert Kennedy	200	250			
" "	93	100			
John Sheffield Jun.	141	150			
" "	50	25			
" "	50	25			
William Right Sr.	100	200			
" "	50	10			
Sherwood Right	135	67	50		
Do Do	66	30			
" "	75	50			
" "	25	12	50		
Eli Callicutt	183	300			
Do Do	100	80			
" "	20	20			
Stephen Davis	100	100			
Do Do	189	40			
" "	150	102			
" "	50	15			
" "	25	69			
" "	16	15			
William McNess Jun.	100	100			
" "	50	50			
Kenneth Murchison	275	225			
	3991	4917	"		

	Land	Dolls	Cents
Amount from Page 1 —	24.666	27.890	
From Do. 2 —	29.027	34.578	
Do. Do. Do. 3 —	27.512	49.885	25
Do. Do. Do. 4 —	23.420½	31.439	50
Do. Do. Do. 5 —	22.117	26287	
Do. Do. Do. 6	24.205	23316	50
Do. Do. Do. 7 —	25660¾	22185	
Do. Do. Do. 8	23649¾	22652	50
Do. Do. Do. 9 —	19290½	20079	16
Do. Do. Do. 10 —	13916	13232	75
Do. Do. Do. 11 —	8992½	6344	85
Do. Do. Do. 12 —	8683½	4499	25
Do. Do. Do. 13	8384	3632	43
Do. Do. Do. 14 —	10,424½	5193	25
Do. Do. Do. 15 —	15554½	13773	25
Do. Do. Do. 16	15402	22252	25
Do. Do. Do. 17	3991	4917	
	304900	332,094	94

Bryan Borough gave in 662 acres of Land and put No Value to it

Names	Land	Value
Autry Fredrick	1050	1050
Autry Elijah	250	170
Autrey Elizabeth	100	120
Autrye Alexander	308	1475
Autry James	282	100
Autrye Alexander Sen	100	50
Allin Mark	300	300
Atkinson James by G.	700	1100
Armstrong Thomas heirs Do.	200	150
Armstrong Do	100	25
Allin Joseph	450	675
Bullock Allin	715	750
Brewer Ambrose	366	530
Brewer Micajah	355	310
Brewer Harmon	30	50
Brady James	100	100
Brady Robert	50	50
Brady Charles	100	50
Burkhead Eleazer	275	450
Burkhead Lewis	100	210
Black Neill	100	110
Black Richard	700	950
Black Hugh	250	200
Brown Tyre	675	500
Brown William	100	200
Bethune Allin	200	120
Buie Mary	300	120
Barrington Samuel	100	100
Blue Daniel	250	230
Brill Bryan	180	90
Brill Rhoday	225	110
Bryan Michael	660	570
Beard Alexander	365	30
Bean Tyre	160	320
Buchannon Daniel	368	200
Barrett William	1603	3660
Bullock Frances Col.	1450	1850
Boroughs Bryan	997	2992
Burkhead Mildred	50	50
Brill Benjamine	100	100
Brewer Elisha	30	100
Brewer William	100	100
Callicutt Eli	225	1100
Comer Adam	460	400
Furry Murdo	200	400

Names	Land	Value
Curry Catharine	150	100
Curry Laughlin	150	150
Cagle George	300	350
Cagle William	265	400
Cagle Jacob	150	200
Cagle Peter	280	200
Cagle Martin	390	44[illegible]
Cagle George	60	50
Cagle Henry	450	[illegible]
Cox William	300	530
Cheek Randol	114	120
Cheek Isaac	300	62[illegible]
Cheek John	1395	18[illegible]
Cheek James	150	17[illegible]
Cheek Richard	635	930
Cuthbertson Joseph	121	140
Cravens John	200	23[illegible]
Cockmon John	100	10[illegible]
Cockmon Catharine	150	12[illegible]
Clark Kenneth	600	90[illegible]
Caddell Benjamine	400	16[illegible]
Caddell Daniel	350	27[illegible]
Carrell Alexander	275	30[illegible]
Craven Henry Lot	330	[illegible]
Campbell Nancy	125	120
Campbell John	250	180
Campbell Angus	307	20[illegible]
Carlton John	130	10[illegible]
Cole Joseph	230	25[illegible]
Campbell Samuel	223	[illegible]
Caddell Jonathan	200	15[illegible]
Davis Peter	919	14[illegible]
Davis James C.	400	76[illegible]
Davis Robert	1300	120
Davis Elizabeth	300	50
Danielly John	450	60[illegible]
Denton Mathew	273	[illegible]
Denton Levy	340	[illegible]
Denton Burrell	220	15[illegible]
Dunlap John Sen	1100	17[illegible]
Dunlap John Jun	183	13[illegible]
Dunlap James	450	6[illegible]
David Patrick	326	[illegible]
David James	250	25[illegible]
Dunn John	135	20[illegible]
Dunn William	100	1[illegible]
Dunn Bartholomew	128	200
Dowdy Amy	[illegible]	[illegible]

Name	Land	Value	Name	Land	Value
Dowdy Amos	220	125	Hannon Reuben	100	35
Duckworth Joseph	200	350	Hugh Samuel by agent	40	160
Davis Stephen	300	300	Harden Wm Heirs	230	230
Dowd Cornelius	1983	2865	Harris Susannah	100	30
Dowd William Capt	550	800	Holland Edmond	200	100
England William 1 Lot	512	923	Jackson Samuel & William	1550	1380
England James	330	620	Jones Allen	390	2000
Elkins Samuel	75	120	Jones William	375	350
Feagins Daniel	50	130	Jackson Margaret	150	80
Feagins William	400	300	Johnston Joseph	526	400
Freeman Reuben	290	450	Johnston Malichi	100	100
Freeman William	217	350	Johnston Michael	250	180
Fry Barsheba	150	150	Johnston James	200	100
Fry George	200	230	Jackson George	2000	1300
Fry William	200	600	Kennedy David	1067	2400
Fry James	200	400	D° for Jacob Carringer	112	112
Fry Joseph	710	420	Kennedy Alexander	360	900
Fry Nathan	380	220	Kennedy Edward	330	300
Furr Leonard	285	400	Kennedy Robert	300	350
Furr Jacob	375	400	Keys Samuel	230	370
Feagins Richardson	1088	1550	Keys John	35	140
Gains James	47½	70	Kendol John	100	60
Gardner Peter	1100	300	Kendol William	60	20
Graham Thomas	600	820	Kennedy John	100	200
Graham George	670	900	Kennedy Hiram	300	400
Graham Margaret	140	130	Kennedy George	100	100
Graham Robert Heirs	300	150	Kelly John 10 Lots	210	520
Gilbert Benjamin	550	1100	Lawhon Joel	420	730
Gilbert Sabra	100	100	Lawhon Lewis	100	100
Gillis Donald	210	200	Lawler Abner	100	180
Glascock Geo Heirs	200	300	Lewis John	230	300
Glascock Patty	100	200	Lewis William	300	190
Glascock Julius	125	250	Leach Malcom & Son	660	660
Griffith William	125	130	Martin William	1890	3000
Gains James	740	2485	D° for A. McLeods Estate	2110	2890
Gains Bradly	1677	1470	Martin Murdock	470	930
Hare John	662	1200	Martin John	930	930
Hare Peter	629	800	Martin Allen	300	300
Hancock John	250	500	Morrison Malcom	274	250
Hains James	50	60	Morrison Normond	450	400
Hundsucker George	208	200	Morrison Allen	2997	900
Holland Richard	642	550	D° B. Bethunes Estate 1 Lot		400
Harvil Thomas	150	100	Morrison John	100	100
Hill Hiram	125	300	Morrison Aleck	170	180
Hannon Thomas	50	60			

List of Taxable Property in Moore County 1818 approximately

Names	Land	Value	Names	Land	Val
Morrison Angus	183	80	McCaskill Alexander	100	30
Muse Silas	600	1330	McCrummen Daniel	493	300
Muse Thomas Jr.	350	400	McCrummen John	84	200
Muse James	90	100	McCrummen Malcom	130	150
Muse Jesse J.	123	150	McDonald Donald	160	200
Muse Thomas	100	100	McDonald Donald Sr.	100	100
Muse James B.	230	500	McDonald Donald Jr.	300	150
Muse Daniel	100	100	McDonald Donald (Blue)	98	100
Matthewson Murdo	310	210	McDonald John	200	400
Matthewson Normond	350	180	McDonald John	284	170
Matthewson Malcom	141	140	McDonald John (M.T.)	133	100
Mclnnis John	100	100	McDonald Angus	133	100
Maness Daniel Sen.	324	470	McDuffie John	100	100
Maness Abednego	200	270	McDaniel Chasraty	180	60
Maness William	150	150	McIver John 4 Lots	1690	2535
Maness Meshack	100	130	McIver Abel	100	100
Maness James Sen.	150	200	McIntosh Neill	519	630
Maness Wm. Nuoly	50	50	McIntosh Alexander	400	330
Miller James	150	200	McIntosh Christian	300	500
Miller Ansel	100	100	McKenzie John	393	440
Miller John	160	100	McKenzie Murdo	330	200
Medlin Alexander	212	250	McKenzie John (by Agent)	150	150
Medlin John Sen.	100	100	McKay John by Do.	1050	1000
Medlin John Jun.	200	200	McKinnon John	430	500
Myrick Francis	300	300	McKinnon Normond	328	250
Moore George	331	370	McKinnon Alexander	74	60
Moore Fanning	75	100	McKinnon Normond Jun.	100	23
Martindale Samuel	330	480	McLeod Neill	150	90
Morgan James	420	620	McLeod Alexander	606	900
Morgan Joseph	250	400	McLeod Alexander	200	250
Morgan Nathan	179	250	McKnight Hugh	400	300
Murchison Kenneth	240	500	McLeod Alexander	300	230
Mash Burn Thomas	200	30	McLeod Daniel	130	150
Murchison John (Esq.)	400	1930	McLeod Mary	125	150
McLeod Nancy	7212	4135	McLeod Normond	200	110
Murchison Rodrick	251	210	McLeod Nancy	100	60
McAulay Roderick	360	550	McLeod Angus	200	135
McAulay Murdo Sr.	200	430	McLain Allen	60	120
McAulay Murdo Esq.	317	260	McLain Hector (Ex.)	300	200
McArthur James	50	50	McLauchlan Dugald	300	300
McCaskill Kenneth	1832	12.00	McNeill Daniel	1527	1500
McCaskill Kenneth Jr.	365	220	McNeill John	930	950
McCaskill Do. Sen.	100	100	McNeill Arch. Esq.	400	800
			McNeill Lauchlan	140	200

Names	Land	Value	Names	Land	Value
McNeill Hector	149	170	Ritter John Jur	50	30
McQueen Angus	525	500	Ritter Jesse	1170	300
McQueen Margaret	200	400	Rowe Joseph	50	100
McRae Gilbert by ag.	130	75	Russell William	180	200
McSween John	325	650	Russell John	24	200
			Russell George	129	210
McSween Murdo	400	400	Richardson Drury	375	250
McMillan Dugald	50	10	Sewell Gideon	1000	2000
McNeill James	128	350	Sewell Joseph	200	320
Maness Thomas	100	170	Smith William	275	400
McKinnon William	100	50	Smith James	379	120
McIver Daniel	600	600	Smith Sarah	230	300
McKinnon Daniel	93	100	Smith John	120	150
McKinnon Angus	60	50	Smith Leonard	200	450
Nall Nicholas	1000	4500	Smith Isham	70	80
Nicholson Meloney	130	150	Smith Nathan	283	300
Ormond Jacob	275	300	Shamburger Peter Senr	750	700
Owen Medford	150	130	Shamburger John Sr & 1 Lot in [illegible]	3040	1990
Patterson John Senr	550	460	Shamburger Peter	360	690
Patterson John Jur	450	470	Shamburger William	100	100
Patterson Daniel	330	250	Sheffield Isham Senr	250	900
Phillips Lewis	200	700	Sheffield John Senr	241	500
Phillips Pretty	160	600	Sheffield John Jur	254	400
Phillips Eli	289	350	Sheffield Ervin	181	310
Phillips Mark	100	220	Sheffield Isham Jur	91	200
Powers Henry for J. [illegible]	100	70	Sheffield Isaac	130	270
Pearce Jesse	100	80	Shields Cornelius	1859	1730
Perry Samuel	610	500	Shields Archibald	270	900
Perry William	40	50	Shields James	260	80
Person William	336	500	Stewart George	225	120
Persons Thomas	300	1150	Stewart Charles	50	25
Person Benjamin	30	110	Stewart George	200	200
Roberts Isaac	1650	1220	Sewell John	1249	1350
Richardson John	1130	653	Sewell Isaac	200	150
Desc. Dr Richardsons Estate	30	160	Sowell Asa	600	130
Richardson Stephen	1100	600	Sowell Jesse	236	360
Richardson Stephen Jr.	300	300	Sowell Charles	172	100
Richardson David	75	100	Smith Samson	200	400
Ritter John	640	900	Sanders Jesse 3 Lots	107	209
Ritter Thomas	550	800	Smith John	200	200
Ritter Jesse	155	260	Stutts Henry	535	750
Ritter Moses Senr	100	100	Stutts Christian	130	400
Ritter Moses Jur	100	60	Stutts Jacob	300	250
			Seal John	50	70

Names	Land	Value
Sisson Elizabeth	100	100
Spivey John	650	610
Spees Peter	100	100
Sears William	50	50
Sears David	100	130
Sears Barnaba	50	30
Street Elizabeth	680	1520
Street Richard	900	250
Tyson William	996	1206
Tyson John 4 Lots	94	2350
Tyson Cornelius	550	550
Do for Thos Tysons Estate	1100	3180
Do for Jas Boroughs	550	1980
Tyson Benjamin	1000	1600
Tucker Nathaniel	250	375
Teague Bruce	30	50
Upton John	220	220
Upton Richard	133	200
Waddell William	480	450
Williams Jeremiah	150	175
Williams Jeremiah	110	140
Williamson William	1116	2000
Williamson Baily	500	250
Williamson William	211	280
Williamson Allen	100	50
Wilson Phillip Harr	223	200
Wilson Robert	600	1100
Do for E. Branson	500	150
Wilson Jeremiah	438	300
Wright Sherwood	385	400
Wright William	215	400
Wade Tinsley	420	630
Wood James	450	430
Do for L. Garners Heirs	425	500
Walker Ewel	100	100
Wadsworth John	130	50
Warner Hardin	440	450
White Adam	475	900
Williams Elizabeth	3930	8716
Williams Thomas	240	240

Names	Land	Value
Yow Henry	200	400
Yow Andrew	292	320
Do C. Yows Estate	100	150
Non Residents by Street		
Duffee William	300	230
Frazier George	110	200
Harden Gabriel	200	200
Latham James	550	460
Murdoch McKenzie	1823	4145
Do for Mary England	300	600
Do for Aaron Tysons Estate	1830	6870
Do for surviving partners of Aaron Tyson & Co	1650	1240
Do for M. McKenzie & Co	790	770
McFuller Peter	230	300
Teague Mary	50	75
Phillips William	200	150
Lawler Eli	150	200
Branson Henry	200	100
Hannah George	300	200
Roberts Owen	230	600
2d District by Reed		
Archd McBryde	696	700
Alexd Clark	1000	900
Alexd Bain	450	500
Archd McMillan & Elder	650	400
Archd McDugalds Estate	600	1000
Alexd McLeod	1116	700
Archd Graham	330	200
Angus McDonald	130	75
Angus McMillan	610	200
Archd Black	130	[illegible]
Alexd McBryde	300	400
Archd McMillan	450	200
Archd Buie	150	50
Archd Cameron	50	25
Archd Wadsworth	570	850
Allen Ellis	100	50
Archd Curry	300	450
Archd Reed	303	600

VI

Names	Land	Value
Angus McDonald	200	300
Angus McDuffie	150	100
Alex & Murdoch Ferguson	250	700
Alex Kaul	440	200
Archd McGilvery	315	250
Angus McGilvery	200	100
Archd Murchison	302	190
Alex McLean	100	75
Alex Campbell	100	80
Archd Cameron	150	100
Andrew Anderson	200	75
Archd Munroe	234	150
Angus McDonald	120	30
Angus Curry	130	50
Amos Hill	30	30
Alex Campbell	337	150
Archd Buchannon	59	25
Archd Ray Esqr	2300	1000
Angus Curry	400	400
Angus McDonald	150	120
Angus Blue	50	50
Allen McDonald	480	232
Archd McDonald	200	100
Ditto	400	280
Angus McDonald	240	120
Anthony Graham	375	185
Abner Harrington	100	80
Angus Shaw	150	150
Archd McDonald	250	120
Angus McIver (tiller)	105	50
Alex Carmicale	100	100
Abraham Cole	475	475
Allen Thomas	140	250
Alex McIver (Miller)	1000	800
Alex McIntosh	100	400
Archd Dalrymple		
Do Alex McIvers Estate	362	200
Averit Baggot Estate	160	80
Abel Douglas	1174	982
Archd McPherson	212	100
Alex Black	150	20
Archd Ray	602	300
Archd Douglas	124	217
Alex Campbell	535	500

Names	Land	Value
Bartholomew McFarland	515	515
Brite Roberts	330	900
Benjamin Thomas	450	800
Britton Wommack	855	575
Benjamin Bishop	100	40
Benjamin Bailey	185	200
Booker Parrish	20	20
Benjamin Wicker	100	100
Benjamin Seler	200	100
Benjamin Graham	307½	307
Barbary Dye	187½	150
Charles Stewart	350	250
Carnaba Stephens for Mordecai Morrison	200	200
Christian McLennon	100	50
Christian Murchison	100	20
Carnaba Stephens	100	400
Crissy Stephens by agent	200	150
Christian Matthews	150	120
Charles Crawford	1100	330
Catharine Black	150	70
Donald McDonald	2000½	2000
Duncan Buie	4000	2950
Duncan McNeill	100	100
Daniel Buie Esqr	700	1300
Duncan McIver (Miller)	741	700
David Wicker	225	600
Duncan Pattison Col.	1935	1500
Daniel Clark	600	350
Daniel McIver	380	500
Daniel McNeill (son of Hector)	150	75
Daniel McRae	180	150
Daniel McDugald	370	370
Daniel Campbell	1500	1000
Daniel Lennon for Jno	125	120
Duncan McDugald	100	80
Duncan Smith	82	30
Duncan McIver	900	500
Duncan McCollum	470	300
Duncan Robeson	86	50
Duncan McPherson	50	50
Duncan Murchison	1840	1400
Daniel Stewart	600	200
Duncan McIver (Hatter)	300	1100
David Thompson	600	400
Dempsey Hathcock	234	200
Duncan McDuffie	130	120
Duncan McIver	743	300
Daniel Nicholson	425	200
Daniel Murchison (Lick)	1109	300

Name	Land	Value	Name	Land	Value
Duncan McRae Hun	100	75	Duncan McMillan	303	150
Daniel Murchison	119	60	Donald McDonald	140	110
Duncan Murchison Big	370	100	Daniel & Peter Kelly	450	300
David Watson	270	200	Dugald Black	800	400
Daniel Stewart	600	300	Daniel Blue	330	210
Duncan Kelly	266	500	Daniel McKinnel	216	100
Daniel Campbell	455	250	Duncan McCollum	175	100
Daniel McIntosh	776	600	Daniel McDonald Sen	124½	100
Daniel Thompson	106	120	Dempsey Hunt	200	150
Daniel Murchison	500	250	Daniel Kelly Sr	450	150
Daniel Shaw Sr	320	250	Duncan Ray	330	128
Daniel McIver (B S)	594	600	Daniel McIntosh	75	75
Daniel Curry	150	75	Daniel McIver	75½	40
Daniel Kitchen	100	210	Daniel Love	300	300
Daniel McDuffie	370	150	Daniel McLean	50	50
Duncan Ray for Son John	125	50	Duncan Cameron	125	60
Daniel McDugald	180	180	David Reid Esqr	1490	240
Daniel Cameron	200	200	Elisha Yarborough	168	250
Daniel McDugald	183	100	Effy Black	100	100
David Graham	250	500	Elizabeth Kitchen	100	100
Daniel Graham	200	100	Edmund Kelly	80	25
Dugald McFarland	550	250	Eleanor Worthington	450	800
Daniel Blue (Tay)	430	200	Edward McIver (Saddler)	275	100
Duncan Black by agent	100	30	Effy McIver	302	200
D. Blue for M. Gilchrist	370	90	Elizabeth McLennan	250	150
Dugald Mathews	200	50	Fredrick Siler	935	1500
Daniel Ray	50	40	Fredrick Thomas	440	610
Daniel Blue (Johnston)	100	50	Finly McDonald Sen	283	128
Daniel McRay	100	40	Florah McIver	60	50
D. Blue for D. Gilchrist	50	25	Gilbert Blue Capt	317	500
Daniel McMillan (Leather)	250	200	Griffeen Hunt	100	100
Daniel Cameron	640	640	George Walker	100	100
Daniel McLeod	200	100	George McRae	100	30
Duncan McLean	100	100	George Brown	100	50
Donald McDonald	88	88	Gilbert McRae	150	150
Daniel Graham	300	200	Hugh Kelly	200	119
Daniel Patterson	450	250	Hugh McDonald	230	100
Duncan Brown	100	80	Hugh McDonald	765	265
Duncan McIntosh	150	150	Henry Morris	283	200
Daniel Kelly	100	50	Kelk Hugh	200	300
Duncan Munroe	100	250	Hugh Cameron	508	250
Duncan McLeod	400	125	Hector Smith	230	150
Daniel McDonald	150	120	Henry Cofer	150	150
Daniel & John Morris	100	100	Henry Cox	400	500
Duncan Curry	50	50	Hugh McLean	1834	5250
Duncan Patterson	475	300	John Gunter	300	200
			John Ray Senr	397	300

Names	Land	Value
John Cameron	50	50
Jacob Gaster Col.	217	325
James Dalrymple	535	520
John Baker	439	400
John Ward	647½	1300
John Shepherd Esq.	200	150
John Cameron (Merit)	2700	1600
John Cameron (Tay Estate)	300	300
John McLeod Esq.	293	200
John McNeill Esq.	2230	830
John Walker	283	200
Jacob Mathews	470	1650
John Morris	1001	800
James McBryde	200	150
John Blue (D. Son)	50	50
John Godfrey	100	50
Jacob Morris	50	50
John Ward	200	300
John McDugald	100	100
John Maples	150	150
James Maples	120	240
John Stewart	670	200
John Gillars	348	348
John McKinnon	100	100
John McIver (one eye)	622	450
John Campbell	125	120
John Worthy	469	850
Daniel McKinzie	200	75
John Baker	500	200
John Blackman	200	300
John Dalrymple	620	350
Joseph Griffin	200	50
Joseph Thompson Mr	119	200
John McIntosh for the heirs of Daniel McIntosh	400	250
John McNeill (by ag.)	175	100
John McFarland	375	600
John Thomas	100	200
John McLeod	100	80
John Welldon Esq.	446	550
John Cole	670	680
John Sinclair Sr.	554	300
John Paterson	480	350

Names	Land	Value
John Stone	185	185
Jesse Walker	115	50
Jonathan Hawly	200	200
John McIver (Paper)	119	100
John Nicholson	250	150
John Spearsfor	100	400
Jonathan Walker	300	200
John McDugald	620	430
John Shephard (Long)	940	1400
John Watson	880	550
John Ray (miller)	460	200
John McCollum	70	50
John Wadsworth	500	250
John Campbell Jun.	250	150
John Smith	345	400
John Kelly	300	30
James Monk	150	70
John McCollum	150	75
Josiah Holloman	797	600
John McInnish	100	30
John Kennedy	60	60
John Blue Esq.	855	400
Joseph Kelly	50	45
John Black	100	100
John Kelly	440	250
John Johnston	200	30
John Cole	700	700
John McIntosh	165	130
Jas. Ray	200	75
John Campbell	250	200
John McNeill (Strong)	400	175
John Campbell	391	200
James Kelly	140	50
John Campbell	50	30
John Worthy for F. Riddle	349	340
Daniel Dalrymple	63	120
Josiah Tyson	539	900
John McLeod (Carpenter)	700	750
John Riddle	100	250
Joseph Kelly	50	60
James Morgan	101	322
John McKinnel	100	73
James Worthy	150	150
John Underwood	90	90
John McDonald	61	61

IX Names	Land	Value
(10) Kenneth Mc[illegible]	519	200
Kenneth McIver	72½	110
Katharine Conley	30	50
Katharine McDonald	200	100
Katharine McIver	75½	40
Kenneth McKinzie	50	30
Kenneth Murchison	830	500
Kenneth McIntosh	200	150
Katharine [illegible]	25	20
Katharine Buchan	312	250
Kinchin Kitchen	450	800
Katharine Black	100	75
Lewis Parham	257	550
Lewis Campbell	50	80
Lauchlin McKinnon	75	50
Lockart Fry	135	100
Lauchlin Curry	550	300
Lauchlin Johnston	50	30
Martin McPherson	567	500
Mary Patterson	350	850
Malcom McFarland	1115	450
Malcom McNeill Estate	2514	700
Murdoch McMillan (Rad)	335	850
Mary Smith	600	500
Malcom Blue Jr	550	300
Malcom Gunter	250	250
Malcom McNeill	300	150
Malcom Blue	100	30
Mondue Morrison	700	1050
Murdoch Ferguson	260	200
Miles McInnish	400	30
Milley Walker	25	200
Murdoch McKinzie	100	50
Malcom Barker	269	170
Margaret Munroe	100	175
Malcom McNeill	180	100
Malcom McGilvery	330	350
Murdoch McIntosh	625	600
Martin Dye	100	100
Martin Thomas	200	150
Malcom McDonald	247	206

Names	Land	Value
Mary McLean	100	60
Malcom Black	468	720
Malcom Black	1030	337
Malcom McMillan	330	150
Malcom Clark	170	170
Malcom Gunter for A. McLennan's Estate	422	150
Malcom Shaw	410	360
Murdoch Ferguson	200	200
Neill McLeod	119	50
Nathan Maples	136	100
Neill Shaw	140	100
Nancy Burr	100	25
Nancy McLeod	95	20
Nathan Allen	200	100
Nancy Campbell	170	170
Neill McDuffie	40	110
Nancy McLeod	100	30
Neill Cameron	320	620
Nevin Clark	310	230
Neill McLeod	500	1125
Neill Patterson	173	575
Neill McLeod	488	300
Neill McMillan	438	70
Neill McFadyen	850	600
Phillip Johnson	1052	1200
Peter Blue Senr	738	375
Peter Blue Jr	1200	800
Peter Morris	200	200
Peter Sexton	300	400
Peter Sinclair G. Ck	550	550
Peter Sinclair	400	350
Phillip Cameron	134	108
Peter Frazure	200	150
Peter Morris	25	200
Rodrick McCrummen	100	50
Robert McLauchlin	250	200
Richd Cole	100	100
Robert Boals	344	300
Robt. Allen (alias Wommack)	100	250
Rodrick Murchison (Hatter)	308	180
Randolph Jackson	124	120
Robert McIver	851	1100
Robert Sterling	320	230
Rebecca Jackson	100	30

Names	Land	Value
Robert Hughes	200	100
Reuben Oliver	550	30
Rebecca Cole	200	200
Tice Harrington	393	300
Spears Ham	977	1350
Isaac Williams	50	20
Stephen Berryman	300	60
Spencer Kelly	100	50
[illegible]	575	1450
Thomas Davis	500	325
Thomas Fry Sen	72	80
Thomas Fry Jun	72	80
Thomas Gilmore	200	120
Thomas Collins Heirs	250	300
Thomas Cox	200	325
Thomas Cole Jun	226	200
Thomas Thompson	800	800
Thomas Cole Senr	300	300
William Dawson	254	100
Wm Dalrymple	913½	800
Wm [illegible]	340	600
Wm Hunt	200	125
Willis Gray	250	50
Wm Murchison	150	150
Wm Shaw	400	290
Wm Olive	100	40
Wm Crawford	300	300
Willis & John Knight	180	150
Wm McCrady	900	800
Wm A. Arnold	200	200
Willis Olive Sen	200	200
Wm Smith	450	250
Wm Brice Esqr	887	666
Wm Lazure	150	120
Walter McBeth	540	600
Willis Dickinson	485	682
Wm Smith	400	250
Wm Campbell	611	307
Warren Jones	100	130
Wm Coffee	50	40
Zachariah Graham	200	200

Non Residents

Names	Land	Value
Archd McFadyen	150	150
Andrew Brown	200	200
Archd McIntire	300	150
Alexr McKay	200	50
Benton Drake	100	100
Benjamin Huckabee	200	200
Charles Blalock	150	150
Daniel McLean	100	100
Daniel McGilvary	50	
Daniel Black	100	
Gilbert Clark	100	
Creasy Stephens	150	
Hector McNeill	700	
Do for Neill McNeill	113½	
Do for John McNeill	175	
Isaac Becker	150	
John McMillan	500	
John McMillan	205	
John McIntire	300	
Kenneth Murchison	615	
Mary Smith	270	
Malcolm Monroe	231	
Malcolm McNeill	1300	
Matthew Morrison	350	
Neill McKay Esqr	400	
Neill McKethan	1100	
Richd Huckabee	330	
Robert Watson	370	
Samuel Howde	160	
Thomas Stokes	130	
William Colvin	400	
John Shaw	200	
William Smith	300	

The End

Amen

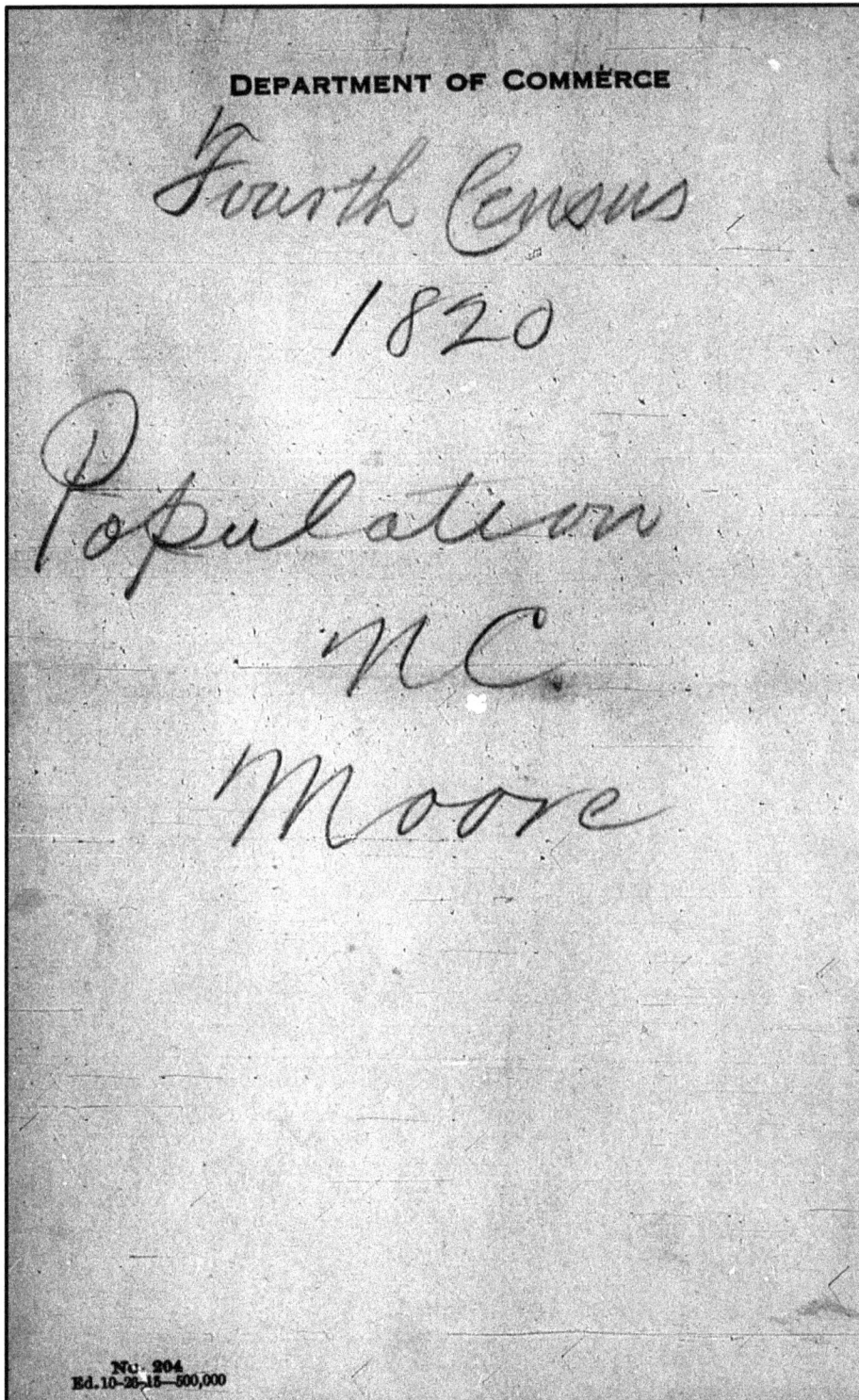

DEPARTMENT OF COMMERCE

Fourth Census

1820

Population

NC

Moore

No. 204
Ed. 10-26-15—500,000

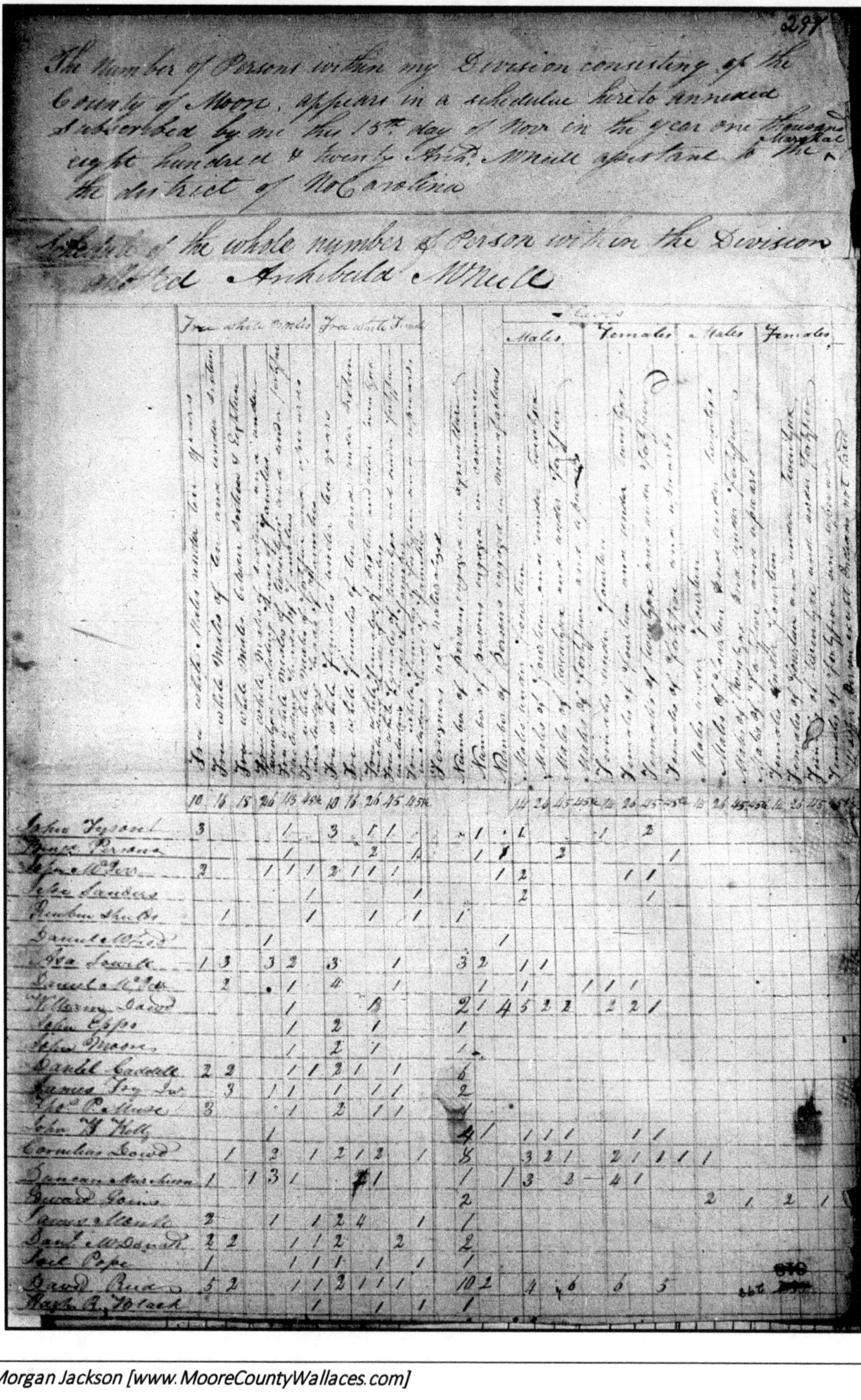

297

The Number of Persons within my Division consisting of the County of Moore, appears in a schedule hereto annexed subscribed by me the 15th day of Nov in the year one thousand eight hundred & twenty Archd. McNeill assistant to the Marshal the district of No Carolina

Schedule of the whole number of Person within the Division allotted Archibald McNeill

John Tyson
Pence Persons
John McGee
John Sanders
Reuben Shields
Daniel Wood
Asa Smith
Daniel McGee
William Dowd
John Epps
John Moore
Daniel Caddell
James Fry Jr
Thos P. Muse
John W. Kelly
Cornelius Dowd
Duncan Murchison
Edward Goins
James Muse
Danl. McDonald
Joel Pope
David Rue
Hugh R. Black

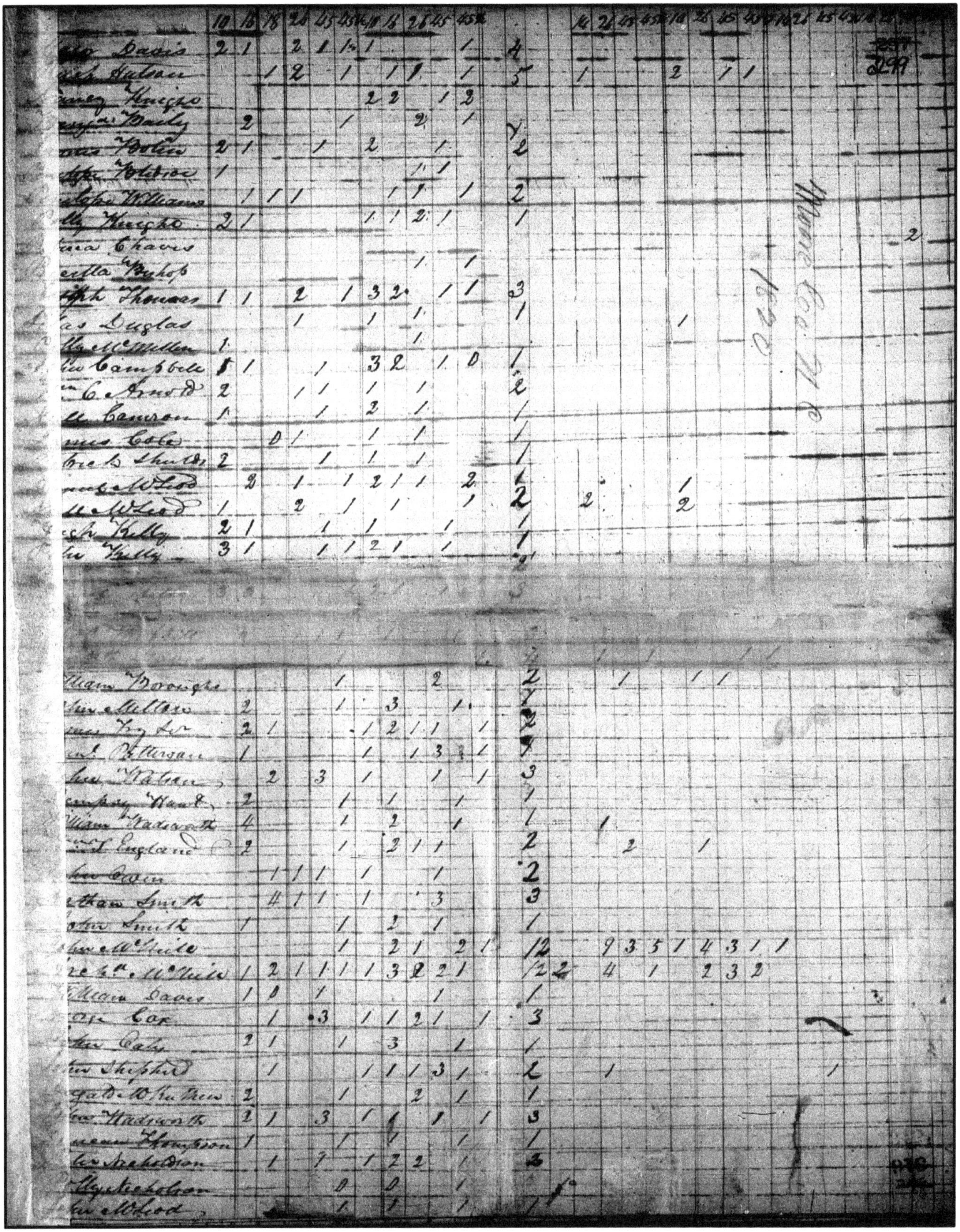

300
315

2	10	16	18	26	45	45+	10	16	26	45	45+					14	26	45	45+	14	26	45	45+	14	26	45	45+	14	26	45	45+
Sally McDonald	1						1			1	1		[illegible]																		
Joseph Stephens	2			1			1		1				1																		
Vincent Sterling	1			1					1				1																		
Robert Sterling	1					1	2				1		1																		
Elizabeth Sterling				1									1																		
William Sterling		1			1								1																		
Hector Smith	1	2		2		1		1			1		3																		
George McRae					1					1	1		1				1														
Warren Lowe	1			1			1			1			1																		
Danl. McDonald	2	1				1	2	1		1			2																		
Lona E. McDonald					1					2	1		1							1											
Jeptha Rannels	1					1	1	1			1		1																		
Duncan Cameron					1		1			1			1																		
Josiah Tyson	3	1			1		3	1		1			3			6	1				1										
Benja Tyson	3				1		3			1			1																		
Robert Boals	2	2		1		1	3	1	1		1		3																		
Edmond Smith					1		1			1			1																		
Andrew Jackson	4	2	1	1		1	1	1	1	1			2																		
Abram Cole	2	1	1	1		1	3				1		2																		
William Dickerson	2	1				1		1	2		1		2																		
Duncan McLeod		1			1		1		1	1	1		1																		
Fedrich Silor			2	2		1	1	1			1		3			1	1	1		3	1	1									
Neill Tyson	2	1			1		1			1			2																		
Alexr. Cameron	3	1			1		3			1			4			2				1											
Daniel Cameron	1			1	1					1	1		1																		
John Lowell				3	2	1	1		1	2	1		2		3																
Isham Lowell	2				1		1		1				[illegible]		1																
Isaac Lowell					1		2		1				[illegible]		1																
John Lowell Jr.	1			1			1		1				[illegible]		1																
Tobias Fry	1				1		2						1																		
Samuel Dew	1				1		1			1			1																		
John Barrot	3				1					1			1																		
William Barrot Jr.				1									2							1											
Lockhart Fry	1			1					1				1																		
Caskill Caddell				1					1				1																		
Susanah Lewis						1			1																						
John Leister					1			1	1		1																				
Julius Glascock						1					1		1																		
Richard Warner	1	1			1		1		1				1																		
Thos. Cox	2	1			1		4			1			1																		
Moses Oliver	1	1	1	1		1	3	1		1			1		1																
John Underwood	1	1			1		2	2		1			1																		
William Kelly						1							1		1									3		1		5	2		
Brittain Thomas	1		1	1			2	2		1			4			1	2	1		1											
William Wright	2					1	2			1			1																		
John Wright		1			1		1			1			1																		
William Watson	1	1		1	1		2	2		1			[illegible]			1	3														
William Ausley					1								6			7	3	4	2	3	5	3	1								
Joseph Griffin						1					1		1			1															

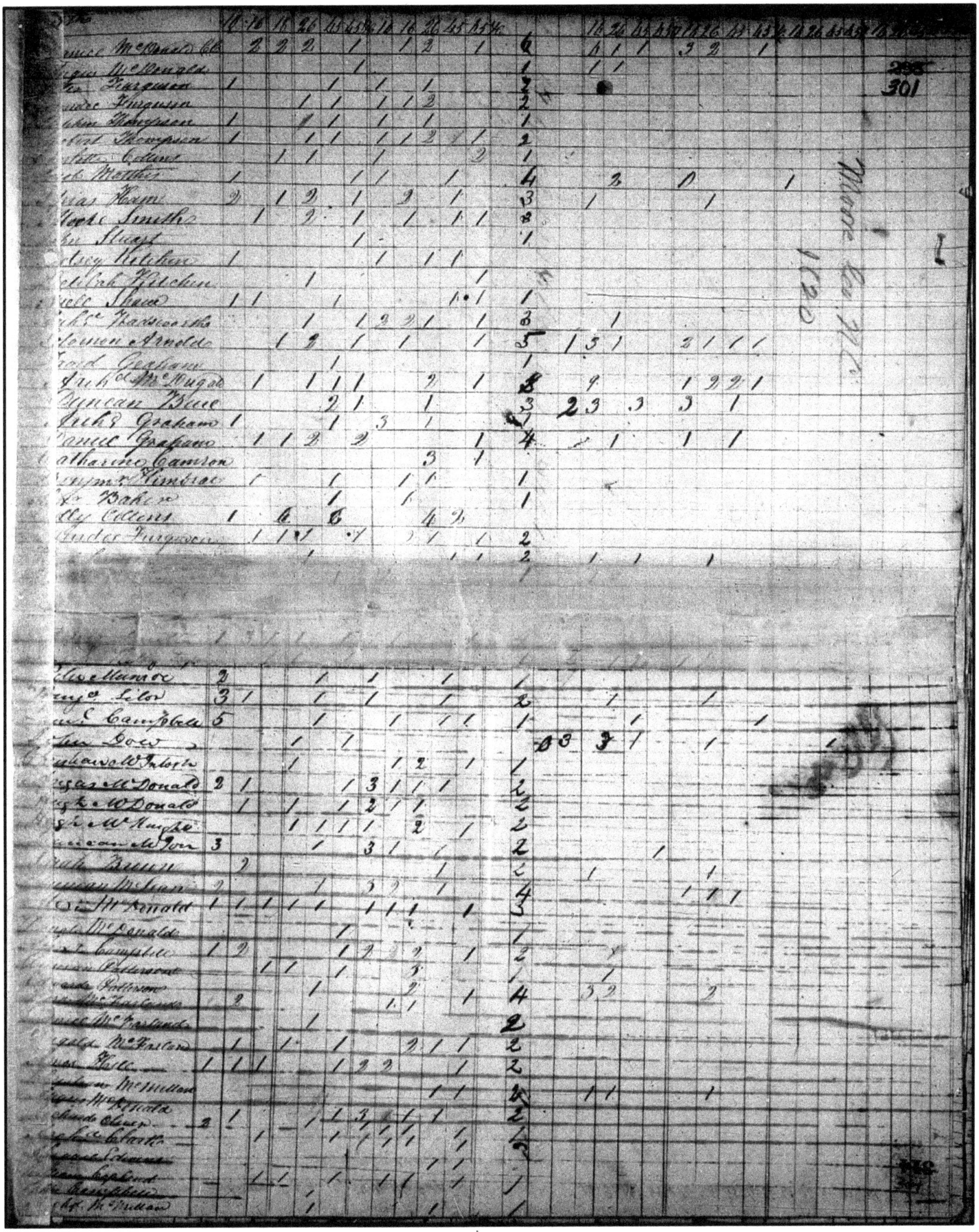

Duncan McDonald Sr
Hugh McDonald
[illegible] Ferguson
Duncan Ferguson
John Thompson
Robert Thompson
[illegible] Collins
[illegible] Matthews
Elias Hayne
[illegible] Smith
John Stuart
Asley Kitchen
Obediah Kitchen
[illegible] Shaw
Richd Wadsworth
Solomon Arnold
David Graham
Archd McDugald
Duncan Blue
Archd Graham
Daniel Graham
Catharine Cameron
Benjamin Kimbrel
[illegible] Baker
Polly Collins
Alexander Ferguson
[illegible] Munroe
Benjn Silor
Danl Campbell
[illegible] Dow
Archibald McIntosh
Angus McDonald
Hugh McDonald
Hugh McNaught
Duncan McIver
[illegible] Bruen
Duncan McInnis
[illegible] McDonald
[illegible] McDonald
[illegible] Campbell
[illegible] Patterson
[illegible] Patterson
[illegible] McFarland
[illegible] McFarland
[illegible] McFarland
[illegible] Hall
[illegible] McMillan
[illegible] McDonald
[illegible] Oliver
[illegible] Clark
[illegible] Edmins
[illegible] Copeland
[illegible] Campbell
[illegible] McMillan
Moore Co NC
1820
301

302

Name	Entries (left to right)
[illegible] McLean	1, 1, 2, 1, 1
[illegible] Clark	4, 2, 2, 1, 3, 1, 1, 5, 2, 2, 1, 1, 1
[illegible] McKenzie	1, 1, 4, 1, 2, 1, 2
[illegible] Campbell	2, 1, 1, 1, 4, 1, 2
[illegible] Morrison	2, 2, 1, 4, 1, 1, 1
Daniel Buchanan	1, 2, 1, 1, 2, 1, 2
William Spoon	1, 1, 1, 1
[illegible] Ray	1, 1, 4, 1, 1, 1, 1, 6, 1
[illegible] Ray	2, 1, 2, 1, 1
[illegible]	1, 1, 1, 1, 1
[illegible] Mathison	1, 1, 1
[illegible]	1, 2, 1, 1
John Campbell	1, 1
Archd McMillan	1, 1, 1, 1, 1
[illegible] McLeod	1, 1, 3, 1, 1
[illegible] McLeod	1, 1, 2, 1, 1, 1
John Blue Esqr	1, 1, 1, 4, 1, 3, 1, 1, 1, 5, 1
Nancy McNeill	2, 2, 1, 1, 1
Archd Buchan	1, 1, 1, 1
Archd Monroe	4, 1, 1, 1, 1, 1, 1
Norman Gillis	2, 7, 1, 1, 3, 2, 5, 2
John Gillis	1, 1, 1, 1, 1
Archd Gillis	1, 1, 1, 1
Archd Blue	1, 1, 2, 2, 1, 2, 1, 1
John Ray	2, 1, 1, 1, 1, 1, 2, 1, 2, 2, 1
Hector McNeill	1, 1, 1, 2, 4, 1, 3, 1, 1, 1
Lauchlin McKinnon	1, 2, 1, 1, 1, 1
Daniel McLean	4, 1, 2, 1, 1, 1
Angus Blue	1, 1, 1, 1, 1, 4, 2, 2, 1
Daniel Blue	2, 1, 1, 1, 3, 1, 2, 2, 2, 1
Daniel Love	1, 1, 1, 1, 1, 1
Patrick Blue Esqr	1, 1, 1, 1, 1, 1
Malcom Blue	2, 1, 1, 1, 1
Peter Blue	1, 1, 1, 1, 1, 4, 1, 1, 3, 2
John McLeod Esqr	2, 1, 2, 4, 1, 1, 2, 1
Daniel Graham	1, 1, 1, 3, 1, 2, 1, 1
Duncan McLeod	1, 1, 2, 1, 1
Christian McLean	2, 1, 2, 1, 3
John Patterson	1, 1, 1, 2, 1, 1, 1
Hugh McDonald Esqr	2, 1, 1, 1
Archd Patterson	1, 1, 1, 1
Donald Patterson	1, 1, 1, 1, 1, 2, 1, 1
John Turner	1, 1, 1, 1, 2
Malcom Clark	2, 1, 2, 2, 1, 1
Angus Clark	1, 1, 1, 2, 1, 1
James Maples	1, 1, 1, 1, 1
Benjamin Stephens	2, 1, 1, 1, 1
Israel Maples	1, 1, 1, 2, 1, 1
John Maples	1, 1, 1
Angus Ferguson	1, 1, 1, 1
Peter McAllen	1, 1, 1
Wm Thomas Gilmore	1, 1, 1, 1, 1, 1
Thomas Maples	1, 1, 1, 1, 4, 1, 2, 2, 1
John McDugald	1, 1, 1, 1
Mary McDugald	1
Archd Cole	1, 3, 1, 2, 1, 1

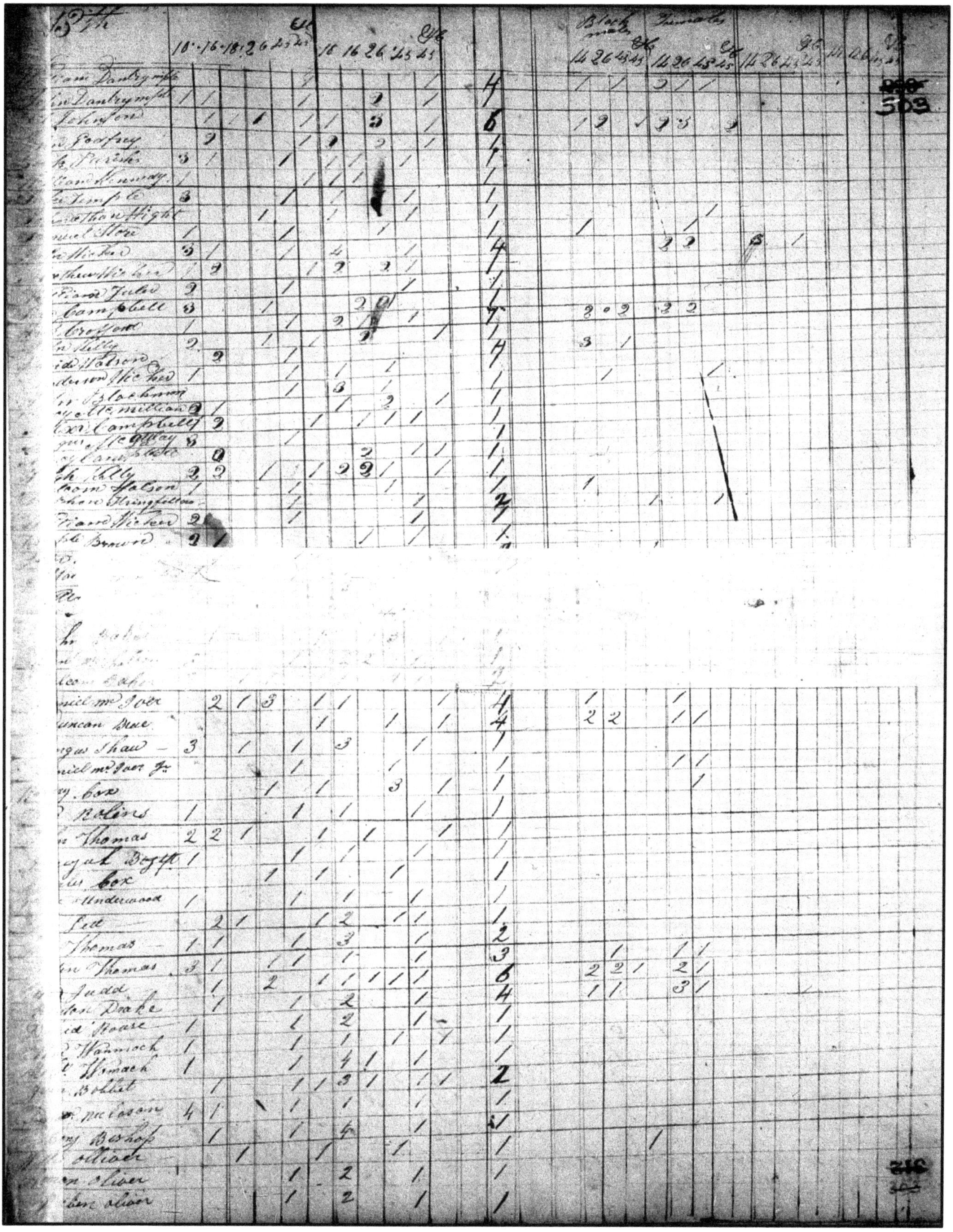

503
Dalrymple
Dalrymple
Johnson
Godfrey
Parish
Kennedy
Temple
Hight
Campbell
Kelly
Watson
Wicker
Blackmon
McMillan
Campbell
McGilvray
Campbell
Kelly
Watson
Stringfellow
Wicker
Brown
Baker
McIver
Duncan
Shaw
McIver Jr
Cox
Bolin
Thomas
Cox
Underwood
Thomas
Thomas
Judd
Drake
Womack
Bishop
Oliver
Oliver

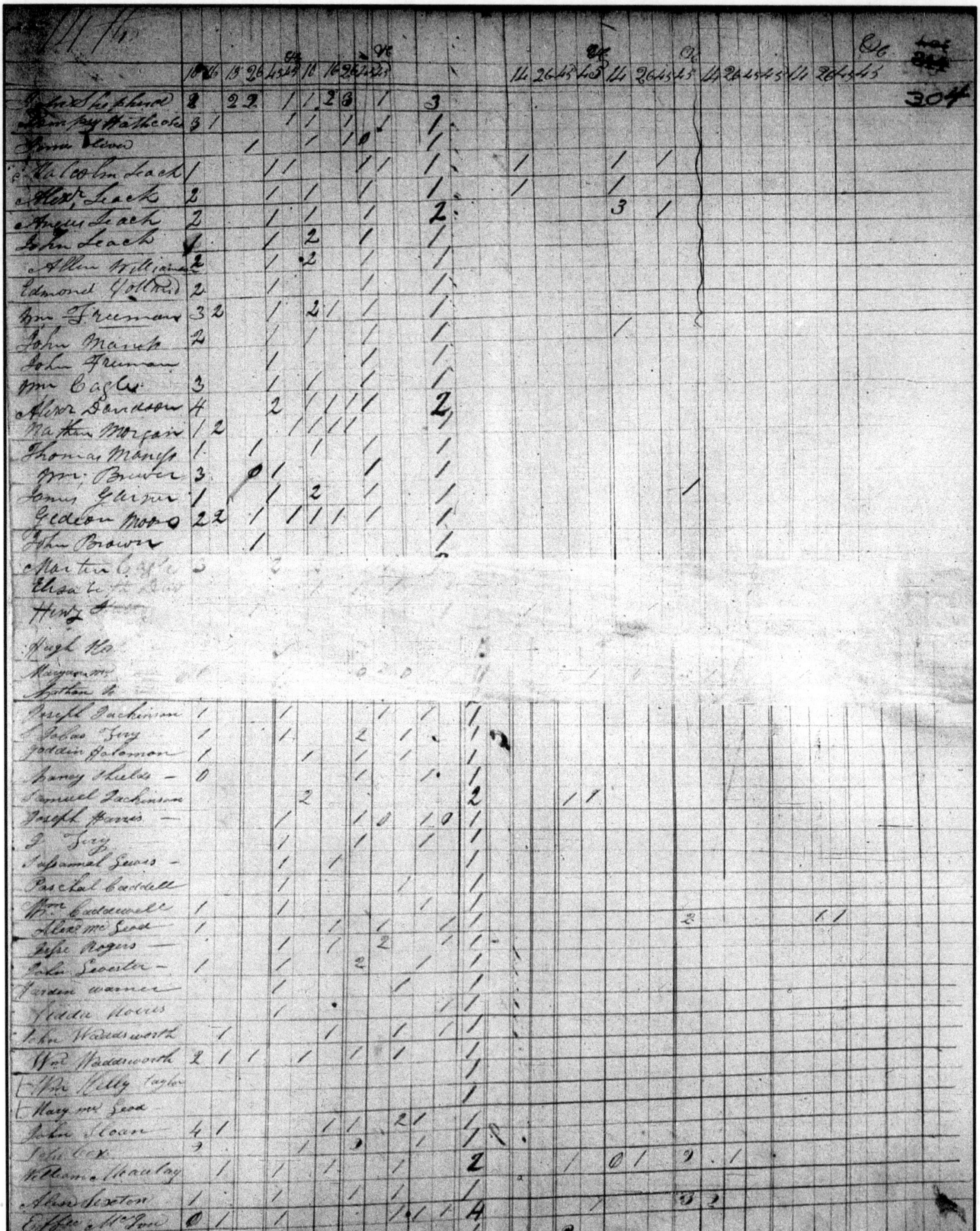
John Shepherd
Pompey Hathcock
Wm. Oliver
Malcolm Leach
Alexr. Leach
Angus Leach
John Leach
Allen Williams
Edmond Yolland
Wm. Freeman
John March
John Freeman
Wm. Cagle
Alexr. Davidson
Nathan Morgan
Thomas Maness
Wm. Brewer
James Garner
Gedeon Moore
John Brown
Martin Cagle
Elsa [illegible]
Henry [illegible]
Hugh Mc[illegible]
Margaret Mc[illegible]
Nathan [illegible]
Joseph Jackinson
Tobias Fry
Jaddin Holoman
Nancy Shields
Samuel Jackinson
Joseph Harris
J. Fry
Jesamnel Lewis
Paschal Caddell
Wm. Caddewell
Alexr. Mc Leod
Jesse Rogers
John Leorter
Harden warner
Jedda Norris
John Wadsworth
Wm. Wadsworth
Wm. Kelly taylor
Mary Mc Leod
John Sloan
John Cox
William Maulay
Alsa Sexton
Effee Mc Iver
Thomas Bobbitt

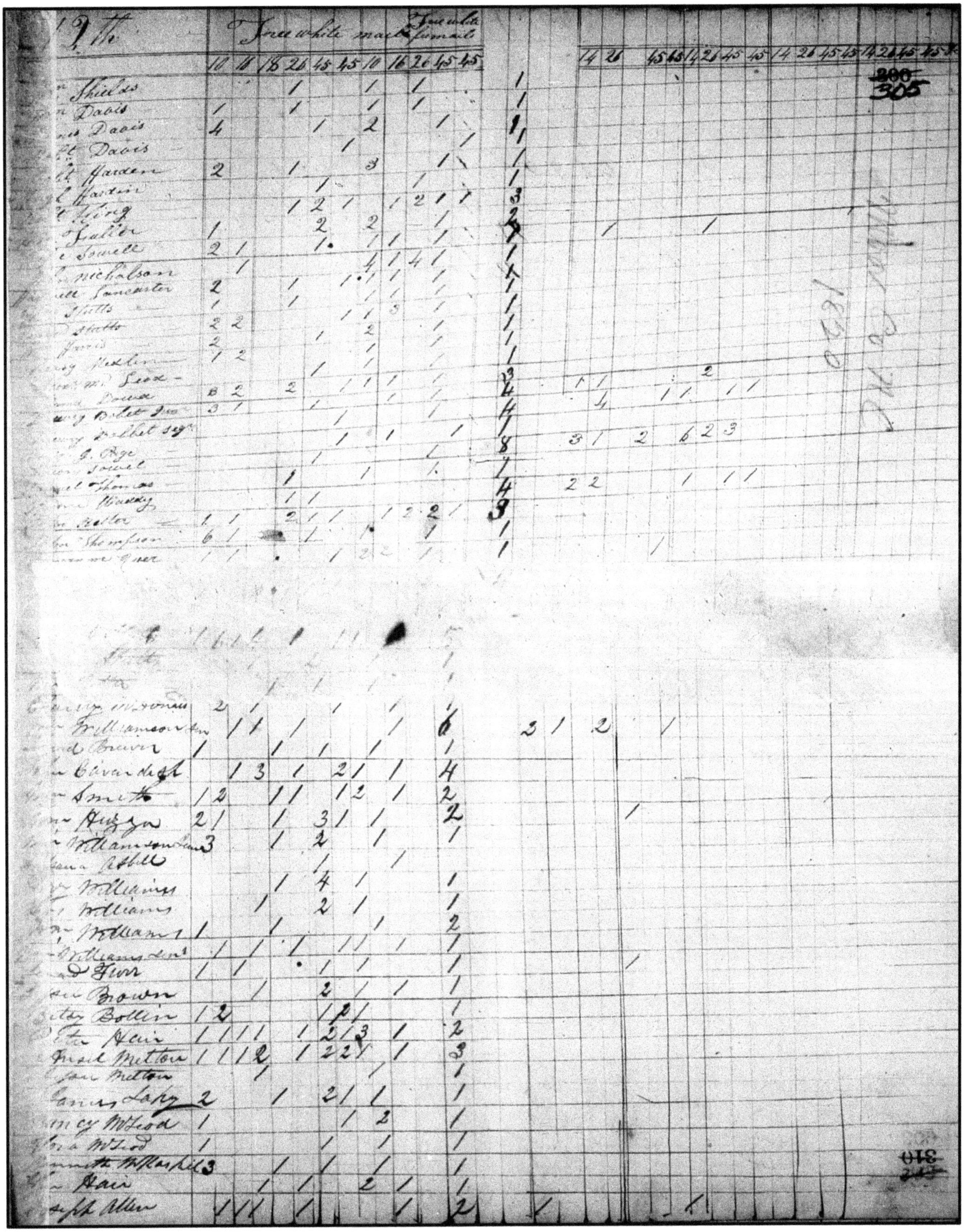
Shields
Davis
Davis
Davis
Harden
Harden
King
Saliker
Sowell
Nicholson
Lancaster
Stutts
Stutts
Harris
Hedlen
Wm. Seox
Dowse
Bulet Jnr
Balbet Snr
G. Rye
Sowel
Thomas
Weddy
Betlor
Thompson
Moore
Maronan
Williamson
Brewer
Cavandesh
Smith
Huggon
Williamson Snr
Cobble
Williams
Williams
Williams
Williams Snr
Fuor
Brown
Bollin
Hair
Mellton
Mellton
Laky
McLeod
McLeod
McKaskel
Hair
Allen

309

[illegible]	10	16	18	26	45	45+	10	16	26	45	45+					14	26	45	45+	14	26	45	45+	14	26	45	45+	14	26	45	45+
[illegible] L. Allen	1				1		1			1			1																		
[illegible] Runnals	1				1		1			1			1																		
Richard Holland						1					1		1																		
Wm Smith, Ch.	1					1	3	1		1			1																		
Oliva Britt	2	1		2	1				2		1		3																		
Bullain Britt					1					1			1																		
Merryman Britt	2				1				1				1																		
Wm Smith Sen	2			1		1					1		1																		
John Smith son of Wm		1			1	1		1					2																		
Everitt Smith	1	1	1	1		1	2	2	1		1		2																		
John Spivey				1		1	1		1		1		2				1					1									
Isaac Spivey	1		1	1	1		2			1			2																		
John McKashell	1	2		1		1	1		1		1		2																		
Susan Bidder	1				1		1		1				1																		
Thomas Williams [illegible]					1		3		1				1																		
Emanuel Yow					1		2		1				1				1			1		1									
Andrew Yow	2				1		4	1		1			1																		
Henry Yow	3	1			1		1			1			1																		
Thomas Ritter	1				1		3			1			1							1		1									
Daniel Manuss	3	1			1			1		1			1																		
Lewis Garner				1			1	1					1			1															
Wm N. Manuss	4	2		1			1	1		1			7																		
Wm Manus Sen						1					1		1																		
James Donald	2	2		2		1		2	1		1		1																		
John Sanborn	3	2			1		1	1		1			1																		
Benj. Phillips	3				1		3			1			1																		
Eli Phillips	3				1		1	2		1			1							1											
John Phillips Sr.	1				1		2		1				1							1											
Sampson D. Smith	1	1			1		4			1			1							1											
Enoch Richardson				1			1		1				1																		
Isaac Sowel					1		1		1				1																		
John Sowel Junior	1			1			1		1				1																		
John Sowel Sen						1			1		1		1																		
John Sowel	2				1		1			1			1																		
Jesse Sowel Junior					1								1																		
Joseph Rouse						1				1	1		1																		
Albert Caddell					1								1																		
Jesse Sanborn				2		1	2			1	2		2																		
Calvin Cox	2			1					1				1																		
Flora Martin	1				1		2	3		1			11			5	4	2		7	1	3									
Daniel McKay	1				1		1		1				1																		
Col. Richd. Street	2	1			1	1	1			1			16			6	3	4		5	3	3									
Charles Haire	1			1		1	2	1	1		1		1																		
Jacob Stutts +																															
Robt. J. Daniel	3	2		4	1	2	1			1			1	e	6	1	2			1	1										
Wm Griffith	1	1			1		1				1					1		1													
Angus McQueen	1				1		1			1			1																		
Kenneth Black					1				1				1																		
Thomas Harmon		1		1		1		1	1		1		1																		
Harden Warner	4	1		3		1			2		3		4																		
George Kennedy x					1				1	1			1																		
Wm Hancock				1					1				1																		

11th	Free white Males 10	16	18	26	45	over 45	Free white females 10	16	26	45	45		14	26	45	45	14	26	45	45	14	26	45	45	14	26	45	45
...ney Buie				2		1						2																
... Silers			1	1					2	2	1	4																
...d Gilbery	2					1	1	1			1	1																
...uel Nicholson	2	1			1	0	4			1		1																
...ert McGoen	1					1	2			1		1																
...llen Saxton	1				1		1		1			1																
...sy Saxton			1	1		0			1		1	1																
...ules Crofford					1		3			1		1																
...m McAuly					1	0						1																
... Oliver				1		1					1	1			2													
...i Gunter				1					1			1																
...niel Campbell	2	1			1		1	1		1		1																
...al Holomon				2		1			3		1	3																
...thaniel Holomon					1						1	1			1													
...Daniel Jackson	2			2		1	2		1	1		3																
...se Goins												4									1	2			1	3	2	1
...n Riddle	3				1		3	1		1		1																
...m Riddle	2				1		2	2		1		1																
...rs G. Riddle	1	1							1		1	1				1												
...n Worthy					1	1	3				1	4			1	1			3	1								
...lis Dickinson	2					1		1	1		1	1																
...ncan McLeod		1				1			1		1	1																
...mon Ferguson					2			1				2																
...n Sinklair	2					1	4			1	0	1	1	1					1									
James Jackson	1	1			1		1		1		1	1																
...n Allen	1	1					1		1	3	1	1																
Daniel ...						1						1																
Solomon Bernot	4					1	1	1		1		1																
James Melton		3	1	2		1	1		1		1	2																
...m Melton	1			1			1		1			1																
...sey Wood		1						2			1																	
Solomon Brewer	1	1			1		2			1		1																
Martin Rouse	2				1					1		1																
...ham Richardson	2				1		1			1		1																
...ham Richardson						1			1		1	1																
...m Lakey					1		1		1			1																
...h Smith	3	1	1	1		1	2			1		2																
...is Williamson		1			1		3			1		1																
James Owens	1				1		3			1		1																
...m Smith R.	1			1			1			1		1																
James Williamson	3	1			1	1			1		1	2																
...y McDonald				1					1			1																
Solomon Dunn	2			1			2			1		1																
...eazy Dunn				1			12	1	2		1	1																
...mon Wilkinson					1	1					1	6			2				3		1							
...mon Wilkinson Sen		1		2		1	1		1		1	3																
...l Wilkinson	1				1		1		1			1			1													
David Jones	1				1		3	1	1			1																
...zekiel Autry	2				1		2		1			1																
Morgan McLean	4				1					1		1																

~~301~~ 307

~~303~~ 307

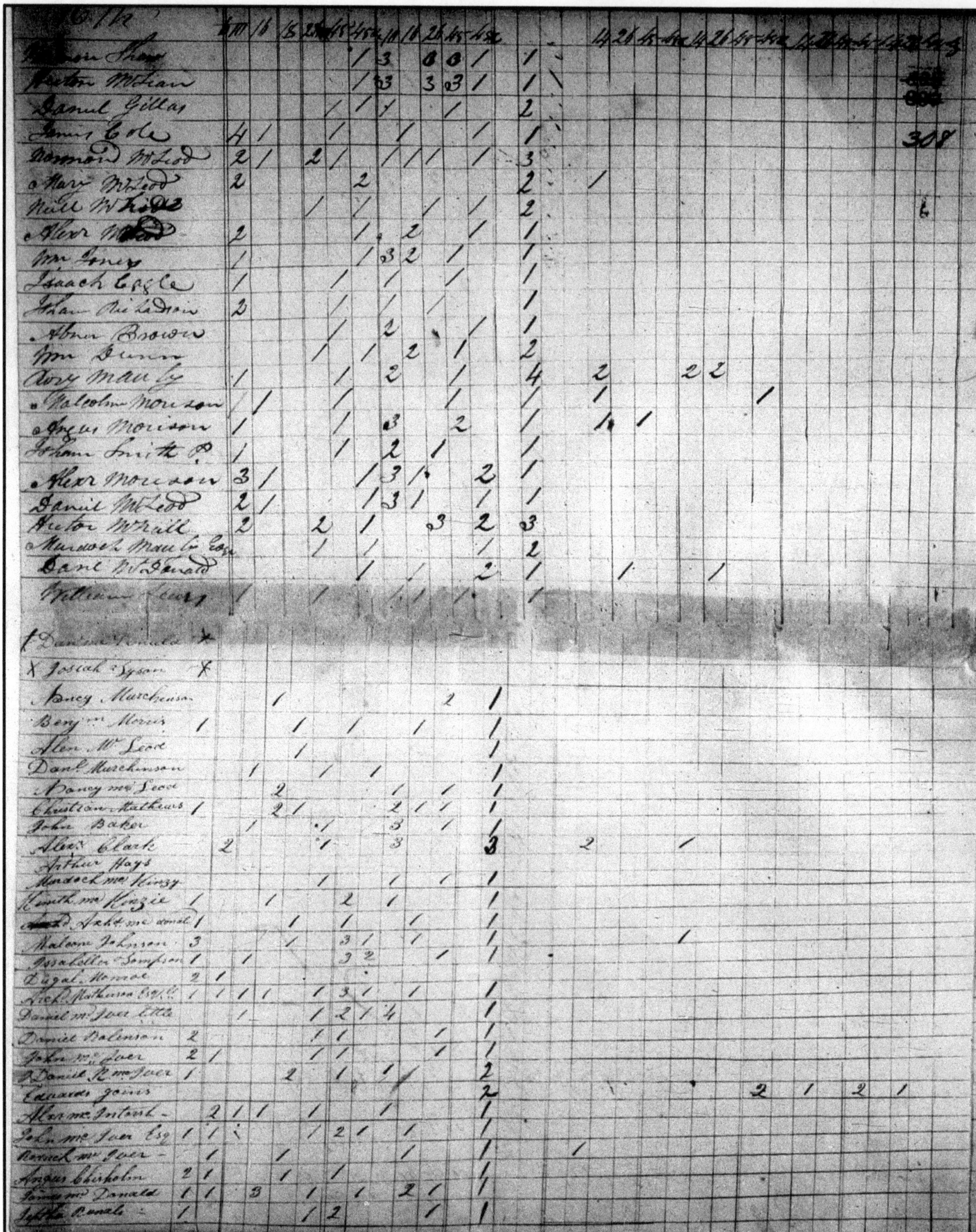

Name	Entries (left to right, as written)
?non Shaw	1, 3, 3, 3, 1, 1
Hector McLean	1, 3, 3, 3, 1, 1
Daniel Gillas	1, 1, 1, 1, 2
James Cole	4, 1, 1, 1, 1, 1
Normond McLeod	2, 1, 2, 1, 1, 1, 1, 1, 3
Mary McLeod	2, 2, 2, 1
Neill McLeod	1, 1, 1, 1, 2
Alexr McLeod	2, 1, 2, 1, 1
Wm Jones	1, 1, 3, 2, 1, 1
Isaach Eagle	1, 1, 1, 1, 1
John Richardson	2, 1, 1, 1
Abner Brown	1, 2, 1, 1
Wm Dunn	1, 1, 2, 1, 2
Rory Manly	1, 1, 2, 1, 4, 2, 2, 2
Malcolm Morrison	1, 1, 1, 1, 1, 1, 1
Angus Morrison	1, 1, 3, 2, 1, 1, 1
John Smith P.	1, 1, 2, 1, 1
Alexr Morrison	3, 1, 1, 3, 1, 2, 1
Daniel McLeod	2, 1, 1, 3, 1, 1, 1
Hector McNeill	2, 2, 1, 3, 2, 3
Murdoch Manly Esqr	1, 1, 1, 2
Danl McDonald	1, 1, 2, 1, 1, 1
William Leary	1, 1, 1, 1, 1, 1
Daniel McDonald X	
X Josiah Tyson X	
Nancy Murchinson	1, 2, 1
Benjm Morris	1, 1, 1, 1, 1
Alen McLeod	1, 1
Danl Murchinson	1, 1, 1, 1
Nancy McLeod	2, 1, 1, 1
Christian Mathews	1, 2, 1, 2, 1, 1, 1
John Baker	1, 1, 3, 1, 1
Alexr Clark	2, 1, 3, 3, 2, 1
Arthur Hays	
Murdoch McKinzy	1, 1, 1, 1
Kenith McKinzie	1, 1, 2, 1, 1
Archd McDonald	1, 1, 1, 1, 1
Malcom Johnson	3, 1, 3, 1, 1, 1, 1
Issabella Simpson	1, 1, 3, 2, 1, 1
Dugal Monroe	2, 1
Archd Matheson Esqr	1, 1, 1, 1, 1, 3, 1, 1, 1
Daniel McIver little	1, 1, 2, 1, 4, 1
Daniel Balenson	2, 1, 1, 1, 1
John McIver	2, 1, 1, 1, 1, 1
Daniel R McIver	1, 2, 1, 1, 2
Edward Goins	2, 2, 1, 2, 1
Alexr McIntosh	2, 1, 1, 1, 1, 1
John McIver Esq	1, 1, 1, 2, 1, 1, 1
Kenneth McIver	1, 1, 1, 1, 1
Angus Chisholm	2, 1, 1, 1, 1
James McDonald	1, 1, 3, 1, 1, 2, 1, 1
Jeptha Ronalds	1, 1, 2, 1, 1

10 the — 10 16 18 26 45 45 10 16 26 45 45 — 14 26 45 45 14 26 45 45 14 26 45 45 14 26 45 45

~~308~~ 309

Name	Entries (left to right)
...n Richardson	3, 1, 1, 1, 1, 1, 1, 2
...ijah Dowd	1, 1, 1
...edunga Morris	1, 2, 1, 1, 3, 3, 1, 3
...ary Spring	1, 1, 1, 1
...nnifer Manes	3, 2, 1, 2, 1, 1, 1, 1, 3
...cholas Nall	1, 1, 1, 1, 1, 1, 11, 1, 5, 2, 6, 1, 5, 2, 3
...ert Tyson	2, 1, 2, 1, 1, 1, 2, 1
...niel McIntosh	1, 1, 1, 1, 2, 1
...rush McCall	1, 1, 1, 1, 1
... Sinkler	1, 1, 1, 1, 1, 1, 2
...me McIver Esq	1, 2, 1, 2, 1, 1, 1, 2, 1, 2, 1, 1, 2, 1, 1
...n Duglas	2, 2, 1, 2, 1, 2, 2, 1, 2
...n Fletcher	1, 2, 2, 1, 1
...n Nicholson	2, 1, 1, 2
...n Sinkler	2, 2, 1, 2, 1, 1, 1, 1, 2
Malcom McGilbera	3, 1, 1, 1
...gus McGilbray	1, 1, 1, 1
...e McInnon	2, 1, 2, 1, 1
...gus McIver x	
...niel Campbell	2, 1, 1, 2, 1, 1, 1
...ncan Campbell	1, 1, 1
...at McKinzie	1, 1, 2, 1, 1
...e McNeill	1, 1, 1, 1, 1, 1
...x McLain	1, 1, 1, 1
...l. Hinchinson	3, 1, 1, 2, 2, 1, 1, 1
...niel Lemons	1, 1, 1, 1, 1
... Lemm...	1, 2, 1
William [illegible]	4, 1, 2, 1, 5
Allen McLean	1, 1, 1, 2, 2, 3
John Kee	1, 1, 1, 1, 1, 2, 1, 1, 2
Vincent Kee	2, 1, 3, 1, 1
James Kee	1, 1, 1, 1
Thomas Kee	1, 2, 1, 1, 1
Neill Morison	1, 1, 2
...neth M[illegible]ill	1, 1, 1, 1, 1, 1
...d Clark	1, 1, 1, 1, 1, 2, 3, 1, 2, 1
John McDuffie	1, 1, 2
Saml McCrimmon	1, 1, 1, 1, 1, 1, 3, 1, 1, 2, 1, 1, 1
James Dunlap	2, 1, 1, 7, 1, 1
John Paterson	1, 1, 1, 1, 1, 1
John Cockman	4, 1, 1, 1, 1, 1, 1, 2
...n Copeland	1, 1, 1, 1, 1, 1, 4
James McKey	1, 1, 4, 1, 1, 1, 2
Fred Ray	1, 1, 1, 1, 1
Alex McKey	1, 1, 3, 2, 1, 1
James Keachy	1, 1, 2, 1, 1
Elizabeth McKey	1, 2, 1, 1
Samuel Barrington	3, 2, 1, 1, 2, 1
James C McGrath	1, 1, 1, 1, 1, 1
Alexander McInnon	3, 1, 1, 1, 1
Henry Hutts	3, 1, 1, 1, 1, 1, 1, 2

~~308~~ 309

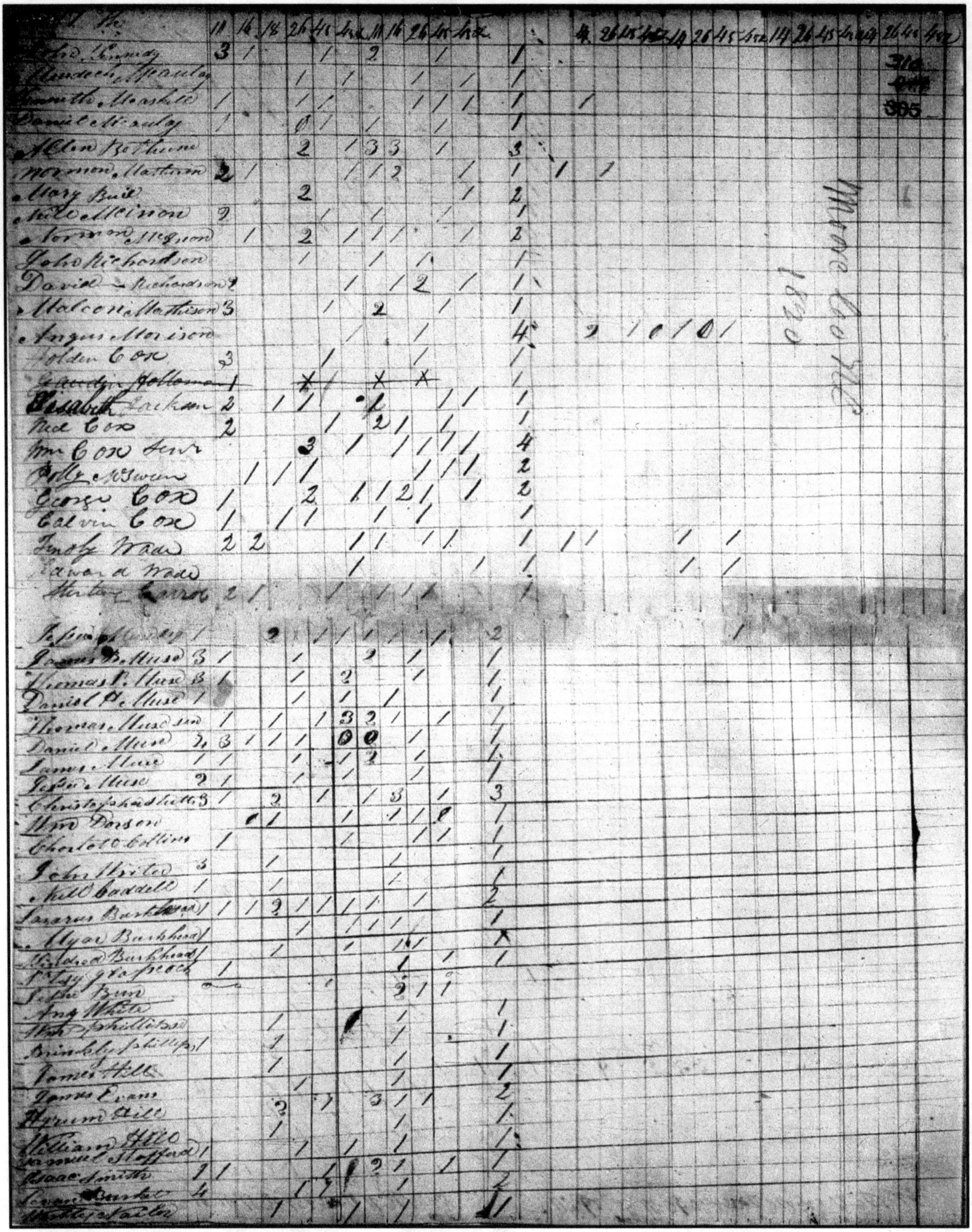
Moore Co NC
1820
John Kennedy
Murdoch McAulay
Kenneth McAskill
Daniel McAulay
Allen Bethune
Norman Mathison
Mary Buie
Neill McInnon
Norman McInnon
John Richardson
David Richardson
Malcolm Mathison
Angus Morison
Holden Cox
Elisabeth Jackson
Ned Cox
Wm Cox Senr
Polly McSwain
George Cox
Calvin Cox
Emily Wade
Edward Wade
James B. Muse
Thomas P. Muse
Daniel P. Muse
Thomas Muse Senr
Daniel Muse
James Muse
Christopher Chaddiell
Wm Dorson
Charlotte Collins
John White
Neill Caddell
Lazarus Burkhead
Alexander Burkhead
Mildred Burkhead
Ang White
Wm Phillips
Brinkley Phillips
James Hill
James Evans
Hyrum Hill
William Hill
Samuel Stafford
Isaac Smith

Name	10	16	18	26	45	45&	10	16	26	45	45&		Agr.	Com.	Man.	14	26	45	45&	14	26	45	45&	14	26	45	45&	14	26	45	45
...ncy Conner	2						1			1	2		1																		
Andrew B Smith	2				1		1		1				1																		
...mes Manes	3	1		1			1		1				1																		
...Kendal						1					1		1																		
...Cagle		2	1	2		1	4	2			1		2																		
...llen Cagle	3				1		2			1			1																		
...a Cagle	2				1		1			1			1																		
...i Cagle	2					1	3	1		1			1																		
...Davis	1				1		3		1				1																		
Nathaniel Tucker	4	1			1			1	4	1			1																		
...Jordan	1				1		2		1				1																		
...Jordan			1	1	1		2		2	1	1		2																		
...lly Leroy	1	1									1		1																		
...Davis	2	2	1	1		1	2		2	1			2								1										
...Culbreath	1	1	1	1	1		2	3		1			2																		
Sarah Culbreath										1			2																		
William Wright	2		0		1	1	3	2	2		1		2			2	1				1										
...Freeman				1						1			1			1															
Samuel Chisholm			1	2	1								3		1	1															
...		2		1		1	1		1	1			1			1				1		1									
...Wallace	3	1			1		1			1			1											1							
George Huntsucker	3		1	3	1	1	1			1			4																		
...Newton						1					1		1																		
...Huntsucker		2		1	1		4	1		1			2																		
John Carlton	1			1			3			1			1																		
...Comuse	2			1			1	1		1			1																		
...hn Carrol							1				1		4							1			1								
Alexr Carrol	2	1	1	1		1	1	1	1	1			2																		
Alexr McIver						1					1		1																		
James England				1			1		1	1	1		4				1		2	3		1									
Carrol Brady	2				1	1	2		1				2																		
...m Person	3			1					1				4			1					2	2									
Robt Wilson		1		2		1	1	2	1		1		4			1		1		1	1										
Wm Mathews	2	1			1		1			1			3																		
Wm Martindale	1	2			1		3			1			1																		
Saml Martindale	1	1				1				1	1		1																		
Josiah Culbreson	4	1		1	1		3		1	1			1																		
...Brown	2	1		1		1		1	3				2																		
Isaach Teague	3	2		1	1		2	1		1			2																		
Polly Smith	1			1			1	1	2				2																		
Wm & Smith	1			1			1			1	1		2				1				1	1		1							
Martha Persons										1			1			1		1			2										
Thomas Person	2					1				1																					
William Waddill	1					1	2	3	2	1½			11				6	2	1		3	5	3								
Polly Kiland	0						1	1	2	1			1																		
...						1		1		1	1		1																		
Lewis Johnstone				3		1			2	1	1		4																		
John Cavendish																															
Polly Kiland									2	1																					
Edith Man...								1	1																						
...rdson	1					1		1		1			1																		
...hn Dam...	2				1	1		1	1	1	1	1	1			1															

~~208~~ 311

~~108~~ 311

342 ~~341~~ ~~308~~

18 7/c	10	16	18	26	45	45+	10	16	26	45	45+					14	26	45	55	14	26	45	45+	14	26	45	45+	14	26	45	45+
Thos Dannelly					1		1		1				1																		
John Upton	1				1		2						1																		
Wm Reaves					1					1			1																		
John Upton						1		1			1		1																		
Drury Brewer						1					1		1																		
[illegible] Myrack				1		1					1		1																		
Nancy Colman											1		1																		
Jacob Stutts	1	1	1	4	2	1		1	1		1		4																		
Rachel Perry				1			4	2		2	2		1																		
Garison Travers											1													1		1	2	1			
James Brewer		2				1	3	2	1	1			1																		
George Moore	1			1					1				1																		
James Hardin		2				1	1		1	2			1																		
John Ritter		1		2		1	1				1		2							3											
Everett Wallace		1		1		1	3	2	1		1		2																		
Daniel McNeill				1		1					1		12			3	1	1	1	6	1	2	2								
John D. Freeman	2				1		1	1		1			1																		
Hardmon Brown	1					1	2	2					1																		
Roderick Bethune		1				1			1	2			1																		
Betsy Dew							1		1		1		1																		
Francis Myrack						1		2	3	1	1		4			3				2	2	1									
Hannah Duckworth											1		4			2	2				2		1								
James McNeill	1					1	4			1			6			5	2			3	2										
Wm. [illegible]	1				1		1		1				1																		
John [illegible]		1			1					1			1																		
William Campbell		1			1		2	1		1			1																		
John Sheffield Sr.	2					1	1	1			2		1																		
John Sheffield Jr.	3	1	1	1		1	2	2		1			2																		
Owen Hare	2				1		2			1			1																		
Cyrel Sheffield		1			1		2	1		1			1																		
Isam Sheffield	1		1	1	1			3		1			2																		
John Garner	3				1		2	1	1				1																		
Isaac Sintery	1	1			1		2			1			1																		
John Shamburger	3	1	1	3		1					1		3			1		1	1												
Silas Wilson	3	1			1		2			1			1																		
Daniel Mann						1							1																		
William Brewer	1				1					1			1																		
Dad Garner	1				1		1		1	1			1			1			1												
Robert Kennedy	2			1	1		3			1			1						1												
Lizzy Wilson						1	3	2			1		2			1	1		1		3	1									
John Dunlap	1				1		2			1			1																		
George Moore	1					1		2			1		1																		
Jacob Cagle	2	1			1		3	1		1			1																		
William Brewer	3				1				1		0		1																		
Alexr Plummer	3				1					1			1																		
James Morgan	2	1	1	1	1		2		1				2				1														
Edward Moore	2			1			1		1				1																		
John Garner Ward	1				1		1	1		1			1				1						1								
Alexr Kennedy	3	1	1	2		1	3	1	1				3			2	2		2		1	1	1								
Absalom Beal			1	2		1	1				1		3																		
John Brown Esq.	2					1	1		1	1			1																		
William Duffy	1				1		2			1			1																		
Peter Shamburger	2				1		3	2		1		1	4				1	1			2	1									

Malcom McDonald
John Blue
Smith Black
Hare
Nathan Maples
Fred. Medlin
William Medlin
Randel Martin
McBrattle
John Blue
McBride
Alex McBride
Daniel McDugald
Duncan Blue
Nancy McLeod
McGilbary
Sandy Walker
Emanuel Marquis
Daniel McLennon
Mary Bobbet
Arrington
Johnson
Daniel McNair
McGill
Malcom McFarland
Baker
McFarland
Saxton
Oliver Phillips
Malcom Phillips
John Phillips
Henry Phillips
Henry Phillips Senr
James Chick
Richard Chick
Sally Phillips
Shields
Shannon Moore
David Shields
Thomas Shields
Jesse Brewer
Bradly Brady
Charles Harden
313
304
302

19 No

314 / 301

Name	WM 10	WM 16	WM 18	WM 26	WM 45	WM 45+	WF 10	WF 16	WF 26	WF 45	WF 45+	Foreign	Agric.	Comm.	Manuf.	SM 14	SM 26	SM 45	SM 45+	SF 14	SF 26	SF 45	SF 45+	FM 14	FM 26	FM 45	FM 45+	FF 14	FF 26	FF 45	FF 45+
John Murchison			1	2	3						1		1		4	3	2		1	2	2		2								
Archd McBryde	3	1			1	1	2		2	2			16	2	2	2	6	3	2	8	1	1	1								
Sally Tyson	2		1	3			1		1	1			13	1	2	6	3	3		13	3	1	1								
Murdoch McMillan	1				1		3	2		1	1		8			5	2		1	3	2	1									
Margaret Tyson				1	1				2		1		1																		
Jam Gilbert							3	1	1		1																				
John Graham	1					1		1		1			1																		
Thomas Mashburn	2	1			1		2	1		1			1																		
William B. Williams				1		1			1		1		70		2	18	16	13	6	20	13	8	4				2				1
Athas Jones	1				1		1			1			11			4	3	1		3	3	1				1					
Joseph Gilbert	1			1					1				1																		
Joab Cheek		2	2	3		1	1		2		1		4			1	1	1		3											
John Cheek		1			1	1							12			4	2		1	3	1	3									
Josiah Cheek				1			2		2				2				1														
Willis Elkins	2	1			1		1	1		1			1																		
Wm Hancock					1			1	1				1																		
John Hancock	3				1				1				1				1														
James Gaines		1				1		2	1		2		16		1	6	3	5	1	7	3	5	1								
H. Bowers						1	1		2		1		2																		
Stephen Yarborough					1	1	1		2		1		4			3				3	1	1									
Thomas Fir[illegible]					1			1		1			1																		
Daniel McLin					1		1		1				1																		
James Kelly						1		1					1			1															
Irvin Cole		1				1							1																		
John Cole					1					1			1																		
[illegible]				1					1				1																		
John McKenzie	2	1				1	1			1			1																		
Archd Black		2		2		1		1	3		1		3								1										
Duncan McCollum	2				1	1	1		1	1	1		2			1					1										
Daniel McKenzie				1	1	1			3		1		3																		
John McLeish	3	2			1		2			2			1																		
Duncan McLeish	3	1			1		2	1		1			1																		
Effemia Black				3							1		3			1			1		2										
Effemia Blackburn		1		1				2	2		1		1							2											
Lauchlin Curry	2	1				1							[illegible]																		
Philip Cameron	1				1								1																		
Daniel McNeill	[illegible]	1	1	1	1		2	1		1			2																		
Helen McMillan			1	1		1		1	3		1		2																		
Daniel Curry				2					1		1		2																		
Hugh McDonald			2	3		1			2		1		4			1															
Sarah McMillan		2	1	1					1		1		1				1														
Daniel McMillan	3				1					1			1									1									
Archd Black	3				1		1			1	1		1																		
Archd Curry	1		1	3		1			1				4																		
Duncan Blue					1								4					1		2		2									
Patrick Blue					1		3			1			4			2				2											
John McPhee				1		1			1	2	1		2																		
John Campbell		2				1	3			1			1																		
Angus McDonald	2		1	3		1	1	1			1		4																		
Jane Black	1	2			1		1	2		1			1																		
Alex McDonald				2		1		2	1		1		3																		
Rachel Ray		1		3	1	1			1		1		1				1														
Archd Bell	2					1	3	2		1			1										1								

Name (as legible)	Tallies (in the order written across the row)
…lisha Bryant	3 1 1 1 1
…argaret Graham	1 1 1 1 1 1
…eorge Graham	1 2 1 1 1 1 1
…ormick Graham	1 1 1
…ert Graham	2 1 1 1
…iam Gilmore	1 1 1 1 1
…orge Fry	2 1 1 1 1 1
…n Spicer	1 1 3 1 1 1
…mas Fry	1 3 1 1
…iam Fry	2 1 1 1 1
…sey Fry	1 1
…den Warner	1 1 1
…es Smith	3 1 2 1 1 1 1
…y Medlin	3 1 1 1
… Patterson	3 2 2 2
…sey Ray	1 2 1
…k McCallum	1 1 2 1 1 1 3
…el Blue	1 1 1 1 1 1
…w Moore	2 1 1 1 1 2 1 1 1 2
…chlen Curry	3 1 2 1 1 1
…nan McLauchlen	1
… Blue	2 1 1 1 1 1
…el Patterson	1 1 3 1 1
… McFether	3 1 1 1 1
…tor Curray	1 1 1 1
…y Black	1
Martin McPherson	1 1 1 2 1 1 1
… Johnston	1 1 1 1
Joseph Johnston	2 1 1 1 1 1 1 6 1 1 2 2
… McMillen	1 1 1 1 1 1 1 1 3
Bryce Roberts	1 1 1 6 3 1 4 1
…bert McLauchlin	1 2 2 1 1
…gald McLauchlin	2 1 1 2 1 2
Angus Curry	2 1 2 1 3 2 * 1 3
…rius Monk	2 1 1 2 1 1 1
Joseph Seawell	1 4 1 2 1 3
Neill Tyson	2 1 1 1 1 1
Alexr McDonald	2 1 1 1 1 1
Thomas Reed	1 2 4 1 1 1
…n McPherson	1 1 1 1 2 2 1 1 2
Dugald McMillen	1 1 1 1
…m Dowdy	1 1 1 1
James Dowdy	1 1 1 2 3 1 2 3 4 1 1 5 2
…dw Gernigan	2 1 1 1 1 1 3 2 5 1 5 3 1
B. Burroughs	1 1 2 1 1 1 1 1 1
Charles Brady	2 1 1 1 1 1 1 1
…vil Cox	2 1 1 2 1 1 4 1 1 1
…m Barrowden	1 2 1 1 2 3 1 2 1 2 1
John McLeod	1 1 1 2 1 1 1 1
Malcolm Patten	1 1 1 1

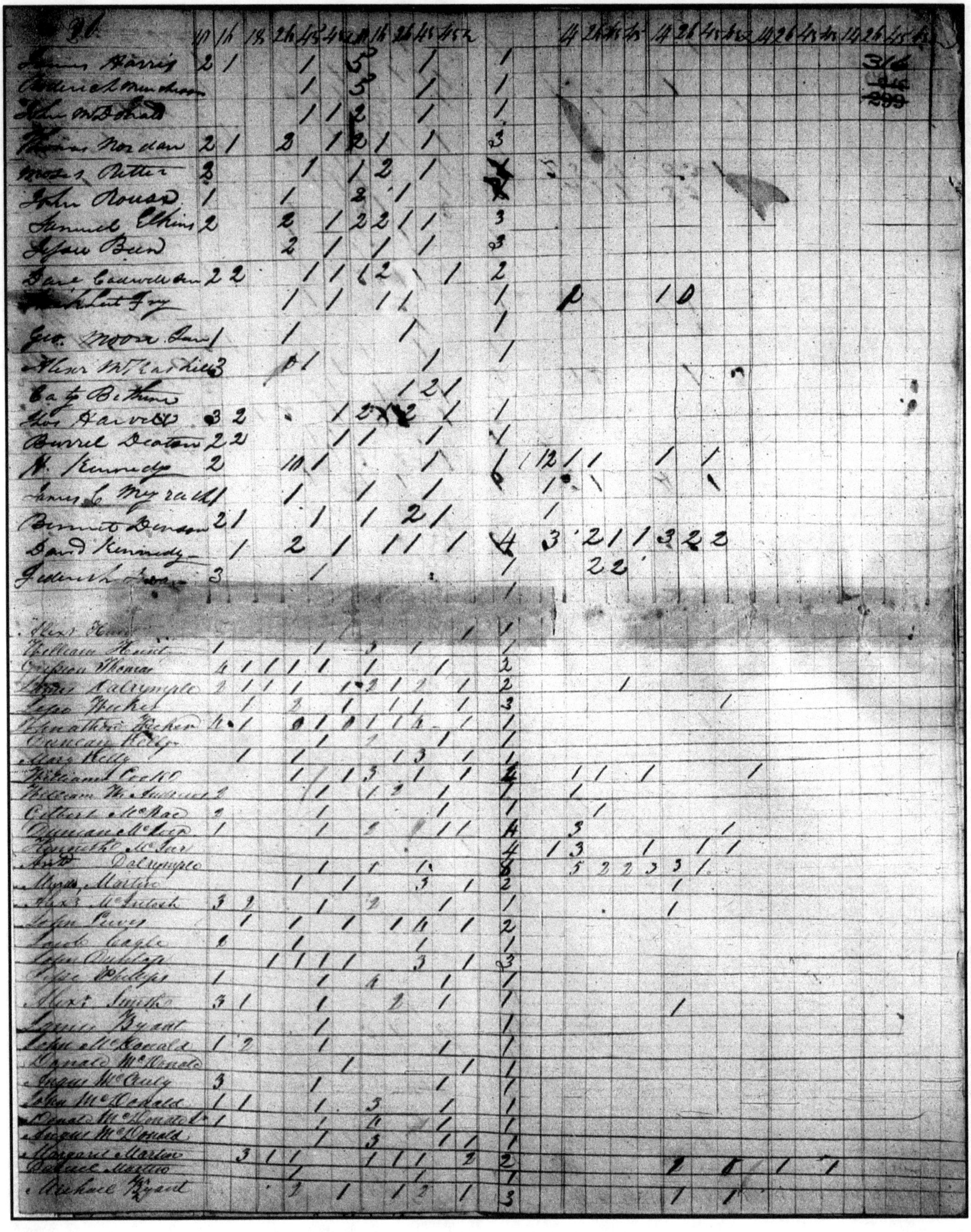

James Harris
Roderick Munderson
John McDonald
Thomas Nordan
Moses Potter
John Rouse
Samuel Elkins
Jesse Bean
Dave Caudwell
[illegible] Fry
Geo. Moore Senr
Alexr McCaskill
Caty Bethune
Thos Harvell
Burrel Deaton
H. Kennedy
James C. Mcgrath
Bennett Denson
David Kennedy
Frederick [illegible]
Alexr [illegible]
William Hewitt
Orpheus Thomas
[illegible] Dalrymple
Jesse Wicker
Jonathan Wicker
Duncan Kelly
[illegible] Kelly
William Cook
William McAuslan
Gilbert McRae
Duncan McLeod
Kenneth McIver
Archd Dalrymple
Moses Martin
Alexr McIntosh
John Pervis
Jacob Cagle
John Phillips
[illegible] Phillips
Alexr Smith
James Bryant
John McDonald
Donald McDonald
Angus McCaly
John McDonald
Donal McDonald
Angus McDonald
Margaret Martin
[illegible] Martin
Michael Bryant

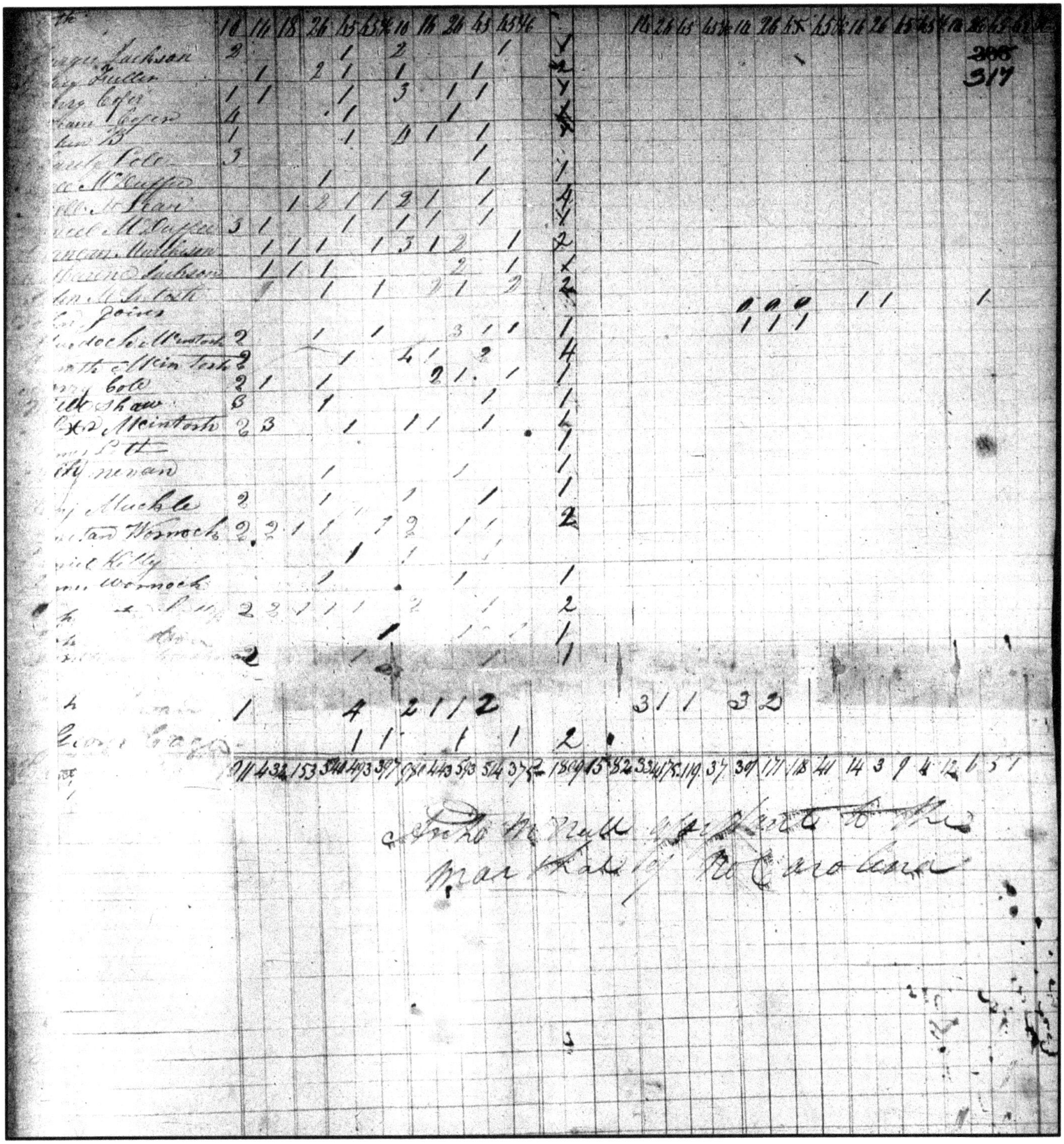

...rge Jackson
...y Fuller
...y Cofer
...am Cofer
...am B
...y Cole
... McDuffie
... McLean
...el McDuffie
...ncan Mathison
...ond Jackson
...n McIntosh
... Joines
...doch McIntosh
...th McIntosh
...y Cole
... Shaw
... McIntosh
... Pitt
... newan
... Muckle
...tan Wormock
...el Kelly
... Wormock
... Cagg...

Archd McNeill Asst to the
Marshal of No Carolina

318

Moore County [illegible] 1821

Col. Beverly Daniel

Sir

I have transmitted you the returns of [illegible]
[illegible]

ERTIFICATE, to be signed by two respectable Inhabitants of the Division, and returned, annexed to the Schedule (No. 1.) by the Assistant to the Marshal.

We hereby certify, that a correct copy of the above Schedule, signed by the said A B McNeill has been set up and remained at two of the most public places within the division, open to the inspection of all concerned.

Daniel McNeill [illegible]
Patrick Dowd Jr.

Name	WM 0-10	WM 10-16	WM 16-18	WM 16-26	WM 26-45	WM 45+	WF 0-10	WF 10-16	WF 16-26	WF 26-45	WF 45+	Foreign	Agric.	Comm.	Manuf.	SM 0-14	SM 14-26	SM 26-45	SM 45+	SF 0-14	SF 14-26	SF 26-45	SF 45+
Alex[illegible]																							
Dan[illegible]																							
Alex McFarlane	1			1			1		1														
Nancy Johnson		2	1	1				1	1		1						1	1					
John McBeath	1			1			1			1			1										
Elizabeth Savage	1			1			1		2		1		1										
Polly Cameron											1		2			3			1			1	
Polly Blue	2	1	1	2		1	2				1		3				1				*		
Moris Morison	1					1	1	1			1		4			2							
Allen Morison	1			1			1		1				1										
Daniel Campbell			1	1		1			1	1			3			1			1		1		
Daniel Shaw						1					1		4										
Peter Morrison		1	1	1		1					1		2										
Benjamin Moris	1				1		1			1			1										
Malcom Blue					1	1			2	2			2			1	1						
William Blue Esqr	2	2				1	3	1		1			1										
Neil McFadin	1	2		1			3	2		1			2						3		1	1	
Duncan McDugald						1			1		1		1				1						
Polly McDugald		2		2	1			2	1		1		3										
John Moris					1		1		1				1										
Stephen Moris	2				1		1	1		1			1										
John Moris Senr	1	1				2	1	1	4		1												
Gideon Edwards		2			1		3			1			1										
William Murchison					1					1			1										
John Dixon		2	1	1	1		1	1	1	1			4						1	1			
William Cole				1			1		1				1										
John Cole		1		1		1	2	2	1		1		2										
Mary Cole	1	1					4			1			1										
Margaret McNeal	3	3					1	1		1													

1830 Census

No. ... by the Marshal of the ... District (or Territory) of North Carolina 444

Slaves Males under 10	Slaves Males 10 to 24	Slaves Males 24 to 36	Slaves Males 36 to 55	Slaves Males 55 to 100	Slaves Males 100, &c.	Slaves Females under 10	Slaves Females 10 to 24	Slaves Females 24 to 36	Slaves Females 36 to 55	Slaves Females 55 to 100	Slaves Females 100, &c.	Free Colored Males under 10	Free Colored Males 10 to 24	Free Colored Males 24 to 36	Free Colored Males 36 to 55	Free Colored Males 55 to 100	Free Colored Males 100, &c.	Free Colored Females under 10	Free Colored Females 10 to 24	Free Colored Females 24 to 36	Free Colored Females 36 to 55	Free Colored Females 55 to 100	Free Colored Females 100, &c.	Total		
1	3	1	1			5	1	1																20		
																								7		
																								10		
1		1	1			4	1	1	1															18		
																								6		
1	2	1	2			3	2			1														20		
	1																							6		
5	8	2				4	2	2																23		
	1																							5		
																								7		
																								7		
																								10		
																								5		
																								5		
1	1					1	1	1																16	17	
1						1	1	1																13		
													1											6		
1	1					1	1																	11		
																								2		
1	1					4	1	1																18		
																								5		
																								8		
							1																	9		
1	1	1	1			1	2																	16	17	13
									1															13	12	12
							1																	7	9	9
1	7	1				3	2	2																24		
[illegible]	23	7	5			27	16	9	9	1			1											298		
																								300		

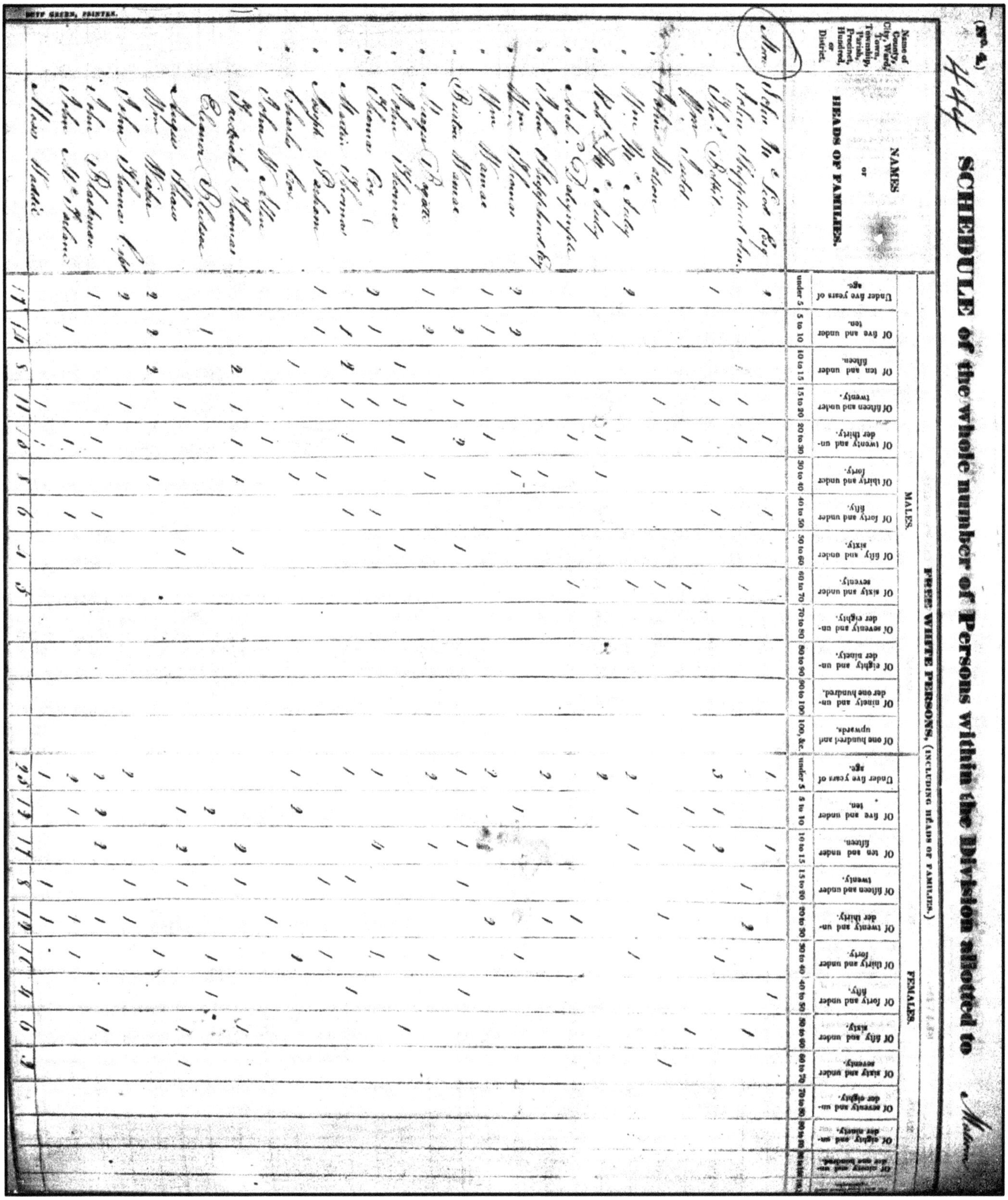

Slaves and Free Persons of Color are continued on the previous page

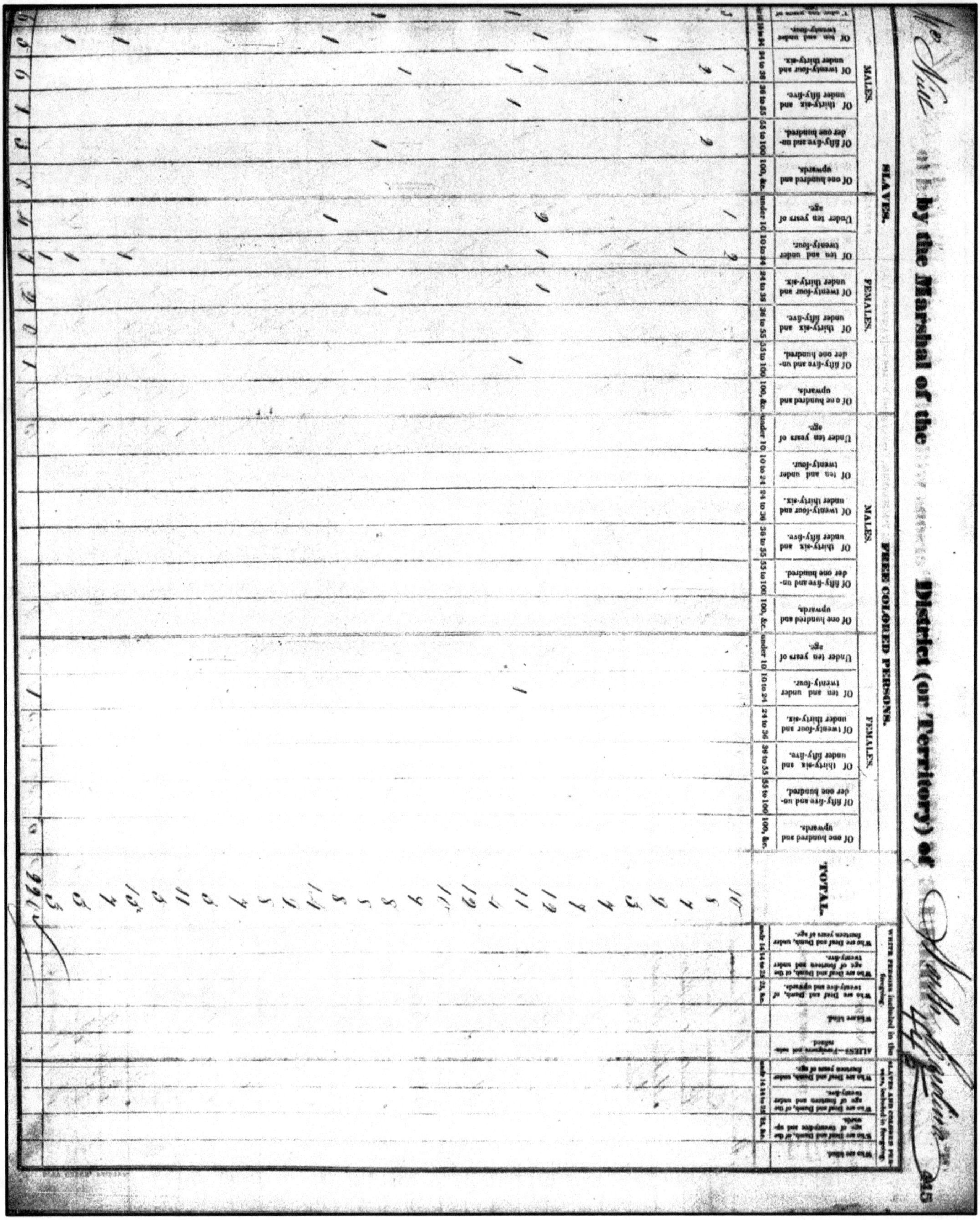
by the Marshal of the District (or Territory) of
SLAVES.
MALES.
FEMALES.
FREE COLORED PERSONS.
MALES.
FEMALES.
TOTAL.
345

(No. 4.) 445 **SCHEDULE of the whole number of Persons within the Division allotted to** [illegible]

FREE WHITE PERSONS, (INCLUDING HEADS OF FAMILIES.)

Name of County, City, Ward, Town, Township, Parish, Precinct, Hundred, or District.	NAMES OF HEADS OF FAMILIES.	MALES: Under five years of age. (under 5)	Of five and under ten. (5 to 10)	Of ten and under fifteen. (10 to 15)	Of fifteen and under twenty. (15 to 20)	Of twenty and under thirty. (20 to 30)	Of thirty and under forty. (30 to 40)	Of forty and under fifty. (40 to 50)	Of fifty and under sixty. (50 to 60)	Of sixty and under seventy. (60 to 70)	Of seventy and under eighty. (70 to 80)	Of eighty and under ninety. (80 to 90)	Of ninety and under one hundred. (90 to 100)	Of one hundred and upwards. (100, &c.)	FEMALES: Under five years of age. (under 5)	Of five and under ten. (5 to 10)	Of ten and under fifteen. (10 to 15)	Of fifteen and under twenty. (15 to 20)	Of twenty and under thirty. (20 to 30)	Of thirty and under forty. (30 to 40)	Of forty and under fifty. (40 to 50)	Of fifty and under sixty. (50 to 60)	Of sixty and under seventy. (60 to 70)	Of seventy and under eighty. (70 to 80)	Of eighty and under ninety. (80 to 90)	Of ninety and under one hundred. (90 to 100)
Moo	Sandy Walker				1					1												1				
〃	Wm Hagardy	1					1								1				1							
〃	John Dickson					3			1									1				1				
〃	Duncan Buie	1				1	1					1			2				2							
〃	Peter Monis					1				1													1			
〃	Malcom Baker			1		1				1								1	1	1		1				
〃	Benjn Marin	1	1	1		1		1										1		1						
〃	Daniel McIver							1							1	2		1			1					
〃	Stephen Davis	2					1								1				1				1			
〃	Wm Rowlands				1	1		1													1					
〃	Benjn Meaker	1	3				1				1				2		1	1		1		1				
〃	Graham Thomas			1	2	2				1					2			1				1				
〃	Saml H Stone		2	1				1							2		1		1							
〃	Jonathan Hight				1	1		1	1																	
〃	Moses Oliver			1	1				1								2	1	1		1					
〃	Daniel Welden		1				1								3			1								
〃	Wm Kelly		2	2					1						2	1		4	1		1					
〃	Wm Hunt	1	2	1			1								1	1		1	1							
〃	Denny Hunt	1	1	2			1									1		1		1						
〃	John Underwood			1		1		1									1	2			1					
〃	John Huckaby	1	1		1													1	1							
〃	Stephen Berryman	1			1				1						1	3	2		1		1					
〃	David Gaster	2					1											1	1							
〃	Wm Watson	1	2	2	2				1						1		3					1				
〃	John Stone			1	2		1										1		1	1						
〃	Jefferson Tuts				1																					
〃	John Welden Esq									1												1				
		13	13	14	18	12	9	6	6	3	1	1			19	8	11	18	13	5	6	7	2			

DUFF GREEN, PRINTER.

Slaves and Free Persons of Color are continued on the previous page

McNiel ... by the Marshal of the ... District (or Territory) of North Carolina 446

446

Slaves, Males: Under ten years of age (under 10)	Slaves, Males: Of ten and under twenty-four (10 to 24)	Slaves, Males: Of twenty-four and under thirty-six (24 to 36)	Slaves, Males: Of thirty-six and under fifty-five (36 to 55)	Slaves, Males: Of fifty-five and under one hundred (55 to 100)	Slaves, Males: Of one hundred and upwards (100, &c.)	Slaves, Females: Under ten years of age (under 10)	Slaves, Females: Of ten and under twenty-four (10 to 24)	Slaves, Females: Of twenty-four and under thirty-six (24 to 36)	Slaves, Females: Of thirty-six and under fifty-five (36 to 55)	Slaves, Females: Of fifty-five and under one hundred (55 to 100)	Slaves, Females: Of one hundred and upwards (100, &c.)	Free Colored Persons, Males: Under ten years of age (under 10)	Free Colored Persons, Males: Of ten and under twenty-four (10 to 24)	Free Colored Persons, Males: Of twenty-four and under thirty-six (24 to 36)	Free Colored Persons, Males: Of thirty-six and under fifty-five (36 to 55)	Free Colored Persons, Males: Of fifty-five and under one hundred (55 to 100)	Free Colored Persons, Males: Of one hundred and upwards (100, &c.)	Free Colored Persons, Females: Under ten years of age (under 10)	Free Colored Persons, Females: Of ten and under twenty-four (10 to 24)	Free Colored Persons, Females: Of twenty-four and under thirty-six (24 to 36)	Free Colored Persons, Females: Of thirty-six and under fifty-five (36 to 55)	Free Colored Persons, Females: Of fifty-five and under one hundred (55 to 100)	Free Colored Persons, Females: Of one hundred and upwards (100, &c.)	TOTAL	White persons included in the foregoing: Who are Deaf and Dumb, under fourteen years of age (under 14)	White persons included in the foregoing: Who are Deaf and Dumb, of the age of fourteen and under twenty-five (14 to 25)	White persons included in the foregoing: Who are Deaf and Dumb, of twenty-five and upwards (25, &c.)	White persons included in the foregoing: Who are blind	Aliens—Foreigners not naturalized	Slaves and colored persons, included in foregoing: Who are Deaf and Dumb, under fourteen years of age (under 14)	Slaves and colored persons, included in foregoing: Who are Deaf and Dumb, of the age of fourteen and under twenty-five (14 to 25)	Slaves and colored persons, included in foregoing: Who are Deaf and Dumb, of the age of twenty-five and upwards (25, &c.)	Slaves and colored persons, included in foregoing: Who are blind
																								5									
																								3									
																								7									
																								3									
																								8									
																								6									
																								10									
																								7									
																								4									
																								5									
1						1	1																	15									
1			1																					8									
																								5									
							2																	14									
																								6									
																								8									
																								8									
																								6									
																								5									
	1						2	1																7									
																								9									
																								10									
																								10									
																								4									
																								6									
1	1					2	2		1															10									
	1						1	1																5									
3	3	0	1			3	8	2	1															194									

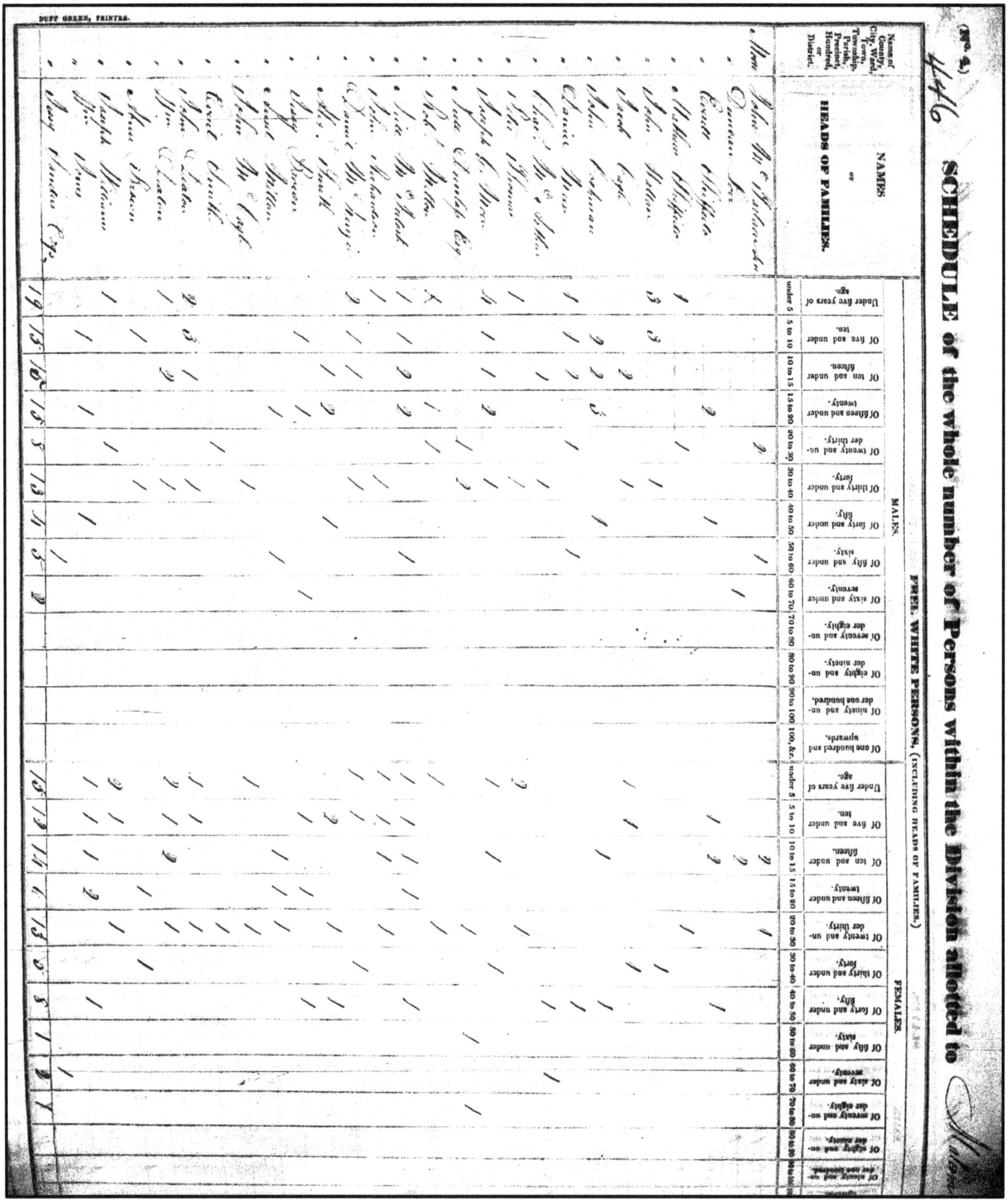

(No. 4.) 446

SCHEDULE of the whole number of Persons within the Division allotted to Malcom

FREE WHITE PERSONS, (INCLUDING HEADS OF FAMILIES.)

Name of County, City, Ward, Town, Township, Parish, Precinct, Hundred, or District.	NAMES OF HEADS OF FAMILIES.	MALES under 5	5 to 10	10 to 15	15 to 20	20 to 30	30 to 40	40 to 50	50 to 60	60 to 70	70 to 80	80 to 90	90 to 100	100, &c.	FEMALES under 5	5 to 10	10 to 15	15 to 20	20 to 30	30 to 40	40 to 50	50 to 60	60 to 70	70 to 80	80 to 90	90 to 100
Moore	John McFarland Sr.					2			1								2		1							
"	Duncan Fox									1							2									
"	Everett Shuffield				2			1								1	2				1					
"	Mathew Shuffield	1				1													1							
"	John Wallace	3	3				1													1						
"	Jacob Cagle			2			1								1	1				1						
"	John Cochman		2	2	3			1									1				1					
"	Daniel Moore	1	1	2		1			1												1					
"	Chas. McLeather			1			1														1		1			
"	Peter Thomas	1					1								2				1							
"	Joseph G. Moore	4	1	1	2		1								1		1			1						
"	Neill Dunlap Esq.					1	2												1			1		1		
"	Robt. Millen	1			1	1									1				1							
"	Neill McIntosh	1	1	2	2				1						1	1	1	1			1					
"	John Richardson	1					1								1	1	1		1							
"	Daniel McKenzie	2	1	1			1								1	1				1						
"	Alex. Smith			1	2			1								2			1		1					
"	Issy Brown		1		1					1						1		1			1					
"	Saml. Millen				1				1								1	1	1							
"	John McCagle						1								1				1							
"	Everit Smith					1													1							
"	John Seaton	2	3	1			1								1	1			1							
"	Wm. Seaton	1		2			1								2	1	2		1							
"	Abner Brown		1				1											1		1						
"	Joseph Williams	1				1									2	1			1							
"	Wm. Jones		1		1			1							1	1	1	2			1					
"	Issy Sanders Esqr.								1														1			
		19	15	15	15	5	13	4	5	2					15	19	14	6	13	5	8	1	2	1		

DUFF GREEN, PRINTER.

Slaves and Free Persons of Color are continued on the previous page

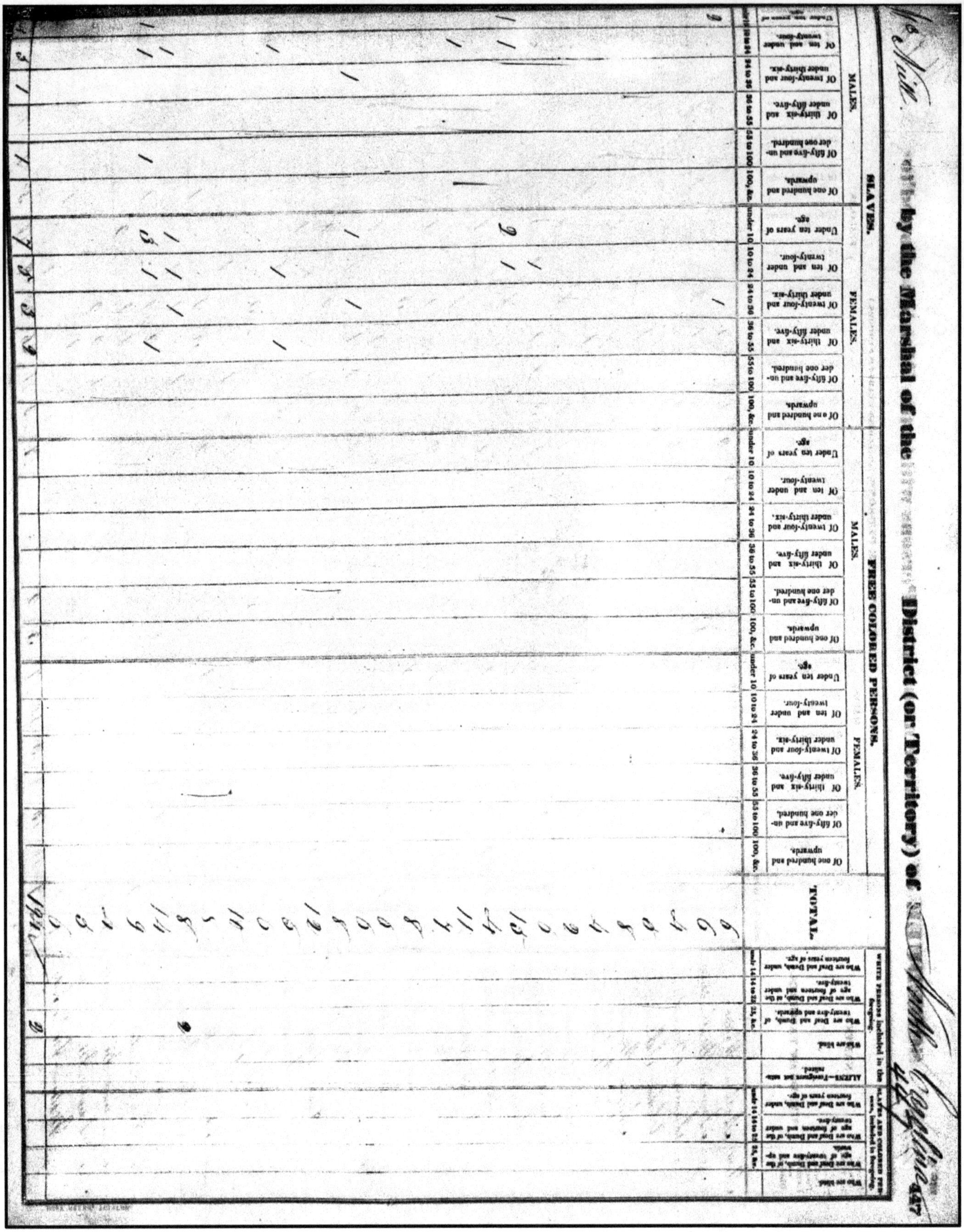
by the Marshal of the District (or Territory) of
447
SLAVES.
MALES.
FEMALES.
FREE COLORED PERSONS.
MALES.
FEMALES.
TOTAL.
WHITE PERSONS included in the foregoing.
Who are blind.
ALIENS—Foreigners not naturalized.
SLAVES AND COLORED PERSONS, included in foregoing.
Who are blind.

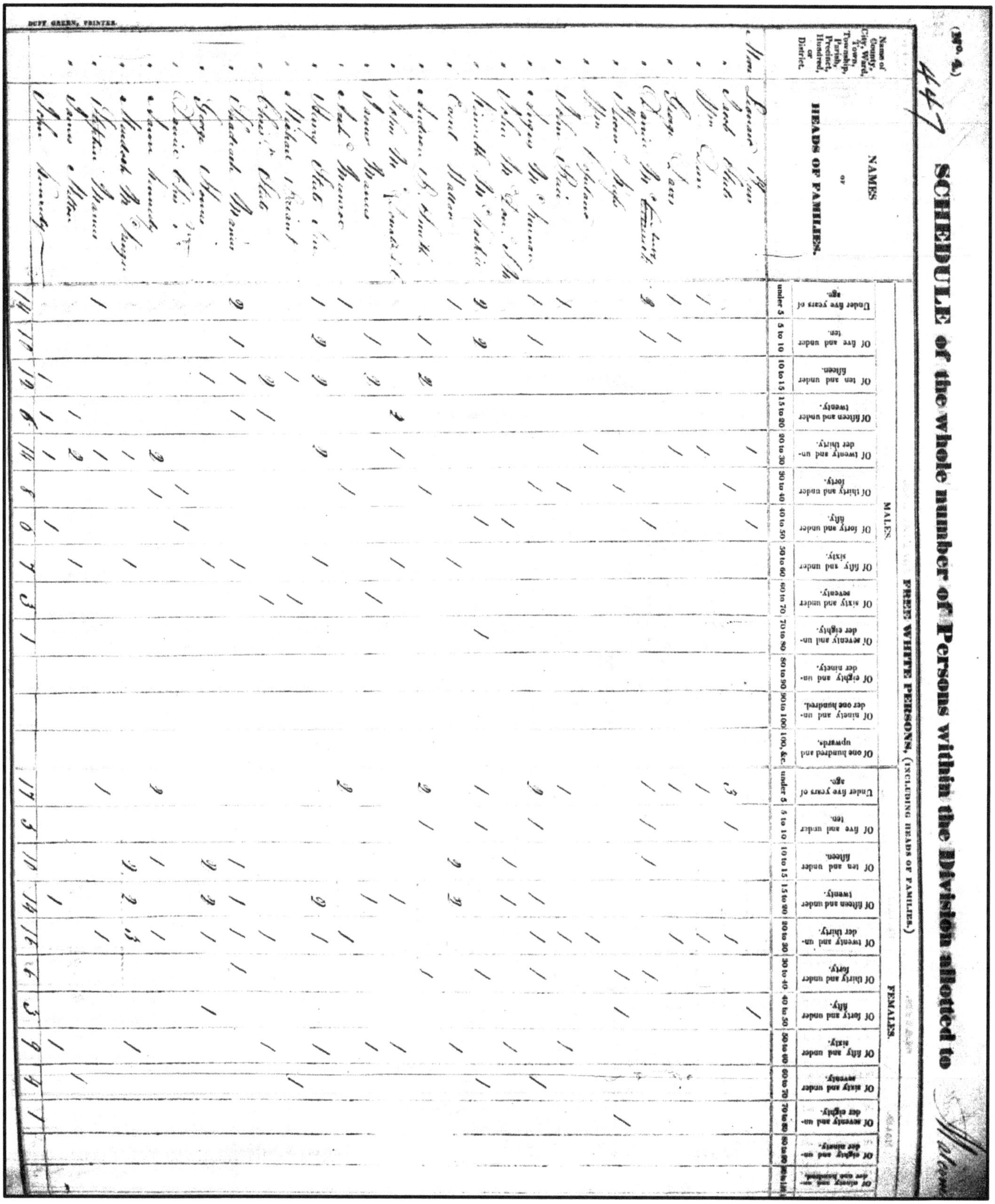

(No. 4.) 447 SCHEDULE of the whole number of Persons within the Division allotted to Malcolm [?]

FREE WHITE PERSONS, (INCLUDING HEADS OF FAMILIES.)

Name of County, City, Ward, Town, Township, Parish, Precinct, Hundred, or District	NAMES or HEADS OF FAMILIES	M under 5	M 5 to 10	M 10 to 15	M 15 to 20	M 20 to 30	M 30 to 40	M 40 to 50	M 50 to 60	M 60 to 70	M 70 to 80	M 80 to 90	M 90 to 100	M 100, &c.	F under 5	F 5 to 10	F 10 to 15	F 15 to 20	F 20 to 30	F 30 to 40	F 40 to 50	F 50 to 60	F 60 to 70	F 70 to 80	F 80 to 90	F 90 to 100
Moore	Leonard Dun [?]					1		1													1					
"	Jacob Stutts [?]						1								3	1			1							
"	Wm Dunn [?]	1				1									1				1							
"	George Davis [?]	1	1			1									1				1							
"	Daniel McIntosh [?]	2	1					1							1	1	1			1						
"	Thomas Wicks [?]						1													1	1			1		
"	Wm Copeland [?]					1													1							
"	John Rice [?]	1					1								1				1			1				
"	Angus McKinnon [?]	1	1				1								2	1		1	1	1			1			
"	John McDonald Sr [?]							1									1	1				1				
"	Kenneth McCaskill [?]	2	2					1			1				1	1				1			1			
"	Carrol Walker [?]	1							1								2	2				1				
"	Andrew B. Smith		1	2			1								2	1				1						
"	John McDonald [?]				2	1			1									1				1				
"	James Mann [?]		1	2						1								1				1				
"	Archd Monroe	1					1								2				1							
"	Henry Stutts Sen	1	2	2		2			1									2	1			1				
"	Michael Bryant [?]			1						1													1			
"	Christn Stutts			2	1					1									1			1				
"	Shadrach Mann [?]	2	1	1	1				1								1	1	1	1						
"	George Mann [?]			1					1								2	2	1		1					
"	Daniel Chisholm [?]						1	1																		
"	Aaron Kennedy [?]					2	1								2		1		1							
"	Murdoch McInnis [?]					1			1								2	2	3			1				
"	Stephen Mann [?]	1				1									1				1							
"	James Melton [?]				1	2			1														1			
	John Kennedy			1	1	1		1										1				1				
		14	10	12	6	14	8	6	7	3	1				17	5	10	14	16	6	3	9	4	1		

DUFF GREEN, PRINTER.

Slaves and Free Persons of Color are continued on the previous page

Slaves and Free Persons of Color are continued on the previous page

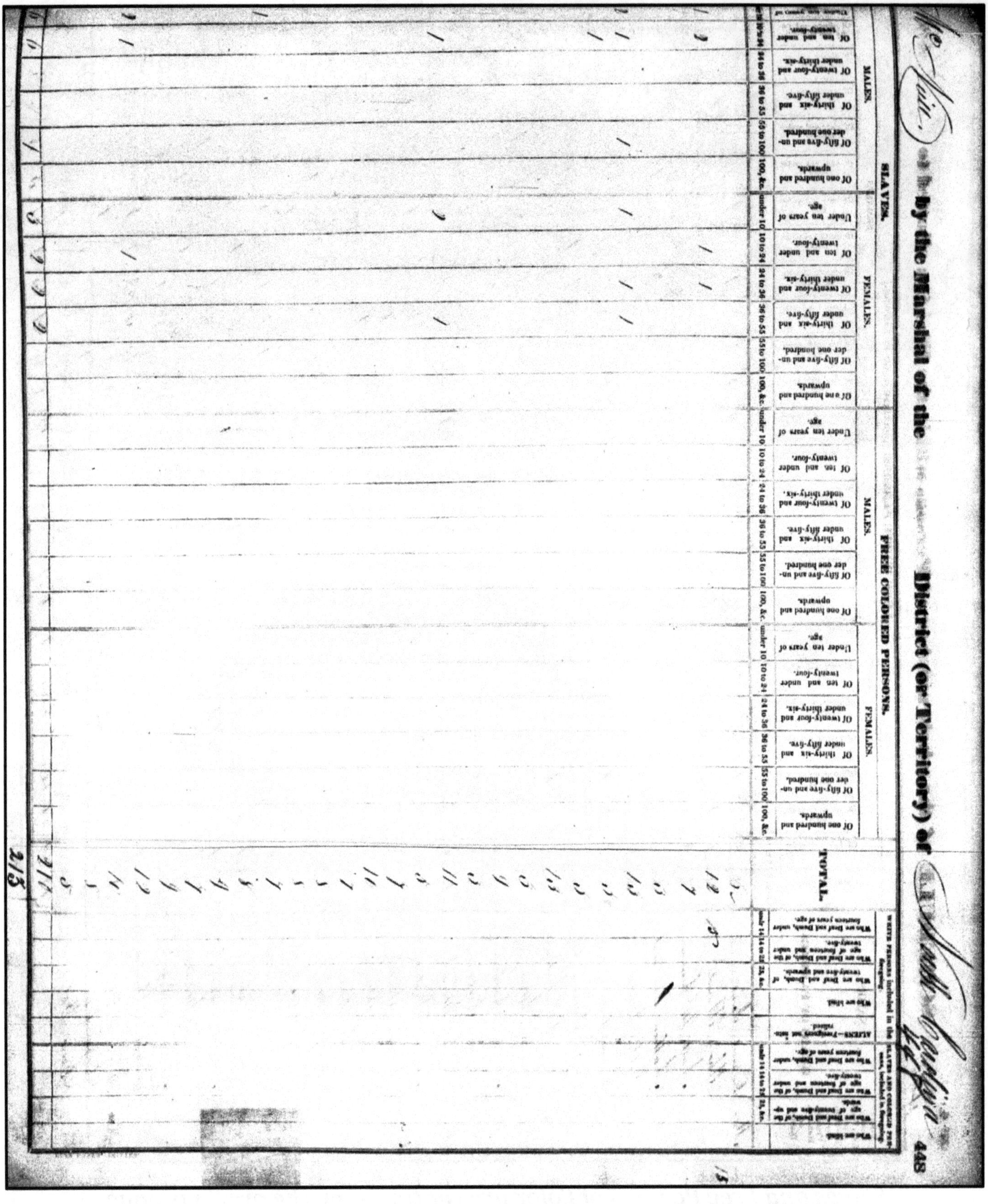
by the Marshal of the District (or Territory) of
448

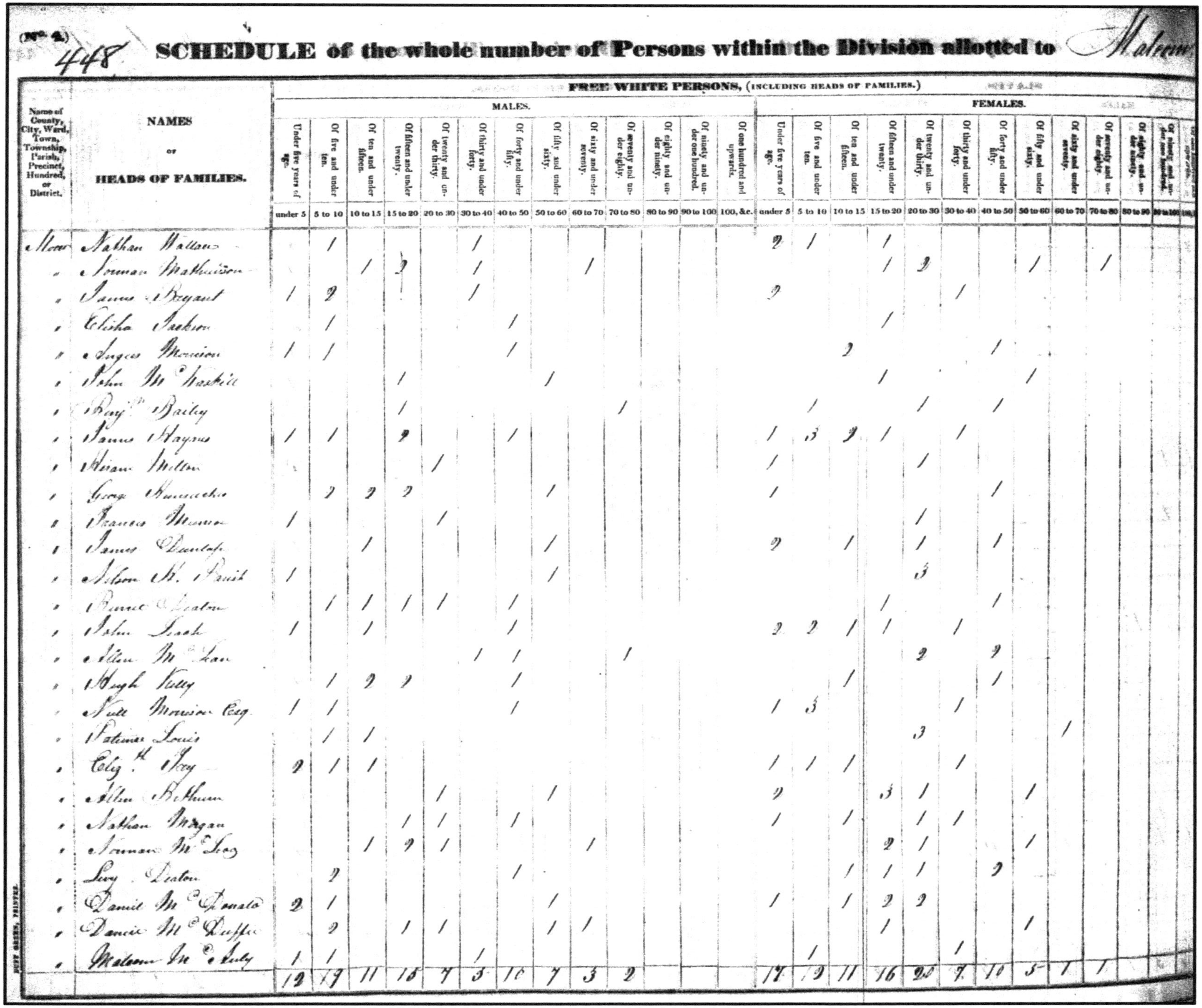

(No. 4) 448 **SCHEDULE of the whole number of Persons within the Division allotted to** Malcom

DUFF GREEN, PRINTER.

Name of County, City, Ward, Town, Township, Parish, Precinct, Hundred, or District.	NAMES OF HEADS OF FAMILIES.	M under 5	M 5 to 10	M 10 to 15	M 15 to 20	M 20 to 30	M 30 to 40	M 40 to 50	M 50 to 60	M 60 to 70	M 70 to 80	M 80 to 90	M 90 to 100	M 100, &c.	F under 5	F 5 to 10	F 10 to 15	F 15 to 20	F 20 to 30	F 30 to 40	F 40 to 50	F 50 to 60	F 60 to 70	F 70 to 80	F 80 to 90	F 90 to 100
Moor	Nathan Wallace		1				1								2	1		1								
"	Norman Mathison			1	2		1			1								1	2			1		1		
"	James Bryant	1	2				1								2					1						
"	Elisha Jackson		1					1										1								
"	Angus Morrison	1	1					1									2				1					
"	John McKaskill				1				1									1				1				
"	Benjn Bailey				1						1					1			1		1					
"	James Haynes	1	1		2			1							1	3	2	1		1						
"	Hiram Melton					1									1				1							
"	George Brunnecke		2	2	2				1						1						1					
"	Francis Munro	1				1													1							
"	James Dunlap			1					1						2		1		1		1					
"	Nelson K. Smith	1							1										3							
"	Bennet Deaton		1	1	1	1		1										1			1					
"	John Seale	1		1				1							2	2	1	1		1						
"	Allen McLean						1	1			1								2		2					
"	Hugh Kelly		1	2	2			1									1				1					
"	Neill Morrison Esq.	1	1					1							1	3				1						
"	Palmer Louis		1	1															3				1			
"	Elizth Kay	2	1	1											1	1	1			1						
"	Allen Bethune					1			1						2			3	1			1				
"	Nathan Morgan				1	1		1							1		1		1	1						
"	Norman McLeod			1	2	1				1								2	1			1				
"	Lucy Deaton		2					1									1	1	1		2					
"	Daniel McDonald	2	1						1						1		1	2	2							
"	Daniel McDuffie		2		1	1			1	1								1				1				
"	Malcom McNeily	1	1				1									1				1						
		12	19	11	15	7	3	10	7	3	2				17	9	11	16	20	7	10	5	1	1		

Slaves and Free Persons of Color are continued on the previous page

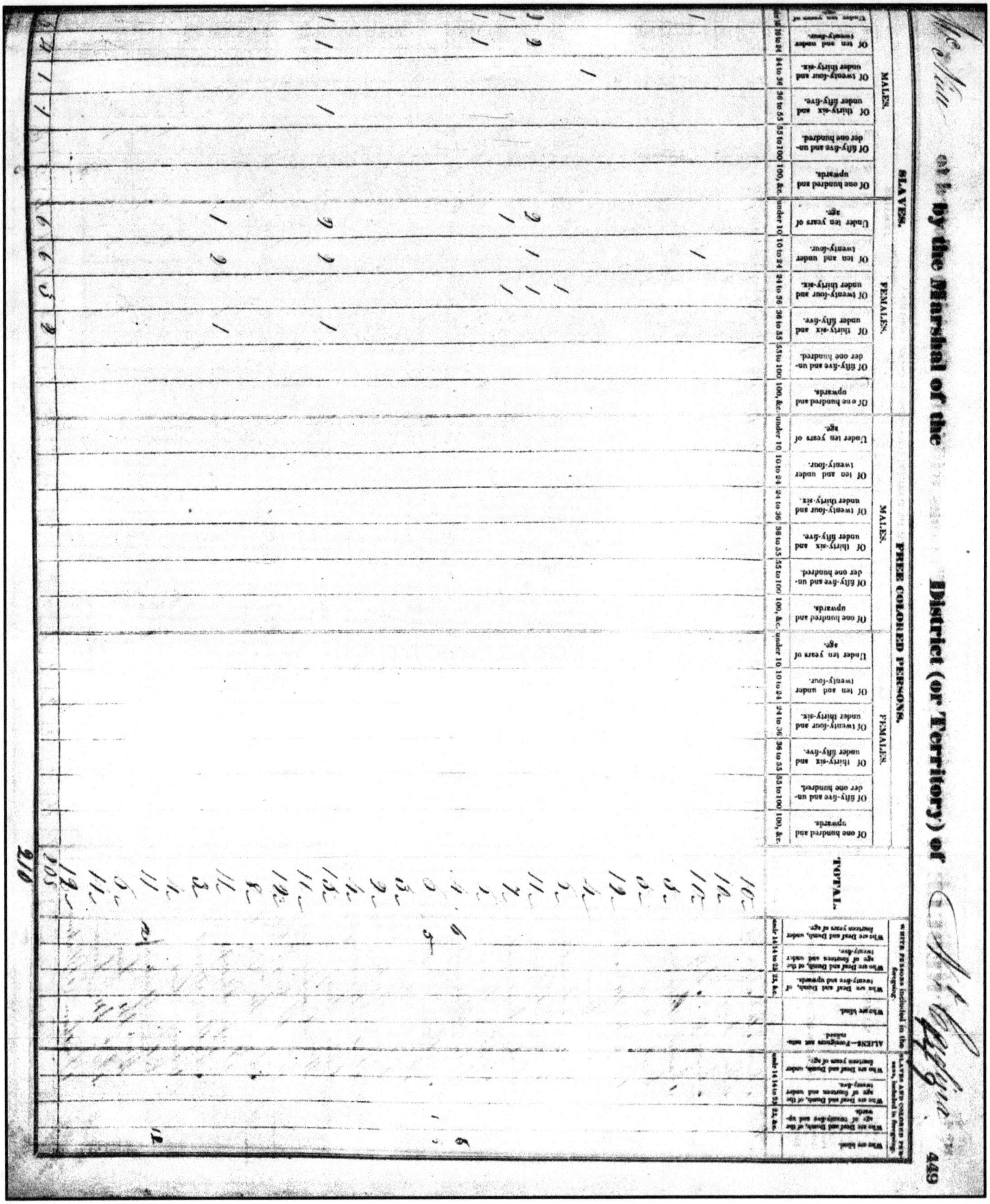

McNeill ... by the Marshal of the ... District (or Territory) of No Carolina 449

Slaves Males under 10	Slaves Males 10 to 24	Slaves Males 24 to 36	Slaves Males 36 to 55	Slaves Males 55 to 100	Slaves Males 100, &c.	Slaves Females under 10	Slaves Females 10 to 24	Slaves Females 24 to 36	Slaves Females 36 to 55	Slaves Females 55 to 100	Slaves Females 100, &c.	Free Colored Males under 10	Free Colored Males 10 to 24	Free Colored Males 24 to 36	Free Colored Males 36 to 55	Free Colored Males 55 to 100	Free Colored Males 100, &c.	Free Colored Females under 10	Free Colored Females 10 to 24	Free Colored Females 24 to 36	Free Colored Females 36 to 55	Free Colored Females 55 to 100	Free Colored Females 100, &c.	TOTAL	White Deaf and Dumb under 14	White Deaf and Dumb 14 to 25	White Deaf and Dumb 25, &c.	White Blind	Aliens—Foreigners not naturalized	Slaves and Colored Deaf and Dumb under 14	Slaves and Colored Deaf and Dumb 14 to 25	Slaves and Colored Deaf and Dumb 25, &c.	Slaves and Colored Blind
																								10									
																								10									
1							1																	10									
																								8									
																								5									
																								12									
		1																						4									
								1																6									
2	2					2	1	1																11									
1						1		1																7									
1	1																							2									
																								4	6								6
																								0	5							1	
																								3									
																								9									
																								4									
1	1		1			2	2		1															13									
																								11									
																								13									
																								8									
						1	2		1															11									
																								3									
																								4									
																								11	2								12
																								6									
																								11									
																								12									
6	4	1	1			6	6	5	2															105									

210

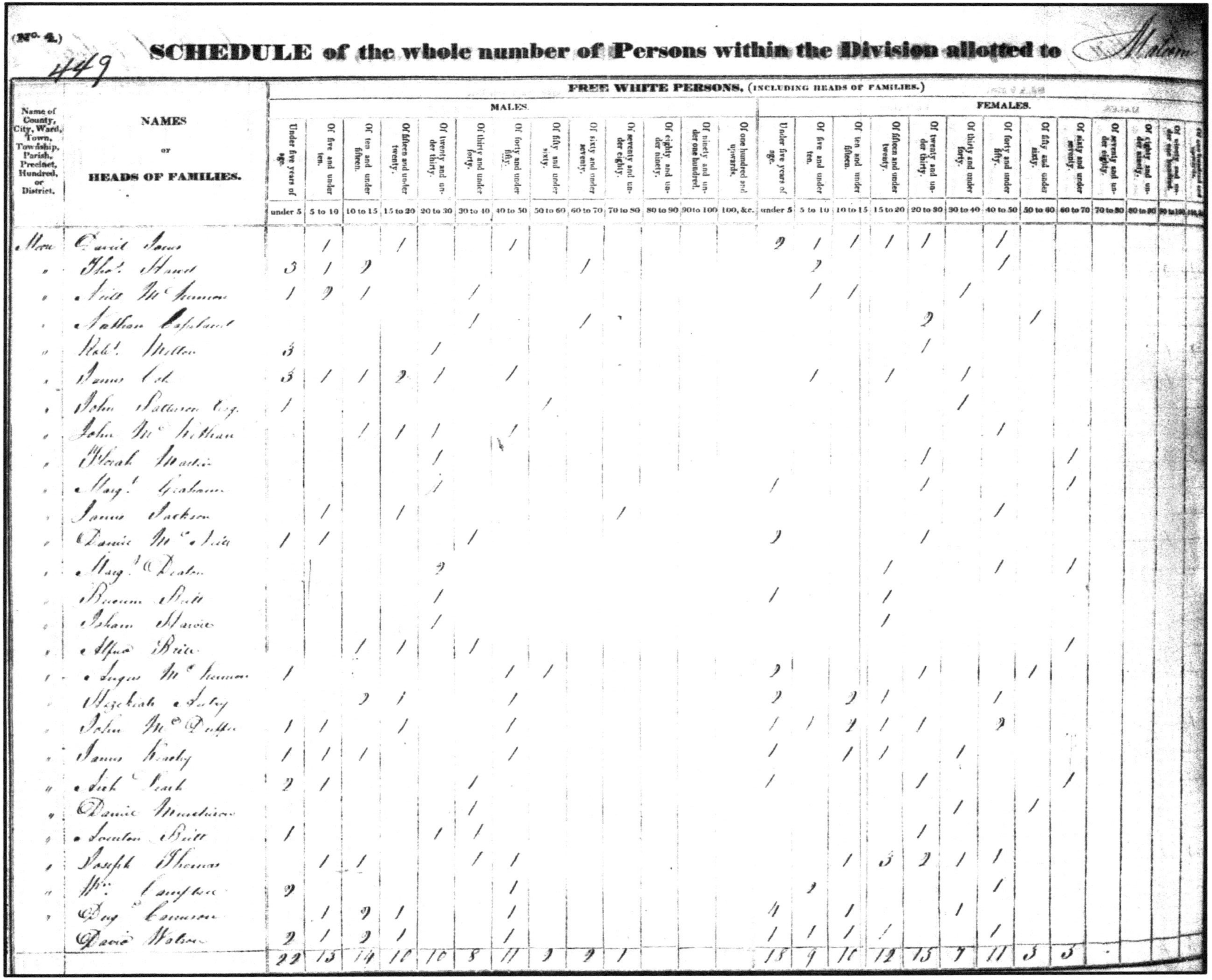

(No. 4.) 449

SCHEDULE of the whole number of Persons within the Division allotted to [illegible]

FREE WHITE PERSONS, (INCLUDING HEADS OF FAMILIES.)

Name of County, City, Ward, Town, Township, Parish, Precinct, Hundred, or District.	NAMES or HEADS OF FAMILIES.	MALES													FEMALES												
		Under five years of age. under 5	Of five and under ten. 5 to 10	Of ten and under fifteen. 10 to 15	Of fifteen and under twenty. 15 to 20	Of twenty and under thirty. 20 to 30	Of thirty and under forty. 30 to 40	Of forty and under fifty. 40 to 50	Of fifty and under sixty. 50 to 60	Of sixty and under seventy. 60 to 70	Of seventy and under eighty. 70 to 80	Of eighty and under ninety. 80 to 90	Of ninety and under one hundred. 90 to 100	Of one hundred and upwards. 100, &c.	Under five years of age. under 5	Of five and under ten. 5 to 10	Of ten and under fifteen. 10 to 15	Of fifteen and under twenty. 15 to 20	Of twenty and under thirty. 20 to 30	Of thirty and under forty. 30 to 40	Of forty and under fifty. 40 to 50	Of fifty and under sixty. 50 to 60	Of sixty and under seventy. 60 to 70	Of seventy and under eighty. 70 to 80	Of eighty and under ninety. 80 to 90	Of ninety and under one hundred. 90 to 100	Of one hundred and upwards. 100, &c.
Moore	David Jones		1		1			1							2	1	1	1	1		1						
"	Thos. Hand	3	1	2						1						2					1						
"	Neill McKinnon	1	2	1			1									1	1			1							
"	Nathan Copeland						1			1									2			1					
"	Robt. Melton	3				1													1								
"	James Cole	3	1	1	2	1		1								1		1		1							
"	John Patterson Esq.	1							1											1							
"	John McMillan			1	1	1		1													1						
"	Micah Martin					1													1				1				
"	Marg. Graham					1									1				1				1				
"	James Jackson		1		1						1										1						
"	Daniel McNeill	1	1				1								2				1								
"	Marg. Deaton					2												1			1		1				
"	Brown Britt					1									1			1									
"	Isham Marcie					1												1									
"	Alfred Britt			1	1		1																1				
"	Angus McKinnon	1						1	1						2				1			1					
"	Hezekiah Seley			2	1			1							2		2	1			1						
"	John McDuffie	1	1		1			1							1	1	2	1	1		2						
"	James Keahy	1	1	1				1							1		1	1		1							
"	Arch. Leach	2	1				1								1				1				1				
"	Daniel Murchison						1													1		1					
"	Lawton Britt	1				1	1												1								
"	Joseph Thomas		1	1			1	1									1	3	2	1	1						
"	Wm. Campbell	2						1								2					1						
"	Dug. Cameron		1	2	1			1							4		1			1							
"	David Wolen	2	1	2	1			1							1	1	1	1			1						
		22	13	14	10	10	8	11	2	2	1				18	9	10	12	15	7	11	3	5	.			

Slaves and Free Persons of Color are continued on the previous page

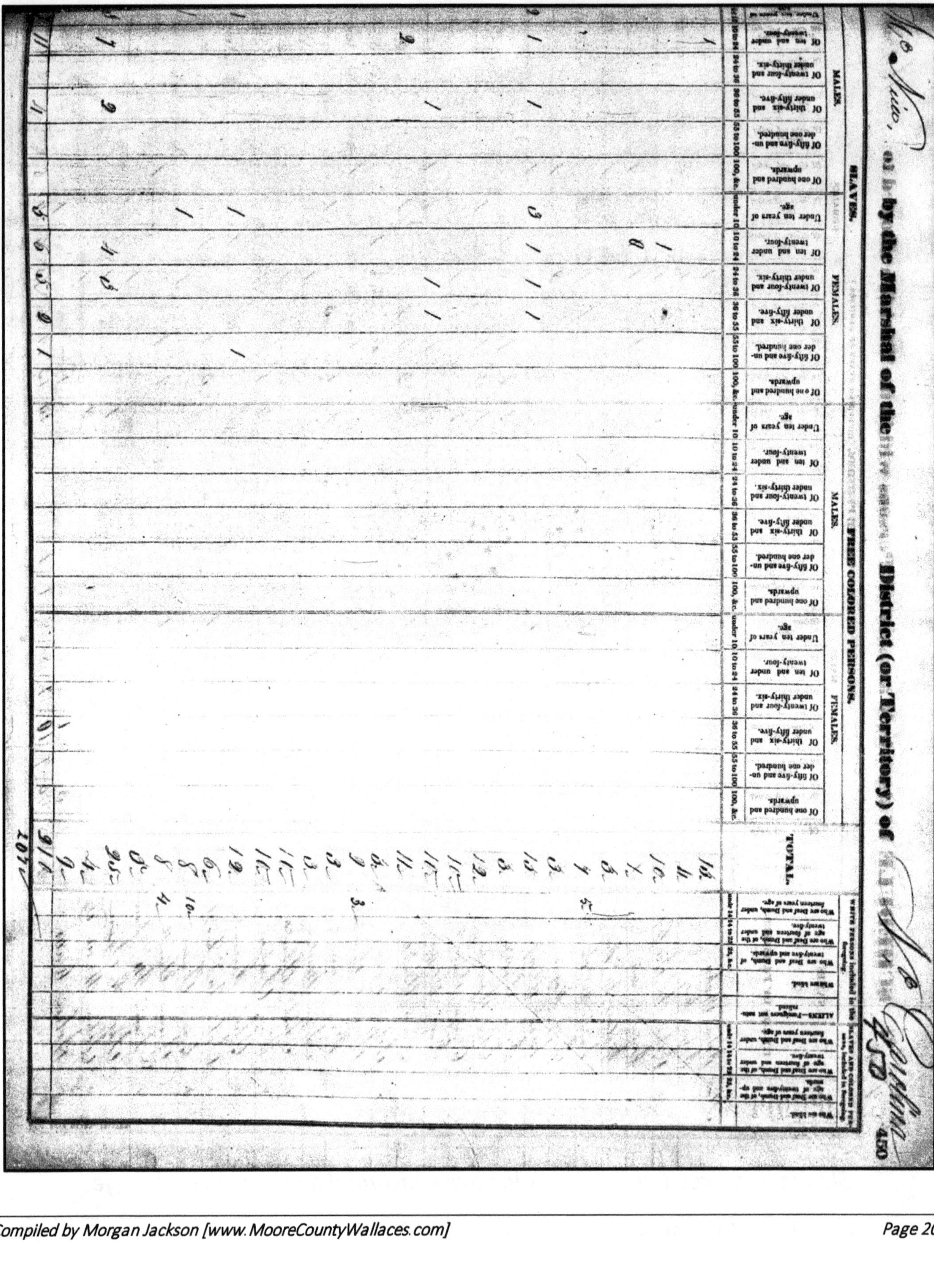
by the Marshal of the District (or Territory) of
SLAVES.
MALES.
FEMALES.
FREE COLORED PERSONS.
MALES.
FEMALES.
TOTAL.
450

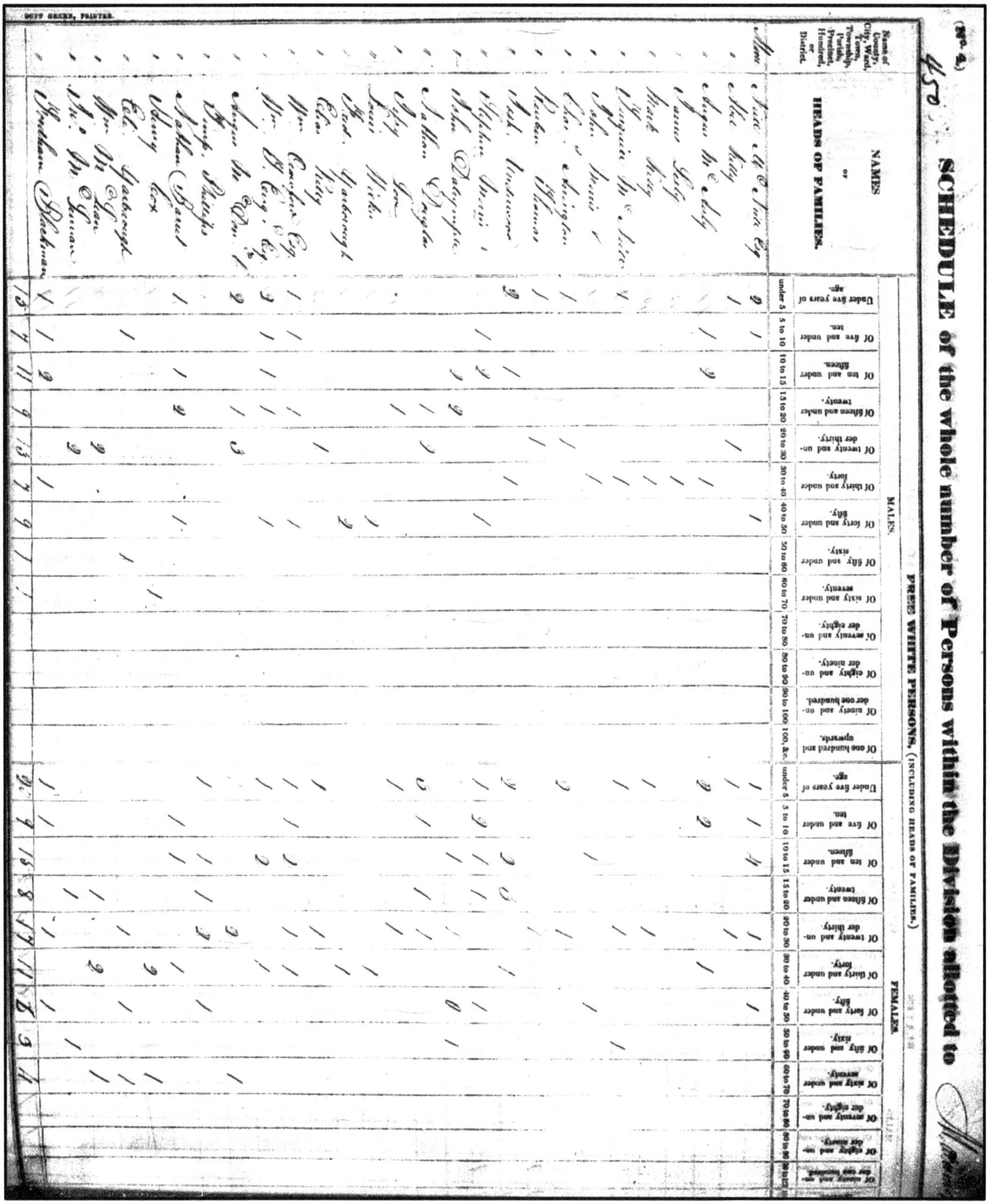

Slaves and Free Persons of Color are continued on the previous page

Mc Nair ... by the Marshal of the ... District (or Territory) of No Carolina 451

Slaves Males under 10	Males 10 to 24	Males 24 to 36	Males 36 to 55	Males 55 to 100	Males 100, &c.	Females under 10	Females 10 to 24	Females 24 to 36	Females 36 to 55	Females 55 to 100	Females 100, &c.	TOTAL
	1											4
												5
	1											5
1												7
2		1				2	2	1				10
1	1					2						10
												10
												9
							1					11
							0					11
							1					5
												9
	2	1										15
	1	1				1		2				11
	3	2		2		3	2	2	3			21
			1									13
	1					1	2					7
												5
		1		1		2	1	1				13
	3	2				1	1		2			16
	2	1	1				2	1				14
		1		1								4
												6
												2
		1					1		1			6
	1	0	2				2					10
						1	1					12
1	16	11	4	4		13	16	7	6			248

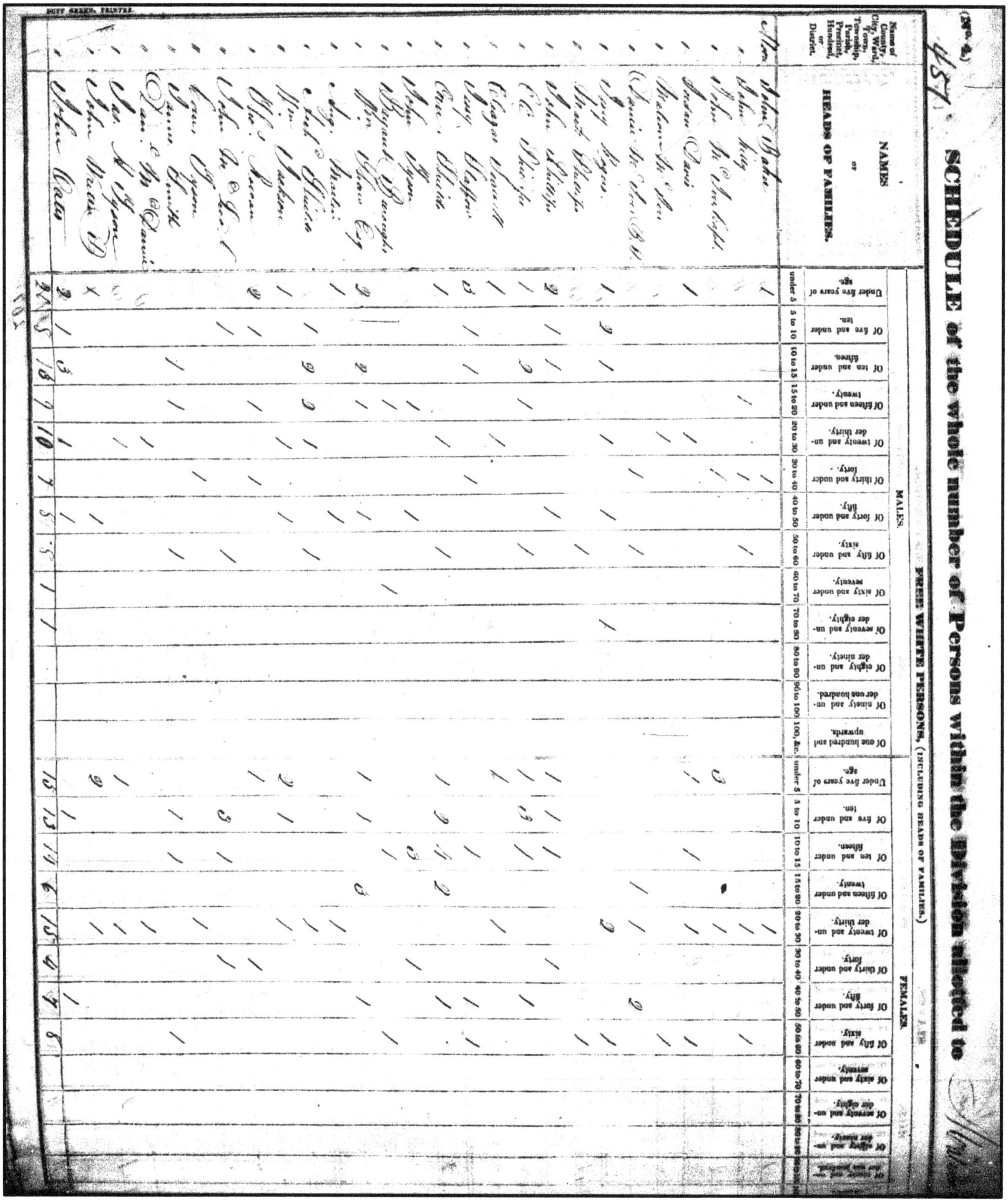

Slaves and Free Persons of Color are continued on the previous page

Mc Niel ... by the Marshal of the ... District (or Territory) of North Carolina 452

SLAVES. Males. Under 10	Males 10 to 24	Males 24 to 36	Males 36 to 55	Males 55 to 100	Males 100, &c.	Females. Under 10	Females 10 to 24	Females 24 to 36	Females 36 to 55	Females 55 to 100	Females 100, &c.	FREE COLORED PERSONS. (Males and Females, all ages)	TOTAL.
													6
													6
													3
										1			9
													10
			1				2	1					15
	3	1	1	1									12
		1					1						6
2		2				2	1						17
													5
													3
													9
1						1	1						9
3			1			2	2						13
													8
													9
													7
													11
													6
	4	1					1						27
													8
3	1	2		1		4	2	1		1			22
1						1			1				9
													5
						4		1					8
	1						1						6
													8
11	9	7	3	2		14	11	3	1	2			250
													257

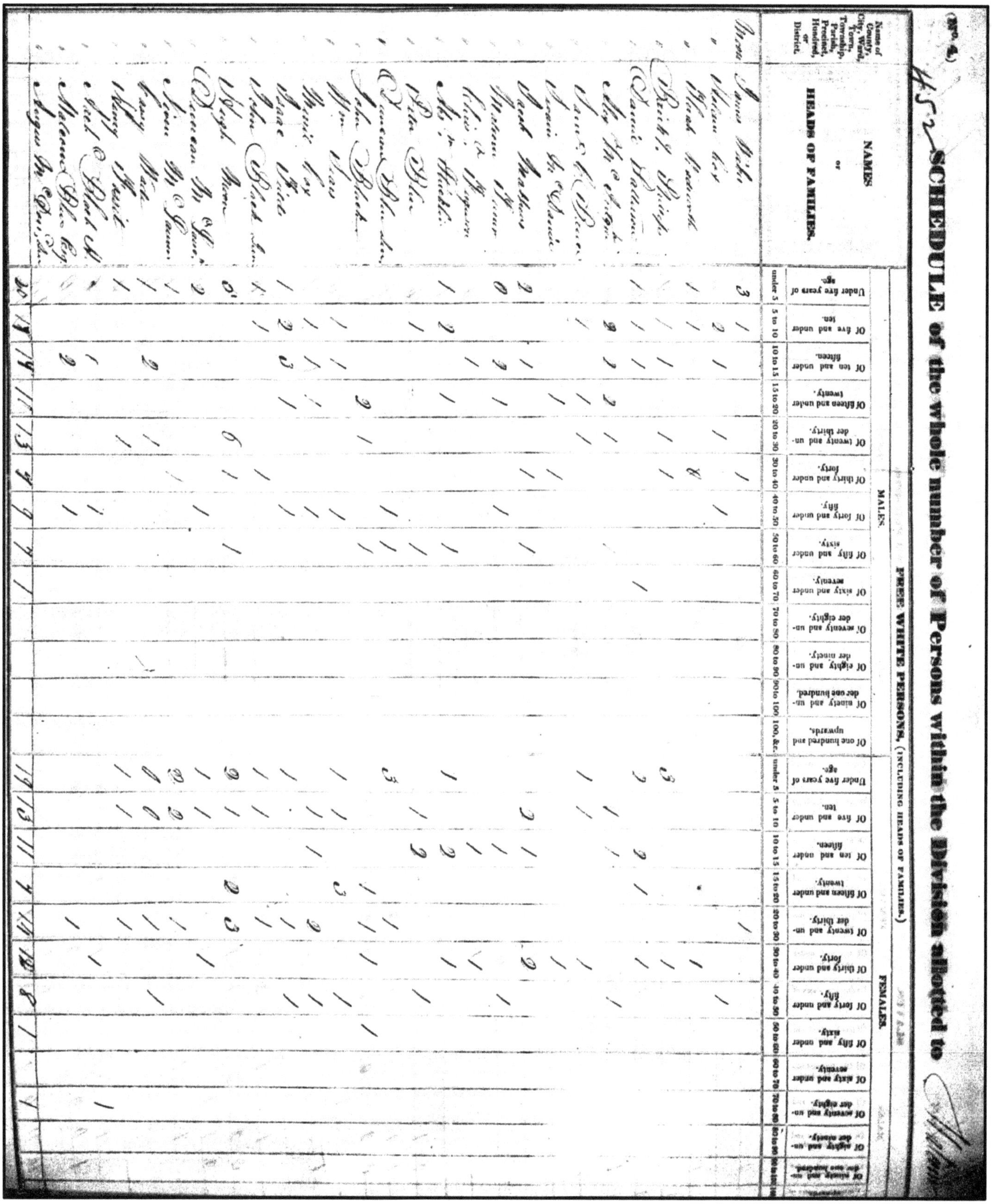

Slaves and Free Persons of Color are continued on the previous page

Mc Neill ... by the Marshal of the ... District (or Territory) of North Carolina 453

Slaves, Males: under 10	Slaves, Males: 10 to 24	Slaves, Males: 24 to 36	Slaves, Males: 36 to 55	Slaves, Males: 55 to 100	Slaves, Males: 100, &c.	Slaves, Females: under 10	Slaves, Females: 10 to 24	Slaves, Females: 24 to 36	Slaves, Females: 36 to 55	Slaves, Females: 55 to 100	Slaves, Females: 100, &c.	Free Colored Persons, Males: under 10	Free Colored Persons, Males: 10 to 24	Free Colored Persons, Males: 24 to 36	Free Colored Persons, Males: 36 to 55	Free Colored Persons, Males: 55 to 100	Free Colored Persons, Males: 100, &c.	Free Colored Persons, Females: under 10	Free Colored Persons, Females: 10 to 24	Free Colored Persons, Females: 24 to 36	Free Colored Persons, Females: 36 to 55	Free Colored Persons, Females: 55 to 100	Free Colored Persons, Females: 100, &c.	TOTAL	White persons included in the foregoing: Deaf and Dumb, under 14	White persons: Deaf and Dumb, 14 to 25	White persons: Deaf and Dumb, 25, &c.	White persons: Who are blind	Aliens—Foreigners not naturalized	Slaves and colored persons included in the foregoing: Deaf and Dumb, under 14	Slaves and colored persons: Deaf and Dumb, 14 to 25	Slaves and colored persons: Deaf and Dumb, 25, &c.	Slaves and colored persons: Who are blind
																								5									
																								8									
																								7									
																								8									
																								3									
																								5									
							1																	4									
																								2									
	2					1	1	1																10									
2	1	4					2			1														11	10								
						0	1																	12									
1	2	1				2	1		1															13									
1	1					3	1	1							1									10									
		1																						11									
																								4									
																								3									
1	1	1				3			1															10									
																								9									
																								6									
																								8	4								
2	1					1	1																	9	10								
																								8									
																								4									
																								3									
1	1					1																		5									
																								7									
	1						1																	6									
8	10	4				11	9	2	2	1					1									184									

184

(Nº 4.) 453 **SCHEDULE of the whole number of Persons within the Division allotted to** Malcom

DUFF GREEN, PRINTER.

Name of County, City, Ward, Town, Township, Parish, Precinct, Hundred, or District.	NAMES OF HEADS OF FAMILIES.	FREE WHITE PERSONS, (INCLUDING HEADS OF FAMILIES.) MALES. Under five years of age. (under 5)	Of five and under ten. (5 to 10)	Of ten and under fifteen. (10 to 15)	Of fifteen and under twenty. (15 to 20)	Of twenty and under thirty. (20 to 30)	Of thirty and under forty. (30 to 40)	Of forty and under fifty. (40 to 50)	Of fifty and under sixty. (50 to 60)	Of sixty and under seventy. (60 to 70)	Of seventy and under eighty. (70 to 80)	Of eighty and under ninety. (80 to 90)	Of ninety and under one hundred. (90 to 100)	Of one hundred and upwards. (100, &c.)	FEMALES. Under five years of age. (under 5)	Of five and under ten. (5 to 10)	Of ten and under fifteen. (10 to 15)	Of fifteen and under twenty. (15 to 20)	Of twenty and under thirty. (20 to 30)	Of thirty and under forty. (30 to 40)	Of forty and under fifty. (40 to 50)	Of fifty and under sixty. (50 to 60)	Of sixty and under seventy. (60 to 70)	Of seventy and under eighty. (70 to 80)	Of eighty and under ninety. (80 to 90)	Of ninety and under one hundred. (90 to 100)
Moore	John McNeill Sen.			1							1								1	1			1			
"	Arch. Ray	2				1									1				1							
"	Edward Patterson	2	1					1							1	1			1							
"	Alex. Ray	1	1	1			1								1		1	1		1						
"	Malcom McInnis	1			1														1							
"	Randell McDonald		3			1													1							
"	Daniel Blue					1									1				1							
"	Arch. Patterson					1												1								
"	John Blue Sr.	1					1									1	1		1							
"	John McLeod Esq.						1			1													2			
"	Lauchlin McKinnon		2					1							2	2	1		1	1					1	
"	Daniel Blue					1	1												2							
"	Alex. Smith Esq.				1		1																			
"	Arch. Buchan	3	1	1			1									2	1			1						
"	Peter Munroe	2					1												1							
"	John McKinnie	1					1												1							
"	George McFarlan					2																			1	
"	Arch. Munroe			1	2	1			1									1	2			1				
"	Malcom Ray		1	1			2								1					1						
"	Daniel McKinnie									1									2				1			
"	Daniel Blue	1				1				1									2							
"	Angus McLean		2	2				1							2					1						
"	Phillip Cameron				1			1										1		1						
"	Daniel McLean				1			1										1								
"	Daniel McDon. Esq.							1											1							
"	John McCallum	1	2	1				1							1					1						
"	Daniel Patterson					1			1								1					1				
		16	13	8	6	10	10	7	2	3	1				10	6	5	5	19	8		2	4		2	

Slaves and Free Persons of Color are continued on the previous page

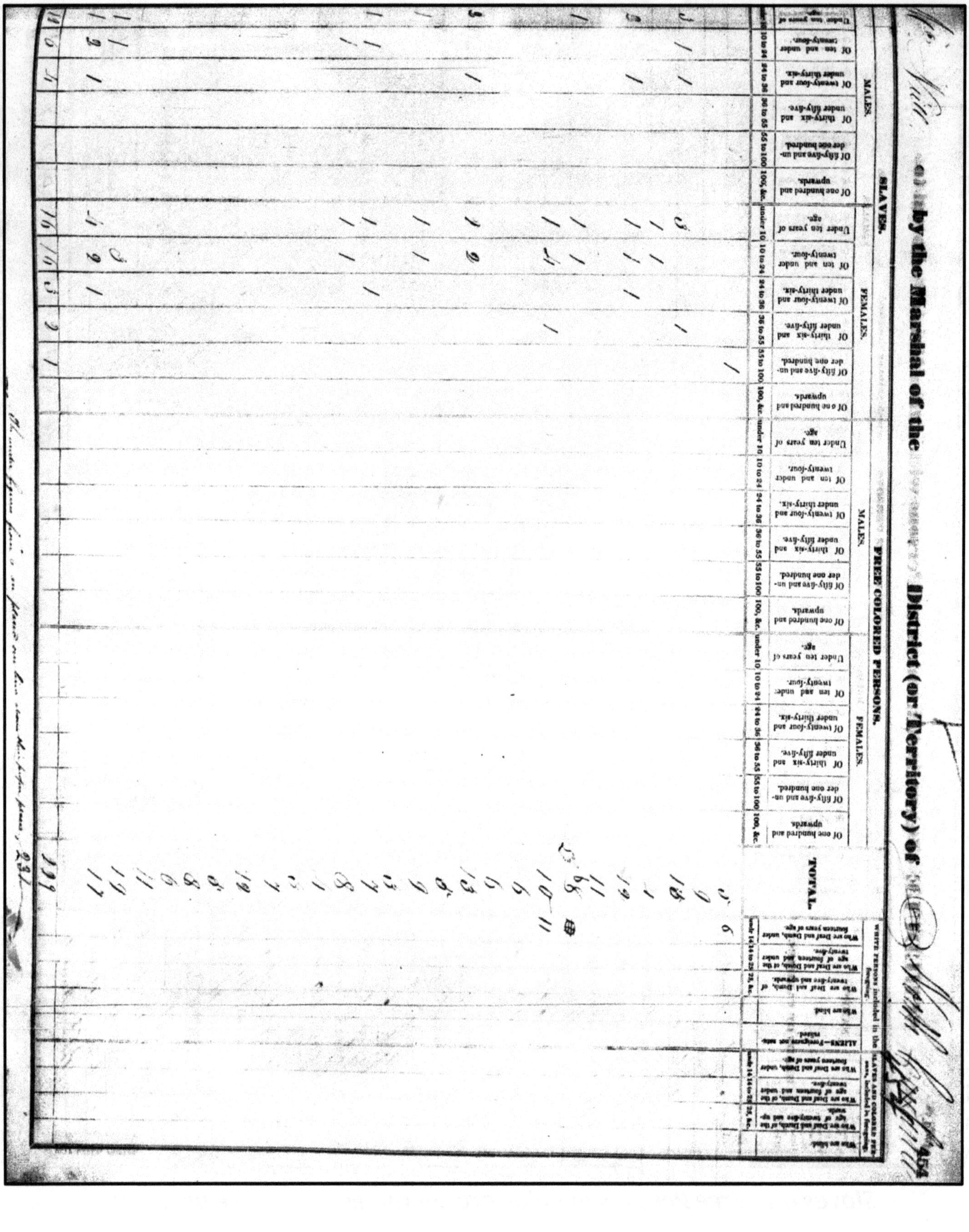

Mc Neill ... by the Marshal of the ... District (or Territory) of North Carolina 454

SLAVES Males under 10	Males 10 to 24	Males 24 to 36	Males 36 to 55	Males 55 to 100	Males 100, &c.	Females under 10	Females 10 to 24	Females 24 to 36	Females 36 to 55	Females 55 to 100	Females 100, &c.	TOTAL	White persons deaf and dumb under 14
										1		5	6
												9	
3	1	1				3			1			15	
						1	1					1	
2		1				1	1	1				19	
												11	
1						1	1					8	
						1	4		1			10	11
												6	
												6	
2		1				1	2					13	
												5	
1						1	1					9	
												13	
1	1					1		1				7	
	1					1	1					8	
												1	
												5	
												7	
												12	
												8	
												8	
												6	
												11	
1	1						3					19	
1	2	1				4	2	1				17	
11	6	4				16	16	3	2	1		199	

The under figures from 5 are placed one line above their proper places, 231

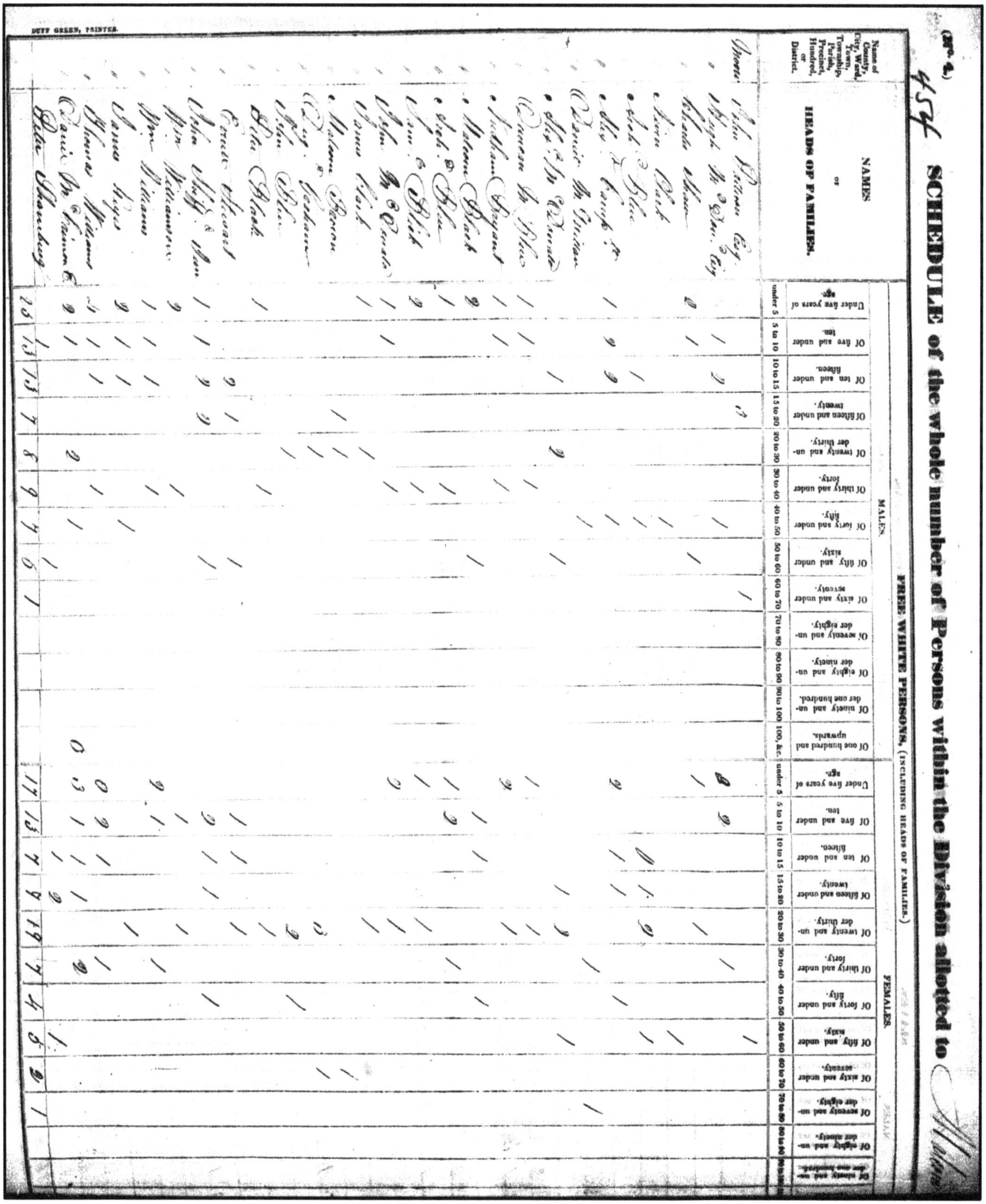

(Nº 4.) 454 SCHEDULE of the whole number of Persons within the Division allotted to Malcom

FREE WHITE PERSONS, (INCLUDING HEADS OF FAMILIES.)

Name of County, City, Ward, Town, Township, Parish, Precinct, Hundred, or District.	NAMES OF HEADS OF FAMILIES.	M under 5	M 5 to 10	M 10 to 15	M 15 to 20	M 20 to 30	M 30 to 40	M 40 to 50	M 50 to 60	M 60 to 70	M 70 to 80	M 80 to 90	M 90 to 100	M 100, &c.	F under 5	F 5 to 10	F 10 to 15	F 15 to 20	F 20 to 30	F 30 to 40	F 40 to 50	F 50 to 60	F 60 to 70	F 70 to 80	F 80 to 90
Moore	John Patterson Esq.				3					1												1			
	Hugh McDonald Esq.		1	2				1							2	2				1					
	Charles Shaw	2	1						1						1				1						
	Aaron Clark							1														1			
	Archd Blue			1				1									0	1	2			1			
	Alexr Campbell	1	2	2				1							2		1	1			1				
	Daniel McMillan							1												1				1	
	Alexd McDonald			1		2			1									1	2			1			
	Duncan M. Blue	1	1				1								1				1						
	Nathan Bryant	1	1				1								2				1						
	Malcom Black	2							1							1	1				1				
	Archd Blue	1					1								1	2				1					
	Saml Black	2					1								1				1						
	John McDonald	1	1				1								2				1						
	James Clark	1				1													1						
	Malcom Bacon				1	1																	1		
	Dugd Graham					1													3				1		
	John Blue					1													2		1				
	Peter Black	1					1												1						
	Ervin Stewart			2	1				1							1	1		1						
	John Shff. Sen.	1	1	2	2				1							2	1	1			1				
	Wm Williamson	2					1									1			1						
	Wm Williams	1	1	1			1								2	1				1					
	James Hayes	2	1	1				1											1						
	Thomas Williams	4	1	1			1								0	2	1			1					
	Daniel McCrimmon	2	1			2		1						0	3	1	1	1		2					
	Peter Shamburg		1						1								1	2				1			
		25	13	13	7	8	9	7	6	1					17	13	7	7	19	7	4	5	2	1	

DUFF GREEN, PRINTER.

Slaves and Free Persons of Color are continued on the previous page

Slaves and Free Persons of Color are continued on the previous page

Mc Nair ... by the Marshal of the ... District (or Territory) of North Carolina 455

455

Slaves: Males under 10	Males 10 to 24	Males 24 to 36	Males 36 to 55	Females under 10	Females 10 to 24	Females 36 to 55	Total	White deaf and dumb, under 14
							11	
							3	
	2	1	1	2	1		12	
	1						13	
1	1	1					14	
							5	
							7	5
							4	
							3	
							4	
							7	
							11	10
							9	
					1		6	
1				3	2	1	13	
							7	
					1		5	
							5	
							11	
2	1				3		13	
							8	
							8	
							13	
							8	
							8	
				1			9	
							11	
4	5	2	1	6	8	1	240	

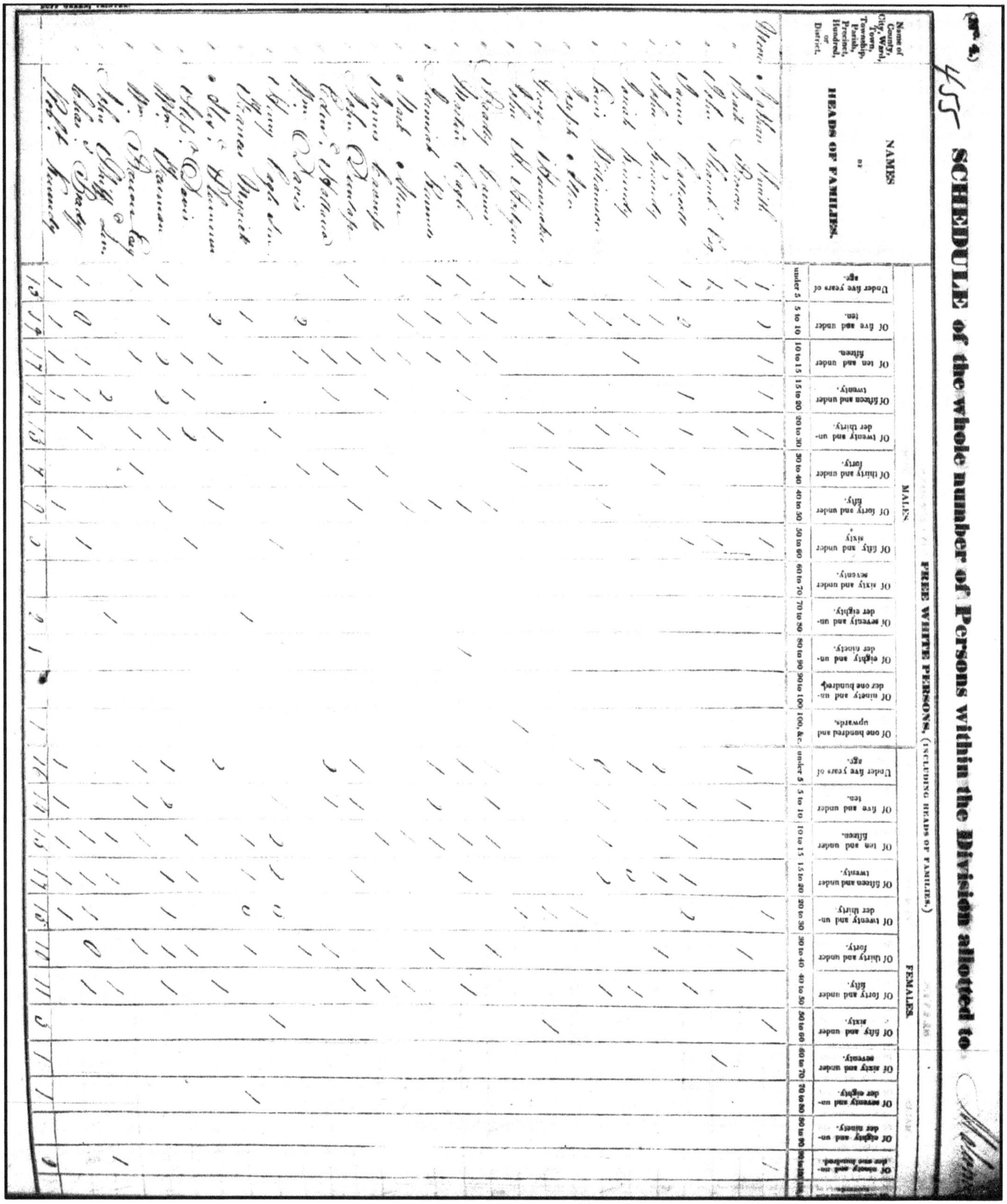

(No. 4.) 455 SCHEDULE of the whole number of Persons within the Division allotted to Moore

Name of County, City, Ward, Town, Township, Parish, Precinct, Hundred, or District	NAMES OF HEADS OF FAMILIES	FREE WHITE PERSONS (including heads of families) — MALES: Under five years of age (under 5)	Of five and under ten (5 to 10)	Of ten and under fifteen (10 to 15)	Of fifteen and under twenty (15 to 20)	Of twenty and under thirty (20 to 30)	Of thirty and under forty (30 to 40)	Of forty and under fifty (40 to 50)	Of fifty and under sixty (50 to 60)	Of sixty and under seventy (60 to 70)	Of seventy and under eighty (70 to 80)	Of eighty and under ninety (80 to 90)	Of ninety and under one hundred (90 to 100)	Of one hundred and upwards (100, &c.)	FEMALES: Under five years of age (under 5)	Of five and under ten (5 to 10)	Of ten and under fifteen (10 to 15)	Of fifteen and under twenty (15 to 20)	Of twenty and under thirty (20 to 30)	Of thirty and under forty (30 to 40)	Of forty and under fifty (40 to 50)	Of fifty and under sixty (50 to 60)	Of sixty and under seventy (60 to 70)	Of seventy and under eighty (70 to 80)	Of eighty and under ninety (80 to 90)	Of ninety and under one hundred (90 to 100)
Moore	Nathan Smith	1	1	1	1	1			1										1			1				1
"	Isaiah Brown	1				1									1	1				1						
"	John Shamb. Esq.	1							1														1			
"	James Cattrell	1	2		1	1			1							1	1	1	2		1					
"	John Kennedy	1	1				1								2	1		1		1						
"	Josiah Kennedy		1	1		1									1			2			1					
"	Louis Williamson		1			1		1							1	1	1	2			1					
"	Joseph Allen		1				1								1				1							
"	George Hancocke	2				1													1			1				
"	John H. Hodges	1					1							1					1							
"	Bradley Cameron		1	1				1								1	1			1						
"	Martin Cagle	1	1	1	1			1				1			1		1	1			1					
"	Jeremiah Kennedy	1	1	1				1							1	1	1			1						
"	Mark Allen		1	1				1													1					
"	James Cameron			1	1		1										1				1					
"	John Dunlap	1		1				1							1	1		1			1					
"	Edwd. Wallace			1	1		1								2	1				1						
"	Wm. Davis		2	1			1													1						
"	Henry Cagle Sen.					1			1								2	2	2			1				
"	Francis Myrick		1								1						1	1	2	1				1		
"	Alexr. Plummer		2	1		1		1							2						1					
"	Stephn. Davis			1	1	2			1								1			1						
"	Wm. Farmer	1	1	2	2	1		1							1	2		1	1	1	1					
"	Wm. Barrow Esq.	1		1		1	1								1	1	1			1						
"	John Shiff Sen.				2						1						1	1			1					1
"	Chas. Brady	1	0	1	1	1			1								1	1	1	0	1					
"	Robt. Kennedy	1	1	1	1			1							1	1	1	1	1							
		13	14	17	12	13	7	9	5		2	1		1	16	14	13	17	15	11	11	5	1	1		9

Slaves and Free Persons of Color are continued on the previous page

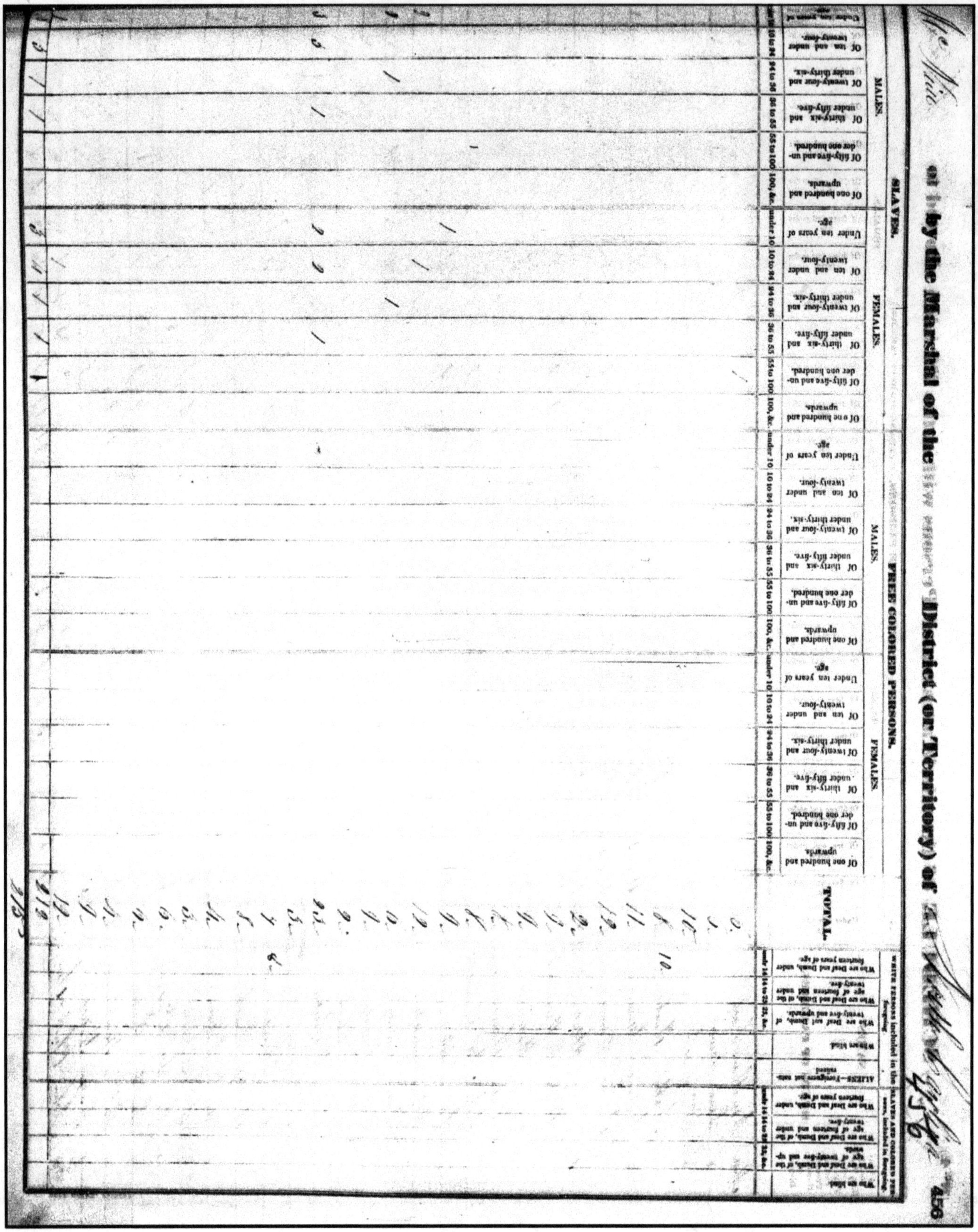
by the Marshal of the District (or Territory) of
SLAVES.
FREE COLORED PERSONS.
TOTAL.
456

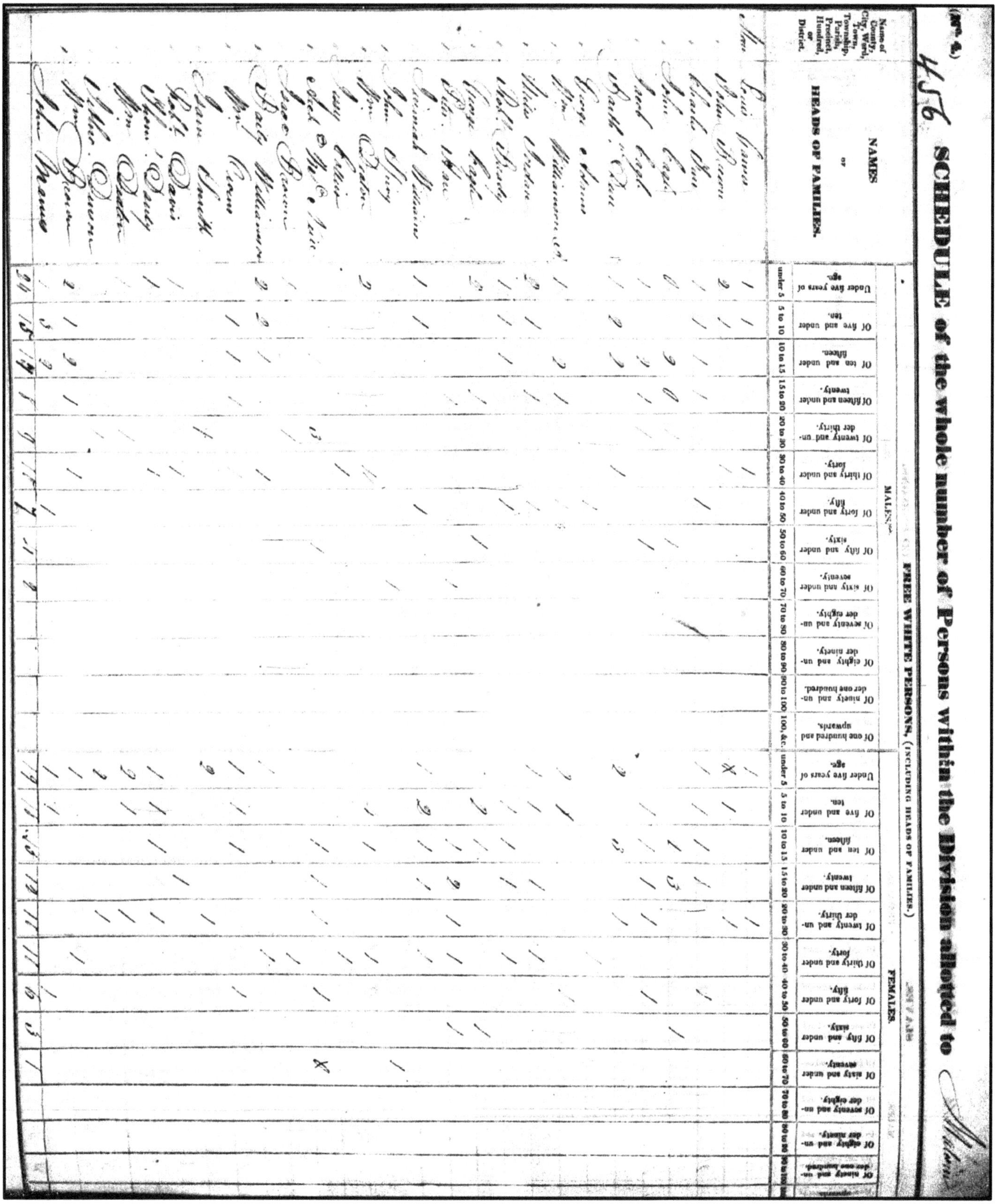

Slaves and Free Persons of Color are continued on the previous page

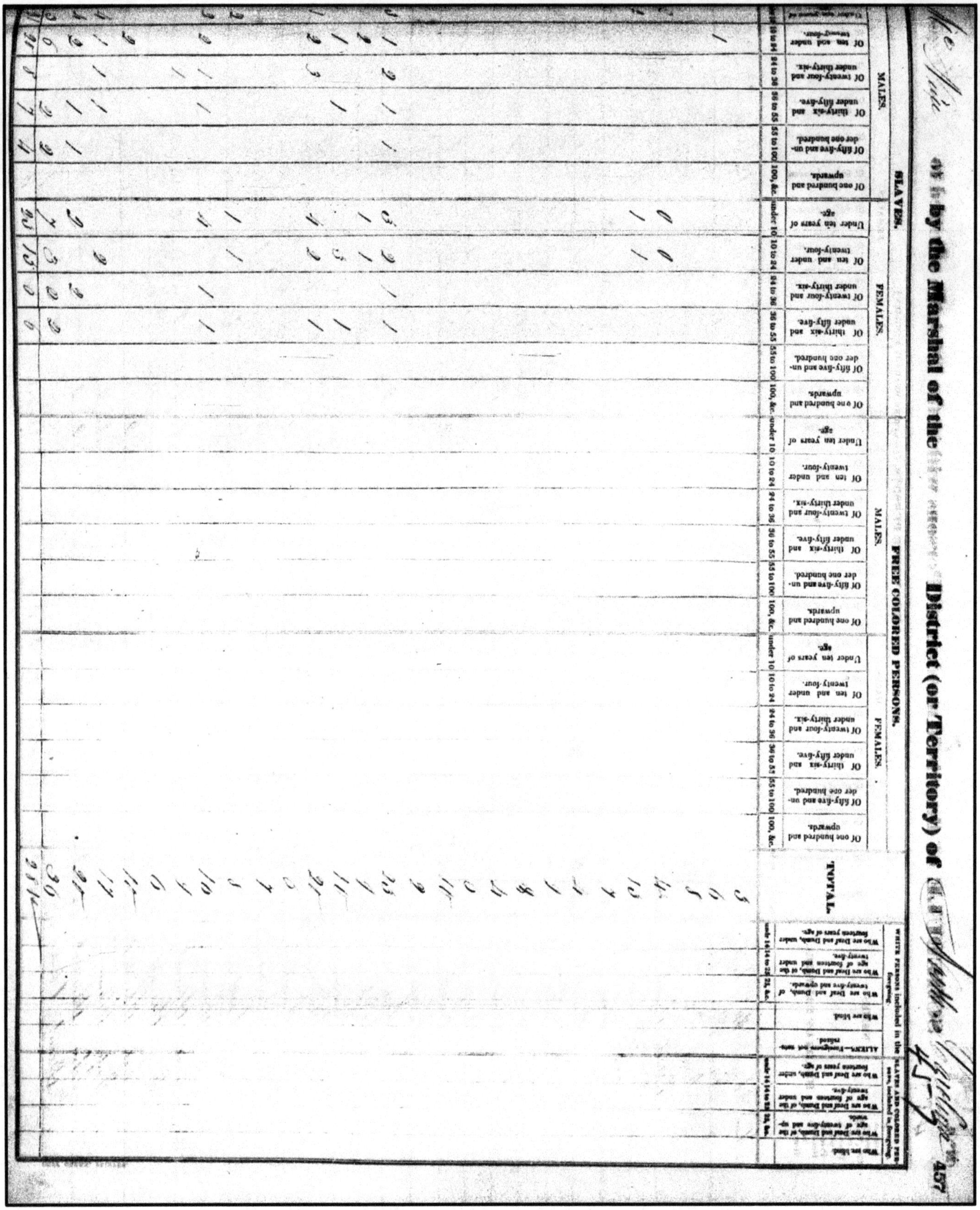

... by the Marshal of the ... District (or Territory) of ...

457

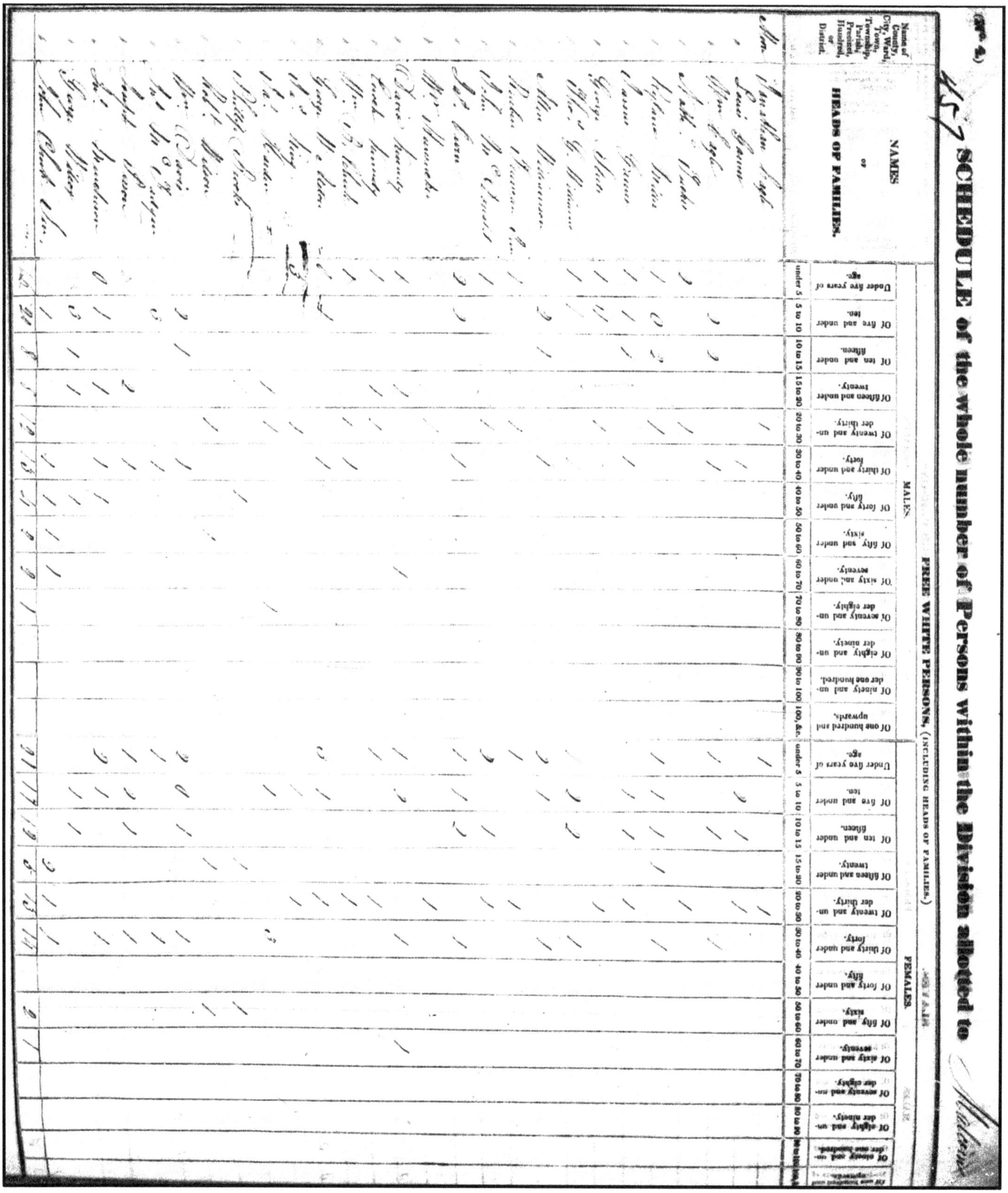

(No. 4.) 457 SCHEDULE of the whole number of Persons within the Division allotted to Malcolm

FREE WHITE PERSONS, (INCLUDING HEADS OF FAMILIES.)

Name of County, City, Ward, Town, Township, Parish, Precinct, Hundred, or District.	NAMES OF HEADS OF FAMILIES.	MALES under 5	5 to 10	10 to 15	15 to 20	20 to 30	30 to 40	40 to 50	50 to 60	60 to 70	70 to 80	80 to 90	90 to 100	100, &c.	FEMALES under 5	5 to 10	10 to 15	15 to 20	20 to 30	30 to 40	40 to 50	50 to 60	60 to 70	70 to 80	80 to 90	90 to 100	100, &c.
Moore	Jonathan Eagle					1									1				1								
"	Louis Garner						1									2	1		1								
"	Wm Eagle		2	2			1								1		1			1							
"	Nath. Tucker	2				1													1								
"	Ryland Miller	1	0	2		1									1	1	1	1		1							
"	James Garner	1	1	1			1									1	1		1								
"	George Stute	1	1			1													1								
"	Thos. G. Williams	1	1												1	2	2			1							
"	Allen Williamson		2	1			1								2	1				1							
"	Reuben Freeman Sen.	1				1									1				1								
"	John McDonald	1				1									2		1		1								
"	Jas. Owen	2	2				1								1	1	2			1							
"	Wm Hunnicutt					1													1								
"	David Kennedy	1			1					1					1	2				1			1				
"	Enoch Kennedy	1			1	1									1				1								
"	Wm B. Clark	1				1	1												1								
"	George Wallace	1	1				1								0	1			1								
"	Jas. King	3				1										1			1								
"	Jas. Harden				1	1					1					1				3							
"	Phillip Brooks							1										1				1					
"	Robt. Wilson					1			1									1				1					
"	Wm Davis		2	1			1								2	0	1			1							
"	Jno. McIntyre		3				1								1					1							
"	Joseph Pearson				2		1								1	2	1			1							
"	Jno. Murchison	0	1		1		1	1							2	1				1							
"	George Wilcox		3	1	1			1								1	1										
"	John Clark Sen.		1				1	1	1	1								2	1	1							
		2	21	8	5	12	13	4	2	2	1				21	17	12	5	13	14		2	1				

Slaves and Free Persons of Color are continued on the previous page

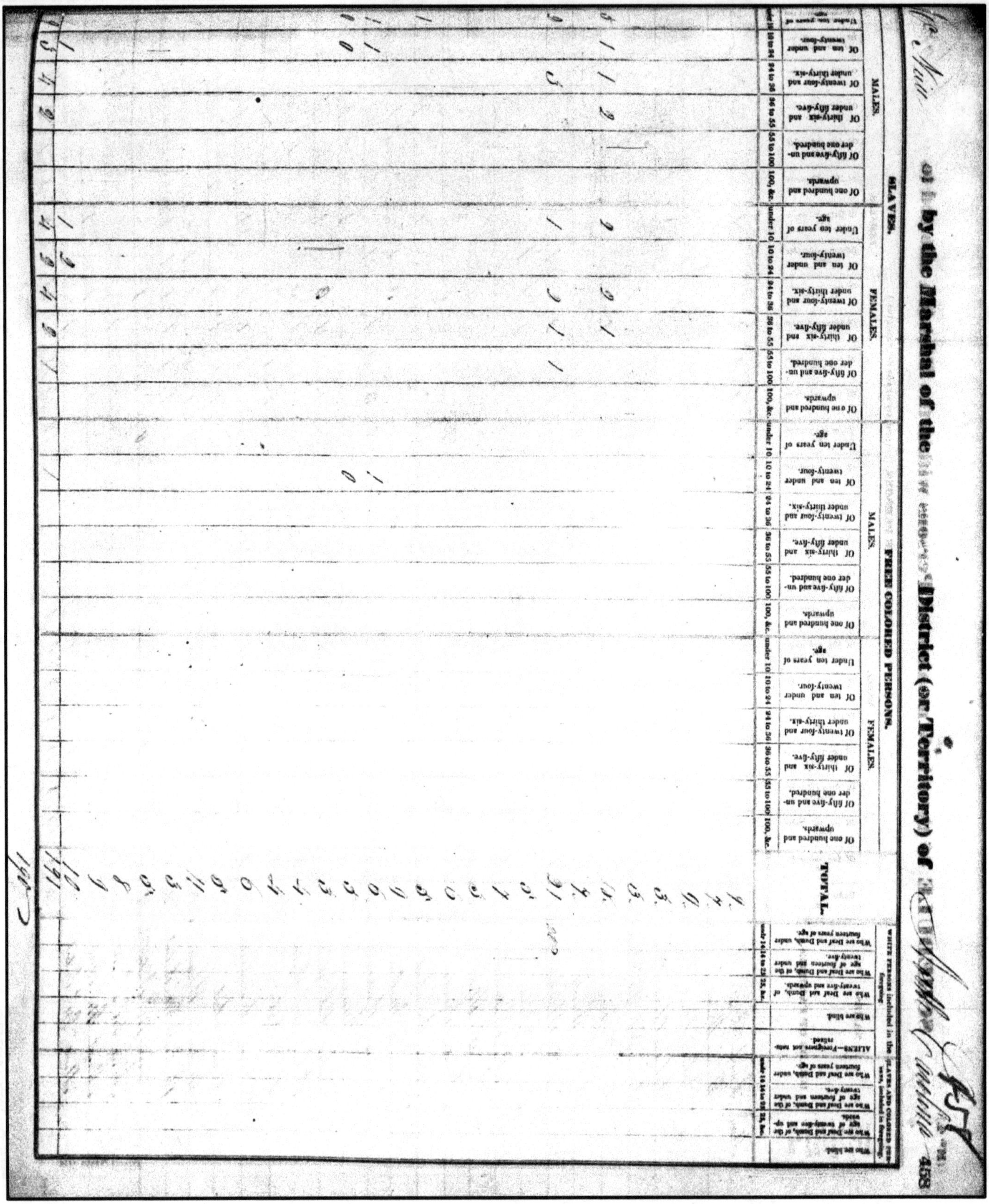
by the Marshal of the District (or Territory) of
SLAVES.
MALES.
FEMALES.
FREE COLORED PERSONS.
MALES.
FEMALES.
TOTAL.
458

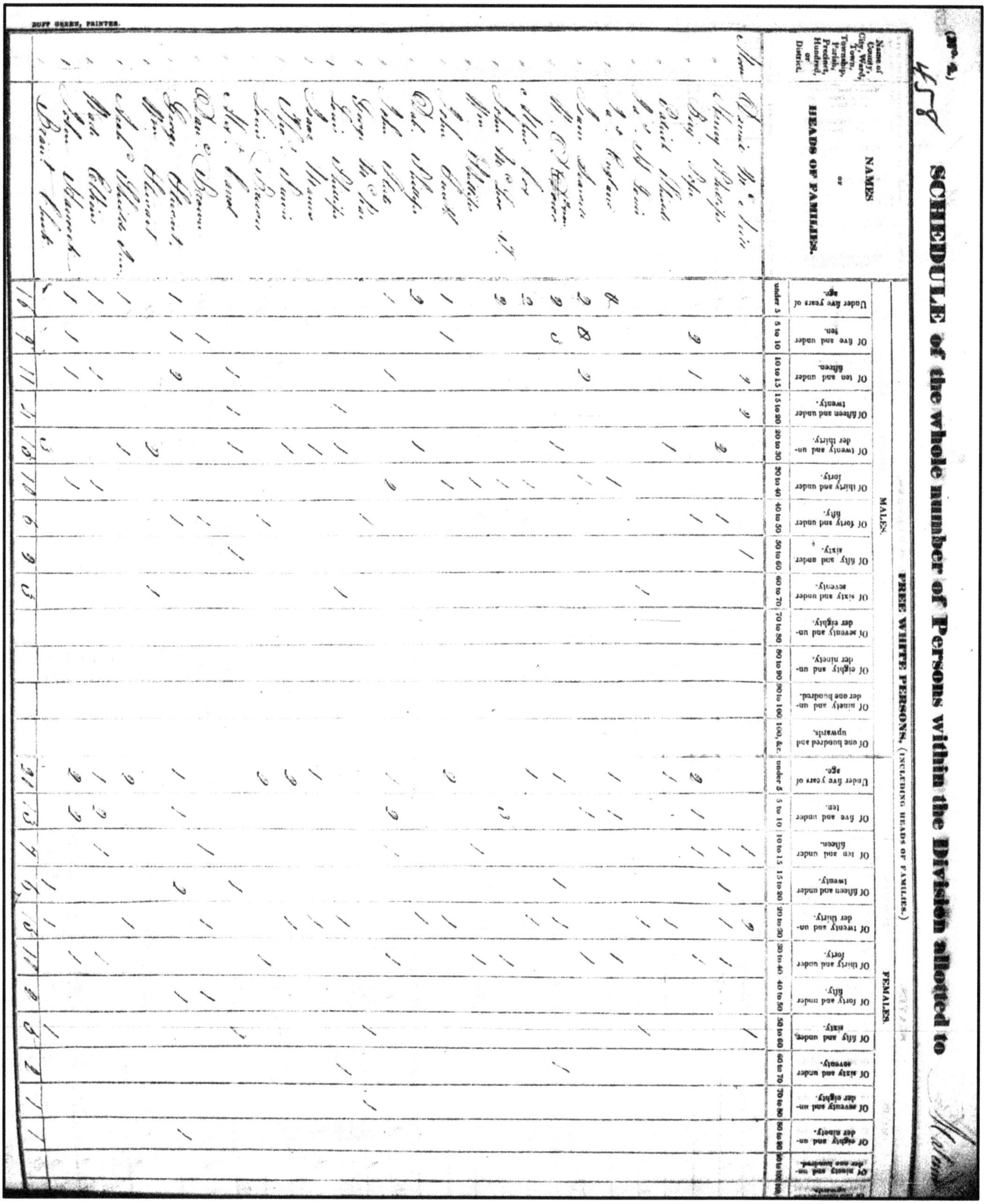

Slaves and Free Persons of Color are continued on the previous page

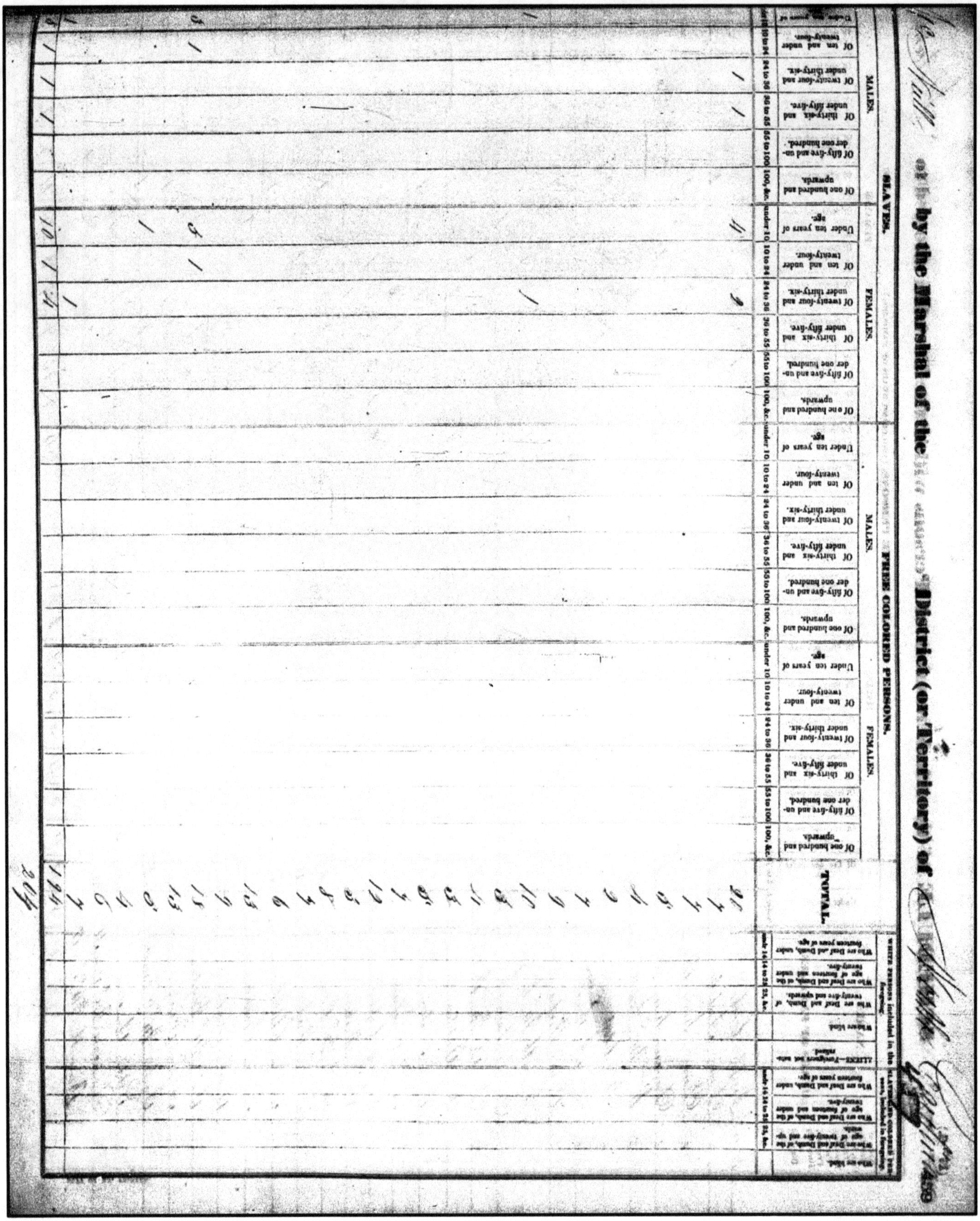
by the Marshal of the
District (or Territory) of
SLAVES.
FREE COLORED PERSONS.
MALES.
FEMALES.
TOTAL.

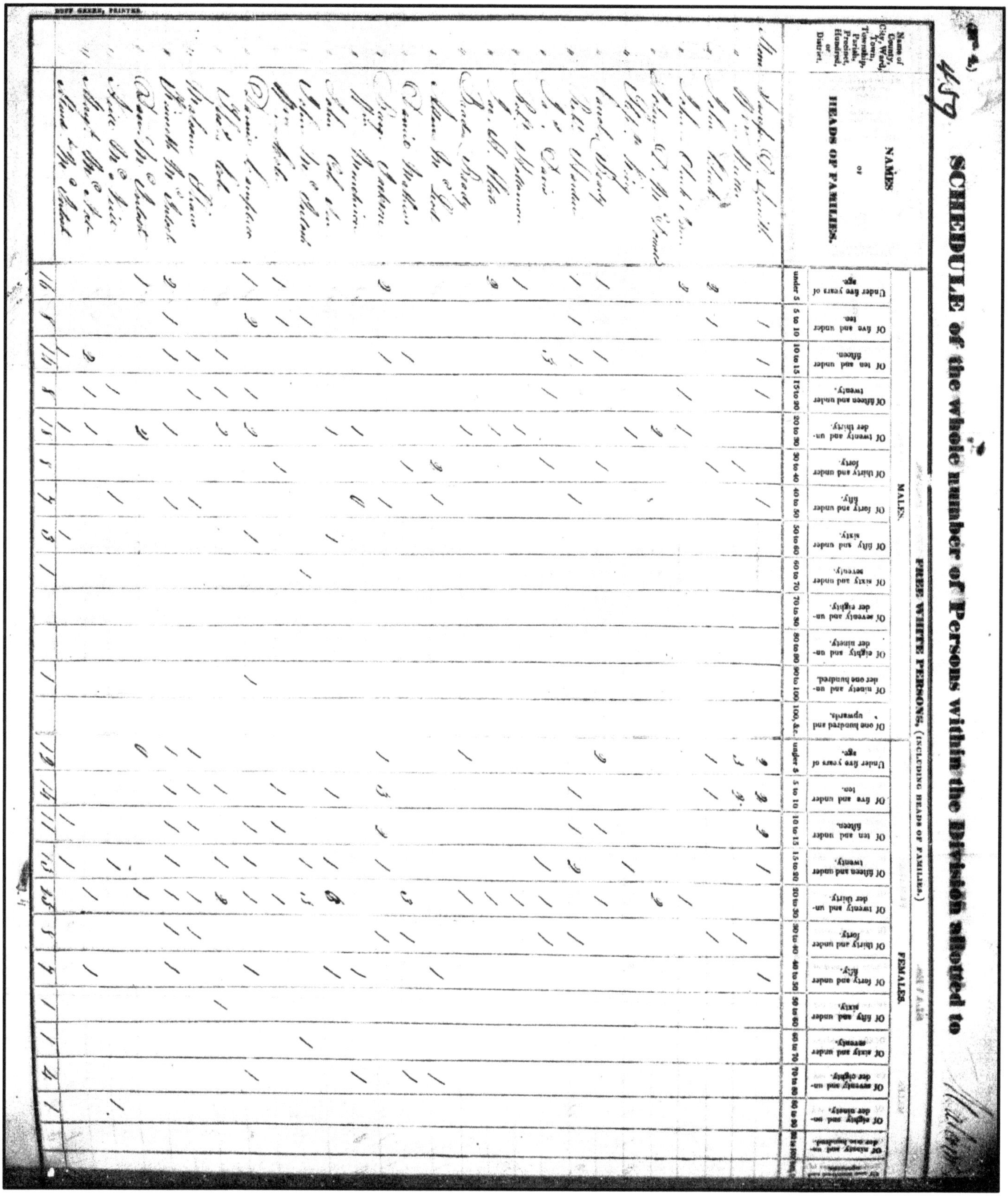

Slaves and Free Persons of Color are continued on the previous page

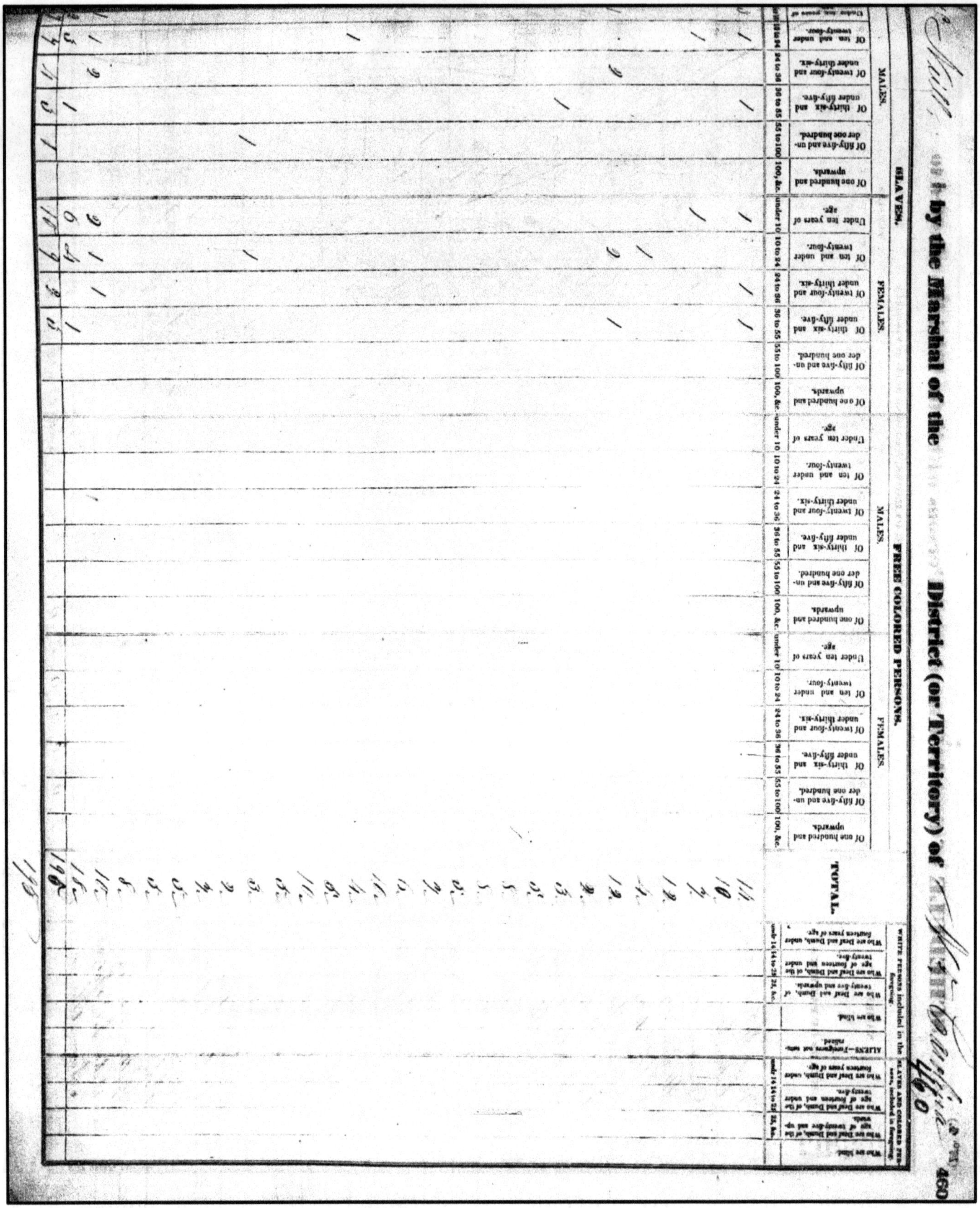
by the Marshal of the District (or Territory) of
SLAVES.
FREE COLORED PERSONS.
TOTAL.
460

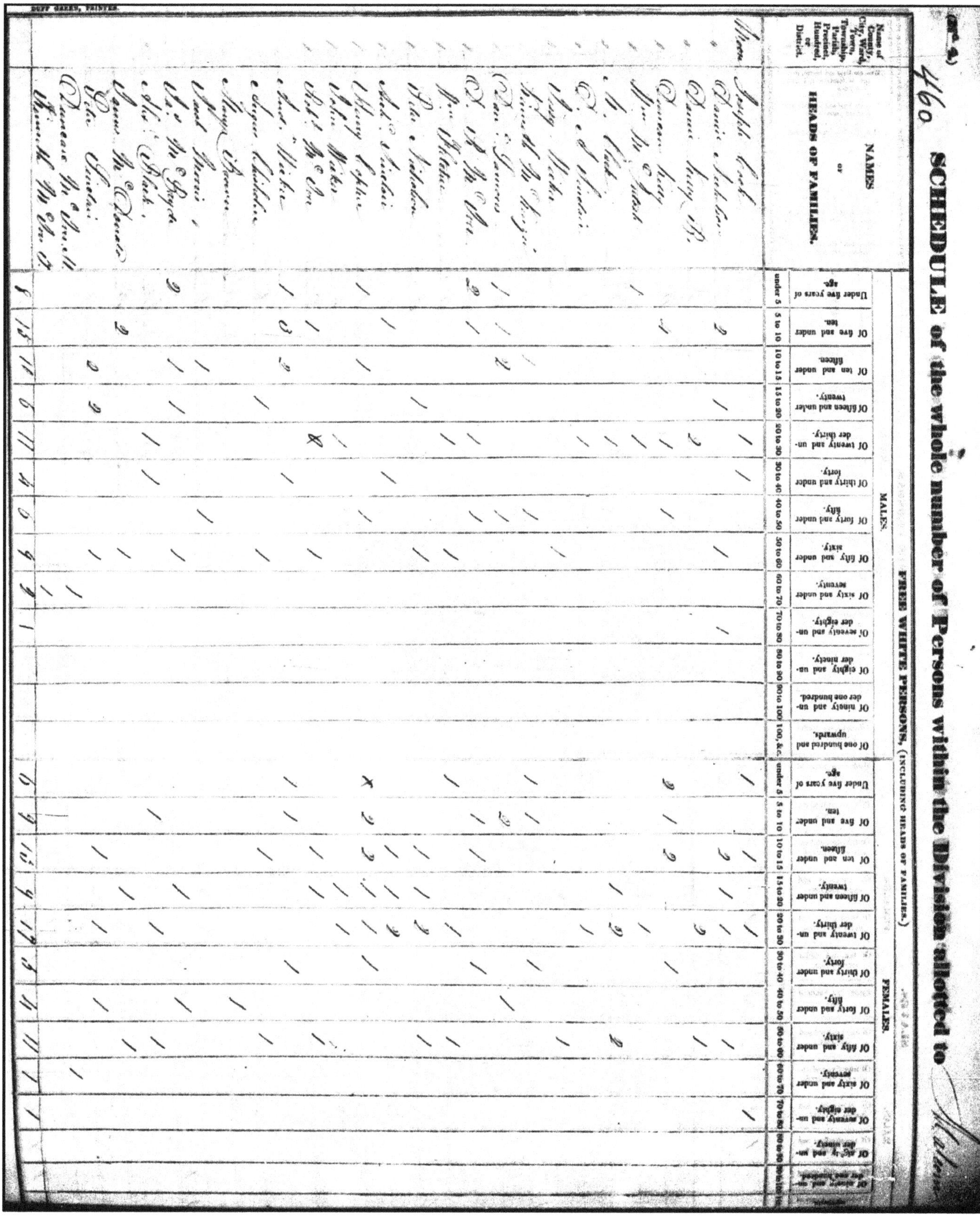

Slaves and Free Persons of Color are continued on the previous page

461

... by the Marshal of the ... District (or Territory) of ... 461

SLAVES. Males. Under ten years of age. (under 10)	Of ten and under twenty-four. (10 to 24)	Of twenty-four and under thirty-six. (24 to 36)	Of thirty-six and under fifty-five. (36 to 55)	Of fifty-five and under one hundred. (55 to 100)	Of one hundred and upwards. (100, &c.)	SLAVES. Females. Under ten years of age. (under 10)	Of ten and under twenty-four. (10 to 24)	Of twenty-four and under thirty-six. (24 to 36)	Of thirty-six and under fifty-five. (36 to 55)	Of fifty-five and under one hundred. (55 to 100)	Of one hundred and upwards. (100, &c.)	FREE COLORED PERSONS. Males. Under ten years of age. (under 10)	Of ten and under twenty-four. (10 to 24)	Of twenty-four and under thirty-six. (24 to 36)	Of thirty-six and under fifty-five. (36 to 55)	Of fifty-five and under one hundred. (55 to 100)	Of one hundred and upwards. (100, &c.)	FREE COLORED PERSONS. Females. Under ten years of age. (under 10)	Of ten and under twenty-four. (10 to 24)	Of twenty-four and under thirty-six. (24 to 36)	Of thirty-six and under fifty-five. (36 to 55)	Of fifty-five and under one hundred. (55 to 100)	Of one hundred and upwards. (100, &c.)	TOTAL.	WHITE PERSONS included in the foregoing. Who are Deaf and Dumb, under fourteen years of age. (undr 14)	Who are Deaf and Dumb, of the age of fourteen and under twenty-five. (14 to 25)	Who are Deaf and Dumb, of twenty-five and upwards. (25, &c.)	Who are blind.	ALIENS.—Foreigners not naturalized.	SLAVES AND COLORED PERSONS, included in foregoing. Who are Deaf and Dumb, under fourteen years of age. (undr 14)	Who are Deaf and Dumb, of the age of fourteen and under twenty-five. (14 to 25)	Who are Deaf and Dumb, of the age of twenty-five and upwards. (25, &c.)	Who are blind.
							1																	6									
																								5									
																								6									
							1																	6									
																								9									
																								1									
6		1				2	2	1		1														21									
5	1					1	1	1																19									
0	0					0	0	0																3									
2	1	2		1		2	2	1		1														24									
3	0			0			1	0		0														11									
																								3									
																								6									
																								6									
												4		1						1				7									
																								11									
																								5									
																								4									
																								8	1								
																								4									
																								3									
																								3									
																								8									
																								3									
			1																					8									
																								4									
																								4									
15	2	3	1	1		5	3	3		2		4		1						1				179									

198

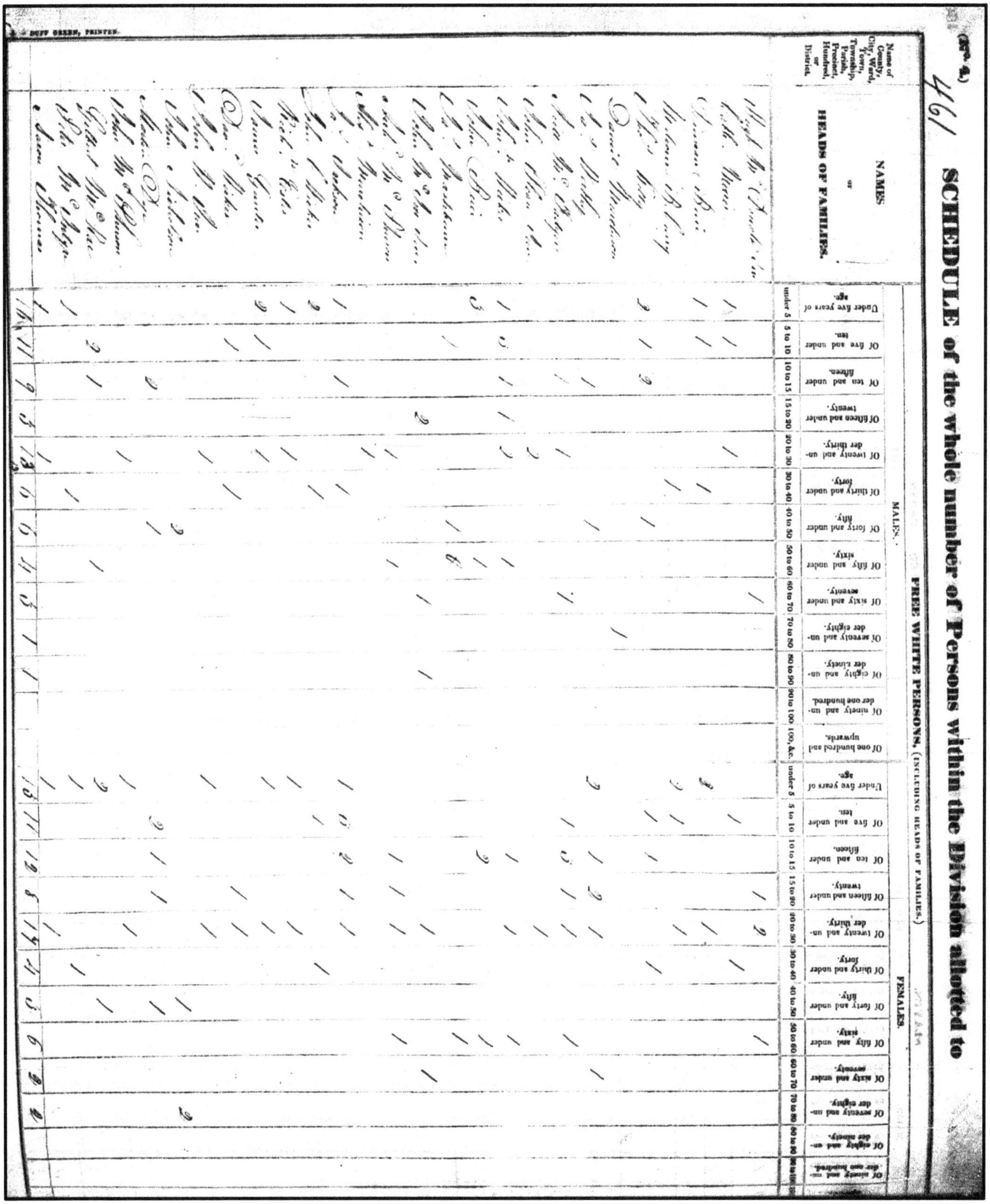

Slaves and Free Persons of Color are continued on the previous page

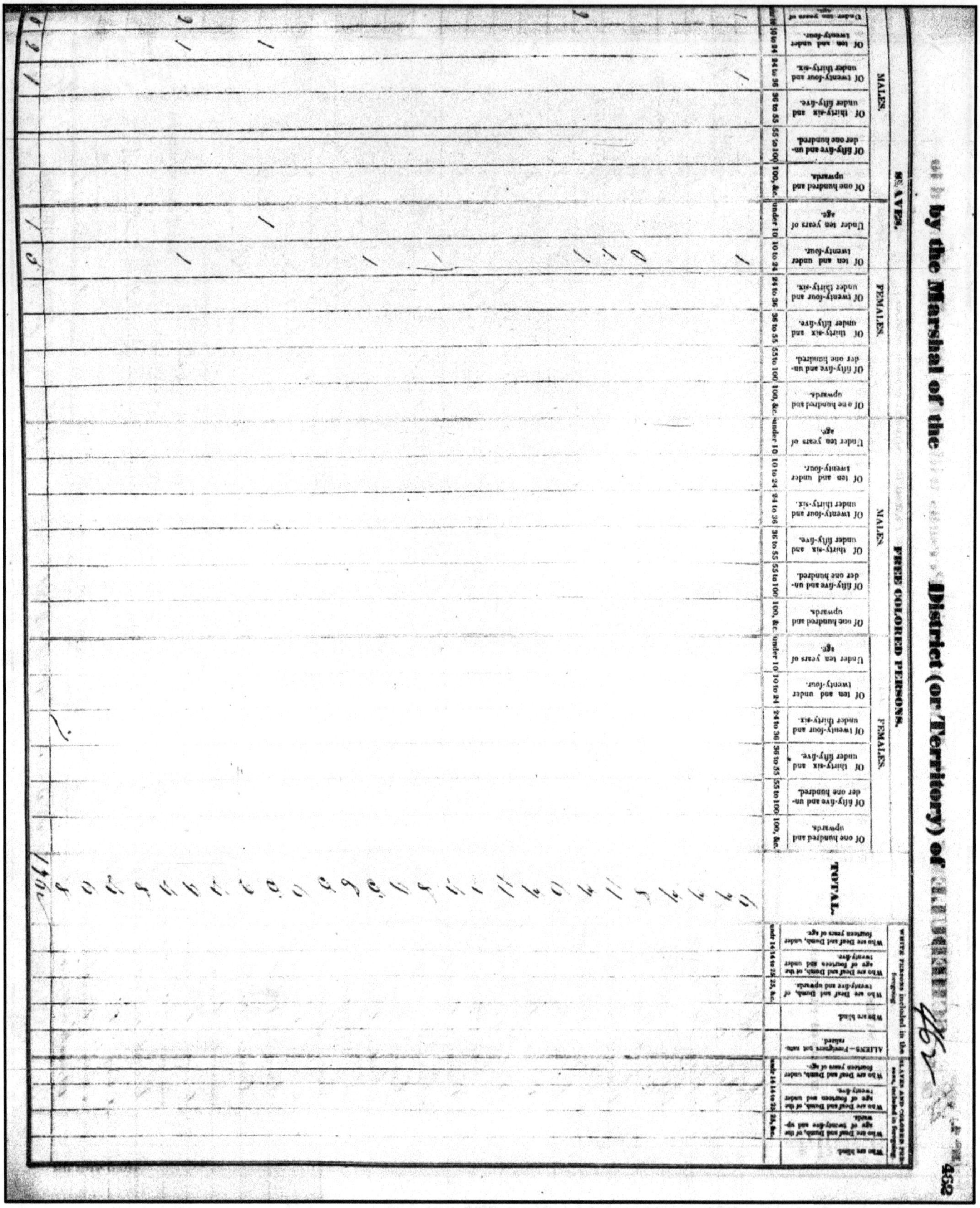
by the Marshal of the District (or Territory) of
452

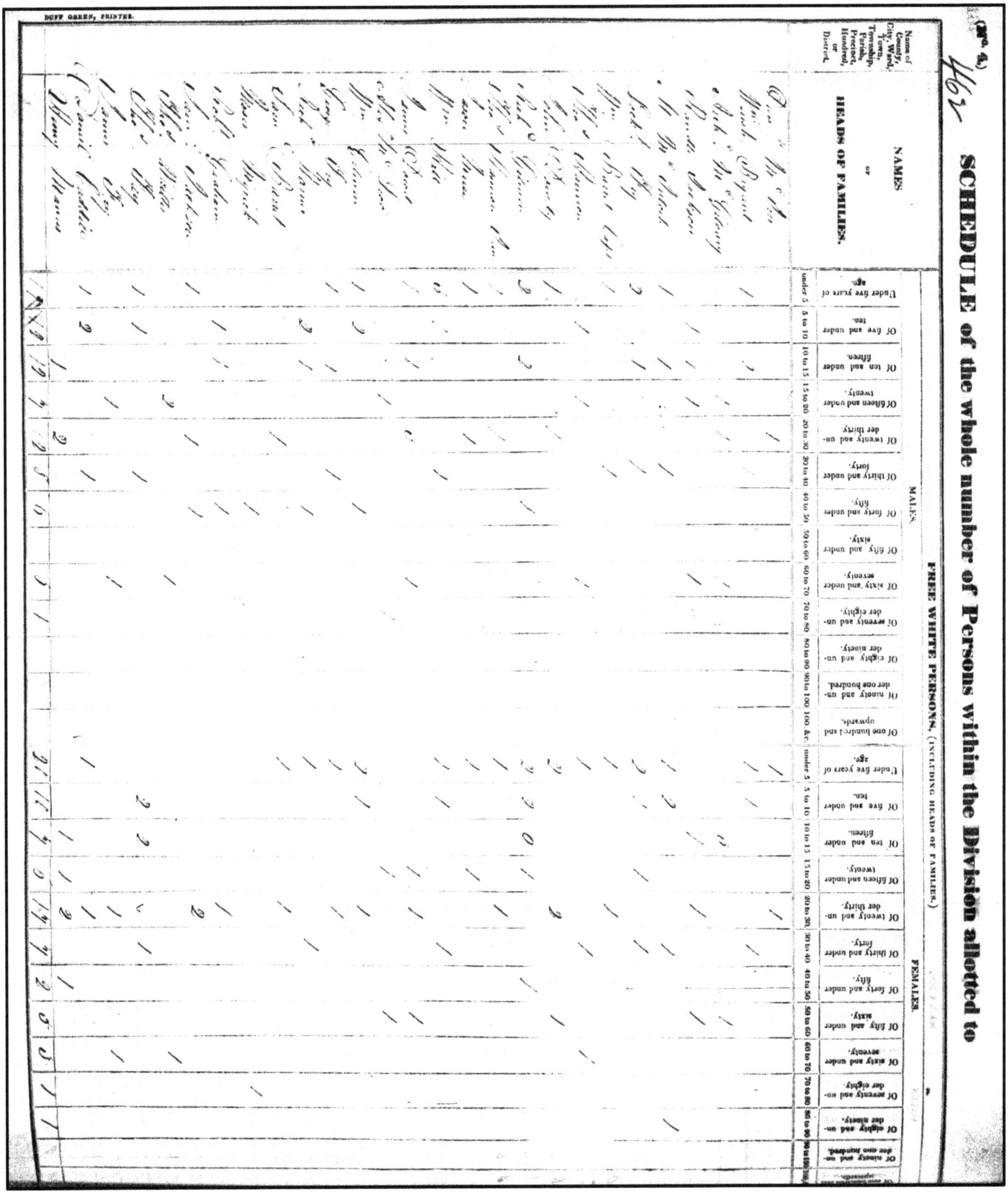

Slaves and Free Persons of Color are continued on the previous page

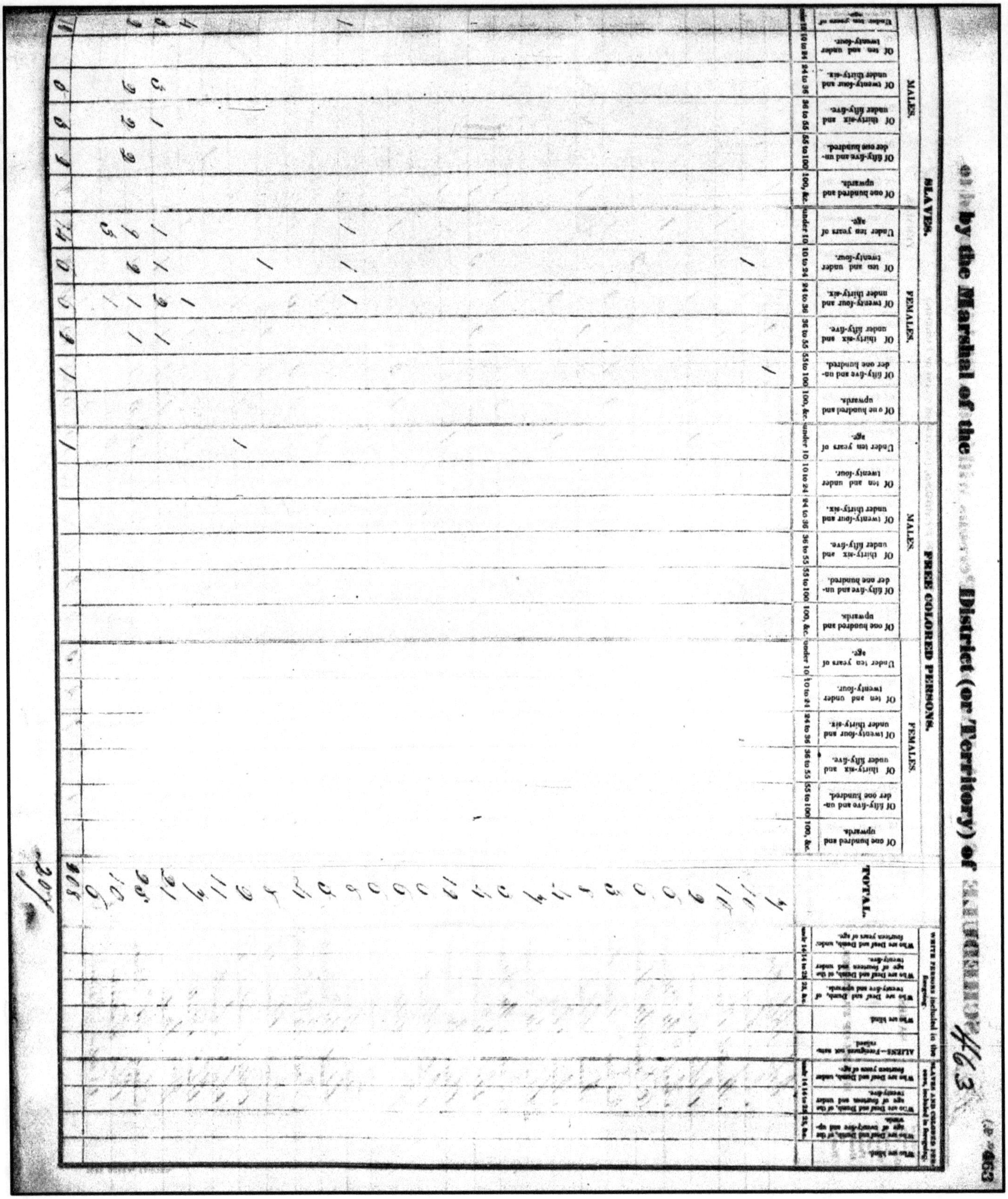
by the Marshal of the District (or Territory) of
SLAVES.
FREE COLORED PERSONS.
MALES.
FEMALES.
TOTAL.
463

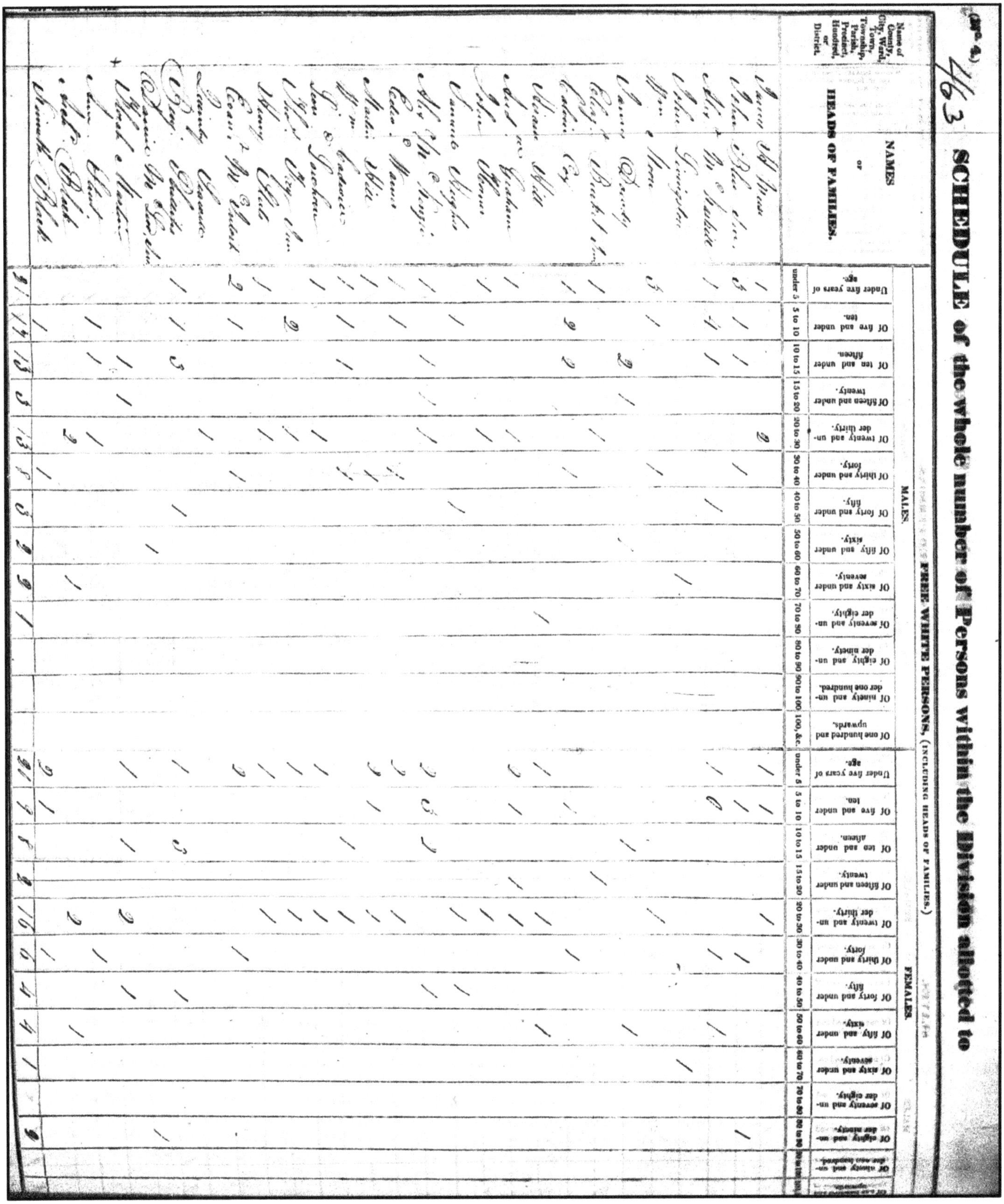

Slaves and Free Persons of Color are continued on the previous page

by the Marshal of the District (or Territory) of 464

Slaves, Males: Under ten years of age (under 10)	Of ten and under twenty-four (10 to 24)	Of twenty-four and under thirty-six (24 to 36)	Of thirty-six and under fifty-five (36 to 55)	Of fifty-five and under one hundred (55 to 100)	Of one hundred and upwards (100, &c.)	Slaves, Females: Under ten years of age (under 10)	Of ten and under twenty-four (10 to 24)	Of twenty-four and under thirty-six (24 to 36)	Of thirty-six and under fifty-five (36 to 55)	Of fifty-five and under one hundred (55 to 100)	Of one hundred and upwards (100, &c.)	Free Colored Persons, Males: Under ten years of age (under 10)	Of ten and under twenty-four (10 to 24)	Of twenty-four and under thirty-six (24 to 36)	Of thirty-six and under fifty-five (36 to 55)	Of fifty-five and under one hundred (55 to 100)	Of one hundred and upwards (100, &c.)	Free Colored Persons, Females: Under ten years of age (under 10)	Of ten and under twenty-four (10 to 24)	Of twenty-four and under thirty-six (24 to 36)	Of thirty-six and under fifty-five (36 to 55)	Of fifty-five and under one hundred (55 to 100)	Of one hundred and upwards (100, &c.)	TOTAL.	White persons included in the foregoing: Who are Deaf and Dumb, under fourteen years of age (under 14)	Who are Deaf and Dumb, of the age of fourteen and under twenty-five (14 to 25)	Who are Deaf and Dumb, of twenty-five and upwards (25, &c.)	Who are blind	Aliens—Foreigners not naturalized	Slaves and colored persons included in the foregoing: Who are Deaf and Dumb, under fourteen years of age (under 14)	Who are Deaf and Dumb, of the age of fourteen and under twenty-five (14 to 25)	Who are Deaf and Dumb, of the age of twenty-five and upwards (25, &c.)	Who are blind
1								1																10									
3						1	1																	11									
																								7									
																								5									
																								3									
							1																	8									
																								11									
1		1	1			2		1		1														13									
		1																						11									
																								9									
																								5									
																								7									
						1	1																	5									
																								1									
																								11	10								
												4	1	2		1		4	3	3		1		19									
												2	2		1			2		2				9									
																								8									
																								14									
																								4									
1	1						1																	9									
4		1				1		1	1	1														11									
																								4									
																								9									
																								9									
																								5									
																								6									
11	1	3	1			3	4	3	1	2		6	3	2	1	1		6	3	5		1		222							2		
																								221									

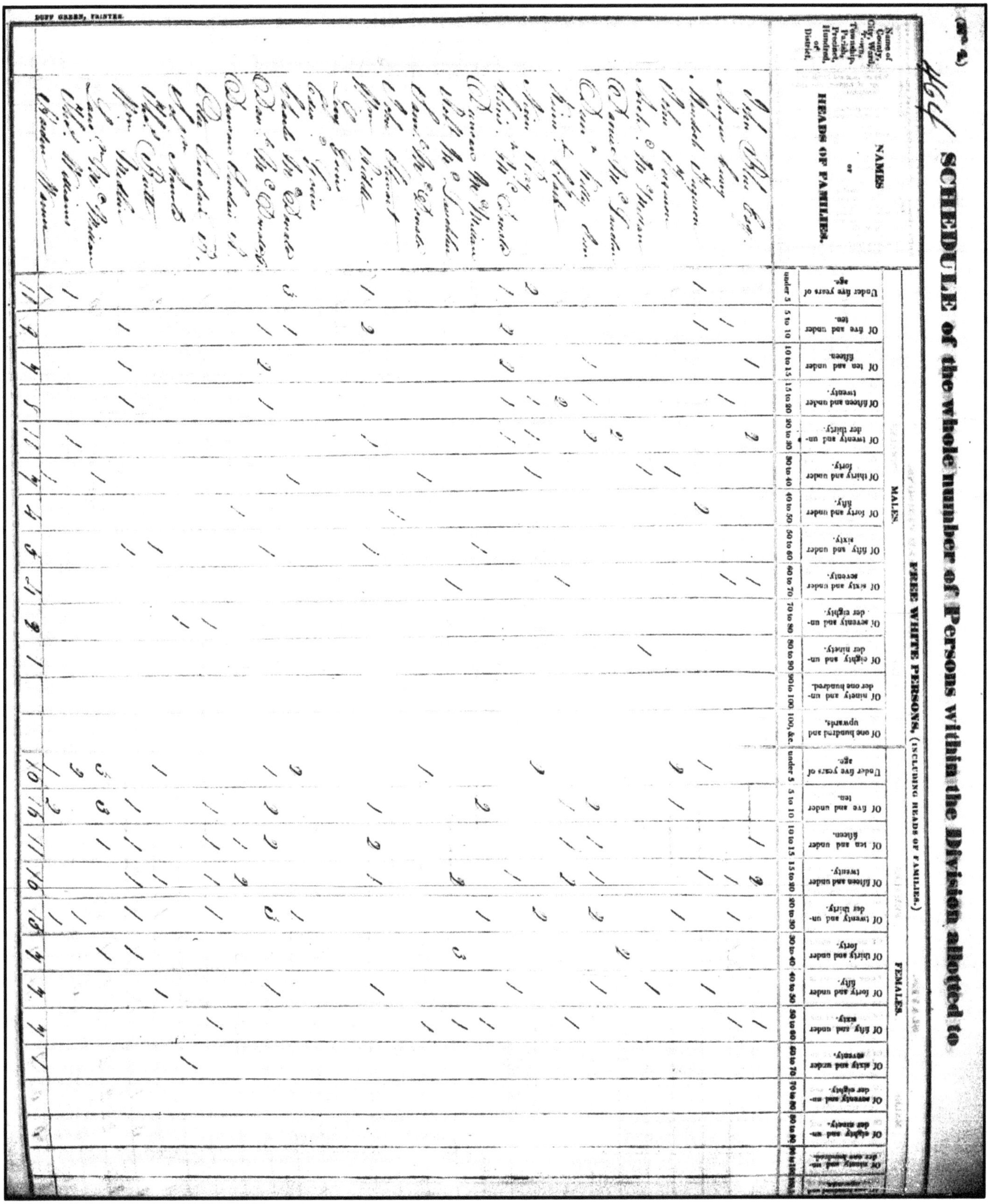

(Nº 4.) 464 SCHEDULE of the whole number of Persons within the Division allotted to

NAMES OR HEADS OF FAMILIES.	M under 5	M 5 to 10	M 10 to 15	M 15 to 20	M 20 to 30	M 30 to 40	M 40 to 50	M 50 to 60	M 60 to 70	M 70 to 80	M 80 to 90	M 90 to 100	M 100, &c.	F under 5	F 5 to 10	F 10 to 15	F 15 to 20	F 20 to 30	F 30 to 40	F 40 to 50	F 50 to 60	F 60 to 70	F 70 to 80	F 80 to 90	F 90 to 100
John Blue Esq.			1		2				1							1	2				1				
Angus Curry		1		1					1								1	1			1				
Murdoch Ferguson	1	1					2							1			1			1					
John Ferguson						1								2	1			1							
Archd McMillan						1					1									1					
Daniel McLauchlin					2														2						
Duncan Kelly Sen.			1	1	2										2	1	1	2		1					
Kennth Clark				2					1						1	1	2				1				
Nevin Ray	2			1	1	1								2				2							
Chris. McDonald	1	2	2	1	1												1			1					
Duncan McMillan								1							2			1			1				
Robt McLauchlin									1								2		3		1				
Saml McDonald						1								1							1				
John Stewart							1																		
Wm Riddle	1	2			1			1							1	2	1			1					
Lucy Goins																									
Edwd Goins																									
Charles McDonald	3	1				1								2				1							
Danl McDonald S.		1	2	1				1						1	2	2		3		1					
Duncan Sinclair R.							1									1	2								
Peter Sinclair B.										1					1	1	1	1			1				
Solmn Arnold										1												1			
Thos Bratt								1						1			1			1					
Wm Medlin		1	1	1				1							1	1	1	1	1						
Laurn McMillan						1								3	3	1			1						
Thos Williams	1				1									2				1							
Harden Warren	1					1								1	2			1							
	11	9	7	8	11	7	4	5	4	2	1			10	16	11	16	15	7	7	7	1			

DUFF GREEN, PRINTER.

Slaves and Free Persons of Color are continued on the previous page

by the Marshal of the District (or Territory) of 465

465

SLAVES. MALES. Under ten years of age.	Of ten and under twenty-four.	Of twenty-four and under thirty-six.	Of thirty-six and under fifty-five.	Of fifty-five and under one hundred.	Of one hundred and upwards.	SLAVES. FEMALES. Under ten years of age.	Of ten and under twenty-four.	Of twenty-four and under thirty-six.	Of thirty-six and under fifty-five.	Of fifty-five and under one hundred.	Of one hundred and upwards.	FREE COLORED PERSONS. MALES. Under ten years of age.	Of ten and under twenty-four.	Of twenty-four and under thirty-six.	Of thirty-six and under fifty-five.	Of fifty-five and under one hundred.	Of one hundred and upwards.	FREE COLORED PERSONS. FEMALES. Under ten years of age.	Of ten and under twenty-four.	Of twenty-four and under thirty-six.	Of thirty-six and under fifty-five.	Of fifty-five and under one hundred.	Of one hundred and upwards.	TOTAL.	WHITE PERSONS included in the foregoing. Who are Deaf and Dumb, under fourteen years of age.	Who are Deaf and Dumb, of the age of fourteen and under twenty-five.	Who are Deaf and Dumb, of twenty-five and upwards.	Who are blind.	ALIENS—Foreigners not naturalized.	SLAVES AND COLORED PERSONS included in foregoing. Who are Deaf and Dumb, under fourteen years of age.	Who are Deaf and Dumb, of the age of fourteen and under twenty-five.	Who are Deaf and Dumb, of the age of twenty-five and upwards.	Who are blind.
under 10	10 to 24	24 to 36	36 to 55	55 to 100	100, &c.	under 10	10 to 24	24 to 36	36 to 55	55 to 100	100, &c.	under 10	10 to 24	24 to 36	36 to 55	55 to 100	100, &c.	under 10	10 to 24	24 to 36	36 to 55	55 to 100	100, &c.		under 14	14 to 25	25, &c.			under 14	14 to 25	25, &c.	
																								6									
																								8									
																								10									
																								4									
																								8									
																								10									
																								8									
																								4									
		1																						9									
1																								11									
	1	1		1		1	1																	11									
																								9									
																								2									
																								9									
									1															14									
																								7									
																								9									
		1																						10									
																								8									
																								8									
																								2									
																								8									
	3			1					1	1														13									
	1			1																				7									
																								9									
	0																							2									
	1																							4									
1	5	6		3		1	1		2	1														192									

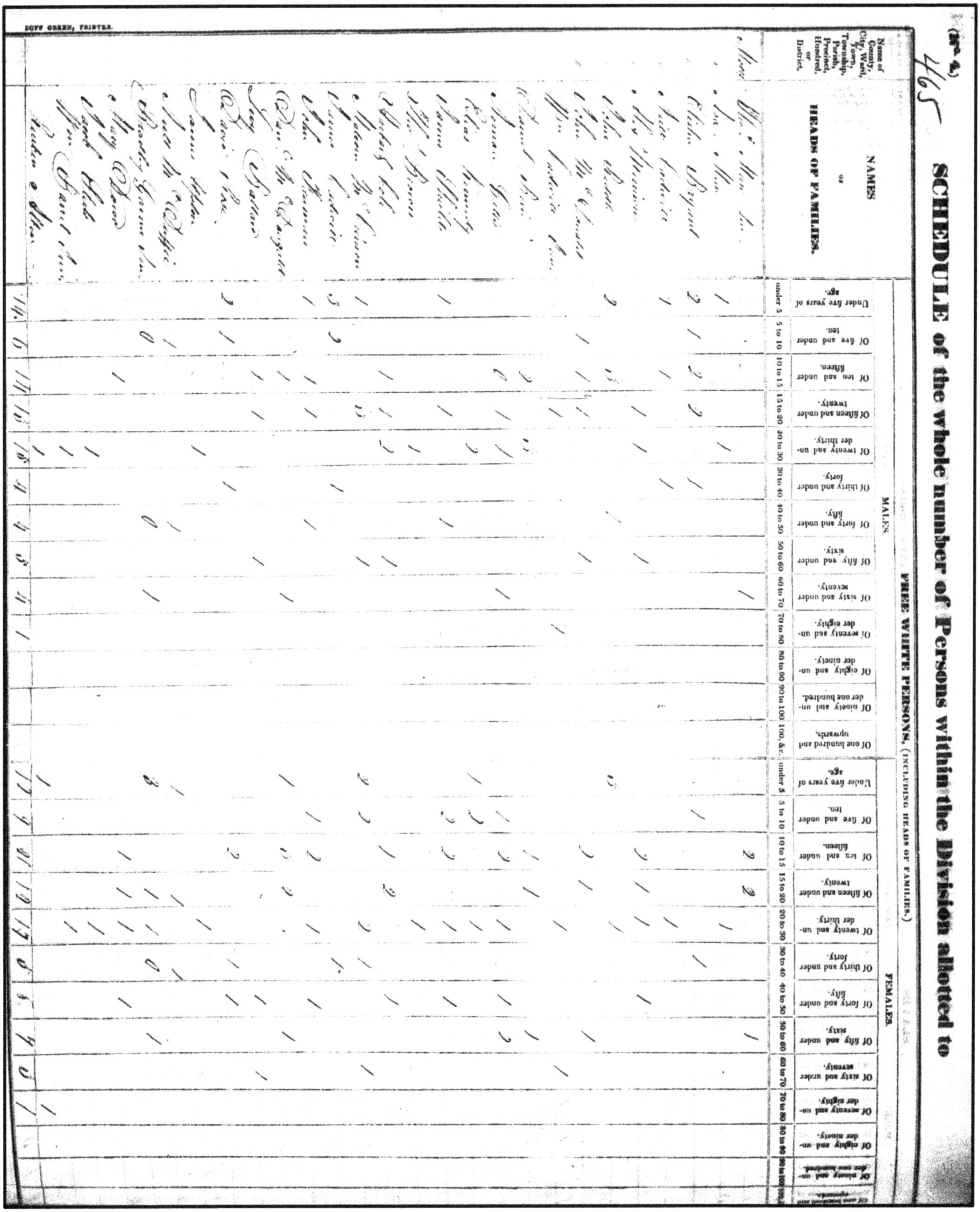
(No. 4.) 465

SCHEDULE of the whole number of Persons within the Division allotted to

DUFF GREEN, PRINTER.

Name of County, City, Ward, Town, Township, Parish, Precinct, Hundred, or District. | NAMES OF HEADS OF FAMILIES. | FREE WHITE PERSONS, (INCLUDING HEADS OF FAMILIES.) MALES: Under five years of age (under 5); Of five and under ten (5 to 10); Of ten and under fifteen (10 to 15); Of fifteen and under twenty (15 to 20); Of twenty and under thirty (20 to 30); Of thirty and under forty (30 to 40); Of forty and under fifty (40 to 50); Of fifty and under sixty (50 to 60); Of sixty and under seventy (60 to 70); Of seventy and under eighty (70 to 80); Of eighty and under ninety (80 to 90); Of ninety and under one hundred (90 to 100); Of one hundred and upwards (100, &c.) | FEMALES: Under five years of age (under 5); Of five and under ten (5 to 10); Of ten and under fifteen (10 to 15); Of fifteen and under twenty (15 to 20); Of twenty and under thirty (20 to 30); Of thirty and under forty (30 to 40); Of forty and under fifty (40 to 50); Of fifty and under sixty (50 to 60); Of sixty and under seventy (60 to 70); Of seventy and under eighty (70 to 80); Of eighty and under ninety (80 to 90); Of ninety and under one hundred (90 to 100); Of one hundred and upwards

Slaves and Free Persons of Color are continued on the previous page

466 ... by the Marshal of the ... District (or Territory) of ... 466

SLAVES. Males: Under ten years of age (under 10)	Of ten and under twenty-four (10 to 24)	Of twenty-four and under thirty-six (24 to 36)	Of thirty-six and under fifty-five (36 to 55)	Of fifty-five and under one hundred (55 to 100)	Of one hundred and upwards (100, &c.)	Females: Under ten years of age (under 10)	Of ten and under twenty-four (10 to 24)	Of twenty-four and under thirty-six (24 to 36)	Of thirty-six and under fifty-five (36 to 55)	Of fifty-five and under one hundred (55 to 100)	Of one hundred and upwards (100, &c.)	TOTAL
												8
3		1					1	1				10
												10
1	1						1					7
												6
1		1				3	1	1				9
												10
1						2	8	1				10
												5
1						1						9
												8
												5
												6
												11
	8											11
												10
4	3	1				2	2		2			23
7	3	4	2	1		2	2	1	2	1		35
												4
5	5		3	1		5	5	5	1	1		80
2								1				11
1								1				14
												8
	1											4
												8
												5
												8
31	16	7	7	9		16	13	11	5	9		318
												304

FREE COLORED PERSONS. Males / Females (all columns blank). WHITE PERSONS included in the foregoing: Deaf and Dumb, Blind; ALIENS; SLAVES AND COLORED PERSONS included in the foregoing: Deaf and Dumb, Blind (blank).

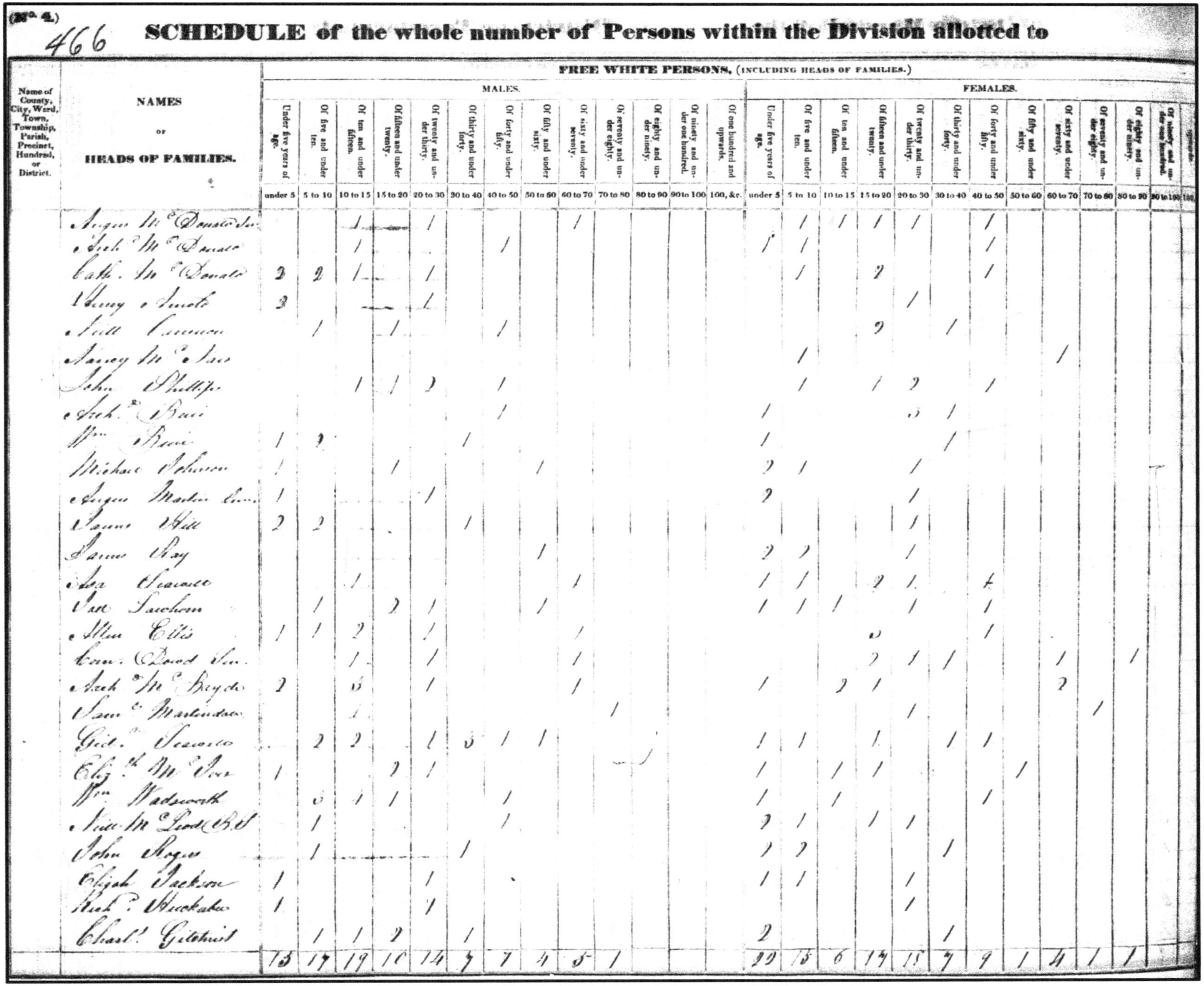

(No. 4.) 466

SCHEDULE of the whole number of Persons within the Division allotted to

FREE WHITE PERSONS, (INCLUDING HEADS OF FAMILIES.)

NAMES OR HEADS OF FAMILIES	M under 5	M 5 to 10	M 10 to 15	M 15 to 20	M 20 to 30	M 30 to 40	M 40 to 50	M 50 to 60	M 60 to 70	M 70 to 80	M 80 to 90	M 90 to 100	M 100, &c.	F under 5	F 5 to 10	F 10 to 15	F 15 to 20	F 20 to 30	F 30 to 40	F 40 to 50	F 50 to 60	F 60 to 70	F 70 to 80	F 80 to 90	F 90 to 100	F 100, &c.
Angus McDonald Sen.			1		1				1						1	1	1	1		1						
Arch. McDonald			1				1							1	1					1						
Cath. McDonald	2	2	1		1										1		2			1						
Henry Smith (?)	2				1													1								
Neill Cameron		1		1			1										2		1							
Nancy McNair (?)															1							1				
John Phillips			1	1	2		1								1		1	2		1						
Archd. Bain (?)							1							1				3	1							
Wm. Rowe (?)	1	2				1								1					1							
Michael Johnson	1			1				1						2	1			1								
Angus Martin Sen.	1				1									2				1								
James Hill	2	2				1												1								
James Ray								1						2	2			1								
Asa Seawell			1						1					1	1		2	1		1						
Neill Jackson		1		2	1			1						1	1	1		1		1						
Allen Ellis	1	1	2		1				1								3			1						
Cam. Dowd Sen.			1		1				1								2	1	1			1		1		
Arch. McBryde	2		3		1				1					1		2	1					2				
Saml. Martindale			1							1								1					1			
Gid. Seawell		2	2		1	3	1	1						1	1		1		1	1						
Elizth. McIver	1			2	1									1		1	1				1					
Wm. Wadsworth		3	1	1			1							1		1				1						
Neill McLeod B.S.		1					1							2	1		1	1								
John Rogers		1				1								2	2				1							
Elijah Jackson	1				1									1	1			1								
Richd. Huckabee	1				1													1								
Charls. Gilchrist		1	1	2		1								2					1							
	13	17	19	10	14	7	7	4	5	1				22	15	6	17	15	7	9	1	4	1	1		

Slaves and Free Persons of Color are continued on the previous page

Mc Niel ... by the Marshal of the ... District (or Territory) of North Carolina 467

SLAVES. MALES.						SLAVES. FEMALES.						FREE COLORED PERSONS. MALES.						FREE COLORED PERSONS. FEMALES.						TOTAL.	White persons included in the foregoing: Who are Deaf and Dumb, under fourteen years of age.
under 10	10 to 24	24 to 36	36 to 55	55 to 100	100, &c.	under 10	10 to 24	24 to 36	36 to 55	55 to 100	100, &c.	under 10	10 to 24	24 to 36	36 to 55	55 to 100	100, &c.	under 10	10 to 24	24 to 36	36 to 55	55 to 100	100, &c.		under 14
																								4	
1									1															6	
																								6	
																								4	
																								3	
						1	1																	10	9
								1																5	
	1		1				1																	8	
																								8	
																								7	
							1																	7	
																								9	
																								12	
4	1		1			3			1	1														15	
						2		1																5	
1							2																	13	
																								7	
																								3	
																								7	
																								7	
1							1																	10	
																								2	
1								1																4	
																								9	
																								12	
		2	1																					6	
																								4	
8	2	2	3			6	9	5	2	1														192	
																								191	

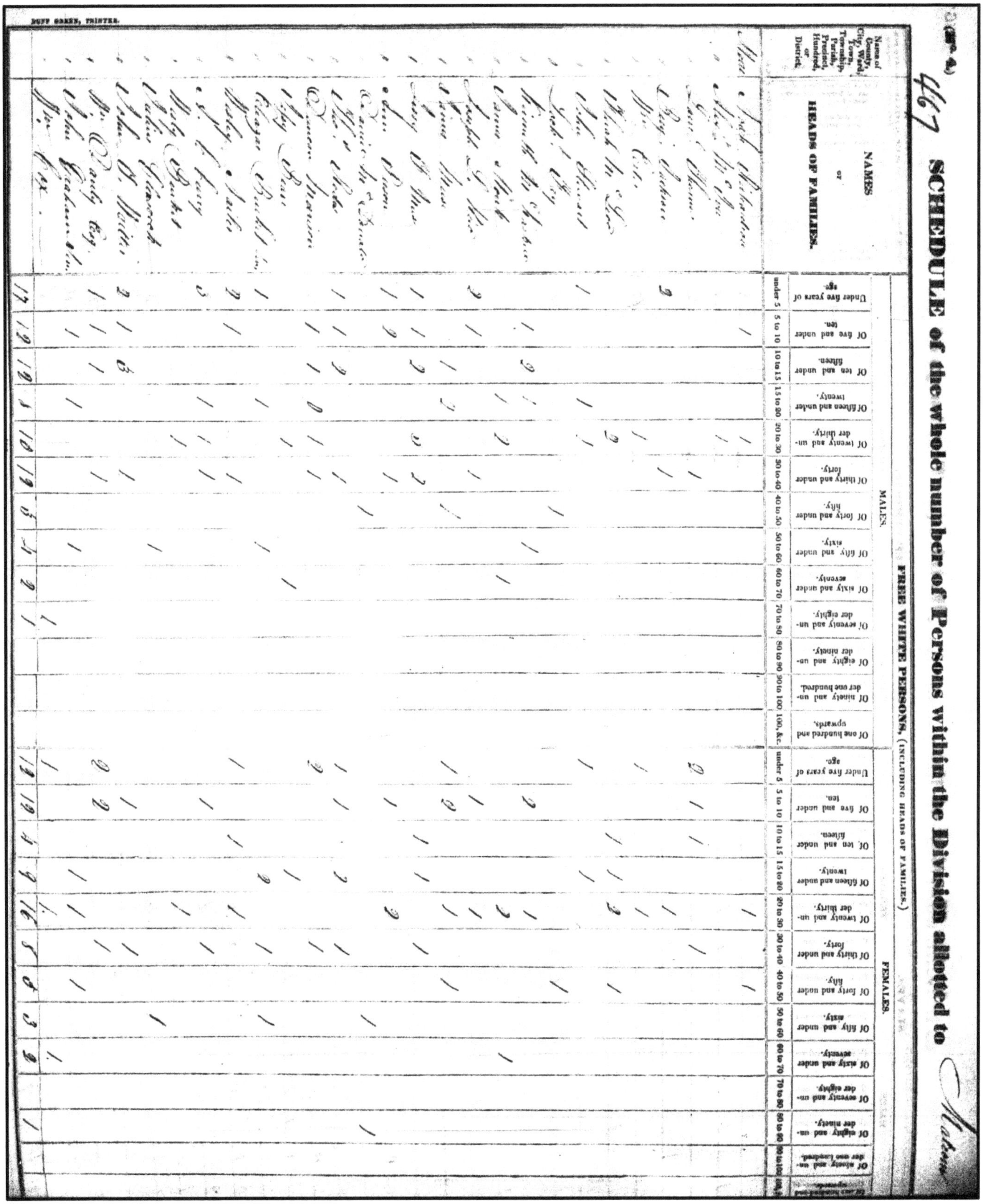

(Nº 4.) 467 SCHEDULE of the whole number of Persons within the Division allotted to Malcom

FREE WHITE PERSONS, (INCLUDING HEADS OF FAMILIES.)

Name of County, City, Ward, Town, Township, Parish, Precinct, Hundred, or District.	NAMES OF HEADS OF FAMILIES.	M under 5	M 5 to 10	M 10 to 15	M 15 to 20	M 20 to 30	M 30 to 40	M 40 to 50	M 50 to 60	M 60 to 70	M 70 to 80	M 80 to 90	M 90 to 100	M 100, &c.	F under 5	F 5 to 10	F 10 to 15	F 15 to 20	F 20 to 30	F 30 to 40	F 40 to 50	F 50 to 60	F 60 to 70	F 70 to 80	F 80 to 90	F 90 to 100	F 100, &c.
Moore	Noah Richardson		1			1													1		1						
"	Alexr McIver					1																					
"	Danl Thomas						1								2	1	1			1							
"	Benj Jackson	2					1												1								
"	Wm Cole					1									1				1								
"	Micah McLeod					2											1	1	2		1						
"	John Stewart	1			1	1									1			1									
"	Lachn Fry							1													1						
"	Kenneth McKenzie		1	2	1				1							2			1								
"	James Monk				1	2				1									2				1				
"	Joseph L. Weir	2	1				1									1			1								
"	James Muse			1	2			1							1	2			1		1						
"	Levy O. Muse	1	1	2		2	2										1	1		1							
"	Ann Pason	1	2				1									1			2								
"	Daniel McDonald							1														1			1		
"	Thos Rhodes	1	1	2			1								1	1		2		1							
"	Duncan Morrison		1	1	0	1	1								2					1							
"	Absy Bean					1				1								1									
"	Eleazar Buckel Sen	1			1				1									2		1		1					
"	Wesley Sailer	2	1				1								1		1		1								
"	A. C. Curry	3			1	1	1									1				1							
"	Wesly Buckel					1													1								
"	Julius Glascock								1													1					
"	John O. Waller	2	1	3			1									1				1							
"	Wm Dauly Esq.	1	1	1			1								2	2				1							
"	John Graham Sen		1		1				1									1	1		1						
"	Wm Cox										1				1				1				1				
		17	12	12	8	10	19	5	4	2	1				12	19	4	9	16	5	8	3	2		1		

DUFF GREEN, PRINTER.

Slaves and Free Persons of Color are continued on the previous page

Mc Neill ... by the Marshal of the ... District (or Territory) of N Carolina 468

Slaves Males: Under ten	Of ten and under twenty-four (10 to 24)	Of twenty-four and under thirty-six (24 to 36)	Of thirty-six and under fifty-five (36 to 55)	Of fifty-five and under one hundred (55 to 100)	Of one hundred and upwards (100, &c.)	Slaves Females: Under ten years of age (under 10)	Of ten and under twenty-four (10 to 24)	Of twenty-four and under thirty-six (24 to 36)	Of thirty-six and under fifty-five (36 to 55)	Of fifty-five and under one hundred (55 to 100)	Of one hundred and upwards (100, &c.)	Free Colored Males: Under ten years of age (under 10)	Of ten and under twenty-four (10 to 24)	Of twenty-four and under thirty-six (24 to 36)	Of thirty-six and under fifty-five (36 to 55)	Of fifty-five and under one hundred (55 to 100)	Of one hundred and upwards (100, &c.)	Free Colored Females: Under ten years of age (under 10)	Of ten and under twenty-four (10 to 24)	Of twenty-four and under thirty-six (24 to 36)	Of thirty-six and under fifty-five (36 to 55)	Of fifty-five and under one hundred (55 to 100)	Of one hundred and upwards (100, &c.)	TOTAL	White persons included in the foregoing: Who are Deaf and Dumb, under fourteen years of age (under 14)	Who are Deaf and Dumb, of the age of fourteen and under twenty-five (14 to 25)	Who are Deaf and Dumb, of twenty-five and upwards (25, &c.)	Who are blind	ALIENS—Foreigners not naturalized	Slaves and colored persons included in the foregoing: Who are Deaf and Dumb, under fourteen years of age (under 14)	Who are Deaf and Dumb, of the age of fourteen and under twenty-five (14 to 25)	Who are Deaf and Dumb, of twenty-five and upwards (25, &c.)	Who are blind
																								10									
																								7									
																								3									
		1						X																3									
																								3									
																								3									
																								4									
	1									1														8									
	1					2																		6									
																								2									
						1																		3									
																								21	21								
4	2					3		2																8									
																								13									
																								6									
																								5									
																								19									
4	2	2																						24									
4	1	1	3			5	2		2	3														11									
1							1		1															8									
																								4									
																								7	4								
																								8									
																								8									
								1																7									
2						1			1															11									
																								26									
3	4	1	1	1		3	3	3	1	1														239	3								
[illegible]	11	3	4	1		13	5	2	3	3																							

335 , 3,

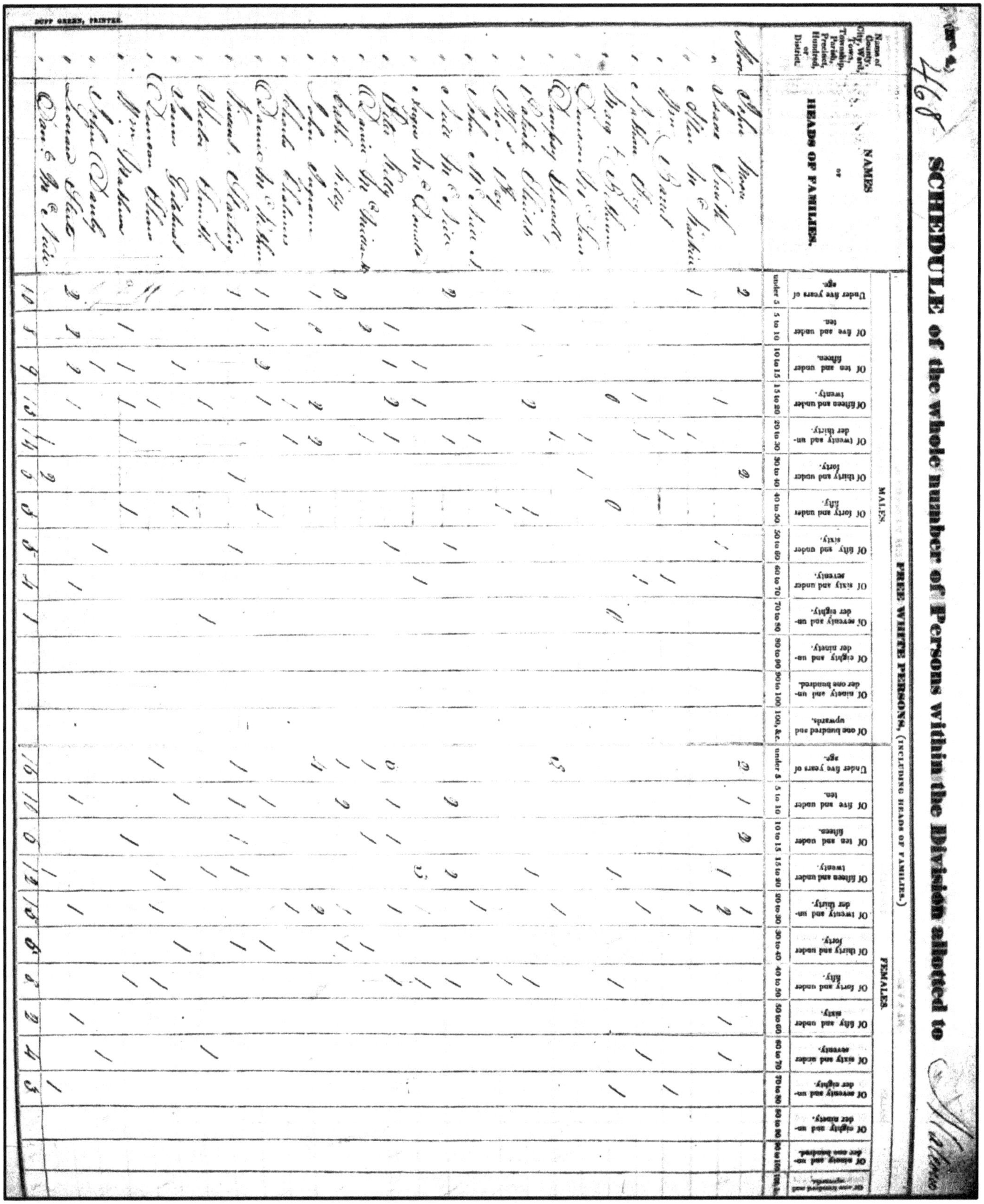

468 SCHEDULE of the whole number of Persons within the Division allotted to Malcom

DUFF GREEN, PRINTER.

Name of County, City, Ward, Town, Township, Parish, Precinct, Hundred, or District.	NAMES of HEADS OF FAMILIES.	FREE WHITE PERSONS, (including heads of families.) MALES. Under five years of age. (under 5)	Of five and under ten. (5 to 10)	Of ten and under fifteen. (10 to 15)	Of fifteen and under twenty. (15 to 20)	Of twenty and under thirty. (20 to 30)	Of thirty and under forty. (30 to 40)	Of forty and under fifty. (40 to 50)	Of fifty and under sixty. (50 to 60)	Of sixty and under seventy. (60 to 70)	Of seventy and under eighty. (70 to 80)	Of eighty and under ninety. (80 to 90)	Of ninety and under one hundred. (90 to 100)	Of one hundred and upwards. (100, &c.)	FEMALES. Under five years of age. (under 5)	Of five and under ten. (5 to 10)	Of ten and under fifteen. (10 to 15)	Of fifteen and under twenty. (15 to 20)	Of twenty and under thirty. (20 to 30)	Of thirty and under forty. (30 to 40)	Of forty and under fifty. (40 to 50)	Of fifty and under sixty. (50 to 60)	Of sixty and under seventy. (60 to 70)	Of seventy and under eighty. (70 to 80)	Of eighty and under ninety. (80 to 90)	Of ninety and under one hundred. (90 to 100)	Of one hundred and upwards. (100, &c.)
Moore	John Moore	2					2								2	1	2		1								
″	Isaac Smith				1				1									1	2			1	1				
″	Allen McKaskill	1				1													1								
″	Wm Barrett					1				1														1			
″	Nathan Fry				1	1				1									1				1				
″	Margt Bethune				0			0			0							1			1			1			
″	Duncan McLean					1	1																				
″	Dempsy Dowell					1									3				1								
″	Patrick Shields		1		2			1										1			1						
″	Thos Fry							1													1						
″	John McNeill Sr					1													1								
″	Neill McNeill	2				1			1							2		2			1						
″	Angus McDonald			1	1					1								3	1		1						
″	Peter Kelly		1	1	2	1			1						0	1	1		1		1						
″	Daniel McMillan		2			1									1		1			1							
″	Cath. Kelly	0													1	2			1	1							
″	John Ingram	1	1		2	2									4				2								
″	Charles Chalmers				1	1													1								
″	Daniel McKethan	1	1	2	1			1								1				1							
″	Vincent Sterling	1					1		1						1	1	1	1		1							
″	Hector Smith				1						1							1					1				
″	James Gilchrist			1				1								1				1							
″	Duncan Shaw				1										1			1	1		1						
″	Wm Mathews		1	1	1	1		1									1				1						
″	John Dauly			1					1														1				
″	Leonard Stutts	2	2	2	1					1						1			1			1					
″	Danl McNeill					1	2											1						1			
		10	8	9	13	14	6	3	5	4	1				16	10	6	12	15	6	6	2	4	3			

Slaves and Free Persons of Color are continued on the previous page

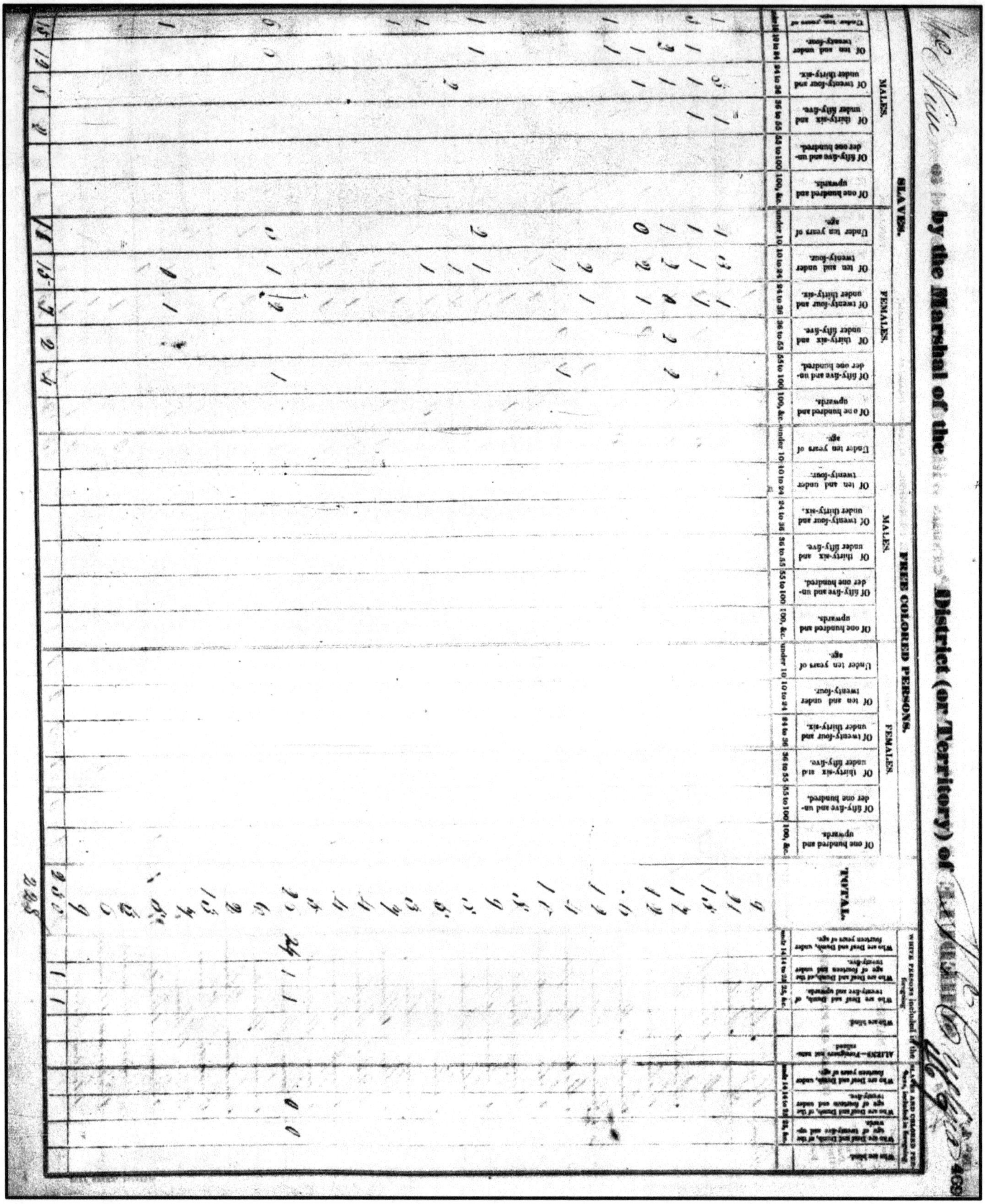

... by the Marshal of the ... District (or Territory) of ... 469

Slaves, Males, under 10	Slaves, Males, 10 to 24	Slaves, Males, 24 to 36	Slaves, Males, 36 to 55	Slaves, Males, 55 to 100	Slaves, Males, 100, &c.	Slaves, Females, under 10	Slaves, Females, 10 to 24	Slaves, Females, 24 to 36	Slaves, Females, 36 to 55	Slaves, Females, 55 to 100	Slaves, Females, 100, &c.	Free Colored, Males, under 10	Free Colored, Males, 10 to 24	Free Colored, Males, 24 to 36	Free Colored, Males, 36 to 55	Free Colored, Males, 55 to 100	Free Colored, Males, 100, &c.	Free Colored, Females, under 10	Free Colored, Females, 10 to 24	Free Colored, Females, 24 to 36	Free Colored, Females, 36 to 55	Free Colored, Females, 55 to 100	Free Colored, Females, 100, &c.	Total	White, Deaf and Dumb, under 14	White, Deaf and Dumb, 14 to 25	White, Deaf and Dumb, 25, &c.	White, Blind	Aliens	Slaves and Colored, Deaf and Dumb, under 14	Slaves and Colored, Deaf and Dumb, 14 to 25	Slaves and Colored, Deaf and Dumb, 25, &c.	Slaves and Colored, Blind
																								9									
1		3	1			1	3	1																21									
1	1	1	1			1	1	1																13									
	2	1				1	2	1	2	2														17									
	1	1				0	2	1																12									
1	1																							6									
							2	1																11									
							1			1														4									
																								10									
																								8									
1	1					2	1																	9									
		2					1																	5									
1							1																	5									
1																								3									
																								7									
																								4									
																								4									
																								5									
6	6					3	1	2		1														25	24	1	1				0	0	
																								6									
																								2									
																								13									
																								7									
1							1	1																5									
																								3									
																								5									
																								9									
15	12	5	2			11	15	7	2	4														230		1	1						
																								228									

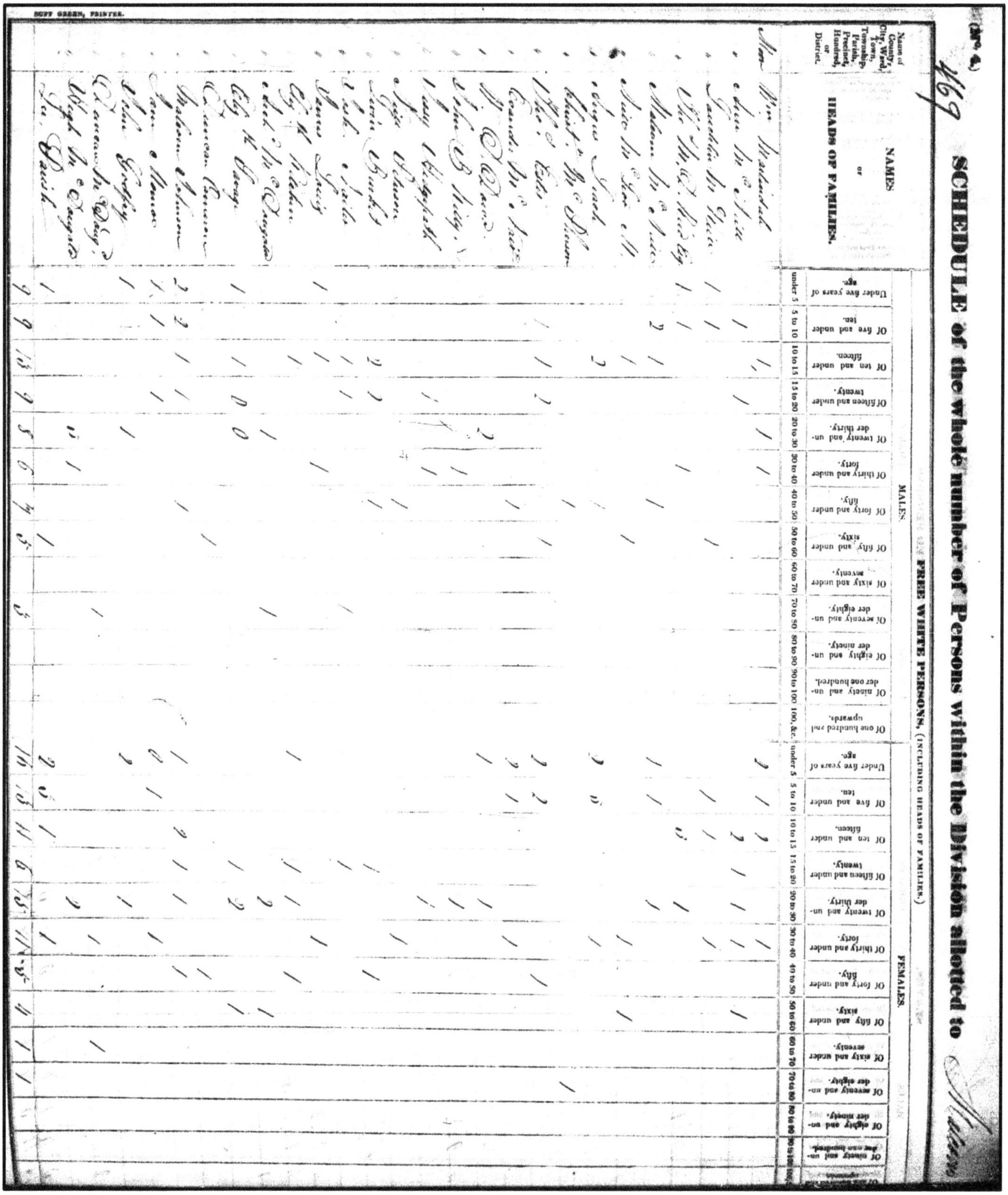

(No. 4.) 469 SCHEDULE of the whole number of Persons within the Division allotted to Malcom

FREE WHITE PERSONS, (INCLUDING HEADS OF FAMILIES.)

Name of County, City, Ward, Town, Township, Parish, Precinct, Hundred, or District.	NAMES OF HEADS OF FAMILIES.	M under 5	M 5 to 10	M 10 to 15	M 15 to 20	M 20 to 30	M 30 to 40	M 40 to 50	M 50 to 60	M 60 to 70	M 70 to 80	M 80 to 90	M 90 to 100	M 100, &c.	F under 5	F 5 to 10	F 10 to 15	F 15 to 20	F 20 to 30	F 30 to 40	F 40 to 50	F 50 to 60	F 60 to 70	F 70 to 80	F 80 to 90	F 90 to 100	F 100, &c.
Moore	Wm Martindale			1		1	1								2	1	2			1							
"	Ann McNeill		1		1												2	1	1	1		1					
"	Laughlin McNeill	1	1						1							1	1			1							
"	Thos M. D. Reid Esq.	1	1				1										3		1								
"	Malcom McNeill		2	1				1							1	1			1								
"	Neill McLeod M.			1					1											1		1					
"	Angus Leach			2				1							2	3				1							
"	Christn McPherson							1																1			
"	Thos Estes		1	1	2				1						2	2					1						
"	Evander McNair							1							2	1				1							
"	W. D. Dowd					2									1				1								
"	John B. Kelly						1												1								
"	Jessy Hedgepath				1		1												1								
"	Nisse Peterson							1												1							
"	Levin Burket			2	2			1										1			1						
"	Josh. Sailor			1	1						1							1									
"	James Lewis	1		1			1													1							
"	Elizth Ritchie			1											1			1	1		1						
"	Arch. McDougald					1					1								2			1					
"	Elizth Savage	1		1	0	0												1	2			1					
"	Duncan Cameron								1												1						
"	Malcom Johnson	2	2	1	1			1							1		2	1	1		1						
"	Jane Monroe	1	1		1										0	1				1							
"	John Godfrey	1				1									2				1								
"	Duncan McDoug.										1									1			1				
"	Hugh McDougald					3	1												2								
"	Jas. Parish	1							1						2	3	1			1							
		9	9	13	9	5	6	7	5		3				16	13	11	6	15	11	5	4	1	1			

DUFF GREEN, PRINTER.

Slaves and Free Persons of Color are continued on the previous page

Slaves and Free Persons of Color are continued on the previous page

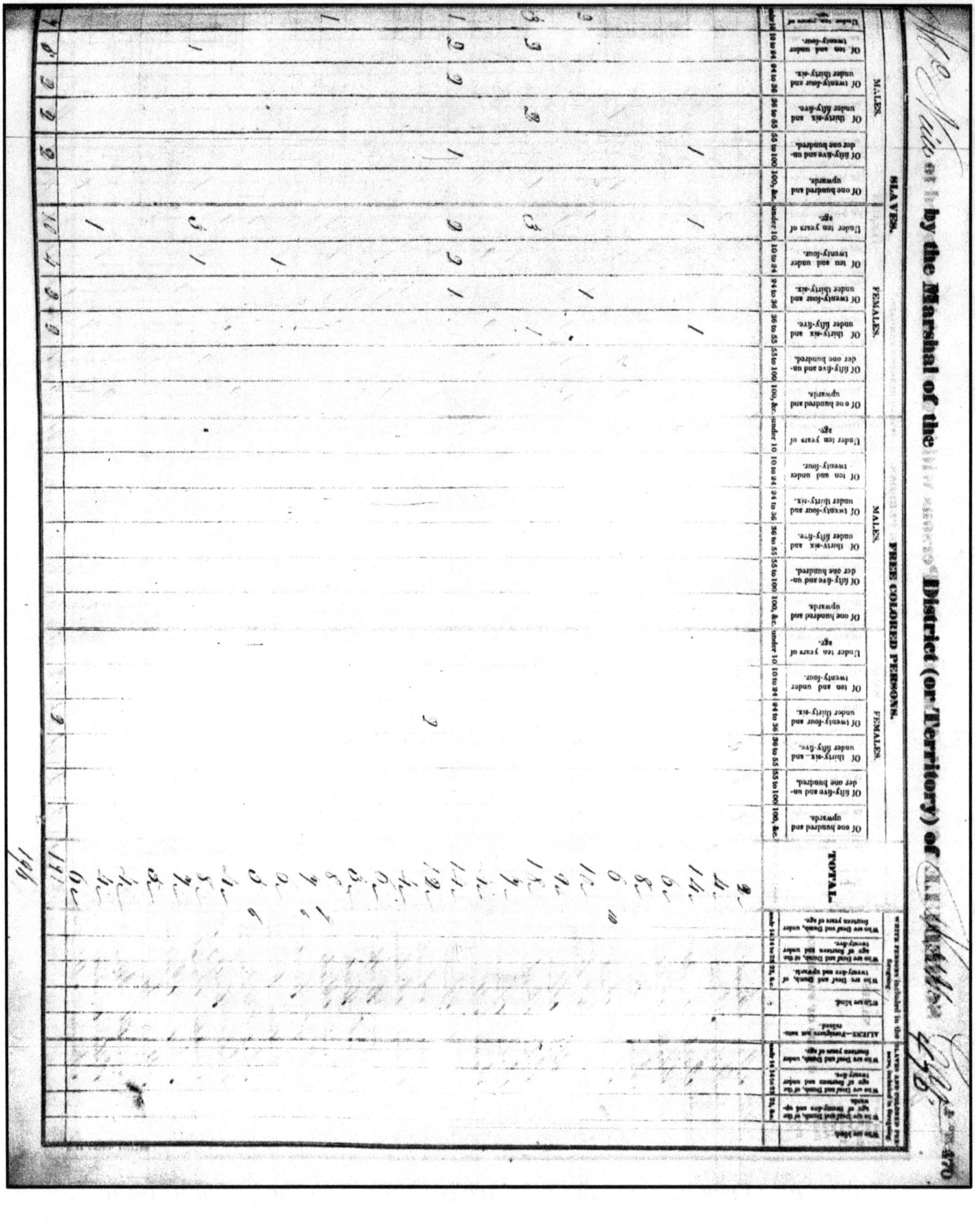

Mc Neil ... by the Marshal of the ... District (or Territory) of N. Carolina 456 470

Sl. M under 10	Sl. M 10 to 24	Sl. M 24 to 36	Sl. M 36 to 55	Sl. M 55 to 100	Sl. M 100, &c.	Sl. F under 10	Sl. F 10 to 24	Sl. F 24 to 36	Sl. F 36 to 55	Sl. F 55 to 100	Sl. F 100, &c.	FC M under 10	FC M 10 to 24	FC M 24 to 36	FC M 36 to 55	FC M 55 to 100	FC M 100, &c.	FC F under 10	FC F 10 to 24	FC F 24 to 36	FC F 36 to 55	FC F 55 to 100	FC F 100, &c.	TOTAL	White deaf and dumb under 14
																								2	
																								4	
				1		1			1															14	
																								6	
																								8	
																								6	10
2								1																10	
																								9	
3	3		2			3			1															18	
																								7	
																								4	
1	2	2		1		2	2	1																14	
																				2				12	
																								4	
																								6	
																								3	
1																								8	
																								7	
							1																	6	
																								3	6
																								4	
	1					3	1																	8	
																								7	
																								5	
																								4	
						1																		4	
																								6	
7	6	2	2	2		10	4	2	2											2				191	

196

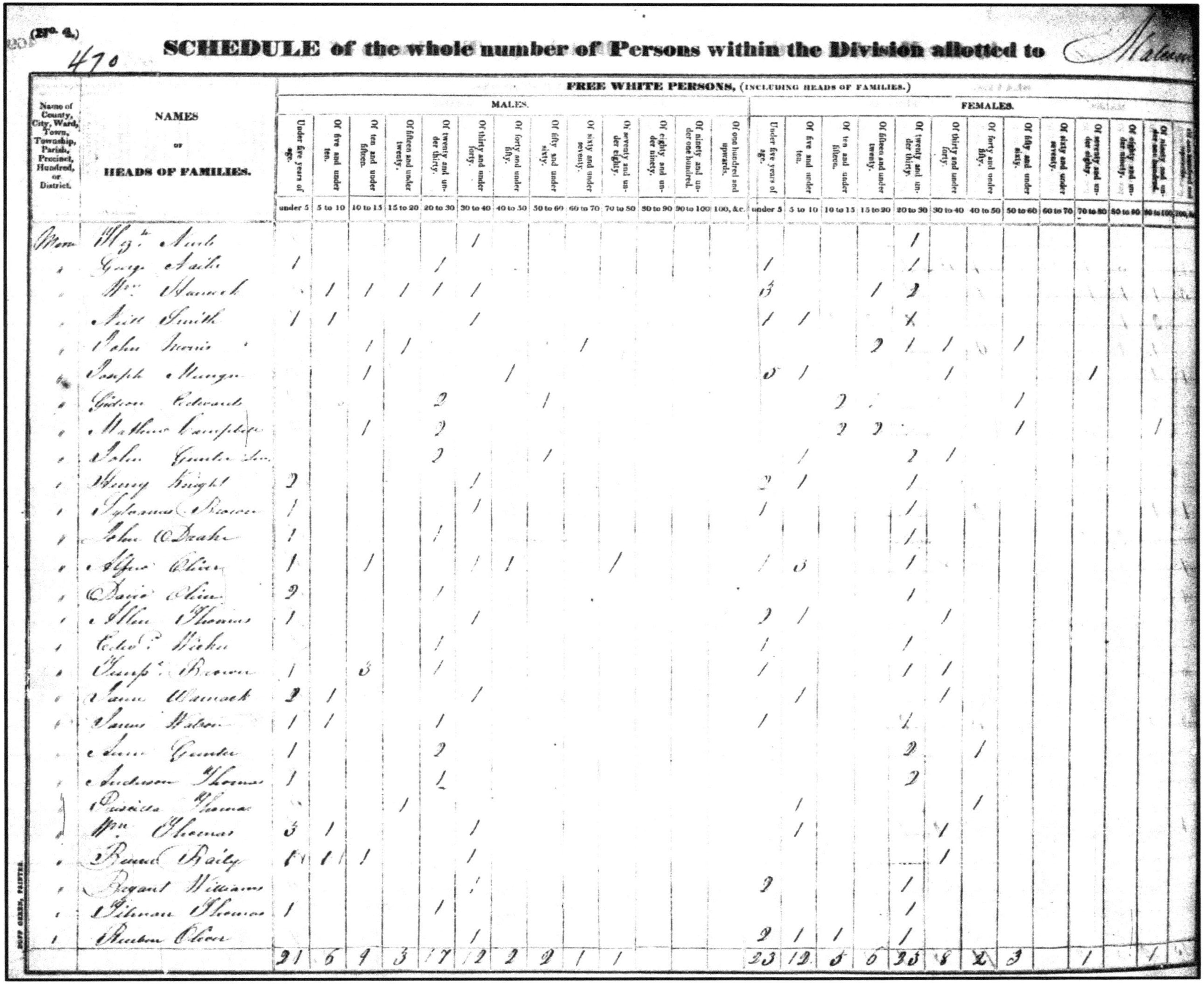

(No. 4.) 470

SCHEDULE of the whole number of Persons within the Division allotted to [illegible]

FREE WHITE PERSONS, (INCLUDING HEADS OF FAMILIES.)

Name of County, City, Ward, Town, Township, Parish, Precinct, Hundred, or District.	NAMES OF HEADS OF FAMILIES.	MALES under 5	M 5 to 10	M 10 to 15	M 15 to 20	M 20 to 30	M 30 to 40	M 40 to 50	M 50 to 60	M 60 to 70	M 70 to 80	M 80 to 90	M 90 to 100	M 100, &c.	FEMALES under 5	F 5 to 10	F 10 to 15	F 15 to 20	F 20 to 30	F 30 to 40	F 40 to 50	F 50 to 60	F 60 to 70	F 70 to 80	F 80 to 90	F 90 to 100	F 100, &c.
Moore	Wm. Auld						1												1								
"	George Auld	1				1									1				1								
"	Wm. Hancock		1	1	1	1	1								3			1	2								
"	Neill Smith	1	1				1								1	1			1								
"	John Morris			1	1					1								2	1	1		1					
"	Joseph Munger			1				1							3	1				1				1			
"	Gideon Edwards					2			1								2					1					
"	Matthew Campbell			1		2											2	2				1				1	
"	John Gunter Sen.					2			1							1			2	1							
"	Henry Knight	2					1								2	1			1								
"	Sylvanus Brown	1					1								1				1								
"	John O Drake	1				1													1								
"	Alfred Oliver	1		1			1	1			1				1	3			1								
"	David Oliver	2				1													1								
"	Allen Thomas	1					1								2	1				1							
"	Edwd. Wicker					1									1				1								
"	Josep. Brown	1		3		1									1				1	1							
"	Jane Warwick	2	1				1									1				1							
"	James Watson	1	1			1									1				1								
"	Ann Gunter	1				2													2		1						
"	Anderson Thomas	1				1													2								
"	Priscilla Thomas				1											1					1						
"	Wm. Thomas	3	1				1									1				1							
"	Bend Baily	1	1	1			1													1							
"	Bryant Williams						1								2				1								
"	Pitman Thomas	1				1													1								
"	Reuben Oliver						1								2	1	1		1								
		21	6	4	3	17	12	2	2	1	1				23	12	5	6	25	8	2	3		1		1	

Duff Green, Printer.

Slaves and Free Persons of Color are continued on the previous page

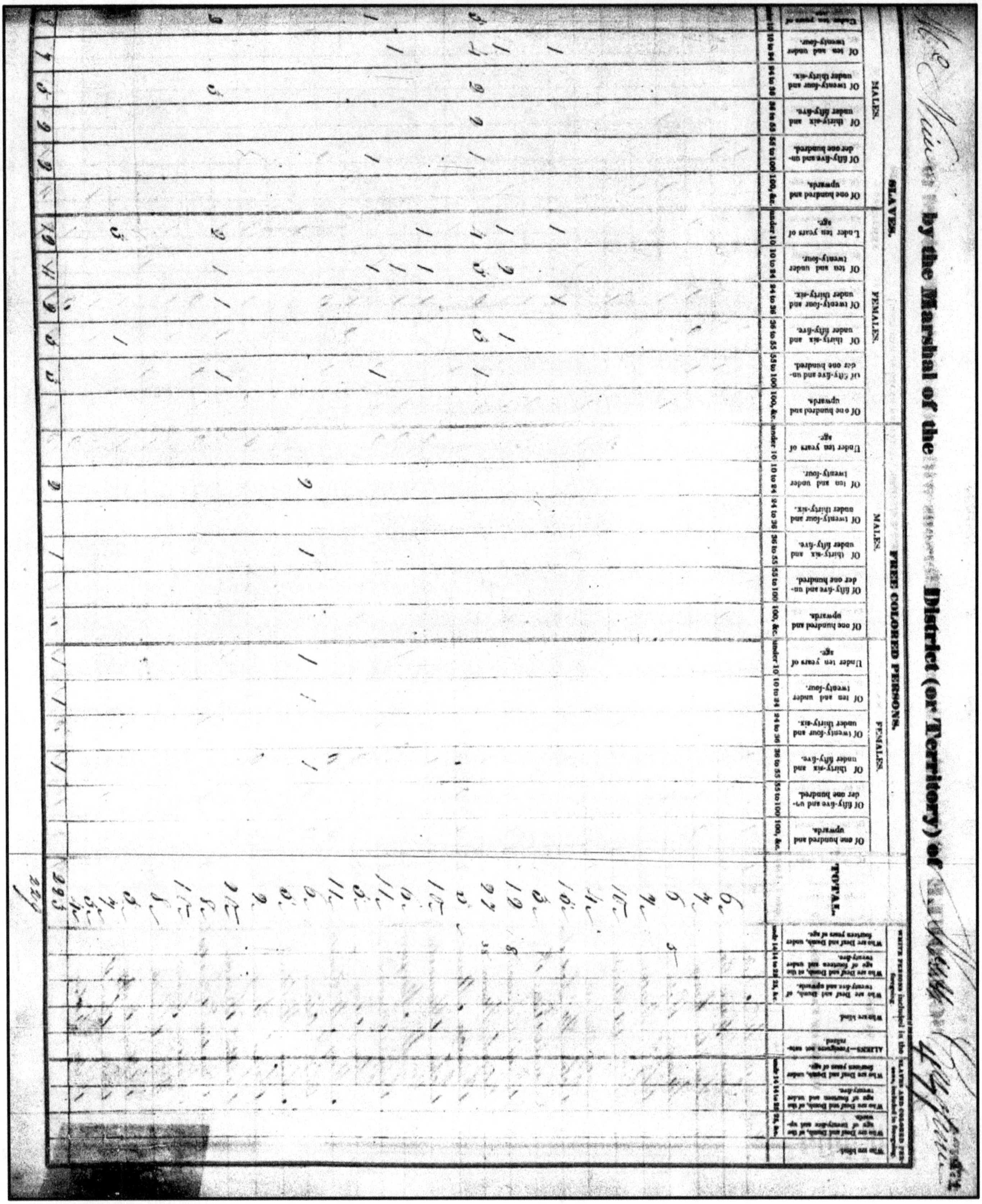
by the Marshal of the District (or Territory) of

SLAVES. MALES. FEMALES. FREE COLORED PERSONS. MALES. FEMALES. TOTAL.

(No. 4.) 471

SCHEDULE of the whole number of Persons within the Division allotted to [illegible]

FREE WHITE PERSONS, (INCLUDING HEADS OF FAMILIES.)

Name of County, City, Ward, Town, Township, Parish, Precinct, Hundred, or District.	NAMES of HEADS OF FAMILIES.	M under 5	M 5 to 10	M 10 to 15	M 15 to 20	M 20 to 30	M 30 to 40	M 40 to 50	M 50 to 60	M 60 to 70	M 70 to 80	M 80 to 90	M 90 to 100	M 100, &c.	F under 5	F 5 to 10	F 10 to 15	F 15 to 20	F 20 to 30	F 30 to 40	F 40 to 50	F 50 to 60	F 60 to 70	F 70 to 80	F 80 to 90	F 90 to 100	F 100, &c.
Moore	Mary Knight			0	1	0		0									1	1	2		2						
"	Wily Vinn	2	2												1				1								
"	Jack Knight				2			1							2	1	1										
"	Charles Pipkin		2	1				2							1					1							
"	Aaron Chin	1					1								1	2	2			1		1		1			
"	Saml Parker								1							1			1		1						
"	Danl McWilliam		1	2	2	2										1	1	1	1		1						
"	Alexr Shaw					1		1														1					
"	John Baker					1				1										1							
"	John Brown		3					1							1		2	2		2							
"	James Mangum					1									3				1								
"	Wm B Arnold		1	1	1			1							1	1	1			1							
"	Harvey Arnold	1				1												1	1								
"	Jacob Johnson														1	2	1		1	1			1				
"	Henry Godfrey	1					1									2			1								
"	Jacob Garter	1		1	1	2				1						1		1	1	1	1						
"	Louis Hicks																										
"	Margt Gunter	1	2													1				1							
"	Andrew Cannon									1											1						
"	Archd Douglas			1	1					1					1	2		3			1						
"	John Godfrey Jr		1			1			1								2		1	1		1					
"	Becker Parish	1		1	1	2			1						1			1	1		1						
"	Andrew Jackson		2	1	1	1			1								1				1						
"	Norris Morrison									1																	
"	R. H. Muse		1	1				1								2	1			1							
"	John Sewell									1								1				1					
"	Norman McLeod						1				1								1					1			
		8	16	9	9	12	4	7	4	6	1				11	16	13	11	13	11	9	4	1	2			

Slaves and Free Persons of Color are continued on the previous page

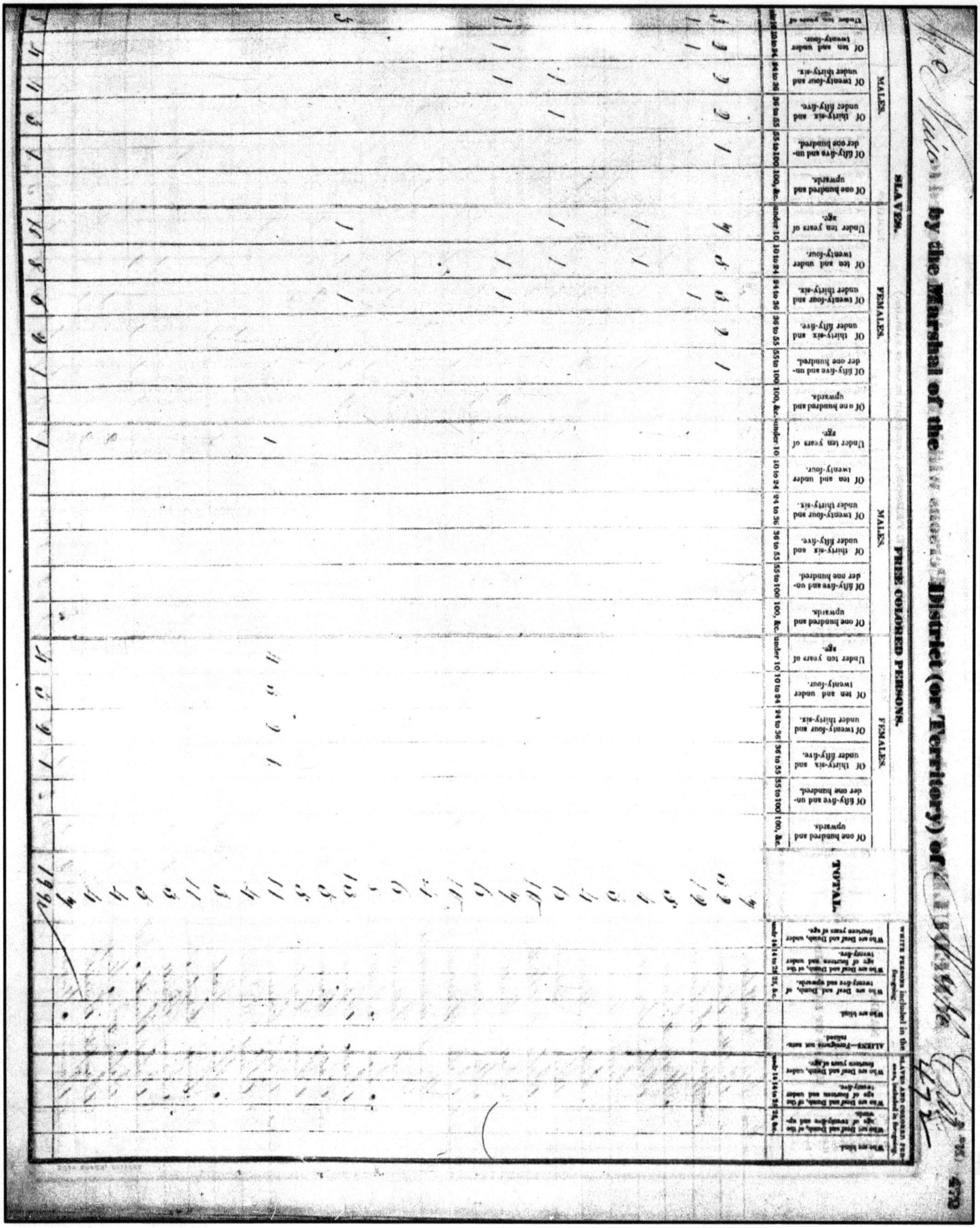
by the Marshal of the District (or Territory) of

SLAVES.

FREE COLORED PERSONS.

TOTAL.

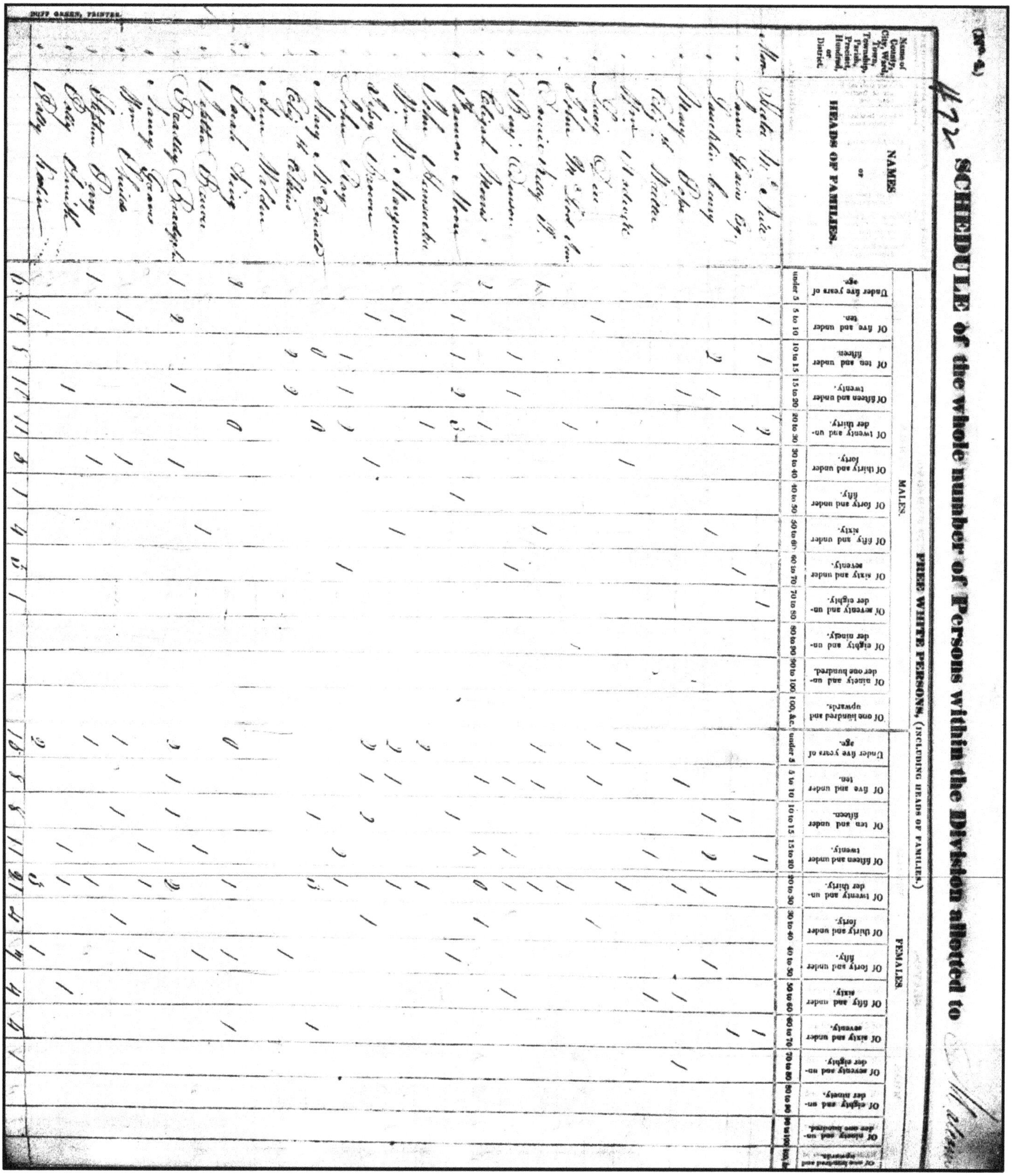

(No. 4.) 472 SCHEDULE of the whole number of Persons within the Division allotted to Malcolm

FREE WHITE PERSONS, (INCLUDING HEADS OF FAMILIES.)

Name of County, City, Ward, Town, Township, Parish, Precinct, Hundred, or District.	NAMES or HEADS OF FAMILIES.	M under 5	M 5 to 10	M 10 to 15	M 15 to 20	M 20 to 30	M 30 to 40	M 40 to 50	M 50 to 60	M 60 to 70	M 70 to 80	M 80 to 90	M 90 to 100	M 100, &c.	F under 5	F 5 to 10	F 10 to 15	F 15 to 20	F 20 to 30	F 30 to 40	F 40 to 50	F 50 to 60	F 60 to 70	F 70 to 80	F 80 to 90	F 90 to 100	F 100, &c.
Moore	Hector McNeill		1	1		2					1							1					1				
"	James Gaines Esq.					1				1							1						1				
"	Laughlin Curry			2	1				1								1	2	1		1						
"	Mary Pope				1											1			1			1		1			
"	Elizth Walker																	1				1					
"	Wm Aldredge						1								1				1								
"	Lucy Lee		1												1	1				1							
"	John McLeod Jun					1													1								
"	Daniel Kelly B.	1							1						1	1			1								
"	Benjn Dunson			1	1					1						1		1	1			1					
"	Elijah Morris	2				1										1		2	1	1							
"	Jamison Moore		1	1	2	3		1									1				1						
"	John Hunsucker					1									2				1								
"	Wm W. Mangum		1						1						2	1			1								
"	Betsy Brown		1				1								2	1	2			1							
"	John Ray			1	1	2				1								2	1								
"	Mary McDonald			1		1											1		3				1				
"	Elizth Atkins			2	2																1						
"	Ann Walden																										
"	Sarah King	1				1									1				1		1		1				
"	Jeptha Brown								1									1			1						
"	Bradley Bradygh	1	2		1		1								3	1	1		2								
"	Nancy Graves																	1	1		1						
"	Wm Shields		1				1								1		1			1							
"	Stephen Perry	1					1								1				1								
"	Polly Smith				1													1	1			1					
"	Polly Walden		1												2				3		1						
		6	9	5	11	11	5	1	4	5	1				15	8	8	11	21	4	7	4	4	1			

Slaves and Free Persons of Color are continued on the previous page

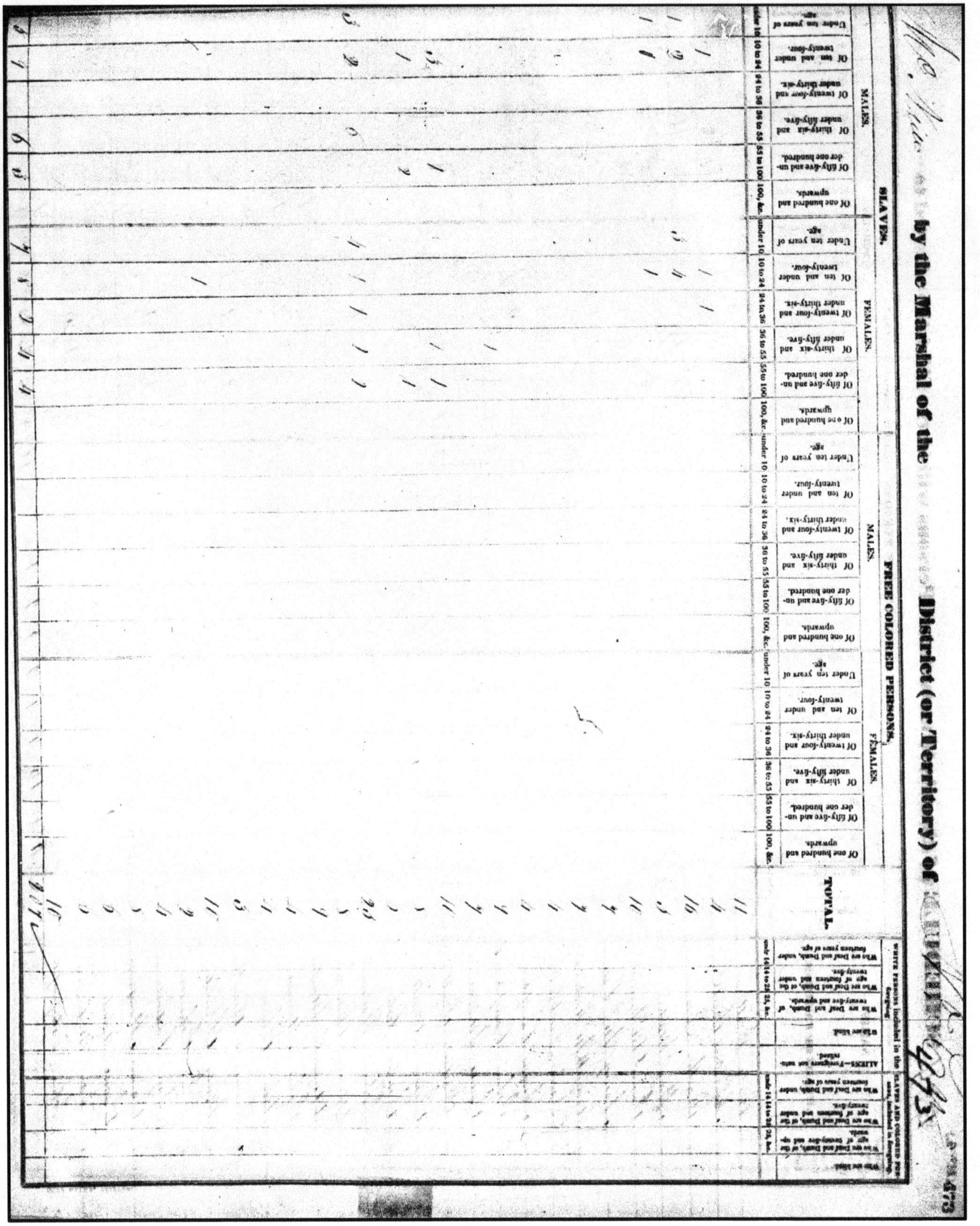

Mo. [illegible] by the Marshal of the [illegible] District (or Territory) of [illegible] 473

Slaves, Males: under 10	Slaves, Males: 10 to 24	Slaves, Males: 24 to 36	Slaves, Males: 36 to 55	Slaves, Males: 55 to 100	Slaves, Males: 100, &c.	Slaves, Females: under 10	Slaves, Females: 10 to 24	Slaves, Females: 24 to 36	Slaves, Females: 36 to 55	Slaves, Females: 55 to 100	Slaves, Females: 100, &c.	Free Colored Persons, Males: under 10	Free Colored Persons, Males: 10 to 24	Free Colored Persons, Males: 24 to 36	Free Colored Persons, Males: 36 to 55	Free Colored Persons, Males: 55 to 100	Free Colored Persons, Males: 100, &c.	Free Colored Persons, Females: under 10	Free Colored Persons, Females: 10 to 24	Free Colored Persons, Females: 24 to 36	Free Colored Persons, Females: 36 to 55	Free Colored Persons, Females: 55 to 100	Free Colored Persons, Females: 100, &c.	TOTAL	White persons included in the foregoing: Deaf and Dumb, under 14	White: Deaf and Dumb, 14 to 25	White: Deaf and Dumb, 25, &c.	White: Blind	Aliens—Foreigners not naturalized	Slaves and colored persons included in the foregoing: Deaf and Dumb, under 14	Slaves and colored: Deaf and Dumb, 14 to 25	Slaves and colored: Deaf and Dumb, 25, &c.	Slaves and colored: Blind
																								11									
	1						1	1																4									
1	2					3	4																	16									
1	1						1																	5									
																								10									
																								7									
																								7									
																								4									
																								4									
									1															4									
																								7									
	3			1					1	1														10									
	1			2						1														5									
																								5									
3	2		6			4	1	1	1	2														23									
																								5									
																								4									
																								4									
																								4									
																								3									
							1																	10									
																								2									
																								4									
																								5									
																								6									
																								9									
																								10									
5	9		6	3		7	8	2	4	4														207									

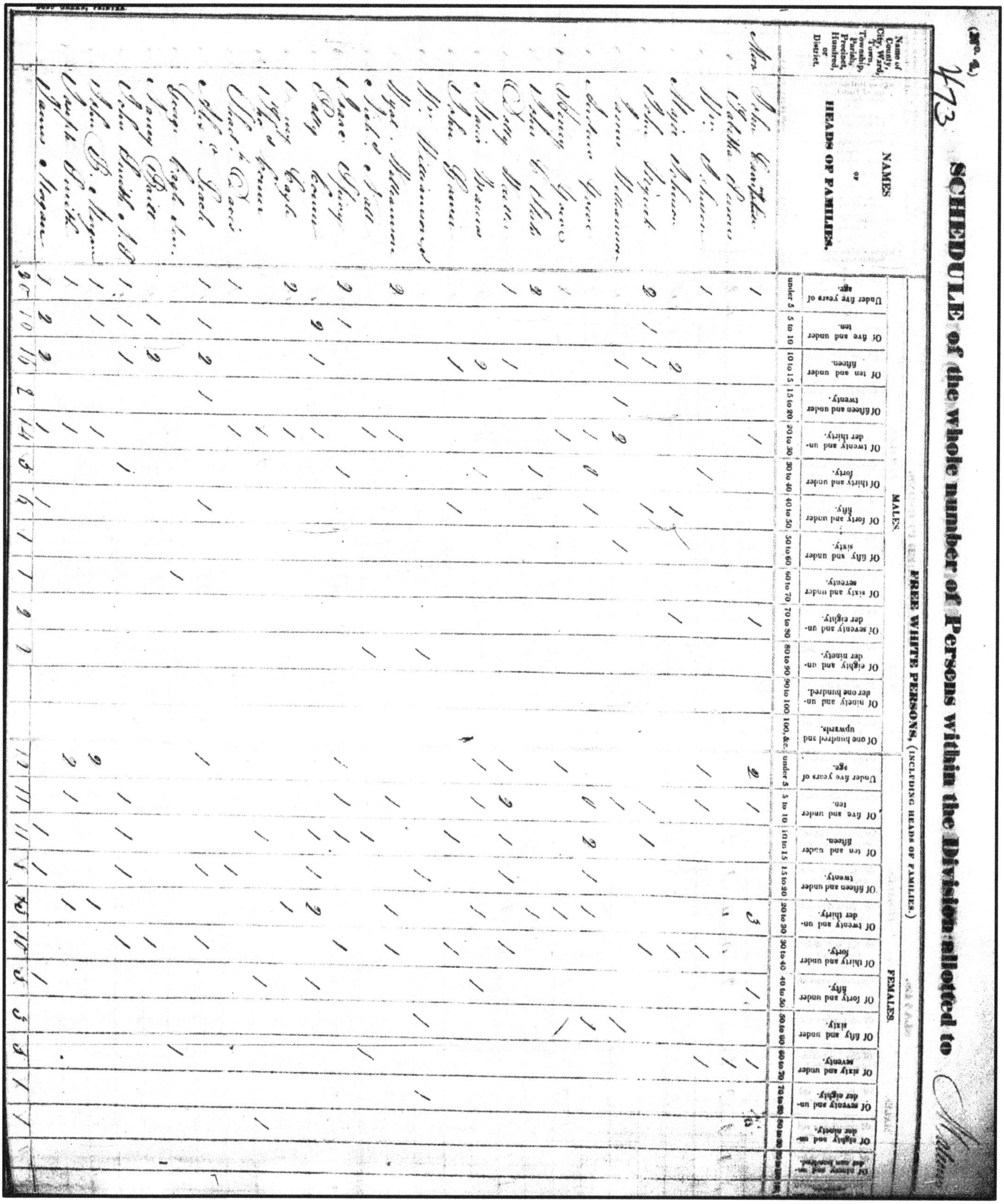

Slaves and Free Persons of Color are continued on the previous page

Mc Neill ... by the Marshal of the ... District (or Territory) of North Carolina 474 / 474

Slaves, Males, under 10	Slaves, Males, 10 to 24	Slaves, Males, 24 to 36	Slaves, Males, 36 to 55	Slaves, Males, 55 to 100	Slaves, Males, 100, &c.	Slaves, Females, under 10	Slaves, Females, 10 to 24	Slaves, Females, 24 to 36	Slaves, Females, 36 to 55	Slaves, Females, 55 to 100	Slaves, Females, 100, &c.	Free Colored, Males, under 10	Free Colored, Males, 10 to 24	Free Colored, Males, 24 to 36	Free Colored, Males, 36 to 55	Free Colored, Males, 55 to 100	Free Colored, Males, 100, &c.	Free Colored, Females, under 10	Free Colored, Females, 10 to 24	Free Colored, Females, 24 to 36	Free Colored, Females, 36 to 55	Free Colored, Females, 55 to 100	Free Colored, Females, 100, &c.	TOTAL	White deaf & dumb under 14	White deaf & dumb 14 to 25	White deaf & dumb 25, &c.	White blind	Aliens	Slaves & colored deaf & dumb under 14	Slaves & colored deaf & dumb 14 to 25	Slaves & colored deaf & dumb 25, &c.	Slaves & colored blind
																								2									
																								1									
																								9									
																								5									
																								5									
																								3									
																								4									
																								7									
																								11									
																								5									
																								8									
																								7									
																								4									
																								9									
																								5									
																								4									
	1					1	1		1															10									
1		1						1																8									
												2	1					1		1	1			5									
																								8									
							1																	6									
																								1									
																								7									
																								3									
2	3		1			2	4	2																11									
	1																							5									
3			1			4	2	2																13									
7	3	1	2			7	8	5	1			2	1					1		1	1			174									

173

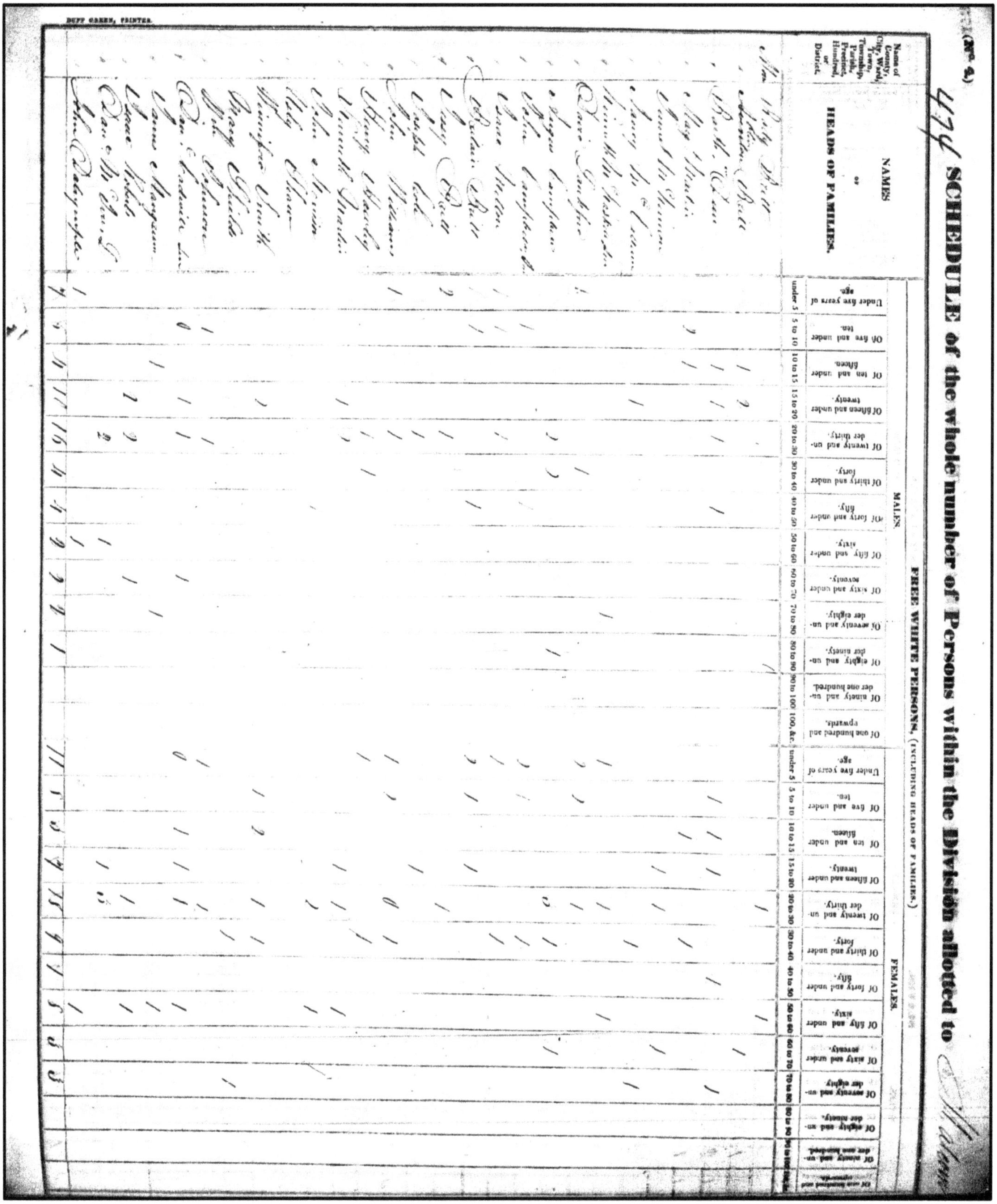

474 SCHEDULE of the whole number of Persons within the Division allotted to [illegible]

FREE WHITE PERSONS, (INCLUDING HEADS OF FAMILIES.)

NAMES OF HEADS OF FAMILIES (handwritten, best reading):

Risty Britt
Ashton Britt
Ruth Dunn
Mary Martin
Samuel McKinnon
Nancy McCrummen
Kenneth McKaskill Sen
Davis Lankford
Angus Campbell
John Campbell Sen
Isaac Melton
Britain Britt
Jesse Britt
Joseph Cole
John Williams
Henry Hawley
Kenneth Martin
John Morrison
Usly Shaw
Winnifred Smith
Mary Shields
Wm Johnson
Danl Cadwell Sen
James Mangum
Isaac Roberts
Danl McDonald
John Dalrymple

Slaves and Free Persons of Color are continued on the previous page

Mc Neill ... by the Marshal of the ... District (or Territory) of North Carolina 475 475

Slaves Males under 10	Slaves Males 10 to 24	Slaves Males 24 to 36	Slaves Males 36 to 55	Slaves Males 55 to 100	Slaves Males 100, &c.	Slaves Females under 10	Slaves Females 10 to 24	Slaves Females 24 to 36	Slaves Females 36 to 55	Slaves Females 55 to 100	Slaves Females 100, &c.	Free Colored Males under 10	Free Colored Males 10 to 24	Free Colored Males 24 to 36	Free Colored Males 36 to 55	Free Colored Males 55 to 100	Free Colored Males 100, &c.	Free Colored Females under 10	Free Colored Females 10 to 24	Free Colored Females 24 to 36	Free Colored Females 36 to 55	Free Colored Females 55 to 100	Free Colored Females 100, &c.	TOTAL	White Deaf and Dumb under 14	White Deaf and Dumb 14 to 25	White Deaf and Dumb 25, &c.	White Blind	Aliens—Foreigners not naturalized	Slaves and Colored Deaf and Dumb under 14	Slaves and Colored Deaf and Dumb 14 to 25	Slaves and Colored Deaf and Dumb 25, &c.	Slaves and Colored Blind
2	2	1	1			3	1	1																16									
7	2	2				1	3	2																27									
																								7									
																								9									
5	1						2																	11									
																								5									
																								4									
																								6									
3	2					2	3		1															15									
																								6									
																								5									
															1							1		2									
																								13									
1								1																14									
	1																							6									
2	4					3	3	2																25									
																								3									
																								4									
																								7									
																								15									
5	4	2				3	2																	35									
																								2									
																								4									
																								4									
																								4									
																								8									
																								7									
22	16	5	1			12	14	6	1						1							1		273									

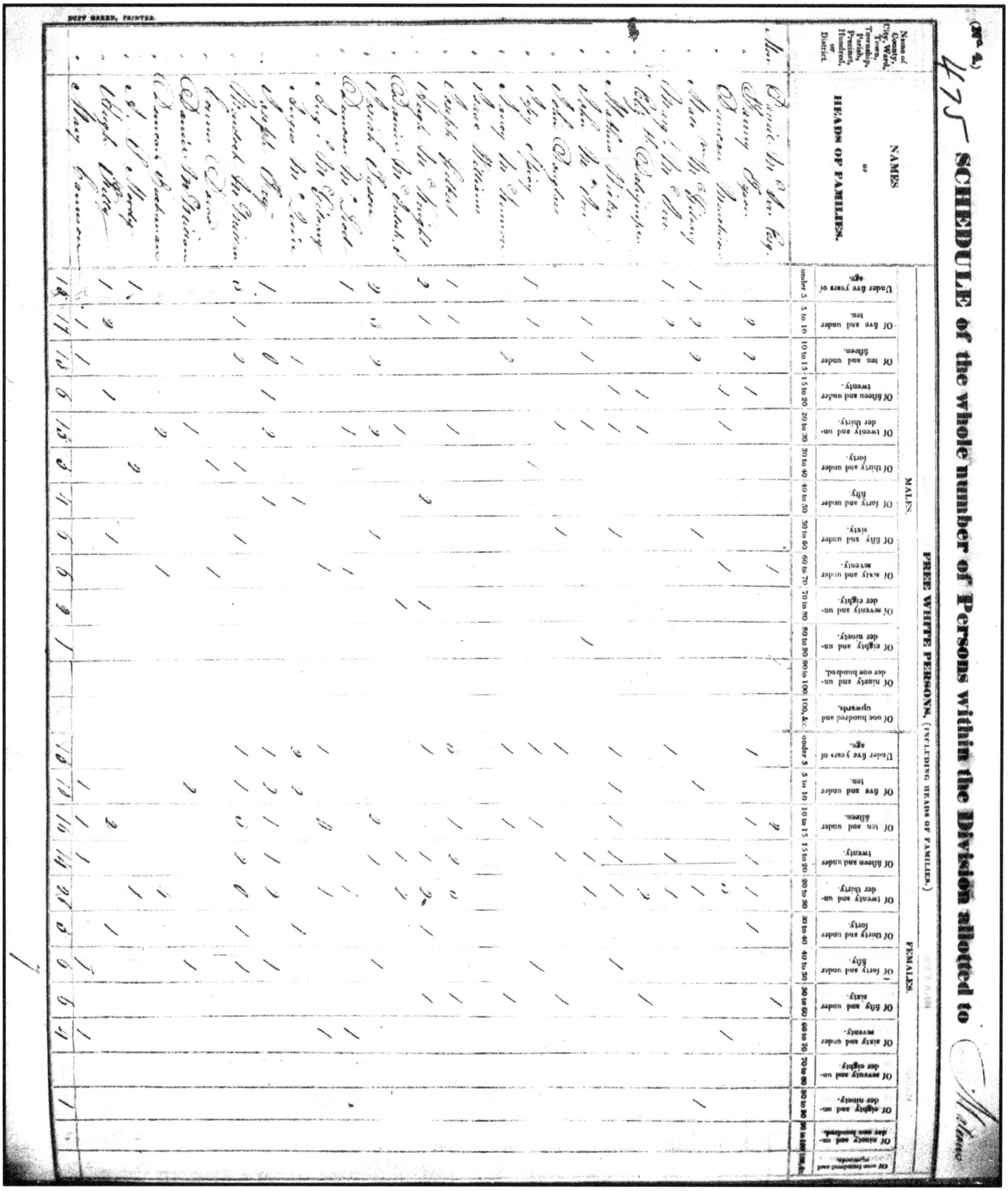

(No. 4.) 475 SCHEDULE of the whole number of Persons within the Division allotted to (McLeans)

FREE WHITE PERSONS, (INCLUDING HEADS OF FAMILIES.)

Name of County, City, Ward, Town, Township, Parish, Precinct, Hundred, or District	NAMES OF HEADS OF FAMILIES	M under 5	M 5 to 10	M 10 to 15	M 15 to 20	M 20 to 30	M 30 to 40	M 40 to 50	M 50 to 60	M 60 to 70	M 70 to 80	M 80 to 90	M 90 to 100	M 100, &c.	F under 5	F 5 to 10	F 10 to 15	F 15 to 20	F 20 to 30	F 30 to 40	F 40 to 50	F 50 to 60	F 60 to 70	F 70 to 80	F 80 to 90	F 90 to 100	F 100, &c.
Moo.	Daniel McIver Esq.									1							2					1					
"	Fanny Tyson		2	2	1										1		1	1	1	1							
"	Duncan Murchison				1	1				1									3				1				
"	Malc. McGilvery	1	2	2					1							1			1						1		
"	Marg. McIver	1	2												1			1	1								
"	Eliz. Dalrymple				1	1													2			1					
"	Mathew Wicker				1	1			1						1	1	1	1	1		1						
"	John McIver		1	1		1						1						1	1								
"	John Douglas					1			1						1			1				1					
"	Peggy Spivy	1	1				1								1		1				1						
"	Nancy McKinnon			2											1		1					1					
"	Isaac Williams																										
"	Joseph Gilbert	1	1			1									3		1	2	3			1					
"	Hugh McKnight	2	1					2			1				1			1	2	1		1					
"	Daniel McIntosh Sr.					1					1							1	2								
"	Josiah Tyson	2	3	2		2			1								2	1			1						
"	Duncan McLeod	1				1				1									1				1				
"	Ang. McGilvery									1					1		3		1				1				
"	Angus McQuin			1				1							2	2				1							
"	Joseph Fry	1		[illegible]	1	2		1							1	2	1	1	2		1						
"	Murdoch McMillan	3	1	2			1		1						1	1	3	2	[illegible]	1	1						
"	Conner Dowd						1			1																	
"	Daniel McMillan					1										2					1						
"	Duncan Buchanan					2				1									1								
"	A. S. Moody	1					2												1								
"	Hugh Kelly	1	2		1				1								2			1							
"	Mary Cameron		1	1												1	1	1			1		1				
		18	17	13	6	13	3	4	5	6	2	1			13	12	16	14	26	5	6	6	4		1		

7

Slaves and Free Persons of Color are continued on the previous page

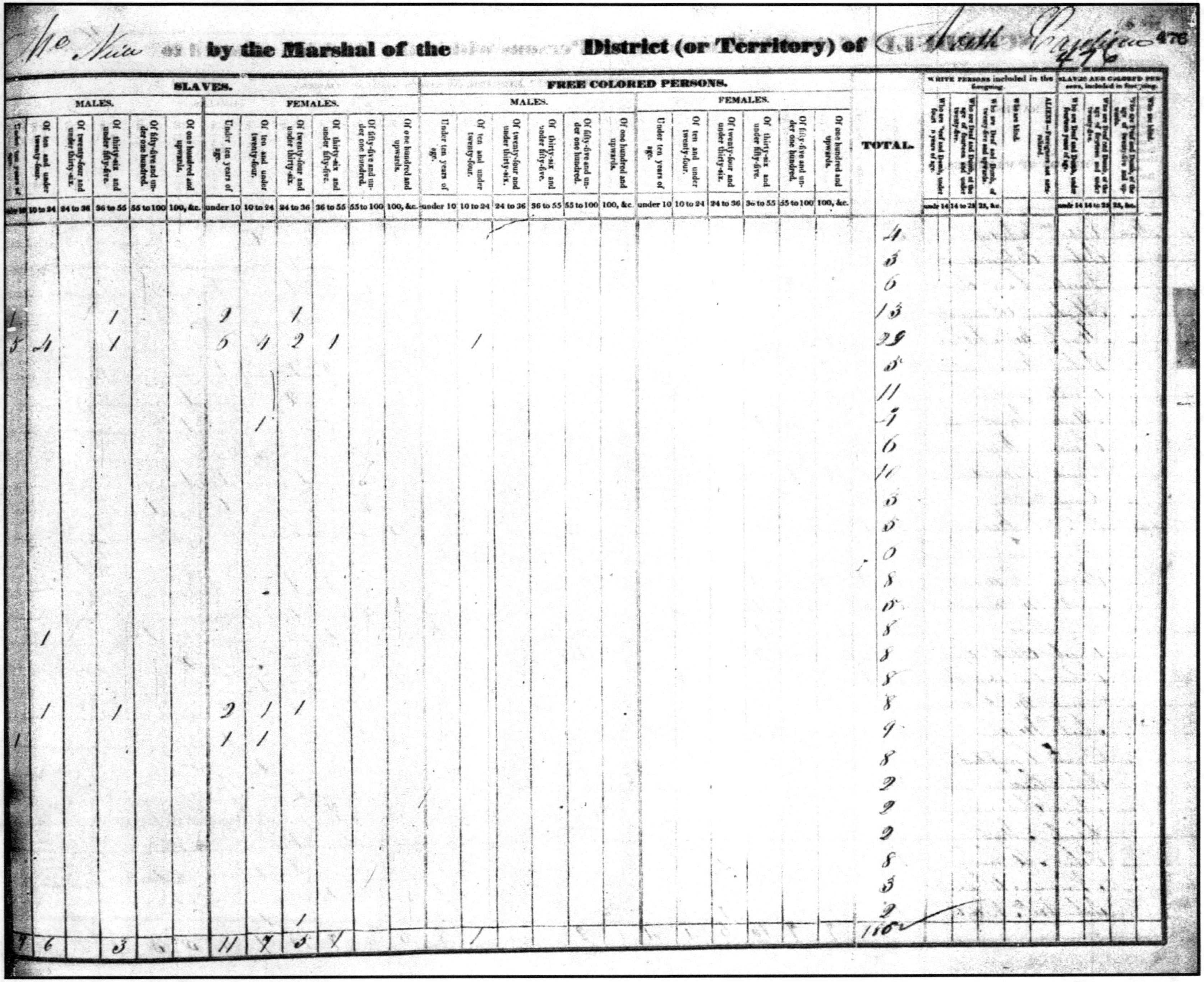

Mc Nia by the Marshal of the District (or Territory) of North Carolina 476

Slaves, Males: Under ten years of age (under 10)	Slaves, Males: Of ten and under twenty-four (10 to 24)	Slaves, Males: Of twenty-four and under thirty-six (24 to 36)	Slaves, Males: Of thirty-six and under fifty-five (36 to 55)	Slaves, Males: Of fifty-five and under one hundred (55 to 100)	Slaves, Males: Of one hundred and upwards (100, &c.)	Slaves, Females: Under ten years of age (under 10)	Slaves, Females: Of ten and under twenty-four (10 to 24)	Slaves, Females: Of twenty-four and under thirty-six (24 to 36)	Slaves, Females: Of thirty-six and under fifty-five (36 to 55)	Slaves, Females: Of fifty-five and under one hundred (55 to 100)	Slaves, Females: Of one hundred and upwards (100, &c.)	Free Colored Persons, Males: Under ten years of age (under 10)	Free Colored Persons, Males: Of ten and under twenty-four (10 to 24)	Free Colored Persons, Males: Of twenty-four and under thirty-six (24 to 36)	Free Colored Persons, Males: Of thirty-six and under fifty-five (36 to 55)	Free Colored Persons, Males: Of fifty-five and under one hundred (55 to 100)	Free Colored Persons, Males: Of one hundred and upwards (100, &c.)	Free Colored Persons, Females: Under ten years of age (under 10)	Free Colored Persons, Females: Of ten and under twenty-four (10 to 24)	Free Colored Persons, Females: Of twenty-four and under thirty-six (24 to 36)	Free Colored Persons, Females: Of thirty-six and under fifty-five (36 to 55)	Free Colored Persons, Females: Of fifty-five and under one hundred (55 to 100)	Free Colored Persons, Females: Of one hundred and upwards (100, &c.)	TOTAL.	White persons included in the foregoing: Who are Deaf and Dumb, under fourteen years of age (under 14)	White persons: Who are Deaf and Dumb, of the age of fourteen and under twenty-five (14 to 25)	White persons: Who are Deaf and Dumb, of twenty-five and upwards (25, &c.)	White persons: Who are blind.	Aliens—Foreigners not naturalized.	Slaves and colored persons included in the foregoing: Who are Deaf and Dumb, under fourteen years of age (under 14)	Slaves and colored persons: Who are Deaf and Dumb, of the age of fourteen and under twenty-five (14 to 25)	Slaves and colored persons: Who are Deaf and Dumb, of the age of twenty-five and upwards (25, &c.)	Slaves and colored persons: Who are blind.
																								4									
																								5									
																								6									
1			1			2		1																13									
5	4		1			5	4	2	1				1											29									
																								5									
																								11									
							1																	7									
																								6									
																								10									
																								5									
																								5									
																								0									
																								8									
																								5									
	1																							8									
																								8									
																								8									
	1		1			2	1	1																8									
1						1	1																	9									
																								8									
																								2									
																								2									
																								2									
																								8									
																								5									
								1																2									
7	6		3			11	7	5	1				1											110									

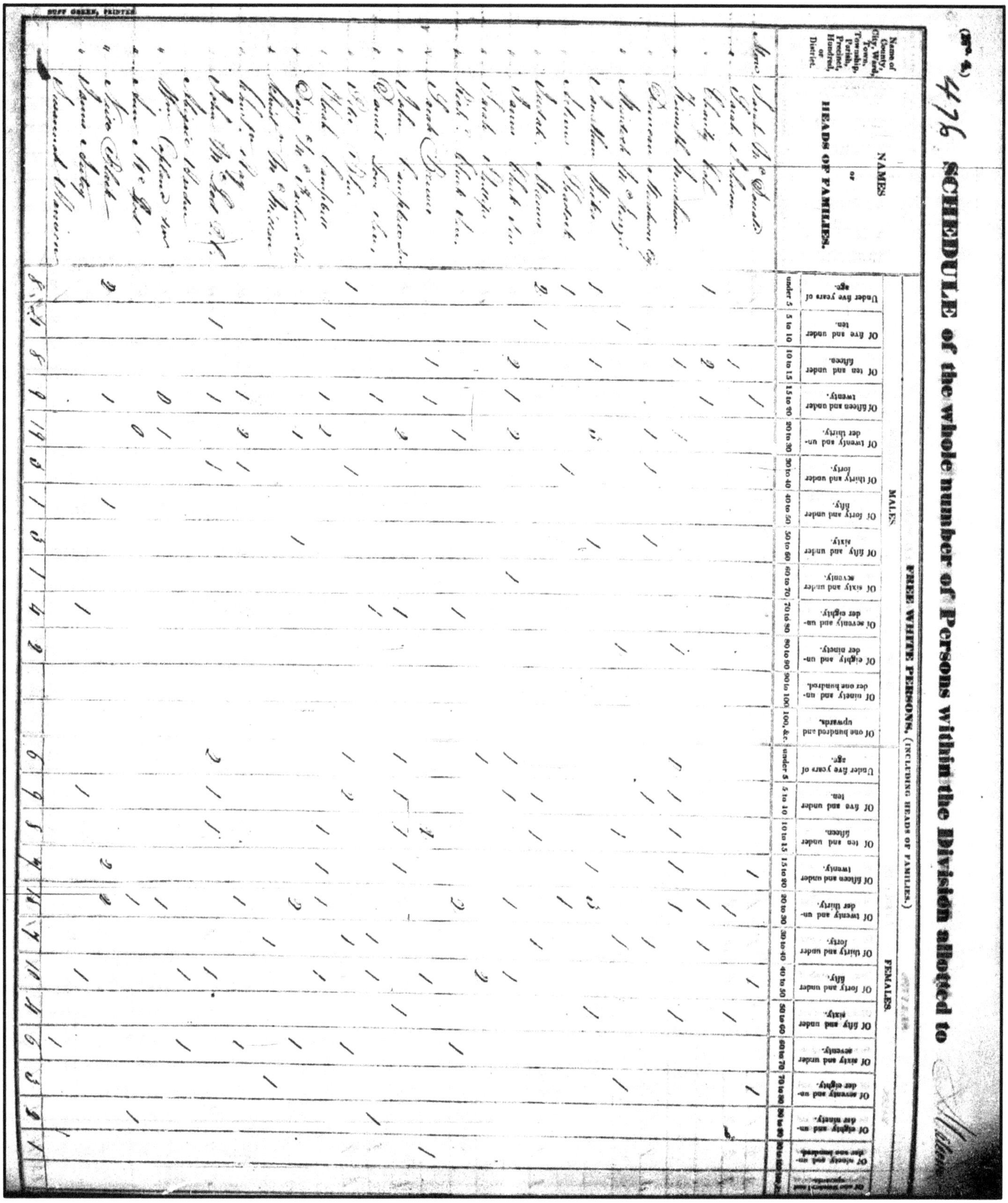

Slaves and Free Persons of Color are continued on the previous page

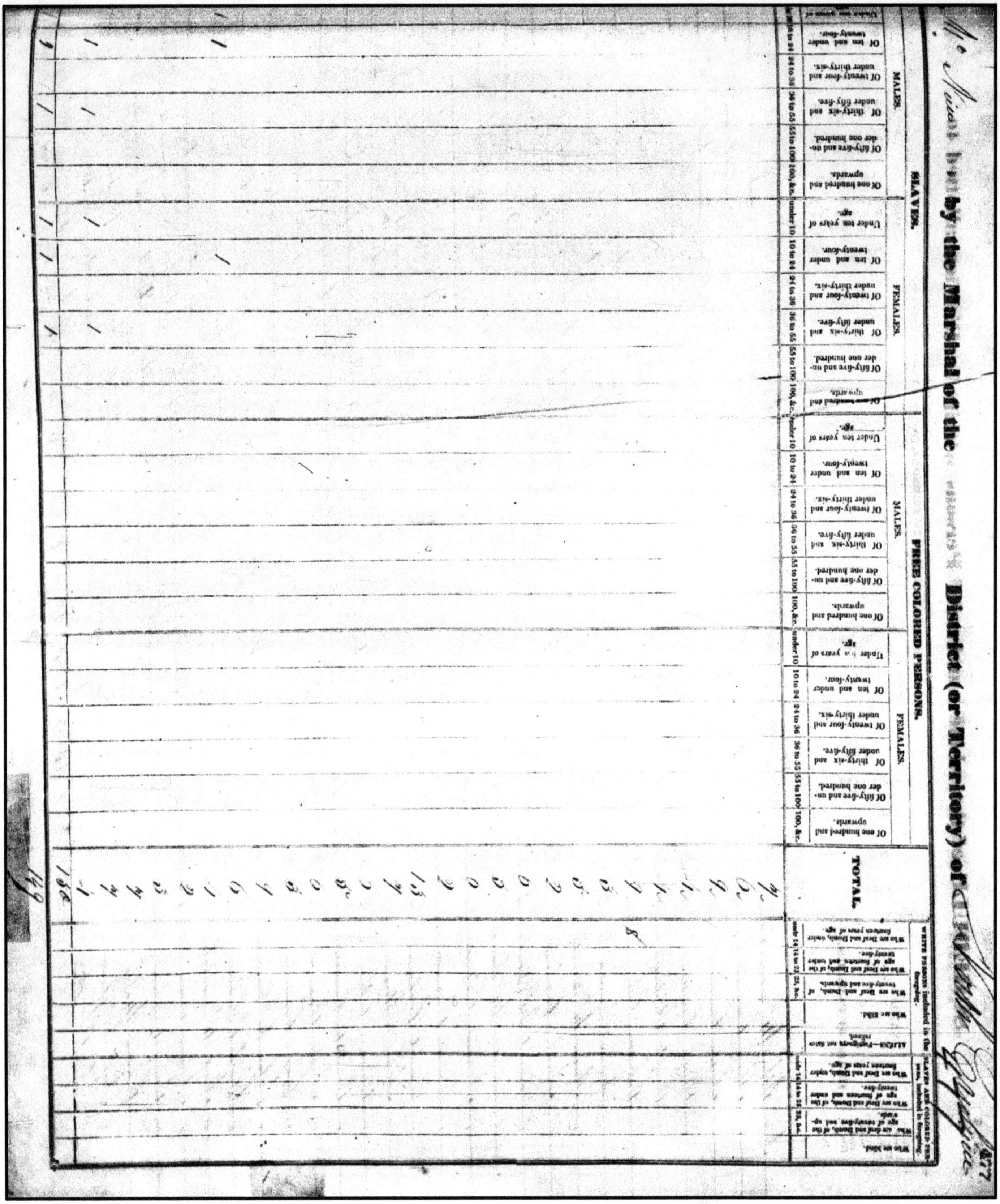

Mc Niven by the Marshal of the District (or Territory) of North Carolina 477

Slaves – Males: under 10	Slaves – Males: 10 to 24	Slaves – Males: 24 to 36	Slaves – Males: 36 to 55	Slaves – Males: 55 to 100	Slaves – Males: 100, &c.	Slaves – Females: under 10	Slaves – Females: 10 to 24	Slaves – Females: 24 to 36	Slaves – Females: 36 to 55	Slaves – Females: 55 to 100	Slaves – Females: 100, &c.	Free Colored – Males (all ages)	Free Colored – Females (all ages)	TOTAL	White persons deaf and dumb, under 14
														4	
														6	
														9	
														4	
														1	
														9	8
														3	
														5	
														2	
														0	
														0	
														0	
														2	
														13	
														4	
														1	
														5	
														0	
														3	
														4	
1	1						1							6	
														1	
														2	
														3	
														4	
	1		1			1			1					4	
														1	
1	9		1			1	1		1					150	
														149	

(No. 4.) 477

SCHEDULE of the whole number of Persons within the Division allotted to Malcom

FREE WHITE PERSONS, (INCLUDING HEADS OF FAMILIES.)

Name of County, City, Ward, Town, Township, Parish, Precinct, Hundred, or District.	NAMES OF HEADS OF FAMILIES.	M under 5	M 5 to 10	M 10 to 15	M 15 to 20	M 20 to 30	M 30 to 40	M 40 to 50	M 50 to 60	M 60 to 70	M 70 to 80	M 80 to 90	M 90 to 100	M 100, &c.	F under 5	F 5 to 10	F 10 to 15	F 15 to 20	F 20 to 30	F 30 to 40	F 40 to 50	F 50 to 60	F 60 to 70	F 70 to 80	F 80 to 90	F 90 to 100
Moore	Ephm Autry	3						1								2				1						
"	John Johnson	1				2									2				1							
"	Zach Cary Sen			1	2	1			1							1	1		1		1					
"	Abraham Hunsucker	1				1									1				1							
"	Margt McArthur			1			1													1				1		
"	John Hayes		1	2					1									2	1		1					
"	Isaiah Graham																		2			1				
"	Martin Martin		1			2					1											1				
"	Samuel Hayes							1												1						
"	David Richardson			1	1					1									1		1	1				
"	Cussey Dunn																2	1			1		1			
"	Wm D. Manus	2	1				1									1			1							
"	Wm Manus Sen												1												1	
"	Augustus Williams	2	1	2	1	2			1							1	1	1	1							
"	Arch McDonald	3	1			1											1		1							
"	Wm Wood	2				1									1			1					1			
"	Jacob Stutts Sen					2					1											2				
"	John Campbell Sen	1	1					1							1	1				1						
"	Daniel McCallum						1												1		1					
"	Arch, Muthis	2	2		1	1			1								1				1					
"	Daniel Campfield				1			1												1						
"	John Collins	2				1													1							
"	Neill Johnson				1													1								
"	Charles Muthis	1				1													1							
"	John McCrery	1					2								1				1	1			1			
"	Norman McDonald					1									1			1								
"	John McNeill S.R.	1					1								1					1						
		22	8	7	7	16	6	4	4	1	2		1		8	6	6	7	14	7	6	5	3	1	1	

Slaves and Free Persons of Color are continued on the previous page

Nile[illegible] by the Marshal of the [illegible] District (or Territory) of N. Carolina 478

SLAVES. MALES. Under ten years of age. (under 10)	Of ten and under twenty-four. (10 to 24)	Of twenty-four and under thirty-six. (24 to 36)	Of thirty-six and under fifty-five. (36 to 55)	Of fifty-five and under one hundred. (55 to 100)	Of one hundred and upwards. (100, &c.)	SLAVES. FEMALES. Under ten years of age. (under 10)	Of ten and under twenty-four. (10 to 24)	Of twenty-four and under thirty-six. (24 to 36)	Of thirty-six and under fifty-five. (36 to 55)	Of fifty-five and under one hundred. (55 to 100)	Of one hundred and upwards. (100, &c.)	FREE COLORED PERSONS. MALES. Under ten years of age. (under 10)	Of ten and under twenty-four. (10 to 24)	Of twenty-four and under thirty-six. (24 to 36)	Of thirty-six and under fifty-five. (36 to 55)	Of fifty-five and under one hundred. (55 to 100)	Of one hundred and upwards. (100, &c.)	FREE COLORED PERSONS. FEMALES. Under ten years of age. (under 10)	Of ten and under twenty-four. (10 to 24)	Of twenty-four and under thirty-six. (24 to 36)	Of thirty-six and under fifty-five. (36 to 55)	Of fifty-five and under one hundred. (55 to 100)	Of one hundred and upwards. (100, &c.)	TOTAL.	WHITE PERSONS included in the foregoing. Who are Deaf and Dumb, under fourteen years of age. (under 14)	Who are Deaf and Dumb, of the age of fourteen and under twenty-five. (14 to 25)	Who are Deaf and Dumb, of twenty-five and upwards. (25, &c.)	Who are blind.	ALIENS—Foreigners not naturalized.	SLAVES AND COLORED PERSONS included in foregoing. Who are Deaf and Dumb, under fourteen years of age. (under 14)	Who are Deaf and Dumb, of the age of fourteen and under twenty-five. (14 to 25)	Who are Deaf and Dumb, of the age of twenty-five and upwards. (25, &c.)	Who are blind.
																								4									
2	2					1	1			1														15									
				1		1	1																	10									
																								5									
																								6									
																								5									
																								5									
																								8 8									
																								7									
																								11									
																								9									
																								4									
																								3									
																								7									
																								8									
																								13									
																								2									
1						2		1	1															11									
1																								9									
																								2									
																								5									
		1					1																	2									
[illegible]	1	1	1				2			1														17 [illegible]									
[illegible]			1							1														10									
																								7									
	2					1	1																	5									
																								9									
7	5	1	2	1		5	6	4	1	3														211									
																								218									

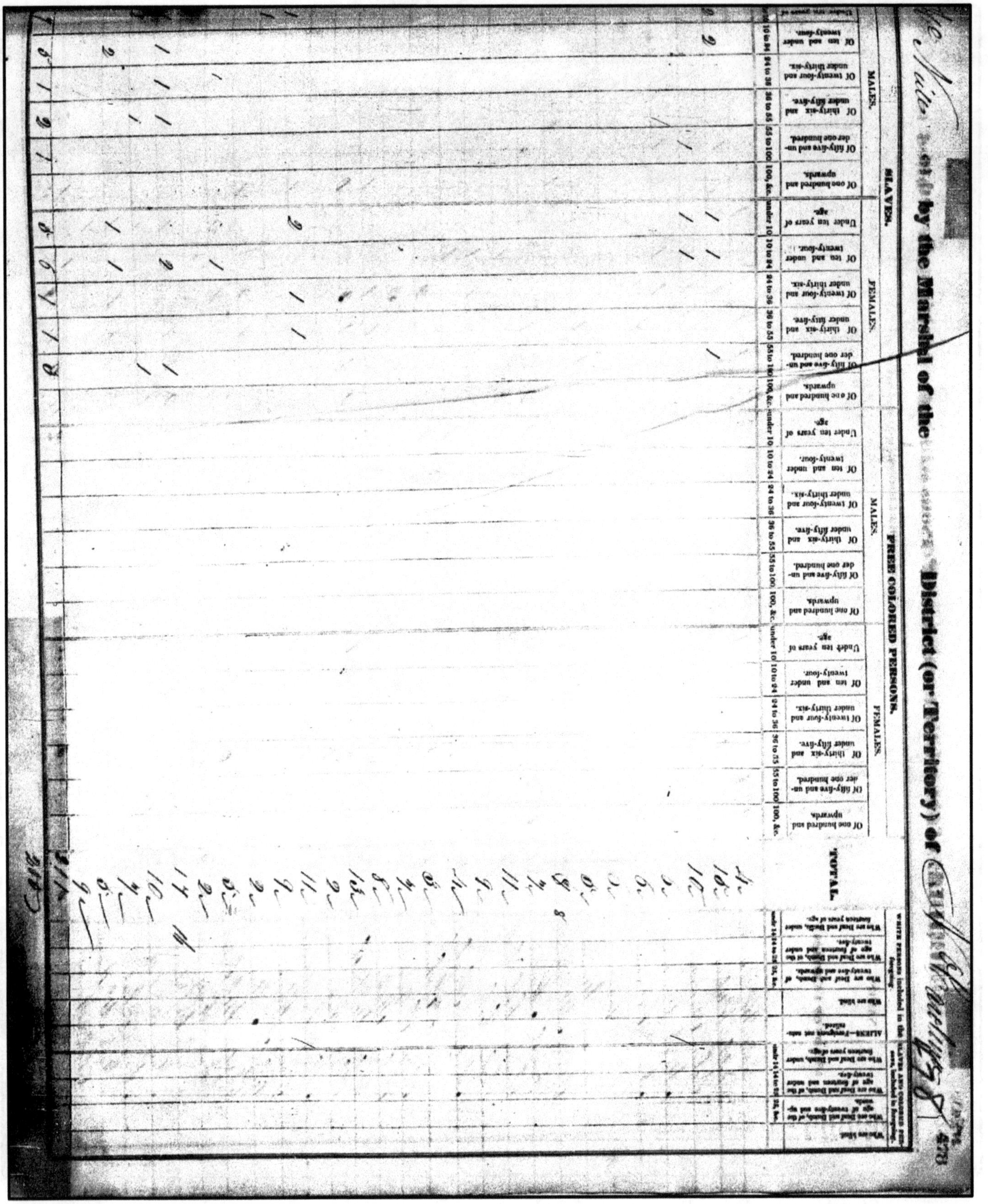

(No. 4.) 478 **SCHEDULE of the whole number of Persons within the Division allotted to** Malcom

FREE WHITE PERSONS, (INCLUDING HEADS OF FAMILIES.)

Name of County, City, Ward, Town, Township, Parish, Precinct, Hundred, or District.	NAMES OF HEADS OF FAMILIES.	MALES: under 5	5 to 10	10 to 15	15 to 20	20 to 30	30 to 40	40 to 50	50 to 60	60 to 70	70 to 80	80 to 90	90 to 100	100, &c.	FEMALES: under 5	5 to 10	10 to 15	15 to 20	20 to 30	30 to 40	40 to 50	50 to 60	60 to 70	70 to 80	80 to 90	90 to 100	100, &c.
Moore	John McDonald Sr.		1				1												1			1					
"	Alexr Cameron				2	2			1								1	1					1				
"	Angus Cameron		1			1		1							1	1			1				1				
"	Hugh Cameron	1	2			1	1													1							
"	Joseph Stubbs	1	2				1										1			1							
"	Johnson Cole		1				1								1	2				1							
"	Bryan Dawson	2					1									1				1							
"	Angus McDonald				3				1								1	1	1				1				
"	Archd Graham		1				1	1								1	2				1						
"	Daniel McDonald	1	1		1	2		1								2	1				2						
"	Duncan McCon Sr.	1		2	1			1								2		1			1						
"	Norman Ferguson	1	1			1	1												1								
"	Daniel Ferguson	1	1			1													1								
"	Daniel Graham	1				3			1												1				1		
"	Allen Morrison	1	2			1									1	1	1			1							
"	Hugh Keith	2	2	2					1						1	1	2	1			1						
"	John T. Cameron			X	1														1								
"	Angus Brown		2	1				1							1					1							
"	George Campbell	2	2			1		1								1			1								
"	John McDougald								1													1					
"	Charles Johnson	2				1												1									
"	Mary McDougald							1															1				
"	Malcom Buie	3	1					1							1	1			1					1			
"	John Shephard									1							1		2	1		1					
"	Thomas Mabbs											1									1	1					
"	Niell McQuin					2													1	1		1					
"	Jessy Thompson	1	1	2				1								1	1		1		1						
		20	20	4	8	15	4	9	5	1		1			6	14	11	5	13	8	8	5	4	1	1		

Slaves and Free Persons of Color are continued on the previous page

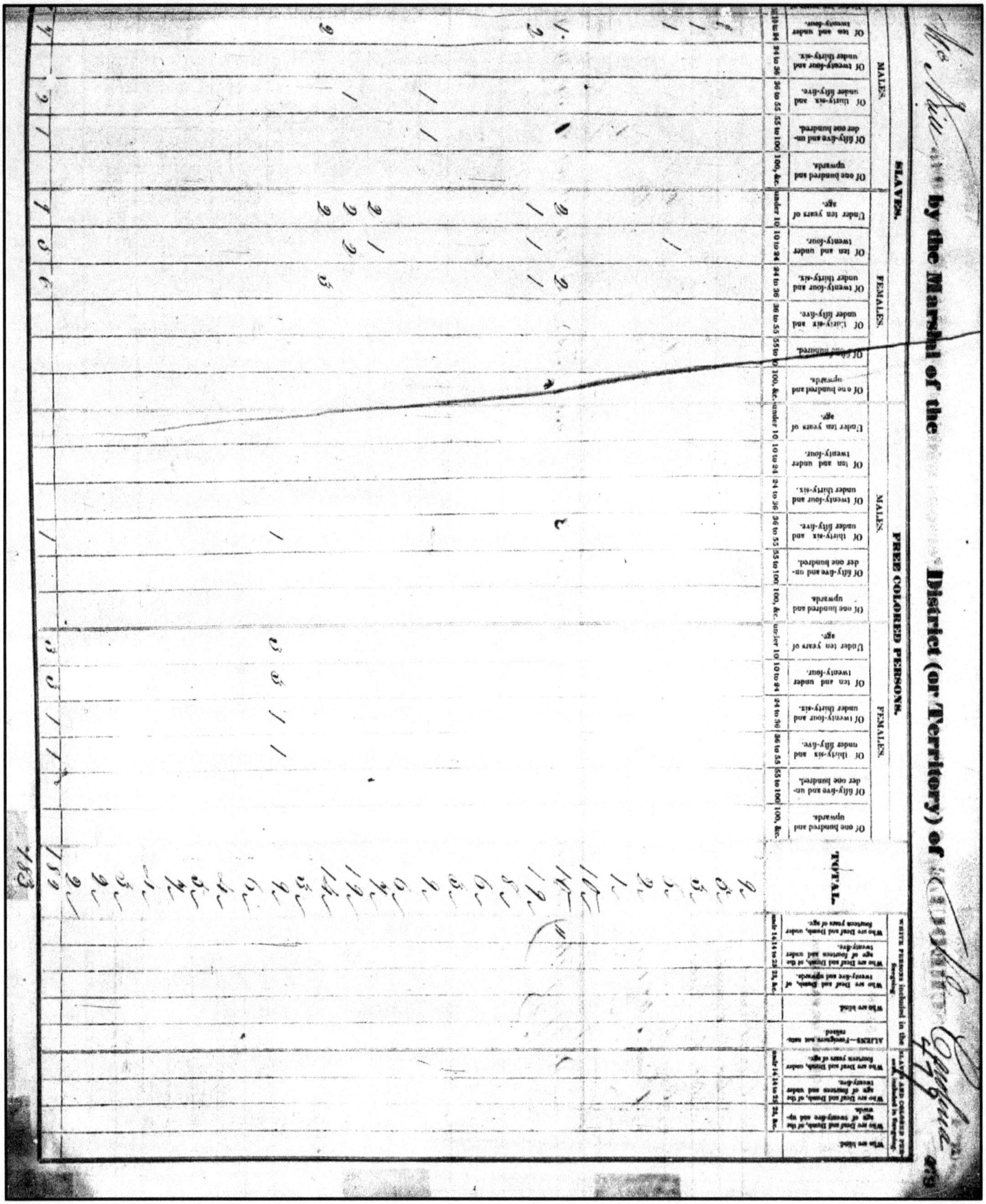

Mc Neill ... by the Marshal of the ... District (or Territory) of N. Carolina 477 479

Slaves, Males: Of ten and under twenty-four (10 to 24)	Slaves, Males: Of twenty-four and under thirty-six (24 to 36)	Slaves, Males: Of thirty-six and under fifty-five (36 to 55)	Slaves, Males: Of fifty-five and under one hundred (55 to 100)	Slaves, Males: Of one hundred and upwards (100, &c.)	Slaves, Females: Under ten years of age (under 10)	Slaves, Females: Of ten and under twenty-four (10 to 24)	Slaves, Females: Of twenty-four and under thirty-six (24 to 36)	Slaves, Females: Of thirty-six and under fifty-five (36 to 55)	Slaves, Females: Of fifty-five and under one hundred (55 to 100)	Slaves, Females: Of one hundred and upwards (100, &c.)	Free Colored Persons, Males: Under ten years of age (under 10)	Free Colored Persons, Males: Of ten and under twenty-four (10 to 24)	Free Colored Persons, Males: Of twenty-four and under thirty-six (24 to 36)	Free Colored Persons, Males: Of thirty-six and under fifty-five (36 to 55)	Free Colored Persons, Males: Of fifty-five and under one hundred (55 to 100)	Free Colored Persons, Males: Of one hundred and upwards (100, &c.)	Free Colored Persons, Females: Under ten years of age (under 10)	Free Colored Persons, Females: Of ten and under twenty-four (10 to 24)	Free Colored Persons, Females: Of twenty-four and under thirty-six (24 to 36)	Free Colored Persons, Females: Of thirty-six and under fifty-five (36 to 55)	Free Colored Persons, Females: Of fifty-five and under one hundred (55 to 100)	Free Colored Persons, Females: Of one hundred and upwards (100, &c.)	TOTAL.	White persons included in the foregoing: Who are Deaf and Dumb, under fourteen years of age (undr 14)	White persons: Who are Deaf and Dumb, of the age of fourteen and under twenty-five (14 to 25)	White persons: Who are Deaf and Dumb, of twenty-five and upwards (25, &c.)	White persons: Who are blind	ALIENS—Foreigners not naturalized	Slaves and colored persons included in the foregoing: Who are Deaf and Dumb, under fourteen years of age (undr 14)	Slaves and colored persons: Who are Deaf and Dumb, of the age of fourteen and under twenty-five (14 to 25)	Slaves and colored persons: Who are Deaf and Dumb, of the age of twenty-five and upwards (25, &c.)	Slaves and colored persons: Who are blind
																							9									
1																							5									
1																							3									
1						1																	5									
																							2									
																							1									
																							10									
1					2		2																10									
2					1	1	1																19									
																							8									
																							6									
																							5									
		1	1																				9									
																							6									
					2	1																	7									
		1			2	2																	19									
2					2		3																14									
																							3									
														1			3	3	1	1			9									
																							6									
																							4									
																							5									
																							7									
																							4									
																							3									
																							2									
																							2									
4		2	1		9	5	6							1			3	3	1	1			189									

183

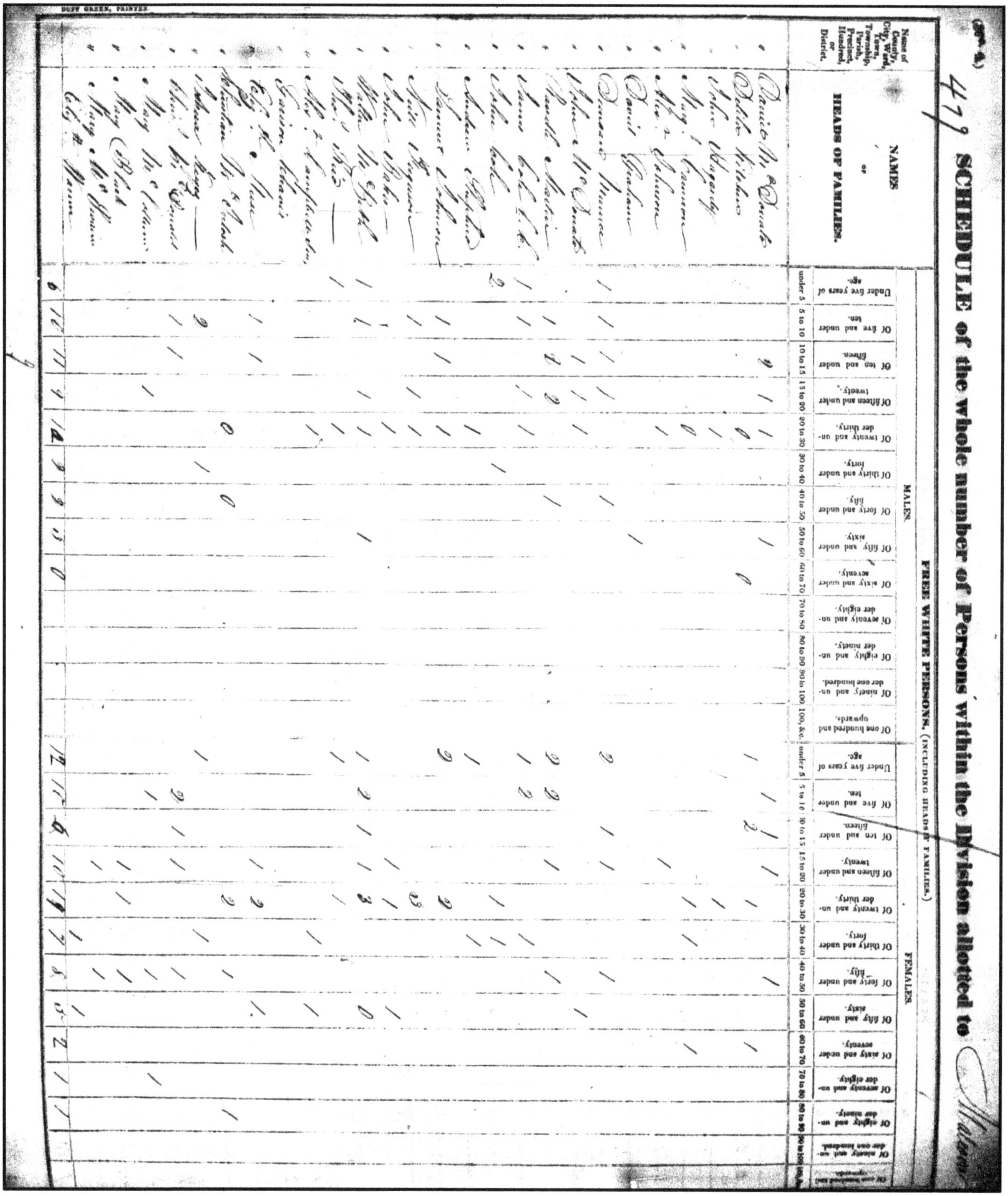

Slaves and Free Persons of Color are continued on the previous page

...by the Marshal of the ... District (or Territory) of No Carolina 480

450

SLAVES Males 10 to 24	Males 24 to 36	Males 36 to 55	Males 55 to 100	Males 100, &c.	Females under 10	Females 10 to 24	Females 24 to 36	Females 36 to 55	Females 55 to 100	Females 100, &c.	FREE COLORED PERSONS Males under 10	Males 10 to 24	Males 24 to 36	Males 36 to 55	Males 55 to 100	Males 100, &c.	Females under 10	Females 10 to 24	Females 24 to 36	Females 36 to 55	Females 55 to 100	Females 100, &c.	TOTAL	White persons included in the foregoing: Who are Deaf and Dumb, under fourteen years of age (under 14)	Who are Deaf and Dumb, of the age of fourteen and under twenty-five (14 to 25)	Who are Deaf and Dumb, of twenty-five and upwards (25, &c.)	Who are blind	ALIENS—Foreigners not naturalized	Slaves and colored persons included in the foregoing: Who are Deaf and Dumb, under fourteen years of age (under 14)	Who are Deaf and Dumb, of the age of fourteen and under twenty-five (14 to 25)	Who are Deaf and Dumb, of the age of twenty-five and upwards (25, &c.)	Who are blind
																							3									
1																							2									
																							2									
1																							4									
																							5									
																							2									
1																							21									
188	116	79	35		330	276	133	79	38		14	9	3	5	1	1	15	11	12	5	1		770[illegible]	3	1	3						
																							7745		1	3				2		

The number of Persons within my division consisting of the County of Moore appears in the foregoing Schedule. Subscribed by me the 16 day of November One thousand eight hundred and thirty

Malcom McNeill Assistant to the Marshal of the District of North Carolina

We hereby certify that a correct copy of the above Schedule Signed by the said Malcom McNeill Assistant to the Marshal of the District of North Carolina has been set up at two of the most publick places within the division open to the inspection of all concerned.

John McNeill

Phi. McDhaid

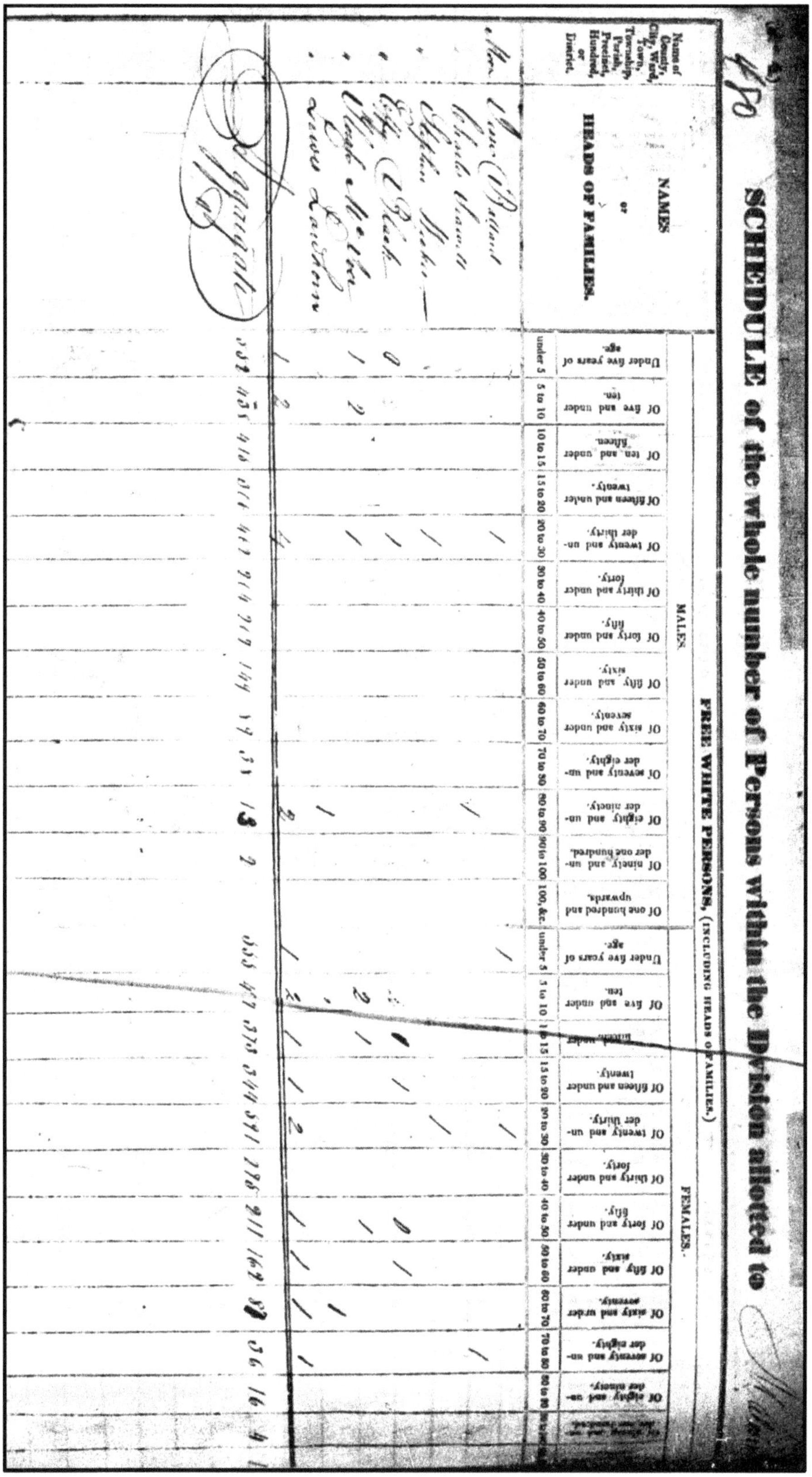

480

SCHEDULE of the whole number of Persons within the Division allotted to

Name of County, City, Ward, Town, Township, Parish, Precinct, Hundred, or District.	NAMES or HEADS OF FAMILIES.	M under 5	M 5 to 10	M 10 to 15	M 15 to 20	M 20 to 30	M 30 to 40	M 40 to 50	M 50 to 60	M 60 to 70	M 70 to 80	M 80 to 90	M 90 to 100	M 100, &c.	F under 5	F 5 to 10	F 10 to 15	F 15 to 20	F 20 to 30	F 30 to 40	F 40 to 50	F 50 to 60	F 60 to 70	F 70 to 80	F 80 to 90	F 90 to 100	F 100, &c.
Moore	Sion Ballard					1									1				1								
	Charles Scarrell											1												1			
	Stephen Walker					1													1								
	Effy C. Black	0				1											1	1			0	1					
	Uriah McIver	1	2			1										2	1				1						
	Lewis Lawhorn											1											1				
		1	2			4						2			1	2	1	1	2		1	1	1	1			
	Aggregate	552	435	416	314	419	264	217	149	97	51	13	2		555	457	373	344	591	276	211	162	87	36	16	4	

Slaves and Free Persons of Color are continued on the previous page

1840 Census

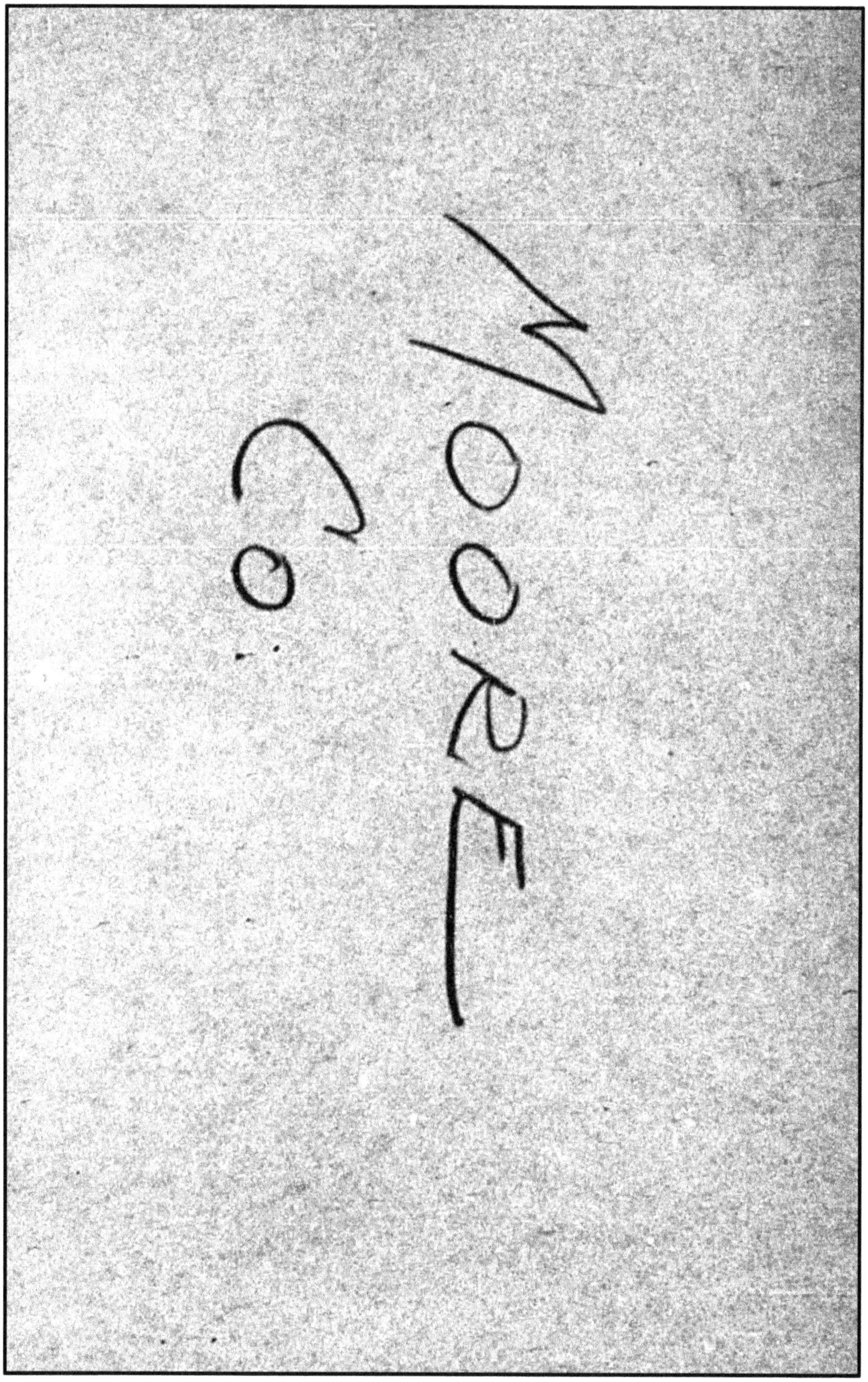
MOORE
CO

by the Marshal of the District (or Territory) of North Carolina

Slaves: Males Under 10	M 10 & under 24	M 24 & under 36	M 36 & under 55	M 55 & under 100	M 100 and upwards	Females Under 10	F 10 & under 24	F 24 & under 36	F 36 & under 55	F 55 & under 100	F 100 and upwards	Total	Mining	Agriculture	Commerce	Manufactures and trades	Navigation of the ocean	Navigation of canals, lakes, and rivers	Learned professions and engineers
												3		2					
												10		2					
												6		1					
2		1				3	1	1	1			11		3					
												6		1					
												7		1					
												4		1					
												5		3					
												2		1					
												6		1					
												3							
												5		1					
												5		1					
												2		1					
												2		1					
												10		2					
												5		2					
												3		2					
							1					6							
												5		3					
												5		2					
												7		2					
												6		2					
												6		2					
												7		3					
												6		3					
												7		3					
												9		4					
2	1	1	..	..		4	3	3	1	..	..	159		50					

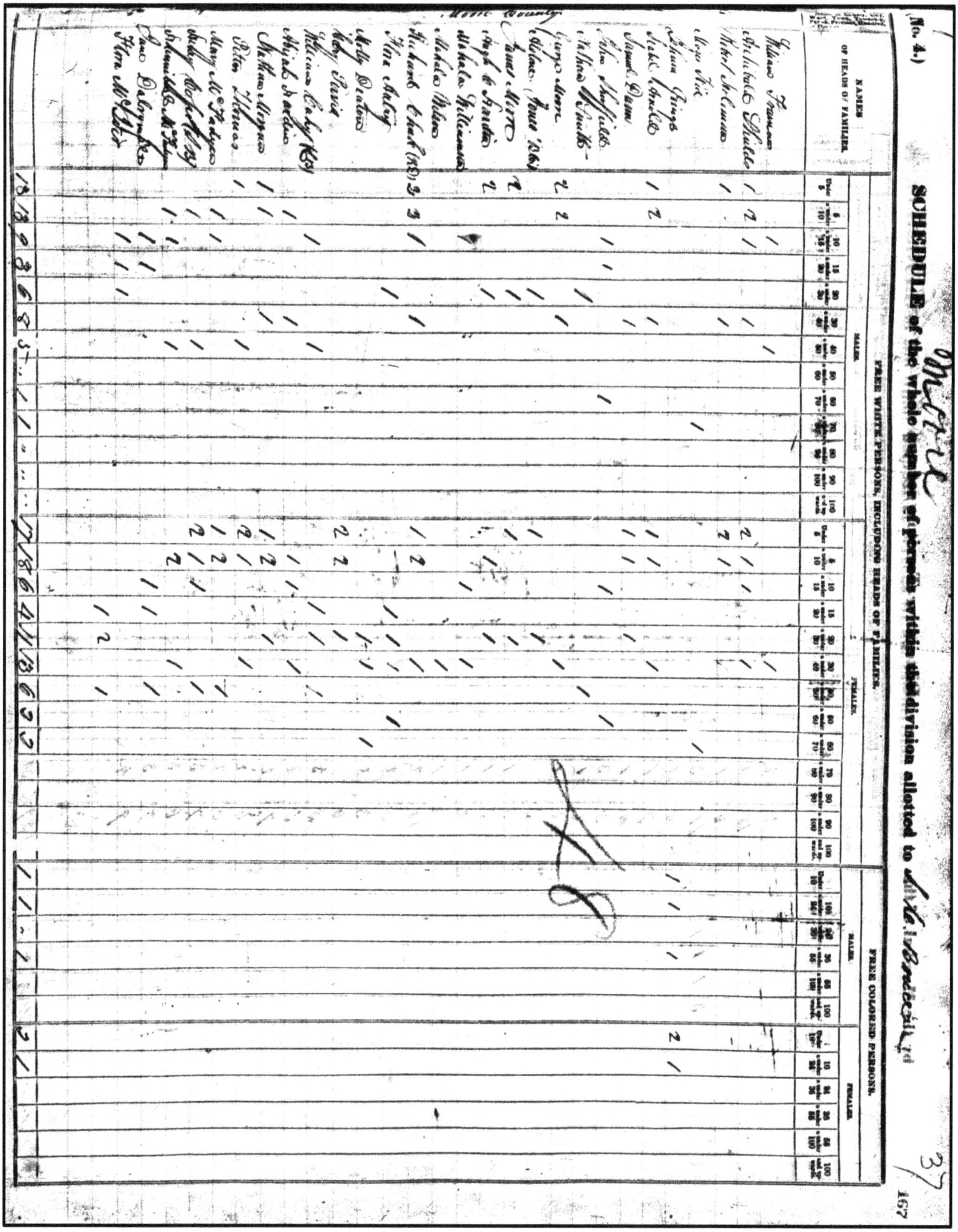
(No. 4.) SCHEDULE of the whole number of persons within the division allotted to [illegible] — Moore — 167 — 37

NAMES OF HEADS OF FAMILIES — FREE WHITE PERSONS, INCLUDING HEADS OF FAMILIES — FREE COLORED PERSONS

William Freeman
Archibald Shields
Robert Holeman
Moses Rice
Johua Grings
Isabel Arnold
Samuel Dunn
John Sheffield
Nathan Smith
George Moore
Abilene Jones (BC)
James Moore
Hugh C Hardin
Mahala Williamson
Mahala Wilson
Richard Clark (RD)
Flora Autry
Molly Deaton
Mary Purvis
William Caby (KS)
Abijah Hardin
Nathan Morgan
Peter Thomas
Mary McFadyen
Sukey Copeland
Schmiddt McFadyen
Jane Dalrymple
Flora McIver

Slaves and Free Persons of Color are located on the previous page

by the Marshal of the District (or Territory) of North Carolina

Slaves, Males, Under 10	10 & under 24	24 & under 36	36 & under 55	55 & under 100	100 & upwards	Slaves, Females, Under 10	10 & under 24	24 & under 36	36 & under 55	55 & under 100	100 & upwards	Total	Agriculture	Other occupations
			1				1	2				10	4	
												3	1	
												7	1	
												12	3	
												6	2	
				1								7	2	
							1					3	3	
												5	1	
	1											5	2	
												7	2	
				1				1		1		6	4	
												3	1	
			1									10	4	
												7	1	
												5	1	
	1											6	2	
												5	2	
												7	3	
							1					8	2	
												2	1	
												6	1	
										1		7	2	
	1								1			6	3	
												8	2	
3		1	2			5	1			1		21	6	
		1					1					8	3	
	1											7	4	
7	7					1	5					23	13	
												13	2	
												6	1	
10	11	2	4	2	-	6	11	3	1	3	-	225	77	

2

(No. 4.) **SCHEDULE** of the whole number of persons within the division allotted to A. C. Bruce 168

Moore County

NAMES OF HEADS OF FAMILIES	Free White Persons, Males: Under 5	5 & under 10	10 & under 15	15 & under 20	20 & under 30	30 & under 40	40 & under 50	50 & under 60	60 & under 70	70 & under 80	80 & under 90	90 & under 100	100 and upwards	Free White Persons, Females: Under 5	5 & under 10	10 & under 15	15 & under 20	20 & under 30	30 & under 40	40 & under 50	50 & under 60	60 & under 70	70 & under 80	80 & under 90	90 & under 100	100 and upwards	Free Colored Persons, Males: Under 10	10 & under 24	24 & under 36	36 & under 55	55 & under 100	100 and upwards	Free Colored Persons, Females: Under 10	10 & under 24	24 & under 36	36 & under 55	55 & under 100	100 and upwards
Daniel Wilder Esqr	1						1									3				1																		
Charles Runnells		1			1														1																			
Daniel C Currie		2	1			1								1	1				1																			
James Jackson	1		1		1		1							1	3	2	1			1																		
John A. Johnson	2					1								2				1																				
David Wicker	2	1	1			1													1																			
John McIver Esqr				1			1																															
James Jackson Jr	2				1									1				1																				
Benjamin Cole					1												1		1				1															
Evander McNair								1						1	1	1	2		1																			
Joseph Cook							1									1			1																			
Nancy Murchison						1																1		1														
Kenneth McIntosh		1	1	1				1								2	1	1			1																	
John Cole Jr	1	1				1								2				1	1																			
Matthew C Wicker	2		2			1																																
Nathan J Knight	2					1								1				1																				
Alexander Black		1						1									1		1				1															
Peter McIntyre		3	1				1									1				1																		
D. M. R. McIntosh	3					1								1	1			1																	1			
Daniel W. McNair					1															1																		
Jordan Wicker	1					1								3					1																			
W. B. Clark	2	1	1			1													1																			
Murdo McIntosh										1								1	1	1																		
Andrew Cole	2	2				1								1				1																				
Mary McIver		1	2	2													2				1																	
John H Dalrymple	1					1								3				1																				
Thomas McKinnish				1	1			1									2				1																	
Johnson Wicker									1													1																
Charles McDonald	1	2	1	1			1							2	2	1	1			1																		
John C Wicker	2	1			1									1				1																				
	25	17	11	6	7	12	6	4	1	1	.	.	.	20	4	11	11	10	11	6	3	2	2	1	[illegible]	.	.	.	.	.	.	.	.	.	1	.	.	.

Slaves and Free Persons of Color are located on the previous page

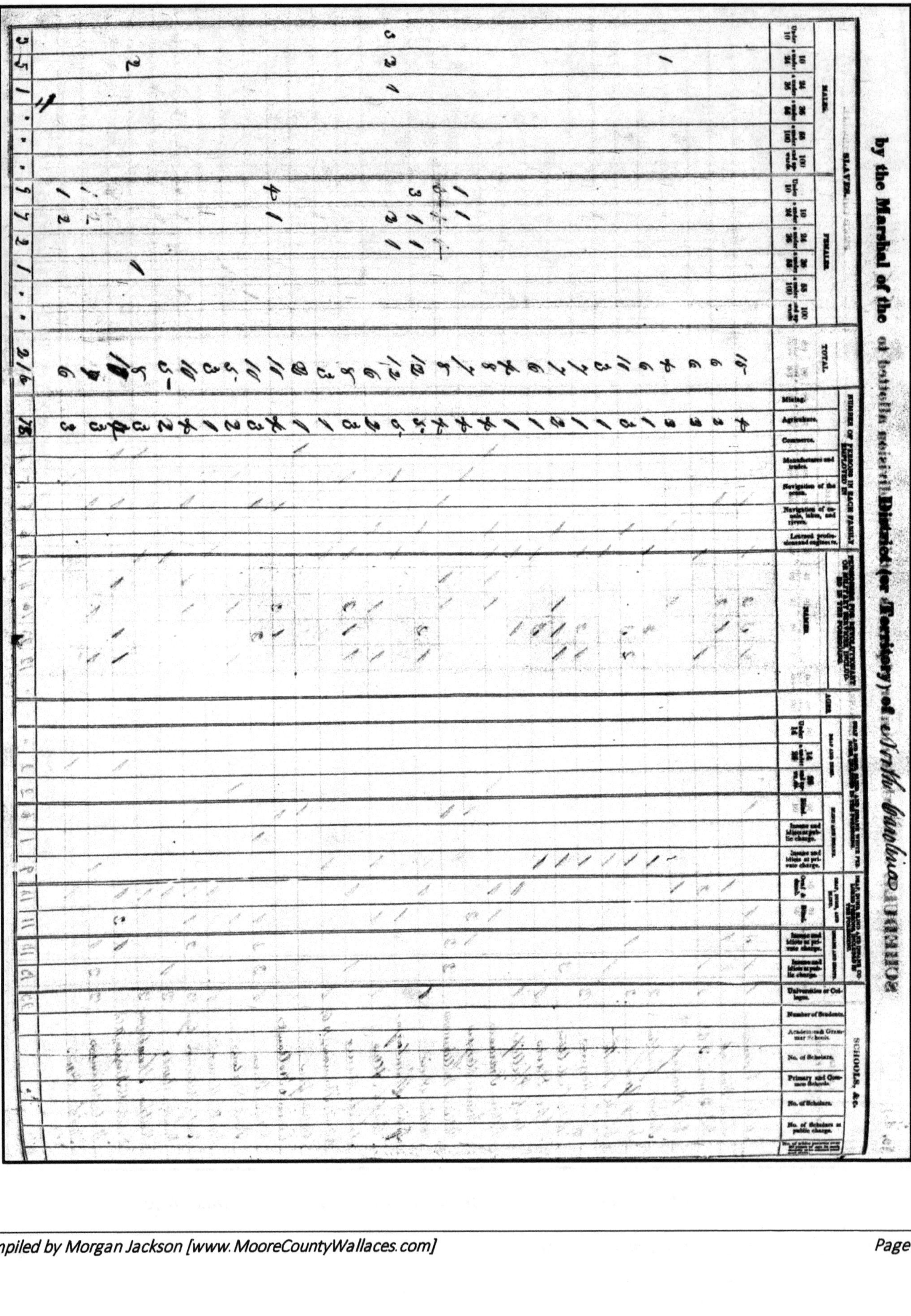
by the Marshal of the District (or Territory) of North Carolina

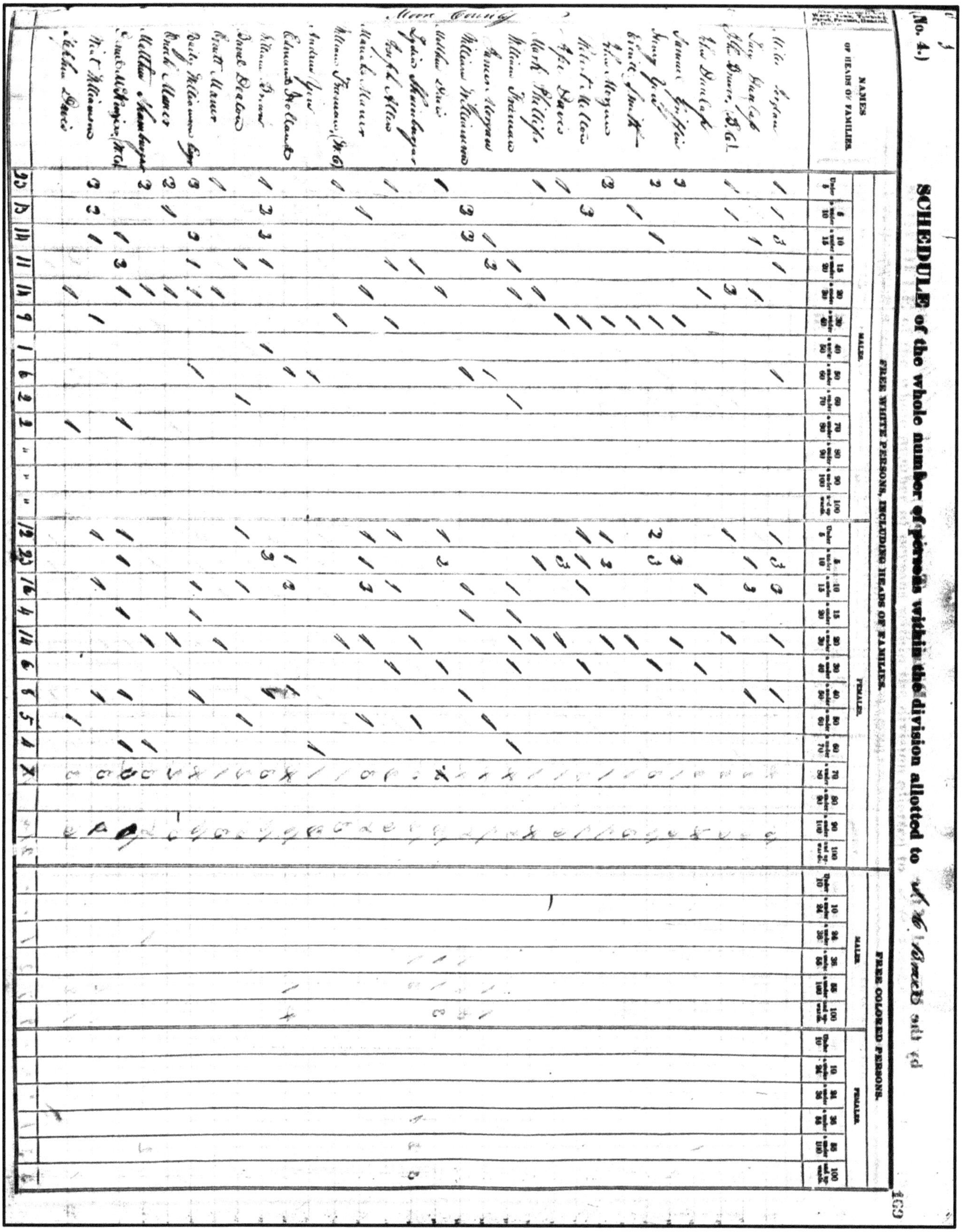

(No. 4.) SCHEDULE of the whole number of persons within the division allotted to A. C. Bruce

Moore County

FREE WHITE PERSONS, INCLUDING HEADS OF FAMILIES.

NAMES OF HEADS OF FAMILIES	M under 5	M 5–10	M 10–15	M 15–20	M 20–30	M 30–40	M 40–50	M 50–60	M 60–70	M 70–80	M 80–90	M 90–100	M 100+	F under 5	F 5–10	F 10–15	F 15–20	F 20–30	F 30–40	F 40–50	F 50–60	F 60–70	F 70–80
Miles Jordan	1	1	3	1				1						1	3	3		1		1			
Lucy Dunlap			1		1										1	3				1			
John Brewer, (B.C.)	1	1			2									1				1					
John Dunlap					1											1			1				
Samuel Griffin	3					1									3			1					
Henry Yow	2		1			1								2	3				1				
Everitt Smith		1				1												1					
John Morgan	2					1								1	2			1					
Robert Mellow		3				1								1	1	1			1				
Asa Davis	1					1									3			1					
Mark Phillips	1				1										1			1					
William Freeman				1	1				1							1	1	1	1			1	
James Morgan			1	2				1													1		
William Williamson		2	2					1								1	1			1			
Matthew Davis	1				1									1	2				1				
Lydia Shamburger				1														1			1		
Joseph Allen	1			1		1								1		1			1				
Mariah Maner		1			1									1	1	3		1			1		
William Freeman, (W.C.)	1					1												1					
Andrew Yow								1														1	
Edmund Holland								1							1	2				1			
William Brown	1	2	2	1			1								3					1			
Daniel Deaton				1					1					1		1					1		
Everitt Maner	1				1													1					
Baily Williamson Esqr	3		2	1	1			1								1	1			1			
Enoch Maner	2	1			1													1					
Matthew Shamburger	2				1													1				1	
Daniel McKenzie, (W.C.)			1	3	1					1				1	1		1			1		1	
Neil Williamson	3	2	1			1								1		1				1			
Nathan Davis					1					1											1		
(Totals)	23	13	14	11	14	9	1	6	2	2	"	"	"	12	23	16	4	14	6	8	5	4	X

Slaves and Free Persons of Color are located on the previous page

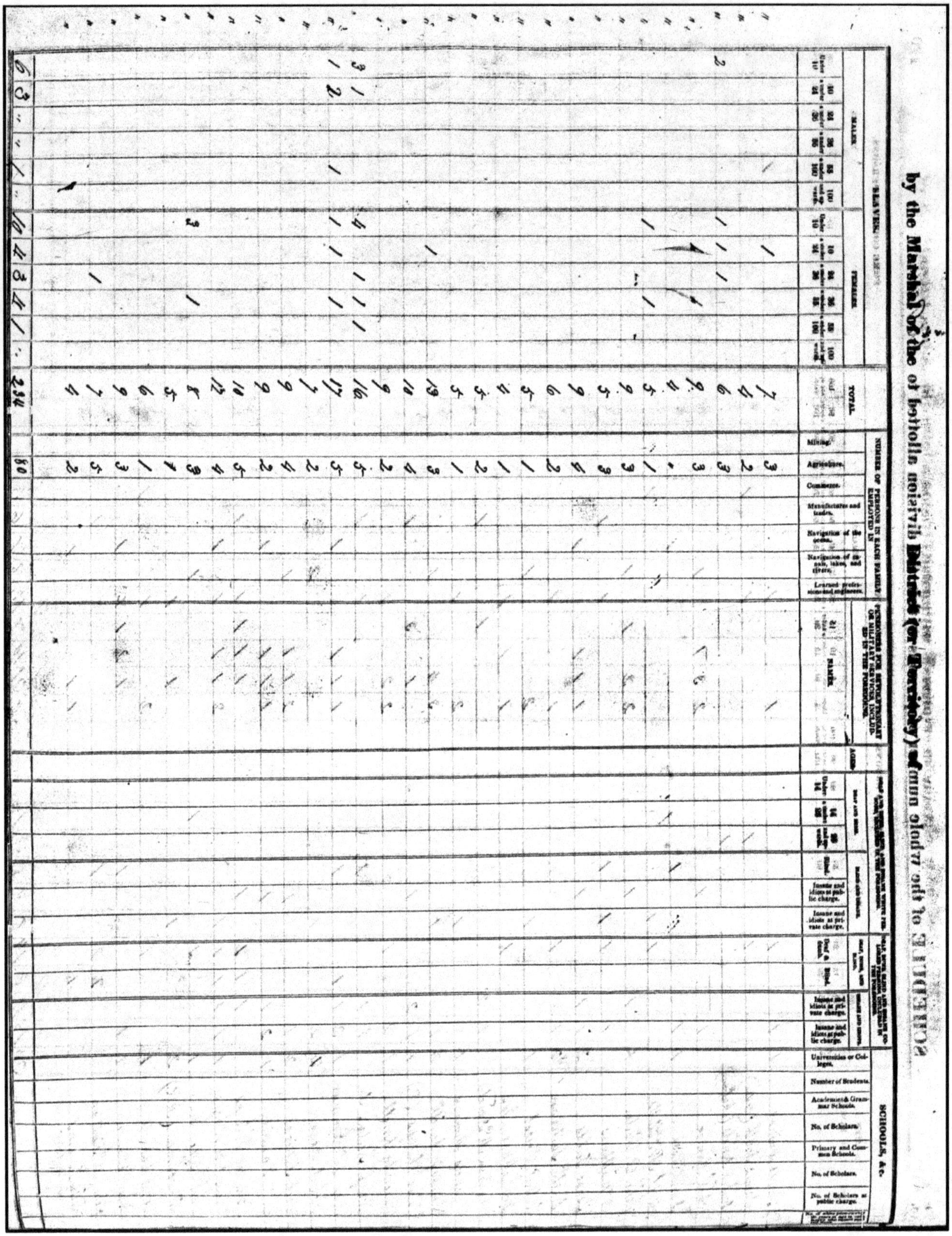

SCHEDULE of the whole number of persons ... allotted to the Marshal of the District (or Territory) of

Slaves: Males under 10	Males 10 & under 24	Males 24 & under 36	Males 36 & under 55	Males 55 & under 100	Males 100 & upwards	Females under 10	Females 10 & under 24	Females 24 & under 36	Females 36 & under 55	Females 55 & under 100	Females 100 & upwards	Total	Agriculture
							1					7	3
												4	2
2						1	1	1				6	3
												9	3
												4	·
						1			1			5	1
												9	3
												5	3
												9	4
												6	2
												5	1
												4	1
												5	2
												5	1
							1					13	3
												10	4
												9	2
3	1					4		1	1	1		16	5
1	2			1		1	1		1			17	5
												7	2
												9	4
												9	2
												10	5
												12	4
						3			1			8	3
												5	1
												6	1
												9	3
								1				7	5
												4	2
6	3	"	"	1	"	10	4	3	4	1	"	234	80

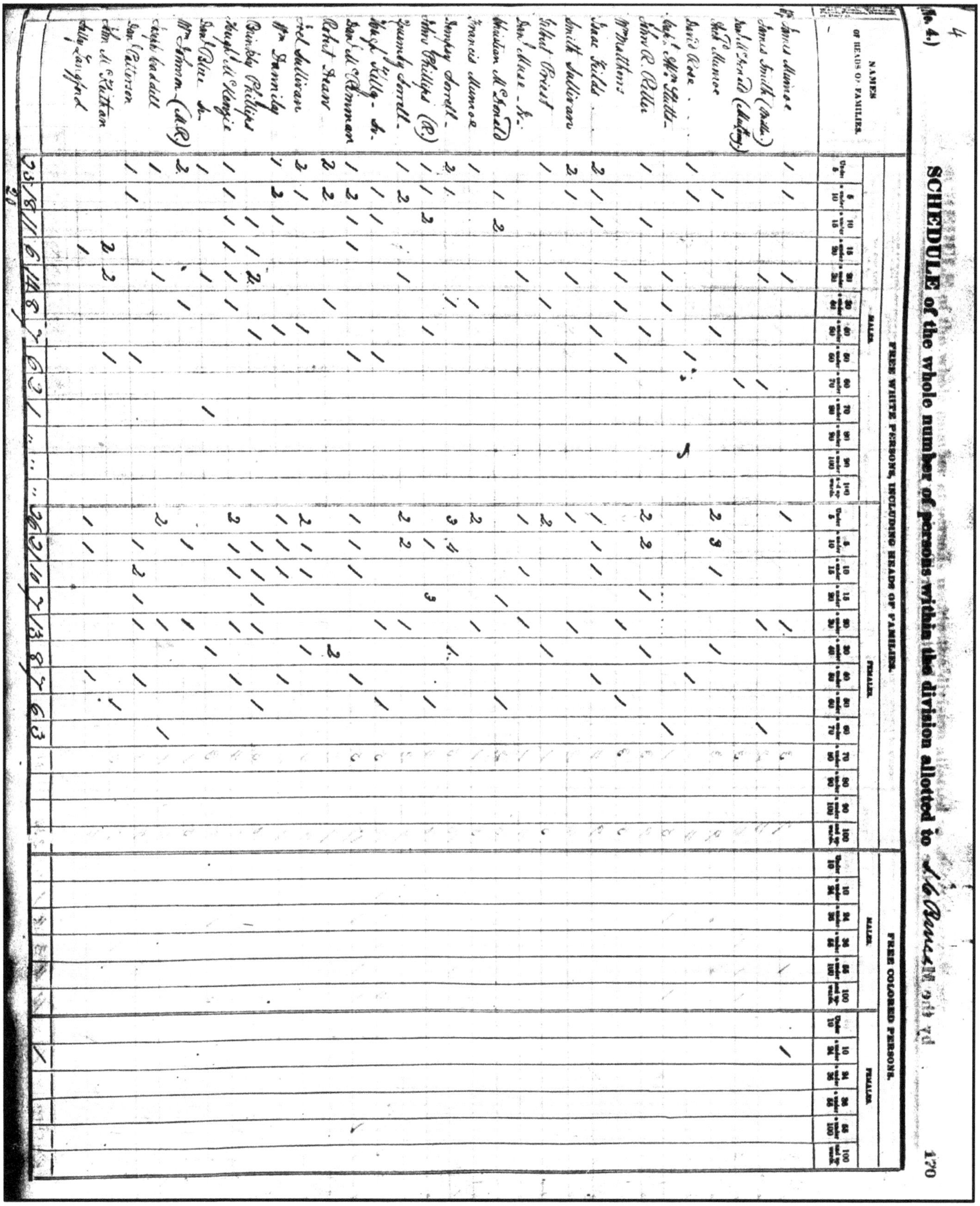
(No. 4.) SCHEDULE of the whole number of persons within the division allotted to [illegible] 170

NAMES OF HEADS OF FAMILIES.

James Munroe
James Smith (Mill.)
Sarah McDonald (Mulatto)
Neil Munroe
David Rose
Capt. Wm. Hill
Alex. R. Ritter
Wm. Matthews
Smith Sullivan
Isaac Fields
Gilbert Priest
Saml. Muse Jr.
Christian McDonald
Francis Munroe
Sampson Sorrell
Alex. Phillips (R.)
Quently Sorrell
Wm. Kelly Jr.
Saml. McKinnon
Robert Sears
Neil Sullivan
Wm. Tunnilay
Brinkley Phillips
Hugh McKenzie
Saml. Blue Jr.
Wm. Johnson (M.R.)
Leah Caddell
Saml. Patterson
Wm. McKeithan
Billy Langford

Slaves and Free Persons of Color are located on the previous page

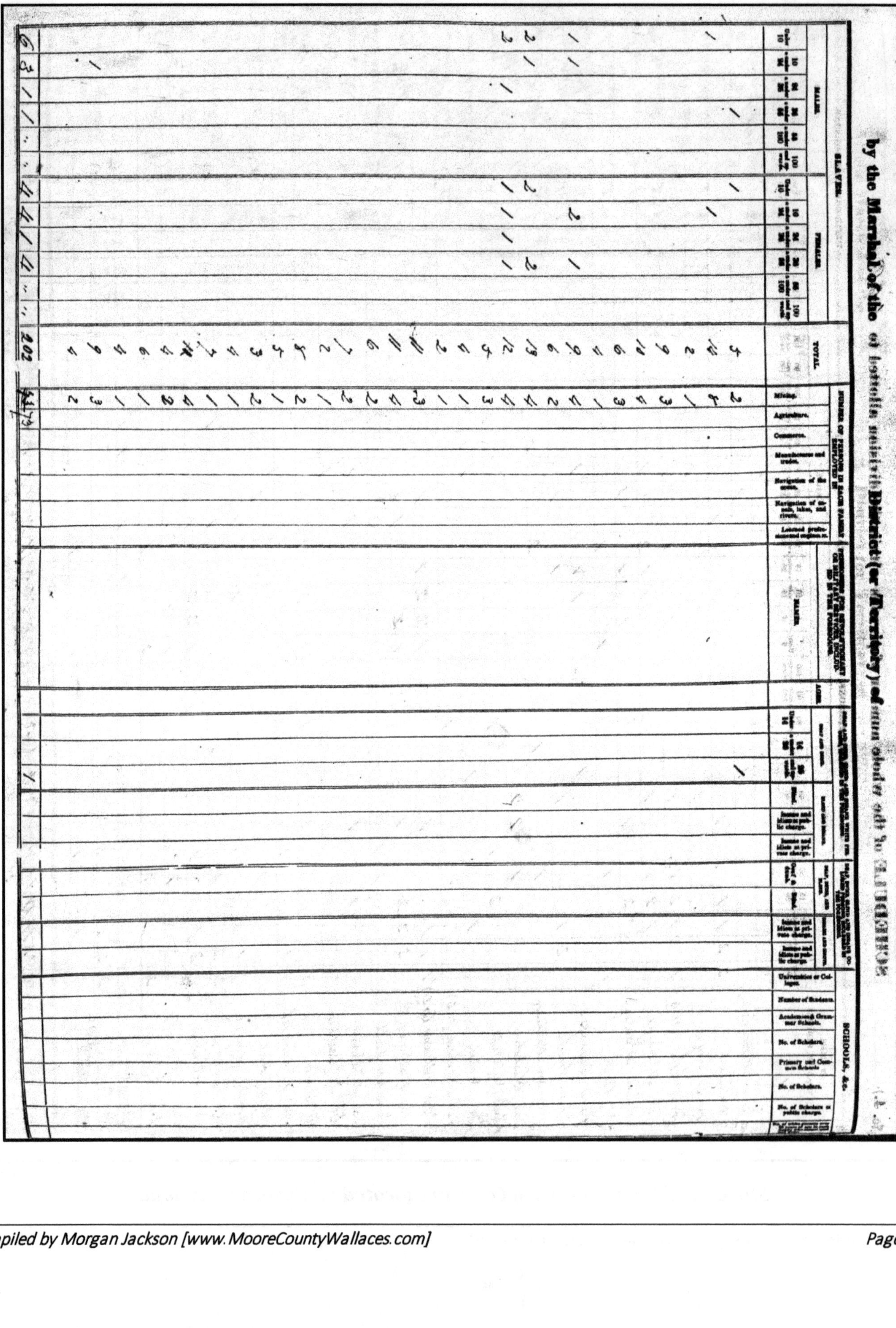

by the Marshal of the District (or Territory) of

Slaves: Males Under 10	Males 10 & under 24	Males 24 & under 36	Males 36 & under 55	Males 55 & under 100	Males 100 and upwards	Females Under 10	Females 10 & under 24	Females 24 & under 36	Females 36 & under 55	Females 55 & under 100	Females 100 and upwards	Total	Employed in: Mining	Agriculture	Commerce	Manufactures and trades	Navigation of the ocean	Navigation of canals, lakes, and rivers	Learned professional engineers, &c.	Pensioners for Revolutionary or military services: Names	Ages	White deaf and dumb: Under 14	14 & under 25	25 and upwards	Blind	Insane and idiots at public charge	Insane and idiots at private charge	Colored: Deaf & dumb	Blind	Insane and idiots at private charge	Insane and idiots at public charge	Universities or Colleges	Number of Students	Academies & Grammar Schools	No. of Scholars	Primary and Common Schools	No. of Scholars	No. of Scholars at public charge
			1			1						5	2											1														
1							1					14	8																									
												2	1																									
												9	3																									
												10	4																									
												6	3																									
												4	1																									
1	1						2		1			9	4																									
												6	2																									
2	1					2			2			13	4																									
2		1				1	1	1	1			12	4																									
												5	3																									
												4	1																									
												2	1																									
												11	3																									
												11	4																									
												6	2																									
												7	2																									
												2	1																									
												8	2																									
												5	1																									
												3	2																									
												4	1																									
												7	1																									
												11	4																									
												4	2																									
												6	1																									
												4	1																									
	1											9	3																									
												4	2																									
6	3	1	1	..	..	4	4	1	4	..	..	202	73											1														

(No. 4.) **SCHEDULE** of the whole number of persons within the division allotted to A. C. Bruce 171

NAMES OF HEADS OF FAMILIES.	FREE WHITE PERSONS, INCLUDING HEADS OF FAMILIES. MALES. Under 5	5 & under 10	10 & under 15	15 & under 20	20 & under 30	30 & under 40	40 & under 50	50 & under 60	60 & under 70	70 & under 80	80 & under 90	90 & under 100	100 and upwards	FEMALES. Under 5	5 & under 10	10 & under 15	15 & under 20	20 & under 30	30 & under 40	40 & under 50	50 & under 60	60 & under 70	70 & under 80	80 & under 90	90 & under 100	100 and upwards	FREE COLORED PERSONS. MALES. Under 10	10 & under 24	24 & under 36	36 & under 55	55 & under 100	100 and upwards	FEMALES. Under 10	10 & under 24	24 & under 36	36 & under 55	55 & under 100	100 and upwards
John Patterson (D.C.)									1							1				1																		
Archd Leach	3	2	1	1			1							1	1	1			1																			
Samuel Key								1													1																	
James Cole (W.C.)	1		1	2	1			1							1			1			1																	
John McDuffie			1	2	1			1								1	1	2			1																	
Malcom McAuley				2			1								1		1			1																		
Wm Britt	1				1									1				1																				
James Dunlap									1							1	1				1																	
Isham Sorrell		2	1					1									1			1																		
Norman Matthison					1					1								2				1		1														
Danl Chisholm					1		2	2																														
Hector McNeill				2		1					1												1															
Levy Deaton			1						1		1										1	1																
James Jackson (W.C.)											1									1																		
John Williams (W.C.)	1	1	1				1							1	2	2	1			1																		
John Wallace		3	3	2			1							1	2				1	1																		
James Campbell					1	1													3				1															
Danl McLean				1			1												1		4																	
Chs McArthur								1													1																	
Wm Deaton	1				1		1				1			1		1		1					1															
Neil McKinnish	1	1				1								1				1																				
Samuel Dye					1				1											1																		
Thomas Hannon		1				1										1			1																			
Pope Hannon	2	2			1														1				1															
James Johnson		2	1			1								1	2	2			1																			
Burrel Ritter					2									1				1																				
Danl McKinnon	2				1									2				1																				
Elias Rose					1														1			1	1															
Danl Blue Jr	2	2	1			1									1				1																			
Alexr Black			1			1								1				1																				
	14	15	11	12	14	7	8	7	4	1	3	..	..	11	10	10	5	11	11	7	10	3	5	1		204												

Slaves and Free Persons of Color are located on the previous page

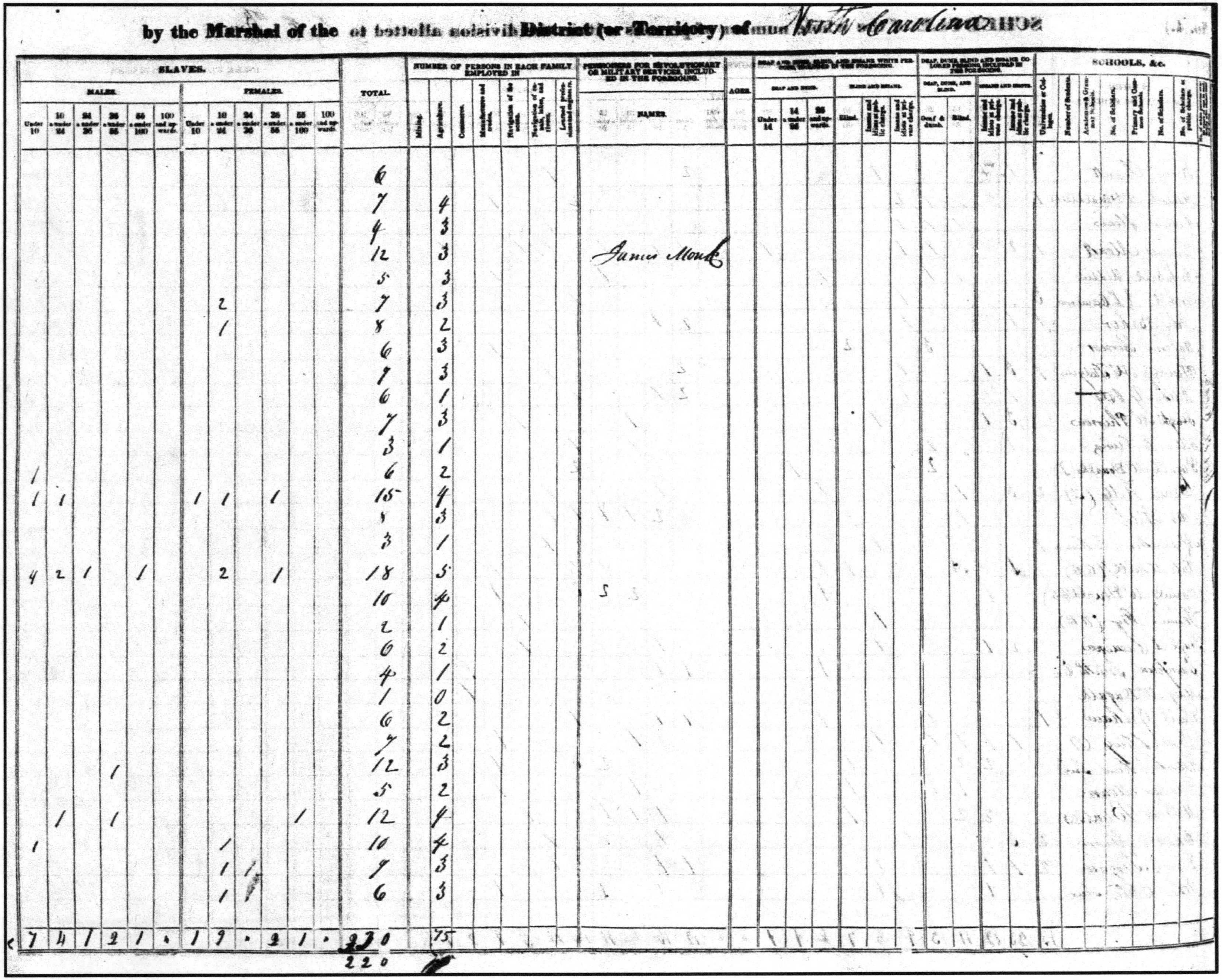

by the Marshal of the District (or Territory) of North Carolina

Slaves, Males: Under 10	10 & under 24	24 & under 36	36 & under 55	55 & under 100	100 and upwards	Slaves, Females: Under 10	10 & under 24	24 & under 36	36 & under 55	55 & under 100	100 and upwards	Total	Mining	Agriculture	Commerce	Manufactures and trades	Navigation of the ocean	Navigation of canals, lakes, and rivers	Learned professional engineers	Pensioners: Names	Ages
												6									
												7		4							
												4		3							
												12		3						James Monk	
												5		3							
							2					7		3							
							1					8		2							
												6		3							
												7		3							
												6		1							
												7		3							
												3		1							
1												6		2							
1	1					1	1		1			15		4							
												8		3							
												3		1							
4	2	1		1			2		1			18		5							
												10		4							
												2		1							
												6		2							
												4		1							
												1		0							
												6		2							
												7		2							
			1									12		3							
												5		2							
	1		1							1		12		4							
1							1					10		4							
							1	1				9		3							
							1	1				6		3							
7	4	1	2	1	•	1	9	•	2	1	•	230		75							
												220									

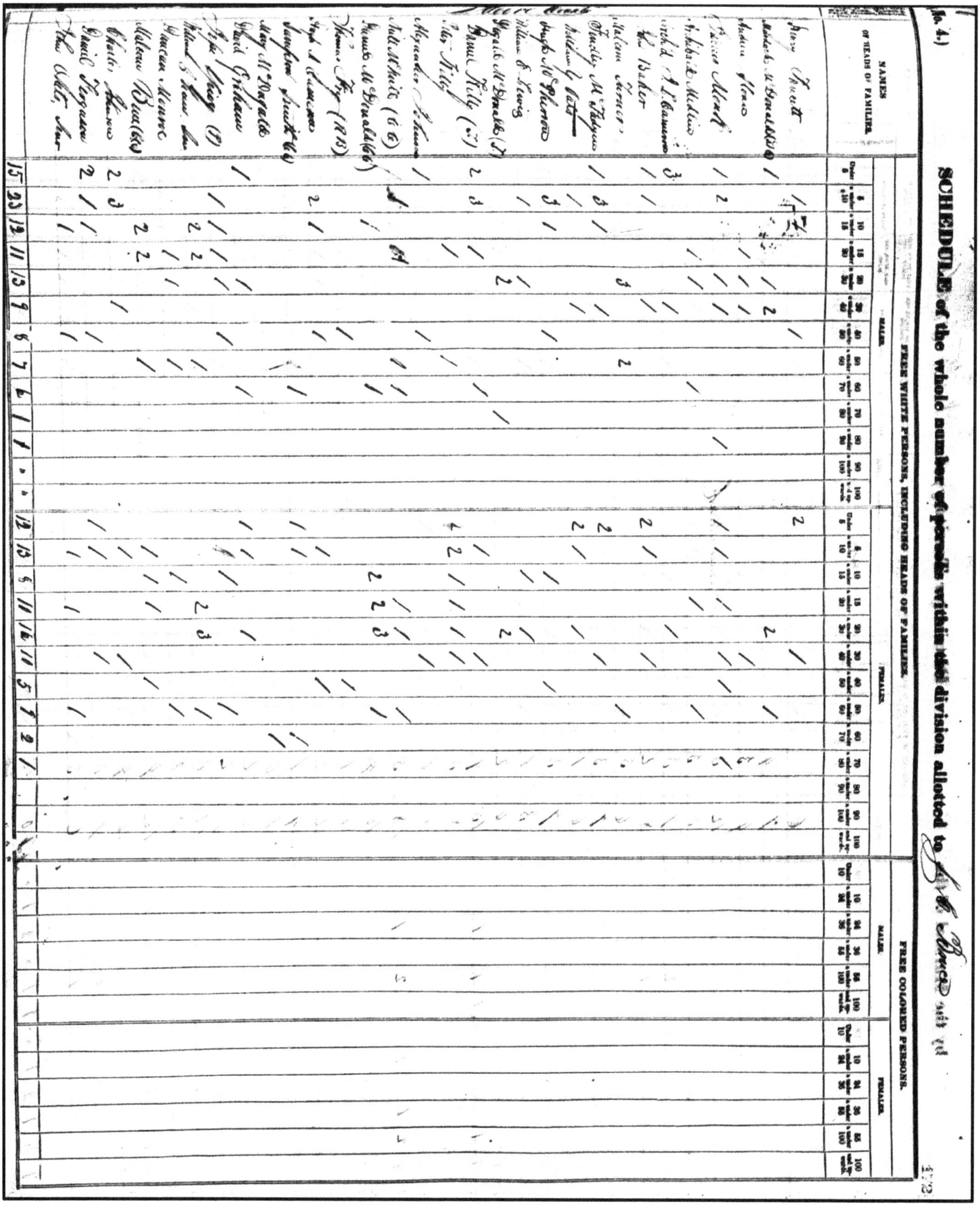

(No. 4.) SCHEDULE of the whole number of persons within the division allotted to J. C. Bruce

472

FREE WHITE PERSONS, INCLUDING HEADS OF FAMILIES. — MALES (columns M) / FEMALES (columns F). FREE COLORED PERSONS — MALES / FEMALES.

NAMES OF HEADS OF FAMILIES	M Under 5	M 5-10	M 10-15	M 15-20	M 20-30	M 30-40	M 40-50	M 50-60	M 60-70	M 70-80	M 80-90	M 90-100	M 100 & up	F Under 5	F 5-10	F 10-15	F 15-20	F 20-30	F 30-40	F 40-50	F 50-60	F 60-70	F 70-80	F 80-90	F 90-100	F 100 & up	FC M Under 10	FC M 10-24	FC M 24-36	FC M 36-55	FC M 55-100	FC M 100 & up	FC F Under 10	FC F 10-24	FC F 24-36	FC F 36-55	FC F 55-100	FC F 100 & up
Henry Fawcett		1					1							2					1																			
Murdock McDonald (CC)	1				1	2												2			1																	
Andrew Flowers				1	1	1													1																			
James Monk	1	2			1	1					1			1	1		1		1	1																		
Archibald Medlin				1	1				1								1				1																	
Arch'd A. L. Cameron	3					1												1																				
John Baker	1	1				1								2	1				1																			
Malcom Turner					3			2													1																	
Findley McFadyen	1	3	1			1								2					1																			
William G. Oats		1				1								2	1			1																				
Hugh McPherson		3	1				1									1				1																		
William E. Lewis		1			1											1		1																				
Dugald McDonald (T)					2					1								2																				
Daniel Kelly (T)	2	3		1					1						1				1																			
Peter Kelly				1				1						4	2	1	1	1	1																			
Alexander Johnson	1						1												1																			
Neill McNeill (CC)		1		1				1	1								1	1			1																	
Daniel McDonald (CC)			1						1							2	2	3			1																	
Thomas Fry (RB)							1													1																		
Hugh A. Cameron		2	1				1								1					1																		
Sampson Smith (CC)									1					1	1							1																
Mary McDugald																						1																
David Graham	1				1				1					1	1			1																				
Jesse Spivey (P)		1	1	1	1		1								1	1					1																	
William G. Shaw Sen			2	2				1									2	3			1																	
Duncan Monroe				1	1			1								1					1																	
Malcom Blue (CC)			2	2				1							1	1	1			1																		
Charles Johnson	2	3				1									1				1																			
Daniel Ferguson	2	1	1				1							1	1				1																			
John Oats, Senr			1				1								1		1				1																	
	15	23	12	11	13	9	8	7	6	1	1	"	"	12	13	8	11	16	11	5	9	2	1															

Slaves and Free Persons of Color are located on the previous page

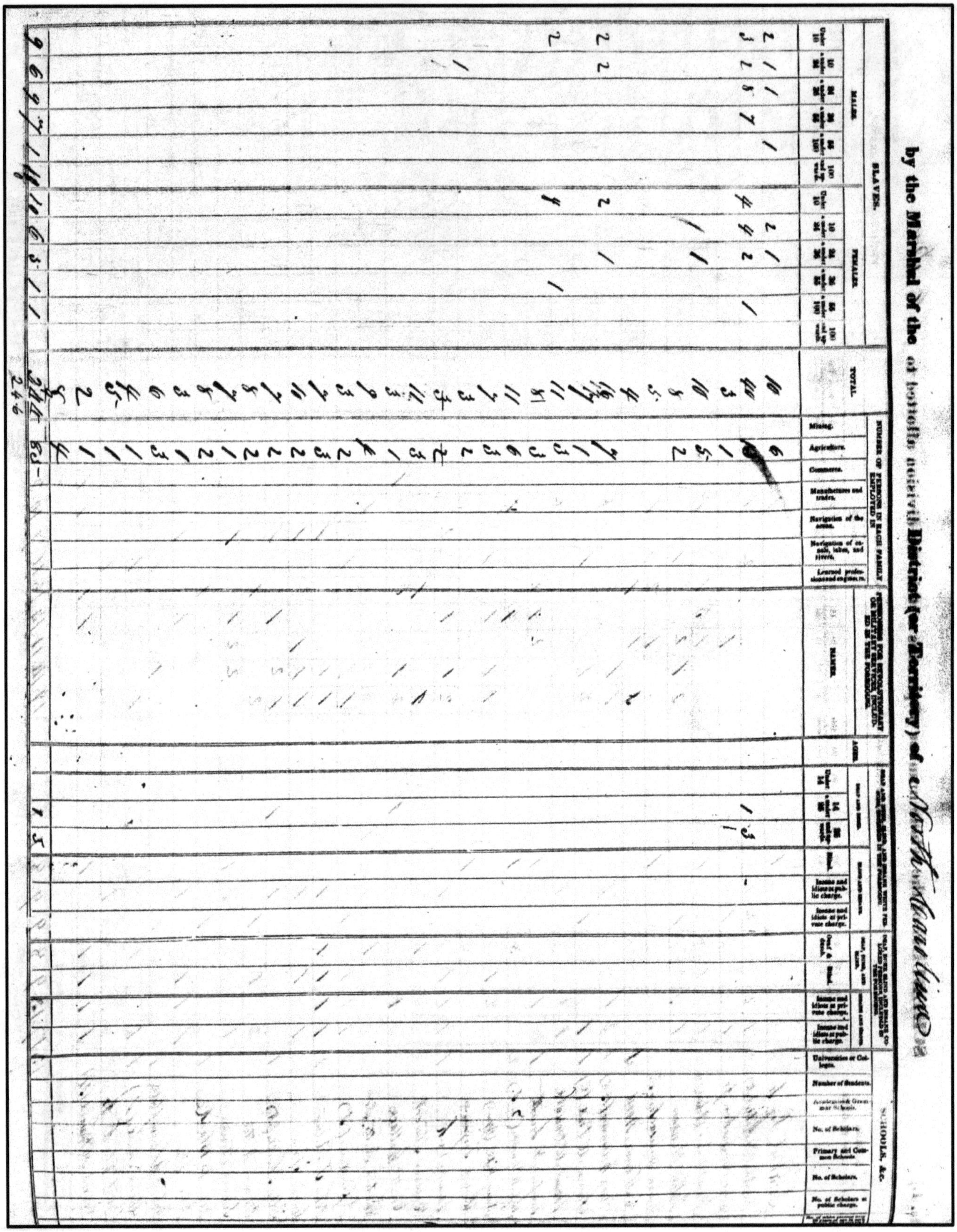

by the Marshal of the District (or Territory) of North Carolina

Slaves, Males, Under 10	Males, 10 & under 24	Males, 24 & under 36	Males, 36 & under 55	Males, 55 & under 100	Males, 100 and upwards	Females, Under 10	Females, 10 & under 24	Females, 24 & under 36	Females, 36 & under 55	Females, 55 & under 100	Females, 100 and upwards	Total	Mining	Agriculture	Commerce	Manufactures and trades	Navigation of the ocean	Navigation of canals, lakes, and rivers	Learned professional engineers, &c.
2	1	1		1			2	1				10		6					
3	2	8	7			4	4	2		1		40		[illegible]					
												3		1					
							1	1				10		5					
												8		2					
												5							
												4							
2	2					2		1				16		7					
												17		1					
2						4			1			11		3					
												81		3					
												11		6					
												7		3					
	1											3		2					
												~~3~~		~~2~~					
												11		3					
												3		1					
												9		4					
												3		2					
												7		3					
												10		2					
												7		2					
												8		2					
												7		1					
												8		2					
												3		1					
												6		3					
												4		1					
												5		1					
												2		1					
												8		4					
9	6	9	7	1	11	10	6	5	1	1		244 / 246		85					

Pensioners for Revolutionary or Military Services, Names	Ages	Deaf and Dumb (White), Under 14	14 & under 25	25 and upwards	Blind	Insane and idiots at public charge	Insane and idiots at private charge	Colored, Deaf & dumb	Colored, Blind	Colored, Insane and idiots at private charge	Colored, Insane and idiots at public charge	Universities or Colleges	Number of Students	Academies and Grammar Schools	No. of Scholars	Primary and Common Schools	No. of Scholars	No. of Scholars at public charge	No. of white persons over 20 who cannot read and write
			1	3															
				1															
			1	5															

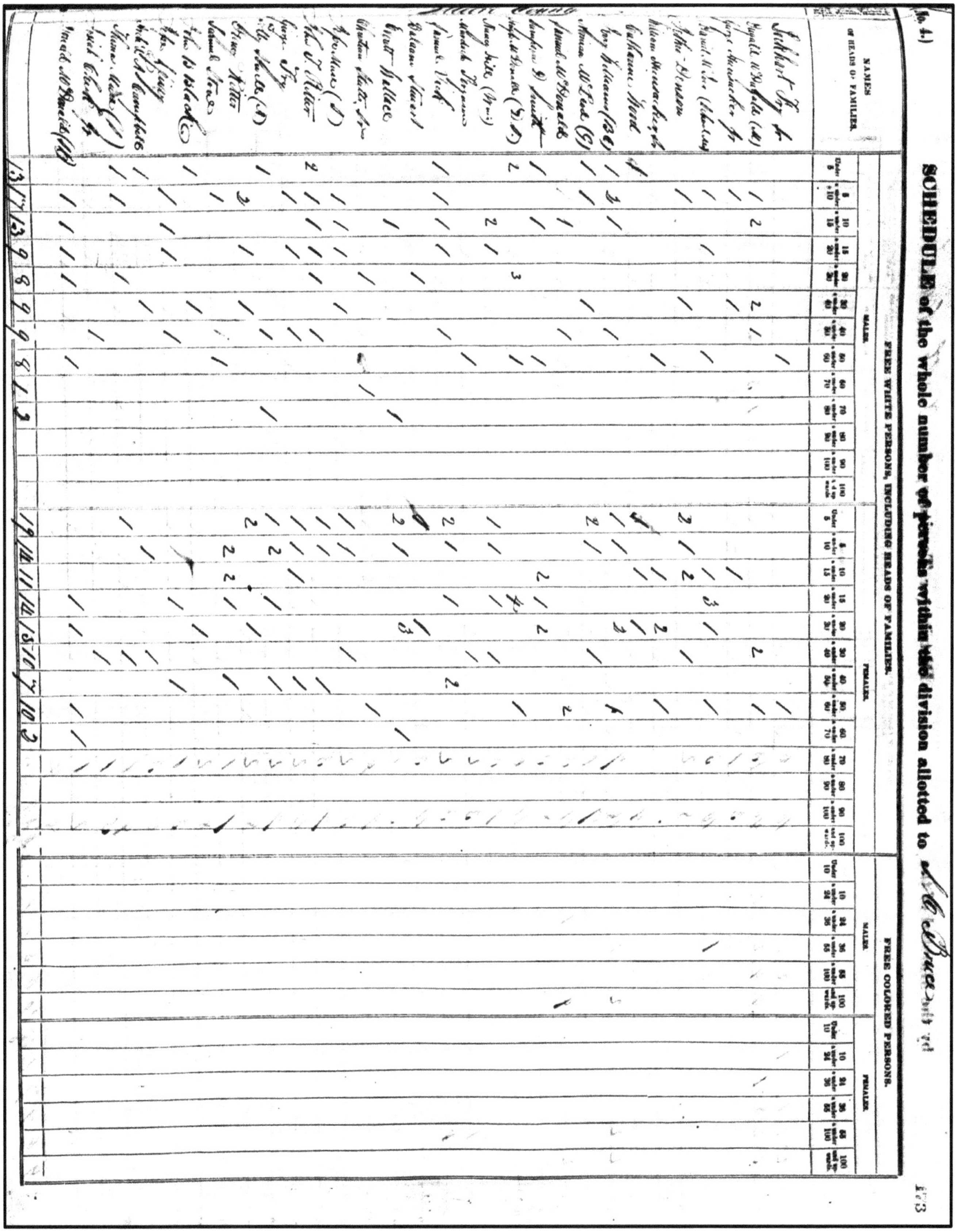

Slaves and Free Persons of Color are located on the previous page

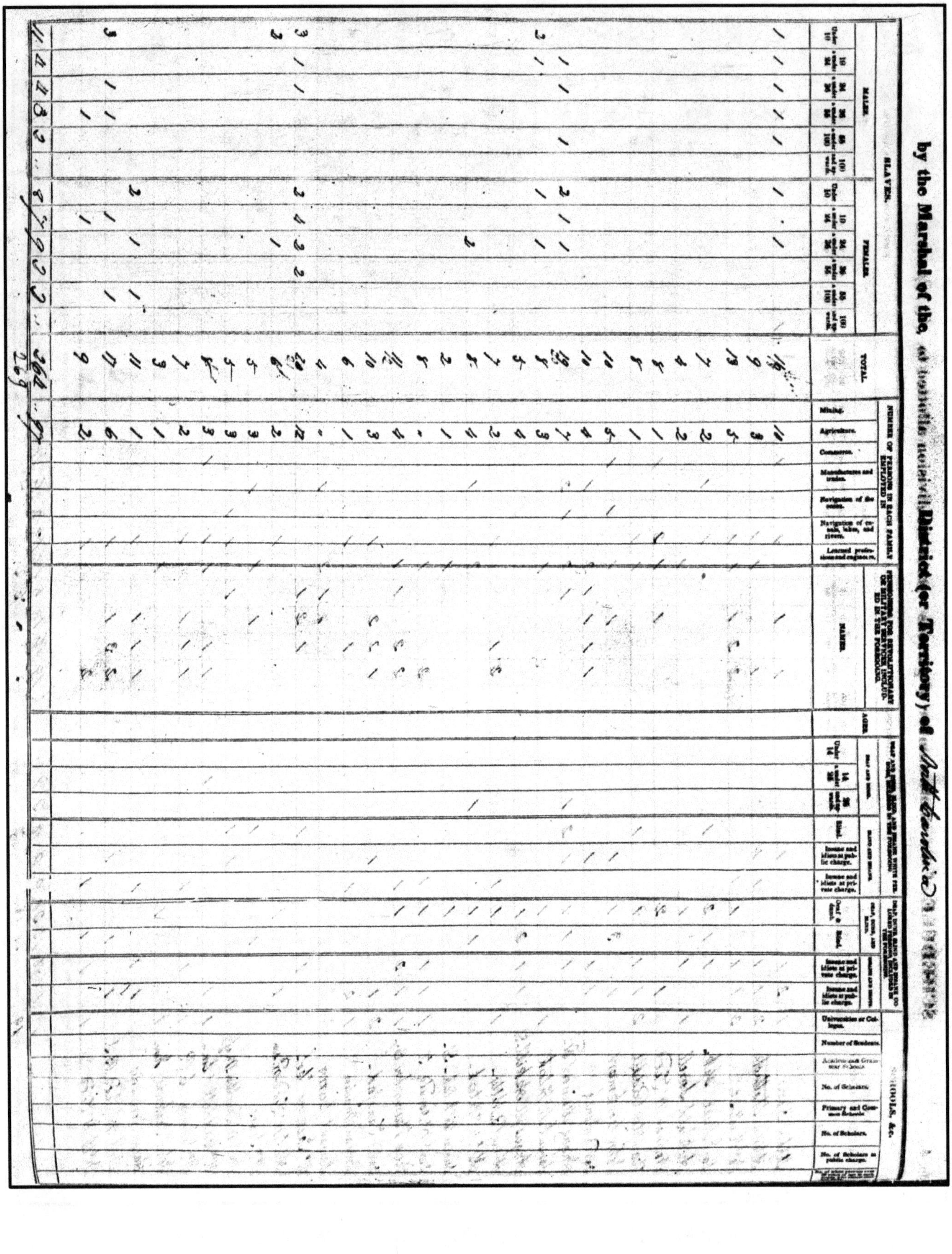

by the Marshal of the District (or Territory) of North Carolina

Slaves, Males: Under 10	10 & under 24	24 & under 36	36 & under 55	55 & under 100	100 and upwards	Slaves, Females: Under 10	10 & under 24	24 & under 36	36 & under 55	55 & under 100	100 and upwards	Total	Mining	Agriculture	Commerce	Manufactures and trades	Navigation of the ocean	Navigation of canals, lakes, and rivers	Learned professions and engineers
1	1	1	1	1		1		1				16		10					
												9		3					
												13		5					
												7		2					
												4		2					
												8		1					
												8		1					
												10		5					
												10		4					
	1	1		1		2	1	1				19		7					
2	1					1		1				8		3					
												5		4					
												7		2					
								2				8		4					
												2		1					
												8		..					
												11/12		4					
												10		3					
												6		1					
												4		..					
3	1	1				2	4	2	2			20/21		12					
2								1				6		2					
												5		3					
												5		3					
												8		3					
												7		2					
												3		1					
						2		1		1		11		1					
3		1	1				1			1		17		6					
			1				1					9		2					
11	4	4	3	2	..	8	7	9	3	2	..	364 / 269	..	97					

Pensioners for Revolutionary or Military Services, included in the foregoing: Names | Ages

Deaf and dumb, blind, and insane white persons, included in the foregoing: Deaf and dumb (Under 14; 14 & under 25; 25 and upwards) | Blind and insane (Blind; Insane and idiots at public charge; Insane and idiots at private charge)

Deaf, dumb, blind and insane colored persons, included in the foregoing: Deaf & dumb, blind (Deaf & dumb; Blind) | Insane and idiots (Insane and idiots at private charge; Insane and idiots at public charge)

Schools, &c.: Universities or Colleges | Number of Students | Academies and Grammar Schools | No. of Scholars | Primary and Common Schools | No. of Scholars | No. of Scholars at public charge

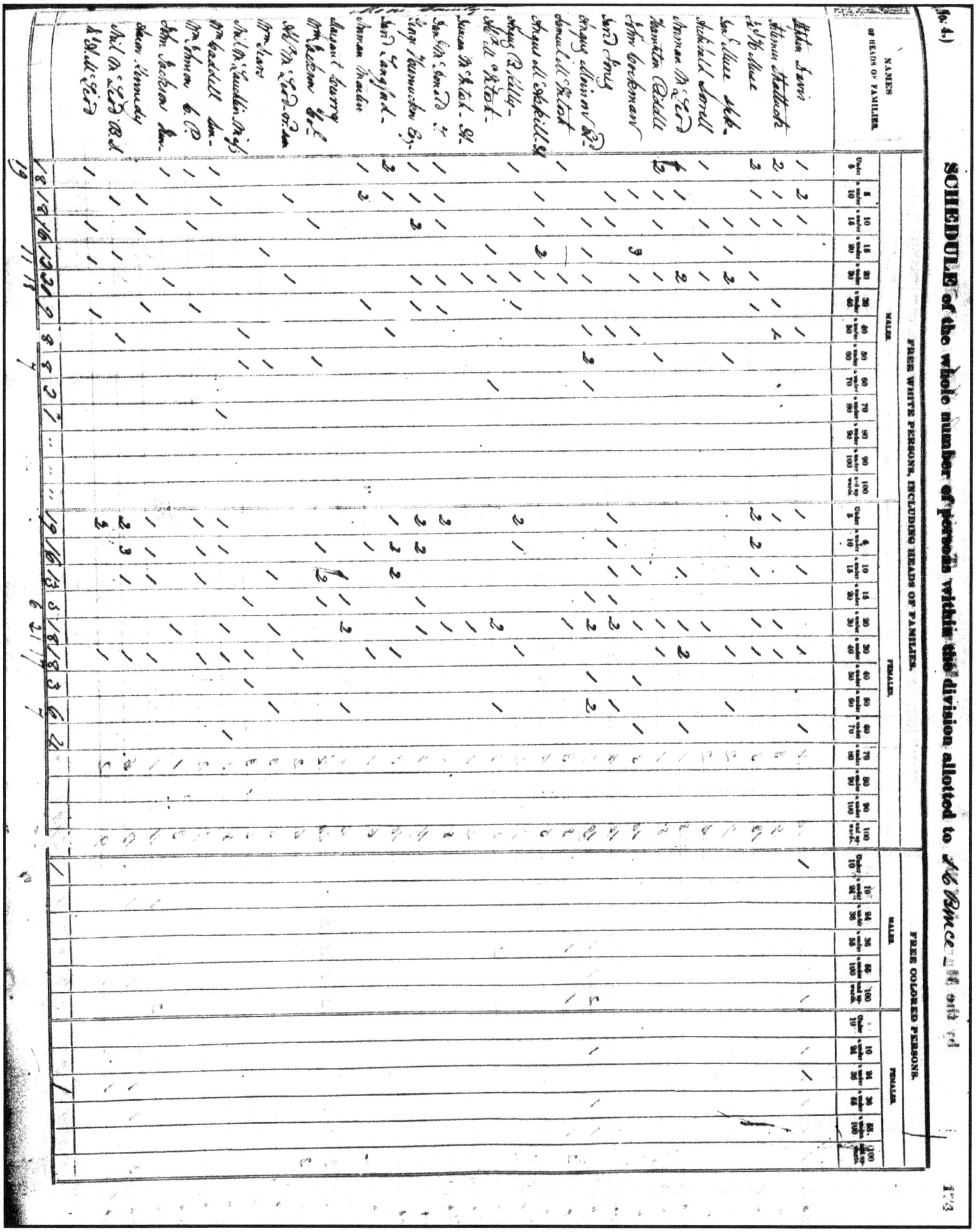

Slaves and Free Persons of Color are located on the previous page

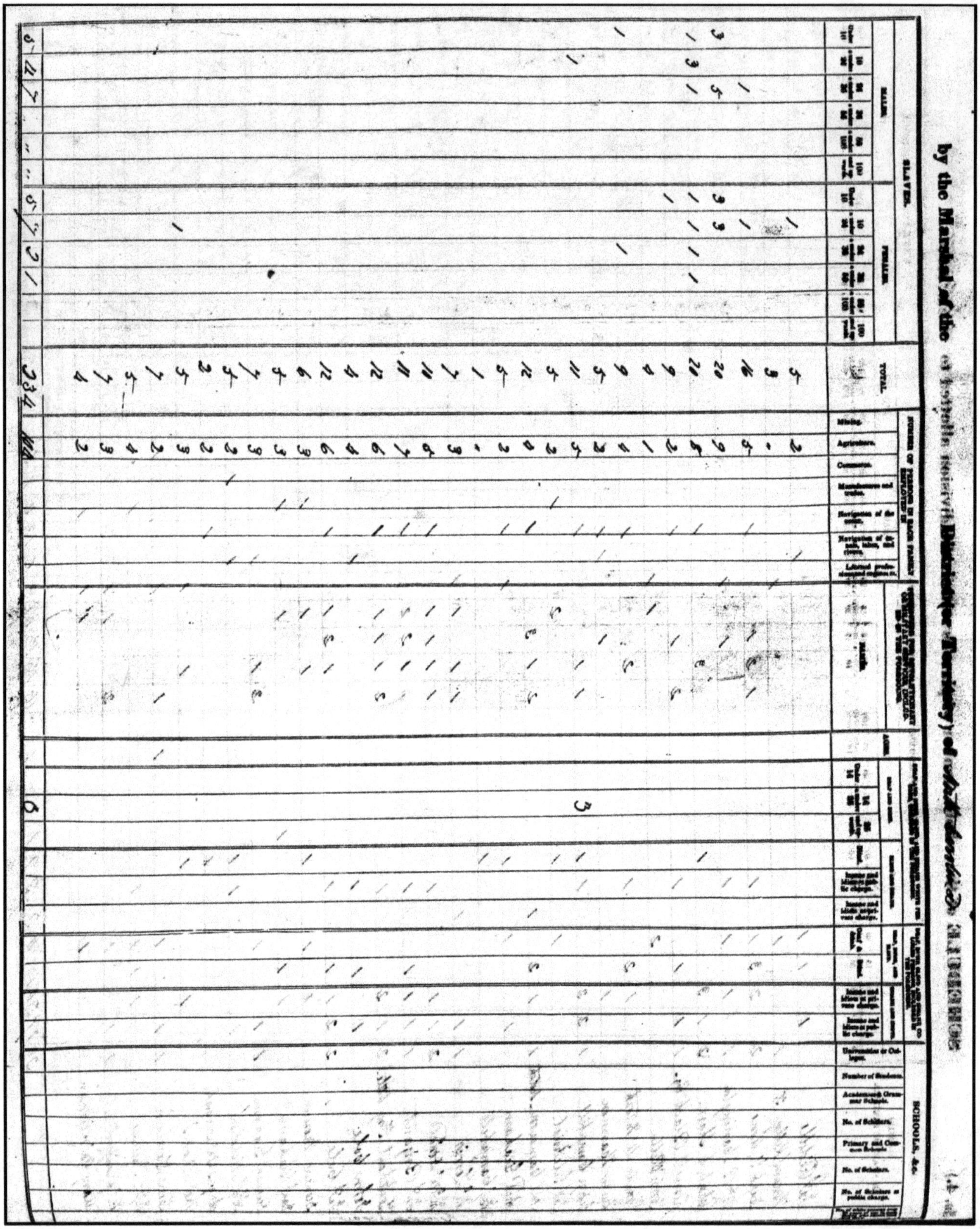
by the Marshal of the District (Territory) of North Carolina
SLAVES.
MALES.
FEMALES.
TOTAL.
SCHOOLS, &c.

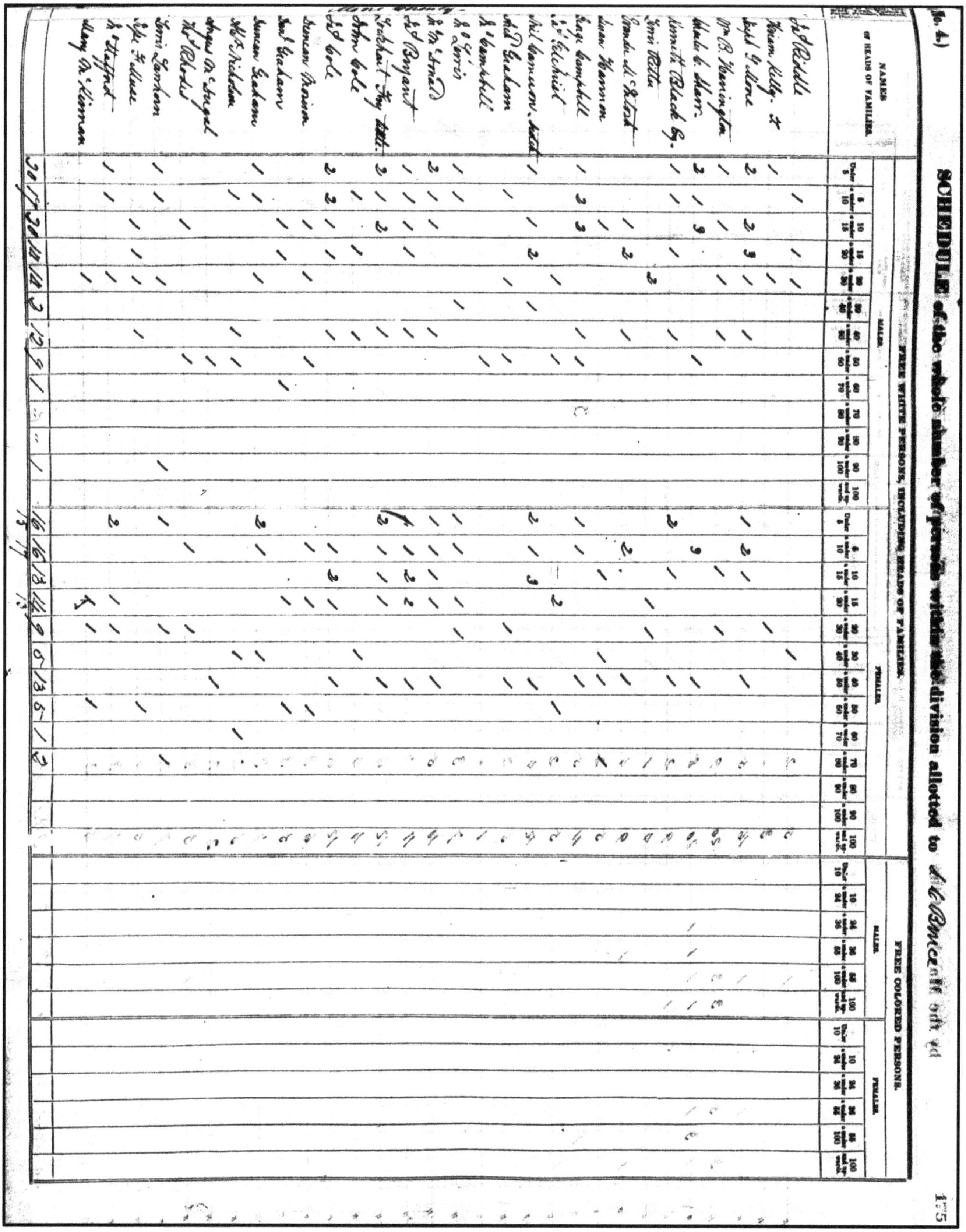

No. 4.) SCHEDULE of the whole number of persons within the division allotted to A. C. Bruce ... 175

NAMES OF HEADS OF FAMILIES	Free White Males Under 5	5 under 10	10 under 15	15 under 20	20 under 30	30 under 40	40 under 50	50 under 60	60 under 70	70 under 80	80 under 90	90 under 100	100 and upwards	Free White Females Under 5	5 under 10	10 under 15	15 under 20	20 under 30	30 under 40	40 under 50	50 under 60	60 under 70	70 under 80	80 under 90	90 under 100	100 and upwards	Free Colored Males Under 10	10 under 24	24 under 36	36 under 55	55 under 100	100 and upwards	Free Colored Females Under 10	10 under 24	24 under 36	36 under 55	55 under 100	100 and upwards
Jas Riddle		1		1	1														1																			
Hiram Kelly	1				1													1																				
Joseph G. Moore	2		2	3	1		1							1	2	1				1																		
Wm B. Harrington	1		1		1		1									1		1																				
Charles C. Sharr	2	1	3					1							3					1																		
Kenneth Black	1	1		1			1							2		1				1																		
Lewis Ritter					2												1	1																				
Evander McIntosh			1	2			1								2					1																		
Susan Hannon			1													1			1	1			1															
George Campbell	1	2	3				1	1						1	1					1																		
Jas Gilchrist					1			1									2				1																	
Neil Cameron, Sketch	1		1	2		1								2	1	3				1																		
Archd Graham		1			1			1										1		1																		
N. Campbell								1																														
N. Lewis	1	1				1								1	1		1	1																				
N. McDonald	2	1	1				1							1	1	1	1			1																		
Jas Bryant	1	1	1	1			1							1	1	2	2			1																		
Lockhart Fry	2	1	2				1							2	1	1	1			1																		
John Cole		1		1			1												1	1																		
Jas Cole	2	2	1	1			1								1	2	1			1																		
Duncan Morison			1		1			1							1		1				1																	
Danl Graham			1	1					1								1				1																	
Duncan Graham	1	1			1									2	1				1																			
Alex Nicholson		1					1	1											1			1																
Angus McDugal								1												1																		
Thos Rhodes			1					1							1			1																				
Lewis Lawhorn	1	1			1							1		1				1					1															
Jesse F. Muse			1	1	1		1														1																	
N. Stafford	1	1			1									2			1	1																				
Mary McKinnon					1												1	1			1																	
	20	17	20	14	14	2	12	9	1	–	–	1		16	16	13	14	9	5	13	5	1	2															
														13	17		13																					

Slaves and Free Persons of Color are located on the previous page

by the Marshal of the District (or Territory) of North Carolina

Slaves, Males: Under 10	10 & under 24	24 & under 36	36 & under 55	55 & under 100	100 and upwards	Slaves, Females: Under 10	10 & under 24	24 & under 36	36 & under 55	55 & under 100	100 and upwards	Total	Employed in Agriculture	Pensioners for Revolutionary or Military Services: Names
						1						15	5	
												3	1	
												8	3	
												8	3	
									1			8	4	
1	1	1				1	1	1	1			16	6	
												6	2	
												10	4	
												2	1	
												4	3	
												5	1	
												6	3	
												8	2	
										1		5	3	
												10	4	
1		1	4			1	1	1				30	7	
	2						1			1		8	4	
2	2	3				1	3	2	1			20	8	
												9	4	
2	1	1	1	1		4	2	2		3		18	10	James Gaines
										1		10	3	
												7	0	
												5	1	
												8	0	
												3	2	
1	1						1					7	3	
	1											4	3	
												10	2	
												4	2	
												2	1	
7	8	6	5	1	..	8	9	6	4	6		359	95	

260

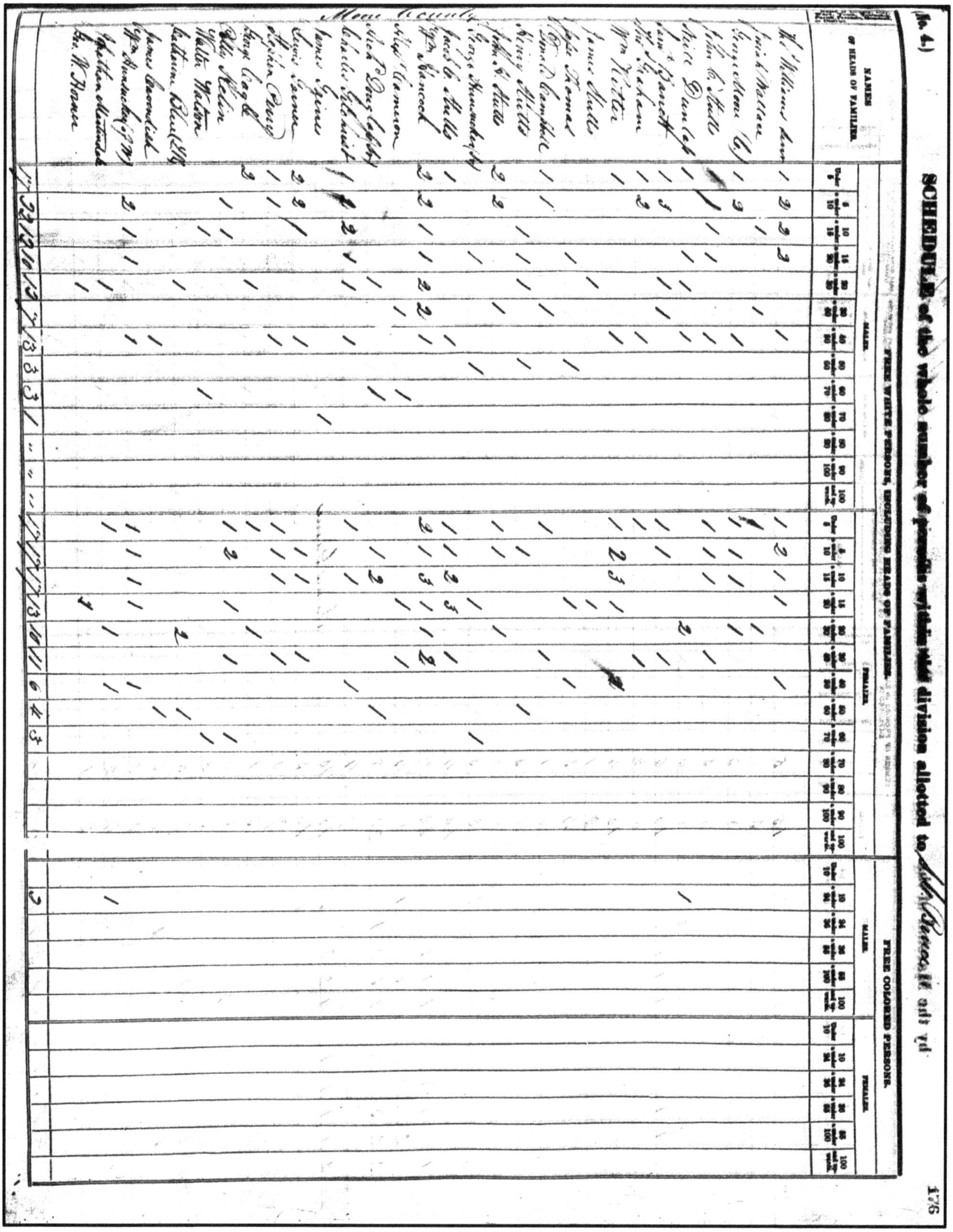

(No. 4.) SCHEDULE of the whole number of persons within the division allotted to [illegible] 176

Moore County

FREE WHITE PERSONS, INCLUDING HEADS OF FAMILIES.

NAMES OF HEADS OF FAMILIES.	Males Under 5	Males 5 under 10	Males 10 under 15	Males 15 under 20	Males 20 under 30	Males 30 under 40	Males 40 under 50	Males 50 under 60	Males 60 under 70	Males 70 under 80	Males 80 under 90	Males 90 under 100	Males 100 and upwards	Females Under 5	Females 5 under 10	Females 10 under 15	Females 15 under 20	Females 20 under 30	Females 30 under 40	Females 40 under 50	Females 50 under 60	Females 60 under 70	Females 70 under 80	Females 80 under 90	Females 90 under 100	Females 100 and upwards
Thos Williams Senr	1	2	2	2			1							1	2	1	1			1						
Josiah Wallace			1			1								1				1								
George Moore (C.)	1	2					1							1	1	1		1								
John C. Stutts	1	1	1	1			1							1	1	1			1							
Neill Dunlap	1			1	1		1											2								
Saml Barrett	1	3			1	1								1	1				1							
Thos Graham	1	2					1							1					1							
Wm Ritter	1						1							1	2	3	1			2						
James Stutts					1												1									
Jesse Thomas				1				1									1			1						
Donald Campbell	1	1				1								1					1							
Henry Stutts			1	1	1			1							1						1					
John H. Stutts	2	2				1								1	1			1								
George Hunsucker (Sr)				1				1									1					1				
Jacob C. Stutts	1						1							1	1	2	3		1							
Wm Hancock	2	2	1	1	2	2	1							2	1	3	1	1	2							
Alexr Cameron						1			1								1		1							
Archd Douglass (Sr)					1				1						1	2					1					
Charles Gilchrist	1	1	2	1	1		1							1		1				1						
James Grimes										1																
Lewis Garner	2	2	1				1								1	1			1							
Stephen Perry	1	1					1							1	1	1			1							
George Cagle	2				1									1				1								
Polly Kelin		1	1											1	2		1		1			1				
Walter Watson			1						1													1				
Catharine Bleu (L.R.)					1													2			1					
James Cavendish							1														1					
Wm Hunsucker (of W)		2	1	1			1							1	1	1	1			1						
Jonathan Martindale					1									1				1		1						
Geo. W. Horner					1												1									
	17	22	12	10	13	7	13	3	3	1	"	"	"	17	17	17	13	10	11	6	4	3				

FREE COLORED PERSONS.

NAMES OF HEADS OF FAMILIES.	Males Under 10	Males 10 under 24	Males 24 under 36	Males 36 under 55	Males 55 under 100	Males 100 and upwards	Females Under 10	Females 10 under 24	Females 24 under 36	Females 36 under 55	Females 55 under 100	Females 100 and upwards
Neill Dunlap		1										
Jonathan Martindale		1										
		2										

Slaves and Free Persons of Color are located on the previous page

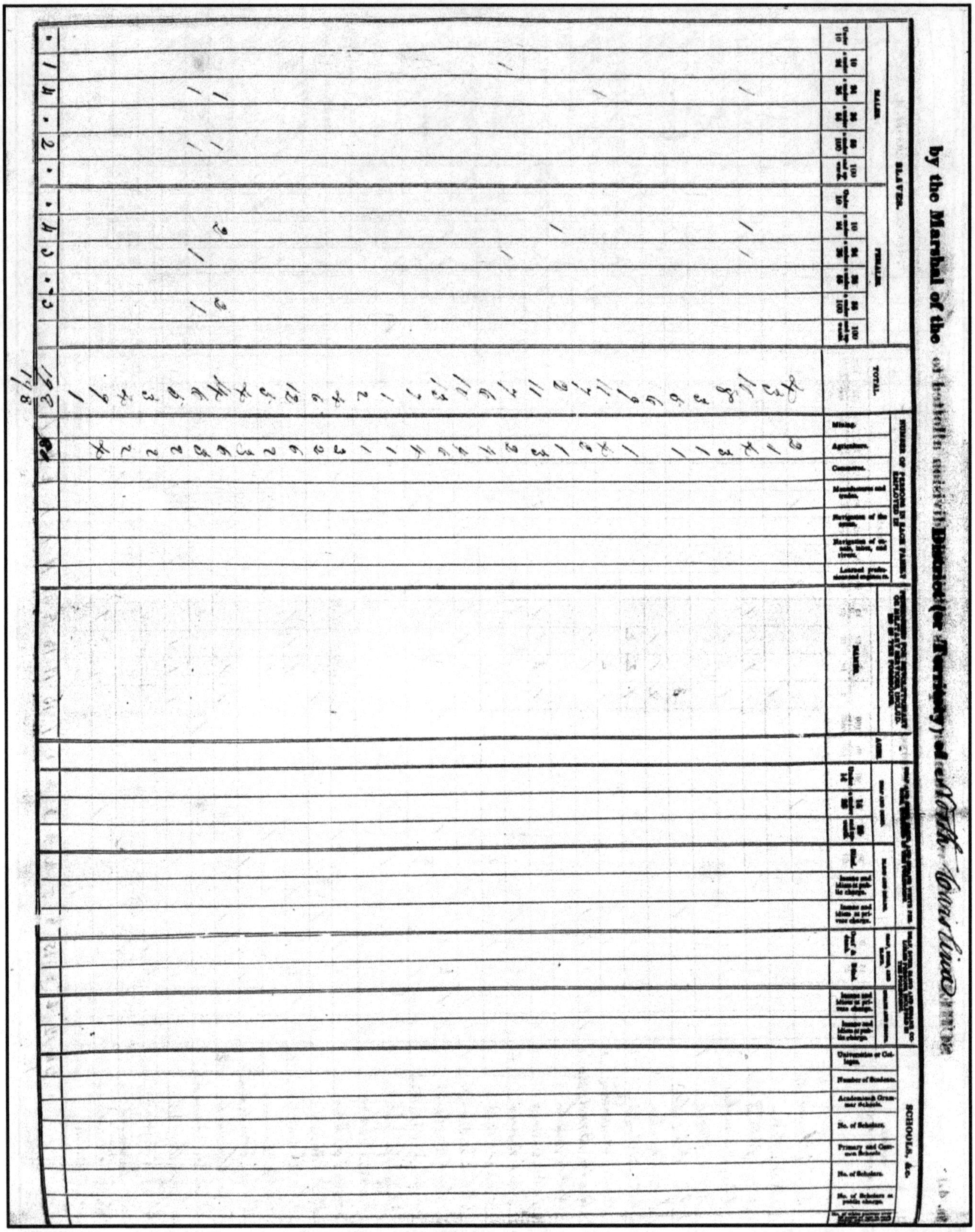

by the Marshal of the District (or Territory) of North Carolina

Slaves, Males: Under 10	10 & under 24	24 & under 36	36 & under 55	55 & under 100	100 and upward	Slaves, Females: Under 10	10 & under 24	24 & under 36	36 & under 55	55 & under 100	100 and upward	Total	Mining	Agriculture	Commerce	Manufactures and trades	Navigation of the ocean	Navigation of canals, lakes, and rivers	Learned professional engineers, &c.
												4		2					
												3		1					
		1					1	1				16		4					
												8		3					
												3		1					
												6		1					
												6							
												9		1					
		1										11		4					
												7		2					
							1					2		1					
												11		3					
	1							1				7		2					
												6		4					
												10		4					
												13		6					
												7		4					
												1		1					
												2		1					
												4		3					
												6		2					
												12		6					
												5		2					
												4		3					
		1		1			2			2		14		6					
		1		1				1		1		6		3					
												5		2					
												3		2					
												4		2					
												9		4					
												1							
•	1	4	•	2	•	•	4	3	•	3		198		[illegible]					

198

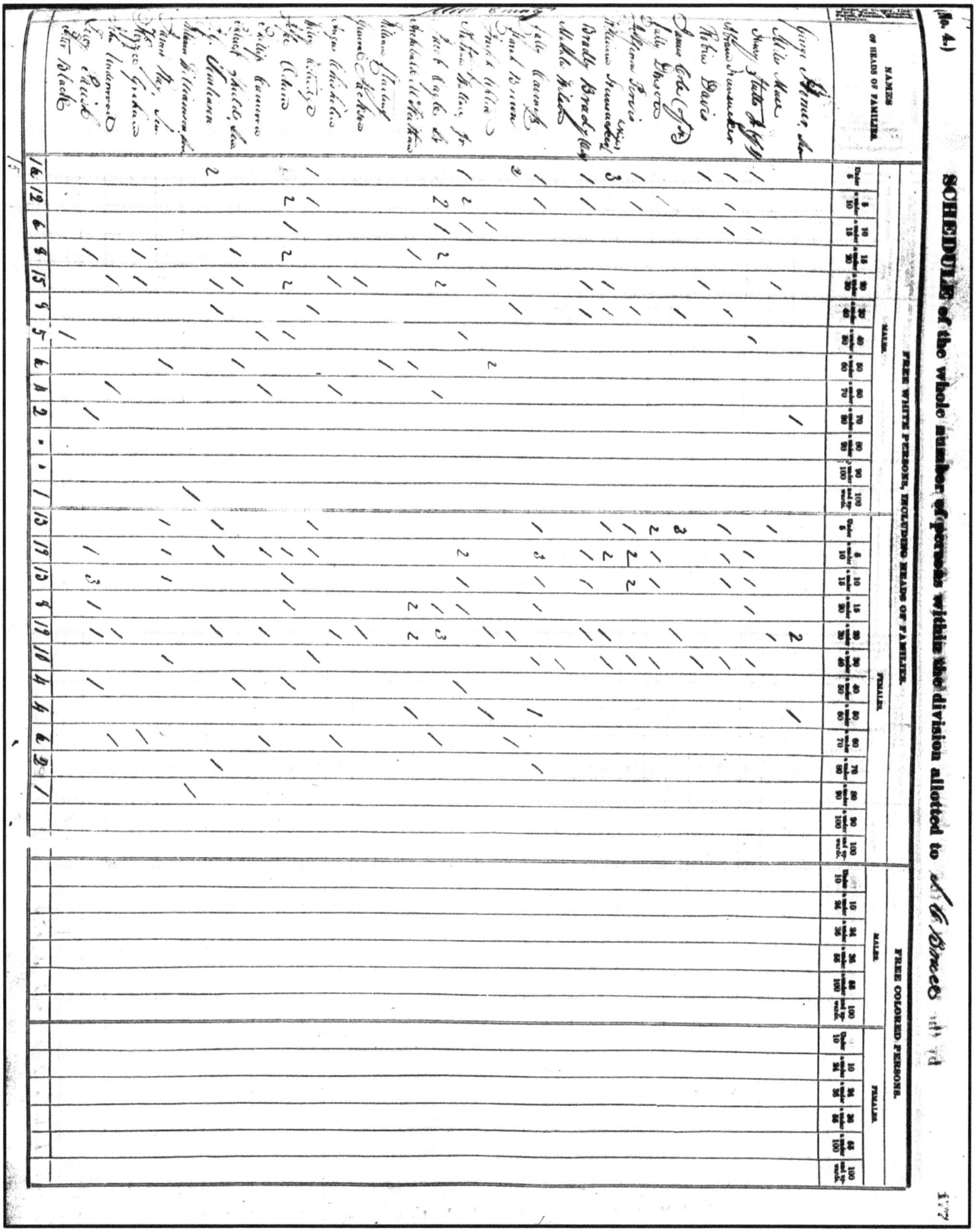

(No. 4.) **SCHEDULE of the whole number of persons within the division allotted to** S. C. Bruce 177

FREE WHITE PERSONS, INCLUDING HEADS OF FAMILIES.

NAMES OF HEADS OF FAMILIES	M Under 5	M 5-10	M 10-15	M 15-20	M 20-30	M 30-40	M 40-50	M 50-60	M 60-70	M 70-80	M 80-90	M 90-100	M 100 & up	F Under 5	F 5-10	F 10-15	F 15-20	F 20-30	F 30-40	F 40-50	F 50-60	F 60-70	F 70-80	F 80-90	F 90-100	F 100 & up
George Homer, Sen										1								2			1					
Milo Muse					1									1				1								
Henry Stutts Jr (of G)	1		1				1								1	1	1		1							
Abram Hunsucker	1	1	1			1								1	1	1			1							
Robin Davis	1				1														1							
James Cole (of Jr)						1								3				1								
Sally Dowson		1												2	1	1			1							
Jefferson Purvis	1	1				1								1	2	2			1							
William Hunsucker (Wil)	3				1	1								1	2			1	1							
Bradly Brady (Cur)	1	1			1	1									1	1		1								
Mikkle Wilson																			1							
Sally Carroll	1	1												1	3	1	1		1		1		1			
Harah Brown	2					1												1				1				
Joseph Wilson			1		1			2										1			1					
Nathan Wallace Jr	1	2	1				1								2	1	1			1						
Jacob Eagle Sr		2	1	2	2				1								1	3				1				
Archibald McKeithan				1				1									2	2			1					
William Starling								1																		
Samuel Jackson					1													1								
Angus Chisholm					1				1									1				1				
Wiley Estridge	1	1				1								1	1				1							
John Collins		2	1	2	2		1								1	1	1			1						
Phillip Cameron							1		1						1			1				1				
Patrick Shields, Sen				1	1			1										1		1						
J. G. Tomlinson	2				1	1								1	1			1					1			
William Williamson, Sen													1											1		
James Hay, Sen								1						1	1	1			1							
Hezza Graham				1	1																	1				
John Underwood					1				1									1				1				
Terry Parish				1						1					1	3	1	1		1						
Peter Black							1																			
	16	12	6	8	15	9	5	6	4	2	.	.	1	13	19	13	8	19	10	4	4	6	2	1		
	15																									

Slaves and Free Persons of Color are located on the previous page

by the Marshal of the District (or Territory) of North Carolina

Slaves, Males: Under 10	10 & under 24	24 & under 36	36 & under 55	55 & under 100	100 and upwards	Slaves, Females: Under 10	10 & under 24	24 & under 36	36 & under 55	55 & under 100	100 and upwards	Total	Persons employed in Mining	Agriculture
3	3	1	1			1		1	1			14		6
												6		2
2	4	2	2			1	4	3	5	1		33		22
												5		2
2	4			2		8	5					30		9
												3		1
												3		1
1			1									10		4
												10		1
												8		4
												4		1
												6		1
	1					3	2	1	1			17		5
	1						1					6		3
												9		3
1	2		2			2		2		1		14		5
							2					9		4
						1						8		4
												5		3
	1					1			1			6		3
1							5		1	1		11		5
												5		2
								1				7		3
												5		3
												6		1
												6		2
												5		2
												5		1
												4		1
							1					8		3
10	16	3	6	2	·	17	20	8	9	3	·	268		47

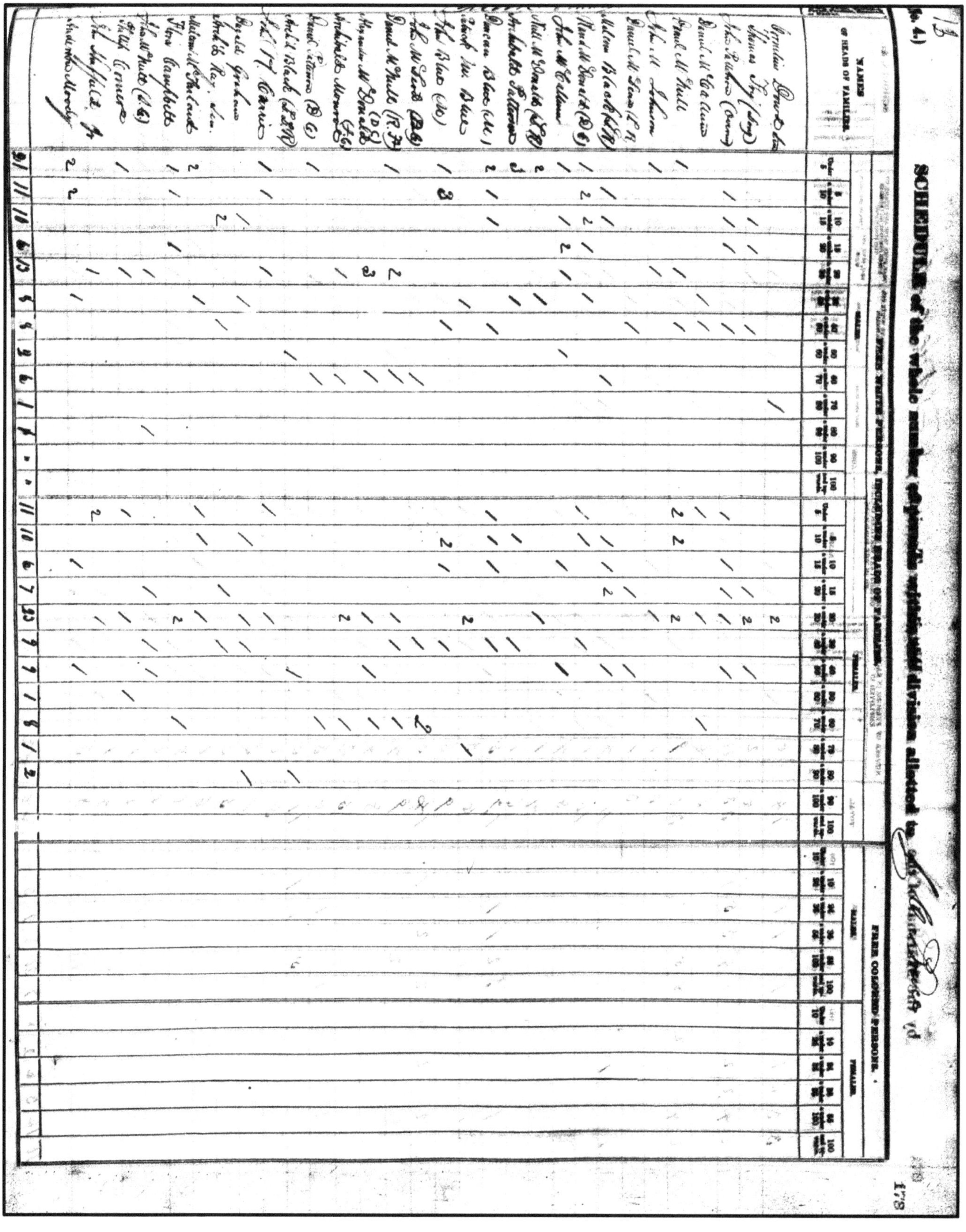

Slaves and Free Persons of Color are located on the previous page

by the Marshal of the District (or Territory) of North Carolina

Slaves, Male: Under 10	Male: 10 & under 24	Male: 24 & under 36	Male: 36 & under 55	Male: 55 & under 100	Male: 100 and upwards	Female: Under 10	Female: 10 & under 24	Female: 24 & under 36	Female: 36 & under 55	Female: 55 & under 100	Female: 100 and upwards	TOTAL	Mining	Agriculture	Commerce	Manufactures and trades	Navigation of the ocean	Navigation of canals, lakes, and rivers	Learned professional engineers, &c.	Universities or Colleges	Number of Students	Academies & Grammar Schools	No. of Scholars	Primary and Common Schools	No. of Scholars	No. of Scholars at public charge
3	1						1					10		4								1	26	1	26	
												3		1								1	18	1	18	
		1										7		2								1	22	1	22	
	1					1						4		2												
							1					8		3												
												10		4												
	1						1					9		3												
	2					2	1		1			10		4												
												5		2												
												5		1												
				1								5		2												
							1					2		2												
												3		1												
												8		1												
												6		1												
												4		1												
	1											3		2												
												7		2												
												5		2												
												4		1												
												6		2												
												11		3												
1		1					1	1				6		3												
												4		1												
												9		4												
												8		2												
												3		2												
												4		2												
												5		3												
												3		3												
4	6	2	..	1	..	3	6	1	1	..	..	176		66								3	66	3	66	

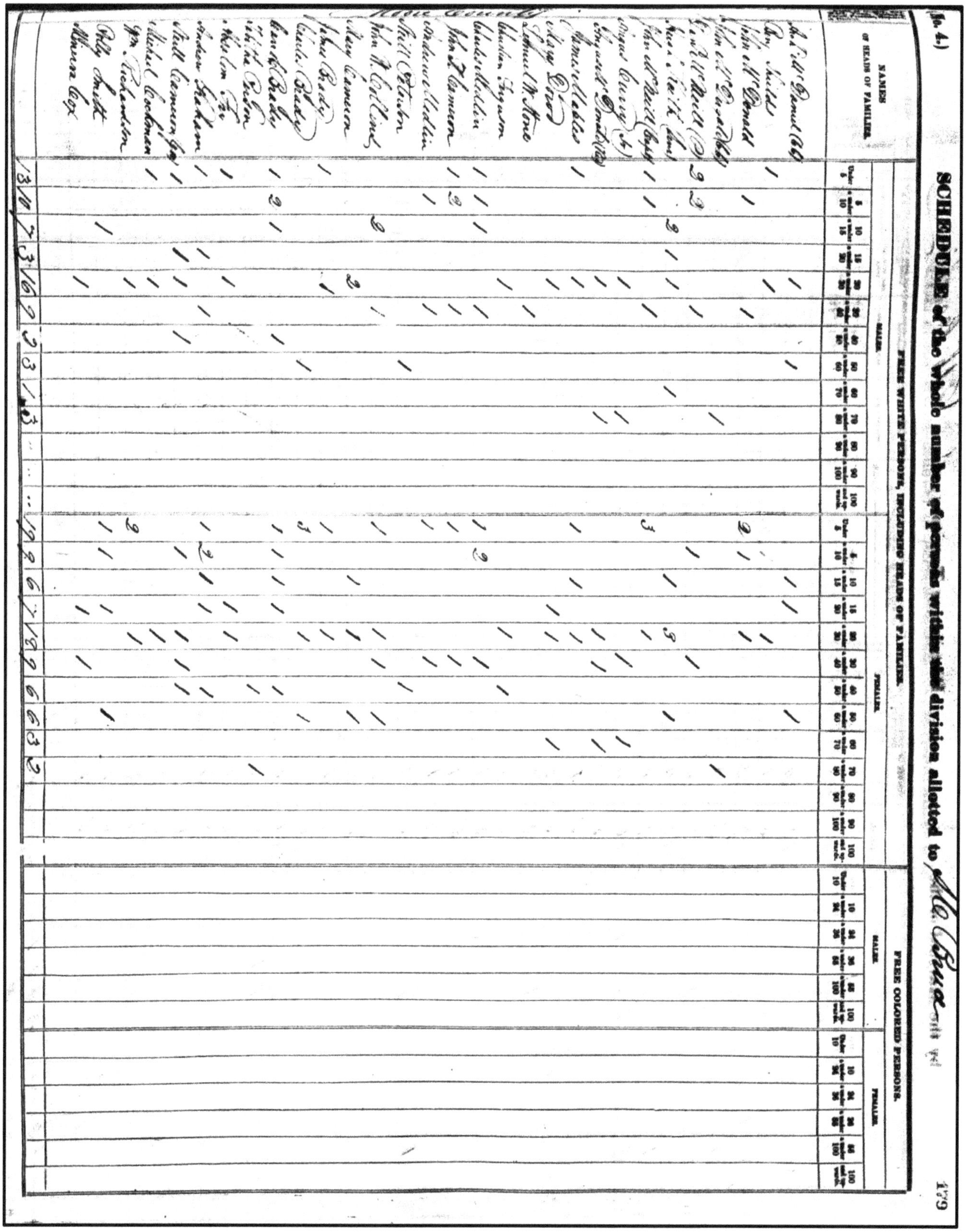

No. 4.) SCHEDULE of the whole number of persons within the division allotted to Al. C. Bruce 179

FREE WHITE PERSONS, INCLUDING HEADS OF FAMILIES. — FREE COLORED PERSONS.

NAMES OF HEADS OF FAMILIES.	M Under 5	M 5-10	M 10-15	M 15-20	M 20-30	M 30-40	M 40-50	M 50-60	M 60-70	M 70-80	M 80-90	M 90-100	M 100+	F Under 5	F 5-10	F 10-15	F 15-20	F 20-30	F 30-40	F 40-50	F 50-60	F 60-70	F 70-80	F 80-90	F 90-100	F 100+
Arch'd McDaniel (Col)					1			1								1	1				1					
Benj Shields	1				1													1								
John McDonald		1				1								2	1			1								
John McDonald (Col)										1													1			
Dan'l McNeill (P)	2	2				1									1				1							
Hugh Keith (Sen)			2	1	1				1							1		3			1					
John McNeill (Capt)	1	1				1								3				1								
Angus Curry (Jr)					1					1									1			1				
Angus McDonald (Ra)					1					1								1	1			1				
James Mables	1				1									1		1		1								
Mary Dowd					1												1	1				1				
Lemuel W. Stone						1																				
Christian Ferguson					1													1		1						
Charles Medlin	1	1	1			1								1	2				1							
John T. Cameron	1	2				1								1					1							
Andrew Medlin		1				1								1					1							
Stell Peterson								1												1						
John W. Collins			2			1								1				1	1		1					
Mary Cameron					2											1		1			1					
James Brady	1				1									1				1								
Charles Brady								1						3				1			1					
Carroll Brady	1	2	1				1							1	1	1	1			1						
Tabitha Person																				1			1			
Absolom Fry	1				1												1	1								
Andrew Graham	1			1		1								1	2	1	1			1						
Stell Cameron (Gov)	1			1	1		1								1			1	1	1						
Michael Cockman	1				1													1								
Wm Richardson					1									2				1								
Polly Smith			1											1	1		1				1					
Minerva Cox					1												1		1							
	13	10	7	3	16	9	2	3	1	3	..	..	..	19	9	6	7	18	9	6	6	3	2			

Slaves and Free Persons of Color are located on the previous page

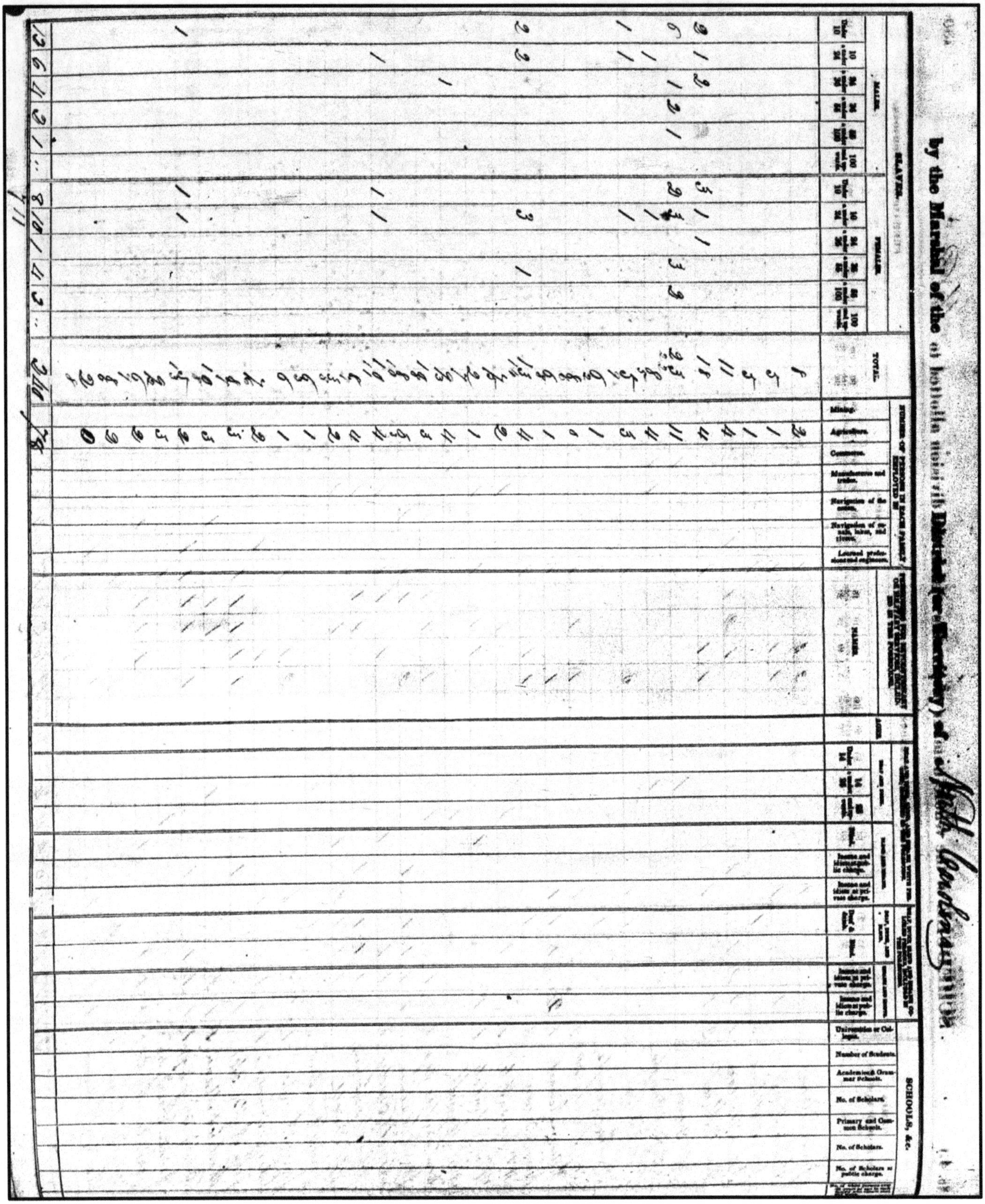

by the Marshal of the District (or Territory) of North Carolina

Slaves: Males Under 10	10 & under 24	24 & under 36	36 & under 55	55 & under 100	100 and upwards	Females Under 10	10 & under 24	24 & under 36	36 & under 55	55 & under 100	100 and upwards	Total	Mining	Agriculture	Commerce	Manufactures and trades	Navigation of the ocean	Navigation of canals, lakes, and rivers	Learned professions and engineers
												8		2					
												5		1					
												5		1					
												11		4					
2	1	2				3	1	1				18		4					
6		1	2	1		2	3		3	2		23		11					
	1						1					8		4					
1	1						1					5		3					
												6		1					
												8		0					
												6		1					
2	2						3		1			13		4					
												5		2					
												2		1					
		1										8		4					
												14		3					
												8		5					
	1					1	1					10		4					
												6		4					
												3		2					
												6		1					
												6		1					
												7		2					
												4		3					
												10		3					
1						1	1					15		2					
												2		3					
												6		2					
												8		2					
												2		0					
13	6	4	2	1	..	8	10	1	4	3	..	240		78					

711

(No. 4.) SCHEDULE of the whole number of persons within the division allotted to Mc Bruce [illegible] 180

Moore County

NAMES OF HEADS OF FAMILIES	Free White Males Under 5	5 & under 10	10 & under 15	15 & under 20	20 & under 30	30 & under 40	40 & under 50	50 & under 60	60 & under 70	70 & under 80	80 & under 90	90 & under 100	100 and upwards	Free White Females Under 5	5 & under 10	10 & under 15	15 & under 20	20 & under 30	30 & under 40	40 & under 50	50 & under 60	60 & under 70	70 & under 80	80 & under 90	90 & under 100	100 and upwards	Free Colored Males Under 10	10 & under 24	24 & under 36	36 & under 55	55 & under 100	100 and upwards	Free Colored Females Under 10	10 & under 24	24 & under 36	36 & under 55	55 & under 100	100 and upwards
James Melton						1								2	3			1					1															
Stephen King		1				1								1	1			1																				
James Matthews	3				1													1																				
Isham Wallace	1	1	2	1			1								1	2	1		1																			
Donald Street	2	1				1								1	1			1										1										
Jeff Brewer										1												1																
Bryant Boroughs										1											1	1																
Phillip Wilson					1	1								3				1																				
Matthew Baroughs					1													1																				
Benjn Shields (Sr)	2					1								1		1		1																				
William Stewart	1	2		1	1	1								1				1																				
Henry Brown	2				1									1	1			1																				
Wm Jones (F.C.)	1			1					1							1					1																	
Wm Martindale	1	1						1							1	1		1			1																	
Alexr Carroll									1													1																
Cornl Shields Esqr	1		1						1					1		1	1	1		1																		
James Garner		1	1	1	1		1							2			1	1		1																		
Robert Brady	1		1	1				1							1		1	1			1																	
John Mann (Senr)			1	1	1		1									1	1				1																	
Jesse Sowell			1	1	1	2		1								1					1																	
James Fry (Senr)					1					1													1															
Jerry Phillips	1					1								2	1			1																				
Eleazer Sowell	1	1	1			1									1				1																			
John Stull (Blk)		1					1							1	1	1	1	1																				
Shadrick Mann	1	1	2							1						1	1			1																		
Bradley Brady (Bkk)	1	1	1	1			1							1			1	1	1																			
James Dowdy Jr									1									1																				
John Kennedy Jr	1	1	1	1				1							1	1	1			1																		
George Williams	1				2									1	1			1																				
Matthew Williams	1	1	1			1								1	2				1																			
	22	13	13	9	11	11	5	4	4	4	..	..	..	19	16	2	9	18	4	4	6	8	3	..	..	..	..	1										

12

Slaves and Free Persons of Color are located on the previous page

SCHEDULE ... by the Marshal of the District (or Territory) of North Carolina

Slaves: Males Under 10	Males 10 & under 24	Males 24 & under 36	Males 36 & under 55	Males 55 & under 100	Males 100 and upwards	Females Under 10	Females 10 & under 24	Females 24 & under 36	Females 36 & under 55	Females 55 & under 100	Females 100 and upwards	TOTAL	Mining	Agriculture	Commerce	Manufactures and trades	Navigation of the ocean	Navigation of canals, lakes, and rivers	Learned professions and engineers
												3		1					
												10		6					
												5		1					
												3		1					
												6		2					
2	1	1				1			1			11		5					
												10		5					
												4		1					
												2							
	1						1					3		2					
												11		4					
												9		2					
												7		2					
		3	1	1		7	3	4	1	1		36		10					
	1					1		2				8		4					
		1						1				5		3					
												8							
												4							
3		2	1	1		2	2	1		1		29		4					
	2						1	1				13		4					
	1					4	1	4				22		6					
	1							1				18		4					
												5		1					
												11		2					
												4		2					
												5		1					
												12		6					
4	1	1	1			2	2		1			26		4					
												3		1					
												3		1					
14	9	8	6	2	"	17	10	14	3	2	"	296		85					

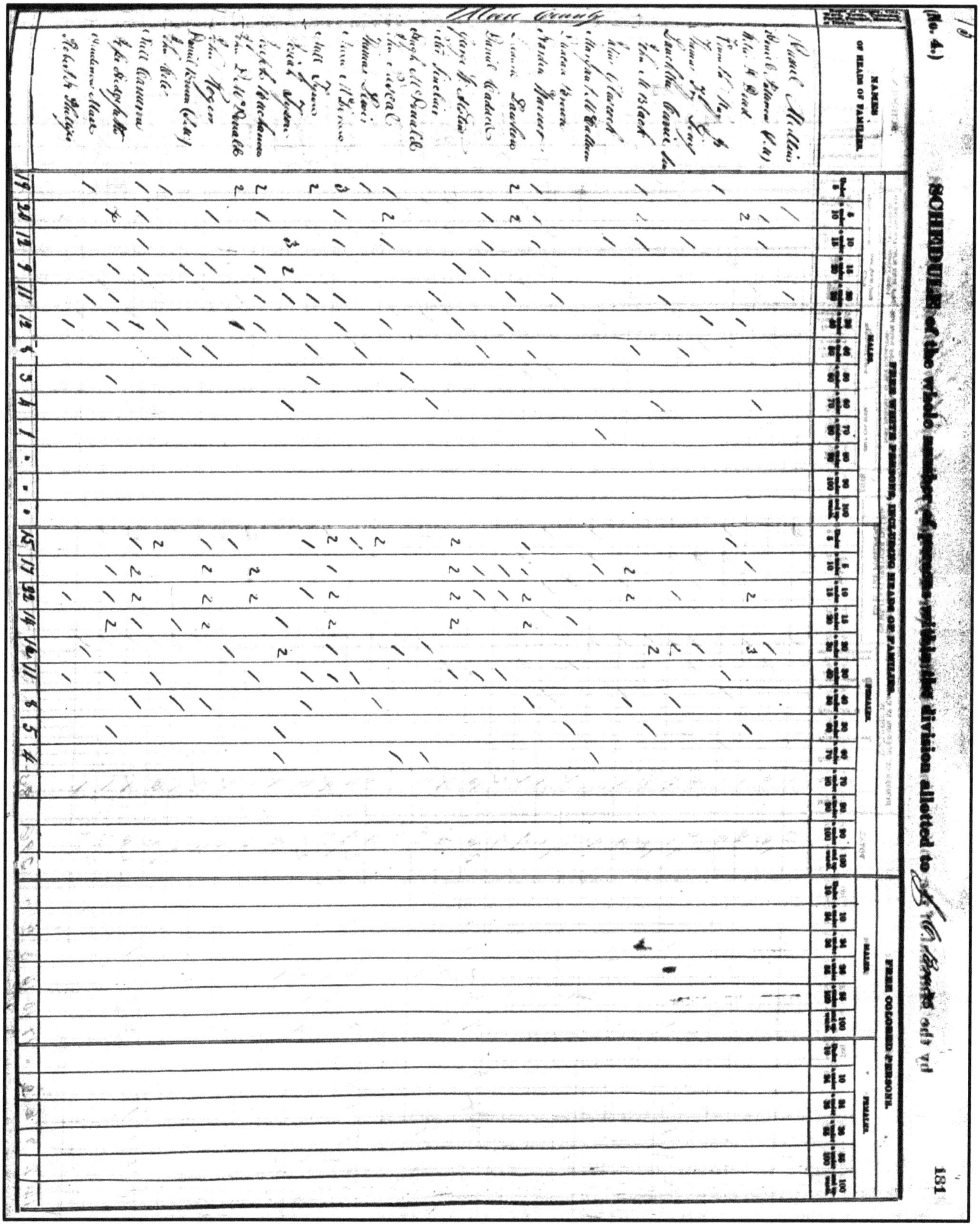

Slaves and Free Persons of Color are located on the previous page

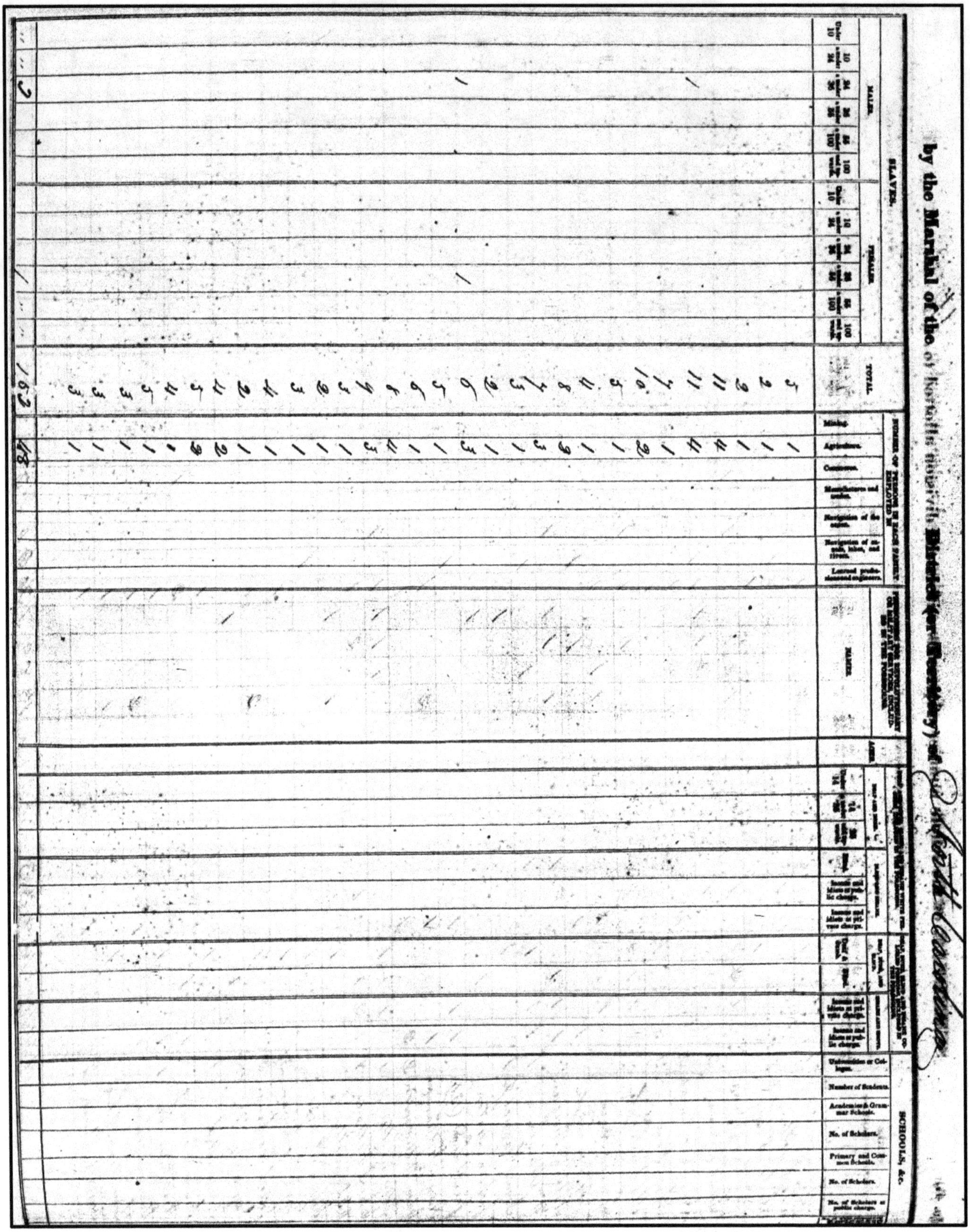

by the Marshal of the District (or Territory) of North Carolina

Slaves, Males, Under 10	Slaves, Males, 10 & under 24	Slaves, Males, 24 & under 36	Slaves, Males, 36 & under 55	Slaves, Males, 55 & under 100	Slaves, Males, 100 and upwards	Slaves, Females, Under 10	Slaves, Females, 10 & under 24	Slaves, Females, 24 & under 36	Slaves, Females, 36 & under 55	Slaves, Females, 55 & under 100	Slaves, Females, 100 and upwards	Total	Employed in: Mining	Agriculture	Commerce	Manufactures and trades	Navigation of the ocean	Navigation of canals, lakes, and rivers	Learned professional engineers	Pensioners for Revolutionary or Military Services: Names	Ages	White Deaf and Dumb: Under 14	14 & under 25	25 and upwards	Blind	Insane and idiots at public charge	Insane and idiots at private charge	Colored Deaf & Dumb	Blind	Insane and idiots at private charge	Insane and idiots at public charge	Universities or Colleges	Number of Students	Academies & Grammar Schools	No. of Scholars	Primary and Common Schools	No. of Scholars	No. of Scholars at public charge
												5		1																								
												2		1																								
												2		1																								
												11		4																								
		1										11		4																								
												7		1																								
												10		2																								
												5		1																								
												4		1																								
												8		3																								
												7		3																								
												3		1																								
												2		1																								
		1							1			6		3																								
												5		1																								
												6		1																								
												8		4																								
												9		3																								
												3		1																								
												2		1																								
												3		1																								
												4		1																								
												2		1																								
												4		2																								
												5		2																								
												4		1																								
												5		1																								
												3		1																								
												3		1																								
												3		1																								
..	..	2							1	..	..	163		48																								

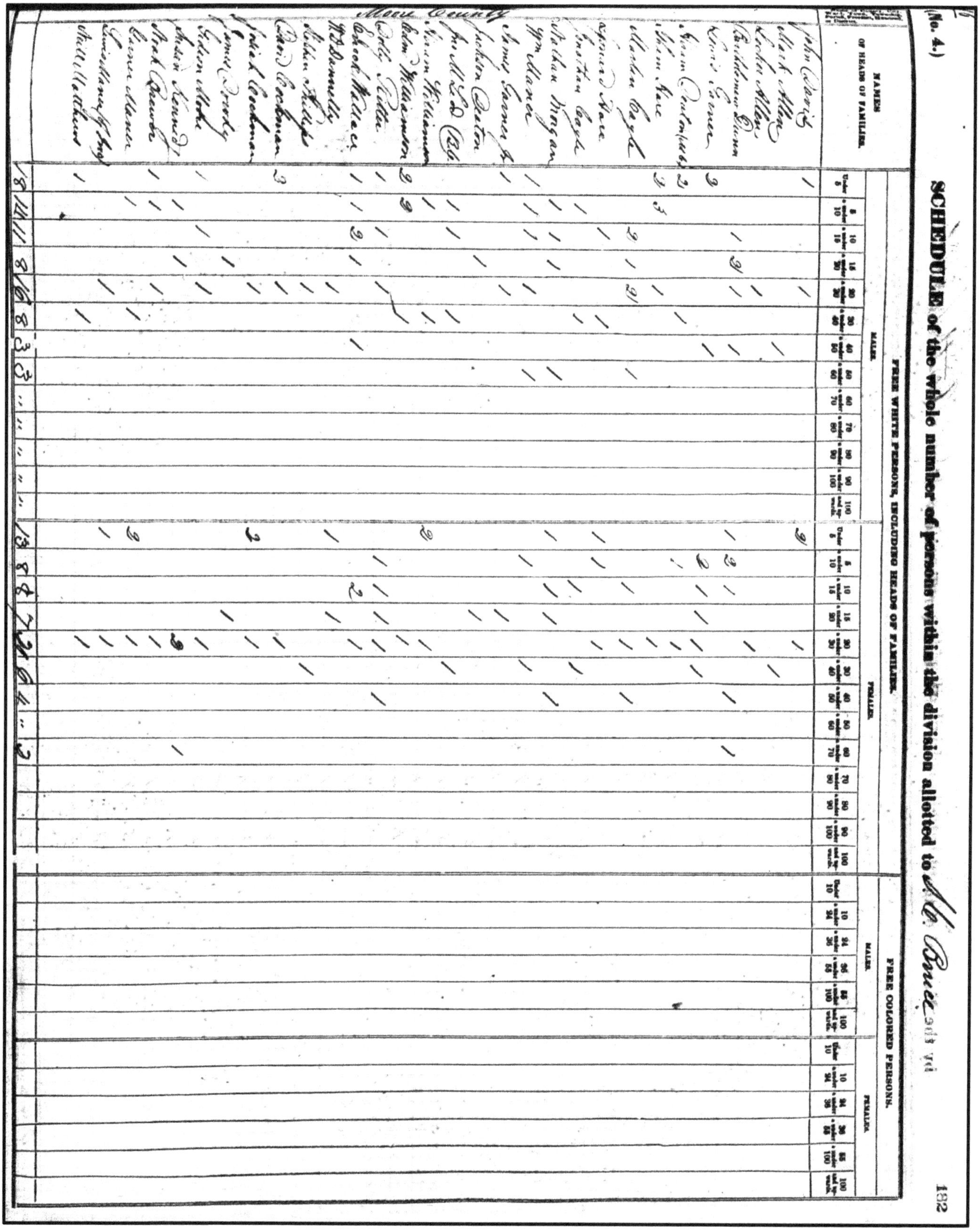

(No. 4.) **SCHEDULE** of the whole number of persons within the division allotted to A. C. Bruce — 182

Moore County

NAMES OF HEADS OF FAMILIES	FREE WHITE PERSONS, INCLUDING HEADS OF FAMILIES. MALES. Under 5	5 & under 10	10 & under 15	15 & under 20	20 & under 30	30 & under 40	40 & under 50	50 & under 60	60 & under 70	70 & under 80	80 & under 90	90 & under 100	100 and upwards	FEMALES. Under 5	5 & under 10	10 & under 15	15 & under 20	20 & under 30	30 & under 40	40 & under 50	50 & under 60	60 & under 70	70 & under 80	80 & under 90	90 & under 100	100 and upwards	FREE COLORED PERSONS. MALES. Under 10	10 & under 24	24 & under 36	36 & under 55	55 & under 100	100 and upwards	FEMALES. Under 10	10 & under 24	24 & under 36	36 & under 55	55 & under 100	100 and upwards
John Davis	1				1									2				1																				
Mark Allen							1												1																			
Locke Allen					1													1																				
Bartholomew Dunn			1	2	1		1							1	2	1				1		1																
Lewis Garner	2						1								2	1	1	1	1																			
Hiram Deaton (Mc6)	2					1									1			1																				
Sherm Hare	2	3			1													1																				
Marten Cagle			2	1	2			1								1		1		1																		
Leonard Hare			1			1								1	1			1																				
Jonathan Cagle		1				1										1			1																			
Nathan Morgan		1	1	1				1						1		1	1			1																		
Wm Maner	1	1	1		1			1							1				1																			
James Garner Jr	1				1												1																					
Jackson Deaton				1													1																					
Jno McLeod (B.G.)		1	1			1													1																			
Hiram Williamson		1				1								2				1																				
Edm Williamson	2	2				1												1																				
Dolly Ritter	1		1		1										1	1	1	1		1																		
Enoch Wallace	1	1	2	1			1									2		1																				
W. D. Donnelly					1									1			1																					
Nathan Phillips					1														1																			
David Cockman	2				1													1																				
Josiah Cockman					1									2				1																				
James Dowdy				1													1																					
Gideon Moore	1		1		1													1																				
Susan Kennedy		1		1														2				1																
Noah Brewer	1	1			1													1																				
Garner Maner		1				1								2				1																				
Lewis Maner (of Ing)					1									1				1																				
Neill Matthews	1					1												1																				
	18	14	11	8	16	8	3	3	"	"	"	"	"	13	8	8	7	21	6	4	"	2																

Slaves and Free Persons of Color are located on the previous page

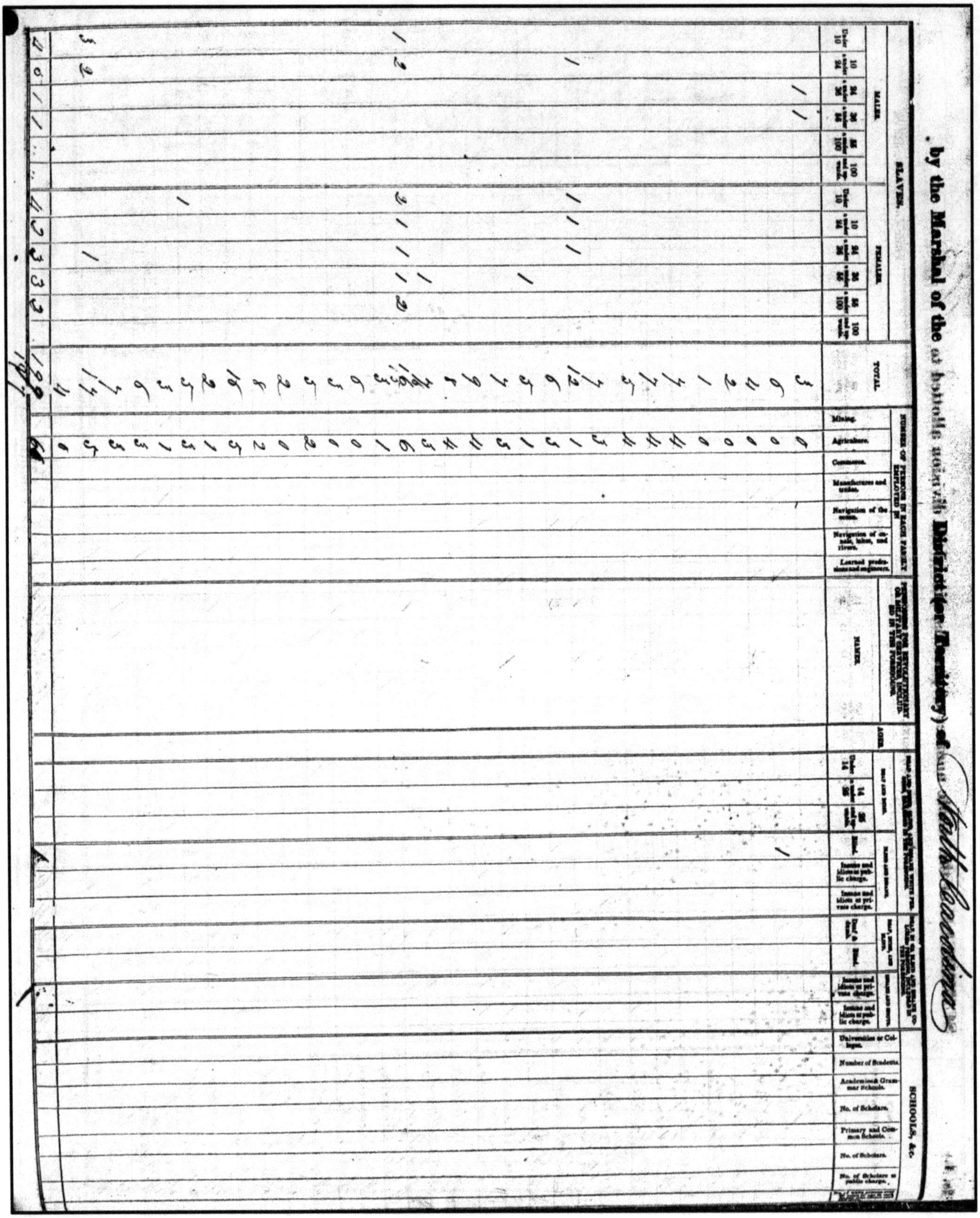

. by the Marshal of the District (or Territory) of North Carolina

Slaves – Males – Under 10	Slaves – Males – 10 & under 24	Slaves – Males – 24 & under 36	Slaves – Males – 36 & under 55	Slaves – Males – 55 & under 100	Slaves – Males – 100 and upwards	Slaves – Females – Under 10	Slaves – Females – 10 & under 24	Slaves – Females – 24 & under 36	Slaves – Females – 36 & under 55	Slaves – Females – 55 & under 100	Slaves – Females – 100 and upwards	Total	Number of persons in each family employed in – Mining	Agriculture	Commerce	Manufactures and trades	Navigation of the ocean	Navigation of canals, lakes, and rivers	Learned professions and engineers	Pensioners for revolutionary or military services, included in the foregoing – Names	Ages	Deaf and dumb white persons – Under 14	14 & under 25	25 and upwards	Blind and insane white persons – Blind	Insane and idiots at public charge	Insane and idiots at private charge	Deaf & dumb colored persons	Blind	Insane and idiots at private charge	Insane and idiots at public charge	Schools – Universities or Colleges	Number of Students	Academies & Grammar Schools	No. of Scholars	Primary and Common Schools	No. of Scholars	No. of Scholars at public charge
		1	1									3		0																								
												6		0											1													
												4		0																								
												2		0																								
												1		0																								
												7		4																								
												7		4																								
												5		4																								
												7		3																								
	1					1	1	1				12		1																								
												6		3																								
									1			5		1																								
												7		3																								
												9		4																								
												8		4																								
									1			7		3																								
1	2					2	1	1	1	2		16		6																								
												3		1																								
												6		0																								
												3		0																								
												5		2																								
												2		0																								
												8		2																								
												16		5																								
												2		1																								
						1						5		3																								
												3		1																								
												6		3																								
												7		3																								
3	2							1				17		5																								
												4		0																								
4	6	1	1	..	..	4	3	3	3	3		199 / 197		66											1													

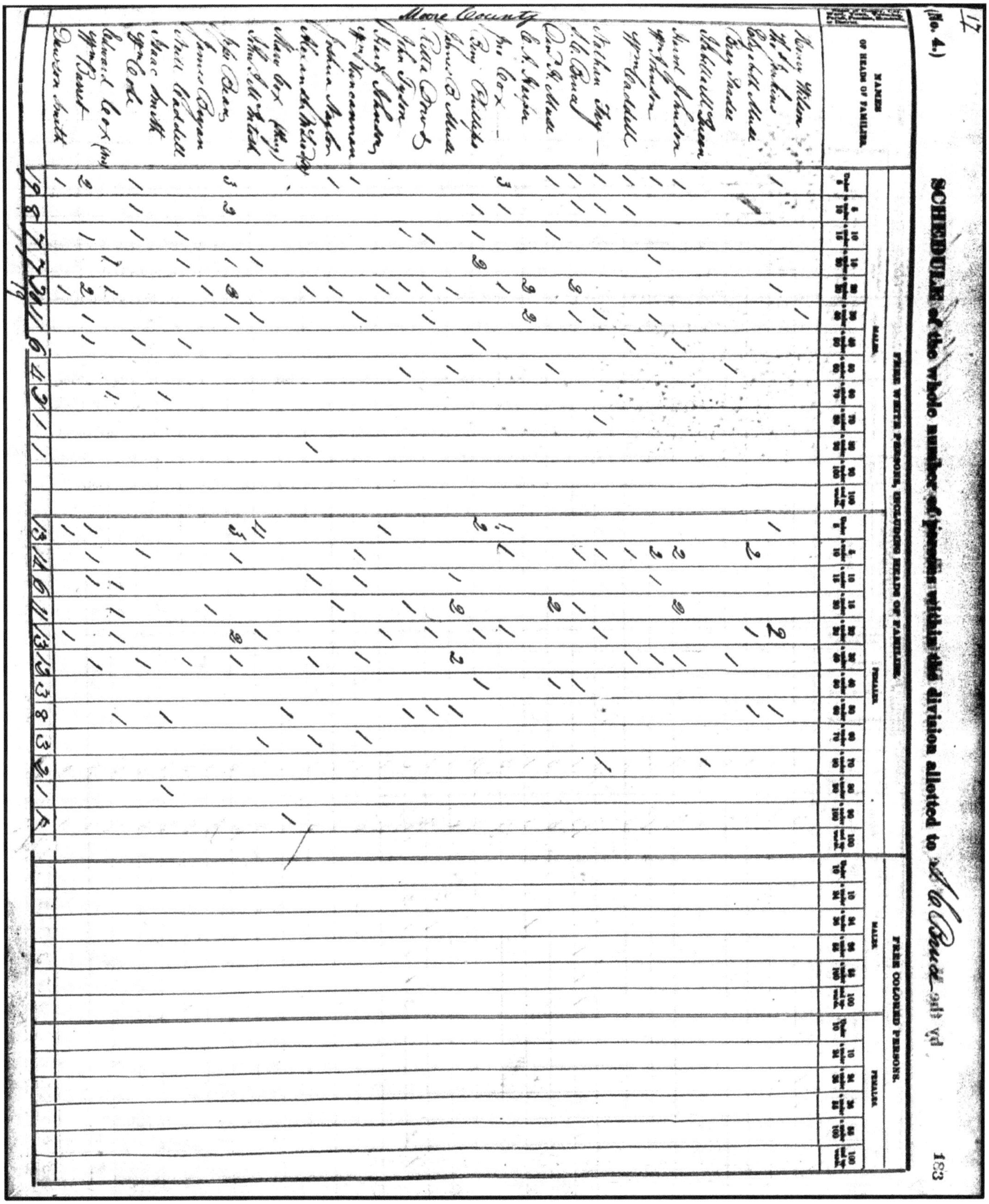
17

(No. 4.) SCHEDULE of the whole number of persons within the division allotted to S. C. Bruce ... 183

Moore County

NAMES OF HEADS OF FAMILIES.

Henry Wilson
Thos Jenkins
Elizabeth Mudd
Bray Pardee
Isabella McQueen
Harrel Johnson
Wm Johnson
Wm Caddell
Nathan Fry
S. C. Bruce
Danl H. Mudd
E. A. Harper
Jno Cox
Benj Phillips
James B. Mudd
Rilla Dowd
John Tyson
Hardy Johnson
Wm Vuncannon
Joshua Naylor
Alexander McLeod
Mary Cox
John J. McIntosh
Jesse Bean
James Bryan
Neill Caddell
Isaac Smith
Wm Cole
Edward Cox
Wm Barret
Dawson Smith

Slaves and Free Persons of Color are located on the previous page

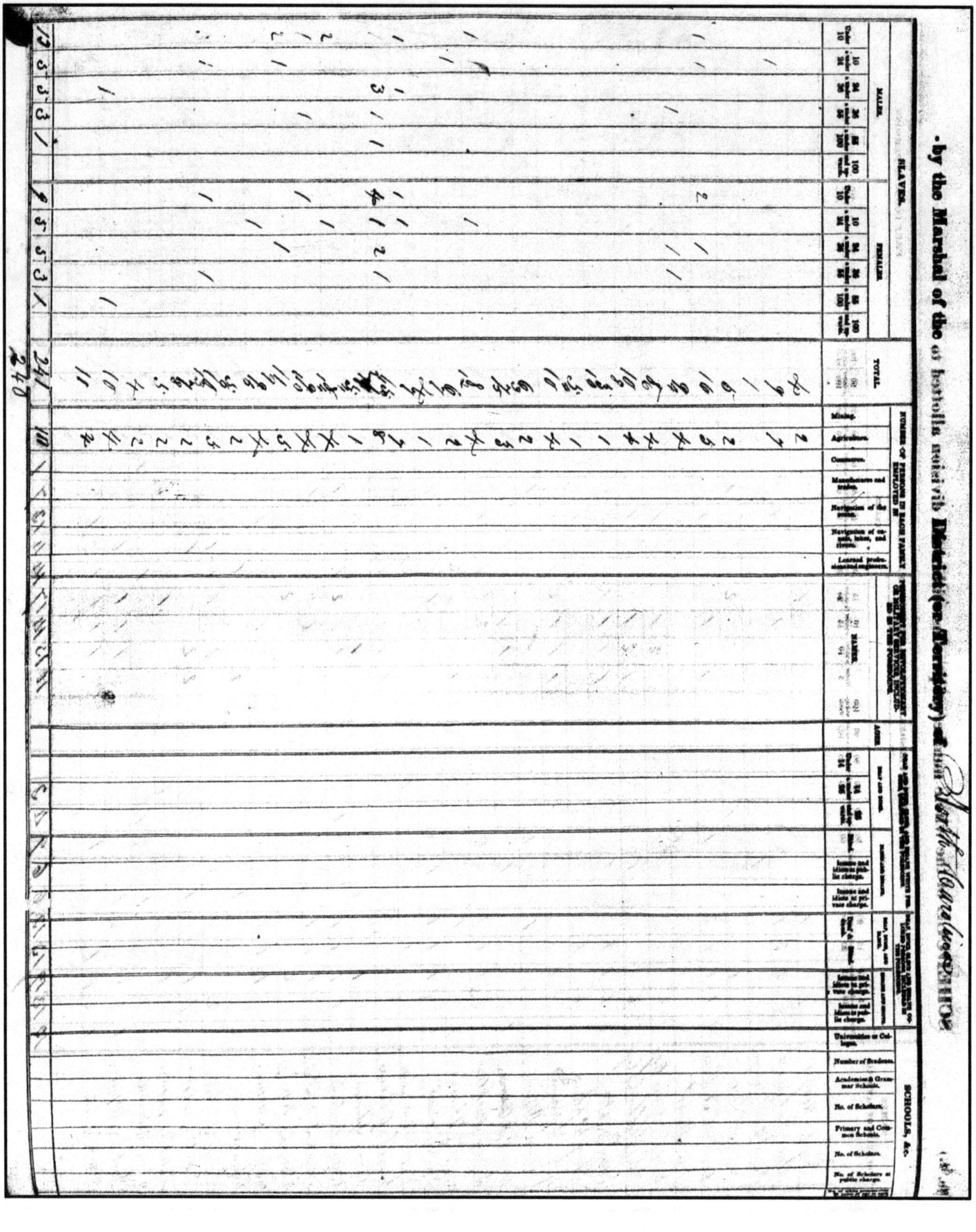

-by the Marshal of the District (or Territory) of North Carolina

Slaves: Males Under 10	Males 10 & under 24	Males 24 & under 36	Males 36 & under 55	Males 55 & under 100	Males 100 and upwards	Females Under 10	Females 10 & under 24	Females 24 & under 36	Females 36 & under 55	Females 55 & under 100	Females 100 and upwards	TOTAL	Mining	Agriculture
												4		2
	1											9		7
												1		
												5		2
1	1					2		1				16		5
			1					1	1			9		4
												6		4
												10		4
												13		1
												5		1
												10		4
												6		2
												7		3
1							1					12		4
	1											6		2
												4		1
1		1				1	1					7		7
		3	1	1		4	1	2	1			15		8
												5		1
2							1					12		4
1			1			1						10		4
2	1							1				11		5
							1					6		4
												5		2
	1					1			1			13		3
												8		2
												5		2
												4		2
		1								1		10		4
												11		4
13	5	5	3	1		9	5	5	3	1		241		10
												240		

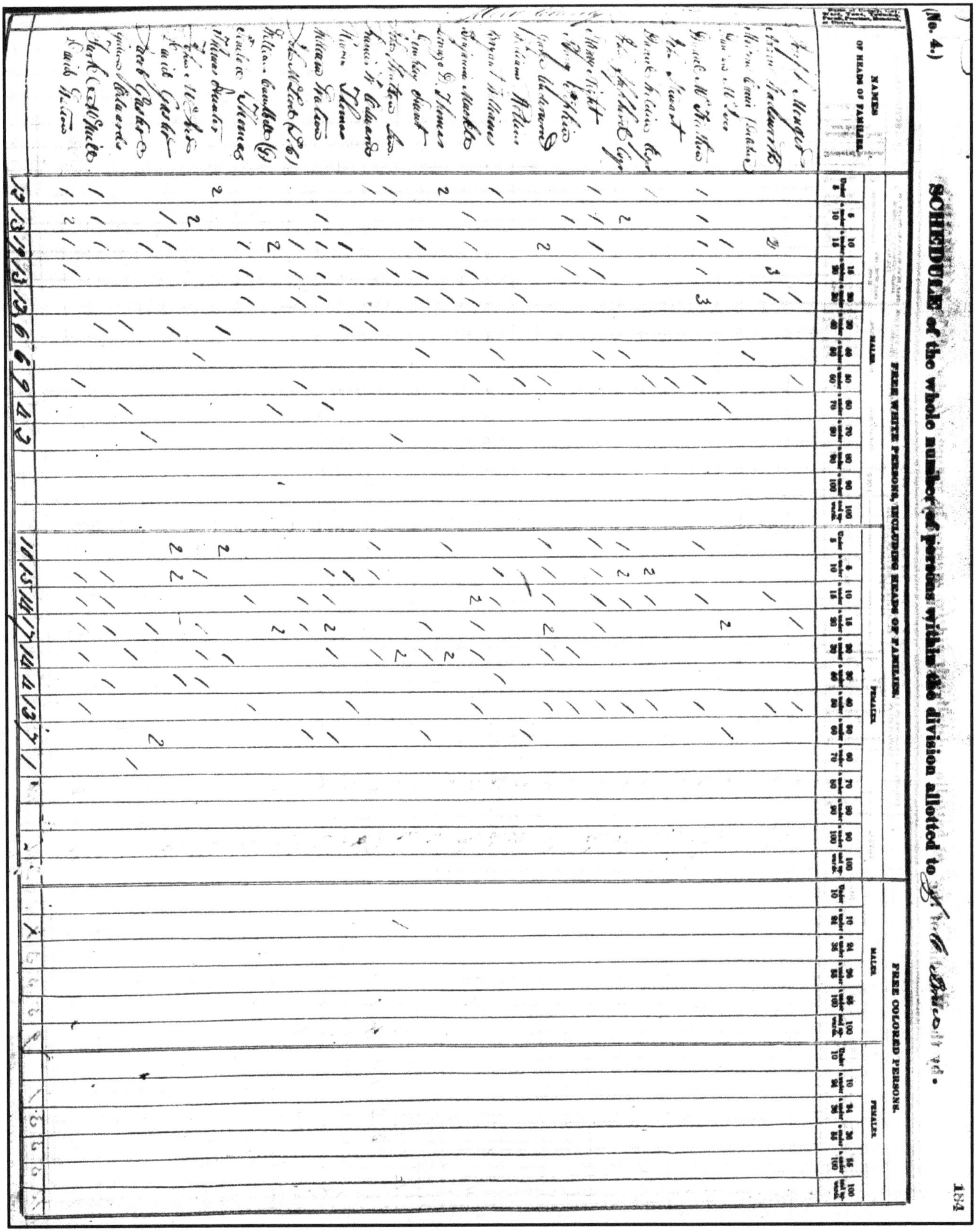

(No. 4.) SCHEDULE of the whole number of persons within the division allotted to [illegible] 184

NAMES OF HEADS OF FAMILIES. — FREE WHITE PERSONS, INCLUDING HEADS OF FAMILIES. (MALES. / FEMALES.) — FREE COLORED PERSONS. (MALES. / FEMALES.)

Joseph Monger
Aaron Wadsworth
Malcom Currie (Bullets)
Duncan McLeod
Daniel McKethan
John Stewart
Daniel Wilcox Esqr
John Shepherd Esqr
Henry Wright
Henry Capshaw
Jacob Underwood
William Rollins
Bryant Williams
Benjamin Mackle
Lorenzo D. Thomas
Dempsey Grant
John Stutton Sen.
Francis W. Edwards
Nixon Thomas
William Watson
John McLeod (P.G)
William Campbell (G)
Tenlow Thomas
Thomas Hunter
John McLeod
David Gaster
Jacob Gaster
Gideon Edwards
Turk McNeill
David Watson

Totals: 12 13 19 13 13 6 6 9 4 2 | 10 15 14 17 14 4 13 7 1

Slaves and Free Persons of Color are located on the previous page

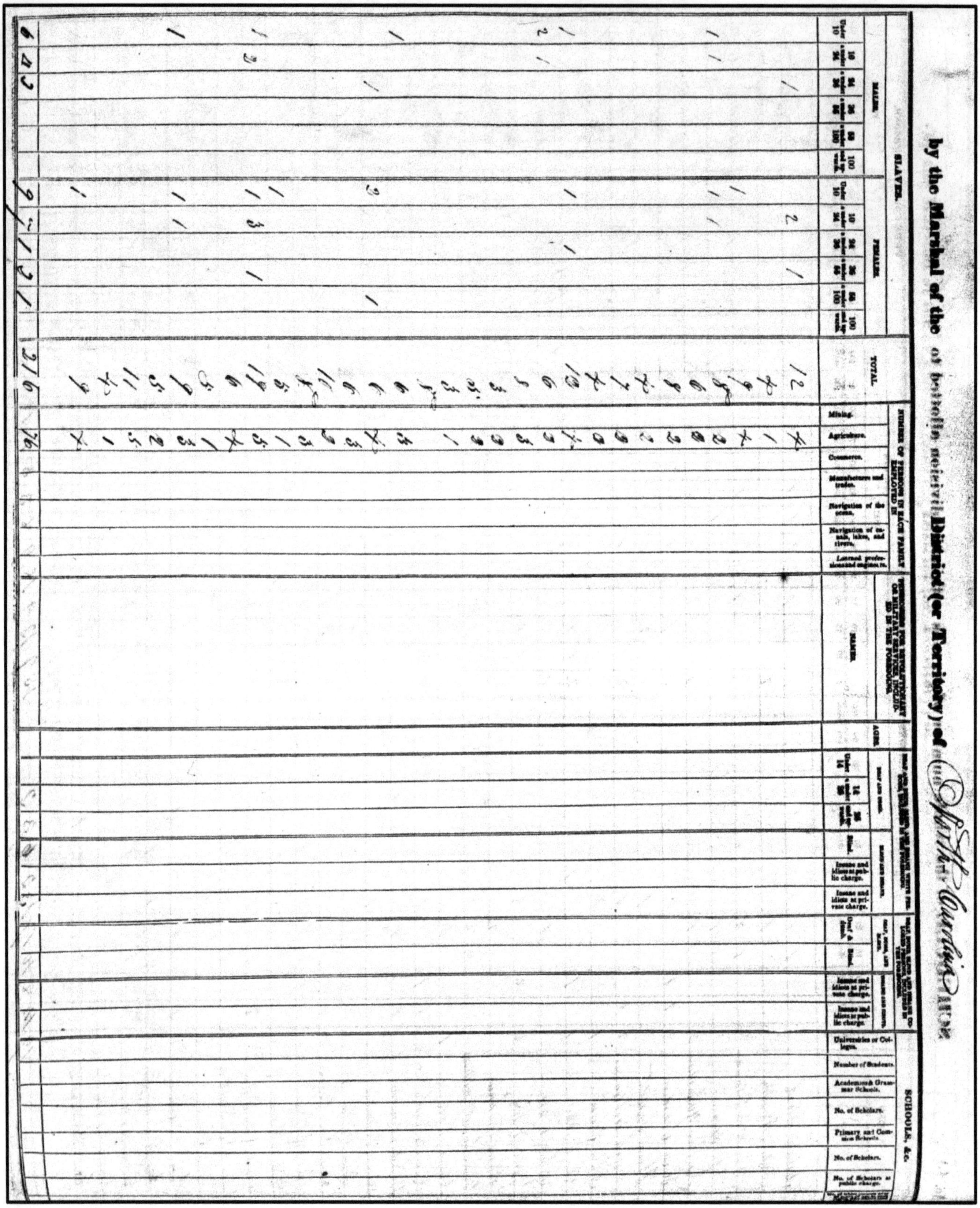

by the Marshal of the District (or Territory) of North Carolina

Slaves, Males, Under 10	Slaves, Males, 10 & under 24	Slaves, Males, 24 & under 36	Slaves, Males, 36 & under 55	Slaves, Males, 55 & under 100	Slaves, Males, 100 and upwards	Slaves, Females, Under 10	Slaves, Females, 10 & under 24	Slaves, Females, 24 & under 36	Slaves, Females, 36 & under 55	Slaves, Females, 55 & under 100	Slaves, Females, 100 and upwards	TOTAL	Mining	Agriculture	Commerce	Manufactures and trades	Navigation of the ocean	Navigation of canals, lakes, and rivers	Learned professional engineers, &c.	Pensioners for Revolutionary or military services: Names	Ages	Deaf and dumb (white): Under 14	14 & under 25	25 and upwards	Blind	Insane and idiots at public charge	Insane and idiots at private charge	Deaf & dumb (colored)	Blind	Insane and idiots at private charge	Insane and idiots at public charge	Universities or Colleges	Number of Students	Academies & Grammar Schools	No. of Scholars	Primary and Common Schools	No. of Scholars	No. of Scholars at public charge
		1					2		1			12		4																								
												4		1																								
						1						9		4																								
1	1					1	1					8		2																								
												6		2																								
												8		2																								
												4		2																								
												7		2																								
												4		0																								
1						1		1				13		7																								
2	1											6		3																								
												8		3																								
												3		2																								
												5		2																								
												3		1																								
												8																										
1												6		3																								
		1				2				1		6		4																								
												6		3																								
												10		2																								
												8		3																								
						1						5		1																								
1	2					1	3		1			17		5																								
												6		4																								
												5		1																								
1						1	1					9		3																								
												5		2																								
												11		5																								
												4		1																								
						1						9		4																								
6	4	3				9	7	1	3	1		216		76																								

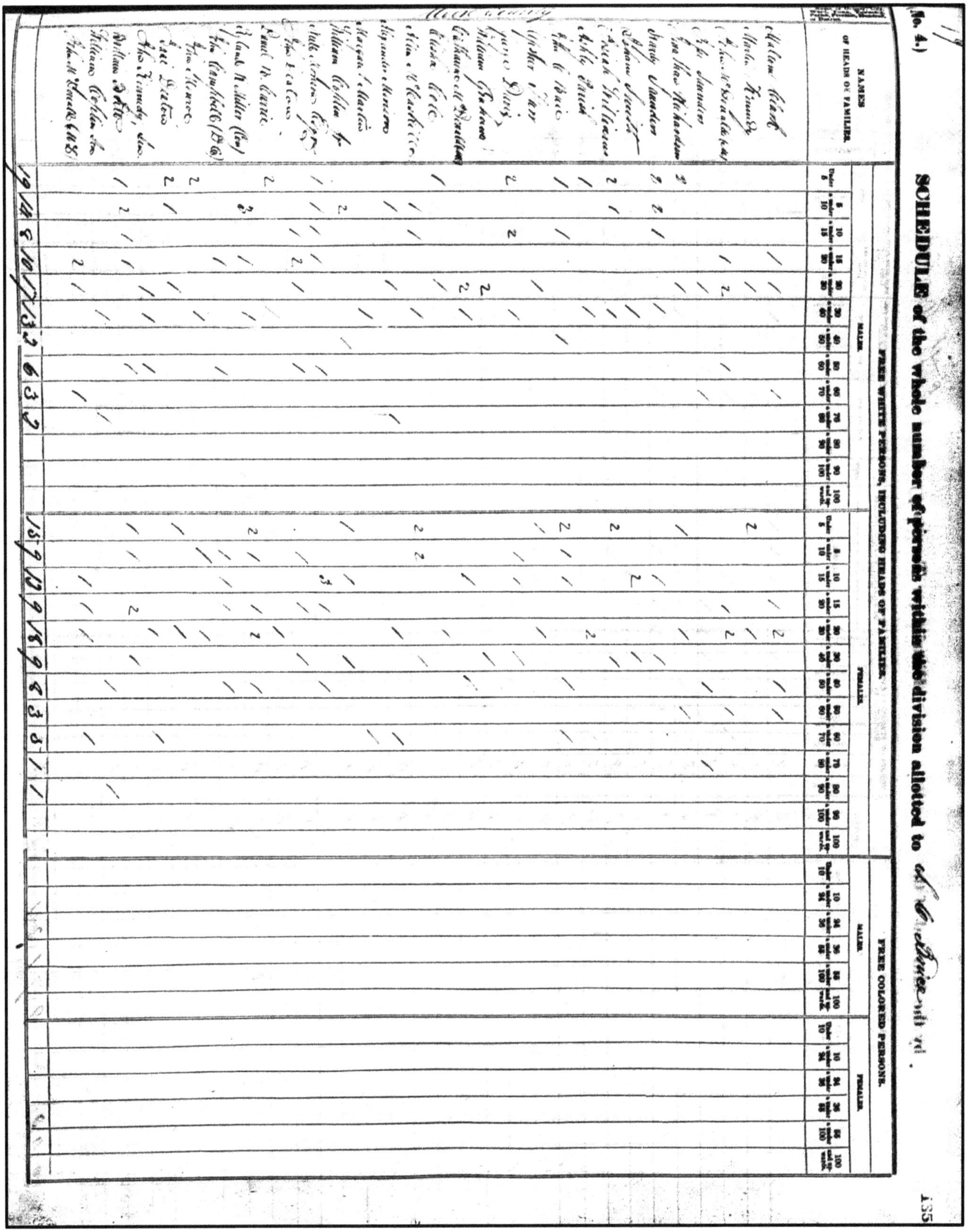
(No. 4.)

SCHEDULE of the whole number of persons within the division allotted to

NAMES OF HEADS OF FAMILIES

FREE WHITE PERSONS, INCLUDING HEADS OF FAMILIES.

FREE COLORED PERSONS.

135

Slaves and Free Persons of Color are located on the previous page

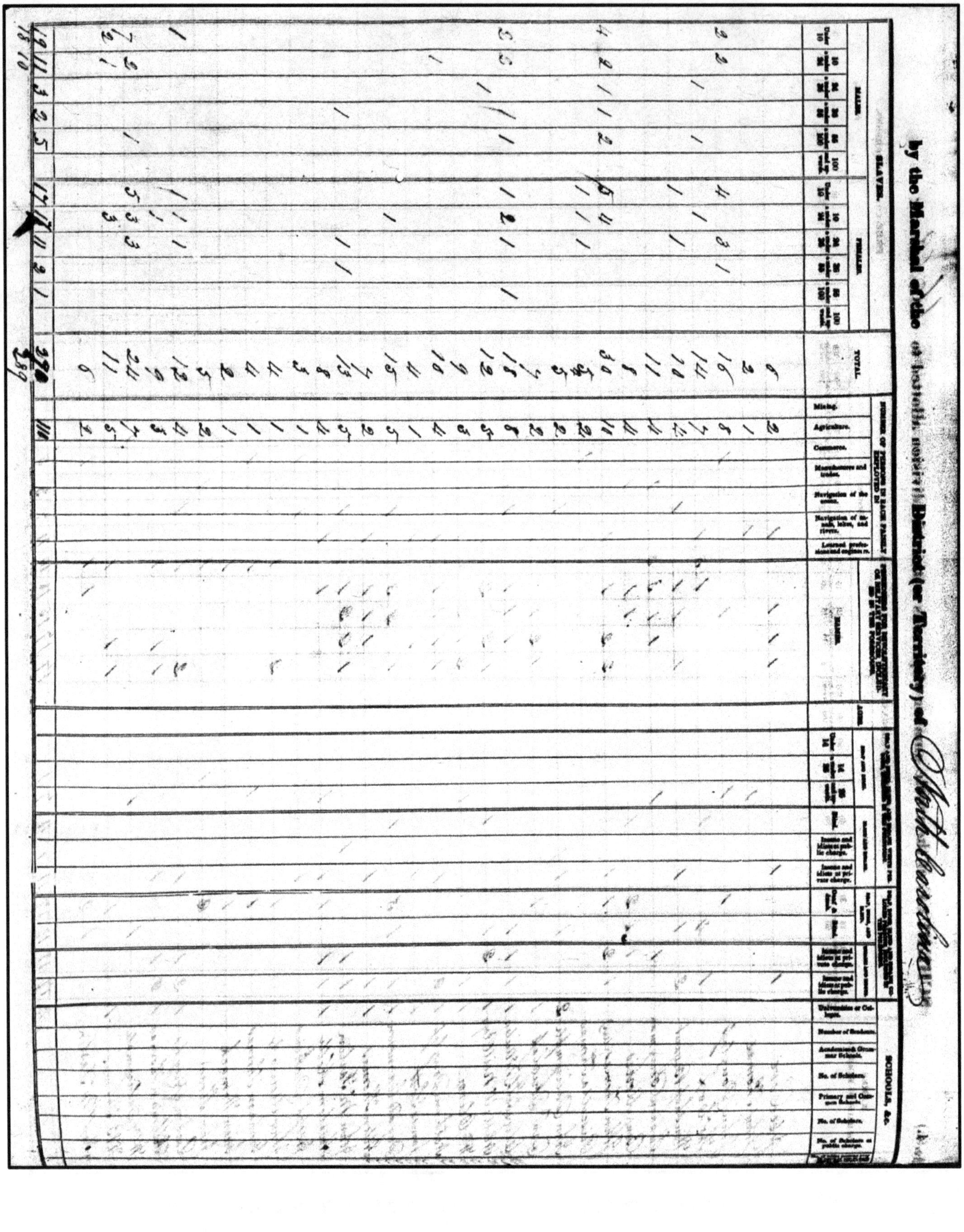
by the Marshal of the … District (or Territory) of North Carolina

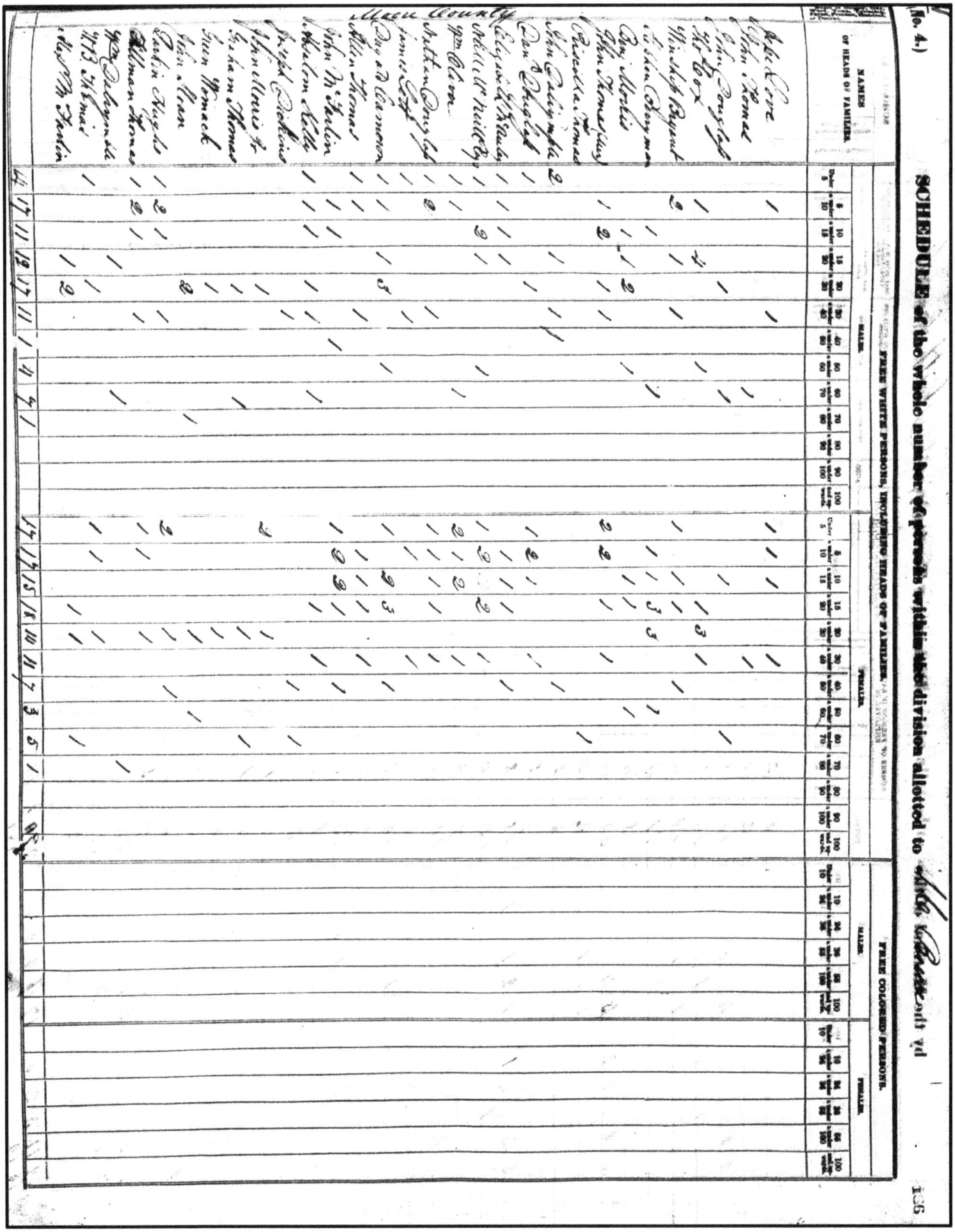

(No. 4.) **SCHEDULE** of the whole number of persons within the division allotted to [illegible] 136

Moore County

FREE WHITE PERSONS, INCLUDING HEADS OF FAMILIES. — MALES.

Names of Heads of Families	Under 5	5 under 10	10 under 15	15 under 20	20 under 30	30 under 40	40 under 50	50 under 60	60 under 70	70 under 80	80 under 90	90 under 100	100 and upwards
Jobe Love		1				1							
John Thomas									1				
John Douglass					1				1				
Thos Cox		1		4				1					
Winship Bryant		2		1		1							
Stephen Berryman			1						1				
Benj Morris			1	1	2			1					
John Thomas (Mer)		1	2		1	1							
Priscilla Thomas													
John Dalrymple	2			1		1	1						
Danl Douglass	1				1								
Elizabeth McAuley	1	1	1	1									
Neill McNeill Esqr	1		2	1				1					
Wm Oliver	1	1							1				
Nathan Douglass	1	2				1							
James Lott	1					1							
Dugald Cameron	1	1		1	3			1					
Allen Thomas	1	1				1							
John McFarlin		1	1				1						
Absalom Kelly	1	1	1		1	1			1				
Joseph Dickins						1							
John Morris Jr					1								
Graham Thomas					1				1				
Green Womack					1								
John Sloan					2					1			
Parkin Hughs	1	2	1			1							
Tillman Thomas	1	2	1			1							
Wm Dalrymple				1					1				
W.B. Thomas	1				1								
Alexr McFarlin				1	2								
	4	17	11	12	17	11	1	4	7	1			

FREE WHITE PERSONS, INCLUDING HEADS OF FAMILIES. — FEMALES.

Names of Heads of Families	Under 5	5 under 10	10 under 15	15 under 20	20 under 30	30 under 40	40 under 50	50 under 60	60 under 70	70 under 80	80 under 90	90 under 100	100 and upwards
Jobe Love	1	1	1			1							
John Thomas						1							
John Douglass			1						1				
Thos Cox				1	3	1							
Winship Bryant	1		1	1			1						
Stephen Berryman		1	1	3	3			1					
Benj Morris			1	1				1					
John Thomas (Mer)	2	2		1		1							
Priscilla Thomas									1				
John Dalrymple							1						
Danl Douglass	1	2	1			1							
Elizabeth McAuley		1	1	1			1						
Neill McNeill Esqr	1	2		2		1							
Wm Oliver	2	1	2			1							
Nathan Douglass	1	1	1	1		1							
James Lott		1				1							
Dugald Cameron	1		2	3			1						
Allen Thomas		1	1	1		1							
John McFarlin	1	2	2	1			1						
Absalom Kelly				1		1							
Joseph Dickins							1		1				
John Morris Jr	2				1								
Graham Thomas					1				1				
Green Womack					1								
John Sloan					1			1					
Parkin Hughs	2				1		1						
Tillman Thomas	1	1			1								
Wm Dalrymple					1					1			
W.B. Thomas	1	1			1								
Alexr McFarlin				1	1				1				
	17	17	15	18	10	11	7	3	5	1			

FREE COLORED PERSONS. — MALES: Under 10; 10 under 24; 24 under 36; 36 under 55; 55 under 100; 100 and upwards. FEMALES: Under 10; 10 under 24; 24 under 36; 36 under 55; 55 under 100; 100 and upwards.

Slaves and Free Persons of Color are located on the previous page

by the Marshal of the District (or Territory) of N. Carolina

Slaves – Males: Under 10	10 & under 24	24 & under 36	36 & under 55	55 & under 100	100 and upwards	Slaves – Females: Under 10	10 & under 24	24 & under 36	36 & under 55	55 & under 100	100 and upwards	Total	Mining	Agriculture	Commerce	Manufactures and trades	Navigation of the ocean	Navigation of canals, lakes, and rivers	Learned professions and engineers
												7		1					
												4		1					
												9		4					
												7		2					
												7		3					
												5		1					
												3		1					
												3		1					
												7		2					
												6		2					
								1				2		2					
												9		4					
												4		1					
												7		2					
												4		1					
												4		1					
												7		1					
												3		1					
												4		1					
												10		3					
												7		2					
												1		1					
		1										8		4					
												5		1					
												8		2					
												4		1					
												9		3					
												4		1					
												10		2					
												6		1					
		1						1				174		53					

Pensioners for Revolutionary or military services, included in the foregoing: Names	Ages	White deaf and dumb: Under 14	14 & under 25	25 and upwards	Blind	Insane and idiots at public charge	Insane and idiots at private charge	Colored deaf, dumb and blind: Deaf & dumb	Blind	Insane and idiots at private charge	Insane and idiots at public charge	Universities or Colleges	Number of Students	Academies & Grammar Schools	No. of Scholars	Primary and Common Schools	No. of Scholars	No. of Scholars at public charge

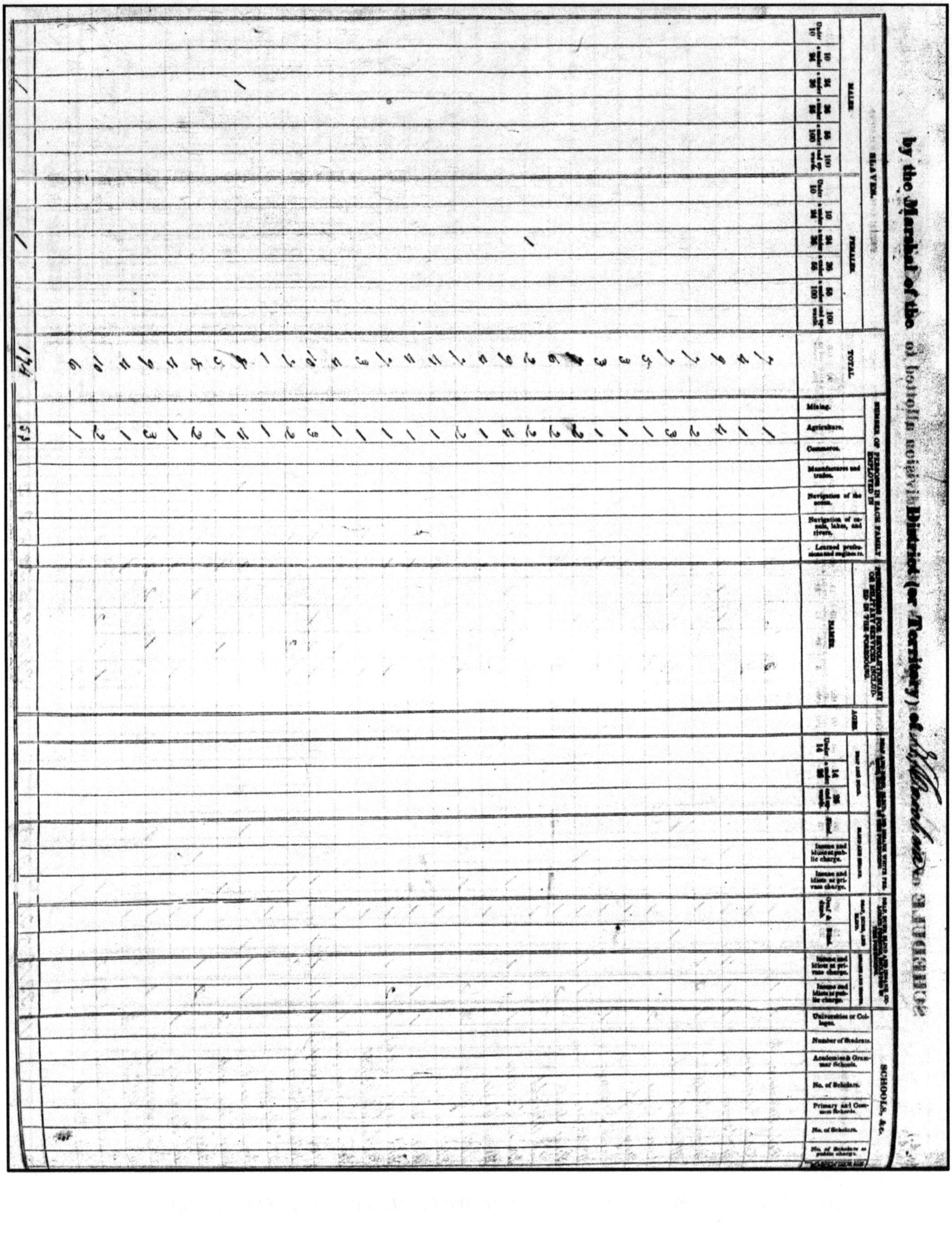

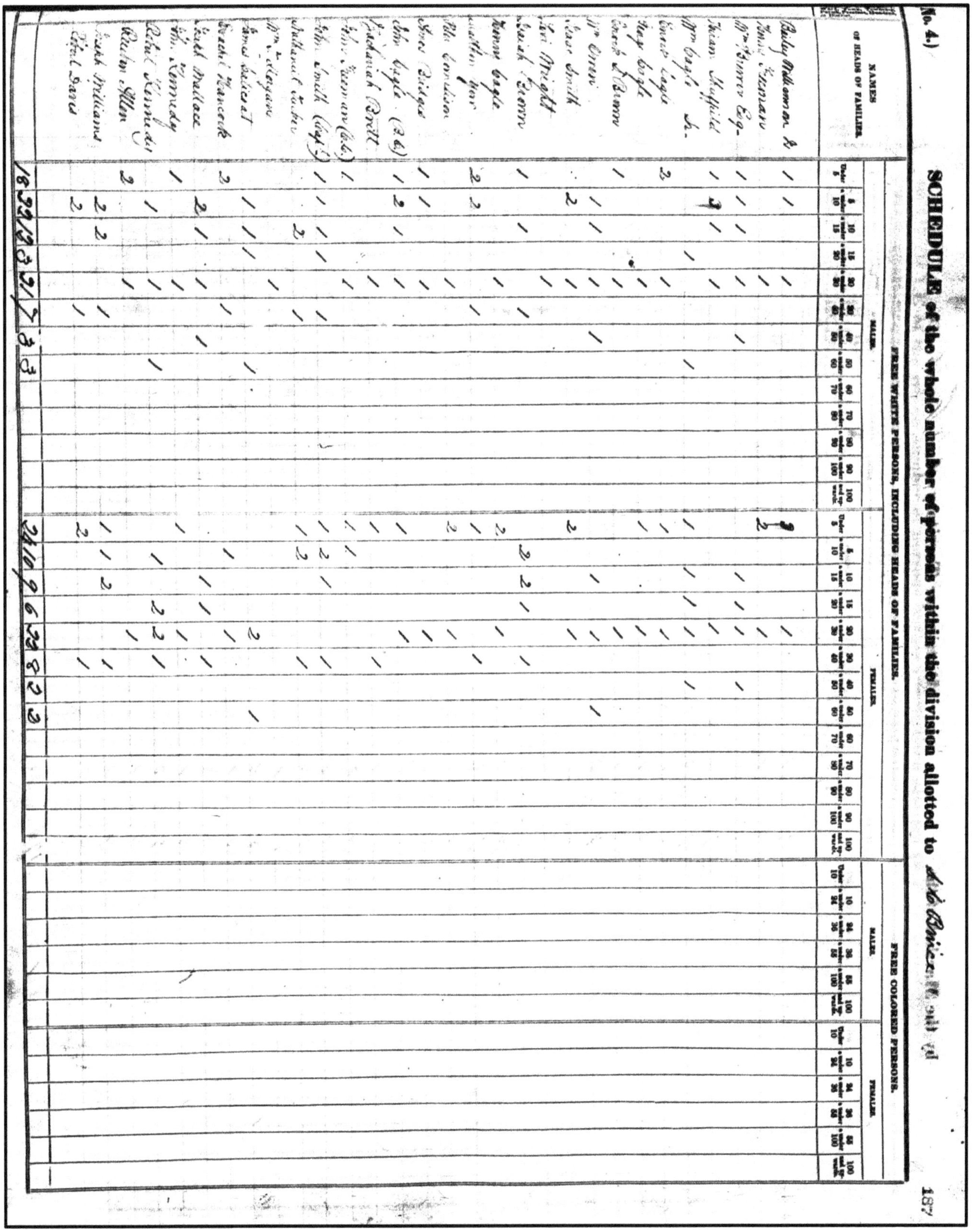

(No. 4.) **SCHEDULE** of the whole number of persons within the division allotted to [illegible] 187

FREE WHITE PERSONS, INCLUDING HEADS OF FAMILIES.

NAMES OF HEADS OF FAMILIES.	M Under 5	M 5–10	M 10–15	M 15–20	M 20–30	M 30–40	M 40–50	M 50–60	M 60–70	M 70–80	M 80–90	M 90–100	M 100 & up	F Under 5	F 5–10	F 10–15	F 15–20	F 20–30	F 30–40	F 40–50	F 50–60	F 60–70	F 70–80	F 80–90	F 90–100	F 100 & up
Bailey Williamson Jr.	1	1			1									3				1								
Henry Freeman					1									2				1								
Wm Burrow Esq.	1	1	1		1		1									1	1	1		1						
Hiram Sheffield	1	3	1		1													1								
Wm Cagle Sr.				1				1						1		1	1	1		1						
Enoch Cagle	2				1									1				1								
Gray Cagle					1									1				1								
Enoch L. Brown	1				1													1								
Wm Owen		1	1		1		1									1		1			1					
Isaac Smith		2			1									2				1								
Levi Wright					1																					
Isaiah Brown	1		1			1									2	2	1		1							
Kenny Cagle					1									2				1								
Matthew Yow	2	2				1								1					1							
Peter Cornelison					1									2				1								
Amos Bridges	1	1			1													1								
John Cagle (B.C.)	1	2	1		1									1				1								
Zachariah Brett					1									1					1							
John Freeman (C.C.)	1				1									1	1											
John Smith (Capt.)	1	1	1	1		1								1	2	1			1							
Nathaniel Tucker			2			1								1	2				1							
Wm T. Morgan					1																					
James Salisbat		1	1	1				1										2			1					
Drachel Hancock	2					1									1			1								
Joseph Wallace		2	1		1		1									1	1		1							
John Kennedy	1				1									1				1								
Robert Kennedy		1			1			1							1		2	2	1							
Reuben Allen	2				1													1								
Joseph Williams		2	2			1								1	1	2			1							
Robert Davis		2				1								2					1							
	18	22	12	3	21	7	3	3						24	10	9	6	22	8	2	2					

FREE COLORED PERSONS. MALES: Under 10, 10–24, 24–36, 36–55, 55–100, 100 and upwards. FEMALES: Under 10, 10–24, 24–36, 36–55, 55–100, 100 and upwards. (no entries)

Slaves and Free Persons of Color are located on the previous page

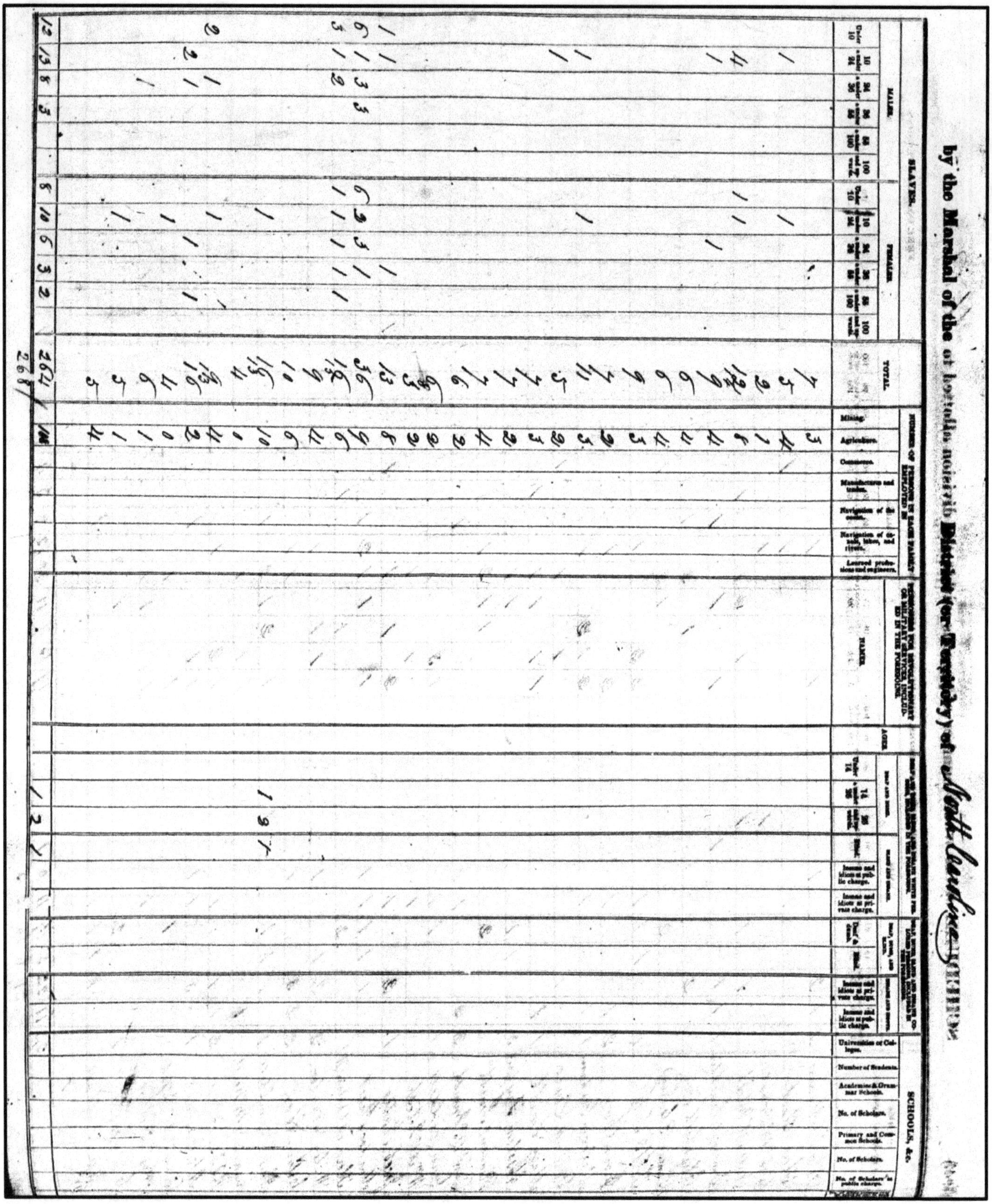

by the Marshal of the District (or Territory) of North Carolina

Slaves, Males, Under 10	Slaves, Males, 10 & under 24	Slaves, Males, 24 & under 36	Slaves, Males, 36 & under 55	Slaves, Males, 55 & under 100	Slaves, Males, 100 and upwards	Slaves, Females, Under 10	Slaves, Females, 10 & under 24	Slaves, Females, 24 & under 36	Slaves, Females, 36 & under 55	Slaves, Females, 55 & under 100	Slaves, Females, 100 and upwards	Total	Employed in Mining	Agriculture	Commerce	Manufactures and trades	Navigation of the ocean	Navigation of canals, lakes, and rivers	Learned professions and engineers	Pensioners for Revolutionary or Military Services: Names	Ages	White Deaf and Dumb, Under 14	White Deaf and Dumb, 14 & under 25	White Deaf and Dumb, 25 and upwards	White Blind	White Insane and idiots at public charge	White Insane and idiots at private charge	Colored Deaf & dumb	Colored Blind	Colored Insane and idiots at private charge	Colored Insane and idiots at public charge	Universities or Colleges	Number of Students	Academies & Grammar Schools	No. of Scholars	Primary and Common Schools	No. of Scholars	No. of Scholars at public charge
												7		3																								
	1						1					5		4																								
												2		1																								
	4					1	1					12		8																								
	1							1				9		4																								
												6		4																								
												6		4																								
												9		3																								
												7		2																								
	1						1					11		3																								
	1											5		2																								
												7		3																								
												7		2																								
												7		4																								
												6		2																								
												6		2																								
												3		2																								
1	1								1			13		8																								
6	1	3	3			6	2	3	1			36		9																								
3	1	2				1	1	1	1	1		16		6																								
												9		4																								
												10		6																								
							1					16		10									1	2	1													
												4		0																								
2		1					1					9		4																								
	2	1						1		1		16		2																								
							1					4		0																								
		1										6		1																								
							1					5		1																								
												5		4																								
12	13	8	3			8	10	6	3	2		264 / 268		108									1	2	1													

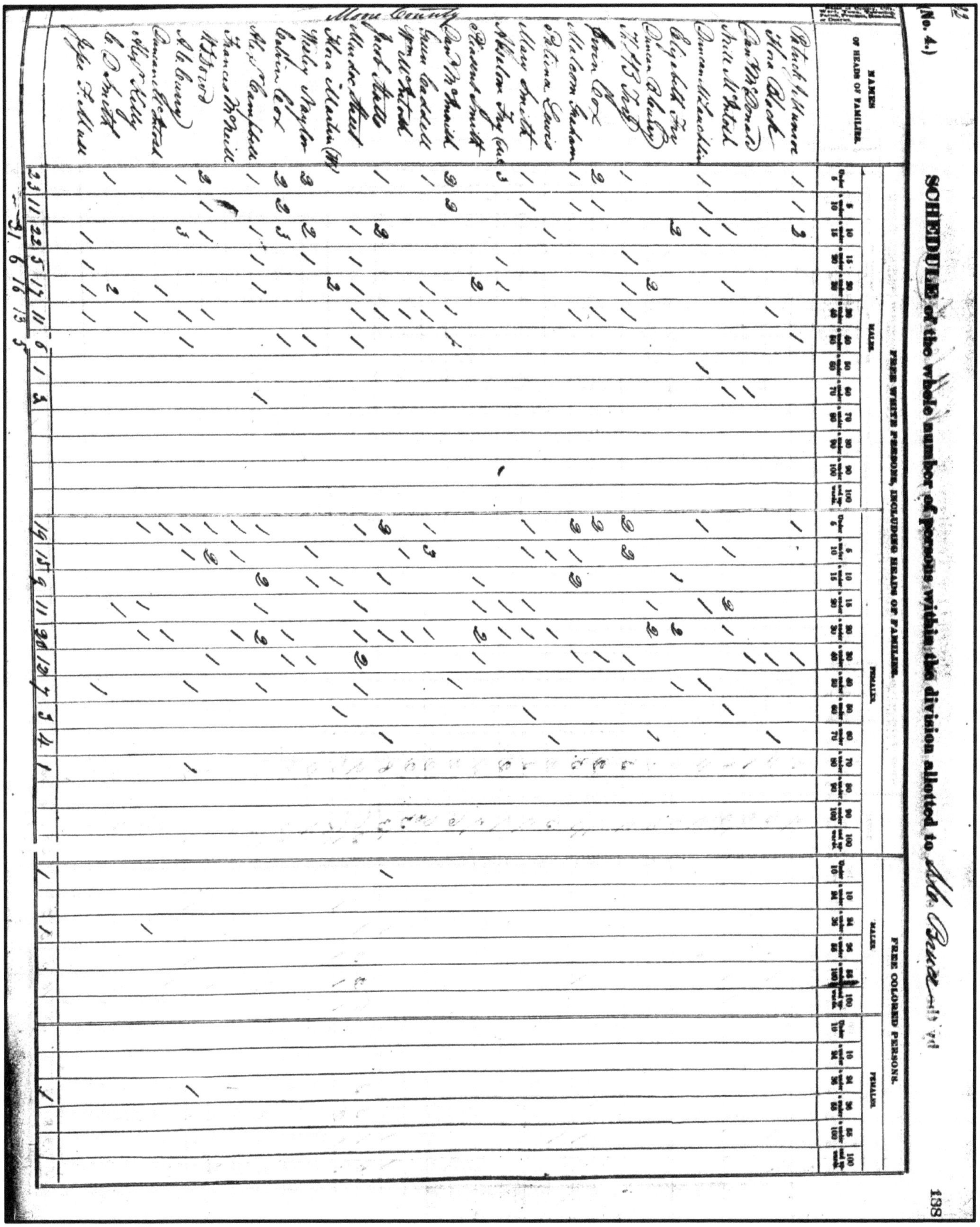

Slaves and Free Persons of Color are located on the previous page

by the Marshal of the District (or Territory) of North Carolina

Slaves, Males: Under 10	10 & under 24	24 & under 36	36 & under 55	55 & under 100	100 and upwards	Slaves, Females: Under 10	10 & under 24	24 & under 36	36 & under 55	55 & under 100	100 and upwards	Total	Agriculture	Academies & Grammar Schools	No. of Scholars	Primary and Common Schools	No. of Scholars
												10	3				
												11 5	1				
	1						1					15	5				
												8	3				
	1						1					4	3				
	1						1					3	3				
1	3					2	1	1				15	6				
	2		1				2	1				15	6				
												7	2				
												8	4				
		1										6	2				
			1									12	5				
												4	1				
												3	3				
												9	4				
	1					2		1				11	5				
	1	1				3		1				10	4				
												29		~~1~~	~~25~~	1	28
2			1			3		1				15	3				
2							1	1				6	3				
	1						1					10	3				
												8	1				
												8	2				
4			1									10	3				
												11					
												11	5				
												1					
												5	2				
												9	4				
	1											5	2				
9	13	1	4			10	8	6				260	88	1		1	28

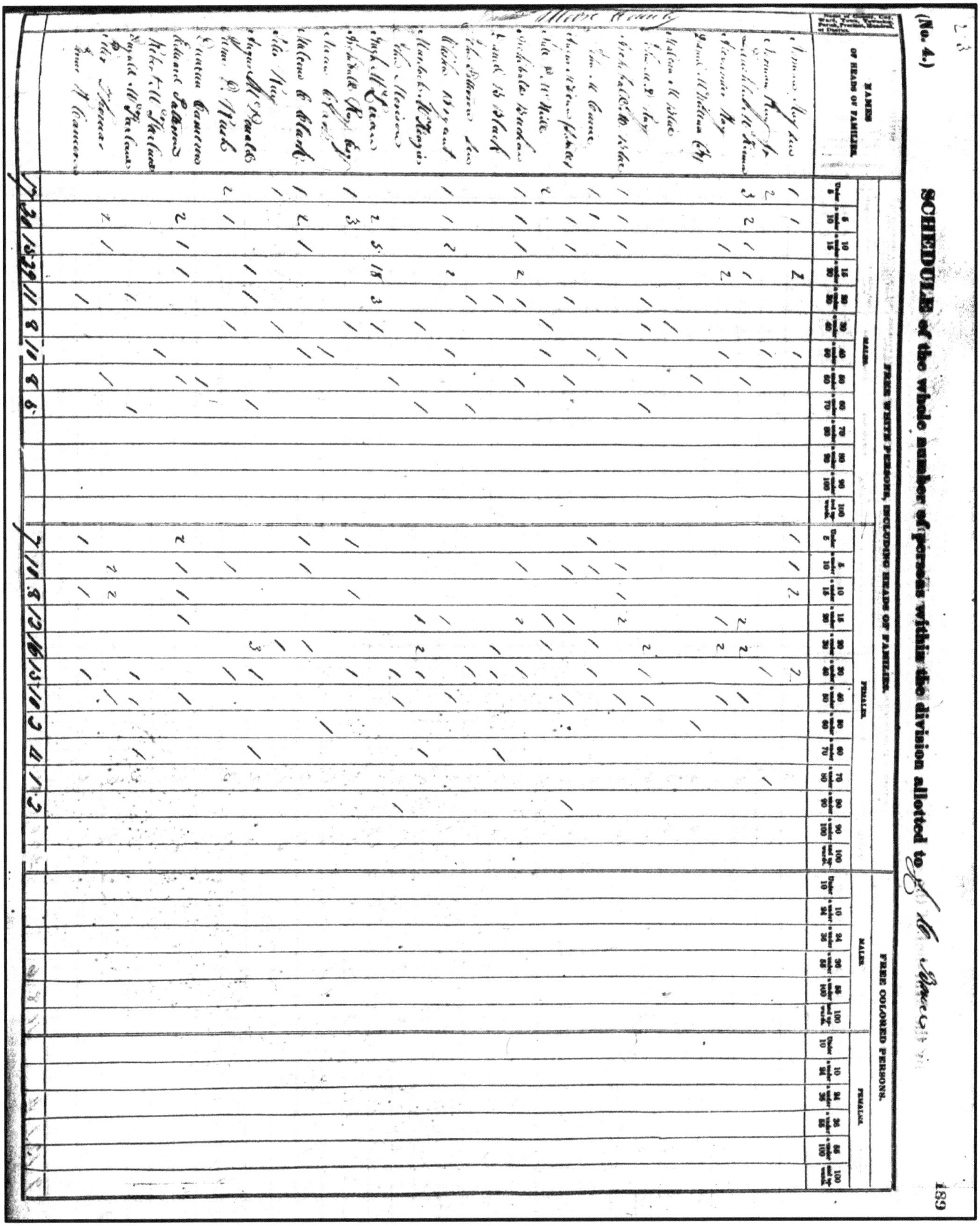

2-3 (No. 4.) SCHEDULE of the whole number of persons within the division allotted to J. C. Bowers [illegible] 189

Moore County

FREE WHITE PERSONS, INCLUDING HEADS OF FAMILIES.

NAMES OF HEADS OF FAMILIES	M Under 5	M 5-10	M 10-15	M 15-20	M 20-30	M 30-40	M 40-50	M 50-60	M 60-70	F Under 5	F 5-10	F 10-15	F 15-20	F 20-30	F 30-40	F 40-50	F 50-60	F 60-70	F 70-80	F 80-90
Norman Ray Sen	1	1		2			1			1	1	2			2					
Norman Ray Jr	2						1								1				1	
Lauchlin McKinnon	3	2	1	1				1					2	2		1				
Alexander Ray			1	2			1						1	2		1				
Daniel McMillan Clk								1									1			
Malcom McBlue						1														
John McD Ray					1	1			1					2	1	1				
Archibald McBlue	1	1	1				1				1	1	2			1				
John McCrum	1	1					1			1	1			1	1					
Angus McDonald (Miller)		1	1		1			1			1		1			1				1
John P. McNeill	2					1	1						1	1						
Archibald Buchan	1	1	1	2	1			1			1		2		1					
Daniel B Black					1									1	1			1		
Thos Patterson Sen					1				1						1					
Walker Bryant	1	1	2	2			1						1			1				
Murdoch McKenzie						1			1				1	2	1			1		
John Morison								1							1	1				1
Hugh McLean		2	5	18	3	1														
Archibald Ray Esq	1	3				1				1		1			1					
Anna Clark							1										1			
Malcom C Clark	1	2	1				1			1	1			1						
Peter Ray	1					1								1						
Angus McDonald				1	1				1					3	1			1		
Duncan D. Nash	2	1				1					1				1					
Duncan Cameron								1												
Edward Patterson		2	1	1				1		2	1	1	1			1				
Robert McFarland							1													
Dugald McFarland					1				1						1	1		1		
Peter Thomas		2	1					1			1	2				1				
Anna A Cameron					1					1		1			1					
Totals	17	30	15	29	11	8	10	8	6	7	11	8	12	16	15	10	3	4	1	2

Slaves and Free Persons of Color are located on the previous page

by the Marshal of the District (or Territory) of North Carolina

Slaves Males Under 10	M 10 under 24	M 24 under 36	M 36 under 55	M 55 under 100	M 100 and upwards	Slaves Females Under 10	F 10 under 24	F 24 under 36	F 36 under 55	F 55 under 100	F 100 and upwards	Total	Agriculture	Colored Insane and idiots at public charge
												12	4	
												6	2	
7	2	2	1	1		5	1	2	1	1		27	10	
3	2	1	2						2	1		14	8	1
												9	4	
												2	2	
2	3					2	3		2			18	8	
												2	1	
												9	4	
												6	2	
												4		
												8	4	
												3	1	
2		3	1				1		1			16	6	
												8	4	
2	6	1	1	1		1	1	1	1			24	10	
												6		
						1						4	3	
												6	2	
												6	2	
												7	2	
												9	4	
							1					7	2	
	2											11	3	
1		1										10	4	
												4	0	
												9	2	
3	2		1				1					14	9	
												5	1	
												4	1	
20	17	8	6	2	"	9	8	3	7	2	.	367 / 266	143	1

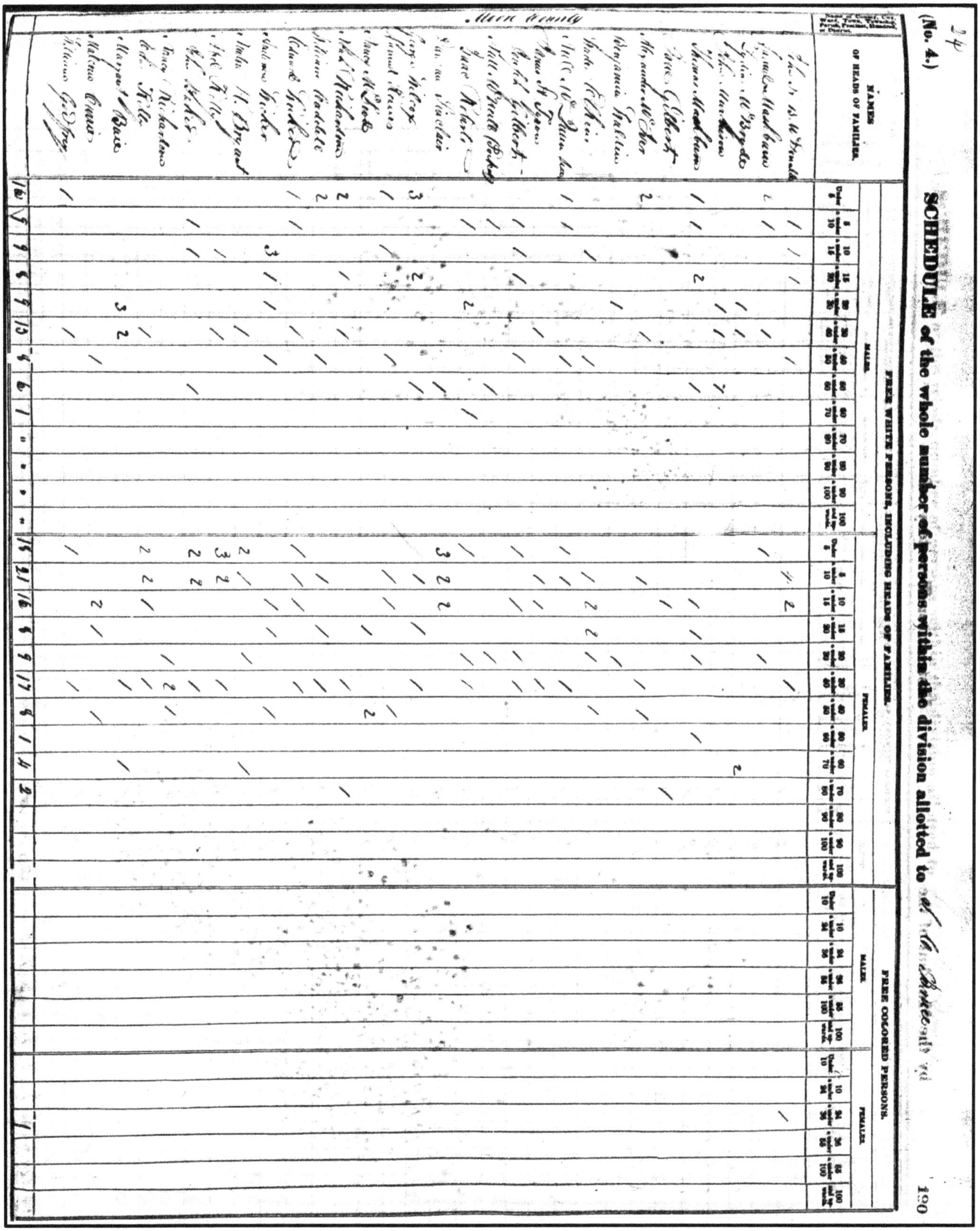

(No. 4.) SCHEDULE of the whole number of persons within the division allotted to

Moore County

Name of County, City, Ward, Town, Township, Parish, Precinct, Hundred, or District.

NAMES OF HEADS OF FAMILIES.

FREE WHITE PERSONS, INCLUDING HEADS OF FAMILIES.

FREE COLORED PERSONS.

190

Slaves and Free Persons of Color are located on the previous page

by the Marshal of the District (or Territory) of North Carolina

Slaves Males Under 10	10 & under 24	24 & under 36	36 & under 55	55 & under 100	100 and upwards	Slaves Females Under 10	10 & under 24	24 & under 36	36 & under 55	55 & under 100	100 and upwards	TOTAL	Mining	Agriculture	Commerce	Manufactures and trades	Navigation of the ocean	Navigation of canals, lakes, and rivers	Learned professions, engineers	Primary and Common Schools	No. of Scholars
												3		1							
5	3	5		3		7	4	3	1	1		41		8							
												8		4							
												6		3							
						6	1					5		2							
1						4		1				10		4							
1	2	1				3	2	2				26		8							
												6		2							
												3		1							
												2		1							
3	1	1	1			2	1		2			13		6							
												6		2							
												[illegible]		3							
												6		3							
				1					1			14		3							
										1		[illegible]		4							
3	1	1				3	2	3				18		8							
												5		2							
												8		2							
1	1	1				2	1	1				14		3							
												5		4							
						3		1				12		4							
												5		1							
												5		1							
	2					3	2					12		4							
												3		1							
												6		3							
												3		1							
												3		1							
												3		1							
												40		0						1	38
19	10	5	1	4	-	27	13	11	4	2		288		91							38
												289									

(No. 4.) 25 | 191

SCHEDULE of the whole number of persons within the division allotted to Samuel C. Bruce

Moore County

NAMES OF HEADS OF FAMILIES.	Free White Males: Under 5	5 & under 10	10 & under 15	15 & under 20	20 & under 30	30 & under 40	40 & under 50	50 & under 60	60 & under 70	70 & under 80	80 & under 90	90 & under 100	100 and upwards	Free White Females: Under 5	5 & under 10	10 & under 15	15 & under 20	20 & under 30	30 & under 40	40 & under 50	50 & under 60	60 & under 70	70 & under 80	80 & under 90	90 & under 100	100 and upwards	Free Colored Males: Under 10	10 & under 24	24 & under 36	36 & under 55	55 & under 100	100 and upwards	Free Colored Females: Under 10	10 & under 24	24 & under 36	36 & under 55	55 & under 100	100 and upwards
Jo. Morgan					2													1																				
John Shaw			1	2				1							1	1	2			1																		
Elizabeth Watson	1	1	1	1											1	1	1			1																		
Charles [illegible]			1	1	1			1								1				1																		
John M Cox	1					1								1				1																				
Elizabeth Dalrymple					1													2				1																
Charles G. Farrington	2	2				1								1	1	2			1																			
Martin Dye		1						1								1	1	1			1																	
Frederick Yarborough									1												1																	
[illegible] Thomas					1									1			1																					
John Gasler					1													1																				
Elizabeth Redd																	1																					
[illegible] Campbell		2				1								1		1	1																					
Elizabeth Morris		2	1				1							1	2	1			1																			
Rosanna Dalrymple					1													2				1																
Patrick Shields Jr	1			1	1	1									1	1		2																				
William Davis		1	1	1	1		1									1	1	1		1																		
William M Johnson			1				1									2				1																		
James Hardin Sen											1						1		1	2																		
Fanny Moore					1				1									1				1																
Moses Kidd										1												1																
John Morgan			1	1	1			1							1	2				1																		
Archibald B Currie	1				1					1								1																				
Elizabeth McLennan		1												2	1			1																				
James D Stone	2				1									1				1																				
Nancy Wright																						1																
Malcolm Morrick								1								1					1																	
Polly Smith	1	1			1										1				1			1																
John Twister										1						1							1															
William Graham					1									1					1																			
Daniel McKenzie	2	7	13	9	1									5	3																							
	11	18	20	16	16	4	5	5	2	5	1	"	"	14	12	16	9	15	5	4	4	6	1															

Slaves and Free Persons of Color are located on the previous page

by the Marshal of the District (or Territory) of North Carolina

Slaves: Males, Under 10	Males, 10 & under 24	Males, 24 & under 36	Males, 36 & under 55	Males, 55 & under 100	Males, 100 and upwards	Females, Under 10	Females, 10 & under 24	Females, 24 & under 36	Females, 36 & under 55	Females, 55 & under 100	Females, 100 and upwards	Total	Mining	Agriculture	Commerce	Manufactures and trades	Navigation of the ocean	Navigation of canals, lakes, and rivers	Learned professions and engineers
		1										3		2					
												5		1					
												8		3					
							1					9		2					
												7		2					
												5		2					
												2		1					
	2	1										10		4					
												5		1					
							1					3		2					
												5		2					
							1					8		3					
2						4		2				13		5					
												7		2					
												6		1					
												10		3					
												6		1					
												2		1					
						3		1				14		4					
												3		1					
												4		1					
												4		1					
												3		1					
												5		2					
							1					5		2					
1				1			1			1		14		4					
												7		2					
												8		2					
												6		3					
1	2						2					12		4					
												5		1					
4	4	2	•	1	•	7	7	3	•	1		197 / 198		64					

36

(No. 4.) **SCHEDULE** of the whole number of persons within the division allotted to A. C. Bruce ... 1?2

Moore County

NAMES OF HEADS OF FAMILIES	FREE WHITE PERSONS, INCLUDING HEADS OF FAMILIES. MALES. Under 5	5 & under 10	10 & under 15	15 & under 20	20 & under 30	30 & under 40	40 & under 50	50 & under 60	60 & under 70	70 & under 80	80 & under 90	90 & under 100	100 and upwards	FEMALES. Under 5	5 & under 10	10 & under 15	15 & under 20	20 & under 30	30 & under 40	40 & under 50	50 & under 60	60 & under 70	70 & under 80	80 & under 90	90 & under 100	100 and upwards
William Buie							1											1								
William McQueen	2				1									1				1								
Daniel McIntosh Sr		3		1	1	1								1					1							
Margaret McNab	2				1	1								2				2			1					
Kenneth Murchison					1	1													2			1				
Charity Cole					1															1						
Archibald Baker					1		1							3				1	1							
Alexander J. McBryde					1									2				1				1				
James S. McBryde					1													1								
William England			1	1				1										2								
Robert M. Leo (B.S.)	2				2									1			1	1								
Malcom McIver						1								1	1			1	1							
Peter Morris	1	1				1								1	1				1				1			
Isaac Phillips Jr	3					1									1			1								
Elisha Morris	1	1	1			1								1	1	2	1		1							
James Morris	1						1							1	1	1			1							
Allen McLeod							1															1				
Angus Leach		1			1			1							1	2	2			1				1		
William Jr. Kimbrough					1									1				1								
John M. Ferguson	1						1												2							
Eli Wadsworth	1				1									1				1								
Stephen Grimes							1							1				1								
Archibald Smith	1					1					1							1	1							
William Keith					1									2				1								
Norman McDonald	2	2			1	1								1	1	1		1								
John McNeill (L.R.)		1	1				1								2	1			1							
John Ferguson	2	3				1										1		1								
Norman Ferguson	1	1	1	1				1											1							
Henry Arnold		1	1			1								2	1			1								
Daniel Graham (C.G.)	1						1							2				1								
	21	14	5	3	15	11	8	3	"	"	1	"	"	24	16	6	4	21	13	2	1	3	1	1		

FREE COLORED PERSONS. MALES. Under 10	10 & under 24	24 & under 36	36 & under 55	55 & under 100	100 and upwards	FEMALES. Under 10	10 & under 24	24 & under 36	36 & under 55	55 & under 100	100 and upwards

Slaves and Free Persons of Color are located on the previous page

by the Marshal of the District (or Territory) of North Carolina

Slaves, Males: Under 10	10 & under 24	24 & under 36	36 & under 55	55 & under 100	100 and upwards	Slaves, Females: Under 10	10 & under 24	24 & under 36	36 & under 55	55 & under 100	100 and upwards	Total	Mining	Agriculture	Commerce	Manufactures and trades	Navigation of the ocean	Navigation of canals, lakes, and rivers	Learned professional engineers, &c.
3	1					2		1		1		21		7					
												16		3					
4	2	1				2	2	3				18		6					
												8		1					
												3							
												4		1					
												7		3					
												6		1					
2	2					2	3					11		3					
												5		2					
							2					9		4					
7	6	2	2	1		4	5		1	3	1	38		16					
												6		2					
												9		2					
						1		1				13		6					
	1											4		2					
	1						1		1			8		4					
							1					7		3					
1			1									5		3					
												3		1					
3	2	2					2		1			12		5					
												12		4					
												3		1					
									1			11		4					
3	2		1			3	2	1				17		5					
												4		2					
												7		2					
	1											4		2					
			1	1								6		2					
1						2	1					6		3					
24	18	5	5	2	"	16	19	6	4	4	1	369		100					
												260							

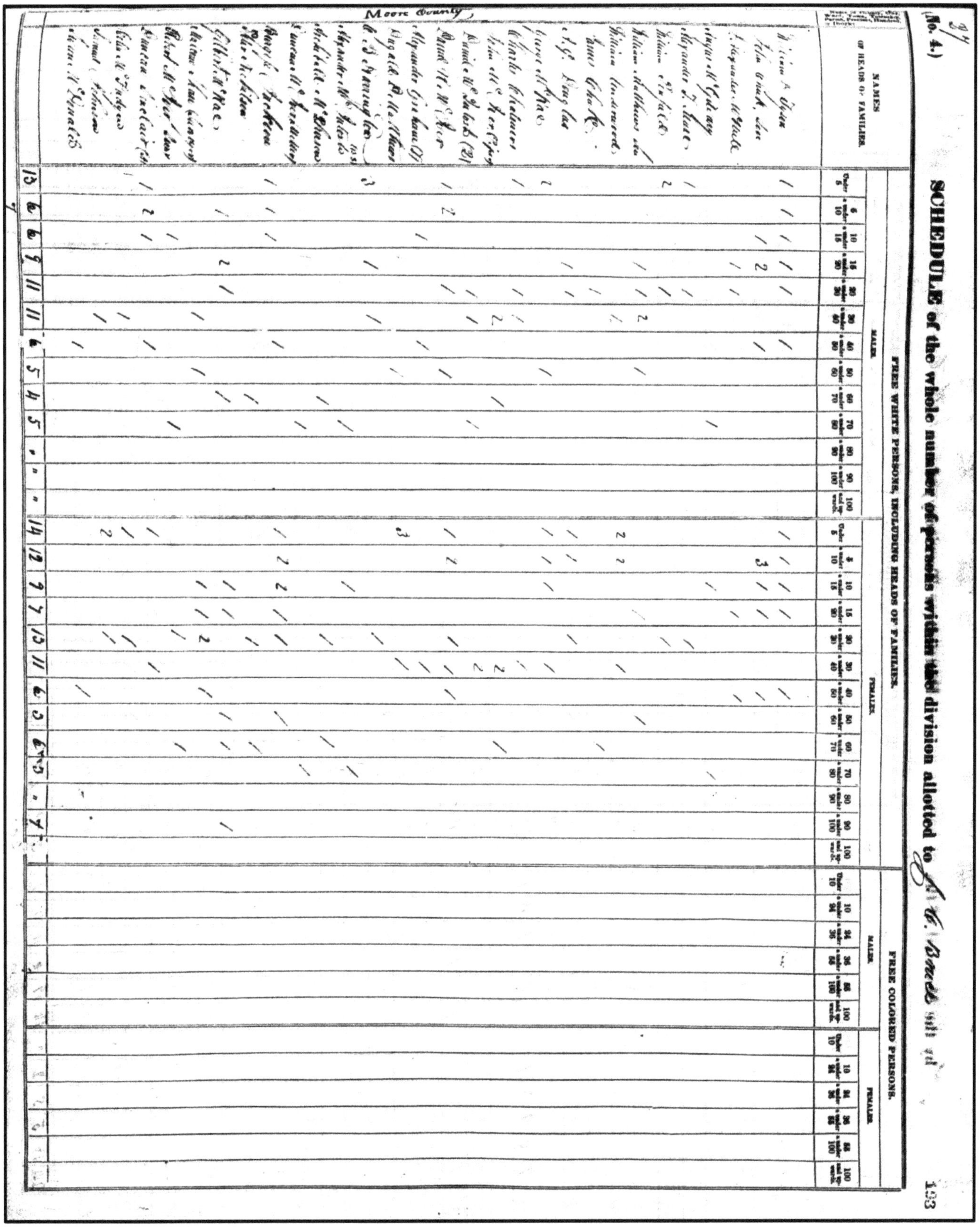

Slaves and Free Persons of Color are located on the previous page

by the Marshal of the District (or Territory) of

Slaves: Males, Under 10	Males, 10 & under 24	Males, 24 & under 36	Males, 36 & under 55	Males, 55 & under 100	Males, 100 and upwards	Females, Under 10	Females, 10 & under 24	Females, 24 & under 36	Females, 36 & under 55	Females, 55 & under 100	Females, 100 and upwards	Total	Employed in: Mining	Agriculture	Commerce	Manufactures and trades	Navigation of the ocean	Navigation of canals, lakes, and rivers	Learned professions and engineers	Pensioners for Revolutionary or military services: Names	Ages	White deaf and dumb: Under 14	14 & under 25	25 and upwards	White: Blind	Insane and idiots at public charge	Insane and idiots at private charge	Colored: Deaf & dumb	Blind	Insane and idiots at private charge	Insane and idiots at public charge	Schools: Universities or Colleges	Number of Students	Academies & Grammar Schools	No. of Scholars	Primary and Common Schools	No. of Scholars	No. of Scholars at public charge	No. of white persons over 20 who cannot read and write
												4		3																									
												8		2																									
												5		1																									
												6		2																									
												6		1																									
												4		1																									
												4		2																									
1	1					2	1	1				12		4																									
												5		1																									
												6		2																									
												4		2																									
												9		2																									
	1											8		3																									
	1						1					7		2																									
												4		1																									
												7		2																									
												9		4																									
8	4	1				4	3	2		1		26		12																									
	1	1					1					8		3																									
												1		-																									
												11		4																									
							1					5		2																									
1	2						1					11		5																									
												2		1																									
												6		2																									
												5		•																									
2	7	2				3	3	2				18		6																									
												3		1																									
												5		2																									
												5		1																									
12	11	4				9	11	5		1		216		[illegible]																									
												214																											

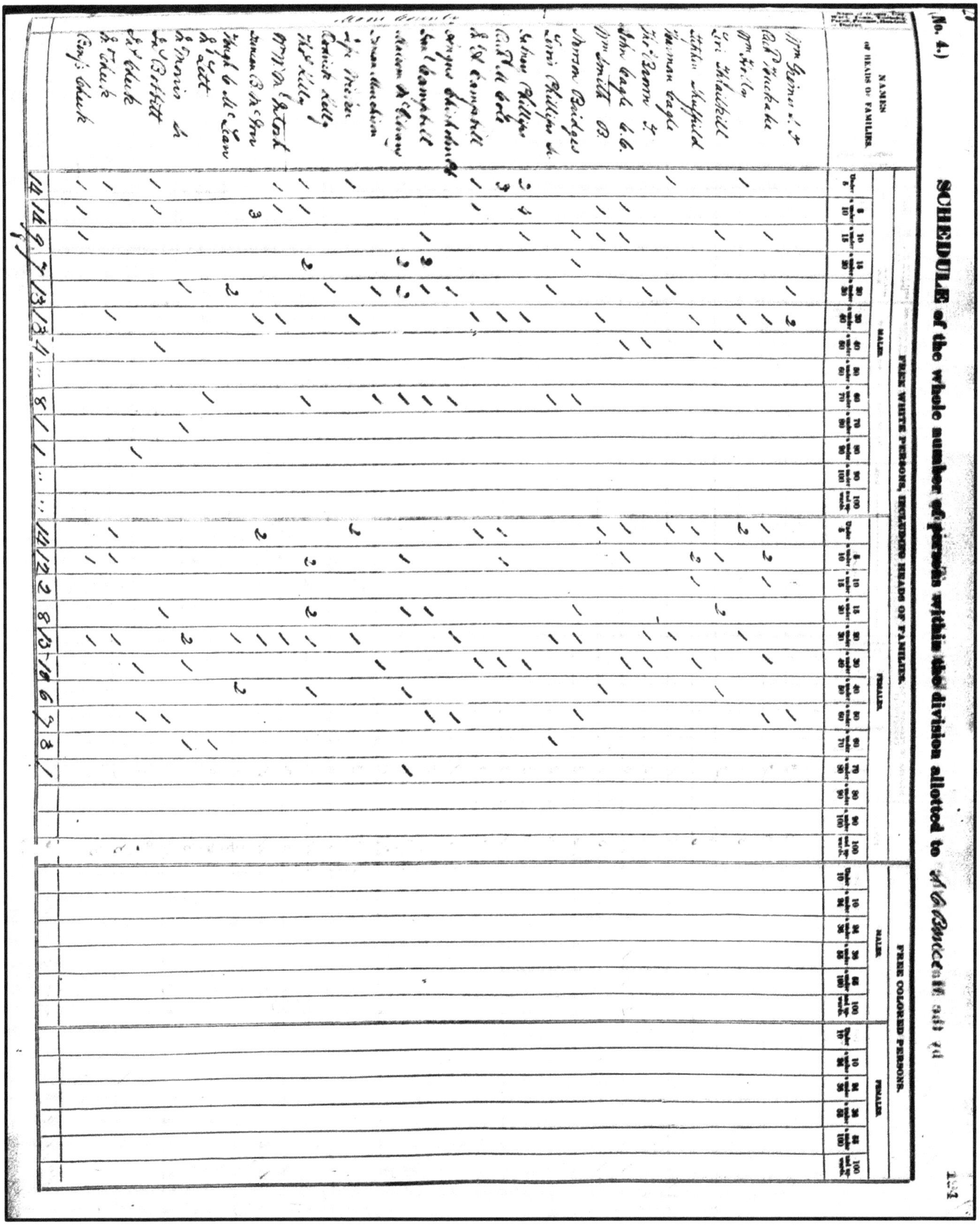

Slaves and Free Persons of Color are located on the previous page

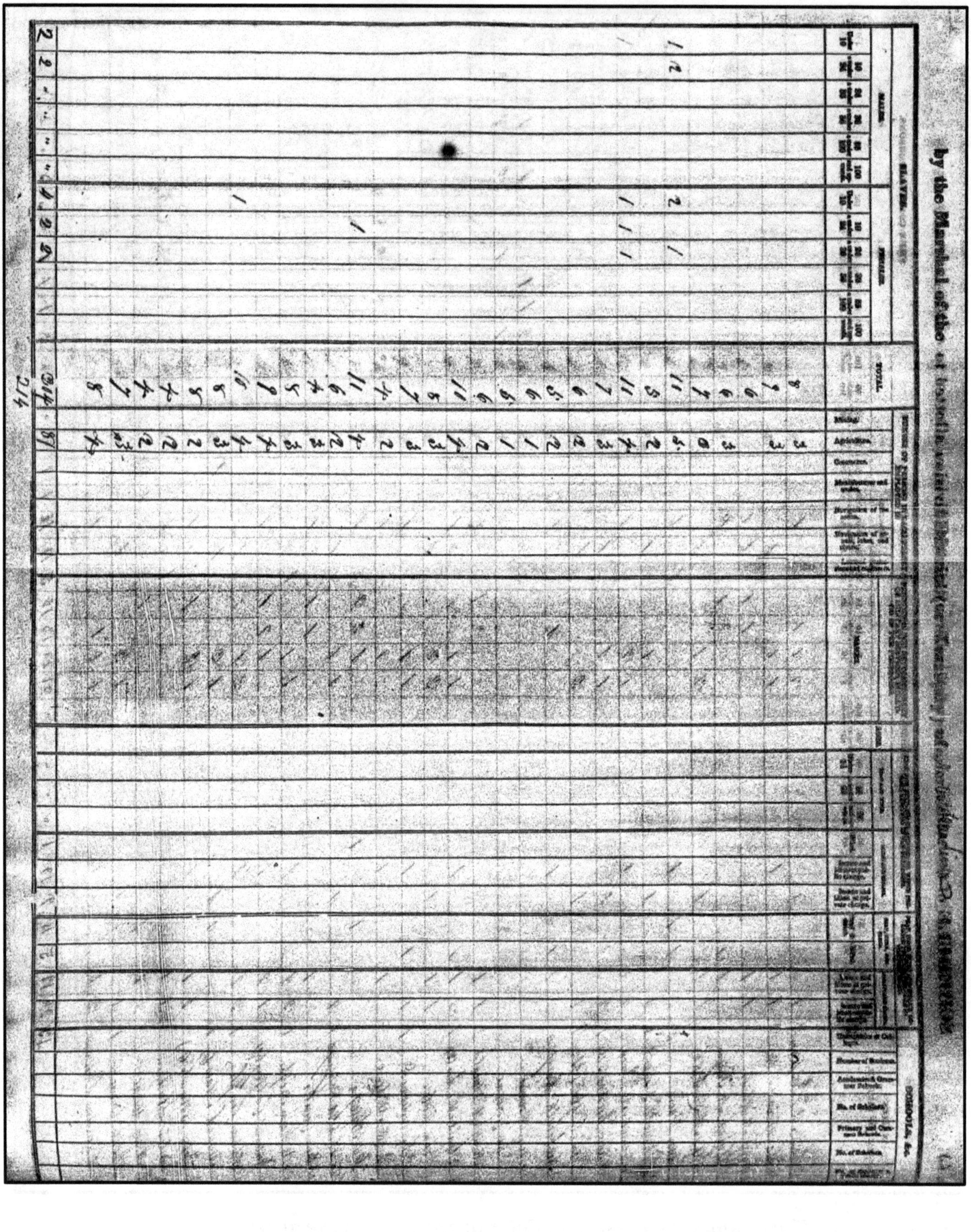

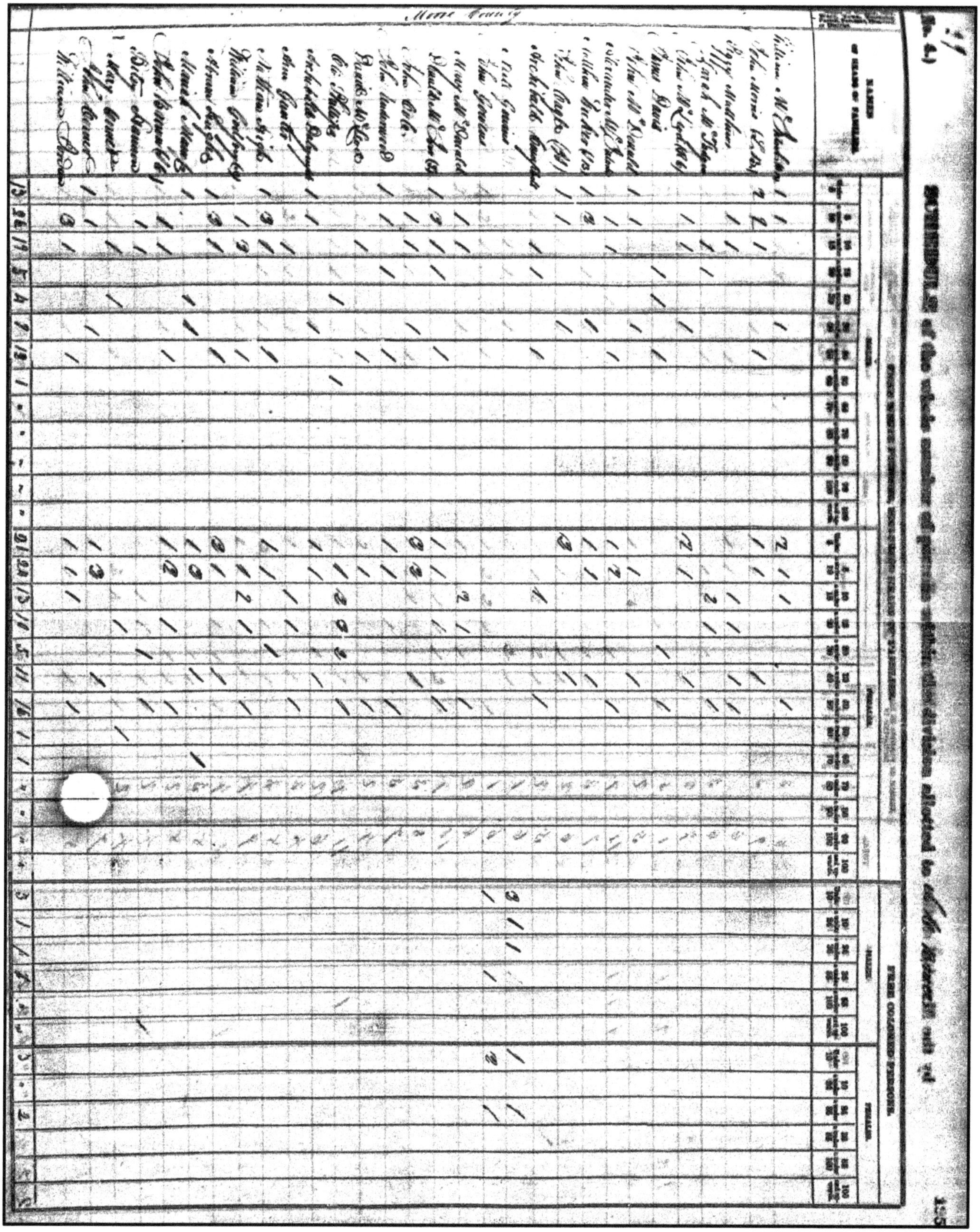

Slaves and Free Persons of Color are located on the previous page

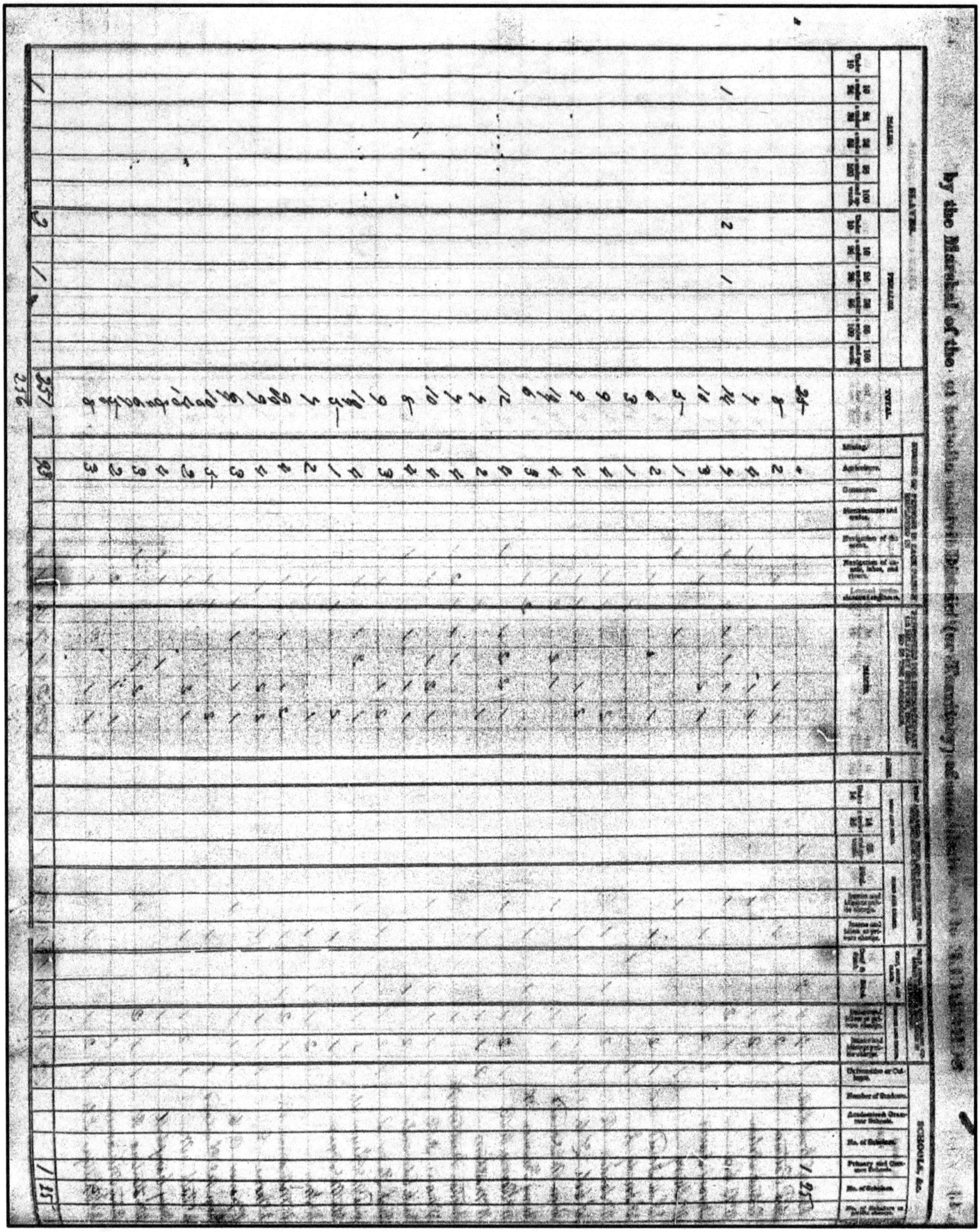

30

No. 4.) **SCHEDULE** of the whole number of persons within the division allotted to A. C. Bruce ... 196

FREE WHITE PERSONS, INCLUDING HEADS OF FAMILIES.

NAMES OF HEADS OF FAMILIES	M Under 5	M 5–10	M 10–15	M 15–20	M 20–30	M 30–40	M 40–50	M 50–60	M 60–70	M 70–80	M 80–90	M 90–100	M 100 & up	F Under 5	F 5–10	F 10–15	F 15–20	F 20–30	F 30–40	F 40–50	F 50–60	F 60–70	F 70–80	F 80–90	F 90–100	F 100 & up
Danl McIver S.M.	1	7	9	7					1																	
Archd Patterson	1	2	1			1								1	1				1							
Rodrick Nelson		2	1				1							1	1					1						
Wm B. Cox	1	1	2				1								1	1	1	1		1						
Neran Davis	2	2	1			1								1	2				1							
Wm Shirg	1	1					1										1			1						
Jno McDonald	1	2				1								1		1			1							
Jno Dowdy L.	1				1													1								
Wm Sanders R.	1	2		1		1								2				1	1							
Jno Cole L.C.	1	1	1			1								2	1			1	1							
Angus McDonald		1	1				1								1	2		2	1							
Henry Freeman M.			1	1		1												2	1							
Wm Reeves R.B.	1	2	1				1							1	2	2	1			1						
Wm Matthews	2	1	1			1								1				1								
Christian Matthews			1													1	1	1	2	1						
Jno Morris D.B.	1	1	1	1			1							1	2	1			1							
Frank Edwards	1	2		1										1	1		1			1						
Buck Zaky L.	1	2	1			1								2	1				1							
Arch McPherson M.		1	1	1			1							1		2	1		1							
Peter McNair		1				1								2				1								
Jno Innes		2	1	1		1								1					1							
Wm Williamson B.		1	2	1		1								2	1		1		1							
Jno Moore G.	1	1	1			1								2	2			1								
Wm Mann B.C.	1	1	1				1							1	1		1	1		1						
George McPharland	1					1								2				1	1							
Jno Keith M.	1	2	1			1								1	2			1	1							
Mary Campbell			1													1			1	1						
Wm Sterling R.	1	1	2				1								2	1				1						
Betsy Williamson	1	1												1	1				2							
Jno Phillips S.G.	1	2	1			1								1	1				1							
	23	43	33	16	1	18	10		1					28	23	11	7	15	21	9						
		42				15	9										18	14								

FREE COLORED PERSONS. (Males: Under 10, 10–24, 24–36, 36–55, 55–100, 100 & upwards; Females: Under 10, 10–24, 24–36, 36–55, 55–100, 100 & upwards) — no entries.

Slaves and Free Persons of Color are located on the previous page

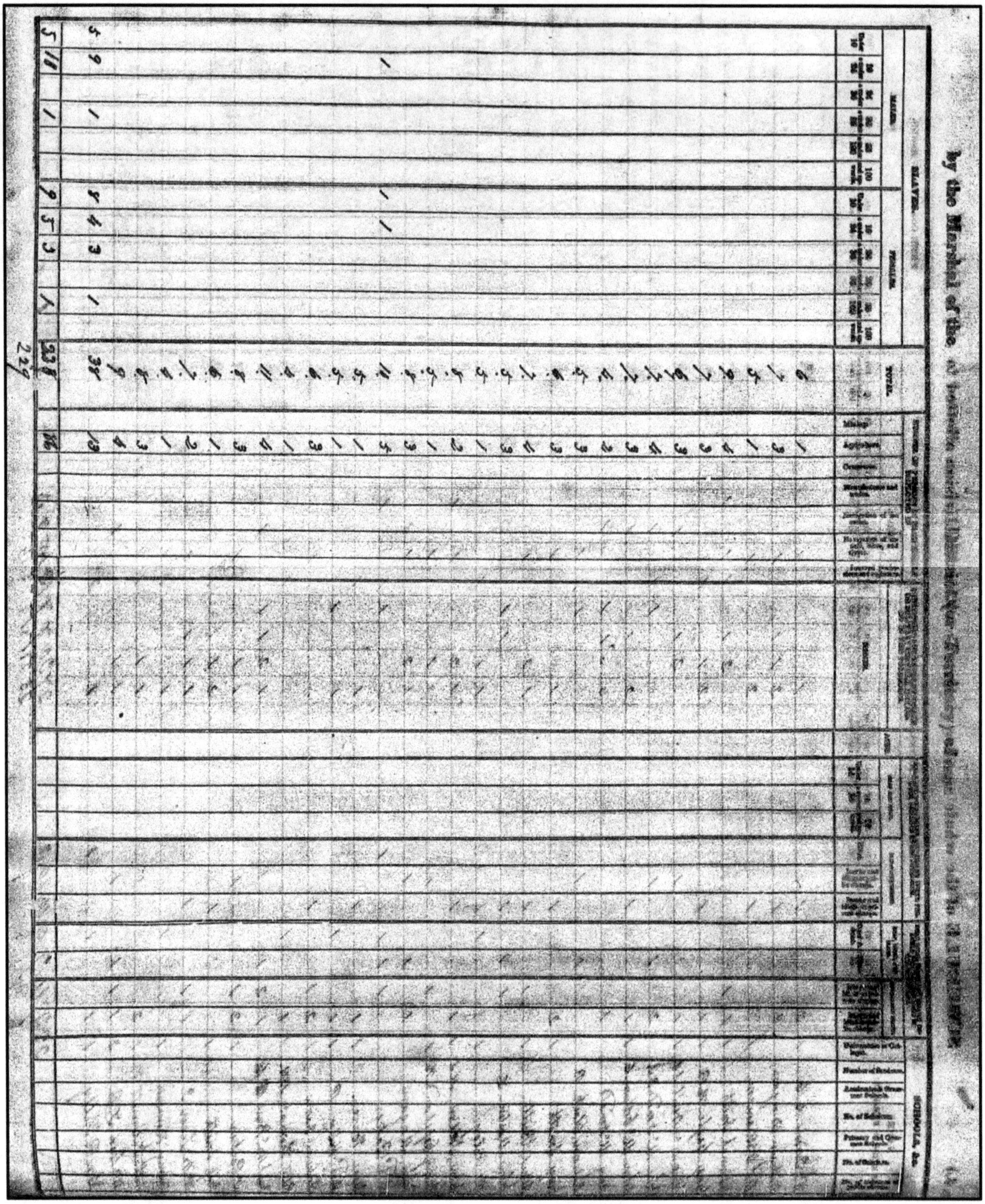
by the Marshal of the

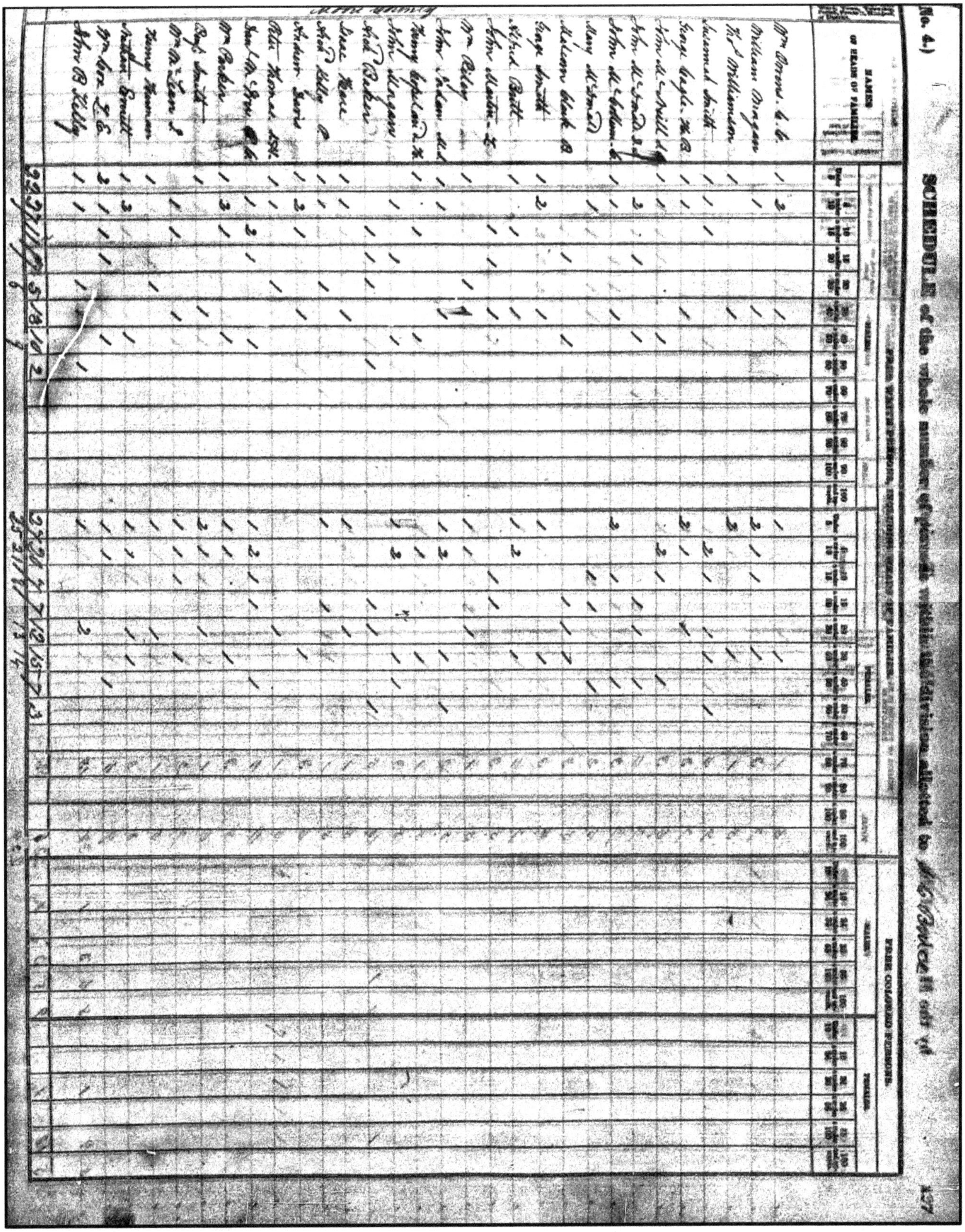

Slaves and Free Persons of Color are located on the previous page

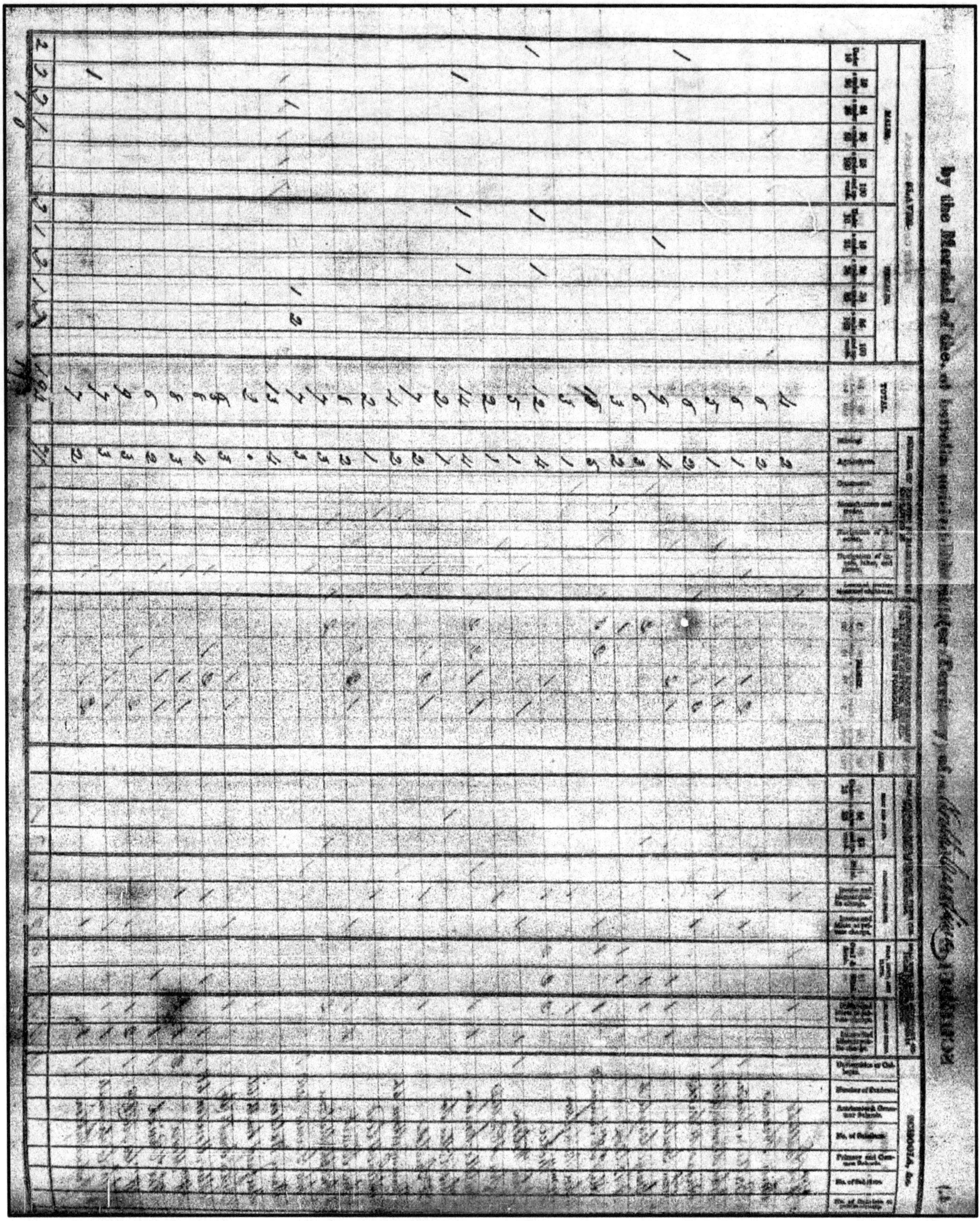

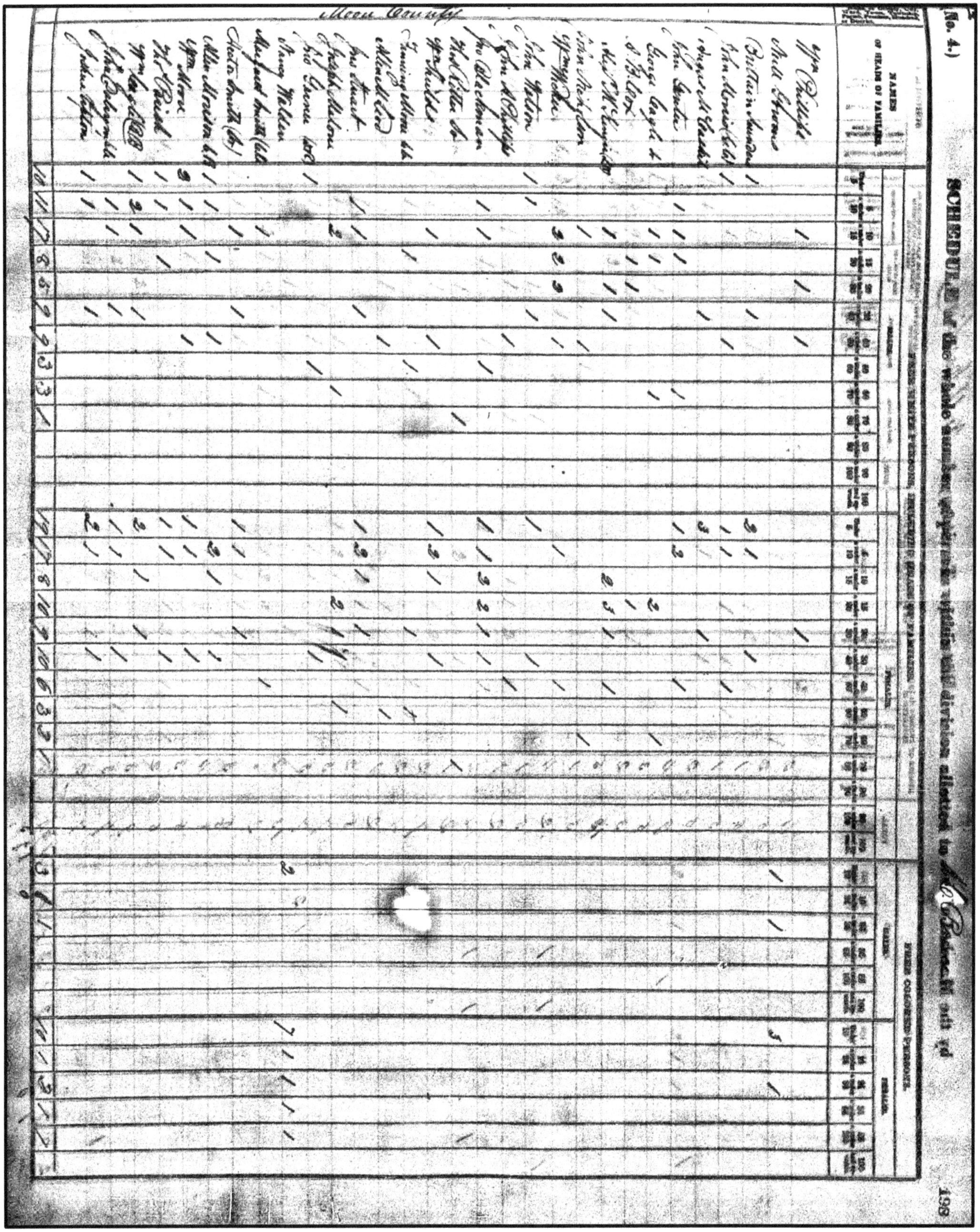

Slaves and Free Persons of Color are located on the previous page

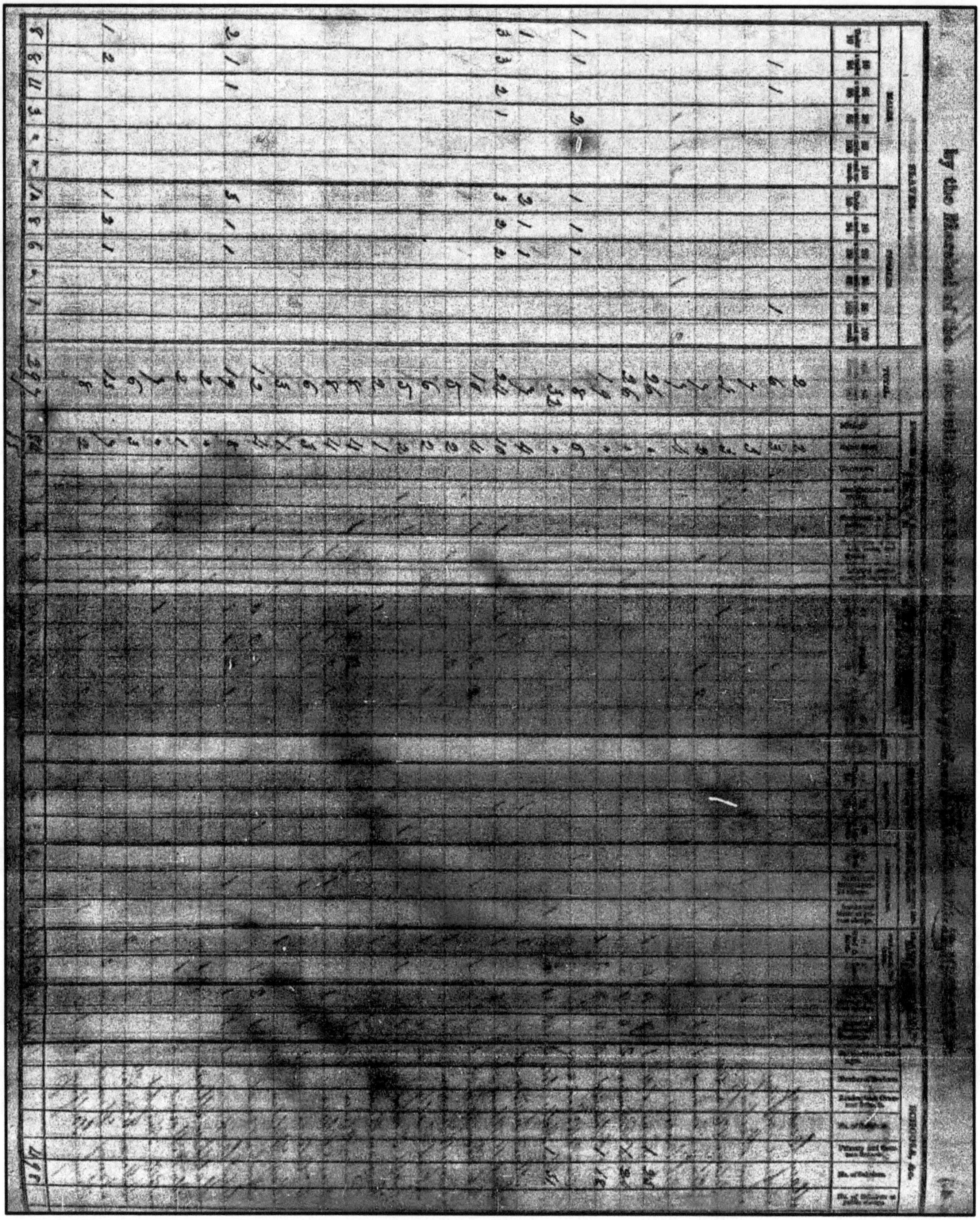

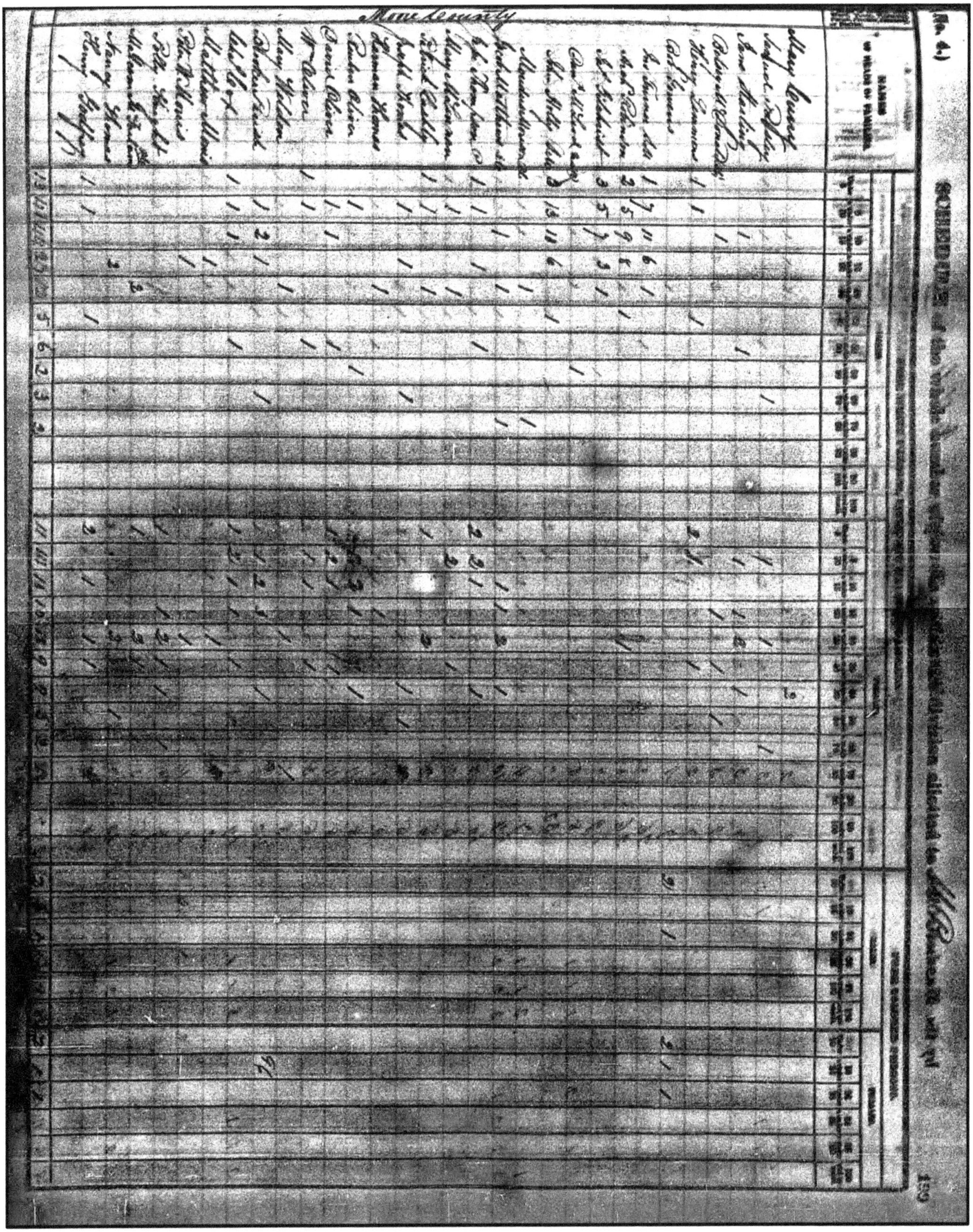

Slaves and Free Persons of Color are located on the previous page

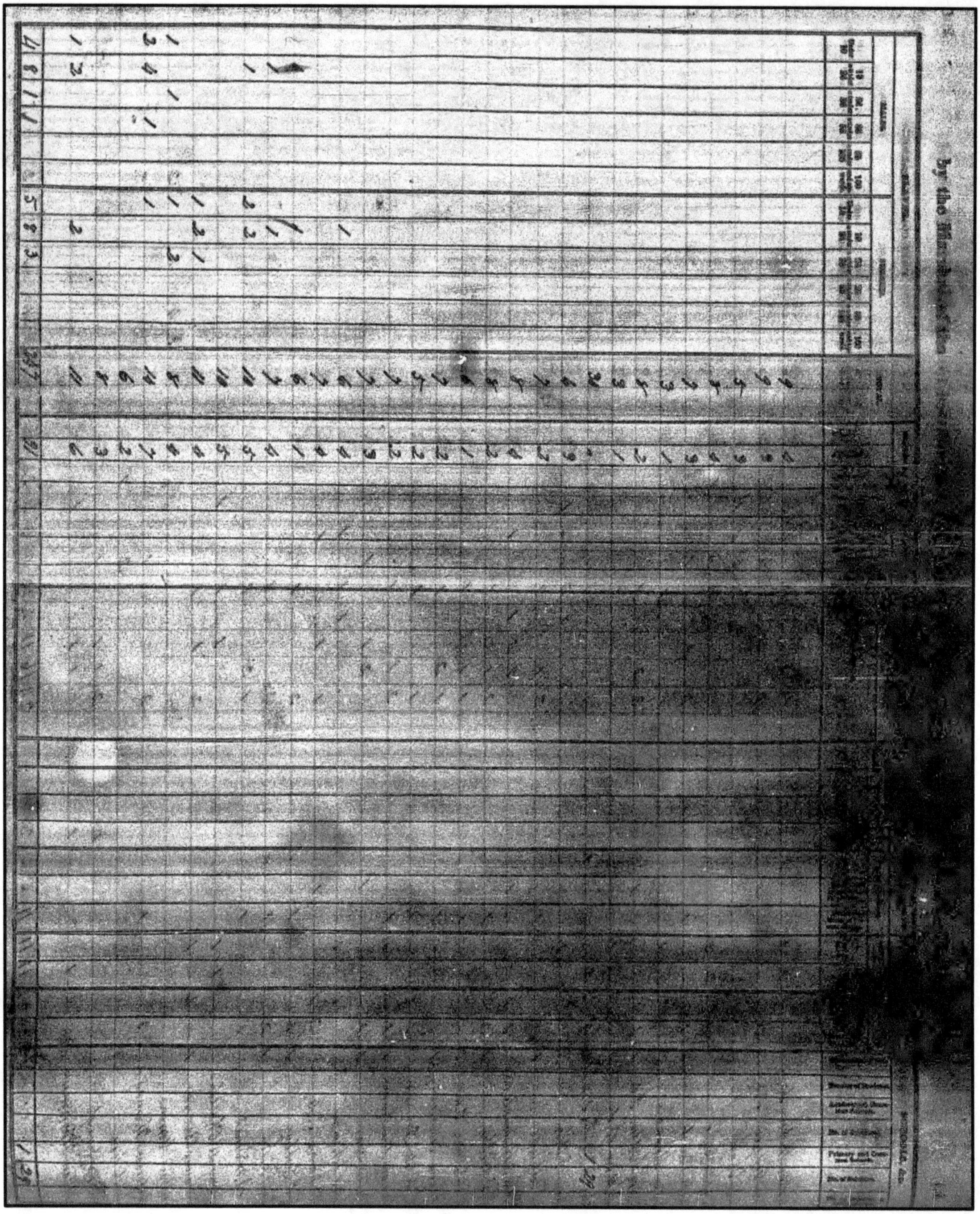

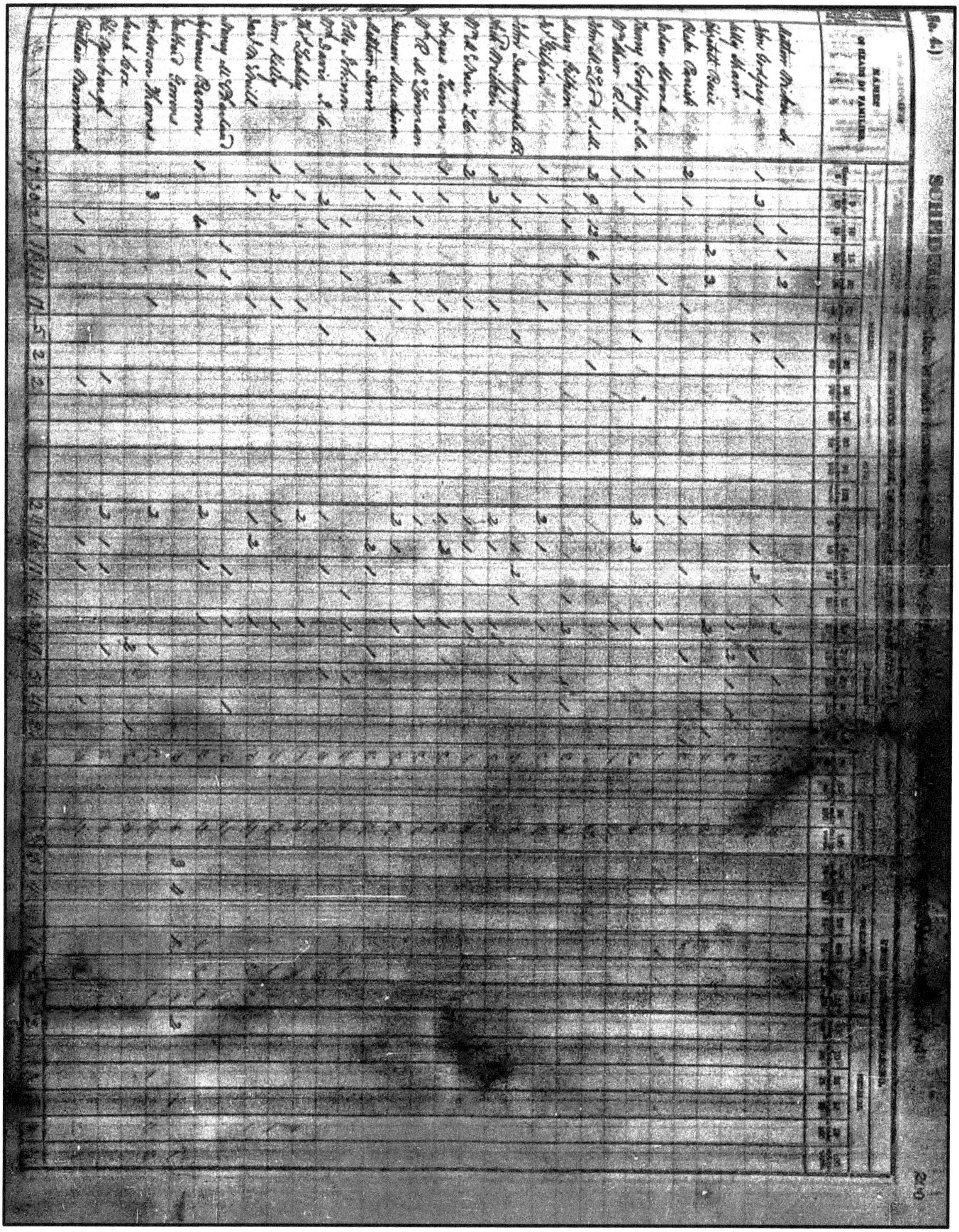

Slaves and Free Persons of Color are located on the previous page

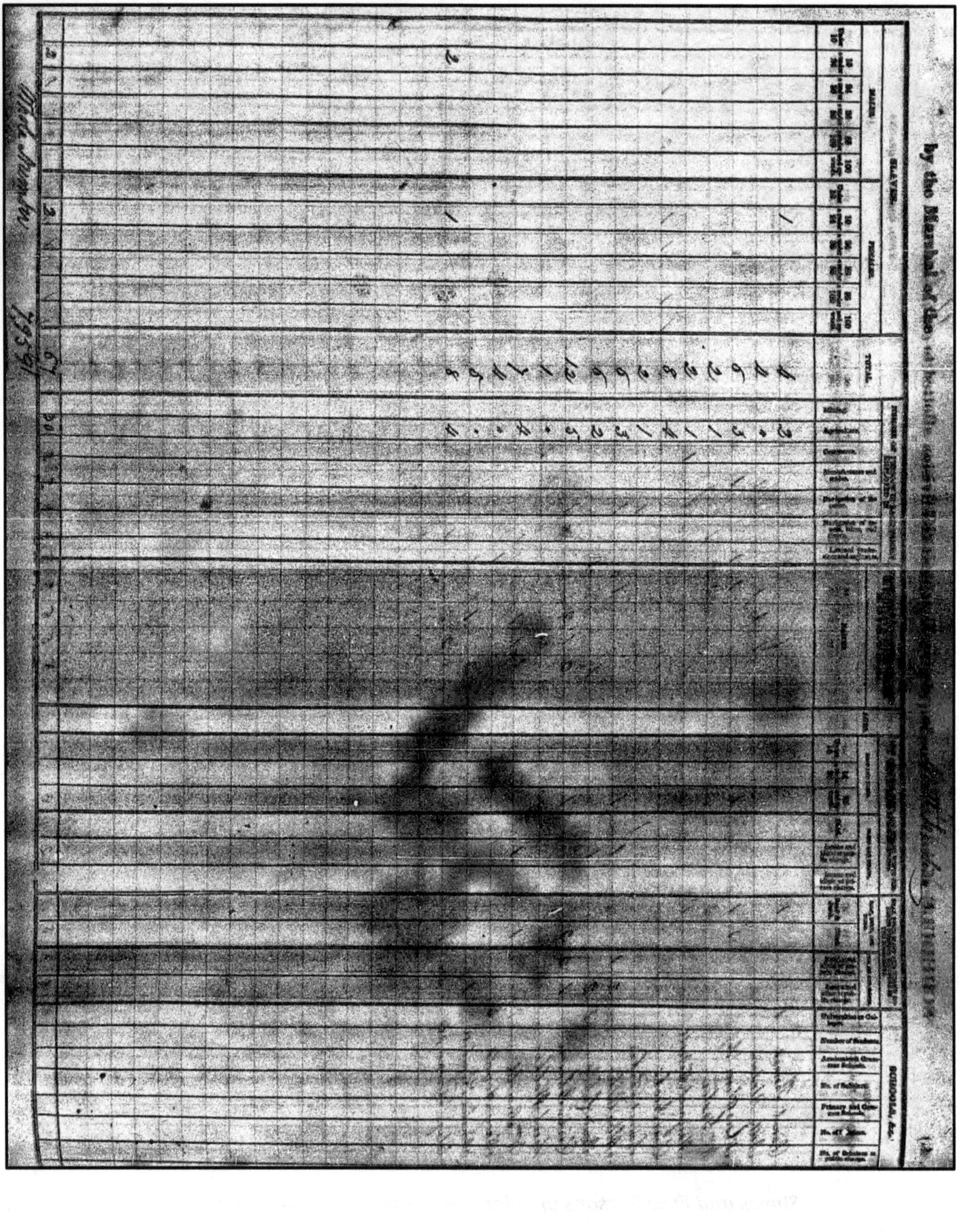

by the Marshal of the

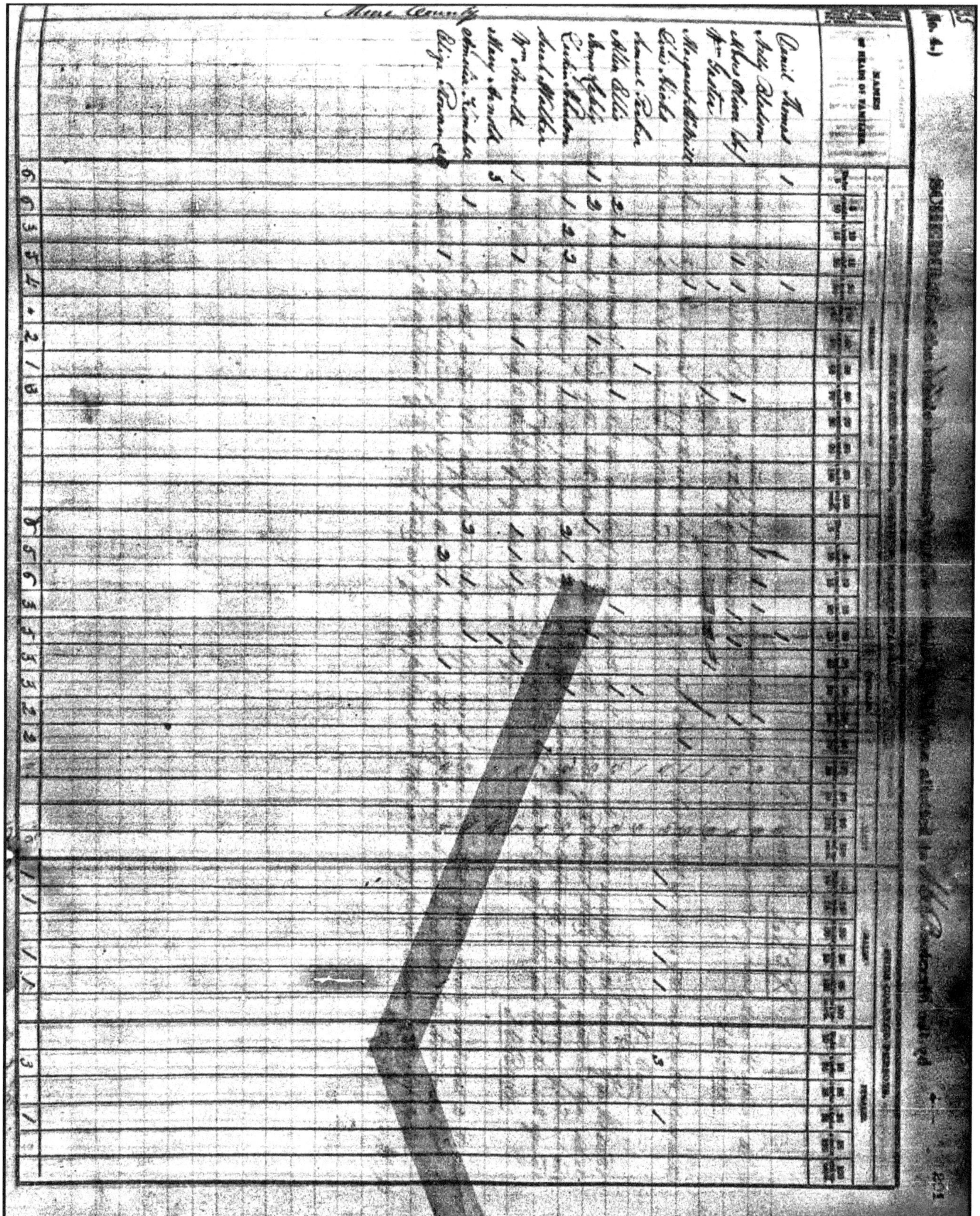

Slaves and Free Persons of Color are located on the previous page

SCHEDULE I.—Free Inhabitants in ______ in the County of Moore State of N. Carolina enumerated by me, on the 6th day of August 1850. N. McCrimmon Ass't Marshal. 165

329

Dwelling-houses numbered in the order of visitation.	Families numbered in the order of visitation.	The Name of every Person whose usual place of abode on the first day of June, 1850, was in this family.	Age.	Sex.	Color, (White, black, or mulatto.)	Profession, Occupation, or Trade of each Male Person over 15 years of age.	Value of Real Estate owned.	Place of Birth. Naming the State, Territory, or Country.	Married within the year.	Attended School within the year.	Persons over 20 y'rs of age who cannot read & write.	Whether deaf and dumb, blind, insane, idiotic, pauper, or convict.
1	2	3	4	5	6	7	8	9	10	11	12	13
1	1	Enoch Wallis	36	M		Farmer		N. Carolina			1	
		Malvina "	28	F				N. Carolina			1	
		Hiram "	15	M				N. Carolina		3		
		Hamilton "	12	M				N. Carolina				
		Isham "	10	M				N. Carolina				
		Spinks "	6	M				N. Carolina				
		Christian "	2	F				N. Carolina				
2	2	Samuel Gilmore	28	M		Farmer		N. Carolina			1	
		Margaret E. "	25	F				N. Carolina			1	
		James A. "	5	M				N. Carolina				
		Angus E. "	4	M				N. Carolina				
		Malvina "	1	F				N. Carolina				
		Pitsey "	45	F				N. Carolina			1	
		Floriday "	14	M				N. Carolina		1		
3	3	Patrick A. McKeithan	31	M		Farmer	350	N. Carolina				
		Margaret "	28	F				N. Carolina				
		Sarah M. "	7	F				N. Carolina				
		Daniel B. "	5	M				N. Carolina				
		Malcom B. "	2	M				N. Carolina				
		Margaret Williams	17	F				N. Carolina				
4	4	John McKeithan	62	M		Farmer	200	N. Carolina				
		Margaret "	67	F				N. Carolina				
		Archibald "	41	M				N. Carolina			1	Idiotic
5	5	John R. McIntosh	49	M		Meth. Clergyman	1200	Scotland				
		Merrel Fry	14	M				N. Carolina				
6	6	Margaret Curry	58	F			150	N. Carolina			1	
		Matilda "	24	F				N. Carolina			1	
		Effy "	7	F				N. Carolina				
7	7	Elizabeth Jones	52	F			30	N. Carolina				
		Lovedy "	30	F				N. Carolina			1	
		Alexander "	22	M		Farmer		N. Carolina				
		Mily E. "	9	F				N. Carolina				
		Duncan D. "	10/12	M				N. Carolina				
8	8	Daniel Patterson	72	M		Farmer	600	N. Carolina				
		Anna "	56	F				Scotland				
		Christian "	31	F				N. Carolina				
		Mary S. "	21	F				N. Carolina				
		Barbara "	19	F				N. Carolina				
		Jane "	17	F				N. Carolina				
		Daniel P. "	15	M				N. Carolina				
9	9	Daniel Caddell	50	M		Farmer	200	N. Carolina				
		Charity	49	F				N. Carolina				

M 21
F 21

Schedule I.—Free Inhabitants in ______________ **in the County of** *Moore* **State of** *N. Carolina* **enumerated by me, on the** *5th* **day of** *August* **1850.** *N. McCrummen* **Ass't Marshal.**

Dwelling-houses numbered in the order of visitation.	Families numbered in the order of visitation.	The Name of every Person whose usual place of abode on the first day of June, 1850, was in this family.	Description: Age.	Description: Sex.	Description: Color, White, black, or mulatto.	Profession, Occupation, or Trade of each Male Person over 15 years of age.	Value of Real Estate owned.	Place of Birth. Naming the State, Territory, or Country.	Married within the year.	Attended School within the year.	Persons over 20 y'rs of age who cannot read & write.	Whether deaf and dumb, blind, insane, idiotic, pauper, or convict.
1	2	3	4	5	6	7	8	9	10	11	12	13
		Tobias Caddell	24	M		Farmer		N. Carolina				
		Mary Caddell	20	F				N. Carolina				
		Barbara "	16	F				N. Carolina				
		Sochart "	25	M		Farmer		N. Carolina				
10	10	John R. Black	55	M		Farmer	825	N. Carolina				
		William M. "	21	M		Student		N. Carolina		1		
		Malcom A. "	18	M		Farmer		N. Carolina				
		Flora "	24	F				N. Carolina				
		Eliza "	22	F				N. Carolina				
		Margaret A. "	16	F				N. Carolina				
		Catharine "	14	F				N. Carolina				
		Murdoch "	13	M				N. Carolina				
		Effy Jane "	5	F				N. Carolina				
11	11	Hugh McKenzie	39	M		Farmer	500	N. Carolina				
		Isabella "	36	F				N. Carolina				
		Flora "	16	F				N. Carolina				
		Kenneth "	14	M				N. Carolina				
		Catharine E.	12	F				N. Carolina				
		Hugh A. "	10	M				N. Carolina				
		Mary J. "	8	F				N. Carolina				
		Nancy "	6	F				N. Carolina				
		Malcom "	4	M				N. Carolina				
		Daniel "	1/2	M				N. Carolina				
		Mary Black	70	F				Scotland			1	
		Kenneth Black	42	M		Laborer		N. Carolina				
12	12	Catharine Black	50	F			75	N. Carolina			1	
		Catharine "	8	F				N. Carolina				
[illegible]	13	Hugh Black	45	M		Farmer	982	N. Carolina				
		Flora "	75	F				Scotland				
		Sarah "	50	F				N. Carolina				
14	14	Merrel Cox	67	M		Miller		N. Carolina				
		Nicy "	44	F				N. Carolina				
		Elizabeth "	5	F				N. Carolina				
15	15	Donald McDonald	75	M		Farmer		Scotland				
		Flora "	40	F				N. Carolina				
16	16	John McKeithan	33	M		Farmer	327	N. Carolina				
		Nancy McKenzie	60	F				Scotland			1	
		Margaret "	34	F				N. Carolina				
		Nancy Sowell	31	F				N. Carolina				
		Mary McKenzie	28	F				N. Carolina				
		Jane McKenzie	27	F				N. Carolina				
		Christian "	26	F				N. Carolina				

M 16
F 26

SCHEDULE I.—Free Inhabitants in ______________ in the County of Moore State 331

of N Carolina enumerated by me, on the 8th day of August 1850. N. McCrimmon Ass't Marshal. 166

Dwelling-houses numbered in the order of visitation.	Families numbered in the order of visitation.	The Name of every Person whose usual place of abode on the first day of June, 1850, was in this family.	Age.	Sex.	Color, White, black, or mulatto.	Profession, Occupation, or Trade of each Male Person over 15 years of age.	Value of Real Estate owned.	Place of Birth. Naming the State, Territory, or Country.	Married within the year.	Attended School within the year.	Persons over 20 years of age who cannot read & write.	Whether deaf and dumb, blind, insane, idiotic, pauper, or convict.	
1	2	3	4	5	6	7	8	9	10	11	12	13	
		Isabella McKenzie	25	F				N. Carolina					1
		Daniel "	24	M		Student		N. Carolina		1			2
		Lovedy "	23	F				N. Carolina					3
		Mary E. Sowell	4	F				N. Carolina					4
		Isabella L. "	3	F				N. Carolina					5
		Margaret A. "	1	F				N. Carolina					6
		Wesley F. Sowell	27	M		Waggoner		N. Carolina					7
17	17	Daniel McKinnon	36	M		Farmer	250	N. Carolina					8
		Catharine "	36	F				N. Carolina					9
		John "	15	M				N. Carolina					10
		William "	13	M				N. Carolina					11
		Margaret J. "	11	F				N. Carolina					12
		Nancy E. "	10	F				N. Carolina					13
		Catharine "	8	F				N. Carolina					14
		Christian "	6	F				N. Carolina					15
		Lyda H. "	5	F				N. Carolina					16
		Alexander "	2	M				N. Carolina					17
		Daniel "	½	M				N. Carolina					18
18	18	Alexander Black	43	M		Farmer	999	N. Carolina					19
		Isabella "	36	F				N. Carolina					20
		Sarah "	12	F				N. Carolina					21
		Flora A. "	10	F				N. Carolina					22
		Archibald M. "	7	M				N. Carolina					23
		William C. "	4	M				N. Carolina					24
19	19	Neill R. Currie	29	M		Farmer	400	N. Carolina					25
		Jennet Currie	26	F				N. Carolina					26
		Angus M. "	4	M				N. Carolina					27
		Sarah A. "	3	F				N. Carolina					28
		Mary E. "	4/12	F				N. Carolina					29
20	20	Kenneth Ray	50	M		Farmer	500	N. Carolina					30
		Margaret "	34	F				N. Carolina					31
		Christian "	13	F				N. Carolina		1			32
		Catharine "	9	F				N. Carolina		1			33
		Sarah "	6	F				N. Carolina					34
		Ann "	4	F				N. Carolina					35
		Mary "	2	F				N. Carolina					36
21	21	Daniel Blue	45	M		Farmer	945	N. Carolina					37
		Anna "	45	F				N. Carolina					38
		John A. "	21	M				N. Carolina			1	Idiotic	39
		Patrick "	20	M		Farmer		N. Carolina					40
		Daniel B. "	17	M		Student		N. Carolina		1			41
		Flora M. "	16	F				N. Carolina		1			42

M 17

SCHEDULE I.—Free Inhabitants in ______________ **in the County of** Moore **State of** N. Carolina **enumerated by me, on the** 6th **day of** August **1850.** N. McInnimee **Ass't Marshal.**

Dwelling-houses numbered in the order of visitation.	Families numbered in the order of visitation.	The Name of every Person whose usual place of abode on the first day of June, 1850, was in this family.	Age.	Sex.	Color, White, black, or mulatto.	Profession, Occupation, or Trade of each Male Person over 15 years of age.	Value of Real Estate owned.	Place of Birth. Naming the State, Territory, or Country.	Married within the year.	Attended School within the year.	Persons over 20 y'rs of age who cannot read & write.	Whether deaf and dumb, blind, insane, idiotic, pauper, or convict.
1	2	3	4	5	6	7	8	9	10	11	12	13
		Malcom Blue	14	m				N. Carolina		1		
		Cornelius C. "	11	m				N. Carolina		1		
		Duncan A. "	9	m				N. Carolina		1		
		Samuel D. "	7	m				N. Carolina				
22	22	Neil McLauchlin	49	m		Farmer	400	Scotland				
		Isabella "	45	F				N. Carolina				
23	23	Donald McLauchlin	47	m		Farmer	400	Scotland			1	
		Catharine "	55	F				Scotland			1	
		Nancy "	53	F				Scotland				
		Sarah "	29	F				N. Carolina				
24	24	George Fry	58	m		Farmer		N. Carolina				
		Temperance "	47	F				N. Carolina				
		Patience "	24	F				N. Carolina				
		William "	21	m		Laborer		N. Carolina		1		
		Emily "	17	F				N. Carolina		1		
		Abpsolem "	16	m		Laborer		N. Carolina		1		
		Nathan "	14	m				N. Carolina		1		
		Eliza "	12	F				N. Carolina		1		
		George F. "	10	m				N. Carolina		1		
25	25	Kenneth Black	57	m		Farmer	750	N. Carolina				
		Mary "	55	F				Scotland				
		Flora "	25	F				N. Carolina				
		Archibald "	14	m				N. Carolina		1		
		Jane E. "	12	F				N. Carolina		1		
		Catharine "	10	F				N. Carolina				
		Donald Blue	85	m		Farmer		Scotland				
26	26	Jesse Hannon	40	m		Farmer	300	N. Carolina			1	
		Anna "	42	F				N. Carolina				
		Daniel O. "	17	m		Farmer		N. Carolina				
		John M. "	16	m		Farmer		N. Carolina				
		William A. "	14	m				N. Carolina				
		Neil "	11	m				N. Carolina				
		Malcom "	9	m				N. Carolina				
		Archibald "	7	m				N. Carolina				
		Flora C. "	2	F				N. Carolina				
		Charles F. Dennis	6	m				N. Carolina				
27	27	Nancy Jackson	60	F				N. Carolina			1	
		Margaret A. "	21	F				N. Carolina				
28	28	Hardin Warner	57	m		Farmer	1300	N. Carolina				
		Margaret M. "	49	F				N. Carolina			1	
		Ailsey "	27	F				N. Carolina				
		Martha A. "	23	F				N. Carolina				

vM23 719

SCHEDULE I.—Free Inhabitants in 2 in the County of Moore State of N. Carolina enumerated by me, on the 7th day of August 1850. N. McCrummen Ass't Marshal.

333

167

Dwelling-houses numbered in the order of visitation.	Families numbered in the order of visitation.	The Name of every Person whose usual place of abode on the first day of June, 1850, was in this family.	Age.	Sex.	Color. White, black, or mulatto.	Profession, Occupation, or Trade of each Male Person over 15 years of age.	Value of Real Estate owned.	Place of Birth. Naming the State, Territory, or Country.	Married within the year.	Attended School within the year.	Persons over 20 y'rs of age who cannot read & write.	Whether deaf and dumb, blind, insane, idiotic, pauper, or convict.
1	2	3	4	5	6	7	8	9	10	11	12	13
		John Warner	20	M		Farmer		N. Carolina				
		Levi S. 〃	18	M		Farmer		〃 〃				
		Margaret 〃	16	F				〃 〃				
		Susannah 〃	13	F				〃 〃				
		Anderson S. 〃	11	M				〃 〃				
		Pity 〃	8	F				〃 〃				
		Patrick D. 〃	4	M				〃 〃				Idiotic
		James Harman	17	M		Laborer		〃 〃				
29	29	Daniel Caddell	89	M		Farmer		〃 〃				
		Emelia 〃	77	F				〃 〃			1	
		Emelia 〃	32	F			50	〃 〃				
		Betsey 〃	15	F				〃 〃				
		Charlotte 〃	11	F				〃 〃		1		
		James N. 〃	10	M				〃 〃		1		
30	30	William Caddell	55	M		Farmer	400	〃 〃				
31	31	John Fox	42	M		Farmer		〃 〃				
		Winniford 〃	38	F				〃 〃			1	
		Francis 〃	19	M		Laborer		〃 〃				
		Benjamin 〃	18	M		Laborer		〃 〃		1		
		Westley 〃	16	M		Laborer		〃 〃		1		
		Dianna 〃	14	F				〃 〃		1		
		Ann M. 〃	11	F				〃 〃				
		Elizabeth 〃	8	F				〃 〃				
		Jacob 〃	6	M				〃 〃				
		Murdo 〃	5	M				〃 〃				
		Margaret 〃	2	F				〃 〃				
		Martha 〃	3/12	F				〃 〃				
32	32	Calvin Cox	50	M		Farmer		〃 〃				
		Susannah 〃	40	F				〃 〃				
		Holcomb 〃	19	M		Farmer		〃 〃				
		John B. 〃	17	M		Farmer		〃 〃				
		Green B. G. 〃	12	M				〃 〃				
		George N. 〃	10	M				〃 〃				
		Emelia 〃	8	F				〃 〃				
		Martha 〃	6	F				〃 〃				
		Mary W. 〃	3	F				〃 〃				
33	33	Alexander Johnson	31	M		Farmer		〃 〃				
		Sarah 〃	25	F				〃 〃				
		Missouri M. C. 〃	2	F				〃 〃				
34	34	James Johnson	46	M		Farmer		〃 〃				
		Elizabeth Warner	21	F				〃 〃				
		Swain Warner	20	M		Farmer		〃 〃				

M 22
Fe 20

SCHEDULE I.—Free Inhabitants in ______ in the County of *Moore* State of *N. Carolina* enumerated by me, on the *7th* day of *August* 1850. *N. McCrummen* Ass't Marshal.

	Dwelling-houses numbered in the order of visitation.	Families numbered in the order of visitation.	The Name of every Person whose usual place of abode on the first day of June, 1850, was in this family.	Age.	Sex.	Color, white, black, or mulatto.	Profession, Occupation, or Trade of each Male Person over 15 years of age.	Value of Real Estate owned.	Place of Birth. Naming the State, Territory, or Country.	Married within the year.	Attended School within the year.	Persons over 20 y'rs of age who cannot read & write.	Whether deaf and dumb, blind, insane, idiotic, pauper, or convict.
	1	2	3	4	5	6	7	8	9	10	11	12	13
1			Huldah Warner	18	F				N Carolina				
2			Edward "	15	M		Farmer		" "		1		
3			Nancy Johnson	12	F				" "		1		
4			Bryant "	9	M				" "		1		
5			Julia "	6	F				" "				
6	35	35	Nathan Fry	48	M		Farmer	700	" "				
7			Elizabeth "	39	F				" "				
8			Harriet "	18	F				" "				
9			Ann C. "	16	F				" "				
10			Alexander N. "	14	M				" "				
11			Jane "	12	F				" "				
12			Ferry "	10	F				" "				
13			Joseph "	7	M				" "				
14			Elizabeth "	4	F				" "				
15			James H. "	10/12	M				" "				
16			Nancy "	81	F				" "			1	
17	36	36	John Jackson	31	M		Farmer		" "			1	
18			Elae "	30	F				" "				
19			William "	13	M				" "				
20			David "	11	M				" "				
21			Mary J. "	9	F				" "				
22			Elizabeth "	9/12	F				" "				
23	37	37	William D. Warner	27	M		Farmer	350	" "				
24			Louisa A. "	31	F				" "				
25			Martha J. "	5	F				" "				
26			John T. "	3	M				" "				
27	38	38	William W. Sears	25	M		Farmer		" "				
28			Temenca Warner	67	F			65	" "			1	
29			Darcus Sears	19	F				" "				
30			Eliza Johnson	17	F				" "				
31			Alexander Campbell	6	M				" "				
32			Jennet E. Sears	4	F				" "				
33	39	39	John Hannon	26	M		Farmer		" "				
34			Amy "	29	F				" "			1	
35			Miley J. "	6/12	F				" "				
36	40	40	Benjamin Barber	33	M		Farmer	50	" "			1	
37			Sarah "	40	F				" "			1	
38			Isabella "	14	F				" "		1		
39			Mary "	12	F				" "		1		
40			Rachel "	10	F				" "		1		
41			Sarah A. "	9	F				" "		1		
42			Penelope "	7	F				" "				

M 15
F 27

335

SCHEDULE I.—Free Inhabitants in in the County of Moore State of N. Carolina enumerated by me, on the 5th day of August 1850. N. McCrummen Ass't Marshal.

168

Dwelling-houses numbered in the order of visitation.	Families numbered in the order of visitation.	The Name of every Person whose usual place of abode on the first day of June, 1850, was in this family.	Age.	Sex.	Color. White, black, or mulatto.	Profession, Occupation, or Trade of each Male Person over 15 years of age.	Value of Real Estate owned.	Place of Birth. Naming the State, Territory, or Country.	Married within the year.	Attended School within the year.	Persons over 20 y'rs of age who cannot read & write.	Whether deaf and dumb, blind, insane, idiotic, pauper, or convict.
1	2	3	4	5	6	7	8	9	10	11	12	13
		Lizzy Barber	4	F				N. Carolina				
41	41	Burrel Ritter	37	M		Farmer		" "			1	
		Catharine "	34	F				" "			1	
		Elizabeth "	11	F				" "				
		Deborah "	9	F				" "				
		Margaret "	6	F				" "				
		Mary "	4	F				" "				
		Susannah "	3	F				" "				
		Martha C. "	1	F				" "				
		Margaret Ritter	88	F				" "			1	
42	42	Benjamin Phillips	63	M		Farmer	250	" "				
		Martha "	57	F				" "			1	
		Mary Stutts	33	F				" "			1	
		Rainy Phillips	30	F				" "				
		Benjamin P. "	20	M		Farmer		" "				
		Simeon P. "	17	M		Ditto		" "				
		Minny Stutts	15	F				" "		1		
		Elizabeth Stutts	11	F				" "		1		
43	43	Nancy Graham	47	F				" "			1	
		Sarah "	10	F				" "		1		
44	44	Jesse Bean	48	M		Farmer	650	" "				
		Barsheba "	28	F				" "				
		A. William "	15	M				" "		1		
		Mary "	12	F				" "		1		
		Annetta "	3	F				" "				
		Arter Davis	19	M		Farmer		" "				
45	45	Angus Martin	53	M		Farmer		" "				
		Murdo L.	20	M		Farmer		" "		1		
		Candis Martin	22	F				" "			1	
		Nancy "	47	F				" "			1	
		Jane "	15	F				" "		1		
		Sarah A. "	13	F				" "		1		
46	46	Jesse Sullivan	27	M		Farmer		" "			1	
		Celia "	30	F				" "				
		William L. "	13	M				" "		1		
		Barbara A. "	11	F				" "		1		
		Martha M. "	10	F				" "		1		
		John B. "	5	M				" "				
47	47	William Cole	53	M		Farmer	750	" "				
		Elizabeth "	42	F				" "			1	
		Richard "	19	M		Farmer		" "				
		Mary A. "	17	F				" "				

M 14
F 28

SCHEDULE I.—Free Inhabitants in ______ in the County of Moore State of N. Carolina enumerated by me, on the 8th day of August 1850. N. McCrummen Ass't Marshal.

	Dwelling-houses numbered in the order of visitation.	Families numbered in the order of visitation.	The Name of every Person whose usual place of abode on the first day of June, 1850, was in this family.	Description: Age.	Description: Sex.	Description: Color, White, black, or mulatto.	Profession, Occupation, or Trade of each Male Person over 15 years of age.	Value of Real Estate owned.	Place of Birth. Naming the State, Territory, or Country.	Married within the year.	Attended School within the year.	Persons over 20 y'rs of age who cannot read & write.	Whether deaf and dumb, blind, insane, idiotic, pauper, or convict.
	1	2	3	4	5	6	7	8	9	10	11	12	13
1			William Cole	8	M				N. Carolina		1		
2			Hiram ″	6	M				″ ″		1		
3			Rosannah ″	4	F				″ ″				
4	48	48	John Tyson	66	M		Farmer	1650	″ ″				
5			Margaret B.	73	F				″ ″				
6			John Crabtree	19	M		Laborer		″ ″				
7	47	47	Isaac Smith	70	M		Farmer	250	″ ″			1	
8			Darcus Hill	80	F				″ ″			1	
9			Elizabeth Hill	65	F				″ ″			1	
10	50	50	Mary Case	61	F				″ ″			1	
11	51	51	William R. Jackson	28	M		Laborer		″ ″				
12			Jerusha	28	F				″			1	
13			Louisa	7	F				″ ″				
14			Catharine E.	5	F				″ ″				
15			Pleasant S.	4	M				″ ″				
16			Jane	3	F				″ ″				
17			William A.	7/12	M				″ ″				
18			Nancy Smith	50	F				″ ″			1	
19	52	52	George D. Ritter	30	M		Farmer	130	″ ″				
20			Emelia Ritter	26	F				″ ″				
21			Nancy ″	2	F				″ ″				
22	53	53	Elizabeth Dowd	38	F			300	″ ″			1	
23			John ″	18	M		Farmer		″ ″		1		
24			Catharine ″	11	F				″ ″		1		
25			George Graham	13	M				″ ″		1		
26	54	54	Sarah Glascock	75	F			400	″ ″				
27			Thomas Dawson	22	M		Farmer		″ ″				
28	55	55	Henry Stutts	41	M		Farmer		″ ″				
29			Patsey ″	45	F				″ ″				
30			Catharine ″	24	F				″ ″			1	
31			Elizabeth ″	18	F				″ ″				
32			Martha ″	14	F				″ ″				
33			Margaret ″	12	F				″ ″				
34			Bethana ″	10	F				″ ″				
35			Julia ″	5	F				″ ″				
36	56	56	William Barrett	56	M		Farmer	975	″ ″				
37			Mary ″	46	F				″ ″				
38			Robert ″	21	M		Farmer		″ ″				
39			Louisa ″	18	F				″ ″		1		
40			Sylvanus ″	16	M		Farmer		″ ″		1		
41			Elizabeth ″	13	F				″ ″		1		
42			William A. ″	10	M				″ ″		1		

ML 17
P 25

SCHEDULE I.—Free Inhabitants in 3 in the County of Moore State 337 of N. Carolina enumerated by me, on the 9th day of August 1850. N. McCrummen Ass't Marshal.

169

Dwelling-houses numbered in the order of visitation.	Families numbered in the order of visitation.	The Name of every Person whose usual place of abode on the first day of June, 1850, was in this family.	Description: Age.	Sex.	Color, White, black, or mulatto.	Profession, Occupation, or Trade of each Male Person over 15 years of age.	Value of Real Estate owned.	Place of Birth. Naming the State, Territory, or Country.	Married within the year.	Attended School within the year.	Persons over 20 y'rs of age who cannot read & write.	Whether deaf and dumb, blind, insane, idiotic, pauper, or convict.
1	2	3	4	5	6	7	8	9	10	11	12	13
57	57	William D. Smith	39	M		Farmer		N. Carolina			1	
		Margaret A. 〃	33	F				〃 〃				
		Neill T. 〃	12	M				〃 〃		1		
		Louisa 〃	11	F				〃 〃		1		
		Mary A. 〃	9	F				〃 〃		1		
		Eliza J. 〃	7	F				〃 〃		1		
		Margaret E. 〃	1	F				〃 〃				
58	58	Bray Pardee	66	M		Tinner	100	Connecticut				
		Elisabeth Pardee	50	F				N. Carolina				
59	59	John T. Dowd	31	M		Farmer	200	〃 〃				
		Fredrick Dowd	31	M		Farmer	280	〃 〃				
		Mary 〃	45	F				〃 〃				
		Elisabeth Dickinson	55	F				〃 〃				
60	60	Bryan Dowd	40	M		Farmer	350	〃 〃				
		Edward Graham	13	M				〃 〃		1		
		William J. Jackson	9	M				〃 〃		1		
61	61	William P. Martin	32	M		Farmer	1300	〃 〃				
		Flora Martin	65	F			600	Scotland				
		Isabella Peacock	20	F				N. Carolina		1		
62	62	Hinson Lone	62	M		Farmer		〃 〃				
		Gincy 〃	38	F				〃 〃			1	
		Richard 〃	11	M				〃 〃		1		
		Edmund 〃	10	M				〃 〃		1		
		Mary A. 〃	9	F				〃 〃				
		Sarah 〃	6	F				〃 〃				
		Hinson 〃	4	M				〃 〃				
		Gincy 〃	2	F				〃 〃				
		Elisabeth 〃	4/12	F				〃 〃				
63	63	Mary Warner	58	F			350	〃 〃				
		John W. 〃	27	M		Farmer	350	〃 〃				
		Neill R. Warner	15	M		Farmer		〃 〃				
64	64	Pleasant Smith	35	M		Farmer		〃 〃				
65	65	Thomas Fry	56	M		Farmer		〃 〃				
		Margaret 〃	56	F				〃 〃				
		Elizabeth 〃	33	F				〃 〃				
		Rodolpha 〃	25	F				〃 〃				
		Alexander McC. 〃	20	M		Farmer		〃 〃		1		
		Hoden J. Love 〃	12	M				〃 〃		1		
		Elizabeth Fry	30	F		Farmer		〃 〃			1	
66	66	Madison J. Fry	30	M		Farmer		〃 〃				
		Nancy J. 〃	22	F				〃 〃				
		W. H. Fry	7	M				〃 〃		1		

M 21 ✓
F 21

SCHEDULE I.—Free Inhabitants in ____________ in the County of Moore State of N Carolina enumerated by me, on the 9th day of August 1850. N. McCrummen Ass't Marshal.

Dwelling-houses numbered in the order of visitation.	Families numbered in the order of visitation.	The Name of every Person whose usual place of abode on the first day of June, 1850, was in this family.	Description: Age.	Sex.	Color, White, black, or mulatto.	Profession, Occupation, or Trade of each Male Person over 15 years of age.	Value of Real Estate owned.	Place of Birth. Naming the State, Territory, or Country.	Married within the year.	Attended School within the year.	Persons over 20 y'rs of age who cannot read & write.	Whether deaf and dumb, blind, insane, idiotic, pauper, or convict.
1	2	3	4	5	6	7	8	9	10	11	12	13
		Mary C. Fry	5	F				N. Carolina				
		Daniel W. Warner	1	M				" "				
67	67	Leonard W. Lawhon	47	M		Farmer	1500	" "				
		Ann R. "	46	F				" "				
		Martha "	21	F				" "		1		
		Andrew D. "	20	M		Farmer		" "		1		
		Ann "	18	F				" "		1		
		Cornelius "	16	M		Farmer		" "		1		
		Nathaniel "	14	M				" "		1		
		Samuel "	13	M				" "		1		
		William H. "	9	M				" "		1		
		Mary "	3	F				" "				
68	68	Wesley Nailor	53	M		Farmer		" "			1	
		Elizabeth "	50	F				" "				
		John "	21	M		Farmer		" "				
		Hezekiah "	19	M		Farmer		" "				
		Catharine "	23	F				" "			1	
		Irene "	16	F				" "				
		W. Alexander "	15	M		Farmer		" "				
		Charles "	10	M				" "				
69	69	Leonard Cheek	42	M		Carpenter		" "				
		Elizabeth Hannon	45	F				" "			1	
		Fanny E. Cheek	23	F				" "			1	
70	70	Zachius Moore	27	M		Farmer		" "				
		Rebecca "	22	F				" "				
		Martha F. "	1	F				" "				
		William "	13	M				" "		1		
71	71	Peter Black	55	M		Farmer		" "				
		Malcom "	21	M		Labourer		" "			1	
		Mary A. "	19	F				" "				
		Margaret "	17	F				" "				
		Dugald "	15	M		Labourer		" "				
		Duncan "	13	M				" "				
72	72	Lockart Fry	57	M		Farmer	500	" "				
		Nancy "	51	F				" "			1	
		Benjamin "	22	M		Farmer		" "		1		
		Daniel "	20	M		Do.		" "		1		
		Emelia "	24	F				" "				
		Mary A. "	25	F				" "		1		
		Jane E. "	17	F				" "		1		
		Margaret E. "	13	F				" "		1		
		William "	11	M				" "		1		

M 23
F 19

SCHEDULE I.—Free Inhabitants in ______________ in the County of Moore State of N. Carolina enumerated by me, on the 10th day of August 1850. N. McCummen Ass't Marshal.

329

170

Dwelling-houses numbered in the order of visitation.	Families numbered in the order of visitation.	The Name of every Person whose usual place of abode on the first day of June, 1850, was in this family.	Description: Age.	Sex.	Color, White, black, or mulatto.	Profession, Occupation, or Trade of each Male Person over 15 years of age.	Value of Real Estate owned.	Place of Birth. Naming the State, Territory, or Country.	Married within the year.	Attended School within the year.	Persons over 20 y'rs of age who cannot read & write.	Whether deaf and dumb, blind, insane, idiotic, pauper, or convict.	
1	2	3	4	5	6	7	8	9	10	11	12	13	
73	73	Hardy Johnson	39	M		Farmer		N. Carolina					1
		Mary "	49	F				" "			1		2
		Mary A. "	19	F				" "		1			3
		Alexander "	7	M				" "		1			4
74	74	Asael Johnson	47	M		Farmer	160	" "					5
		Elizabeth "	38	F				" "			1		6
		Westley "	18	M		Farmer		" "		1			7
		Barbara "	16	F				" "		1			8
		Martha J. "	11	F				" "		1			9
		Mary A. "	9	F				" "		1			10
		Catharine "	7	F				" "		1			11
		John A. "	3	M				" "					12
75	75	Edmund Johnson	24	M		Farmer		" "					13
		Elizabeth "	21	F				" "					14
		Fanny H. "	19	F				" "					15
		Flora A. "	15	F				" "					16
		Thomas "	10	M				" "					17
76	76	Samuel Vick	54	M		Farmer		" "			1		18
		Duncan "	18	M		Laborer		" "					19
		Absolom "	13	M				" "					20
		Sarah "	39	F				" "			1		21
		Catharine "	20	F				" "			1		22
		Christian "	15	F				" "					23
		Flora "	10	F				" "					24
		Nancy "	8	F				" "					25
		Mary McCollum	13	F				" "					26
77	77	Isaac Cox	43	M		Laborer		" "					27
		Nancy "	50	F				" "					28
		John "	15	M		none		" "					29
		William "	14	M				" "					30
		Susan "	12	F				" "					31
		MacDonald "	10	M				" "					32
78	78	Mary Smith	66	F				" "			1		33
		Matilda "	37	F				" "			1		34
		Ann "	21	F				" "					35
		Winney A. "	10	F				" "					36
		Willis H. "	2	M				" "					37
77	77	Thomas Fay	47	M		Farmer		" "					38
		Philadelpha "	46	F				" "			1		39
		Eliza "	20	F				" "					40
		Margaret "	18	F				" "					41
		Caroline "	13	F				" "					42

m 16
f 26

SCHEDULE I.—Free Inhabitants in ____________ in the County of Moore State of N. Carolina enumerated by me, on the 12th day of August 1850. N. McCrummen Ass't Marshal.

Dwelling-houses numbered in the order of visitation.	Families numbered in the order of visitation.	The Name of every Person whose usual place of abode on the first day of June, 1850, was in this family.	Age.	Sex.	Color, White, black, or mulatto.	Profession, Occupation, or Trade of each Male Person over 15 years of age.	Value of Real Estate owned.	Place of Birth, Naming the State, Territory, or Country.	Married within the year.	Attended School within the year.	Persons over 20 y'rs of age who cannot read & write.	Whether deaf and dumb, blind, insane, idiotic, pauper, or convict.
1	2	3	4	5	6	7	8	9	10	11	12	13
		Selina Fry	11	F				N. Carolina				
		Jennet ″	4	F				″ ″				
		Joseph ″	2	M				″ ″				
80	80	Calvin Welch	23	M		Farmer		″ ″				
		Emeline ″	23	F				″ ″				
81	81	Rebecca Williams	42	F				″ ″			1	
		Catharine ″	13	F				″ ″				
		Sarah E. ″	7	F				″ ″				
		William S. ″	5	M				″ ″				
82	82	Charity Cox	40	F				″ ″				
		Louisa R. ″	9	F				″ ″				
		Mary J. ″	5	F				″ ″				
83	83	Lockert Fry	32	M		Farmer	120	″ ″				
		Rosetta ″	29	F				″ ″				
		Lydia ″	8	F				″ ″				
		Betsey ″	5	F				″ ″				
		Idona ″	3	F				″ ″				
		William ″	9/12	M				″ ″				
84	84	Samuel Dice	75	M		Farmer		″ ″			1	
		Nancy ″	60	F				″ ″				
		Betsey ″	20	F				″ ″			1	
		Thomas ″	9	M				″ ″				
85	85	Jno. D. Patterson	46	M		Farmer		″ ″				
		Margaret ″	38	F				″ ″				
		William ″	6	M				″ ″				
		Frances ″	4	F				″ ″				
		John ″	1/12	M				″ ″				
86	86	Elizabeth McDonald	23	F				″ ″			1	
		Ann ″	20	F				″ ″		1	1	
		Ann ″	18	F				″ ″		1		
		Noah ″	10	M				″ ″		1		
		Neill ″	9	M				″ ″		1		
87	87	Aaron Willis	24	M		Laborer		″ ″			1	
		Sarah ″	24	F				″ ″			1	
		Winniford ″	4	F				″ ″				
		Mary ″	3	F				″ ″				
88	88	Fanny Smith	30	F				″ ″			1	
		William ″	3	M				″ ″				
88	89	James Bryant	56	M		Farmer	2000	″ ″				
		Ann ″	56	F				″ ″			1	
		George ″	21	M		Farmer		″ ″				
		Deborah ″	17	F				″ ″				

m 16
f 26

347

171

SCHEDULE I.—Free Inhabitants in 4 in the County of Moore State of N. Carolina enumerated by me, on the 13th day of August 1850. N. McCrummen Ass't Marshal.

Dwelling-houses numbered in the order of visitation.	Families numbered in the order of visitation.	The Name of every Person whose usual place of abode on the first day of June, 1850, was in this family.	Age.	Sex.	Color, { White, black, or mulatto. }	Profession, Occupation, or Trade of each Male Person over 15 years of age.	Value of Real Estate owned.	Place of Birth. Naming the State, Territory, or Country.	Married within the year.	Attended School within the year.	Persons over 20 y'rs of age who cannot read & write.	Whether deaf and dumb, blind, insane, idiotic, pauper, or convict.
1	2	3	4	5	6	7	8	9	10	11	12	13
		Burgy A. Bryant	14	F				N. Carolina				
		Littleton "	11	M				" "				
		Prudy "	1/12	F				" "				
89	89	Jacob Stutts	50	M		Farmer	1500	" "				
		Elizabeth "	42	F				" "				
		Henry "	24	M		Farmer		" "				
		William B. "	21	M		Farmer		" "				
		George W. "	19	M		Ditto		" "				
		Lucy "	15	F				" "		1		
		Mary "	13	F				" "		1		
		Walter "	9	M				" "		1		
		Samuel "	8	M				" "		1		
		Nancy "	5	F				" "				
		Martin "	1	M				" "				
		Lindsey Moore	28	M		Laborer		" "				
90	90	William M. Person	24	M		Farmer	3600	" "				
		Margaret "	20	F				" "				
		Colin A. Munroe	55	M		Farmer		" "				
		Ann "	48	F				" "				
		John A. "	17	M		Student		" "		1		
		Sarah C. "	10	F				" "		1		
		Benjamin P. "	9	M				" "		1		
91	91	Catharine Jackson	43	F			500	" "				
		John A. "	21	M		Farmer		" "				
		Mary A. "	19	F				" "		1		
		Martha R. "	17	F				" "		1		
		Thomas "	13	M				" "		1		
92	92	Samuel Barrett	47	M		Farmer	3000	" "				
		Elizabeth "	44	F				" "				
		Robert "	19	M		Meth. Clergyman		" "		1		
		William "	18	M		Farmer		" "		1		
		Alexander "	16	M		Farmer		" "		1		
		Mary E. "	14	F				" "		1		
		John A. "	13	M				" "		1		
		Junius A. "	11	M				" "				Idiotic
		David "	9	M				" "		1		
		Doctor "	4	M				" "				
93	93	Temperance Bratton	28	F				" "			1	
		William A. "	11	M				" "				
		Sally C. "	8	F				" "				
		Elizabeth "	6	F				" "				
		Mary F. "	2	F				" "				

M 24
F 18

SCHEDULE I.—Free Inhabitants in ______ in the County of Moore State of N. Carolina enumerated by me, on the 14th day of August 1850. N. McCrummen Ass't Marshal.

Dwelling-houses numbered in the order of visitation.	Families numbered in the order of visitation.	The Name of every Person whose usual place of abode on the first day of June, 1850, was in this family.	Description: Age.	Description: Sex.	Description: Color, White, black, or mulatto.	Profession, Occupation, or Trade of each Male Person over 15 years of age.	Value of Real Estate owned.	Place of Birth. Naming the State, Territory, or Country.	Married within the year.	Attended School within the year.	Persons over 20 y'rs of age who cannot read & write.	Whether deaf and dumb, blind, insane, idiotic, pauper, or convict.
1	2	3	4	5	6	7	8	9	10	11	12	13
		Henry T. S. Castlin	1	m				N. Carolina				
94	94	Sarah Castlin	40	F				South Carolina			1	
		Ellen "	18	F				N. Carolina				
95	95	Angus B. Kelly	40	m		Farmer	100	N. Carolina				
		Nancy "	40	F				" "				
		Mary C. "	15	F				" "				
		Isabella "	14	F				" "				
		Hugh "	12	m				" "				
		Margaret "	10	F				" "				
		Sarah F. "	8	F				" "				
		Catharine E. "	6	F				" "				
		Jane E.	4	F				" "				
		Ann E.	1	F				" "				
96	96	Daniel C. Kelly	37	m		Farmer	150	" "				
		Christian "	31	F				" "				
		Peter J. Ballard	12	m				" "		1		
		Sarah A. Brown	5	F				" "		1		
97	97	William J. McIntosh	44	m		Farmer	500	" "				
		Margaret "	31	F				" "				
		Elizabeth "	19	F				" "				
		Mary A. "	9	F				" "		1		
		Martha J. "	5	F				" "		1		
		Mary McIntosh	69	F				" "				
98	98	Neill Dowdy	34	m		Farmer		" "				
		Fraincy "	35	F				" "				
		Margaret J. "	10	F				" "				
		Rebecca "	8	F				" "				
		James S. "	5/12	m				" "				
99	99	Sarah Ross	54	F				" "			1	
		Elisha "	16	m		Basket making		" "				
100	100	Benjamin Medlin	35	m		Farmer		" "			1	
		Rosetta "	25	F				" "			1	
		William T. "	9	m				" "		1		
		Archibald "	8	m				" "		1		
		Riley "	7	m				" "				
		John "	2	m				" "				
101	101	Daniel Medlin	35	m		Farmer		" "			1	
		Rebecca "	35	F				" "			1	
		William "	15	m		Farmer		" "		1		
		Agmlina "	12	F				" "				
		John A. "	10	m				" "		1		
		Jane "	8	F				" "				

+ m 17
F 25

343

SCHEDULE I.—Free Inhabitants in ______ **in the County of** Moore **State of** N. Carolina **enumerated by me, on the** 14th **day of** August **1850.** N. McCummins **Ass't Marshal.** 172

Line	Dwelling-houses numbered in the order of visitation.	Families numbered in the order of visitation.	The Name of every Person whose usual place of abode on the first day of June, 1850, was in this family.	Age.	Sex.	Color, White, black, or mulatto.	Profession, Occupation, or Trade of each Male Person over 15 years of age.	Value of Real Estate owned.	Place of Birth. Naming the State, Territory, or Country.	Married within the year.	Attended School within the year.	Persons over 20 yr's of age who cannot read & write.	Whether deaf and dumb, blind, insane, idiotic, pauper, or convict.
	1	2	3	4	5	6	7	8	9	10	11	12	13
1			Benjamin Medlin	6	M				N. Carolina				
2			Elisabeth "	4	F				" "				
3			James "	2	M				" "				
4			Henry Rose	25	M		Farmer		" "			1	
5	102	102	Thomas Rose	23	M		Ditto		" "			1	
6			Mary "	35	F				" "			1	
7			Elina J. "	14	F				" "		1		
8			Catharine A. "	12	F				" "		1		
9			John T. "	9	M				" "		1		
10			William D. "	1	M				" "				
11	103	103	William Medlin	73	M		Farmer		" "			1	
12			Happy "	60	F				" "			1	
13			Christian "	12	F				" "		1		
14			Swain "	10	M				" "		1		
15	104	104	Niell McIntosh	28	M		Farmer	400	" "				
16			Caroline "	20	F				" "				
17			Sarah F. "	4	F				" "				
18			Alexander "	2	M				" "				
19			Mary E. "	2	F				" "				
20			Mahala Smith	26	F				" "				
21	105	105	Duncan McIntosh	38	M		Farmer	200	" "				
22			Sarah "	36	F				" "				
23			Duncan Smith	10	M				" "		1		
24	106	106	Samuel McIntosh	40	M		Farmer	500	" "				
25			Ann "	38	F				" "				
26			Samuel S. "	10	M				" "		1		
27			Mary A. "	8	F				" "		1		
28			Martha "	6	F				" "		1		
29			William "	4	M				" "				
30			Kitty "	3	F				" "				
31			Sarah "	1	F				" "				
32	107	107	Mary McIntosh	63	F			400	" "			1	
33			Daniel "	20	M		Farmer		" "				
34			Niell Milton	29	M		Farmer		" "				
35			Hannah Ham	30	F				" "				
36	108	108	John S. McIntosh	47	M		Farmer	800	" "				
37			Elisabeth "	37	F				" "			1	
38			Mary S. "	14	F				" "				
39			Sarah "	10	F				" "		1		
40			Niell "	9	M				" "		1		
41			Asah "	8	M				" "		1		
42			William A. "	6	M				" "		1		

m21
721

SCHEDULE I.—Free Inhabitants in ______________ **in the County of** Moore **State of** N Carolina **enumerated by me, on the** 14th **day of** August **1850.** N McCummens **Ass't Marshal.**

Dwelling-houses numbered in the order of visitation.	Families numbered in the order of visitation.	The Name of every Person whose usual place of abode on the first day of June, 1850, was in this family.	Age.	Sex.	Color, white, black, or mulatto.	Profession, Occupation, or Trade of each Male Person over 15 years of age.	Value of Real Estate owned.	Place of Birth. Naming the State, Territory, or Country.	Married within the year.	Attended School within the year.	Persons over 20 y'rs of age who cannot read & write.	Whether deaf and dumb, blind, insane, idiotic, pauper, or convict.
1	2	3	4	5	6	7	8	9	10	11	12	13
		Alexander McIntosh	5	m				N Carolina		1		
		Elizabeth "	3	F				" "				
		Rutha A "	1	F				" "				
109	109	William Bryant	26	m		Farmer	550	" "				
		Leah "	22	F				" "				
		Noah Smith	15	m		Farmer		" "		1		
		Hamilton	13	m				" "		1		
		William Hunsucker	22	m		Farmer		" "				
110	110	William B Fry	29	m		Ditto	500	" "				
		William Fry	22	m		Laborer		" "				
111	111	Neill Caddell	38	m		Farmer	500	" "				
		Elizabeth "	30	F				" "			1	
		Robert Graham	50	m		Laborer		" "			1	
112	112	Catharine Lawhon	63	F				" "			1	
		Thomas Hunsucker	20	m		Farmer		" "				
113	113	Isaiah Lawhon	27	m		Ditto	225	" "			1	
		Margaret J "	26	F				" "			1	
		Joel "	3	m				" "				
		Rufus "	2	m				" "				
		Charles Manly "	11/12	m				" "				
114	114	Stephen Davis	57	m		Farmer	1450	" "				
		Jane "	35	F				" "				
		Nancy "	23	F				" "				
		Dewitton "	21	m		Teacher		" "				
		John "	19	m		Farmer		" "		1		
		Edmund "	18	m		Ditto		" "		1		
		Mary A "	12	F				" "		1		
		Harrison "	10	m				" "		1		
		Malcom "	7	m				" "		1		
		Stephen "	5	m				" "				
115	115	Lydia Busnell	41	F	B			" "				
		William "	19	m	B			" "				
		Thomas "	17	m	B			" "				
		Ann "	16	F	B			" "				
		Betsy "	10	F	B			" "				
116	116	William Moore	32	m		Farmer	600	" "				
		Serepta A "	25	F				" "				
		Mary E "	7	F				" "		1		
		Sarah A "	5	F				" "				
		Martha "	3	F				" "				
		Margaret J "	11/12	F				" "				
		Anthony Evans	38	m	m	Carpenter		Virginia		1		

1 m 26 ~~48~~ 3 m
F 16 27 3 F

345

SCHEDULE I.—Free Inhabitants in 5 in the County of Moore State of N. Carolina enumerated by me, on the 15th day of August 1850. N. McCrummen Ass't Marshal. 173

	Dwelling-houses numbered in the order of visitation.	Families numbered in the order of visitation.	The Name of every Person whose usual place of abode on the first day of June, 1850, was in this family.	Description: Age.	Sex.	Color, White, black, or mulatto.	Profession, Occupation, or Trade of each Male Person over 15 years of age.	Value of Real Estate owned.	Place of Birth. Naming the State, Territory, or Country.	Married within the year.	Attended School within the year.	Persons over 20 y'rs of age who cannot read & write.	Whether deaf and dumb, blind, insane, idiotic, pauper, or convict.	
	1	2	3	4	5	6	7	8	9	10	11	12	13	
1	117	117	Alvin Smith	29	m		Farmer		N. Carolina			/		1
2			Patsey "	29	F				" "			/		2
3			Elizabeth "	11	F				" "		/			3
4			Mary A. "	8	F				" "		/			4
5			William "	6	m				" "		/			5
6			Caroline "	2	F				" "					6
7	118	118	Mary B. Sowell	49	F			250	" "					7
8			Martha J. "	17	F				" "					8
9			Lydia F. "	15	F				" "		/			9
10			Eli P. "	12	m				" "		/			10
11	119	119	John Medlin	25	m		Farmer		" "			/		11
12			Mary "	22	F				" "			/		12
13			Nancy A. "	4	F				" "					13
14			Sarah C. "	2	F				" "					14
15			Ruth "	4/12	F				" "					15
16			Sarah Richardson	45	F				" "			/		16
17	120	120	George McIntosh	32	m		Farmer	800	" "					17
18			Susannah "	19	F				" "					18
19			Mary J. "	1	F				" "					19
20			Jesse Ballard	42	m		Farmer		" "			/		20
21	121	121	Dempsey Sowell	45	m		Farmer		" "					21
22			Mary "	40	F				" "					22
23			Jason "	16	m		Farmer		" "		/			23
24			James W. "	14	m				" "		/			24
25			Sarah M. "	12	F				" "					25
26			Catharine "	12	F				" "		/			26
27			Emiline "	10	F				" "		/			27
28			Elizabeth "	8	F				" "					28
29			Thomas S. L. "	5	m				" "					29
30	122	122	Eli Oldham	32	m		Farmer		" "			/		30
31			Betsey "	27	F				" "					31
32			Emily "	7	F				" "					32
33			Ashley "	6	m				" "					33
34			Asa "	4	m				" "					34
35			Margaret "	2/12	F				" "					35
36			Rebecca Hardin	39	F				" "					36
37	123	123	Daniel H. Muse	60	m		Farmer	300	" "					37
38			Jennett R. "	51	F				" "					38
39			Kindred "	14	m				" "		/			39
40			Patience Muse	25	F				" "	—				40
41	[illegible]	124	Henry B. Pitts	39	m		Farmer		" "					41
42			Olive "	39	F				" "					42

m 16
F 26

SCHEDULE I.—Free Inhabitants in ______ in the County of Moore State of N. Carolina enumerated by me, on the sixth day of August 1850. N. McL. E. Cromma Ass't Marshal.

	Dwelling-houses numbered in the order of visitation.	Families numbered in the order of visitation.	The Name of every Person whose usual place of abode on the first day of June, 1850, was in this family.	Age.	Sex.	Color, White, black, or mulatto.	Profession, Occupation, or Trade of each Male Person over 15 years of age.	Value of Real Estate owned.	Place of Birth. Naming the State, Territory, or Country.	Married within the year.	Attended School within the year.	Persons over 20 y'rs of age who cannot read & write.	Whether deaf and dumb, blind, insane, idiotic, pauper, or convict.
	1	2	3	4	5	6	7	8	9	10	11	12	13
1			Cherry Ritter	15	F				N. Carolina		1		
2			Presley "	12	m				" "		1		
3			Lindsay T. "	10	m				" "		1		
4			Betsey "	5	F				" "				
5	125	125	John T. Ritter	59	m		Farmer		" "				
6			Mary "	54	F				" "			1	
7			Archibald "	26	m		Carpenter		" "				
8			Margaret "	16	F				" "		1		
9			Darcus J. "	15	F				" "		1		
10			Thomas H. "	17	m		Laborer		" "		1		
11			Leonard H. "	12	m				" "		X		
12			Malcom A. "	11	m				" "		1		
13			Christian "	7	F				" "		1		
14			Archibald Jr. "	6	m				" "				
15	126	126	Alexander Kelly	39	m		Farmer	10500	" "				
16			Sarah "	30	F				" "				
17			Catharine J. "	9	F				" "		1		
18			Duncan "	7	m				" "		1		
19			Mary A. "	5	F				" "		1		
20			John M. "	4	m				" "				
21			Patrick "	2	m				" "				
22			Murdoch "	1/10	m				" "				
23			Isabella Kelly	36	F			500	" "				
24			Daniel J. "	15	m		Student		" "		1		
25			Catharine A. "	13	F				" "		1		
26			John B. "	11	m				" "		1		
27			Margaret Morrison	35	F			300	" "				
28	127	127	Thomas Cole	28	m		Coachmaker	350	" "				
29			Margaret "	28	F				" "				
30			Jacob "	1	m				" "				
31	128	128	Samuel Jackson	35	m		Blacksmith		" "				
32			Mary "	29	F				" "			1	
33			Archibald J. "	11	m				" "		1		
34			William H. "	9	m				" "		1		
35			Flora A. "	7	F				" "		1		
36			George M. "	5	m				" "				
37			John L. "	2	m				" "				
38			Nancy "	2	F				" "				
39			Alexander "	1/12	m				" "				
40	129	129	George G. Muse	31	m		Farmer	230	" "				
41			Jane "	29	F				" "				
42			James H. "	7	m				" "		1		

m 25
F 17

SCHEDULE I.—Free Inhabitants in ______ in the County of Moore State 347
of N. Carolina enumerated by me, on the 17th day of August 1850. N. McCrummen Ass't Marshal. 174

Dwelling-houses numbered in the order of visitation.	Families numbered in the order of visitation.	The Name of every Person whose usual place of abode on the first day of June, 1850, was in this family.	Description: Age.	Sex.	Color, White, black, or mulatto.	Profession, Occupation, or Trade of each Male Person over 15 years of age.	Value of Real Estate owned.	Place of Birth. Naming the State, Territory, or Country.	Married within the year.	Attended School within the year.	Persons over 20 yr's of age who cannot read & write.	Whether deaf and dumb, blind, insane, idiotic, pauper, or convict.
1	2	3	4	5	6	7	8	9	10	11	12	13
		John C. Muse	5	m				N. Carolina		1		
		Alexander D. "	4	m				" "				
		Andrew H.	4/12	m				" "				
~~130~~	~~130~~	Margaret Gilchrist	55	F				Scotland				Deaf & Dumb
130	130	James B. Muse	65	m		Farmer	400	N. Carolina			1	
		Elizabeth "	65	F				" "				
		Margaret R. "	43	F				" "				
		Lydia C. "	41	F				" "				
		Milly C. "	24	F				" "				
		Martha E. "	22	F				" "				
		Sarah F. "	9	F				" "		1		
		Lucian "	3	m				" "				
		Crawford Key	19	m		Farmer		" "				
		Pinckney Deaton	12	m				" "		1		
131	131	Jesse Thomas	82	m				" "				Poverty
		Mary Rose	80	F				" "			1	Poverty
		Celia Burrantine	54	F				" "			1	Paralysis
		Mary John	35	F				" "			1	Insanity
		Mary Fry	37	F				" "			1	Rheumatism
		Elias Ballard	18	m		none		" "				Idiotic
		Lydia Chavis	13	F				" "				Idiotic
		Fanny	85	F	B			Virginia				Blind
132	132	Henderson Muse	36	m		Farmer	400	N. Carolina				
		Nancy E. "	31	F				" "			1	
		Chapel B. "	11	m				" "		1		
		Julia A. "	9	F				" "		1		
		Mary E. "	6	F				" "		1		
		Margaret "	7/12	F				" "				
133	133	Nancy Campbell	59	F				Scotland				
		Alexander W. "	21	m				N. Carolina				
		Mary "	20	F				" "			1	
		Isabella Gilchrist	60	F				Scotland				Deaf & Dumb
		Mary "	51	F				"				Deaf & Dumb
		George Campbell	10	m				N. Carolina		1		
		John Wicker	24	m		Laborer		" "				
134	134	Laughlin Kelly	33	m		Farmer	300	" "				
		Christian "	58	F				" "				
		Christian "	27	F				" "				
		Daniel M. S. "	3	m				" "				
		William J. "	1	m				" "				
		Murdoch Matt McLeod	18	m		Student		" "		1		
135	135	Jesse F. Muse	57	m		Farmer		" "				

Poor House

m 19
f 23
17

SCHEDULE I.—Free Inhabitants in ______ in the County of *Moore* State of *N Carolina* enumerated by me, on the *19th* day of *August*, 1850. *N. McCrummen* Ass't Marshal.

Dwelling-houses numbered in the order of visitation.	Families numbered in the order of visitation.	The Name of every Person whose usual place of abode on the first day of June, 1850, was in this family.	Age.	Sex.	Color, White, black, or mulatto.	Profession, Occupation, or Trade of each Male Person over 15 years of age.	Value of Real Estate owned.	Place of Birth. Naming the State, Territory, or Country.	Married within the year.	Attended School within the year.	Persons over 20 y'rs of age who cannot read & write.	Whether deaf and dumb, blind, insane, idiotic, pauper, or convict.
1	2	3	4	5	6	7	8	9	10	11	12	13
		Mary Muse	59	F				N. Carolina			1	
		Fanny McNeill	35	F			100	" "			1	
		Samuel Muse	23	m		Farmer		" "	—			
		Mary McNeill	17	F				" "				
		Martha A.	13	F				" "				
136	136	Mary J. Nailor	26	F				" "				
		Sarah "	9	F				" "		1		
137	137	Augustus McNeill	37	m		O.S.P. Clergyman	1000	" "				
		Harriet A. "	31	F				New York				
		Mary A. "	13	F				N. Carolina		1		
		Catherine E. "	5	F				" "		1		
		Ann E. "	9	F				" "		1		
		Margaret J. "	7	F				" "		1		
		James McNeill	22	m		Student		Alabama		1		
		David T. "	18	m		Student		"		1		
		Eveline T. "	15	F				"		1		
		Cyrus Harrington	23	m		Student		N. Carolina		1		
		E. Sparks Eagle	15	m		Student		" "		1		
138	138	Thomas Jenkins	36	m		Merchant	1000	" "				Blind
		Milbury "	36	F				" "				
		Mary R. "	14	F				" "				
		Alfred F. "	11	m				" "				
		John R. "	9	m				" "				
		Sarah J. "	6	F				" "				
		Henry H. "	4	m				" "				
		Charles P. "	1	m				" "				
		Mary H. Jenkins	67	F				" "				
139	139	Thomas W. Postell	37	m		Meth. Clergyman		South Carolina				
		Emma "	38	F				" "				
		Winiford Jenkins	35	F				N. Carolina				
		Julian A. Burnett	16	m				" "				
140	140	John C. Jenkins	22	m		Merchant	1500	" "				
		Eliza "	25	F				" "				
		Catherine J. "	23	F				" "				
		Mary E. "	17	F				" "		1		
141	141	Thomas B. Tyson	36	m		Merchant	2500	" "				
		Mary "	26	F				" "				
		Lucian B. "	7	m				" "		1		
		John Shaw	26	m		Physician		" "				
		Geo. S. Cole	21	m		Clerk		" "				
		Eliza A. McIntosh	11	F				" "		1		
		John H. McGilvary	8	m				" "		1		

m 19
F 23

SCHEDULE I.—Free Inhabitants in 6 in the County of Moore State of N. Carolina enumerated by me, on the 19th day of August 1850. N. McCrummen Ass't Marshal. 349

175

Dwelling-houses numbered in the order of visitation.	Families numbered in the order of visitation.	The Name of every Person whose usual place of abode on the first day of June, 1850, was in this family.	Description: Age.	Description: Sex.	Description: Color. White, black, or mulatto.	Profession, Occupation, or Trade of each Male Person over 15 years of age.	Value of Real Estate owned.	Place of Birth. Naming the State, Territory, or Country.	Married within the year.	Attended School within the year.	Persons over 20 y'rs of age who cannot read & write.	Whether deaf and dumb, blind, insane, idiotic, pauper, or convict.
1	2	3	4	5	6	7	8	9	10	11	12	13
142	142	Phillip Cameron	62	M		Blacksmith		N. Carolina				
		Mary "	73	F				" "				
		Catharine Patterson	20	F				" "			1	
143	143	Hugh McDonald	65	M		Farmer	500	" "				
		Catharine "	56	F				" "				
		Allen C. "	29	M		Farmer	250	" "				
		Mary E. "	27	F				" "				
		Betsey A. "	25	F				" "				
		Margaret E. "	23	F				" "		1		
		Marion E. "	21	F				" "		1		
		Daniel W. "	18	M		Farmer		" "		1		
		Malcom J. A. "	16	M		Ditto		" "		1		
144	144	John McDonald	47	M		Farmer	400	" "				
		Mary "	37	F				" "				
		Catharine "	8	F				" "				
		Alexander "	6	F				" "				
		Murdoch "	5	M				" "				
		Mary M. "	3	F				" "				
		John C. "	1	M				" "				
145	145	Daniel McDonald	43	M		Farmer	250	" "				
		Isabella "	36	F				" "				
		Christian "	4	F				" "				
		Daniel N. "	3	M				" "				
		John A. "	5/12	M				" "				
146	146	Alexander McDonald	73	M		Farmer	240	" "				
		Alexander C. "	38	M		Farmer		" "				
		Mary "	38	F				" "				
		Effy "	50	F				" "			1	
		Mary "	40	F				" "			1	
		William A. "	1	M				" "				
147	147	Daniel McMillan	30	M		Farmer	300	" "				
		Anna "	29	F				" "				
		Flora J. "	4	F				" "				
		Daniel C. "	2	M				" "				
		Archibald "	1	M				" "				
148	148	Robert McFarland	53	M		Farmer	600	" "				
		Eleanor "	50	F				" "				
		John Davidson	14	M				" "		1		
149	149	Malcom McFarland	41	M		Farmer		" "				
		Catharine "	39	F				" "				
		Catharine "	16	F				" "		1		
		Margaret "	14	F				" "		1		

M 20
F 22

SCHEDULE I.—Free Inhabitants in ______ in the County of Moore State of N. Carolina enumerated by me, on the 19th day of August 1850. N. McCrummen Ass't Marshal.

	Dwelling-houses numbered in the order of visitation.	Families numbered in the order of visitation.	The Name of every Person whose usual place of abode on the first day of June, 1850, was in this family.	Description: Age.	Description: Sex.	Description: Color, White, black, or mulatto.	Profession, Occupation, or Trade of each Male Person over 15 years of age.	Value of Real Estate owned.	Place of Birth. Naming the State, Territory, or Country.	Married within the year.	Attended School within the year.	Persons over 20 y'rs of age who cannot read & write.	Whether deaf and dumb, blind, insane, idiotic, pauper, or convict.
	1	2	3	4	5	6	7	8	9	10	11	12	13
1			Dugald McFarland	12	M				N. Carolina		1		
2			Neil "	11	M				" "		1		
3			Elizabeth "	9	F				" "		1		
4			Eliza "	7	F				" "		1		
5			Emeline "	5	F				" "				
6			Dianna "	3	F				" "				
7	150	150	Edward Patterson	63	M		Farmer	500	" "				
8			Sarah "	51	F				" "				
9			Duncan "	29	M		Student		" "		1		
10			Mary "	27	F				" "				
11			Allen D. "	23	M		Farmer		" "		1		
12			Archibald "	20	M		Ditto		" "		1		
13			Marion A. "	16	F				" "		1		
14			John "	18	M		Farmer		" "		1		
15			Barbara E. "	13	F				" "		1		
16			Amelia M. "	10	F				" "		1		
17			Daniel E. "	6	M				" "				
18			Calvin Buie	25	M		Student		" "		1		
19			William Doakin	21	M		Ditto		" "		1		
20	151	151	Mary Clark	60	F			350	Scotland				
21			Catharine "	31	F				N Carolina				
22			Archibald "	34	M		none		" "				
23			Christian "	28	F				" "				
24			Donald "	26	M		Farmer		" "				
25			Anna Ray	3	F				" "				
26	152	152	Patrick Ray	44	M		Farmer	250	" "				
27			Mary A. "	31	F				" "				
28			John C. "	12	M				" "		1		
29			Archibald "	8	M				" "		1		
30			Mary L. "	7	F				" "		1		
31			Malcom "	3	M				" "				
32	153	153	Duncan Black	37	M		Farmer	50	" "				
33			Christian "	30	F				" "				
34			Margaret "	9	F				" "		1		
35			Mary A. "	6	F				" "		1		
36			Sarah "	2	F				" "				
37	154	154	Daniel McFarland	55	M		Farmer	400	" "				
38			Mary "	58	F				" "				
39	155	155	Sarah McDonald	50	F			200	" "				
40			Nancy Brown	18	F				" "		1		
41	156	156	Archibald Ray	48	M			450	" "				
42			Flora "	50	F				Scotland				

m 19
F 23

SCHEDULE I.—Free Inhabitants in ______ in the County of *Moore* State of *N. Carolina* enumerated by me, on the *30th* day of *August* 1850. *N. McCrummen* Ass't Marshal.

387

176

Dwelling-houses numbered in the order of visitation.	Families numbered in the order of visitation.	The Name of every Person whose usual place of abode on the first day of June, 1850, was in this family.	Description: Age.	Description: Sex.	Description: Color. White, black, or mulatto.	Profession, Occupation, or Trade of each Male Person over 15 years of age.	Value of Real Estate owned.	Place of Birth. Naming the State, Territory, or Country.	Married within the year.	Attended School within the year.	Persons over 20 y'rs of age who cannot read & write.	Whether deaf and dumb, blind, insane, idiotic, pauper, or convict.
1	2	3	4	5	6	7	8	9	10	11	12	13
		Mary Ray	20	F				N. Carolina				
		John "	17	M		Student		" "		1		
		Joseph "	15	M		Farmer		" "		1		
		Catharine "	13	F				" "		1		
		David "	11	M				" "		1		
		Sarah E. "	6	F				" "		1		
157	157	Hugh McLauren	50	M		O.S.P. Clergyman	600	South Carolina				
		Eliza "	31	F				Scotland				
		Cornelius M. "	6	M				N. Carolina				
		Anna B. "	4	F				" "				
		Thomas C. "	2	M				" "				
		Catharine "	1/12	F				" "				
158	158	James D. Rush	41	M		Farmer	700	" "				
		Jannet "	39	F				" "				
		Catharine "	18	F				" "		1		
		Benjamin "	17	M		Farmer		" "		1		
		Alexander "	14	M				" "		1		
		Martin "	12	M				" "		1		
		Harrison "	9	M				" "		1		
		John "	6	M				" "				Blind
159	159	Nathan Copeland	49	M		Farmer	350	" "	—			
		Clarkey A. "	21	F				" "	—			
		Rebecca "	51	F				" "			1	
		Eli P. Dannelly	23	M		Farmer		" "				
160	160	Daniel McInnis	43	M		Farmer		" "				
		Anna "	44	F				" "				
		Neil "	17	M		Laborer		" "				
		John "	15	M		Ditto		" "				
		Duncan "	13	M				" "				
		Ann "	12	F				" "				
		Malcom "	11	M				" "				
		Sarah "	7	F				" "				
		Margaret "	4	F				" "				
		William "	1	M				" "				
161	161	Catharine Campbell	58	F				" "			1	
		Ann "	26	F				" "				
		Angus "	23	M		Farmer	75	" "				
		Sarah "	22	F				" "				
		Isaac Stutts	31	M		Farmer		" "			1	
		Margaret "	30	F				" "			1	
162	162	Nancy McLeod	50	F			100	" "			1	
		Margaret "	30	F				" "			1	

M22
F20 V

SCHEDULE I.—Free Inhabitants in ______ in the County of Moore State of N. Carolina enumerated by me, on the 28th day of August 1850. N. McCrimmon Ass't Marshal.

	Dwelling-houses numbered in the order of visitation.	Families numbered in the order of visitation.	The Name of every Person whose usual place of abode on the first day of June, 1850, was in this family.	Description: Age.	Description: Sex.	Description: Color, (White, black, or mulatto.)	Profession, Occupation, or Trade of each Male Person over 15 years of age.	Value of Real Estate owned.	Place of Birth. Naming the State, Territory, or Country.	Married within the year.	Attended School within the year.	Persons over 20 y'rs of age who cannot read & write.	Whether deaf and dumb, blind, insane, idiotic, pauper, or convict.
	1	2	3	4	5	6	7	8	9	10	11	12	13
1			Catharine McLeod	27	F				N. Carolina			1	
2			Anna "	24	F				" "				
3			Jane "	21	F				" "				
4			John A. "	16	M		Farmer		" "		1		
5	163	163	Margaret McMillan	66	F			50	" "			1	
6			Jennet "	38	F				" "			1	
7			Anna "	27	F				" "			1	
8			Mary "	25	F				"				
9			Archibald "	17	M		Farmer		" "		1		
10	164	164	Peter Thomas	58	M		Farmer	280	" "				
11			Ann "	52	F				" "				
12			John C. "	23	M		Farmer		" "				
13			Murdo M. "	18	M		Farmer		" "				
14			Eliza "	21	F				" "				
15			Daniel A. "	17	M		Farmer		" "		1		
16			E. Anna "	12	F				" "		1		
17			Mary B. "	11	F				" "		1		
18			Joseph P. "	9	M				" "		1		
19	165	165	Murdoch McKenzie	78	M		Farmer	500	Scotland				
20			Sarah "	50	F				N. Carolina				
21			Elizabeth "	35	F				" "				
22			Jane "	30	F				" "				
23			Sarah "	25	F				" "				
24			Emeline "	13	F				" "		1		
25			Alexander McLeod	35	M		Farmer		" "				
26			Jarret Graham	22	M		Farmer		" "			1	
27			William A. "	8	M				" "		1		
28	166	166	Daniel McKenzie	43	M		Farmer	700	" "				
29			Flora "	35	F				" "				
30			Alexander M. "	9	M				" "		1		
31			Murdoch G. "	7	M				" "		1		
32			John C. "	4	M				" "				
33			Sarah L. "	8/12	F				" "				
34			Eliza McDonald	18	F				" "				
35			Alexander W. McLennan	20	M		Student		" "		1		
36	167	167	Neill McKinnon	33	M		Farmer		" "	—			
37			Margaret "	25	F				" "	—			
38	168	168	Catharine McDonald	50	F			200	" "				
39			Margaret "	33	F				" "				
40			Effy "	27	F				" "				
41			Mary "	25	F				" "				
42			John "	24	M		Farmer		" "				

m 18
f 24

SCHEDULE I.—Free Inhabitants in 07 in the County of Moore State 363 of N. Carolina enumerated by me, on the 21st day of August 1850. N. McCrummen Ass't Marshal. 177

Dwelling-houses numbered in the order of visitation.	Families numbered in the order of visitation.	The Name of every Person whose usual place of abode on the first day of June, 1850, was in this family.	Age.	Sex.	Color, White, black, or mulatto.	Profession, Occupation, or Trade of each Male Person over 15 years of age.	Value of Real Estate owned.	Place of Birth. Naming the State, Territory, or Country.	Married within the year.	Attended School within the year.	Persons over 20 y'rs of age who cannot read & write.	Whether deaf and dumb, blind, insane, idiotic, pauper, or convict.	
1	2	3	4	5	6	7	8	9	10	11	12	13	
		John P. Graham	2	m				N. Carolina					1
169	169	Malcom C. Clark	52	m		Farmer	450	" "					2
		Jane "	43	F				" "					3
		George W. "	21	m		Student		" "					4
		N. Daniel I. "	19	m		Student		" "					5
		John B. "	17	m		Farmer		" "		1			6
		Archibald A. "	13	m				" "		1			7
		Sarah I. "	11	F				" "		1			8
		William K. "	8	m				" "		1			9
		Cornelius H. "	5	m				" "		1			10
		Mary C. "	3	F				" "					11
170	170	Malcom Brown	40	m		Farmer	250	" "					12
		Mary "	37	F				" "					13
		William "	12	m				" "		1			14
		Alexander "	10	m				" "		1			15
		Emiline "	8	F				" "		1			16
		Margaret "	5	F				" "		1			17
		Duncan "	3	m				" "					18
		Malcom "	2/12	m				" "					19
171	171	Flora Campbell	54	F			350	Scotland			1		20
		Mary A. "	30	F			200	N. Carolina					21
		Isabella "	27	F			200	" "			1		22
		Randal "	16	m		Farmer		" "		1			23
		John A "	15	m		Ditto		" "		1			24
		William A. "	8	m				" "		1			25
172	172	Margaret Black	43	F				" "			1		26
		John "	20	m		Laborer		" "					27
		Mary "	16	F				" "					28
		Elizabeth "	12	F				" "		1			29
		Isabella "	8	F				" "					30
173	173	Nancy Autry	50	F				" "			1		31
		Anna "	22	F				" "			1		32
174	174	Sarah Eddings	62	F			50	" "			1		33
175	175	Duncan Shaw	47	m		Farmer	200	" "					34
		Flora "	49	F				" "			1		35
		Sarah I. "	19	F				" "		1			36
		Duncan C. "	17	m		Farmer		" "		1			37
		Alexander "	10	m				" "		1			38
176	176	Duncan Brown	30	m				" "					39
		Loveday M. "	39	F				" "					40
177	177	Archibald Patterson	47	m		Farmer	75	" "					41
		Sarah E. "	17	F				" "		1			42

M22
722

SCHEDULE I.—Free Inhabitants in ______ in the County of Moore State of N. Carolina enumerated by me, on the 22nd day of August 1850. N. McCrummen Ass't Marshal.

	Dwelling-houses numbered in the order of visitation.	Families numbered in the order of visitation.	The Name of every Person whose usual place of abode on the first day of June, 1850, was in this family.	Description: Age.	Sex.	Color, (White, black, or mulatto.)	Profession, Occupation, or Trade of each Male Person over 15 years of age.	Value of Real Estate owned.	Place of Birth. Naming the State, Territory, or Country.	Married within the year.	Attended School within the year.	Persons over 20 y'rs of age who cannot read & write.	Whether deaf and dumb, blind, insane, idiotic, pauper, or convict.
	1	2	3	4	5	6	7	8	9	10	11	12	13
1			John A. Patterson	15	m		Farmer		N. Carolina		1		
2			Archibald "	13	m				" "		1		
3			William D. "	11	m				" "		1		
4			Margaret "	8	F				" "				
5			Duncan "	4	m				" "				
6	178	178	John McKinnon	23	m		Farmer	300	" "				
7			Kisander "	29	F				" "				
8	179	179	Daniel Patterson	75	m		Farmer	700	" "				
9			Emilia "	79	F				Scotland			1	
10			Caroline McDonald	24	F				N. Carolina				
11	180	180	John McLeod	48	m		Hatter		" "				
12			Flora "	42	F				" "				
13			William "	17	m		Farmer		" "				
14			Duncan J. "	16	m		Farmer		" "				
15			Daniel "	15	m		Ditto		" "				
16			Alexander "	11	m				" "				
17			Evander "	10	m				" "				
18			Samuel "	9	m				" "				
19			Sarah A. "	7	F				" "				
20			Emiline "	5	F				" "				
21			Margaret "	4	F				" "				
22			Flora A. "	1	F				" "				
23			John C. McLeod	19	m				" "				
24	181	181	Ronald C. McDonald	50	m		Farmer	150	Scotland				
25			Nancy "	40	F				"			1	
26			Sarah "	20	F				"		1		
27			Catharine "	18	F				"		1		
28			John "	16	m		Farmer		North Carolina		1		
29			Mary "	13	F				" "		1		
30			Effy "	9	F				" "		1		
31			Archibald "	5	m				" "				
32			Christian "	4	F				" "				
33	182	182	Randolph McDonald	49	m		Farmer	300	" "				
34			Mary "	48	F				" "				
35			John A. "	24	m		Farmer		" "				
36			Archibald "	22	m		Farmer		" "				
37			Daniel "	19	m		Farmer		" "				
38			Loveday "	17	F				" "				
39			Mary A. "	15	F				" "				
40			Daniel "	13	m				" "				
41			William "	13	m				" "				
42			Martin "	11	m				" "				

M24
F 18

SCHEDULE I.—Free Inhabitants in ______ in the County of Moore State of N. Carolina enumerated by me, on the 23d day of August 1850. Neill McCrummen Ass't Marshal.

178

Dwelling-houses numbered in the order of visitation.	Families numbered in the order of visitation.	The Name of every Person whose usual place of abode on the first day of June, 1850, was in this family.	Description: Age.	Sex.	Color, (White, black, or mulatto.)	Profession, Occupation, or Trade of each Male Person over 15 years of age.	Value of Real Estate owned.	Place of Birth. Naming the State, Territory, or Country.	Married within the year.	Attended School within the year.	Persons over 20 y'rs of age who cannot read & write.	Whether deaf and dumb, blind, insane, idiotic, pauper, or convict.
1	2	3	4	5	6	7	8	9	10	11	12	13
		Catharine J. McDonald	8	F				N. Carolina				
183	183	James Caddell	58	m		Farmer	700	" "				
		Catharine "	55	F				" "			1	
		Dugald B. "	26	m		Farmer		" "				
		Malcom "	25	m		Tailor		" "				
		John "	23	m		Farmer		" "				
		Archibald "	22	m		Farmer		" "				
		Daniel P. "	21	m		Farmer		" "				
		Margaret A "	14	F				" "				
		Catharine "	12	F				" "		1		
184	184	Mary Ray	54	F			70	" "				
		Martha A. "	21	F				" "				
		Mary J. "	18	F				" "		1		
185	185	Mary McNatt	60	F				" "			1	
		Edward "	23	m		Farmer		" "			1	
186	186	Peter McCaskill	60	m		Farmer		Scotland				
		Mary "	40	F				"				
		Nancy "	19	F				Upper Canada		1		
		Catharine "	17	F				" "		1		
		Donald "	12	m				Novascotia		1		
		Malcom "	9	m				"		1		
187	187	Angus McLean	66	m		Farmer	300	Scotland			1	
		Nancy "	60	F				"			1	
		Christian "	23	F				N. Carolina				
		Anna "	21	F				" "		1		
		Kenneth "	19	m		Farmer		" "		1		
188	188	John McLeod	82	m		Farmer	450	Scotland				
		Neill "	52	m		Physician		N. Carolina				
		Nancy McKinnon	28	F				South Carolina				
		Mary A. "	4	F				N. Carolina				
189	189	Ann Graham	89	F				Scotland			1	
		Dugald "	45	m		Farmer	900	N. Carolina				
		Nancy "	47	F				" "				
		Sarah "	16	F				" "		1		
		Flora Gillis	60	F				" "			1	
		Mary "	15	F				" "		1		
190	190	Laughlin McKinnon	67	m		Farmer	660	" "				
		Mary "	52	F				" "				
		Mary "	22	F				" "				
		William "	17	m		Farmer		" "		1		
		Martin "	15	m				" "		1		
		Laughlin J. "	13	m				" "		1		

m 19
F 23

368

SCHEDULE I.—Free Inhabitants in ______ **in the County of** *Moore* **State of** *N. Carolina* **enumerated by me, on the** *24th* **day of** *August* **1850.** *N. McCrummen* **Ass't Marshal.**

Dwelling-houses numbered in the order of visitation.	Families numbered in the order of visitation.	The Name of every Person whose usual place of abode on the first day of June, 1850, was in this family.	Age.	Sex.	Color, White, black, or mulatto.	Profession, Occupation, or Trade of each Male Person over 15 years of age.	Value of Real Estate owned.	Place of Birth. Naming the State, Territory, or Country.	Married within the year.	Attended School within the year.	Persons over 20 y'rs of age who cannot read & write.	Whether deaf and dumb, blind, insane, idiotic, pauper, or convict.
1	2	3	4	5	6	7	8	9	10	11	12	13
		Colin B. McKinnon	12	m				N. Carolina		1		
191	191	Alexander Ray	60	m		Farmer	300	Scotland				
		Barbara "	62	F				N. Carolina				
		Sarah "	34	F				" "				
		Mary "	32	F				" "				
		John "	28	m		Farmer		" "				
		Neill "	26	m		Farmer		" "				
		Archibald "	23	m		Farmer		" "				
		Christian "	21	F				" "				
192	192	Charles C. Shaw	69	m		Farmer	3000	" "				
		Mary "	50	F				" "				
		Eliza "	21	F				" "				
		Thomas "	20	m		Farmer		" "				
		Margaret "	17	F				" "		1		
		Mary J. "	15	F				" "		1		
		Daniel "	13	m				" "		1		
		Charles W. "	11	m				" "		1		
		Christian "	9	F				" "		1		
193	193	Duncan Shaw	38	m		Farmer	1460	" "				
		C. Jane "	24	F				" "				
		M. Jenett "	3	F				" "				
		Harriet A. "	1	F				" "				
194	194	Alexander Munroe	33	m		Farmer	300	" "				
		Nancy "	47	F				" "				
		Effy "	45	F				" "				
195	195	John McD. Ray	48	m		Farmer	210	" "				
		Sarah A. "	25	F				" "				
		John A. J. "	3	m				" "				
		Samuel J. "	2	m				" "				
		William Johnson	13	m				South Carolina				
196		Archibald Ray	33	m		Farmer	770	N. Carolina				
		Ann "	28	F				" "				
		Sarah A. "	3	F				" "				
		Daniel Ray	69	m		Gunsmith	15	" "				
		Catharine "	72	F				" "				
		Mary "	39	F				" "				
197	197	Archibald Campbell	43	m		Farmer	300	" "				
		Nancy "	36	F				" "				
		Margaret C. "	17	F				" "				
		John "	15	M				" "				
		Daniel J. "	2	m				" "				
		Mary A. "	12	F				" "				

m 20
F 22

SCHEDULE I.—Free Inhabitants in 8 **in the County of** Moore **State of** N. Carolina **enumerated by me, on the** 26th **day of** August **1850.** N. McCrummen **Ass't Marshal.**

367

179

Line	Dwelling-houses numbered in the order of visitation.	Families numbered in the order of visitation.	The Name of every Person whose usual place of abode on the first day of June, 1850, was in this family.	Age.	Sex.	Color, {White, black, or mulatto.	Profession, Occupation, or Trade of each Male Person over 15 years of age.	Value of Real Estate owned.	Place of Birth. Naming the State, Territory, or Country.	Married within the year.	Attended School within the year.	Persons over 20 y'rs of age who cannot read & write.	Whether deaf and dumb, blind, insane, idiotic, pauper, or convict.
	1	2	3	4	5	6	7	8	9	10	11	12	13
1			Nancy Campbell	68	F				Scotland				
2			Jane E. "	5	F				N. Carolina				
3			John Shaw	5	M				" "				
4	198	198	Malcom McBlue	47	M		Farmer	1000	" "				
5			Flora "	36	F				" "				
6			Margaret "	6	F				" "				
7			Sarah A. "	5	F				" "				
8			John C. "	3	M				" "				
9			Catharine "	2	F				" "				
10			Malcom J. "	1/12	M				" "				
11	199	199	Daniel McNeill	72	M		Farmer	1200	Scotland				
12			Margaret "	65	F				N. Carolina			1	
13			Mary "	42	F				" "				
14			Catharine "	31	F				" "				
15			Mary McKinnon	62	F				Scotland			1	
16	200	200	Malcom McNeill	35	M		Farmer		N. Carolina				
17			Flora "	27	F				" "				
18			Sarah E. "	2	F				" "				
19			Daniel A. "	4/12	M				" "				
20	201	201	Archibald Buchan	61	M		Farmer	1000	" "				
21			Mary "	40	F				" "				
22			Danl. McL. "	32	M		Farmer		" "				
23			Sarah	18	F				" "				
24			James A. J.	11	M				" "		1		
25			Mary J.	9	F				" "		1		
26			Jonathan E.	5	M				" "				
27			Harriet A.	2	F				" "				
28			Frances E.	3/12	F				" "				
29			Margaret E.	3/12	F				" "				
30			Murdo J. McSween	14	M				" "		1		
31	202	202	John M. Johnson	34	M		Farmer	500	" "				
32			Margaret "	41	F				" "				
33			Evander McN. "	10	M				" "		1		
34			Sarah A. "	5	F				" "				
35			Margaret A. "	2	F				" "				
36	203	203	Christian McDonald	66	F				Scotland				
37	204	204	Archibald Blue	53	M		Farmer	2000	N. Carolina				
38			Jannet "	52	F				" "				
39			Daniel "	23	M		Farmer	50	" "		1		
40			Margaret "	21	F				" "		1		
41			Mary E. "	19	F				" "		1		
42			Evander McN. "	16	M		Farmer		" "		1		

m 17
f 25

SCHEDULE I.—Free Inhabitants in ______ in the County of Moore State of N Carolina enumerated by me, on the 27th day of August 1850. N McCrummen Ass't Marshal.

Dwelling-houses numbered in the order of visitation.	Families numbered in the order of visitation.	The Name of every Person whose usual place of abode on the first day of June, 1850, was in this family.	Description: Age.	Description: Sex.	Description: Color, White, black, or mulatto.	Profession, Occupation, or Trade of each Male Person over 15 years of age.	Value of Real Estate owned.	Place of Birth. Naming the State, Territory, or Country.	Married within the year.	Attended School within the year.	Persons over 20 y'rs of age who cannot read & write.	Whether deaf and dumb, blind, insane, idiotic, pauper, or convict.
1	2	3	4	5	6	7	8	9	10	11	12	13
		John A. B. Blue	11	M				N Carolina		1		
205	205	Patrick J. Munroe	51	M		Farmer	400	" "				
		Catharine "	48	F				" "				
		Alexander "	22	M		Farmer		" "				
		Archibald B. "	20	M		Farmer		" "				
		William B. "	18	M		Farmer		" "				
		Sarah "	15	F				" "		1		
		Hugh B. "	12	M				" "		1		
		Flora M. "	7	F				" "		1		
		Daniel R. "	3	M				" "				
206	206	Duncan M. Blue	51	M		Farmer	600	" "				
		John S. "	22	M		Farmer		" "				
		Christian "	20	F				" "				
		Catharine "	19	F				" "				Idiotic
		Sarah "	15	F				" "		1		
		Duncan C. "	13	M				" "		1		
		Patrick H. C. "	11	M				" "				
		William C. "	9	M				" "		1		
207	207	Nancy McDonald	50	F			400	" "				
		Margaret "	45	F				" "				
		Catharine "	40	F				" "				
		Mary Black	31	F			500	" "				
		Archibald Caddell	31	M		Farmer	100	" "			1	
208	208	Neill McDonald	43	M		Farmer	350	" "				
		Margaret A. "	32	F				" "				
		Daniel "	10	M				" "		1	-	
		Sarah J. "	8	F				" "		1		
		Mary A. "	6	F				" "		1		
		Eliza C. "	4	F				" "				
		Angus	3	M				" "				
209	209	Angus McDonald	82	M		Farmer	350	Scotland			1	
		Dugald "	50	M		Tailor	54	Ditto				
		Catharine "	45	F				N. Carolina				
		Mary "	43	F				" "				
		William Caddell	17	M		Tailor		" "				
210	210	John McN. Ferguson	31	M		Farmer	300	" "				
		Margaret McNeill	55	F				" "				
		Mary "	50	F				" "				
211	211	John B. Black	44	M		Farmer	250	" "				
		Catharine "	32	F				" "				
		George W.	11	M				" "		1		
		Ann E.	7	F				" "		1		

M 22
F 20

SCHEDULE I.—Free Inhabitants in ____________ in the County of *Moore* State of *N Carolina* enumerated by me, on the *27th* day of *August* 1850. *N. McCrummen* Ass't Marshal. *369*

180

Dwelling-houses numbered in the order of visitation.	Families numbered in the order of visitation.	The Name of every Person whose usual place of abode on the first day of June, 1850, was in this family.	Description: Age.	Description: Sex.	Description: Color, White, black, or mulatto.	Profession, Occupation, or Trade of each Male Person over 15 years of age.	Value of Real Estate owned.	Place of Birth. Naming the State, Territory, or Country.	Married within the year.	Attended School within the year.	Persons over 20 y'rs of age who cannot read & write.	Whether deaf and dumb, blind, insane, idiotic, pauper, or convict.	
1	2	3	4	5	6	7	8	9	10	11	12	13	
		Eugenia E. Black	5	F				N Carolina					1
		Mary E. "	4	F				" "					2
212	212	Effie Black	75	F				" "					3
		Margaret "	47	F				" "					4
		Flora E. "	35	F				" "					5
213	213	Patrick M. Blue	43	M		Farmer	800	" "					6
		Sarah E. "	34	F				" "					7
		Mary J. "	4	F				" "					8
		John A. "	1	M				" "					9
214	214	Daniel B. Black	39	M		Farmer	350	" "					10
		Ann "	35	F				" "					11
		Mary J. McDonald	26	F				" "					12
		Margaret "	2	F				" "					13
		John F. "	1	M				" "					14
215	215	Ann Currie	53	F			305	" "					15
		Archibald C.	25	M		Student		" "		1			16
		Duncan A.	23	M		Farmer		" "		1			17
216	216	Duncan C. Blue	69	M		Farmer	1200	" "					18
		Sarah "	44	F				" "					19
		Margaret "	25	F				" "					20
		Catharine J. "	22	F				" "					21
		Sarah E. "	20	F				" "		1			22
		Mary E. "	18	F				" "		1			23
		Martha "	16	F				" "		1			24
		John P. "	15	M				" "		1			25
		Duncan "	12	M				" "		1			26
		Malcom P. N. "	10	M				" "		1			27
		Talitha "	8	F				" "					28
		William D. "	6	M				" "					29
		Mardo J. "	4	M				" "					30
217	217	Daniel McKeithen	60	M		Farmer	2000	" "					31
		Scinthy "	56	F				" "					32
		Archibald "	35	M		Teacher		" "					33
		Alexander J. "	26	M		Farmer		" "					34
		Martha A. S. "	25	F				" "					35
		Daniel P. "	21	M		Farmer		" "					36
		Neill "	18	M		Farmer		" "		1			37
		James P. B. "	14	M				" "		1			38
		Lydia "	10	F				" "					39
218	218	John McNeill	53	M		Farmer	325	" "					40
		Nancy "	37	F				" "					41
		William "	22	M		Farmer		" "		1			42

M 20
F 22

SCHEDULE I.—Free Inhabitants in ________ in the County of Moore State of N. Carolina enumerated by me, on the 28th day of August 1850. N. McCrimmon Ass't Marshal.

	Dwelling-houses numbered in the order of visitation.	Families numbered in the order of visitation.	The Name of every Person whose usual place of abode on the first day of June, 1850, was in this family.	Description: Age.	Sex.	Color, White, black, or mulatto.	Profession, Occupation, or Trade of each Male Person over 15 years of age.	Value of Real Estate owned.	Place of Birth. Naming the State, Territory, or Country.	Married within the year.	Attended School within the year.	Persons over 20 yrs of age who cannot read & write.	Whether deaf and dumb, blind, insane, idiotic, pauper, or convict.
	1	2	3	4	5	6	7	8	9	10	11	12	13
1			Catharine McNeill	20	F				N. Carolina				
2			Margret "	18	F				" "				
3			Angus McNeill	16	M		Farmer		" "		1		
4	219	219	John D. McDonald	42	M		Farmer	300	" "				
5			Jane "	32	F				" "				
6			Daniel E. "	14	M				" "		1		
7			Adam "	11	M				" "		1		
8			Margaret "	10	F				" "		1		
9			William "	8	M				" "				
10			John A. "	5	M				" "				
11			Hiram D. "	3	M				" "				
12			Lydia J. "	1	F				" "				
13	220	220	Daniel McDonald	64	M		Farmer	1097	" "				
14			Margaret "	67	F				" "			1	
15			Anna "	22	F				" "				
16	221	221	Christian McDonald	50	F			400	Scotland			1	
17			Donald B. McDonald	28	M		Farmer		N. Carolina				
18			Catharine "	26	F				" "				
19			Archibald "	24	M		Farmer		" "				
20			Catharine "	8	F				" "		1		
21	222	222	Margaret McCallum	67	F				" "				
22			Elizabeth "	27	F				" "				
23	223	223	John M. Curry	50	M		Farmer	100	" "				
24			Mary "	39	F				" "				
25			Flora "	52	F				" "			1	
26			Catharine A. "	21	F				" "				
27			Neill B. "	14	M				" "		1		
28			Betsey "	11	F				" "		1		
29			John H. "	9	M				" "				
30			Daniel A. "	7	M				" "		1		
31			Jane "	7	F				" "		1		
32			Effy E. "	5	F				" "				
33			Helena "	3	F				" "				
34			Duncan B. "	1	M				" "				
35	224	224	John Patterson	81	M		Farmer	600	" "				
36			Mary "	45	F				" "				
37			Samuel D. "	8	M				" "				
38	225	225	John M. Blue	50	M		Farmer	300	" "				
39			Margaret "	37	F				" "				
40			Mary A. "	21	F				" "		1		
41			Malcom "	19	M		Farmer		" "		1		
42			Archibald "	17	M		Farmer		" "		1		

M 20
F 22

361

SCHEDULE I.—Free Inhabitants in 9 in the County of Moore State of N. Carolina enumerated by me, on the 28th day of August 1850. Neill McCrummen Ass't Marshal. 181

Dwelling-houses numbered in the order of visitation.	Families numbered in the order of visitation.	The Name of every Person whose usual place of abode on the first day of June, 1850, was in this family.	Age.	Sex.	Color, White, black, or mulatto.	Profession, Occupation, or Trade of each Male Person over 15 years of age.	Value of Real Estate owned.	Place of Birth. Naming the State, Territory, or Country.	Married within the year.	Attended School within the year.	Persons over 20 y'rs of age who cannot read & write.	Whether deaf and dumb, blind, insane, idiotic, pauper, or convict.
1	2	3	4	5	6	7	8	9	10	11	12	13
		Catharine Blue	16	F				N. Carolina		1		
		Eliza "	14	F				" "		1		
		John "	12	m				" "		1		
		Patrick "	11	m				" "		1		
		Elizabeth "	8	F				" "		1		
		Daniel "	2	m				" "				
226	226	Neven Ray	50	m		Farmer	250	" "				
		Effy "	47	F				" "				
		Archibald "	12	m				" "		1		
		Malcom "	10	m				" "		1		
		Catharine "	8	F				" "		1		
227	227	Daniel McCallum	53	m		Farmer	75	" "	—			
		Effy "	40	F				" "	—			
		Flora "	80	F				Scotland			1	
228	228	Mary McKinnel	52	F				N. Carolina				
		Effy "	45	F			65	" "			1	
		James K. Black	22	m		Farmer	40	" "				
229	229	Daniel McLean	61	m		Farmer	125	Scotland				
		Isabella "	69	F				N. Carolina			1	
		John K. "	31	m		Merchant	80	" "				
		Archibald "	38	m		Farmer		" "			1	
		Catharine "	27	F				" "				
230	230	Neven Ray	58	m		Farmer	600	" "				
		Effy "	47	F				" "				
		John "	25	m		Student		" "		1		
		Christiane	23	F				" "		1		
		Flora J. "	22	F				" "		1		
		Malcom "	20	m		Farmer		" "		1		
		Mary A. "	18	F				" "		1		
		Hugh M. "	16	m		Farmer		" "		1		
		Sarah "	14	F				" "		1		
		Archibald "	12	m				" "		1		
		William A. "	10	m				" "		1		
		Duncan "	7	m				" "		1		
		Nancy Ray	50	F				" "				
231	231	Malcom Black	76	m		Farmer	800	" "				
		Sarah "	60	F				Scotland			1	
		Catharine "	30	F				N. Carolina				
		Lauchlin "	22	m		Farmer		" "		1		
		Jane "	20	F				" "		1		
		John W. Smith	15	m		Labor		" "		1		
		James L. Cunningham	20	m		Student		South Carolina		1		

372

SCHEDULE I.—Free Inhabitants in ______ in the County of Moore State of N. Carolina enumerated by me, on the 29th day of August 1850. N. McCrummen Ass't Marshal.

Dwelling-houses numbered in the order of visitation.	Families numbered in the order of visitation.	The Name of every Person whose usual place of abode on the first day of June, 1850, was in this family.	Age.	Sex.	Color, White, black, or mulatto.	Profession, Occupation, or Trade of each Male Person over 15 years of age.	Value of Real Estate owned.	Place of Birth. Naming the State, Territory, or Country.	Married within the year.	Attended School within the year.	Persons over 20 y'rs of age who cannot read & write.	Whether deaf and dumb, blind, insane, idiotic, pauper, or convict.
1	2	3	4	5	6	7	8	9	10	11	12	13
232	232	John McCollum	67	m		Farmer	505	N. Carolina				
		Christian "	51	F				" "				
		John "	30	m		Farmer	75	" "				
		Hugh "	27	m		Teacher	50	" "				
		Archibald "	25	m		Farmer		" "				
		Flora A. "	23	F				" "				
		Malcom "	21	m		Farmer		" "		1		
		Angus "	14	m				" "		1		
233	233	James Ray	69	m		Farmer	500	" "				
		Flora "	45	F				" "			1	
		Catharine "	25	F				" "				
		Nancy "	18	F				" "		1		
		Elizabeth "	10	F				" "		1		
		Malcom "	2	m				" "				
234	234	James R. Cameron	37	m		Blacksmith		" "				
		Sarah "	42	F				" "				
		Harriet "	11	F				" "				
		Evander McMillan	7	m				" "				
235	235	John H. B. McDonald	56	m		Farmer	325	" "				
		Christian "	46	F				" "			1	
		James W. "	26	m		Farmer		" "				
		Jane M. "	23	F				" "				
		Mary E. "	22	F				" "		1		
		Allen "	19	m		Farmer		" "		1		
		Malcom "	17	m		Farmer		" "		1		
		Christian "	15	F				" "		1		
		Norah "	12	F				" "		1		
		Lexa "	12	F				" "		1		
		Nancy "	10	F				" "		1		
		Loveday "	8	F				" "		1		
		Betsey "	4	F				" "				
		Effy "	1	F				" "				
236	236	Archibald Curry	35	m		Farmer	600	" "				
		Sarah "	44	F				" "				
		Lauchlin B. "	11	m				" "				
		Flora A. "	9	F				" "				
		Daniel A. "	5	m				" "				
		John A. "	2	m				" "				
		James Allen	44	m	B.	Farmer		" "			1	
237	237	Daniel B. Curry	40	m	-	Farmer	200	" "				
		Jane "	32	F				" "				
		Duncan "	12	m				" "				

m 21 1 B. m

363
182

SCHEDULE I.—Free Inhabitants in ________ in the County of Moore State of N. Carolina enumerated by me, on the 30th day of August 1850. N. McCrummen Ass't Marshal.

	Dwelling-houses numbered in the order of visitation.	Families numbered in the order of visitation.	The Name of every Person whose usual place of abode on the first day of June, 1850, was in this family.	Description: Age.	Description: Sex.	Description: Color, White, black, or mulatto.	Profession, Occupation, or Trade of each Male Person over 15 years of age.	Value of Real Estate owned.	Place of Birth. Naming the State, Territory, or Country.	Married within the year.	Attended School within the year.	Persons over 20 y'rs of age who cannot read & write.	Whether deaf and dumb, blind, insane, idiotic, pauper, or convict.	
	1	2	3	4	5	6	7	8	9	10	11	12	13	
1			Lauchlin A. Curry	9	m				N. Carolina					1
2			Sarah C. "	6	F				" "					2
3			Rebecca J. "	4	F				" "					3
4	238	238	Duncan B. Curry	35	m		Farmer	150	" "					4
5			Nancy "	38	F				" "					5
6			Sarah A. "	7	F				" "					6
7			Barbara "	4	F				" "					7
8			Margaret "	3	F				" "					8
9			William C. "	1	m				" "					9
10	239	239	Green B. Fields	32	m		Farmer		" "		1	1		10
11			Ann B. "	33	F				" "					11
12			Tobias "	7	m				" "					12
13			Anderson "	6	m				" "					13
14			William "	2	m				" "					14
15	240	240	Sarah Curry	66	F			335	" "					15
16			Flora "	42	F				" "			1		16
17			Nancy B. "	34	F				" "					17
18			Jane B. "	29	F				" "					18
19			Aaron Murchison	19	m		Farmer		" "					19
20	241	241	Elizabeth Fry	40	F			300	" "					20
21			Walter A. "	21	m		Farmer		" "					21
22			Jane P. "	19	F				" "					22
23	242	242	Malcom Graham	46	m		Farmer	500	" "					23
24			Sarah A. "	19	F				" "					24
25			Henry W. "	17	m		Farmer		" "					25
26			Emiline "	16	F				" "					26
27			John W. "	14	m				" "					27
28			Margaret J. "	12	F				" "					28
29			Elizabeth A. "	10	F				" "					29
30			Noah P. "	8	m				" "					30
31			David W. "	6	m				" "					31
32			Lurina "	3	F				" "					32
33	243	243	John R. Curry	37	m		Farmer	325	" "					33
34			Jane "	40	F				" "					34
35			Flora M. "	12	F				" "					35
36			Lauchlin "	10	m				" "				Insane	36
37			Archibald "	7	m				" "					37
38			Lydia "	4	F				" "					38
39			Murdoch "	1	m				" "					39
40	244	244	Joseph Wallis	52	m		Farmer		" "			1		40
41			Chaney "	50	F				" "			1		41
42			Ruffin "	18	m		Farmer		" "					42

M 20
F 22

SCHEDULE I.—Free Inhabitants in ______ in the County of Moore State of N. Carolina enumerated by me, on the 30th day of August 1850. N. McCrummen Ass't Marshal.

Dwelling-houses numbered in the order of visitation.	Families numbered in the order of visitation.	The Name of every Person whose usual place of abode on the first day of June, 1850, was in this family.	Description: Age.	Sex.	Colour, White, black, or mulatto.	Profession, Occupation, or Trade of each Male Person over 15 years of age.	Value of Real Estate owned.	Place of Birth. Naming the State, Territory, or Country.	Married within the year.	Attended School within the year.	Persons over 20 y'rs of age who cannot read & write.	Whether deaf and dumb, blind, insane, idiotic, pauper, or convict.
1	2	3	4	5	6	7	8	9	10	11	12	13
		Seaborn Wallis	17	m		Farmer		N. Carolina				
		Alexander "	15	m		Ditto		" "				
245	245	John McKinnie	37	m		Farmer	300	" "			1	
		Ann "	30	F				" "				
		Sarah "	60	F				" "				
		Duncan "	25	m		Farmer		" "				
246	246	Norman McDonald	22	m		Farmer	300	" "				
		Anna "	38	F				" "				
		Mary "	36	F				" "				
		Catharine "	33	F				" "				
		Margaret "	20	F				" "				
		Christian "	17	F				" "				
		Allen E. "	12	m				" "				
		Malcom A. "	10	m				" "				
		Daniel C. "	7	m				" "				
247	247	John McDonald	72	m		Farmer	260	" "				
		Catharine "	64	F				" "				
		Allen "	32	m		Farmer		" "				
248	248	Andrew Graham	48	m		Farmer	900	" "				
		Martha "	22	F				" "				
		Loveday "	21	F				" "				
		Effy "	18	F				" "				
		Terry "	16	F				" "				
		Alexander "	12	M				" "				
		Deborah "	7	F				" "				
		Mary "	3	F				" "				
249	249	Sarah Graham	47	F			50	" "				
		Sarah Lancaster	22	F				" "			1	
250	250	Angus McDonald	42	m		Farmer	400	" "				
		Christian "	28	F				" "				
		Kenneth "	7	m				" "				
		Kitty M. "	5	F				" "				
		Catharine "	58	F				" "			1	
		Neill McDonald	27	m		O. S. P. Clergyman		N. C. —				
		Laura "	20	F				S Carolina —				
		Nancy Jackson	19	F				N. Carolina				
251	251	Green B. Caddell	40	m		Blacksmith		" "				
		Margaret "	38	F				" "				
		Ann J. "	18	F				" "				
		Drusilla C. "	16	F				" "		1		
		Patience "	13	F				" "				
		Neill B. "	11	m				" "				

365

SCHEDULE I.—Free Inhabitants in 10 in the County of Moore State of N. Carolina enumerated by me, on the 31st day of August 1850. W. M. Crummen Ass't Marshal. 183

Dwelling-houses numbered in the order of visitation.	Families numbered in the order of visitation.	The Name of every Person whose usual place of abode on the first day of June, 1850, was in this family.	Age.	Sex.	Color, (White, black, or mulatto.)	Profession, Occupation, or Trade of each Male Person over 15 years of age.	Value of Real Estate owned.	Place of Birth. Naming the State, Territory, or Country.	Married within the year.	Attended School within the year.	Persons over 20 y'rs of age who cannot read & write.	Whether deaf and dumb, blind, insane, idiotic, pauper, or convict.
1	2	3	4	5	6	7	8	9	10	11	12	13
		Elizabeth Caddell	9	F				N. Carolina				
		John F. 〃	6	M				〃 〃				
		Daniel 〃	1	M				〃 〃				
252	252	William Hunucker	50	M		Farmer		〃 〃				
		Celia 〃	52	F				〃 〃			1	
		Thomas 〃	21	M		Farmer		〃 〃		1		
		Margaret 〃	16	F				〃 〃		1		
		John 〃	15	M				〃 〃		1		
		Nancy 〃	12	F				〃 〃		1		
		Elizabeth 〃	12	F				〃 〃		1		
		William 〃	10	M				〃 〃				
253	253	Ephraim Oldham	35	M		Farmer		〃 〃			1	
		Sarah A. 〃	25	F				〃 〃			1	
		Nancy 〃	9	F				〃 〃				
		Green 〃	7	M				〃 〃				
		Archibald Hunucker	8	M				〃 〃				
		Mary F. Oldham	5	F				〃 〃				
		Margaret J. Hunucker	3	F				〃 〃				
		Robert D. Oldham	3	M				〃 〃				
254	254	Patience Lewis	91	F			500	〃 〃				
		Mary Martin	38	F			100	〃 〃				
		John Foy	26	M		Farmer		〃 〃				
255	255	John Lewis	45	M		Farmer	256	〃 〃				
		Elizabeth 〃	37	F				〃 〃			1	
		Sarah 〃	18	F				〃 〃				
		Patience C. 〃	16	F				〃 〃				
		Mary A. 〃	15	F				〃 〃				
		William E. 〃	13	M				〃 〃		1		
		Benjamin C. 〃	11	M				〃 〃		1		
		Martha J. 〃	9	F				〃 〃				
		John C. 〃	6	M				〃 〃				
		Margaret J. 〃	4	F				〃 〃				
		Daniel C. 〃	2/12	M				〃 〃				
256	256	Laughlin Curry	32	M		Farmer	75	〃 〃				
		Ann 〃	29	F				〃 〃				
		Sarah E. 〃	8	F				〃 〃		1		
		Henry B. 〃	6	M				〃 〃		1		
		John C. 〃	3	M				〃 〃				
		Ann C. 〃	1	F				〃 〃				
		Manna Brandine	8	M	M			〃 〃				
[illegible]	257	Cornelius Dunlap	54	M		Farmer	2900	〃 〃				
		Margaret 〃	34	F				〃 〃				

M 21 1 B m
F 21

374

SCHEDULE I.—Free Inhabitants in ________ in the County of Moore State of N. Carolina enumerated by me, on the 31st day of August 1850. N. McCrummen Ass't Marshal.

Line	Dwelling-houses numbered in the order of visitation.	Families numbered in the order of visitation.	The Name of every Person whose usual place of abode on the first day of June, 1850, was in this family.	Age.	Sex.	Color, White, black, or mulatto.	Profession, Occupation, or Trade of each Male Person over 15 years of age.	Value of Real Estate owned.	Place of Birth. Naming the State, Territory, or Country.	Married within the year.	Attended School within the year.	Persons over 20 y'rs of age who cannot read & write.	Whether deaf and dumb, blind, insane, idiotic, pauper, or convict.
	1	2	3	4	5	6	7	8	9	10	11	12	13
1			Alexander Dunlap	10	M				N. Carolina		1		
2			Daniel 〃	8	M				〃 〃		1		
3			John 〃	5	M				〃 〃		1		
4			Sarah 〃	3	F				〃 〃				
5			Cornelius 〃	2	M				〃 〃				
6			Angus 〃	1/12	M				〃 〃				
7			Anderson Moore	15	M				〃 〃		1		
8			William Chavis	12	M	M			〃 〃				
9			Mary Jones	27	F				〃 〃			1	
10			Neill Haily	19	M		Farmer		〃 〃				
11	258	258	Angus Cary	35	M		Ditto	350	〃 〃				
12			Christian 〃	28	F				〃 〃				
13			Daniel M. 〃	7	M				〃 〃		1		
14			Flora J. 〃	5	F				〃 〃				
15			Angus Mc 〃	3	M				〃 〃				
16			Hugh C. 〃	2	M				〃 〃				
17			Elizabeth Gillis	19	F				〃 〃				
18	259	259	John S. McLeod	45	M		Farmer	400	〃 〃				
19			James W. 〃	19	M		Ditto		〃 〃		1		
20			Eliza J. 〃	17	F				〃 〃		1		
21			Angus G. 〃	15	M				〃 〃		1		
22			Harriet 〃	13	F				〃 〃		1		
23			John D. 〃	11	M				〃 〃		1		
24			Mary A. 〃	8	F				〃 〃		1		
25			Lauchlin 〃	4	M				〃 〃				
26	260	260	Neill Peterson	67	M		Farmer	500	〃 〃				
27	261	261	James Monk	90	M		Farmer	150	Scotland			1	
28			Sarah 〃	45	F				N. Carolina				
29			Alexander 〃	38	M		none		〃 〃				
30	262	262	Allen McDonald	50	M		Farmer	236	Scotland			1	
31			Mary 〃	40	F				Ditto			1	
32			Alexander 〃	20	M		Farmer		Ditto		1	1	
33			Mary 〃	18	F				Ditto				
34			Sarah 〃	16	F				Ditto		1		
35			John 〃	14	M				N. Carolina		1		
36			Margaret 〃	12	F				〃 〃		1		
37			Donald 〃	10	M				〃 〃		1		
38			Christian 〃	8	F				〃 〃		1		
39			Neill 〃	6	M				〃 〃				
40	263	263	Isabella McLauchlin	80	F			170	Scotland			1	
41			Catharine 〃	48	F				Ditto			1	
42			Isabella 〃	46	F				Ditto				

M 25 — 1B M
F 17

367
184

SCHEDULE I.—Free Inhabitants in ________ **in the County of** Moore **State of** N. Carolina **enumerated by me, on the** 23 **day of** September **1850.** N. McCrummen **Ass't Marshal.**

Dwelling-houses numbered in the order of visitation.	Families numbered in the order of visitation.	The Name of every Person whose usual place of abode on the first day of June, 1850, was in this family.	Description: Age.	Sex.	Color, White, black, or mulatto.	Profession, Occupation, or Trade of each Male Person over 15 years of age.	Value of Real Estate owned.	Place of Birth. Naming the State, Territory, or Country.	Married within the year.	Attended School within the year.	Persons over 20 y'rs of age who cannot read & write.	Whether deaf and dumb, blind, insane, idiotic, pauper, or convict.
1	2	3	4	5	6	7	8	9	10	11	12	13
		Christian McLauchlin	34	F				N. Carolina				
		Lovedy "	32	F				" "				
264	264	Murde McDonald	35	M		Farmer	500	Scotland				
		Mary "	30	F				N. Carolina				
		Mary "	1	F				" "				
		Catharine "	3/12	F				" "				
265	265	Mary McDonald	70	F				Scotland			1	
		Alexander "	35	M		Farmer		Scotland				
		Sarah "	23	F				Scotland				
		John "	14	M				N. Carolina		1		
266	266	Eliza M. Rowan	53	F			1600	" "				
		Eliza J.	18	F				" "				
267	267	Isaac H. Rowan	26	M		Farmer		" "				
		Sarah "	26	F				" "				
		Richard T. "	5	M				" "				
		Archibald E. "	4	M				" "				
		William G. "	4	M				" "				
		Isaac H. "	2	M				" "				
		Robert D. "	1/12	M				" "				
		Mary McIver	58	F		Farmer	100	" "			1	
268	268	Andrew Sloan	42	M		Farmer	130	" "				
		Lydia "	45	F			130	" "				
269	269	Hugh Leach	34	M		Farmer	550	" "				
		Sarah "	23	F			100	" "				
		Martin "	19	M		Student	850	" "		1		
		Ann E. "	17	F				" "				
270	270	John A. McLeod	47	M		Carriagemaker	300	" "				
		James A. "	15	M		Farmer		" "		1		
		Lydia M. "	13	F				" "		1		
		Catharine "	11	F				" "		1		
		Sarah E. "	8	F				" "		1		
		Catharine McLeod	76	F				" "			1	
		Alexander Kelly	34	M		Farmer		" "				
271	271	John Strickland	38	M		Laborer		" "			1	
		Nancy "	27	F				" "			1	
		Ann A. "	9	F				" "		1		
		Henry W. "	6	M				" "		1		
		Christian "	2	F				" "				
272	272	Daniel C. Curry	45	M		Laborer		" "				
		Catharine "	40	F				" "				
		Kenneth "	21	M		Laborer		" "		1		
		Angus "	19	M		Laborer		" "				

m 20
F 22

SCHEDULE I.—Free Inhabitants in ___ in the County of Moore State of N. Carolina enumerated by me, on the 10th day of September 1850. N. McCrummen Ass't Marshal.

Dwelling-houses numbered in the order of visitation.	Families numbered in the order of visitation.	The Name of every Person whose usual place of abode on the first day of June, 1850, was in this family.	Description: Age.	Sex.	Color, (White, black, or mulatto.)	Profession, Occupation, or Trade of each Male Person over 15 years of age.	Value of Real Estate owned.	Place of Birth. Naming the State, Territory, or Country.	Married within the year.	Attended School within the year.	Persons over 20 years of age who cannot read & write.	Whether deaf and dumb, blind, insane, idiotic, pauper, or convict.
1	2	3	4	5	6	7	8	9	10	11	12	13
273	273	Catharine McLauchlin	50	F			600	N. Carolina				
		Martha "	23	F				" "				
		Dugald "	21	M		Farmer		" "		1		
		Robert A. "	18	M		Ditto		" "		1		
		Niell "	16	M		Ditto		" "		1		
		Nancy C. "	13	F				" "		1		
274	274	Samuel W. Stone	60	M		Farmer	130	" "				
		Catharine "	39	F				" "				
275	275	Daniel McIntosh	56	M		Hatter		" "				
		Isabella "	40	F			99	" "				
		Mary "	35	F				" "				
276	276	William Graham	36	M		Farmer	40	" "			1	
		Flora "	45	F				" "			1	
277	277	John Graham	35	M		Farmer		" "			1	
		Ann J. "	31	F				" "			1	
		Allen "	4	M				" "				
		Mary J. "	4/12	F				" "				
278	278	James Graham	45	M		Farmer	30	" "			1	
279	279	Donald Kelly	72	M		Farmer	900	Scotland			1	
		Donald "	21	M		Farmer		N. Carolina				
		Mary "	19	F				" "				
		James "	18	M		Farmer		" "		1		
		Angus "	15	M		Ditto		" "		1		
		John "	13	M				" "		1		
		Cornelius "	11	M				" "		1		
280	280	John N. Ferguson	51	M		Farmer	600	Scotland				
		Christian "	40	F				N. Carolina				
		John "	11	M				" "		1		
		Nancy McDonald	40	F				" "				
281	281	Duncan M. Munroe	31	M		Farmer	240	" "				
		Rebecca A. "	28	F				" "			1	
		William E. "	7	M				" "		1		
		Martha J. "	6	F				" "				
		John T. "	5	M				" "				
		James A. "	3	M				" "				
		Patrick R. "	2	M				" "				
		Rebecca E. "	11/12	F				" "				
282	282	John McNeill "	43	M		Farmer	700	" "				
		Martha E. "	38	F				" "				
		Malcom A. "	19	M		Farmer		" "		1		
		John N. "	16	M		Farmer		" "		1		
		Sarah J. "	13	F				" "		1		

M-25
F-17

11 369

SCHEDULE I.—Free Inhabitants in ____________ in the County of Moore State 185
of N. Carolina enumerated by me, on the 4th day of Septem 1850. Neill McCrummen Ass't Marshal.

Line	Dwelling-houses numbered in the order of visitation	Families numbered in the order of visitation	The Name of every Person whose usual place of abode on the first day of June, 1850, was in this family.	Age	Sex	Color, (White, black, or mulatto)	Profession, Occupation, or Trade of each Male Person over 15 years of age.	Value of Real Estate owned.	Place of Birth. Naming the State, Territory, or Country.	Married within the year.	Attended School within the year.	Persons over 20 y'rs of age who cannot read & write.	Whether deaf and dumb, blind, insane, idiotic, pauper, or convict.
	1	2	3	4	5	6	7	8	9	10	11	12	13
1			Mary C. McNeill	12	F				N. Carolina		1		
2			Martha N. "	8	F				" "		1		
3			Isabella "	4	F				" "		1		
4			Neill D. "	3	m				" "				
5			James A. "	1	m				" "				
6			William Miller	40	m		Laborer		Pennsylvania				
7	283	283	Parham Y. Oats	33	m		Farmer	400	N. Carolina				
8			Nancy "	20	F				" "				
9			Quincy A. "	1	m				" "				
10	284	284	Lockart Fry	66	m		Farmer	4000	" "				
11			Annette "	2	F				" "				
12	285	285	Stephen Graham	52	m		Farmer	60	" "				
13			Mary "	37	F				" "			1	
14			Margaret "	12	F				" "				
15	286	286	Andrew Medlin	27	m		Farmer		" "			1	
16			Deborah "	44	F				" "				
17			Alexander "	17	m		Farmer	30	" "				
18			Sarah A. "	11	F				" "				
19			Andrew "	6	m				" "				
20	287	287	Kizza Graham	72	F			20	" "			1	
21	287	287	Alexander McIntosh	25	m		Farmer	20	" "	—		1	
22			Matricia "	19	F				" "	—			
23	288	288	John C. Ferguson	25	m		Farmer		" "				
24			Sarah "	40	F				" "				
25	289	289	Mary McNeill	68	F			1000	" "				
26			Neill K. "	25	m		Farmer		" "				
27			Thomas J. "	20	m				" "				Idiot
28			Catharine McDonald	22	F				" "				
29	290	290	Peter Kelly	70	m		Farmer	1000	Scotland			1	
30			Christian "	29	F				N. Carolina				
31			Daniel "	26	m		Farmer		" "				
32			Flora "	23	F				" "				
33			Margaret Robertson	31	F				" "				
34			Mary C. "	4	F				" "				
35			Noah Jackson	8	m				" "				
36	291	291	Archibald McDonald	66	m		Farmer	800	Scotland			1	
37			Margaret "	65	F				"			1	
38			Donald "	31	m		Farmer	600	N. Carolina				
39			Nancy "	25	F				" "				
40			Celia "	23	F				" "				
41	292	292	Nancy McLeod	60	F			450	Scotland				
42			Dorothy McIver	56	F				"				

M 19
F 23

SCHEDULE I.—Free Inhabitants in ______ in the County of Moore State of N. Carolina enumerated by me, on the 5th day of September 1850. A. McCrummen Ass't Marshal.

Dwelling-houses numbered in the order of visitation.	Families numbered in the order of visitation.	The Name of every Person whose usual place of abode on the first day of June, 1850, was in this family.	Age.	Sex.	Color, {White, black, or mulatto.	Profession, Occupation, or Trade of each Male Person over 15 years of age.	Value of Real Estate owned.	Place of Birth. Naming the State, Territory, or Country.	Married within the year.	Attended School within the year.	Persons over 20 y'rs of age who cannot read & write.	Whether deaf and dumb, blind, insane, idiotic, pauper, or convict.
1	2	3	4	5	6	7	8	9	10	11	12	13
293	293	Angus McDonald	81	m		Farmer	100	Scotland				
		Sarah "	78	F				"			1	
		Allen I. "	36	m		Farmer	50	N. Carolina				
		Malvina "	18	F				" "				
		Nelly "	38	F				" "				
		William In	2	m				" "				
294	294	Charles Medlin	50	m		Farmer	100	" "				
		Mary "	43	F				" "			1	
		Angus "	20	m		Farmer		" "				
		Melinda "	17	F				" "				
		Letha "	16	F				" "				
		Neill "	11	m				" "				
		Nelly "	11	F				" "				
		Jacob "	7	m				" "				
		Emeline "	3	F				" "				
295	295	Daniel McDonald	40	m		Farmer	1107	" "				
		Christian "	15	F				" "		1		
		Margaret "	13	F				" "		1		
		Donald P. "	10	m				" "		1		
		Murdoch McS. "	8	m				" "		1		
296	296	John McDonald	45	m		Farmer	3000	" "				
		Nancy "	37	F				" "				
		Daniel R. "	18	m		Farmer		" "		1		
		Margaret "	16	F				" "		1		
		Catharine "	14	F				" "		1		
		Mary I. "	11	F				" "		1		
		Kenneth "	9	m				" "		1		
		Elizabeth "	6	F				" "		1		
		James K. P. "	3	m				" "				
		John "	4/12	m				" "				
297	297	Archibald McMillan	35	m		Farmer		" "				
		Sarah A. "	31	F				" "				
		Eliza I. "	8	F				" "				
		Louisa B. "	7	F				" "				
		John A. "	5	m				" "				
		Christian M. "	2	F				" "				
		John A. Ferguson	28	m		Farmer		" "				
298	298	Murdoch Ferguson	60	m		Farmer		Scotland			1	
299	299	John Ferguson	50	m		Farmer	25	"				
		Christian "	45	F				N. Carolina				
		Catharine "	20	F				" "		1		
		William "	18	m		Farmer		" "		1		

M 21
F 21

SCHEDULE I.—Free Inhabitants in ______ in the County of Moore State of N. Carolina enumerated by me, on the 5th day of September 1850. N. McCrummen Ass't Marshal.

371

186

Dwelling-houses numbered in the order of visitation.	Families numbered in the order of visitation.	The Name of every Person whose usual place of abode on the first day of June, 1850, was in this family.	Description: Age.	Sex.	Color, White, black, or mulatto.	Profession, Occupation, or Trade of each Male Person over 15 years of age.	Value of Real Estate owned.	Place of Birth. Naming the State, Territory, or Country.	Married within the year.	Attended School within the year.	Persons over 20 y'rs of age who cannot read & write.	Whether deaf and dumb, blind, insane, idiotic, pauper, or convict.	
1	2	3	4	5	6	7	8	9	10	11	12	13	
		Angus Ferguson	16	m		Farmer		N. Carolina					1
		Peter "	14	m				" "					2
		James "	12	m				" "					3
		Archibald "	9	m				" "		/			4
		Sarah "	8	F				" "					5
		Flora McDonald	50	F				" "			/		6
300	300	Mary Collins	68	F				" "			/		7
		Margaret "	39	F				" "			/		8
		Nancy "	37	F				" "			/		9
		Jane "	30	F				" "			/		10
		James H. "	9	m				" "					11
		Sarah Collins	66	F				" "			/		12
		Margaret "	26	F				" "			/		13
		John T. "	1	m				" "					14
301	301	Joseph H. M. Bynum	22	m		Farmer		" "	—				15
		Mary A. M. "	17	F				" "	—				16
302	302	Malcom Turner	66	m		Farmer	316	Scotland					17
		Isabella "	64	F				"			/		18
		Daniel "	35	m		Farmer		"					19
		Lydia "	34	F				N. Carolina					20
		Alexander "	30	m		Physician		Scotland					21
303	303	Archibald Smith	45	m		Farmer		N. Carolina			/		22
		Mary "	45	F				" "					23
		Daniel A. S. "	17	m		Farmer	75	" "		/			24
		James "	16	m		Farmer		" "		/			25
		Neill "	12	m				" "		/			26
		Anabella "	11	F				" "		/			27
		Stephen "	8	m				" "		/			28
304	304	Sarah Smith	75	F				" "			/		29
		Margaret "	24	F				" "			/		30
		Sarah "	20	F				" "		/			31
		Winniford "	16	F				" "		/			32
		William "	1	m				" "					33
305	305	William Johnson	46	m		Millwright	1200	" "					34
		Sarah J. "	32	F				" "					35
		Mary E. "	15	F				" "					36
		John A. "	13	m				" "					37
		Archibald "	11	m				" "					38
		Isabella "	10	F				" "					39
		Samuel "	7	m				" "					40
		Ann M. "	4	F				" "					41
		William B. "	11/12	m				" "					42

m 21
Fe 21

SCHEDULE I.—Free Inhabitants in ______ in the County of Moore State of N. Carolina enumerated by me, on the 6th day of September 1850. N. McCrummen Ass't Marshal.

Dwelling-houses numbered in the order of visitation.	Families numbered in the order of visitation.	The Name of every Person whose usual place of abode on the first day of June, 1850, was in this family.	Age.	Sex.	Color, White, black, or mulatto.	Profession, Occupation, or Trade of each Male Person over 15 years of age.	Value of Real Estate owned.	Place of Birth. Naming the State, Territory, or Country.	Married within the year.	Attended School within the year.	Persons over 20 y'rs of age who cannot read & write.	Whether deaf and dumb, blind, insane, idiotic, pauper, or convict.
1	2	3	4	5	6	7	8	9	10	11	12	13
306	306	Hugh Keith	74	m		Farmer	700	Scotland				
		Catharine "	59	F				"				
		Duncan "	38	m		Farmer		N. Carolina				
		Elizabeth A. "	36	F				" "				
		Mary "	34	F				" "				
		Margaret "	32	F				" "				
		Effy J. "	24	F				" "				
		Hugh "	22	m		Farmer		" "				
		John "	20	m		Farmer		" "				
307	307	Peter Munroe	40	m		Farmer	600	" "				
		Mary "	38	F				" "				
		Sarah A. "	11	F				" "		1		
		John "	9	m				" "		1		
		Mary "	5	F				" "		1		
		Hector "	3	m				" "				
308	308	Finlay McFadyen	50	m		Farmer	430	" "				
		Effy "	39	F				" "				
		Neill "	20	m		Farmer		" "		1		
		Duncan "	18	m		Farmer		" "		1		
		Colin "	16	m		Farmer		" "		1		
		Archibald "	14	m				" "		1		
		Christian M. "	12	F				" "		1		
		Mary A. "	10	F				" "		1		
		Loveday J. "	8	F				" "		1		
		Sarah C. "	6	F				" "		1		
		Martha E. "	5	F				" "				
		Lydia J. "	2	F				" "				
309	309	Mary Cameron	69	F				" "				
		Mary "	32	F				" "				
		John "	30	m		Millwright	600	" "				
		Margaret "	24	F				" "				
310	310	Archibald Johnson	33	m		Farmer	25	" "				
		Emma "	24	F				" "				
311	311	Frances Johnson	40	F			120	" "				
		Catharine "	24	F				" "				
312	[illegible]	Hugh A. Cameron	55	m		Farmer	800	" "				
		Catharine "	45	F				Scotland				
		Daniel "	21	m		Farmer		N. Carolina				
		Sarah "	19	F				" "				
313	313	Archibald L. Cameron	43	m		Farmer	500	" "				
		Isabella "	32	F				" "				
		Archibald "	14	m				" "		1		

M 18
F 24

12 373 187

Schedule I.—Free Inhabitants in ______________ **in the County of** *Moore* **State of** *N. Carolina* **enumerated by me, on the** *7th* **day of** *September* **1850.** *N. McCrummen* **Ass't Marshal.**

Dwelling-houses numbered in the order of visitation.	Families numbered in the order of visitation.	The Name of every Person whose usual place of abode on the first day of June, 1850, was in this family.	Description. Age.	Sex.	Color, White, black, or mulatto.	Profession, Occupation, or Trade of each Male Person over 15 years of age.	Value of Real Estate owned.	Place of Birth. Naming the State, Territory, or Country.	Married within the year.	Attended School within the year.	Persons over 20 y'rs of age who cannot read & write.	Whether deaf and dumb, blind, insane, idiotic, pauper, or convict.
1	2	3	4	5	6	7	8	9	10	11	12	13
		John Cameron	12	M				N. Carolina		1		
		James "	12	M				" "		1		
		Mary A. "	10	F				" "		1		
		Catharine J. "	8	F				" "		1		
		Neill "	6	M				" "				
		Adelaid "	3	F				" "				
314	314	Stokes Roberts	47	M		Farmer		" "			1	
		Kitsey "	34	F				" "				
		Mary M. "	14	F				" "				
		Franklin "	12	M				" "				
		John T. "	3	M				" "				
		Alexander J. "	1	M				" "				
315	315	John T. Cameron	43	M		Farmer	800	" "				
		Mary "	42	F				" "				
		Daniel "	18	M		Farmer		" "		1		
		Patrick "	15	M		Farmer		" "		1		
		Mary "	13	F				" "		1		
		John A. "	11	M				" "		1		
		Alexander "	9	M				" "		1		
		Nancy "	6	F				" "		1		
316	316	Isabella Baker	60	F			334	" "				
317	317	Neill Cameron	47	M		Farmer	300	" "				
		Flora "	25	F				" "				
		John Shaw	26	M		Carpenter		" "				
318	318	Alexander Cameron	73	M		Farmer	350	" "				
		Flora "	47	F				" "				
319	319	Paul Allen	65	M		Farmer	300	" "			1	
		Sarah "	55	F				" "			1	
		William "	17	M		Farmer		" "				
320	320	John McD. Cameron	32	M		Farmer	150	" "				
		Jennet "	27	F				" "				
		John "	7	M				" "				
		Mary "	5	F				" "				
		Benjamin "	3	M				" "				
		William A.	6/12	M				" "				
321	321	Thomas Fry	74	M		Farmer	100	" "			1	
		Malinda Medlin	17	F				" "		1		
322	322	Jesse Thompson	63	M		Farmer	2000	" "				
		Louisa "	43	F				" "			1	
		Gilbert "	22	M		Farmer		" "				
		Gaston "	19	M		Ditto		" "		1		
		Isaac "	17	M		Farmer		" "		1		

M 26
F 16

SCHEDULE I.—Free Inhabitants in ____________ in the County of *Moore* State of *N Carolina* enumerated by me, on the *7th* day of *September* 1850. *N. McCrummen* Ass't Marshal.

Dwelling-houses numbered in the order of visitation.	Families numbered in the order of visitation.	The Name of every Person whose usual place of abode on the first day of June, 1850, was in this family.	Description: Age.	Sex.	Color, White, black, or mulatto.	Profession, Occupation, or Trade of each Male Person over 15 years of age.	Value of Real Estate owned.	Place of Birth. Naming the State, Territory, or Country.	Married within the year.	Attended School within the year.	Persons over 20 y'rs of age who cannot read & write.	Whether deaf and dumb, blind, insane, idiotic, pauper, or convict.
1	2	3	4	5	6	7	8	9	10	11	12	13
		J. William Thompson	15	M		Farmer		N Carolina		1		
		Bryant "	12	M				" "		1		
		Rufus "	10	M				" "		1		
		Harriet "	7	F				" "		1		
		Narcissa "	3	F				" "				
		Zachary Taylor "	5/12	M				" "				
323	323	Daniel Graham	55	M		Farmer	50	" "				
		Nancy "	39	F				" "			1	
		David "	12	M				" "		1		
		Mary J. "	10	F				" "		1		
324	324	Garret Thompson	26	M		Farmer		" "				
		Elizabeth "	17	F				" "				
		Phebe Thompson	29	F				" "				
		Patience Grant	65	F				" "				
325	325	Thomas Matthews	31	M		Farmer	115	" "				
		Elizabeth J. "	21	F				" "				
		James C. "	2	M				" "				
326	326	John Baker	43	M		Farmer	700	" "				
		Elizabeth "	45	F				" "				
		John McF. "	18	M		Farmer		" "		1		
		Nancy "	16	F				" "		1		
		Margaret "	14	F				" "		1		
		James "	12	M				" "		1		
		Mary A. "	10	F				" "		1		
		Elizabeth "	8	F				" "		1		
		Alexander "	6	M				" "				
		Catharine "	2	F				" "				
327	327	Peyton Stokes	26	M		Farmer	65	" "			1	
		Nancy "	33	F				" "			1	
		Angus M. D.	7	M				" "		1		
		Nancy F.	3	F				" "				
		John W.	2	M				" "				
328	328	Jacob Matthews	78	M		Farmer	2200	" "				
		Catharine "	56	F				" "				
		Catharine "	26	F				" "				
		John G. "	23	M		Physician		" "				
		Joel A. "	21	M		Farmer		" "		1		
		Mary M. "	18	F				" "				
329	329	William C. Rogers	38	M		Farmer		" "				
		Jemima "	34	F				" "				
		Sarah C. "	16	F				" "		1		
		Hiram "	14	M				" "		1		

M 21
F 21

SCHEDULE I.—Free Inhabitants in ______ in the County of Moore State of N Carolina enumerated by me, on the 9th day of September 1850. N. McCrummen Ass't Marshal.

375

188

Dwelling-houses numbered in the order of visitation.	Families numbered in the order of visitation.	The Name of every Person whose usual place of abode on the first day of June, 1850, was in this family.	Age.	Sex.	Color, White, black, or mulatto.	Profession, Occupation, or Trade of each Male Person over 15 years of age.	Value of Real Estate owned.	Place of Birth. Naming the State, Territory, or Country.	Married within the year.	Attended School within the year.	Persons over 20 yr's of age who cannot read & write.	Whether deaf and dumb, blind, insane, idiotic, pauper, or convict.	
1	2	3	4	5	6	7	8	9	10	11	12	13	
		John C. Rogers	12	M				N. Carolina		1			1
		Joseph "	10	M				" "		1			2
		Priscilla "	7	F				" "		1			3
		Aaron C "	4	M				" "					4
		Rubin N "	2	M				" "					5
		Susan	1	F				" "					6
330	330	James Worthy	63	M		Farmer	1750	" "					7
		Sarah "	48	F				" "					8
		Innmanda "	17	F				" "					9
		Nancy "	14	F				" "		1			10
		John A. "	13	M				" "		1			11
		William A. Phillips	26	M		Farmer	400	" "	—				12
		Mary A. "	24	F				" "	—				13
331	331	Henry Arnold	47	M		Farmer	900	" "					14
		Mary "	36	F				" "					15
		Mary A. "	17	F				" "					16
		Sarah C. "	11	F				" "		1			17
		Elizabeth A. "	9	F				" "		1			18
		Neill T. "	7	M				" "					19
		Henry A. "	5	M				" "					20
		James	4/12	M				" "					21
		William Arnold	22	M		Merchant		" "					22
332	332	Sween M. McL McDonald	52	M		Farmer	95	" "					23
		Hannah "	52	F				" "					24
333	333	Norman McDonald	47	M		Farmer		" "					25
		Sarah K. "	39	F				" "					26
		Daniel "	19	M		Farmer		" "		1			27
		Neill "	17	M		Ditto		" "		1			28
		Mary A. "	15	F				" "		1			29
		John "	12	M				" "		1			30
		James "	12	M				" "		1			31
		Christian M. "	10	F				" "		1			32
		Elizabeth J. "	7	F				" "		1			33
		Thomas A. "	4	M				" "					34
		Norman "	2	M				" "					35
334	334	William Keith	39	M		Farmer	350	" "					36
		Sarah J. "	32	F				" "					37
		Mary J. "	13	F				" "		1			38
		Catharine "	10	F				" "		1			39
		Flora A. "	7	F				" "		1			40
		Andrew J. "	4	M				" "					41
		Jacob M. "	11/12	M				" "					42

M 23
F 19

SCHEDULE I.—Free Inhabitants in ______ **in the County of** Moore **State of** N. Carolina **enumerated by me, on the** 9th **day of** September **1850.** N. McCrummen **Ass't Marshal**

Dwelling-houses numbered in the order of visitation.	Families numbered in the order of visitation.	The Name of every Person whose usual place of abode on the first day of June, 1850, was in this family.	Description: Age.	Description: Sex.	Description: Color, White, black, or mulatto.	Profession, Occupation, or Trade of each Male Person over 15 years of age.	Value of Real Estate owned.	Place of Birth. Naming the State, Territory, or Country.	Married within the year.	Attended School within the year.	Persons over 20 y'rs of age who cannot read & write.	Whether deaf and dumb, blind, insane, idiotic, pauper, or convict.
1	2	3	4	5	6	7	8	9	10	11	12	13
335	335	Malcom McLean	60	M		Farmer	177	Scotland				
		Catharine "	40	F				N. Carolina				
		Flora "	21	F				Scotland				
		John "	19	M		Farmer		Ditto				
		Peter "	18	M		Farmer		Scotland				
		James "	13	M				Ditto		1		
336	336	John McDugald	80	M		Farmer	200	Scotland			1	
		Margaret "	81	F				Ditto			1	
337	337	Angus McDugald	66	M		Farmer	60	Ditto			1	
		Julia Kitchen	63	F				N. Carolina			1	
338	338	Margaret J. Cameron	52	F			179	" "				
		Christian "	57	F				" "				
339	339	Charles C. Johnson	46	M		Farmer	350	" "				
		Harriet A. "	43	F				" "				
		James "	23	M		Farmer		" "				
		John W. "	21	M		Ditto		" "		1		
		William J. "	18	M		Ditto		" "		1		
		Mary A. "	16	F				" "		1		
		Samuel "	13	M				" "		1		
		Charles A. "	10	M				" "		1		
		Martha J. "	6	F				" "		1		
		Richard H. "	2	M				" "				
340	340	James A. Medlin	34	M		Laborer		" "				
		Mary A. "	19	F				" "				
		Green "	1	M				" "				
341	341	Rebecca Medlin	65	F				" "			1	
		John "	36	M		Farmer		" "			1	
342	342	Margaret Medlin	40	F				" "			1	
		Emily E. "	6	F				" "				
		Archibald "	4	M				" "				
343	343	James Gilchrist	28	M		Farmer	325	" "				
		Rachael "	26	F				" "				
344	344	Duncan Munroe	55	M		Farmer	300	" "			1	
		Jane "	54	F				" "				
		Sarah "	25	F				" "			1	
		Niell "	16	M		Farmer		" "				
345	345	Willis Medlin	37	M		Shoemaker		" "			1	
		Nancy "	35	F				" "			1	
		Susannah "	8	F				" "				
		Scintha "	3	F				" "				
346	346	Allison Pierce	25	M		Farmer		" "				
		Nancy "	35	F				" "			1	

√ M 22
F 20

SCHEDULE I.—Free Inhabitants in ________ in the County of Moore State of N. Carolina enumerated by me, on the 10th day of September 1850. N. McCrummen Ass't Marshal. 377

189

Dwelling-houses numbered in the order of visitation.	Families numbered in the order of visitation.	The Name of every Person whose usual place of abode on the first day of June, 1850, was in this family.	Description: Age.	Description: Sex.	Description: Color, (White, black, or mulatto.)	Profession, Occupation, or Trade of each Male Person over 15 years of age.	Value of Real Estate owned.	Place of Birth. Naming the State, Territory, or Country.	Married within the year.	Attended School within the year.	Persons over 20 y'rs of age who cannot read & write.	Whether deaf and dumb, blind, insane, idiotic, pauper, or convict.
1	2	3	4	5	6	7	8	9	10	11	12	13
		Eliza Oats	20	F				N. Carolina				
		Elizabeth J. Allison	[illegible]	F				" "				
347	347	Neill McDonald	48	m		Hatter		" "				
		Nancy "	40	F				" "			/	
		John W. "	18	m		Laborer		" "		/		
		Margaret "	16	F				" "		/		
		James A. "	14	m				" "		/		
348	348	James Maples	42	m		Farmer		" "				
		Mary "	42	F				" "			/	
		Loveday "	12	F				" "				
		John "	10	m				" "				
		Mary C. "	9	F				" "				
		Duncan J. "	7	m				" "				
		Dugald McD. "	5	m				" "				
		Westley "	4	m				" "				
		William H.	1	m				" "				
349	349	Margaret Graham	74	F				" "			/	
		Duncan "	48	m		Farmer		" "				
350	350	Neill Graham	45	m		Farmer	200	" "				
		Catharine "	33	F				" "				
		Mary E. "	9	F				" "				
		Effy J. "	7	F				" "				
		Daniel A. "	5	m				" "				
		John M. "	4	F				" "				
		Archibald W. "	2	m				" "				
		Nancy	4/12	F				" "				
351	351	David Graham	76	m		Farmer	[illegible]	Scotland				
352	352	Alfred Willis	45	m		Ditto	350	N. Carolina				
		Eleanor "	40	F				" "				
		Mary J. "	17	F				" "		/		
		Sarah C. "	13	F				" "		/		
		Henrietta "	10	F				" "		/		
		William J. "	8	m				" "		/		
		John W. "	4	m				" "				
353	353	Dugald McDugald	47	m		Farmer	4000	" "				
		Elizabeth J. "	27	F				" "				
		Rebecca "	4	F				" "				
		Archibald "	3	m				" "				
		Neill "	5/12	m				" "				
		Daniel B. McDugald	54	m		none		" "				Deaf&Dumb
		Mary "	52	F				" "				
		Margaret "	49	F				" "				

M 21
F 21

SCHEDULE I.—Free Inhabitants in [illegible] in the County of Moore State of N. Carolina enumerated by me, on the 11th day of September 1850. N. McCrummen Ass't Marshal.

Dwelling-houses numbered in the order of visitation.	Families numbered in the order of visitation.	The Name of every Person whose usual place of abode on the first day of June, 1850, was in this family.	Age.	Sex.	Color, White, black, or mulatto.	Profession, Occupation, or Trade of each Male Person over 15 years of age.	Value of Real Estate owned.	Place of Birth. Naming the State, Territory, or Country.	Married within the year.	Attended School within the year.	Persons over 20 y'rs of age who cannot read & write.	Whether deaf and dumb, blind, insane, idiotic, pauper, or convict.
1	2	3	4	5	6	7	8	9	10	11	12	13
		Uriah Skemerhorn	30	m		Sawyer		New York				
354	354	John Jackson	34	F				N. Carolina				
		Christian "	33	F				" "			1	
		Sophia "	13	F				" "				
		Noah "	11	m				" "				
		Joseph "	1	m				" "				
355	355	Daniel McNeill	42	m		Farmer		" "				
		Nancy "	39	F				" "				
		Neill "	19	m		Laborer		" "		1		
		Mary A. "	18	F		[illegible]		" "		1		
		William "	16	m		Farmer		" "				
		John "	13	m				" "		1		
		Henry "	11	m				" "				
		Margaret "	9	F				" "		1		
		Sarah "	6	F				" "				
356	356	Archibald Graham	65	m		Farmer	350	Scotland				
		Elizabeth "	28	F				N. Carolina				
		Duncan "	26	m		Farmer		" "				
		Mary "	24	F				" "				
		Margaret "	4	F				" "				
357	357	James Gilchrist	60	m		Farmer	350	Scotland				
		George "	32	m		Farmer		"				Deaf & Dum[b]
		Catharine "	30	F				"				Deaf & dum[b]
		Elizabeth "	26	F				N. Carolina				Deaf & dum[b]
		Duncan Shaw	8	m				N. C.				
358	358	Allen B. Morrison	56	m		Farmer	250	" "				
		Flora "	51	F				Scotland			1	
		Catharine "	32	F				N. Carolina				
		Duncan "	31	m		Farmer		" "				
		William "	26	m		Farmer		" "				
		Margaret "	25	F				" "				
		Malcom "	24	m		Farmer		" "				
		Christian "	22	F				" "		1		
		Nancy "	20	F				" "		1		
		Mary "	18	F				" "		1		
		Horace "	12	m				" "		1		
359	359	George Campbell	49	m		Farmer	600	Scotland				
		John "	23	m		Farmer		N. Carolina		1		
		Hugh "	21	m		Farmer		N. C.		1		
		Daniel "	19	m		Farmer		" "		1		
		Alexander "	17	m		Farmer		" "		1		
		Flora A. "	15	F				" "		1		

M 23
F 19

SCHEDULE I.—Free Inhabitants in ________ in the County of Moore State of N. Carolina enumerated by me, on the 11th day of September 1850. N. McCrummen Ass't Marshal.

379

190

Dwelling-houses numbered in the order of visitation.	Families numbered in the order of visitation.	The Name of every Person whose usual place of abode on the first day of June, 1850, was in this family.	Age.	Sex.	Color, (White, black, or mulatto.)	Profession, Occupation, or Trade of each Male Person over 15 years of age.	Value of Real Estate owned.	Place of Birth. Naming the State, Territory, or Country.	Married within the year.	Attended School within the year.	Persons over 20 y'rs of age who cannot read & write.	Whether deaf and dumb, blind, insane, idiotic, pauper, or convict.	
1	2	3	4	5	6	7	8	9	10	11	12	13	
		Elizabeth Campbell	11	F				N. Carolina		1			1
		John Campbell	65	m		none		Scotland					2
		Hugh "	63	m		Farmer		"					3
		Mary "	52	F				"					4
360	360	Elizabeth Starling	28	F			50	N. Carolina			1		5
		William R. "	21	m		Farmer		" "					6
		Margaret "	18	F				" "					7
		James A. "	2	m				" "					8
361	361	Thomas Cole	37	m		Farmer	50	" "					9
		Eleanor "	36	F				" "			1		10
362	362	Hartart Cole	33	m		Farmer	50	" "					11
		Catharine "	27	F				" "			1		12
		Elizabeth "	7	F				" "		1			13
		John C. "	6	m				" "					14
		James "	4	m				" "					15
		Lucinda "	3	F				" "					16
		Jesse "	1	m				" "					17
363	363	Archibald Smith	40	m		Farmer	250	" "					18
		Anna "	35	F				" "					19
		Malcam "	12	m				" "					20
		Hector "	9	m				" "					21
		Margaret "	6	F				" "					22
		Mary A. "	12	F				" "					23
		Nancy Smith	42	F				" "					24
364	364	David J. Wicker	38	m		Farmer		" "					25
		Priscilla "	26	F				" "			1		26
		Mary "	7	F				" "					27
		Eliza "	4	F				" "					28
365	365	Alexander Johnson	45	m		Cooper		" "					29
		Sarah J. "	37	F				" "					30
		Nancy "	18	F				" "					31
		Mary J. "	16	F				" "					32
		Dugald "	14	m			150	" "					33
366	366	Malcom Johnson	64	m		Farmer	500	" "					34
		Ann "	62	F				" "			1		35
		Margaret "	42	F				" "					36
		Flora "	38	F				" "					37
		Eliza "	24	F				" "					38
		Daniel "	22	m		Farmer		" "					39
		Westley "	18	m		Farmer		" "					40
		Eleanor "	7	F				" "					41
		Malcom "	4	m				" "					42

m 19
F 23

SCHEDULE I.—Free Inhabitants in ______ in the County of Moore State of N. Carolina enumerated by me, on the 12 day of September 1850. N. McCrummen Ass't Marshal.

Dwelling-houses numbered in the order of visitation.	Families numbered in the order of visitation.	The Name of every Person whose usual place of abode on the first day of June, 1850, was in this family.	Description: Age.	Description: Sex.	Description: Color, White, black, or mulatto.	Profession, Occupation, or Trade of each Male Person over 15 years of age.	Value of Real Estate owned.	Place of Birth. Naming the State, Territory, or Country.	Married within the year.	Attended School within the year.	Persons over 20 y'rs of age who cannot read & write.	Whether deaf and dumb, blind, insane, idiotic, pauper, or convict.
1	2	3	4	5	6	7	8	9	10	11	12	13
367	367	John A. Johnson	39	m		Farmer	250	N. Carolina				
		Sarah "	24	F				" "				
		Daniel "	16	m		Farmer		" "				
		Mary A. "	13	F				" "				
		Margaret "	12	F				" "				
		John "	10	m				" "				
		Jane "	8	F				" "				
		Jennet J. "	6	F				" "				
		Samuel "	2	m				" "				
368	368	Malcom Johnson	39	m		Farmer	210	" "				
		Mary "	38	F				" "				
369	369	Elizabeth Savage	74	F			25	" "				
		Barbara "	44	F				" "			1	
		Hector McKinnon	15	m				" "				
370	370	Sarah Pierce	35	F				" "			1	
		John "	28	m		Laborer		" "			1	
		David B. M.	1	M				" "				
		Margaret J. "	3/12	F				" "				
371	371	Neill Savage	35	m		Farmer	50	" "				
		Isabella "	26	F				" "			1	
		Ann M. "	7	F				" "				
		Thomas J. "	5	m				" "				
		Mary J. "	2	F				" "				
		Uriah S. "	6/12	m				" "				
372	372	Mirriam Savage	39	F			50	" "			1	
		Tidings Cameron	19	m		Farmer		" "				
		Elizabeth McDonald	13	F				" "				
373	373	Duncan Cameron	73	m		Farmer	40	" "				
		Catharine "	60	F				" "				
		Jennet Johnson	11	F				" "				
374	374	Hardy Pierce	28	m		Farmer		" "				
		Catharine "	32	F				" "				
		Thomas B. "	2	m				" "				
		Malcom "	7/12	m				" "				
		Duncan "	7/12	m				" "				
375	375	Jane Pierce	47	F			75	" "			1	
		Archibald "	18	m		Farmer		" "				
		James "	16	m		Farmer		" "				
376	376	Daniel Buie	58	m		Farmer	300	" "				
		Lucy "	50	F				" "			1	
		Fanny "	23	F				" "				
		Sarah "	21	F				" "				

m 20
F 22

14

191

381

SCHEDULE I.—Free Inhabitants in ______ in the County of Moore State of N. Carolina enumerated by me, on the 12th day of September 1850. A. McCrummen Ass't Marshal.

Dwelling-houses numbered in the order of visitation.	Families numbered in the order of visitation.	The Name of every Person whose usual place of abode on the first day of June, 1850, was in this family.	Age.	Sex.	Color, white, black, or mulatto.	Profession, Occupation, or Trade of each Male Person over 15 years of age.	Value of Real Estate owned.	Place of Birth. Naming the State, Territory, or Country.	Married within the year.	Attended School within the year.	Persons over 20 y'rs of age who cannot read & write.	Whether deaf and dumb, blind, insane, idiotic, pauper, or convict.
1	2	3	4	5	6	7	8	9	10	11	12	13
		Selbey Buie	19	F				N. Carolina				
		Daniel "	17	M		Farmer		" "				
		John D. "	15	M				" "				
		Baily "	13	M				" "				
		Lucy "	10	F				" "				
377	377	Allen Buie	38	M		Farmer	250	" "				
378	378	William Buie	33	M		Farmer	280	" "				
		Ann "	30	F				" "				
		Mary "	28	F				" "				
379	379	Christian Johnson	51	F			125	" "				
		John K. Johnson	29	M		Farmer		" "				
		Anna	22	F				" "				
380	380	Samuel Johnson	47	M		Farmer	300	" "				
		Martha E. "	30	F				" "				
		Mary A. "	11	F				" "		1		
		Sarah C. "	9	F				" "		1		
		Thomas "	7	M				" "		1		
		Frances "	5	F				" "		1		
		Jennet "	4	F				" "				
		Margaret "	3	F				" "				
		Martha E. "	3/12	F				" "				
381	381	Archibald Buie	58	M		Farmer	500	" "				
		Sarah "	53	F				" "			1	
		Isabella "	51	F				" "			1	
		Jennet A. "	20	F				" "				
382	382	William Buie	53	M		Teacher	300	" "				
		Mary "	48	F				" "				
383	383	Collin McFadyen	49	M		Farmer	1000	" "				
		Linda "	32	F				" "				
		Mary J. "	11	F				" "				
		Annabella "	9	F				" "				
		Niell "	8	M				" "				
		John "	6	M				" "				
		Gideon "	4	M				" "				
		Sarah "	2	F				" "				
[illegible]	384	Brooks Parish	75	M		Farmer		" "			1	
		Christian "	64	F				" "			1	
		Sarah "	35	F				" "			1	
		Elizabeth "	24	F				" "				
		Thomas "	22	M		Farmer		" "				
[illegible]	385	Catharine McDugald	36	F			100	" "				
		Flora McDugald	16	F				" "				

M16

SCHEDULE I.—Free Inhabitants in ______ in the County of Moore State of N Carolina enumerated by me, on the 13th day of September 1850. N. McCrummen Ass't Marshal.

	Dwelling-houses numbered in the order of visitation.	Families numbered in the order of visitation.	The Name of every Person whose usual place of abode on the first day of June, 1850, was in this family.	Age.	Sex.	Color, White, black, or mulatto.	Profession, Occupation, or Trade of each Male Person over 15 years of age.	Value of Real Estate owned.	Place of Birth, Naming the State, Territory, or Country.	Married within the year.	Attended School within the year.	Persons over 20 y'rs of age who cannot read & write.	Whether deaf and dumb, blind, insane, idiotic, pauper, or convict.
	1	2	3	4	5	6	7	8	9	10	11	12	13
1			Martha McDugald	10	F				N. Carolina		1		
2			Sarah C. "	8	F				" "		1		
3			Elizabeth "	1	F				" "				
4			Nancy McDugald	13	F				" "		1		
5			Leroy Parish	80	M		Farmer		" "			1	
6			Daniel Morris	21	M		Farmer		" "				
7	386	386	Jane Munroe	60	F			100	" "			1	
8			Dugald "	22	M		Laborer		" "				
9	387	387	Alexander McBryde	38	M		Farmer	207	" "				
10			Catharine "	41	F				" "				
11			Mary "	12	F				" "		1		
12			Rachel "	10	F				" "		1		
13			Margaret J. "	8	F				" "		1		
14			James "	7	M				" "				
15			Christian "	4	F				" "				
16			Catharine "	11/12	F				" "				
17			Margaret Bruce	74	F			60	" "			1	
18	388	388	James McBryde	77	M		Farmer	75	" "				
19			Mary "	60	F				" "			1	
20			Christian "	37	F				" "				
21	389	389	John McBryde	28	M		Farmer	50	" "	—			
22			Thomas "	25	M		Do.		" "				
23			Teresa "	26	F				" "	—		1	
24	390	390	James S McBryde	36	M		Farmer	100	" "				
25			Margaret "	37	F				" "				
26			William "	9	M				" "				
27			Catharine "	8	F				" "				
28			Margaret "	5	F				" "				
29	391	391	Sarah Shaw	57	F				" "				
30			Barbara "	27	F				" "				
31			Margaret J. "	23	F				" "				
32			Neill W. "	23	M		Farmer		" "				
33	392	392	John McDuffie	25	M		Farmer	50	" "	—			
34			Catharine "	32	F				" "	—			
35	393	393	William A. Baker	34	M		Farmer	375	" "				
36			Sarah L. "	31	F				" "				
37			Barbara L. "	6	F				" "				
38			Malcom "	4	M				" "				
39			Neill A. "	2	M				" "				
40			Margaret J.	7/12	F				" "				
41	394	394	Mary McIver	78	F			400	" "			1	
42			Daniel McGilvary	37	M		Farmer	350	" "				

m16

SCHEDULE I.—Free Inhabitants in ______ in the County of Moore State of N. Carolina enumerated by me, on the 14th day of September 1850. N. McCrummen Ass't Marshal. 383

192

Dwelling-houses numbered in the order of visitation.	Families numbered in the order of visitation.	The Name of every Person whose usual place of abode on the first day of June, 1850, was in this family.	Age.	Sex.	Color, White, black, or mulatto.	Profession, Occupation, or Trade of each Male Person over 15 years of age.	Value of Real Estate owned.	Place of Birth. Naming the State, Territory, or Country.	Married within the year.	Attended School within the year.	Persons over 20 y'rs of age who cannot read & write.	Whether deaf and dumb, blind, insane, idiotic, pauper, or convict.
1	2	3	4	5	6	7	8	9	10	11	12	13
		Nancy McGilvary	35	F				N. Carolina				
		Duncan A. "	3	M				" "				
		Daniel C. "	2	M				" "				
		John A. "	1/12	M				" "				
395	395	Alexander McGilvary	38	M		Farmer	200	" "				
		Archibald "	87	M		Do.	402	Scotland			1	
396	396	Thomas Mashburn	30	M		Carpenter	50	N. Carolina				
		Elizabeth "	28	F				" "				
		M. Elizabeth "	5	F				" "				
		Malissa A. "	6	F				" "				
		Rebecca C. "	1	F				" "				
397	397	Thomas Mashburn	66	M		Farmer	50	" "				
398	398	John Godfrey	45	M		Farmer		N. C.			1	
		Nancy "	43	F				" "				
		Richard "	19	M		Farmer		" "				
		Elizabeth "	15	F				" "		1		
		Rebecca "	14	F				" "		1		
		James "	13	M				" "		1		
		Mary "	12	F				" "		1		
		John "	11	M				" "		1		
		Lacy "	5	F				" "				
399	399	Peter Morris	45	M		Farmer	190	" "				
		Rebecca "	50	F				" "			1	
		Sarah "	17	F				" "				
		Benjamin "	15	M		Farmer		" "				
		Joseph "	13	M				" "		1		
		Temperance "	11	F				" "		1		
		Martha "	7	F				" "		1		
		Jordan "	6	M				" "				
400	400	Joel Pore	52	M		Farmer	83	" "				
		Susan "	32	F				" "				
		Sovat "	9	M				" "		1		
		Elizabeth "	7	F				" "		1		
		Nicy "	5	F				" "				
		Anna "	3	F				" "				
		Hardy "	1	M				" "				
401	401	John Underwood	73	M		Farmer		" "				
		Anna "	75	F				" "			1	
		Mary "	38	F				" "				
402	402	William Underwood	46	M		Farmer		" "				
		Elizabeth "	44	F				" "				
		Reasaw "	15	F				" "		1		

M20

SCHEDULE I.—Free Inhabitants in ______________ in the County of Moore State of N. Carolina enumerated by me, on the 14th day of September 1850. N. McCrimmon Ass't Marshal.

Dwelling-houses numbered in the order of visitation.	Families numbered in the order of visitation.	The Name of every Person whose usual place of abode on the first day of June, 1850, was in this family.	Age.	Sex.	Color, (White, black, or mulatto.)	Profession, Occupation, or Trade of each Male Person over 15 years of age.	Value of Real Estate owned.	Place of Birth. Naming the State, Territory, or Country.	Married within the year.	Attended School within the year.	Persons over 20 y'rs of age who cannot read & write.	Whether deaf and dumb, blind, insane, idiotic, pauper, or convict.
1	2	3	4	5	6	7	8	9	10	11	12	13
		Darcus M. Underwood	16	F				N. Carolina		1		
		Martha E. "	13	F				" "		1		
		Nancy "	11	F				" "		1		
		John A. "	9	M				" "		1		
		Mary A. "	7	F				" "				
		W. Daniel "	6	M				" "				
		Abel D. "	4	M				" "				
		Sarah C. "	1	F				" "				
403	403	William McDugald	50	M		Farmer	106	Scotland				
		Catharine "	45	F				"				
		Dugald "	17	M		Farmer		"		1		
		Alexander "	15	M		Do.		"		1		
		Duncan "	13	M				"		1		
		Donald "	11	M				"		1		
		Catharine "	9	F				N. Carolina				
		Mary "	4	F				" "				
		Margaret "	1	F				" "				
404	404	James Morris	52	M		Farmer	200	" "				
		Mathew "	16	M		Do.		" "				
		Margaret "	13	F				" "				
		Sophia "	3	F				" "				
405	405	John Cameron	36	M		Farmer	40	" "				
		Daniel "	32	M		Do.		" "				
		Sarah "	22	F				" "				
		Dugald "	1	M				" "				
		John "	2/12	M				" "				
406	406	Dugald Cameron	67	M		Farmer	700	" "				
		Hugh "	28	M		Ditto		" "				
		Mary "	25	F				" "				
		Catharine "	21	F				" "				
		Allen "	18	M		Clerk		" "				
		Sarah "	13	F				" "	1			
		Dugald "	12	M				" "	1			
407	407	Nancy Morris	31	F				" "				
		Barbara J. Edwards	1	F				" "				
		John Swan	66	M		Farmer	300	" "				
		Frances M.	39	F				" "				
		Mary A.	37	F				" "				
		Frances	30	F				" "				
		Ann	26	F				" "				
		Lucy	18	F				" "				
		Tambell	32	M		Farmer		" "				

M20

15 385

Schedule I.—Free Inhabitants in ______ **in the County of** Moore **State of** N. Carolina **enumerated by me, on the** 16th **day of** September **1850.** N. McCrummen **Ass't Marshal.**

193

Dwelling-houses numbered in the order of visitation.	Families numbered in the order of visitation.	The Name of every Person whose usual place of abode on the first day of June, 1850, was in this family.	Description: Age.	Sex.	Color, (White, black, or mulatto.)	Profession, Occupation, or Trade of each Male Person over 15 years of age.	Value of Real Estate owned.	Place of Birth. Naming the State, Territory, or Country.	Married within the year.	Attended School within the year.	Persons over 20 y'rs of age who cannot read & write.	Whether deaf and dumb, blind, insane, idiotic, pauper, or convict.	
1	2	3	4	5	6	7	8	9	10	11	12	13	
		Frederick A. Swann	25	M		Farmer		N. Carolina					1
		Frederick Waddell	10	M				" "					2
		James Swann	3	M				" "					3
		Frances "	2	F				" "					4
		John "	3/12	M				" "					5
408	408	Margaret Buie	73	F			1000	" "					6
		Margaret "	50	F				" "					7
		Hector "	48	M		Farmer	300	" "					8
		Daniel "	45	M		Ditto	200	" "					9
		Malcom "	42	M		none		" "			1		10
		John "	40	M		none		" "			1		11
		Alexander "	38	M		Farmer		" "					12
409	409	John Cose	41	M		Farmer	600	" "					13
		Delila "	31	F				" "					14
		Mary "	14	F				" "					15
		W. Joseph "	11	M				" "		1			16
		John L. "	9	M				" "		1			17
		Alexander "	6	M				" "					18
		Duncan M. "	3	M				" "					19
		Alexander "	24	M		Farmer		" "					20
410	410	Thomas Cose	65	M		Farmer	2000	" "			1		21
		Martha "	37	F				" "					22
		Easther "	7	F				" "		1			23
		Isaac W. "	6	M				" "		1			24
		Rufus "	9/12	M				" "					25
		Benton P. Cose	21	M		Farmer		" "			1		26
		William A.	18	M		Farmer		" "					27
411	411	Henry Cose	20	M		Farmer		" "					28
		Isabella "	20	F				" "					29
		Elizabeth C. "	2/12	F				" "					30
412	412	John Morris	36	M		Farmer	300	" "					31
		Candis "	34	F				" "					32
		Margaret "	14	F				" "		1			33
		Sarah "	11	F				" "		1			34
		Fanny "	7	F				" "		1			35
		William Goins	27	M		Farmer		" "			1		36
413	413	John Morris	82	M		Farmer	950	" "					37
		Nancy "	75	F				" "			1		38
		Nancy "	54	F				" "			1		39
		Sarah "	51	F				" "					40
414	414	Peter W. Morris	47	M		Farmer	200	" "					41
		Sarah "	45	F				" "					42

M 25

SCHEDULE I.—Free Inhabitants in ______ in the County of Moore State of N. Carolina enumerated by me, on the 16th day of September 1850. N. McCrummen Ass't Marshal.

Dwelling-houses numbered in the order of visitation.	Families numbered in the order of visitation.	The Name of every Person whose usual place of abode on the first day of June, 1850, was in this family.	Age.	Sex.	Color, White, black, or mulatto.	Profession, Occupation, or Trade of each Male Person over 15 years of age.	Value of Real Estate owned.	Place of Birth. Naming the State, Territory, or Country.	Married within the year.	Attended School within the year.	Persons over 20 y'rs of age who cannot read & write.	Whether deaf and dumb, blind, insane, idiotic, pauper, or convict.
1	2	3	4	5	6	7	8	9	10	11	12	13
		Edmund M. Morris	2	m		~~Farmer~~		N. Carolina				
415	415	L. Daw Thomas	38	m		Farmer		" "			1	
		Barbara "	35	F				" "			1	
		John W. "	13	m				" "		1		
		Eliza J. "	11	F				" "		1		
		Asa P. "	10	m				" "		1		
		Sarah A. "	9	F				" "		1		
		Charles F. "	4	m				" "				
		Sophia C. "	1	F				" "				
416	416	Catharine Morris	55	F			100	" "				
		Ann J. "	28	F				" "				
		William "	26	m		Farmer	70	" "	—			
		Thomas "	23	m		Farmer		" "				
		Gideon Edwards	70	m		Farmer	300	" "				
417	417	Spence W. "	40	m		Farmer	350	" "				
		Jane "	30	F				" "				
418	418	Francis Edwards	43	m		Farmer	500	" "				
		Sarah J. "	15	F				" "		1		
		William "	13	m				" "		1		
		Elizabeth "	10	F				" "		1		
		Nancy "	8	F				" "		1		
		John "	5	m				" "				
419	417	John W. Scoggin	53	m		Farmer	200	Virginia				
		Mary "	43	F				N. Carolina			1	
		Stephen "	21	m		Farmer		" "				
		Mary "	15	F				" "		1		
		John "	13	m				" "		1		
		James "	11	m				" "		1		
		Lucy "	4	F				" "				
420	420	John H. Dalrymple	41	m		Farmer	1200	" "				
		Elizabeth "	35	F				" "				
		Mary "	15	F				" "		1		
		Elizabeth "	14	F				" "		1		
		William "	12	m				" "		1		
		Jennet A. "	10	F				" "		1		
		John "	8	m				" "		1		
		Margarett "	6	F				" "		1		
		David C. "	5	m				" "				
		Sarah C. "	2	F				" "				
		Archibald "	½	m				" "				
421	421	Donald McLeod	80	m		Farmer	500	Scotland				
422	422	Larkin Hughes	39	m		Farmer		N. Carolina			1	

m 23
f 19

SCHEDULE I.—Free Inhabitants in ______________ in the County of Moore State of N. Carolina enumerated by me, on the 27th day of September 1850. N. McCrummen Ass't Marshal.

387

194

Dwelling-houses numbered in the order of visitation.	Families numbered in the order of visitation.	The Name of every Person whose usual place of abode on the first day of June, 1850, was in this family.	Age.	Sex.	Color, (White, black, or mulatto.)	Profession, Occupation, or Trade of each Male Person over 15 years of age.	Value of Real Estate owned.	Place of Birth. Naming the State, Territory, or Country.	Married within the year.	Attended School within the year.	Persons over 20 y'rs of age who cannot read & write.	Whether deaf and dumb, blind, insane, idiotic, pauper, or convict.
1	2	3	4	5	6	7	8	9	10	11	12	13
		Margaret Hughes	49	F				N. Carolina				
		John "	19	M		Farmer		" "				
		Murphy "	17	M		Ditto		" "				
		Mary A. "	14	F				" "				
		Catharine "	12	F				" "				
423	423	Effy McIver	29	F				" "				
		Daniel "	23	M		Farmer	300	" "				
424	424	Dempsey Hunt	56	M		Ditto		" "				
		Sarah "	68	F				" "			1	
		Demaris "	37	F				" "			1	
		Henry "	32	M		Farmer		" "				
		George "	28	M		Farmer		" "				
		Sarah "	25	F				" "			1	
		Kearney "	22	M		Farmer		" "				
425	425	John Hunt	34	M		Farmer		" "				
		Charity "	29	F				" "				
		Sarah A. E. "	4	F				" "				
426	426	Elizabeth Dalrymple	81	F			400	Scotland				
		Jannet "	49	F				N. Carolina				
		Margaret "	47	F				" "				
		Archibald "	37	M		Farmer	300	" "				
427	427	William Dalrymple	77	M		Farmer	700	Scotland				
		Henry Godfrey	21	M		Ditto		N. Carolina				
428	428	John McIver	55	M		Farmer	1000	" "				
		Margaret "	48	F				" "				
		Caroline "	23	F				" "				
		James D. "	16	M		Farmer		" "		1		
		Alexander "	13	M				" "		1		
		Rosanna "	10	F				" "		1		
		John A. "	6	M				" "				
429	429	Allen Ellis	72	M		Farmer	200	" "				
		Nancy "	65	F				" "			1	
		Winiford "	34	F				" "				
430	430	Daniel McPhaul	27	M		Farmer	30	" "				
		Mary "	37	F				" "			1	
		William "	17	M		Farmer		" "		1		
		Ann "	14	F				" "		1		
		Thomas A. "	12	M				" "		1		
		John	9	M				" "		1		
431	431	William Hawley	44	M		Farmer	250	" "				
		Margaret "	36	F				" "				
		John A. "	15	M		Farmer		" "		1		

M 22
F 20

SCHEDULE I.—Free Inhabitants in [illegible] **in the County of** Moore **State of** N. Carolina **enumerated by me, on the** 17th **day of** September **1850.** W. McCrummen **Ass't Marshal.**

Line	Dwelling-houses numbered in the order of visitation. (1)	Families numbered in the order of visitation. (2)	The Name of every Person whose usual place of abode on the first day of June, 1850, was in this family. (3)	Age. (4)	Sex. (5)	Color, white, black, or mulatto. (6)	Profession, Occupation, or Trade of each Male Person over 15 years of age. (7)	Value of Real Estate owned. (8)	Place of Birth. Naming the State, Territory, or Country. (9)	Married within the year. (10)	Attended School within the year. (11)	Persons over 20 yr's of age who cannot read and write. (12)	Whether deaf and dumb, blind, insane, idiotic, pauper, or convict. (13)
1			Mary A. Hawley	14	F				N. Carolina		1		
2			Barbara "	11	F				" "		1		
3			Jamima E. "	6	F				" "				
4			David M. "	3	M				" "				
5			Nancy A. "	1	F				" "				
6	432	432	Elizabeth McLennon	37	F			300	" "				
7			Allen "	17	M		none		" "		1		
8			Jane "	16	F				" "				
9			Sarah A. "	13	F				" "		1		
10			Elizabeth "	11	F				" "		1		
11	433	433	Archibald G. Douglas	38	M		Farmer	300	" "				
12			Sarah "	33	F				" "				
13			Nancy "	12	F				" "		1		
14			Sarah "	10	F				" "		1		
15			Archibald "	7	M				" "		1		
16			Martha E. "	5	F				" "				
17			Rosa "	2	F				" "				
18	434	434	David Gaster	47	M		Farmer	1000	" "				
19			Jamima "	46	F				" "				
20			Andrew A. "	21	M		Farmer		" "				
21			John M. "	20	M		Ditto		" "				
22			Ann S. "	19	F				" "		1		
23			Margaret E. "	16	F				" "		1		
24			Mary D. "	14	F				" "		1		
25			Jemima A. "	12	F				" "		1		
26			Nancy V. "	9	F				" "		1		
27			William D. "	4	M				" "				
28			David P. Morris	33	M		Farmer		" "				
29	435	435	John May	27	M		Ditto	300	" "				
30			Jennet "	24	F				" "				
31			Barbara "	1	F				" "				
32	436	436	Charles G. Harrington	45	M		Farmer	800	" "				
33			Penelopy "	43	F				" "			1	
34			Jennet "	23	F				" "				
35			Simon "	20	M		Farmer		" "		1		
36			Benjamin "	17	M				" "		1		
37			Elizabeth "	15	F				" "		1		
38			John "	13	M				" "		1		
39			William "	11	M				" "		1		
40			Mary "	10	F				" "		1		
41			Nancy "	8	F				" "		1		
42			Thomas "	6	M				" "				

m 16
f. 9 6

16

SCHEDULE I.—Free Inhabitants in ______ in the County of Moore State of N. Carolina enumerated by me, on the 18th day of September 1850. N. McCrummen Ass't Marshal.

389

495

Dwelling-houses numbered in the order of visitation.	Families numbered in the order of visitation.	The Name of every Person whose usual place of abode on the first day of June, 1850, was in this family.	Age.	Sex.	Color, (White, black, or mulatto.)	Profession, Occupation, or Trade of each Male Person over 15 years of age.	Value of Real Estate owned.	Place of Birth. Naming the State, Territory, or Country.	Married within the year.	Attended School within the year.	Persons over 20 y'rs of age who cannot read & write.	Whether deaf and dumb, blind, insane, idiotic, pauper, or convict.
1	2	3	4	5	6	7	8	9	10	11	12	13
		James K. Harrington	4	M		[illegible]		N. Carolina				
		Henry Godfrey	52	M		Farmer		" "				
		Mary "	47	F				" "			1	
		Nelly "	22	F				" "				
		Henry "	21	M		Farmer		" "				
		Jane "	18	F				" "				
		John "	15	M		Farmer		" "				
		Marshal "	5	M	~~M~~			" "				
		Andrew J. "	2/12	M				" "				
437	437	Daniel Gaster	22	M		Farmer		" "				
		Margaret "	23	F				" "				
		Telitha A. Thomas	13	F				" "				
438	438	David Sloan	31	M		Farmer	225	" "				
		Anna "	20	F				" "				
		William E. "	2	M				" "				
		John R. "	3/12	F				" "				
439	439	Martha Johnson	54	F				" "			1	
		Mary A. "	25	F				" "				
		Martha "	20	F				" "				
		Emeline "	5	F				" "				
		Nancy C. "	3	F				" "				
		William "	1	M				" "				
440	440	John Gaster	36	M		Farmer	50	" "				
		Sarah "	32	F				" "				
		Martha A. "	9	F				" "		1		
		Nancy "	7	F				" "				
		Sarah J. "	5	F				" "				
		Evander "	1	M				" "				
441	441	Blake Parish	43	M		Farmer	136	" "			1	
		Anna "	43	F				" "			1	
		Lucinda "	19	F				" "				Idiotic
		John M. "	18	M		Farmer		" "				
		Christian "	14	F				" "				
		Joseph B. "	12	M				" "		1		
		Darius R. "	11	M				" "		1		
		Elizabeth "	9	F				" "		1		
		David "	6	M				" "				
		Martha "	4	F				" "				
		Catharine "	3	F				" "				
442	442	Jesse Love	49	M		Farmer	175	" "			1	
		Susan "	33	F				" "			1	
		Mary C. "	22	F				" "				

m 18 1 B m
f 24

SCHEDULE I.—Free Inhabitants in ______ in the County of *Moore* State of *N. Carolina* enumerated by me, on the *18th* day of *September* 1850. *N. McCrummen* Ass't Marshal.

Dwelling-houses numbered in the order of visitation.	Families numbered in the order of visitation.	The Name of every Person whose usual place of abode on the first day of June, 1850, was in this family.	Age.	Sex.	Color, {White, black, or mulatto.	Profession, Occupation, or Trade of each Male Person over 15 years of age.	Value of Real Estate owned.	Place of Birth. Naming the State, Territory, or Country.	Married within the year.	Attended School within the year.	Persons over 20 y'rs of age who cannot read & write.	Whether deaf and dumb, blind, insane, idiotic, pauper, or convict.
1	2	3	4	5	6	7	8	9	10	11	12	13
		Andrew Love	18	M		Farmer		N. Carolina				
		Eliza "	14	F				" "		1		
		Candis "	12	F				" "		1		
		Westley "	10	M				" "		1		
		Margaret "	6	F				" "				
		Alexander "	2	M				" "				
443	443	Rebecca Godfrey	45	F				" "				
		Mary A. "	11	F				" "				
444	444	Patrick Sashley	42	M		Farmer	200	" "				
		Scynthia "	42	F				" "			1	
		John L. "	18	M		Farmer		" "				
		Mary A. "	14	F				" "				
		Joseph Thomas	78	M		Farmer		" "			1	
		James Mashburn	17	M		Farmer		" "				
445	445	Jacob Gaster	36	M		Farmer	100	" "			1	
		Mary A. "	37	F				" "				
		Emeline "	13	F				" "		1		
		Ambers "	14	M				" "		1		
		John C. "	8	M				" "		1		
		Henry D. "	2	M				" "				
		Nancy Shaw	26	F				" "			1	
446	446	Jacob Gaster	85	M		Farmer		" "				
		Nancy "	64	F				" "				
		Henry "	43	M				" "				
		Barbara Die	62	F				" "				
447	447	Green H. Sloan	28	M		Farmer	200	" "				
		Sopha C. "	23	F				" "				
		David H. "	8	M				" "		1		
		John A. "	5	M				" "				
		Sarah A. M. "	4	F				" "				
		Samanthra "	2	F				" "				
		Mary Blackman	30	F				" "				
448	448	William Rollins	63	M		Farmer	400	" "				
		Mary "	62	F				" "				
		Thomas "	30	M		Farmer	730	" "				
449	449	Emily Kimball	45	F				" "			1	
		Barbara "	23	F				" "			1	
		Mary "	17	F				" "				
		Isabella "	12	F				" "		1		
457	450	Sarah J. Wicker	26	F				" "			1	
		Elizabeth	8	F				" "				
		Fanny	6	F				" "				

m 18
fe 24

SCHEDULE I.—Free Inhabitants in ______________ **in the County of** *Moore* **State of** *N. Carolina* **enumerated by me, on the** *19th* **day of** *September* **1850.** *N. McCrimmon* **Ass't Marshal.** 391

198

Dwelling-houses numbered in the order of visitation.	Families numbered in the order of visitation.	The Name of every Person whose usual place of abode on the first day of June, 1850, was in this family.	Description: Age.	Sex.	Color, White, black, or mulatto.	Profession, Occupation, or Trade of each Male Person over 15 years of age.	Value of Real Estate owned.	Place of Birth. Naming the State, Territory, or Country.	Married within the year.	Attended School within the year.	Persons over 20 y'rs of age who cannot read & write.	Whether deaf and dumb, blind, insane, idiotic, pauper, or convict.
1	2	3	4	5	6	7	8	9	10	11	12	13
		Nancy Walker	4	F				N. Carolina				
		Archibald "	2	M				" "				
451	451	John Baker	58	M		Farmer	600	" "				
		Neill A. "	21	M		Ditto		" "				
		Margaret "	18	F				" "				
		Catharine "	17	F				" "				
		Daniel "	16	M		Farmer		" "		1		
		Isabella "	14	F				" "		1		
		Margaret "	12	F				" "		1		
452	452	John McFarland	50	M		Farmer	150	" "				
		Margaret "	49	F				" "				
		Caroline "	19	F				" "				
		John B. "	17	M		Farmer		" "		1		
		Mary "	15	F				" "		1		
		Margaret "	14	F				" "		1		
		Antonette "	12	F				" "		1		
		Aronette "	12	F				" "		1		
453	453	William Pepkin	26	M		Farmer		" "				
		Elizabeth "	24	F				" "			1	
		Archibald "	1	M				" "				
		John Marshal "	2	M				" "				
454	454	Turquill McNeill	50	M		Farmer	400	" "				
		Margaret "	51	F				" "				
		Ann E. "	24	F				" "				
		John "	19	M		Farmer		" "		1		
		Alexander "	17	M				" "		1		
		Mary M. "	13	F				" "		1		
		Sarah C. "	10	F				" "		1		
		Jennet A. "	8	F				" "		1		
455	455	Louis McLeod	24	M		Farmer	400	" "				
		Eliza "	26	F				" "				
		Angelette "	1	F				" "				
		David Kelly	15	M				" "				
		Mary Brown	18	F				" "				
456	456	Margaret Mann	33	F				" "				
		Caroline "	7	F	M			" "				
		Calvin "	5	M	M			" "				
		Ann "	1	F	M			" "				
457	457	Nancy McFarland	69	F			345	" "				
		Alexander	30	M		Farmer		" "				
		Catharine	25	F				" "				
458	458	Neill McNeill	62	M		Farmer	1500	" "				

m 17 : 13
F 25 27

SCHEDULE I.—Free Inhabitants in ____________ in the County of Moore State of N Carolina enumerated by me, on the 19th day of September 1850. N McCrummen Ass't Marshal.

	Dwelling-houses numbered in the order of visitation.	Families numbered in the order of visitation.	The Name of every Person whose usual place of abode on the first day of June, 1850, was in this family.	Age.	Sex.	Color, White, black, or mulatto.	Profession, Occupation, or Trade of each Male Person over 15 years of age.	Value of Real Estate owned.	Place of Birth. Naming the State, Territory, or Country.	Married within the year.	Attended School within the year.	Persons over 20 y'rs of age who cannot read & write.	Whether deaf and dumb, blind, insane, idiotic, pauper, or convict.
	1	2	3	4	5	6	7	8	9	10	11	12	13
1			Sophia McNeill	59	F				N. Carolina				
2			Lovedy "	25	F				" "				
3			Sarah "	23	F				" "				
4			Sophia "	21	F				" "		1		
5			Margaret "	18	F				" "		1		
6			Turquill "	15	M				" "		1		
7			Elizabeth "	13	F				" "				
8	459	459	William Buchannon	29	M		Farmer	250	" "				
9			Delilah "	32	F				" "			1	
10			John W. "	9	M				" "				
11			Andrew "	7	M				" "				
12			Mary A. "	5	F				" "				
13			Thomas R. "	3	M				" "				
14			James B. "	1	M				" "				
15			Catharine "	20	F				" "			1	
16	460	459	Fredrick Yarbrough	56	M		Farmer	250	" "				
17	461	461	Penelopy Pipkin	61	F				" "			1	
18			Dicy Yarbrough	37	F				" "				
19			Elinder E. "	9	F				" "				
20	462	462	Joseph Stuart	67	M		Farmer		" "				
21			Mary "	51	F				" "			1	
22			Martha A. "	14	F				" "				
23			Andrew A. "	13	M				" "				
24			Elizabeth C. "	10	F				" "				
25			Murdock Mc. "	4	M				" "				
26	463	463	Benjamin Muckle	57	M		Farmer		" "			1	
27			Sarah "	55	F				" "			1	
28			Elizabeth "	32	F				" "			1	
29			Mary "	30	F				" "			1	
30			Andrew "	28	M		Farmer		" "				
31			James "	25	M		Farmer		" "				
32			Benjamin "	23	M		Farmer		" "				
33			Isaac "	22	M		Ditto		" "				
34			Jane "	19	F				" "				
35			Anna "	17	F				" "				
36	464	464	Sylvanus Brown	43	M		Farmer		" "			1	Cann
37			Elizabeth "	36	F				" "			1	
38			Margret "	22	F				" "			1	
39			Rebecca "	14	F				" "				
40			Greenwood "	13	M				" "				
41			Neill A. "	11	M				" "				
42			Eliza "	6	F				" "				

m 18
fe 24

393

SCHEDULE I.—Free Inhabitants in ______________ in the County of *Moore* State of *N. Carolina* enumerated by me, on the *19th* day of *September* 1850. *N. McCrummen* Ass't Marshal.

197

Dwelling-houses numbered in the order of visitation.	Families numbered in the order of visitation.	The Name of every Person whose usual place of abode on the first day of June, 1850, was in this family.	Description: Age.	Sex.	Color, White, black, or mulatto.	Profession, Occupation, or Trade of each Male Person over 15 years of age.	Value of Real Estate owned.	Place of Birth. Naming the State, Territory, or Country.	Married within the year.	Attended School within the year.	Persons over 20 years of age who cannot read & write.	Whether deaf and dumb, blind, insane, idiotic, pauper, or convict.
1	2	3	4	5	6	7	8	9	10	11	12	13
		Andrew Brown	2	m				N. Carolina				
		Elizabeth "	6/12	F				" "				
465	465	Daniel Thomas	36	m		Farmer	150	" "			/	
		Priscilla "	36	F				" "				
		Payton "	11	m				" "				
		Mahalah "	8	F				" "				
		Cassa "	6	F				" "				
		Delilah "	4	F				" "				
		Telitha "	4	F				" "				
		John "	2	m				" "				
		Andrew "	3/12	m				" "				
		Benjamin "	20	m		Farmer		" "			/	
466	466	Hiram Thomas	40	m		Farmer	50	" "				
		Eliza "	32	F				" "				
		John W. "	8	m				" "				
		Mary I. "	4	F				" "				
		James M. "	10/12	m				" "				
467	467	William Thomas	26	m		Farmer	125	" "				
		Mary	35	F				" "			/	
468	468	Grissum Thomas	67	m		Farmer	150	Virginia			/	
		Sarah "	62	F				N. Carolina			/	
469	469	Eli Yarbrough	62	m		none		" "				
		Mary "	43	F				" "				
		Ann E. "	16	F				" "		/		
		Elizabeth J. "	14	F				" "		/		
		Nancy C. "	12	F				" "		/		
		Eleanor S. "	9	F				" "				
		Sarah G. "	6	F				" "				
470	470	George Howard	58	m		Farmer	282	" "				
		Elizabeth "	57	F				" "				
		Matilda J. "	23	F				" "				
		Susan "	22	F				" "				
		Caswell S. "	20	m		Farmer		" "				
		Elizabeth "	18	F				" "				
		Julia "	16	F				" "				
471	471	Absalom Kelly	34	m		Farmer	200	" "				
		Nancy "	27	F				" "				
		John T. "	10	m				" "		/		
		Fanny "	8	F				" "		/		
		Henry L. M. "	5	m				" "				
		Sarah "	2	F				" "				
		William A. "	5/12	m				" "				

M 18
F 24

SCHEDULE I.—Free Inhabitants in ______ in the County of Moore State of N. Carolina enumerated by me, on the 20th day of September 1850. N. McCrummen Ass't Marshal.

Line	Dwelling-houses numbered in the order of visitation.	Families numbered in the order of visitation.	The Name of every Person whose usual place of abode on the first day of June, 1850, was in this family.	Description: Age.	Description: Sex.	Description: Color, White, black, or mulatto.	Profession, Occupation, or Trade of each Male Person over 15 years of age.	Value of Real Estate owned.	Place of Birth. Naming the State, Territory, or Country.	Married within the year.	Attended School within the year.	Persons over 20 y'rs of age who cannot read & write.	Whether deaf and dumb, blind, insane, idiotic, pauper, or convict.
	1	2	3	4	5	6	7	8	9	10	11	12	13
1			Martha Siley	45	F				N. Carolina			1	
2			John Goings	24	m	m	Farmer		" "			1	
3	472	472	John Sheppard	57	m		Farmer	600	" "				
4			Mary "	51	F				" "				
5			Nancy "	22	F				" "				
6			Mahalah "	21	F				" "				
7			Elizabeth "	19	F				" "				
8			James L. "	17	m		Farmer		" "		1		
9			John A. "	15	m		Ditto		" "		1		
10			Mary J. "	13	F				" "		1		
11			Altha W. "	7	F				" "				
12	473	473	John Dalrymple	45	m		Farmer	475	" "				
13			Flora "	34	F				" "				
14			James "	14	m				" "				
15			Malcom "	12	m				" "				
16			Rosanna "	8	F				" "		1		
17			William "	6	m				" "		1		
18			Elizabeth "	5	F				" "				
19			John G. "	3	m				" "				
20			Neill A. "	1	m				" "				
21	474	474	Nancy Oliver	60	F			150	Virginia			1	
22			Elizabeth "	33	F				N. Carolina				
23			Eleanor "	26	F				" "				
24			Moses "	25	m		Farmer		" "				
25	475	475	George Underwood	62	m		Farmer	530	" "			1	
26			Sarah "	62	F				Virginia			1	
27			Winniford "	32	F				N. Carolina			1	
28			Elizabeth "	30	F				" "				
29			Loveday "	28	F				" "			1	
30			James "	25	M		Farmer		" "			1	
31			William "	23	M		Farmer		" "			1	
32			Eliza "	18	F				" "				
33			Nancy "	16	F				" "				
34			Thomas Jasper	14	m				" "				
35	476	476	Joseph Thomas	34	m		Farmer	300	" "			1	
36			Elizabeth "	23	F				" "				
37			Nancy "	5	F				" "				
38			Matilda "	2	F				" "				
39			Alexander Bowlin	13	m				" "				
40	477	477	Bryant Williams	51	m		Farmer	280	" "				
41			Sarah "	35	F				" "				
42			Pattie "	20	F				" "			1	

m 18 13 m
F 24

395

SCHEDULE I.—Free Inhabitants in ____________ in the County of Moore State of North Carolina enumerated by me, on the 20th day of September 1850. N. McCrummen Ass't Marshal.

198

Dwelling-houses numbered in the order of visitation	Families numbered in the order of visitation	The Name of every Person whose usual place of abode on the first day of June, 1850, was in this family.	Age	Sex	Color (White, black, or mulatto)	Profession, Occupation, or Trade of each Male Person over 15 years of age.	Value of Real Estate owned.	Place of Birth. Naming the State, Territory, or Country.	Married within the year.	Attended School within the year.	Persons over 20 y'rs of age who cannot read & write.	Whether deaf and dumb, blind, insane, idiotic, pauper, or convict.	
1	2	3	4	5	6	7	8	9	10	11	12	13	
		James H. Williams	11	m				N. Carolina					1
		Nancy "	9	F				" "					2
		Thomas "	6	m				" "					3
478	478	Joseph Buchanan	22	m		Farmer		" "			/		4
		Mary S. "	23	F				" "					5
		Sion H. "	1	m				" "					6
479		Rosanna Dalrymple	76	F			600	" "					7
		Archibald "	43	m		Farmer		" "					8
480 (482)	480 (479)	Abner Wommack	25	m		Miller		" "					9
		Sarah "	23	F				" "			/		10
		Isaac B. "	4	m				" "					11
		Gaston "	2	m				" "					12
		Sarah A. "	1/10	F				" "					13
		Mary A. Wommack	21	F				" "			/		14
481 (480)	481 (480)	Samuel McAulay	21	m		Farmer		" "					15
482	482	Darius Thomas	34	m		Farmer	533	" "					16
		Martha "	26	F				" "			/		17
483	483	Reubin Oliver	56	m		Farmer		" "					18
		Elizabeth "	50	F				" "			/		19
		Dicy "	26	F				" "			/		20
		Sepathia "	24	F				" "			/		21
		Jane "	22	F				" "					22
		Delilah "	18	F				" "					23
		James H. "	11	m				" "					24
484	484	Tillman Thomas	45	m		Farmer	400	" "					25
		Harriet "	42	F				" "					26
		William J. "	21	m		Farmer		" "					27
		Macklin "	19	m		Farmer		" "					28
		Jefferson "	17	m		Farmer		" "					29
		Henderson B. "	14	m				" "					30
		Mary A. "	12	F				" "					31
		Elizabeth E. "	10	F				" "					32
		John M. B. "	8	m				" "					33
		Henry F. "	6	m				" "					34
		James K. P. "	4	m				" "					35
		Harriet M. "	1	F				" "					36
485	485	Temperance Knight	57	F				" "			/		37
		Martha A. "	36	F				" "			/		38
		Dicy "	34	F				" "			/		39
		Nancy "	11	F				" "					40
486	486	Mary Knight	70	F				Virginia			/		41
		Sarah "	38	F				N. Carolina			/		42

m 20
Fe 22

SCHEDULE I.—Free Inhabitants in ______ in the County of *Moore* State of *N. Carolina* enumerated by me, on the *21st* day of *September* 1850. *N. McCrummen* Ass't Marshal.

	Dwelling-houses numbered in the order of visitation.	Families numbered in the order of visitation.	The Name of every Person whose usual place of abode on the first day of June, 1850, was in this family.	Age.	Sex.	Color, (White, black, or mulatto.)	Profession, Occupation, or Trade of each Male Person over 15 years of age.	Value of Real Estate owned.	Place of Birth. Naming the State, Territory, or Country.	Married within the year.	Attended School within the year.	Persons over 20 y'rs of age who cannot read & write.	Whether deaf and dumb, blind, insane, idiotic, pauper, or convict.
	1	2	3	4	5	6	7	8	9	10	11	12	13
1			Lucinda Knight	32	F				N. Carolina			1	
2			John M. "	2	m				" "				
3	487	487	Daniel Douglas	40	m		Carpenter	600	" "				
4			Saney "	41	F				" "				
5			Delany "	24	F				" "				
6			Lucinda "	22	F				" "				
7			Dorcas "	15	F				" "				
8			Elizabeth A. "	13	F				" "				
9			James "	9	m				" "				
10			Nancy "	7	F				" "				
11	488	488	Archibald Douglas	72	m		Farmer	2000	" "				
12			Rosanna "	65	F				" "			1	
13			Sarah "	26	F				" "				
14	489	489	Henry Knight	56	m		Farmer		" "			1	
15			Mary "	47	F				" "			1	
16			John "	17	m		Farmer		" "				
17			Telitha "	13	F				" "				
18	490	490	John Douglas	77	m		Farmer	1200	" "				
19	491	491	Kisaiah Bolin	46	F				" "				
20			Nancy Stone	20	F				" "			1	
21	492	492	Mary Ward	35	F				" "			1	
22			Flora A. Bletcher	20	F				" "			1	
23	493	493	Green Thomas	30	m		Farmer	300	" "				
24			Nancy "	24	F				" "				
25			Napoleon "	[illegible]	m				" "				
26			Penelope Thomas	50	F				" "			1	
27			Isabella "	23	F				" "				
28			Henry "	27	m		Tailor		" "				
29	494	494	Henderson Gaddo	44	m		Farmer		" "				
30			Elizabeth "	74	F				" "				
31	495	495	Priscilla Thomas	50	F			100	" "			1	
32			William Brown	47	m		Farmer		" "			1	
33			Elizabeth Dickins	45	F				" "			1	
34	496	496	Sarah Cox	82	F			400	" "			1	
35			Elizabeth "	50	F				" "			1	
36			Celia "	45	F				" "			1	
37	497	497	Lewis Hicks	60	m	m	Farmer		" "			1	
38			Libby "	45	F	m			" "			1	
39			Malvina "	30	F	m			" "			1	
40			Luther "	26	m	m	Farmer		" "			1	
41			Nancy "	20	F	m			" "			1	
42			Jane "	17	F	m			" "				

m 14 2B
F 28 17

1K 397

SCHEDULE I.—Free Inhabitants in ____________ in the County of Moore State of N. Carolina enumerated by me, on the 23rd day of September 1850. W. McCrummen Ass't Marshal.

199

Dwelling-houses numbered in the order of visitation.	Families numbered in the order of visitation.	The Name of every Person whose usual place of abode on the first day of June, 1850, was in this family.	Description: Age.	Sex.	Color, (White, black, or mulatto.)	Profession, Occupation, or Trade of each Male Person over 15 years of age.	Value of Real Estate owned.	Place of Birth. Naming the State, Territory, or Country.	Married within the year.	Attended School within the year.	Persons over 20 y'rs of age who cannot read & write.	Whether deaf and dumb, blind, insane, idiotic, pauper, or convict.
1	2	3	4	5	6	7	8	9	10	11	12	13
		Andrew Hicks	15	M	M			N. Carolina				
		Elizabeth "	13	F	M			" "				
		Isabella "	11	F	M			" "				
		Ellis "	9	M	M			" "				
		Middy "	6	F	M			" "				
		John "	2	M	M			" "				
498	498	Charles Cox	52	M		Farmer	250	" "				
		Rebecca "	50	F				" "				
		Sarah "	22	F				" "			1	
		John W. "	20	M		Farmer		" "				
		William O.B. "	16	M		Farmer		" "				
		Andrew L. "	16	M		Ditto		" "				
		Isabella C. "	13	F				" "		1		
		Mary A. "	9	F				" "				
499	499	Abner E. Yarbrough	29	M		Farmer	300	" "				
		Isabella C. "	30	F				" "				
		Benjamin W. Hunter	13	M			250	" "		1		
		Jane E. "	11	F				" "		1		
		Martha "	9	F				" "		1		
		John M. "	7	M				" "		1		
		Charles A. "	5	M				" "				
		James Easton Yarbro.	3	M				" "				
		Abner N. "	1	M				" "				
500	500	Gideon Dickins	62	M		Farmer		" "			1	
		Temperance "	58	F				Virginia				
		James "	24	M		Farmer		N. Carolina			1	
501	501	Daniel Wildon	53	M		Farmer	880	" "				
		Sarah "	50	F				" "				
		Catharine "	20	F				" "				
		Sarah A. "	16	F				" "				
		Caroline F. "	14	F				" "				
		John A. "	10	M				" "				
502	502	Thomas A. Yarbrough	30	M		Farmer	125	" "				
		Barbara A. "	23	F				" "				
		Marinda "	23	F				" "			1	
		Margaret A. "	3	F				" "				
		Delilah F. "	1	F				" "				
503	503	Anderson Thomas	43	M		Farmer		" "			1	
		Temperance "	39	F				" "			1	
		William "	19	M		Farmer		" "		1		
		Mary A. "	17	F				" "				
		John "	14	M				" "				

M 21 33
F 21 0

SCHEDULE I.—Free Inhabitants in ______________ **in the County of** *Moore* **State of** *N Carolina* **enumerated by me, on the** *23d* **day of** *September* **1850.** *N. M. McCrimmon* **Ass't Marshal.**

	Dwelling-houses numbered in the order of visitation.	Families numbered in the order of visitation.	The Name of every Person whose usual place of abode on the first day of June, 1850, was in this family.	Age.	Sex.	Color, (White, black, or mulatto.)	Profession, Occupation, or Trade of each Male Person over 15 years of age.	Value of Real Estate owned.	Place of Birth. Naming the State, Territory, or Country.	Married within the year.	Attended School within the year.	Persons over 20 y'rs of age who cannot read & write.	Whether deaf and dumb, blind, insane, idiotic, pauper, or convict.
	1	2	3	4	5	6	7	8	9	10	11	12	13
1			Robert Thomas	12	M				N. Carolina				
2			David "	10	M				" "				
3			Sarah "	9	F				" "				
4			Sackfield "	7	M				" "				
5			Catharine "	6	F				" "				
6			Alexander "	3	M				" "				
7	504	504	Robert T. Johnson	34	M		Farmer		" "			1	
8			Flora "	30	F				" "				
9			Duncan "	3	M				" "				
10			William A. "	1	M				" "				
11			John Thomas	31	M		Farmer		" "				
12	505	505	John McLeod	67	M		Farmer	1550	" "				
13			Elizabeth "	62	F				" "				
14			Nancy A. "	22	F				" "				
15			Nancy Buchannan	30	F				" "			1	
16			James Parham	22	M		Farmer		" "				
17			Andrew Brown	12	M				" "		1		
18	506	506	Elizabeth Wicker	58	F			400	" "				
19			James B. "	31	M		Farmer		" "				
20			Benjamin "	21	M		Ditto		" "				
21			Elizabeth "	17	F				" "				
22	507	507	Sarah Thomas	45	F			2000	" "				
23			Isabella C. "	20	F				" "				
24			Mary A. "	18	F				" "				
25			William A. "	17	M				" "				
26			Emeline "	15	F				" "		1		
27			Sarah E. "	12	F				" "		1		
28			Delitha "	8	F				" "		1		
29			Delany "	8	F				" "		1		
30			William Berryman	37	M				" "				
31			Eliza J. "	25	F				" "				
32			Ann E. "	8	F				" "		1		
33			Samantha "	6	F				" "				
34			Alexander C. "	3	M				" "				
35			Louisa F. "	1	F				" "				
36			George Goins	13	M				" "				
37	508	508	Anna Gunter	60	F			150	" "			1	
38			Kearny Buchannan	20	M		Farmer		" "				
39			Isabella C. Huckaby	13	F				" "		1		
40	509	509	John Buchannan	36	M		Farmer	175	" "			1	
41			Catharine "	35	F				" "				
42			Elizabeth "	16	F				" "		1		

M-19

399

SCHEDULE I.—Free Inhabitants in ______________ **in the County of** Moore **State of** N. Carolina **enumerated by me, on the** 24th **day of** September **1850.** N. McCrummen **Ass't Marshal.**

200

Line	Dwelling-houses numbered in the order of visitation.	Families numbered in the order of visitation.	The Name of every Person whose usual place of abode on the first day of June, 1850, was in this family.	Age.	Sex.	Color, (White, black, or mulatto.)	Profession, Occupation, or Trade of each Male Person over 15 years of age.	Value of Real Estate owned.	Place of Birth. Naming the State, Territory, or Country.	Married within the year.	Attended School within the year.	Persons over 20 y'rs of age who cannot read & write.	Whether deaf and dumb, blind, insane, idiotic, pauper, or convict.
	1	2	3	4	5	6	7	8	9	10	11	12	13
1			Riley Buchannon	15	M				N. Carolina				
2			William H. "	12	M				" "				
3			Ann "	12	F				" "				
4			Nancy "	7	F				" "				
5			John R. "	6	M				" "				
6	510	510	John Miller	39	M	M	Farmer		" "			1	
7			Susan "	40	F	M			" "			1	
8			Ann "	14	F	M			" "				
9			James "	12	M	M			" "				
10			Elizabeth "	9	F	M			" "				
11			Wiley J. "	7	M	M			" "				
12			Mary A. "	6	F	M			" "				
13			Nancy "	4	F	M			" "				
14			John "	2	M	M			" "				
15	511	511	Kissiah Thomas	47	F			268	" "			1	
16			Benjamin "	21	M		Farmer		" "				
17			Mary "	20	F				" "				
18			John "	18	M		Farmer		" "				
19			Silpha "	16	F				" "				
20			Martha A. "	13	F				" "				
21	512	512	Sarah Sloan	80	F			300	" "			1	
22			Gaston "	38	M		Farmer		" "				
23			Turner "	32	M				" "				
24			Sarah "	32	F				" "				
25			Joseph "	4	M				" "				
26			John A. "	1	M				" "				
27	513	513	Jordan Sloan	36	M		Merchant	180	" "				
28			Sophia "	40	F				" "				
29			John "	14	M				" "				
30			Sarah "	12	F				" "				
31			Nancy "	9	F				" "				
32			Sophia "	7	F				" "				
33			David "	5	M				" "				
34			Jordan "	2	M				" "				
35			Alvis "	2/12	M				" "				
36			Robert Gains	23	M		Laborer		" "			1	
37	514	514	Robert McAuley	56	M		Farmer	100	" "				
38			Peggy "	44	F				" "				
39			Margaret "	23	F				" "				
40			William "	17	M		Farmer		" "		1		
41			John "	15	M		Ditto		" "		1		
42			Mary C. "	13	F				" "		1		

M22 4B

SCHEDULE I.—Free Inhabitants in ______ **in the County of** Moore **State of** N. Carolina **enumerated by me, on the** 24th **day of** September **1850.** N. McCrimmon **Ass't Marshal.**

Line	Dwelling-houses numbered in the order of visitation.	Families numbered in the order of visitation.	The Name of every Person whose usual place of abode on the first day of June, 1850, was in this family.	Age.	Sex.	Color, White, black, or mulatto.	Profession, Occupation, or Trade of each Male Person over 15 years of age.	Value of Real Estate owned.	Place of Birth. Naming the State, Territory, or Country.	Married within the year.	Attended School within the year.	Persons over 20 years of age who cannot read & write.	Whether deaf and dumb, blind, insane, idiotic, pauper, or convict.
	1	2	3	4	5	6	7	8	9	10	11	12	13
1			Barbara A. McAuly	9	F				N. Carolina				
2			James P. "	5	M				" "				
3	515	515	Elias Case	25	M		Farmer	250	" "				
4			Nancy "	22	F				" "				
5			Thomas "	1	M				" "				
6			Mary A. "	3/12	F				" "				
7	516	516	Malcom McFarland	49	M		Farmer	300	" "				
8			Ann "	35	F				" "				
9			John A. "	8	M				" "				
10			William M. "	6	M				" "				
11			James A. "	3	M				" "				
12			Elizabeth McFarland	47	F			60	" "				
13			John Abbott	86	M		none		" "				
14	517	517	Daniel McFarland	40	M		Farmer	350	" "				
15			Nancy "	33	F				" "				
16	518	518	Elizabeth Watson	50	F			200	" "			1	
17			Nancy "	33	F				" "			1	
18			Andrew "	26	M		Farmer		" "			1	
19			Jane "	20	F				" "			1	
20			Neill "	19	M		Farmer		" "				
21			Mathew "	18	M		Ditto		" "				
22			Arabella "	12	F				" "				
23	519	519	Allan Thomas	50	M		Farmer	150	" "				
24			Nancy F. "	49	F				" "				
25			Emeline "	23	F				" "				
26			Susan "	22	F				" "				
27			John "	21	M		Farmer		" "				
28			Calvin "	11	M				" "				
29			Flora J.	9	F				" "				
30	520	520	William Collins	67	M		Cooper	100	" "				
31			Nancy "	48	F				" "				
32			Margaret "	25	F				" "			1	
33			Sarah "	23	F				" "				
34			Mary "	22	F				" "				
35			John "	21	M		Carpenter		" "				
36			Nancy "	17	F				" "		1		
37			Willis "	14	M				" "		1		
38			Catharine "	11	F				" "		1		
39			Alfred C. "	7	M				" "		1		
40			John M. Thomas	29	M		Farmer	76	" "			1	
41	521	521	Nancy "	26	F				" "				
42			Mahalah H. "	2/12	F				" "				

m 20
f 22

19 401

201

SCHEDULE I.—Free Inhabitants in ______ in the County of Moore State of N. Carolina enumerated by me, on the 25th day of September 1850. N. McCrummen Ass't Marshal.

Dwelling-houses numbered in the order of visitation.	Families numbered in the order of visitation.	The Name of every Person whose usual place of abode on the first day of June, 1850, was in this family.	Description: Age.	Description: Sex.	Description: Color, white, black, or mulatto.	Profession, Occupation, or Trade of each Male Person over 15 years of age.	Value of Real Estate owned.	Place of Birth. Naming the State, Territory, or Country.	Married within the year.	Attended School within the year.	Persons over 20 y'rs of age who cannot read & write.	Whether deaf and dumb, blind, insane, idiotic, pauper, or convict.
1	2	3	4	5	6	7	8	9	10	11	12	13
		Henry Spivey	9	m				N. Carolina				
522	522	Mary Shaw	38	F.			15	" "				
		Flora A. "	6	F.				" "				
523	523	John Campbell	24	m		Farmer	105	" "				
		Kissiah E. "	28	F.				" "				
		Mary M. "	25	F.				" "				
		William "	1	m				" "				
524	524	John Hawley	32	m		Farmer	160	" "				
		Lucinda "	27	F.				" "				
		Marshal H. "	3	m				" "				
		Isabella C. "	2	F.				" "				
525	525	Alfred Oliver	54	m		Farmer	1000	" "				
		Elizabeth "	54	F.				" "				
		Barbara McAulay	26	F.				" "				
		Nancy "	18	F.				" "		1		
		Sarah "	16	F.				" "		1		
		Sion "	14	m				" "		1		
		James McAulay	24	m		Farmer		" "				
		Thomas Campbell	20	m		Farmer		" "				
526	526	William Buchanan	36	m				" "			1	
		Eliza "	36	F.				" "				
		Mathew G. "	8	m				" "		1		
		Martha E. "	6	F.				" "				
		Benjamin F. "	4	m				" "				
		Mary A. "	1	F.				" "				
527	527	David Oliver	48	m		Carpenter	300	" "				
		Nancy "	44	F.				" "				
		John M. "	23	m		Carpenter		" "				
		Malcom "	21	m		Farmer		" "		1		
		Margaret "	18	F.				" "		1		
		Elizabeth "	16	F.				" "		1		
		Sarah "	13	F.				" "		1		
		Nancy G. "	10	F.				" "		1		
		Marionah "	8	F.				" "		1		
		David A. "	4	m				" "				
		Louisa "	6/12	F.				" "				
528	528	Penelope Chavis	72	F.	m			" "				
		Rebecca "	67	F.	m			" "				
529	529	James Lett	50	m		Farmer	250	" "				
		Mary E. "	40	F.				" "				
		Elizabeth "	14	F.				" "				
		William "	12	m				" "			1	

m 18
F 24 0 7

14 **SCHEDULE I.—Free Inhabitants in** ________________ **in the County of** *Moore* **State of** *N. Carolina* **enumerated by me, on the** *25th* **day of** *Septem* **1850.** *N. McCrummen* **Ass't Marshal.**

Dwelling-houses numbered in the order of visitation.	Families numbered in the order of visitation.	The Name of every Person whose usual place of abode on the first day of June, 1850, was in this family.	Age.	Sex.	Color, White, black, or mulatto.	Profession, Occupation, or Trade of each Male Person over 15 years of age.	Value of Real Estate owned.	Place of Birth. Naming the State, Territory, or Country.	Married within the year.	Attended School within the year.	Persons over 20 y'rs of age who cannot read & write.	Whether deaf and dumb, blind, insane, idiotic, pauper, or convict.
1	2	3	4	5	6	7	8	9	10	11	12	13
		Louisa Lott	10	F				N. Carolina		1		
		Nancy "	7	F				" "				
		Mary "	5	F				" "				
		Lavina "	2	F				" "				
530	530	Abel Kelly	46	m		Blacksmith	4000	" "				
		Elizabeth "	42	F				" "				
		Alfred "	22	m		Miller		" "	—			
		Frances "	20	F				" "				
		Martha "	19	F				" "		1		
		Nancy "	16	F				" "		1		
		Mary A. "	13	F				" "		1		
		Delilah J. "	8	F				" "		1		
		James H. "	5	m				" "				
		Abel A. "	2	m				" "				
531	531	Thomas Harrington	71	m		Farmer	1160	" "				
		Lydia "	46	F				" "			1	
		Thomas "	29	m		Farmer	160	" "				
		William D. Harrington	24	m		Constable		" "				
532	532	Hugh Kelly	83	m		Wagonmaker		" "				
		Archibald "	30	m		Mechanic		" "			1	
		Elizabeth "	35	F				" "			1	
		Telitha A. "	30	F				" "				
		Margaret "	8	F				" "		1		
		Mary A. "	6	F				" "				
		John "	4	m				" "				
		Celia "	9/12	F				" "				
533	533	Hugh Kelly	33	m		Laborer		" "			1	
		Elizabeth "	30	F				" "			1	
		Anabella "	7	F				" "				
		Nancy "	4	F				" "				
534	534	Archibald Harrington	30	m		Farmer	700	" "				
		Hesper A. "	19	F				" "				
		Nancy J. "	3	F				" "				
		Abner A. "	1	m				" "				
		Henry Kelly	22	m		Farmer		" "				
		Jane Goings	12	F				" "				
535	535	Joseph J. McIntire	23	m		Farmer	1100	" "				
536	536	William Watson	74	m		Farmer	3000	" "				
		Elizabeth "	62	F				" "			1	
		Jane "	39	F				" "				
		Malcom "	34	m		Farmer		" "			1	
		William	24	m		Farmer	200	" "				

m 18
F 24

403

SCHEDULE I.—Free Inhabitants in ______________ in the County of Moore State of N. Carolina enumerated by me, on the 26th day of Septem 1850. N. McCrummen Ass't Marshal. 202

Dwelling-houses numbered in the order of visitation.	Families numbered in the order of visitation.	The Name of every Person whose usual place of abode on the first day of June, 1850, was in this family.	Age.	Sex.	Color, White, black, or mulatto.	Profession, Occupation, or Trade of each Male Person over 15 years of age.	Value of Real Estate owned.	Place of Birth. Naming the State, Territory, or Country.	Married within the year.	Attended School within the year.	Persons over 20 y'rs of age who cannot read & write.	Whether deaf and dumb, blind, insane, idiotic, pauper, or convict.	
1	2	3	4	5	6	7	8	9	10	11	12	13	
		Elizabeth Watson	22	F.				N. Carolina		1			1
		Margarett J. "	18	F.				" "		1			2
537	537	David Watson	70	m		Farmer	300	" "					3
		Jane "	48	F.				" "					4
		Calvin "	23	m		Farmer		" "					5
		Cilvia Watson	27	F.				" "					6
		Margaret "	20	F.				" "					7
		Sallie "	18	F.				" "					8
		Henry "	17	m		Farmer		" "					9
		Alexander "	13	m				" "					10
538	538	Nancy Mathis	63	F.			25	" "			1		11
		Mary "	23	F.				" "			1		12
		Telitha A. "	6	F.				" "					13
		William R. "	21	m		Farmer		" "					14
539	539	Lewis Wicker	48	m		Farmer	200	" "			1		15
		Jane "	38	F.				Scotland					16
		Nancy "	19	F.				N. Carolina					17
		Archibald "	11	m				" "		1			18
		Sarah "	10	F.				" "		1			19
		Benjamin L. "	9	m				" "		1			20
		Frances C. "	7	F.				" "		1			21
		Mary J. "	5	F.				" "					22
		Margaret J. "	4	F.				" "					23
		William M. "	2	m				" "					24
		James "	1/2	m				" "					25
540	640	Nancy Wicker	52	F.			265	" "			1		26
		Daniel "	22	m		Farmer		" "			1		27
		Louis "	19	m		Farmer		" "					28
		Eli "	17	m		Farmer		" "					29
		Sarah "	14	F.				" "					30
		Susan "	12	F.				" "					31
		Elizabeth "	10	F.				" "					32
		William "	8	m				" "					33
[illegible]	541	Charles Wicker	34	m		Blacksmith		" "					34
		Jane "	35	F.				" "					35
		Martha "	14	F.				" "					36
		Robert "	12	m				" "					37
		Jane "	9	F.				" "					38
		Alvis "	4	m				" "					39
		Josiah "	2	m				" "					40
		Mathew Watson	21	m		Blacksmith		" "					41
[illegible]	[illegible]	Jonathan Wicker	32	m		Farmer	300	" "					42

M 20
F 22

SCHEDULE I.—Free Inhabitants in ____________ in the County of Moore State of N. Carolina enumerated by me, on the 26th day of Septem. 1850. Neill McCrummen Ass't Marshal.

Dwelling-houses numbered in the order of visitation.	Families numbered in the order of visitation.	The Name of every Person whose usual place of abode on the first day of June, 1850, was in this family.	Age.	Sex.	Color, { White, black, or mulatto.	Profession, Occupation, or Trade of each Male Person over 15 years of age.	Value of Real Estate owned.	Place of Birth. Naming the State, Territory, or Country.	Married within the year.	Attended School within the year.	Persons over 20 y'rs of age who cannot read & write.	Whether deaf and dumb, blind, insane, idiotic, pauper, or convict.
1	2	3	4	5	6	7	8	9	10	11	12	13
		Nancy Wicker	32	F				N. Carolina				
		Stephen "	6	m				" "		1		
		Emeline "	4	F				" "		1		
		Jonathan "	2	m				" "				
		Evander "	1	m				" "				
543	543	Benjamin Wicker	41	m		Farmer	150	" "				
		Susan "	49	F				" "			1	
		Thomas "	17	m		Farmer		" "				
		Warren "	16	m		Farmer		" "		1		
		Elijah "	12	m				" "		1		
		Nancy "	10	F				" "		1		
		Benjamin R. "	7	m				" "				
544	544	Mary Wicker	54	F				" "			1	
		Mary "	52	F				" "			1	
		Nisey "	38	F				" "				
		Zilpha "	37	F				" "				
545	545	Stephen Wicker	43	m		none	200	" "				
		Elizabeth "	55	F				" "				
		Mathew "	14	m				" "				
546	546	Edward Wicker	46	m		Farmer	200	" "			1	
		Martha "	40	F				" "				
		Martha "	19	F				" "		1		
		Sallie J. "	7	F				" "		1		
		Rebecca "	3	F				" "				
		Evander "	6/12	m				" "				
		William Wicker	16	m		Farmer		" "		1		
547	547	Cherry Wicker	48	F			62	" "			1	
		Sallie "	36	F				" "			1	
		Nancy "	34	F				" "			1	
		Mary "	28	F				" "			1	
		Jane "	23	F				" "			1	
		William "	13	m				" "		1		
		Green B. "	9	m				" "		1		
		Mathew "	1	m				" "				
548	548	Elias Kelly	45	m		Waggonmaker	160	" "			1	
		Penelope "	41	F				" "				
		Celia "	16	F				" "				
		Elizabeth "	16	F				" "				
		Flora A. "	13	F				" "				
		M. Jane "	10	F				" "				
		Nancy "	5	F				" "				
		Zilpha Kelly	19	F				" "				

m 17

20

SCHEDULE I.—Free Inhabitants in ____________ in the County of Moore State of N. Carolina enumerated by me, on the 27th day of September 1850. N. McCrummen Ass't Marshal.

2405

203

Dwelling-houses numbered in the order of visitation.	Families numbered in the order of visitation.	The Name of every Person whose usual place of abode on the first day of June, 1850, was in this family.	DESCRIPTION. Age.	Sex.	Color, White, black, or mulatto.	Profession, Occupation, or Trade of each Male Person over 15 years of age.	Value of Real Estate owned.	Place of Birth. Naming the State, Territory, or Country.	Married within the year.	Attended School within the year.	Persons over 20 y'rs of age who cannot read & write.	Whether deaf and dumb, blind, insane, idiotic, pauper, or convict.
1	2	3	4	5	6	7	8	9	10	11	12	13
		Hugh A. Kelly	1	m				N. Carolina				
549	549	John Kelly	78	m		Farmer	130	" "				
		Mack "	52	m		Farmer	200	" "				
		Elizabeth "	42	F				" "				
550	550	Sion Campbell	43	m		Farmer	400	" "				
		Nancy "	43	F				" "				
		James A. "	18	m		Farmer		" "		/		
		John "	17	m		Farmer		" "		/		
		Ann E. "	14	F				" "		/		
551	551	Reuben Thomas	52	m		Farmer	100	" "			/	
		Charity "	48	F				" "			/	
		John "	20	m		Farmer		" "		/		
		Nancy "	17	F				" "				
552	552	John Blackman	62	m		Farmer	387	" "				
		Candice "	42	F				" "				
		Mary "	32	F				" "				
		Nancy "	19	F				" "				
		Frances C. "	13	F				" "				
		Susan "	10	F				" "				
		Jafe F. "	8	m				" "				
		Philpena A. "	5	F				" "				
		Benjamin "	3	m				" "				
553	553	Nathan Hight	46	m		Farmer	265	" "				
		James "	14	m				" "				
		Elizabeth "	12	F				" "				
		Joseph "	10	m				" "				
		Lydia "	8	F				" "				
		Fanny "	5	F				" "				
554	554	John Watson	49	m		Farmer	360	" "				
		Mary "	44	F				" "				
		Robert "	15	m				" "		/		
		Malcom "	14	m				" "		/		
		Flora A. "	12	F				" "		/		
		Garner "	9	m				" "		/		
		Catharine "	7	F				" "		/		
		Mary J. "	2	F				" "				
…5	555	Malcom B. Watson	43	m		Farmer	400	" "				
		Barbara "	33	F				" "				
		Elizabeth "	8	F				" "		/		
		David "	5	m				" "				
		Robert "	3	m				" "				
		Margaret "	9/12	F				" "				

m 21
f 21

Schedule I.—Free Inhabitants in ______ **in the County of** Moore **State of** N. Carolina **enumerated by me, on the** 27th **day of** Septem. **1850.** N. McCrummen **Ass't Marshal.**

	Dwelling-houses numbered in the order of visitation.	Families numbered in the order of visitation.	The Name of every Person whose usual place of abode on the first day of June, 1850, was in this family.	Age.	Sex.	Color, White, black, or mulatto.	Profession, Occupation, or Trade of each Male Person over 15 years of age.	Value of Real Estate owned.	Place of Birth. Naming the State, Territory, or Country.	Married within the year.	Attended School within the year.	Persons over 20 y'rs of age who cannot read & write.	Whether deaf and dumb, blind, insane, idiotic, pauper, or convict.
	1	2	3	4	5	6	7	8	9	10	11	12	13
1			Anna Watson	49	F				N. Carolina				
2	556	556	Richard Morris	16	m		Farmer		" "				
3	557	557	James Stone	34	m		Farmer		" "				
4			Judy "	31	F				" "				
5			Sallie "	12	F				" "				
6			Parker "	11	m				" "		/		
7			James M. "	10	m				" "		/		
8			Martha "	5	F				" "				
9			David "	4	m				" "				
10			Frances "	3	F				" "				
11			A. Jane "	1	F				" "				
12	558	558	Mathew B. Morris	42	m		Tailor	100	" "				
13			Margaret "	30	F				" "				
14			Archibald I. "	9	m				" "		/		
15			Flora A. E. "	7	F				" "		/		
16			Allen J. "	5	m				" "				
17			Daniel H. "	3	m				" "				
18			Effy J. "	1	F				" "				
19			Allen Ellis	21	m		Farmer		" "			/	
20	559	559	William Godfrey	38	m		Farmer	40	" "				
21			Mathew "	14	m				" "		/		
22			William "	12	m				" "		/		
23	560	560	Matilda Gunter	51	F			250	" "			/	
24			John A. "	19	m		Farmer		" "				
25			Joseph "	18	m		Farmer		" "				
26			Hesper A. "	16	F				" "		/		
27			Lucy E. "	14	F				" "		/		
28			Kesander J. "	12	F				" "		/		
29			Lucy Tetley	79	F				" "			/	
30			Lydia Godfrey	57	F				" "			/	
31	561	561	Elisha Watson	26	m		Farmer	414	" "				
32			Ann E. "	37	F				" "				
33	562	562	Anderson Wicker	56	m		Farmer	126	" "			/	
34			Nancy "	58	F				" "				
35			Jane "	30	F				" "				
36			Charles "	20	m		Farmer		" "				
37			Niah A. "	19	F				" "				
38			Elizabeth A. "	3	F				" "				
39			Charles A. "	1/12	m				" "				
40			Allen Parish	16	m		Farmer		" "				
41	563	563	Mathew Wicker	34	m		Farmer	50	" "			/	
42			Sallie "	29	F				" "				

M 21
F 21

SCHEDULE I.—Free Inhabitants in ________ in the County of *Moore* State of *N. Carolina* enumerated by me, on the *25th* day of *Septem.* 1850. *N. McCrummen* Ass't Marshal. 497

204

Dwelling-houses numbered in the order of visitation.	Families numbered in the order of visitation.	The Name of every Person whose usual place of abode on the first day of June, 1850, was in this family.	Description: Age.	Sex.	Color, (White, black, or mulatto.)	Profession, Occupation, or Trade of each Male Person over 15 years of age.	Value of Real Estate owned.	Place of Birth. Naming the State, Territory, or Country.	Married within the year.	Attended School within the year.	Persons over 20 y'rs of age who cannot read & write.	Whether deaf and dumb, blind, insane, idiotic, pauper, or convict.	
1	2	3	4	5	6	7	8	9	10	11	12	13	
		William L. Wicker	8	m				N. Carolina					1
		Eliza L. "	6	F				" "					2
		Elizabeth "	4	F				" "					3
		Charles F. "	2	m				" "					4
		Martha A. "	9/12	F				" "					5
564	564	Priscilla Kelly	27	F				" "			1		6
		Roderick "	33	m		Cooper		" "					7
		Martha "	9	F				" "					8
565	565	John A. Wicker	36	m		Farmer	75	" "			1		9
		Margaret "	29	F				" "					10
		Nancy "	3	F				" "					11
		Sarah J. "	1	F				" "					12
		Robert A. "	2/12	m				" "					13
566	566	Thomas Kelly	63	m		Farmer		" "			1		14
		Elizabeth "	50	F				" "					15
		Mariah "	28	F				" "			1		16
		Mary "	20	F				" "			1		17
		Margaret "	13	F				" "					18
		Thomas "	11	m				" "					19
		Spencer "	9	m				" "					20
		Stephen Morris	83	m		none		" "			1		21
567	567	Jane McIver	60	F			640	Scotland					22
		Mary "	24	F				N. Carolina					23
		John "	22	m		Farmer		" "					24
		Andrew "	20	m		Farmer		" "		1			25
		Williamson "	14	m				" "		1			26
568	568	Levi Gunter	39	m		Farmer	550	" "					27
		Mary "	31	F				" "					28
		Martha "	6	F				" "					29
		Mary "	2	F				" "					30
569	569	Martin Dye	63	m		Farmer		" "					31
		Sallie "	63	m				" "					32
		Martin E. "	17	m				" "					33
		Loveday Johnson	30	F				" "			1		34
570	570	W. Westley Dye	32	m		Farmer	200	" "					35
		Jane "	27	F				" "			1		36
		Johnell "	10	m				" "		1			37
		Dalaney "	8	F				" "		1			38
		David "	6	m				" "		1			39
		Martin E. "	4	m				" "					40
		Jane "	2	F				" "					41
	571	Archibald McIver	40	m		Farmer	800	" "					42

M 21
Fe 21

SCHEDULE I.—Free Inhabitants in ______ in the County of Moore State of N. Carolina enumerated by me, on the 25th day of Septem 1850. Neill McCrummen Ass't Marshal.

Dwelling-houses numbered in the order of visitation.	Families numbered in the order of visitation.	The Name of every Person whose usual place of abode on the first day of June, 1850, was in this family.	Age.	Sex.	Color, White, black, or mulatto.	Profession, Occupation, or Trade of each Male Person over 15 years of age.	Value of Real Estate owned.	Place of Birth. Naming the State, Territory, or Country.	Married within the year.	Attended School within the year.	Persons over 20 y'rs of age who cannot read & write.	Whether deaf and dumb, blind, insane, idiotic, pauper, or convict.
1	2	3	4	5	6	7	8	9	10	11	12	13
		Nancy McIver	25	F				N. Carolina				
		John T. "	13	m				" "		1		
		Abel "	11	m				" "		1		
		Sarah "	5	F				" "				
		Mathew "	2	m				" "				
		Catharine "	2/12	F				" "				
		Angus McIver	27	m	Laborer			" "				
572	572	Daniel R. McIver	60	m	Farmer	850		" "				
		Catharine "	53	F				" "				
		Christian "	30	F				" "				
		Lydia "	25	F				" "				
		Jennet "	17	F				" "		1		
		Mary A. "	14	F				" "		1		
		Edward "	11	m				" "		1		
		Mary Bradley	83	F				Scotland				Blind
573	573	Mary McIver	60	F			2500	N. Carolina				
		Eliza "	27	F				" "				
		Mary A. "	25	F				" "				
		John D. "	23	m		Farmer		" "				
		Archibald "	20	m		Farmer		" "		1		
		William "	19	m		None		" "				Idiotic
		Evander J. "	16	m		Student		" "		1		
574	574	Duncan D. McIver	49	m		Farmer	1050	" "				
		Flora "	46	F				" "				
		John D. "	18	m		None		" "				Blind
		Daniel N. "	16	m		Farmer		" "		1		
		Duncan M. "	14	m				" "		1		
		Isabella "	11	F				" "		1		
		Mary J. "	9	F				" "		1		
		Murdoch "	7	m				" "		1		
		Kenneth "	5	m				" "		1		
575	575	John McIver	78	m		Farmer	150	Scotland			1	
		Kenneth "	45	m		Farmer		N. Carolina				
		Catharine "	12	F				" "		1		
		Neill A. "	8	m				" "		1		
		Neill McIver	51	m		Tailor		Scotland				
576	576	John R. McIver	39	m		Farmer		N. Carolina				
		Lucinda "	33	F				" "			1	
		John W. "	12	m				" "		1		
		William N. "	6	M				" "		1		
		Kenneth "	4	m				" "				
		George "	2	m				" "				

m 25
F 17

21 409

SCHEDULE I.—Free Inhabitants in ______________ in the County of *Moore* State of *N. Carolina* enumerated by me, on the *30th* day of *September* 1850. *N. McCrummen* Ass't Marshal. 205

Dwelling-houses numbered in the order of visitation.	Families numbered in the order of visitation.	The Name of every Person whose usual place of abode on the first day of June, 1850, was in this family.	Description: Age.	Sex.	Color, {White, black, or mulatto.	Profession, Occupation, or Trade of each Male Person over 15 years of age.	Value of Real Estate owned.	Place of Birth. Naming the State, Territory, or Country.	Married within the year.	Attended School within the year.	Persons over 20 y'rs of age who cannot read & write.	Whether deaf and dumb, blind, insane, idiotic, pauper, or convict.	
1	2	3	4	5	6	7	8	9	10	11	12	13	
		Mathew McIver	72	M				N. Carolina					1
577	577	Archibald McPherson	78	M		Farmer	80	Scotland			1		2
		Sarah "	75	F				Ditto			1		3
		Catharine "	30	F				N. Carolina			1		4
		Flora Campbell	8	F				" "		1			5
578	578	Hastin Gilmore	34	M		Farmer	500	" "					6
		Frances A. "	36	F				" "					7
		Mildred "	13	F				" "		1			8
		Nathan A. "	10	M				" "		1			9
		John A. "	8	M				" "					10
		Robert "	5	M				" "					11
		Baxter "	3	M				" "					12
		Ann E. "	$\frac{10}{12}$	F				" "					13
579	579	Mary McIver	70	F			500	" "			1		14
		Jesse Wicker	9	M				" "					15
580	580	Daniel B. McIver	31	M		Farmer	1500	" "	—				16
		Mary A. "	16	F				" "	—				17
		John McIver	19	M				" "		1			18
581	581	David W. Wicker	49	M		Farmer	800	" "					19
		Christian "	40	F				" "					20
		Alexander "	18	M		Farmer		" "					21
		Kenneth "	13	M				" "					22
		Jesse "	12	M				" "					23
		Elizabeth "	8	F				" "		1			24
582	582	Elisha Wicker	26	M		Farmer	200	" "			1		25
		Anna "	22	F				" "			1		26
		Alexander "	3	M				" "					27
		Archibald "	2	M				" "					28
		Martha "	$\frac{1}{365}$	F				" "					29
		William Brown	16	M		Farmer		" "					30
		John McIntosh	24	M		Carpenter		" "					31
583	583	Elizabeth Jackson	45	F			5	" "			1		32
		Sarah C. "	15	F				" "					33
584	584	Mathew C. Wicker	49	M		Farmer	125	" "					34
		Christian "	50	F				" "					35
		John "	18	M		Farmer		" "		1			36
		Jesse C. "	13	M				" "					37
		William G. "	15	M				" "					38
		David S. "	12	M				" "					39
		Elizabeth "	8	F				" "					40
		John M. "	6	M				" "					41
585	585	Newton R. Bryan	40	M		Farmer	700	" "					42

M 26
F 16 ✓

SCHEDULE I.—Free Inhabitants in ______ in the County of Moore State of N. Carolina enumerated by me, on the 1st day of October 1850. N. McCrummen Ass't Marshal.

Dwelling-houses numbered in the order of visitation.	Families numbered in the order of visitation.	The Name of every Person whose usual place of abode on the first day of June, 1850, was in this family.	Description: Age.	Sex.	Color, White, black, or mulatto.	Profession, Occupation, or Trade of each Male Person over 15 years of age.	Value of Real Estate owned.	Place of Birth, Naming the State, Territory, or Country.	Married within the year.	Attended School within the year.	Persons over 20 y'rs of age who cannot read & write.	Whether deaf and dumb, blind, insane, idiotic, pauper, or convict.
1	2	3	4	5	6	7	8	9	10	11	12	13
		Ann C. Bryant	37	F				N. Carolina				
		Margaret "	14	F				" "				
		Mary J. "	12	F				" "				
		Ruth "	10	F				" "				
		Francina "	8	F				" "				
		Reddin "	6	M				" "				
		John "	4	M				" "				
		Flora A. "	2	F				" "				
		Roderick N. "	4/12	M				" "				
586	586	George W. Watson	30	M		Physician		" "				
		Mary S. "	31	F				" "				
		Melvina Riddle	20	F				" "			1	
		Mary A. "	19	F				" "				
587	587	Joseph Cook	52	M		Farmer	1000	" "				
		Tabitha "	38	F				" "				
		John M. Campbell	15	M		Farmer		" "		1		
588	588	Winship Bryant	48	M		Farmer	500	" "				
		Nancy "	53	F				" "				
		Margaret "	20	F				" "				
		Winship N. "	16	M		Farmer		" "				
		Elizabeth "	8	F				" "				
		Reddin Bryant	80	M		none		" "				
		John Hughs	18	M		Farmer		" "				
		Sheba Bryan	75	F				" "				
		Jemima Sett	75	F				" "				
589	589	Flora Baker	79	F			200	" "				
		Mary Buie	69	F				" "			1	
590	590	Evander S. McIver	31	M		Merchant	700	" "				
		Jesse S. Bryan	23	M		Ditto		" "				
		Mary A. "	25	F				" "				
		Archibald Hughs	16	M		Farmer		" "				
		Albert Wicker	16	M		Ditto		" "				
591	591	Margaret Mathews	49	F			100	" "			1	
		Isabella "	35	F				" "			1	
592	592	Wesley McIver	29	M		Farmer	700	" "				
		Jane C. "	24	F				" "				
593	593	Margaret Shaw	40	F				" "			1	
		Catharine "	26	F				" "			1	
		Mary "	4/12	F				" "				
594	594	Catharine Black	57	F			50	" "			1	
		John "	16	M		Farmer		" "				
595	595	John C. Wicker	43	M		Farmer		" "				

M 17
7025

411

SCHEDULE I.—Free Inhabitants in ______ in the County of Moore State of N Carolina enumerated by me, on the 9th day of October 1850. N. McCummen Ass't Marshal. 206

Dwelling-houses numbered in the order of visitation.	Families numbered in the order of visitation.	The Name of every Person whose usual place of abode on the first day of June, 1850, was in this family.	Age.	Sex.	Color, White, black, or mulatto.	Profession, Occupation, or Trade of each Male Person over 15 years of age.	Value of Real Estate owned.	Place of Birth. Naming the State, Territory, or Country.	Married within the year.	Attended School within the year.	Persons over 20 y'rs of age who cannot read & write.	Whether deaf and dumb, blind, insane, idiotic, pauper, or convict.	
1	2	3	4	5	6	7	8	9	10	11	12	13	
		Flora Wicker	43	F				N. Carolina					1
		Martha "	17	F				" "					2
		Pleasant "	10	M				" "					3
		Mary J. "	6	F				" "					4
		Archibald "	3	M				" "					5
		Ann C. "	4/12	F				" "					6
596	596	William Gaster	34	M		Farmer	90	" "					7
		Nancy "	36	F				" "					8
		Frances "	9	F				" "					9
		Sarah "	8	F				" "					10
		Lucy J "	6	F				" "					11
		Isabella "	3	F				" "					12
		Alexander "	1	M				" "					13
597	597	Daniel Matthews	54	M		Farmer	475	" "					14
		Nancy "	42	F				" "					15
		Isabella C. "	15	F				" "		1			16
		John B. "	13	M				" "		1			17
		Christian "	11	F				" "		1			18
		Margaret "	9	F				" "		1			19
		Louisa F. "	7	F				" "		1			20
598	598	Thomas Wicker	27	M		Farmer	400	" "					21
		Penelope "	23	F				" "					22
		James "	2	M				" "					23
		Nancy "	4/12	F				" "					24
		Martha Wicker	70	F				" "			1		25
		Haywood Bobbitt	25	M		Farmer		" "					26
599	599	Mary Mathews	60	F				" "					27
		Stephen Wicker	23	M		Farmer		" "					28
		Mary "	26	F				" "			1		29
		Evander "	1	M				" "					30
		Daniel "	2/12	M				" "					31
600	600	William Walden	50	M		Farmer	330	" "			1		32
		Winnifred "	45	F				" "					33
		Eliza "	24	F				" "			1		34
		Delany "	21	F				" "			1		35
		Nancy Walden	22	F				" "			1		36
		Polly "	18	F				" "					37
		Ann "	13	F				" "					38
		William "	12	M				" "					39
611	611	Duncan McPherson	40	M		Farmer		" "					40
		Mary "	30	F				" "					41
		Donald "	12	M				" "		1			42

m 16
F 26

SCHEDULE I.—Free Inhabitants in ______________ in the County of *Moore* State of *N Carolina* enumerated by me, on the *2d* day of *October* 1850. *N McCrummen* Ass't Marshal.

Dwelling-houses numbered in the order of visitation.	Families numbered in the order of visitation.	The Name of every Person whose usual place of abode on the first day of June, 1850, was in this family.	Description: Age.	Sex.	Color, White, black, or mulatto.	Profession, Occupation, or Trade of each Male Person over 15 years of age.	Value of Real Estate owned.	Place of Birth. Naming the State, Territory, or Country.	Married within the year.	Attended School within the year.	Persons over 20 y'rs of age who cannot read & write.	Whether deaf and dumb, blind, insane, idiotic, pauper, or convict.
1	2	3	4	5	6	7	8	9	10	11	12	13
		Archibald D. McPherson	10	M				N Carolina		1		
		Dawson "	7	M				" "		1		
		Sarah "	4	F				" "				
		Murdock A. "	2	M				" "				
		Mary C. "	1/12	F				" "				
602	602	William B. Petty	29	M		Farmer	350	" "				
		Melinda "	28	F				" "				
		William H. "	2	M				" "				
		Henry T. "	5/12	M				" "				
603	603	Flora McIver	61	F			[illegible]	Scotland				
		Catharine McIver	30	F			143	N Carolina				
		Isabella "	25	F			143	N Carolina				
		Kenneth "	23	M		Farmer	486	" "				
604	604	John A. Gilmore	32	M		Ditto	1550	" "				
		Phebe "	35	F				" "				
		David C. "	5	M				" "				
		Jackson C. "	5	M				" "				
605	605	Green B. Gilmore	25	M		Farmer	350	" "	—			
		Elizabeth "	17	F				" "	—			
606	606	James Burns	25	M		Farmer		" "				
		Flora A. "	25	F				" "				
		Francis M. "	2	M				" "				
		Sarah C. "	7/12	F				" "				
607	607	Jordan Wicker	43	M		Farmer	300	" "				
		Margaret "	45	F				" "				
		Ambers "	15	M		Farmer		" "		1		
		Mary "	14	F				" "		1		
		Margaret "	13	F				" "		1		
		Sarah "	11	F				" "		1		
		Warren "	6	M				" "				
		Andrew Burns	16	M		Farmer		" "				
608	608	John W. Stedman	47	M		Farmer	400	" "				
		Mary "	43	F				" "				
		William "	17	M		Farmer		" "		1		
		Permelia H. "	10	F				" "		1		
		David B. "	9	M				" "		1		
		Henry C. "	6	M				" "		1		
		Happy "	4	F				" "				
609	609	James Bridges	56	M		Farmer	150	" "				
		Catharine "	48	F				" "			1	
		William "	27	M		Farmer		" "				
		Ann "	25	F				" "				

M 23
F 19

22 423

SCHEDULE I.—Free Inhabitants in ______________ in the County of Moore State of N. Carolina enumerated by me, on the 3d day of October 1850. Neill McCrummen Ass't Marshal. 207

Dwelling-houses numbered in the order of visitation.	Families numbered in the order of visitation.	The Name of every Person whose usual place of abode on the first day of June, 1850, was in this family.	Age.	Sex.	Color, (White, black, or mulatto.)	Profession, Occupation, or Trade of each Male Person over 15 years of age.	Value of Real Estate owned.	Place of Birth. Naming the State, Territory, or Country.	Married within the year.	Attended School within the year.	Persons over 20 y'rs of age who cannot read & write.	Whether deaf and dumb, blind, insane, idiotic, pauper, or convict.	
1	2	3	4	5	6	7	8	9	10	11	12	13	
		Mary Bridges	18	F				N. Carolina					1
		Joseph "	16	m		Farmer		" "					2
		Catharine Gilmore	4	F				" "					3
610	610	William Dowdy	65	m		Laborer		" "	—				4
		Lettice "	23	F				" "	—				5
611	611	Peter McIntyre	50	m		Farmer	340	" "					6
		Isabella "	53	F				" "					7
		Mary "	22	F				" "					8
		Daniel "	20	m		Teacher		" "					9
		John "	18	m		Farmer		" "					10
		Kenneth "	14	m				" "		/			11
612	612	John McIver	54	m		Farmer	460	" "					12
		Harriet Walden	16	F	m			" "					13
613	613	Catharine McIntosh	52	F			150	" "					14
		Eliza "	25	F				" "					15
		Margaret J. "	22	F				" "					16
		Mary J. "	20	F				" "					17
		John "	13	m				" "					18
		Roderick "	10	m				" "					19
614	614	John McDonald	30	m		Farmer		" "					20
		Lucy "	37	F				" "					21
		Henry C. "	6	m				" "		/			22
		Elizabeth "	3	F				" "					23
		David "	1	m				" "					24
615	615	Duncan McR. McIntosh	41	m		Farmer	53	" "					25
		Temperance "	38	F				" "					26
		John A. "	18	m		Farmer		" "					27
		Margaret "	16	F				" "		/			28
		Mary "	15	F				" "		/			29
		Archibald "	13	m				" "		/			30
		Daniel "	12	m				" "		/			31
		Frances M. "	10	F				" "		/			32
		Christian M. "	8	F				" "		/			33
		William D. "	5	m				" "					34
		Elizabeth "	5	F				" "					35
		George A. "	1	m				" "					36
616	616	William McIntosh	48	m		Farmer	50	" "					37
		Catharine "	46	F				" "					38
		Daniel "	21	m		Farmer		" "		/			39
		Jennet "	19	F				" "		/			40
		Mary "	14	F				" "		/			41
		Christian McIntosh	70	F			1500	Scotland			/		42

m 20 ✓
F 22 . 17

424

SCHEDULE I.—Free Inhabitants in ______ **in the County of** Moore **State of** N. Carolina **enumerated by me, on the** 3d **day of** October **1850.** N. McCrimmon **Ass't Marshal.**

	Dwelling-houses numbered in the order of visitation.	Families numbered in the order of visitation.	The Name of every Person whose usual place of abode on the first day of June, 1850, was in this family.	Age.	Sex.	Color, (White, black, or mulatto.)	Profession, Occupation, or Trade of each Male Person over 15 years of age.	Value of Real Estate owned.	Place of Birth. Naming the State, Territory, or Country.	Married within the year.	Attended School within the year.	Persons over 20 y'rs of age who cannot read & write.	Whether deaf and dumb, blind, insane, idiotic, pauper, or convict.
	1	2	3	4	5	6	7	8	9	10	11	12	13
1	617	617	Richard M. Cole	46	m		Farmer	300	N. Carolina				
2			Mary "	41	F.				" "				
3			Mary "	16	F.				" "		1		
4			Green B. "	15	m				" "		1		
5			William B. "	13	m				" "		1		
6			Stephen "	11	m				" "		1		
7			Margaret "	11	F.				" "		1		
8			Martha E. "	9	F.				" "		1		
9			Esther D. "	6	F.				" "		1		
10			Richard F. "	3	m				" "				
11			George "	1	m				" "				
12	618	618	John A. Phillips	57	m		Carpenter	250	" "				
13			Isabella "	48	F.				" "				
14			Eliza A. "	9	F.				" "		1		
15			John H. "	7	m				" "		1		
16			Daniel McIntosh	86	m		Farmer		Scotland			1	
17	619	619	Evander McGilvary	34	m		Farmer	800	N. Carolina				
18			Mary A. "	23	F.				" "				
19			William	3	m				" "				
20	620	620	Thomas Cole	47	m		Farmer	712	" "				
21			Nancy "	48	F.				" "				
22			Thomas W. "	18	m		Farmer		" "		1		
23			Mary "	17	F.				" "		1		
24			Andrew "	15	m				" "		1		
25			Margaret "	13	F.				" "		1		
26			George W. "	9	m				" "		1		
27			Isabella "	6	F.				" "		1		
28			John B. "	2	m				" "				
29			Sylvia Cole	49	F.				" "				
30	621	621	Benjamin Cole	32	m		Farmer	250	" "				
31			Mahalah "	24	F.				" "				
32	622	622	Alexander N. McRae	28	m		Farmer	1000	" "				
33			Mary "	21	F.				" "				
34			Daniel R. "	2/12	m				" "				
35	623	623	John Nicholson	80	m		Farmer		Scotland				
36			Nancy E. Sheppard	59	F.				N. Carolina			1	
37			David Baker	11	m				" "		1		
38			Malcom Brown	7	m				" "		1		
39	624	624	Elizabeth Baker	40	F.				" "				
40			Flora "	14	F.				" "		1		
41			Jennet "	12	F.				" "		1		
42			Margaret "	10	F.				" "		1		

M 22
F 20

415

SCHEDULE I.—Free Inhabitants in ______________ in the County of Moore State of N. Carolina enumerated by me, on the 8th day of October 1850. N. McCrummen Ass't Marshal. 208

Dwelling-houses numbered in the order of visitation.	Families numbered in the order of visitation.	The Name of every Person whose usual place of abode on the first day of June, 1850, was in this family.	Age.	Sex.	Color, white, black, or mulatto.	Profession, Occupation, or Trade of each Male Person over 15 years of age.	Value of Real Estate owned.	Place of Birth. Naming the State, Territory, or Country.	Married within the year.	Attended School within the year.	Persons over 20 y'rs of age who cannot read & write.	Whether deaf and dumb, blind, insane, idiotic, pauper, or convict.
1	2	3	4	5	6	7	8	9	10	11	12	13
		Catharine Baker	8	F				N. Carolina		1		
		Mary "	6	F				" "		1		
625	625	Peter Sinclair	75	m		Farmer	300	" "				
		Jennet "	73	F				" "			1	
		Mary "	45	F				" "				
		Andrew "	33	m		Carpenter	400	" "				
		Nancy "	29	F				" "				Idiotic
		William George	13	m	m			" "				
626	626	Malcom Black	28	m		Farmer		" "				
		Margaret "	34	F				" "				
		Catharine "	7	F				" "				
		Archibald "	6	m				" "				
		Nancy "	4	F				" "				
		John "	1	m				" "				
627	627	Catharine McQueen	50	F			70	Scotland			1	
628	628	William McQueen	43	m		Farmer		" "				
		Elizabeth "	38	F				" "				
		Mary "	13	F				" "				
		John "	11	m				" "				
		Catharine "	8	F				" "				
		Archibald "	1	m				" "				
		Duncan "	1	m				" "				
629	629	Christian McLeod	76	F			100	N. Carolina			1	
630	630	Daniel McLeod	64	m		Farmer	100	" "			1	
631	631	Alexander Black	59	m		Farmer	60	Scotland				Convict
		Sylvia "	50	F				N. Carolina				
632	632	Louis Brown	21	m		Laborer		" "	—		1	
		Catharine "	22	F				" "	—		1	
633	633	Neill McDuffie	34	m		Farmer	100	" "			1	
		Ann "	24	F				" "			1	
		John "	6	m				" "				
		Margaret "	5	F				" "				
		Daniel "	2	m				" "				
		Rebecca "	4/12	F				" "				
634	634	Nancy McDuffie	56	F			300	" "				
		Flora "	16	F				" "				
635	635	John Morris	38	m		Farmer	150	" "				
		Mary "	27	F				" "				
		Jane "	8	F				" "				
		Catharine "	6	F				" "				
		David "	5	m				" "				
		Isabella "	3	F				" "				

m 18 1 B
F 21

Schedule I.—Free Inhabitants in ______ in the County of *Moore* State of *N. Carolina* enumerated by me, on the *4th* day of *October* 1850. *N. McCrummen* Ass't Marshal.

Dwelling-houses numbered in the order of visitation	Families numbered in the order of visitation	The Name of every Person whose usual place of abode on the first day of June, 1850, was in this family	Age	Sex	Color (White, black, or mulatto)	Profession, Occupation, or Trade of each Male Person over 15 years of age	Value of Real Estate owned	Place of Birth, Naming the State, Territory, or Country	Married within the year	Attended School within the year	Persons over 20 y'rs of age who cannot read & write	Whether deaf and dumb, blind, insane, idiotic, pauper, or convict
1	2	3	4	5	6	7	8	9	10	11	12	13
		Henry Morris	1	m				N. Carolina				
		Robert "	7/12	m				" "				
		Frances Oldham	34	F				" "			/	
636	636	Stephen Morris	63	m		Farmer		" "				
		Jennet "	63	F				" "			/	
		Eliza "	39	F				" "				
		Lucy "	35	F				" "				
		Stephen "	24	m		Farmer		" "			/	
		Nancy "	22	F				" "			/	
		Daniel "	17	m		Farmer		" "				
637	637	Daniel McIntosh	49	m		Farmer	1000	" "				
		Margaret "	44	F				" "				
		Duncan "	18	m		Farmer		" "		/		
		John W. "	16	m		Farmer		" "		/		
		David "	14	m				" "		/		
		Mary A. "	11	F				" "		/		
638	638	Duncan Murchison	70	m		Farmer	8000	" "				
		Frances "	22	F				" "				
		Nancy Rogers	24	F				" "				
		Owen Oldham	18	m		Farmer		" "				
		Anderson Walker	24	m		Farmer		" "				
639	639	Henry Oldham	45	m		Farmer	187	" "				
		Lydia "	42	F				" "			/	
		Jane "	19	F				" "				
		Margaret "	14	F				" "				
		Thomas "	12	m				" "				
		William "	8	m				" "				
		Westley "	6	m				" "				
		John A. "	4	m				" "				
640	640	Margaret Berryman	64	F			130	" "			/	
		Barbara "	33	F				" "				
		Epatha "	31	F				" "				
		Sarah "	29	F				" "				
		John W. "	22	m		Farmer		" "				
		Statira "	19	F				" "		/		
		Richard Gaines	17	m	m	Farmer		" "				
641	641	John McDuffie	25	m		Farmer	77	" "				
		Jennet "	21	F				" "			/	
		Elizabeth "	2	F				" "				
		Mary "	11/12	F				" "				
		Joseph Oldham	16	m		Farmer		" "				
642	642	Charles McDonald	54	m		Farmer	300	Scotland				

m 22 F 20 13 m.

23 417

SCHEDULE I.—Free Inhabitants in ______ in the County of Moore State of N. Carolina enumerated by me, on the 6th day of October 1850. N. McCrummen Ass't Marshal. 209

Dwelling-houses numbered in the order of visitation.	Families numbered in the order of visitation.	The Name of every Person whose usual place of abode on the first day of June, 1850, was in this family.	Description: Age.	Sex.	Color, White, black, or mulatto.	Profession, Occupation, or Trade of each Male Person over 15 years of age.	Value of Real Estate owned.	Place of Birth. Naming the State, Territory, or Country.	Married within the year.	Attended School within the year.	Persons over 20 y'rs of age who cannot read & write.	Whether deaf and dumb, blind, insane, idiotic, pauper, or convict.	
1	2	3	4	5	6	7	8	9	10	11	12	13	
		Mary McDonald	47	F				N. Carolina					1
		Nancy "	21	F				" "					2
		John "	20	m		Carpenter		" "		/			3
		Angus "	18	m		Farmer		" "		/			4
		Flora "	16	F				" "		/			5
		Mary "	14	F				" "		/			6
		Sarah "	12	F				" "		/			7
		Elizabeth "	10	F				" "		/			8
		Catharine "	8	F				" "		/			9
643	643	Margaret Nicholson	43	F				" "			/		10
		Mary	13	F				" "					11
		Calvin H. Smith	23	m		Laborer		" "					12
644	644	Nancy Morris	39	F			50	" "					13
		Kenneth "	4	m				" "					14
		Sarah "	1	F				" "					15
645	645	Nill Morris	34	m		Farmer	75	" "			-		16
		Martha "	26	F				" "			/		17
		Nathaniel "	5	m				" "					18
		Sarah E. "	4	F				" "					19
		Murdoch "	2	m				" "					20
		Mary A. "	1	F				" "					21
646	646	Christian Gillis	55	F				" "					22
		Cynthia "	22	F				" "					23
		Mary "	19	F				" "					24
		Margaret "	15	F				" "					25
		Martha "	12	F	m			" "					26
		Nancy "	10	F	m			" "					27
647	647	Benjamin Morris	57	m		Farmer	200	" "					28
		Margaret "	50	F				" "					29
		Jemina "	35	F				" "					30
		Jonathan "	26	m		Farmer		" "			/		31
		Thomas "	24	m		Farmer		" "			/		32
		John A. "	19	m		Farmer		" "					33
		Margaret "	15	F				" "					34
		Martha A. "	10	F				" "					35
648	648	Duncan Lamont	31	m		Farmer	250	" "					36
		Sarah "	21	F				" "					37
		John "	1	m				" "					38
		William "	5/12	m				" "					39
[illegible]	649	John Cole	76	m		Farmer	300	" "					40
		Nancy "	70	F				" "			/		41
		Temperance "	30	F				" "			/		42

m 15
727 27

SCHEDULE I.—Free Inhabitants in ______ in the County of Moore State of N. Carolina enumerated by me, on the 5th day of October 1850. N. McCrummen Ass't Marshal.

	Dwelling-houses numbered in the order of visitation.	Families numbered in the order of visitation.	The Name of every Person whose usual place of abode on the first day of June, 1850, was in this family.	Description: Age.	Sex.	Color, (White, black, or mulatto.)	Profession, Occupation, or Trade of each Male Person over 15 years of age.	Value of Real Estate owned.	Place of Birth. Naming the State, Territory, or Country.	Married within the year.	Attended School within the year.	Persons over 20 y'rs of age who cannot read & write.	Whether deaf and dumb, blind, insane, idiotic, pauper, or convict.
	1	2	3	4	5	6	7	8	9	10	11	12	13
1			Elizabeth Cole	11	F				N. Carolina		1		
2	650	650	Alexander Graham	62	m		Farmer	210	Scotland				
3			Sarah "	43	F				N. Carolina				
4			Flora A. "	6	F				" "		1		
5	651	651	Henry Cafer	60	m		Farmer	300	" "				
6			Margaret "	53	F				" "				
7			Celia "	40	F				" "			1	
8			Elizabeth "	37	F				" "			1	
9			Sallie "	25	F				" "		1		
10			Kenneth "	19	m		Farmer		" "		1		
11			John "	17	m		Farmer		" "		1		
12			Isabella "	14	F				" "		1		
13			Flora "	13	F				" "		1		
14	652	652	William Goings	50	m	m	Farmer		" "			1	
15			Martha "	39	F	m			" "			1	
16			Sarah A. "	17	F	m			" "				
17			David "	13	m	m			" "				
18			Sidney "	11	m	m			" "				
19			Lucinda "	8	F	m			" "				
20			Elizabeth "	6	F	m			" "				
21			Andrew "	1	m	m			" "				
22	653	653	Andrew Cole	41	m		Farmer	350	" "				
23			Catharine "	38	F				" "				
24			John "	18	m		Farmer		" "				
25			Enoch "	15	m				" "				
26			George "	13	m				" "				
27			Nancy "	11	F				" "				
28			Andrew "	9	m				" "				
29			Frances "	5	F				" "				
30			Martha "	3	F				" "				
31			Jennet "	2	F				" "				
32			Thomas "	1	m				" "				
33	654	654	Malcom Curry	53	m		Blacksmith	375	" "				
34			Margaret "	57	F				" "				
35			Mary J. "	27	F				" "				
36			Isabella "	19	F				" "				
37			James Johnson	24	m		Farmer		" "			1	
38	655	655	James Jackson	34	m		Farmer	200	" "				
39			Jennet "	40	F				" "				
40			Archibald "	14	m				" "				
41			Dicy A. "	12	F				" "				
42			Burges C. "	10	m				" "				

m 19 4B
F 23 47

SCHEDULE I.—Free Inhabitants in ___ in the County of *Moore* State *419*
of *N. Carolina* enumerated by me, on the *7th* day of *October* 1850. *N. McCrummen* Ass't Marshal. 210

Dwelling-houses numbered in the order of visitation.	Families numbered in the order of visitation.	The Name of every Person whose usual place of abode on the first day of June, 1850, was in this family.	Description: Age.	Description: Sex.	Description: Color. White, black, or mulatto.	Profession, Occupation, or Trade of each Male Person over 15 years of age.	Value of Real Estate owned.	Place of Birth. Naming the State, Territory, or Country.	Married within the year.	Attended School within the year.	Persons over 20 y'rs of age who cannot read & write.	Whether deaf and dumb, blind, insane, idiotic, pauper, or convict.
1	2	3	4	5	6	7	8	9	10	11	12	13
		Effy Jackson	8	F				N. Carolina				
		Gerry "	4	m				" "				
		Mary J. "	2	F				" "				
56	656	William R. Spivey	21	m		Farmer	100	" "				
		Lavina "	22	F				" "				
		Jesse D. "	2	m				" "				
		Burges J. "	2/12	m				" "				
57	657	Esther Strickland	60	F				" "			1	
		Nathan "	25	m		Laborer	100	" "				
		Jennet "	20	F				" "				
58	658	Neill T. Lamont	29	m		Farmer	50	" "				
		Mary "	28	F				" "			1	
		James D. "	3	m				" "				
		Joseph J. "	4/12	m				" "				
		Nancy Cole	12	F				" "				
659	659	Bird Jackson	60	m		Farmer	550	" "				
		Dicy "	56	F				" "			1	
		Elizabeth "	26	F				" "			1	
		Eleanor "	18	F				" "				
		Melinda "	16	F				" "				
		Herbert Jackson	20	m		Farmer		" "				
		David Jackson	18	m		Farmer		" "				
60	660	John Cole	41	m		Farmer	300	" "				
		Flora "	40	F				" "				
		James "	16	m				" "		1		
		Mary "	13	F				" "		1		
		Neill "	11	m				" "		1		
		Margaret "	10	F				" "		1		
		Nancy "	8	F				" "		1		
		Thomas "	6	m				" "				
		Elizabeth "	5	F				" "				
		Duncan "	2	m				" "				
		Flora "	2/12	F				" "				
661	661	Jesse Spivey	55	m		Farmer	800	" "				
		Sarah "	32	F				" "			1	
		Benjamin "	26	m		Laborer		" "				
		Margaret "	24	F				" "			1	
		Murdoch "	20	m		Farmer		" "				
		Martha J. Jackson	5	F				" "				
62	662	John Stuart	61	m		Farmer	300	Scotland				
63	663	Nathan Graham	37	m		Farmer	150	N. Carolina			1	
		Mary A. "	37	F				" "			1	

M 21
F 21

SCHEDULE I.—Free Inhabitants in ______ in the County of Moore State of N. Carolina enumerated by me, on the 7th day of October 1850. N. McCrummen Ass't Marshal.

	Dwelling-houses numbered in the order of visitation.	Families numbered in the order of visitation.	The Name of every Person whose usual place of abode on the first day of June, 1850, was in this family.	Description: Age.	Sex.	Color, (White, black, or mulatto.)	Profession, Occupation, or Trade of each Male Person over 15 years of age.	Value of Real Estate owned.	Place of Birth. Naming the State, Territory, or Country.	Married within the year.	Attended School within the year.	Persons over 20 y'rs of age who cannot read & write.	Whether deaf and dumb, blind, insane, idiotic, pauper, or convict.
	1	2	3	4	5	6	7	8	9	10	11	12	13
1			Elizabeth J. Graham	11	F				N. Carolina		1		
2			Benjamin "	4	m				" "				
3			Daniel "	7/12	F				" "				
4	664	664	Archibald McKithan	66	m		Farmer	40	" "				
5			Frances "	35	F				" "			1	
6			Neill "	11	m				" "		1		
7			Duncan "	4	m				" "				
8			Sarah M. "	1	F				" "				
9	665	665	Catharine Chisholm	74	F			100	" "				
10			Effy "	37	F				" "				
11			Alexander "	31	m		Teacher		" "				
12	666	666	Dawson R. Tyson	26	m		Farmer		" "				
13			Rebecca "	28	F				" "				
14			William J. "	3/12	m				" "				
15	667	667	Elias B. Harrington	42	m		Farmer	600	" "				
16			Mary "	39	F				" "				
17			Isaiah "	14	M				" "		1		
18			Abner "	12	m				" "		1		
19			Thomas "	10	m				" "		1		
20			John McM. "	7	m				" "		1		
21			Margaret E. "	5	F				" "		1		
22			James A. "	3	m				" "				
23			Mary A. "	2/12	F				" "				
24	668	668	James R. Patterson	49	m		Merchant	350	" "				
25			Elizabeth D. "	39	F				" "				
26			Frances "	16	F			200	" "				
27			Drury "	8	m				" "		1		
28	667	669	James Riddle	41	m		Waggonmaker	500	" "				
29			Flora "	43	F				" "				
30			Daniel "	9	m				" "		1		
31			Eliza "	7	F				" "		1		
32			Mary A. "	6	F				" "		1		
33			James "	4	m				" "		1		
34			John McIver	38	m		Farmer		" "				
35			Kenneth Wicker	21	m		Waggoner		" "				
36			Daniel L. Riddle	18	m		Farmer		" "				
37			Daniel Morris	18	m		Farmer		" "				
38			Mary Gillis	19	F				" "				
39	670	670	James McDonald	79	m		Farmer		" "				
40			Catharine "	35	F				" "			1	
41			Thomas "	26	m		Laborer		" "				
42	671	671	Wiley Riddle	25	m		Farmer	100	" "				

M 25
F 17

SCHEDULE I.—Free Inhabitants in 24 in the County of Moore State #21
of N. Carolina enumerated by me, on the 8th day of October 1850. N. McCrummon Ass't Marshal.

211

Dwelling-houses numbered in the order of visitation.	Families numbered in the order of visitation.	The Name of every Person whose usual place of abode on the first day of June, 1850, was in this family.	Description. Age.	Sex.	Color, White, black, or mulatto.	Profession, Occupation, or Trade of each Male Person over 15 years of age.	Value of Real Estate owned.	Place of Birth. Naming the State, Territory, or Country.	Married within the year.	Attended School within the year.	Persons over 20 y'rs of age who cannot read & write.	Whether deaf and dumb, blind, insane, idiotic, pauper, or convict.	
1	2	3	4	5	6	7	8	9	10	11	12	13	
		Elizabeth A. Riddle	20	F				N. Carolina					1
		Archibald "	1	m				" "					2
		Mariam Core	65	F				" "			/		3
		David "	16	m		Farmer		" "		/			4
672	672	Neill Thompson	25	m		Farmer		" "			/		5
		Christian "	26	F				" "					6
		Flora A. "	3	F				" "					7
673	673	John Jackson	26	m		Farmer	160	" "	—				8
		Mary "	28	F				" "	—		/		9
674	674	John Riddle	30	m		Waggonmaker	200	" "					10
		Margaret "	30	F				" "					11
		Lydia "	4	F				" "					12
		Mary "	2	F				" "					13
		Elizabeth "	5/12	F				" "					14
675	675	William H. Kimbrel	35	m		Farmer	150	" "					15
		Nancy "	31	F				" "					16
		William B. "	9	m				" "					17
		Lavina "	5	F				" "					18
		Samuel R. "	3	m				" "					19
		Anna M. "	1	F				" "					20
676	676	Samuel Paisley	77	m		O.S.P. Clergyman	550	" "					21
		Eleanor "	70	F				" "					22
		Sidney Goings	10	m	m			" "					23
677	677	Angus McDonald	28	m		Waggonmaker	125	" "			/		24
		Catharine "	26	F				" "					25
		John B. "	3/12	m				" "					26
678	678	Josiah Tyson	70	m		Farmer	2500	" "					27
		Elizabeth "	64	F				" "					28
		Elizabeth "	27	F				" "					29
		Margaret "	25	F				" "					30
		John "	24	m		Farmer		" "					31
		Benjamin "	22	m		Farmer		" "					32
679	679	John F. Underwood	30	m		Farmer	400	" "					33
		Margaret "	22	F				" "					34
		Daniel McL. "	1	m				" "					35
680	680	Lavina Johnson	42	F			150	" "			/		36
		John Johnson	15	m				" "					37
681	681	Daniel Lamont	67	m		Farmer	200	" "					38
		Deborah "	55	F				" "			/		39
		Jane "	26	F				" "					40
		Alexander "	23	m				" "				Insane	41
		Daniel "	19	m		Farmer		" "					42

m 21 16
f 21
✓

SCHEDULE I.—Free Inhabitants in ______ in the County of Moore State of N. Carolina enumerated by me, on the 5th day of October 1850. Niell McCrummen Ass't Marshal.

	Dwelling-houses numbered in the order of visitation.	Families numbered in the order of visitation.	The Name of every Person whose usual place of abode on the first day of June, 1850, was in this family.	Age.	Sex.	Color, White, black, or mulatto.	Profession, Occupation, or Trade of each Male Person over 15 years of age.	Value of Real Estate owned.	Place of Birth. Naming the State, Territory, or Country.	Married within the year.	Attended School within the year.	Persons over 20 y'rs of age who cannot read & write.	Whether deaf and dumb, blind, insane, idiotic, pauper, or convict.
	1	2	3	4	5	6	7	8	9	10	11	12	13
1			Catharine Lamont	64	F			37	N. Carolina			1	
2	682	682	Kenneth Murchison	40	m		Farmer	510	" "				
3			Martha J. "	25	F				" "				
4			Margaret F. "	3	F				" "				
5			Oscar B. "	1	m				" "				
6			Margaret Murchison	86	F				Scotland			1	
7			Annabella "	53	F				N. Carolina				
8			Flora "	43	F				" "				
9	683	683	Kenneth McIntosh	66	m		Farmer	400	" "				
10			Catharine "	64	F				" "				
11			Margaret "	44	F				" "				
12			Rebecca "	36	F				" "				
13			Jennet "	33	F				" "				
14			Alexander "	31	m		Book seller	50	" "				
15			Nancy "	29	F				" "				
16			John "	26	m		Carpenter		" "				
17			Kenneth F. "	24	m		Farmer		" "				
18			Lancaster G. McIver	14	m				" "				
19	684	684	John A. Campbell	43	m		Farmer	200	" "				
20			Mary "	43	F				" "				
21			William B. "	16	m		Farmer		" "		1		
22			Mary A. "	14	F				" "		1		
23			John R. "	12	m				" "		1		
24			George W. "	10	m				" "		1		
25			Thomas C. "	8	m				" "		1		
26			Elizabeth J. "	6	F				" "				
27			James A. "	4	m				" "				
28			Martha A. "	9/12	F				" "				
29	685	685	Neill Smith	32	m	m	Farmer		" "			1	
30			Nancy Griffin	48	F	m			" "			1	
31			James "	20	m	m	Farmer		" "			1	
32			Gifford Griffin	47	m	m	Laborer		" "			1	
33	686	686	Catharine Murchison	70	F			250	" "			1	
34			Rebecca "	33	F				" "				
35			Lydia "	30	F				" "				
36	687	687	Gilbert McRae	70	m		Farmer	1200	" "				
37			Margaret "	61	F				" "				
38			John "	29	m		Farmer		" "				
39			Catharine "	21	F				" "				
40			Murdoch "	18	m		Farmer		" "		1		
41			Martha Brewer	13	F				" "				
42	688	688	Daniel Campbell	70	m		Farmer	425	" "				

m 20 33
F 22 17

Schedule I.—Free Inhabitants in ______ in the County of Moore State of N. Carolina enumerated by me, on the 4th day of October 1850. Neill McCrummen Ass't Marshal.

433

212

Dwelling-houses numbered in the order of visitation	Families numbered in the order of visitation	The Name of every Person whose usual place of abode on the first day of June, 1850, was in this family	Age	Sex	Color	Profession, Occupation, or Trade of each Male Person over 15 years of age	Value of Real Estate owned	Place of Birth, Naming the State, Territory, or Country	Married within the year	Attended School within the year	Persons over 20 y'rs of age who cannot read & write	Whether deaf and dumb, blind, insane, idiotic, pauper, or convict	
1	2	3	4	5	6	7	8	9	10	11	12	13	
		Nancy Campbell	69	F				Scotland			/		1
		James "	28	m		none		N. Carolina			/		2
		Peter M "	21	m		Farmer		" "					3
		Margaret McCallum	71	F			288	Scotland			/		4
		David Goings	14	m	m			N. Carolina					5
689	689	Neill McNeill	66	m		Farmer	168	Scotland					6
		Nancy "	37	F				N. Carolina					7
		Daniel Ca "	17	m		Farmer		" "					8
690	690	Levi Goings	87	m	m	Farmer	130	" "			/		9
		Amy "	77	F	m			" "			/		10
		Nutty "	47	F	m			" "			/		11
		Joseph "	10	m	m			" "					12
691	691	Neill Goings	37	m	m	Farmer	105	" "			/		13
		Mary "	36	F	m			" "			/		14
		Delilah "	16	F	m			" "					15
		Amy "	15	F	m			" "					16
		Chaney "	12	F	m			" "					17
		Sarah "	10	F	m			" "					18
		Celia "	8	F	m			" "					19
		Catharine "	6	F	m			" "					20
		Eliza "	3	F	m			" "					21
692	692	Elizabeth Goings	46	F	m			" "					22
		Barbara "	2	F	m			" "					23
693	693	Levi Goings	26	m	m	Farmer	50	" "			/		24
		Mary "	26	F	m			" "			/		25
		Flora A "	2	F	m			" "					26
		Jennet "	1	F	m			" "					27
694	694	John Goings	58	m	m	Farmer		" "			/		28
		Lydia "	45	F				" "			/		29
		John "	21	m	m	Farmer		" "			/		30
		Benjamin "	18	m	m	Farmer		" "					31
		Lydia "	14	F	m			" "					32
		Rachel "	73	F				" "					33
695	695	Martha Goings	35	F	m			" "					34
		Wiley "	7	m	m			" "					35
		Haywood "	3	m	m			" "					36
696	696	Thomas Goings	20	m	m	Farmer		" "	—		/		37
		Celicia "	27	F	m			" "	—		/		38
		Telitha "	8	F	m			" "					39
		James "	5	m	m			" "					40
		Green "	3	m	m			" "					41
		Henry "	2	m	m			" "					42

M 18 14B
F 24 197

SCHEDULE I.—Free Inhabitants in ________ **in the County of** Moore **State of** N. Carolina **enumerated by me, on the** 9th **day of** October **1850.** N. McCrummen **Ass't Marshal.**

Dwelling-houses numbered in the order of visitation.	Families numbered in the order of visitation.	The Name of every Person whose usual place of abode on the first day of June, 1850, was in this family.	Description: Age.	Sex.	Color, White, black, or mulatto.	Profession, Occupation, or Trade of each Male Person over 15 years of age.	Value of Real Estate owned.	Place of Birth. Naming the State, Territory, or Country.	Married within the year.	Attended School within the year.	Persons over 20 y'rs of age who cannot read & write.	Whether deaf and dumb, blind, insane, idiotic, pauper, or convict.
1	2	3	4	5	6	7	8	9	10	11	12	13
697	697	David Goings	23	M	M	Farmer	135	N. Carolina	—		1	
		Mary "	40	F	M			" "	—		1	
		William H. "	16	M	M	Farmer		" "				
		Eliza J. "	13	F	M			" "				
		Berry "	11	M	M			" "				
		Emuline "	8	F	M			" "				
		Eli "	6	M	M			" "				
		Marticia "	3	F	M			" "				
		Laurince "	6/12	M	M			" "				
698	698	Nancy Walden	72	F	M		100	" "			1	
		Rebecca "	48	F	M			" "				
		Elizabeth "	38	F	M			" "				
		Leanna "	31	F	M			" "				
		Emily "	29	F	M			" "				
		Hays "	7	M	M			" "				
		Adaline "	10	F	M			" "				
		Henry "	7	M	M			" "				
		Augusta "	6	F	M			" "				
		Leanidas "	4	M	M			" "				
		Joseph J. "	1	M	M			" "				
699	699	Lucy Goings	29	F	M			" "			1	
		Mary A. "	10	F	M			" "				
		Rebecca "	8	F	M			" "				
		Lucian "	3	M	M			" "				
		Edmund "	2	M	M			" "				
700	700	Rebecca Walden	47	F	M			" "				
		Elizabeth "	22	F	M			" "				
		Mary "	20	F	M			" "				
		Pattie "	18	F	M			" "				
		Louisa "	16	F	M			" "				
		Margaret "	12	F	M			" "				
701	701	Tyrrel Gordon	40	M	M	Carpenter	400	" "				
		Celia "	23	F	M			" "				
		Adalaid "	7	F	M			" "				
		Nancy Goings	24	F	M			" "				
		William "	5	M	M			" "				
702	702	Duncan A Sinclair	48	M		Farmer	500	" "				
		Effy "	47	F				" "				
		Daniel "	19	M		Farmer		" "				
		John "	17	M		Farmer	160	" "				
		Peter "	15	M				" "				
		Mary "	12	F				" "				

M 17
F 25

130
237

SCHEDULE I.—Free Inhabitants in ______ in the County of *Moore* State of *N. Carolina* enumerated by me, on the *10th* day of *October* 1850. *Neill McCrummen* Ass't Marshal. *425*

213

Dwelling-houses numbered in the order of visitation.	Families numbered in the order of visitation.	The Name of every Person whose usual place of abode on the first day of June, 1850, was in this family.	Age.	Sex.	Color, (White, black, or mulatto.)	Profession, Occupation, or Trade of each Male Person over 15 years of age.	Value of Real Estate owned.	Place of Birth. Naming the State, Territory, or Country.	Married within the year.	Attended School within the year.	Persons over 20 y'rs of age who cannot read & write.	Whether deaf and dumb, blind, insane, idiotic, pauper, or convict.
1	2	3	4	5	6	7	8	9	10	11	12	13
		Archibald Sinclair	10	m				N. Carolina				
		James "	7	m				" "				
		George "	9/12	m				" "				
703	703	Joab McDonald	38	m		Farmer		" "				
		Sarah "	30	F				" "			1	
		Daniel "	7	m				" "				
		Flora A. "	6	F				" "				
		Mary J. "	3	F				" "				
		Charlotte "	2	F				" "				
		Sarah C. "	1/12	F				" "				
704	704	William C. Campbell	41	m		Farmer	3000	" "				
		Cynthia D. "	40	F				" "				
		Anna J. "	13	F				" "				
705	705	Pendleton Walden	26	m	m	Laborer		" "			1	
		Eliza "	24	F	m			" "			1	
		Ann "	7	F	m			" "				
		Mary "	2	F	m			" "				
		Sarah "	1	F	m			" "				
		Henry Walden	25	m	m	Laborer		" "			1	
706	706	Robert A. Stuart	28	m		Merchant		" "				
		Catharine "	25	F				" "				
		Caroline "	4	F				" "				
		Charles "	2	m				" "				
707	707	Charity Roberts	43	F			4000	" "				
		Isaac "	15	m				" "		1		
		Mary "	10	F				" "		1		
		John "	8	m				" "		1		
		Bright "	6	m				" "		1		
		Charlotte Cox	34	F				" "				
		John A. McDonald	23	m		Merchant		" "				
		William "	18	m		Clerk		" "				
708	708	Allen W. Jones	31	m		Merchant	1000	" "				
		Velina "	17	F				" "				
		Hannah M. "	2	F				" "				
		Mary "	6/12	F				" "				
		Baldy H. Jones	24	m		Merchant		" "				
		Elizabeth "	20	F				" "				
		Reddick H. Davis	25	m		Tailor		" "				
709	707	George Wilcox	64	m		Farmer	3000	" "				
		William "	25	m		Student		" "		1		
		Mary "	17	F				" "				
		George "	14	m				" "				

m 21 2B
F 21 47

SCHEDULE I.—Free Inhabitants in ______________ in the County of *Moore* State of *N. Carolina* enumerated by me, on the *10th* day of *October* 1850. *N. McCrummen* Ass't Marshal.

Dwelling-houses numbered in the order of visitation.	Families numbered in the order of visitation.	The Name of every Person whose usual place of abode on the first day of June, 1850, was in this family.	Age.	Sex.	Color, { White, black, or mulatto.	Profession, Occupation, or Trade of each Male Person over 15 years of age.	Value of Real Estate owned.	Place of Birth. Naming the State, Territory, or Country.	Married within the year.	Attended School within the year.	Persons over 20 y'rs of age who cannot read & write.	Whether deaf and dumb, blind, insane, idiotic, pauper, or convict.
1	2	3	4	5	6	7	8	9	10	11	12	13
		Martin Wilcox	12	m				N. Carolina				
		Robert "	10	m				" "				
		Harman "	6	m				" "				
		Ann E. Brewer	16	F				" "				
710	710	Margaret McDonald	27	F				" "			1	
		William H. "	9	m				" "				
		Sarah "	7	F				" "				
711	711	Joseph Malone	76	m		Farmer	100	" "			1	
		Jane "	60	F				" "			1	
		Amy "	29	F				" "			1	
		Jane "	26	F				" "			1	
		John "	23	m		Farmer		" "			1	
		Benjamin "	20	m		Farmer		" "			1	
		Cyntharis "	8	F				" "				
		Mary A. "	6	F				" "				
		Jane "	5	F				" "				
		Henry "	4	m				" "				
712	712	Calvin Oldham	28	m		Blacksmith		" "				
		Mary "	30	F				" "				
		Margaret "	4	F				" "				
		Thomas "	2	m				" "				
		Mary "	9/12	F				" "				
713	713	William Watson	36	m		Farmer	2750	" "				
		Susan "	36	F				" "				
		Jane C. "	8	F				" "		1		
		Ann E. "	6	F				" "		1		
		Sarah R. "	4	F				" "				
		Monterey "	2	F				" "				
		Don Charles "	1	m				" "				
		Isaac W. Greer	14	m				" "		1		
714	714	Marmaduke Malone	47	m		Farmer		" "			1	
		Matilda "	43	F				" "				
		Jane "	18	F				" "				
		William "	15	m		Farmer		" "				
		Willis "	13	m				" "				
		Mary "	11	F				" "				
		Daniel "	8	m				" "				
		Rosanna "	5	F				" "				
		Margaret "	1	F				" "				
715	715	Mary McFadyen	55	F			300	Scotland			1	
		Dugald "	16	m		Farmer		N. Carolina				
716	716	Duncan McFadyen	26	m		Farmer		" "				

m 19
F 23

SCHEDULE I.—Free Inhabitants in ____________ in the County of *Moore* State of *N. Carolina* enumerated by me, on the *10th* day of *October* 1850. *Neill McCrummen* Ass't Marshal. *927*

214

Dwelling-houses numbered in the order of visitation.	Families numbered in the order of visitation.	The Name of every Person whose usual place of abode on the first day of June, 1850, was in this family.	Age.	Sex.	Color, White, black, or mulatto.	Profession, Occupation, or Trade of each Male Person over 15 years of age.	Value of Real Estate owned.	Place of Birth. Naming the State, Territory, or Country.	Married within the year.	Attended School within the year.	Persons over 20 y'rs of age who cannot read & write.	Whether deaf and dumb, blind, insane, idiotic, pauper, or convict.
1	2	3	4	5	6	7	8	9	10	11	12	13
		A. M. McFadyen	19	F				N. Carolina				
		John D. "	10/12	m				" "				
717	717	Catharine McDonald	64	F			300	Scotland			1	
		Mary "	35	F				N. Carolina				
		Christian "	33	F				" "				
		Flora "	25	F				" "				
		Ronald "	23	m	Farmer		150	" "				
718	718	William Gilmore	27	m		Farmer		" "			1	
		Ann E. "	29	F				" "				
		James "	6	m				" "				
		John "	4	m				" "				
		Miles "	2	m				" "				
		Eli "	1/12	m				" "				
719	719	Samuel McDonald	66	m		Farmer	150	Scotland			1	
		Margaret "	68	F				"			1	
		Flora "	71	F				"			1	Blind
720	720	Edward McIntosh	57	m		Farmer		"				
		Margaret "	57	F				N. Carolina				
		Angus "	20	m		Farmer		" "				
		Flora "	17	F				" "				
		Nancy "	17	F				" "				
721	721	Hugh McDonald	79	m		Farmer	100	Scotland			1	
		Mary "	70	F				"			1	
		Isabella Barber	15	F				N. Carolina		1		
722	722	Flora McLeod	43	F			200	" "				
		Daniel L. McLeod	20	m		Farmer		" "				
723	723	Margaret McLeod	56	F			300	" "				
		Nepsy "	30	F				" "				
		Mary "	26	F				" "				
		Duncan "	23	m		Farmer		" "				
		Angus "	20	m		Farmer		" "				
		Flora "	17	F				" "				
724	724	John Morris	53	m		Farmer	150	" "				
		Margaret "	50	F				" "				
		Flora A. "	14	F				" "		1		
		John D. "	12	m				" "		1		
		Mary "	10	F				" "		1		
		Margaret "	8	F				" "		1		
		George "	6	m				" "				
725	725	Joseph Maunger	66	m		Farmer	300	" "				
		Nancy "	50	F				" "			1	
		Mary A. "	24	F				" "				

m 18
f 24

SCHEDULE I.—Free Inhabitants in ________ in the County of Moore State of N. Carolina enumerated by me, on the 10th day of October 1850. N. Mc Crummen Ass't Marshal.

Dwelling-houses numbered in the order of visitation.	Families numbered in the order of visitation.	The Name of every Person whose usual place of abode on the first day of June, 1850, was in this family.	Description: Age.	Sex.	Color, White, black, or mulatto.	Profession, Occupation, or Trade of each Male Person over 15 years of age.	Value of Real Estate owned.	Place of Birth. Naming the State, Territory, or Country.	Married within the year.	Attended School within the year.	Persons over 20 y'rs of age who cannot read & write.	Whether deaf and dumb, blind, insane, idiotic, pauper, or convict.
1	2	3	4	5	6	7	8	9	10	11	12	13
726	726	Alexander Robertson	56	m		Farmer	200	Scotland				
		Alexis "	31	f				"				
		Malcom Wheeler	7	m				N. Carolina				
727	727	Duncan M. Johnson	35	m		Farmer	200	" "				
		Eliza "	32	f				" "				
		Martha J. "	7	f				" "		1		
		Neill A "	5	m				" "		1		
		John C. "	3	m				" "				
		Duncan M. "	1	m				" "				
728	728	Angus McKaskill	44	m		Farmer		" "				
		Elizabeth "	35	f				" "				
		Jennet "	15	f				" "		1		
		Celia A. "	14	f				" "		1		
		Catharine "	11	f				" "		1		
		John W. "	8	m				" "		1		
		Elizabeth "	4	f				" "				
729	729	Joseph J. Mounger	32	m		Farmer	300	" "				
		Margaret B. "	33	f				" "				
		Jane "	5	f				" "				
		John "	4	m				" "				
		Nancy "	3	f				" "				
		Mary "	1	f				" "				
		James "	4/12	m				" "				
730	730	Norman McLeod	46	m		Farmer		" "				
		Sarah "	45	f				" "				
		Murdock "	18	m		Student		" "		1		
		Barbara "	15	f				" "		1		
		Duncan "	13	m				" "		1		
		Catharine "	11	f				" "		1		
		Celia "	8	f				" "		1		
		John A. "	3	m				" "				
731	731	Margery McKenzie	82	f				Scotland			1	
732	732	Eli Wadsworth	35	m		Farmer	600	N. Carolina				
		Mary "	33	f				" "				
		Margaret J. "	12	f				" "				
		Peter S. "	9	m				" "				
		Sarah A. "	7	f				" "				
		William "	5	m				" "				
		Catharine "	2	f				" "				
		Mary F. "	1	f				" "				
733	733	Kenneth H. Worthy	30	m		Constable	200	" "				
		Margaret "	27	f				" "				

m 19
fe 23

26.5 429

SCHEDULE I.—Free Inhabitants in ______ in the County of Moore State of N. Carolina enumerated by me, on the 12th day of October 1850. N. McLennan Ass't Marshal. 215

Line	Dwelling-houses numbered in the order of visitation.	Families numbered in the order of visitation.	The Name of every Person whose usual place of abode on the first day of June, 1850, was in this family.	Age.	Sex.	Color, White, black, or mulatto.	Profession, Occupation, or Trade of each Male Person over 15 years of age.	Value of Real Estate owned.	Place of Birth. Naming the State, Territory, or Country.	Married within the year.	Attended School within the year.	Persons over 20 y'rs of age who cannot read & write.	Whether deaf and dumb, blind, insane, idiotic, pauper, or convict.
	1	2	3	4	5	6	7	8	9	10	11	12	13
1			Jane Worthy	1	F				N. Carolina				
2	737	737	Daniel J. Shaw	35	m		Farmer	360	N. Carolina				
3			Nancy "	34	F				N. Carolina				
4			Mary J. "	11	F				N. Carolina				
5			William H. "	9	m				N. Carolina				
6	738	738	William Starling	60	m		Farmer		N. Carolina			1	
7	739	739	William Riddle	75	m		Farmer		N. Carolina			1	
8			Rebecca "	65	F				N. Carolina				Blind
9			Jane "	28	F				N. Carolina			1	
10			George W. "	10	m				N. Carolina				
11			Rebecca "	8	F				N. Carolina				
12			Russel "	1	m				N. Carolina				
13	740	740	William Shaw	65	m		Farmer	1500	Scotland				
14			Mary "	64	F				N. Carolina				
15			Alexander "	34	m		Farmer		N. Carolina				
16			Mary "	30	F				N. Carolina				
17			Jane "	28	F				N. Carolina				
18			Catharine "	26	F				N. Carolina				
19			Eliza "	20	F				N. Carolina				
20			Dugald "	12	m				N. Carolina		1		
21	741	741	Mary Cole	45	F			400	N. Carolina				
22			John B. "	23	m		Farmer		N. Carolina				
23			James A. "	21	m		Farmer		N. Carolina				
24			Catharine Shaw	50	F				N. Carolina			1	
25	742	742	Hardy Patterson	55	m		Farmer	292	N. Carolina				
26			Lucy "	52	F				N. Carolina			1	
27			Elizabeth "	26	F				N. Carolina				
28			Susan "	22	F				N. Carolina				
29			Robert "	21	m		Farmer		N. Carolina				
30			Martha "	19	F				N. Carolina				
31			Sallie "	16	F				N. Carolina				
32	743	743	Rachel Jackson	46	F			25	N. Carolina			1	
33			Samuel "	22	m		Laborer		N. Carolina			1	
34			Rachel "	21	F				N. Carolina			1	
35			Nancy "	15	F				N. Carolina				
36	744	744	Norman Ferguson	59	m		Farmer	1431	Scotland				
37			Nancy "	46	F				N. Carolina				
38			Murdoch "	24	m		Millwright		N. Carolina				
39			Fergus "	19	m		Farmer		N. Carolina		1		
40			Angus "	13	m				N. Carolina		1		
41			Daniel "	9	m				N. Carolina		1		
42			Catharine "	8	F				N. Carolina		1		

442

SCHEDULE I.—Free Inhabitants in ______ **in the County of** Moore **State of** N. Carolina **enumerated by me, on the** 12th **day of** October **1850.** N. McCrummen **Ass't Marshal.**

Dwelling-houses numbered in the order of visitation.	Families numbered in the order of visitation.	The Name of every Person whose usual place of abode on the first day of June, 1850, was in this family.	Age.	Sex.	Color, {White, black, or mulatto.	Profession, Occupation, or Trade of each Male Person over 15 years of age.	Value of Real Estate owned.	Place of Birth, Naming the State, Territory, or Country.	Married within the year.	Attended School within the year.	Persons over 20 y'rs of age who cannot read & write.	Whether deaf and dumb, blind, insane, idiotic, pauper, or convict.
1	2	3	4	5	6	7	8	9	10	11	12	13
		William A. Ferguson	6	m				N. Carolina		1		
		Samuel N. "	2	m				N. Carolina				
745	745	Neill Cameron	64	m		Farmer	600	N. Carolina				
		Mary "	57	F				N. Carolina				
		Alexander H. "	15	m				N. Carolina		1		
		Margaret Tyson	35	F				N. Carolina				
746	746	Wiley R. Foster	44	m		Farmer		N. Carolina				
		Sarah "	44	F				N. Carolina			1	
		William "	17	m		Farmer		N. Carolina				
		Julia E. "	6	F				N. Carolina				
		Candice "	2	F				N. Carolina				
		Elizabeth "	1/12	F				N. Carolina				
		Nancy Riddle	46	F				N. Carolina				Deaf & Dumb
747	747	Richard Riddle	22	m		Farmer		N. Carolina			1	
		Jane "	28	F				N. Carolina			1	
748	748	Martha Hancock	20	F			500	N. Carolina				
		Mary "	17	F				N. Carolina				
		Elizabeth "	10	F				N. Carolina		1		
749	749	Alexander C. Curry	53	m		Clerk of Court	1000	N. Carolina				
		Christian B. "	55	F				N. Carolina				
		Neill A. "	24	m		Carpenter		N. Carolina				
		Angus "	22	m		Student		N. Carolina		1		
		Benjamin R. "	20	m		Clerk		N. Carolina				
		Margaret "	17	F				N. Carolina				
		Mary "	14	F				N. Carolina				
		John B. "	12	M				N. Carolina		1		
		Cornelius H. Dowd	47	m		Merchant	1500	N. Carolina				
		John Morrison	47	m		Clerk of Court	8000	N. Carolina				
		Hector Turner	32	m		Physician		N. Carolina				
		Archibald McDonald	22	m		Student		N. Carolina		1		
		William "	20	m		Student		N. Carolina		1		
		Malcom Shaw	20	m		Student		N. Carolina		1		
		Caleb C. Bryant	20	m		Student		N. Carolina		1		
		James D. Thomas	23	m		Student		N. Carolina		1		
		Alexander Smyth	45	m		Tailor		England				
		William H. Harper	21	M		Student		N. Carolina		1		
		John Munroe	17	M		Student		N. Carolina		1		
		Benjamin "	11	M		Student		N. Carolina		1		
		Haywood Caddell	16	M		Student		N. Carolina		1		
		Daniel W. McDonald	24	M		Carpenter		N. Carolina				
		David K. Parnell	21	M		Carpenter		N. Carolina			1	
		Benjamin Fry	21	M		Laborer		N. Carolina				

M 28

431

216

SCHEDULE I.—Free Inhabitants in ________________ in the County of Moore State of N. Carolina enumerated by me, on the 10th day of October 1850. N. McCrummen Ass't Marshal.

Dwelling-houses numbered in the order of visitation.	Families numbered in the order of visitation.	The Name of every Person whose usual place of abode on the first day of June, 1850, was in this family.	Age.	Sex.	Color, White, black, or mulatto.	Profession, Occupation, or Trade of each Male Person over 15 years of age.	Value of Real Estate owned.	Place of Birth, Naming the State, Territory, or Country.	Married within the year.	Attended School within the year.	Persons over 20 y'rs of age who cannot read & write.	Whether deaf and dumb, blind, insane, idiotic, pauper, or convict.
1	2	3	4	5	6	7	8	9	10	11	12	13
		Noah Criscoe	22	m		Carpenter		N. Carolina				
		Martin Black	25	m		Teacher		N. Carolina				
750	750	Elizabeth Muse	41	F				N. Carolina			1	
		Catharine "	20	F				N. Carolina				
		Mary "	16	F				N. Carolina				
		Frances "	9	F				N. Carolina				
		Elizabeth Muse	55	F				N. Carolina			1	
		William R. "	1	m				N. Carolina				
751	751	Alexander T. Muse	32	m		Farmer	325	N. Carolina				
		Nancy "	33	F				N. Carolina			1	
		William "	10	m				N. Carolina		1		
		Jesse W. "	8	m				N. Carolina		1		
		Malcom "	6	m				N. Carolina		1		
		Isaiah "	4	m				N. Carolina	1			
		Robert S. "	2	m				N. Carolina				
		Susan E. "	1/12	F				N. Carolina				
752	752	Flora Wadsworth	60	F			516	N. Carolina				
		Sarah E. "	26	F				N. Carolina				
		Neill M. "	24	m		Farmer		N. Carolina				
		Mary E. "	6	F				N. Carolina				
753	753	Lewis Lawhon	36	m		Farmer	400	N. Carolina				
		Minny "	36	F				N. Carolina				
		Archibald "	15	m		Farmer		N. Carolina				
		Catharine "	13	F				N. Carolina				
		John "	11	m				N. Carolina				
		Joel "	9	m				N. Carolina				
		William S. "	5	m				N. Carolina				
		Martha E. "	1	F				N. Carolina				
754	754	Evander McNair	60	m		Farmer		S. Carolina				
		Elianor "	54	F				Scotland				
		Nancy "	24	F				N. Carolina				
		Catharine "	19	F				N. Carolina				
		Margaret "	17	F				N. Carolina				
		Sarah "	13	F				N. Carolina				
56	755	John W. Shields	39	m		Farmer	350	N. Carolina				
		Margaret "	32	F				N. Carolina				
		Neill Shields	8	m				N. Carolina				
		Mary "	2	F				N. Carolina				
		Martha "	2	F				N. Carolina				
6	756	William S. Shields	29	m		Farmer	258	N. Carolina				
		Emeline "	22	F				N. Carolina				
		Catharine Shields	60	F				N. Carolina				

m 19

SCHEDULE I.—Free Inhabitants in ______________ in the County of Moore State of N. Carolina enumerated by me, on the 15th day of October 1850. N. McCrummen Ass't Marshal.

Dwelling-houses numbered in the order of visitation.	Families numbered in the order of visitation.	The Name of every Person whose usual place of abode on the first day of June, 1850, was in this family.	Age.	Sex.	Color, White, black, or mulatto.	Profession, Occupation, or Trade of each Male Person over 15 years of age.	Value of Real Estate owned.	Place of Birth, Naming the State, Territory, or Country.	Married within the year.	Attended School within the year.	Persons over 20 y'rs of age who cannot read & write.	Whether deaf and dumb, blind, insane, idiotic, pauper, or convict.
1	2	3	4	5	6	7	8	9	10	11	12	13
757	757	Benjamin J. Shields	37	m		Farmer	193	N. Carolina				
		Mariah "	36	F				N. Carolina			1	
		Dugan P. "	14	m				N. Carolina		1		
		Daniel S. "	9	m				N. Carolina		1		
		William "	5	m				N. Carolina				
758	758	Peter Sinclair	43	m		Farmer	600	N. Carolina				
		Elizabeth "	41	F				N. Carolina				
		Thomas W. "	17	m		Farmer		N. Carolina				
		Sylvia J. "	15	F				N. Carolina		1		
		Mary A. "	11	F				N. Carolina		1		
		Jennet J. "	10	F				N. Carolina		1		
		Daniel "	6	m				N. Carolina				
		Stephen Morris	27	m		Farmer		N. Carolina				
759	759	Brinkley Philips	60	m		Farmer	350	N. Carolina				
		Elizabeth "	59	F				N. Carolina				
		Ann E. "	23	F				N. Carolina				
760	760	Flora McLeod	60	F			300	N. Carolina				
		Mary "	30	F				N. Carolina				
761	761	John A. McKeithen	32	m		Farmer	500	N. Carolina				
		Christiana C. "	33	F				N. Carolina				
		Cynthia A. "	2	F				N. Carolina				
		Loveday "	4/12	F				N. Carolina				
		Thomas Shaw	20	m		Labourer		N. Carolina				
762	762	Richard Dowd	31	m		Farmer	400	N. Carolina				
		Nancy "	34	F				N. Carolina				
		Mary "	30	F				N. Carolina				
763	763	Gilbert Priest	47	m		Labourer		N. Carolina				
		Lucy "	42	F				N. Carolina				
		Loveday "	10	F				N. Carolina		1		
		Owen "	9	m				N. Carolina		1		
		Catharine "	6	F				N. Carolina		1		
		Alexander "	5	m				N. Carolina				
		Mariah "	1/2	F				N. Carolina				
764	764	Malcom Currie	61	m		Farmer	225	Scotland				
		Catharine "	46	F				Scotland			1	
765	765	Nancy McIntosh	57	F				Scotland			1	
		Margaret "	49	F				Scotland				
		Mary "	47	F				N. Carolina				
766	766	Dugan McIver	79	m		Farmer	300	N. Carolina				7
		Effy "	66	F				N. Carolina				
		John B. "	22	m		Farmer		N. Carolina				
		Tally McIver	25	F				N. Carolina				

M 18

SCHEDULE I.—Free Inhabitants in ______ in the County of Moore State of N. Carolina enumerated by me, on the 16th day of October 1850. N. M. Crummer Ass't Marshal.

438 217

Dwelling-houses numbered in the order of visitation.	Families numbered in the order of visitation.	The Name of every Person whose usual place of abode on the first day of June, 1850, was in this family.	Age.	Sex.	Color, (White, black, or mulatto.)	Profession, Occupation, or Trade of each Male Person over 15 years of age.	Value of Real Estate owned.	Place of Birth. Naming the State, Territory, or Country.	Married within the year.	Attended School within the year.	Persons over 20 y'rs of age who cannot read & write.	Whether deaf and dumb, blind, insane, idiotic, pauper, or convict.
1	2	3	4	5	6	7	8	9	10	11	12	13
		John J. Shepperd	18	m		Farmer		N. Carolina				
764	764	Iven Kelly	33	m		Farmer	620	" "				
		Eliza "	42	F				" "			1	
		Eliza "	8	F				" "		1		
		Elizabeth "	5	F				" "		1		
		Evander J. "	3	m				" "				
		Daniel D. "	8/12	m				" "				
		Catharine Kelly	70	F				Scotland			1	
		Margaret "	27	F				N. Carolina				
765	765	David Rhodes	34	m		Farmer	200	" "				
		Lucretia "	37	F			200	" "				
		Mary "	26	F			200	" "				
		Elizabeth "	22	F			200	" "				
766	766	John Oats	63	m		Farmer	1000	" "				
		Sarah A. "	18	F				" "				
767	767	Westley W. Oats	25	m		Farmer		" "				
		Martha J. "	20	F				" "				
		Leander "	1	m				" "				
768	768	Daniel Ferguson	55	m		Farmer	300	Scotland				
		Jennet "	47	F				N. Carolina				
		Murdoch "	23	m		Carpenter		" "				
		Daniel "	19	m		Farmer		" "		1		
		Mary A. "	17	F				" "				
		Margaret "	14	F				" "		1		
		Neill "	12	m				" "		1		
		John "	6	m				" "		1		
		Elizabeth A. "	5	F				" "		1		
769	769	Young Oats	42	m		Farmer	232	" "				
		Martha "	39	F				" "				
		John R. "	18	m		Farmer		" "		1		
		Mary A. "	16	F				" "		1		
		Sarah E. "	14	F				" "				
		Temperance "	12	F				" "				
		James A. "	9	m				" "				
		Julia A. "	6	F				" "				
[illegible]70	770	Charles Gilchrist	58	m		Farmer	350	Scotland				
		Nancy "	58	F				"				
		Charles "	17	m		Farmer		N. Carolina		1		
		Catharine Gilchrist	22	F				" "				
[illegible]1	771	William Wadsworth	26	m		Farmer		" "				
		Margaret "	26	F				" "				
		Flora A. "	2	F				" "				

m 19
F 23
✓

444

Schedule I.—Free Inhabitants in ______________ **in the County of** Moore **State of** N. Carolina **enumerated by me, on the** 17th **day of** October **1850.** N. McCrummen **Ass't Marshal.**

Dwelling-houses numbered in the order of visitation.	Families numbered in the order of visitation.	The Name of every Person whose usual place of abode on the first day of June, 1850, was in this family.	Description: Age.	Sex.	Color, White, black, or mulatto.	Profession, Occupation, or Trade of each Male Person over 15 years of age.	Value of Real Estate owned.	Place of Birth. Naming the State, Territory, or Country.	Married within the year.	Attended School within the year.	Persons over 20 y'rs of age who cannot read & write.	Whether deaf and dumb, blind, insane, idiotic, pauper, or convict.
1	2	3	4	5	6	7	8	9	10	11	12	13
772	772	William Wadsworth	59	m		Farmer	1000	N. Carolina				
		Margaret "	59	F				" "				
		Hiram "	23	m		Farmer		" "				
		George "	19	m		Farmer		" "				
		Adam Wadsworth	36	m		Sheriff	250	" "				
		Jane "	24	F				" "				
		Catherine "	1/12	F				" "				
773	773	Harbard Cole	78	m		Farmer		" "				
		Temperance "	29	F				" "			1	
		Margaret Brewer	13	F				" "		1		
		Eleanor Cole	9	F				" "		1		
774	774	David Johnson	29	m		Farmer		" "				
		Eliza "	28	F				" "				
775	775	James Goings	58	m	m	Farmer	100	" "			1	
		Andrew "	22	m	m	Farmer		" "			1	
		Henry "	21	m	m	Farmer		" "			1	
		Ursula "	15	F	m			" "				
		Amy "	12	F	m			" "				
		John "	8	m	m			" "				
		James "	6	m	m			" "				
		Mary "	4	F	m			" "				
776	776	Archibald Kelly	31	m		Farmer	100	" "				
		Ann "	33	F				" "				
		William K. "	2	m				" "				
		Hugh A. "	10/12	m				" "				
777	777	Samuel Stone	60	m		Farmer	300	" "				
		Priscilla "	60	F				" "				
		Emeline "	26	F				" "				
		Martha "	18	F				" "				
		Rosanna "	15	F				" "				
		Archibald "	12	m				" "				
778	778	William Duncannon	46	m		Laborer		" "				
		Zilpha "	42	F				" "				
		Susannah E. "	20	F				" "				
		Delitha "	17	F				" "				
		William A. "	12	m				" "				
779	779	Daniel Short	70	m		Farmer	1400	" "				
		Margaret "	50	F				" "				
		Sarah "	19	F				" "		y		
		Brinkley "	17	m		Farmer		" "		1		
		Eliza "	16	F				" "		1		
		Frances "	15	F				" "		1		

m 20 5-B.
fe 22 37
✓

SCHEDULE I.—Free Inhabitants in ________ in the County of *Moore* State of *N. Carolina* enumerated by me, on the *17th* day of *October* 1850. *Neill McCrummen* Ass't Marshal.

635

218

Dwelling-houses numbered in the order of visitation	Families numbered in the order of visitation	The Name of every Person whose usual place of abode on the first day of June, 1850, was in this family	Age	Sex	Color (White, black, or mulatto)	Profession, Occupation, or Trade of each Male Person over 15 years of age	Value of Real Estate owned	Place of Birth, Naming the State, Territory, or Country	Married within the year	Attended School within the year	Persons over 20 y'rs of age who cannot read & write	Whether deaf and dumb, blind, insane, idiotic, pauper, or convict	
1	2	3	4	5	6	7	8	9	10	11	12	13	
		Margaret Short	13	F				N. Carolina		1			1
		Ellen "	11	F				" "		1			2
		Caroline "	10	F				" "		1			3
		Samuel "	6	m				" "		1			4
780	780	George McRae	63	m		Farmer	1360	" "					5
		Jennet "	50	F				" "					6
		Margaret "	21	F				" "					7
		Nancy "	15	F				" "		1			8
		Mary "	14	F				" "		1			9
		Roderick "	13	m				" "		1			10
		Daniel "	12	m				" "		1			11
		Alexander "	10	m				" "		1			12
		John "	8	m				" "		1			13
		Angus McGilvary	87	m		none	267	Scotland			1		14
		Mary McRae	72	F				N. Carolina			1		15
781	781	John Rogers	50	m		Laborer		So. Carolina					16
		Mary "	50	F				N. Carolina			1		17
		Sarah "	20	F				" "			1		18
		Margaret "	18	F				" "					19
		Elizabeth "	16	F				" "					20
		John "	14	m				" "					21
		Lavina "	12	F				" "					22
		William Oldham	30	m		Laborer		" "			1		23
		Mary "	20	F				" "			1		24
		Riley "	5	m				" "					25
		Lindsay "	3	m				" "					26
782	782	Balaam Stuart	34	m		Farmer	138	" "					27
		Mary "	36	F				" "					28
		Louisa C. "	10	F				" "		1			29
		Angus L. "	8	m				" "		1			30
		Emily A. "	6	F				" "		1			31
		Clarissa "	4	F				" "					32
		George "	2	m				" "					33
		Ann E. Smith	21	F				" "					34
785	785	Neill McLeod	56	m		Farmer	1800	Scotland					35
		Catharine "	56	F				N. Carolina					36
		Mary "	27	F				" "					37
		Nancy "	16	F				" "		1			38
		William McLeod	19	m		Farmer		" "		1			39
		Jane "	14	F				" "		1			40
		Isabella "	11	F				" "		1			41
		Frances "	8	F				" "		1			42

m 17
F 25

SCHEDULE I.—Free Inhabitants in ______ in the County of Moore State of N. Carolina enumerated by me, on the 18th day of October 1850. Neill McCrummen Ass't Marshal.

	Dwelling-houses numbered in the order of visitation.	Families numbered in the order of visitation.	The Name of every Person whose usual place of abode on the first day of June, 1850, was in this family.	Description: Age.	Sex.	Color, (White, black, or mulatto.)	Profession, Occupation, or Trade of each Male Person over 15 years of age.	Value of Real Estate owned.	Place of Birth. Naming the State, Territory, or Country.	Married within the year.	Attended School within the year.	Persons over 20 y'rs of age who cannot read & write.	Whether deaf and dumb, blind, insane, idiotic, pauper, or convict.
	1	2	3	4	5	6	7	8	9	10	11	12	13
1			Duncan McLeod	7	m				N. Carolina		1		
2			Sarah "	4	F				" "				
3			Lydia "	4/12	F				" "				
4	784	784	Jeremiah Barber	40	m		Farmer	25	" "				
5			Nancy "	30	F				" "			1	
6			Martha "	22	F				" "			1	
7			Hiram "	20	m		Farmer		" "		1	1	
8			Andrew "	17	m		Farmer		" "		1		
9			Drusilla "	14	F				" "				
10			William "	12	m				" "		1		
11			Elizabeth "	10	F				" "				
12			Jeremiah "	8	m				" "		1		
13			Nancy "	6	F				" "				
14			Mary "	1	F				" "				
15	785	785	Rachel Cole	57	F			1400	" "				
16			John A. "	21	m		Farmer		" "				
17			Telitha "	17	F				" "				
18			James McC "	17	m		Farmer		" "		1		
19			William B. "	15	m				" "		1		
20			Benjamin "	13	m				" "		1		
21			George W. "	11	m				" "		1		
22			Richard "	9	m				" "		1		
23	786	786	Thomas W. Lewis	57	m		Teacher		" "				
24			Evira "	46	F				" "				
25			Martha A. "	13	F				" "		1		
26			George H. "	11	m				" "		1		
27			Charlotte A. "	8	F				" "		1		
28			James H. "	6	m				" "		1		
29	787	787	Daniel Campbell	38	m		Carpenter	650	" "				
30			Isabella "	30	F				" "				
31			John "	16	m		Farmer		" "		1		
32			Mary J. "	12	F				" "		1		
33			Angus "	10	m				" "		1		
34			Kenneth "	7	m				" "				
35			Catherine "	3	F				" "				
36			Murdoch "	1	m				" "				
37	788	788	William Jackson	23	m		Laborer		" "			1	
38			Catherine "	23	F				" "			1	
39			William W. "	2	m				" "				
40	789	789	Jane Campbell	65	F			900	" "				
41			Nancy "	40	F				" "				
42			Christian "	35	F				" "				

M 22
F 20

SCHEDULE I.—Free Inhabitants in ______ **in the County of** *Moore* **State of** *N. Carolina* **enumerated by me, on the** *19th* **day of** *October* **1850.** *N. McCrimmon* **Ass't Marshal.**

219 87

Dwelling-houses numbered in the order of visitation.	Families numbered in the order of visitation.	The Name of every Person whose usual place of abode on the first day of June, 1850, was in this family.	Description: Age.	Description: Sex.	Description: Color, White, black, or mulatto.	Profession, Occupation, or Trade of each Male Person over 15 years of age.	Value of Real Estate owned.	Place of Birth. Naming the State, Territory, or Country.	Married within the year.	Attended School within the year.	Persons over 20 y'rs of age who cannot read & write.	Whether deaf and dumb, blind, insane, idiotic, pauper, or convict.
1	2	3	4	5	6	7	8	9	10	11	12	13
		Findlay Campbell	32	M		Farmer	75	N. Carolina				
		John C. "	30	M		Teacher		" "				
		William W. "	28	M		Merchant	75	" "				
790	790	Margaret Sinclair	72	F			1500	" "				
		Duncan M. "	32	M		Farmer		" "				
		Jane A. "	30	F				" "				
		Duncan C. McDonald	5	M				" "				
791	791	William D. Harrington	51	M		Farmer	4000	" "				
		Lydia M. "	34	F				" "				
		Ann E. "	21	F				" "				
		James "	11	M				" "		1		
		Mary "	9	F				" "		1		
		Sarah A. "	7	F				" "		1		
		William A. "	5	M				" "				
		Ugenia "	4	F				" "				
		Julius "	2	M				" "				
		Elisha Harrington	23	M		Farmer		" "				
		Henrietta	70	F	B			Virginia				
792	792	Dawson Tyson	51	M		Farmer	3000	N. Carolina				
		Joseph "	25	M		Ditto		" "				
		William A. "	20	M		Farmer		" "		1		
		Lydia "	16	F				" "				
		Neill "	14	M				" "		1		
		Mabala "	10	F				" "		1		
		George "	8	M				" "		1		
		Pleasan Sorrell	22	M		Cabinetmaker		" "				
		Margaret "	30	F				" "				
793	793	Lydia Roberts	32	F			1800	" "				
		Lucy A. "	13	F				" "		1		
		Benjamin "	12	M				" "		1		
		Charles "	9	M				" "		1		
		Sallie "	8	F				" "				
		Henry "	6	M				" "				
		Robert "	3	M				" "				
		Wiley "	11/12	M				" "				
		Sallie Elkins	19	F				" "				
[illegible]4	794	Neill Tyson	64	M		Farmer	1700	" "				
		Mary "	57	F				" "				
		Margaret Grimes	19	F				" "				
[illegible]5	795	Nancy McIver	49	F			600	" "				
		Langston "	14	M				" "		1		
[illegible]6	796	Wade Elkins	52	M		Farmer	300	" "			1	

M 24
F 18 17

SCHEDULE I.—Free Inhabitants in ____________ in the County of *Moore* State of *N. Carolina* enumerated by me, on the *21st* day of *October* 1850. *N. McCrummen* Ass't Marshal.

Dwelling-houses numbered in the order of visitation.	Families numbered in the order of visitation.	The Name of every Person whose usual place of abode on the first day of June, 1850, was in this family.	Age.	Sex.	Color, White, black, or mulatto.	Profession, Occupation, or Trade of each Male Person over 15 years of age.	Value of Real Estate owned.	Place of Birth. Naming the State, Territory, or Country.	Married within the year.	Attended School within the year.	Persons over 20 y'rs of age who cannot read & write.	Whether deaf and dumb, blind, insane, idiotic, pauper, or convict.
1	2	3	4	5	6	7	8	9	10	11	12	13
		Mary Elkins	53	F				N. Carolina			1	
		John "	30	M		Farmer		" "				
		Dicy "	19	F				" "				
		Rebecca "	15	F				" "				
		Hezekiah Grace	28	M		Farmer		" "				
		Lydia "	27	F				" "				
		Dilla "	2	F				" "				
		Eliza Elkins	25	F				" "				
797	797	Joseph Gilbert	52	M		Farmer		" "				
		Mary "	49	F				" "				
		Benjamin "	26	M		Farmer		" "				
		James "	19	M		Farmer		" "				
		Celia A. "	10	F				" "		1		
		Joseph "	7	M				" "		1		
798	798	Amy Bingham	70	F			1650	Virginia				
799	799	John Murchison	69	M		Farmer	2000	N. Carolina				
		Kenneth B. "	50	M		Lawyer		" "				
800	800	Joseph L. Reid	54	M		Farmer		" "				
		Grace "	54	F				" "				
801	801	Charles Chalmers	42	M		Physician	8000	" "				
		Mary "	44	F				" "				
		Charlotte "	45	F				" "				
		Margaret "	41	F				" "				
		John A. "	34	M		Physician		" "				
802	802	Jesse Hedspeth	47	M		Farmer	1300	" "				
		Bethana "	36	F				" "			1	
		Josiah "	18	M		Farmer		" "				
		John "	16	M		Ditto		" "				
803	803	Munde Mashburn	28	M		Laborer		" "				
		Nancy "	22	F				" "				
		Robert H. "	3	M				" "				
804	804	Mary Cheek	74	F				" "				
		Joseph "	44	M		Carpenter		" "				
		James "	39	M		Farmer		" "				
805	805	Jesse Womble	60	M		Farmer	2000	" "				
		Elizabeth "	52	F				" "				
		Joseph "	24	M		Farmer		" "				
		Thomas "	22	M		Ditto		" "				
		Candice "	20	F				" "				
		Lydia "	17	F				" "				
		Cornelius "	12	M				" "		1		
		Emeliza "	12	F				" "		1		

m22
620

SCHEDULE I.—Free Inhabitants in ______ in the County of *Moore* State of *N. Carolina* enumerated by me, on the *2nd* day of *October* 1850. *N. McCrummen* Ass't Marshal. 439

220

Dwelling-houses numbered in the order of visitation.	Families numbered in the order of visitation.	The Name of every Person whose usual place of abode on the first day of June, 1850, was in this family.	Age.	Sex.	Color, White, black, or mulatto.	Profession, Occupation, or Trade of each Male Person over 15 years of age.	Value of Real Estate owned.	Place of Birth. Naming the State, Territory, or Country.	Married within the year.	Attended School within the year.	Persons over 20 y'rs of age who cannot read & write.	Whether deaf and dumb, blind, insane, idiotic, pauper, or convict.
1	2	3	4	5	6	7	8	9	10	11	12	13
		Robert Paschal	19	M		Farmer		N. Carolina				
806	806	Lewis Phillips	43	M		Farmer	450	"				
		Nancy "	41	F				"				
		Emeline "	17	F				"				
		Malphus "	15	M				"		/		
		Martin C. "	14	M				"		/		
		Emory C. "	13	M				"		/		
		Alpha "	11	F				"		/		
		Baxter C. "	8	M				"				
		Nancy C. "	7	F				"		/		
		Elmina "	5	F				"		/		
		Eliza A. "	2	F				"				
		Martha A. "	1	F				"				
807	807	Charles A. Phillips	34	M		Farmer	700	"				
		Mary "	40	F				"				
808	808	Robert A. Phillips	46	M		Farmer	250	"				
		Lydia A. "	20	F				"				
		Elias Phillips	10	M	M			"				
809	809	William Curtis	34	M		Farmer	300	"			/	
		Martha "	34	F				"				
		William D. "	6	M				"				
		Esther A. "	5	F				"				
		Margaret E. "	4	F				"				
		Nancy E. "	8	F				"				
810	810	Stephen Phillips	39	M		Laborer		"			/	
		Nancy "	40	F				"			/	
811	811	William Phillips	57	M		Metho. Clergyman	300	"				
		Esther "	35	F				"				
		Charles W. "	3	M				"				
		James L. "	2	M				"				
		Joseph P. "	1	M				"				
812	812	Dabney Phillips	50	M		Farmer	640	"				
		Amy "	47	F				"				
		Lewis L. "	22	M		Farmer		"				
		John W. "	20	M		Farmer		"				
		Allen "	18	M		Farmer		"				
		William "	16	M		Ditto		"				
		Charles "	14	M				"				
		Chalmers "	10	M				"				
		Brinkley "	8	M				"				
		Albert "	6	M				"				
		Dabney "	3	M				"				

25 m m 26
16 f f 16
1 m Col

SCHEDULE I.—Free Inhabitants in ________ in the County of Moores State of N. Carolina enumerated by me, on the 22d day of October 1850. N. McCrummen Ass't Marshal.

	Dwelling-houses numbered in the order of visitation.	Families numbered in the order of visitation.	The Name of every Person whose usual place of abode on the first day of June, 1850, was in this family.	Age.	Sex.	Color, White, black, or mulatto.	Profession, Occupation, or Trade of each Male Person over 15 years of age.	Value of Real Estate owned.	Place of Birth. Naming the State, Territory, or Country.	Married within the year.	Attended School within the year.	Persons over 20 y'rs of age who cannot read & write.	Whether deaf and dumb, blind, insane, idiotic, pauper, or convict.
	1	2	3	4	5	6	7	8	9	10	11	12	13
1	813	813	Donald Street	40	M		Farmer	2500	N. Carolina		.		
2			Lydia "	36	F				" "				
3			Hugh "	17	M		Student		" "		/		
4			Mary "	15	F				" "				
5			Anna "	13	F				" "		/		
6			Charles "	12	M				" "		/		
7			Archibald "	10	M				" "		/		
8			Richard "	8	M				" "		/		
9			Donald "	5	M				" "		/		
10			Augusta "	3/12	F				" "				
11			Mary Ballard	19	F				" "				
12			Olivia "	4/12	F				" "				
13	814	814	James C. Davis	59	M		Farmer	1750	" "				
14			Sarah "	60	F				" "				
15	815	815	Joshua Phillips	30	M		Hatter		" "			/	
16			Elizabeth "	32	F				" "			/	
17			Chloe "	10	F				" "				
18			William "	8	M				" "				
19			Berry "	3	M				" "				
20	816	816	Berry Phillips	25	M		Farmer		" "				
21			Mary "	24	F				" "				
22			Archibald "	1	M				" "				
23	817	817	Archibald Shields	50	M		Farmer	150	" "				
24			Miriam "	45	F				" "			/	
25			Martha "	22	F				" "				
26			Hannah "	20	F				" "				
27			Enoch "	21	M		Farmer		" "				
28			Orren "	16	M		Farmer		" "		/		
29			Mahala "	14	F				" "		/		
30			Nancy "	12	F				" "		/		
31			Lucy "	10	F				" "		/		
32			Neill "	8	M				" "		/		
33			Margaret "	6	F				" "		/		
34			Lydia "	4	F				" "				
35			Leander "	1	M				" "				
36	818	818	John Cheek	56	M		Farmer	1000	" "				
37			Lydia "	55	F				" "				
38			Lewis "	24	M		Farmer		" "				
39			Nancy "	22	F				" "				
40			Richard "	21	M		Farmer		" "				
41			Charity "	18	F				" "				
42			Elizabeth "	18	F				" "				

M 20
Fe 22
✓

39 941

SCHEDULE I.—Free Inhabitants in ______ in the County of *Moore* **State** of *N. Carolina* enumerated by me, on the *23d* day of *October* 1850. *N. McCrummen* Ass't Marshal.

221

Line	Dwelling-houses numbered in the order of visitation.	Families numbered in the order of visitation.	The Name of every Person whose usual place of abode on the first day of June, 1850, was in this family.	Description: Age.	Sex.	Color, White, black, or mulatto.	Profession, Occupation, or Trade of each Male Person over 15 years of age.	Value of Real Estate owned.	Place of Birth. Naming the State, Territory, or Country.	Married within the year.	Attended School within the year.	Persons over 20 y'rs of age who cannot read & write.	Whether deaf and dumb, blind, insane, idiotic, pauper, or convict.	Line
	1	2	3	4	5	6	7	8	9	10	11	12	13	
1			Rubama Cheek	15	F				N. Carolina					1
2	819	819	Elizabeth Cheek	58	F				"					2
3	820	820	James Davis	29	M		Farmer	350	"					3
4			Mary "	29	F				"					4
5			Charles "	7	M				"					5
6			Lydia "	3	F				"					6
7			Louisa A. "	1	F				"					7
8			James Jackson	12	M				"		1			8
9	821	821	William C. Davis	56	M		Farmer	100	"			1		9
10			Phebe "	55	F				"			1		10
11			Enoch "	16	M		Farmer		"		1			11
12			Nancy "	23	F				"					12
13	822	822	John Hancock	30	M		Farmer	300	"					13
14			Nancy "	24	F				"					14
15			James M. "	1	M				"					15
16	823	823	Archibald Shields	30	M		Farmer		"					16
17			Finaly "	31	F				"					17
18			Ann "	9	F				"				Deaf & Dumb	18
19			Susan "	4	F				"				Deaf & Dumb	19
20			Charles C. "	3	M				"				Deaf & Dumb	20
21			George Moore	21	M		Farmer		"					21
22	824	824	James Shields	67	M		Farmer	1250	"					22
23			Susannah "	62	F				"					23
24			Austin "	22	M		Farmer		"			1		24
25	825	825	John Hancock	64	M		Farmer	600	"					25
26			Clarkey "	54	F				"					26
27			Martha A. "	26	F				"					27
28			Clarkey "	24	F				"					28
29			Margaret "	22	F				"			1		29
30			William "	20	M		none		"					30
31			Nancy "	17	F				"					31
32			Lydia "	17	F				"					32
33			Rhody "	14	F				"					33
34			Josephine "	12	F				"					34
35			James Brewer	15	M				"					35
36	[illegible]	826	Augustus B. Phar	29	M		Farmer	3252	"					36
37			Jane "	23	F				"					37
38			Alice "	2	F				"					38
39			James A. Phar	31	M		Merchant		"					39
40	[illegible]	827	William Davis	30	M		Laborer		"			1		40
41			Clarkey "	30	F				"					41
42			Westley "	6	M				"					42

m 19
F 23

SCHEDULE I.—Free Inhabitants in ______ in the County of Moore State of N. Carolina enumerated by me, on the 23d day of October 1850. N. McCrummen Ass't Marshal.

	Dwelling-houses numbered in the order of visitation.	Families numbered in the order of visitation.	The Name of every Person whose usual place of abode on the first day of June, 1850, was in this family.	Description: Age.	Description: Sex.	Description: Color, White, black, or mulatto.	Profession, Occupation, or Trade of each Male Person over 15 years of age.	Value of Real Estate owned.	Place of Birth. Naming the State, Territory, or Country.	Married within the year.	Attended School within the year.	Persons over 20 y'rs of age who cannot read & write.	Whether deaf and dumb, blind, insane, idiotic, pauper, or convict.
	1	2	3	4	5	6	7	8	9	10	11	12	13
1			Martin Davis	4	M				N. Carolina				
2			Taylor "	2	M				" "				
3	828	828	Nathaniel Brown	27	M		Laborer		" "				
4			Elizabeth "	22	F				" "				
5			Albert "	1	M				" "				
6	829	829	Daniel Brown	65	M		Farmer		" "				
7			Sarah "	60	F				" "				
8	830	830	Michael Phillips	47	M		Miller		" "			1	
9			Eliza "	41	F				" "				
10			Sabra "	21	F				" "				
11			Martha "	13	F				" "				
12			Amanda "	10	F				" "				
13			James "	8	M				" "				
14	831	831	John Paschal	47	M		Blacksmith		" "				
15			Elizabeth "	49	F				" "				
16			Nathan "	20	M		Laborer		" "				
17			Robert "	19	M		Laborer		" "				
18			Harper A. "	17	F				" "				
19			John L "	13	M				" "				
20			Catharine "	11	F				" "				
21			David "	8	M				" "				
22	832	832	John Phillips	49	M		Farmer		" "			1	
23			Elizabeth "	38	F				" "			1	
24			James "	15	M				" "				
25			Kenneth "	13	M				" "				
26			Mary "	11	F				" "				
27			Jane "	9	F				" "				
28			Neill "	6	M				" "				
29			Joseph "	2	M				" "				
30	833	833	Ann Street	59	F			4300	" "				
31			Murdo "	34	M		Physician		" "				
32			Richard "	29	M		Farmer		" "				
33	834	834	George Hackee	25	M		Farmer	6000	" "				
34			Anderson Jones	27	M		Farmer		" "				
35			Ann M. "	19	F				" "				
36			Mary J. "	1	F				" "				
37			Frances "	2/12	F				" "				
38	835	835	Neill Mathews	41	M		Farmer	50	" "				
39			Elizabeth "	41	F				" "			1	
40			Enoch W. "	11	M				" "		1		
41			William A "	7	M				" "		1		
42			Mary J. "	4	F				" "				

m 24
F 18

443

SCHEDULE I.—Free Inhabitants in ______ in the County of Moore State of N. Carolina enumerated by me, on the 24th day of October 1850. N. McCrummen Ass't Marshal.

222

Dwelling-houses numbered in the order of visitation.	Families numbered in the order of visitation.	The Name of every Person whose usual place of abode on the first day of June, 1850, was in this family.	Age.	Sex.	Color, white, black, or mulatto.	Profession, Occupation, or Trade of each Male Person over 15 years of age.	Value of Real Estate owned.	Place of Birth. Naming the State, Territory, or Country.	Married within the year.	Attended School within the year.	Persons over 20 y'rs of age who cannot read & write.	Whether deaf and dumb, blind, insane, idiotic, pauper, or convict.
1	2	3	4	5	6	7	8	9	10	11	12	13
836	836	Charles H. Stewart	29	M		Farmer	200	N. Carolina				
		Rebecca "	23	F				" "				
		Camilla "	1	F				" "				
837	837	Martha A. Alston	41	F				" "				
		Margaret "	21	F				" "				
		Elizabeth "	15	F				" "				
		Olivia "	14	F				" "				
		Pamelia "	10	F				" "				
		Brantly Jones	71	M		Millwright		" "				
		George Moore	14	M				" "				
838	838	Hardy Knight	35	M		Farmer		" "			1	
		Nancy "	23	F				" "			1	
		William B. "	2	M				" "				
		Flora A. "	1	F				" "				
839	839	George Stewart	61	M		Meth. Clergyman	950	" "				
		Sophia "	36	F				" "				
		Elizabeth "	26	F				" "				
		Samuel D. "	21	M		Farmer		" "		1		
		Albert "	16	M		Ditto		" "		1		
		Clarissa "	57	F				" "				
		Laurence "	8	M				" "		1		
840	840	Josiah Cheek	45	M		Laborer		" "				
		Lucinda "	30	F				" "				
		James Jackson	14	M				" "		1		
841	841	Jeremiah Tinnison	23	M		Farmer	150	" "				
		Charity "	33	F				" "				
		George "	3	M				" "				
		Margaret "	6/12	F				" "				
		John Tinnison	51	M		None		" "				
842	842	Fanning Moore	74	M		Farmer	250	" "			1	
		Frances "	78	F				" "			1	
		Mary "	30	F				" "			1	
843	843	Nancy Cheek	60	F			60	Virginia			1	
		Jane Brewer	45	F				N. Carolina			1	
		Elizabeth "	41	F				" "				
		Noah "	2	M				" "				
844	844	Benjamin Shields	47	M		Farmer	200	" "				
		Lydia "	42	F				" "			1	
		William T. "	14	M				" "		1		
		Mary E. "	12	F				" "		1		
		Robert D. "	11	M				" "		1		
		Martha "	8	F				" "		1		

Schedule I.—Free Inhabitants in ______ in the County of *Moore* State of *N. Carolina* enumerated by me, on the *25th* day of *October* 1850. *N. McCrummen* Ass't Marshal.

Dwelling-houses numbered in the order of visitation.	Families numbered in the order of visitation.	The Name of every Person whose usual place of abode on the first day of June, 1850, was in this family.	Age.	Sex.	Color, White, black, or mulatto.	Profession, Occupation, or Trade of each Male Person over 15 years of age.	Value of Real Estate owned.	Place of Birth. Naming the State, Territory, or Country.	Married within the year.	Attended School within the year.	Persons over 20 y'rs of age who cannot read & write.	Whether deaf and dumb, blind, insane, idiotic, pauper, or convict.
1	2	3	4	5	6	7	8	9	10	11	12	13
		Catherine Shields	7	F				N. Carolina		1		
		John "	5	M				" "				
		Malcom "	2	M				" "				
		Lydia Shields	21	F				" "				
		Luther Paschal	22	M		Laborer		" "			1	
		Nathan "	21	M		Laborer		" "			1	
845	845	Ann McNeill	69	F				" "				
		Mary "	31	F				" "				
		Malcom D. "	28	M		Farmer		" "				
		Adalaid "	4	F				" "		1		
		Martha "	3	F				" "				
846	846	Patrick Shields	44	M		Farmer		" "				
		Martha "	40	F				" "				
		Sophronia "	21	F				" "				
		Emily "	15	F				" "				
		Bryan "	7	M				" "		1		
		Rosanna "	5	F				" "		1		
		Mary "	3	F				" "				
		Sophia "	6/12	F				" "				
847	847	Phillip Wilson	40	M		Farmer	1000	" "				
		Lydia "	38	F				" "				
		Mary "	14	F				" "		1		
		Nancy "	13	F				" "		1		
		Emily "	11	F				" "		1		
		Robert "	9	M				" "		1		
		Daniel "	7	M				" "		1		
		Sarah "	1	F				" "				
848	848	Mahala Wilson	50	F			400	" "				
		Bradley Brady	46	M		Farmer		" "				
		Rebecca "	32	F				" "			1	
		Mary "	21	F				" "				
		Alexander "	18	M		Farmer		" "				
		Dicy "	16	F				" "				
		Christentery "	12	M				" "				
		Susannah "	2	F				" "				
		Mariah "	2	F				" "				
		Nancy "	2	F				" "				
849	849	Robert W. Colston	24	M		Farmer	2800	" "				
		Louisa A. "	20	F				" "				
850	850	Joseph Beal	35	M		Farmer	75	" "				
		Elizabeth "	25	F				" "				
		Emily "	6	F				" "				

38 445

Schedule I.—Free Inhabitants in ______ in the County of *Moore* State of *N. Carolina* enumerated by me, on the *26th* day of *October* 1850. *N. McCrummen* Ass't Marshal.

223

Dwelling-houses numbered in the order of visitation.	Families numbered in the order of visitation.	The Name of every Person whose usual place of abode on the first day of June, 1850, was in this family.	Age.	Sex.	Color, White, black, or mulatto.	Profession, Occupation, or Trade of each Male Person over 15 years of age.	Value of Real Estate owned.	Place of Birth. Naming the State, Territory, or Country.	Married within the year.	Attended School within the year.	Persons over 20 y'rs of age who cannot read & write.	Whether deaf and dumb, blind, insane, idiotic, pauper, or convict.
1	2	3	4	5	6	7	8	9	10	11	12	13
		Mary Beal	5	F				N. Carolina				
		Martha "	3	F				" "				
		Robert "	1	m				" "				
851	851	James Brady	37	m		Farmer	50	" "				
		Mary "	35	F				" "			/	
		Lucas "	12	m				" "		/		
		James C. "	10	m				" "		/		
		Elizabeth "	8	F				" "		/		
		Charles "	6	m				" "				
		Martha A. "	4	F				" "				
		Robert W. "	2/12	m				" "				
852	852	Carrel Brady	56	m		Farmer		" "			/	
		Lydia "	55	F				" "			/	
		Martha "	22	F				" "			/	
		William "	15	m				" "				
		Samuel "	12	m				" "				
		Catharine "	10	F				" "				
		Napoleon "	6	m				" "				
853	853	Margaret Taylor	24	F				" "			/	
		Charlotte "	1	F				" "				
		Lucretia Brady	2	F				" "				
		John Brady	24	m		Laborer		" "			/	
854	854	Stephen Phillips	40	m		Farmer		" "			/	
		Nancy "	45	F				" "			/	
855 / 854	855 / 854	Charles Brady	75	m		Farmer		" "				
		Amy "	46	F			50	" "			/	
		Julia "	18	F				" "				
		Lucy A. "	15	F				" "		/		
		Eliza "	14	F				" "				
856	856	Charles Brady	30	m		Farmer		" "	—		/	
		Pimpernel "	22	F				" "	—		/	
857	857	Milley Moore	35	F				" "			/	
		Mary "	16	F				" "				
		Pattie "	12	F				" "				
		Anna "	9	F				" "				
		Bryant "	7	m				" "				
		Lydia "	3	F				" "				
		Sarah "	1	F				" "				
858	858	Hugh C. Hardin	36	m		Farmer	1000	" "				
		Sallie "	35	F				" "			/	
		Jane "	16	F				" "		/		
		Joab C. "	10	m				" "				

m 17
F 25

SCHEDULE I.—Free Inhabitants in ____________ in the County of Moore State of N. Carolina enumerated by me, on the 26th day of October 1850. N. McCrummen Ass't Marshal.

Dwelling-houses numbered in the order of visitation.	Families numbered in the order of visitation.	The Name of every Person whose usual place of abode on the first day of June, 1850, was in this family.	Description: Age.	Description: Sex.	Description: Color, White, black, or mulatto.	Profession, Occupation, or Trade of each Male Person over 15 years of age.	Value of Real Estate owned.	Place of Birth. Naming the State, Territory, or Country.	Married within the year.	Attended School within the year.	Persons over 20 y'rs of age who cannot read & write.	Whether deaf and dumb, blind, insane, idiotic, pauper, or convict.
1	2	3	4	5	6	7	8	9	10	11	12	13
		Winston Hardin	8	m				N. Carolina				
		Clementine "	5	F				" "				
		Lewis "	4	m				" "				
		Martha "	3	F				" "				
859	859	Major S. Johnson	60	m		Farmer		Virginia				
		Mary "	44	F				N. Carolina			1	
		Malcom "	1	m				" "				
860	860	James Cole	45	m		Farmer	170	" "				
		Eliza "	45	F				" "				
		Mary "	13	F				" "		1		
		Elizabeth "	12	F				" "		1		
		Alpha "	10	F				" "		1		
		Sarah F. "	8	F				" "		1		
		Eliza "	6	F				" "		1		
		James "	4	m				" "				
861	861	Nimrod R. Brady	27	m		Farmer		" "				
		Martha "	24	F				" "			1	
		Sarah F. "	3/12	F				" "				
862	862	Bradley Brady	51	m		Farmer	600	" "				
		Hester "	48	F				" "			1	
		Jane "	28	F				" "			1	
		Ann E. "	22	F				" "			1	
		Bradley "	20	m		Farmer		" "		1		
		Martha "	18	F				" "				
		Jesse "	16	m		Farmer		" "		1		
		Hester "	13	F				" "		1		
		Daniel "	11	m				" "		1		
		Winniford "	9	F				" "		1		
		Manly "	6	m				" "		1		
863	863	Jeremiah Phillips	48	m		Farmer	220	" "				
		Martha "	36	F				" "			1	
		Lydia "	17	F				" "		1		
		Martha "	15	F				" "		1		
		Amy "	14	F				" "		1		
		William H. "	12	m				" "		1		
		Rebecca "	10	F				" "		1		
		Joab "	8	m				" "		1		
		Mary "	6	F				" "				
		Jeremiah "	5	m				" "				
		Charles "	3	m				" "				
864	864	Mathew Manes	21	m				" "			1	
		Martha "	21	F				" "			1	

m 18
F 24

SCHEDULE I.—Free Inhabitants in ______________ in the County of Moore State of N. Carolina enumerated by me, on the 26th day of October 1850. N. M. McCrummen Ass't Marshal. 447

224

Dwelling-houses numbered in the order of visitation.	Families numbered in the order of visitation.	The Name of every Person whose usual place of abode on the first day of June, 1850, was in this family.	Description: Age.	Sex.	Color, White, black, or mulatto.	Profession, Occupation, or Trade of each Male Person over 15 years of age.	Value of Real Estate owned.	Place of Birth. Naming the State, Territory, or Country.	Married within the year.	Attended School within the year.	Persons over 20 years of age who cannot read & write.	Whether deaf and dumb, blind, insane, idiotic, pauper, or convict.	
1	2	3	4	5	6	7	8	9	10	11	12	13	
		Zachariah T. McManis	1	m				N. Carolina					1
865	865	William Shields	53	m		Farmer	300	" "					2
		Westley "	23	m		Laborer		" "					3
		Arsina "	20	F				" "		1			4
		Sarah "	17	F				" "		1			5
		Mary "	10	F				" "		1			6
866	866	Hiram Johnson	35	m		Laborer		" "			1		7
		Lydia "	34	F				" "					8
		Mary "	12	F				" "		1			9
		Phebe "	10	F				" "		1			10
		Benjamin "	8	m				" "		1			11
		Lydia "	6	F				" "					12
		William "	3	m				" "					13
867	867	Susannah Brown	34	F			150	" "					14
		Mary "	16	F				" "		1			15
		Catharine "	13	F				" "		1			16
		Marshal "	11	m				" "		1			17
		Henry "	9	m				" "		1			18
		Ann R. "	8	F				" "		1			19
		John "	6	m				" "		1			20
		Cornelius "	5	m				" "					21
868	868	Benjamin R. Person	29	m		Farmer	1000	" "	—				22
		Lucinda "	22	F				" "	—				23
869	869	Elias A. Brewer	38	m		Farmer		" "			1		24
		Mary "	34	F				" "			1		25
		Lydia "	2	F				" "					26
		Elizabeth "	3/12	F				" "					27
870	870	Charles McManis	25	m		Farmer		" "			1		28
		Clarky "	35	F				" "			1		29
		Emory "	4	m				" "					30
		Alexander "	3	m				" "					31
		Jefs "	1	m				" "					32
		Benjamin "	8/12	m				" "					33
871	871	James Moore	40	m		Farmer	100	" "			1		34
		Elizabeth "	33	F				" "					35
		Mary "	11	F				" "		1			36
		Joseph "	9	m				" "		1			37
		Frances "	7	F				" "		1			38
		Nancy "	6	F				" "					39
		Elizabeth "	3/12	F				" "					40
		Eleanor Parsons	63	F				" "			1		41
872		Jonathan Martindale	33	m		Farmer	400	" "					42

M 20
F 22

SCHEDULE I.—Free Inhabitants in ______ in the County of Moore State of N. Carolina enumerated by me, on the 28th day of October 1850. N. McCrummen Ass't Marshal.

Dwelling-houses numbered in the order of visitation.	Families numbered in the order of visitation.	The Name of every Person whose usual place of abode on the first day of June, 1850, was in this family.	Description: Age.	Description: Sex.	Description: Color, White, black, or mulatto.	Profession, Occupation, or Trade of each Male Person over 15 years of age.	Value of Real Estate owned.	Place of Birth. Naming the State, Territory, or Country.	Married within the year.	Attended School within the year.	Persons over 20 y'rs of age who cannot read & write.	Whether deaf and dumb, blind, insane, idiotic, pauper, or convict.
1	2	3	4	5	6	7	8	9	10	11	12	13
		Lydia M. Martindale	30	F				N. Carolina				
		Agnes "	12	F				" "				
		Nancy "	10	F				" "				
		John "	8	m				" "				
		James "	6	m				" "				
		Mary E. "	3/12	F				" "				
		Nancy Martindale	65	F				" "				
873	873	Alston Brewer	23	m	m	Farmer		" "			1	
		Hannah "	20	F	m			" "			1	
		Mary "	2	F	m			" "				
		Alston "	4/12	m	m			" "				
874	874	William Martindale	70	m		Farmer	150	" "				
		Jude "	53	F				" "			1	
		Ann M. "	17	F				" "				
		Mary "	13	F				" "				
		Thomas Morris	13	m				" "				
		Henry Manis	19	m		Farmer		" "				
875	875	Enoch S. Powers	27	m		Farmer	250	" "				
		Agnes "	30	F				" "				
		James "	4	m				" "				
		John H. "	3	m				" "				
		Lydia S. "	1	F				" "				
876	876	Jacob Stutts	50	m		Farmer	300	" "			1	
		Hannah "	46	F				" "			1	
		Adam Kivlin	24	m		Farmer		" "				
		Anna "	22	F				" "				
877	877	Robert L. Purvis	39	m		Farmer	470	" "				
		Sarah "	22	F				" "			1	
		Andrew J. "	17	m		Farmer		" "		1		
		Cornelius "	16	m		Farmer		" "		1		
		McQueen A. "	15	F				" "		1		
		Franklin H. "	13	m				" "		1		
		Joseph "	9	m				" "		1		
		George "	6	m				" "		1		
		John M. "	1	m				" "				
878	878	Winey A. Cavendish	31	F				" "			1	
		Harrison "	8	m	m			" "				
		Mary "	7	F	m			" "				
		Ann "	3	F	m			" "				
		Frances "	4/12	F	m			" "				
879	879	John Little	36	m	m	Farmer		" "			1	
		Martha "	26	F	m			" "			1	

m 21 4B
F 21 6 F

449

SCHEDULE I.—Free Inhabitants in ______ in the County of Moore State of N. Carolina enumerated by me, on the 27th day of October 1850. N. McCrummen Ass't Marshal.

225

Dwelling-houses numbered in the order of visitation.	Families numbered in the order of visitation.	The Name of every Person whose usual place of abode on the first day of June, 1850, was in this family.	Age.	Sex.	Color, White, black, or mulatto.	Profession, Occupation, or Trade of each Male Person over 15 years of age.	Value of Real Estate owned.	Place of Birth. Naming the State, Territory, or Country.	Married within the year.	Attended School within the year.	Persons over 20 y'rs of age who cannot read & write.	Whether deaf and dumb, blind, insane, idiotic, pauper, or convict.
1	2	3	4	5	6	7	8	9	10	11	12	13
880	880	Samuel Beck	60	m		Miller		N. Carolina			1	
		Jane "	40	F				" "			1	
		Elenor "	17	F				" "				
881	881	Sallie Kelam	32	F				" "			1	
		Bettie "	22	F				" "			1	
		Alfred "	15	m	m			" "				
		Nicy "	11	F	m			" "				
		Mary Kealin	60	F				" "				
882	882	Mariah Cavendish	49	F				" "			1	
		Isiah "	26	m		Laborer		" "			1	
		Alexander "	13	m				" "				
		Dicy "	10	F	m			" "				
		Marley "	3	m	m			" "				
883	883	Dolly Cavendish	47	F				" "				
		Eliza "	18	F				" "				
		William "	13	m				" "				
884	884	William Johnson	60	m		Farmer	2500	" "				
		Mary E. "	60	F				" "				
		Elvira "	22	F				" "				
		Mary A. Tyson	1	F				" "				
885	885	James Cavendish	52	m		Farmer	475	" "				
		Susannah "	70	F				" "			1	
		Frances "	15	F				" "		1		
886	886	John M. Myrick	65	m		Farmer	150	" "				
		Margaret "	51	F				" "				
		John "	20	m		Farmer		" "			1	
		Susannah "	18	F				" "		1		
		William L. "	15	m				" "		1		
		Margaret "	11	F				" "		1		
887	887	James Gaines	88	m		Farmer	2500	Virginia				
		Cary "	70	F				N. Carolina		1		
888	888	Lewis Garner	55	m		Gunsmith	250	" "				
		Mary "	44	F				" "				
		Henry "	21	m		Farmer		" "		1		
		Lucy "	17	F				" "		1		
		Edison "	15	m				" "		1		
		William "	13	m				" "		1		
		John "	10	m				" "		1		
		Samuel "	8	m				" "		1		
		Marcus "	7	m				" "		1		
		Elizabeth "	4	F				" "				
889	889	John Ritter	34	m		Farmer	350	" "				

M 20 2 B
F 22 2 F

SCHEDULE I.—Free Inhabitants in ________ in the County of Moore State of N. Carolina enumerated by me, on the 28th day of October 1850. N. McCrummen Ass't Marshal.

	Dwelling-houses numbered in the order of visitation.	Families numbered in the order of visitation.	The Name of every Person whose usual place of abode on the first day of June, 1850, was in this family.	Age.	Sex.	Color, White, black, or mulatto.	Profession, Occupation, or Trade of each Male Person over 15 years of age.	Value of Real Estate owned.	Place of Birth. Naming the State, Territory, or Country.	Married within the year.	Attended School within the year.	Persons over 20 y'rs of age who cannot read & write.	Whether deaf and dumb, blind, insane, idiotic, pauper, or convict.
	1	2	3	4	5	6	7	8	9	10	11	12	13
1			Sarah A. Ritter	32	F				N. Carolina				
2			Marion "	10	M				" "		1		
3			Thomas "	9	M				" "		1		
4			Martha "	7	F				" "		1		
5			John S. "	5	M				" "		1		
6			Mary "	3	F				" "				
7			Judy "	2	F				" "				
8			Cynthia "	4/12	F				" "				
9			Huldah Myrick	54	F				" "				
10			Addison Ritter	1	M				" "				
11	890	890	Elias Manis	31	M		Farmer	130	" "				
12			Elizabeth "	28	F				" "			1	
13			Julia A. "	8	F				" "		1		
14			Sarah "	6	F				" "		1		
15			Amandes "	4	F				" "				
16			Dicy J. "	2	F				" "				
17			Letty Manis	20	F				" "			1	
18			Elizabeth Manis	39	F				" "			1	
19	891	891	Margery "	18	F				" "				
20			Lewis Manis	19	M		Farmer		" "				
21			Mary "	12	F	M			" "				
22			Enoch "	6	M				" "				
23			Dumas "	5	M				" "				
24			Mascah Manis	68	F			75	" "			1	
25	892	892	Enoch Manis	31	M		Farmer	150	" "				
26			Amelia "	35	F				" "			1	
27			Emaly "	13	M				" "		1		
28			Francis "	10	M				" "		1		
29			Robertis "	8	M				" "		1		
30			John "	6	M				" "		1		
31			Elizabeth "	1	F				" "				
32			Eliza "	3	F				" "				
33	893	893	James Garner	32	M		Farmer	150	" "				
34			Molsey "	25	F				" "			1	
35			John F. "	11	M				" "		1		
36			Adams "	10	M				" "		1		
37			Lydia "	9	F				" "		1		
38			Eli "	7	M				" "				
39			Pickney "	4	M				" "				
40			Catharine "	3	F				" "				
41	894	894	John Garner	60	M		Farmer	700	" "				
42			Jude "	30	F				" "			1	

M 19
F 23 17

451

SCHEDULE I.—Free Inhabitants in ______________ in the County of Moore State of N. Carolina enumerated by me, on the 28th day of October 1850. N. McCrummen Ass't Marshal.

226

Dwelling-houses numbered in the order of visitation.	Families numbered in the order of visitation.	The Name of every Person whose usual place of abode on the first day of June, 1850, was in this family.	Age.	Sex.	Color, White, black, or mulatto.	Profession, Occupation, or Trade of each Male Person over 15 years of age.	Value of Real Estate owned.	Place of Birth. Naming the State, Territory, or Country.	Married within the year.	Attended School within the year.	Persons over 20 y'rs of age who cannot read & write.	Whether deaf and dumb, blind, insane, idiotic, pauper, or convict.	
1	2	3	4	5	6	7	8	9	10	11	12	13	
		Emeline Garner	12	F				N. Carolina		1			1
		Abel "	10	M				" "		1			2
		John "	9	M				" "		1			3
		Eliza A. "	6	F				" "		1			4
		William B.	3	M				" "					5
895	895	Elias Ritter	21	M		Farmer	40	" "	—				6
		Lydia "	18	F				" "	—				7
896	896	George Moore	25	M		Laborer		" "			1		8
		Mary "	24	F				" "			1		9
		William L. "	5	M				" "					10
		Andrew "	3	M				" "					11
		Sarah "	3	F				" "					12
		Elias "	1	M				" "					13
897	897	Lewis Garner	57	M		Farmer	500	" "			1		14
		Elizabeth "	48	F				" "					15
		Margaret "	17	F				" "		1			16
		Lewis O. "	10	M				" "		1			17
898	898	Riley Moore	30	M		Laborer		" "			1		18
		Eliza J. "	25	F				" "			1		19
		John "	4	M				" "					20
		Adaline "	2	F				" "					21
		Sallie Moore	60	F				" "			1		22
899	899	Enoch S. Brown	32	M		Farmer	200	" "					23
		Eliza "	32	F				" "			1		24
		Eli "	10	M				" "		1			25
		Mary "	8	F				" "					26
		Sarah A. "	3	F				" "					27
		Martha J. "	3	F				" "					28
900	900	Margaret Williamson	76	F				" "			1		29
		Lewis Williamson	33	M		Farmer	100	" "			1		30
		Sarah "	25	F				" "					31
901	901	Baily Brown	36	M		Farmer		" "			1		32
		Francy "	33	F				" "					33
		Elias "	10	M				" "		1			34
		Sarah "	6	F				" "					35
		Elina A. "	5	F				" "					36
902	902	John Manus	63	M		Farmer	800	" "			1		37
		Sarah "	60	F				" "			1		38
		John "	26	M		Farmer		" "		1			39
		Mark Manus	37	M		Farmer		" "			1		40
903	903	Lewis G. Manus	33	M		Farmer		" "					41
		Rebecca "	33	F				" "			1		42

M 21
F 21

SCHEDULE I.—Free Inhabitants in ______________ **in the County of** *Moore* **State of** *N. Carolina* **enumerated by me, on the** *26th* **day of** *October* **1850.** *N. McCrummen* **Ass't Marshal.**

Dwelling-houses numbered in the order of visitation.	Families numbered in the order of visitation.	The Name of every Person whose usual place of abode on the first day of June, 1850, was in this family.	Age.	Sex.	Color, White, black, or mulatto.	Profession, Occupation, or Trade of each Male Person over 15 years of age.	Value of Real Estate owned.	Place of Birth. Naming the State, Territory, or Country.	Married within the year.	Attended School within the year.	Persons over 20 yrs of age who cannot read & write.	Whether deaf and dumb, blind, insane, idiotic, pauper, or convict.
1	2	3	4	5	6	7	8	9	10	11	12	13
		Elizabeth Manis	10	F				N. Carolina		1		
		Sarah "	9	F				" "		1		
		John W. "	7	M				" "				
		Cary "	5	F				" "				
		Margaret "	2/12	F				" "				
904	904	Robartus Manis	27	M		Farmer		" "				
		Sarah "	27	F				" "				
		John W. "	4	M				" "				
		Sarah "	2	F				" "				
905	905	James M. Garner	30	M		Farmer		" "			1	
		Susannah "	32	F				" "			1	
		John "	3	M				" "				
		Rebecca Myrick	48	F				" "			1	
906	906	Mathew Yow	42	M		Farmer	375	" "				
		Malony "	43	F				" "			1	
		Henry "	19	M		Farmer		" "		1		
		Andrew "	16	M		Do.		" "		1		
		David "	14	M				" "		1		
		William "	12	M				" "		1		
		Celia "	10	F				" "		1		
		Sallie "	8	F				" "		1		
		Lydia "	6	F				" "				
		Mary "	3	F				" "				
907	907	Andrew Yow	69	M		Farmer		" "				
		Julian A. "	20	F				" "				
		Mary Manis	3	F				" "				
908	908	William B. Freeman	37	M		Carpenter		" "				
		Elizabeth "	32	F				" "				
		James A. "	9	M				" "		1		
		John W. "	6	M				" "		1		
909	909	William Williamson	56	M		Farmer		" "				
		James "	24	M		Farmer		" "			1	
		Wyatt "	22	M		Farmer		" "				
		John "	20	M		Ditto		" "		1		
		Mathew "	12	M				" "		1		
		Lewis "	9	M				" "				
		Henry "	5	M				" "				
		Jemima Williamson	50	F				" "				
		Nancy "	26	F				" "				
		Margaret "	18	F				" "			1	
		Rebecca "	11	F				" "			1	
910	910	Hiram Williamson	42	M		Farmer	250	" "				

M 22

32 453

SCHEDULE I.—Free Inhabitants in ______ in the County of Moore State of N. Carolina enumerated by me, on the 26th day of October 1850. Neill McCrummen Ass't Marshal.

227

Dwelling-houses numbered in the order of visitation.	Families numbered in the order of visitation.	The Name of every Person whose usual place of abode on the first day of June, 1850, was in this family.	Description: Age.	Sex.	Color, White, black, or mulatto.	Profession, Occupation, or Trade of each Male Person over 15 years of age.	Value of Real Estate owned.	Place of Birth. Naming the State, Territory, or Country.	Married within the year.	Attended School within the year.	Persons over 20 y'rs of age who cannot read & write.	Whether deaf and dumb, blind, insane, idiotic, pauper, or convict.	
1	2	3	4	5	6	7	8	9	10	11	12	13	
		Lotty Williamson	32	F				N.C.					1
		David "	16	m		Farmer		N.C.		1			2
		Eliza "	13	F				N.C.		1			3
		Mary "	11	F				N.C.		1			4
		James "	9	m				N.C.		1			5
		Bradley "	6	m				N.C.					6
		Eli "	1	m				N.C.					7
911	911	Isaac Williams	25	m		Farmer		N.C.					8
		Martha "	24	F				N.C.					9
912	912	William Jordan	34	m		Farmer	350	N.C.					10
		Francey "	32	F				N.C.			1		11
		Miles "	4	m				N.C.					12
		John "	3	m				N.C.					13
		Mary "	2	F				N.C.					14
		Martha "	6/12	F				N.C.					15
913	913	James Moore	35	m		Laborer		N.C.			1		16
		Bathana "	40	F				N.C.			1		17
		Larkins "	14	m				N.C.					18
		Candice "	10	F				N.C.					19
		Balaam "	7	m				N.C.					20
		George "	6	m				N.C.					21
[illegible]14	914	Wyatt Williamson	48	m		Farmer	700	N.C.					22
		Mary "	53	F				N.C.					23
		Wiley "	21	m		Farmer		N.C.					24
		Windrick "	18	m		Farmer		N.C.					25
		William W. "	17	m				N.C.					26
		Mary E. "	13	F				N.C.					27
		John "	10	m				N.C.					28
[illegible]15	915	Henry Yow	44	m		Farmer	595	N.C.					29
		Elizabeth "	43	F				N.C.			1		30
		Mathew "	22	m		Farmer		N.C.		1			31
		Rebecca "	20	F				N.C.		1			32
		Elizabeth "	18	F				N.C.		1			33
		Julia A. "	16	F				N.C.		1			34
		Amelia "	15	F				N.C.		1			35
		Sarah "	12	F				N.C.		1			36
		Isaac "	10	m				N.C.		1			37
		Simeon "	8	m				N.C.		1			38
		Mary "	6	F				N.C.		1			39
		William "	4	m				N.C.					40
		Lydia "	2	F				N.C.					41
	916	Nancy Brewer	22	F				N.C.					42

M 22

SCHEDULE I.—Free Inhabitants in ______ in the County of *Moore* State of *N. Carolina* enumerated by me, on the *28th* day of *October* 1850. *N. McCrummen* Ass't Marshal.

Dwelling-houses numbered in the order of visitation.	Families numbered in the order of visitation.	The Name of every Person whose usual place of abode on the first day of June, 1850, was in this family.	Age.	Sex.	Color, (White, black, or mulatto.)	Profession, Occupation, or Trade of each Male Person over 15 years of age.	Value of Real Estate owned.	Place of Birth. Naming the State, Territory, or Country.	Married within the year.	Attended School within the year.	Persons over 20 y'rs of age who cannot read & write.	Whether deaf and dumb, blind, insane, idiotic, pauper, or convict.
1	2	3	4	5	6	7	8	9	10	11	12	13
		William Brewer	5	m				N.C.				
		Alfred "	4	m				N.C.				
		Mary "	1	F				N.C.				
		Elizabeth Craven	13	F				N.C.				
917	917	E. Gardner Moffitt	35	m		Physician	125	N.C.				
918	918	Gideon Moore	35	m		Farmer		N.C.			1	
		Mary "	26	F				N.C.			1	
		Bryant "	10	m				N.C.				
		Alexander "	4	m				N.C.				
		Malcom "	2	F				N.C.				
		Lindsay "	3/12	m				N.C.				
919	919	Elizabeth Morris	43	F				N.C.			1	
		John "	25	m				N.C.			1	
		Sallie "	23	F				N.C.			1	
		Enoch "	22	m		Farmer		N.C.			1	
		Alfred "	20	m		Ditto		N.C.			1	
		James D. "	11	m				N.C.				
		Mary "	4	F				N.C.				
		David "	6/12	m				N.C.				
920	920	Elizabeth Spencer	49	F			650	N.C.				
		Elizabeth Pool	8	F				N.C.				
		William Wilborn	14	m				N.C.				
921	921	Clarkson Spencer	25	m		Labourer		N.C.				
		Martha "	17	F				N.C.				
		James "	3/12	m				N.C.				
922	922	Wesley Mattle	23	m		Labourer		N.C.				
		Margaret "	20	F				N.C.			1	
923	923	Goodin Hussey	37	m		Farmer	500	N.C.				
		Mary "	33	F				N.C.				
		William "	16	m				N.C.		1		
		Martha "	13	F				N.C.		1		
		Judiah "	11	F				N.C.		1		
		Robertes "	10	m				N.C.				
		Mary "	9	F				N.C.				
		Sarah "	7	F				N.C.				
		Lucy "	5	F				N.C.				
		Lydia "	2	F				N.C.				
		Andrew Hussey	15	m				N.C.		1		
924	924	Parham K. Maynard	31	m		Farmer	150	N.C.				
		Nancy "	32	F				N.C.				
		Ann E. "	9	F				N.C.		1		
		Columbus "	7	m				N.C.				

M22

455

SCHEDULE I.—Free Inhabitants in ________ in the County of Moore State of N. Carolina enumerated by me, on the 31st day of October 1850. N. McLennan Ass't Marshal.

228

Dwelling-houses numbered in the order of visitation.	Families numbered in the order of visitation.	The Name of every Person whose usual place of abode on the first day of June, 1850, was in this family.	Age.	Sex.	Color, (White, black, or mulatto.)	Profession, Occupation, or Trade of each Male Person over 15 years of age.	Value of Real Estate owned.	Place of Birth. Naming the State, Territory, or Country.	Married within the year.	Attended School within the year.	Persons over 20 y'rs of age who cannot read & write.	Whether deaf and dumb, blind, insane, idiotic, pauper, or convict.	
1	2	3	4	5	6	7	8	9	10	11	12	13	
		Martha A. Alyrick	5	F.				N.C.					1
		Margaret E. "	2	F.				N.C.					2
725	[illegible]	Jeremiah Williams	70	m		Farmer		N.C.			1		3
		Susannah "	60	F.				N.C.			1		4
		Dicy "	19	F.				N.C.					5
		Elias "	17	m		Farmer		N.C.					6
		Abram "	15	m				N.C.					7
		Kelly "	13	m				N.C.					8
		Martha J. "	17	F.				N.C.					9
726	726	William Kennedy	31	m		Farmer	800	N.C.					10
		Eliza "	30	F.				N.C.			1		11
		Julia "	12	F.				N.C.					12
		Mary "	10	F.				N.C.					13
		Enoch "	8	m				N.C.					14
		Elias "	6	m				N.C.					15
		Duncan "	3	m				N.C.					16
727	727	Mathew Davis	39	m		Farmer	700	N.C.					17
		Nancy "	38	F.				N.C.					18
		Mary A. "	16	F.				N.C.					19
		Martha E. "	14	F.				N.C.					20
		Susannah "	12	F.				N.C.					21
		Windsors "	10	m				N.C.					22
		Jane "	8	F.				N.C.					23
728	728	William Brown	57	m		Farmer	475	N.C.					24
		Elizabeth "	54	F.				N.C.			1		25
		Anabeth "	21	F.				N.C.			1		26
		Eliza "	19	F.				N.C.		1			27
		Noah R. "	14	m				N.C.		1			28
		Stephen Davis	5	m				N.C.					29
729	729	Thomas Williams	55	m		Farmer	800	N.C.			1		30
		Elizabeth "	53	F.				N.C.			1		31
		Elizabeth "	24	F.				N.C.			1		32
		Noah "	20	m		Farmer		N.C.					33
		Raleigh "	18	m		Farmer		N.C.					34
		Elias "	16	m		Farmer		N.C.					35
		Darcus "	14	F.				N.C.					36
		David "	12	m				N.C.					37
		Elizabeth Williams	74	F.				N.C.					38
		Sarah "	40	F.				N.C.			1		39
[illegible]	730	Bailey Williamson	59	m		Farmer	635	N.C.					40
		Elizabeth "	53	F.				N.C.					41
		Martha "	29	F.				N.C.					42

m 19
f 23

48

SCHEDULE I.—Free Inhabitants in ______ in the County of Moore State of N Carolina enumerated by me, on the 21st day of October 1850. N. McCrummen Ass't Marshal.

Dwelling-houses numbered in the order of visitation	Families numbered in the order of visitation	The Name of every Person whose usual place of abode on the first day of June, 1850, was in this family	Age	Sex	Color (White, black, or mulatto)	Profession, Occupation, or Trade of each Male Person over 15 years of age	Value of Real Estate owned	Place of Birth, Naming the State, Territory, or Country	Married within the year	Attended School within the year	Persons over 20 y'rs of age who cannot read & write	Whether deaf and dumb, blind, insane, idiotic, pauper, or convict
1	2	3	4	5	6	7	8	9	10	11	12	13
		Anderson Williamson	21	m		Farmer		N Carolina				
		Nancy "	19	F				"				
		Kearney C. "	17	m		Farmer		"		1		
		Alexander "	13	m				"		1		
		Cornelius "	10	m				"		1		
931	931	William J. Williamson	31	m		Gunsmith		"				
		Martha "	21	F				"			1	
		Caroline "	11	F				"		1		
		Elizabeth "	9	F				"		1		
		Noah R. "	7	m				"				
		Mary H. "	5	F				"				
		Madison C. "	2	m				"				
		Sarah J. "	1/12	F				"				
932	932	John Cagle	35	m		Farmer	50	N C				
		Zilpha "	40	F				N C				
		Martha "	14	F				N C				
		Mathew "	13	m				"		1		
		Spinks "	11	m				"		1		
		William "	4/12	m				"				
933	933	Ashley Parish	48	m		Farmer	140	"				
		Deborah "	20	F				"			1	
		Nelson "	13	m				"		1		
		Jeffe "	8	m				"		1		
		Eli "	4	m				"				
934	934	Jane Parish	52	F				"			1	
		Elizabeth "	43	F				"				
935	935	Dolly Jones	40	F				"			1	
		Elias Rose	36	m		Farmer		"			1	
936	936	John Kennedy	59	m		Gun smith		"				
		Sallie "	55	F				"				
		David "	16	m		Farmer		"				
		Enoch "	13	m				"				
		Powell "	11	m				"				
937	937	Edmund Williamson	40	m		Gunsmith		"				
		Margaret "	30	F				"				
		Isaac "	17	m		Farmer		"				
		Jesse "	15	m				"				
		Hiram "	13	m				"				
		Kelly "	10	m				"				
		Margaret "	8	F				"				
938	938	William Williamson	65	m		Farmer	50	"				
		Elizabeth "	61	F				"			1	

m 26
F 16

SCHEDULE I.—Free Inhabitants in ______________ in the County of Moore State of N. Carolina enumerated by me, on the 1st day of November 1850. N. McCommon Ass't Marshal.

657

229

Dwelling-houses numbered in the order of visitation.	Families numbered in the order of visitation.	The Name of every Person whose usual place of abode on the first day of June, 1850, was in this family.	Age.	Sex.	Color, (White, black, or mulatto.)	Profession, Occupation, or Trade of each Male Person over 15 years of age.	Value of Real Estate owned.	Place of Birth. Naming the State, Territory, or Country.	Married within the year.	Attended School within the year.	Persons over 20 y'rs of age who cannot read & write.	Whether deaf and dumb, blind, insane, idiotic, pauper, or convict.	Line
1	2	3	4	5	6	7	8	9	10	11	12	13	
		Tryam McWilliamson	18	M		Farmer		N. Carolina					1
		Wright W. "	18	M		Farmer		" "					2
		Sypthia Williamson	23	F				" "					3
		Martha "	5	F				" "					4
939	939	Asa Williamson	32	M		Farmer		" "	—				5
		Mary "	18	F				" "	—				6
		Isaac Williamson	23	M		Farmer	800	" "					7
940	940	William W. Williams	51	M		Farmer	436	" "					8
		Mary "	45	F				" "			/		9
		Martha "	24	F				" "					10
		Margaret "	22	F				" "			/		11
		Elizabeth "	20	F				" "					12
		Alfred "	18	M		Farmer		" "		/			13
		Wyatt "	17	M		Ditto		" "		/			14
		Marshal "	14	M				" "		/			15
		Asa "	13	M				" "		/			16
		Levi "	10	M				" "		/			17
		Kiya "	8	M				" "					18
		William "	6	M				" "					19
941	941	William Stinson	54	M		Hatter	128	" "					20
		Margaret "	44	F				" "			/		21
942	942	Edward L. Stewart	21	M		Wheelwright		" "					22
		Martha "	20	F				" "					23
		William "	1	M				" "					24
943	943	Anderson S. Moody	50	M		Hatter	800	" "					25
		Sallie "	44	F				" "					26
		William "	18	M		Farmer		" "		/			27
		Peter "	16	M		Farmer		" "		/			28
		Franklin "	13	M				" "		/			29
		Quimby "	12	M				" "		/			30
		John "	9	M				" "		/			31
		Daniel "	5	M				" "					32
		Alexander "	1	M				" "					33
944	944	Richmond Nall	42	M		Laborer		" "					34
		Mary "	42	F				" "			/		35
		Martha "	18	F				" "		/			36
		Chestley "	16	M		Laborer		" "		/			37
		Willis "	12	M				" "		/			38
		Elizabeth "	8	F				" "		/			39
		Absalom "	6	M				" "		/			40
		Mary "	3	F				" "					41
945	945	Porscilla Brewer	26	F				" "			/		42

M 27
F 15

SCHEDULE I.—Free Inhabitants in ______ **in the County of** Moore **State of** N Carolina **enumerated by me, on the** 1st **day of** November **1850.** N McCrummen **Ass't Marshal.**

Dwelling-houses numbered in the order of visitation.	Families numbered in the order of visitation.	The Name of every Person whose usual place of abode on the first day of June, 1850, was in this family.	Description: Age.	Description: Sex.	Description: Color, (White, black, or mulatto.)	Profession, Occupation, or Trade of each Male Person over 15 years of age.	Value of Real Estate owned.	Place of Birth. Naming the State, Territory, or Country.	Married within the year.	Attended School within the year.	Persons over 20 y'rs of age who cannot read & write.	Whether deaf and dumb, blind, insane, idiotic, pauper, or convict.
1	2	3	4	5	6	7	8	9	10	11	12	13
		Amy Brewer	23	F				N. Carolina			1	
		Washington "	12	M				" "		1		
		Mahalah "	8	F				" "		1		
		Mark "	3	M				" "				
		Barnabas Criscoe	22	M		Laborer		" "			1	
946	946	William Bird	35	M		Laborer		" "			1	
		Keraley "	35	F				" "			1	
		Ann "	17	F				" "		1		
		Sarah "	15	F				" "		1		
		Creey "	12	F				" "		1		
		Susan "	10	F				" "		1		
		Phebe "	8	F				" "		1		
		John "	6	M				" "				
		Drusilla Brewer	70	M				" "			1	
947	947	William Wright	30	M		Farmer	850	" "				
		Lovedy "	23	F				" "				
		Sarah "	4	F				" "				
		Julia A. "	6/12	F				" "				
		Elizabeth Dunlap	68	F				" "			1	
		Frances "	30	F				" "				
948	948	Lewis Phillips	36	M		Laborer		" "			1	
		Mary "	39	F				" "				
		William "	15	M				" "		1		
		James "	12	M				" "		1		
		John "	10	M				" "		1		
		Pattie "	8	F				" "				
		Sarah "	5	F				" "				
		Mary "	3	F				" "				
		Eli "	2	M				" "				
949	949	Kiza Owens	25	M		Farmer	50	" "				
		Mary "	27	F				" "				
		Sunday "	2	F				" "				
		Eli "	1	M				" "				
		John Sheffield	14	M				" "				
950	950	John Teague	33	M		Farmer		" "				
		Pamelia "	37	F				" "				
		Eli "	13	M				" "		1		
		Willis "	11	M				" "		1		
		Susannah "	9	F				" "		1		
		Elizabeth "	7	F				" "				
		Mahala "	2	F				" "				
		Lydia J. Gilbert	22	F				" "				

m 18
f 24

459

230

SCHEDULE I.—Free Inhabitants in ____________ **in the County of** *Moore* **State of** *N. Carolina* **enumerated by me, on the** *2d* **day of** *November* **1850.** *N. McCrummen* **Ass't Marshal.**

Dwelling-houses numbered in the order of visitation.	Families numbered in the order of visitation.	The Name of every Person whose usual place of abode on the first day of June, 1850, was in this family.	Age.	Sex.	Color, (White, black, or mulatto.)	Profession, Occupation, or Trade of each Male Person over 15 years of age.	Value of Real Estate owned.	Place of Birth. Naming the State, Territory, or Country.	Married within the year.	Attended School within the year.	Persons over 20 y'rs of age who cannot read & write.	Whether deaf and dumb, blind, insane, idiotic, pauper, or convict.
1	2	3	4	5	6	7	8	9	10	11	12	13
		Manda Gilbert	17	F				N. Carolina				
951	951	Jesse Davis	43	M		Farmer	210	" "				
		Lydia "	33	F				" "				
		Martha "	17	F				" "				
		Eliza "	16	F				" "				
		Elizabeth "	13	F				" "				
		John "	11	M				" "				
		Jockey "	9	M				" "				
		Sarepta "	6	F				" "				
952	952	John Brewer	39	M		Farmer	150	" "				
		Susannah "	39	F				" "			1	
		William "	15	M				" "		1		
		Mary "	14	F				" "				
		Eliza "	12	M				" "		1		
		Henry "	9	M				" "		1		
		Wesley "	7	M				" "		1		
		Adams "	5	M				" "		1		
		John "	4	M				" "				
		Isaac Teague	20	M		Laborer		" "			1	
953	953	Miles Jordan	65	M		Farmer	350	" "			1	
		Mary "	53	F				" "			1	
		Elizabeth "	35	F				" "			1	
		Winniford "	24	F				" "			1	
		Jesse "	21	M		Farmer		" "				
		Mary "	18	F				" "				
		Matilda "	16	F				" "				
		Sarah "	14	F				" "				
		Enoch "	10	M				" "				
		Louisa "	10	F				" "				
954	954	Joseph Owens	27	M		Farmer		" "				
		Malvina "	30	F				" "			1	
		Mary "	6	F				" "				
		Daniel W. "	4	M				" "				
		Franklin "	2	M				" "				
		Adaline "	2/12	F				" "				
955	955	James Owen	65	M		Farmer	400	" "			1	
		Susannah "	65	F				" "			1	
		Francy "	25	F				" "			1	
		Hannah "	30	F				" "				
		Susannah "	20	F				" "			1	
		James "	19	M		Farmer		" "				
		Martha "	17	F				" "				

M 19
F 23

SCHEDULE I.—Free Inhabitants in ____________ in the County of Moore State of N Carolina enumerated by me, on the 8 day of November 1850. N. McCrummen Ass't Marshal.

Dwelling-houses numbered in the order of visitation	Families numbered in the order of visitation	The Name of every Person whose usual place of abode on the first day of June, 1850, was in this family.	Age	Sex	Color, (White, black, or mulatto.)	Profession, Occupation, or Trade of each Male Person over 15 years of age.	Value of Real Estate owned.	Place of Birth. Naming the State, Territory, or Country.	Married within the year.	Attended School within the year.	Persons over 20 y'rs of age who cannot read & write.	Whether deaf and dumb, blind, insane, idiotic, pauper, or convict.
1	2	3	4	5	6	7	8	9	10	11	12	13
		Mily Owens	13	F				N Carolina				
956	956	Jonathan Eagle	46	M		Farmer	900	"				
		Sarah "	44	F				"			1	[illegible]
		Dempsey "	17	M		Farmer		"				
		William Sheffield	12	M				"				Deaf & Dumb
957	957	Aaron E. Kennedy	24	M		Farmer		"				
		Olive "	23	F				"				
		Lucinda "	2	F				"				
		Sarah F. "	1	F				"				
958	958	Jesse Eagle	31	M		Farmer	550	"			1	
		Sarah "	25	F				"			1	
		Neill Eagle	36	M		Farmer		"			1	
		Mary "	29	F				"			1	
		Lindsay "	21	M		Farmer		"			1	
		Charles "	18	M		~~[illegible]~~						Idiot
		Tyson "	16	M		Farmer		"				
		Margaret "	13	F				"				
		Noah "	10	M				"				
		Catharine "	6	F				"				
959	959	George W. Eagle	36	M		Farmer	175	"				
		Maranda "	35	F				"				
		Lucy A. "	15	F				"				
		Madison "	5	M				"				
		Enoch "	6/12	M				"				
		Sarah Reader	70	F				"			1	
960	960	George Eagle	62	M		Farmer	650	"			1	
		Nancy "	60	F				"			1	
		Gilliam "	25	M		Farmer		"			1	
		Adaline "	18	F				"				
961	961	Henry Brown	25	M		Farmer		"				
		Sarah "	24	F				"			1	
		Adaline "	3	F				"				
		Elisha "	1	M				"				
962	962	John Dunlap	32	M		Farmer	1525	"				
		Mary "	36	F				"				
		James H. "	6	M				"				
		William C.D.	4	M				"				
		Henry C. "	2	M				"				
		Mary A.E.	5/12	F				"				
		John McKenzie	28	M		Laborer		"				
963	963	Newson Bridges	75	M		Miller		"			1	
		Elizabeth "	58	F				"			1	

M 23
F 19
1 B. M.

34 461

231

SCHEDULE I.—Free Inhabitants in ______ in the County of Moore State of N. Carolina enumerated by me, on the 2nd day of November 1850. N. McCrummen Ass't Marshal.

Dwelling-houses numbered in the order of visitation.	Families numbered in the order of visitation.	The Name of every Person whose usual place of abode on the first day of June, 1850, was in this family.	Description: Age.	Sex.	Color, (White, black, or mulatto.)	Profession, Occupation, or Trade of each Male Person over 15 years of age.	Value of Real Estate owned.	Place of Birth. Naming the State, Territory, or Country.	Married within the year.	Attended School within the year.	Persons over 20 y'rs of age who cannot read & write.	Whether deaf and dumb, blind, insane, idiotic, pauper, or convict.
1	2	3	4	5	6	7	8	9	10	11	12	13
		Elizabeth Bridges	24	F				N. Carolina			1	
		Luticia "	14	F				" "				
		Adaline "	12	F				" "				
		Martha J. "	2	F				" "				
964	964	Spencer Brown	21	m		Farmer		" "	—		1	
		Sarah "	17	F				" "				
965	965	Alsey Maris	24	m		Farmer	150	" "			1	
		Catharine "	17	F				" "				
		Bethuel "	1	m				" "				
966	966	Henry Cagle	38	m		Farmer	100	" "				
		Elizabeth "	35	F				" "			1	
		Deborah "	15	F				" "		1		
		Sarah "	12	F				" "				
		Wincy "	10	F				" "				
		Nancy J. "	4	F				" "				
967	967	Everet Smith	46	m		Farmer	50	" "				
		Malaney "	42	F				" "				
		William Barrentine	15	m				" "				
968	968	Isaiah Brown	47	m		Farmer	125	" "				
		Martha "	25	F				" "				
		Malaney "	21	F				" "				
		Delitha "	19	F				" "				
		Mary A "	16	F				" "				
		Amy "	14	F				" "				
		Jesse "	11	m				" "				
		Francy "	9	F				" "				
969	969	Isham Smith	45	m		Farmer	125	" "				
		Mary "	41	F				" "				
		Lydia "	23	F				" "				
		Nancy "	5/12	F				" "				
970	970	George Smith	33	m		Laborer		" "			1	
		Clarissa "	33	F				" "			1	
		Nathan "	13	m				" "				
		Everet "	11	m				" "				
		Lydia "	7	F				" "				
		Hardy "	4	m				" "				
971	971	Thomas Richardson	24	m		Farmer	100	" "			1	
		Nancy "	24	F				" "			x	
		Lydia M. "	5	F				" "				
		John D. "	3	m				" "				
		Isham T. "	1	m				" "				
972	972	William W. Brown	23	m		Farmer		" "				

477

SCHEDULE I.—Free Inhabitants in ______________ in the County of Moore State of N. Carolina enumerated by me, on the 4th day of November 1850. N. McCrummen Ass't Marshal.

Dwelling-houses numbered in the order of visitation.	Families numbered in the order of visitation.	The Name of every Person whose usual place of abode on the first day of June, 1850, was in this family.	Age.	Sex.	Color, White, black, or mulatto.	Profession, Occupation, or Trade of each Male Person over 15 years of age.	Value of Real Estate owned.	Place of Birth. Naming the State, Territory, or Country.	Married within the year.	Attended School within the year.	Persons over 20 y'rs of age who cannot read & write.	Whether deaf and dumb, blind, insane, idiotic, pauper, or convict.
1	2	3	4	5	6	7	8	9	10	11	12	13
		Margaret Brown	26	F				N. Carolina			1	
		Lydia "	1	F				" "				
		Mary "	3/12	F				" "				
973	973	Thomas Brown	51	m		Tailor	600	" "				
		Matilda "	49	F				" "			1	
974	974	Riland Key	34	m		Laborer		" "			1	
		Temperance "	32	F				" "				
		Sarah "	9	F				" "				
		Louisa "	6	F				" "				
		Jane "	4	F				" "				
		Mary "	3/12	F				" "				
975	975	Thomas Brown	18	m		Laborer	50	" "				
		Rebecca "	22	F				" "				
		Lucinda "	11/12	F				" "				
		Aaron Brown	22	m		Student		" "				
976	976	William Smith	50	m		Farmer		" "			1	
		Elizabeth "	49	F				" "			1	
		Francy "	21	F				" "				Idiot
		Elias "	20	m		Laborer		" "			1	
		Hiram "	13	m				" "				
		Amanda "	11	F				" "				
		Hannah "	10	F				" "				
977	977	Upshur Sowell	21	m		Farmer	300	" "				
		Julia A. "	17	F				" "				
		Alfonza "	11/12	m				" "				
978	978	Stephen Sheffield	37	m		Laborer		" "	—		1	
		Pattie "	34	F				" "	—			
		Bethana "	17	F				" "				
		Martha "	15	F				" "				
		Amanda "	13	F				" "				
		Calvin "	3/12	m				" "				
979	979	William Stutts	31	m		Miner	100	" "				
		Clarkey "	31	F				" "			1	
		Dumas "	8	m				" "		1		
		Noah R. "	4	m				" "				
980	980	Noah Brewer	36	m		Blacksmith	100	" "			1	
		Martha "	36	F				" "			1	
		Whitson "	16	m		Clerk		" "				
		Alexander "	11	m				" "		>		
		William S. "	2	m				" "				
981	981	James Gordon	41	m		Miner		" "				
		Ann "	41	F								

M-19 /

463

SCHEDULE I.—Free Inhabitants in ______________ in the County of Moore State of N. Carolina enumerated by me, on the 4th day of November 1850. Neill McCrummen Ass't Marshal.

232

Dwelling-houses numbered in the order of visitation.	Families numbered in the order of visitation.	The Name of every Person whose usual place of abode on the first day of June, 1850, was in this family.	Age.	Sex.	Color, White, black, or mulatto.	Profession, Occupation, or Trade of each Male Person over 15 years of age.	Value of Real Estate owned.	Place of Birth. Naming the State, Territory, or Country.	Married within the year.	Attended School within the year.	Persons over 20 y'rs of age who cannot read & write.	Whether deaf and dumb, blind, insane, idiotic, pauper, or convict.
1	2	3	4	5	6	7	8	9	10	11	12	13
		William Gordon	18	m		Laborer		N. Carolina				
		Rowan "	16	F				" "				
		James "	13	m				" "				
		George "	10	m				" "				
		Thomas "	7	m				" "				
		Robert "	2	m				" "				
		John "	3/12	m				" "				
982	982	Bethuel Coffin	30	m		Merchant	1200	" "				
		Camilla "	21	F				" "				
983	983	John Cagle	57	m		Farmer	5000	" "				
		Martha "	46	F			371	" "				
		Elizabeth Cagle	90	F		~~Far~~		" "			1	
984	984	Levi Deaton	25	m		Farmer	100	" "				
		Nancy "	20	F				" "				
		Rebecca "	7/12	F				" "				
985	985	Mary Rouse	48	F				" "			1	
		Enoch "	18	m		Farmer		" "				
986	986	Upshur Furr	42	m		Farmer	650	" "				
		Rebecca "	33	F				" "				
		Lundy J. "	11	F				" "		1		
		Emily A. "	9	F				" "		1		
		Sarah M. "	6	F				" "		1		
		John R. "	4	m				" "				
		William B. "	3	m				" "				
		Mary E. "	1	F				" "				
987	987	William Richardson	44	m		Farmer		" "			1	
		Sallie "	14	F				" "				
		Lucinda "	10	F				" "				
		Nancy J. "	8	F				" "				
		David D. "	5	m				" "				
		Hiram R. "	4	m				" "				
988	988	Nathaniel Morley	32	m		Miner		" "				
		Catherine "	34	F				" "			1	
		James N. "	2	m				" "				
989	989	William Hunsucker	75	m		~~Farmer~~ none		" "				
		Livicy "	78	F				" "			1	
		Elizabeth "	36	F				" "			1	
		Bethuel "	5	m				" "				
990	990	Stephen Davis	23	m		Farmer		" "				
		Francy "	22	F				" "			1	
991	991	George Davis	48	m		Farmer	400	" "			1	
		Elizabeth "	49	F				" "				

SCHEDULE I.—Free Inhabitants in ______ in the County of Moore State of N. Carolina enumerated by me, on the 5th day of November 1850. N. McCrummen Ass't Marshal.

Dwelling-houses numbered in the order of visitation.	Families numbered in the order of visitation.	The Name of every Person whose usual place of abode on the first day of June, 1850, was in this family.	Age.	Sex.	Color, (White, black, or mulatto.)	Profession, Occupation, or Trade of each Male Person over 15 years of age.	Value of Real Estate owned.	Place of Birth. Naming the State, Territory, or Country.	Married within the year.	Attended School within the year.	Persons over 20 y'rs of age who cannot read & write.	Whether deaf and dumb, blind, insane, idiotic, pauper, or convict.
1	2	3	4	5	6	7	8	9	10	11	12	13
		Martha Davis	21	F				N. Carolina			1	
		Raleigh "	13	m				" "		1		
		Baxter "	9	m				" "		1		
		John "	9	m				" "		1		
		Elizabeth "	7	F				" "				
992	992	James Davis	27	m		Farmer		" "				
		Lydia "	27	F				" "				
		Mary "	3	F				" "				
		Sarah "	1	F				" "				
993	993	Turner Samuel	22	m		Farmer	600	" "				
		Catherine "	22	F				" "			1	
		Albert "	3	m				" "				
		Alexander "	1	m				" "				
994	994	Nancy Furr	61	F				" "			1	
995	995	James Williams	65	m		Laborer		" "				
		Nancy "	60	F				" "			1	
		Elizabeth "	15	F				" "		1		
		Spane Williams	18	m		Farmer		" "				
		Nancy "	12	F				" "				
		Headman "	8	m				" "		1		
		Avant "	3	m				" "				
996	996	Nancy Shaw	43	F				" "				
		Flora "	41	F				" "				
		Sarah "	39	F				" "				
997	997	John Williams	50	m		Farmer	320	" "				
		Lydea "	50	F				" "			1	
		Milly "	21	F				" "			1	
		Mary "	18	F				" "				
		Jerry "	16	m		Farmer		" "		1		
		Rebecca "	15	F				" "		1		
		Edward "	11	m				" "		1		
		Elias "	9	m				" "		1		
		Franey Williams	14	F				" "				
		Harman Brown	19	m		Farmer		" "				
998	998	John Richardson	57	m		Farmer	200	" "			1	
		Nancy "	50	F			75	" "			1	
		Rosanna "	31	F				" "			1	
		Angelica "	29	F				" "			1	
		Catharine "	21	F				" "			1	
		Eliza "	16	F				" "				
		Deborah "	14	F				" "				
		Lydia "	8	F				" "				

35   465

SCHEDULE I.—Free Inhabitants in ____________ **in the County of** Moore **State of** N. Carolina **enumerated by me, on the** 6th **day of** November **1850.** N. McCrummen **Ass't Marshal.**

233

Dwelling-houses numbered in the order of visitation.	Families numbered in the order of visitation.	The Name of every Person whose usual place of abode on the first day of June, 1850, was in this family.	Age.	Sex.	Color, {White, black, or mulatto.	Profession, Occupation, or Trade of each Male Person over 15 years of age.	Value of Real Estate owned.	Place of Birth. Naming the State, Territory, or Country.	Married within the year.	Attended School within the year.	Persons over 20 years of age who cannot read & write.	Whether deaf and dumb, blind, insane, idiotic, pauper, or convict.
1	2	3	4	5	6	7	8	9	10	11	12	13
		Sallie Moore	25	F				N. Carolina	—		1	
999	999	Enoch Richardson	22	m		Farmer		" "			1	
		Martha "	25	F				" "			1	
		John "	1	m				" "				
		James W. Moore	19	m		Farmer		" "				
1000	1000	Joseph Deaton	52	m		Farmer	100	" "				
		Mary "	47	F				" "				
		Elias M. "	20	m		Farmer		" "				
		Martha "	15	F				" "		1		
		James "	12	m				" "		1		
		Henry H. "	9	m				" "		1		
1001	1001	Daniel McLean	55	m		Farmer	600	" "				
		Margaret "	70	F				" "				
		Nancy "	66	F				" "			1	
		Christian "	66	F				" "			1	
		Jennet "	62	F				" "			1	
		Flora A. "	8	F				" "				
		Allen C. "	6	m				" "				
		Hugh A. "	2	m				" "				
		William Williams	21	m		Laborer		" "			1	
1002	1002	John Kennedy	68	m		Farmer	120	Scotland			1	
		Margery "	63	F				N. Carolina				
		Duncan "	30	m		Constable	1000	" "				
		Margery "	1	F				" "				
		Laurence Williams	19	m		Farmer		" "				
1003	1003	Alexander Kennedy	41	m		Farmer	600	" "				
		Neill "	5	m				" "				
		John A. "	3	m				" "				
1004	1004	Margaret Richardson	45	F				" "		[illegible]		
		John McRouse	30	m		Farmer	270	" "				
		Lydia "	28	F				" "			1	
		Archibald McNeill	6	m				" "				
1005	1005	Noah Williams	23	m		Farmer	100	" "			1	
		Mary "	17	F				" "				
1006	1006	Archibald McNeill	32	m		Farmer	175	" "			1	
		Jennet "	27	F				" "			1	
		Mary "	7	F				" "				
		Elizabeth "	5	F				" "				
		John R. "	1	m				" "				
1007	1007	Enoch Williams	24	m		Laborer		" "			1	
		Jane "	20	F				" "			1	
1008	1008	William Bremer	57	m		Carpenter		" "				

M 24
F 18

SCHEDULE I.—Free Inhabitants in ______ in the County of Moore State of N. Carolina enumerated by me, on the 5th day of November 1850. N. McLennan Ass't Marshal.

Dwelling-houses numbered in the order of visitation.	Families numbered in the order of visitation.	The Name of every Person whose usual place of abode on the first day of June, 1850, was in this family.	Description: Age.	Sex.	Color, White, black, or mulatto.	Profession, Occupation, or Trade of each Male Person over 15 years of age.	Value of Real Estate owned.	Place of Birth. Naming the State, Territory, or Country.	Married within the year.	Attended School within the year.	Persons over 20 years of age who cannot read & write.	Whether deaf and dumb, blind, insane, idiotic, pauper, or convict.
1	2	3	4	5	6	7	8	9	10	11	12	13
		Elizabeth Brewer	56	F				N. Carolina			1	
		Sampson "	27	m		Farmer	100	" "			1	
		Winey "	24	F				" "			1	
		Celia "	20	F				" "				
		Martin "	15	m				" "		1		
1009	1009	John D. Bethune	37	m		Carpenter		" "				
		Christian "	22	F				" "				
		Catharine Bethune	72	F			250	" "			1	
1010	1010	Joseph Williams	47	m		Farmer		" "				
		Nancy "	40	F				" "				
		Nancy "	21	F				" "			1	
		William "	20	m		Farmer		" "			1	
		Mathew "	15	m				" "				
		Upshur "	13	m				" "				
		Ann "	12	F				" "				
		Lewis "	8	m				" "				
		Louisa "	8	F				" "				
1011	1011	Jennet McKenzie	58	F			300	" "			1	
		Kenneth "	24	m		Farmer		" "				
		Murdoch "	20	m		Ditto		" "		1		
		Anna McKenzie	26	F				" "			1	
		Christian "	18	F				" "				
		Catharine "	15	F				" "				
		Kenneth "	9	m				" "				
		Anna E. "	3	F				" "				
1012	1012	Noah Britt	22	m		Farmer	340	" "			1	
		Elizabeth "	26	F				" "			1	
		Margaret "	4	F				" "				
		Sarah "	1	F				" "				
1013	1013	Neill Morrison	65	m		Farmer	400	" "				
		Mary "	50	F				" "				
		Norman "	28	m		Farmer		" "				
		Margaret "	27	F				" "				
		Mary A. "	25	F				" "				
		Sarah J. "	23	F				" "				
		Samuel N. "	21	m		Farmer		" "				
		Catharine E. "	19	F				" "				
		Alexander "	17	m		Farmer		" "				
		John C. "	15	m				" "				
1014	1014	Arrington Britt	43	m		Farmer	220	" "			1	
		Sallie "	46	F				" "			1	
		Noah "	16	m		Farmer		" "				

M 19
F 23

SCHEDULE I.—Free Inhabitants in ______ in the County of Moore State 467
of N. Carolina enumerated by me, on the 5th day of November 1850. N. McCrummen Ass't Marshal.

234

Dwelling-houses numbered in the order of visitation.	Families numbered in the order of visitation.	The Name of every Person whose usual place of abode on the first day of June, 1850, was in this family.	Description: Age.	Sex.	Color, White, black, or mulatto.	Profession, Occupation, or Trade of each Male Person over 15 years of age.	Value of Real Estate owned.	Place of Birth. Naming the State, Territory, or Country.	Married within the year.	Attended School within the year.	Persons over 20 y'rs of age who cannot read & write.	Whether deaf and dumb, blind, insane, idiotic, pauper, or convict.	
1	2	3	4	5	6	7	8	9	10	11	12	13	
1015	1015	Mary Deaton	75	F			330	N. Carolina			1		1
		George Deakins	32	m		Farmer		" "					2
		Elizabeth Dunnan	49	F				" "			1		3
16	1016	Nathan Wallis	50	m		Farmer		" "			1		4
		Emily "	50	F				" "					5
		Nancy "	27	F				" "					6
		Frances "	21	F				" "					7
		Mary "	19	F				" "					8
		Enoch "	13	m				" "					9
		Benjamin "	10	m				" "					10
17	1017	Catharine McDonald	28	F			150	" "					11
		Catharine "	6	F				" "					12
		John E. "	4	m				" "					13
		Sophia "	1	F				" "					14
		Martin McNair	21	m		Farmer		" "					15
18	1018	Mathew Deaton	28	m		Farmer	150	" "					16
		Margaret "	20	F				" "					17
		Mary A. "	1	F				" "					18
		Lydia Smith	23	F				" "			1		19
19	1019	Isaac Deaton	39	m		Farmer	525	" "					20
		Mimy "	35	F				" "					21
		Lockey "	17	m		Farmer		" "					22
		William "	14	m				" "		1			23
		John "	12	m				" "		1			24
		Margaret "	11	F				" "		1			25
		Mathew "	9	m				" "		1			26
		Reuben "	7	m				" "		1			27
		Terry A. "	4	F				" "					28
		Deborah "	2	F				" "					29
20	1020	Elisha Cole	38	m		Farmer	558	" "					30
		Frances "	34	F				" "					31
		Stokes "	11	m				" "		1			32
		Elizabeth "	9	F				" "		1			33
		Barbara "	7	F				" "		1			34
		Franklin "	5	m				" "					35
		Sampson "	3	m				" "					36
		William "	1	m				" "					37
1	1021	John Munroe	48	m		Farmer	400	" "					38
		Mary "	42	F				" "					39
		Amanda "	16	F				" "					40
		Malcom "	14	m				" "					41
		Benjamin F. "	12	m				" "					42

m 21
F 21

477

SCHEDULE I.—Free Inhabitants in ______________ in the County of *Moore* State of *N. Carolina* enumerated by me, on the *6th* day of *November* 1850. *N. McCrummen* Ass't Marshal.

Dwelling-houses numbered in the order of visitation.	Families numbered in the order of visitation.	The Name of every Person whose usual place of abode on the first day of June, 1850, was in this family.	Description: Age.	Description: Sex.	Description: Color, (White, black, or mulatto.)	Profession, Occupation, or Trade of each Male Person over 15 years of age.	Value of Real Estate owned.	Place of Birth. Naming the State, Territory, or Country.	Married within the year.	Attended School within the year.	Persons over 20 y'rs of age who cannot read & write.	Whether deaf and dumb, blind, insane, idiotic, pauper, or convict.
1	2	3	4	5	6	7	8	9	10	11	12	13
		Levi Munroe	10	m				N. Carolina				
		Mary C. "	8	F				" "				
		William "	6	m				" "				
		John C. "	4	m				" "				
		Lauchlin "	2	m				" "				
		Robert "	1/12	m				" "				
1022	1022	Francis Munroe	46	m		Farmer	680	" "				
		Catharine "	36	F				" "				
		Lauchlin R. "	22	m		Farmer		" "				
		Mary A. "	12	F				" "				
		Eliza "	11	F				" "				
		Catharine "	8	F				" "				
		James "	6	m				" "				
		John "	3	m				" "				
		Jannet "	1/12	F				" "				
1023	1023	Christian Sanders	48	F			600	" "			1	
		John McIntosh	25	m		Merchant		" "				
		Sarah Craig	45	F				" "			1	
		Mary Morris	47	F				" "			1	
		Martha "	12	F				" "				
		Ann "	7	F				" "				
1024	1024	Joseph Deaton	26	m		Farmer	250	" "			1	
		Isabella "	23	F				" "				
		Lydia "	3	F				" "				
		Christian "	2	F				" "				
		Mary J. "	6/12	F				" "				
1025	1025	Joseph Cole	42	m		Farmer	200	" "			1	
		Mary "	38	F				" "			1	
		Telitha "	19	F				" "				
		Riland R. "	13	m				" "				
		Julia "	11	F				" "				
		Duncan "	9	m				" "				
		Malcom "	7	m				" "				
		George "	5	m				" "				
		Nancy "	2	F				" "				
1026	1026	Angus McKinnon	65	m		Farmer	800	" "				
		John "	22	m		Farmer		" "		1		
		Ann "	20	F				" "				
		Mary "	17	F				" "				
		Jennet "	16	F				" "				
		Catharine "	14	F				" "				
		Norman McKinnon	70	m		Farmer	25	" "				

m 19
F 23

36 469

SCHEDULE I.—Free Inhabitants in ____ in the County of Moore State of N. Carolina enumerated by me, on the 6th day of November 1850. [illegible] Ass't Marshal.

235

Dwelling-houses numbered in the order of visitation.	Families numbered in the order of visitation.	The Name of every Person whose usual place of abode on the first day of June, 1850, was in this family.	Age.	Sex.	Color, White, black, or mulatto.	Profession, Occupation, or Trade of each Male Person over 15 years of age.	Value of Real Estate owned.	Place of Birth. Naming the State, Territory, or Country.	Married within the year.	Attended School within the year.	Persons over 20 y'rs of age who cannot read & write.	Whether deaf and dumb, blind, insane, idiotic, pauper, or convict.
1	2	3	4	5	6	7	8	9	10	11	12	13
1027	1027	Alexander Morrison	83	m		Farmer	500	Scotland				
		Nancy "	74	F				N. Carolina				
		Elizabeth "	27	F				" "				
		Allen "	25	m		Farmer		" "				
		Neill McCaskill	16	m		Farmer		" "				
		Edmund Denson	18	m	m	Farmer		" "				
1028	1028	Samuel Key	62	m		Miller		" "			1	
		Abigail "	50	F				" "			1	
1029	1029	William Copeland	48	m		Farmer	50	" "			1	
		Mary "	48	F				" "			1	
		Tabitha "	18	F				" "				
		John N. "	17	m		Farmer		" "				
		William "	15	m				" "				
		Jane "	9	F				" "				
		Mary E. "	7	F				" "				
1030	1030	Sallie Landcaster	45	F				" "				
		Mary "	17	F	m			" "				
1031	1031	James Cole	66	m		Farmer	335	" "				
		Jane "	58	F				" "			1	
		Nancy "	38	F				" "			1	
		John "	33	m		Farmer		" "				
		William "	24	m		Farmer		" "		1		
		James "	22	m		Farmer		" "		1		
		Calvin "	20	m		Farmer		" "		1		
		Jane "	18	F				" "		1		
		John "	13	m				" "		1		
		William "	11	m				" "		1		
1032	1032	Joshua Williamson	38	m		Laborer		" "			1	
		Sarah "	28	F				" "			1	
		Allen C. "	3/12	m				" "				
		Eliza Dockins	36	F				" "				
		Bethuel "	5	m				" "				
1033	1033	Angus Morrison	67	m		Farmer	1500	" "				
		Sarah "	60	F				" "				
		Margaret "	36	F				" "				
		Malcom "	28	m		Farmer		" "				
1034	1034	William Patteson	20	m		Farmer	800	" "				
		Angeline Smith	60	F				" "			1	
1035	1035	Flora McLeod	67	F				" "			1	
1036	1036	Mary McLeod	76	F			200	" "			1	
		Christian "	64	F				" "			1	
		Flora "	44	F				" "				

m 21 F 15

SCHEDULE I.—Free Inhabitants in ______________ in the County of Moore State of N. Carolina enumerated by me, on the 7th day of November 1850. N. McCormmick Ass't Marshal.

Line	Dwelling-houses numbered in the order of visitation.	Families numbered in the order of visitation.	The Name of every Person whose usual place of abode on the first day of June, 1850, was in this family.	Age.	Sex.	Color, White, black, or mulatto.	Profession, Occupation, or Trade of each Male Person over 15 years of age.	Value of Real Estate owned.	Place of Birth. Naming the State, Territory, or Country.	Married within the year.	Attended School within the year.	Persons over 20 years of age who cannot read & write.	Whether deaf and dumb, blind, insane, idiotic, pauper, or convict.
	1	2	3	4	5	6	7	8	9	10	11	12	13
1			Nancy McLeod	39	F				N. Carolina				
2			Daniel "	36	m		Farmer		" "				
3	1037	1037	Daniel McNeill	57	m		Farmer	110	" "				
4			Martha "	44	F				" "			1	
5			Alexander "	27	m		Farmer	112	" "				
6			Loveday "	25	F				" "			1	
7			Hector "	21	m		Farmer		" "				
8			Margaret "	19	F				" "				
9			Daniel "	17	m		Farmer		" "				
10			John "	14	m				" "				
11			Noah "	11	m				" "				
12	1038	1038	Mary Parish	41	F			30	" "				
13			John "	20	m		Farmer		" "				
14	1039	1039	John Stutts	52	m		Farmer	2100	" "				
15			Nancy "	46	F				" "				
16			Andrew "	21	m		Farmer		" "		1	1	
17			John "	19	m		Farmer		" "		1		
18			Sarah "	13	F				" "		1		
19			Lydia "	10	F				" "		1		
20			Hugh "	9	m				" "				
21			Noah "	6	m				" "				
22	1040	1040	John H. Stutts	47	m		Farmer	90	" "				
23			Sallie "	37	F				" "				
24			Lydia "	18	F				" "		1		
25			Henry "	17	m		Farmer		" "		1		
26			Mary "	15	F				" "		1		
27			Andrew "	12	m				" "		1		
28			Lucy "	9	F				" "		1		
29			George "	6	m				" "				
30	1041	1041	Isabella Matheson	76	F			667	Scotland			1	
31			Christina "	42	F				N. Carolina				
32			Catharine "	37	F				" "				
33			Kenneth "	35	m		Farmer	15	" "				
34			Isabella "	1	F				" "				
35	1042	1042	James Garner	56	m		Farmer		" "				
36			Margaret "	53	F				" "			1	
37			Elizabeth "	30	F				" "			1	
38			Edmund "	20	m		Farmer		" "				
39			William "	17	m		Farmer		" "		1		
40			Jude "	16	F				" "				
41			Mary "	10	F				" "				
42			Steadman "	8	m				" "				

m 22

477

236

SCHEDULE I.—Free Inhabitants in ______ in the County of Moore State of N. Carolina enumerated by me, on the 8th day of November 1850. Neill McLennan Ass't Marshal.

Dwelling-houses numbered in the order of visitation.	Families numbered in the order of visitation.	The Name of every Person whose usual place of abode on the first day of June, 1850, was in this family.	Description: Age.	Sex.	Color, (White, black, or mulatto.)	Profession, Occupation, or Trade of each Male Person over 15 years of age.	Value of Real Estate owned.	Place of Birth. Naming the State, Territory, or Country.	Married within the year.	Attended School within the year.	Persons over 20 y'rs of age who cannot read & write.	Whether deaf and dumb, blind, insane, idiotic, pauper, or convict.
1	2	3	4	5	6	7	8	9	10	11	12	13
1043	1043	Fanny Wallis	32	F				N. Carolina				
		Mary "	14	F				" "				
		Rebecca "	8	F				" "				
		John "	4	m				" "				
		Julia "	6/12	F				" "				
1044	1044	Mathew Williams	45	m		Farmer	200	" "				
		Lydia "	44	F				" "			1	
		Lindsay "	21	m		Farmer		" "		1		
		Elizabeth "	19	F				" "		1		
		Henry "	16	m		Farmer		" "				
		Lydia "	14	F				" "				
		Mary "	13	F				" "				
		Herbert "	11	m				" "				
		John "	8	m				" "				
		Celia "	5	F				" "				
		James Hunsucker	30	m		Farmer		" "				
1045	1045	Christopher Mattle	91	m		Farmer		" "			1	
		Celia "	81	F				" "			1	
		Leonard "	33	m		Farmer	150	" "				
		Margaret "	21	F				" "				
		Elias "	1	m				" "				
1046	1046	Susannah Muse	60	F				" "			1	
		William H. "	24	m		Farmer		" "				
		Westley B. "	23	m		Farmer		" "			1	
1047	1047	John R. Ritter	57	m		Farmer	1000	" "			1	
		Mary "	48	F				" "				
		Westley "	21	m		Merchant		" "				
		Jane "	15	F				" "		1		
		Shinks "	18	m		Farmer		" "				
		Sarah "	13	F				" "				
		Mary "	11	F				" "				
		Henry L. "	9	F				" "				
		Anna A. "	6	F				" "				
		William L. "	10/12	m				" "				
1048	1048	Hiram R. Kelly	34	m		Tailor		" "				
		Harriet "	38	F				" "				
		Sophia "	12	F				" "		1		
		Andrew "	9	m				" "		1		
		Catharine "	6	F				" "				
		Joseph "	1	m				" "				
	1049	Noah Richardson	46	m		Bapt. Clergyman	1000	" "				
		Elizabeth "	48	F				" "				

m 20
7 23

SCHEDULE I.—Free Inhabitants in ______ in the County of Moore State of N. Carolina enumerated by me, on the 8th day of November 1850. N. McCrimmon Ass't Marshal.

Dwelling-houses numbered in the order of visitation. (1)	Families numbered in the order of visitation. (2)	The Name of every Person whose usual place of abode on the first day of June, 1850, was in this family. (3)	Age. (4)	Sex. (5)	Color, White, black, or mulatto. (6)	Profession, Occupation, or Trade of each Male Person over 15 years of age. (7)	Value of Real Estate owned. (8)	Place of Birth. Naming the State, Territory, or Country. (9)	Married within the year. (10)	Attended School within the year. (11)	Persons over 20 y'rs of age who cannot read & write. (12)	Whether deaf and dumb, blind, insane, idiotic, pauper, or convict. (13)
		William B. Richardson	25	m		Farmer	200	N. Carolina	—			
		Margaret "	20	F				" "	—			
		Judson S. "	14	m				" "		1		
		James B. "	9	m				" "		1		
		Lucinda Rogers	5	F				" "				
1050	1050	John Stutts	56	m		Farmer	600	" "				
		Elizabeth "	22	F				" "			1	
		John A. "	18	m		Farmer		" "		1		
		Julia "	17	F				" "		1		
		Martha "	14	F				" "		1		
1051	1051	George Hunsucker	75	m		Farmer		" "				
		Sarah "	74	F				" "				
1052	1052	Henry Stutts	75	m		Farmer	200	" "			1	
		Lucy "	65	F				" "			1	
		Mary "	7	F				" "		1		
1053	1053	Shadrach Maness	80	m		Farmer	62	" "				
		Celia "	70	F				" "			1	
		Lucretia "	25	F				" "			1	
		Ireley "	16	m		Farmer		" "		1		
1054	1054	John Riddell	32	m		Mechanic	350	" "				
		Lydia "	32	F				" "				
		Sarah "	5	F				" "				
		Mary "	2	F				" "				
		Eliza Stutts	22	F				" "				
1055	1055	John McLeod	44	m		Farmer	1000	" "				
		Mary "	45	F				" "				
		David Wood	17	m		Farmer		" "				
1056	1056	Stephen D. Williams	25	m		Farmer	700	" "				
		Francy "	24	F				" "				
		William T. "	2	m				" "				
		Richard M. "	1	m				" "				
		Lorenzo Williams	21	m		Farmer		" "			1	
1057	1057	Mariah Stutts	50	F			600	" "				
		Mary "	22	F				" "				
		Celia "	20	F				" "		1		
		Sarah "	18	F				" "		1		
		Elizabeth "	17	F				" "		1		
		Lotty "	15	F				" "		1		
		Spinks "	12	m				" "		1		
		Dempsey "	10	m				" "				
		James W. "	8	m				" "				
10		Sarah McNeill	23	F								

m 14 ✓

37 473

SCHEDULE I.—Free Inhabitants in ________ in the County of Moore State of N Carolina enumerated by me, on the 8th day of November 1850. N McClennen Ass't Marshal. 237

Dwelling-houses numbered in the order of visitation.	Families numbered in the order of visitation.	The Name of every Person whose usual place of abode on the first day of June, 1850, was in this family.	Description: Age.	Description: Sex.	Description: Color, (White, black, or mulatto.)	Profession, Occupation, or Trade of each Male Person over 15 years of age.	Value of Real Estate owned.	Place of Birth. Naming the State, Territory, or Country.	Married within the year.	Attended School within the year.	Persons over 20 y'rs of age who cannot read & write.	Whether deaf and dumb, blind, insane, idiotic, pauper, or convict.	
1	2	3	4	5	6	7	8	9	10	11	12	13	
1058	1058	Andrew Hunsucker	32	m		Farmer	125	N Carolina					1
		Clarkey "	31	f				" "					2
		Amelia "	10	f				" "		1			3
		William "	7	m				" "		1			4
		Westley "	6	m				" "					5
		James "	5	m				" "					6
		Nancy "	1	f				" "					7
1059	1059	Jesse Murray	55	m		Mechanic		" "			1		8
		Pennet "	40	f				" "			1		9
		John W. "	15	m				" "		1			10
		Mary "	13	f				" "		1			11
		Campbell "	12	f				" "		1			12
		Narcissa "	11	f				" "					13
		Miley "	10	f				" "					14
		Andrew "	8	m				" "					15
[illegible]	1060	William Hunsucker	46	m		Farmer	246	" "					16
		Elizabeth "	46	f				" "			1		17
		Martha "	20	f				" "					18
		Nelson "	17	m		Farmer		" "		1			19
		Huston "	13	m				" "		1			20
		Thomas H "	10	m				" "		1			21
		Sarah F "	8	f				" "		1			22
[illegible]	1061	William L Wallis	27	m		Farmer		" "			1		23
		Josiah "	16	m		Farmer		" "					24
		Celia "	15	f				" "					25
		Everett "	12	m				" "					26
		William J "	10	m				" "					27
		Mary Davis	40	f				" "			1		28
		James "	1	m				" "					29
		Elizabeth Smith	32	f				" "					30
		Mary "	2	f				" "					31
		Missourie "	1	f				" "					32
[illegible]	1062	William Stutts	30	m		Farmer	250	" "					33
		Margaret "	31	f				" "					34
		Murdoch "	4	m				" "					35
		Robert "	2	m				" "					36
		George "	2/12	m				" "					37
	1063	George Hunsucker	46	m		Farmer	400	" "					38
		Martha "	38	f				" "					39
		Asa "	22	m		Farmer	1000	" "					40
		Enoch W "	20	m		Farmer		" "					41
		Sarah E "	17	f				" "					42

m 23

48

Schedule I.—Free Inhabitants in ______ **in the County of** Moore **State of** N. Carolina **enumerated by me, on the** 8th **day of** November **1850.** N. McCrummen **Ass't Marshal.**

Dwelling-houses numbered in the order of visitation.	Families numbered in the order of visitation.	The Name of every Person whose usual place of abode on the first day of June, 1850, was in this family.	Description: Age.	Sex.	Color, (White, black, or mulatto.)	Profession, Occupation, or Trade of each Male Person over 15 years of age.	Value of Real Estate owned.	Place of Birth. Naming the State, Territory, or Country.	Married within the year.	Attended School within the year.	Persons over 20 y'rs of age who cannot read & write.	Whether deaf and dumb, blind, insane, idiotic, pauper, or convict.
1	2	3	4	5	6	7	8	9	10	11	12	13
		Cary J. Hunsucker	14	F				N. Carolina				
		Martha "	12	F				" "				
1064	1064	Catharine Wood	46	F				" "			1	
		Winnaford "	24	F				" "			1	
		James "	21	M		Laborer		" "				
		Elizabeth "	15	F				" "				
		Mary A. "	9	F				" "				
		Samuel Wood	13	M				" "				
		Westley Wood	19	M		Laborer		" "				
1065	1065	Susannah Wallis	35	F	M			" "				
1066	1066	Robert Davis	34	M		Laborer		" "			1	
		Elizabeth "	24	F				" "			1	
		Thomas "	2	M				" "				
1067	1067	Mary Campbell	30	F				" "				
		Sween "	10	M				" "				
		Sundy "	8	F				" "				
		Leander "	6	F				" "				
		Alexander "	4	M				" "				
		Shedrach "	3	M				" "				
		Mary C. "	1	F				" "				
1068	1068	Kinchen Fields	34	M		Laborer		" "				
1069	1069	George Cagle	36	M		Farmer	200	" "				
		Elizabeth "	36	F				" "				
		Mathew "	12	M				" "				
		Branson "	10	M				" "				
		Elizabeth "	8	F				" "				
		Julia "	6	F				" "				
		Lydia "	4	F				" "				
		Emily "	2	F				" "				
1070	1070	George M. Hunsucker	48	M		Farmer	800	" "				
		Elizabeth "	38	F				" "				
		Lauretta "	7	F				" "		1		
		Clarkson "	4	M				" "				
		Missouria "	2	F				" "				
		Rejina "	5/12	F				" "				
		Eli Wallis	12	M	M			" "				
		Calvin "	9	M	M			" "				
1071	1071	Cornelius Shields	71	M		Farmer	5500	" "				
		Jane "	51	F				" "				
		John W. "	24	M		Farmer		" "	—			
		Martha "	23	F				" "	—			
		James M. "	13	M				" "		1		

M. 19 2 B

475

SCHEDULE I.—Free Inhabitants in ______ in the County of Moore State of N. Carolina enumerated by me, on the 9th day of November 1850. N. McCrummen Ass't Marshal. 238

Dwelling-houses numbered in the order of visitation.	Families numbered in the order of visitation.	The Name of every Person whose usual place of abode on the first day of June, 1850, was in this family.	Age.	Sex.	Color, White, black, or mulatto.	Profession, Occupation, or Trade of each Male Person over 15 years of age.	Value of Real Estate owned.	Place of Birth. Naming the State, Territory, or Country.	Married within the year.	Attended School within the year.	Persons over 20 y'rs of age who cannot read & write.	Whether deaf and dumb, blind, insane, idiotic, pauper, or convict.	
1	2	3	4	5	6	7	8	9	10	11	12	13	
		Elizabeth J. Shields	10	F				N. Carolina		1			1
		Casander "	7	m				" "					2
1072	1072	Sampson Deaton	42	m		Miller		" "					3
		Mary "	40	F				" "			1		4
		Nancy "	14	F				" "					5
		Sarah "	11	F				" "					6
		George "	9	m				" "					7
		Henry C. "	6	m				" "					8
		Thalany "	3	m				" "					9
1073	1073	David Jones	62	m		Farmer	400	" "					10
		Dorothy "	61	F				" "			1		11
		Rebecca "	37	F				" "					12
		Frany "	34	F				" "			1		13
		Sarah "	24	F				" "					14
		Martha "	22	F				" "					15
		Lydia "	20	F				" "					16
		Elkin "	18	m		Farmer		" "					17
		Rany "	15	F				" "					18
1074	1074	James Deaton	30	m		Farmer		" "					19
		Catharine "	30	F				" "					20
		Marion "	3	m				" "					21
		Jane "	1	F				" "					22
		William "	6/12	m				" "					23
1075	1075	Amelia Jones	65	F			500	" "			1		24
		Nancy Brown	38	F				" "			1		25
		Westley "	11	m				" "		1			26
		Gaston Hunsucker	10	m				" "		1			27
1076	1076	Edmund Gardiner	95	m		Farmer		" "					28
1077	1077	James Gribble	46	m		Miner		England	—				29
		Gilley "	20	F				N. Carolina	—		1		30
1078	1078	Manda Wallis	40	F				" "			1		31
		Sarah "	10	F				" "					32
		Cornelius "	5	m	m			" "					33
		Anderson "	3	m	m			" "					34
		Spinks "	2	m	m			" "					35
1079	1079	James Dicks	50	m		Cabinetmaker		" "					36
		Elizabeth Ballard	38	F				" "					37
		Westley "	10	m				" "		1			38
		Daniel Kennedy	80	m	B			" "					39
1080	1080	Hugh Kelly	66	m		Farmer	1000	Scotland					40
		Nancy "	66	F				Ditto					41
		Kenneth "	27	m		Farmer		N. Carolina					42

m 22 4B w

SCHEDULE I.—Free Inhabitants in ______ in the County of *Moore* State of *N Carolina* enumerated by me, on the *12th* day of *November* 1850. *N. McKinnon* Ass't Marshal.

Dwelling-houses numbered in the order of visitation.	Families numbered in the order of visitation.	The Name of every Person whose usual place of abode on the first day of June, 1850, was in this family.	Description: Age.	Description: Sex.	Description: Color, (White, black, or mulatto.)	Profession, Occupation, or Trade of each Male Person over 15 years of age.	Value of Real Estate owned.	Place of Birth. Naming the State, Territory, or Country.	Married within the year.	Attended School within the year.	Persons over 20 y'rs of age who cannot read & write.	Whether deaf and dumb, blind, insane, idiotic, pauper, or convict.
1	2	3	4	5	6	7	8	9	10	11	12	13
		Mary J. Kelly	15	F				N. Carolina				
		Murdoch McLeod	46	m		Carpenter		" "				
1081	1081	Isham Wallis	49	m		Farmer	1600	" "			1	
		Nancy "	44	F				" "		1		
		Waltby "	21	m		Farmer		" "		1		
		Quinby "	18	m		Farmer		" "		1		
		Socky "	14	m				" "		1		
		Emsley "	12	F				" "				
		Samuel "	9	m				" "				
		Jane "	6	F				" "				
		Sampson "	5	m				" "				
		Virgil "	4	m				" "				
		John "	3/12	m				" "				
1082	1082	John Gardiner	24	m		Farmer	140	" "				
		Sarah "	20	F				" "			1	
		Stephen "	1/12	m				" "				
1083	1083	James Milton	46	m		Farmer	250	" "				
		Temperance "	36	F				" "			1	
		Elizabeth "	19	F				" "				
		Manda "	17	F				" "				
		Priscilla "	15	F				" "				
		Lydia "	12	F				" "		1		
		Temperance "	11	F				" "		1		
		Nancy "	8	F				" "		1		
		George "	6	m				" "		1		
		Lucinda "	4	F				" "				
		James W. "	2	m				" "				
		Margaret "	4/12	F				" "				
		John Jones	35	m		Wheelwright	250	" "				
		Margaret "	22	F				" "				
		Emmerson "	4	m				" "				
		Orren "	3	m				" "				
		Nelson "	4/12	m				" "				
1084	1084	Winey Jones	16	F				" "				
1085	1085	George W. Horner	33	m		Farmer	200	" "			1	
		Mary A. "	29	F				" "			1	
		Thomas "	9	m				" "		1		
		James W. "	7	m				" "		1		
		Elizabeth "	5	F				" "				
		Catharine "	3	F				" "				
1086	1086	George Cockman	32	m		Farmer	200	" "				
		Clarkey "	26	F				" "				

m 22

38 477

SCHEDULE I.—Free Inhabitants in ______ in the County of Moore State of N. Carolina enumerated by me, on the 29th day of November 1850. [illegible] Ass't Marshal. 239

Dwelling-houses numbered in the order of visitation.	Families numbered in the order of visitation.	The Name of every Person whose usual place of abode on the first day of June, 1850, was in this family.	DESCRIPTION. Age.	Sex.	Color, White, black, or mulatto.	Profession, Occupation, or Trade of each Male Person over 15 years of age.	Value of Real Estate owned.	PLACE OF BIRTH. Naming the State, Territory, or Country.	Married within the year.	Attended School within the year.	Persons over 20 y'rs of age who cannot read & write.	Whether deaf and dumb, blind, insane, idiotic, pauper, or convict.
1	2	3	4	5	6	7	8	9	10	11	12	13
		William M. Cockman	8	m				N. Carolina		/		
		Mary E. "	6	f				N. Carolina		/		
		Sarah L. "	4	f				N. Carolina				
		Isham W. "	2	m				N. Carolina				
		Nancy Cockman	3/12	f				N. Carolina				
087	1087	John Cockman	64	m		Farmer	350	N. Carolina				
		Mary "	66	f				N. Carolina				
		Isaac Richardson	18	m		Farmer		N. Carolina				
088	1088	Noah Cockman	24	m		Farmer		N. Carolina				
		Mary "	22	f				N. Carolina			/	
		George "	3	m				N. Carolina				
		John "	2	m				N. Carolina				
089	1089	Isaac Williams	34	m		Farmer	100	N. Carolina			/	
		Lydia "	38	f				N. Carolina			/	
		Louisa "	18	f				N. Carolina		/		
		Henry "	17	m		Farmer		N. Carolina		/		
		Temperance "	16	f				N. Carolina		/		
		Missouri "	12	f				N. Carolina		/		
		Susan "	11	f				N. Carolina		/		
		George "	9	m				N. Carolina		/		
		Mary "	5	f				N. Carolina				
		Haywood "	5/12	m				N. Carolina				
090	1090	Sampson Cockman	31	m		Farmer		N. Carolina				
		Elizabeth "	26	f				N. Carolina			/	
		Clarkey "	8	f				N. Carolina				
		Noah "	6	m				N. Carolina				
		Sarah "	4	f				N. Carolina				
		Isham "	4/12	m				N. Carolina				
091	1091	Lydia Cockman	34	f			100	N. Carolina			/	
		Martha "	13	f				N. Carolina		/		
		W. Jane "	11	f				N. Carolina		/		
		Alexander "	9	m				N. Carolina		/		
		Mark "	7	m				N. Carolina				
		Matilda "	5	f				N. Carolina				
092	1092	David Cockman	38	m		Farmer	100	N. Carolina				
		Sarah "	30	f				N. Carolina			/	
		Elizabeth "	10	f				N. Carolina				
		Mary "	8	f				N. Carolina				
		Angeline "	6	f				N. Carolina				
		David "	5	m				N. Carolina				
3	1093	George Williams	36	m		Farmer		N. Carolina			/	
		Dory "	33	f				N. Carolina			/	

m 14
f 23

SCHEDULE I.—Free Inhabitants in ______ in the County of Moore State of N. Carolina enumerated by me, on the 13th day of November 1850. N. McCrimmen Ass't Marshal.

Dwelling-houses numbered in the order of visitation.	Families numbered in the order of visitation.	The Name of every Person whose usual place of abode on the first day of June, 1850, was in this family.	Age.	Sex.	Color, White, black, or mulatto.	Profession, Occupation, or Trade of each Male Person over 15 years of age.	Value of Real Estate owned.	Place of Birth. Naming the State, Territory, or Country.	Married within the year.	Attended School within the year.	Persons over 20 y'rs of age who cannot read & write.	Whether deaf and dumb, blind, insane, idiotic, pauper, or convict.
1	2	3	4	5	6	7	8	9	10	11	12	13
		Candice Williams	16	F				N. Carolina		1		
		Jefferson "	14	M				N. Carolina		1		
		Julia A. "	12	F				N. Carolina		1		
		Temperance "	10	F				N. Carolina		1		
		Hannah J. "	8	F				N. Carolina		1		
		Rebecca E. "	5	F				N. Carolina				
		Priscilla "	2	F				N. Carolina				
		Chestley F. Horner	21	M		Farmer	300	N. Carolina				
1094	1094	Franklin Muse	34	M		Farmer	75	N. Carolina			1	
		Joziah "	34	F				N. Carolina			1	
		Archibald "	8	M				N. Carolina				
		John W. "	5	M				N. Carolina				
		Candice "	4	F				N. Carolina				
		Lavina C. "	1	F				N. Carolina				
1095	1095	Daniel Muse	42	M		Farmer		N. Carolina			1	
		Elizabeth "	37	F				N. Carolina			1	
		Martha J. "	11	F				N. Carolina				
		Margaret E. "	10	F				N. Carolina				
		Susannah "	8	F				N. Carolina				
		Rebecca "	4	F				N. Carolina				
1096	1096	Miles Muse	33	M		Farmer	30	N. Carolina				
		Priscilla "	28	F				N. Carolina			1	
		Ann "	11	F				N. Carolina				
		Temperance "	6	F				N. Carolina				
		Elizabeth "	2	F				N. Carolina				
		George "	1/12	M				N. Carolina				
1097	1097	James Dowdy	38	M		Farmer	50	N. Carolina				
		Rainy "	35	F				N. Carolina				
1098	1098	Neill Black	34	M		Farmer	100	N. Carolina				
		Margaret "	34	F				N. Carolina				
		Martha "	5	F				N. Carolina				
1099	1099	William "	3	M				N. Carolina				
		Alexander "	1	M				N. Carolina				
		Williams Sowell	34	M		Farmer	275	N. Carolina				
		Martha "	27	F				N. Carolina				
		John "	1	M				N. Carolina				
1100	1100	Nancy Furr	60	F				N. Carolina			1	
		Lenard "	20	M		Laborer		N. Carolina			1	
		Emberline Wallis	19	F				N. Carolina				
1101	1101	Ames Dowdy	71	M		Farmer	400	N. Carolina				
		Rachel "	34	F				N. Carolina			1	
		Archibald "	8	M				N. Carolina		1		

M 17

479

SCHEDULE I.—Free Inhabitants in ________ in the County of Moore State of N. Carolina enumerated by me, on the 13th day of November 1850. N. McCrummen Ass't Marshal.

240

Dwelling-houses numbered in the order of visitation.	Families numbered in the order of visitation.	The Name of every Person whose usual place of abode on the first day of June, 1850, was in this family.	Age.	Sex.	Color, White, black, or mulatto.	Profession, Occupation, or Trade of each Male Person over 15 years of age.	Value of Real Estate owned.	Place of Birth. Naming the State, Territory, or Country.	Married within the year.	Attended School within the year.	Persons over 20 y'rs of age who cannot read & write.	Whether deaf and dumb, blind, insane, idiotic, pauper, or convict.	
1	2	3	4	5	6	7	8	9	10	11	12	13	
		Rachel C. Dowdy	6	F				N. Carolina		1			1
		Jane "	3	F				N. Carolina					2
1102	1102	William Caddell	50	M		Farmer	100	N. Carolina					3
		Rainy "	47	F				N. Carolina					4
		Artimus "	14	M				N. Carolina					5
		Cornelius "	11	M				N. Carolina					6
1103		Quimby Sowell	41	M		Farmer		N. Carolina					7
		Emeline "	36	F				N. Carolina			1		8
		Anderson S. "	15	M				N. Carolina		1			9
		Rebeca "	17	F				N. Carolina		1			10
		Mary "	14	F				N. Carolina		1			11
		Malinda "	12	F				N. Carolina		1			12
		Clarkey A. "	10	F				N. Carolina		1			13
		Asa G. "	8	M				N. Carolina		1			14
		Joseph P. "	6	M				N. Carolina		1			15
		Archibald W. "	4	M				N. Carolina					16
		Jason W. "	2	M				N. Carolina					17
		John B. D. "	6/12	M				N. Carolina					18
1104	1104	James Muse	48	M		Farmer		N. Carolina					19
		Patience "	47	F				N. Carolina					20
		Jane "	21	F				N. Carolina		1			21
		Sophia "	15	F				N. Carolina		1			22
		Miranda "	13	F				N. Carolina		1			23
		John "	11	M				N. Carolina		1			24
1105	1105	James Fry	82	M		Farmer		N. Carolina					25
1106	1106	Pope Muse	46	M		Farmer	450	N. Carolina					26
		Nancy "	39	F				N. Carolina					27
		William "	23	M		Farmer		N. Carolina		1			28
		Candice "	20	F				N. Carolina		1			29
		Noah "	16	M		Farmer		N. Carolina		1			30
		Susan "	14	F				N. Carolina		1			31
		Archibald "	11	M				N. Carolina		1			32
		Ashley "	9	M				N. Carolina		1			33
		Comodore "	7	M				N. Carolina		1			34
1107	1107	Pauley Caddell	29	M		Farmer	862	N. Carolina					35
		Hannah "	23	F				N. Carolina					36
		Julia Ann "	4	F				N. Carolina					37
		Mary A. "	2	F				N. Carolina					38
		John "	1/12	M				N. Carolina					39
1108	1108	Absolam Fry	37	M		Farmer		N. Carolina					40
		Clarissa "	35	F				N. Carolina			1		41
		Joseph "	13	M				N. Carolina		1			42

M 23
F 19

SCHEDULE I.—Free Inhabitants in ________ in the County of Moore State of N. Carolina enumerated by me, on the 13th day of November 1850. N. McCrummen Ass't Marshal

Dwelling-houses numbered in the order of visitation.	Families numbered in the order of visitation.	The Name of every Person whose usual place of abode on the first day of June, 1850, was in this family.	Age.	Sex.	Color, White, black, or mulatto.	Profession, Occupation, or Trade of each Male Person over 15 years of age.	Value of Real Estate owned.	Place of Birth. Naming the State, Territory, or Country.	Married within the year.	Attended School within the year.	Persons over 20 y'rs of age who cannot read & write.	Whether deaf and dumb, blind, insane, idiotic, pauper, or convict.
1	2	3	4	5	6	7	8	9	10	11	12	13
		Patrick S. Fry	12	M				N. Carolina		1		
		Thomas M. "	10	M				N. Carolina		1		
		Nicy E. "	8	F				N. Carolina		1		
		Grafton R. "	6	M				N. Carolina		1		
		William A. "	4	M				N. Carolina				
		Jesse "	3	M				N. Carolina				
		Mary "	1	F				N. Carolina				
		Alexander A. "	2	M				N. Carolina				
1109	1109	Joseph Caddell	38	M		Farmer	500	N. Carolina				
		Sarah "	34	F				N. Carolina			1	
		Bryan "	15	M				N. Carolina		1		
		Jane "	14	F				N. Carolina				
		Martha "	13	F				N. Carolina		1		
		Nancy "	12	F				N. Carolina		1		
		Evander "	11	M				N. Carolina		1		
		Mary "	5	F				N. Carolina				
		James B. "	4	M				N. Carolina				
		Presley T. "	1	M				N. Carolina				
		Elizabeth Caddell	82	F				N. Carolina				
1110	1110	Elizabeth Upton	75	F			100	N. Carolina			1	
		Mary "	36	F				N. Carolina			1	
		William Reaves	50	M		Farmer	100	N. Carolina				
1111	1111	Joseph Upton	33	F		Farmer	95	N. Carolina				
		Catharine "	30	F				N. Carolina			1	
		Thomas W. "	2	M				N. Carolina				
		Neill W. "	1/12	M				N. Carolina				
1112	1112	Mark Russel	40	M		Meth. Clergyman	500	N. Carolina				
		Eliza "	16	F				N. Carolina		1		
		Westley S. "	11	M				N. Carolina		1		
		Caroline "	9	F				N. Carolina		1		
		Thomas "	7	M				N. Carolina		1		
		Sarah "	5	F				N. Carolina				
		William "	3	M				N. Carolina				
1113	1113	Nathan Smith	55	M		Farmer		N. Carolina			1	
		Jennet "	56	F				N. Carolina			1	
		Lucy Brown	38	F			200	N. Carolina				
		William A. "	18	M		Farmer		N. Carolina		1		
		Abner "	15	M				N. Carolina		1		
1114	1114	Elisha Cagle	34	M		Farmer	225	N. Carolina				
		Ann "	35	F				N. Carolina				
		John R. "	10	M				N. Carolina		1		
		Abraham "	8	M				N. Carolina		1		

M 24
F 18

39 481

SCHEDULE I.—Free Inhabitants in ______ in the County of Moore State of N. Carolina enumerated by me, on the 14th day of November 1850. N. McCrummen Ass't Marshal.

241

Dwelling-houses numbered in the order of visitation.	Families numbered in the order of visitation.	The Name of every Person whose usual place of abode on the first day of June, 1850, was in this family.	Age.	Sex.	Color, White, black, or mulatto.	Profession, Occupation, or Trade of each Male Person over 15 years of age.	Value of Real Estate owned.	Place of Birth. Naming the State, Territory, or Country.	Married within the year.	Attended School within the year.	Persons over 20 y'rs of age who cannot read & write.	Whether deaf and dumb, blind, insane, idiotic, pauper, or convict.
1	2	3	4	5	6	7	8	9	10	11	12	13
		Nancy J. Cagle	6	F				N. Carolina		1		
		Julia A. "	4	F				" "				
		Sarah "	1	F				" "				
1115	1115	Richard Phillips	40	M		Laborer		" "				
		Nancy "	50	F				" "				
		Ann D. "	10	F				" "				
1116	1116	Thomas Williams	62	M		Farmer	1000	" "			1	
		Mary "	52	F				" "			1	
		Alston "	19	M		Farmer		" "		1		
		Pattie "	18	F				" "				
		Branson "	16	M		Farmer		" "		1		
		Alexander "	12	M				" "		1		
		Andrew "	8	M				" "		1		
1117	1117	James Stutts	33	M		Farmer	500	" "				
		Ann R. "	30	F				" "				
		Cornelius "	9	M				" "		1		
		Benjamin "	8	M				" "		1		
		James A. "	6	M				" "				
		Don Lewis "	3	M				" "				
		Alina "	1	F				" "				
1118	1118	Lindsay Stutts	28	M		Farmer	200	" "				
		Isabella "	21	F				" "				
1119	1119	Henry Brown	29	M		Farmer	150	" "			1	
		Mary "	23	F				" "				
		James "	4	M				" "				
		John A. "	2	M				" "				
		Martha "	11/12	F				" "				
1120	1120	Garner Manis	44	M		Farmer	300	" "				
		Catharine "	36	F				" "			1	
		James A. "	15	M				" "		1		
		Mary "	14	F				" "		1		
		Lydia "	8	F				" "				
		Sadberry "	6	M				" "				
		A. Spinks "	4	M				" "				
1121	1121	Josiah "	2	M				" "				
		Mathew Williams	32	M		Farmer	700	" "				
		Elizabeth "	26	F				" "				
		Pleasant "	7	M				" "		1		
		Mary E. "	6	F				" "				
		Emeline "	4	F				" "				
		Murdoch "	2	M				" "				
		Jane "	6/12	F				" "				

M 23
F 19

SCHEDULE I.—Free Inhabitants in ______________ **in the County of** Moore **State of** N Carolina **enumerated by me, on the** 14th **day of** November **1850.** N. McCrummen **Ass't Marshal.**

	Dwelling-houses numbered in the order of visitation.	Families numbered in the order of visitation.	The Name of every Person whose usual place of abode on the first day of June, 1850, was in this family.	Description: Age.	Sex.	Color, White, black, or mulatto.	Profession, Occupation, or Trade of each Male Person over 15 years of age.	Value of Real Estate owned.	Place of Birth. Naming the State, Territory, or Country.	Married within the year.	Attended School within the year.	Persons over 20 y'rs of age who cannot read & write.	Whether deaf and dumb, blind, insane, idiotic, pauper, or convict.
	1	2	3	4	5	6	7	8	9	10	11	12	13
1	1122	1122	Mary Manus	32	F			200	N. Carolina			1	
2			Ann "	22	F				" "			1	
3			Thomas "	15	M				" "				
4			Reuben "	14	M				" "				
5			Windsor "	7	M				" "				
6			Lydia "	6	F				" "				
7	1123	1123	Elizabeth Manus	38	F				" "			1	
8			William "	17	M		Laborer		" "				
9			Frances "	13	F				" "				
10			Dorcus "	10	F				" "				
11	1124	1124	Henry Stutts	58	M		Farmer	500	" "			1	
12			Edmund "	20	M		Farmer		" "		1		
13			Pleasant "	17	M		Ditto		" "		1		
14			Duncan McIntosh	40	M		Tailor	200	" "				
15			Emeline "	28	F				" "				
16	1125	1125	Bryan Boroughs	86	M		Farmer	2000	" "				
17			Sallie "	76	F				" "				
18			Nancy Waddill	62	F				" "				Idiot
19	1126	1126	Stephen Perry	60	M		Farmer		" "			1	
20			Elizabeth "	50	F				" "			1	
21			William "	20	M		Laborer		" "			1	
22			Mary "	18	F				" "				
23			Benjamin "	15	M				" "				
24			Elizabeth "	13	F				" "				
25			Lincy "	6	F	M			" "				
26	1127	1127	William Stuart	46	M		Wheelwright		" "				
27			Ann "	31	F				" "				
28			Robert "	15	M				" "		1		
29			Arabella "	13	F				" "		1		
30			Enoch R. "	11	M				" "		1		
31			George T. "	8	M				" "		1		
32			Emeline "	6	F				" "				
33			Mary "	4	F				" "				
34			Anna "	2	F				" "				
35			Charles "	1	M				" "				
36	1128	1128	Sarah Stutts	77	F				" "			1	
37			Leonard "	25	M		Laborer		" "				
38	1129	1129	Abraham Stutts	46	M		Farmer	250	" "				
39			Cary "	37	F				" "				
40			Mary L. "	12	F				" "		1		
41			Sarah L. "	12	F				" "		1		
42			Elizabeth "	11	F				" "				

m 19

483

SCHEDULE I.—Free Inhabitants in ______________ in the County of Moore State of N. Carolina enumerated by me, on the 15th day of November 1850. N. McCrummen Ass't Marshal.

242

Dwelling-houses numbered in the order of visitation.	Families numbered in the order of visitation.	The Name of every Person whose usual place of abode on the first day of June, 1850, was in this family.	Description: Age.	Sex.	Color, {White, black, or mulatto.	Profession, Occupation, or Trade of each Male Person over 15 years of age.	Value of Real Estate owned.	Place of Birth. Naming the State, Territory, or Country.	Married within the year.	Attended School within the year.	Persons over 20 y'rs of age who cannot read & write.	Whether deaf and dumb, blind, insane, idiotic, pauper, or convict.	
1	2	3	4	5	6	7	8	9	10	11	12	13	
130	1130	Sarah Denson	46	F				N. Carolina			1		1
		Francy "	24	F				" "			1		2
		Rebecca "	16	F				" "					3
		David "	14	m				" "					4
		William "	8	m				" "					5
		Kearny "	3	m				" "					6
		Duncan "	3	m				" "					7
		Spinks "	3/12	m				" "					8
131	1131	William Ritter	51	m		Farmer	400	" "			1		9
		Catharine "	50	F				" "			1		10
		Elizabeth "	29	F				" "			1		11
		Lydia "	19	F				" "					12
		Nancy "	17	F				" "					13
		Emily C. "	15	F				" "					14
		William "	14	m				" "					15
		Miley F. "	12	F				" "					16
		John H. "	10	m				" "					17
		Wright "	6	m				" "					18
		Bruce "	3	m				" "					19
132	1132	Robert Brady	66	m		Farmer	50	" "			1		20
		Jennet "	63	F				" "			1		21
		Westley "	22	m		Farmer		" "					22
		Ellis "	18	F				" "		1			23
		John "	13	m				" "		1			24
		Susan Stutts	38	F				" "					25
133	1133	John Cole	49	m		Laborer		" "					26
		Jane "	38	F				" "					27
		Manda "	17	F				" "		1			28
		Lucy A. "	14	F				" "		1			29
		John "	13	m				" "		1			30
		James "	10	m				" "					31
		Jane "	6	F				" "					32
		Selina "	4	F				" "					33
		Harbard "	1	m				" "					34
34	1134	Henry Manes	36	m		Laborer		" "			1		35
		Amy "	25	F				" "			1		36
		Nancy "	9	F				" "					37
		Adaline "	7	F				" "					38
5	1135	John Moore	37	m		Laborer		" "			1		39
		Elizabeth Perry	23	F				" "			1		40
		Henry "	1	m				" "					41
	1136	James Mathis	31	M		Wheelwright		" "					42

M 21

SCHEDULE I.—Free Inhabitants in ________________ in the County of Moore State of N. Carolina enumerated by me, on the 15th day of November 1850. N. McCrummen Ass't Marshal.

	Dwelling-houses numbered in the order of visitation.	Families numbered in the order of visitation.	The Name of every Person whose usual place of abode on the first day of June, 1850, was in this family.	Age.	Sex.	Color, White, black, or mulatto.	Profession, Occupation, or Trade of each Male Person over 15 years of age.	Value of Real Estate owned.	Place of Birth. Naming the State, Territory, or Country.	Married within the year.	Attended School within the year.	Persons over 20 years of age who cannot read & write.	Whether deaf and dumb, blind, insane, idiotic, pauper, or convict.
	1	2	3	4	5	6	7	8	9	10	11	12	13
1			Lydia Mathis	41	F				N. Carolina				
2			Isaah "	13	M				" "		1		
3			Malfus "	12	M				" "		1		
4			Patrick "	11	M				" "		1		
5			Thomas "	8	M				" "		1		
6			Martha "	6	F				" "		1		
7			James "	4	M				" "				
8	1137	1137	William Mathis	65	M		Farmer	40	" "			1	
9			Mary "	64	F				" "			1	
10			Jane "	27	F				" "				
11			William "	4	M				" "				
12	1138	1138	Stephen King	45	M		Labourer		" "				
13			Delilah "	38	F				" "				
14			Mary "	17	F				" "		1		
15			William "	16	M				" "		1		
16	1139	1139	Isaac Lowell	41	M		Wheelwright	800	" "				
17			Catharine "	29	F				" "				
18			Ann "	8	F				" "		1		
19			Jesse "	7	M				" "				
20			Nancy "	4	F				" "				
21			Ashley "	2	M				" "				
22			William A. "	2/12	M				" "				
23			Josiah Lakey	18	M		Farmer		" "				
24	1140	1140	Nancy Phillips	63	F			1000	" "				
25			Ann "	22	F				" "				
26			Sophia "	18	F				" "				
27			Flora A. "	17	F				" "				
28			Amelia "	15	F				" "				
29			Orin Scovill	45	M		Farmer		Connecticut				
30			Hugh Moore	18	M				N. Carolina		1		
31			Joseph Browne	7	M				" "		1		
32	1141	1141	James McIlwain	28	M		Labourer		" "				
33			Caroline "	25	F				" "				
34			Mary "	4	F				" "				
35			Ann "	3	F				" "				
36			Patience "	1	F				" "				
37	1142	1142	Eli Davis	21	M		Labourer		" "			1	
38			Sarah "	27	F				" "			1	
39			Ruth "	6/12	F				" "				
40	1143	1143	William Mathis	26	M		Farmer		" "	1			
41			Mary "	21	F				" "	1		1	
42	1144	1144	Josiah Wallis	43	M		Farmer		" "			1	

M21

4 5
485

Schedule I.—Free Inhabitants in ______ **in the County of** Moore **State of** N. Carolina **enumerated by me, on the** 16th **day of** Novem, **1850.** N. McCrummen **Ass't Marshal.**

243

Dwelling-houses numbered in the order of visitation.	Families numbered in the order of visitation.	The Name of every Person whose usual place of abode on the first day of June, 1850, was in this family.	Description. Age.	Sex.	Color, White, black, or mulatto.	Profession, Occupation, or Trade of each Male Person over 15 years of age.	Value of Real Estate owned.	Place of Birth. Naming the State, Territory, or Country.	Married within the year.	Attended School within the year.	Persons over 20 y'rs of age who cannot read & write.	Whether deaf and dumb, blind, insane, idiotic, pauper, or convict.	
1	2	3	4	5	6	7	8	9	10	11	12	13	
		Catharine Wallis	42	F				N. Carolina			1		1
1145	1145	Elias Moore	30	m		Farmer		" "	—		1		2
		Elizabeth "	26	F				" "	—		1		3
1146	1146	Drusilla Moore	60	F				" "			1		4
		Sarah "	16	F				" "		1			5
		John "	13	m				" "					6
		Albert Moore	18	m		Laborer		" "					7
1147	1147	Kearney Fields	27	m		Farmer		" "			1		8
		Martha "	26	F				" "			1		9
		Henry "	10	m				" "		1			10
		Louisa "	7	F				" "					11
		Sarah "	5	F				" "					12
		Catharine "	1/12	F				" "					13
1148	1148	Eleazer Sewell	42	m		Farmer	1000	" "					14
		Mary "	41	F				" "					15
		Cornelius "	21	m		Farmer		" "					16
		Rvina "	20	F				" "					17
		Samuel W. "	16	m		Farmer		" "		1			18
		Virgil "	10	m				" "		1			19
		Charles M. "	5	m				" "					20
		Robert H. "	2	m				" "					21
		Josiah "	3/12	m				" "					22
1149	1149	Donald McDonald	46	m		Tailor		" "					23
		Mary "	38	F				" "					24
		Alexander "	17	m		Farmer		" "					25
		Angus "	15	m				" "		1			26
		Christian "	13	F				" "		1			27
		Sarah A. "	11	F				" "		1			28
		Hugh M. "	8	m				" "		1			29
		Mary E. "	4	F				" "					30
150	1150	Martha Smith	75	F			262	" "			1		31
		Rachel "	27	F				" "			1		32
151	1151	Daniel Short	23	m		Farmer	560	" "					33
		Elizabeth "	25	F				" "					34
		Devotion D. "	1	m				" "					35
152	1152	William Dowd	32	m		Farmer		" "					36
		Jane "	27	F				" "					37
		Emiline "	7	F				" "					38
		Elizabeth J. "	3	F				" "					39
3	1153	Eli Rogers	30	m		Laborer		" "					40
		Eliza "	30	F				" "					41
		Joseph "	7	m				" "					42

M 21
F 21

SCHEDULE I.—Free Inhabitants in ______ **in the County of** *Moore* **State of** *N. Carolina* **enumerated by me, on the** *16th* **day of** *Novem* **1850.** *N. McCrummen* **Ass't Marshal.**

	Dwelling-houses numbered in the order of visitation.	Families numbered in the order of visitation.	The Name of every Person whose usual place of abode on the first day of June, 1850, was in this family.	Age.	Sex.	Color, White, black, or mulatto.	Profession, Occupation, or Trade of each Male Person over 15 years of age.	Value of Real Estate owned.	Place of Birth. Naming the State, Territory, or Country.	Married within the year.	Attended School within the year.	Persons over 20 y'rs of age who cannot read & write.	Whether deaf and dumb, blind, insane, idiotic, pauper, or convict.
	1	2	3	4	5	6	7	8	9	10	11	12	13
1			Alvery Rogers	4	m				N. Carolina				
2	1154	1154	Burrel H. Short	30	m		Farmer	500	" "				
3			Mary "	32	F				" "				
4			Martha "	2	F				" "				
5			Pleasant W. "	6/12	m				" "				
6	1155	1155	Isaac Stafford	29	m		Farmer		" "				
7			Sarah "	30	F				" "				
8			Mary A. "	6	F				" "				
9			Thomas W. "	4	m				" "				
10			Jesse R. "	1	m				" "				
11	1156	1156	Bryant Stafford	26	m		Farmer	1000	" "			1	
12			Mary "	25	F				" "			1	
13			Henry C. Brewer	12	m				" "				
14			Rebecca Cockman	30	F				" "			1	
15	1157	1157	Henry Fields	27	m		Farmer	850	" "				
16			Martha "	22	F				" "				
17			Charles "	6/12	m				" "				
18			Nancy Fields	60	F				" "				
19			Richard "	23	m		Farmer		" "				
20			Edward "	20	m		Farmer		" "				
21			James "	18	m		Farmer		" "				
22			Isaac "	16	m		Farmer		" "		1		
23			Mary "	14	F				" "		1		
24	1158	1158	John Fields	25	m		Farmer		" "	—	—		
25			Nancy "	26	F				" "	—	—		
26	1159	1159	Alexander Carrell	75	m		Farmer	260	" "				
27			Phebe "	73	F				" "				
28	1160	1160	Neill McPherson	37	m		Farmer		" "			1	
29			Zabra "	35	F				" "			1	
30			Alexander "	13	m				" "		1		
31			Mary "	10	F				" "		1		
32			John "	8	M				" "		1		
33			H. Catharine "	5	F				" "				
34			Hugh "	3	m				" "				
35			Joseph "	1	m				" "				
36	1161	1161	John Brewer	45	m		Farmer		" "				
37			Sarah "	40	F				" "			1	
38			Mary "	17	F				" "		1		
39			Margaret "	15	F				" "		1		
40			Dicy "	14	F				" "		1		
41			Ann "	12	F				" "		1		
42			Samuel "	6	m				" "				

m 23
F 19

SCHEDULE I.—Free Inhabitants in _______ in the County of *Moore* State of *N. Carolina* enumerated by me, on the *16th* day of *Novem.* 1850. *N. McCrummen* Ass't Marshal. 487

244

Dwelling-houses numbered in the order of visitation.	Families numbered in the order of visitation.	The Name of every Person whose usual place of abode on the first day of June, 1850, was in this family.	Description: Age.	Sex.	Color, White, black, or mulatto.	Profession, Occupation, or Trade of each Male Person over 15 years of age.	Value of Real Estate owned.	Place of Birth. Naming the State, Territory, or Country.	Married within the year.	Attended School within the year.	Persons over 20 y'rs of age who cannot read & write.	Whether deaf and dumb, blind, insane, idiotic, pauper, or convict.
1	2	3	4	5	6	7	8	9	10	11	12	13
		Melinda Brewer	2	F				N. Carolina				
162	1162	Hugh Mathis	34	M		Laborer		" "				
		Candice "	26	F				" "				
		Arnold "	7	M				" "		1		
		Ennice "	4	F				" "				
		Julia "	3	F				" "				
		Absalom "	1/12	M				" "				
163	1163	Hiram W. Biggelow	19	M		Farmer		" "	—			
		Ruhama "	23	F				" "	—			
164	1164	Joel Sillivan	59	M		Farmer	1000	" "				
		Nancy "	31	F				" "				
		Lydia M. "	14	F				" "				
		Zada "	12	F				" "				
		Isaac "	11	M				" "		1		
		Green "	9	M				" "		1		
		Eli "	8	M				" "		1		
		Minnetta "	6	F				" "				
		Julia "	4	F				" "				
165	1165	Jesse G. Sowell	25	M		Farmer	200	" "				
		Ruthe "	21	F				" "				
166	1166	Eli R. Sowell	29	M		Wheelwright		" "				
		Nancy "	22	F				" "			1	
		Frances "	7	F				" "				
		Taylor "	4	M				" "				
		Rebecca Patterson	30	F				" "			1	
167	1167	Jesse Sowell	65	M		Mechanic		" "				
		Nancy "	55	F				" "			1	
		Ann M. "	24	F				" "				
		Joshua L. Sowell	21	M		Farmer	150	" "				
168	1168	William Donnelly	54	M		Farmer		" "				
		Sarah "	53	F				" "			1	
		Mahalah "	25	F				" "				
		Wiley "	19	M		Farmer		" "		1		
		Swaim "	17	M		Farmer		" "		1		
		Dillon J. "	15	M				" "		1		
		John P. "	8	M				" "		1		
9	1169	Michael Cockman	41	M		Laborer		" "				
		Alamina "	31	F				" "				
		William "	13	M				" "		1		
		Wesley "	9	M				" "		1		
		Lovday "	5	F				" "		1		
		Eli "	3	M				" "				

M 22
F 20

SCHEDULE I.—Free Inhabitants in ____________ **in the County of** *Moore* **State of** *N. Carolina* **enumerated by me, on the** *16th* **day of** *Novem.* **1850.** *N. McCrummen* **Ass't Marshal.**

Line	Dwelling-houses numbered in the order of visitation	Families numbered in the order of visitation	The Name of every Person whose usual place of abode on the first day of June, 1850, was in this family	Age	Sex	Color, White, black, or mulatto	Profession, Occupation, or Trade of each Male Person over 15 years of age	Value of Real Estate owned	Place of Birth, Naming the State, Territory, or Country	Married within the year	Attended School within the year	Persons over 20 y'rs of age who cannot read & write	Whether deaf and dumb, blind, insane, idiotic, pauper, or convict
	1	2	3	4	5	6	7	8	9	10	11	12	13
1	1170	1170	Eli Oldham	30	m		Laborer		N. Carolina			1	
2			Nancy "	30	F				" "			1	
3			Mary "	9	F				" "				
4			John "	6	m				" "				
5			Margaret "	4	F				" "				
6			Jesse "	7/12	m				" "				
7	1171	1171	Angus McCaskill	30	m		Farmer	470	" "				
8			Mary "	30	F				" "				
9			Alexander "	3	m				" "				
10			Neill "	1	m				" "				
11			Kenneth McCaskill	30	m		Farmer		" "				
12			Alexander "	18	m		Farmer		" "				
13			Jane McIntosh	8	F				" "		1		
14	1172	1172	Cornelius D. Smith	41	m		Farmer		" "				
15			Flora A. "	24	F				" "				
16			William "	11	m				" "		1		
17			Catharine "	9	F				" "		1		
18			Henry "	7	m				" "				
19			Mary "	5	F				" "				
20			Alexander "	3	m				" "				
21			John "	1	m				" "				
22	1173	1173	Bluford Simmons	48	m		Farmer	400	" "				
23			Moley "	41	F				" "				
24			Kirwin "	20	m		Farmer		" "				
25			Berilla "	18	F				" "				
26			Love "	16	m		Farmer		" "				
27			Martha "	14	F				" "				
28			Gainey "	12	m				" "				
29			Cada "	10	m				" "				
30			Eveline "	8	F				" "				
31	1174	1174	William C. Thagard	26	m		Farmer	700	" "	—			
32			Lucy "	21	F				" "	→			
33			Nancy Thagard	53	F				" "				
34			Eliza D. "	25	F				" "				
35			Hazzeltine "	18	F				" "		1		
36	1175	1175	Willis D. Dowd	44	m		Farmer	1250	" "				
37			Martha "	19	F				" "				
38			Clement "	17	m		Student		" "		1		
39			Ann M. "	16	F				" "				
40			James C. "	14	m				" "		1		
41			William P. "	12	m				" "		1		
42			Eliza "	11	F				" "				

m 23
f 19

41

489

SCHEDULE I.—Free Inhabitants in ______ in the County of Moore State of N. Carolina enumerated by me, on the 16th day of November 1850. N. McCrimmon Ass't Marshal.

245

Dwelling-houses numbered in the order of visitation.	Families numbered in the order of visitation.	The Name of every Person whose usual place of abode on the first day of June, 1850, was in this family.	Age.	Sex.	Color, White, black, or mulatto.	Profession, Occupation, or Trade of each Male Person over 15 years of age.	Value of Real Estate owned.	Place of Birth. Naming the State, Territory, or Country.	Married within the year.	Attended School within the year.	Persons over 20 y'rs of age who cannot read & write.	Whether deaf and dumb, blind, insane, idiotic, pauper, or convict.
1	2	3	4	5	6	7	8	9	10	11	12	13
		Emily M. Dowd	8	F				N.C.				
		Henry C. "	5	m				"				
		Charles D. "	5	m				"				
1176	1176	John Stuart	45	m		Farmer	800	"				
		Dicy "	40	F				"				
		Elias "	17	m		Farmer		"		/		
		Sarah "	15	F				"		/		
		Margaret "	11	F				"		/		
		Ellen "	9	F				"		/		
		Martha "	7	F				"		/		
		Mary E. "	4	F				"				
		Catharine "	1	F				"				
1177	1177	Martin Kennedy	40	m		Labourer		"				
		Margaret "	35	F				"			/	
		Mary "	12	F				"				
		Margaret "	11	F				"				
		William "	7	m				"				
		Elizabeth "	5	F				"				
1178	1178	Jofe Sanders	21	m		Farmer		"	—		/	
		Mary "	20	F				"	—			
1179	1175	Hardy Sanders	45	m		Blacksmith	300	"				
		Sallie "	42	F				"			/	
		Boitian "	19	m		Farmer		"		/		
		Isham "	17	m		Farmer		"		/		
		Simon "	14	m				"		/		
		John "	12	m				"		/		
		Lydia "	8	F				"				
		Mary "	7	F				"				
1180	1180	Allen McCaskill	45	m		Farmer	150	"				
		Nancy "	43	F				"				
		John "	22	m		Farmer		"				
		Martha "	18	F				"				
		Kenneth "	16	m		Farmer		"				
		Jennet "	14	F				"				
		Margaret "	12	F				"				
		Christian "	10	F				"				
		Alexander "	8	m				"				
		Sarah "	2	F				"				
81	1181	Henry Foreman	42	m		Farmer	171	"			/	
		Martha "	30	F				"				
		Mary "	16	F				"		/		
		Nancy "	12	F				"		/		

M 17 v

SCHEDULE I.—Free Inhabitants in ______________ **in the County of** *Moore* **State of** *N. Carolina* **enumerated by me, on the** *12th* **day of** *November* **1850.** *N. McCrummen* **Ass't Marshal.**

	Dwelling-houses numbered in the order of visitation.	Families numbered in the order of visitation.	The Name of every Person whose usual place of abode on the first day of June, 1850, was in this family.	Description: Age.	Sex.	Color, White, black, or mulatto.	Profession, Occupation, or Trade of each Male Person over 15 years of age.	Value of Real Estate owned.	Place of Birth. Naming the State, Territory, or Country.	Married within the year.	Attended School within the year.	Persons over 20 yrs of age who cannot read & write.	Whether deaf and dumb, blind, insane, idiotic, pauper, or convict.
	1	2	3	4	5	6	7	8	9	10	11	12	13
1			Emeline Freeman	6	F				N. Carolina				
2			Elias „	3	m				„				
3			Lydia „	2	F				„				
4	1182	1182	John Morgan	46	m		Farmer	300	„				
5			Malinda „	40	F				„			1	
6			Susan „	18	F				„				
7			Nathan „	15	m				„				
8			Ann „	13	F				„				
9			John „	12	m				„				
10			Lucinda „	12	F				„				
11			Elizabeth „	10	F				„				
12			John „	8	F				„				
13			William „	6	m				„				
14			Thomas „	4	m				„				
15			Loveday „	1	F				„				
16			George „	1	m				„				
17			William Morgan	40	m		Farmer		„				
18	1183	1183	Webby Morgan	64	F			225	„			1	
19			Pleasant „	23	m		Farmer		„				
20			Elizabeth „	18	F				„				
21			William „	1	m				„				
22	1184	1184	George T. Morgan	27	m		Farmer	50	„				
23			Elizabeth „	20	F				„				
24			Reuben J. „	10	m				„				
25	1185	1185	Joseph B. Morgan	29	m		Farmer	125	„				
26			Elizabeth „	26	F				„				
27			Lydia „	5	F				„				
28			Priscilla J. „	3	F				„				
29			Martha L. „	1	F				„				
30	1186	1186	William T. Morgan	45	m		Farmer	160	„				
31			James T. „	19	m		Farmer		„		1		
32			William B. „	17	m		Farmer		„		1		
33			Emma Smith	38	F				„			1	
34	1187	1187	James G. Morgan	30	m		Farmer	65	„				
35			Mary „	27	F				„			1	
36			Francy „	10	F				„		1		
37			Elizabeth „	9	F				„		1		
38			Edmund D. „	8	m				„				
39			Rebecca „	5	F				„				
40			George B. „	4	m				„				
41			James „	1	m				„				
42	1188	1188	William R. Britt	35	m		Farmer	30	„				

M 21

SCHEDULE I.—Free Inhabitants in ... in the County of Moore State N. Carolina enumerated by me, on the 20th day of November 1850. N. McCrummen Ass't Marshal.

491

246

Dwelling-houses numbered in the order of visitation.	Families numbered in the order of visitation.	The Name of every Person whose usual place of abode on the first day of June, 1850, was in this family.	Age.	Sex.	Color, {White, black, or mulatto.	Profession, Occupation, or Trade of each Male Person over 15 years of age.	Value of Real Estate owned.	Place of Birth. Naming the State, Territory, or Country.	Married within the year.	Attended School within the year.	Persons over 20 y'rs of age who cannot read & write.	Whether deaf and dumb, blind, insane, idiotic, pauper, or convict.
1	2	3	4	5	6	7	8	9	10	11	12	13
		Selena Britt	25	F.				N. Carolina				
		Marimon "	12	m				" "				
		Elizabeth "	10	F.				" "				
		Jackson "	7	m				" "				
		Hardy "	3	m				" "				
7	1189	Sarah Smith	48	F.				" "				
		Jennet "	13	F.				" "				
		Nancy "	13	F.				" "				
10	1190	John Freeman	37	m		Farmer	275	" "			/	
		Nancy "	48	F.				" "			/	
		Sarah "	14	F.				" "				
		Isaac "	13	m				" "		/		
		Detitha "	11	F.				" "		/		
		Mary A. "	9	F.				" "		/		
11	1191	Zachariah Britt	36	m		Farmer	50	" "			/	
		Nancy "	42	F.				" "			/	
		Elizabeth "	11	F.				" "				
		Enoch "	9	m				" "				
		Henry "	6	m				" "				
		Ezekiel "	4	m				" "				
		William "	1	m			~~[illegible]~~	" "				
	1192	Edmund Holland	59	m		Farmer	1000	" "				
		Priscilla "	58	F.				" "			/	
		Margaret "	16	F.				" "				
3	1193	Reuben Allen	45	m		Farmer	450	" "				
		Mahalah "	38	F.				" "			/	
		Mark "	14	m				" "		/		
		Martha "	6	F.				" "				
4	1194	Joseph Allen	47	m		Farmer	400	" "				
		Francy "	46	F.				" "				
		Raleigh "	27	m		Farmer	50	" "				
		John "	15	m				" "		/		
		Margaret "	12	F.				" "				
		Joseph "	7	m				" "				
	1195	Jonathan Richardson	37	m		Farmer	100	" "				
		Elizabeth "	34	F.				" "			/	
		Maloney "	14	F.				" "				
		John "	12	m				" "				
		David "	9	m				" "				
		Sampson "	8	m				" "				
		Lydia "	6	F.				" "				
		Elizabeth "	3	F.				" "				

M 21
F 21

SCHEDULE I.—Free Inhabitants in ________ in the County of Moore State of N. Carolina enumerated by me, on the 20th day of November 1850. N. H. McCrummen Ass't Marshal.

Dwelling-houses numbered in the order of visitation.	Families numbered in the order of visitation.	The Name of every Person whose usual place of abode on the first day of June, 1850, was in this family.	Age.	Sex.	Color, White, black, or mulatto.	Profession, Occupation, or Trade of each Male Person over 15 years of age.	Value of Real Estate owned.	Place of Birth. Naming the State, Territory, or Country.	Married within the year.	Attended School within the year.	Persons over 20 y'rs of age who cannot read & write.	Whether deaf and dumb, blind, insane, idiotic, pauper, or convict.
1	2	3	4	5	6	7	8	9	10	11	12	13
		Everett S. Richardson	1	m				N. Carolina				
		Hiram P. "	1/12	m				" "				
1196	1196	Levicy Richardson	60	F				" "			1	
1197	1197	Eleanor Key	72	F				" "			1	
		Sallie "	70	F				" "				
1198	1198	Burrel Deaton	73	m		Farmer	500	" "			1	
		Patience "	66	F				" "			1	
		Buzzle "	27	m		Farmer		" "			1	
1199	1199	Jackson Deaton	29	m		Farmer	75	" "			1	
		Elizabeth "	27	F				" "			1	
		Nancy "	9	F				" "		1		
		Madison "	7	m				" "				
		Dyson "	6	m				" "				
		Patience "	2	F				" "				
1200	1200	William Deaton	37	m		Farmer		" "				
		Flora "	35	F				" "				
		Noah "	12	m				" "		1		
		Sarah "	10	F				" "		1		
		Catharine "	3	F				" "				
1201	1201	Hiram Deaton	43	m		Farmer	200	" "			1	
		Harriet "	34	F				" "				
		Burrel "	13	m				" "		1		
		John "	12	m				" "		1		
		Rebecca "	10	F				" "		1		
		Sarah A. "	8	F				" "		1		
		Margaret "	5	F				" "				
		William "	3	m				" "				
		Patience "	7/12	F				" "				
1202	1202	Sarah Wallis	24	F				" "			1	
		Eli "	6	m				" "				
		Loveday "	1	F				" "				
1203	1203	Pleasant Key	24	m		Farmer	160	" "				
		Mary "	24	F				" "				
		Eleanor "	17	F				" "				
		Samuel "	11	m				" "		1		
		Martha "	8/12	F				" "				
1204	1204	Thomas Key	60	m		Farmer		" "				
		Bellison "	48	F				" "			1	
1215	1215	Lockey Allen	31	m		Farmer	250	" "				
		Martha "	32	F				" "				
		Margaret "	10	F				" "		1		
		Mark "	6	m				" "		1		

m 19
F 23

42 493 247

SCHEDULE I.—Free Inhabitants in ______ in the County of Moore State of N. Carolina enumerated by me, on the 21st day of November 1850. N. McCrummen Ass't Marshal.

Dwelling-houses numbered in the order of visitation.	Families numbered in the order of visitation.	The Name of every Person whose usual place of abode on the first day of June, 1850, was in this family.	Age.	Sex.	Color, White, black, or mulatto.	Profession, Occupation, or Trade of each Male Person over 15 years of age.	Value of Real Estate owned.	Place of Birth. Naming the State, Territory, or Country.	Married within the year.	Attended School within the year.	Persons over 20 y'rs of age who cannot read & write.	Whether deaf and dumb, blind, insane, idiotic, pauper, or convict.
1	2	3	4	5	6	7	8	9	10	11	12	13
		John S. Allen	4	m				N. Carolina				
		William "	2	m				" "				
1206	1206	Nicholas Nall	48	m		Farmer	200	" "				
		Lydia "	29	F				" "				
		Emily "	10	F				" "		1		
		William A. "	8	m				" "		1		
		John "	7	m				" "		1		
		Nancy "	6	F				" "				
		Mary "	4	F				" "				
		Rebecca "	2	F				" "				
		Joseph "	7/12	m				" "				
		Bennet Owen	33	m		Farmer		" "			1	
		Elizabeth "	30	F				" "				
		Telitha "	6	F				" "				
		Nancy "	4	F				" "				
		Catharine "	2	F				" "				
		William "	2/12	m				" "				
		Martha Allen	62	F				" "			1	
1207	1207	Alexander Leach	66	m		Farmer	500	Scotland				
		Christian "	55	F				N. Carolina				
		Mary "	26	F				" "				
		Angus B. "	20	m		Farmer		N. Carolina				
		Alexander "	17	m		Farmer		" "				
		Jane M. "	10	F				" "		1		
1208	1208	Archibald Leach	55	m		Farmer	500	Scotland				
		Catharine "	48	F				N. Carolina				
		Alexander "	20	m		Farmer		" "				
		Daniel "	18	m		Farmer		" "				
		Mary "	19	F				" "				
		Angus "	16	m		Farmer		" "				
		John "	14	m				" "				
		Neill "	12	m				" "				
		Ann "	10	F				" "				
		Sarah "	8	F				" "				
1209	1209	Sarah Patterson	54	F				" "				
		Duncan Patterson	24	m				" "				Blind
		Margaret "	19	F				" "				
		Emily "	14	F				" "				
1210	1210	Bartholomew Dunn	58	m		Farmer	325	" "				
		Mary "	57	F				" "		1		
		Darcus "	19	F				" "				
		Margaret "	17	F				" "	1			

m 19

523

SCHEDULE I.—Free Inhabitants in ___ **in the County of** Moore **State of** N. Carolina **enumerated by me, on the** 21st **day of** November **1850.** N. McCrummen **Ass't Marshal.**

Dwelling-houses numbered in the order of visitation.	Families numbered in the order of visitation.	The Name of every Person whose usual place of abode on the first day of June, 1850, was in this family.	DESCRIPTION. Age.	Sex.	Color, White, black, or mulatto.	Profession, Occupation, or Trade of each Male Person over 15 years of age.	Value of Real Estate owned.	PLACE OF BIRTH. Naming the State, Territory, or Country.	Married within the year.	Attended School within the year.	Persons over 20 y'rs of age who cannot read & write.	Whether deaf and dumb, blind, insane, idiotic, pauper, or convict.
1	2	3	4	5	6	7	8	9	10	11	12	13
		Green B. Dunn	12	m				N. Carolina		1		
		Seynthia "	7	F				" "				
1211	1211	Jesse Smetherman	32	m		Farmer	700	" "				
		Hannah "	32	F				" "				
		Jesse Spencer	14	m				" "		1		
1212	1212	James Collicot	25	m		Farmer	400	" "				
		Elizabeth "	30	F				" "			1	
		Clarissa "	27	F				" "			1	
		Archibald "	23	m		Farmer		" "				
1213	1213	Margaret Deaton	36	F				" "			1	
		Emeline "	14	F				" "		1		
		Mary J. "	12	F				" "		1		
		Jane "	10	F				" "				
1214	1214	Riland R. Miller	54	m		Farmer	166	" "				
		Elizabeth "	56	F				" "				
		Martha "	21	F				" "				
		Newnan "	18	m		Farmer		" "		1		
		Noah "	16	m		Ditto		" "		1		
		Frances A. "	14	F				" "		1		
		Rebecca "	9	F				" "		1		
1215	1215	Hagman Miller	24	m		Farmer		" "				
		Martha "	21	F				" "				
		Wiley "	6/12	m				" "				
1216	1216	Levi Wright	25	m		Farmer	450	" "				
		Elizabeth "	25	F		~~Ditto~~		" "				
		Lovedy H. "	5	F				" "		1		
		James M.	4	m				" "				
		Martecca	3	F				" "				
		Sarah Milton	50	F		[illegible]		" "			1	
1217	1217	Stephen Davis	77	m		Farmer		" "			1	
		Elizabeth "	68	F				" "			1	
		Archibald "	29	m		Farmer	430	" "				
		Mary "	25	F				" "				
		John "	2	m				" "				
1298	1218	Hiram Sheffield	39	m		Gunsmith		" "			1	
		Elizabeth "	39	F				" "				
		Dempsey "	20	m		Farmer		" "		1		
		Isaac "	14	m				" "				
		William "	12	m				" "				
		Jonathan "	10	m				" "				
		Levi "	8	m				" "				
		Sarah "	6	F				" "				

m 21
F 21

495

SCHEDULE I.—Free Inhabitants in ______________ in the County of Moore State of N. Carolina enumerated by me, on the 21st day of November 1850. N. McCrummen Ass't Marshal. 248

Dwelling-houses numbered in the order of visitation.	Families numbered in the order of visitation.	The Name of every Person whose usual place of abode on the first day of June, 1850, was in this family.	Age.	Sex.	Color, White, black, or mulatto.	Profession, Occupation, or Trade of each Male Person over 15 years of age.	Value of Real Estate owned.	Place of Birth. Naming the State, Territory, or Country.	Married within the year.	Attended School within the year.	Persons over 20 y'rs of age who cannot read & write.	Whether deaf and dumb, blind, insane, idiotic, pauper, or convict.
1	2	3	4	5	6	7	8	9	10	11	12	13
		Calvin Sheffield	4	m				N. Carolina				
		Martha "	2	f				" "				
1219	1219	John Davis	37	m		Farmer	300	" "				
		Zylpha "	35	f				" "			1	
		Elizabeth "	12	f				" "				
		Jane "	11	f				" "				
		George "	9	m				" "				
		Levi "	8	m				" "				
		Letitia "	7	f				" "				
		Leanda "	6	f				" "				
		Mary "	4	f				" "				
		Hayman "	3	m				" "				
		Martha "	1	f				" "				
1220	1220	Robert Davis	45	m		Farmer	325	" "				
		Mary "	37	f				" "				
		Emery "	20	m		Farmer		" "		1		
		Aaron "	18	m		Farmer		" "		1		
		Ann E. "	15	f				" "		1		
		Mary "	12	f				" "		1		
		Wincy J. "	9	f				" "		1		
		Stephen "	7	m				" "				
		William "	3	m				" "				
1221	1221	Isham Hare	37	m		Farmer	600	" "				
		Mary "	36	f				" "				
		Kendrick "	13	m				" "				
		John "	11	m				" "				
		Lydia "	7	f				" "				
		Rebecca "	5	f				" "				
		Lucy "	2	f				" "				
1222	1222	William Freeman	66	m		Farmer	100	" "				
		Elizabeth "	66	f				" "			1	
		Mary "	33	f				" "			1	
		Reubin "	30	m		Farmer		" "			1	
		Elizabeth "	28	f				" "			1	
		Martha "	25	f				" "			1	
		Enoch Freeman	26	m		Farmer	300	" "			1	
		Mary "	22	f				" "			1	
		Alexander "	3	m				" "				
		Aaron "	2	m				" "				
		Louisa "	3/12	f				" "				
1223	1223	Jacob Teague	64	m		Farmer	150	" "				
		Nancy "	28	f				" "			1	

m 19
fe 23

5??

SCHEDULE I.—Free Inhabitants in ______________ **in the County of** Moore **State of** N. Carolina **enumerated by me, on the** 22d **day of** November **1850.** N. McCrummen **Ass't Marshal**

	Dwelling-houses numbered in the order of visitation.	Families numbered in the order of visitation.	The Name of every Person whose usual place of abode on the first day of June, 1850, was in this family.	DESCRIPTION. Age.	Sex.	Color, White, black, or mulatto.	Profession, Occupation, or Trade of each Male Person over 15 years of age.	Value of Real Estate owned.	PLACE OF BIRTH. Naming the State, Territory, or Country.	Married within the year.	Attended School within the year.	Persons over 20 y'rs of age who cannot read & write.	Whether deaf and dumb, blind, insane, idiotic, pauper, or convict.
	1	2	3	4	5	6	7	8	9	10	11	12	13
1			Elizabeth Teague	26	F				N. Carolina			1	
2			Susan "	23	F				" "			1	
3			Mary "	17	F				" "				
4			Atkins "	16	m		Farmer		" "				
5			William "	7	m				" "				
6			Scynthia "	5	F				" "				
7	1224	1224	Phillip Comer	36	m		Farmer	75	" "			1	
8			Margaret "	34	F				" "			1	
9			Peter S "	13	m				" "				
10			Elizabeth "	10	F				" "				
11			Lydia "	7	F				" "				
12			William "	5	m				" "				
13			Martin "	2	m				" "				
14	1223	1225	Susannah Asbell	80	F				" "			1	
15	1225	1225	Susannah Comer	46	F			200	" "			1	
16			Malony Dunn	34	F				" "				
17			William "	10	m				" "				
18			Hannah "	8	F				" "				
19			Margaret "	6	F				" "				
20			James "	3	m				" "				
21	1226	1226	Peter Shamburger	38	m		Farmer	1200	" "				
22			Elvira "	32	F				" "				
23			Francina "	8	F				" "		1		
24			Margaret "	11	F				" "		1		
25			Anna A "	1	F				" "				
26	1227	1227	Lydia Shamburger	72	F				" "			1	
27			Mary Lawrence	38	F				" "				Insane
28	1228	1228	Elijah Spivey	33	m		Farmer		" "			1	
29			Susannah "	34	F				" "			1	
30			Martha "	10	F				" "		1		
31			Mark "	8	m				" "		1		
32			Josiah "	6	m				" "		1		
33			Spencer "	4	m				" "				
34			Isaac "	3	m				" "				
35	1227	1227	Isaac Coghe	25	m		Farmer	200	" "			1	
36			Francy "	26	F				" "			1	
37			John W. "	1	m				" "				
38			Anna Hare	50	F				" "				
39	1230	1230	Adam Comer	28	m		Farmer	100	" "			1	
40			Elizabeth "	50	F				" "			1	
41			Mary "	30	F				" "			1	
42	1231	1231	Lucy Comer	28	F			80	" "			1	

m 17
F 25

43   497

SCHEDULE I.—Free Inhabitants in ______________ **in the County of** *Moore* **State of** *N. Carolina* **enumerated by me, on the** *22nd* **day of** *November* **1850.** *N. McCrummen* **Ass't Marshal.** 249

Dwelling-houses numbered in the order of visitation.	Families numbered in the order of visitation.	The Name of every Person whose usual place of abode on the first day of June, 1850, was in this family.	Description: Age.	Sex.	Color, white, black, or mulatto.	Profession, Occupation, or Trade of each Male Person over 15 years of age.	Value of Real Estate owned.	Place of Birth. Naming the State, Territory, or Country.	Married within the year.	Attended School within the year.	Persons over 20 y'rs of age who cannot read & write.	Whether deaf and dumb, blind, insane, idiotic, pauper, or convict.	
1	2	3	4	5	6	7	8	9	10	11	12	13	
		Thomas Comer	6	M				N. Carolina					1
		Marticia "	2	F				" "					2
1232	1232	Enoch Cagle	39	M		Farmer		" "					3
		Nancy "	36	F				" "			/		4
		James "	15	M				" "					5
		Lewis "	14	M				" "		/			6
		Elizabeth "	12	F				" "					7
		George "	10	M				" "					8
		Henry "	8	M				" "					9
		Gilliam	5	M				" "					10
		Mary "	2	F				" "					11
1233	1233	Thomas McNeill	50	M				" "					12
		Elizabeth "	48	F				" "			/		13
		Daniel "	13	M				" "					14
		Lydia "	12	F				" "					15
		Elizabeth "	10	F				" "					16
		Malcom "	8	M				" "					17
		William "	6	M				" "					18
		Enoch "	6/12	M				" "					19
		Thomas "	6/12	M				" "					20
1234	1234	Elizabeth Cagle	40	F			400	" "			/		21
		Sallie "	35	F				" "			/		22
		Henry "	11	M				" "					23
1235	1235	Anna Woodle	70	F				South Carolina			/		24
		Larkey "	35	F				" "			/		25
		Duncan "	21	M		Laborer		" "			/		26
		Epsey "	16	F	M			" "					27
		Terry "	13	M	M			" "					28
		John "	10	M	M			" "					29
		Elsevan "	8	M				N. Carolina					30
		Jane "	4	F				" "					31
		John Medlin	29	M		Farmer		" "					32
1236	1236	Nathaniel Tucker	45	M		Farmer	350	" "					33
		Clergyman "	49	F				" "			/		34
		Beacon "	22	M		Farmer		" "					35
		Jesse "	20	M		Do		" "					36
		Amy "	18	F				" "					37
		Martha "	16	F				" "					38
		Rhody "	13	F				" "					39
		John "	11	M				" "					40
		Nathaniel "	8	M				" "					41
1237	1237	John Comer	30	M		Farmer	100	" "					42

M 25 2 B
F 17 1 F

SCHEDULE I.—Free Inhabitants in ________ **in the County of** *Moore* **State of** *N. Carolina* **enumerated by me, on the** *22nd* **day of** *November* **1850.** *N. McCrummen* **Ass't Marshal.**

	Dwelling-houses numbered in the order of visitation.	Families numbered in the order of visitation.	The Name of every Person whose usual place of abode on the first day of June, 1850, was in this family.	Description: Age.	Sex.	Color, White, black, or mulatto.	Profession, Occupation, or Trade of each Male Person over 15 years of age.	Value of Real Estate owned.	Place of Birth. Naming the State, Territory, or Country.	Married within the year.	Attended School within the year.	Persons over 20 y'rs of age who cannot read & write.	Whether deaf and dumb, blind, insane, idiotic, pauper, or convict.
	1	2	3	4	5	6	7	8	9	10	11	12	13
1			Elizabeth Comer	40	F				N. Carolina			1	
2			William "	20	M		Farmer		" "				
3			Enoch "	14	M				" "				
4			Hannah "	12	F				" "				
5			Lucy "	9	F				" "				
6			Hindrick "	8	M				" "				
7			Henry "	1	M				" "				
8	1238	1238	James Dunlap	33	M		Farmer	200	" "				
9			Caroline "	21	F				" "				
10			Phebe "	18	F				" "				
11			Daniel "	1	M				" "				
12	1239	1239	Mary Spivey	52	F			1000	" "			1	
13			Mary "	35	F				" "			1	
14			Sallie "	20	F				" "				
15			Mary "	17	F				" "				
16			Eliza "	16	F				" "				
17			Spencer "	12	M				" "				
18	1240	1240	Joseph Hogan	30	M		Laborer		" "			1	
19			Elizabeth "	25	F				" "			1	
20			Jane "	1	F				" "				
21	1241	1241	William Owens	50	M		Farmer	250	" "			1	
22			Mary "	65	F				" "				
23			Eliza "	22	F				" "				
24			William "	19	M		Farmer		" "		1		
25	1242	1242	Temple Spivey	25	M		Farmer		" "				
26	1243	1243	John Sheffield	34	M		Wheelwright	75	" "			1	
27			Sallie "	38	F				" "			1	
28			Martha "	12	F				" "				
29			Mary "	10	F				" "				
30			Delilah "	7	F				" "				
31			Lydia "	6	F				" "				
32			Hannah "	4	F				" "				
33			Rebecca "	2	F				" "				
34			Jane "	7/12	F				" "				
35	1244	1244	Martin Sheffield	37	M		Farmer	1000	" "			1	
36			Jane "	30	F				" "			1	
37			Sarah "	15	F				" "				
38			Isaac "	13	M				" "				
39			John "	11	M				" "				
40			Jane "	9	F				" "				
41			Elija "	7	M				" "				
42			Mathew "	5	M				" "				

M 17

499

SCHEDULE I.—Free Inhabitants in ____________ in the County of Moore State of N. Carolina enumerated by me, on the 22nd day of November 1850. N. McInnmen Ass't Marshal. 250

Dwelling-houses numbered in the order of visitation.	Families numbered in the order of visitation.	The Name of every Person whose usual place of abode on the first day of June, 1850, was in this family.	Age.	Sex.	Color, white, black, or mulatto.	Profession, Occupation, or Trade of each Male Person over 15 years of age.	Value of Real Estate owned.	Place of Birth. Naming the State, Territory, or Country.	Married within the year.	Attended School within the year.	Persons over 20 y'rs of age who cannot read & write.	Whether deaf and dumb, blind, insane, idiotic, pauper, or convict.
1	2	3	4	5	6	7	8	9	10	11	12	13
		William Sheffield	2	m				N. Carolina				
		Everett Smith	74	m		Miller		" "			1	
		Henry Brewer	25	m		Laborer		" "				
1245	1245	Isham Sheffield	21	m		Carpenter		" "			1	
		Anna "	30	F				" "			1	
		William "	2	m				" "				
1246	1246	Sarah Brewer	10	F				" "		1		
1246	1246	Everett Sheffield	23	m		Wheelwright	75	" "			1	
		Catharine "	60	F				" "			1	
1247	1247	William Eagle	62	m		Farmer	300	" "				
		Sarah "	50	F				" "			1	
1248	1248	Robert Mitton	47	m		Farmer	1000	" "				
		Christian "	45	F				" "				
		Nill "	20	m		Farmer		" "		1		
		James "	17	m		Farmer		" "				
		Nancy "	16	F				" "				
		Mary "	12	F				" "		1		
		Hannah Hass	34	F				" "				
1249	1249	Beacom Britt	45	m		Farmer	250	" "			1	
		Deborah "	22	F				" "			1	
		Benjamin "	15	m				" "				
		Nathaniel "	12	m				" "				
		Mary A. "	10	F				" "				
		Temperance "	8	F				" "				
		Sallie "	6	F				" "				
		Pattie "	1	F				" "				
		Rhody Britt	72	F				" "			1	
1250	1250	David Kennedy	25	m		Laborer		" "				
		Amy "	28	F				" "				
		Mary "	6	F				" "				
		Robert "	3	M				" "				
		Elizabeth "	1/12	F				" "				
		Lydia "	26	F				" "			1	
1251	1251	Eli Smith	35	m		Farmer	180	" "				
		Dorothy "	23	F				" "			1	
		Angus "	3	m				" "				
		Mary "	2	F				" "				
		Christina "	2/12	F				" "				
		Olive Britt	83	F				" "				
[illegible]	1252	Joseph Smith	33	m		Farmer	100	" "				
		Temperance "	21	F				" "			1	
		Lucinda "	3	F				" "				

M 18
504

SCHEDULE I.—Free Inhabitants in ______________ in the County of Moore State of N. Carolina enumerated by me, on the 23d day of November 1850. N. McCrimmon Ass't Marshal.

	Dwelling-houses numbered in the order of visitation.	Families numbered in the order of visitation.	The Name of every Person whose usual place of abode on the first day of June, 1850, was in this family.	Age.	Sex.	Color, { White, black, or mulatto.	Profession, Occupation, or Trade of each Male Person over 15 years of age.	Value of Real Estate owned.	Place of Birth. Naming the State, Territory, or Country.	Married within the year.	Attended School within the year.	Persons over 20 y'rs of age who cannot read & write.	Whether deaf and dumb, blind, insane, idiotic, pauper, or convict.
	1	2	3	4	5	6	7	8	9	10	11	12	13
1			Catharine Smith	1	F				N. Carolina				
2	1253	1253	Duncan Leach	26	M		Farmer		" "				
3			Lydia "	27	F				" "				
4			Archibald "	2	M				" "				
5			Martin "	3/12	M				" "				
6	1254	1	Eliza Patterson	17	F				" "				
7	1254	1254	Eli McLeod	28	M		Farmer		" "				
8			Ann	25	F				" "				
9	1255	1255	Daniel McIver	63	M		Farmer	500	" "				
10			Nancy "	64	F				" "				
11			Jennet "	30	F				" "				
12			Margaret "	27	F				" "				
13			Jennet Kidd	11	F				" "				
14			Cary "	7	M				" "				
15			Kenneth McCaskill	30	M		Laborer		" "				
16			Catharine "	25	F				" "				
17			Christian "	1	F				" "				
18	1256	1256	Bryant Britt	30	M		Farmer	80	" "				
19			Barbara "	25	F				" "			1	
20			Anna "	5	F				" "				
21			Jane "	4	F				" "				
22			John C. "	2	M				" "				
23	1257	1257	Britain Britt	62	M		Farmer	250	" "				
24			Sallie "	47	F				" "			1	
25			Elizabeth "	20	F				" "				
26			Levi "	18	M		Farmer		" "		1		
27			Britain D. "	16	M		Farmer		" "		1		
28			William "	13	M				" "		1		
29			Patience "	11	M				" "				
30			Joseph "	10	M				" "				
31			Jonathan "	8	M				" "				
32			Sallie "	7	F				" "				
33	1258	1258	Zacheus Britt	24	M		Farmer		" "				
34			Lydia "	20	F				" "			1	
35			Daniel "	3	M				" "				
36			Edmund "	10/12	M				" "				
37	1257	1259	John McDuffee	70	M		Farmer	200	" "			1	
38			Effy "	60	F				" "			1	
39			Flora "	35	F				" "			1	
40			Angus "	26	M		Laborer		" "				
41			Neill "	23	M		Farmer		" "				
42			Effy "	28	F				" "				

m 21

44 591

251

Schedule I.—Free Inhabitants in ______ in the County of *Moore* State of *N. Carolina* enumerated by me, on the *23d* day of *Novem.* 1850. *N. McCrummen* Ass't Marshal.

Dwelling-houses numbered in the order of visitation.	Families numbered in the order of visitation.	The Name of every Person whose usual place of abode on the first day of June, 1850, was in this family.	Age.	Sex.	Color, White, black, or mulatto.	Profession, Occupation, or Trade of each Male Person over 15 years of age.	Value of Real Estate owned.	Place of Birth. Naming the State, Territory, or Country.	Married within the year.	Attended School within the year.	Persons over 20 y'rs of age who cannot read & write.	Whether deaf and dumb, blind, insane, idiotic, pauper, or convict.
1	2	3	4	5	6	7	8	9	10	11	12	13
		Mary McDuffee	35	F				N. Carolina				
		Catharine "	30	F				" "				
		Anna "	28	F				" "			1	
		Christian "	24	F				" "				
1260	1260	Charles McArthur	55	m		Farmer	150	" "			1	
1261	1261	John L. Martin	35	m		Farmer	300	" "			1	
		Catharine "	47	F				" "				
		Alexander C. "	13	m				" "		1		
		Mary A. "	9	F				" "		1		
		Flora J. "	7	F				" "		1		
1262	1262	Malcom McAulay	57	m		Farmer	130	" "				
		Catharine "	61	F				" "			1	
		Mary "	26	F				" "			1	
		John "	25	m		Farmer		" "				
		Catharine "	18	F				" "				
1263	1263	Alexander McKinzie	40	m		Farmer		" "				
		Elizabeth "	30	F				" "			1	
		John "	4	m				" "				
		Daniel "	2	m				" "				
		Malcom "	1	m				" "				
		Simon "	1/12	m				" "				
		Isabella Sowell	56	F			150	" "				
		Simon "	20	m		Farmer		" "		1		
		Delilah Chavis	24	F				" "				
		Charlotte Brewer	14	F				" "		1		
1264	1264	John Bice	50	m		Farmer	240	" "				
		Margaret "	49	F				" "				
		Sarah E. "	20	F				" "				
		Margard "	18	F				" "				
		Regina M. "	16	F				" "		1		
		John "	14	m				" "		1		
		Mary J. "	12	F				" "		1		
		Martin "	9	m				" "				
1265	1265	Benjamin Bailey	37	m		Farmer	150	" "				
		Nancy "	45	F				" "				
		Christian "	17	F				" "		1		
		Daniel "	15	m				" "		1		
		John "	14	m				" "		1		
		Russel "	12	m				" "		1		
		Jafe "	9	m				" "		1		
		Angus "	7	m				" "		1		
		Jane "	5	F				" "				

m 20
f 22

SCHEDULE I.—Free Inhabitants in ____________ in the County of Moore State of N. Carolina enumerated by me, on the 25th day of Novem. 1850. N. McCrummen Ass't Marshal.

	Dwelling-houses numbered in the order of visitation.	Families numbered in the order of visitation.	The Name of every Person whose usual place of abode on the first day of June, 1850, was in this family.	Description: Age.	Sex.	Color, White, black, or mulatto.	Profession, Occupation, or Trade of each Male Person over 15 years of age.	Value of Real Estate owned.	Place of Birth. Naming the State, Territory, or Country.	Married within the year.	Attended School within the year.	Persons over 20 y'rs of age who cannot read & write.	Whether deaf and dumb, blind, insane, idiotic, pauper, or convict.
	1	2	3	4	5	6	7	8	9	10	11	12	13
1			Margaret Bailey	1	F				N. Carolina				
2	1266	1266	Jane Bailey	70	F			20	" "			1	
3			Rebecca "	50	F				" "			1	
4	1267	1267	John Campbell	66	m		Farmer	240	" "				
5			Catharine "	55	F				" "			1	
6			Daniel B. "	26	m		Student		" "		1		
7			Mary A. "	24	F				" "		1		
8			Margaret C. "	21	F				" "		1		
9			Sarah J. "	16	F				" "		1		
10	1268	1268	Asa Smith	30	m		Farmer	50	" "			1	
11			Sallie "	40	F				" "			1	
12	1269	1269	James Campbell	50	m		Farmer	275	" "				
13			Margaret "	56	F				" "				
14			Catharine "	54	F				" "				
15			Samuel "	48	m		Farmer		" "				
16	1270	1270	John Morrison	63	m		Farmer	350	" "				
17			Christian "	52	F				" "			1	
18			Mary McQueen	15	F				" "				
19	1271	1271	Mary Morrison	59	F				" "				
20			Isabella "	52	F				" "				
21	1272	1272	Westley Graham	24	m		Farmer		" "				
22			Sarah "	25	F				" "			1	
23			Margaret "	1	F				" "				
24	1273	1273	Norman McDuffee	39	m		Farmer	400	" "				
25			Catharine "	24	F				" "				
26			Malcom "	3/12	m				" "				
27	1274	1274	Daniel Chisholm	70	m		Farmer	950	Scotland				
28			Murdoch "	60	m		Farmer		"				
29			Alexander "	58	m				"				Deaf & Dumb
30	1275	1275	Joseph Britt	31	m		Farmer	21	N. Carolina				
31			Nancy "	31	F				" "				
32			Allen "	10	m				" "				
33			Ann "	8	F				" "				
34			Daniel "	3	m				" "				
35	1276	1276	Thomas Cole	27	m		Farmer		" "	—			
36			Christian "	24	F				" "	—			
37	1277	1277	Marion Armstrong	59	F			1000	" "				Deaf
38			Melinda "	30	F				" "				
39			Henry C. "	29	m		Merchant		" "				
40			John F. "	23	m		Farmer		" "				
41	1278	1278	Charles Muse	29	m		Farmer	130	" "				
42			Effy "	26	F				" "				

m 19
F 23

SCHEDULE I.—Free Inhabitants in ______ in the County of Moore State of N. Carolina enumerated by me, on the 25th day of Novem. 1850. N. McCrummen Ass't Marshal.

503

252

Dwelling-houses numbered in the order of visitation.	Families numbered in the order of visitation.	The Name of every Person whose usual place of abode on the first day of June, 1850, was in this family.	Age.	Sex.	Color, (White, black, or mulatto.)	Profession, Occupation, or Trade of each Male Person over 15 years of age.	Value of Real Estate owned.	Place of Birth. Naming the State, Territory, or Country.	Married within the year.	Attended School within the year.	Persons over 20 y'rs of age who cannot read & write.	Whether deaf and dumb, blind, insane, idiotic, pauper, or convict.
1	2	3	4	5	6	7	8	9	10	11	12	13
		John Muse	8	m				N. Carolina		1		
		Samuel "	5	m				" "				
		David "	3	m				" "				
		Mary A. "	1	f				" "				
1279	1279	Haywood Muse	26	m		Farmer		" "				
		Flora "	26	f				" "			1	
		Emily A. "	5/12	f				" "				
1280	1280	Lewis Ritter	34	m		Carpenter	100	" "			1	
		Viney "	28	f				" "				
		Archibald Ritter	28	m		Carpenter		" "				
1281	1281	Malcom Kelly	28	m		Merchant	1600	" "				
		Angus R. "	35	m		Lawyer	600	" "				
		Nancy "	18	f				" "		1		
		John B. McLeod	22	m		Student		" "		1		
		Malcom McIntosh	23	m		Merchant		" "				
1282	1282	Duncan Keith	36	m		Shoemaker	400	Scotland				
		Elizabeth "	36	f				"			1	
		James "	15	m				"		1		
		John R. "	11	m				"				
		Ann "	9	f				"				
		Catharine "	7	f				"				
		Mary "	5	f				N. Carolina				
		William "	3	m				" "				
		Duncan M. "	1	m				" "				
1283	1283	Robert McNab	45	m		Bapt. Clergyman	6500	Scotland				
		Elizabeth "	39	f				N. Carolina				
		Edwin L. "	1	m				" "				
		Alexander McAllester	11	m			3000	" "				
		Mary J. "	9	f			3000	" "				
		Elizabeth A. Colvin	32	f			2000	" "				
		Ellen Wood	9	f				" "				
		John Black	21	m		Student		" "		1		
		David A. Powell	18	m		Student		" "		1		
		William "	15	m				" "		1		
		Daniel O. Warner	23	m		Merchant		" "				
		William D. Wiley	19	m		Student		" "		1		
1284	1284	Samuel C. Bruce	48	m		Physician	4000	" "				
		Martha "	56	f				" "				
		Jerome "	15	m				" "				
		Samuel J. Person	26	m		Lawyer	2000	" "				
		Mary "	24	f				" "				
		Murdoch B. Person	24	m			2000	" "				

Hotel

m 27
f 15

SCHEDULE I.—Free Inhabitants in ________ in the County of Moore State

504 of N. Carolina enumerated by me, on the 25th day of Novem. 1850. N. McCrummen Ass't Marshal.

Dwelling-houses numbered in the order of visitation.	Families numbered in the order of visitation.	The Name of every Person whose usual place of abode on the first day of June, 1850, was in this family.	Age.	Sex.	Color, White, black, or mulatto.	Profession, Occupation, or Trade of each Male Person over 15 years of age.	Value of Real Estate owned.	Place of Birth. Naming the State, Territory, or Country.	Married within the year.	Attended School within the year.	Persons over 20 y'rs of age who cannot read & write.	Whether deaf and dumb, blind, insane, idiotic, pauper, or convict.
1	2	3	4	5	6	7	8	9	10	11	12	13
		Lydia Person	17	F.				N. Carolina				
		Chales Bruce	50	m		none		" "				
1285	1285	Malcom McCrummen	75	m			1000	Scotland				
		Christian "	59	F.				N. Carolina				
		Catharine "	82	F.				Scotland			1	
		Catharine "	46	F.				N. Carolina				
		Sarah M. "	44	F.				" "				
		Charles C. "	39	m		Newspaper Agt		" "				
		Norman "	37	m		" "		" "				
		Eliza "	31	F.				" "				
		Isabella "	29	F.				" "				
		Ann "	25	F.				" "				
		Malcom "	22	m		Farmer		" "				
		Lucinda "	21	F.				" "				
		John "	19	m		Farmer		" "				
1286	1286	Catharine Kelly	55	F.				Scotland			1	

Total [illegible]
White males 3676
[illegible] Fem 3621
Col. Males 79
[illegible] [illegible]
7366

m 6
f 10

58
42
176
152

44 Sheets

SCHEDULE 3.—Persons who Died during the Year ending 1st June, 1850, in ________ 433 in the County of Moore State of North Carolina, enumerated by me, N. McCrummen Ass't Marshal.

NAME OF EVERY PERSON WHO DIED during the Year ending 1st June, 1850, whose usual Place of Abode at the Time of his Death was in this Family.	DESCRIPTION. Age.	Sex.	Colour (White, black, or mulatto.)	Free or Slave.	Married or widowed.	PLACE OF BIRTH. Naming the State, Territory, or Country.	The Month in which the Person died.	PROFESSION, OCCUPATION, OR TRADE.	DISEASE, OR CAUSE OF DEATH.	Number of DAYS ILL.
1	2	3	4	5	6	7	8	9	10	11
John M. Sowell	31	m			m	N. Carolina	August	Farmer	Bellious Fever	8 days
William A. Sowell	1	m				" "	"		" "	12 days
Anna R. Dowd	20	F			wd	" "	July		Cancer	2 years
John R. Martin	37	m				" "	February	Miner	Appoplexy	Sudden
Dolly McDonald	55	F			wd	" "	September		Consumption	3 months
Jinnet	30	F	B	S		" "	March		Consumption	8 weeks
John Caddell	21	m				" "	November	Farmer	Putrid sore throat	3 weeks
Samuel James	34	m				England	February	Miner	Consumption	5 weeks
Ruina Sowell	16	F				N. Carolina	August		Bellious Fever	9 days
Benjamin	1	m	B	S		" "	May		Unknown	6 weeks
David Rose	65	m			m	" "	July	None	Unknown	2 weeks
Lucy	85	F	B	S		" "	August		Unknown	Sudden
Allen	7/12	m	B	S		" "	August		Accident	Sudden
Malcom C. Ray	19	m				" "	April	Farmer	Rheumatism	[illegible] weeks
Sarah Brown	84	F			wd	Scotland	February		Asthma	[illegible]
Abigail Eddings	80	F			wd	N. Carolina	September		Dropsy	6 months
Anna Blue	47	F			m	" "	August		Consumption	[illegible] months
Patience Graham	45	F			m	" "	March		Typhus Fever	3 weeks
Jack	23	m	m	S		" "	July		Typhus Fever	9 days
Neill McDonald	27	m				" "	August	Farmer	Typhus Fever	12 days
Nancy Graham	47	F			m	" "	October		Child Bed	Sudden
Isaac Graham	8	m				" "	June		Typhus Fever	[illegible] weeks
Celia Patterson	56	F			m	" "	May		Scrofula	2 years
Willis	23	m	B	S		" "	August		Inflamation of Brain	8 days
Duncan McLaughlin	74	m			m	Scotland	March	Farmer	Cholic	3 days
Mariah	22	F	B	S		N. Carolina	August		Died in Child Bed	Sudden
Neill	5	m	B	S		" "	March		Burned	[illegible] weeks
Mary McDugald	10	F				" "	April		Dropsy	1 year
Ned	1	m	B	S		" "	March		Fever	3 days
William	2/12	m	B	S		" "	January		Accident	Sudden
John Thomas	60	m			m	" "	November	Farmer	Consumption	[illegible] months
William Weaker	54	m			m	" "	August	Farmer	Appoplexy	
John Thomas	45	m			m	" "	Jany	Farmer	Dropsy	5 months
James Lett	10 days	m				" "	March		Croup	10 days
Jane	15 yr	F				" "	November		— Fever	15 days

Remarks. In a portion of this District Typhus Fever prevailed to some extent during the past year proving fatal in several cases — Cause unknown. — The soil is diversified — the northern portion is inclined to be Clayey with a growth of Oak, hickory &c. — The southern part is sandy with neverfailing streams of pure water — growth, pitch or long leaf pine. In the North and North western parts Gold mines have been discovered, and wrought to some extent. Iron Ore, Soap stone, Granite, Slate, Quartz and Coal abounds — especially on Deep River.

SCHEDULE 3.—Persons who Died during the Year ending 1st June, 1850, in ______________ **in the County of** *Moore* **State of** *N. Carolina*, **enumerated by me,** *N. McCrummen* **Ass't Marshal.**

	NAME OF EVERY PERSON WHO DIED during the Year ending 1st June, 1850, whose usual Place of Abode at the Time of his Death was in his Family.	DESCRIPTION. Age.	Sex.	Colour (White, black, or mulatto).	Free or Slave.	Married or widowed.	PLACE OF BIRTH. Naming the State, Territory, or Country.	The Month in which the Person died.	PROFESSION, OCCUPATION, OR TRADE.	DISEASE, OR CAUSE OF DEATH.	Number of DAYS ILL.
	1	2	3	4	5	6	7	8	9	10	11
1	Matthew Wicker	22	m			m	N. Carolina	November	Farmer	Unknow	3 year
2	Nancy Haight	70	F			wd	N. Carolina	June		Bilious Fever	5 week
3	H. Ann Haight	38	F			m	Tennessee	May		Consumption	3 year
4	John A. McIver	19	m				N. Carolina	January	Farmer	Pleurisy	28 days
5	Priscilla	7/12	F				N. Carolina	August		Accident	Sudden
6	Malcom Baker	73	m			m	Scotland	October	Farmer	Dropsy / Unknown	3 month
7	Sarah A. Lamont	3	F				N. Carolina	June		Unknown	3 month
8	Peter	78	m	B	S		N. Carolina	July		Unknown	2 month
9	Sarah McDonald	62	F				N. Carolina	January		Dropsy of Heart	a week
10	John McLeod	59	m			m	Scotland	June	Farmer	Dropsy of Heart	3 month
11	John	1/12	m	B	S		N. Carolina	February		Unknown	3 days
12	Rose	3/12	F	B	S		N. Carolina	Feby		Accidental	Sudden
13	James Cole	44	m			m	N. Carolina	May	Farmer	Pneumonia	7 days
14	Richard	78	m	B	S		N. Carolina	December		Appoplexy	
15	Mary	1/12	F	B	S		N. Carolina	January		Croup	1 day
16	Elizabeth Phillips	28	F			m	N. Carolina	Feby		Childbed	Sudden
17	Lydia Street	1/12	F				N. Carolina	September		— Fever	3 days
18	Mary Phillips	7/12	F				N. Carolina	Septem		Diarhea	2 week
19	Mary Davis	2	F				N. Carolina	Septem		— Fever	1 week
20	Dorothian Hancock	7/12	m				N. Carolina	Septem		Diarhea	2 week
21	Mary Tyson	22	F			m	N. Carolina	July		Child Bed Fev	3 week
22	Eli Cagle	22	m			m	N. Carolina	August	Farmer	Inflam of Brain	3 days
23	Elizabeth	3/12	F	B	S		N. Carolina	Jany		Whooping Cough	3 week
24	Winny Brewer	1/12	F				N. Carolina	Jany		Hives	1 day
25	Martha Richardson	3	F				N. Carolina	July		Croup	3 week
26	Norman Shaw	85	m			wd	Scotland	August	Farmer	Typhoid Fev	6 days
27	Margaret Kennedy	36	F			m	N. Carolina	Septem		Typhus Fev	8 days
28	Daniel McDonald	76	m			wd	Scotland	August	Farmer	Bilious Fev	2 week
29	John McNeill	46	m				N. Carolina	August	Farmer	Appoplexy	
30	Daniel McDonald	39	m			m	N. Carolina	Septem	Farmer	Typhus Fev	2 week
31	Mary A. McDonald	7	F				N. Carolina	October		Typhus Fev	3 week
32	James Reynolds	25	m				N. Carolina	July	Farmer	Typhus Fev	2 week
33	Josiah P. Ritter	1/12	m				N. Carolina	Jany		Croup	1 day
34	Josiah Cockman	36	m			m	N. Carolina	August	Farmer	Hernia	1 week
35	Sarah A. Russell	36	F			m	N. Carolina	March		Consumption	1 year

Remarks:

17 m
18 f
35

SCHEDULE 3.—Persons who Died during the Year ending 1st June, 1850, in ______ in the County of Moore State of North Carolina, enumerated by me, N. McCrummen Ass't Marshal. 437

NAME OF EVERY PERSON WHO DIED during the Year ending 1st June, 1850, whose usual Place of Abode at the Time of his Death was in this Family.	DESCRIPTION. Age.	Sex.	Colour (White, black, or mulatto.)	Free or Slave.	Married or widowed.	PLACE OF BIRTH. Naming the State, Territory, or Country.	The Month in which the Person died.	PROFESSION, OCCUPATION, OR TRADE.	DISEASE, OR CAUSE OF DEATH.	Number of DAYS ILL.
1	2	3	4	5	6	7	8	9	10	11
Elizabeth Stutts	42	F			m	N. Carolina	October		Pneumonia	2 weeks
William R. Mathis	4/12	m				" "	Septem.		Unknown	2 months
Ruthe	4/12	F	B	S		" "	July		Accident	Sudden
Isaac Spivey	58	m			m	" "	Novem.	Farmer	Dropsy	1 year
Norman McLeod	1/12	m				" "	Septem.		Inflam of Bowels	2 weeks

Remarks.

3 m

21

SCHEDULE 2.—Slave Inhabitants in ______ in the County of *Moore* State of *N. Carolina*, enumerated by me, on the *5th* day of *August*, 1850. *N. McCrummen* Ass't Marshal.

	Names of Slave Owners.	Number of Slaves.	Description. Age.	Sex.	Colour.	Fugitives from the State.	Number manumitted.	Deaf & dumb, blind, insane, or idiotic.
	1	2	3	4	5	6	7	8
1	Patrick A. McKeithan	1	13	M	B			
2	John McKeithan	1	44	F	B			
3	John McIntosh	1	40	F	B			
4		1	9	M	B			
5	Hugh Black	1	25	F	B			
6		1	23	F	B			
7		1	21	F	B			
8		1	3	F	B			
9		1	1	F	B			
10		1	1	M	B			
11		1	1	M	B			
12		1	35	M	B			
13	Neill Curry	1	28	M	B			
14		1	10	F	B			
15	Kenneth Ray	1	15	M	M			
16	Daniel Blue	1	23	M	B			
17	Neill McLauchlin	1	19	M	B			
18		1	17	F	B			
19		1	16	F	B			
20	Donald McLauchlin	1	20	F	B			
21		1	6	M	B			
22		1	3	M	B			
23	Kenneth Black	1	18	F	B			
24		1	11/12	M	B			
25	[illegible] Bean	1	27	F	B			
26		1	6	F	B			
27		1	4	M	B			
28		1	3	F	B			
29	William Cole	1	50	M	B			
30		1	40	F	B			
31		1	10	F	B			
32		1	8	M	B			
33		1	4	M	B			
34	John Tyson	1	80	F	B			
35		1	60	F	M			
36		1	55	F	B			
37		1	40	F	B			
38		1	21	M	M			
39		1	21	F	M			
40		1	20	F	M			
41		1	13	M	B			
42		1	14	F	B			

	Names of Slave Owners.	Number of Slaves.	Description. Age.	Sex.	Colour.	Fugitives from the State.	Number manumitted.	Deaf & dumb, blind, insane, or idiotic.
	1	2	3	4	5	6	7	8
1		1	9	M	M			
2		1	4	F	B			
3		1	3/12	M	B			
4		1	1/12	F	B			
5		1	45	M	B			
6	Sarah Glascock	1	50	M	B			
7	William D. Smith	1	18	F	B			
8		1	12	F	B			
9		1	9	F	B			
10		1	2/12	F	B			
11	John D. Dowd	1	22	M	B			
12		1	20	F	B			
13		1	12	M	B			
14		1	8	F	B			
15		1	4	M	B			
16		1	2	M	B			
17	Bryan Dowd	1	54	F	B			
18	William P. Martin	1	65	F	B			
19		1	51	F	M			
20		1	47	F	M			
21		1	36	F	B			
22		1	46	M	B			
23		1	20	M	M			
24		1	18	F	B			
25		1	14	F	B			
26		1	16	M	B			
27		1	15	M	B			
28		1	9	F	B			
29		1	7	F	B			
30		1	6	F	B			
31		1	26	M	B			
32		1	8	F	B			
33		1	6	F	B			
34		1	4	F	B			
35		1	3	F	B			
36		1	8/12	F	B			
37		1	3	M	B			
38		1	11/12	M	B			
39	Mary Warner	1	20	F	B			
40		1	8	M	B			
41		1	1	F	B			
42	Madison L. Fry	1	6	F	B			

SCHEDULE 2.—Slave Inhabitants in ____________ in the County of *Moore* **State of** *N Carolina*, **enumerated by me, on the** *12th* **day of** *August*, **1850.** *N. McCrummen* **Ass't Marshal.**

	Names of Slave Owners.	Number of Slaves.	Description. Age.	Sex.	Colour.	Fugitives from the State.	Number manumitted.	Deaf & dumb, blind, insane, or idiotic.
	1	2	3	4	5	6	7	8
1	Leonard W. Lawhon	1	3	M	B			
2	Iver D. Patterson	1	36	F	B			
3		1	24	F	B			
4		1	19	M	B			
5		1	18	F	B			
6		1	16	M	B			
7		1	2	M	B			
8	Jacob Stutts	1	21	M	B			
9		1	8	M	M			
10		1	3	F	M			
11	William M. Person	1	39	M	B			
12		1	28	M	B			
13		1	28	F	B			
14		1	27	M	B			
15		1	18	M	B			
16		1	18	F	B			
17		1	16	M	B			
18		1	11	M	[illegible]			
19		1	3	F	B			
20		1	2	M	M			
21	Samuel Barrett	1	55	F	B			
22		1	44	F	B			
23		1	44	F	B			
24		1	35	M	B			
25		1	30	F	B			
26		1	30	M	M			
27		1	24	F	M			
28		1	22	F	B			
29		1	20	M	B			
30		1	18	M	B			
31		1	16	M	B			
32		1	12	M	B			
33		1	12	F	B			
34		1	10	F	M			
35		1	10	M	B			
36		1	10	M	B			
37		1	7	M	B			
38		1	6	M	B			
39		1	5	M	B			
40		1	5	M	B			
41		1	4	F	B			
42		1	3	M	B			

	Names of Slave Owners.	Number of Slaves.	Description. Age.	Sex.	Colour.	Fugitives from the State.	Number manumitted.	Deaf & dumb, blind, insane, or idiotic.
	1	2	3	4	5	6	7	8
1		1	3	F	B			
2		1	2	M	B			
3		1	2	F	B			
4		1	½	F	B			
5	William J. McIntosh	1	25	F	B			
6		1	7	F	B			
7	Samuel McIntosh	1	16	F	B			
8		1	14	F	B			
9		1	13	F	B			
10	Mary McIntosh	1	22	M	B			
11	John J. McIntosh	1	22	F	B			
12		1	2	M	B			
13	William B. Fry	1	30	M	B			
14		1	45	M	B			
15		1	28	M	B			
16		1	20	F	B			
17		1	28	F	B			
18		1	23	M	B			
19		1	16	M	B			
20		1	16	M	B			
21		1	11	M	B			
22		1	1	F	B			
23		1	5	F	B			
24		1	5	M	B			
25		1	4	F	B			
26		1	2	F	B			
27		1	5/12	M	B			
28	Neill Caddell	1	30	M	B			
29		1	26	F	B			
30		1	4	F	B			
31		1	3	M	B			
32		1	2	M	B			
33	Stephen Davis	1	45	M	M			
34	George McIntosh	1	35	F	B			
35		1	8	M	B			
36	Daniel A. Muse	1	16	F	B			
37	Lochart Fry	1	19	F	B			
38		1	12	F	B			
39	John Morison	1	34	F	M			
40		1	7	F	B			
41		1	4	F	B			
42		1	1	F	B			

SCHEDULE 2.—Slave Inhabitants in ______ in the County of *Moore* 3 State of *N. Carolina*, enumerated by me, on the *16th* day of *August*, 1850. *N. McCrummen* Ass't Marshal.

Line	Names of Slave Owners.	Number of Slaves.	Age.	Sex.	Colour.	Fugitives from the State.	Number manumitted.	Deaf & dumb, blind, insane, or idiotic.
	1	2	3	4	5	6	7	8
1	Alexander Kelly	1	53	m	B			
2		1	52	m	B			
3		1	51	m	B			
4		1	51	m	B			
5		1	45	F	M			
6		1	30	F	B			
7		1	18	F	B			
8		1	18	M	B			
9		1	28	m	B			
10		1	12	m	B			
11		1	9	m	B			
12		1	7	F	B			
13		1	7	m	B			
14		1	5	m	M			
15		1	5	m	B			
16		1	3	m	B			
17		1	3	m	B			
18		1	2/12	F	B			
19		1	75	m	B			
20		1	60	F	B			
21		1	30	m	B			
22		1	28	m	B			
23		1	24	m	B			
24		1	17	m	B			
25		1	26	F	M			
26		1	13	F	B			
27		1	6	m	B			
28		1	4	m	B			
29		1	1/12	m	B			
30		1	9/12	F	B			
31	Thomas Cole	1	22	m	B			
32		1	26	F	B			
33		1	3	F	B			
34	James B. Muse	1	70	F	B			
35	Lauchlin Kelly	1	27	F	B			
36		1	9	F	M			
37		1	8	m	M			
38		1	5	m	B			
39		1	2	F	B			
40		1	1	F	B			
41	Efa F. Muse	1	30	m	B			
42	Angus C. McNeill	1	24	m	B			

m 26 f 16

Line	Names of Slave Owners.	Number of Slaves.	Age.	Sex.	Colour.	Fugitives from the State.	Number manumitted.	Deaf & dumb, blind, insane, or idiotic.
	1	2	3	4	5	6	7	8
1		1	64	F	B			
2		1	40	m	B			
3		1	14	F	M			
4	Thomas Jenkins	1	25	F	B			
5	John C. Jackson	1	85	F	B.			
6		1	35	F	B.			
7		1	12	F	B			
8		1	2	m	m			
9		1	1	m	B			
10	Thomas B. Tyson	1	34	F	m			
11		1	20	F	B			
12		1	18	F	m			
13		1	12	m	B			
14		1	2	F	m			
15		1	1	m	B			
16	Lewis H. Ritter	1	30	F	B.			
17	Malcom Kelly	1	40	F	B			
18		1	25	m	B			
19	Angus R. Kelly	1	8	m	m			
20	Robert McNabb	1	35	F	B			
21		1	22	m	B			
22		1	20	F	B			
23		1	13	F	B			
24		1	10	m	B			
25		1	6	F	B			
26		1	3	m	B			
27		1	1	F	B			
28		1	2/12	m	B			
29		1	16	F	B			
30		1	16	F	B			
31		1	22	m	B			
32		1	70	m	B			Blind
33	Samuel C. Bruce	1	46	m	B			
34		1	42	F	B			
35		1	28	F	B			
36		1	16	m	B			
37		1	14	m	B			
38		1	8	F	B			
39		1	6	F	B			
40		1	6	F	B			
41		1	4	m	B			
42		1	2	m	B			

m 11 f

m 18 f 2

SCHEDULE 2.—Slave Inhabitants in ______ **in the County of** Moore **State of** N. Carolina**, enumerated by me, on the** 17th **day of** August **, 1850.** N. McCrummen **Ass't Marshal.**

	Names of Slave Owners.	Number of Slaves.	Description. Age.	Sex.	Colour.	Fugitives from the State.	Number manumitted.	Deaf & dumb, blind, insane, or idiotic.
	1	2	3	4	5	6	7	8
1	William Barrett	1	35	F	B			
2		1	28	m	m			
3		1	22	m	B			
4		1	23	F	B			
5		1	22	F	m			
6		1	20	m	B			
7		1	17	m	B			
8		1	14	m	B			
9		1	10	m	B			
10		1	8	m	B			
11		1	8	m	B			
12		1	7	F	B			
13		1	6	m	B			
14		1	5	m	B			
15		1	3	m	B			
16		1	3	F	B			
17		1	6/12	F	B			
18	Daniel Chisholm	1	58	F	B			
19		1	35	m	B			
20		1	28	F	B			
21		1	26	F	B			
22		1	18	F	B			
23		1	14	m	B			
24		1	12	m	B			
25		1	7	F	B			
26		1	5	F	B			
27		1	2	m	B			
28		1	2	F	B			
29		1	3/12	m	B			
30	John Buie	1	45	F	B			
31		1	19	m	B			
32		1	16	F	B			
33	Wright Cotton	1	30	m	B			
34		1	15	m	B			
35	Mary Morrison	1	45	F	B			
36		1	23	m	B			
37	Marion Armstrong	1	50	F	B			
38		1	32	F	B			
39		1	29	m	B			
40		1	13	F	B			
41		1	10	m	B			
42		1	8	F	B			

M 22
F 20

	Names of Slave Owners.	Number of Slaves.	Description. Age.	Sex.	Colour.	Fugitives from the State.	Number manumitted.	Deaf & dumb, blind, insane, or idiotic.
	1	2	3	4	5	6	7	8
1		1	5	m	B			
2		1	2/12	F	B			
3								
4								
5								
6								
7								
8								
9								
10								
11								
12								
13								
14								
15								
16								
17								
18								
19								
20								
21								
22								
23								
24								
25								
26								
27								
28								
29								
30								
31								
32								
33								
34								
35								
36								
37								
38								
39								
40								
41								
42								

M 1
F 1

SCHEDULE 2.—Slave Inhabitants in ____________ in the County of Moore 325 State of N. Carolina, enumerated by me, on the 20th day of August, 1850. N. McCrummen Ass't Marshal.

Line	NAMES OF SLAVE OWNERS.	Number of Slaves.	DESCRIPTION. Age.	Sex.	Colour.	Fugitives from the State.	Number manumitted.	Deaf & dumb, blind, insane, or idiotic.
	1	2	3	4	5	6	7	8
1	Mary Clark	1	60	F	B.			
2		1	38	m	B.			
3		1	12	F	B.			
4	Archibald Ray	1	65	m	B.			
5		1	45	F	B.			
6		1	17	F	B.			
7		1	10	m	B.			
8		1	9	F	B.			
9		1	6	F	B.			
10	Hugh McLaurin	1	27	F	B.			
11		1	10	m	B.			
12		1	9	m	B.			
13		1	6	m	B.			
14		1	4	m	B.			
15		1	2	F	B.			
16		1	6/12	F	B.			
17	James D. Rush	1	9	F	B.			
18	Jane McKenzie	1	40	m	B.			
19		1	13	F	B.			
20	Daniel McKenzie	1	18	F	B.			
21		1	17	F	B.			
22		1	4	m	m			
23		1	2/12	m	B.			
24	Malcom C. Clark	1	24	F	B.			
25		1	7	F	B.			
26		1	4/12	m	B.			
27	Malcom Brown	1	23	F	B.			
28	Duncan Brown	1	45	F	B.			
29		1	38	F	B.			
30		1	25	m	B.			
31		1	8	F	B.			
32		1	5	m	B.			
33	John McKinnon	1	6	F	B.			
34	Daniel Patterson	1	45	F	B.			
35		1	21	m	B.			
36		1	11	F	B.			
37		1	7	F	B.			
38	John McLeod	1	36	F	B.			
39		1	18	F	B.			
40	John McLeod	1	52	m	B.			
41		1	27	F	B.			
42		1	17	F	B.			

Line	NAMES OF SLAVE OWNERS.	Number of Slaves.	DESCRIPTION. Age.	Sex.	Colour.	Fugitives from the State.	Number manumitted.	Deaf & dumb, blind, insane, or idiotic.
	1	2	3	4	5	6	7	8
1		1	18	m	B.			
2	Angus Graham	1	30	F	B.			
3		1	25	F	B.			
4		1	10	m	B.			
5		1	4	m	B.			
6	Laughlin McKinnon	1	22	F	B.			
7		1	2	F	B.			
8		1	4/12	F	B.			
9	Charles C. Shaw	1	60	F	B.			
10		1	45	m	B.			
11		1	40	F	B.			
12		1	22	F	B.			
13		1	22	m	B.			
14		1	18	F	B.			
15		1	11	m	B.			
16		1	9	F	B.			
17		1	7	m	B.			
18		1	4	m	B.			
19		1	2	m	B.			
20		1	1	F	B.			
21	Duncan Shaw	1	40	F	B.			
22		1	10	F	B.			
23	John M. D. Ray	1	27	m	B.			
24		1	8	F	B.			
25	Archibald Ray	1	60	F	B.			
26		1	22	m	B.			
27		1	20	m	B.			
28		1	15	m	B.			
29		1	17	F	B.			
30		1	10	F	B.			
31		1	7	F	B.			
32		1	10	F	B.			
33		1	5	F	B.			
34	Archibald Campbell	1	25	m	B.			
35		1	25	F	B.			
36		1	4	F	B.			
37	Malcom McBlue	1	37	m	B.			
38		1	37	F	B.			
39		1	30	m	B.			
40		1	26	F	B.			
41		1	2	m	B.			
42		1	1	F	B.			

m 15

2 m 1

SCHEDULE 2.—Slave Inhabitants in ______ **in the County of** *Moore* **State of** *N. Carolina*, **enumerated by me, on the** *26th* **day of** *August*, **1850.** *N. McCrummen* **Ass't Marshal.**

	Names of Slave Owners.	Number of Slaves.	Age.	Sex.	Colour.	Fugitives from the State.	Number manumitted.	Deaf & dumb, blind, insane, or idiotic.
	1	2	3	4	5	6	7	8
1	Daniel McNeill	1	22	m	B			
2		1	22	F	B			
3		1	19	F	B			
4		1	17	m	B			
5		1	4	m	B			
6		1	3	m	B			
7	Archibald Buchan	1	45	m	m			
8		1	14	m	B			
9	Christian McDonald	1	30	F	B			
10		1	10	F	B			
11		1	9	F	B			
12		1	7	F	B			
13		1	5	m	B			
14		1	3	m	B			
15	Archibald M Blue	1	47	m	B			
16		1	46	F	B			
17		1	29	F	B			
18		1	28	F	B			
19		1	27	m	B			
20		1	12	F	B			
21		1	10	m	B			
22		1	8	F	B			
23		1	6	m	B			
24		1	5	m	B			
25		1	5	m	B			
26		1	2	F	B			
27		1	2	F	B			
28		1	21	m	B			
29	Duncan M Blue	1	60	F	B			
30		1	40	F	B			
31		1	20	F	B			
32		1	20	m	B			
33		1	18	m	B			
34		1	18	F	B			
35		1	10	F	B			
36		1	7	m	B			
37		1	1	F	B			
38	Mary Black	1	28	F	B			
39		1	2	m	m			
40		1	[illegible]	m	m			
41	Dugald McDonald	1	16	m	B			
42	Daniel McNeill	1	1	m	B			

	Names of Slave Owners.	Number of Slaves.	Age.	Sex.	Colour.	Fugitives from the State.	Number manumitted.	Deaf & dumb, blind, insane, or idiotic.
	1	2	3	4	5	6	7	8
1	Effy Black	1	26	F	B			
2		1	5/12	m	B			
3	Patrick M Blue	1	27	m	B			
4		1	22	F	B			
5		1	15	F	B			
6		1	2	m	B			
7		1	1/12	m	B			
8	Daniel B. Black	1	19	F	B			
9		1	12	F	B			
10		1	6/12	F	B			
11	Mary J. McDonald	1	65	m	B			
12		1	16	F	B			
13	Ann Curry	1	16	F	B			
14	Duncan C. Blue	1	50	F	B			
15		1	26	m	B			
16		1	24	m	B			
17		1	24	F	B			
18		1	20	F	B			
19		1	6	F	B			
20		1	3	F	B			
21		1	1	F	M			
22	Daniel McKeithan	1	39	F	B			
23		1	21	m	B			
24		1	18	F	B			
25		1	16	F	B			
26		1	11	m	B			
27		1	9	m	B			
28		1	6	F	B			
29		1	4	m	B			
30		1	2	F	B			
31	Malcom Black	1	45	m	B			
32		1	19	m	B			
33	Patrick Ray	1	37	F	B			
34		1	2	F	B			
35	Archibald Curry	1	44	F	B			
36		1	14	F	B			
37		1	10	F	B			
38		1	2	m	B			
39		1	10/12	m	B			
40	Daniel B. Curry	1	18	F	B			
41	Duncan B. Curry	1	52	F	B			
42		1	9	F	B			

SCHEDULE 2.—Slave Inhabitants in ________ **in the County of** *Moore* 329 **State of** *N. Carolina*, **enumerated by me, on the** *29th* **day of** *August*, **1850.** *N. McCrummen* **Ass't Marshal.**

	Names of Slave Owners.	Number of Slaves.	Description. Age.	Sex.	Colour.	Fugitives from the State.	Number manumitted.	Deaf & dumb, blind, insane, or idiotic.
	1	2	3	4	5	6	7	8
1	Sarah Curry	1	51	F	B			
2		1	8	m	B			
3		1	6	F	B			
4		1	2	F	B			
5	Malcom Graham	1	26	F	B			
6		1	2	m	B			
7	Allen McDonald	1	12	m	B			
8	Andrew Graham	1	16	m	B			
9	John M. Fry	1	40	m	B			
10		1	1	F	B			
11	Cornelius Dunlap	1	60	F	B			
12		1	54	m	B			
13		1	45	F	B			
14	Angus Curry	1	19	m	B			
15		1	13	F	B			
16	John L. McLeod	1	19	F	m			
17		1	3	m	B			
18		1	1	m	B			
19	Neill Peterson	1	46	m	B			
20		1	25	F	B			
21	Eliza M. Rowan	1	59	F	B			
22		1	28	F	B			
23		1	14	m	B			
24		1	10	m	B			
25		1	7	m	B			
26		1	5	F	B			
27		1	2	F	B			
28	Hugh Leach	1	20	F	B			
29		1	18	F	B			
30		1	17	F	B			
31		1	9	F	B			
32		1	1	m	B			
33		1	1/12	F	m			
34	John A. McLeod	1	23	F	B			
35		1	6	F	B			
36		1	3	m	B			
37		1	1/12	m	B			
38	Catharine McLauchlin	1	42	F	B			
39		1	22	F	B			
40		1	21	m	B			
41		1	9	F	B			
42		1	7	m	B			

M 18

	Names of Slave Owners.	Number of Slaves.	Description. Age.	Sex.	Colour.	Fugitives from the State.	Number manumitted.	Deaf & dumb, blind, insane, or idiotic.
	1	2	3	4	5	6	7	8
1		1	5	m	B			
2	Lemuel W. Stone	1	8	m	B			
3	Donald Kelly	1	50	F	B			
4		1	33	m	B			
5		1	25	m	B			
6		1	27	F	B			
7		1	14	m	B			
8		1	13	F	B			
9		1	10	F	B			
10		1	8	F	B			
11		1	6	F	B			
12		1	8/12	m	B			
13	John N. Ferguson	1	45	m	B			
14	John McNeill	1	24	F	B			
15		1	20	m	B			
16		1	4	F	B			
17		1	3	F	B			
18		1	4/12	m	B			
19	Lochart Fry	1	31	F	B			
20		1	31	m	B			
21		1	18	F	B			
22		1	16	m	B			
23		1	15	F	B			
24		1	13	m	B			
25		1	11	m	B			
26		1	4	F	B			
27	Mary McNeill	1	32	m	B			
28		1	18	m	B			
29		1	14	m	B			
30		1	10	F	B			
31		1	50	F	B			
32	Peter Kelly	1	14	F	B			
33	Archibald McDonald	1	40	F	B			
34		1	20	m	B			
35		1	18	m	B			
36		1	16	m	B			
37		1	17	F	B			
38		1	8	F	B			
39		1	6	m	B			
40		1	6	m	B			
41		1	3	m	B			
42	Nancy McLeod	1	38	m	B			

M 23

SCHEDULE 2.—Slave Inhabitants in ______ **in the County of** Moore **State of** N. Carolina, **enumerated by me, on the** 6th **day of** September, **1850.** N. McCrummen **Ass't Marshal.**

	NAMES OF SLAVE OWNERS.	Number of Slaves.	DESCRIPTION. Age.	Sex.	Colour.	Fugitives from the State.	Number manumitted.	Deaf & dumb, blind, insane, or idiotic.
	1	2	3	4	5	6	7	8
1	Allen J. McDonald	1	10	m	B			
2	Donald McDonald	1	22	m	B			
3		1	20	F	B			
4		1	19	F	B			
5		1	10	F	B			
6		1	10	F	B			
7		1	7	F	B			
8		1	5	m	B			
9	John McDonald	1	50	F	B			
10		1	20	m	B			
11	Murdoch Ferguson	1	23	m	B			
12	Daniel Turner	1	20	F	B			
13		1	3	F	B			
14	Hugh Keith	1	12	m	B			
15	Mary Cameron	1	12	F	B			
16	Archibald J. L. Cameron	1	25	F	B			
17		1	2	F	B			
18	Isabella Baker	1	17	F	B			
19	Neill Cameron	1	22	m	B			
20		1	22	F	B			
21		1	10	F	B			
22		1	5	m	B			
23	Alexander Cameron	1	30	m	B			
24		1	4	m	B			
25		1	78	F	B			
26	Jesse Thompson	1	20	F	m			
27	Thomas Mathis	1	13	F	B			
28		1	21	m	B			
29	Jacob Mathis	1	45	F	B			
30		1	27	m	B			
31		1	21	m	B			
32		1	16	F	B			
33		1	14	F	B			
34		1	12	F	B			
35		1	10	m	B			
36		1	8	F	B			
37		1	8	m	B			
38		1	6	m	B			
39	James Worthy	1	40	F	B			
40		1	27	m	B			
41		1	25	F	B			
42		1	23	F	B			

m 17
F 25

	NAMES OF SLAVE OWNERS.	Number of Slaves.	DESCRIPTION. Age.	Sex.	Colour.	Fugitives from the State.	Number manumitted.	Deaf & dumb, blind, insane, or idiotic.
	1	2	3	4	5	6	7	8
1		1	19	m	B			
2		1	17	m	B			
3		1	13	F	B			
4		1	11	m	B			
5		1	9	m	B			
6		1	7	F	B			
7		1	7	F	B			
8		1	6	F	B			
9		1	5	m	B			
10		1	4	m	B			
11		1	3	m	B			
12		1	3	F	B			
13		1	2	F	B			
14		1	2/12	m	m			
15	Henry Arnold	1	31	m	B			
16		1	27	F	B			
17		1	25	F	m			
18		1	23	m	B			
19		1	8	m	B			
20		1	8	F	B			
21		1	6	F	m			
22		1	4	F	B			
23		1	4	F	B			
24		1	9/12	m	B			
25	Susan M. S. McDonald	1	35	F	B			
26		1	15	m	B			
27		1	9	F	B			
28		1	5	F	B			
29		1	3	m	B			
30		1	1	m	B			
31	Norman McDonald	1	37	F	B			
32		1	10	m	B			
33		1	9	m	B			
34		1	7	m	B			
35		1	4	m	B			
36		1	2	F	B			
37		1	10/12	m	B			
38	William Keith	1	22	F	B			
39		1	7	F	B			
40		1	1	m	B			
41	John McDugald	1	51	F	B			
42		1	20	F	m			

m 21
F 21

SCHEDULE 2.—Slave Inhabitants in ______________ in the County of *Moore* 33 State of *N. Carolina*, enumerated by me, on the *9th* day of *September*, 1850. *N. McCrummen* Ass't Marshal.

NAMES OF SLAVE OWNERS.	Number of Slaves.	DESCRIPTION. Age.	Sex.	Colour.	Fugitives from the State.	Number manumitted.	Deaf & dumb, blind, insane, or idiotic.
1	2	3	4	5	6	7	8
John McDugald	1	4	F.	B.			
	1	7/12	F.	M			
James Gilchrist	1	12	F.	B.			
Neill Graham	1	14	F.	B.			
Alfred Willis	1	25	F.	B.			
	1	3	M	B.			
	1	6/12	M	B.			
Dugald McDugald	1	55	F.	B.			
	1	52	F.	B.			
	1	42	M.	B.			
	1	32	M	B.			
	1	27	M	B.			
	1	26	M	B.			
	1	25	M	B.			
	1	22	M	B.			
	1	18	M	B.			
	1	22	F.	B.			
	1	22	F	B.			
	1	33	F	B.			
	1	17	F.	B.			
	1	16	F.	B.			
	1	14	M	B.			
	1	10	F	B.			
	1	12	M	B.			
	1	12	M	B.			
	1	9	F.	B.			
	1	9	F.	B.			
	1	7	M	B.			
	1	9	F	B.			
	1	7	F	B.			
	1	4	M	B.			
	1	2	M	B.			
	1	7	M	B.			
	1	2	F	B.			
Allen B. Morrison	1	19	F	B.			
Malcom Johnson	1	23	F	B.			
	1	21	M	B.			
	1	5	M	B.			
Malcom Johnson	1	11	M	B.			
Allen Buie	1	39	F	B.			
	1	22	M	B.			
	1	12	M	B.			

m 21
f 21

1st 6f

NAMES OF SLAVE OWNERS.	Number of Slaves.	DESCRIPTION. Age.	Sex.	Colour.	Fugitives from the State.	Number manumitted.	Deaf & dumb, blind, insane, or idiotic.
1	2	3	4	5	6	7	8
	1	4	F.	B.			
	1	1	F	B.			
William Buie	1	18	F.	B.			
	1	16	M	B.			
	1	33	M	B.			
	1	11	M	B.			
	1	8	F.	B.			
	1	5	F.	B.			
Archibald Buie	1	54	F	B.			
	1	31	F	M			
	1	23	M	B.			
	1	22	F	B.			
	1	19	F	B.			
	1	16	M	B.			
	1	12	M	B.			
	1	5	F	B.			
	1	5	F.	B.			
	1	3	M	B.			
	1	2	F	B.			
Jane Munroe	1	55	F	B.			
	1	20	M	B.			
	1	18	M	B.			
	1	16	F	B.			
	1	14	F	B.			
	1	12	F	B.			
	1	10	M	B.			
	1	8	F	B.			
	1	4	M	B.			
	1	1	F.	B.			
Sarah Shaw	1	27	M	B.			
	1	20	F	B.			
	1	17	F	B.			
	1	9	M	B.			
	1	4	F.	B.			
	1	4/12	F	B.			
	1	3/12	F.	B.			
William H. Baker	1	42	F	B.			
	1	26	F.	B.			
	1	7	M	B.			
	1	5	F	B.			
	1	3	F	B.			
	1	2/12	F.	B.			

m 14
f 28

SCHEDULE 2.—Slave Inhabitants in ____________ **in the County of** *Moore* **S**

of *N. Carolina*, **enumerated by me, on the** *14th* **day of** *September*, **1850.** *N. McCrummen* **Ass't Ma**

Line	NAMES OF SLAVE OWNERS. (1)	Number of Slaves. (2)	DESCRIPTION. Age. (3)	Sex. (4)	Colour. (5)	Fugitives from the State. (6)	Number manumitted. (7)	Deaf & dumb, blind, insane, or idiotic. (8)
1		1	1/12	F	B.			
2	Mary McIver	1	40	F	B.			
3		1	40	m	B.			
4		1	14	F	B.			
5		1	13	F	B			
6		1	10	m	B			
7		1	5	F	B			
8		1	6/12	F	B			
9		1	22	m	m			
10	Alexander McGilvary	1	20	F	B			
11		1	1	F	B.			
12	John Cameron	1	55	F	B.			
13		1	12	m	B.			
14		1	40	F	B.			
15		1	12	m	B			
16	Dugald Cameron	1	22	m	B			
17		1	21	F	B.			
18		1	20	F	B			
19		1	6	F	B.			
20		1	4	m	B			
21		1	2	F	B			
22		1	1	m	B.			
23	John Swann	1	80	F	B			
24		1	70	m	B			
25		1	50	F	B			
26		1	40	F	B			
27		1	28	m	m			
28		1	28	m	B.			
29		1	27	F	m			
30		1	20	m	m			
31		1	21	m	B			
32		1	20	m	B			
33		1	17	F	B			
34		1	17	F	B			
35		1	12	F	B			
36		1	12	m	B			
37		1	12	m	B			
38		1	12	m	B			
39		1	10	m	B			
40		1	10	F	B			
41		1	10	F	B			
42		1	8	m	B			

m 19
F 23

Line	NAMES OF SLAVE OWNERS. (1)	Number of Slaves. (2)	DESCRIPTION. Age. (3)	Sex. (4)	Colour. (5)	Fugitives from the State. (6)	Number manumitted. (7)	Deaf & dumb, blind, or id…
1		1	2	m	m			
2		1	8	F	B			
3		1	3	F	B			
4		1	10	m	B.			
5	Margaret Buie	1	56	m	B.			
6		1	25	F	B			
7		1	22	F	B.			
8		1	18	m	B.			
9		1	16	m	B.			
10		1	12	F	B			
11		1	11	F	B.			
12		1	9	F	B.			
13		1	4	m	B.			
14		1	2	F	B			
15		1	3	F	B			
16		1	1	m	B			
17		1	3/12	m	B.			
18		1	2/12	F	B.			
19		1	17	m	B			
20	John M. Cox	1	21	m	B.			
21		1	10	F	B			
22		1	4	m	B.			
23	Thomas Cox	1	70	m	B			
24		1	35	m	m			
25		1	21	F	B.			
26		1	20	m	B			
27		1	20	F	B.			
28		1	14	m	B.			
29		1	7	F	B			
30		1	4	m	B			
31		1	2	m	B			
32	Henry Cox	1	3	m	B			
33	John Morris	1	5	F	B.			
34		1	22	m	B			
35	Catharine Morris	1	14	F	B.			
36	Gideon Edwards	1	50	F	B			
37		1	23	m	B			
38		1	16	F	B.			
39		1	14	m	B			
40		1	12	m	B.			
41	John H. Dalrymple	1	45	m	B			
42		1	26	m	m			

m 24
F 18

SCHEDULE 2.—Slave Inhabitants in in the County of *Moore* State of *N. Carolina*, enumerated by me, on the *16th* day of *September*, 1850. *N. McCrummen* Ass't Marshal. *33*

	Names of Slave Owners. (1)	Number of Slaves. (2)	Description. Age. (3)	Sex. (4)	Colour. (5)	Fugitives from the State. (6)	Number manumitted. (7)	Deaf & dumb, blind, insane, or idiotic. (8)
1	[illegible]h H. Dalrymple	1	32	F	B			
2		1	12	F	M			
3		1	7	M	B			
4		1	26	M	B			
5	[D]aniel McLeod	1	60	F	B			
6		1	31	M	B			
7		1	29	M	B			
8		1	22	M	B			
9	[A]bby McIver	1	30	F	B			
10		1	11	M	B			
11		1	9	F	B			
12		1	6	F	B			
13		1	3	F	B			
14		1	1	M	B			
15	[E]lizabeth Dalrymple	1	27	F	B			
16		1	17	M	B			
17		1	16	F	B			
18		1	14	F	B			
19		1	12	F	B			
20		1	10	F	B			
21	[W]illiam Dalrymple	1	45	F	B			
22		1	22	F	B			
23		1	20	M	B			
24		1	18	M	B			
25		1	16	M	B			
26		1	11	F	B			
27		1	8	M	B			
28		1	4	M	B			
29		1	2/12	M	B			
30		1	1	M	B			
31	[J]ohn McIver	1	47	F	B			
32		1	22	M	B			
33		1	19	M	B			
34		1	10	M	B			
35		1	8	M	B			
36	[A]rchibald F. Douglas	1	13	M	B			
37	[D]avid Kester	1	8	F	B			
38	[J]ohn May	1	56	F	B			
39		1	15	M	B			
40	[C]harles B. Harrington	1	40	F	B			
41		1	35	M	B			
42		1	27	M	B			

M 23
F 19

	Names of Slave Owners. (1)	Number of Slaves. (2)	Description. Age. (3)	Sex. (4)	Colour. (5)	Fugitives from the State. (6)	Number manumitted. (7)	Deaf & dumb, blind, insane, or idiotic. (8)
1		1	23	F	B			
2		1	22	M	B			
3		1	21	M	B			
4		1	17	M	B			
5		1	17	M	B			
6		1	23	F	B			
7		1	16	F	B			
8		1	14	M	B			
9		1	12	F	B			
10		1	10	F	B			
11		1	8	F	B			
12		1	5	M	B			
13		1	3	F	B			
14	Martha Johnson	1	90	F	B			
15	William Rollins	1	25	M	B			
16		1	25	M	B			
17		1	25	F	B			
18		1	21	F	B			
19		1	7	F	B			
20		1	4	M	B			
21		1	2	F	B			
22		1	2	F	B			
23		1	1	F	B			
24		1	11	F	B			
25	John Baker	1	35	M	B			
26		1	18	F	B			
27		1	17	M	B			
28	Torquill McNeill	1	46	M	B			
29	Lewis McLeod	1	8	M	B			
30	Nancy McFarland	1	25	M	B			
31		1	23	F	B			
32	Neill McNeill	1	36	M	B			
33	Benjamin Muckle	1	35	F	B			
34		1	5	M	B			
35		1	3	F	B			
36		1	1	F	B			
37	John Sheppard	1	25	F	B			
38		1	11	M	B			
39		1	2	F	B			
40		1	3	M	B			
41	John Dalrymple	1	27	F	B			
42		1	8	M	B			

M 19
F 23

SCHEDULE 2.—Slave Inhabitants in in the County of *Moore* **State of** *N. Carolina*, **enumerated by me, on the** *20th* **day of** *September*, **1850.** *N. McCrummen* **Ass't Marshal.**

	NAMES OF SLAVE OWNERS.	Number of Slaves.	DESCRIPTION. Age.	Sex.	Colour.	Fugitives from the State.	Number manumitted.	Deaf & dumb, blind, insane, or idiotic.
	1	2	3	4	5	6	7	8
1		1	7	F	B			
2		1	4	F	B			
3		1	2	F	B			
4		1	9/12	F	B			
5	Joseph Thomas	1	25	m	B			
6		1	14	F	B			
7		1	9	m	B			
8	Rosanna Dalrymple	1	65	m	m			
9		1	60	F	B			
10		1	16	F	m			
11		1	13	F	B			
12		1	11	m	B			
13		1	4	m	B			
14	Samuel McAulay	1	44	m	B			
15		1	33	F	B			
16		1	5	m	B			
17		1	4/12	F	B			
18	Darias Thomas	1	37	F	B			
19		1	30	F	B			
20		1	25	F	B			
21		1	20	F	B			
22		1	6	F	B			
23		1	5	F	B			
24		1	8	m	B			
25		1	8	m	m			
26		1	5	F	B			
27	Tillman Thomas	1	27	F	B			
28		1	1	F	B			
29	Daniel Douglas	1	29	F	B			
30		1	15	m	B			
31		1	2	F	B			
32	Archibald Douglas	1	54	F	B			
33		1	50	m	B			
34		1	48	m	B			
35		1	27	m	B			
36		1	22	m	B			
37		1	20	F	B			
38		1	18	m	B			
39		1	15	m	B			
40		1	6	m	B			
41		1	4	F	B			
42		1	2	m	B			

M 18
F 24

	NAMES OF SLAVE OWNERS.	Number of Slaves.	DESCRIPTION. Age.	Sex.	Colour.	Fugitives from the State.	Number manumitted.	Deaf & dumb, blind, insane, or idiotic.
	1	2	3	4	5	6	7	8
1		1	14	F	B			
2	John Douglas	1	52	F	B			
3		1	35	F	B			
4		1	35	m	B			
5		1	32	m	B			
6		1	23	F	B			
7		1	18	F	B			
8		1	13	F	B			
9		1	13	m	B			
10		1	9	F	B			
11		1	5	F	B			
12		1	6	m	B			
13		1	4	m	m			
14		1	1	F	B			
15		1	8	F	B			
16		1	2	m	B			
17		1	31	F	B			
18	Penelope Thomas	1	23	F	B			
19		1	20	m	B			
20		1	19	m	B			
21		1	1	m	B			
22	Henderson Judd	1	60	F	B			
23		1	55	m	B			
24		1	24	m	B			
25		1	20	F	B			
26		1	17	m	B			
27		1	13	F	B			
28		1	12	m	B			
29		1	7	m	m			
30		1	8/12	m	m			
31	Sarah Cox	1	40	m	B			
32		1	30	F	B			
33		1	26	F	B			
34		1	11	m	B			
35		1	10	F	B			
36		1	10	F	B			
37		1	8	F	B			
38		1	4	m	B			
39		1	1	F	B			
40		1	6/12	m	B			
41	Charles Cox	1	24	m	B			
42		1	21	F	B			

M 20
F 22

SCHEDULE 2. Slave Inhabitants in ____________ in the County of Moore 344 State of N. Carolina, enumerated by me, on the 23d day of September, 1850. N. McCrummen Ass't Marshal.

	NAMES OF SLAVE OWNERS.	Number of Slaves.	DESCRIPTION. Age.	Sex.	Colour.	Fugitives from the State.	Number manumitted.	Deaf & dumb, blind, insane, or idiotic.
	1	2	3	4	5	6	7	8
1	Charles Cox	1	10	m	m			
2		1	9	m	m			
3		1	13	F	B			
4		1	2	F	B			
5	Abner E. Yarbrough	1	18	F	B			
6		1	10	F	B			
7		1	1	m	B			
8	Hugh C. McLean	1	38	m	B			
9		1	38	F	B			
10		1	32	F	B			
11		1	18	F	B			
12		1	13	m	B			
13		1	10	m	B			
14		1	6	F	m			
15		1	5	F	B			
16		1	4	m	B			
17		1	2	F	m			
18		1	2/12	m	m			
19	John McLeod	1	65	m	B			
20		1	40	m	B			
21		1	36	m	B			
22		1	50	F	B			
23		1	34	m	B			
24		1	25	m	B			
25		1	23	F	B			
26		1	20	F	B			
27		1	18	m	B			
28		1	16	m	B			
29		1	13	F	B			
30		1	6	m	B			
31		1	4	m	B			
32		1	2	F	B			
33	Elizabeth Wicker	1	35	F	m			
34		1	1	F	m			
35	Sarah Thomas	1	46	m	m			
36		1	48	F	m			
37		1	70	m	B			
38	William Berryman	1	28	F	m			
39		1	8	m	B			
40		1	6	m	B			
41		1	4	m	m			
42		1	1	F	m			

m 22
F 20

	NAMES OF SLAVE OWNERS.	Number of Slaves.	DESCRIPTION. Age.	Sex.	Colour.	Fugitives from the State.	Number manumitted.	Deaf & dumb, blind, insane, or idiotic.
	1	2	3	4	5	6	7	8
1	Robert McAulay	1	27	F	B			
2		1	5	m	B			
3		1	3	F	B			
4		1	1	m	B			
5	Elias Cox	1	9	F	B			
6	John Campbell	1	7	m	B			
7	Barbara McAulay	1	20	m	B			
8		1	60	F	B			
9		1	40	m	B			
10		1	30	F	B			
11		1	17	F	B			
12	Abel Kelly	1	50	m	B			
13	Thomas Harrington	1	37	m	B			
14		1	30	m	B			
15		1	27	m	B			
16		1	25	F	B			
17		1	24	F	B			
18		1	22	m	B			
19		1	22	m	B			
20		1	22	F	B			
21		1	11	F	B			
22		1	3	F	B			
23		1	3	F	B			
24		1	1	m	B			
25		1	6/12	F	B			
26		1	6/12	F	B			
27	Archibald Harrington	1	40	F	B			
28		1	17	m	B			
29		1	1	m	B			
30	Thomas I. Minter	1	55	F	B			
31		1	35	m	m			
32		1	17	m	B			
33		1	13	F	B			
34		1	6	F	B			
35	William Watson	1	32	F	B			
36		1	22	F	B			
37		1	20	m	B			
38		1	18	F	B			
39		1	1	F	B			
40		1	2/12	m	B			
41		1	27	m	B			
42	David Watson	1	20	F	B			

11m 8f

SCHEDULE 2.—Slave Inhabitants in ______ in the County of *Moore* State of *N. Carolina*, enumerated by me, on the *26th* day of *September* 1850. *N. McCrummen* Ass't Marshal.

	NAMES OF SLAVE OWNERS.	Number of Slaves.	Age.	Sex.	Colour.	Fugitives from the State.	Number manumitted.	Deaf & dumb, blind, insane, or idiotic.
	1	2	3	4	5	6	7	8
1	Sian Campbell	1	35	F	B			
2		1	5	F	B.			
3		1	3	m	B			
4	John Blackman	1	35	F	B.			
5		1	20	m	B			
6		1	16	F	B			
7		1	8	F	B			
8		1	5	m	B			
9		1	3	F	B			
10	Nathan Haight	1	43	F	B			
11		1	21	m	B			
12		1	16	F	B			
13		1	14	F	B.			
14		1	12	F	B			
15	Malcom B Watson	1	7	F	B.			
16	Elisha Watson	1	15	F	B			
17	Levi Gunter	1	13	F	B.			
18	W. Westley Dye	1	49	m	B.			
19	Evander McIver	1	52	F	B			
20		1	48	m	B.			
21		1	31	m	B			
22		1	26	F	B.			
23		1	18	m	B			
24		1	16	m	B			
25		1	13	m	B.			
26		1	7	m	B			
27		1	5	m	B.			
28		1	4	m	B.			
29		1	3/12	m	B.			
30	Daniel R. McIver	1	45	F	B.			
31	Mary McIver	1	50	m	B			
32		1	45	m	B.			
33		1	38	F	B			
34		1	22	F	B			
35		1	20	F	B			
36		1	35	m	B			
37		1	17	m	B			
38		1	15	F	B.			
39		1	12	F	B			
40		1	10	F	B.			
41		1	3	F	m			
42		1	2/12	m	B.			

m 19
F 23

	NAMES OF SLAVE OWNERS.	Number of Slaves.	Age.	Sex.	Colour.	Fugitives from the State.	Number manumitted.	Deaf & dumb, blind, insane, or idiotic.
	1	2	3	4	5	6	7	8
1	Duncan McIver	1	65	m	B.			
2		1	23	m	B			
3		1	18	F	B			
4		1	9	m	B.			
5	Hastin Gilmore	1	13	m	B.			
6	Mary McIver	1	46	m	B			
7		1	14	F	B			
8		1	7	F	B.			
9	Daniel B. McIver	1	30	m	B.			
10		1	18	F	B.			
11		1	12	F	B			
12	David W. Wicker	1	65	m	B.			
13	Newton Bryan	1	50	F	B.			
14		1	18	F	B.			
15		1	11/12	m	B			
16	George W. Watson	1	53	F	B.			
17		1	21	m	B.			
18	Joseph Cook	1	62	F	B.			
19		1	20	m	B			
20		1	7	m	B.			
21	Winship Bryant	1	36	F	B.			
22		1	23	m	B			
23		1	11	F	B.			
24		1	9	m	B.			
25		1	7	m	B			
26		1	3	m	B			
27		1	11/12	F	B.			
28	Evander S. McIver	1	40	F	B.			
29		1	21	m	B			
30		1	14	F	B.			
31	Wesley McIver	1	24	F	B.			
32		1	20	m	B			
33		1	16	m	B.			
34		1	14	F	B			
35		1	42	F	B.			
36		1	4	m	B.			
37		1	1	F	B			
38	Daniel Mathews	1	24	F	B			
39		1	13	F	B			
40		1	3	F	B			
41		1	1	m	B			
42	Thomas Wicker	1	46	F	B			

m 20
F 22

SCHEDULE 2.—Slave Inhabitants in ______________ **in the County of** Moore **State of** N. Carolina **enumerated by me, on the** 2nd **day of** October **, 1850.** N. McCrummen **Ass't Marshal.**

	NAMES OF SLAVE OWNERS.	Number of Slaves.	DESCRIPTION. Age.	Sex.	Colour.	Fugitives from the State.	Number manumitted.	Deaf & dumb, blind, insane, or idiotic.
	1	2	3	4	5	6	7	8
1	Thomas Wicker Sr.	1	40	m	B.			
2		1	15	m	B.			
3		1	12	F	B.			
4		1	8	m	B.			
5	William Petty	1	15	F	B.			
6	Flora McIver	1	26	F	B.			
7		1	21	m	B.			
8	John J. Gilmore	1	27	m	B.			
9		1	21	F	B.			
10		1	17	F	B.			
11		1	17	F	B.			
12		1	16	F	B.			
13		1	14	F	B.			
14		1	9	m	B.			
15		1	9	m	B.			
16		1	7	m	B.			
17		1	6	m	B.			
18	Green B. Gilmore	1	12	F	B.			
19	Jordan Wicker	1	13	m	B.			
20	John W. Stedman	1	74	F	B.			
21		1	13	F	B.			
22		1	10	m	B.			
23		1	6	m	B.			
24		1	17	m	B.			
25	Peter McIntyre	1	22	m	B.			
26	John McIver	1	50	m	B.			
27		1	40	m	B.			
28		1	24	F	B.			
29		1	24	F	B.			
30		1	7	F	B.			
31		1	5	m	B.			
32		1	4	F	B.			
33		1	4	F	B.			
34		1	2	m	B.			
35		1	2	m	B.			
36		1	1	m	B.			
37	Duncan M. R. McIntosh	1	24	F	B.			
38		1	13	F	B.			
39		1	1	m	B.			
40	William M. McIntosh	1	32	F	B.			
41		1	[illegible]2	F	B.			
42		1	8	F	B.			

m 21

	NAMES OF SLAVE OWNERS.	Number of Slaves.	DESCRIPTION. Age.	Sex.	Colour.	Fugitives from the State.	Number manumitted.	Deaf & dumb, blind, insane, or idiotic.
	1	2	3	4	5	6	7	8
1		1	7	F	B.			
2		1	4	F	m			
3		1	3	m	B.			
4		1	2	m	B.			
5		1	1/12	m	B.			
6		1	4/12	F	B.			
7	Richard M. Cole	1	23	F	B.			
8	Evander McGilvary	1	28	m	B.			
9	Thomas Cole	1	36	F	B.			
10		1	11	m	B.			
11		1	10	F	B.			
12		1	8	m	B.			
13		1	3	m	B.			
14		1	1	m	B.			
15	Benjamin Cole	1	14	m	B.			
16	Daniel M. McIntosh	1	22	F	B.			
17		1	18	F	B.			
18		1	15	m	B.			
19		1	9	F	B.			
20		1	7	F	B.			
21		1	3/12	F	B.			
22	Duncan Murchison	1	52	F	B.			
23		1	45	m	B.			
24		1	42	m	B.			
25		1	38	m	B.			
26		1	35	F	B.			
27		1	24	m	B.			
28		1	20	F	B.			
29		1	19	m	B.			
30		1	19	m	B.			
31		1	16	F	B.			
32		1	15	m	B.			
33		1	15	F	B.			
34		1	16	m	B.			
35		1	73	F	B.			
36		1	14	m	B.			
37		1	13	m	B.			
38		1	11	m	B.			
39		1	11	m	B.			
40		1	7	m	B.			
41		1	6	m	B.			
42		1	5	F	B.			

2f

SCHEDULE 2.—Slave Inhabitants in ________ **in the County of** Moore **State of** N. Carolina, **enumerated by me, on the** 5th **day of** October, **1850.** N. McCrummen **Ass't Marshal.**

	Names of Slave Owners. (1)	Number of Slaves. (2)	Description. Age. (3)	Description. Sex. (4)	Description. Colour. (5)	Fugitives from the State. (6)	Numbermanumitted. (7)	Deaf & dumb, blind, insane, or idiotic. (8)
1		1	2	F	B			
2	Charles McDowall	1	28	F	B			
3		1	8	m	m			
4		1	5	m	B			
5		1	2	m	m			
6		1	5/12	m	m			
7	Alexander Graham	1	20	m	B.			
8	Duncan Murchison	1	42	F	B.			
9		1	6	F	m			
10		1	4	m	B.			
11		1	2	m	m			
12	Dawson Tyson	1	11	F	B			
13	Elias B. Harrington	1	8	F	m			
14	James R. Patterson	1	40	F	B			
15		1	4	m	B.			
16		1	1	m	m			
17	Neill Thompson	1	16	F	B.			
18	Samuel Paisley	1	53	F	B.			
19		1	33	m	B.			
20		1	24	m	B.			
21	Josiah Tyson	1	50	F	B.			
22		1	29	F	B			
23		1	27	F	B			
24		1	13	F	B.			
25		1	12	F	B.			
26		1	11	F	B.			
27		1	11	F	B.			
28		1	7	m	B			
29		1	5	m	B.			
30		1	4	m	B.			
31		1	1	m	B.			
32		1	7	F	B			
33		1	6	F	B			
34	Catharine Murchison	1	18	F	B.			
35		1	17	F	B			
36		1	13	m	B.			
37	Gilbert McRae	1	70	F	B.			
38		1	24	m	B			
39	Daniel Campbell	1	32	F	B.			
40		1	9	F	B			
41		1	6	F	B			
42	William C. Campbell	1	31	m	B			

m 18

	Names of Slave Owners. (1)	Number of Slaves. (2)	Description. Age. (3)	Description. Sex. (4)	Description. Colour. (5)	Fugitives from the State. (6)	Numbermanumitted. (7)	Deaf & dumb, blind, insane, or idiotic. (8)
1		1	24	F	B.			
2		1	24	F	B.			
3		1	24	F	B.			
4		1	20	m	B.			
5		1	8	F	B.			
6		1	6	F	B.			
7		1	4	F	B.			
8		1	2	F	B.			
9	Robert A. Stuart	1	24	F	B.			
10		1	20	m	B.			
11		1	6	F	B			
12		1	3/12	F	B.			
13	Charity Roberts	1	60	m	m			
14		1	55	F	B.			
15		1	40	m	B.			
16		1	40	m	B.			
17		1	40	F	B.			
18		1	40	m	B.			
19		1	28	F	B.			
20		1	13	F	B.			
21		1	7	F	B.			
22		1	5	m	B.			
23		1	3	m	B.			
24		1	7/12	m	B.			
25	Allen W. Jones	1	85	F	B			
26		1	22	m	B			
27		1	19	F	B.			
28		1	19	m	B.			
29		1	13	m	B.			
30		1	19	F	B.			
31		1	12	F	B.			
32	George Wilcox	1	24	m	B			
33		1	57	F	B.			
34		1	26	m	B			
35		1	22	F	B.			
36		1	19	F	B.			
37		1	18	m	B.			
38		1	4	F	B			
39		1	2	F	B			
40		1	2	m	B			
41		1	1	m	B			
42	William Watson	1	37	m	B.			

m 18

SCHEDULE 2. — Slave Inhabitants in in the County of Moore State of N. Carolina, enumerated by me, on the 11th day of October, 1850. N. McCrummen Ass't Marshal.

	NAMES OF SLAVE OWNERS.	Number of Slaves.	Age.	Sex.	Colour.	Fugitives from the State.	Number manumitted.	Deaf & dumb, blind, insane, or idiotic.
	1	2	3	4	5	6	7	8
1	William Watson Sr	1	20	F.	B			
2		1	18	F.	B			
3		1	8	m	B			
4		1	4	m	B			
5		1	1	m	B			
6	Harry McFadyen	1	18	m	B			
7	Samuel McDonald	1	39	F.	B			
8		1	21	F.	B			
9		1	20	F.	B			
10		1	12	m	B			
11		1	8	m	B			
12		1	6	F.	B			
13		1	4	F.	B			
14		1	1	m	B			
15	Hugh McDonald	1	35	m	B			
16		1	23	m	B			
17		1	2	m	B			
18	Joseph Mounger	1	12	m	B			
19	Kenneth Worthy	1	36	m	B			
20		1	10	F.	B			
21	Hardy Patterson	1	29	m	B			
22		1	14	m	B			
23	Norman Ferguson	1	30	m	B			
24		1	29	F.	B			
25		1	25	F.	B			
26		1	12	m	B			
27		1	7	m	B			
28		1	6	F.	B			
29		1	4	F.	B			
30		1	1	F.	B			
31	Martha Hancock	1	45	F.	B			
32		1	9	m	B			
33		1	7	F.	B			
34		1	5	F.	B			
35	Evander C. Curry	1	90	m	B			
36		1	80	F.	B			
37		1	50	F.	B			
38		1	50	m	B			
39		1	45	F.	B			
40		1	13	m	B			
41		1	11	F.	B			
42		1	9	m	B			

m 22 f 20

	NAMES OF SLAVE OWNERS.	Number of Slaves.	Age.	Sex.	Colour.	Fugitives from the State.	Number manumitted.	Deaf & dumb, blind, insane, or idiotic.
	1	2	3	4	5	6	7	8
1		1	13	m	B			
2	Evander McNair	1	21	F.	B			
3		1	3	F.	m			
4	Brinkley Phillips	1	17	m	B			
5	Flora McLeod	1	40	F.	B			
6		1	12	m	B			
7		1	10	F.	B			
8		1	4	F.	B			
9		1	3	m	B			
10		1	4/12	m	B.			
11	John A. McKithen	1	37	F.	B			
12		1	19	F.	B			
13		1	12	F.	B			
14		1	10	F.	B			
15		1	8	m	B			
16		1	5	F.	B			
17	Malcom Curry	1	55	m	B			
18	Duncan McIver	1	12	F.	B			
19	Lucretia Rhodes	1	20	F.	B			
20		1	11	m	B			
21		1	3	F.	B			
22	John Oats	1	58	m	B			
23		1	28	m	B			
24		1	27	F.	B			
25		1	2	m	B			
26		1	10	F.	B			
27	Charles Gilchrist	1	20	F.	B			
28		1	15	m	m			
29		1	9	F.	B			
30		1	5/12	m	B			
31	William Wadsworth	1	30	F.	B			
32		1	20	F.	B			
33		1	23	m	B			
34		1	9	F.	B			
35		1	7	F.	B			
36		1	5	m	B			
37		1	3	m	B			
38		1	3	m	B			
39		1	2/12	m	B			
40	William Wadsworth	1	13	m	B			
41	David Johnson	1	4	m	B.			
42	Daniel Short	1	38	F.	B			

7m 0f

m 20 f 22

SCHEDULE 2.—Slave Inhabitants in in the County of *Moore* State of *N. Carolina*, enumerated by me, on the *17th* day of *October*, 1850. *N. McCrummen* Ass't Marshal.

	Names of Slave Owners.	Number of Slaves.	Age.	Sex.	Colour.	Fugitives from the State.	Number manumitted.	Deaf & dumb, blind, insane, or idiotic.
	1	2	3	4	5	6	7	8
1		1	23	m	B			
2		1	21	m	B			
3		1	17	m	B			
4		1	15	m	B			
5		1	4	F	B			
6	George McRae	1	22	m	B			
7	Neill McLeod	1	40	m	B			
8		1	32	F	B.			
9		1	27	m	B			
10		1	19	m	B			
11		1	18	m	B			
12		1	16	F	B			
13		1	15	m	B			
14		1	13	m	B			
15		1	11	m	B			
16		1	10	F	B			
17		1	8	F	B			
18		1	6	F	B			
19		1	3	F	B			
20		1	1/10	F	B			
21	Daniel Campbell	1	37	m	B.			
22	Finlay Campbell	1	35	F	B			
23	Margaret Sinclair	1	45	F	B			
24		1	40	F	B			
25		1	40	m	B			
26		1	22	F.	B			
27		1	21	m	B			
28		1	17	m	B			
29		1	11	F	B			
30		1	7	m	B			
31		1	4	F	B			
32		1	1	F	B			
33	William D. Harrington	1	40	m	B			
34		1	40	m	M			
35		1	37	m	B			
36		1	36	m	B			
37		1	30	m	B			
38		1	60	m	B			
39		1	33	F	B			
40		1	30	F	B			
41		1	24	F	B			
42		1	19	F.	B			

M 23
F 19

	Names of Slave Owners.	Number of Slaves.	Age.	Sex.	Colour.	Fugitives from the State.	Number manumitted.	Deaf & dumb, blind, insane, or idiotic.
	1	2	3	4	5	6	7	8
1		1	16	F	B			
2		1	13	m	B			
3		1	12	m	B			
4		1	10	m	B			
5		1	6	F	B			
6		1	5	F	B			
7		1	3	m	B			
8		1	6	m	B			
9		1	5	F	m			
10		1	5	m	B			
11		1	2	F	B			
12		1	3	m	m			
13		1	2	F	m			
14		1	2	F	m			
15		1	1	m	B			
16		1	1	F	B			
17		1	4/12	m	B			
18	William D. Tyson	1	35	F	B			
19		1	21	m	B.			
20		1	19	m	B			
21		1	18	F	B			
22		1	17	m	B			
23		1	15	m	m			
24		1	11	F	B.			
25		1	4	m	M			
26		1	1	F	B			
27	Lydia Roberts	1	35	m	B.			
28		1	23	m	B			
29		1	25	m	B.			
30		1	20	m	B			
31		1	16	m	B			
32		1	13	m	B			
33		1	20	F	B.			
34		1	15	F	B			
35		1	13	F	B			
36		1	12	F	B			
37		1	1	F	B			
38	Neill Tyson	1	50	F.	B			
39		1	23	m	B			
40		1	23	m	B.			
41		1	20	F	B			
42		1	4	F	B			

M 22
F 20

SCHEDULE 2.—Slave Inhabitants in ______ in the County of Moore State of N. Carolina, enumerated by me, on the 19th day of October, 1850. N. McCrummen Ass't Marshal.

Line	Names of Slave Owners. (1)	Number of Slaves. (2)	Age. (3)	Sex. (4)	Colour. (5)	Fugitives from the State. (6)	Number manumitted. (7)	Deaf & dumb, blind, insane, or idiotic. (8)
1		1	2	m	B			
2		1	1/12	F	B			
3	Nancy McIver	1	30	F	m			
4		1	8	m	B			
5		1	8	m	B			
6		1	4	F	m			
7		1	2	m	m			
8	M Bingham	1	73	m	B			
9		1	70	F	B			
10		1	52	F	B			
11		1	40	m	B			
12		1	32	m	B			
13		1	24	F	B			
14		1	22	F	B			
15		1	21	m	B			
16		1	12	m	B			
17		1	11	F	B			
18		1	8	F	B			
19		1	6	m	B			
20		1	5	m	B			
21		1	6	m	B			
22		1	4	m	B			
23		1	2	m	B			
24		1	6/12	m	B			
25		1	1	m	B			
26	John Murchison	1	80	F	B			
27		1	70	m	B			
28		1	60	F	B			
29		1	50	m	B			
30		1	48	m	B			
31		1	40	F	B			
32		1	28	m	B			
33		1	25	m	B			
34		1	22	m	B			
35		1	19	m	B			
36		1	19	m	B			
37		1	9	m	B			
38		1	7	m	B			
39		1	15	F	B			
40	Charles Chalmers	1	85	F	B			
41		1	75	F	B			
42		1	60	m	B			

Line	Names of Slave Owners. (1)	Number of Slaves. (2)	Age. (3)	Sex. (4)	Colour. (5)	Fugitives from the State. (6)	Number manumitted. (7)	Deaf & dumb, blind, insane, or idiotic. (8)
1		1	60	m	B			
2		1	58	m	B			
3		1	56	F	B			
4		1	51	m	B			
5		1	43	m	B			
6		1	36	m	B			
7		1	26	m	B			
8		1	24	m	B			
9		1	25	m	B			
10		1	28	m	B			
11		1	26	m	B			
12		1	23	m	B			
13		1	22	m	B			
14		1	20	m	B			
15		1	20	m	B			
16		1	17	m	B			
17		1	14	m	B			
18		1	10	m	B			
19		1	9	m	B			
20		1	8	m	B			
21		1	7	m	B			
22		1	2	m	B			
23		1	2	F	B			
24		1	17	F	B			
25		1	9	F	B			
26		1	6	F	B			
27		1	5	F	B			
28		1	4	F	B			
29		1	2	F	B			
30		1	1	F	B			
31		1	65	F	B			
32	Jepe Hedgepeth	1	34	F	B			
33		1	28	F	B			
34		1	15	m	B			
35		1	12	m	B			
36		1	11	F	B			
37		1	7	m	B			
38		1	6	m	B			
39		1	5	m	B			
40		1	3	m	B			
41		1	4	m	B			
42		1	4	F	B			

SCHEDULE 2.—Slave Inhabitants in ______________ **in the County of** Moore **State of** N. Carolina, **enumerated by me, on the** 22nd **day of** October, **1850.** N. McCrummen **Ass't Marshal.**

	NAMES OF SLAVE OWNERS.	Number of Slaves.	DESCRIPTION. Age.	Sex.	Colour.	Fugitives from the State.	Numbermanumitted.	Deaf & dumb, blind, insane, or idiotic.
	1	2	3	4	5	6	7	8
1		1	1	m	B			
2		1	9/12	m	B.			
3	Mary Cheek	1	40	F.	B.			
4		1	35	F.	B.			
5		1	31	m	B			
6		1	28	F	B			
7		1	16	F	m			
8		1	14	m	B			
9		1	12	F	B			
10		1	11	m	B			
11		1	11	F	B			
12		1	8	F	B			
13		1	7	F	B			
14		1	7	m	m			
15		1	1	F	B			
16		1	9/12	m	B.			
17		1	1	m	B			
18	Jesse Womble	1	44	m	B			
19		1	32	m	B.			
20		1	30	F	B			
21		1	19	F	B			
22		1	18	m	B			
23		1	11	F	B			
24		1	8	m	B			
25		1	7	m	B			
26		1	6	m	B			
27		1	5	F	B			
28		1	4	m	B			
29		1	2	m	B			
30		1	2	m	B			
31	Donald Street	1	65	m	B			
32		1	65	F	B			
33		1	45	m	B			
34		1	42	m	B			
35		1	40	m	B			
36		1	36	F	B			
37		1	12	F	B			
38		1	12	m	B			
39		1	10	F	B			
40		1	8	m	B			
41		1	8	m	B			
42		1	5	F	B			

	NAMES OF SLAVE OWNERS.	Number of Slaves.	DESCRIPTION. Age.	Sex.	Colour.	Fugitives from the State.	Numbermanumitted.	Deaf & dumb, blind, insane, or idiotic.
	1	2	3	4	5	6	7	8
1		1	4	m	B			
2		1	3	F	B			
3		1	1	m	B			
4	James C. Davis	1	55	F	B			
5		1	21	m	m			
6		1	19	F.	B			
7		1	6/12	m	m			
8	Augustus B. Pharr	1	45	F	B			
9		1	20	m	B			
10		1	15	m	B			
11		1	12	F	B			
12		1	12	F	B			
13		1	12	m	B			
14	Ann Street	1	65	m	B.			
15		1	65	m	B.			
16		1	34	F	B.			
17		1	24	F	B.			
18		1	18	m	B.			
19		1	16	m	B.			
20		1	13	F	B.			
21		1	11	m	B.			
22		1	9	F	B.			
23		1	8	m	B			
24		1	8	m	B			
25		1	8	F.	B.			
26		1	5	F	B			
27		1	5	F	B.			
28		1	5	F	B.			
29		1	5	m	B			
30		1	3	m	B			
31		1	3	m	B			
32		1	2	F.	B			
33	Richard Street	1	70	F	B.			
34		1	7	m	B.			
35		1	7	F	B.			
36		1	6	F	B.			
37		1	4	F	B.			
38		1	4	F	B			
39		1	2	m	B.			
40	Anderson Jones	1	9	F	B			
41	George Facher	1	60	m	B			
42								

SCHEDULE 2.—Slave Inhabitants in ______ **in the County of** Moore **State of** N. Carolina**, enumerated by me, on the** 24th **day of** October**, 1850.** N. McCrummen **Ass't Marshal.**

	NAMES OF SLAVE OWNERS.	Number of Slaves.	DESCRIPTION. Age.	Sex.	Colour.	Fugitives from the State.	Number manumitted.	Deaf & dumb, blind, insane, or idiotic.
	1	2	3	4	5	6	7	8
1	George Foshee	1	28	m	B.			
2		1	23	m	B.			
3		1	32	F	B.			
4		1	28	F	B.			
5		1	20	F	B.			
6		1	19	F	B.			
7		1	18	m	B.			
8		1	12	m	B.			
9		1	11	F	B.			
10		1	3	m	m			
11		1	2	m	m			
12	Martha H. Alston	1	49	m	B.			
13		1	50	F.	B.			
14		1	18	F.	B.			
15		1	16	F.	B.			
16	Nathaniel Alston	1	21	m	B.			
17		1	20	m	B.			
18		1	20	m	B.			
19		1	20	m	B.			
20		1	36	F	B.			
21	Isaac N. Clegg	1	30	F	B.			
22		1	26	m	B.			
23		1	23	F	B.			
24		1	21	m	B.			
25		1	19	F	B.			
26		1	15	m	B.			
27		1	20	m	B.			
28		1	8	F	B.			
29		1	6	m	m			
30		1	4	F	B.			
31		1	2	F	B.			
32		1	1	m	B.			
33	Ann McNeill	1	39	m	B.			
34		1	31	m	B.			
35		1	27	F	B.			
36		1	1	m	B.			
37		1	7/12	m	B.			
38	Robert Goldston	1	40	m	B.			
39		1	25	m	B.			
40		1	21	F	B.			
41		1	18	F	B.			
42		1	16	F	B.			

	NAMES OF SLAVE OWNERS.	Number of Slaves.	DESCRIPTION. Age.	Sex.	Colour.	Fugitives from the State.	Number manumitted.	Deaf & dumb, blind, insane, or idiotic.
	1	2	3	4	5	6	7	8
1		1	13	m	B.			
2		1	8	F	B.			
3		1	2	m	B.			
4	Benjamin P. Person	1	60	m	B.			
5		1	45	F	B.			
6		1	34	m	B.			
7		1	18	F	B.			
8		1	16	F	B.			
9		1	7	F	B.			
10		1	4	F	B.			
11		1	3	F	B.			
12	William M. Johnson	1	40	F.	B.			
13		1	30	m	B.			
14		1	20	F	B.			
15		1	17	F	B.			
16		1	14	m	m			
17		1	12	m	B.			
18		1	12	F.	B.			
19		1	9	F	B.			
20		1	9	m	B.			
21		1	8	m	B.			
22		1	5	F	B.			
23		1	2	m	B.			
24		1	4/12	m	m			
25		1	38	F	m			
26	James Cavendish	1	60	F	B.			
27		1	22	m	B.			
28	John Myrick	1	40	F	B.			
29		1	18	F.	B.			
30		1	10	m	B.			
31	James Gaines	1	74	m	B.			
32		1	70	F	B.			
33		1	45	m	B.			
34		1	49	F	B.			
35		1	25	F	B.			
36		1	18	m	B.			
37		1	16	F	B.			
38		1	15	F	B.			
39		1	4	m	B.			
40		1	2	F	B.			
41	Huldah Myrick	1	53	F.	B.			
42		1	11	m	B.			

8 m 2f

SCHEDULE 2.—Slave Inhabitants in in the County of *Moore* **State of** *N. Carolina*, **enumerated by me, on the** *28th* **day of** *October*, **1850.** *N. McCrummen* **Ass't Marshal.**

Line	NAMES OF SLAVE OWNERS.	Number of Slaves.	DESCRIPTION. Age.	Sex.	Colour.	Fugitives from the State.	Number manumitted.	Deaf & dumb, blind, insane, or idiotic.
	1	2	3	4	5	6	7	8
1	John Garner	1	80	F	B.			
2		1	70	F	B.			
3		1	57	F	m			
4		1	40	m	m			
5	Lewis Garner	1	35	m	B.			
6	Enoch S. Brown	1	76	m	B.			
7	John Maness	1	38	F	B.			
8		1	23	m	B.			
9		1	18	F	B			
10		1	5	F	B.			
11		1	3	m	B.			
12		1	2	F	B			
13		1	2/12	F	B			
14	James M. Garner	1	18	F	B.			
15	Wyatt Williamson	1	38	F	m			
16		1	8	m	B.			
17		1	6	m	B			
18		1	3	F	B			
19		1	4/12	m	B			
20	Henry Yow	1	21	F	B.			
21		1	2	m	B			
22		1	2/12	F	B			
23	Mathew Davis	1	25	m	B			
24		1	20	F	B			
25		1	11	m	B.			
26		1	9	m	B			
27		1	3	F	B			
28		1	1	m	B.			
29	Jeremiah Williams	1	40	F	B			
30		1	23	m	B.			
31		1	20	m	B			
32		1	15	F	B.			
33		1	12	F	B			
34		1	10	m	B			
35		1	8	F	B			
36	Bailey Williamson	1	103	m	B			
37		1	80	F	B			
38	Anderson S. Moody	1	24	F	B			
39		1	20	F	B.			
40		1	4	m	B			
41		1	2	F	B.			
42		1	2/12	m	B			

m 19

Line	NAMES OF SLAVE OWNERS.	Number of Slaves.	DESCRIPTION. Age.	Sex.	Colour.	Fugitives from the State.	Number manumitted.	Deaf & dumb, blind, insane, or idiotic.
	1	2	3	4	5	6	7	8
1	A. S. Moody Dec	1	6	F	m			
2	William Wright	1	50	F	B.			
3		1	28	F	B.			
4		1	25	F	B.			
5		1	8	m	B			
6		1	6	F	B			
7		1	1	F	B.			
8	John Dunlap	1	40	F	B.			
9		1	29	m	B.			
10		1	5	F	B.			
11	Thomas Brown	1	11	m	B.			
12	Bethuel Coffin	1	7	F	B.			
13	John Cagle	1	65	F	B.			
14		1	37	F	B.			
15		1	35	m	B.			
16		1	20	F	B.			
17		1	18	m	B.			
18		1	16	F	B.			
19		1	13	F	B.			
20		1	11	F	B			
21		1	9	F	B.			
22		1	6	F	B			
23		1	3	m	B.			
24		1	1	m	B			
25	Upshur Furr	1	48	F	B.			
26		1	30	m	B.			
27		1	21	m	B.			
28		1	15	F	B.			
29		1	13	m	B.			
30	Nathaniel Marley	1	9	m	B.			
31		1	9	F	B.			
32	Alexander Kennedy	1	15	F	B.			
33	Avington Britt	1	15	F	B.			
34	Mary Deaton	1	9	F	B.			
35	Catharine McDonald	1	7	F	B.			
36	Catharine McDonald	1	18	m	B.			
37	Isaac Deaton	1	30	m	B.			
38		1	12	F	B			
39	Angus McKinnon	1	41	F	B.			
40		1	36	F	B.			
41		1	30	m	B			
42		1	18	m	B			

m 15

SCHEDULE 2.—Slave Inhabitants in ______________ in the County of *Moore* 869 **State of** *N. Carolina*, **enumerated by me, on the** *6th* **day of** *November*, **1850.** *N. McCrummen* **Ass't Marshal.**

NAMES OF SLAVE OWNERS.	Number of Slaves.	Age.	Sex.	Colour.	Fugitives from the State.	Number manumitted.	Deaf & dumb, blind, insane, or idiotic.
1	2	3	4	5	6	7	8
Norman McKinnon	1	24	F	B.			
	1	22	F.	B.			
	1	13	m	B.			
	1	9	m	B.			
	1	3	F.	B.			
	1	2	F.	B.			
Alexander Morrison	1	34	F.	B.			
	1	13	F.	m			
	1	11	m	m			
	1	8	m	B.			
	1	6	F.	B.			
	1	4	F	B.			
	1	2	m	B			
Angus Morrison	1	38	m	B.			
Ifabella Mathison	1	50	F	B.			
	1	48	F.	B.			
	1	21	m	B.			
	1	19	F.	B.			
	1	13	m	B.			
	1	10	m	B.			
	1	10	m	B.			
	1	8	F.	B.			
	1	8	F.	B.			
	1	7	F	B.			
John R. Ritter	1	35	m	B.			
	1	30	m	B			
	1	30	F	M			
	1	25	m	B			
	1	12	F.	m			
	1	10	m	m			
	1	8	m	m			
	1	5	m	m			
Noah Richardson	1	26	F	B.			
	1	25	m	B.			
	1	24	F.	B.			
	1	16	F	B.			
	1	9	F.	B.			
	1	4	m	B.			
	1	3	m	B.			
	1	2/12	F.	B.			
John McLeode	1	60	F.	B.			
	1	45	m	B.			

NAMES OF SLAVE OWNERS.	Number of Slaves.	Age.	Sex.	Colour.	Fugitives from the State.	Number manumitted.	Deaf & dumb, blind, insane, or idiotic.
1	2	3	4	5	6	7	8
	1	24	F	B			
	1	3	m	B.			
	1	5/12	m	B.			
Marah Stutts	1	35	m	B.			
George M. Hunsucker	1	32	F	B.			
	1	2	m	B.			
	1	1/12	F	B			
Cornelius Sheilds	1	44	m	B.			
	1	32	m	B			
	1	30	F.	B			
	1	10	F.	B.			
	1	8	m	B.			
	1	6	F.	B.			
	1	5	m	B.			
	1	2	m	B.			
Amelia Jones	1	26	F.	B.			
Hugh Kelly	1	40	F	B.			
	1	16	F	B.			
	1	13	M	B.			
Lydia Cockman	1	8	F.	B.			
William Sewell	1	10	m	B.			
James Dowdy	1	25	F	B.			
	1	13	F	B.			
	1	11	m	B			
	1	5	m	B.			
	1	1	m	B.			
Presley Caddell	1	18	F.	B.			
	1	12	F	B.			
	1	10	m	B.			
	1	1	m	B.			
Mark Russell	1	29	F	B.			
	1	20	m	B.			
	1	18	F	B.			
Henry Stutts	1	45	m	B.			
	1	22	F	B.			
Bryant Borroughs	1	65	F.	B.			
	1	60	F.	B.			
	1	60	m	B.			
	1	50	m	B.			
	1	50	F.	m			
	1	27	F.	B.			
	1	36	m	B.			

m 20 f 22 5m 7f m 21 f 21

SCHEDULE 2.—Slave Inhabitants in ______ **in the County of** *Moore* **State of** *N. Carolina*, **enumerated by me, on the** *14th* **day of** *November*, **1850.** *N. McCrummen* **Ass't Marshal**

	Names of Slave Owners.	Number of Slaves.	Description: Age.	Description: Sex.	Description: Colour.	Fugitives from the State.	Number manumitted.	Deaf & dumb, blind, insane, or idiotic.
	1	2	3	4	5	6	7	8
1		1	33	F	B.			
2		1	22	F	B.			
3		1	20	m	B.			
4		1	14	F	B.			
5		1	12	m	B.			
6		1	8	F	B.			
7		1	8	m	B.			
8		1	7	m	B.			
9		1	5	F	B.			
10		1	5	F	B.			
11		1	3	m	B.			
12		1	3	m	B.			
13		1	3	F	B.			
14		1	5/12	F	B.			
15		1	3/12	m	B.			
16	Abram Stutts	1	55	F	B.			
17		1	21	F	B.			
18		1	4	F	B.			
19	William Ritter	1	10	F	B.			
20	Eleazer Sowell	1	24	m	B.			
21	Jesse G. Sowell	1	8	F	B.			
22		1	6	m	B.			
23	Angus McCaskill	1	11	F	B.			
24	Willis D. Dowd	1	25	F	B.			
25		1	16	m	B.			
26		1	14	m	B.			
27		1	5	m	B.			
28	John Stutts	1	40	F	B.			
29		1	4	m	B.			
30		1	2	F	B.			
31	George T. Morgan	1	18	F	m			
32	Edmund Holland	1	30	F	B.			
33		1	16	F	B.			
34		1	14	F	B.			
35		1	12	F	B.			
36		1	10	F	B.			
37		1	8	m	B.			
38		1	6	F	B.			
39		1	4	m	B.			
40		1	1	F	B.			
41	Reuben Allen	1	30	m	B.			
42	Lockey Allen	1	27	F	B.			

	Names of Slave Owners.	Number of Slaves.	Description: Age.	Description: Sex.	Description: Colour.	Fugitives from the State.	Number manumitted.	Deaf & dumb, blind, insane, or idiotic.
	1	2	3	4	5	6	7	8
1	Alexander Leach	1	55	F	B.			
2		1	35	F	B.			
3		1	29	F	B.			
4		1	17	F	B.			
5	Jesse Smitherman	1	45	m	m			
6		1	45	F	B.			
7		1	26	F	m			
8		1	23	F	m			
9		1	22	F	m			
10		1	21	F	m			
11		1	20	F	m			
12		1	18	F	B.			
13		1	16	m	B.			
14		1	13	F	B.			
15		1	12	m	B.			
16		1	11	F	B.			
17		1	9	F	B.			
18		1	8	m	m			
19		1	7	m	m			
20		1	6	F	B.			
21		1	5	F	B.			
22		1	4	m	B.			
23		1	2	m	B.			
24		1	3	F	m			
25		1	3	m	m			
26		1	1	F	B.			
27	Hayman Miller	1	26	F	B.			
28		1	8	F	B.			
29	Stephen Davis	1	24	F	B.			
30		1	21	F	B.			
31		1	9	F	B.			
32		1	7	m	B.			
33		1	7	F	B.			
34		1	6	m	B.			
35		1	4	m	B.			
36		1	4/12	m	B.			
37		1	1/12	m	B.			
38	Peter Shamburger	1	23	m	B.			
39		1	21	F	B.			
40		1	16	m	B.			
41		1	1	m	B.			
42	Lydia Shamburger	1	28	m	B.			

12 Sheets

Schedule 5.—Products of Industry in ______ in the County of Moore 421 State N. Carolina during the Year ending June 1, 1850, as enumerated by me, N. McCrummen Ass't Marshal.

Name of Corporation, Company, or Individual, producing Articles to the Annual Value of $500.	Name of Business, Manufacture, or Product.	Capital invested in Real and Personal Estate in the Business.	Raw Material used, including Fuel. Quantities.	Kinds.	Values.	Kind of motive power, machinery, structure, or resource.	Average number of hands employed. Male.	Female.	Wages. Average monthly cost of male labor.	Average monthly cost of female labor.	Annual Product. Quantities.	Kinds.	Values.
1	2	3	4	5	6	7	8	9	10	11	12	13	14
Duncan Keith	Shoemaker	$ 250	100 sides	Leather	$ 200	Hand	2		$45		300 Prs	Shoes & boots	$ 900
J. C. Gardner	Flour & corn mill	1000	2000 Bu	Wheat	1600	Water	1		20		500 Bls	Flour	2000
" "	" "		500 Bu	Corn	300	Runstones	"		"		500 Bush	Meal	375
H. C. Kelly	Flour & Corn mill	2000	3000 Bu	Wheat	2400	Water	1		20		600 Bls	Flour	3000
" "	" "		3000 Bu	Corn	1800	Runstones	"		"		3000 Bush	Meal	2250
" "	Saw mill	300	500	Stocks	300	Water & steam	4		60		190000 feet	Lumber	1520
J. B. & A. Kearn	Flour & corn mill	1200	2500 Bu	Wheat	2000	Water	1		10		510 Bls	Flour	2500
" "	" "		500 Bu	Corn	300	Runstones	"		"		500 Bush	Meal	350
		4-750			8-950		9		155				12-595

5

SCHEDULE 4.—Productions of Agriculture in [illegible] **in the**
enumerated by me, on the 12th **day of** August **1850.**

	Name of Owner, Agent, or Manager of the Farm.	Acres of Land. Improved.	Unimproved.	Cash value of Farm.	Value of Farming Implements and Machinery.	Live Stock, June 1st, 1850. Horses.	Asses and Mules.	Milch Cows.	Working Oxen.	Other Cattle.	Sheep.	Swine.	Value of Live Stock.	Wheat, bushels of.	Rye, bushels of.	Indian Corn, bushels of.	Oats, bushels of.	Rice, lbs. of.	Tobacco, lbs. of.
	1	2	3	4	5	6	7	8	9	10	11	12	13	14	15	16	17	18	19
1	Lockart Fry	30	45	100	10	1		1					50	30		150	60		
2	Ivor D. Patterson	110	1190	600	25	3		4		4		24	290	14		300	150	600	
3	Elizabeth McDonald	25	75	100	6	2		4		2		10	147			150	15		
4	James Bryant	135	265	2000	65	3		4		15	9	32	304	40		375	100		
5	Jacob Settle	150	450	1500	200	4		5		4	5	50	300	42		500	30		
6	William M. Person	190	500	4000	90	5		4		4		25	201	100		200	35		
7	John E. Jackson	40	100	400	50	2		3		2			156	30		300	20		
8	Samuel Barrett	500	500	2000	250	8	5	12		10	26	80	976	250		2000	400		
9	William J. McIntosh	50	152	200	100	2		3		4	6	10	175	40		300	100		20
10	Benjamin Medlin	200	257	1400	15	3		6		10	40	32	212	40		400	60		20
11	Neill McIntosh	50	200	500	12	1		3		2	4	9	135			175	60		
12	Duncan McIntosh	30	40	300	5	1		2		1	15	12	92			150	30		
13	Samuel McIntosh	40	288	300	50	3		3		6		20	150			200	75		
14	Mary McIntosh	60	140	150	10	1		4		3		28	171	50		500	50		
15	John J. McIntosh	100	460	600	65	3		8			8	30	205	55		400	25		
16	William Bryant	40	150	300	15	3		3		4		20	222	45		300	15		
17	William R. Fry	350	600	4000	175	1	4	6		30	3	40	213	50		1000	200		
18	Neill Caddell	80	150	550	35	3		6		9	13	36	287	22		400	100		
19	Catharine Lawhon	40	200	1000	6	2		2		3		10	108	12		300			
20	Isaiah Lawhon	30	100	250	3	1		2		4		8	117	15		100	10		
21	Stephen Davis	100	285	750	75	4		4		6	10	50	270	50		400	30		
22	William Moore	40	200	650	70	4		3		4	20	12	221	30		200	100		
23	Mary A. Sewell	40	50	350	10	2		2		2	10	12	178			200	25		
24	George McIntosh	40	149	500	35	5		4		8		15	218	20		400	75		
25	Dempsey Sewell	100	600	2000	5	3		7		3	25	32	209	50		250	75		
26	Daniel H. Muse	50	100	400	60	2		2		4	8	9	161	37		150	50		
27	John T. Ritter	12	72	200	15	1		3		1		22	78			100			
28	Alexander Kelly	400	2300	8500	350	8	5	14		35	7	100	1147	300		3100	400		
29	George E. Muse	30	48	300	55	2		1		2		17	210	22		100	100		
30	James B. Muse	40	60	400	20	3		5		2	20	10	200	25		100	75		
31	Henderson	40	220	400	12	2		2		3	5	5	127	47		175	20		
32	Alexander W. Campbell	50	250	600	10	2		5		8	15	14	228	41		500	20		
33	Laughlin Kelly	100	465	800	100	3		7		10	14	25	275	71		400	200		
34	Lemuel Muse	25	110	250	10	2		1		5	15	15	150	12		105	10		
35	Augustus McNeill	35	150	1000	75	2		3		2	[illegible]	12	263			200			
36	Samuel C. Bruce	30	400	1000	200	3		3				40	400			100			
37	William Barrett	300	400	975	30	6		4		8	40	55	495	25		1000	400		
38	Hugh McDonald	60	750	500	100	2		5		16	20	50	376	14		250	10		
39	John McDonald	20	300	300	5	1		4		7	10	12	187			50			
40	Daniel McDonald	25	700	300	10	2		1		4	7	22	187			105	10		
41	Alexander McDonald	60	180	300	25	1		12		8	20	8	241	1640		11	[illegible]		
		3747	13581	41625	2511	112	14	174		257	383	1019	11775			10[illegible]	[illegible]		48

County of *Moore* State of *North Carolina* during the Year ending June 1, 1850, as

N. McCrummen Ass't Marshal.

Year ending June 1, 1850.

	Ginned Cotton, bales of 400 lbs. each.	Wool, lbs. of.	Peas & Beans, bush. of.	Irish Potatoes, bush. of.	Sweet Potatoes, bush. of.	Barley, bushels of.	Buckwheat, bushels of.	Value of Orchard Products in dollars.	Wine, gallons of.	Value of Produce of Market Gardens.	Butter, lbs. of.	Cheese, lbs. of.	Hay, tons of.	Clover Seed, bush. of.	Other Grass Seeds, bushels of.	Hops, lbs. of.	Hemp. Dew Rotted, tons of.	Hemp. Water Rotted, tons of.	Flax, lbs. of.	Flaxseed, bushels of.	Silk Cocoons, lbs. of.	Maple Sugar, lbs. of.	Cane Sugar, hhds. of 1,000 lbs.	Molasses, gallons of.	Beeswax and Honey, lbs. of.	Value of Home-made Manufactures.	Value of Animals slaughtered.
	20	21	22	23	24	25	26	27	28	29	30	31	32	33	34	35	36	37	38	39	40	41	42	43	44	45	46
1			1		25																					10	50
2			10	12	100						25															10	105
3			5		50						20															50	130
4		20	10	4	100						100															50	158
5	3	15	4	3	75						50								5	1					20	20	204
6				10	100						100															25	105
7			7	3	50																					20	
8	37	45	70	30	250						260															100	400
9				10	50						50															30	50
10	6	22	1	4	50						150															70	90
11	1	6		3	40						104															50	41
12	1	35			20						40															40	33
13	1		6	3	30						10								10	2						10	30
14	1		2								40															47	81
15		16		13	100														20	2						50	100
16	1		8	6	75						30															50	80
17	7		5		50						30								1							8	101
18		35			50						60								10	1						30	111
19				5	200						50								15	3						35	40
20	1				25						50															10	30
21		6		30	30						36															35	88
22		26		25	30						50															68	50
23	1			6	30						100															50	60
24			10	10	100						40		1													20	176
25		70	5	15	300						100															118	100
26		11	6		20						100								40	1						40	30
27			5	15	75						10														3	50	30
28	6	20	50	25	300						225		1						20	5						60	300
29			10	10	30						30															90	45
30		30	30	15	100						50								30						102	150	43
31		14	6	5	60																					75	30
32		30	15	10	50						40								10	1						22	68
33	2	28	8	10	60						104	50														30	70
34		20		2	5																					5	40
35			10	5	10						50															7	36
36			20	10	25																					15	55
37	8	100	40		75						75															60	[illegible]
38		60	30	10	100						50	20							15	2						160	180
39		35	4		35						20															2	35
40		20	12		100						10															14	47
41		30	10		100						100															10	54

963

SCHEDULE 4.—Productions of Agriculture in ____________ **in the** ____________ **enumerated by me, on the** 19th **day of** August **1850.**

	Name of Owner, agent, or Manager of the Farm.	Acres of Land. Improved.	Unimproved.	Cash value of Farm.	Value of farming Implements and Machinery.	Live Stock, June 1st, 1850. Horses.	Asses and Mules.	Milch Cows.	Working Oxen.	Other Cattle.	Sheep.	Swine.	Value of Live Stock.	Produce during the — Wheat, bushels of.	Rye, bushels of.	Indian Corn, bushels of.	Oats, bushels of.	Rice, lbs. of.	Tobacco, lbs. of.
	1	2	3	4	5	6	7	8	9	10	11	12	13	14	15	16	17	18	19
1	Daniel McMillan	20	180	200	6	2		4		4	7	20	157	4		130	4		
2	Robert McFarland	30	200	500	5	1		10		20	50	45	420	7		120			
3	Malcom McFarland	20	200	200	5	2		10		14	35	12	250			100	2		
4	Edward Patterson	80	140	300	90	4		9		13	35	60	379	25	12	350	50		
5	Mary Clark	50	210	300	16	2		3		16	75	18	290	14	10	230			
6	Patrick Ray	25	225	250	5	1		2		4	20	6	106		6	100			
7	Daniel McFarland	20	200	100	45	1		3		7	20	20	180			100			
8	Archibald Ray	100	250	450	20	2		8		6	15	17	239	30	6	350			
9	Hugh McLaurin	20	242	600	20	1		4		6	3	7	120	20		100			
10	James D. Rush	100	300	700	100	3		4		10	13	6	305	50		500	50		
11	Nathan Copeland	50	300	350	10	1		2		1	10	9	150	20	6	200	50		
12	Angus Campbell	25	50	125	3	2		3		1	2	9	91	5		100			
13	Nancy McLeod	25	75	200	4	1		1		3	3	8	70			125			
14	Peter Thomas	50	175	400	10	2		5		11	20	15	261	20		300	40		
15	Murdoch McKenzie	100	400	1000	100	6		15		30	40	30	795	30	30	350	50		
16	Daniel McKenzie	200	900	700	100	3		7	2	10	10	10	390	25	12	400	50		
17	Neill McKinnon	30	75	400	10	1		4		3	2	10	124	20		200	50		
18	John McDonald	25	150	200	70	4		6		12	20	20	404	26		300			
19	Malcom C. Clark	60	363	450	100	2		9		4	20	25	262	12	10	350			
20	Malcom Brown	40	297	250	15	3	1	8		16	20	30	492	4	[illegible]	150	20		
21	Flora Campbell	45	555	600	5	1		1		6	10	20	125	40	5	150			
22	Duncan Brown	50	200	200	15	3		14		12	30	30	378	7		150			
23	Archibald Patterson	40	80	75	20	1		10		15	11	30	236			150			
24	John McKinnon	30	290	300	10	2		1		1		20	84			150			
25	Daniel Patterson	80	1310	650	100	2		14		20	25	50	445		12	200	20		
26	John McLeod	120	1180	500	100	4		9		20	50	35	550	18	6	340		180	
27	Ranald McDonald	35	137	150	5	1		8		17	17	45	378	5	2	100			
28	Randolph McDonald	140	700	500	30	3		12		15	20	50	480			300			
29	James Caddell	70	1080	700	15	4		10		15	80	60	445	6	20	250			
30	Angus McLean	50	240	200	25	3		6		7	5	45	219		6	140			
31	John McLeod	50	240	400	20	4		8	2	20	10	20	405		5	200			
32	Dugald Graham	80	360	400	100	4		14		13	30	50	497		35	350			
33	Laughlin McKinnon	70	900	650	30	4		5		10	80	50	455		10	450	10		
34	Alexander Ray	50	650	500	30	4		4		11	14	20	340	8	2	150			
35	Charles C. Shaw	100	900	1000	100	6		6		24	25	45	555	10	75	1000			
36	Duncan Shaw	80	455	1000	50	3		3		12	30	50	390	35	20	400	30		
37	Alexander Monroe	50	160	600	25	1		4		15	50	40	200			300			
38	John M. D. Ray	50	160	500	15	1		2		6		20	124			250	10		
39	Archibald Ray	100	600	1000	50	4		13	2	20	25	85	616	15	40	700			
40	Archibald Campbell	60	940	300	100	2	1	7	2	15	35	60	380	10	15	175	10		
41	Malcom M. Blue	100	1550	2500	50	4		18		27	75	60	557	15	60	800			
		2510	18969	20320	1629	105	2	268	6	516	1162	1302	13655	493	425	10520	432	160	

County of *Moore* State of *North Carolina* during the Year ending June 1, 1850, as

Norman McCrimmon Ass't Marshal.

Year ending June 1, 1850.

	Ginned Cotton, bales of 400 lbs. each.	Wool, lbs. of.	Peas & Beans, bush. of.	Irish Potatoes, bush. of.	Sweet Potatoes, bush. of.	Barley, bushels of.	Buckwheat, bushels of.	Value of Orchard Products in dollars.	Wine, gallons of.	Value of Produce of Market Gardens.	Butter, lbs. of.	Cheese, lbs. of.	Hay, tons of.	Clover Seed, bush. of.	Other Grass Seeds, bushels of.	Hops, lbs. of.	Hemp. Dew Rotted, tons of.	Hemp. Water Rotted, tons of.	Flax, lbs. of.	Flaxseed, bushels of.	Silk Cocoons, lbs. of.	Maple Sugar, lbs. of.	Cane Sugar, hhds. of 1,000 lbs.	Molasses, gallons of.	Beeswax and Honey, lbs. of.	Value of Home-made Manufactures.	Value of Animals slaughtered.
	20	21	22	23	24	25	26	27	28	29	30	31	32	33	34	35	36	37	38	39	40	41	42	43	44	45	46
1		12	20	1	20						10															16	60
2		100	50		20						200															12	70
3		75	4	1	30						40															20	47
4		30	30		160						30															60	185
5		150	8		75						100															60	77
6		30	13	10	80						6															11	30
7		30	20		20						5															10	27
8	1	30	20		160						80															68	70
9		5	30	5	60						75																65
10		20	30	30	150						200															50	79
11		20	5		20						10															10	40
12		5	2		25						10															10	34
13		7																								30	11
14		30	20	16	30						100														5	88	85
15	1	200	100	100	200						250															150	190
16	2	20	25	10	102						106															50	129
17	1				25						30															10	60
18	1	42			25						40															65	100
19		60	30	6	20						80															30	50
20		40	20	6	40						20															50	72
21		10	20																							5	30
22		60	20		20						150															12	75
23		40	30		30						10															10	50
24		15	3		20						28															20	50
25		50	20		100						75															18	75
26		200	20		200						60														14	65	150
27		31	20		60						48	20														35	80
28		40	20		120						124															30	200
29		250	100	1	100						106															30	140
30		5	40		100						20															31	50
31		20		10	150						50															7	87
32		60	30		200						50															50	125
33		300	100		50						50															100	79
34		20	6	10	30						30															50	100
35		50	50		50						30															50	200
36		75	30		100						50															30	115
37		100	75		25						30															50	140
38			50	10	30						30															30	75
39		75	150	10	60						100															100	220
40		50	20	6	200						25															40	75
41		150	100	10	100						150															45	215

965

SCHEDULE 4.—Productions of Agriculture in ______ in the ______ enumerated by me, on the 7th day of September 1850.

	Name of Owner, Agent, or Manager of the Farm.	Acres of Land. Improved.	Acres of Land. Unimproved.	Cash value of Farm.	Value of farming Implements and Machinery.	Live Stock, June 1st, 1850. Horses.	Asses and Mules.	Milch Cows.	Working Oxen.	Other Cattle.	Sheep.	Swine.	Value of Live Stock.	Produce during the year. Wheat, bushels of.	Rye, bushels of.	Indian Corn, bushels of.	Oats, bushels of.	Rice, lbs. of.	Tobacco, lbs. of.
	1	2	3	4	5	6	7	8	9	10	11	12	13	14	15	16	17	18	19
1	John M. D. Cameron	20	160	150	5	1		1		5		30	115	4	4	100	20		
2	Jesse Thompson	100	1214	2000	25	4		5		20	26	35	361	45	4	500	20		
3	Thomas Mathews	50	50	800	15	2		4		3		25	230	15		310	40		
4	John Baker	50	184	700	20	1		4		6	16	10	126	20		300	75		
5	Jacob Mathews	160	334	2200	100	5		4		8	26	38	418	32	32	900	70	400	
6	James Worthy	100	460	1000	100	5		5		7	6	14	225	15	2	500	60		
7	Henry Arnolds	130	414	800	60	4		6		7	5	14	336	8	9	600	100		
8	Norman McDonald	60	300	300	15	2		3		4		20	170		15	400	38		
9	William Keich	20	105	250	20	2		3		6	9	16	145			200	30		
10	John McDugald	30	84	200	20	1		4		6	15	13	123		15	100	8		
11	Margaret E. Cameron	20	100	120	3			1	1			6	40			100			10
12	Charles C. Johnson	40	185	350	40	1		4		3		8	110			200	30	110	40
13	Duncan Munroe	40	60	200	75	2		4		5	8	35	208	5	15	100	20		
14	Neill Graham	30	170	200	25	2		4		5	4	10	117		4	80			
15	Dugald McDugald	300	3700	13750	400	8	4	6	12	15		75	1330			1500	200		
16	Archibald Graham	60	292	350	15	2		4		9	7	20	232		8	275	20		
17	James Gilchrist	50	300	350	25	3		4		4	3	15	142			200	20		
18	Allen B. Morrison	45	240	250	25	2	1	9		11	35	40	525		4	400	10		
19	George Campbell	64	689	650	50	4		8		4	14	13	301			150	40		
20	Archibald Smith	25	281	250	12	1		4		4	8	10	113			90	10		
21	Malcom Johnson	30	470	500	15	3		8		7	20	30	300	5	12	200	15	600	
22	John A. Johnson	30	158	[illegible]	30	2		6		7	12	32	227			125	75	300	
23	Malcom Johnson	20	190	210	5	1		2		4	3	30	150	5		25	10	300	
24	Daniel Buie	70	280	300	20	3		9		20	25	30	325	14	6	300	10		
25	Allen Buie	50	40	250	4	1		3		3	9	15	124	15		100	10	50	
26	William Buie	50	200	280	19	2		7		11	10	15	246	10	20	150	10	300	
27	John K. Johnson	15	135	125	4	2		3		4	12	11	153	8	6	150	7		
28	William Buie	40	210	200	10	1		3		4	9	20	139	10	5	156			
29	Collen McFadyen	40	1060	600	60	2		5		10	15	35	340	30	20	200			
30	Jane Munroe	40	60	100	3	2		4		4	12	15	169	4		150			
31	Alexander McBryde	40	250	207	10	1		5		8	6	23	156	14		200	6		
32	James McBryde	30	210	75	3	1		4		6	15	7	125	4		75	5		
33	Sarah Shaw	61	439	500	35	2		6		8	15	20	230		10	520	30		
34	William H. Baker	30	263	400	5	1		3		8	7	11	157			200	10		
35	Mary McIver	50	350	400	20	1		3		3	8	5	106	4		150	5		
36	Daniel McGilivray	55	343	350	7	1	1	3		1		14	131	8		130	10		
37	Alexander McGilivray	25	100	200	25	1	2	3		2		17	163			60	25		
38	Peter Morris	35	345	190	15	2		6		13	9	21	202		15	150			
39	Joel Pore	30	84	83	12	1		2		8	4	10	144	5	15	150	10		
40	William McDugald	40	205	200	20	2		10		9	3	28	255		4	250	10		
41	John Cameron	25	53	40	75	3		7		6		35	261	25		[illegible]	[illegible]		

County of Moore **State of** North Carolina **during the Year ending June 1, 1850,** &c.

Norman McCrimmon Ass't Marshal.

Year ending June 1, 1850.

	Ginned Cotton, bales of 400 lbs. each.	Wool, lbs. of.	Peas & Beans, bush. of.	Irish Potatoes, bush. of.	Sweet Potatoes, bush. of.	Barley, bushels of.	Buckwheat, bushels of.	Value of Orchard Products in dollars.	Wine, gallons of.	Value of Produce of Market Gardens.	Butter, lbs. of.	Cheese, lbs. of.	Hay, tons of.	Clover Seed, bush. of.	Other Grass Seeds, bushels of.	Hops, lbs. of.	Hemp: Dew Rotted, tons of.	Hemp: Water Rotted, tons of.	Flax, lbs. of.	Flaxseed, bushels of.	Silk Cocoons, lbs. of.	Maple Sugar, lbs. of.	Cane Sugar, hhds. of 1,000 lbs.	Molasses, gallons of.	Beeswax and Honey, lbs. of.	Value of Home-made Manufactures.	Value of Animals slaughtered.
	20	21	22	23	24	25	26	27	28	29	30	31	32	33	34	35	36	37	38	39	40	41	42	43	44	45	46
1			10		100						20															15	450
2		52	25	15	180						25															50	113
3			50	4	25						32		1													12	49
4		30	30		100						32														25	35	67
5		30	100	20	60						60		1												32	50	160
6	3	15	49		100						100		1													65	111
7		10	30		20						104		3													50	93
8			30		30						32															20	85
9		18	10	10	30						52															24	62
10		15	10	5	30						12															6	31
11			40	6	30						10															8	17
12			20	30	125						52															40	60
13		16	10	5	50						40														100	25	113
14		4	10	30	50						40															25	75
15			150	100	500						104		3													100	500
16		15	12		25						40															15	50
17		3			100						20															6	30
18		70	30		100						104															76	98
19		28	10		50						104																91
20		16	22	5	30						40															25	25
21		36	20		100						32															25	78
22		16	15		100						52															6	68
23		4	5		20						15															13	38
24		30	20		100						50															60	128
25		20	10		50						20															15	73
26		20	25		50						75															40	68
27		15		1	20						15															9	31
28		20			20						20																50
29		50	20		150						25															30	96
30		12	4		12						4															5	41
31		12	6	10	50						10															30	60
32		15		5	30						25															9	45
33	1	30	5	40	20						100															40	102
34		15	8		30						52	10													10	30	72
35		14	5		50						30															15	25
36	1		10	3	60																					10	40
37	1		6	5	35						5																36
38		18	5		100						100	50														50	63
39		6	8	5	50						30															3	50
40		5	15	3	30						50															7	67
41					50						25															10	140

76

SCHEDULE 4.—Productions of Agriculture in ______ in the ______ enumerated by me, on the 16th day of September 1850.

Name of Owner, Agent, or Manager of the Farm.	Acres of Land: Improved.	Acres of Land: Unimproved.	Cash value of Farm.	Value of farming Implements and Machinery.	Live Stock, June 1st, 1850: Horses.	Asses and Mules.	Milch Cows.	Working Oxen.	Other Cattle.	Sheep.	Swine.	Value of Live Stock.	Wheat, bushels of.	Rye, bushels of.	Indian Corn, bushels of.	Oats, bushels of.	Rice, lbs. of.	Tobacco, lbs. of.
1	2	3	4	5	6	7	8	9	10	11	12	13	14	15	16	17	18	19
Duigald Cameron	70	680	700	155	4		14	2	40	[illegible]	[illegible]	667	91	3	550	30		
Margaret Buie	50	600	1500	201	1	2	12	2	35	50	100	610			400	50		
John M. Cox	100	400	600	95	1	2	4	1	11	13	31	393	72		421	125		
Thomas Cox	100	1060	1500	150	3	2	6		5	12	30	377	60		500	124		
John Morris	60	180	300	70	2		4		5	9	15	196	40	1	270	30		
John Morris	30	610	950	20	2		4		8	15	30	165	18		100	25		
Peter Morris	30	109	300	10	1		1		1	4	12	64	12		175	4		
Catharine Morris	30	80	100	50	2		3		4	7	24	179	19		175	12		
Gideon Edwards	70	140	300	75	5		4		7	10	25	310	20		410	15		
Francis Edwards	50	200	500	10	1		4		5	7	30	162			300	30		
John W. Scoggins	35	170	200	10	1	1	1		4	6	30	148			400	21		
John H. Dalrymple	150	847	1200	75	2	3	10		13	16	33	520	44		[illegible]	100		
Daniel McIver	50	300	450	15	2		2		1		12	110			201			
Henry Hunt	100	279	500	70	5		3		6	11	32	231	30		400	100		
Archibald Dalrymple	125	332	600	57	3		10		18	30	27	360	75		400	25		
William Dalrymple	60	654	800	25	2	1	5		15	10	40	260	9		350	15		
John McIver	80	420	1000	145	5		7		9	32	27	432	20		400	80	75	
William Hanly	50	100	250	35	2		4		6	12	20	192		25	210	15		
Elizabeth McLennon	16	134	320	5			1		1	6	18	49			50			
Archibald E. Douglass	30	132	300	10	2		4		4	7	7	144	21		250	40		
David Gaster	200	422	1000	150	4	1	7		8	10	30	392	67		400	105		
John May	40	260	300	8	1		3		6		16	156			300			
Charles G. Harrington	200	590	800	100	5	2	15		20	35	100	730	200		[illegible]	[illegible]		
Henry Godfrey	25	45	70	15	2	2	2		1		15	138	12		100			
Blake Parish	50	86	136	10	2		2		4		21	100	11	3	[illegible]	[illegible]		
Jesse Love	50	80	175	24	2	1	4		4	9	30	188	10	11	175	[illegible]		
Patrick Lashley	40	160	200	20	2		1		5	6	30	196	14	12	200	[illegible]		
Jacob Gaster	30	85	100	8	1		2		4		10	145	15		150	10		
Green H. Sloan	30	108	200	8	2		2		4	6	12	163			200	12		
William Rollins	80	522	817	40	4		4	2	2	11	32	328	20	4	300	20		
John Baker	50	430	600	30	3		4	2	5	4	30	279	15	10	330	30		
John McFarland	35	54	200	8	1		2		1	1	9	98	5		125	10		
William Pipkin	25	75	100	5	1		2		1		16	88			150	75		
Torquil McNeill	80	90	400	10	3		4		6	2	30	207	45		150	40		
Louis McLeod	50	54	400	38	1		5		1		30	150			350	100		
Nancy McFarland	50	295	345	20	2		3	1	2	10	25	220	55	[illegible]	350	12		
Neill McNeill	150	1050	1000	20	3	1	4	2	4	13	40	324			[illegible]	[illegible]		
William Buchanan	25	87	250	12	1		4		5		33	181			[illegible]	[illegible]		
Benjamin Muckle	50	700	530	50	5		8		12	36	40	271	80	4	[illegible]	[illegible]		
Daniel Thomas	40	145	150	6	1		2		[illegible]	[illegible]	[illegible]	[illegible]	8		[illegible]			
George Hayward	40	500	282	23	2		1		5									

County of Moore State of N. Carolina during the Year ending June 1, 1850, as

Norman McCrummen, Ass't Marshal.

Year ending June 1, 1850.

	Ginned Cotton, bales of 400 lbs. each.	Wool, lbs. of.	Peas & Beans, bush. of.	Irish Potatoes, bush. of.	Sweet Potatoes, bush. of.	Barley, bushels of.	Buckwheat, bushels of.	Value of Orchard Products in dollars.	Wine, gallons of.	Value of Produce of Market Gardens.	Butter, lbs. of.	Cheese, lbs. of.	Hay, tons of.	Clover Seed, bush. of.	Other Grass Seeds, bushels of.	Hops, lbs. of.	Hemp: Dew Rotted, tons of.	Hemp: Water Rotted, tons of.	Flax, lbs. of.	Flaxseed, bushels of.	Silk Cocoons, lbs. of.	Maple Sugar, lbs. of.	Cane Sugar, hhds. of 1,000 lbs.	Molasses, gallons of.	Beeswax and Honey, lbs. of.	Value of Home-made Manufactures.	Value of Animals slaughtered.
	20	21	22	23	24	25	26	27	28	29	30	31	32	33	34	35	36	37	38	39	40	41	42	43	44	45	46
1		40	20	5	150						107	80	7													46	220
2	8	50	20	20	200						150															50	175
3	2	31	30	5	75						150															75	108
4	1	11	3		15						52															28	115
5	1	15	10		50						50															26	80
6		15	7		30						20															5	43
7	1	6			20						10															6	32
8	2	12	3		50						20															20	80
9	4	21	20	5	50						52		1													30	61
10	4	14		5	30						50																50
11		8		5	200						52															3	157
12	5	25		10	600						104	20													15	40	122
13			10								10															15	20
14	1	30			75						50															20	97
15	4	60	6		600						104															37	75
16	3	15	10		30						50															8	80
17	3	40	20	5	30						100		1													52	85
18	2	24		10	60						104	50														30	32
19	1	12	4		50																					20	32
20		14	6		30						52														20	25	43
21	5	20	20		75						104															65	103
22			20		50						75															21	30
23	6	32	100	20	50						200															60	270
24	1				15						5															5	25
25	1		30	20	60																					13	55
26	1	12	25	10	80						30															20	65
27	1	2			130						30														10	45	50
28	1		20	8	140						30															12	35
29	1	10	15	10	60						100															10	60
30		17	20	2	50						10															15	47
31	2	6	10		200						10															4	76
32					50						20															20	72
33					6						10															4	35
34	2			15	10						50															40	54
35			50		20						20															10	50
36	1	12			60						50															6	94
37		33	25	20	200						104															30	120
38	1				20						30															22	68
39		50			50						50															40	100
40			6		10						20															5	36
41			50	4	30						60															100	35

SCHEDULE 4.—Productions of Agriculture in ______ 7th in the ______ enumerated by me, on the 26th day of August 1850.

	Name of Owner, Agent, or Manager of the Farm.	Acres of Land. Improved.	Unimproved.	Cash value of Farm.	Value of farming Implements and Machinery.	Live Stock, June 1st, 1850. Horses.	Asses and Mules.	Milch Cows.	Working Oxen.	Other Cattle.	Sheep.	Swine.	Value of Live Stock.	Produce during the year ending June 1, 1850. Wheat, bushels of.	Rye, bushels of.	Indian Corn, bushels of.	Oats, bushels of.	Rice, lbs. of.	Tobacco, lbs. of.	
	1	2	3	4	5	6	7	8	9	10	11	12	13	14	15	16	17	18	19	
1	Daniel McNeill	75	435	1200	75	5	1	13		40	51	65	711	35	35	800				1
2	Archibald Buchanan	150	2090	1124	75	3		11		17	15	60	475	15	40	300				2
3	John M. Johnson	35	215	400	35	1		5		9	35	25	245			175	10			3
4	Archibald M. Blue	225	3447	2500	65	9		15		45	110	175	1140	40	100	1500				4
5	Patrick S. Munroe	60	540	400	40	3		8		5	25	40	305			200				5
6	Duncan M. Blue	130	1470	600	50	4		10		11	50	60	555	30	60	400				6
7	Nancy McDonald	50	350	500	12	1		8		11		75	385	10	7	200				7
8	Neill McDonald	40	432	350	25	1		3		5	12	20	162	5	10	125	35			8
9	Angus McDonald	40	587	500	35	2		6		12	11	20	236		11	160				9
10	John McN. Ferguson	60	397	300	60	2		7		23	50	60	435	6	10	140				10
11	John B. Black	50	200	230	25	2		4		8	30	15	192			130	10			11
12	Patrick M. Blue	100	1090	1000	25	4		6		12	14	40	364	30	10	300				12
13	Daniel B. Black	50	300	350	60	4		5		10	40	16	360	12		150	30			13
14	Ann Curry	30	270	500	10	1		4		6		20	130			100				14
15	Duncan C. Blue	40	1000	500	25	3		7	6	11	20	35	510		50	100				15
16	Daniel McKeithan	80	1937	1800	25	5		12		13	31	57	656	75	8	600	15			16
17	John McNeill	50	300	350	25	2		7		14	22	20	282	20	20	300	10			17
18	John D. McDonald	25	310	300	10	1		4		8	20	20	195	10		175	8			18
19	Daniel McDonald	55	1042	1097	10	2		5		10	15	33	210			300	10			19
20	Christian McDonald	40	287	400	15	2		4		7	15	35	324	15	15	150	20			20
21	John M. Curry	40	60	100	3	3		4		6	19	7	255	30		200				21
22	John M. Blue	20	380	300	15	2		6		10	6	21	186	51		200	20			22
23	Nevin Ray	12	205	217	5	2		8		7	12	20	192	12		150				23
24	Daniel McCallum	50	200	125	75	2		3		18	4	9	269	16		100				24
25	Daniel McLean	30	270	500	5	2		5		12		15	217	4	8	100				25
26	Nevin Ray	60	400	600	75	3		7		6	50	25	305	20	30	300				26
27	Malcom Black	100	1600	800	30	5		10		20	20	30	565	40	21	300	10			27
28	John McCollum	45	490	580	35	4		3		12	10	30	330	30	5	250				28
29	John F. B. McDonald	30	279	250	12	1		10	1	15	30	50	305			300				29
30	Archibald B. Curry	80	720	570	75	3		5		18	30	20	269	20	7	250	25			30
31	Daniel B. Curry	35	65	200	15	2		3		6	4	20	169	30		250				31
32	Duncan B. Curry	75	200	250	10	2		3		7	15	18	305	32		250	10			32
33	Green B. Fields	100	251	300	6	2		2		8	5	100	290	20		150	200			33
34	Sarah Curry	50	190	335	5	1		3		7	12	15	137	14		250	10			34
35	Elizabeth Fry	50	173	400	20	2		4		4	10	15	160			100	15			35
36	Malcom Graham	80	170	400	25	3		3		2		40	206	42		250	24			36
37	John McInnis	40	250	350	5	2		2		1	9	16	130		13	125	57			37
38	Norman McDonald	30	270	300	5	4		4		3	4	15	204	27		150	12			38
39	John McDonald	60	131	500	35	3		2		4	17	43	252	30		100	30			39
40	Andrew Graham	80	210	600	70	3		4		2	8	16	178	60		300	50			40
41	Angus McDonald	50	750	600	45	3		4		6	22	28	275	13		150	30			41
		2522	19775	2678	1258	115	1	238	7	457	914	1453	13189	793	[illegible]	1350	460			

County of Moore State of North Carolina during the Year ending June 1, 1850, as

Norman McCrummen Ass't Marshal.

Year ending June 1, 1850.

Line	Ginned Cotton, bales of 400 lbs. each (20)	Wool, lbs. of (21)	Peas & Beans, bush. of (22)	Irish Potatoes, bush. of (23)	Sweet Potatoes, bush. of (24)	Barley, bushels of (25)	Buckwheat, bushels of (26)	Value of Orchard Products in dollars (27)	Wine, gallons of (28)	Value of Produce of Market Gardens (29)	Butter, lbs. of (30)	Cheese, lbs. of (31)	Hay, tons of (32)	Clover Seed, bush. of (33)	Other Grass Seeds, bushels of (34)	Hops, lbs. of (35)	Hemp: Dew Rotted, tons of (36)	Hemp: Water Rotted, tons of (37)	Flax, lbs. of (38)	Flaxseed, bushels of (39)	Silk Cocoons, lbs. of (40)	Maple Sugar, lbs. of (41)	Cane Sugar, hhds. of 1,000 lbs. (42)	Molasses, gallons of (43)	Beeswax and Honey, lbs. of (44)	Value of Home-made Manufactures (45)	Value of Animals slaughtered (46)
1	1	22	30	10	250						231															30	201
2		25	30	15	200						100															56	177
3		70	15	10	30						50															27	65
4		275	400		200						100															75	442
5		67	15		150						20															33	77
6		125	102	10	300						100															40	156
7	1		40	5	200						100								12							85	130
8		15	10	4	100						25														6	40	65
9		22	5		150						60															20	19
10		100	30		100						52															40	99
11		60	10		50						25															20	63
12		30	10		50						52														10	30	60
13		80	40		125						52															20	57
14			20		40						30																35
15		50	20	25	100						72															80	261
16		60	150	5	175						104															47	165
17		50	70	5	40						50															65	75
18		25	20		75						15															34	52
19		30	150		40						30															17	83
20		30	20		80						50	20														36	83
21		38	40	8	100						10															25	20
22		10	10		75						15															25	75
23		15	5	5	75						30	15														25	35
24			10	10	50						20															6	35
25			20	10	100						25															25	42
26		100	25		130						100															51	121
27		40	20		150						50								30							20	126
28		20	13		100						30															20	75
29		30	5	10	60						75															30	100
30		20	10	5	50						100															40	102
31	2	10	25	8	50						100															25	72
32		25	30		35						50															24	62
33		6	20	4	30						50															13	38
34		24	13	5	50						50															37	69
35		25			40						10															8	35
36	1			5	80																					20	22
37		12	5	7	60						10	2														11	40
38		10			30						20															30	35
39		30		10	100						50													10			50
40	2	18	5								20	1														25	30
41	1	30	4	3	50						60															12	58

42 25 1290 19

971

SCHEDULE 4.—Productions of Agriculture in ______________ **in the** ______ **enumerated by me, on the** *31st* **day of** *August* **1850.**

#	Name of Owner, Agent, or Manager of the Farm.	Acres of Land: Improved.	Acres of Land: Unimproved.	Cash value of Farm.	Value of farming implements and machinery.	Live Stock, June 1st, 1850: Horses.	Asses and Mules.	Milch Cows.	Working Oxen.	Other Cattle.	Sheep.	Swine.	Value of Live Stock.	Produce during the year: Wheat, bushels of.	Rye, bushels of.	Indian Corn, bushels of.	Oats, bushels of.	Rice, lbs. of.	Tobacco, lbs. of.
	1	2	3	4	5	6	7	8	9	10	11	12	13	14	15	16	17	18	19
1	Patience Lewis	65	365	500	100	4		4		11	30	30	360	11		550	120		
2	John Lewis	40	206	296	6	1		3		1		10	57			150	100		
3	Cornelius Dunlap	200	1300	1500	240	6		8		15	11	50	516	40		625	300		
4	Angus Curry	70	230	500	30	2		5		7	13	25	210	50	15	175	20		
5	John S. McLeod	30	270	100	10	2		5		8	9	12	205	12		125	30		
6	Neill Peterson	70	360	500	30	4		5		8	5	70	455	3	20	150	70		
7	Allen McDonald	50	186	230	6	2		5		7	9	21	267	10	10	100	10		
8	Isabella McLauchlin	60	210	270	5	2		2		8	23	20	248	8		100	100		
9	Murdo McDonald	40	210	250	10	2		5		6		18	208	22	16	450	18		
10	Alexander McDonald	40	210	250	10	1		7		4	40	18	250	8	17	200	40		
11	Elizabeth M. Rowan	100	825	2000	50	4		3		12	3	28	335	30	25	500	30		
12	Andrew Sloan	80	235	370	50	3	1	6		14	6	20	330		4	150	30		
13	Hugh Leach	70	850	1300	100	3		4		9	10	18	276	5	3	150	40		
14	John A. McLeod	35	215	300	20	2		1		3	7	11	187			100	30		
15	Catharine McLauchlin	60	535	680	25	4		6		10	18	15	348	18		300	20		
16	Donald Kelly	50	278	900	75	3		7		7	14	10	320	16		300	30		
17	John N. Ferguson	70	215	600	75	3		4		10	15	40	255	60	5	350	35		
18	John McNeill	40	500	700	75	5		5	4	3	13	14	411	15	6	500	30		
19	Parham G. Oats	36	184	400	25	3		1		7	13	8	230	5		300	40		
20	Richard Fry	100	500	3000	150	2		2	3	4	12	35	237	30		160	37		
21	John C. Ferguson	60	355	415	25	2		4		4		12	194	20		300	15		
22	Mary McNeill	100	400	1000	75	4		4		8		12	390	60	20	750	50		
23	Peter Kelly	60	490	1000	100	4		5		12	9	23	330	12	35	150	60		
24	Archibald McDonald	100	675	1400	115	7		13	4	15	32	50	677	80	20	800	100		
25	Nancy McLeod	28	272	400	20	1		4		6	4	11	157	10	2	110	5		
26	Angus McDonald	33	377	200	75	2		5		9	25	12	228	7	7	90	30		
27	Charles Medlin	20	90	100	4	1							40			130			
28	Donald McDonald	150	950	1107	80	1	2	3		12	15	50	400	25	25	400			
29	John McDonald	200	900	2000	75	3		7	2	10	8	30	318	18	18	250	20		
30	Malcom Turner	60	140	600	23	3		9		9	3	30	358	10		275	30		
31	Archibald Smith	25	425	450	5	1		3		3		5	85			200			
32	William Johnson	60	520	1200	5	2		4		6	16	20	256			150			
33	Hugh Keith	30	545	700	20	6		6		16	10	15	365	5	5	300			
34	Peter Munroe	30	150	400	10	2		4		4	25	6	187	4	10	100	6		
35	Finlay McFadyen	75	416	430	20	3		9		20	30	40	380	11		400	15		
36	John A. Cameron	40	360	500	15	1	1	3		10	8	20	278	20		200			
37	Hugh A. Cameron	35	688	800	20	3		4		8		20	207	6		175	50		
38	Archibald A. F. Cameron	75	400	475	40	4		5		10	30	20	295	25		350	12		
39	John T. Cameron	30	420	700	40	1	1	4	4	5	30	15	295	5		175	10		
40	Neill Cameron	40	510	500	50	6		8		10	10	25	365		20	350	30		
41	Alexander Cameron	10	140	150	70	2		5		7	8	15	205	10		200			
		2588	17187	[illegible]	1979	117	5	157	17	[illegible]	[illegible]	[illegible]	11721	671	[illegible]	[illegible]	[illegible]		

County of Moore **State of** North Carolina **during the Year ending June 1, 1850, as**

Norman McCrummen **Ass't Marshal.**

Year ending June 1, 1850.

	Ginned Cotton, bales of 400 lbs. each.	Wool, lbs. of.	Peas & Beans, bush. of.	Irish Potatoes, bush. of.	Sweet Potatoes, bush. of.	Barley, bushels of.	Buckwheat, bushels of.	Value of Orchard Products in dollars.	Wine, gallons of.	Value of Produce of Market Gardens.	Butter, lbs. of.	Cheese, lbs. of.	Hay, tons of.	Clover Seed, bush. of.	Other Grass Seeds, bushels of.	Hops, lbs. of.	Hemp: Dew Rotted, tons of.	Hemp: Water Rotted, tons of.	Flax, lbs. of.	Flaxseed, bushels of.	Silk Cocoons, lbs. of.	Maple Sugar, lbs. of.	Cane Sugar, hhds. of 1,000 lbs.	Molasses, gallons of.	Beeswax and Honey, lbs. of.	Value of Home-made Manufactures.	Value of Animals slaughtered.
	20	21	22	23	24	25	26	27	28	29	30	31	32	33	34	35	36	37	38	39	40	41	42	43	44	45	46
1		30	25	12	30						30															24	203
2				2	20						50															37	40
3	4	50	5	5	100						150															50	200
4		26	15	6	150						50															30	84
5		18	12	3	50						35															20	70
6		10	15		50						35	15														10	107
7		20	100		120						50															40	90
8		70			100						15															30	64
9			8	7	50						25															10	31
10		80	15		50						100	20														30	67
11		6	40	20	200						30															42	116
12		20	2	10	30						20																65
13		4	5		100						10														2	30	94
14		12	4	10	50						5														3	20	73
15		20	5	5	100						50															30	128
16		30	12		12						40															30	75
17		20	1	20	150						40															50	85
18		30	20		50						50															30	105
19		20	10		50						30															20	60
20	3	25		5	300						100															25	140
21	2		12	8	20						30															15	40
22			40		20						100																100
23	1	20	30		100						200															50	64
24	1	64	10	8	250						200															65	120
25		10		2	20						40														2	16	30
26		40	10	8	70						70															40	45
27			15	6	100																					25	
28			20		50								1														98
29		14	10	45	75						30															30	77
30		5	25		75						75															20	85
31			4								26																20
32		24	20		30																						75
33		15	20	10	100						104															50	60
34		30	30	5	100						40															15	46
35		30	40		200						32															60	115
36		8	20		25						30															44	60
37			10		100						30															15	120
38		30	20	20	60						32	20														51	90
39		20	20		40						50		1														70
40		10	20		100						40		1														100
41		20	20	5	30						30	10														10	78

SCHEDULE 4.—Productions of Agriculture in ______ 77 **in the**

enumerated by me, on the *20th* **day of** *September* **1850.**

	Name of Owner, Agent, or Manager of the Farm.	Acres of Land.				Live Stock, June 1st, 1850.								Produce during the					
		Improved.	Unimproved.	Cash value of Farm.	Value of farming Implements and Machinery.	Horses.	Asses and Mules.	Milch Cows.	Working Oxen.	Other Cattle.	Sheep.	Swine.	Value of Live Stock.	Wheat, bushels of.	Rye, bushels of.	Indian Corn, bushels of.	Oats, bushels of.	Rice, lbs. of.	Tobacco, lbs. of.
	1	2	3	4	5	6	7	8	9	10	11	12	13	14	15	16	17	18	19
1	John Sheppard	30	364	364	68	4		6		5	10	29	205	8		400			
2	John Dalrymple	60	435	475	20	2	1	4		2	10	12	226	10		300		300	
3	George Underwood	60	470	530	14	4	1	6	2	6	14	60	439	60	10	400	30		
4	Joseph Thomas	100	200	300	10	3		4	2	6	6	37	349	61		600	100		
5	Bryant Williams	40	240	280	22	1		2		3		18	85	23		200	20		
6	Archibald Dalrymple	100	310	600	30	3	2	5	2	3	15	24	307	7		400	60		
7	Darius Thomas	60	400	630	70	2		3		4	12	60	222	64		600	75		
8	Tilman Thomas	40	160	230	108	3		3	2	4	15	20	260	40		600	60		4
9	Daniel Douglas	40	200	600	10	1		4		3		15	116			300			
10	Archibald Douglas	100	360	2000	105	5	4	10		12	13	15	758	60		1500	400		200
11	John Douglas	160	332	1200	145	4	3	5		16	15	64	679	140		1050	260		
12	Green Thomas	50	250	300	30	4		3		4	12	35	167	40		400	60		
13	Henderson Judd	50	200	300	10	2		2		10		10	125	50		375	100		
14	Priscilla Thomas	30	70	100	5	1		2	2	1		19	130	10		150	8		
15	Sarah Cox	100	300	440	20	3		2	1	4	6	24	170	30		300	15		
16	Charles Cox	80	270	400	25	4		4	2	4	20	35	380	60		450	20		
17	Abner E. Yarbrough	130	350	660	50	2		3		7		16	185	50		325	30		
18	Daniel Weldon	50	230	280	3	1		2		7		20	110			300			
19	Thomas Yarbrough	25	72	125	5	1		2		1		10	57	18		100			
20	Anderson Thomas	50	120	200	10	2		2		3	7	20	172	35		300	10		
21	Hugh C. McLean	200	1000	4000	200	4	6	6	2	14	15	20	609	180		1000	300		
22	John McLeod	160	471	1650	415	8	1	5	2	14	16	76	643	160		750	200		
23	Elizabeth Walker	30	110	400	15	2		3	1	1		18	162	53		90	20		
24	William R. Berryman	150	200	1250	100	6	1	6	2	12		60	675	145		1500	90		
25	Anna Gunter	16	72	160	6	1		2		1	1	12	81	16		105	20		
26	John Buchannon	50	100	175	25	3		2		4	7	15	147	50		100			
27	Keziah Thomas	50	218	268	20	2		3				13	143	18		125	20		
28	Sarah Sloan	45	100	200	45	4		5		2		30	[illegible]			200	80		
29	Jordan Sloan	50	40	180	200	4		4		3	5	15	215	20		450	200		
30	Robert McAulay	40	62	100	15	2	1	1				8	67	15		200	30		
31	Malcom McFarland	25	116	300	12	1		2		3		14	107			300	200		
32	Daniel McFarland	50	240	360	35	2	1	1		1		40	180	16		325	200		
33	Elizabeth Watson	70	130	200	25	2		2		7	8	22	270	8		250	16		
34	Allen Thomas	40	100	150	15	1	1	4		6	4	25	181	7		200	5		
35	John Hawley	50	110	160	10	1		1		2		12	86			150			
36	Alfred Oliver	100	600	800	25	4		4		5	3	30	298	50		375	200		
37	David Oliver	50	165	300	65	2	1	4		4		16	196	40		200	200		
38	Abel Kelly	24	460	4000	100	2	3	4		3		7	400			100	200		
39	Thomas Harrington	165	583	1160	116	6	3	9		12	15	71	721	209		1590	400		
40	Archibald Harrington	100	195	700	100	3		5		1	3	35	287	46		450	195	400	
41	Thomas I. Minter	100	210	1100	15	2	1	2		2		30	315	30		400	130		
		2690	11410	6335	[illegible]	116	26	148	20	214	234	1152	11444	1781	10	17660	[illegible]	[illegible]	204

County of *Moore* State of *North Carolina* during the Year ending June 1, 1850, as *Norman McCrummen* Ass't Marshal.

Year ending June 1, 1850.

	Ginned Cotton, bales of 400 lbs. each.	Wool, lbs. of.	Peas & Beans, bush. of.	Irish Potatoes, bush. of.	Sweet Potatoes, bush. of.	Barley, bushels of.	Buckwheat, bushels of.	Value of Orchard Products in dollars.	Wine, gallons of.	Value of Produce of Market Gardens.	Butter, lbs. of.	Cheese, lbs. of.	Hay, tons of.	Clover Seed, bush. of.	Other Grass Seeds, bushels of.	Hops, lbs. of.	Hemp. Dew Rotted, tons of.	Hemp. Water Rotted, tons of.	Flax, lbs. of.	Flaxseed, bushels of.	Silk Cocoons, lbs. of.	Maple Sugar, lbs. of.	Cane Sugar, hhds. of 1,000 lbs.	Molasses, gallons of.	Beeswax and Honey, lbs. of.	Value of Home-made Manufactures.	Value of Animals slaughtered.
	20	21	22	23	24	25	26	27	28	29	30	31	32	33	34	35	36	37	38	39	40	41	42	43	44	45	46
1		20	30		100						32															60	73
2	1	30			100						100															30	36
3	2	15			150						60															25	63
4	1	10	20		60						20															30	76
5	1		10		40						30															12	60
6	2	30			60						75		2													6	75
7	2	33	6		80						50															50	112
8	3	26		10	80						40															20	70
9					10						104														30	50	30
10	3	26	40		100						60															20	132
11	3	25	60		300						50															8	13[illegible]
12	3	15			20						10															10	63
13	2		10		10						16															10	30
14					10						10															6	30
15	1	8	2		8						10															12	70
16	1	8	2	10	60						50															80	93
17	1		20	12	20						52															40	60
18																											30
19			8	2	10																						60
20		6		10	40																				10	30	85
21			100	25	200						100																100
22	3	8	30	10	40						30														10	37	182
23	1			10	30						32								10						25	20	48
24			20		20						100															45	16[illegible]
25		6	5	6	40						15															5	30
26		7	3		20																					5	23
27	1		5		30						30															20	67
28			4		10						20																55
29		15	20		200						32	100													16	15	70
30			20	10	70						10															40	60
31				13	10						60	13													200	16	35
32			10		100						20																30
33		8	10	8	100						20															10	62
34	1	4	15		30						30															32	30
35			10	30	75						40															20	25
36	1		30		100						60															40	107
37			30	10	40						166															26	73
38					30						150															37	68
39	3	32	100	15	60						136	1														70	163
40	2	6	100	10	30						50															30	110
41	2				25						25																40

SCHEDULE 4.—Productions of Agriculture in ____________ 975 in the
enumerated by me, on the 26th day of September 1850.

	Name of Owner, Agent, or Manager of the Farm.	Acres of Land: Improved.	Unimproved.	Cash value of Farm.	Value of farming Implements and Machinery.	Live Stock, June 1st, 1850: Horses.	Asses and Mules.	Milch Cows.	Working Oxen.	Other Cattle.	Sheep.	Swine.	Value of Live Stock.	Produce during the year: Wheat, bushels of.	Rye, bushels of.	Indian Corn, bushels of.	Oats, bushels of.	Rice, lbs. of.	Tobacco, lbs. of.
	1	2	3	4	5	6	7	8	9	10	11	12	13	14	15	16	17	18	19
1	William Watson	150	270	3000	250	4	4	12	2	25	40	100	875	100		1250	300	120	250
2	David Watson	45	255	300	50	4	2	4	2	10	15	40	470	40		400	25		50
3	Louis Wicker	30	330	200	30	2		4		4	13	25	194	48		125	30		
4	Nancy Wicker	150	150	265	35	3		4		4	17	42	269	100		200	300		
5	Jonathan Wicker	25	275	300	10	1		4		2	12	11	131	26		150	10		
6	Benjamin Wicker	65	50	150	30	2	1	5		8	3	33	293	36		200	20		
7	Mary Wicker	30	120	150	28	1		5		2	7	28	162	22		150	30		
8	Edward Wicker	40	160	200	20	2	1	2		2		10	180	15		200	20		
9	Cherry Wicker	50	76	62	15	1		4		4	4	14	153	15		200	30		
10	John Kelly	25	105	130	10		1	2		6	18	20	130	13		100	40		
11	Sion Campbell	60	250	330	100	4	1	3		3	3	35	348	60		235	100		
12	Reuben Thomas	30	70	100	2	1		2		2		16	64	14		100			20
13	John Blackman	70	317	387	45	2	1	3		3	11	20	188			300	40	60	
14	Nathan Haight	30	222	220	5	1				3		13	114			150	10		
15	John Watson	50	250	350	35	2		4	2	8	15	35	200	15	10	200	25		
16	Malcom B. Watson	40	360	400	10	2		3		4	11	20	179	16	8	200			
17	Matilda Curles	50	200	250	25	2	1	3	2	6	9	16	219	25		300	5		
18	Elisha Watson	50	206	404	10	1	1	2		2		30	185	38		75	60		
19	Anderson Wicker	70	56	126	20	3		4	2	8	7	22	212	20		175	25		
20	Mathew Wicker	20	80	50	5	1		1			5	2	44	10		60	30		
21	Jane McIver	40	281	640	20	1		2		3	3	10	98	20		105	30		
22	Martin Dye	50	87	140	50	3		4		8	25	15	205	41		300	75		
23	W. Westley Dye	50	60	200	370	3		2		7	12	19	294	41		250	75		
24	Archibald McIver	25	362	400	50	2		3		8	6	10	166	20		100	15		
25	Evander McIver	100	1595	2450	35	—	3	5	2	13	20	25	390	60		300	200		
26	Daniel R. McIver	80	130	850	60	3		2		13	25	20	290	10		400	40		30
27	Mary McIver	150	930	2500	200	7		9		10	30	50	570	250		875	200		
28	Duncan D. McIver	90	310	1050	55	5		7	2	7	12	30	430	85		900	440		50
29	John McIver	30	120	150	25	1		4		3	6	9	77	25		150	25		
30	Mastin Gilmore	50	450	600	60	2	2	3		3		12	260	85		400	40		
31	Mary McIver	50	150	300	80	3		7		4	12	45	332	45		500	80		
32	Daniel B. McIver	30	370	1500	5	2		2				20	90	36		200	20		
33	David W. Wicker	80	240	300	175	3	2	6		15	10	20	452	130		200	100		
34	Elisha Wicker	30	108	200	7	2		1		3		16	125	40		125	75		
35	Mathew Wicker	30	200	300	60	2		3		6	12	23	212	30		350	100		[illegible]
36	Newton Bryant	40	160	450	300	1	3	6		8	20	20	310	55		200	75		
37	Joseph Cook	30	425	1000	100	3		5		6	5	15	305	40		350	20		
38	Winship Bryant	100	700	300	75	3		7		3	18	11	241	80		400	23		
39	Flora Baker	30	160	200	5	1		2		2	3	8	45	5		200	50		
40	Isabella Mathis	15	85	100	2	1		1		7	2	13	98			105	5		
41	Westley McIver	30	250	700	70	3		6		4	23	30	200	90		250	25		
		[illegible]	[illegible]	9449	[illegible]	80	32	161	11	246	450	964	[illegible]	1791	18	[illegible]	3015	160	410

County of *Moore* State of *North Carolina* during the Year ending June 1, 1850, as

Norman McCrummen Ass't Marshal.

Year ending June 1, 1850.

	Ginned Cotton, bales of 400 lbs. each.	Wool, lbs. of.	Peas & Beans, bush. of.	Irish Potatoes, bush. of.	Sweet Potatoes, bush. of.	Barley, bushels of.	Buckwheat, bushels of.	Value of Orchard Products in dollars.	Wine, gallons of.	Value of Produce of Market Gardens.	Butter, lbs. of.	Cheese, lbs. of.	Hay, tons of.	Clover Seed, bush. of.	Other Grass Seeds, bushels of.	Hops, lbs. of.	Hemp. Dew Rotted, tons of.	Hemp. Water Rotted, tons of.	Flax, lbs. of.	Flaxseed, bushels of.	Silk Cocoons, lbs. of.	Maple Sugar, lbs. of.	Cane Sugar, hhds. of 1,000 lbs.	Molasses, gallons of.	Beeswax and Honey, lbs. of.	Value of Home-made Manufactures.	Value of Animals slaughtered.
	20	21	22	23	24	25	26	27	28	29	30	31	32	33	34	35	36	37	38	39	40	41	42	43	44	45	46
1	6	30	100		400						150								20	4						100	209
2	2	20	10		50						104															43	108
3		20	3	3	20						30															30	36
4	2	24	10		19						52								10	1						70	60
5	1	22		2	40						104								3							8	44
6		3	10	10	70						100															12	75
7	1	10		3	30						104															60	60
8	2			3	12						30															15	60
9	1	10	10	4	50						104								10							22	66
10	1	20	4		20						20															8	41
11	3	6	10	10	50						100															40	62
12	1				25						15															5	35
13	1	12	30	3	25						40														20	15	75
14			10	3	40						5															4	30
15	2	25	12		80						104															27	78
16	1	8	8		20						25															15	70
17	2	13	20	1	20						104														12	45	46
18	1		12								20																78
19		10	3	6	50						104															37	113
20	1	8		5	12						30															7	40
21	1	4			10						13															15	52
22	1	30	8		40						150															18	32
23		25			100						25														100		75
24		10		10	30						52																40
25	4	40	20	5	100						100	40	2													30	100
26	2	30	4	30	100						125								15							62	90
27	2	60	20	10	300						200															52	130
28		24	6	20	40						52															10	103
29	1	10		4	10																						43
30					30						20															18	58
31		12			19						150																110
32	2				10																						30
33	1	20	20		100						150															10	86
34	2				40						20															20	29
35		12		5	100						50														54	20	57
36		40	20	10	40						25															20	77
37	1	12	10	2	40						60															22	55
38		21			100						75														23	37	25
39		10	8	3	20						52																43
40		3			[illegible]						5															4	25
41	4	20	12	7	75						75														20	20	27

SCHEDULE 4.—Productions of Agriculture in ______ 977 in the ______ **enumerated by me, on the** [illegible] **day of** October **1850.**

Name of Owner, Agent, or Manager of the Farm.	Acres of Land. Improved.	Acres of Land. Unimproved.	Cash value of Farm.	Value of farming Implements and Machinery.	Live Stock, June 1st, 1850. Horses.	Asses and Mules.	Milch Cows.	Working Oxen.	Other Cattle.	Sheep.	Swine.	Value of Live Stock.	Produce during the year. Wheat, bushels of.	Rye, bushels of.	Indian Corn, bushels of.	Oats, bushels of.	Rice, lbs. of.	Tobacco, lbs. of.
1	2	3	4	5	6	7	8	9	10	11	12	13	14	15	16	17	18	19
1 Daniel McWilliams	75	105	475	100	4		5		5	[illegible]	11	324	47		315	35		
2 Thomas Wicker	50	150	400	135	3		8		5		20	335	20		625	30		
3 William Walden	30	170	480	5	1		1				2	35	75		300	25		1
4 William B. Kelly	40	350	350	30	1		2		8	6	15	125	80		300	30		
5 Flora McInnis	100	700	800	70	2		7		11	23	40	365	100		500	20		
6 John A. Gilmore	150	800	1350	260	4	1	3	2	10	12	40	432	245		575	75		
7 James Burns	25	100	250	5	1		2		2		1	75	10		100	20		15
8 Jordan Wicker	90	95	300	100	3		7		13	12	30	373	107		500	100		
9 John Stedman	35	97	400	40	2		2	2	4	6	7	201	40		300	20		
10 James Bridges	30	120	150	30	2		3		3	6	3	183			225			
11 Peter McIntyre	30	227	640	5	3		7		8	5	17	282	12		300	35		
12 John McIver	150	297	700	50	5		7	2	10	10	34	475	130		600	240		
13 Catharine McColskey	40	90	150	6	1		2		2		15	68	10		150	20		300
14 Duncan McK. McColskey	125	475	1200	34	3		3		3	13	25	327	35		300	75		
15 William McColskey	50	280	1000	79	2	1	4		8	4	14	287	30		300	30		
16 Richard M. Cole	75	61	300	60	4		8		11	19	47	388	50		450	20		100
17 Evander McGilvary	50	330	400	38	1	1	5		7	14	21	227	70		225	125		
18 Thomas Cole	70	210	713	75	3		2		14	14	35	371	26		450	40		
19 Benjamin Cole	25	138	250	60	2		2		1	15	7	107	19		175	25		
20 Alexander N. McIver	30	350	1000	50	3		4		10	23	28	262	50		300	30		
21 Peter Sinclair	60	305	668	60	3	1	3		5	8	11	321	17		150	10		
22 John Morris	70	125	150	6	2		3	2	10	30	32	277	38		250	11		
23 Daniel M. McColskey	80	370	1000	495	4		7		8	30	30	370	100		500	300		
24 Duncan Murchison	200	1800	4000	510	4	10	12		40	30	50	1281	355		1700	130		
25 Margaret Bergman	35	95	130	6	2		3		2	14	12	161	32		350	50		30
26 Charles McDonald	100	203	300	50	3		7		17	15	10	280	40		350	40		
27 Duncan Lamont	46	369	350	6	2		2		3		11	155	45		100			
28 Alexander Graham	60	27	180	60	2		4		4	6	15	183	26		200	20		
29 Henry Cofer	60	240	300	30	2		4		3	5	7	136	37		150	35		
30 Andrew Cole	30	310	330	55	2	1	3		2	19	20	227	80		175			
31 Malcom Curry	30	345	375	3	2		3		4	7	30	177			150			
32 James Jackson	30	170	200	25	2		2		5	10	24	246	42		130	10		
33 Bird Jackson	100	263	550	170	2	2	6		8	30	26	346	77		300	20		
34 John Cole	45	110	350	20	1		4		5			115	40		250	40		
35 Jesse Spivey	45	255	300	100	3		3		3	12	25	333	35		100	40		
36 Nathan Graham	35	165	150	15	2		2		3	9	7	103			100	10		
37 Elias B. Harrington	65	375	600	75	2		4		3		12	230	60		200	30		
38 James Riddle	40	210	500	25	3		6		15		34	300	35		300	45	500	
39 William H. Kimbrell	30	70	150	40	1		3		3		6	114	20		100			
40 Samuel Paisley	65	203	350	100	6		6		7	5	24	342	75		400	150		
41 Josiah Tyson	50	1450	2500	20	4		2		6		30	241			2[illegible]	50		
	2695	12574	25160	3155	106	21	181	8	286	405	810	11190	2293		12515	[illegible]	540	343

County of [illegible] State of [illegible] during the Year ending June 1, 1850, as [illegible] Ass't Marshal.

Year ending June 1, 1850.

	Ginned Cotton, bales of 400 lbs. each.	Wool, lbs. of.	Peas & Beans, bush. of.	Irish Potatoes, bush. of.	Sweet Potatoes, bush. of.	Barley, bushels of.	Buckwheat, bushels of.	Value of Orchard Products in dollars.	Wine, gallons of.	Value of Produce of Market Gardens.	Butter, lbs. of.	Cheese, lbs. of.	Hay, tons of.	Clover Seed, bush. of.	Other Grass Seeds, bushels of.	Hops, lbs. of.	Hemp: Dew Rotted, tons of.	Hemp: Water Rotted, tons of.	Flax, lbs. of.	Flaxseed, bushels of.	Silk Cocoons, lbs. of.	Maple Sugar, lbs. of.	Cane Sugar, hhds. of 1,000 lbs.	Molasses, gallons of.	Beeswax and Honey, lbs. of.	Value of Home-made Manufactures.	Value of Animals slaughtered.
	20	21	22	23	24	25	26	27	28	29	30	31	32	33	34	35	36	37	38	39	40	41	42	43	44	45	46
1	2	15			40						52								15	1						20	77
2	3		15		10						100								20	2						12	110
3	1			2	25						20															11	20
4	3	6		5	25						32															10	45
5	2	40	15	10	30						38															20	72
6	12	23		5	75						50															20	130
7	1				25						30															5	19
8	3	24	10	3	30						102								20	1						20	48
9		1	12		30						100															15	60
10		20		7	30						32															12	30
11	3	10			30						104															20	103
12	3	16		3	75						50															25	114
13	1			10	20						30															60	46
14	1	30	10	6	75						102															50	48
15	3		2		200						32															40	61
16	1	38	20	1	70						100															50	65
17	3	20	10	5	40						32															15	57
18	3	25	10	5	100						100														5	40	110
19	1	40	3	5	50						30														20	37	35
20	3	25		3	6						15															10	90
21		13		4	15						25															10	62
22	1	30									20															30	72
23	2	35		20	200						100														26	40	93
24	18	100	20	15	150						300	2														30	120
25	1	30	4	2	40						100															50	41
26	1	30	5	10	100						40															75	78
27				2	40						30															10	33
28		12		10	25						25															20	57
29	1	8	10	15	100						50															25	58
30		20		10	100						32														25		52
31		8	12	2	75						12															10	37
32		17		5	10						20															40	87
33		40		15	300						100															40	83
34		15	23	15	30						100															10	48
35		15	20	12	50						50	2														10	60
36		18	15		20						15	15													15	15	41
37				20	30						104															30	50
38			12	7	75						75	30														20	73
39					30						30															5	20
40		10		5	50						200	1														2	70
41			10	28	50						200															60	60

SCHEDULE 4.—Productions of Agriculture in ______ 979 in the
enumerated by me, on the 8th day of October 1850.

Name of Owner, Agent, or Manager of the Farm.	Acres of Land. Improved.	Unimproved.	Cash value of Farm.	Value of farming Implements and Machinery.	Live Stock, June 1st, 1850. Horses.	Asses and Mules.	Milch Cows.	Working Oxen.	Other Cattle.	Sheep.	Swine.	Value of Live Stock.	Produce during the year. Wheat, bushels of.	Rye, bushels of.	Indian Corn, bushels of.	Oats, bushels of.	Rice, lbs. of.	Tobacco, lbs. of.	
1	2	3	4	5	6	7	8	9	10	11	12	13	14	15	16	17	18	19	
1 John T. Underwood	20	375	375	30	1		1		2		7	86	11		125	15			1
2 Savinor Johnson	40	160	150	10	2		2		3	10	8	150	20		100	15		10	2
3 Daniel Lamont	25	175	200	5	2		4		6	5	9	170	18		125	10		10	3
4 Kenneth Murchison	45	465	500	65	3		5		6	12	30	282	35		250				4
5 Kenneth McAlar	60	344	404	100	4	1	4		5	21	25	368	43		300	100		15	5
6 John A. Campbell	60	100	300	60	4	1	4		8	27	15	315	27		175	50			6
7 Rebecca Murchison	50	200	250	30		1	6		8	5	30	221	30		120	40			7
8 Gilbert McRae	80	631	1200	165	4		6		12	50	25	477	60		450	100			8
9 Daniel Campbell	70	343	413	50	2		5		3	12	14	255	54		250	25		45	9
10 Levi Saingo	30	75	130	5			1		1			16	30		150				10
11 Duncan A. Sinclair	85	315	600	85	3		4		4	10	15	195	50		300				11
12 William C. Campbell	100	336	3000	250	3		6		8	30	40	430	50		500				12
13 Charriel Roberts	120	1000	4000	80	3	3	6		3	1	30	321	250		750				13
14 Allen W. Jones	100	200	1000	98	4	2	4		2		40	315	76	6	450				14
15 George Wilcox	75	775	3000	30	2	1	6		10		35	365	75		850	150			15
16 William Watson	100	1100	2750	120	5		2	2	10	3	20	528	183		400	100			16
17 Catharine McDonald	30	570	450	6	3	1	7		3	10	20	225	37		200	30			17
18 Samuel McDonald	40	160	150	10	3		5		7	4	13	244	35		150	15			18
19 Edward McIntosh	30	135	250	6	1		3		5	6	6	107	9		100	20			19
20 Hugh McDonald	30	136	150	15	4		6		6	3	6	201	15	6	150	8			20
21 Margaret McLeod	40	160	300	60	3		4		8	4	16	296	45		160	40			21
22 John Morris	20	105	150	15	1		2		2		10	75	10		100	25			22
23 Joseph Maunger	20	183	300	20	1		3		3	10	12	120	8		150	7		20	23
24 Angus McCaskill	30	375	700	22	1		4		4		16	150	28		200	11			24
25 Joseph J. Maunger	25	200	300	15	1		2		2	10	14	110	25		200	15			25
26 Eli Wadsworth	35	265	600	100	1		3		3	9	7	111	42		150	10			26
27 Daniel Shaw	25	125	360	6	2		2		3	6	12	131	15		200	20			27
28 William Shaw	50	300	1500	110	5		6		5	10	30	360	50		300	50			28
29 Mary Cole	50	350	400	15	4		2		9	8	15	235	30	5	300	4			29
30 Hardy Patterson	60	232	400	95	2		6		3		24	248			600				30
31 Norman Ferguson	100	268	1000	150	5		11		20	20	35	550	137		400	30			31
32 Neil Cameron	31	219	600	12	3		2		8	12	7	230	26		240	10			32
33 Alexander C. Curry	30	205	300	15	4		1	2	6		25	341			150	150			33
34 Alexander T. McLee	45	100	325	85	3		3		2		9	218	60		300	50			34
35 John W. Shields	20	250	350	20	1		4		6	20	20	170	18		150	40			35
36 William J. Shields	40	100	150	20	1		4		6	14	30	157	15		125	50		5	36
37 Benjamin J. Shields	20	135	150	15	3		3		4	20	28	225	22		125	11			37
38 Peter Sinclair	70	310	600	45	3		3		4	17	13	212	63		300	150			38
39 Brinkley Phillips	60	140	340	100	3		4		4	6	21	261	67		400	150			39
40 Flora McLeod	65	235	300	15	3		3		7	25	10	335	100	20	200	40			40
41 John A. McKeithen	30	490	500	100	2		6		12		40	355	23		570	30			41
	2066	12232	26232	2235	104	10	170	4	255	390	794	10033	1892	57	11045	1455		103	

County of Moore State of North Carolina during the Year ending June 1, 1850, as [illegible] Ass't Marshal.

Year ending June 1, 1850.

	Ginned Cotton, bales of 400 lbs. each.	Wool, lbs. of.	Peas & Beans, bush. of.	Irish Potatoes, bush. of.	Sweet Potatoes, bush. of.	Barley, bushels of.	Buckwheat, bushels of.	Value of Orchard Products in dollars.	Wine, gallons of.	Value of Produce of Market Gardens.	Butter, lbs. of.	Cheese, lbs. of.	Hay, tons of.	Clover Seed, bush. of.	Other Grass Seeds, bushels of.	Hops, lbs. of.	Hemp. Dew Rotted, tons of.	Hemp. Water Rotted, tons of.	Flax, lbs. of.	Flaxseed, bushels of.	Silk Cocoons, lbs. of.	Maple Sugar, lbs. of.	Cane Sugar, hhds. of 1,000 lbs.	Molasses, gallons of.	Beeswax and Honey, lbs. of.	Value of Home-made Manufactures.	Value of Animals slaughtered.
	20	21	22	23	24	25	26	27	28	29	30	31	32	33	34	35	36	37	38	39	40	41	42	43	44	45	46
1	1		5	10	30						25															10	30
2		10		5	70						50															10	40
3		8		5	100						32															30	33
4	1	24	20	25	60						136															60	80
5	3	33		10	100						32															75	91
6	3	20	5	5	20						50														42	36	56
7	3	20	10		15						104								30	2						48	52
8	3	100	20	15	100						130	40	2						10							78	128
9	4	24		10	40						104	10														30	57
10					15						10															6	5
11	1	15	8	4	10						15															15	34
12	10	30	40	20	100						150														30	50	140
13	2	3	20	10	30						75															10	122
14	6		10	5	25						75								10								81
15	1		20	10	100						50															24	124
16	1	6	30	25	150						75															5	150
17	2	12			20						32	10														20	70
18		12			20						20															10	55
19	1	12			10						10															30	47
20		12	4	6	10						30															2	30
21	2	6		10	25						104															60	58
22	1			8	20																					10	45
23	1	7			12						50															20	38
24			10	10	25						32															20	55
25	2	10	10	15	30						25															20	57
26	1	7			60																					10	30
27		19		5	30						15														23	10	40
28	2	15		20	45						70															30	63
29		9	4		30						20															10	63
30			13	2	25						30															67	40
31	6	30		20	60						136															30	127
32		20		10	20						25														15	20	47
33				30	130																						170
34					30						40															60	50
35		40	1	5	20						30															6	40
36		20	8	13	40						20															15	50
37		14	3	10	30						15															15	48
38	1	30	1	3	30						42															45	57
39	1	10	10		100						30								10							30	33
40	1	42	10	10	60						52														30	43	173
41			75	25	75						104															22	140

981

SCHEDULE 4.—Productions of Agriculture in ______ **in the** ______ **enumerated by me, on the** 23rd **day of** October **1850.**

Name of Owner, Agent, or Manager of the Farm.	Acres of Land. Improved.	Unimproved.	Cash value of Farm.	Value of farming implements and machinery.	Live Stock, June 1st, 1850. Horses.	Asses and Mules.	Milch Cows.	Working Oxen.	Other Cattle.	Sheep.	Swine.	Value of Live Stock.	Produce during the year. Wheat, bushels of.	Rye, bushels of.	Indian Corn, bushels of.	Oats, bushels of.	Rice, lbs. of.	Tobacco, lbs. of.
1	2	3	4	5	6	7	8	9	10	11	12	13	14	15	16	17	18	19
1 James Davis	40	262	350	50	1		1		4	4	12	83	50		250	40		
2 William C. Davis	80	362	500	70	2		2		3	13	24	144	50		200	80		
3 John Hancock	20	130	300	50	1		1				12	65	1		55	5		
4 James Sheilds	80	479	1250	100	3		5		11		26	275	65		275	10		
5 John Hancock	70	330	600	70	4		3		6	20	100	290	90		250			
6 Angus B. Pharr	150	500	2250	80	4		3		4	6	30	206			900	100		
7 Nere Street	260	900	4000	200	6		9		22	20	40	660	300	15	1070	50		
8 George Foshee	180	464	4000	250	3	3	7	1	12		30	650	300		500			
9 Charles F. Stewart	25	75	200	30	2		2		2	8	10	148	15		150	15		
10 Nathaniel Alston	100	3200	5000	50	2	2	3		7		10	245	30		450	10		
11 Isaac Clegg	150	996	300	600	1	4	9		20		80	795			750	100		
12 George Stewart	20	630	950	67	3		5		5	15	12	228	40		400	20		
13 Benjamin Sheilds	70	160	200	50	4		5		11		17	225	65		450	130		
14 Ann McNeill	60	100	550	35	2		4		6			122	13		160	50		
15 Patrick Sheilds	30	220	300	10	1		3		3		6	132	15		200	20		
16 Mahalah Wilson	50	89	400	60	4		6		5	4	50	255	20		325	50		
17 Philip Wilson	50	210	1000	10	3		5		7		20	202	17		200	30		40
18 Robert W. Goldston	65	185	650	100	5		5		14		20	410			400	50		
19 James Brady	22	70	150	62	2		5		4	6	18	160	42		150	5		15
20 James Cole	40	130	170	10	1		3		2	4	12	100	30		125	40		50
21 N. R. Brady	25	91	100	5	1					2	25	100	15		225	10		
22 Bradly Brady	75	886	500	75	4		6		5	6	40	241	64		370	30		
23 Benjamin R. Person	100	229	1000	165	3	1	3		5	4	20	280	85		635	100		125
24 James Moore	25	25	100	10	3		3		4		40	265	25		150			
25 Jonathan J. Martindale	50	175	400	15	2		2		4	8	20	175	80		260	25		
26 William Martindale	20	130	150	5	1		4		3		2	85	10		200	15		20
27 Jeremiah Phillips	30	98	200	6	2		3		2		14	125	2		240	25		
28 Enoch S. Powers	44	206	150	10	3		3		1	2	30	217	62		290	60		
29 Jacob Stutts	50	150	300	8	2		2		3	8	15	150	55		200			
30 Robert L. Person	70	330	470	80	4		3		4	6	35	251	70		450	50		
31 William M. Johnson	120	480	1750	115	3	2	6		5	12	26	317	130		500	100		
32 James Cavendish	60	240	475	75	3		4		2	5	30	239	100	1	400	25		
33 John Myrick	25	135	150	4	1		2		3	7	25	161	20		370	10		
34 James Gaines	100	220	2500	70	4		2		4	5	25	415	60		500	70		
35 Lewis Garner	50	182	250	50	3				5	10	30	175	40		300	10		
36 John Ritter	40	260	350	20	5		4		4	20	15	225	50		340	50		
37 Elias Morris	25	85	130	50	2		2			7	12	102	37		150	25		
38 Enoch Morris	40	35	150	30	2		2		4	11	12	105	20		125	25		
39 James Garner	30	70	150	6	1		3		4	10	14	115	10		100	50		
40 John Garner	55	305	700	50	2		2		5	14	25	244	8		250	20		
41 Elias Ritter	12	38	40	12	1						15	55			100	15		
	2628	1524	1015	9655	108	12	141	1	204	251	918	9530	2095	16	1364	1890		25

County of *Moore* State of *N. Carolina* during the Year ending June 1, 1850, as

Norman McCrummen Ass't Marshal.

Year ending June 1, 1850.

	Ginned Cotton, bales of 400 lbs. each.	Wool, lbs. of.	Peas & Beans, bush. of.	Irish Potatoes, bush. of.	Sweet Potatoes, bush. of.	Barley, bushels of.	Buckwheat, bushels of.	Value of Orchard Products in dollars.	Wine, gallons of.	Value of Produce of Market Gardens.	Butter, lbs. of.	Cheese, lbs. of.	Hay, tons of.	Clover Seed, bush. of.	Other Grass Seeds, bushels of.	Hops, lbs. of.	Hemp: Dew Rotted, tons of.	Hemp: Water Rotted, tons of.	Flax, lbs. of.	Flaxseed, bushels of.	Silk Cocoons, lbs. of.	Maple Sugar, lbs. of.	Cane Sugar, hhds. of 1,000 lbs.	Molasses, gallons of.	Beeswax and Honey, lbs. of.	Value of Home-made Manufactures.	Value of Animals slaughtered.
	20	21	22	23	24	25	26	27	28	29	30	31	32	33	34	35	36	37	38	39	40	41	42	43	44	45	46
1		8	5	7	30						20															18	40
2		24	3	3	60						60															10	70
3			4		15																					5	30
4				10	70						100														25	40	132
5		22	25		10						50															105	102
6		10	8	4	40						50		1													10	110
7	3	25	5	20	40						100		1												20	20	800
8	3		15	3	25						100																170
9		10	1	4	40						30														20	22	45
10	1		10		20						75															20	100
11	6				160						200																135
12		20	12	10	30						25								10							60	41
13	1		20	20	60						75	20													40	60	108
14				10							20															20	70
15				13	30						75								20	1						40	37
16		8		12							50	60														30	85
17			6	4	25						30	5													24	30	60
18			3	12	15						30																60
19		10	8	7	50						52	20							10	1						36	76
20		10	2	10	50						30															10	43
21		6	10	5	30																					10	46
22		6	20	5	30						30	20							10							60	60
23		14	5		50						75								10	1						20	53
24											40	10														10	36
25		10			25						20														24	10	50
26			3		10						40	20							10							10	10
27			4	6	30						30															12	41
28		4	2	20	10						20															10	86
29		5																								9	45
30		6		15							40															10	40
31		15		10							100								20							100	83
32		8		5	40						5								3	1							103
33		7	10	4	20						20								3	1						20	32
34		5		8							20															20	85
35		20	7	4	25						20															15	42
36		11	4	5	30						60														10	10	33
37		15	4	4	35						5								10	1					15	22	40
38		15		12							20								10	1						10	45
39		15	3	5	8						40								8	1						12	21
40		15	6	12	12						30								12	1					40	30	70
41																											60
	[illegible]	[illegible]	[illegible]	[illegible]	[illegible]						1553	[illegible]							89							[illegible]	

913

SCHEDULE 4.—Productions of Agriculture in ______________ **in the** ______________ **enumerated by me, on the** 16th **day of** October **1850.**

	Name of Owner, Agent, or Manager of the Farm.	Acres of Land. Improved.	Unimproved.	Cash value of Farm.	Value of farming Implements and Machinery.	Live Stock, June 1st, 1850. Horses.	Asses and Mules.	Milch Cows.	Working Oxen.	Other Cattle.	Sheep.	Swine.	Value of Live Stock.	Produce during the year. Wheat, bushels of.	Rye, bushels of.	Indian Corn, bushels of.	Oats, bushels of.	Rice, lbs. of.	Tobacco, lbs. of.	
	1	2	3	4	5	6	7	8	9	10	11	12	13	14	15	16	17	18	19	
1	Richard Dowd	30	265	450	15	2		4		6	4	30	204	12		200	50			1
2	Malcom Curry	25	410	225	15	2		3		3	3	10	163	3		165				2
3	Duncan McIver	60	85	300	12	3		5		3	12	10	227	60		200	15			3
4	Evander Kelly	100	277	620	125	5		5		6	18	12	295	60	20	275	25			4
5	David Rhodes	55	628	800	10	4		2		5	9	10	229	15		125				5
6	John Oats	100	1000	1000	100	9	1	7		10	36	45	671	25	20	550	60			6
7	Daniel Ferguson	65	137	300	100	3	2	6		6	15	20	401	80		350	15			7
8	Young Oats	35	197	235	10	2	1	6		1	6	20	225	20	10	200		200		8
9	Charles Gilchrist	40	290	330	50	4		2		6	27	12	301	60		300	12			9
10	William Wadsworth	100	1100	1000	150	6	1	8		8	15	60	735	90		600	100			10
11	Daniel Short	75	1450	1400	150	3		7		25	25	60	445	100		375	75			11
12	George McRae	100	898	1300	90	4		8		17	30	40	490	75		450	100			12
13	Balaam Stewart	50	88	138	10	2		4		3	3	13	131	32		165	50			13
14	Neill McLeod	130	1645	1865	189	5	3	10		26	20	60	690	100		1250	150			14
15	Jeremiah Barber	40	109	250	5	2		2		2		18	133	35		250	30			15
16	Rachel Cole	120	650	1400	55	3	4	4		15	30	40	542	82		400				16
17	Daniel Campbell	25	275	500	8	1		2	2	4	7	10	188	21		175	40			17
18	Findlay Campbell	80	459	1050	48	4		2	2	4	40	10	289	30	3	350	100			18
19	Duncan McSinclair	100	649	1500	86	4		10		15		35	427	98		400	150			19
20	William D. Harrington	375	1475	4500	205	3	6	10	2	12	27	100	1212	190		2000	200			20
21	William D. Tyson	150	550	3500	300	2	8	2		20	20	20	1580	200		800	100			21
22	Lydia Roberts	130	150	1800	100	1	2	5		3		35	287	130		750	50			22
23	Neill Tyson	85	120	1200	125	2	4	5		12	28	40	613	96		600	100			23
24	Nancy McIver	30	320	600	8			2		4		10	65	40		250				24
25	Wade Elkins	60	90	300	43	5		7		3	4	20	290			400	200			25
26	Amy Bingham	80	366	1655	180	5	2	6	2	6	14	30	474	160		750	70		51	26
27	John Murchison	300	215	2000	200	7	4	12		26		75	802	140		650	200			27
28	Charles Chalmers	660	600	8000	500	12	7	10	6	35	80	150	1475	950		1500	400			28
29	Jesse Hedgepeth	150	950	1500	195	7	1	7		6		35	560	160		850				29
30	Jesse Womble	100	640	2000	237	7		12		5	13	55	633	215	14	1000	40			30
31	James Cheek	125	500	1400	50	7		8		16		60	580	180		500	50			31
32	Lewis Phillips	50	250	450	40	3		5		3	8	35	238	96		375	30			32
33	Charles H. Phillips	25	225	700	12	3		2		3		6	167	25		250				33
34	Robert Phillips	25	75	250	30	2		2		4	6	30	206	30		100	30			34
35	William Curtis	40	176	300	100	3		2		8	7	41	237	31		500	100		15	35
36	William Phillips	30	120	300	10	1		2		3	8	12	95	20		200	15			36
37	Dabney Phillips	130	340	990	115	5		5		8	28	30	418	120		1000	30			37
38	Donald Street	150	1400	2250	270	4	3	7		15	14	35	487	100		1250	500			38
39	James C. Davis	100	1140	1750	120	4		6		7	19	50	404	150		750	200			39
40	Archibald Shields	65	75	150	46	3		2		5	27	21	253	64		500	125			40
41	John Cheek	50	200	1000	75	3		1		5	10	21	211	65		500	200			41
		4365	[illegible]	[illegible]	4118	[illegible]	[illegible]	[illegible]	[illegible]	[illegible]	[illegible]	[illegible]	17969	[illegible]	[illegible]	[illegible]	[illegible]	[illegible]	[illegible]	

County of *Moore* State of *North Carolina* during the Year ending June 1, 1850, as *Norman McCrummen* Ass't Marshal.

Year ending June 1, 1850.

	Ginned Cotton, bales of 400 lbs. each.	Wool, lbs. of.	Peas & Beans, bush. of.	Irish Potatoes, bush. of.	Sweet Potatoes, bush of.	Barley, bushels of.	Buckwheat, bushels of.	Value of Orchard Products in dollars.	Wine, gallons of.	Value of Produce of Market Gardens.	Butter, lbs. of.	Cheese, lbs. of.	Hay, tons of.	Clover Seed, bush. of.	Other Grass Seeds, bushels of.	Hops, lbs. of.	Hemp: Dew Rotted, tons of.	Hemp: Water Rotted, tons of.	Flax, lbs. of.	Flaxseed, bushels of.	Silk Cocoons, lbs. of.	Maple Sugar, lbs. of.	Cane Sugar, hhds. of 1,000 lbs.	Molasses, gallons of.	Beeswax and Honey, lbs. of.	Value of Home-made Manufactures.	Value of Animals slaughtered.
	20	21	22	23	24	25	26	27	28	29	30	31	32	33	34	35	36	37	38	39	40	41	42	43	44	45	46
1	2	6	6		10						52															22	43
2		4	4	6	30						60															5	35
3	1	15			15						50															25	60
4	1	20	10	20	30						52															20	11
5		20		20	30						30															50	50
6		30	100		400						25															10	119
7	2	20		5	30						10															45	50
8		10	10		80						50															40	58
9	1	30		8	30						50															30	75
10	2	28	20	7	20						30														12	25	119
11	1	30		15	30						100															60	180
12	3	45	20		100						104		1						10	1						60	165
13			2	2	30						30															14	30
14	10	20	15	6	100						200								75	1						60	144
15	2			5	30						5								5							10	60
16	5	30			125						200	20							5							32	71
17		10	15		40																						72
18	1	40	10		60						25														36	60	78
19	5				20						75	25														24	80
20	8	42	15	20	200						200														15	100	235
21	1	40	20	15	100						200														10	60	206
22	8		15		25						50															15	120
23	1	36	5	20	100						208								20	2						60	170
24			4	10	30						30															21	85
25			40		20						50															45	75
26	1	15	25	20	90						100															60	120
27	4		12	10	30						125															25	260
28	18	200	10	25	250						300														35	150	460
29	1		10	5	200						30		1													30	100
30	1	20	12	10	75						100															60	181
31	2		2	30	100						32	26							20	1					30	40	135
32		16	5	5	120						50								15							28	134
33			8		10						40														30	10	48
34		12	3	10	40						32								15						50	10	61
35		10		5	50						20														25	10	61
36		10		10	20						25															15	51
37		35		10	100						30								25	1						15	78
38	4	24	5	100	300						300								100	3					100	70	230
39		20		100	60						50															30	255
40		40		20	100						31															90	90
41	1	18	6	30	100						80								30	2						60	105

SCHEDULE 4.—Productions of Agriculture in ______ 983 in the ______ enumerated by me, on the 28th day of October 1850.

Name of Owner, Agent, or Manager of the Farm.	Acres of Land: Improved.	Acres of Land: Unimproved.	Cash value of Farm.	Value of farming Implements and Machinery.	Live Stock, June 1st, 1850: Horses.	Asses and Mules.	Milch Cows.	Working Oxen.	Other Cattle.	Sheep.	Swine.	Value of Live Stock.	Produce during the year: Wheat, bushels of.	Rye, bushels of.	Indian Corn, bushels of.	Oats, bushels of.	Rice, lbs. of.	Tobacco, lbs. of.
1	2	3	4	5	6	7	8	9	10	11	12	13	14	15	16	17	18	19
1 Lewis Garner	35	270	300	60	3		4		4	18	21	210	29		226	20		
2 Enoch Brown	50	50	200	37	2		1		8	5	11	155	13		250	100		
3 Lewis Williamson	25	55	150	6	1		3		2	5	10	73	25		150	20		
4 John Manis	70	117	400	100	4		7		6	35	40	425	65	3	300	100		
5 Lewis Manis	35	95	150	50	2		4		6	24	29	224	30		150	20		
6 Robert Manis	20	30	100	10	2		3		3	7	35	162	25		150	20		
7 Mathew Yow	75	225	375	60	4		4		5	20	20	235	50		300	100		
8 Andrew Yow	50	150	200	30	4		4		3	10	15	172	25		300	20		20
9 Hiram Williamson	30	81	230	25	3		4		11	19	9	219	30		250	75		
10 Wyatt Williamson	100	460	700	95	3		3		13	40	60	362	86		425	500		50
11 Henry Yow	80	89	170	75	6		5		9	20	35	600	114		500	25		
12 James E. Hussey	60	254	500	100	4		5		8	30	35	290	75		405	20		15
13 Mathew Davis	60	390	450	20	3		3		2	5	30	215			250			
14 Jeremiah Williams	130	670	800	120	7		2		3	16	15	271	80		520	40		
15 William Brown	40	365	350	25	4		2		10	10	20	210	45		150	15		
16 Thomas E. Williams	100	725	825	125	6		5		4	60	55	419	70		400	200		40
17 Bailey Williamson	60	640	635	100	3		3		3	50	25	300	72		400	60		30
18 John Eagle	50	150	200	50	3		2		5	20	20	215	15		200	200		
19 Ashley Parish	25	146	145	40	2		2		1		6	110	13		125	30		15
20 William W. Williamson	40	600	150	3	1		2		3	15	10	110	39		250	25		
21 Isaac Williamson	40	310	600	50	4		1				15	175	17		225	50		
22 William B. Williams	75	122	436	60	6		6		6	9	30	405	80		400	150		
23 Anderson McCloudy	50	1400	800	60	6		5		12	50	75	465	30		225	50		
24 William Wright	80	550	850	100	3		4		10	13	30	315	86		600	100		200
25 Kiza Owens	15	35	50	50	1		2		3	10	19	130	6		125	20		20
26 Jesse Davis	25	103	210	10	2		3		3	3	9	104	10		125	40		
27 John Brewer	25	47	150	10	2		3		3	7	8	135	12		125	50		1
28 Miles Jordan	60	290	350	75	4		3		7	20	12	254	37		275	30		
29 Joseph Owen	25	50	100	10	2		2		3	3	10	120	26		200	10		
30 James Owen	50	125	200	12	1		3		5	12	40	192	80		400			
31 Jonathan Eagle	65	635	900	90	4		4	2	12	29	71	534	80		500	100		100
32 Aaron Kennedy	30		150	6	2		2		2	2	35	152	30		200	40		
33 Jesse Eagle	70	690	650	40	3		3		9	23	15	235	35		275	121		120
34 George W. Eagle	20	280	175	10	1		2		2	6	14	82	27		80			
35 George Eagle	80	425	650	100	3		4		5	22	24	432	100		125	50		
36 John Dunlap	75	1464	1525	124	6	1	2		4	25	60	409	60		300	60		
37 Alsey Manis	25	108	150	3	2		1		1		7	92	20		175	5		
38 Isaiah Brown	30	170	125	25	2		2		1	10	17	106	20		150			
39 Everet Smith	30	70	150	10	2		2		2	20	16	147	25		125	30		
40 Isham Smith	30	95	125	8	2		3		3	12	35	170	17		175	20		
41 Thomas Brown	50	940	600	40	1		3		4	60	50	155	22		150	20		
	2094	957	09	2024	130	1	12	2	212	57	1050	9797	1816	3	10955	1029		620

County of *Moore* State of *North Carolina* during the Year ending June 1, 1850, as

[illegible] Ass't Marshal.

Year ending June 1, 1850.

	Ginned Cotton, bales of 400 lbs. each.	Wool, lbs. of.	Peas & Beans, bush. of.	Irish Potatoes, bush. of.	Sweet Potatoes, bush. of.	Barley, bushels of.	Buckwheat, bushels of.	Value of Orchard Products in dollars.	Wine, gallons of.	Value of Produce of Market Gardens.	Butter, lbs. of.	Cheese, lbs. of.	Hay, tons of.	Clover Seed, bush. of.	Other Grass Seeds, bushels of.	Hops, lbs. of.	Hemp: Dew Rotted, tons of.	Hemp: Water Rotted, tons of.	Flax, lbs. of.	Flaxseed, bushels of.	Silk Cocoons, lbs. of.	Maple Sugar, lbs. of.	Cane Sugar, hhds. of 1,000 lbs.	Molasses, gallons of.	Beeswax and Honey, lbs. of.	Value of Home-made Manufactures.	Value of Animals slaughtered.
	20	21	22	23	24	25	26	27	28	29	30	31	32	33	34	35	36	37	38	39	40	41	42	43	44	45	46
1		2	1	4	20						5														20	30	42
2		3		10	20																					10	49
3		3		3							15															6	40
4		30	5	12	20						164								10	2						20	76
5		23	10	6	40						30								3	1						10	44
6		12	2	3							15															8	50
7		40	3	3	72						20		1						10	1						60	70
8		22	4	3	20						13								12								51
9		22	3	15							20								3							10	72
10		30	2	40	30						40		1													26	128
11		60	6	20	50						32		1													80	133
12		20	20	23	40						30		1						15	1						37	112
13			5	2	10						10															30	20
14		30		3							30		1													62	28
15		17			20						20															10	30
16		140	4	15	60						100		1						12	2						40	70
17		30		10	10						30								10	1						25	60
18		20		5	20						20								5							10	30
19				10	15						10															20	30
20		12		3							5								15	1						25	26
21			3																								40
22		18	1	30	30						30															30	80
23		130		10							30														25	37	105
24		30	50	40	30						200		1						10							100	100
25		13	10	3	11						40								8							29	62
26		10	3	3	30						20								20	1						20	46
27		20		5	3						20								5							10	32
28		20		4	30						100								10	1						23	40
29		4		3	60						20								3							16	25
30		20		3	50						20								4							20	61
31		20	6	15	20						100														100	24	105
32			6	7	1						13								10	1					10	10	33
33		30	5	25	40						30								4	1						10	29
34		16		8	20						25								10							22	28
35		60		20	10						6								20	3						25	37
36		30	3	10							20															48	83
37			3	10	30																					10	25
38		20	5	10	30																					40	
39		40	5	10	20						30								13	1						15	34
40		22	2								40															20	31
41		120		10	30						30															8	18

97

SCHEDULE 4.—Productions of Agriculture in ______________ in the ______________ enumerated by me, on the *4th* day of *November* 1850.

	Name of Owner, Agent, or Manager of the Farm.	Acres of Land. Improved.	Acres of Land. Unimproved.	Cash value of Farm.	Value of farming implements and Machinery.	Live Stock, June 1st, 1850. Horses.	Asses and Mules.	Milch Cows.	Working Oxen.	Other Cattle.	Sheep.	Swine.	Value of Live Stock.	Produce during the year. Wheat, bushels of.	Rye, bushels of.	Indian Corn, bushels of.	Oats, bushels of.	Rice, lbs. of.	Tobacco, lbs. of.
	1	2	3	4	5	6	7	8	9	10	11	12	13	14	15	16	17	18	19
1	Upshur Sewell	18	65	100	2	1		1				6	45			100	10		
2	John Cagle	70	371	671	100	6	1	6		3	7	40	243	40		400	50		
3	Upshur Furr	130	460	650	60	6	1	6		6	12	50	427	100		500	150		
4	Stephen Davis	18	88	100	3	1		1				1	65			100	10		
5	George Davis	60	340	400	100	2		5		6	20	70	250	60		350	100		
6	James Davis	20		60	5	1		3		3	2	10	117	10		175	50		
7	Turner Sewell	20	175	650	5	2		1		3	8	14	153			240	100		
8	John Williams	70	250	325	8	3		3		8		20	257	60		650	20		
9	Daniel McLean	40	324	600	75	3		5		7	20	25	260	35		120	20		100
10	John Kennedy	40	174	300	100	2		6		10	9	15	249	15		250	25		
11	Alexander Kennedy	40	220	600	20	2		2		10	15	20	225	55		120	75		
12	John McRanee	20	115	270	8	1		1		1		17	104	26		325	7		40
13	Noah Williams	20	80	100	5	1		1				12	100	18		175	10		
14	Archibald McNeill	30	145	175	70	1		2		2	8	20	120	20		130	50		
15	John Bethune	50	200	250	10			3		2	6	16	57			125	60		
16	Joseph Williams	80	620	1000	3	2						10	80			350	150		
17	Kenneth McKenzie	40	260	300	10	2		6		6	10	25	230	45		200	60		20
18	Neill Morrison	80	170	400	100	4		4		4	24	30	314	50		250	75		
19	Arrington Britt	90	110	225	140	2		4		7	22	30	282	120		375			30
20	Catharine McDonald	35	135	150	10	2		3		5	18	12	137	40		250	100		
21	Mathew Deaton	30	78	150	10	2		1		1	3	27	97	41		150	60		
22	Isaac Deaton	75	523	525	200	4		6		12	13	30	373	87		600	50		
23	Elisha Cole	30	528	558	85	2		3		3	6	30	176	20		125	60		
24	John Munroe	60	159	400	100	3		5		4	4	21	224	65		325	60		
25	Francis Munroe	20	25	500	110	2		2		8		14	178	10		100	25		
26	Christian Sanders	90	235	600	40	1		2		5	18	30	188	46		300	20		
27	Joseph Deaton	40	160	250	40	1		1		4		20	121	24		240	35		
28	Joseph Cole	50	150	200	10	2				7	7	35	189	50		200	25		
29	Angus McKinnon	100	550	925	100	5		5		12	30	30	200			200	15		60
30	Allen Morrison	75	425	500	120	3		4		10	30	25	320	70		400	200		
31	James Cole	100	230	335	20	3		6		9	18	30	328	50		350	100		
32	Angus Morrison	100	1100	1000	100	8		11		7	40	60	520	65		375	70		
33	William Patterson	50	350	800	10	1		1		3		12	97	20		115	20		20
34	Daniel McNeill	60	50	110	10	5		3		8	20	30	400	103		200	40		
35	Kenneth Mathison	25	665	692	52	4		6		10	12	40	402	32	5	400	40		
36	James Tanner	25	130	155	8	3		2		3	1	11	166	40		150	15		
37	Mathew Williams	30	120	200	20	2		2		2		30	120	30		150	20		
38	John R. Ritter	135	475	1000	100	4		8		7	20	12	420	75		450	30		
39	Noah Richardson	200	1100	1400	150	6		10		14	40	80	604	140		500	100		
40	John Stutts	70	230	400	100	2		4		12		14	250	65		300	200		
41	John Ridder	35	305	200	6	1		2		2		60	135	50		175	25		

County of Moore State of North Carolina during the Year ending June 1, 1850, as
Norman [illegible] Ass't Marshal.

Year ending June 1, 1850.

	Ginned Cotton, bales of 400 lbs. each	Wool, lbs. of	Peas & Beans, bush. of	Irish Potatoes, bush. of	Sweet Potatoes, bush. of	Barley, bushels of	Buckwheat, bushels of	Value of Orchard Products in dollars	Wine, gallons of	Value of Produce of Market Gardens	Butter, lbs. of	Cheese, lbs. of	Hay, tons of	Clover Seed, bush. of	Other Grass Seeds, bushels of	Hops, lbs. of	Hemp: Dew Rotted, tons of	Hemp: Water Rotted, tons of	Flax, lbs. of	Flaxseed, bushels of	Silk Cocoons, lbs. of	Maple Sugar, lbs. of	Cane Sugar, hhds. of 1,000 lbs.	Molasses, gallons of	Beeswax and Honey, lbs. of	Value of Home-made Manufactures	Value of Animals slaughtered
	20	21	22	23	24	25	26	27	28	29	30	31	32	33	34	35	36	37	38	39	40	41	42	43	44	45	46
1				2							5															8	10
2		10		20	30						100		1													8	113
3		15		25	200						100															45	170
4			3	3	10																					5	4
5		40		12	30						100															15	97
6		3		5	20						25															10	25
7		8		5	25						50															20	85
8				20	130						50															30	87
9		20			25						75														5	30	68
10		20		5							100								10	2						3	55
11		30		20	30						50														50		50
12			2	2	15						10															10	35
13					12						15															8	20
14		16	5	5	30						15															10	21
15		4	4	20	60						30	10														20	35
16			10																							20	35
17		15		10							50								13	3						25	67
18	1	20	6	30	30						100								40	2						50	95
19		21	3	4	100						100															30	78
20		20		20	25						50															25	37
21	1	6	1	10							15								40	2						10	35
22	1	30	5	10	30						104															20	65
23		12		6	20						20															20	70
24		8	3	12	40						100								20	1						30	50
25			1	15	20						40															15	25
26		35		10	75						50															60	100
27				5	25						50															15	40
28		25	10	6	100						30														7	30	120
29		25	1	6	10						20								3							25	65
30		60	10		50						200															50	65
31		25			100						104								20	3						25	66
32	1	60		10	30						104															60	136
33			2		15						20															10	22
34		40			60						40															60	90
35		30	20	5	50						400								20	1						60	113
36			3	2	10						10															10	35
37				13	20						20								5							15	40
38		40		5	20						62															15	27
39	3	80		40	60						300		1												15	75	135
40				10	20						52								20	1						30	75
41				10															30	3						30	40

981

SCHEDULE 4.—Productions of Agriculture in ______ in the ______ enumerated by me, on the 8th day of November 1850.

	Name of Owner, Agent, or Manager of the Farm.	Acres of Land. Improved.	Unimproved.	Cash value of Farm.	Value of farming implements and machinery.	Live Stock, June 1st, 1850. Horses.	Asses and Mules.	Milch Cows.	Working Oxen.	Other Cattle.	Sheep.	Swine.	Value of Live Stock.	Produce during the year. Wheat, bushels of.	Rye, bushels of.	Indian Corn, bushels of.	Oats, bushels of.	Rice, lbs. of.	Tobacco, lbs. of.
	1	2	3	4	5	6	7	8	9	10	11	12	13	14	15	16	17	18	19
1	John McLeod	60	690	1000	100	3		8		10	30	17	274	75		500			
2	Stephen Williams	10	274	700	5	3		1		1			144	86		125	40		
3	Hannah Stutts	50	550	600	10	3		7		6	30	17	230	40		250	10		
4	William Hunsucker	35	189	340	10	2		3		6	6	20	150	25		300	50		
5	Asa Hunsucker	40	240	1000	30	2		3		8	40	15	235	150		150	40		
6	George W. Hunsucker	50	335	800	65	2		4		8		20	210	30		250			
7	Cornelius Shields	90	1110	3000	350	6		7		11		50	375	50		600	200		
8	James Horne	50	230	700	10	2		4		3		40	196	35		250	70		
9	James Deaton	20	30	75	6	1		2		5		8	93	35		100	50		
10	Hugh Kelly	130	380	800	100	4		7		5	10	35	330	70		300	100		
11	Johnson Wallis	200	975	800	75	3		3		6	50	100	360	247		600			
12	James Milton	70	105	300	75	2		5		9	40	16	310	70		400	50		
13	George W. Horner	40	43	300	25	1	1	3		4	7	8	141	30		150	15		
14	Sampson Cockman	30	79	100	3	2		2		2	5	25	75	35		150			
15	George Cockman	50	150	300	4	2		1			12	30	112	17		300	30		
16	John Cockman	40	460	350	20	2		3		5	1	40	181	50		300	30		
17	Lydia Cockman	50	50	100	5	1		2		1	20	15	100	50		160	15		
18	William Sowell	60	118	275	75	2		1		8	[illegible]	20	175	35		250	100		
19	James Dowdy	35	88	400	30	3		4		9	7	24	212	30		150	20		100
20	William Caddell	40	110	100	5	1		4		3	20	10	150			150	40		
21	Isaac Muse	60	290	350	75	5		4		7	13	15	265	100		250	100		
22	Presley Caddell	100	350	862	75	3		2		5	15	30	350	30		400	100		
23	Joseph Caddell	50	230	500	10	2		5		4	35	40	235	46		300	200		20
24	Mark Russell	40	410	500	75	2		3		4		26	180	75		150	20		
25	Elisha Cagle	20	75	225	55	2		3		6	20	20	195	70		250	30		
26	Thomas Williams	100	390	1000	150	8		7		7		20	520	160		1200	200		
27	James Stutts	50	183	500	6	1		3		6		11	131	81		175	30		
28	James Marsh	25	218	300	45	3		2		4	12	25	142	45		225			
29	Henry Stutts	60	366	500	100	4		4		4		14	284	100		250	25		
30	Bryant Boroughs	160	400	3000	200	8		2		12	8	40	358	140		1000	200		
31	William Stewart	50	250	300	10	1		3				20	90	40		300	100		
32	Abram Stutts	50	200	250	75	2		4			15	55	245	60		325	12		
33	William Ritter	50	350	400	50	3		4		7	11	20	226	50		400	30		
34	Robert Brady	40	10	101	5	2		6		12		40	280	53		250	20		
35	Nancy Phillips	90	450	1020	80	2		5		8	22	20	262	40		150	60		
36	Eleazer Sowell	75	245	1000	75	3		6		7	10	10	245	75		325	45		
37	Daniel Short	35	135	500	100	1	2			3		8	315	60		135	30		
38	William Dowd	25	140	500	50	1		3		8	2	12	112	3		150	40		
39	Basil Short	30	300	500	10	1		3		5	2	15	127	12		135	15		
40	Bryant Stafford	40	704	1000	50	2		2		3	8	16	145	35		150	12		
41	Henry Fields	250	850	500	100	5		10		10		30	530	70		[illegible]			
		2500	[illegible]	[illegible]	2349	107	3	54		[illegible]	[illegible]	[illegible]	9042	9473		14605	[illegible]		

County of Moores State of North Carolina during the Year ending June 1, 1850, as

Norman McC[illegible] Ass't Marshal.

Year ending June 1, 1850.

Line	Ginned Cotton, bales of 400 lbs. each. (20)	Wool, lbs. of. (21)	Peas & Beans, bush. of. (22)	Irish Potatoes, bush. of. (23)	Sweet Potatoes, bush. of. (24)	Barley, bushels of. (25)	Buckwheat, bushels of. (26)	Value of Orchard Products in dollars. (27)	Wine, gallons of. (28)	Value of Produce of Market Gardens. (29)	Butter, lbs. of. (30)	Cheese, lbs. of. (31)	Hay, tons of. (32)	Clover Seed, bush. of. (33)	Other Grass Seeds, bushels of. (34)	Hops, lbs. of. (35)	Hemp. Dew Rotted, tons of. (36)	Hemp. Water Rotted, tons of. (37)	Flax, lbs. of. (38)	Flaxseed, bushels of. (39)	Silk Cocoons, lbs. of. (40)	Maple Sugar, lbs. of. (41)	Cane Sugar, hhds. of 1,000 lbs. (42)	Molasses, gallons of. (43)	Beeswax and Honey, lbs. of. (44)	Value of Home-made Manufactures. (45)	Value of Animals slaughtered. (46)
1		30		15	15						156															40	120
2				3	50																					5	
3	1	80		20	30						100															30	[illegible]
4		6	5	10	30						32															5	60
5		35	10	21	40						50															100	172
6				50	50						75															20	52
7			4	40	100						30															40	165
8		26	2	10	20						104															50	70
9				4	15						50		1													15	35
10	2	10	3	10	40						40															8	77
11		100			40						20															40	170
12		40	6		80						50															70	60
13		19	00	25	20						30															15	36
14		10		3	50						30															15	32
15			1	6							20															20	28
16			3	3	12						6																30
17	1			4	5						20															20	52
18	4		4	10	30						40															20	35
19	1	14		8	100						10								12	1						21	61
20		40	4	3	10						50															10	42
21	1	20	6	[illegible]	40						30															80	93
22		25		6	25						40															15	65
23		30	10	5	50						75															61	115
24			5	8	25						104																45
25		35		12	40						100														6	30	88
26	1		10	25	25						100		1													30	120
27					50						30															20	45
28		12	2		35						30															10	37
29				10	50						30								10							18	55
30	1	12	25	12	30						30		1						20	6						60	132
31					100						50															20	
32		30		4	25						30		1						10	1						15	31
33		15		4	50						50															30	32
34				10	40						60															25	30
35	1	40		4	40						104		1												40	60	46
36	2	20			75						30															20	30
37			4	10	25						50														20	10	35
38	1			3	30						40															10	60
39	2	4	5	10	25						25															10	57
40	1	16			6						30															10	57
41	2		10	15	20						100															30	73

SCHEDULE 4.—Productions of Agriculture in ______________ 991 in the

enumerated by me, on the 16th **day of** November **1850.**

Name of Owner, Agent, or Manager of the Farm.	Acres of Land. Improved.	Unimproved.	Cash value of Farm.	Value of farming implements and machinery.	Live Stock, June 1st, 1850. Horses.	Asses and Mules.	Milch Cows.	Working Oxen.	Other Cattle.	Sheep.	Swine.	Value of Live Stock.	Produce during the year. Wheat, bushels of.	Rye, bushels of.	Indian Corn, bushels of.	Oats, bushels of.	Rice, lbs. of.	Tobacco, lbs. of.	
1	2	3	4	5	6	7	8	9	10	11	12	13	14	15	16	17	18	19	
Joel Sullivan	30	270	1500	200	3		5		6	16	6	232	15		150	50			1
Angus McCaskill	50	236	470	60	3		4		6		25	250			450				2
Bluford Simmons	30	170	450	25	1		3		6	5	40	190			150	15			3
William C. Thagard	40	210	500	30	2		3		4		12	217			175	10			4
Ollin D. Dowd	75	625	1500	50	3		6	2	14	75	10	410	35		450	50			5
John Street	50	180	800	60	3		6		6	20	20	300	60		500	200			6
Henry Freeman	30	141	171	5	1		2		3	8	17	103	20		150	50		30	7
John Morgan	50	150	300	20	3		2		4	13	16	169	20		225	15			8
Pleasant Morgan	40	96	225	8	2		2		7	3	25	228	40		200	10			9
George T. Morgan	35	35	80	15	2		2		2		20	110	20		300	25			10
Joseph Morgan	25	50	125	10	2		2		4	7	18	157	8		200	30			11
William T. Morgan	35	145	140	5	2		3		3		20	150	20		200	20			12
John Freeman	35	230	275	10	2		3		3	3	20	170	25		200	20			13
Edmund Holland	40	400	400	75	4		3		6	10	40	255	18		200	10			14
Reuben Allen	50	400	450	80	2		3		12	25	30	275	34		400	40			15
Joseph Allen	50	350	450	125	3		3		5	28	20	323	42		450	50		50	16
Jonathan Richardson	40	100	100	10	2		2		4	1	24	113	18		175	30			17
Daniel Deaton	25	265	300	8	2		3		4	13	27	163	37		150	100			18
Hiram Deaton	40	258	200	50	3		2		4	26	35	216	31		250	20			19
Lockey Allen	50	445	750	100	3		5		4	4	30	236	40		300	150		50	20
Nicholas Nall	30	170	200	65	3		4		2		10	154	19		225	75			21
Alexander Leach	100	400	500	100	6		6		11	40	100	605	120		300	200			22
Archibald Leach	100	400	500	25	4		4		8	12	40	352	20		350	25			23
Bartholomew Dunn	80	260	325	100	3		4		6	4	50	266	76		400	50			24
Jesse Smith Thomas	125	1375	700	100	5		9	2	50	30	50	725	74	5	300	50			25
James Wallicot	50	350	400	70	5		5		9	10	20	335	55		400	40			26
Richard R. Miller	60	106	166	30	3		2		8	36	50	426	70		350	30			27
Levi Wright	40	380	450	30	2	1	3		3	4	20	314	20		300	60			28
Stephen Davis	29	201	430	30	3		4		1	8	17	195	20		202	50		40	29
John Davis	40	210	300	60	3		4		1	10	12	147	30		200	50		15	30
Robert Davis	40	206	325	30	2		5		5	20	35	260	33		225	90		20	31
Enoch Freeman	40	660	500	100	4		4		5		75	275	23		275	60		20	32
Isham Hare	50	450	600	55	4		4		5	20	25	294	50		300	90		200	33
Peter Shamburgher	100	1300	1000	150	7		7		4	8	15	224	60		500	25			34
Enoch Cagle	50	120	150	65	3		2		2	36	30	221	49		400	50			35
Nathaniel Tucker	50	100	250	100	3		3		4	9	14	207	45		150	50			36
James Dunlap	20	280	200	40	2		2		2		8	135	10		150	30		20	37
William Owens	35	195	250	60	4		3		5	30	40	330	20		250	100		20	38
Martin Sheffield	60	140	600	70	3		6		7	15	30	227	8		300	50			39
Robert Milton	70	440	1000	50	6		2		5	13	13	321	21		500	40		25	40
Beacom Britt	40	160	250	80	3		2		2		30	186	45		250				41
	1019	[illegible]	[illegible]	2956	[illegible]		[illegible]		[illegible]		[illegible]	10354	1404	[illegible]	11500	[illegible]		[illegible]	

County of Moore State of North Carolina during the Year ending June 1, 1850, as

Norman McGr[illegible] Ass't Marshal.

Year ending June 1, 1850.

	Ginned Cotton, bales of 400 lbs. each.	Wool, lbs. of.	Peas & Beans, bush. of.	Irish Potatoes, bush. of.	Sweet Potatoes, bush. of.	Barley, bushels of.	Buckwheat, bushels of.	Value of Orchard Products in dollars.	Wine, gallons of.	Value of Produce of Market Gardens.	Butter, lbs. of.	Cheese, lbs. of.	Hay, tons of.	Clover Seed, bush. of.	Other Grass Seeds, bushels of.	Hops, lbs. of.	Hemp: Dew Rotted, tons of.	Hemp: Water Rotted, tons of.	Flax, lbs. of.	Flaxseed, bushels of.	Silk Cocoons, lbs. of.	Maple Sugar, lbs. of.	Cane Sugar, hhds. of 1,000 lbs.	Molasses, gallons of.	Beeswax and Honey, lbs. of.	Value of Home-made Manufactures.	Value of Animals slaughtered.
	20	21	22	23	24	25	26	27	28	29	30	31	32	33	34	35	36	37	38	39	40	41	42	43	44	45	46
1		28		25	50						50															10	50
2			5	4	40						15															20	50
3		8	7		30						5																25
4			4		40						32																40
5		100		10	50						30														40	40	140
6	1	40			130						60								20	2						40	113
7		16			30						30															16	50
8		20			20														20	1						20	20
9		6	3	5	30						15															10	37
10				6							20															15	25
11		17	2	2	30						25								10	1						10	20
12				5	12						20								3	1						10	73
13		6	4	10	20						10														30	20	37
14		10			15																					10	50
15		30	3		20						15															10	50
16		60		5	20						20															15	53
17			3	2	40						40															15	30
18		26		15	50						60								30	2					26	6	40
19		30			40						20								8							30	37
20		7		2	10						30								3	2						5	52
21			5	2	15						100															10	52
22		70		10	200						30															60	360
23		30		40	15						30															20	21
24		8	3	10							30								23	4						90	51
25		60	10	15	3						200		1													100	122
26		12		15	40						30								20	2						75	100
27		40		10	40						5		1						4	1						60	80
28		5	8	3	20						30		1													12	25
29		8		8	20						20								15	2						10	40
30		15		6	7						20															20	50
31		32	1	10	40						70															21	76
32				6	50						40								10	1						20	68
33		40		8	25						40								10	1						20	60
34		15		15	20						30		1						5	1						20	85
35		30	4	30	50						10								30	2						30	75
36		27			15						15								23	2						20	50
37											20								30	2						10	50
38		30		25	10						30								15	1						40	60
39		30	2	12							50															20	60
40		20		15							50								25	3						40	76
41	1				50						40															50	40

SCHEDULE 4.—Productions of Agriculture in ______________ 793 in the
enumerated by me, on the 5th day of November 1850.

	Name of Owner, Agent, or Manager of the Farm.	Acres of Land. Improved.	Unimproved.	Cash value of Farm.	Value of farming Implements and Machinery.	Live Stock, June 1st, 1850. Horses.	Asses and Mules.	Milch Cows.	Working Oxen.	Other Cattle.	Sheep.	Swine.	Value of Live Stock.	Wheat, bushels of.	Rye, bushels of.	Indian Corn, bushels of.	Oats, bushels of.	Rice, lbs. of.	Tobacco, lbs. of.	
	1	2	3	4	5	6	7	8	9	10	11	12	13	14	15	16	17	18	19	
1	Enoch Wallis	20	230	300	3	1						30	80			100	25			1
2	Patrick A. McKeithan	60	332	600	30	2		2		5	8	17	187	7		200	100			2
3	John McKeithan	50	96	500	30	1				8		30	140	7		200	100			3
4	John R. McIntosh	25	195	400	60	2						14	120			100				4
5	Margaret Curry	25	313	200	5	1		3		2	25	15	117	7		50				5
6	Daniel Patterson	100	695	600	100	2		12		50	30	40	500	50	25	350	100			6
7	Daniel Caddell	40	360	200	100	4		7		18	12	20	332	12		200	20			7
8	John M. Black	50	600	600	100	4		8		25	30	25	405	30	10	275				8
9	Hugh McKenzie	75	607	800	40	3		7		12	60	30	314	40		250	100		10	9
10	Hugh Black	100	780	780	75	3	1	11		19	13	50	715	32	30	300	30		20	10
11	John McKenzie	75	325	600	75	2		10		10	15	35	305	6	12	250	15		50	11
12	Daniel McKinnon	40	160	250	10	1		3		8		13	129	10	5	100			50	12
13	Alexander Black	100	899	500	10	4		3		10	4	40	284	45	26	300				13
14	Neill McCurry	50	200	400	100	2		2		7	6	20	180	12		250	10			14
15	Kenneth Ray	30	470	400	50	3		2		6	14	15	230	32		140				15
16	Daniel Blue	100	750	800	100	2		10		15	30	30	375	20	10	450	20			16
17	Neill McLauchlen	32	368	300	6	2		3		12	8	25	221	6	10	140				17
18	Donald McLauchlen	40	360	200	10	1		2		8	6	28	168	6	20	160				18
19	Kenneth Black	60	360	600	100	3		7		8	16	40	270	15	4	200	60			19
20	Jesse Hannon	60	400	200	40	1		7		7	13	28	170	13	12	300	50			20
21	Hardin Warner	100	700	1000	70	3		6		7	40	36	390	20	17	400	100	10		21
22	William Caddell	40	216	200	5			2		3		20	60			125	30			22
23	John Frey	15	35	75	4	1				5		7	90	10	20	85				23
24	Calvin Cox	27		75	3			1		3			25			150				24
25	Alexander Johnson	30	120	250	2							2	2			150	50		60	25
26	James Johnson	30	262	300	10	2		1		1	8	15	114	18		200	20			26
27	Nathan Frey	60	432	500	50	4		4		8	12	28	200	10		300	30			27
28	William D. Warner	23	69	100	25	1		2		2		7	76	11	1	200				28
29	William W. Sears	25	75	100	5	1		3		4		15	132	16		100				29
30	John Hannon	17	130	100	4	1		2		1	8	16	80	6		175				30
31	Benjamin Barber	32	150	200	10	1		4		5			135	25		185	30			31
32	Burrel Ritter	18	130	100	10	1		1		2		12	60			50				32
33	Benjamin Phillips	75	125	500	5	2		3		4	8	26	175	50		300	60		100	33
34	Jesse Bean	150	130	650	100	3		7		12	15	28	310	30		400	30			34
35	Jesse Sullivan	20		100	5	2		1		1	2	12	73	20		150	10		50	35
36	William Cole	70	180	750	130	5		6		4	15	12	226	47		375	150			36
37	John Tyson	100	550	3300	100	4		8	4	15	15	30	431	50		600	90			37
38	Isaac Smith	30	145	100	6	1		2				14	60	12		30	5			38
39	Elizabeth Dowd	40	70	300	60	3		1		5	8	13	170	25		300	30			39
40	Sarah Glasscock	25	100	600	10	2		2		4	5	15	141	30		150				40
41	Henry Stutts	30	145	250	60	2		2		2		13	210			175	20			41
		[illegible]	3211	8730	1519	62		157	4	315	427	867	8494	[illegible]	292	8655	2415		810	

County of Moore State of North Carolina during the Year ending June 1, 1850, as

Norman McCrummen Ass't Marshal.

Year ending June 1, 1850.

	Ginned Cotton, bales of 400 lbs. each.	Wool, lbs. of	Peas & Beans, bush. of.	Irish Potatoes, bush. of.	Sweet Potatoes, bush. of.	Barley, bushels of.	Buckwheat, bushels of.	Value of Orchard Products in dollars.	Wine, gallons of.	Value of Produce of Market Gardens.	Butter, lbs. of	Cheese, lbs. of	Hay, tons of.	Clover Seed, bush. of.	Other Grass Seeds, bushels of.	Hops, lbs. of.	Hemp: Dew Rotted, tons of.	Hemp: Water Rotted, tons of.	Flax, lbs. of.	Flaxseed, bushels of.	Silk Cocoons, lbs. of.	Maple Sugar, lbs. of.	Cane Sugar, hhds. of 1,000 lbs.	Molasses, gallons of.	Beeswax and Honey, lbs. of.	Value of Home-made Manufactures.	Value of Animals slaughtered.
	20	21	22	23	24	25	26	27	28	29	30	31	32	33	34	35	36	37	38	39	40	41	42	43	44	45	46
1			10		30																					12	36
2		30	10		150																					12	88
3		30			100																					12	70
4			10	2	30																						30
5		15	4	3	20						24															13	40
6		[illegible]	40		300						100	20														25	186
7		24	40		150						30								10	1						20	61
8		40	20		150						100															60	131
9		100	15		100						100															25	125
10		60	100	5	300						150	30	4												22	26	149
11		40	15		50						100															50	115
12			11	4	100						30	10														25	40
13		10	20	4	150						20	40															72
14		12	3		30						30															12	90
15		25	20	2	70						20															15	55
16		40	50	10	100						50								15	2					60	26	175
17		6			40						60															10	85
18		20			200						48															40	80
19		30	20		300						75															50	100
20		25	10	3	75						50															25	75
21		30	25		85						100															60	130
22								100																			
23				8	50						30															40	50
24			15	1	50																						
25			20																							5	37
26		12	4		40																					25	55
27	1	30			100						50															20	95
28			10		20						25															15	46
29			25		75						30																40
30		2	10		10																					23	43
31	2			2	12						40															8	50
32																										15	30
33	2	15	2		100						100								25	1						150	50
34	4	20	5	10	25						60								30	2						50	134
35	2	5	4	3	50						10								5	1						10	25
36	2	25	10	30	150						150															75	75
37		30		3	80						100															50	100
38					20						8															6	35
39		20	2	3	40						20															15	50
40		10			20						5																60
41			10		100						50															50	20

SCHEDULE 4.—Productions of Agriculture in ______ 975 ______ **in the** ______ **enumerated by me, on the** 15th **day of** November **1850.**

Name of Owner, Agent, or Manager of the Farm.	Acres of Land: Improved.	Acres of Land: Unimproved.	Cash value of Farm.	Value of farming Implements and Machinery.	Live Stock, June 1st, 1850: Horses.	Asses and Mules.	Milch Cows.	Working Oxen.	Other Cattle.	Sheep.	Swine.	Value of Live Stock.	Produce during the year: Wheat, bushels of.	Rye, bushels of.	Indian Corn, bushels of.	Oats, bushels of.	Rice, lbs. of.	Tobacco, lbs. of.
1	2	3	4	5	6	7	8	9	10	11	12	13	14	15	16	17	18	19
William D. Smith	30	390	600	6	1		2		4	4	25	149			325	10		
John D. Dowd	40	130	160	40	2		4		3	9	12	190	15		350	20		10
Brian Dowd	60	140	600	100	2		4		4	12	25	120	35		400	40		
William P. Martin	300	1700	2250	200	5		8		20	15	50	605			600	200		
Hinson Cline	30	420	600	35	1		1				2	35	25		125	10		
Mary Brewer	30	350	800	6	1					4	12	65	13		200	40		
John Warner	40	23	400	100	2		5		10	7	70	300	20		375	60		
Madison McFry	45	38	500	25	3				7	4	6	188	15		200	75		
Leonard W. Cawker	130	330	1500	120	4		9		15		60	370	180		900	150		
Westley Naylor	30	60	100	10	1		1		1		13	50			130			
Harvel Johnson	30	130	100	10	3		3		4	12	30	140	10	6	200			
Cochart Fry	80	320	500	50	3		7		13	24	24	354	6		400			30
Daniel McIver	40	460	500	20	3	1	5		6	3	20	253	50		200	30		
Britian Britt	50	250	250	6	2		4		3	11	20	116	45		150	30		
John McDuffie	50	210	200	100	2		7		7	12	90	367	37		200	140		
Malcom McAulay	30	90	130	75	4		4		8	35	50	300	32		250	60		
Alexander McKenzie	30	210	275	75	2		3		4	7	24	176	35	22	250	32		
John C. Bruce	65	175	240	15	4		8		8	25	50	355	65		400	100		50
John Morrison	50	300	350	10	4		10		20	12	30	417	40	20	300			
Marion Armstrong	75	400	1000	75	3		2		4		25	365			700	100		
Malcom McCrummen	120	300	700	120	6		19		30	60	68	815	10		600	50		

176 105 1197

County of Moore State of N. Carolina during the Year ending June 1, 1850, as
Norman McCrimmon Ass't Marshal.

Year ending June 1, 1850.

	Ginned Cotton, bales of 400 lbs. each.	Wool, lbs. of.	Peas & Beans, bush. of.	Irish Potatoes, bush of.	Sweet Potatoes, bush of.	Barley, bushels of.	Buckwheat, bushels of.	Value of Orchard Products in dollars.	Wine, gallons of.	Value of Produce of Market Gardens.	Butter, lbs. of.	Cheese, lbs. of.	Hay, tons of.	Clover Seed, bush. of.	Other Grass Seeds, bushels of.	Hops, lbs. of.	Hemp. Dew Rotted, tons of.	Hemp. Water Rotted, tons of.	Flax, lbs. of.	Flaxseed, bushels of.	Silk Cocoons, lbs. of.	Maple Sugar, lbs. of.	Cane Sugar, hhds. of 1,000 lbs.	Molasses, gallons of.	Beeswax and Honey, lbs. of.	Value of Home-made Manufactures.	Value of Animals slaughtered.
	20	21	22	23	24	25	26	27	28	29	30	31	32	33	34	35	36	37	38	39	40	41	42	43	44	45	46
1					40																						60
2		16	2	6	[illegible]						[illegible]															25	46
3		20	[illegible]	5	40						[illegible]															15	50
4				[illegible]	[illegible]						[illegible]															50	150
5			4		[illegible]																						60
6		1	10		[illegible]						[illegible]															25	40
7		[illegible]																									176
8		[illegible]	1	1	[illegible]						[illegible]															30	72
9			10	[illegible]	[illegible]						200															84	325
10					150						[illegible]															25	60
11		20	10		100						[illegible]															30	82
12		50	40	12	200						[illegible]															100	155
13				[illegible]	40						[illegible]															10	32
14		20		5	50						10															20	32
15		20			40						100															40	102
16		70		10	15																					20	75
17			10	6	150						10															25	55
18		30	40	30	[illegible]						[illegible]								50	2					16	62	100
19		24									200															50	60
20			30	[illegible]	[illegible]						100																100
21		50	40		200						150	40														60	220
22																											
23																											
24																											
25																											
26																											
27																											
28																											
29																											
30																											
31																											
32																											
33																											
34																											
35																											
36																											
37																											
38																											
39																											
40																											
41																											

Full Name Index

Barrett, Samuel...226, 283, 346, 514, 538
Barrett, Solomon...15, 25, 52, 60, 70, 76, 78, 111, 149, 177
Barrett, Sylvanus...341
Barrett, William...3, 14, 51, 60, 64, 76, 86, 125, 143, 157, 238, 297, 341, 346, 516, 538
Barrett, William (Capt.)...226
Barrett, William A....341
Barrett, William Jr....170, 232
Barrett, William Sr....185
Barrington, Samuel...126, 157, 179
Barrington, William...24, 52
Bates, Andrew...3, 14, 23, 52
Beal, Elizabeth...449
Beal, Emily...449
Beal, Joseph...449
Beal, Martha...450
Beal, Mary...450
Beal, Robert...450
Bean, A. William...340
Bean, Annetta...340
Bean, Barsheba...340
Bean, Elijah...65
Bean, Jesse...66, 78, 87, 108, 143, 157, 180, 186, 236, 297, 340, 513, 570
Bean, Mary...340
Bean, Richard...64
Beard, Alexander...118, 157
Beason, Edward...105, 141, 161
Beck, Eleanor...454
Beck, Jane...454
Beck, Samuel...454
Bell, Linsey...18
Bennerman, William...10, 11
Bennett, Thomas...81
Berryman, Alexander C....403
Berryman, Ann E....403
Berryman, Barbara...421
Berryman, Eliza J....403
Berryman, Epatha...421
Berryman, John...90
Berryman, John W....421
Berryman, Louisa F....403
Berryman, Margaret...421, 554
Berryman, Matilda...421
Berryman, Samantha...403
Berryman, Sarah...421
Berryman, Stephen...127, 144, 166, 192, 303
Berryman, William...58, 68, 87, 135, 403, 525
Berryman, William R....550
Bethune, ?...158
Bethune, Allen...126, 147, 157, 180, 198
Bethune, Angus...21, 32, 46
Bethune, Catherine...76, 90, 471
Bethune, Caty...125, 186
Bethune, Christian...471
Bethune, Christopher...66, 90
Bethune, Colin...16, 76
Bethune, Farquard...4, 16, 51, 76
Bethune, John...66, 86, 564
Bethune, John D....471
Bethune, Margaret...238
Bethune, Murdoch...21, 59, 76, 78, 96, 104, 105, 112
Bethune, P....62
Bethune, Peter...4, 20, 32
Bethune, Roderick...182
Bettis, E....62
Bettis, Elijah...7, 18, 26, 55, 64, 65
Bettis, Elijah Jr....86
Bettis, Elijah Sr....90
Bettis, Elisha...82
Biggelow, Hiram W....492
Biggelow, Ruhama...492
Billings, Jasper...70, 100
Bingham, Amy...443, 560
Bingham, M....531
Bird, Abner...125
Bird, Ann...463
Bird, Benjamin...86, 125
Bird, Crecy...463
Bird, Fereby...463
Bird, John...463
Bird, Phebe...463
Bird, Richard...3, 16, 23, 49, 59, 76
Bird, Robert...59, 70, 76, 99
Bird, Sarah...463
Bird, Susan...463
Bird, William...463
Bishop, Benjamin...95, 105, 132, 162, 173
Bishop, Priscilla...169
Black, Alexander...162, 222, 267, 273, 336, 420, 483, 570
Black, Ann...364
Black, Ann E....363
Black, Archibald...65, 82, 143, 150, 161, 184, 228, 337, 420
Black, Archibald (H.)...206
Black, Archibald (Herds)...184
Black, Archibald (L.L.R.)...287
Black, Archibald M....336
Black, Catherine...144, 162, 165, 335(3), 337, 363, 415, 420
Black, Caty...119, 135
Black, Christian...355
Black, Daniel...166
Black, Daniel B....309, 364, 518, 546
Black, Dugald...151, 163, 343
Black, Duncan...150, 163, 343, 355
Black, Effemia...184
Black, Effemia (Dugald)...184
Black, Effy...123, 149, 163, 262, 364, 518
Black, Effy Jane...335
Black, Eliza...335
Black, Elizabeth...358
Black, Eugenia E....364
Black, Flora...307, 335(2), 337
Black, Flora A....336
Black, Flora E....364
Black, George W....363
Black, Hugh...87, 88, 114, 143, 157, 335, 513, 570
Black, Hugh R....168
Black, Isabel...76
Black, Isabella...336, 358
Black, James K....366
Black, Jane...366
Black, Jane E....337
Black, John...20, 33, 47, 68, 120, 125, 150, 164, 184, 206, 358, 415, 420, 508
Black, John B....277, 363, 546
Black, John Jr....206
Black, John M....293, 335, 570
Black, Kenneth...176, 183, 228, 335, 337, 513, 570
Black, Kenneth (Esq.)...281
Black, Lauchlin...366
Black, Malcolm...88, 89, 108, 119, 150(2), 151, 165(2), 210, 343, 366, 420, 518, 546
Black, Malcolm (L.R.)...287
Black, Malcolm A....335
Black, Margaret...76, 343, 355, 358, 364, 420, 483
Black, Margaret A....335
Black, Martha...483
Black, Martin...436
Black, Mary...260, 335, 337, 358, 363, 518
Black, Mary A....343, 355
Black, Mary E....364
Black, Murdoch...335
Black, Nancy...420
Black, Neill...143, 157, 254, 483
Black, Peter...21, 33, 210, 285, 343
Black, Richard...157
Black, Sally...185
Black, Sarah...335, 336, 355, 366
Black, Sylvia...420
Black, William...483
Black, William C....336
Black, William M....335
Blackman, Benjamin...410
Blackman, Candace...410
Blackman, Fordham...202
Blackman, Frances C....410
Blackman, Jesse F....410
Blackman, John...147, 164, 173, 190, 327, 410, 526, 552
Blackman, Mary...395, 410
Blackman, Nancy...410
Blackman, Philpena A....410
Blackman, Susan...410
Blake, Samuel...210
Blalock, Charles...147, 166
Blanchard, John...19
Blanchett, J....62
Blanchett, J. Jr....62
Blanchett, John...7, 26(2), 54, 57, 70
Blanchett, John Sr....69
Blanchett, Robert...68
Bledsoe, Eleanor...190
Bledsoe, Nelly...333
Bledsoe, Penelope...169
Bletcher, Flora A....401
Blue, Angus...150, 162, 172
Blue, Anna...336, 510
Blue, Archibald...172, 210(2), 362, 365
Blue, Archibald M....309, 518, 546
Blue, Catherine...362, 363, 366
Blue, Catherine (L.R.)...283
Blue, Catherine J....364
Blue, Christian...363
Blue, Cornelius C....337
Blue, Daniel...81, 109, 119, 143, 157, 163, 172, 185, 208(3), 336, 362, 366, 513, 570
Blue, Daniel (Johnston)...163
Blue, Daniel B....336
Blue, Daniel Jr....273
Blue, Daniel Sr....150, 271
Blue, Donald...337
Blue, Duncan...30, 41, 65, 88, 115, 173, 184, 364
Blue, Duncan (M.)...287
Blue, Duncan A....337
Blue, Duncan C....363, 364, 518, 546
Blue, Duncan M....210, 363, 518, 546
Blue, Duncan Sr....206
Blue, Eliza...366
Blue, Elizabeth...366
Blue, Evander McN....362
Blue, Flora...362
Blue, Flora M....336

Blue, Isabella...88
Blue, Jennet...362
Blue, John...65, 78, 84, 119, 152, 183, 185, 210, 366
Blue, John (D.C.)...208
Blue, John (Esq.)...164, 172, 230
Blue, John (M.)...287
Blue, John A....336, 364
Blue, John A.B....363
Blue, John C....362
Blue, John M....365, 546
Blue, John P....364
Blue, John S....363
Blue, John Sr....228
Blue, Malcolm...152, 165, 172, 337, 365
Blue, Malcolm (C.C)...275
Blue, Malcolm (Esq.)...206
Blue, Malcolm J....362
Blue, Malcolm M....309, 362, 517, 540
Blue, Malcolm P.N....364
Blue, Margaret...362(2), 364, 365
Blue, Martha...364
Blue, Mary A....365
Blue, Mary E....362, 364
Blue, Mary J....364
Blue, Murdo J....364
Blue, Patrick...184, 336, 366
Blue, Patrick (tailor)...172
Blue, Patrick H.C....363
Blue, Patrick Jr....152
Blue, Patrick M....287, 364, 518, 546
Blue, Peter...65, 88, 115, 172, 206, 254
Blue, Peter Jr....165
Blue, Peter Sr....151, 165
Blue, Polly...188
Blue, Samuel D....337
Blue, Sarah...363, 364
Blue, Sarah A....362
Blue, Sarah E....364(2)
Blue, Tabitha...364
Blue, William D....364
Blue, William P....363
Bobbitt, ?...169
Bobbitt, Drury Jr....175
Bobbitt, Drury Sr....175, 183
Bobbitt, Haywood...416
Bobbitt, James...319
Bobbitt, Jesse...173
Bobbitt, Thomas...174, 190
Bohannan, David...5, 21
Bohannan, John...4, 21
Bohannan, Sarah...32
Boles, Robert...65, 92, 129, 140, 165, 170
Boles, Robert Sr....92
Boling, Alexander...399
Boling, Betsy...175
Boling, James...169
Boling, Kisaiah...401
Booker, Malcolm...165
Bookers, Joseph...146
Boqutte, Meager...190
Boroughs, B....185
Boroughs, Bryan...78, 87, 108, 141, 156, 157, 204, 291, 487, 535, 566
Boroughs, James...161
Boroughs, Matthew...291
Boroughs, Sallie...487
Boroughs, William...169
Bostick, Levi...118, 130
Bowzer, James...70
Boyd, Alexander...127
Boyd, Frances...69
Boyd, John...91, 106
Boyette, John...139
Bradley, Mary...413
Brady, Alexander...449
Brady, Amy...450
Brady, Ann E....451
Brady, Bradley...183, 220, 449, 451(2), 558
Brady, Bradley (Big)...291
Brady, Bradley (O.H.?)...285
Brady, Bradley Jr....246
Brady, Carroll...181, 220, 289, 450
Brady, Catherine...450
Brady, Charles...85, 109, 153, 157, 185, 212, 289, 450(3)
Brady, Chistenberry...449
Brady, Daniel...451
Brady, Dicy...449
Brady, Eliza...450
Brady, Elizabeth...450
Brady, Ellen...488
Brady, Hester...451(2)
Brady, James...66, 99, 141, 157, 289, 450, 558
Brady, James C....450
Brady, Jane...451
Brady, Jennet...488
Brady, Jesse...451
Brady, John...450, 488
Brady, Julia...450
Brady, Lucas...450
Brady, Lucretia...450
Brady, Lucy J....450
Brady, Lydia...450
Brady, Manly...451
Brady, Mariah...449
Brady, Martha...450, 451(2)
Brady, Martha H....450
Brady, Mary...449, 450
Brady, N.R....558
Brady, Nancy...449
Brady, Napoleon...450
Brady, Nimrod R....451
Brady, Rebecca...449
Brady, Robert...157, 214, 291, 488, 566
Brady, Robert W....450
Brady, Samuel...450
Brady, Sarah F....451
Brady, Susannah...449
Brady, Temperance...450
Brady, Westley...488
Brady, William...450
Brady, Winniford...451
Branson, Henry...161
Brazel, George...14, 24, 52, 71
Brewer, Adam...464
Brewer, Alexander...467
Brewer, Alfred...459
Brewer, Alston...453(2)
Brewer, Ambrose...69, 74, 84, 105, 122, 141, 157
Brewer, Amy...463
Brewer, Ann...491
Brewer, Ann E....431
Brewer, Celia...471
Brewer, Charlotte...506
Brewer, David...124, 175
Brewer, Dicy...491
Brewer, Drury...70, 84, 121, 182
Brewer, Druscilla...463
Brewer, Elias A....452
Brewer, Elisha...157
Brewer, Eliza...464
Brewer, Elizabeth...98, 448, 452, 471
Brewer, Frederick...115
Brewer, George...6, 17, 27, 57
Brewer, Hannah...453
Brewer, Harmon...82, 116, 142, 157, 182, 469
Brewer, Henry...116, 464, 504
Brewer, Henry C....491
Brewer, Howell...123
Brewer, James...446
Brewer, Jane...448
Brewer, Jeff...291
Brewer, Jeptha...246
Brewer, Jesse...183
Brewer, John...464(2), 491, 562
Brewer, John (B.C.)...269
Brewer, Lanier/Near...7, 69, 182
Brewer, Lewis...218
Brewer, Lydia...452
Brewer, Mahalah...463
Brewer, Malcolm...419
Brewer, Margaret...439, 491
Brewer, Mark...463
Brewer, Martha...427, 467
Brewer, Martin...471
Brewer, Mary...452, 453, 459, 464, 491
Brewer, Melinda...492
Brewer, Micajah/Cagor...82, 115, 142, 157, 181
Brewer, Nancy...458
Brewer, Nimrod...70
Brewer, Noah...295, 448, 467
Brewer, Priscilla...462
Brewer, S....140, 160
Brewer, Sampson...471
Brewer, Samuel...491
Brewer, Sarah...254, 491, 504
Brewer, Sarah A. ...347
Brewer, Solomon...116, 177
Brewer, Susannah...464
Brewer, Viley...149
Brewer, Washington...463
Brewer, Westley...464
Brewer, Whitson...467
Brewer, William...82, 157, 174, 182, 459, 464, 470
Brewer, William (Esq.)...212, 305
Brewer, William Jr....182
Brewer, William S....467
Brewer, Willis...110
Brewer, Wincy...471, 511
Bridges, Adaline...466
Bridges, Amos...305
Bridges, Ann...417
Bridges, Catherine...417
Bridges, Elizabeth...465, 466
Bridges, James...417, 554
Bridges, Joseph...418
Bridges, Luticia...466
Bridges, Martha J....466
Bridges, Mary...418
Bridges, Newsom...176, 319, 465
Bridges, William...417
Britt, Alfred...200, 325
Britt, Allen...507
Britt, Ann...507
Britt, Anna...505
Britt, Avington...182, 200, 471, 534, 564
Britt, Barbara...505

Buie, Calvin...355
Buie, D....61(2), 163(2)
Buie, D. (blacksmith)...61
Buie, D. (tailor)...61
Buie, Daniel...68, 93, 108, 139, 232, 385, 386, 390, 542
Buie, Daniel (Esq.)...162
Buie, Daniel (tailor)...163
Buie, Duncan...29, 40, 58, 68, 69, 94, 112, 122, 140, 162, 171, 183, 192, 224
Buie, Duncan (Red)...69
Buie, Duncan (tailor)...70, 146
Buie, Duncan Jr....10, 12, 40
Buie, Duncan Sr....10, 12
Buie, Elizabeth...331
Buie, Fanny...385
Buie, Flora...135
Buie, G....61
Buie, Gilbert...65, 106, 131
Buie, Gilbert (Capt.)...145, 163
Buie, Gilbert (Mil)...131
Buie, Gilbert Jr....94
Buie, Gilbert Sr....93
Buie, Hector...390
Buie, Isabella...386
Buie, J....61
Buie, J. Sr....61
Buie, Jennet A....386
Buie, John...97, 122, 183, 196, 224, 390, 506(2), 516
Buie, John (D son)...164
Buie, John (tailor)...146
Buie, John C....301, 572
Buie, John D....386
Buie, Laney...385, 386
Buie, Lelhey...386
Buie, M. (Juniper)...61
Buie, Malcolm...76, 94, 110, 146, 188, 258, 390
Buie, Malcolm (Juniper)...70
Buie, Malcolm Jr....165
Buie, Margaret...311, 390(2), 506(2), 522, 544
Buie, Martin...506
Buie, Mary...118, 147, 157, 180, 386(2), 415
Buie, Mary J....506
Buie, Nancy...165
Buie, Regina M....506
Buie, Sarah...385, 386
Buie, Sarah E....506
Buie, William...93, 94, 234, 315, 386(2), 521, 542(2)
Buie, William (Esq.)...146, 166, 188
Bulling, Thomas...71
Bullock, Allen...113, 157
Bullock, Francis...65, 82, 112, 154
Bullock, Francis (Col.)...157
Bullock, John...65
Bullock, Jonathan...86
Burgwyn, John...18
Burk, William...129
Burkhead, Eleazor...112, 142, 157, 180
Burkhead, Eleazor Jr....228
Burkhead, Eleazor Sr....236
Burkhead, James...91
Burkhead, Kindred...157, 180
Burkhead, Lazarus...93, 180
Burkhead, Leven...142, 157, 180, 240
Burkhead, Nehemiah...143
Burkhead, Wesley...236
Burnett, Ann...349
Burnett, Betsy...349
Burnett, Julian A....353
Burnett, Lydia...349
Burnett, Thomas...349
Burnett, William...349
Burns, Andrew...417
Burns, Flora A....417
Burns, Francis M....417
Burns, James...417, 554
Burns, Margaret...17
Burns, Sarah C....417
Busby (Busbee), Isaac...26, 55
Busby (Busbee), John...7, 17
Busby (Busbee), M....62
Busby (Busbee), Thomas...26, 55
Butler, Polly...118
Butt, Thomas...230
Bynum, Joseph H.M....376
Bynum, Mary A.M....376
Caddell, Albert...176
Caddell, Ann J....369
Caddell, Archibald...360, 363
Caddell, Artimus...484
Caddell, Barbara...335
Caddell, Benjamin...78, 89, 118, 148, 157
Caddell, Betsy...338
Caddell, Bryan...485
Caddell, Catherine...360(2)
Caddell, Charity...334
Caddell, Charlotte...338
Caddell, Cornelius...484
Caddell, Daniel...78, 82, 110, 143, 157, 168, 226, 293, 334, 338, 370, 570
Caddell, Daniel P....360
Caddell, Daniel Sr....186, 250
Caddell, Drusilla C....369
Caddell, Dugald B....360
Caddell, Elizabeth...349, 370, 485
Caddell, Emelia...338(2)
Caddell, Evander...485
Caddell, Green...307
Caddell, Green B....369
Caddell, Hannah...484
Caddell, Haywood...435
Caddell, J....62(3)
Caddell, J. Jr....62
Caddell, James...20, 21, 33, 42, 64, 73, 87, 232, 360, 540
Caddell, James B....485
Caddell, James Jr....4
Caddell, James N....338
Caddell, Jane...485
Caddell, John...4, 66, 360, 484, 510
Caddell, John F....370
Caddell, Jonathan...4, 32, 43, 64, 89, 105, 112, 141, 157
Caddell, Joseph...271, 485, 566
Caddell, Julia Ann...484
Caddell, Lochart...335
Caddell, Malcolm...360
Caddell, Margaret...369
Caddell, Margaret A....360
Caddell, Martha...485
Caddell, Mary...335, 485
Caddell, Mary A....484
Caddell, Nancy...485
Caddell, Neill...180, 232, 297, 349, 514, 538
Caddell, Neill B....369
Caddell, Paschal...170, 174
Caddell, Patience...369
Caddell, Presley...484, 535, 566
Caddell, Presley T....485
Caddell, Rainy...484
Caddell, Sarah...485
Caddell, Tobias...335
Caddell, William...65, 86, 109, 174, 179, 228, 246, 297, 311, 338, 363, 484, 566, 570
Caddell, William Jr....232
Caddell, William Sr....142, 279
Cagle, Abraham...485
Cagle, Adaline...465
Cagle, Ann...485
Cagle, Branson...479
Cagle, Catharine...96, 465
Cagle, Caty...117, 118
Cagle, Charles...465
Cagle, Christian...65, 117
Cagle, David...65
Cagle, Deborah...466
Cagle, Dempsey...465
Cagle, E. Spinks...353
Cagle, Eli...511
Cagle, Elisha...485, 566
Cagle, Elizabeth...466, 468, 479(2), 502(2)
Cagle, Emily...479
Cagle, Enoch...305, 465, 502, 568
Cagle, Franey...501
Cagle, George...3, 15, 24, 52, 59, 66, 67, 96, 117, 123, 148, 153, 157(2), 187, 214, 283, 305, 465, 479, 502, 562
Cagle, George (H.B.)...325
Cagle, George Sr....248, 327
Cagle, George W....465, 562
Cagle, Gilliam...465, 502
Cagle, Harmon...319
Cagle, Henry...3, 14, 24, 52, 59, 65, 73, 84, 117, 118, 142, 157, 181, 248, 305, 466, 502(2)
Cagle, Henry Jr....85
Cagle, Henry Sr....212
Cagle, Isaac...178, 501
Cagle, Jacob...69, 78, 99, 117, 154, 157, 182, 186, 194, 214
Cagle, Jacob Sr....285
Cagle, James...502
Cagle, Jesse...465, 562
Cagle, John...3, 14, 23, 49, 59, 65, 117, 123, 153, 181, 214, 461, 468, 534, 562, 564
Cagle, John (B.C.)...305
Cagle, John (C.C.)...319
Cagle, John (J.S.)...321
Cagle, John M....194
Cagle, John R....485
Cagle, John W....501
Cagle, Jonathan...216, 295, 465, 562
Cagle, Julia...479
Cagle, Julia A....486
Cagle, Leonard...15, 24, 52, 59, 65, 85
Cagle, Lewis...502
Cagle, Lindsay...465
Cagle, Lucy A....465
Cagle, Lydia...479
Cagle, Madison...465
Cagle, Maranda...465
Cagle, Margaret...465
Cagle, Martha...461, 468
Cagle, Martin...153, 157, 174, 181, 212, 295
Cagle, Mary...465, 502
Cagle, Matthew...461, 479
Cagle, Nancy...465, 502
Cagle, Nancy J....466, 486
Cagle, Neill...465

Cagle, Noah...465
Cagle, Peter...85, 117, 154, 157, 181
Cagle, Roger...66
Cagle, Sallie...502
Cagle, Sarah...465(2), 466, 486, 504
Cagle, Spinks...461
Cagle, Tyson...465
Cagle, William...71, 84, 157, 174, 216, 461, 504
Cagle, William (B.B.)...327
Cagle, William Sr....305
Cagle, Wincy...466
Cagle, Zilpha...461
Callicutt, Archibald...499
Callicutt, Clarissa...499
Callicutt, Eli...118, 154, 157
Callicutt, Elizabeth...499
Callicutt, James...85, 181, 212, 305, 499, 568
Callicutt, Sarah...181
Calton, George...89
Cameron, A....62
Cameron, Adelaide...378
Cameron, Alexander...131, 170, 258, 283, 378(2), 520, 548
Cameron, Alexander H....435
Cameron, Allen...389
Cameron, Angus...258
Cameron, Archibald...123, 136, 144, 161, 162, 377
Cameron, Archibald A.J....548
Cameron, Archibald J.L....275, 377, 520
Cameron, Benjamin...378
Cameron, Catherine...140, 171, 377, 385, 389
Cameron, Catherine J....378
Cameron, Christian...381
Cameron, Daniel...140(2), 144, 163(2), 170, 377, 378, 389
Cameron, Dugald...146, 200, 303, 389(3), 522, 544
Cameron, Duncan...140, 145, 163, 170, 240, 309, 385
Cameron, Evander McN....367
Cameron, Flora...378(2)
Cameron, Harriet...367
Cameron, Hugh...87, 136, 144, 163, 258, 389
Cameron, Hugh A....275, 377, 548
Cameron, Isabella...377
Cameron, James...378
Cameron, James R....309, 367
Cameron, Jennet...378
Cameron, John...13, 29, 39, 69, 91, 100, 112, 140(2), 164, 377, 378(2), 389(2), 522, 542
Cameron, John (merchant)...164
Cameron, John (tailor)...58, 68, 99, 164
Cameron, John A....378, 548
Cameron, John Jr....81
Cameron, John M.D....378, 542
Cameron, John Sr....68
Cameron, John T....258, 289, 378, 548
Cameron, Margaret...260, 377
Cameron, Margaret G....381, 542
Cameron, Mary...252, 289, 354, 377(2), 378(3), 389, 435, 520
Cameron, Mary A....378
Cameron, Nancy...378
Cameron, Neill...139, 165, 169, 234, 293, 378(2), 435, 520, 548, 556
Cameron, Neill (G.)...289
Cameron, Neill (scotch)...281
Cameron, Norman...12
Cameron, Patrick...378
Cameron, Phillip...123, 151, 165, 184, 208, 285, 354
Cameron, Polly...188
Cameron, Sarah...367, 377, 389(2)
Cameron, Tidings...385
Cameron, William H....378
Campbell, ?...173
Campbell, A....61, 62
Campbell, Alexander...66, 113, 133, 145, 150(2), 162(3), 171, 173, 188, 210, 307, 339, 383, 479
Campbell, Alexander Jr....260
Campbell, Alexander W....352, 538
Campbell, Angus...5, 15, 21, 22, 32, 43, 59, 60, 67(2), 97, 123, 147, 157, 172, 250, 356, 441, 540
Campbell, Ann...356
Campbell, Ann E....410
Campbell, Anna J....430
Campbell, Archibald...321, 361, 517, 540
Campbell, Archibald A....277
Campbell, Catherine...356, 441, 507(2)
Campbell, Charles...67, 68, 90
Campbell, Charles (Esq.)...68
Campbell, Christian...441
Campbell, Colin...9, 13, 30, 41, 58, 78
Campbell, Cynthia D....430
Campbell, D....61
Campbell, Daniel...3, 16, 20, 24, 52, 69, 70, 72, 135, 140, 144, 162, 163, 177, 179, 188, 220, 256, 319, 383, 427, 441, 528, 530, 556, 560
Campbell, Daniel B....507
Campbell, Daniel J....361
Campbell, Donald...283
Campbell, Duncan...10, 12, 29, 30, 38, 41, 65(2), 87, 88, 179
Campbell, Duncan Sr....13
Campbell, Elizabeth...384
Campbell, Elizabeth J....427
Campbell, Findley...442, 530, 560
Campbell, Flora...254, 287, 358, 414, 540
Campbell, Flora A....383
Campbell, George...258, 281, 352, 383, 542
Campbell, George W....427
Campbell, Hugh...383, 384
Campbell, Isabella...358, 441
Campbell, J....61
Campbell, James...67, 87, 273, 428, 507
Campbell, James A....410, 427
Campbell, Jane...441
Campbell, Jane E....362
Campbell, John...64, 70, 88, 108, 120, 121 (2), 126, 133, 134, 141, 144, 145, 149(2), 157, 164(4), 169, 171, 172, 184, 281, 361, 383, 384, 406, 410, 441, 507, 525
Campbell, John (D.C.)...301
Campbell, John A....319, 358, 427, 556
Campbell, John C....442
Campbell, John Jr....250, 256
Campbell, John M....415
Campbell, John P....427
Campbell, John Sr....148, 164, 254
Campbell, Kenneth...21, 441
Campbell, Kissiah E....406
Campbell, L....62
Campbell, Leanda...479
Campbell, Lewis ...165
Campbell, Lundy...479
Campbell, Margaret...97, 507
Campbell, Margaret C....361
Campbell, Margaret J....507
Campbell, Martha A....427
Campbell, Mary...323, 352, 384, 427, 479
Campbell, Mary A....358, 361, 427, 507
Campbell, Mary C....479
Campbell, Mary J....441
Campbell, Mary M....406
Campbell, Matthew...65, 242
Campbell, Murdoch...69, 441
Campbell, Nancy...82, 119, 147, 157, 165, 173, 352, 361, 362, 410, 428, 441
Campbell, Peter M....428
Campbell, Randall...358
Campbell, Samuel...121, 141, 157, 171, 507
Campbell, Sarah...356
Campbell, Sarah J....507
Campbell, Shadrach...479
Campbell, Sion...313, 410, 526, 552
Campbell, Sween...479
Campbell, Thomas...406
Campbell, Thomas C....427
Campbell, William...76, 133, 147, 166, 182, 200, 406
Campbell, William (G.)...299
Campbell, William A....358
Campbell, William B....427
Campbell, William C....430, 528, 556
Campbell, William W....442
Carlisle, Horah...69
Carlisle, Robert...69(2), 94
Carlisle, Thomas...69
Carlton, John...125, 157, 181
Carmichael, Alexander...105, 145, 162
Carmichael, Graziel/Grisson...65, 78, 93, 105
Caroman, John...58
Carpenter, Adam...85
Carpenter, Elizabeth...76
Carpenter, John...15, 25, 53
Carpenter, Owen...2, 16, 23, 48, 59, 67, 76, 86
Carraway, John...68
Carraway, Moses...82
Carringer, Christopher...15
Carringer, David...85
Carringer, George...2, 15, 23, 48, 59, 66, 76, 90, 122
Carringer, George Jr....78
Carringer, Jacob...158
Carroll, Alexander...82, 140, 157, 181, 218, 291, 491
Carroll, Allen...111
Carroll, J.B. ...112
Carroll, Jesse...83, 101, 112
Carroll, John...8, 19, 26, 55, 65, 69, 110, 181
Carroll, John Esq....67
Carroll, John Jr....83, 104, 109
Carroll, John Sr....82
Carroll, Phebe...491
Carroll, Sterling...7, 17, 180
Carter, Joseph...28, 36
Caviness, Alexander...454
Caviness, Ann...453
Caviness, Dicy...454
Caviness, Dolly...454
Caviness, Eliza...454
Caviness, Frances...453, 454
Caviness, Harrison...453
Caviness, Isaiah...454
Caviness, James...212, 283, 454, 533, 558

Caviness, John...85, 123, 153, 157, 175, 181, 248
Caviness, Mariah...454
Caviness, Marley...454
Caviness, Mary...453
Caviness, Richard...17
Caviness, Sally...285
Caviness, Susannah...454
Caviness, Wiley A....453
Caviness, William...454
Chalmers, Charles...238, 317, 443, 531, 560
Chalmers, Charlotte...443
Chalmers, John A....443
Chalmers, Margaret...443
Chalmers, Mary...443
Chapman, Abner...64, 72
Chavis, Delilah...506
Chavis, Garrison...182, 260
Chavis, J....61
Chavis, Lydia...352
Chavis, Penelope...406
Chavis, Rebecca...169, 406
Chavis, William...72, 371
Cheek, Benjamin...319
Cheek, Brantly...218
Cheek, Charity...445
Cheek, Elizabeth...445, 446
Cheek, Fanny E....343
Cheek, James...98, 130, 141, 157, 183, 317, 319, 443, 560
Cheek, James Sr....254
Cheek, Joab...78, 83, 130, 141, 157, 184
Cheek, John...73, 87, 110, 142, 157, 184, 220, 319, 445, 560
Cheek, John Jr....220
Cheek, John Sr....216, 317
Cheek, Joseph...443
Cheek, Josiah...184, 448
Cheek, Josiah Jr....277
Cheek, Leonard...343
Cheek, Lewis...445
Cheek, Lucinda...448
Cheek, Lydia...445
Cheek, Mary...443, 532
Cheek, Nancy...445, 448
Cheek, Phillip...27, 57, 70, 81
Cheek, R....63
Cheek, Randolph...6, 19, 68, 86, 109, 141, 157
Cheek, Richard...27, 57, 66, 98, 124, 157, 183, 445
Cheek, Richard (R.D.)...265
Cheek, Richard Sr....254
Cheek, Robert...7, 19, 27, 57, 65, 98
Cheek, Ruhania...446
Cheek, W.B....267
Cheek, William B....216
Chisholm, Alexander...425, 507
Chisholm, Angus...144, 178, 222, 285
Chisholm, Angus (P.C.)...319
Chisholm, Catherine...425
Chisholm, Daniel...147, 181, 196, 273, 507, 516
Chisholm, Effy...425
Chisholm, Murdoch...507
Chriscoe, Barnabas...463
Chriscoe, Noah...436
Clark, A....61
Clark, Alexander...135, 144, 161, 178
Clark, Archibald...91, 119, 151, 171, 179, 355
Clark, Archibald A....358
Clark, Catherine...355
Clark, Christian...355
Clark, Cornelius H....358
Clark, D....61(2)
Clark, Daniel...88, 119, 152, 162
Clark, Donald...355
Clark, G....61
Clark, George W....358
Clark, Gilbert...144, 166
Clark, J....61
Clark, J. (Muddy Creek)...61
Clark, J. (sailor)...61
Clark, Jabas...64
Clark, James...210
Clark, Jane...358
Clark, John B....358
Clark, Katy...70
Clark, Kenneth...69, 119, 147, 157, 172, 230
Clark, M....61, 222
Clark, Malcolm...88, 119, 165, 172, 301
Clark, Malcolm (B.)...325
Clark, Malcolm C....309, 358, 517, 540
Clark, Mary...355, 517, 540
Clark, Mary C....358
Clark, N. Daniel J....358
Clark, Nevin...151, 165, 172, 210, 309
Clark, Sarah J....358
Clark, William K....358
Clegg, Isaac...558
Clegg, Isaac N....533
Coats, Patsy...96
Cochran, William...58
Cockman, Alamina...492
Cockman, Alexander...482
Cockman, Angeline...482
Cockman, Catherine...116, 149, 157
Cockman, Clarkey...481, 482
Cockman, David...295, 482(2)
Cockman, Eli...492
Cockman, Elizabeth...482(2)
Cockman, George...481, 482, 566
Cockman, Isham...482
Cockman, Isham W....482
Cockman, John...112, 148, 157, 179, 194, 279, 482(2), 566
Cockman, Joseph...59, 65, 76, 86, 91
Cockman, Josiah...295, 511
Cockman, Loveday...492
Cockman, Lydia...482, 535, 566
Cockman, Mark...482
Cockman, Martha...482
Cockman, Mary...482(3)
Cockman, Mary E....482
Cockman, Matilda...482
Cockman, Michael...289, 492
Cockman, Nancy J....482
Cockman, Noah...482(2)
Cockman, Rebecca...491
Cockman, Sampson...482, 566
Cockman, Sarah...482(2)
Cockman, Sarah L....482
Cockman, W. Jane...482
Cockman, Westley...492
Cockman, William...492
Cockman, William M....482
Coffee, William...58, 92
Coffer, Celia...423
Coffer, Elizabeth...423
Coffer, Flora...423
Coffer, Henry...127, 145, 163, 187, 222, 423, 554
Coffer, Henry (S.B.)...265
Coffer, Isabella...423
Coffer, John...423
Coffer, Kenneth...423
Coffer, Margaret...423
Coffer, Sallie...423
Coffer, William...144, 166, 187
Coffin, Bethuel...468, 534
Coffin, Camilla...468
Coggin, Mathew...66
Cole, Abraham...10, 11, 28, 36, 58, 69, 91, 110, 144, 162, 170
Cole, Alexander...58
Cole, Alpha...451
Cole, Andrew...11, 36, 67, 91, 124, 267, 419, 423(2), 554
Cole, Barbara...472
Cole, Benjamin...267, 419, 441, 527, 554
Cole, Calvin...474
Cole, Catherine...384, 423
Cole, Charity...254, 315
Cole, Christian...507
Cole, Daniel...68
Cole, Dickson...139
Cole, Duncan...424, 473
Cole, Eleanor...384, 439
Cole, Elisha...301, 472, 564
Cole, Eliza...451(2)
Cole, Elizabeth...340, 384, 423, 424, 451, 472
Cole, Enoch...423
Cole, Esther J....419
Cole, Flora...424(2)
Cole, Frances...423, 472
Cole, Franklin...472
Cole, George...419, 423, 473
Cole, George S....353
Cole, George W....419, 441
Cole, Green B....419
Cole, Harbard...92, 124, 232, 384, 439, 488
Cole, Hiram...341
Cole, Isabella...419
Cole, Jacob...351
Cole, James...126, 169, 178, 200, 281, 384, 424, 451(2), 474(2), 488, 511, 558, 564
Cole, James (C.K.)...260
Cole, James (L.C.)...323
Cole, James (of H.)...285
Cole, James (W.C.)...273
Cole, James A....434
Cole, James M.C....441
Cole, Jane...474(2), 488(2)
Cole, Jennet...423
Cole, Jesse...384
Cole, John...11, 28, 37, 58, 67, 92, 109, 124, 126, 127, 144, 164, 184, 188, 260, 281, 293, 321, 422, 423, 424, 474(2), 488(2), 554
Cole, John A....441
Cole, John B....419, 434
Cole, John C....384
Cole, John Jr....91, 267
Cole, John Sr....92, 220
Cole, Johnson...258
Cole, Joseph...126, 148, 157, 250, 473, 564
Cole, Julia...473
Cole, Lucinda...384
Cole, Lucy...28, 38
Cole, Lucy A....488
Cole, Mahalah...419

Cole, Malcolm...473
Cole, Manda...488
Cole, Margaret...351, 419(2), 424
Cole, Martha...423
Cole, Martha E....419
Cole, Mary...187, 188, 419(3), 424, 434, 451, 473, 556
Cole, Mary J....340
Cole, Nancy...419, 422, 423, 424(2), 473, 474
Cole, Neill...424
Cole, Rachel...441, 560
Cole, Rebecca...145
Cole, Reuben...166
Cole, Richard...165, 172, 340, 441
Cole, Richard F....419
Cole, Richard M....319, 419, 527, 554
Cole, Riland R....473
Cole, Rosannah M....341
Cole, Salina...488
Cole, Sampson...472
Cole, Sarah F....451
Cole, Silvy...128, 140, 184
Cole, Stephen...419
Cole, Stokes...472
Cole, Sylvia...419
Cole, Telitha...441, 473
Cole, Temperance...422, 439
Cole, Thomas...9, 13, 28, 58, 67, 92, 110, 220, 351, 384, 419, 423, 424, 507, 515, 527, 554
Cole, Thomas Jr....37, 144, 166
Cole, Thomas Sr....144, 166
Cole, Thomas W....419
Cole, William...11, 28, 35, 118, 127, 188, 220, 297, 340, 341, 472, 474(2), 513, 570
Cole, William B....419, 441
Cole, Willis...76, 82
Collier, Jesse...214
Collins, ?--lly...171
Collins, Charlotte...171, 180
Collins, Henrietta...70
Collins, James...7, 18, 66, 78, 81, 83
Collins, James H....376
Collins, Jane...376
Collins, Jeremiah...10, 12
Collins, Jesse...6, 19
Collins, John...256
Collins, John T....376
Collins, John W....289
Collins, Margaret...376(2)
Collins, Mary...376
Collins, Mourning...119
Collins, Nancy...376
Collins, Sarah...376
Collins, Stephen...66, 92
Collins, Thomas...58, 83, 166
Collins, Thomas Jr....10, 11, 28, 37, 58, 66, 84
Collins, Thomas Sr....10, 11, 28, 37, 68
Collins, William...10
Colquhoon, Anguish...87
Colvin, Elizabeth A....508
Colvin, William...166
Comer, Adam...15, 24, 52, 59, 68, 105, 111, 143, 157, 501
Comer, Elizabeth...501(2), 503
Comer, Enoch...503
Comer, Hannah...503
Comer, Henry...503
Comer, John...76, 118, 321, 502
Comer, Kendrick...503
Comer, Lucy...501, 503
Comer, Lydia...501
Comer, Margaret...501
Comer, Marticia...502
Comer, Martin...501
Comer, Mary...321, 501
Comer, Nancy...181
Comer, Peter L....501
Comer, Phillip...287, 501
Comer, Polly...248
Comer, Susannah...501
Comer, Thomas...248, 502
Comer, William...501, 503
Conley, Catherine...146, 165
Cook, Joseph...222, 267, 415, 526, 552
Cook, Tabitha...415
Cook, William...65, 73, 186
Cooper, Benjamin...66
Cooper, Harrison...74
Cooper, Jesse...58, 70
Copeland, Clarkey A....356
Copeland, Henry (H.)...325
Copeland, Jane...474
Copeland, John...69
Copeland, John N....474
Copeland, Mary...93, 474
Copeland, Mary E....474
Copeland, Nathan...200, 356, 540
Copeland, Rebecca...23, 50, 59, 356
Copeland, Tabitha...474
Copeland, William...65, 120, 147, 171, 179, 196, 474(2)
Copeland, William Jr....254, 301
Copeland, William Sr....301
Copher/Cosher, William...67
Core, David...426
Core, Mariam...426
Cornelison, Peter...305
Cotton, Wright...516
Cox, A.B....327
Cox, Alexander...390(2)
Cox, Alfred...218
Cox, Andrew L....402
Cox, Benton P....390
Cox, Calvin...176, 180, 228, 307, 338, 570
Cox, Celia...401
Cox, Charity...345
Cox, Charles...173, 190, 329, 402, 524, 525, 550
Cox, Charlotte...430
Cox, Delila...390
Cox, Duncan M....390
Cox, E....62
Cox, Easther...390
Cox, Edward...5, 22, 33, 42, 67, 90
Cox, Edward (Ned)...297
Cox, Elias...405, 525
Cox, Elizabeth...335, 401
Cox, Elizabeth C....390
Cox, Emelia...338
Cox, George...67, 82, 130, 169, 180
Cox, George N....338
Cox, Green B.G....338
Cox, Henry...66, 95, 133, 146, 163, 173, 202, 390, 522
Cox, Holcomb...338
Cox, Holden...113, 143, 180, 206
Cox, Holden S....342
Cox, Irvin...307, 344
Cox, Isaac W....390
Cox, Isabella...390
Cox, Isabella C....402
Cox, John...3, 23, 50, 60, 70, 174, 297, 344, 390
Cox, John B....338
Cox, John L....390
Cox, John M....313, 522, 544
Cox, John W....402
Cox, Louisa R....345
Cox, MacDonald...344
Cox, Martha...338, 390
Cox, Mary...341, 390
Cox, Mary (Shug)...297
Cox, Mary A....405
Cox, Mary J....345, 402
Cox, Mary W....338
Cox, Merrill...130, 185, 206, 335
Cox, Minerva...289
Cox, Moses...67, 95
Cox, Nancy...344, 405
Cox, Ned...180
Cox, Nicy...335
Cox, Rebecca...402
Cox, Robert...2, 25, 53
Cox, Rufus...390
Cox, S....62
Cox, Sarah...331, 401, 402, 524, 550
Cox, Susan...344
Cox, Susannah...338
Cox, Thomas...133, 146, 166, 170, 190, 303, 390, 405, 522, 544
Cox, W. Joseph...390
Cox, William...65, 82, 114, 157, 236, 344
Cox, William (L.E.)...325
Cox, William A....390
Cox, William B....323
Cox, William O.B....402
Cox, William Sr....180
Crabtree, Elizabeth...346
Crabtree, Ellen...347
Crabtree, Henry T.S....347
Crabtree, John...341
Crabtree, Mary F....346
Crabtree, Sally C....346
Crabtree, Sarah...347
Crabtree, Temperance...346
Crabtree, William A....346
Craig, John...71
Craig, Sarah...473
Craven, Elizabeth...459
Craven, Henry...142, 157
Crawford, ?...173
Crawford, Charles...146, 162, 177
Crawford, William...146, 166
Crawford, William (Esq.)...202
Creas, Calnon...58
Culbertson, Jacob...142
Culbertson, Joseph...157
Culbertson, Josiah...116, 181
Cunningham, James L....366
Currie (Curry), A.C. ...236, 307
Currie (Curry), Alexander...139
Currie (Curry), Alexander C....435, 529, 556
Currie (Curry), Angus...16, 51, 87, 109, 139, 162(2), 185, 230, 371, 372, 435, 519, 548
Currie (Curry), Angus M....336
Currie (Curry), Angus Mc....371
Currie (Curry), Angus Sr....289
Currie (Curry), Ann...364, 370, 518, 546
Currie (Curry), Ann C....370
Currie (Curry), Archibald...92, 94, 124, 139, 161, 184, 367, 368, 518

Currie (Curry), Archibald B....313, 546
Currie (Curry), Archibald C....364
Currie (Curry), Barbara...368
Currie (Curry), Benjamin R....435
Currie (Curry), Betsey...365
Currie (Curry), Catherine...157, 372, 437
Currie (Curry), Catherine A....365
Currie (Curry), Christian...371
Currie (Curry), Christian B....435
Currie (Curry), Daniel...163, 184
Currie (Curry), Daniel A....365, 367
Currie (Curry), Daniel B....301, 367, 518, 546
Currie (Curry), Daniel C....267, 372
Currie (Curry), Daniel M....371
Currie (Curry), Duncan...120, 151, 163, 367
Currie (Curry), Duncan B....307, 365, 368, 518, 546
Currie (Curry), Duncan J....364
Currie (Curry), Effy...334
Currie (Curry), Effy E....365
Currie (Curry), Flora...365, 368
Currie (Curry), Flora A....367
Currie (Curry), Flora J....371
Currie (Curry), Flora M....368
Currie (Curry), Hector...185
Currie (Curry), Helena...365
Currie (Curry), Henry B....370
Currie (Curry), Hugh C....371
Currie (Curry), Isabella...423
Currie (Curry), James...139
Currie (Curry), Jane...365, 367, 368(2)
Currie (Curry), Jane B....368
Currie (Curry), Jennet...336
Currie (Curry), John A....367
Currie (Curry), John B....435
Currie (Curry), John C....370
Currie (Curry), John H....365
Currie (Curry), John M....256, 309, 365, 546
Currie (Curry), John R....287, 368
Currie (Curry), Kenneth...372
Currie (Curry), Lauchlin...16, 51, 87, 119, 123, 143, 149, 157, 165, 184, 185, 246, 368, 370
Currie (Curry), Lauchlin A....368
Currie (Curry), Lauchlin B....367
Currie (Curry), Lauchlin Sr....256, 293
Currie (Curry), Lydia...368
Currie (Curry), Malcolm...311, 423, 437, 529, 554, 560
Currie (Curry), Malcolm (Ditcher?)...299
Currie (Curry), Malcolm B....224
Currie (Curry), Margaret...279, 334, 368, 423, 435, 570
Currie (Curry), Mary...125, 329, 365, 435
Currie (Curry), Mary E....336
Currie (Curry), Mary J....423
Currie (Curry), Matilda...334
Currie (Curry), Murdoch...87, 129, 143, 157, 368
Currie (Curry), Nancy...368
Currie (Curry), Nancy B....368
Currie (Curry), Neill...513
Currie (Curry), Neill A....435
Currie (Curry), Neill B....365
Currie (Curry), Neill R....336, 570
Currie (Curry), Rebecca J....368
Currie (Curry), Sarah...367, 368, 519, 546
Currie (Curry), Sarah A....336, 368
Currie (Curry), Sarah C....368
Currie (Curry), Sarah E....370
Currie (Curry), William C....368
Curtis, Esther A....444
Curtis, Margaret E....444
Curtis, Martha...444
Curtis, Nancy E....444
Curtis, William...444, 560
Curtis, William D....444
Dale, Martin...72
Dalrymple, Archibald...68, 72, 81, 136, 145, 162, 186, 190, 321, 391, 392, 400, 544, 550
Dalrymple, David E....391
Dalrymple, Elizabeth...252, 313, 391(2), 392, 399, 523
Dalrymple, Flora...399
Dalrymple, J....61
Dalrymple, James...94, 131, 146, 164, 186, 399
Dalrymple, Jane...265
Dalrymple, Jennet...145, 164, 391, 392
Dalrymple, John...68, 94, 131, 145, 164, 173, 202, 250, 303, 327, 391, 399, 523, 550
Dalrymple, John (B.)...331
Dalrymple, John G....399
Dalrymple, John H....267, 391, 522, 523, 544
Dalrymple, Malcolm...399
Dalrymple, Margaret...392
Dalrymple, Margaret A....391
Dalrymple, Mary...391
Dalrymple, Neill A....399
Dalrymple, Rosanna...313, 399, 400, 524
Dalrymple, Sarah C....391
Dalrymple, William...131, 145, 166, 173, 303, 391, 392, 399, 523, 544
Daniel, Robert J....176
Dannelly, Dillon J....492
Dannelly, Eli P. ...356
Dannelly, John...87, 111, 142, 157, 181, 238
Dannelly, John P....492
Dannelly, Mahala...492
Dannelly, Sarah...492
Dannelly, Swain...492
Dannelly, Thomas...182, 214
Dannelly, W.D....295
Dannelly, Wiley...492
Dannelly, William...65, 271, 492
Dannelly, William (Esq.)...236
Dark, Joseph...124
Dark, Samuel...70, 72, 81
Dark, Sarah...127
Davidson, Alexander...174
Davidson, David...69
Davidson, John...9, 354
Davis, Aaron...84, 500
Davis, Andrew...325
Davis, Ann...28, 37
Davis, Ann E....500
Davis, Archibald...499
Davis, Arthur...10, 12, 68
Davis, Artn...340
Davis, Baxter...469
Davis, Burgess...87
Davis, Charles...446
Davis, Clarkey...446
Davis, Devotion...123, 349
Davis, Edmund...349
Davis, Eli...489
Davis, Eliza...464
Davis, Elizabeth...157, 169, 464, 468, 469, 479, 499, 500
Davis, Emory...500
Davis, Enoch...446
Davis, Franey...468
Davis, George...196, 301, 468, 500, 564
Davis, Hardy...25, 53, 59, 67, 78, 85
Davis, Harrison...349
Davis, Hayman...500
Davis, James...68, 86, 108, 141, 175, 220, 321, 446, 469, 478, 558, 564
Davis, James C....157, 445, 532, 560
Davis, Jane...349, 460, 500
Davis, Jesse...269, 464, 562
Davis, John...295, 349, 464, 469, 499, 500, 568
Davis, Jordan...204
Davis, Leanda...500
Davis, Letitia...500
Davis, Levi...500
Davis, Lockey...464
Davis, Louisa J....446
Davis, Lydia...446, 464, 469
Davis, M....62
Davis, Malcolm...349
Davis, Martha...464, 469, 500
Davis, Martha E....460
Davis, Martin...447
Davis, Mary...446, 469, 478, 499, 500(3), 511
Davis, Mary A....349, 460
Davis, Matthew...10, 12, 29, 39, 68, 73, 84, 169, 269, 331, 460, 534, 562
Davis, Nancy...349, 446, 460
Davis, Nevin...323
Davis, Peter...110, 154, 157, 181
Davis, Phebe...446
Davis, R....62
Davis, Raleigh...469
Davis, Ralph...11, 30, 40, 58, 64, 84, 87, 115
Davis, Reddick H....430
Davis, Robert...66, 69, 72, 99, 122, 141, 157, 175, 214, 305, 479, 500, 568
Davis, Robin...285
Davis, Ruth...489
Davis, Sarah...70, 445, 469, 489
Davis, Serepta...464
Davis, Shadrach...248
Davis, Stephen...97, 136, 154, 158, 181, 192, 212, 269, 279, 349(2), 460, 468, 499, 500, 514, 536, 538, 564, 568
Davis, Susannah...117, 460
Davis, Taylor...447
Davis, Thomas...13, 67, 84, 139, 166, 479
Davis, Vincent...65
Davis, Westley...446
Davis, William...19, 65, 169, 175, 182, 212, 216, 313, 446, 500
Davis, William (J.C.)...331
Davis, William C....446, 558
Davis, Wincy J....500
Davis, Windsor...460
Davis, Zachariah...78
Davis, Zilpha...500
Dawkins, Bethuel...474
Dawkins, Eliza...474
Dawkins, George...472
Dawson, Bryan...258
Dawson, Isaac...133
Dawson, Thomas...341
Dawson, William...119, 140, 166
Dawson, Wilson...128
Dean, Henry...4
Dean, Jeremiah...97
Dean, Robert...271

Deaton, Bazel...497
Deaton, Burrell...85, 114, 136, 149, 157, 186, 198, 269, 497(2), 568
Deaton, Catherine...480, 497
Deaton, Christian...473
Deaton, Deborah...472
Deaton, Dison...497
Deaton, Elias M....470
Deaton, Elizabeth...497
Deaton, Emeline...499
Deaton, Flora...497
Deaton, Harriett...497
Deaton, Henry H....470
Deaton, Hiram...497, 568
Deaton, Hiram (M.C.)...295
Deaton, Isaac...301, 472, 534, 564
Deaton, Isabella...473
Deaton, Jackson...295, 497
Deaton, James...470, 480, 566
Deaton, Jane...480, 499
Deaton, John...194, 301, 472
Deaton, John ...497
Deaton, Joseph...470, 473, 564
Deaton, Levi...91, 136, 148, 157, 198, 273, 468
Deaton, Lockey...472
Deaton, Lydia...473
Deaton, Madison...497
Deaton, Margaret...200, 472(2), 497, 499
Deaton, Marion...480
Deaton, Martha...470
Deaton, Mary...470, 472, 534
Deaton, Mary A....472
Deaton, Mary J....499
Deaton, Matthew...85, 136, 147, 157, 181, 472(2), 564
Deaton, Mimy J....473
Deaton, Minny...472
Deaton, Molly...265
Deaton, Nancy...468, 497
Deaton, Noah...497
Deaton, Patience...497(3)
Deaton, Pinckney...352
Deaton, Rebecca...468, 497
Deaton, Reuben...472
Deaton, Sarah...497
Deaton, Sarah A....497
Deaton, Terry A....472
Deaton, William...194, 214(2), 273, 472, 480, 497(2)
Demby, Joshua...70, 95
Dennis, Charles F....337
Denson, Benjamin...246
Denson, Bennett...186
Denson, David...488
Denson, Duncan...488
Denson, Edmund...474
Denson, Franey...488
Denson, Jethro...214, 277
Denson, Kearny...488
Denson, Rebecca...488
Denson, Sally...285
Denson, Sarah...488
Denson, Spinks...488
Denson, William...488
Denson/Dovson, William...180
Dey, Ann...70
Dickens, Elizabeth...401
Dickens, Gideon...402
Dickens, James...402
Dickens, Joseph...303
Dickens, Temperance...402
Dickinson (Dickerson), Elizabeth...342
Dickinson (Dickerson), James...58
Dickinson (Dickerson), Jeremiah...109
Dickinson (Dickerson), Michael...81
Dickinson (Dickerson), R....62
Dickinson (Dickerson), Robert...66, 82, 105, 124
Dickinson (Dickerson), Thomas...101
Dickinson (Dickerson), W....62
Dickinson (Dickerson), William...124, 140, 170
Dickinson (Dickerson), Willis...8, 19, 26, 54, 66, 83, 140, 166, 177
Dicks, James...480
Diffie, John...85
Diffie, William...161, 182
Dixon, John...188, 192
Dobbins, F....61
Dockins, William...355
Doland, Felen...58
Donald, James...176
Douglas, A.G....317
Douglas, Abel...145, 162
Douglas, Archibald...145, 162, 244, 393, 401, 524, 550
Douglas, Archibald G....393, 523, 544
Douglas, Archibald Sr....283
Douglas, Daniel...303, 401, 524, 550
Douglas, Delaney...401
Douglas, Dorcas...401
Douglas, Elizabeth A....401
Douglas, James...401
Douglas, John...179, 252, 303, 401, 524, 550
Douglas, Lavicey...401
Douglas, Lucinda...401
Douglas, Martha E....393
Douglas, Nancy...393, 401
Douglas, Nathan...202, 303
Douglas, Rosa...393
Douglas, Rosanna...401
Douglas, Sarah...393(2), 401
Douglas, Silas...169
Dowd, Ann M....493
Dowd, Anna R....510
Dowd, Bryan...342, 513, 572
Dowd, Catherine...341
Dowd, Charles D....494
Dowd, Clement...493
Dowd, Connor...7, 18, 26, 56, 252
Dowd, Cornelius...68, 81, 100, 101, 136, 142, 158, 168
Dowd, Cornelius H....435
Dowd, Cornelius Sr....234, 287
Dowd, Eliza...493
Dowd, Elizabeth...341, 570
Dowd, Elizabeth J....490
Dowd, Emeline...490
Dowd, Emily M....494
Dowd, Henry C....494
Dowd, James...82, 105, 110, 157, 175, 226
Dowd, James C....493
Dowd, Jane...490
Dowd, John...171, 341
Dowd, John D....342, 513, 572
Dowd, Kendrick...342
Dowd, M....62
Dowd, Martha...493
Dowd, Mary...64, 80, 232, 289, 342, 437
Dowd, Nancy...437
Dowd, Patrick...68, 93, 110, 143, 157, 179
Dowd, Retta...297
Dowd, Richard...437, 560
Dowd, W.D....240, 307
Dowd, William...142, 168, 490, 566
Dowd, William (Capt.)...158
Dowd, William P....493
Dowd, Willis D....293, 493, 536, 568
Dowdy, Amos...115, 142, 158, 483
Dowdy, Archibald...483
Dowdy, Daniel...89
Dowdy, Franey...347
Dowdy, James...89, 114, 125, 143, 157, 185, 228, 295, 483, 535, 566
Dowdy, James Jr....323
Dowdy, James S....347
Dowdy, James Sr....291
Dowdy, Jane...484
Dowdy, John...226
Dowdy, Lettice...418
Dowdy, Margaret J....347
Dowdy, Neill...347
Dowdy, Rachel...483
Dowdy, Rachel C....484
Dowdy, Rainy...483
Dowdy, Rebecca...347
Dowdy, William...185, 418
Drake, Benton...146, 166, 173
Drake, John...242
Duckworth, Hannah...182
Duckworth, J....62
Duckworth, Jacob...8, 19
Duckworth, Jesse...69
Duckworth, Joseph...7, 18, 27, 57, 70, 83, 112, 158
Due (Dew), Betsy...345
Due (Dew), Elizabeth/Betsy...174, 182
Due (Dew), Lucy...246
Due (Dew), Nancy...345
Due (Dew), Samuel...170, 273, 345
Due (Dew), Thomas...345
Due/Dye, John...87
Duffie, William...154
Dunlap, Alexander...371
Dunlap, Angus...371
Dunlap, Caroline...503
Dunlap, Cornelius...370, 371, 519, 548
Dunlap, Daniel...371, 503
Dunlap, Elizabeth...463
Dunlap, Frances...463
Dunlap, Henry C....465
Dunlap, J....62
Dunlap, James...112, 148, 157, 179, 198, 273, 503, 568
Dunlap, James H....465
Dunlap, John...6, 17, 27, 57, 70, 77, 93, 131, 142, 182, 186, 212, 269, 371, 465, 534, 562
Dunlap, John Jr....154, 157
Dunlap, John Sr....157
Dunlap, Lucy...269
Dunlap, Margaret...370
Dunlap, Mary...465
Dunlap, Mary A.E....465
Dunlap, Neill...283
Dunlap, Neill (Esq.)...194
Dunlap, Phebe...503
Dunlap, Sarah...371
Dunlap, William C.D....465
Dunn, B....59
Dunn, B. Sr....59
Dunn, Bartholomew...2, 14, 23, 48, 96(2), 126, 149, 157, 177, 214, 250, 295, 498, 568

Dunn, Bartholomew Jr...67
Dunn, Bartholomew Sr...67
Dunn, Creasy...177, 256
Dunn, Cynthia...499
Dunn, Darcus...498
Dunn, George...480
Dunn, Green B...499
Dunn, Hannah...501
Dunn, Henry C...480
Dunn, Hezekiah...24, 52, 59, 66
Dunn, Isaac...2, 14, 23, 52, 59, 71, 78
Dunn, James...501
Dunn, John...86, 96, 113, 126, 147, 157
Dunn, Joseph...8, 18
Dunn, Joseph Jr...68
Dunn, Joseph Sr...68
Dunn, Maloney...501
Dunn, Margaret...498, 501
Dunn, Mary...480, 498
Dunn, Nancy...480
Dunn, Ptolemy...480
Dunn, Richard...2(2), 14, 23, 59, 66
Dunn, Richard Jr...14, 23, 52
Dunn, Richard Sr...52
Dunn, Sampson...480
Dunn, Samuel...67, 78, 81, 104, 129, 265
Dunn, Sarah...480
Dunn, Thomas...67, 84
Dunn, W...62
Dunn, William...2, 8, 14, 18, 23, 27, 50, 57, 59, 65, 67, 84, 96, 117, 126, 148, 157, 178, 196, 501
Dunn, William Esq...76
Dunnan, Elizabeth...472
Dye, Barbara...395
Dye, Barbary...139, 162
Dye, David...412
Dye, Delaney...412
Dye, Elizabeth...26, 55, 58
Dye, Jane...412(2)
Dye, John M...412
Dye, Martin...58, 133, 146, 165, 224, 313, 412, 552
Dye, Martin E...412(2)
Dye, Sallie...412
Dye, W. Westley...412, 526, 552
Dye, William...7, 18
Dye, William Sr...7
Eddins, Abigail...510
Eddins, Sarah...358
Eddins, Theophilus...66, 74
Edwards, Abigail...171
Edwards, Barbara J...389
Edwards, Elizabeth...391
Edwards, Francis...391, 544
Edwards, Francis W...299
Edwards, Frank...323
Edwards, Gideon...188, 242, 299, 391, 522, 544
Edwards, Jacob...68
Edwards, Jane...391
Edwards, John...391
Edwards, Joshua...68
Edwards, Nancy...391
Edwards, Sarah J...391
Edwards, Spence W...391
Edwards, William...391
Egelton, Thomas...37, 58, 65
Egerton, Thomas...10, 11, 28
Elkins, Benjamin...7, 69, 99
Elkins, Dicy...443
Elkins, Eliza...443
Elkins, Elizabeth...246
Elkins, James...27, 57, 69, 98
Elkins, John...74, 443
Elkins, Mary...443
Elkins, Rebecca...443
Elkins, Sallie...442
Elkins, Samuel...78, 98, 112, 142, 158, 186
Elkins, Stephen...81
Elkins, Wade...218, 311, 442, 560
Elkins, Willis...184
Elliott, John...92
Elliott, Thomas...11
Elliott, William...92, 127
Ellis, Allen...146, 161, 234, 333, 392, 411
Ellis, Nancy...392
Ellis, Winnifred...392
Elmore, William...59
England, James...140, 158, 181, 218
England, Mary...161
England, William...141, 158, 315
England, William T...169
England, William T. (Esq.)...202
English, Joseph...60
Epps, Edward...82, 115
Epps, John...168
Estes, Candace...435
Estes, Elizabeth...435
Estes, Julia E...435
Estes, Richardson...224
Estes, Sarah...435
Estes, Thomas...240
Estes, Wiley R...435
Estes, William...236, 435
Estridge, Wiley...285
Evans, Anthony...349
Evans, James...180
Evans, John...28, 35, 67, 86
Everett, Nathan...325
Falsom, Malcolm...173
Farrar, James...338
Faucett, Henry...206, 275
Feagan, A...62
Feagan, Aaron...4, 17, 32, 44
Feagan, Daniel...111, 143
Feagan, David...158
Feagan, John...89
Feagan, R...62
Feagan, Richardson...4, 20, 32, 43, 64, 73, 76, 78(2), 86, 111, 143, 158
Feagan, William...91, 111, 149, 158
Felsom, William W...81
Ferguson, Alexander...2, 14, 42, 162, 171
Ferguson, Angus...172, 258, 376, 434
Ferguson, Archibald...376
Ferguson, Catherine...375, 434
Ferguson, Christian...289, 373, 375
Ferguson, Christopher...206
Ferguson, Daniel...258, 275, 434, 438(2), 560
Ferguson, Elizabeth J...438
Ferguson, Fergus...434
Ferguson, James...376
Ferguson, Jennet...438
Ferguson, John...128, 230, 315, 373, 375, 438
Ferguson, John A...375
Ferguson, John C...374, 548
Ferguson, John M...315
Ferguson, John McN...363, 546
Ferguson, John N...373, 519, 548
Ferguson, Margaret...438
Ferguson, Mary A...438
Ferguson, Murdoch...119, 129, 139(2), 162, 165(2), 171, 230, 277, 375, 434, 438, 520
Ferguson, Nancy...434
Ferguson, Neill...260, 438
Ferguson, Norman...177, 258, 315, 434, 529, 556
Ferguson, Peter...171, 376
Ferguson, Samuel N...435
Ferguson, Sarah...374, 376
Ferguson, William...375
Ferguson, William A...435
Fields, Anderson...368
Fields, Ann B...368
Fields, Catherine...490
Fields, Charles...491
Fields, Edward...491
Fields, Green B...368, 546
Fields, Henry...490, 491, 566
Fields, Isaac...206, 271, 491
Fields, James...491
Fields, John...15, 52, 59, 491
Fields, Kearney...490
Fields, Kinchen...479
Fields, Louisa...490
Fields, Martha...490, 491
Fields, Mary...491
Fields, Nancy...491(2)
Fields, Richard...491
Fields, Sarah...490
Fields, Susannah...70
Fields, Tobias...368
Fields, William...368
Filly, Daniel...30
Finch, Mary...166
Finelson, John...15, 59
Finley, Daniel...41
Finnison, Charity...448
Finnison, George...448
Finnison, Jeremiah...448
Finnison, John...448
Finnison, Margaret...448
Fletcher, Anguish...51
Fletcher, William...179, 222
Floyd, John...7
Floyd, John Jr...17
Floyd, John Sr...18
Folsom, William...93
Ford, William...10
Foushee, George...447, 532, 533, 558
Frazier, George...140, 161
Frazier, Peter...165
Frazier, Thomas...105
Frazier, William...130, 139, 166
Freeman, Aaron...500
Freeman, Alexander...500
Freeman, Delitha...496
Freeman, Elias...495
Freeman, Elizabeth...457, 500(2)
Freeman, Emeline...495
Freeman, Enoch...500, 568
Freeman, Henry...305, 494, 568
Freeman, Henry (W.)...323
Freeman, Isaac...496
Freeman, James A...457
Freeman, John...174, 181, 232, 496, 568
Freeman, John (C.C.)...305
Freeman, John H...182
Freeman, John W...457
Freeman, Louisa...500

Gilbert, Benjamin...100, 140, 158, 443
Gilbert, Celia A....443
Gilbert, James...443
Gilbert, Jane...184, 311
Gilbert, Joseph...8, 19, 27, 57, 184, 252, 311, 443(2)
Gilbert, Lydia J....463
Gilbert, Manda...464
Gilbert, Mary...443
Gilbert, Sabra...70, 158
Gilbery, ?...177
Gilchrist, Benjamin...70
Gilchrist, Catherine...383, 438
Gilchrist, Charles...234, 283, 438(2), 529, 560
Gilchrist, D....163
Gilchrist, Elizabeth...383
Gilchrist, George...383
Gilchrist, Isabella...352
Gilchrist, James...238, 281, 329, 381, 383, 521, 542
Gilchrist, John...91
Gilchrist, M....163
Gilchrist, Malcolm...9, 12, 30, 41, 69, 72, 75, 83, 140
Gilchrist, Margaret...352
Gilchrist, Mary...352
Gilchrist, Nancy...438
Gilchrist, Rachel...381
Gilliam, John...85
Gilliam, John Sr....86
Gillis, Archibald...71, 89, 119, 172
Gillis, Christian...422
Gillis, Cynthia...422
Gillis, Daniel...83, 89, 126, 135, 141, 149, 178
Gillis, Donald...158
Gillis, Elizabeth...371
Gillis, Flora...360
Gillis, John...172
Gillis, Margaret...422
Gillis, Martha...422
Gillis, Mary...360, 422, 425
Gillis, Nancy...422
Gillis, Norman...172, 232
Gilmore, Angus G....334
Gilmore, Ann E....414, 432
Gilmore, Baxter...414
Gilmore, Catherine...418
Gilmore, Charles...29, 38
Gilmore, Charles H....9, 11
Gilmore, David C....417
Gilmore, Eli...432
Gilmore, Elizabeth...417
Gilmore, Floriday...334
Gilmore, Frances A....414
Gilmore, George...10, 11
Gilmore, Green B....417, 527
Gilmore, Hastin...414, 526, 552
Gilmore, Hugh...10, 11
Gilmore, Hugh Sr....28
Gilmore, Humphrey...10, 11
Gilmore, Isabelle...9, 12
Gilmore, Jackson C....417
Gilmore, James...432
Gilmore, James...4, 10, 11, 17, 28, 35
Gilmore, James H....334
Gilmore, John...9(2), 10, 432
Gilmore, John J....414, 417, 527, 554
Gilmore, John Jr....11, 28, 37
Gilmore, John Sr....11, 29, 36
Gilmore, Malvina...334
Gilmore, Margaret E....334
Gilmore, Mildred...414
Gilmore, Miles...432
Gilmore, Nathan A....414
Gilmore, Phebe...417
Gilmore, Pitsey...334
Gilmore, Polly...125
Gilmore, Richard...226
Gilmore, Robert...414
Gilmore, Samuel...9, 29, 38, 334
Gilmore, Thomas...9, 11, 29, 39, 58, 67, 83, 140(2), 166, 172
Gilmore, William...432
Gilmore, William...149, 185, 226
Gilpin, James...331
Gilpin, Mary...331
Glascock, George...109, 143, 158
Glascock, John Melton...64
Glascock, Julius...142, 158, 170, 236, 293
Glascock, Martin...78
Glascock, Patty...64, 99, 111, 158, 180
Glascock, Sarah...341, 513, 570
Godfrey, Andrew J....394
Godfrey, Elizabeth...388
Godfrey, Henry...244, 329, 392, 394(2), 544
Godfrey, Henry (J.C.)...331
Godfrey, James...388
Godfrey, Jane...394
Godfrey, John...95, 146, 164, 173, 240, 331, 388(2), 394
Godfrey, John Sr....244
Godfrey, Laney...388
Godfrey, Lydia...411
Godfrey, Marshal...394
Godfrey, Mary...388, 394
Godfrey, Mary A....395
Godfrey, Matthew...411
Godfrey, Nancy...388
Godfrey, Nelly...394
Godfrey, Rebecca...388, 395
Godfrey, Richard...388
Godfrey, Thomas...15
Godfrey, William...311, 321, 411(2)
Goins, Amy...428(2), 439
Goins, Andrew...423, 439
Goins, Barbara...428
Goins, Benjamin...428
Goins, Berry...429
Goins, Bob...329
Goins, Catherine...428
Goins, Celia...428
Goins, Celicia...428
Goins, Chaney...428
Goins, David...423, 428, 429
Goins, Delilah...428
Goins, Edmund...429
Goins, Edward...127, 168, 178, 230
Goins, Eli...429
Goins, Eliza...428
Goins, Eliza J....429
Goins, Elizabeth...423, 428
Goins, Emeline...429
Goins, Flora A....428
Goins, George...403
Goins, Green...428
Goins, Haywood...428
Goins, Henry...76, 91, 127, 428, 439
Goins, Hubbard...331
Goins, James...428, 439(2)
Goins, Jane...407
Goins, Jennet...428
Goins, John...187, 321, 399, 428(2), 439
Goins, Joseph...428
Goins, Lawrence...429
Goins, Levi...76, 92, 127, 177, 230, 428(2), 556
Goins, Lucian...429
Goins, Lucinda...423
Goins, Lucy...429
Goins, Lydia...428(2)
Goins, Margaret...442
Goins, Martha...423, 428
Goins, Marticia...429
Goins, Mary...428(2), 429, 439
Goins, Mary A....429
Goins, Nancy...429
Goins, Neill...321, 327, 428
Goins, Nutty...428
Goins, Rachel...428
Goins, Rebecca...429
Goins, Richard...421
Goins, Robert...404
Goins, Sarah...428
Goins, Sarah A....423
Goins, Sidney...423, 426
Goins, Telitha...428
Goins, Thomas...428
Goins, Ursula...439
Goins, Wiley...428
Goins, William...9, 11, 37, 58, 65, 68, 91, 127, 390, 420, 423, 429
Goins, William H....429
Gold, Daniel...8, 19
Goldston, John...7, 17, 70
Goldston, Louisa A....449
Goldston, Robert...533
Goldston, Robert W....449, 558
Gordon, Adalaide...429
Gordon, Ann...467
Gordon, Celia...429
Gordon, George...468
Gordon, James...467, 468
Gordon, John...18, 468
Gordon, Robert...468
Gordon, Rowan...468
Gordon, Thomas...468
Gordon, Tyrrel...429
Gordon, William...468
Graham (Grimes), Alexander...369, 423, 528, 554
Graham (Grimes), Alexander (T.)...317
Graham (Grimes), Allen...373
Graham (Grimes), Andrew...228, 289, 369, 519, 546
Graham (Grimes), Ann...360
Graham (Grimes), Ann J....373
Graham (Grimes), Anna...517
Graham (Grimes), Anthony...152, 162
Graham (Grimes), Archibald...139, 161, 171, 258, 281, 383, 542
Graham (Grimes), Archibald W....382
Graham (Grimes), Benjamin...10, 12, 30, 41, 58, 70, 98, 119, 152, 162, 425
Graham (Grimes), Catherine...382
Graham (Grimes), D....61(2)
Graham (Grimes), Daniel...65, 72, 89, 119, 139, 151, 163(2), 171, 172, 258, 281, 379, 425
Graham (Grimes), Daniel (C.C.)...315
Graham (Grimes), Daniel A....382

Graham (Grimes), David...139, 163, 171, 260, 275, 379, 382
Graham (Grimes), David W....368
Graham (Grimes), Deborah...369
Graham (Grimes), Dugald...210, 287, 360, 540
Graham (Grimes), Duncan...281, 382, 383
Graham (Grimes), Edward...342
Graham (Grimes), Effy...369
Graham (Grimes), Effy J....382
Graham (Grimes), Elizabeth...383
Graham (Grimes), Elizabeth A....368
Graham (Grimes), Elizabeth J....425
Graham (Grimes), Emeline...368
Graham (Grimes), Flora...373
Graham (Grimes), Flora A....423
Graham (Grimes), George...67, 90, 125, 149, 158, 185, 341
Graham (Grimes), Harmon...185
Graham (Grimes), Henry W....368
Graham (Grimes), Isaac...510
Graham (Grimes), James...373
Graham (Grimes), Jarret...357
Graham (Grimes), John...128, 184, 373
Graham (Grimes), John M....382
Graham (Grimes), John P....358
Graham (Grimes), John Sr....236
Graham (Grimes), John W....368
Graham (Grimes), Kizzie...285, 374
Graham (Grimes), Loveday...369
Graham (Grimes), Lurina...368
Graham (Grimes), M....61
Graham (Grimes), Malcolm...307, 368, 519, 546
Graham (Grimes), Margaret...126, 158, 185, 200, 374, 382, 383, 507
Graham (Grimes), Margaret J....368
Graham (Grimes), Martha...369
Graham (Grimes), Mary...369, 374, 383
Graham (Grimes), Mary A....424
Graham (Grimes), Mary E....382
Graham (Grimes), Mary J....373, 379
Graham (Grimes), Nancy...340, 360, 379, 382, 510
Graham (Grimes), Nathan...424, 554
Graham (Grimes), Neill...128, 382, 521, 542
Graham (Grimes), Noah P....368
Graham (Grimes), Patience...510
Graham (Grimes), Robert...3, 14, 51, 60, 64, 86, 99, 147, 158, 185, 226, 349
Graham (Grimes), Sarah...256, 340, 360, 369, 423, 507
Graham (Grimes), Sarah A....368
Graham (Grimes), Stephen...315, 374
Graham (Grimes), Terry...369
Graham (Grimes), Thomas...25, 53, 60, 64, 86, 109, 143, 158, 283
Graham (Grimes), Westley...507
Graham (Grimes), William...301, 313, 373
Graham (Grimes), William (S.T.)...319
Graham (Grimes), William H....357
Graham (Grimes), Zachariah...119, 139, 166
Grant, Patience...379
Graves, Nancy...246
Graves, Peter...8, 17
Gray, Willis...84, 127, 166
Greenhill, Joseph...69
Gribble, Gilley...480
Gribble, James...480
Grice, Isaac W....431
Griffin, Gifford...427
Griffin, James...427
Griffin, Jesse...66
Griffin, John...126, 132
Griffin, Joseph...132, 164, 170
Griffin, Lawrence...132
Griffin, Nancy...427
Griffin, Samuel...269
Griffin, Yanee...132
Griffith, William...95, 133, 143, 158, 176
Gringe, Isham...265
Groce, Dilla...443
Groce, Hezekiah...443
Groce, Lydia...443
Gunter, Ann...242, 321
Gunter, Anna...403, 550
Gunter, Cassandra J....411
Gunter, Charnal...95
Gunter, Elizabeth...133
Gunter, Hesper A....411
Gunter, James...224
Gunter, John...114, 146, 163, 327
Gunter, John A....411
Gunter, John Jr....93
Gunter, John Sr....93, 242
Gunter, Joseph...411
Gunter, Levi...412, 526
Gunter, Lewis...177
Gunter, Lucy E....411
Gunter, Malcolm...134, 146, 165(2)
Gunter, Margaret...244
Gunter, Martha...412
Gunter, Mary...412(2)
Gunter, Matilda...411, 552
Hagardy, John...260
Hagardy, William...192
Hagwood, Josiah...132
Haily, Neill...371
Haines (Hines, Hynes), James...97, 148, 158, 198
Hall, Ignatius...69
Ham, Speas...139, 166, 171
Hancock, Clarkey...446(2)
Hancock, Devotion...511
Hancock, Elizabeth...69, 83, 435
Hancock, Evachel...305
Hancock, James...82
Hancock, James M....446
Hancock, John...6, 17, 140, 158, 184, 218, 446(2), 558(2)
Hancock, Josephine...446
Hancock, Lydia...446
Hancock, Margaret...446
Hancock, Martha...435, 529
Hancock, Martha A....446
Hancock, Mary...435
Hancock, Nancy...446(2)
Hancock, Patsay...93
Hancock, Rhody...446
Hancock, S....63
Hancock, Susannah...6, 17, 26, 54
Hancock, William...7, 17, 26, 54, 68, 176, 184, 242, 283, 446
Hanley/Hundley, Jonathan...146
Hannah, George...161
Hannon, Amy...339
Hannon, Anna...337
Hannon, Archibald...337
Hannon, Asa...89
Hannon, Betsy...321
Hannon, Daniel O....337
Hannon, Elizabeth...343
Hannon, Flora J....337
Hannon, Jesse...273, 337, 570
Hannon, John...339, 570
Hannon, John M....337
Hannon, Malcolm...337
Hannon, Miley J....339
Hannon, Neill...337
Hannon, Rebecca...142
Hannon, Reuben...158
Hannon, Susan...281
Hannon, Thomas...89, 111, 125, 158, 226, 273
Hannon, Thomas Jr....65, 226
Hannon, Thomas Sr....66, 89
Hannon, William A....337
Hardin, Abigail...147, 254
Hardin, Abijah...265
Hardin, Charles...183
Hardin, Clementine...451
Hardin, G....62
Hardin, Gabriel...19, 26, 54, 69, 122, 161
Hardin, Gabriel Jr....6, 70
Hardin, Gabriel Sr....6
Hardin, Hugh...175
Hardin, Hugh C....265, 450
Hardin, Jacob...28
Hardin, James...8, 17, 69, 99, 122, 182, 216
Hardin, James Sr....313
Hardin, Jane...450
Hardin, Joab C....450
Hardin, John...6
Hardin, Lewis...451
Hardin, Martha...451
Hardin, Rebecca...350
Hardin, Robert...122, 175, 220
Hardin, Sallie...450
Hardin, W....62, 63
Hardin, William...19, 27, 57, 62, 70, 76, 78, 90, 158
Hardin, William (Buck)...70
Hardin, William Sr....27, 57
Hardin, Winston...451
Hardison, Collins...9, 11
Hardison, Jacob...9, 12
Hardy, Collins...58
Hardy, Colonel...28, 37
Hardy, Jacob...35, 58
Hare (Hair), Anna...501
Hare (Hair), Hannah...348, 504
Hare (Hair), Isaac...325
Hare (Hair), Isham...295, 500, 568
Hare (Hair), John...59, 66, 85, 111, 158, 175, 500
Hare (Hair), John Jr....111
Hare (Hair), John Sr....153
Hare (Hair), Kendrick...500
Hare (Hair), Leonard...295
Hare (Hair), Lucy...500
Hare (Hair), Lydia...500
Hare (Hair), Mary...500
Hare (Hair), Owen...182
Hare (Hair), Peter...59, 66, 85(2), 158, 175, 214
Hare (Hair), Peter Sr....153
Hare (Hair), Rebecca...500
Hargrove, John...66
Harmon, Henry...325
Harper, E.A....297
Harper, William H....435
Harrington, Abner...145, 162, 425

Harrington, Abner A....407
Harrington, Ann E....442
Harrington, Archibald...407, 525, 550
Harrington, Benjamin...393
Harrington, C.B....317
Harrington, Charles G....313, 393, 523, 544
Harrington, Cyrus...353
Harrington, Elias B....425, 528, 554
Harrington, Elisha...442
Harrington, Elizabeth...393
Harrington, Eugenia...442
Harrington, Henrietta...442
Harrington, Hesper A....407
Harrington, James...442
Harrington, James A....425
Harrington, James K....394
Harrington, Jennet...393
Harrington, John...393
Harrington, John M.M....425
Harrington, Josiah...425
Harrington, Julius...442
Harrington, Lydia...407
Harrington, Lydia M....442
Harrington, Margaret E....425
Harrington, Mary...393, 425, 442
Harrington, Mary A....425
Harrington, Nancy...393
Harrington, Nancy J....407
Harrington, Penelope...393
Harrington, Sarah J....442
Harrington, Sion...65, 94, 130, 146, 166, 393
Harrington, Thomas...393, 407(2), 425, 525, 550
Harrington, William...393
Harrington, William B....281
Harrington, William D....407, 442, 530, 560
Harrington, William H....442
Harris, James...28, 35, 186
Harris, Joseph...174
Harris, Susannah...125, 158
Harris, William...175
Harrison, Susannah...254
Harrison, Thomas...176
Hart, Simon...15, 25, 53, 59
Harvel, Isham...200
Harvel, Thomas...136, 148, 158, 186, 200
Harwick, Jacob...67
Hathcock, Dempsey...95, 132, 146, 162, 174
Hawley, Barbara...393
Hawley, David M....393
Hawley, Henry...250
Hawley, Isabella C....406
Hawley, Jemima E....393
Hawley, John...406, 550
Hawley, John A....392
Hawley, Jonathan...164
Hawley, Lucinda...406
Hawley, Margaret...392
Hawley, Marshal H....406
Hawley, Mary A....393
Hawley, Nancy J....393
Hawley, William...392, 544
Hayes, Arthur...178
Hayes, James...69
Hayes, John...69
Haygood, George...18
Haygood, Partin/Partain...7, 18
Haynes, Xpher...18
Heard, Charles...176
Heard, Stephen...10, 29, 39
Hedgepath, Bethania...443
Hedgepath, Jesse...240, 293, 443, 531, 560
Hedgepath, John...443
Hedgepath, Josiah...443
Held, John...24
Henley, Jesse...78
Hewings, Cornelius...70
Heyia/Huer, John...89
Hicks, Andrew...402
Hicks, Elizabeth...402
Hicks, Ellis...402
Hicks, Howell...121
Hicks, Isabella...402
Hicks, Jane...401
Hicks, John...84, 402
Hicks, Lethy...401
Hicks, Lewis...244, 333, 401
Hicks, Luther...401
Hicks, Malvina...401
Hicks, Middy...402
Hicks, Nancy...401
Hight, Elizabeth...410
Hight, Fanny...410
Hight, H. Ann...511
Hight, James...410
Hight, Jonathan...173, 192
Hight, Joseph...410
Hight, Lydia...410
Hight, Nancy...313, 511
Hight, Nathan...321, 410, 526, 552
Hight, Nathan J....267
Hill, Amos...92, 123, 140, 162, 171
Hill, Camp...76
Hill, Dorcus...341
Hill, Elizabeth...341
Hill, Hemerick...98
Hill, Hiram...143, 158, 180, 228
Hill, Isaac...7, 18, 26, 56
Hill, J....62
Hill, James...4, 20, 31, 43, 64, 72, 110, 180, 234
Hill, Martin...228
Hill, Michael...59
Hill, Nancy (Wms.)...277
Hill, William...226
Hilliard, John...70, 78, 87
Hilliard, Silas...124
Hinton, Dempsey...26, 55
Hinton, James...26, 55
Hodges, Edmund...66
Hodges, John...2, 14
Hodgin, John H....212
Hogan, Elizabeth...503
Hogan, Jane...503
Hogan, Joseph...503
Holcombe, James...83
Holden, John...146
Holder/Holden, Charles...85
Holland, Edmond...153, 158, 174, 212, 269, 496, 536, 568
Holland, Margaret...496
Holland, Priscilla...496
Holland, Richard...97, 136, 154, 158, 176
Holloman, Goddin...100, 174, 180
Holloman, Joseph...164
Holloman, Josiah...68, 100, 110, 141, 177
Holloman, Nathaniel...177
Holloman, Robert...220, 265
Holly, John (S.M.)...329
Holly, William...319
Holmes, David...74
Hone, Isaac...58
Hood, Abraham...67
Hooton, Elijah...27, 57
Hooton, John...7
Horner, Catherine...481
Horner, Chestley T....483
Horner, Elizabeth...481
Horner, George...196
Horner, George Sr....285
Horner, George W....283, 481, 566
Horner, James W....481
Horner, Mary A....481
Horner, Thomas...481
Horser, Joab...183
Horser, Joseph...27, 57
Horser, William...139
Houghton, Littleton...70
Howard, Caswell S....398
Howard, Elizabeth...398(2)
Howard, George...398, 544
Howard, Julia...398
Howard, Susan...398
Howard, Utilda J....398
Howell, Hardin/Hardy...4, 21, 47
Howell, John...5, 22, 31, 43
Howle, Samuel...144, 166
Hubbard, James...85
Huckabee, Benjamin...113, 146, 166
Huckabee, Isabella C....403
Huckabee, John...95, 192
Huckabee, Richard...146, 166, 234, 319
Hudson, Rush...169
Hugh, Heth...163
Hugh, Samuel...158
Hughes, Abram...321
Hughes, Archibald...415
Hughes, Catherine...392
Hughes, John...65, 392, 415
Hughes, Larkin...303, 391
Hughes, Margaret...392
Hughes, Mary A....392
Hughes, Murphy...392
Hughes, Neil...68
Hughes, Robert...166
Hughes, Samuel...78, 228
Hughes, William...66, 93, 145
Humphrey, William...65
Hunnicutt, H....62
Hunnicutt, Hartwell...7, 18, 27, 57
Hunnicutt, J. Jr....62
Hunnicutt, John Jr....7, 18, 26, 55
Hunnicutt, R....63
Hunnicutt, Randolph...10, 26, 31, 54
Hunnicutt, Robert...70
Hunsucker, Abraham...256, 285
Hunsucker, Amelia...478
Hunsucker, Andrew...478
Hunsucker, Archibald...370
Hunsucker, Asa...478, 566
Hunsucker, Bethuel...468
Hunsucker, Cary J....479
Hunsucker, Celia...370
Hunsucker, Clarkey...478
Hunsucker, Clarkson...479
Hunsucker, Elizabeth...370, 468, 478, 479
Hunsucker, Enoch W....478
Hunsucker, Gaston...480
Hunsucker, George...84, 109, 147, 158, 181, 198, 212, 477, 478
Hunsucker, George (Esq.)...279
Hunsucker, George Jr....277
Hunsucker, George M....479, 535, 566

Johnson, Major...248
Johnson, Major S....451
Johnson, Malcolm...140, 178, 240, 384(2), 385, 451, 521(2), 542(2)
Johnson, Margaret...362, 384, 385, 386
Johnson, Margaret A....362
Johnson, Martha...394(2), 523
Johnson, Martha E....386(2)
Johnson, Martha J....344, 381, 433
Johnson, Mary...344, 385, 451, 452
Johnson, Mary A....344(2), 381, 385, 386
Johnson, Mary E....376, 454
Johnson, Mary J....384, 394
Johnson, Michael...143, 234
Johnson, Missouri M.P....338
Johnson, Nancy...339, 384
Johnson, Nancy (widow)...188
Johnson, Nancy C....394
Johnson, Neill...256
Johnson, Neill A....433
Johnson, Phebe...452
Johnson, Phillip...93, 147, 165
Johnson, Polly...331
Johnson, Randolph...139
Johnson, Richard H....381
Johnson, Robert T....403
Johnson, Samuel...9, 12, 260, 317, 376, 381, 385, 386
Johnson, Sarah...244, 254, 338, 385
Johnson, Sarah A....362
Johnson, Sarah C....386
Johnson, Sarah J....376, 384
Johnson, Thomas...344, 386
Johnson, Westley...344, 384
Johnson, William...248, 250, 297, 361, 376, 394, 452, 454, 548
Johnson, William (C.P.)...279
Johnson, William (M.R.)...271
Johnson, William A....403
Johnson, William B....376
Johnson, William M....313, 533, 558
Johnson, William S....381
Johnston, ?...173
Johnston, Arthur...125
Johnston, Catherine...144
Johnston, Daniel...29, 40
Johnston, Duncan...66, 70
Johnston, Hartwell...58
Johnston, Hezekiah...69, 99
Johnston, James...121, 143, 158
Johnston, John...67, 124, 164
Johnston, Joseph...113, 142, 158, 185
Johnston, Lauchlin...120, 123, 165
Johnston, Lewis...115, 181
Johnston, Malachi...158
Johnston, Michael...125, 158
Johnston, Phillip...65, 72, 135
Johnston, Rebecca...144
Johnston, Sally...128
Johnston, Samuel...30, 40, 58, 140
Johnston, W....61
Johnston, William...124, 185
Jones, Alexander...334
Jones, Allen W....430, 528, 556
Jones, Alston (B.C.)...265
Jones, Amelia...480, 535
Jones, Anderson...447, 532
Jones, Ann M....447
Jones, Atlas...136, 142, 158, 184
Jones, Baldy H....430
Jones, Brantley...448
Jones, D....62
Jones, David...92, 121, 123(2), 177, 200, 279, 480, 566
Jones, David Sr....92
Jones, Dolly...461
Jones, Dorothy...480
Jones, Duncan D....334
Jones, Elizabeth...334, 430
Jones, Elkin...128, 152, 480
Jones, Emerson...481
Jones, Frances...447
Jones, Franey...480
Jones, Hannah M....430
Jones, John...323, 481
Jones, Lovedy...334
Jones, Lucy...64, 100
Jones, Lydia...480
Jones, Margaret...481
Jones, Marshal...123
Jones, Martha...480
Jones, Mary...371, 430
Jones, Mary J....447
Jones, Mily E....334
Jones, Nelson...481
Jones, Orren...481
Jones, Rany...480
Jones, Rebecca...69, 480
Jones, Sarah...480
Jones, Shadrick...123
Jones, Silvanus...71
Jones, Solomon...58
Jones, Velina...430
Jones, Warren...166, 170
Jones, William...121, 148, 158, 178, 194
Jones, William (F.C.)...291
Jones, Wincy...481
Jordan, Elizabeth...464
Jordan, Enoch...464
Jordan, Franey...458
Jordan, Jesse...464
Jordan, John...458
Jordan, John (M.S.)...325
Jordan, Levica...464
Jordan, Martha...458
Jordan, Mary...458, 464(2)
Jordan, Matilda...464
Jordan, Mead...70
Jordan, Miles...181, 214, 269, 458, 464, 562
Jordan, Sarah...464
Jordan, William...321, 458
Jordan, Winniford...464
Joyner (Joiner), Drury...78, 86
Judd, Elizabeth...313, 401
Judd, Henderson...401, 524, 550
Judd, Jefferson...192
Judd, William...94, 133, 145, 166, 173, 190
Keahey (Keachey), James...179, 200
Keahey (Keachey), William (C.B.)...265
Kealin (Keeling), A....62
Kealin (Keeling), Adam...6, 18, 26, 56, 453
Kealin (Keeling), Alfred...454
Kealin (Keeling), Anna...453
Kealin (Keeling), Betsy...181
Kealin (Keeling), Bettie...454
Kealin (Keeling), Elizabeth...122
Kealin (Keeling), Mary...454
Kealin (Keeling), Nicy...454
Kealin (Keeling), Polly...181, 246, 283
Kealin (Keeling), Sallie...454
Keith, Andrew J....380
Keith, Ann...508
Keith, Catherine...377, 380, 508
Keith, Duncan...377, 508, 537
Keith, Duncan M....508
Keith, Effy J....377
Keith, Elizabeth...508
Keith, Elizabeth A....377
Keith, Flora A....380
Keith, Hugh...119, 139, 174, 258, 377(2), 520, 548
Keith, Hugh Sr....289
Keith, Jacob M....380
Keith, James...508
Keith, John...377
Keith, John (W.)...323
Keith, John R....508
Keith, Margaret...377
Keith, Mary...377, 508
Keith, Mary J....380
Keith, Sarah J....380
Keith, William...315, 380, 508, 520, 542
Kelly, ?...169, 171
Kelly, Abel...202, 311, 407, 525, 550, 537
Kelly, Abel A....407
Kelly, Absalom...303, 398
Kelly, Alexander...307, 351, 372, 515, 538
Kelly, Alfred...407
Kelly, Andrew...476
Kelly, Angus...373
Kelly, Angus B....279, 347
Kelly, Angus R....508, 515
Kelly, Ann...439
Kelly, Ann E....347
Kelly, Arabella...407
Kelly, Archibald...407, 439
Kelly, Archibald (P.)...325
Kelly, Catherine...238, 438, 476, 509
Kelly, Catherine E....347
Kelly, Catherine J....351(2)
Kelly, Celia...407, 409
Kelly, Christian...347, 352(2), 374
Kelly, Cornelius...373
Kelly, Daniel...121, 129, 135, 139, 163(2), 187, 374
Kelly, Daniel (B.)...222
Kelly, Daniel (T.)...246, 275
Kelly, Daniel C....347
Kelly, Daniel D....438
Kelly, Daniel Jr....163
Kelly, Daniel McS....352
Kelly, Daniel T....351
Kelly, David...396
Kelly, Delilah J....407
Kelly, Donald...373(2), 519, 548
Kelly, Duncan...144, 163, 186, 222, 351
Kelly, Duncan Jr....230
Kelly, Edmond...134, 145, 163
Kelly, Elias...202, 311, 409
Kelly, Eliza...438(2)
Kelly, Elizabeth...407(3), 409, 410, 412, 438
Kelly, Evander...560
Kelly, Evander J....438
Kelly, Fancy...398
Kelly, Flora...374
Kelly, Flora A....409
Kelly, Frances...407
Kelly, Harriett...476
Kelly, Henry...407
Kelly, Henry L.M....398
Kelly, Hiram (T.)...281
Kelly, Hiram K....476

Kelly, Hugh...69, 93, 134, 139, 146, 163, 169, 173, 198, 252, 347, 407(2), 480, 535, 566
Kelly, Hugh A....410, 439
Kelly, Hugh Sr....271
Kelly, Isabella...347, 351
Kelly, Isom...331
Kelly, Iver...438
Kelly, James...120, 124, 139, 164, 184, 373
Kelly, James H....407
Kelly, Jane E....347
Kelly, John...93, 124, 134, 140, 145, 158, 164(2), 173, 204, 373, 407, 410, 552
Kelly, John B....168, 240, 325, 351
Kelly, John M....351
Kelly, John T....398
Kelly, Joseph...133, 134, 145, 164(2), 476
Kelly, Kenneth...480
Kelly, Lauchlin...352, 515, 538
Kelly, M. Jane...409
Kelly, Malcolm...508, 515
Kelly, Margaret...347, 407, 412, 438
Kelly, Mariah...412
Kelly, Mark...202, 410
Kelly, Martha...407, 412
Kelly, Mary...93, 134, 186, 373, 412
Kelly, Mary A....351, 407(2)
Kelly, Mary J....347, 481
Kelly, Murdoch...351
Kelly, Nancy...347, 398, 407(2), 409, 480, 508
Kelly, Neil...9, 13, 30, 40
Kelly, Patrick...351
Kelly, Penelope...409
Kelly, Peter...124, 140, 163, 169, 238, 275, 374, 519, 548
Kelly, Priscilla...412
Kelly, Roderick...319, 412
Kelly, Sarah...351, 398
Kelly, Sarah F....347
Kelly, Sophia...476
Kelly, Spencer...166, 412
Kelly, Telitha A....407
Kelly, Thomas...224, 319, 412(2)
Kelly, William...133, 170, 192
Kelly, William (tailor)...174
Kelly, William A....398
Kelly, William C. ...134
Kelly, William J....352
Kelly, William K....439
Kelly, Zilpha...409
Kendall (Kendle), John...158
Kendall (Kendle), William...117, 158, 181
Kendall (Kendle), William Jr....153
Kennedy, Aaron...196, 279, 562
Kennedy, Aaron E....465
Kennedy, Alexander...51, 59, 67, 85, 129, 153, 158, 182, 470, 534, 564
Kennedy, Amy...504
Kennedy, Daniel...480
Kennedy, David...67, 85, 115, 154, 158, 186, 216, 461, 504
Kennedy, Duncan...460, 470
Kennedy, Edward...117, 153, 158
Kennedy, Elias...232, 460
Kennedy, Eliza...460
Kennedy, Elizabeth...494, 504
Kennedy, Enoch...216, 460, 461
Kennedy, George...116, 149, 158, 176
Kennedy, H....186
Kennedy, Hiram...154, 158
Kennedy, J....62
Kennedy, John...120, 148, 153, 158, 164, 180, 196, 212, 305, 461, 470, 564
Kennedy, John A....470
Kennedy, John Jr....291
Kennedy, John Sr....301
Kennedy, Josiah...212
Kennedy, Julia...460
Kennedy, Lucinda...465
Kennedy, Lydia...504
Kennedy, Margaret...494(2), 511
Kennedy, Margery...470(2)
Kennedy, Martin...301, 494
Kennedy, Mary...460, 494, 504
Kennedy, Neill...470
Kennedy, Olive...465
Kennedy, Powell...461
Kennedy, Robert...112, 154, 158, 182, 212, 305 , 504
Kennedy, Sallie...461
Kennedy, Sarah F....465
Kennedy, Susan...295
Kennedy, W....61
Kennedy, William...173, 460, 494
Key, Abigail...474
Key, Bellison...497
Key, Cornelius...85
Key, Crawford...352
Key, Eleanor...497(2)
Key, James...179, 210
Key, Jane...467
Key, John...2, 14, 23, 49, 59, 66, 96, 109, 118, 148, 158, 179, 256
Key, Joshua...260
Key, Louisa...467
Key, Martha...497
Key, Mary...467, 497
Key, Moses...71
Key, Pleasant...497
Key, Riland...467
Key, Sallie...497
Key, Samuel...149, 158, 256, 273, 474, 497
Key, Sarah...118, 467
Key, Temperance...467
Key, Thomas...2, 59, 66, 96, 179, 196, 497
Key, Vincent...179
Key, William...14, 23, 49, 74, 96
Kidd, Cary...505
Kidd, Jennet...505
Kidd, Moses...265, 313
Kimball, Amelia...333
Kimball, Barbara...395
Kimball, Emily...395
Kimball, Isabella...395
Kimball, Mary...395
Kimbrell, Anna M....426
Kimbrell, Benjamin...171
Kimbrell, Lavina...426
Kimbrell, Nancy...426
Kimbrell, Samuel R....426
Kimbrell, William B....426
Kimbrell, William H....426, 554
Kimbrough, William H....315
King, D....61
King, Delilah...489
King, James...216
King, Mary...489
King, Robert...83, 108, 175
King, Sarah...246
King, Stephen...58, 66, 220, 291, 489
King, William...66, 81(2), 82, 489
Kinney (Kenney), John...10, 28, 36, 58, 64, 92
Kitchen, Betsey...171
Kitchen, Delilah...171, 260
Kitchen, Elizabeth...128, 139, 163, 240
Kitchen, Kinchen...28, 36, 67, 81, 128, 139, 165
Kitchen, Malcolm...58
Kitchen, Mathew...70
Kitchen, Zabra...381
Knight, Flora A....448
Knight, Hardy...448
Knight, Henry...242, 299, 401
Knight, Jack...244
Knight, John...132, 166, 170, 401
Knight, John M....401
Knight, Lucinda...401
Knight, Martha A....400
Knight, Mary...244, 400, 401
Knight, Nancy...169, 400, 448
Knight, Polly...169, 329
Knight, Sarah...400
Knight, Telitha...401
Knight, Temperance...400
Knight, Vicy...400
Knight, William...145
Knight, William B....448
Knight, Willis...166
Knight, Wilson...170
Lakey, Buck (S.)...323
Lakey, James...116, 175
Lakey, Josiah...489
Lakey, William...177
Laman, Neill...135
Lamb, Benjamin...76
Lamb, Joseph...81, 110
Lambert ?, Nicy...133
Lammonds (Lemmonds, Lamont), Alexander...426
Lammonds (Lemmonds, Lamont), Catherine...427
Lammonds (Lemmonds, Lamont), Daniel...144, 162, 179, 222, 426(2), 556
Lammonds (Lemmonds, Lamont), Deborah...426
Lammonds (Lemmonds, Lamont), Duncan...422, 554
Lammonds (Lemmonds, Lamont), Henry...329
Lammonds (Lemmonds, Lamont), James D....424
Lammonds (Lemmonds, Lamont), Jane...426
Lammonds (Lemmonds, Lamont), John...422
Lammonds (Lemmonds, Lamont), John...145, 179
Lammonds (Lemmonds, Lamont), Joseph J....424
Lammonds (Lemmonds, Lamont), Mary...424
Lammonds (Lemmonds, Lamont), N....62
Lammonds (Lemmonds, Lamont), Neill T....424
Lammonds (Lemmonds, Lamont), Sarah...422
Lammonds (Lemmonds, Lamont), Sarah A....511
Lammonds (Lemmonds, Lamont), William...422
Lancaster, Hartwell...9, 67, 91(2), 135, 175

McArthur, Charles...194, 273, 506
McArthur, James...117, 147, 159
McArthur, John...70
McArthur, Margaret...256
McArty, James...96
McAulay, Angus...69, 186, 202
McAulay, Barbara...406, 525
McAulay, Barbara J....405
McAulay, Catherine...506(2)
McAulay, Daniel...180, 196
McAulay, Elizabeth...303
McAulay, James...406
McAulay, James R....405
McAulay, John...38, 59, 71, 77, 96, 141, 177, 404, 506
McAulay, John Sr....67
McAulay, Malcolm...198, 273, 506
McAulay, Malcom...572
McAulay, Margaret...404
McAulay, Mary...506
McAulay, Mary C....404
McAulay, Murdoch...67, 69, 91, 97, 109, 117(2), 148(2), 180
McAulay, Murdoch (Esq.)...159, 178
McAulay, Murdoch Jr....159
McAulay, Nancy...81, 406
McAulay, Peany...404
McAulay, Robert...190, 404, 525, 550
McAulay, Roderick...118, 148, 159
McAulay, Rory...178
McAulay, Samuel...400, 524
McAulay, Sarah...406
McAulay, Sion...406
McAulay, William...65, 78, 104, 105, 147, 174, 190, 404
McAulay, William C....94
McBath, John...188
McBath, Walter...91, 108, 139, 166, 183, 260
McBryde (McBride), A....61
McBryde (McBride), Alexander...68, 94, 122, 145, 161, 183, 387, 542
McBryde (McBride), Alexander G....315
McBryde (McBride), Archibald...64, 84, 108, 145, 161, 184, 234
McBryde (McBride), Catherine...387(3)
McBryde (McBride), Christian...387(2)
McBryde (McBride), Fereba...387
McBryde (McBride), James...122, 146, 164, 183, 222, 387(2), 542
McBryde (McBride), James S....315, 387
McBryde (McBride), John...387
McBryde (McBride), Lydia...311
McBryde (McBride), Margaret...387(2)
McBryde (McBride), Margaret J....387
McBryde (McBride), Mary...387(2)
McBryde (McBride), Rachel...387
McBryde (McBride), Thomas...387
McBryde (McBride), William...387
McCain, Duncan...11
McCall, Angus...145, 179
McCall, Duncan...144
McCall, James...74
McCallum (McCollum), Angus...367
McCallum (McCollum), Archibald...367
McCallum (McCollum), Christian...367
McCallum (McCollum), Daniel...256, 287, 366, 546
McCallum (McCollum), Duncan...68, 72, 88, 92, 120, 144, 150, 162, 163, 184
McCallum (McCollum), Effy...366
McCallum (McCollum), Elizabeth...365
McCallum (McCollum), Flora...185
McCallum (McCollum), Flora A....367
McCallum (McCollum), Hugh...367
McCallum (McCollum), John...77, 88, 150, 164(2), 208, 287, 367(2), 546
McCallum (McCollum), John (C.)...325
McCallum (McCollum), Malcolm...367
McCallum (McCollum), Margaret...293, 365, 428
McCallum (McCollum), Mary...260, 344
McCallum (McCollum), Nancy...250
McCamler, John...12
McCaskill, A....62
McCaskill, Alexander...136, 143, 159, 186, 228, 493(2), 494
McCaskill, Allen...238, 301, 494
McCaskill, Angus...20, 32, 46, 66, 90, 327, 433, 493, 536, 556, 568
McCaskill, Angus (A.)...279
McCaskill, Catherine...360, 433, 505
McCaskill, Celia A....433
McCaskill, Christian...494, 505
McCaskill, Donald...360
McCaskill, Elizabeth...433(2)
McCaskill, Jennet...433, 494
McCaskill, John...90, 123, 176, 198, 494
McCaskill, John W....433
McCaskill, Kenneth...126, 129, 141, 147, 148(2), 159, 175, 179, 180, 196, 236, 493, 494, 505
McCaskill, Kenneth Jr....159
McCaskill, Kenneth Sr....159, 250
McCaskill, Malcolm...360
McCaskill, Margaret...494
McCaskill, Martha...494
McCaskill, Mary...360, 493
McCaskill, Nancy...360, 494
McCaskill, Neill...474, 493
McCaskill, Peter...360
McCaskill, Sarah...494
McClellan, ?...76
McClendon, Francis...4, 20
McClendon, Joel...20
McClendon, John...21
McColshey, D....61
McColy, John...29
McCrane, Alexander...18, 21
McCrane, Christopher...38
McCrane, Daniel...18
McCrane, Gilchrist...11
McCrane, John...4, 5(2), 31, 32
McCrane, John (MC)...21
McCraney, D....61
McCrimmon (McCrummen), Ann...509
McCrimmon (McCrummen), Catherine...509(2)
McCrimmon (McCrummen), Charles C....509
McCrimmon (McCrummen), Christian...509
McCrimmon (McCrummen), Daniel...129, 159, 179, 271
McCrimmon (McCrummen), Daniel (E.)...210
McCrimmon (McCrummen), David...148
McCrimmon (McCrummen), Eliza...509
McCrimmon (McCrummen), Isabella...509
McCrimmon (McCrummen), John...5, 21, 31, 148, 159, 509
McCrimmon (McCrummen), Lucinda...509
McCrimmon (McCrummen), Malcolm...66, 108, 143, 159, 232, 509(2), 572
McCrimmon (McCrummen), Norman...66, 108, 509
McCrimmon (McCrummen), Roderick...149, 165
McCrimmon (McCrummen), Sarah M....509
McCruly, William...166
McDaniel, Alexander...87
McDaniel, Allen...88
McDaniel, Anguish...86
McDaniel, Archibald (C.C.)...289
McDaniel, Charity...142, 159
McDaniel, Daniel...69, 81, 88, 96, 97, 204
McDaniel, Findley...88
McDaniel, Hugh...81, 89
McDaniel, James...97
McDaniel, John...60, 65, 90
McDaniel, Kenneth...59
McDaniel, Milley...64
McDaniel, Sandy...5
McDaniel, Swain...206
McDonald, ?...171
McDonald, A....61, 62(2)
McDonald, Adam...365
McDonald, Affey...58
McDonald, Alexander...13, 33, 65, 119, 124, 171, 185, 210, 354(2) 371, 372, 490, 538, 548
McDonald, Alexander (D.C.)...287
McDonald, Alexander C....354
McDonald, Allen...12, 29, 40, 68, 162, 184, 367, 369, 371, 519, 548
McDonald, Allen C....354
McDonald, Allen E....369
McDonald, Allen J....375, 520
McDonald, Angus...32(2), 45, 77, 120 (2), 126, 128, 144, 148, 159, 161, 162(4), 171(2), 184, 186, 238, 258, 309, 323, 363(2), 369, 375, 422, 426, 490, 546(2), 548
McDonald, Angus (C.)...202
McDonald, Angus (Red)...289
McDonald, Angus Jr....206
McDonald, Angus Sr....234
McDonald, Ann...345(2)
McDonald, Anna...365, 369
McDonald, Archibald...144, 150, 162(2), 178, 234, 359(2), 365, 374, 435, 519, 548
McDonald, Archibald (C.)...256
McDonald, Betsy...329, 367
McDonald, Betsy A....354
McDonald, Capt.'s Widow...21
McDonald, Caroline...359
McDonald, Catherine...41, 130, 165, 234, 354(2), 357, 359, 363(2), 365(2), 369(3), 372, 374, 375, 422, 425, 426, 432, 472(2), 534, 556, 564
McDonald, Catherine (M.)...301
McDonald, Catherine J....360
McDonald, Caty...137
McDonald, Celia...374
McDonald, Charity...175
McDonald, Charles...230, 267, 421, 528, 554
McDonald, Charlotte...430
McDonald, Christian...230, 260, 271, 354, 359, 362, 365, 367(2), 369(2), 371, 375, 432, 490, 518, 546
McDonald, Christian M....380
McDonald, D....61
McDonald, Daniel...24, 52, 59, 98, 109(2), 110, 118, 119(2), 121, 126, 128, 139, 147, 148, 149(2), 163, 168, 170, 178(2), 198, 230,

236, 258, 260, 307, 354, 359(2), 363, 365, 375, 380, 430, 511(2), 538, 546
McDonald, Daniel (C.C.)...171, 275
McDonald, Daniel (Esq.)...208
McDonald, Daniel (Mullony?)...271
McDonald, Daniel (T.)...279
McDonald, Daniel C....369
McDonald, Daniel E....365
McDonald, Daniel N....354
McDonald, Daniel R....375
McDonald, Daniel Sr....163
McDonald, Daniel W....354, 435
McDonald, David...418
McDonald, Dolly...510
McDonald, Donald...67, 71, 126, 144, 148, 149, 151(2), 152, 159, 162, 163(2), 171, 186, 335, 371, 374, 490, 520, 548
McDonald, Donald (Blue)...159
McDonald, Donald (S.K.)...277
McDonald, Donald B....365
McDonald, Donald Jr....159, 186
McDonald, Donald P....375
McDonald, Donald Sr....159
McDonald, Dugald...363, 518
McDonald, Dugald (T.)...275
McDonald, Duncan C....442
McDonald, Effie/Effy...78, 354, 357, 359, 367
McDonald, Eliza...357
McDonald, Eliza C....363
McDonald, Elizabeth...345, 375, 385, 418, 422, 538
McDonald, Elizabeth J....380
McDonald, Findley...13, 69
McDonald, Findley Sr....163
McDonald, Flora...66, 335, 376, 422, 432(2)
McDonald, Flora A....430
McDonald, Hannah...380
McDonald, Henry C....418
McDonald, Hiram D....365
McDonald, Hugh...11, 29, 40, 65, 70, 119, 125, 139, 145, 149, 163(2), 171, 184, 293, 354, 432, 529, 538, 556
McDonald, Hugh (D.S.)...277
McDonald, Hugh (Esq.)...172, 210
McDonald, Hugh M....490
McDonald, Hugh Sr....224
McDonald, Isabella...354
McDonald, J....61
McDonald, James...5, 22, 33, 72, 128, 178, 222, 323, 380, 425
McDonald, James A....382
McDonald, James K.P....375
McDonald, James W....367
McDonald, Jane...33, 365, 367
McDonald, Jane M....367
McDonald, Joab...430
McDonald, John...12, 20, 28, 32, 35, 45, 58, 66(2), 72, 78, 105, 113, 119, 126(2), 142, 144, 149, 152, 159(2), 164, 177, 186(3), 210, 216, 232, 260, 281, 289, 321, 354, 357, 359, 369, 371, 372, 375(2), 380, 418, 422, 520, 538, 540, 546, 548
McDonald, John (D.C.)...196
McDonald, John (D.S.)...325
McDonald, John (M.)...301
McDonald, John (M.L.)...301
McDonald, John (M.T.)...149, 159
McDonald, John (Pocket Cr)...13
McDonald, John (S.M.)...196
McDonald, John (S.R.)...258
McDonald, John A....354, 359, 365, 430
McDonald, John B....426
McDonald, John C....354
McDonald, John D....220, 293, 365, 546
McDonald, John E....472
McDonald, John H.B....311, 367, 546
McDonald, John Jr....143
McDonald, John K....364
McDonald, John W....382
McDonald, Katy...68
McDonald, Kenneth...21, 24, 52, 67, 99, 369, 375
McDonald, Kitty M....369
McDonald, Laura...369
McDonald, Lexa...367
McDonald, Loveday...367
McDonald, Lovedy...359
McDonald, Lucy...418
McDonald, Lydia J....365
McDonald, Malcolm...112, 149, 165, 183, 367
McDonald, Malcolm A....369
McDonald, Malcolm J.A....354
McDonald, Malvina...375
McDonald, Margaret...357, 363, 364, 365(2), 369, 371, 374, 375(2), 382, 431, 432
McDonald, Margaret A....363
McDonald, Margaret E....354
McDonald, Marion C....354
McDonald, Marquis...22
McDonald, Martia...359
McDonald, Mary...20, 31, 42, 68, 246, 321, 325, 354(3), 357, 359(2), 363, 369, 371(2), 372(3), 422(2), 432(2), 490
McDonald, Mary A....359, 363, 380, 511
McDonald, Mary E....354, 367, 490
McDonald, Mary J....364, 375, 430, 518
McDonald, Mary M....354
McDonald, Murdo...372, 548
McDonald, Murdoch...354
McDonald, Murdoch (D.C.)...275
McDonald, Murdoch McS....375
McDonald, Nancy...359, 363, 367, 373, 374, 375, 382, 422, 546
McDonald, Neill...121, 126, 345, 363, 369, 371, 380, 382, 510, 546
McDonald, Neill (L.R.)...287
McDonald, Nelly...375
McDonald, Noah...345
McDonald, Nora...367
McDonald, Norman...9, 12, 29, 39, 58, 68, 256, 315, 369, 380(2), 520, 542, 546
McDonald, Phillip...149
McDonald, Randall...208
McDonald, Randolph...9, 540
McDonald, Randolph (D.C.)...287
McDonald, Randolph C....359
McDonald, Ronald...432, 540
McDonald, Ronald L....359
McDonald, Sally...170
McDonald, Samuel...170, 230, 277, 432, 529, 556
McDonald, Sanders...20
McDonald, Sarah...67, 254, 355, 359, 371, 372, 375, 422, 430, 431, 511
McDonald, Sarah A....490
McDonald, Sarah C....430
McDonald, Sarah J....363
McDonald, Sarah K....380
McDonald, Sophia...472
McDonald, Swain M.S....520
McDonald, Sween...317
McDonald, Sween M.S....380
McDonald, Thomas...425
McDonald, Thomas A....380
McDonald, Widow...5(2)
McDonald, William...66, 72, 359, 365, 430, 435
McDonald, William A....354
McDonald, William H....431
McDonald, William J....375
McDuffie, Angus...71, 162, 505
McDuffie, Ann...420
McDuffie, Anna...506
McDuffie, Catherine...387, 506, 507
McDuffie, Christian...506
McDuffie, Daniel...131, 144, 163, 187, 198, 420
McDuffie, Duncan...94, 135, 144, 162
McDuffie, Effy...505(2)
McDuffie, Elizabeth...421
McDuffie, Flora...420, 505
McDuffie, Jennet...421
McDuffie, John...20, 47, 58, 66, 117, 124, 148, 159, 179, 200, 273, 387, 420, 421, 505, 572
McDuffie, Malcolm...507
McDuffie, Margaret...420
McDuffie, Mary...77, 421, 506
McDuffie, Nancy...420
McDuffie, Neill...92, 135, 145, 165, 187, 232, 420, 505
McDuffie, Norman...70, 507
McDuffie, Rebecca...420
McDugald, Alexander...389
McDugald, Allen...94
McDugald, Angus...58, 70, 149, 150, 281, 381
McDugald, Archibald...82, 108, 139, 171, 240, 382
McDugald, Archibald (Col.)...161
McDugald, Catherine...386, 389(2)
McDugald, D....61
McDugald, Daniel...128, 131, 139, 146, 162, 163(2), 183, 232
McDugald, Daniel B....382
McDugald, Donald...389
McDugald, Dugald...382, 389, 521, 542
McDugald, Dugald (M.)...277
McDugald, Duncan...70, 93, 122, 146, 162, 188, 240, 389
McDugald, Elizabeth...387
McDugald, Elizabeth J....382
McDugald, Fanny...386
McDugald, Hugh...240
McDugald, John...70, 93, 122, 128, 139, 146, 164(2), 172, 258, 381, 520, 521, 542
McDugald, John (C.C.)...289
McDugald, Margaret...258, 381, 382, 389
McDugald, Martha...387
McDugald, Mary...172, 275, 382, 389, 510
McDugald, Nancy...387
McDugald, Neill...382
McDugald, Polly...188
McDugald, Rebecca...382
McDugald, Sarah C....387
McDugald, William...389, 542
McEachern, Alexander...188
McEachern, Peter...90, 101
McFadyen, A.M....432
McFadyen, Annabella...386
McFadyen, Archibald...166, 377

McKinnon, Neill...32, 46, 180, 200, 357, 540
McKinnon, Norman...69, 88, 97(2), 117, 148(2), 159, 177, 180, 473, 535
McKinnon, Norman Jr....159
McKinnon, Norman Sr....177
McKinnon, Peter...179
McKinnon, William...160, 336, 360
McKnight, Hugh...110, 140, 159, 171, 252
McLaughlin (McLauchlin), Catherine...337, 371, 373, 519, 548
McLaughlin (McLauchlin), Christian...372
McLaughlin (McLauchlin), Daniel...230
McLaughlin (McLauchlin), Donald...337, 513, 570
McLaughlin (McLauchlin), Dugald...114, 142, 159, 185, 373
McLaughlin (McLauchlin), Duncan...185, 307, 510
McLaughlin (McLauchlin), Isabella...337, 371(2), 548
McLaughlin (McLauchlin), Loveday...372
McLaughlin (McLauchlin), Martha...373
McLaughlin (McLauchlin), Nancy...337
McLaughlin (McLauchlin), Nancy C....373
McLaughlin (McLauchlin), Neill...337, 373, 513, 570
McLaughlin (McLauchlin), Neill (Maj.)...279
McLaughlin (McLauchlin), Robert...108, 140, 165, 185, 230
McLaughlin (McLauchlin), Robert A....373
McLaughlin (McLauchlin), Sarah...337
McLaurin, Anna B....356
McLaurin, Catherine...356
McLaurin, Cornelius M....356
McLaurin, Duncan...206
McLaurin, Eliza...356
McLaurin, Hugh...309, 356, 517, 540
McLaurin, Nevin...206, 293
McLaurin, Thomas C....356
McLean (McLain), Alexander...92, 131, 145, 162, 170
McLean (McLain), Allen...97, 136, 159, 179, 198
McLean (McLain), Allen C....470
McLean (McLain), Angus...148, 177, 208, 360, 540
McLean (McLain), Angus (S. Hill)...309
McLean (McLain), Anna...360
McLean (McLain), Archibald...90, 108, 366
McLean (McLain), Asa...88
McLean (McLain), Catherine...366, 381
McLean (McLain), Christian...360, 470
McLean (McLain), Christian (H.C.)...172
McLean (McLain), D....61(2)
McLean (McLain), D. (small)...61
McLean (McLain), Daniel...12, 29, 40, 58, 69, 152, 163, 166, 208, 273, 366, 470, 546, 564
McLean (McLain), Daniel (L.R.)...287
McLean (McLain), Donald...70, 172
McLean (McLain), Duncan...119, 120, 123, 149, 163, 171, 238
McLean (McLain), Effy...119
McLean (McLain), Flora...381
McLean (McLain), Flora A....470
McLean (McLain), Hector...60, 67, 69, 97(2), 126, 148(2), 159, 178
McLean (McLain), Hugh...147, 163
McLean (McLain), Hugh A....470
McLean (McLain), Hugh C....319, 525, 550
McLean (McLain), Isabella...366
McLean (McLain), J....61
McLean (McLain), J. (boatman)...61
McLean (McLain), J. (Ind. Branch)...61
McLean (McLain), James...381
McLean (McLain), Jennet...470
McLean (McLain), John...65, 70, 78, 93, 381
McLean (McLain), John (Gasters)...70
McLean (McLain), John K....366
McLean (McLain), Kenneth...360
McLean (McLain), Lauchlin...5, 20, 94
McLean (McLain), M....62(2)
McLean (McLain), Malcolm...381
McLean (McLain), Margaret...470
McLean (McLain), Mary...77, 165
McLean (McLain), Nancy...360, 470
McLean (McLain), Neill...5, 21, 66, 77, 120, 131, 187
McLean (McLain), Neill Sr....70
McLean (McLain), Norman...15, 60, 69
McLean (McLain), Peter...381
McLean (McLain), Sarah...131, 146
McLean (McLain), William...202
McLean (McLain), William (J.)...325
McLendon, Francis...32, 44
McLendon, John...21
McLennon, A....165
McLennon, Alexander W. ...357
McLennon, Allen...114, 393
McLennon, Christian...162
McLennon, Elizabeth...163, 313, 393(2), 544
McLennon, Jane...393
McLennon, Jennet...183
McLennon, John...73, 83, 202
McLennon, Mary...64, 329
McLennon, Sarah A....393
McLennon, William R....331
McLeod, (of John McClendon Place)...21
McLeod, (Schoolmaster)...22
McLeod, A....61, 158
McLeod, Alexander...32(2), 43, 66, 71, 77, 82, 92, 94, 113, 117, 122, 140, 148, 159(3), 161, 174, 175, 178, 226, 357, 359
McLeod, Alexander (Wd. Son)...279
McLeod, Alexander Sr....297
McLeod, Allen...144, 178, 220, 315, 327
McLeod, Angelette...396
McLeod, Anguish...95
McLeod, Angus...159, 432
McLeod, Angus G....371
McLeod, Ann...43, 147, 148, 254, 505
McLeod, Anna...67, 357
McLeod, Barbara...433
McLeod, Caller...47
McLeod, Catherine...357, 372(2), 433, 440
McLeod, Celia...433
McLeod, Charles...69, 84
McLeod, Christian...420, 474
McLeod, Daniel...5, 9, 22, 24(2), 52(2), 59, 60, 69, 72, 87, 91, 97(2), 118, 121, 145, 159, 163, 168, 169, 178, 321, 329, 359, 420, 475, 523
McLeod, Daniel L....432
McLeod, Daniel Sr....228
McLeod, Donald...391
McLeod, Duncan...140, 163, 170, 172, 177, 252, 432, 433, 441
McLeod, Duncan J....359
McLeod, Eli...505
McLeod, Eliza...396
McLeod, Eliza J....371
McLeod, Elizabeth...403
McLeod, Emeline...359
McLeod, Evander...359
McLeod, Flora...175, 236, 359, 432(2), 437, 474(2), 529, 556
McLeod, Flora A....359
McLeod, Frances...440
McLeod, Harriet...371
McLeod, Isabella...440
McLeod, James A....372
McLeod, James W....371
McLeod, Jane...357, 440
McLeod, John...5, 15, 21, 33, 53, 66, 88, 105, 119, 130, 136, 139, 150, 151, 164, 169, 172(2), 185, 359, 360, 403, 477, 511, 517(2), 525, 535, 540(2), 550, 566
McLeod, John (B.C.)...287, 295
McLeod, John (C.)...204
McLeod, John (Carpenter)...164
McLeod, John (D.C.)...254
McLeod, John (Esq.)...164, 172, 190, 208
McLeod, John (L.C.)...299
McLeod, John (R.C.)...321
McLeod, John (S.M.)...331
McLeod, John (T.)...218
McLeod, John A....279, 357, 372, 433, 519, 548
McLeod, John B....508
McLeod, John C....359
McLeod, John D....371
McLeod, John Jr....25, 246
McLeod, John L....371, 519, 548
McLeod, Kenneth...59, 69, 71
McLeod, Lauchlin...371
McLeod, Louis...396, 523, 544
McLeod, Lydia...441
McLeod, Lydia M....372
McLeod, M....59
McLeod, Malcolm...69, 71
McLeod, Margaret...356, 359, 432, 556
McLeod, Mary...118, 148, 159, 174, 178, 432, 437, 440, 474, 477
McLeod, Mary A....371
McLeod, Mrs....5, 33
McLeod, Mrs. (RC)...21
McLeod, Murdoch...69, 97, 433, 481
McLeod, Murdoch M....352
McLeod, N....62
McLeod, Nancy...69, 77, 96, 127, 159(2), 165(2), 172, 175, 178, 183, 311, 356, 374, 440, 475, 519, 540, 548
McLeod, Nancy A....403
McLeod, Neill...5, 68, 69, 77, 78(3), 84, 86, 92, 94, 97, 110, 113, 117, 121, 139, 144, 148, 159, 165(3), 169, 178, 360, 440, 530, 560
McLeod, Neill (B.S.)...234, 279
McLeod, Neill (Esq.)...72
McLeod, Neill (M.)...240
McLeod, Neill (merchant)...105
McLeod, Neill (surveyor)...104
McLeod, Nepsy...432
McLeod, Norman...15, 32, 60, 66, 69, 81, 90, 98, 126, 147, 159, 178, 198, 244, 279, 433, 512
McLeod, Norman (G.)...277
McLeod, Samuel...359
McLeod, Sandy...5
McLeod, Sarah...433, 441
McLeod, Sarah A....359
McLeod, Sarah E....372
McLeod, W....61
McLeod, William...5, 22, 47, 149, 359, 440
McMillan, Alexander...77, 134

McRae, Mary...58, 64, 68, 440(2)
McRae, Murdoch...8, 18, 44, 58, 65, 427
McRae, Nancy...440
McRae, Phillip...47
McRae, Roderick...440
McSwain (McSween), ?...77
McSwain (McSween), Daniel...5, 20, 33, 45, 51, 59, 126
McSwain (McSween), Hugh...4, 20, 46
McSwain (McSween), John...5, 130, 143, 160
McSwain (McSween), Mary...260
McSwain (McSween), Murdo J....362
McSwain (McSween), Murdoch...77, 143, 160
McSwain (McSween), N....62
McSwain (McSween), Nancy...65, 89
McSwain (McSween), Neill...32
McSwain (McSween), Polly...180
McWadsworth, Daniel...98
Mears, John...70
Mears, William...65, 87
Medford, Jeptha...14, 24, 52, 59, 98
Medlin, Alexander...143, 159, 374
Medlin, Andrew...289, 374(2)
Medlin, Angeline...347
Medlin, Angus...375
Medlin, Archibald...139, 183, 256, 275, 347, 381
Medlin, Benjamin...347, 348, 538
Medlin, Charles...256, 289, 375, 548
Medlin, Christian...348
Medlin, Daniel...184, 293, 347
Medlin, Deborah...374
Medlin, Elizabeth...348
Medlin, Emaline...375
Medlin, Emily E....381
Medlin, Green...381
Medlin, Happy...348
Medlin, Hugh...99
Medlin, Jacob...375
Medlin, James...348
Medlin, James A....381
Medlin, Jane...347
Medlin, Jesse...175
Medlin, Jesse (Cooper)...41
Medlin, Joel...13, 30(2), 41, 62, 67, 99
Medlin, John...68, 99, 105, 110, 185, 347, 350, 381, 502
Medlin, John A....347
Medlin, John Jr....143, 159
Medlin, John Sr....159
Medlin, Letha...375
Medlin, Malinda...375, 378
Medlin, Margaret...381
Medlin, Mary...350, 375
Medlin, Mary A....381
Medlin, Nancy...381
Medlin, Nancy A....350
Medlin, Neill...375
Medlin, Nelly...375
Medlin, Rebecca...67, 347, 381
Medlin, Riley...347
Medlin, Rosetta...347
Medlin, Ruth...350
Medlin, Sarah A....374
Medlin, Sarah C....350
Medlin, Scintha...381
Medlin, Susannah...381
Medlin, Swain...348
Medlin, William...183, 230, 347, 348
Medlin, William T....347
Medlin, Willie...381
Melton, Ansel...23, 50 , 59, 69, 72, 96, 110, 159, 175, 194
Melton, Benjamin...77
Melton, Christian...504
Melton, David...7, 17, 26, 56
Melton, Elizabeth...481
Melton, George...481
Melton, Hiram...198
Melton, Isaac...250
Melton, James...65, 77, 86, 90, 111, 148, 159, 177, 196, 291, 481, 504, 566
Melton, James W....481
Melton, Jesse...175
Melton, John...147, 159, 169
Melton, Lucinda...481
Melton, Lydia...481
Melton, Manda...481
Melton, Margaret...481
Melton, Mary...504
Melton, Nancy...481, 504
Melton, Nathaniel...64, 90
Melton, Neill...348, 504
Melton, Priscilla...481
Melton, Robert...194, 200, 269, 504
Melton, Sarah...499
Melton, Temperance...481(2)
Melton, William...177
Merritt, Ann...82
Merritt, James...67
Merritt, John...68, 91
Merritt, Mark...70, 91
Miles, J....62
Miles, Jesse...68
Miller, ?...76
Miller, Ann...404
Miller, Elizabeth...404, 499
Miller, Frances A....499
Miller, Hayman...499, 536
Miller, James...404
Miller, John...404(2)
Miller, Martha...499(2)
Miller, Mary A....404
Miller, Nancy...404
Miller, Newman...499
Miller, Noah...499
Miller, Rebecca...499
Miller, Riland...216
Miller, Riland R....499, 568
Miller, Riland R. (Con.)...301
Miller, Susan...404
Miller, Wiley...499
Miller, Wiley J....404
Miller, William...374
Mills, Joshua...69
Minter, Joseph J....407
Minter, Thomas J....525, 550
Minyard, John...71
Mishal, John...58
Mitchell, John...9, 13, 30, 40
Moffitt, E. Gardner...459
Monger, James...433
Monger, Jane...433
Monger, John...433
Monger, Joseph...242, 299, 432, 529, 556
Monger, Joseph J....433, 556
Monger, Margaret B....433
Monger, Mary...433
Monger, Mary A....432
Monger, Nancy...432, 433
Monk, Alexander...371
Monk, Archibald...16
Monk, Asbel...69
Monk, Daniel...66
Monk, James...68, 81, 115, 139, 164, 168, 185, 236, 275, 371
Monk, Sarah...371
Monroe, Alexander...69, 361, 363, 540
Monroe, Amanda...472
Monroe, Ann...346
Monroe, Archibald...125, 152, 162, 172, 196, 208, 271
Monroe, Archibald (J.C.)...287
Monroe, Archibald B....363
Monroe, Benjamin...435
Monroe, Benjamin F....472
Monroe, Benjamin P....346
Monroe, Catherine...363, 473(2)
Monroe, Colin A....346
Monroe, Daniel...66, 88
Monroe, Daniel R....363
Monroe, Dugald...115, 178, 387
Monroe, Duncan...128, 139, 163, 260, 275, 381, 542
Monroe, Duncan M....373
Monroe, Effy...361
Monroe, Eliza...473
Monroe, Flora M....363
Monroe, Francis...198, 271, 473, 564
Monroe, Hector...377
Monroe, Hugh B....363
Monroe, James...271, 473
Monroe, James H....373
Monroe, Jane...240, 381, 387, 521, 542
Monroe, Jennet...473
Monroe, John...88, 301, 377, 435, 472, 473, 564
Monroe, John A....346
Monroe, John C....473
Monroe, John T....373
Monroe, Lauchlin...473
Monroe, Lauchlin B....473
Monroe, Levi...473
Monroe, Malcolm...69, 73, 76, 78, 82, 115, 152, 166, 472
Monroe, Margaret...64, 144, 165
Monroe, Martha J....373
Monroe, Mary...377(2), 472
Monroe, Mary A....473
Monroe, Mary C....473
Monroe, Nancy...361
Monroe, Neill...69, 381
Monroe, Patrick J....307, 363, 546
Monroe, Patrick R....373
Monroe, Peter...140, 171, 208, 377, 548
Monroe, Rebecca A....373
Monroe, Rebecca E....373
Monroe, Robert...473
Monroe, Sarah...363, 381
Monroe, Sarah A....377
Monroe, Sarah C....346
Monroe, William...473
Monroe, William B....363
Monroe, William E....373
Moody, A.S. ...252
Moody, Alexander...462
Moody, Anderson...287
Moody, Anderson S....462, 534, 562
Moody, Daniel...462
Moody, Franklin...462
Moody, John...462
Moody, Peter...462

Moody, Quimby...462
Moody, Sallie...462
Moody, William...462
Moore, Adaline...456
Moore, Albert...490
Moore, Alexander...459
Moore, Anderson...371
Moore, Andrew...456
Moore, Anna...450
Moore, Balaam...458
Moore, Bethana...458
Moore, Bryant...450, 459
Moore, Candace...458
Moore, David...68
Moore, Drusilla...490
Moore, Edward...8, 17, 26, 55, 130, 182
Moore, Edward Jr....65, 69
Moore, Edward Sr....71
Moore, Elias...456, 490
Moore, Eliza...456
Moore, Elizabeth...452(2), 490
Moore, Fanning...122, 159, 183, 246, 313, 448
Moore, Fanning (C.C)...327
Moore, Frances...448, 452
Moore, George...115, 154, 159, 182(2), 265, 446, 448, 456, 458
Moore, George (C.)...283
Moore, George Jr....186
Moore, Gideon...116, 174, 295, 459
Moore, Hugh...206, 489
Moore, Irwin...67
Moore, James...27, 57, 67, 265, 452, 458, 558
Moore, James W....470
Moore, John...98, 114, 168, 185, 238, 456, 488, 490
Moore, John (G.)...323
Moore, Joseph...452
Moore, Joseph G....194, 281
Moore, Larkins...458
Moore, Lindsey...346, 459
Moore, Lydia...450
Moore, Malcolm...459
Moore, Margaret T....349
Moore, Martha F....343
Moore, Martha J....349
Moore, Mary...448, 450, 452, 456, 459
Moore, Mary E....349
Moore, Milley...450
Moore, Nancy...452
Moore, Pattie...450
Moore, Rebecca...343
Moore, Riley...456
Moore, Robert...17, 78, 122
Moore, Sallie...456, 470
Moore, Sarah...450, 456, 490
Moore, Sarah A....349
Moore, Serepta A....349
Moore, Thomas...28, 37
Moore, William...19, 59, 77, 78, 228, 327, 343, 349, 538
Moore, William S....456
Moore, Zacheus...343
Morgan, Ann...495
Morgan, Edmund D....495
Morgan, Elizabeth...495(5)
Morgan, Franey...495
Morgan, George...14, 85, 495
Morgan, George B....495
Morgan, George T....495, 536, 568
Morgan, James...2, 15, 24, 52, 96, 136, 154, 159, 164, 182, 248, 269, 495
Morgan, James G....495
Morgan, James T....495
Morgan, Jesse...313
Morgan, John...2, 16, 24, 52, 59, 66, 68, 269, 313, 325, 495(3), 568
Morgan, John B....248
Morgan, John Jr....69
Morgan, Joseph...84, 136, 153, 159, 568
Morgan, Joseph B....495
Morgan, Loveday...495
Morgan, Lucinda...495
Morgan, Lydia...495
Morgan, Malinda...495
Morgan, Martha L....495
Morgan, Mary...495
Morgan, Nathan...96, 136, 148, 159, 174, 198, 265, 295, 495
Morgan, Pleasant...495, 568
Morgan, Polly...116
Morgan, Priscilla J....495
Morgan, Rebecca...495
Morgan, Reuben J....495
Morgan, Susan...495
Morgan, Thomas...495
Morgan, Webby...495
Morgan, William...2, 14, 24, 52, 59, 66, 67, 84, 85, 325, 495(3)
Morgan, William B....495
Morgan, William T....305, 495, 568
Morris, A....62
Morris, Allen D....411
Morris, Ann...473
Morris, Ann J....391
Morris, Archibald J....411
Morris, Benjamin...178, 188, 192, 303, 388, 422
Morris, Candis...390
Morris, Catherine...224, 391, 420, 522, 544
Morris, Daniel...163, 387, 421, 425
Morris, Daniel H....411
Morris, David...420
Morris, David P....393
Morris, Edmund M....391
Morris, Effy J....411
Morris, Elijah...246
Morris, Elisha...315
Morris, Eliza...421
Morris, Elizabeth...313
Morris, F....61
Morris, Fanny...390
Morris, Flora A....432
Morris, Flora A.E....411
Morris, Frederick...65, 68, 93, 121
Morris, George...432
Morris, H....61
Morris, Henry...93, 121, 146, 163, 421
Morris, Henry Jr....68
Morris, Henry Sr....68
Morris, Isabella...420
Morris, Jacob...121, 146, 164, 222
Morris, James...315, 389
Morris, James (D.B.)...323
Morris, Jane...420
Morris, Jemima...422
Morris, Jennet...421
Morris, John...71, 121, 146, 163, 164, 188, 202, 242, 390(2), 420, 432, 522, 544, 544, 554, 556
Morris, John (G.C.)...327
Morris, John (L.B.)...321
Morris, John A....422
Morris, John D....432
Morris, John Jr....94, 303
Morris, John Sr....93, 188, 319
Morris, Jonathan...422
Morris, Jordan...388
Morris, Joseph...388
Morris, Kenneth...422
Morris, Lucy...421
Morris, Margaret...389, 390, 411, 422(2), 432(2)
Morris, Martha...388, 422, 473
Morris, Martha A....422
Morris, Mary...134, 146, 420, 432, 473
Morris, Mary A....422
Morris, Matthew...69, 146, 329, 389
Morris, Matthew B....411
Morris, Murdoch...422
Morris, Nancy...389, 390(2), 421, 422
Morris, Nathaniel...422
Morris, Neill...422
Morris, Peter...68, 93, 131, 146, 165(2), 192, 315, 388, 542, 544
Morris, Peter W....329, 390
Morris, Rebecca...388
Morris, Richard...411
Morris, Robert...421
Morris, Sarah...388, 390(3), 422
Morris, Sarah E....422
Morris, Sophia...389
Morris, Stephen...65, 69, 94, 131, 188, 202, 412, 421(2), 437
Morris, Temperance...388
Morris, Thomas...391, 422, 453
Morris, William...391
Morrison, Adam...5
Morrison, Alexander...69, 91, 110, 148, 158, 178, 232, 301, 471, 474, 535
Morrison, Allen...59, 78, 147, 158, 188, 258, 474, 564
Morrison, Allen (C.B.)...327
Morrison, Allen B....383, 521, 542
Morrison, Angus...149, 159, 178, 180, 198, 474, 535, 564
Morrison, Angus (Eld.)...279
Morrison, Archibald...32, 43
Morrison, Cain...11, 29, 38
Morrison, Catherine...383
Morrison, Catherine E....471
Morrison, Christian...71, 383, 507
Morrison, Daniel...45
Morrison, Duncan...236, 281, 383
Morrison, Elizabeth...474
Morrison, Flora...383
Morrison, Horace...383
Morrison, Isabella...507
Morrison, John...20, 32, 45, 88, 147, 158, 250, 309, 435, 507, 514, 572
Morrison, John C....471
Morrison, Kenneth...43, 67
Morrison, Malcolm...60, 69, 98, 120, 147, 158, 178, 383, 474
Morrison, Malcolm C....97
Morrison, Margaret...351, 383, 471, 474
Morrison, Mary...383, 471, 507, 516
Morrison, Mary A....471
Morrison, Mathew...166
Morrison, Maurice...65, 114
Morrison, Mondell...162, 165
Morrison, Monders (P.C.)...329

Morrison, Morris...82, 140, 188, 244
Morrison, Mrs....5, 33
Morrison, Nancy...383, 474
Morrison, Neill...179, 471, 564
Morrison, Neill (Esq.)...198, 301
Morrison, Norman...4, 24, 45, 52, 59, 69, 91, 118, 148, 158, 471
Morrison, Penelope...21
Morrison, Peter...188
Morrison, Rodham...21
Morrison, Samuel N....471
Morrison, Sarah...172, 474
Morrison, Sarah J....471
Morrison, William...383
Muckle, Andrew...397
Muckle, Anna...397
Muckle, Benjamin...146, 187, 192, 299, 397(2), 523, 544
Muckle, Elizabeth...397
Muckle, Isaac...397
Muckle, James...397
Muckle, Jane...397
Muckle, Mary...397
Muckle, Sarah...397
Munn, A....62
Munn, Angus...58
Munn, Ann...396
Munn, Calvin...396
Munn, Carolina...396
Munn, D....61
Munn, Margaret...396
Murchison, Alexander...127, 145, 224
Murchison, Annabella...427
Murchison, Archibald...162
Murchison, Barbara...65, 78
Murchison, Catherine...427, 528
Murchison, Christian...76, 92, 127, 162
Murchison, D....62
Murchison, Daniel...92, 127, 135, 144(2), 145, 163(2), 178, 200, 224
Murchison, Daniel (Red)...162
Murchison, Duncan...65, 92, 109, 124, 144, 162, 168, 187, 252, 319, 331, 421, 527, 528, 554
Murchison, Duncan (Big)...163
Murchison, Duncan (Esq.)...254
Murchison, Elizabeth...68
Murchison, Finley...30
Murchison, Flora...427
Murchison, Frances...421
Murchison, Isabell...76
Murchison, John...29, 39, 92, 104, 105, 141, 184, 216, 311, 443, 531, 560
Murchison, John (tailor)...159
Murchison, K....62
Murchison, Kenneth...11, 30, 41, 58, 64, 66, 87, 89, 127, 143, 144, 154, 159, 165, 166, 179, 254, 315, 427, 556
Murchison, Kenneth B....443
Murchison, Lydia...427
Murchison, Margaret...427
Murchison, Margaret F....427
Murchison, Martha J....427
Murchison, Murdock...65
Murchison, Nancy...144, 178, 267
Murchison, Oscar B....427
Murchison, Rebecca...427, 556
Murchison, Roderick...104, 105, 139, 142, 159, 186
Murchison, Roderick (hatter)...165
Murchison, William...114, 122, 146, 166, 188, 220
Murchsion, Aaron...368
Murley, Samuel...141
Murray, Andrew...478
Murray, Campbell...478
Murray, Duncan...66
Murray, Jennet...478
Murray, Jesse...478
Murray, John W....478
Murray, Mary...478
Murray, Miley...478
Murray, Narcissa...478
Muse, Alexander D....352
Muse, Alexander T....317, 436, 556
Muse, Andrew H....352
Muse, Ann...483
Muse, Archibald...483, 484
Muse, Asa...232
Muse, Ashley...484
Muse, C....63
Muse, Candace...483, 484
Muse, Catherine...436
Muse, Chapel B....352
Muse, Charity...44, 65
Muse, Charles...507
Muse, Commodore...484
Muse, D.H....244
Muse, Daniel...8, 19, 114, 142, 159, 180, 194, 483
Muse, Daniel (Spk.)...279
Muse, Daniel H....180, 297, 350, 514, 538
Muse, Daniel Jr....271
Muse, David...508
Muse, Effy...507
Muse, Elizabeth...260, 297, 352, 436(2), 483(2)
Muse, Emily A....508
Muse, Flora...508
Muse, Frances...436
Muse, Franklin...483
Muse, George...483
Muse, George G....351, 538
Muse, Haywood...508
Muse, Henderson...293, 352, 538
Muse, J....62
Muse, James...7, 17, 66, 74, 89, 121, 159, 180, 236, 484
Muse, James B....143, 159, 180, 297, 352, 515, 538
Muse, James H....228, 279, 351
Muse, James Jr....31, 42, 142
Muse, James Sr....33
Muse, Jane...351, 484
Muse, Jason...121, 226
Muse, Jennet K....350
Muse, Jesse...65, 90, 112, 159, 180, 484, 566
Muse, Jesse (Esq.)...143, 180
Muse, Jesse (S.)...277
Muse, Jesse F....143, 181, 236, 281, 307, 352, 515
Muse, Jesse J....159
Muse, Jesse W....436
Muse, John...484, 508
Muse, John C....352
Muse, John W....483
Muse, Josiah...436, 483
Muse, Julia A....352
Muse, Kendrick...83
Muse, Kindred...350
Muse, Lavina C....483
Muse, Lemuel...353, 538
Muse, Lucian...352
Muse, Lydia C....352
Muse, Malcolm...436
Muse, Maranda...484
Muse, Margaret...352
Muse, Margaret B....352
Muse, Margaret E....483
Muse, Martha E....352
Muse, Martha J....483
Muse, Mary...353, 436
Muse, Mary A....508
Muse, Mary E....352
Muse, Miles...285, 483
Muse, Milly C....352
Muse, Nancy...436, 484
Muse, Nancy E....352
Muse, Noah...484
Muse, Patience...350, 484
Muse, Priscilla...483
Muse, Rebecca...483
Muse, Robert S....436
Muse, Samuel...508
Muse, Sarah F....352
Muse, Sophia...484
Muse, Susan...484
Muse, Susan E....436
Muse, Susannah...476, 483
Muse, Temperance...483
Muse, Thomas...68, 83, 109, 137, 159
Muse, Thomas (S?)...277
Muse, Thomas P....143, 168, 180
Muse, Thomas Sr....143, 159, 180, 232
Muse, Westley B....476
Muse, William...436, 484
Muse, William H....476
Muse, William R....436
Myrick, ?...182
Myrick, Ann E....459
Myrick, Columbus...459
Myrick, Francis...69, 99, 111, 141, 159, 182, 212
Myrick, Huldah...455, 533
Myrick, James C....179, 186
Myrick, John...248, 454, 533, 558
Myrick, John M....454
Myrick, Margaret...454(2)
Myrick, Margaret E....460
Myrick, Martha J....460
Myrick, Moses...226, 313
Myrick, Nancy...459
Myrick, Parham K....459
Myrick, Rebecca...457
Myrick, Susannah...454
Myrick, William L....454
Nailor, Catherine...343
Nailor, Charles...343
Nailor, Elizabeth...343
Nailor, George...242
Nailor, Hezekiah...343
Nailor, Irene...343
Nailor, John...343
Nailor, Joshua...240, 297
Nailor, Mary J....353
Nailor, Sarah...353
Nailor, W. Alexander...343
Nailor, Wesley...180, 236, 307, 343, 572
Nall, Absalom...462
Nall, Chestley...462
Nall, Elizabeth...462
Nall, Emily...498

Phillips, Lewis S....444
Phillips, Lewis Sr....319
Phillips, Lydia...451
Phillips, Lydia A....444
Phillips, Malphus...444
Phillips, Mark...67, 83, 110, 143, 160, 204, 269
Phillips, Martha...340, 447, 451(2)
Phillips, Martha J....444
Phillips, Mary...444, 445, 447, 451, 463(2), 511
Phillips, Mary A....380
Phillips, Mastin C....444
Phillips, Mathew...124, 141
Phillips, Michael...447
Phillips, Nancy...444(2), 450, 486, 489, 566
Phillips, Nancy C....444
Phillips, Neill...447
Phillips, Patience...83
Phillips, Pattie...463
Phillips, Patty...141, 160
Phillips, Rainy...340
Phillips, Rebecca...451
Phillips, Richard...486
Phillips, Robert...560
Phillips, Robert H....293, 444
Phillips, Sally...183
Phillips, Sarah...254, 463
Phillips, Sebra...447
Phillips, Simon P....340
Phillips, Sophia...489
Phillips, Stephen...295, 444, 450
Phillips, Sybil...130
Phillips, Temperance...202
Phillips, William...137, 142, 161, 180, 218, 327, 444(2), 445, 463, 560
Phillips, William A....380
Phillips, William H....451
Pike, Benjamin...95
Piles, S....61
Pinfield, William...317
Pipkin, Archibald...396
Pipkin, Charles...244, 313
Pipkin, Elizabeth...396
Pipkin, John Marshal...396
Pipkin, Penelope...397
Pipkin, Penny...299
Pipkin, William...396, 544
Pittman, Dempsey...65
Pittman, Jesse...12
Pittman, John...12
Pittman, Joseph...12
Plummer, Alexander...182, 212
Poe, William...26
Poole, Elizabeth...459
Poole, William...56
Pope, Benjamin...141, 218
Pope, Joel...141, 168
Pope, Mary...246
Pope, Uriah...125
Poplin, William...26, 56, 58
Pore, Anna...388
Pore, Elizabeth...388
Pore, Hardy...388
Pore, Joel...388, 542
Pore, Lovet...388
Pore, Nicy...388
Pore, Susan...388
Porter, John...130
Postell, Emma...353
Postell, Thomas W....353
Potter, William...6
Powell, David A....508
Powell, William...508
Powers, Agnes...453
Powers, Enoch S....453, 558
Powers, Henry...160, 184
Powers, James...453
Powers, John H....453
Powers, Lydia J....453
Price, Lewis...67, 94, 121
Priest, Alexander...437
Priest, Catherine...437
Priest, Gilbert...271, 437
Priest, Loveday...437
Priest, Lucy...437
Priest, Mariah...437
Priest, Owen...437
Purnal, James...68
Purvis, Andrew J....453
Purvis, Cary...265
Purvis, Cornelius...453
Purvis, Franklin H....453
Purvis, George...453
Purvis, Jefferson...285
Purvis, John M....453
Purvis, Joseph...453
Purvis, Missouri A....453
Purvis, Robert L....453, 558
Purvis, Sarah...453
Purvis, Thomas...218
Quimby, John...64, 78
Ragland, John...58
Ragland, Richard...58
Ragsdale, Abner...91
Ragsdale, Benjamin...67, 84
Ragsdale, Daniel...70, 87
Ragsdale, John...67, 92
Ragsdale, Richard...67, 87, 104, 105
Ramage, Darius...66, 97
Ray, Alexander...147, 172, 208, 309, 361, 540
Ray, Ann...336, 361
Ray, Anna...355
Ray, Archibald...65, 72, 76, 78, 84, 88, 89, 120, 129, 152, 162, 172, 179, 208, 355(2), 361(2), 366(2), 517(2), 540(2)
Ray, Archibald (Esq.)...162, 309
Ray, Archibald Sr....287
Ray, Barbara...361
Ray, Betsy...185
Ray, Catherine...336, 356, 361, 366, 367
Ray, Christian...254, 336, 361, 366
Ray, Daniel...163, 361
Ray, David...356
Ray, Duncan...88, 111, 112, 163(2), 366
Ray, Duncan Jr....150
Ray, Duncan Sr....151
Ray, Effy...366(2)
Ray, Elizabeth...367
Ray, Flora...355, 367
Ray, Flora J....366
Ray, Hugh...61
Ray, Hugh M....366
Ray, J....61
Ray, James...65, 150, 164, 234, 367
Ray, James Sr....285
Ray, John...20, 33, 76, 88, 89, 120(2), 163, 172, 184, 246, 356, 361, 366
Ray, John (Miller)...164
Ray, John A.J....361
Ray, John C....355
Ray, John M.D....309, 361, 517, 540
Ray, John Sr....151, 163
Ray, Joseph...356
Ray, Kenneth...336, 513, 570
Ray, Kenneth Jr....293
Ray, Malcolm...208, 355, 366(2), 367
Ray, Malcolm C....510
Ray, Margaret...336
Ray, Martha A....360
Ray, Mary...336,356, 360, 361(2)
Ray, Mary A....355, 366
Ray, Mary J....360
Ray, Mary L....355
Ray, Nancy...366, 367
Ray, Neill...361
Ray, Nevin...230, 366(2), 546(2)
Ray, Norman Jr....309
Ray, Norman Sr....309
Ray, Patrick...355, 518, 540
Ray, Peter...309
Ray, Samuel J....361
Ray, Sarah...336, 361, 366
Ray, Sarah A....361
Ray, Sarah E....356
Ray, Sarah J....361
Ray, William A....366
Ray, Wilson...122
Record, John...66, 82
Reddin, Levi...121
Reeder, Sarah...465
Reeves (Reives, Reaves), Lucinda...477
Reeves (Reives, Reaves), Samuel...311
Reeves (Reives, Reaves), William...182, 485
Reeves (Reives, Reaves), William (R.B.)...323
Reid (Reed), Archibald...91, 109, 139, 161, 184
Reid (Reed), David...131, 147, 168
Reid (Reed), David (Esq.)...163
Reid (Reed), Grace...443
Reid (Reed), Joseph L....443
Reid (Reed), Thomas...185, 260
Reid (Reed), Thomas M.D....261
Reid (Reed), Thomas M.D. (Esq.)...240
Reid (Reed), William...66, 70
Reynolds, Charles...267
Reynolds, Fanny...69
Reynolds, James...511
Reynolds, Jeffery...128
Reynolds, Jeptha...81, 91, 145, 170, 178
Reynolds, Jeremiah...212
Reynolds, Jerry...176
Reynolds, Luvay...90
Reynolds, Mary...128
Reynolds, Peter...58
Reynolds, Sally...124
Reynolds, Sarah...69
Rhodes, David...438, 560
Rhodes, Elizabeth...438
Rhodes, Lucretia...438, 529
Rhodes, Mary...438
Rhodes, Thomas...124, 139, 236, 281
Rhodes, William...98
Rice, Joseph L....236
Richardson, Abraham...6, 17
Richardson, Angelica...469
Richardson, Catherine...469
Richardson, D....160
Richardson, David...23, 50, 59, 66, 96, 136, 148, 160, 180, 256, 496
Richardson, David D....468

Shaw, Daniel J...434
Shaw, Daniel Sr...145, 163
Shaw, Dugald...434
Shaw, Duncan...238, 358, 361, 383, 517, 540
Shaw, Duncan C...358
Shaw, Eliza...361, 434
Shaw, Flora...358, 469
Shaw, Flora A...406
Shaw, Harriet A...361
Shaw, Jane...434
Shaw, John...54, 22(2), 31, 32, 45 166, 313, 353, 362, 378
Shaw, L. Jane...361
Shaw, M. Jennet...361
Shaw, Malcolm...4, 20, 32, 45, 146, 165, 220, 435
Shaw, Malcolm (Surveyor)...317
Shaw, Margaret...361, 415
Shaw, Margaret J...387
Shaw, Mary...361, 406, 415, 434(2)
Shaw, Mary J...361, 434
Shaw, Nancy...395, 434, 469
Shaw, Neill...10, 13, 30, 41, 140, 165, 171, 187
Shaw, Neill W...387
Shaw, Norman...178, 511
Shaw, Peter...21, 32
Shaw, Sally...182, 331
Shaw, Sarah...387, 469, 521, 542
Shaw, Sarah J...358
Shaw, Shion...128
Shaw, Thomas...361, 437
Shaw, Usly...250
Shaw, William...131, 166, 434, 556
Shaw, William (Capt.)...146
Shaw, William (Esq.)...204
Shaw, William (R.S.)...331
Shaw, William H...434
Shaw, William Sr...275
Shears, John...132
Sheffield, Amanda...467
Sheffield, Anna...504
Sheffield, Bethana...467
Sheffield, Calvin...467, 500
Sheffield, Catherine...504
Sheffield, Delilah...503
Sheffield, Dempsey...499
Sheffield, Eliza...503
Sheffield, Elizabeth...499
Sheffield, Everet...85, 118, 153, 160, 182, 194, 504
Sheffield, Hannah...503
Sheffield, Hiram...305, 499
Sheffield, Isaac...160, 499, 503
Sheffield, Isham...84, 112, 118, 153(2), 182, 504
Sheffield, Isham Jr...160
Sheffield, Isham Sr...160
Sheffield, Jane...503(3)
Sheffield, John...2, 51, 59, 84, 109, 118, 265, 463, 503(2)
Sheffield, John Jr...15, 25, 53, 59, 67, 154, 160, 182, 210, 287
Sheffield, John Sr...15, 67, 154, 160, 182, 212
Sheffield, Jonathan...499
Sheffield, Levi...499
Sheffield, Lydia...503
Sheffield, Martha...467, 500, 503
Sheffield, Martin...503, 568
Sheffield, Mary...503
Sheffield, Matthew...194, 503
Sheffield, Pattie...467
Sheffield, Rebecca...503
Sheffield, Sallie...503
Sheffield, Sarah...499, 503
Sheffield, Stephen...319, 467
Sheffield, William...465, 499, 504(2)
Sheffield, William Sr...15
Shepherd (Sheppard), Altha V...399
Shepherd (Sheppard), Andrew...260
Shepherd (Sheppard), Elizabeth...399
Shepherd (Sheppard), James L...399
Shepherd (Sheppard), John...65, 93, 132, 145, 146, 169, 174, 258, 399, 523, 550
Shepherd (Sheppard), John (Esq.)...164, 190, 299
Shepherd (Sheppard), John (Long)...164
Shepherd (Sheppard), John A...399
Shepherd (Sheppard), John J...438
Shepherd (Sheppard), John Jr...95
Shepherd (Sheppard), John Sr...68, 94, 190
Shepherd (Sheppard), Mahalah...399
Shepherd (Sheppard), Mary...399
Shepherd (Sheppard), Mary J...399
Shepherd (Sheppard), Nancy...399
Shepherd (Sheppard), Nancy E...419
Shields, Ann...446
Shields, Archibald...108, 141, 160, 183, 204, 265, 445, 446, 560
Shields, Archibald Jr...218
Shields, Arsina...452
Shields, Austin...446
Shields, B...62
Shields, Benjamin...7, 19, 26, 54, 67, 82, 289, 448, 558
Shields, Benjamin (D.R.)...291
Shields, Benjamin J...437, 556
Shields, Bryan...449
Shields, Cassander...445, 480
Shields, Catherine...436, 449
Shields, Charles C...446
Shields, Cornelius...81, 141, 160, 204, 479, 535, 566
Shields, Cornelius Esq...291
Shields, Daniel J...437
Shields, Duncan P...437
Shields, Elizabeth J...480
Shields, Emeline...436
Shields, Emily...449
Shields, Enoch...445
Shields, Finity...446
Shields, Hannah...445
Shields, James...142, 160, 183, 232, 446, 558
Shields, James M...479
Shields, Jane...479
Shields, John...449
Shields, John W...436, 479, 556
Shields, Lucy...445
Shields, Lydia...445, 448, 449
Shields, Mahala...445
Shields, Malcolm...449
Shields, Margaret...436, 445
Shields, Mariah...437
Shields, Martha...436, 445, 448, 449, 479
Shields, Mary...250, 436, 449, 452
Shields, Mary E...448
Shields, Miriam...445
Shields, Nancy...174, 445
Shields, Neill...122, 183, 436, 445
Shields, Orren...445
Shields, Patrick...130, 169, 218, 238, 449, 558
Shields, Patrick Jr...313
Shields, Patrick Sr...285
Shields, Reuben...17, 26, 54, 68, 96, 104, 115, 168
Shields, Robert D...448
Shields, Rosanna...449
Shields, Sarah...452
Shields, Sophia...449
Shields, Sophronia...449
Shields, Susan...446
Shields, Susannah...446
Shields, Westley...452
Shields, William...175, 246, 327, 437, 452
Shields, William J...436, 556
Shields, William T...448
Short, Brinkley...439
Short, Burrel...566
Short, Burrel H...491
Short, Caroline...440
Short, Daniel...439, 490, 529, 560, 566
Short, Devotion D...490
Short, Eliza...439
Short, Elizabeth...490
Short, Ellen...440
Short, Frances...439
Short, Margaret...439, 440
Short, Martha...491
Short, Mary...491
Short, Pleasant W...491
Short, Samuel...440
Short, Sarah...439
Siler, Benjamin...110, 139, 162, 171
Siler, Frederick...99, 139, 163, 170
Siler, John...177(2)
Silvy, Martha...399
Simmons, Berilla...493
Simmons, Bluford...493, 568
Simmons, Cade...493
Simmons, Eveline...493
Simmons, Gainey...493
Simmons, Kirvin...493
Simmons, Love...493
Simmons, Martha...493
Simmons, Molcy...493
Simmons, William...16
Sinclair, Andrew...420
Sinclair, Archibald...222, 430
Sinclair, D.A. ...222
Sinclair, Daniel...429, 437
Sinclair, Duncan...128, 311
Sinclair, Duncan (A.)...317
Sinclair, Duncan (R.)...230
Sinclair, Duncan A...429, 556
Sinclair, Duncan M...442, 560
Sinclair, Effy...429
Sinclair, Elizabeth...437
Sinclair, George...430
Sinclair, James...430
Sinclair, Jane J...442
Sinclair, Jennet...420
Sinclair, Jennet J...437
Sinclair, John...64, 92, 127, 144, 179, 429
Sinclair, John (Sr.)...164
Sinclair, Margaret...442, 530
Sinclair, Mary...420, 429
Sinclair, Mary A...437
Sinclair, Nancy...420
Sinclair, Peter...76, 134, 139, 145, 165, 177, 179, 222, 293, 420, 429, 437, 554, 556

Stutts, Minny...340
Stutts, Murdoch...478
Stutts, Nancy...346, 475
Stutts, Noah...475
Stutts, Noah B....467
Stutts, Patsy...341
Stutts, Pleasant...487
Stutts, Robert...478
Stutts, Sallie...475
Stutts, Samuel...346
Stutts, Sarah...475, 477, 487
Stutts, Sarah L....487
Stutts, Spinks...477
Stutts, Susan...488
Stutts, Walter...346
Stutts, Wesley...459
Stutts, William...175, 467, 478
Stutts, William B....346
Suggs, Solomon...133
Sullivan, Barbara A....340
Sullivan, Celia...340
Sullivan, Eli...492
Sullivan, Green...492
Sullivan, Isaac...492
Sullivan, Jesse...340, 570
Sullivan, Joel...271, 492, 568
Sullivan, John B....340
Sullivan, Joseph...95, 133
Sullivan, Julia...492
Sullivan, Lydia M....492
Sullivan, Martha M....340
Sullivan, Minnetta...492
Sullivan, Nancy...492
Sullivan, Smith...271
Sullivan, William L....340
Sullivan, Zada...492
Sumer, David...58
Sutton, James...64
Swann, Ann...389
Swann, Frances...389, 390
Swann, Frances H....389
Swann, Frederick...186
Swann, Frederick J....390
Swann, James...390
Swann, James M....389
Swann, John...244, 389, 390, 522
Swann, Lucy...389
Swann, Mary H....389
Tarleton, Sion...74
Taylor, Aaron...145
Taylor, Charlotte...450
Taylor, Margaret...450
Taylor, Shadrach...6
Taylor, Zachary...379
Teague, Atkins...501
Teague, Cynthia...501
Teague, Eli...463
Teague, Elizabeth...463, 501
Teague, Isaac...122, 161, 181, 464
Teague, Isaac Jr....142
Teague, Isaac Sr....142
Teague, Jacob...500
Teague, John...463
Teague, Mahala...463
Teague, Mary...161, 501
Teague, Matthias...99
Teague, Moses...130
Teague, Nancy...500
Teague, Permelia...463
Teague, Susan...501
Teague, Susannah...463
Teague, William...64, 66, 501
Teague, William (Black)...69
Teague, William (Preacher)...69
Teague, Willis...463
Teastor, Robert...98
Teastor, Sarah...98
Tedwell, Francis...2, 14, 23, 48, 59
Tedwell, Jenny...65
Tedwell, Samuel...15, 59, 65
Temple, Dickson...70
Temple, Lewis...69, 83
Temple, Luke...135, 173
Temple, Needham...64
Thagard, Eliza J....493
Thagard, Hasseltine...493
Thagard, Lucy...493
Thagard, Nancy...493
Thagard, William C....493, 568
Thomas, ?...173
Thomas, Aaron...224
Thomas, Alexander...403
Thomas, Allen...145, 162, 242, 303, 405, 550
Thomas, Anderson...242, 331, 402, 550
Thomas, Andrew...398
Thomas, Ann...357
Thomas, Asa P....391
Thomas, Barbara...391
Thomas, Benjamin...133, 146, 162, 398, 404
Thomas, Calvin...405
Thomas, Cassa...398
Thomas, Catherine...403
Thomas, Charity...410
Thomas, Charles F....391
Thomas, Daniel...333, 398, 544
Thomas, Daniel A....357
Thomas, Darius...400, 524, 550
Thomas, David...403
Thomas, Delaney...403
Thomas, Delilah...398
Thomas, Delitha...403
Thomas, Dora...123
Thomas, E. Ann...357
Thomas, Eliza...357, 398
Thomas, Eliza J....391
Thomas, Elizabeth...399
Thomas, Elizabeth E....400
Thomas, Emeline...403, 405
Thomas, Flora J....405
Thomas, Frederick...145, 163, 190
Thomas, Graham...303
Thomas, Green...401, 550
Thomas, Grissom...186, 192, 398
Thomas, Harriet...400
Thomas, Harriet M....400
Thomas, Henderson...313
Thomas, Henderson B....400
Thomas, Henry...401
Thomas, Henry F....400
Thomas, Herman...329
Thomas, Hiram...398
Thomas, Isabella...401
Thomas, Isabella C....403
Thomas, James D....435
Thomas, James K.P....400
Thomas, James M....398
Thomas, Jefferson...400
Thomas, Jesse...283, 352
Thomas, John ...74, 132, 145, 164, 173, 190, 228, 303, 398, 402, 403, 404, 405, 410, 510(2)
Thomas, John (Capt.)...190
Thomas, John (Mer.)...303
Thomas, John C....357
Thomas, John M....405
Thomas, John M.B....400
Thomas, John W....391, 398
Thomas, Joseph...93, 134, 146, 169, 200, 329, 395, 399, 524, 550
Thomas, Joseph P....357
Thomas, Keziah...66, 404, 550
Thomas, L. Dow...391
Thomas, Lorenzo D....299
Thomas, Macklin...400
Thomas, Mahalah...398
Thomas, Malinda H....405
Thomas, Martha...400
Thomas, Martha A....404
Thomas, Martin...145, 165, 173, 190
Thomas, Mary...398, 404
Thomas, Mary A....400, 402, 403
Thomas, Mary B....357
Thomas, Mary J....398
Thomas, Matilda...399
Thomas, Micajah...112
Thomas, Murdo M....357
Thomas, Nancy...329, 399, 401, 405, 410
Thomas, Nancy F....405
Thomas, Napoleon...401
Thomas, Nathan...83, 108
Thomas, Penelope...299, 401, 524
Thomas, Peter...194, 265, 309, 357, 540
Thomas, Peter (S.H.)...325
Thomas, Peyton...398
Thomas, Priscilla...170, 242, 303, 398, 401, 550
Thomas, Reuben...202, 299, 410, 552
Thomas, Robert...403
Thomas, Sackfield...403
Thomas, Samuel...175, 236
Thomas, Sarah...398
Thomas, Sarah A....391
Thomas, Sarah E....403
Thomas, Silpha...404
Thomas, Sophia C....391
Thomas, Susan...405
Thomas, Telitha...398
Thomas, Telitha A....394
Thomas, Temperance...402
Thomas, Thomas...68
Thomas, Tillman...242, 303, 400, 524, 550
Thomas, W.B....303
Thomas, William...190, 242, 398, 402
Thomas, William A.J....403
Thomas, William J....400
Thompson, Bryant...379
Thompson, Christian...426
Thompson, Daniel...135(2), 144, 145, 163
Thompson, David...162, 188
Thompson, Duncan...145, 169
Thompson, Elizabeth...379
Thompson, Flora A....426
Thompson, Garret...379
Thompson, Gaston...378
Thompson, Gilbert...378
Thompson, Harriet...379
Thompson, Isaac...378
Thompson, Jesse...258, 378, 520, 542
Thompson, Jesse (P.)...329
Thompson, John...175
Thompson, Joseph (M)...164
Thompson, Louisa...378
Thompson, Narcissa...379

Wallace, Celia...478
Wallace, Chaney...368
Wallace, Christian...334
Wallace, Cornelius...480
Wallace, Eli...479, 497
Wallace, Emberline...483
Wallace, Emsley...481
Wallace, Enoch...295, 334, 570
Wallace, Everet...65, 90, 116, 148, 161, 182, 196, 277, 472, 478
Wallace, Finity...472
Wallace, Franey...472, 476
Wallace, Hamilton...334
Wallace, Hiram...334
Wallace, Isham...291, 334, 481, 566
Wallace, Jane...481
Wallace, John...194, 273, 476, 481
Wallace, Joseph...305, 368
Wallace, Josiah...283, 478, 489
Wallace, Julia...476
Wallace, Lockey...481
Wallace, Loveday...497
Wallace, Malvina...334
Wallace, Manda...480
Wallace, Mary...345, 472, 476
Wallace, Nancy...472, 481
Wallace, Nathan...198, 472
Wallace, Nathan Jr....285
Wallace, Nicholas...111, 181
Wallace, Quimby...481
Wallace, Rebecca...476
Wallace, Ruffin...368
Wallace, Sampson...481
Wallace, Samuel...481
Wallace, Sarah...345, 480, 497
Wallace, Seaborn...369
Wallace, Spinks...334, 480
Wallace, Susannah...479
Wallace, Virgil...481
Wallace, Westley...481
Wallace, William J....478
Wallace, William L....478
Wallace, Winniferd...345
Walton, David...133
Walton, William...133
Ward, Edy...95
Ward, Ellen...508
Ward, John...94, 113, 133, 146, 164(2)
Ward, John L....139
Ward, Mary...401
Ward, Thomas...97
Warner, Anderson S....338
Warner, Daniel O....508
Warner, Daniel W....343
Warner, Edward...228, 339
Warner, Elizabeth...260, 338
Warner, Hardin...121, 142, 161, 174, 176, 230, 293, 337, 570
Warner, Hardin Jr....185
Warner, Huldah...339
Warner, J....62
Warner, John...83, 338, 572
Warner, John T....339
Warner, John W....342
Warner, Levi S....338
Warner, Levincia...339
Warner, Louisa A....339
Warner, Margaret...338
Warner, Margaret M....337
Warner, Martha J....337, 339
Warner, Mary...342, 513, 572
Warner, Neill R....342
Warner, Patrick D....338
Warner, Pirty...338
Warner, Richard...170, 226
Warner, Silsey...337
Warner, Susannah...338
Warner, Swain...338
Warner, William D....339, 570
Watkins, Ewell/Newell...15, 24, 52
Watkins, Neill...2
Watson, Alexander...408
Watson, Andrew...405
Watson, Ann E....411, 431
Watson, Anna...411
Watson, Arabella...405
Watson, Barbara...410
Watson, Calvin...408
Watson, Catherine...93, 410
Watson, David...146, 163, 173, 200, 299, 408, 410, 525, 552
Watson, Don Charles...431
Watson, Elisha...411, 526, 552
Watson, Elizabeth...313, 405, 407, 408, 410, 550
Watson, Flora A....410
Watson, Garner...410
Watson, George W....415, 526
Watson, Henry...408
Watson, Hugh...65
Watson, James...242
Watson, Jane...405, 407, 408
Watson, Jane C....431
Watson, John...70, 93, 109, 145, 164, 169, 190, 327, 410, 552
Watson, John Sr....299
Watson, Malcolm...407, 410
Watson, Malcolm B....410, 526, 552
Watson, Margaret...408, 410
Watson, Margaret J....408
Watson, Mary...410
Watson, Mary J....410, 415
Watson, Matthew...134, 405, 408
Watson, Monterey...431
Watson, Nancy...405
Watson, Neill...405
Watson, Robert...65, 93, 144, 166, 410(2)
Watson, Sallie...408
Watson, Sarah R....431
Watson, Susan...431
Watson, Sylvia...408
Watson, Walter...129, 283
Watson, William...68, 93, 146, 170, 192, 299, 407(2), 431, 525, 528, 529, 552, 556
Watts, J....61
Watts, Mary...64
Webb, Milly...146
Weightat, John...18
Welch, Calvin...345
Welch, Emeline...345
Weldon, Caroline T....402
Weldon, Catherine...402
Weldon, Daniel...192, 402, 550
Weldon, Daniel (Esq.)...267, 299
Weldon, John...133
Weldon, John (Esq.)...146, 164, 192
Weldon, John J....402
Weldon, Sarah...402
Weldon, Sarah J....402
Weldon, William...145
Wells, Isaac...142
Wells, Sally...142
Wheeler, Malcolm...433
White, Adam...82, 98, 109, 142, 161
White, Andrew...81, 114
White, Ann...143, 180
White, James...76
White, John...19, 115
White, Josiah...114
White, Phillip...90
White, William...21, 33, 136
Whitford, William...12
Whitford, William B....28, 39, 69, 71
Whitford, William Bastin...10, 12, 58
Whittle, James...8
Wicker, Albert...415
Wicker, Alexander...414(2)
Wicker, Alvis...408
Wicker, Ambers...417
Wicker, Anderson...173, 222, 311, 411, 421, 552
Wicker, Ann...70
Wicker, Ann C....416
Wicker, Anna...414
Wicker, Archibald...331, 396, 408, 414, 416
Wicker, Benjamin...67, 93, 162, 403, 409, 552
Wicker, Benjamin F....408
Wicker, Benjamin P....409
Wicker, Brittan M....408
Wicker, Charles...408, 411
Wicker, Charles A....411
Wicker, Charles F....412
Wicker, Cherry...409, 552
Wicker, Christian...414(2)
Wicker, Daniel...408, 416
Wicker, David...68(2), 134, 162, 224, 267
Wicker, David (Esq.)...145
Wicker, David J....384
Wicker, David S....414
Wicker, David W....414, 526, 552
Wicker, Edward...242, 311, 409, 552
Wicker, Eli...408
Wicker, Elijah...409
Wicker, Elisha...414, 552
Wicker, Eliza...384
Wicker, Eliza J....412
Wicker, Elizabeth...395, 403(2), 408, 409, 412, 414(2), 525, 550
Wicker, Elizabeth A....411
Wicker, Evander...409(2), 416
Wicker, Eveline...409
Wicker, Fanny...395
Wicker, Flora...416
Wicker, Frances C....408
Wicker, Green B....409
Wicker, James...206, 408, 416
Wicker, James B....403
Wicker, Jane...408(3), 409, 411
Wicker, Jesse...134, 145, 164, 186, 222, 319, 414(2)
Wicker, Jesse C....414
Wicker, John...164, 173, 222, 414
Wicker, John A....412
Wicker, John C....224, 267, 415
Wicker, John M....414
Wicker, Johnson...134, 224, 267
Wicker, Johnston...145
Wicker, Jonathan...67, 93, 134, 146, 164, 186, 254, 408, 409, 552
Wicker, Jordan...267, 417, 527, 554
Wicker, Josiah...408
Wicker, Kenneth...414, 425

Wicker, Lewis...202, 408(2), 552
Wicker, Margaret...412, 417(2)
Wicker, Margaret J....408
Wicker, Martha...408, 409(2), 414, 416(2)
Wicker, Martha A....412
Wicker, Mary...384, 409(2), 416, 417, 552
Wicker, Mary J....408, 416
Wicker, Matthew...93, 134, 173, 252, 409(2), 411, 511, 552(2)
Wicker, Matthew (S.B.)...321
Wicker, Matthew C....267, 414
Wicker, Matthew Sr....331
Wicker, Milly...134, 165
Wicker, Minny...409
Wicker, Nancy...396, 408(2), 409(3), 411, 412, 416, 552
Wicker, Nepsey...409
Wicker, Niah A....411
Wicker, Penelope...416
Wicker, Pleasant...93, 416
Wicker, Priscilla...384
Wicker, Rebecca...409
Wicker, Robert...408
Wicker, Robert A....412
Wicker, Sallie...409, 411
Wicker, Sallie J....409
Wicker, Sarah...408(2), 417
Wicker, Sarah J....395, 412
Wicker, Stephen...262, 409(2), 416
Wicker, Susan...408, 409
Wicker, Thomas...409, 416, 526, 527, 554
Wicker, Warren...409, 417
Wicker, William...173, 190, 327, 408, 409(2), 510
Wicker, William F....412
Wicker, William G....414
Wicker, Zilpha...409
Wilborn, William...459
Wilcox, George...216, 311, 430(2), 528, 556
Wilcox, Harmon...431
Wilcox, Martin...431
Wilcox, Mary...430
Wilcox, Robert...431
Wilcox, William...430
Wiley, William D....508
Wilkinson, Robert...91
Willey, James...83
Williams, Abram...460
Williams, Alexander...486
Williams, Alfred...462
Williams, Alston...486
Williams, Andrew...486
Williams, Ann...471
Williams, Asa...462
Williams, Avant...469
Williams, Benjamin...83, 108
Williams, Branson...486
Williams, Bryant...242, 299, 399, 550
Williams, Candace...483
Williams, Catherine...345
Williams, Celia...476
Williams, Darcus...460
Williams, David...460
Williams, Dicy...460
Williams, Doxy...482
Williams, Edward...469
Williams, Elias...460(2), 469
Williams, Eliza...140
Williams, Elizabeth...111, 161, 460(3), 462, 469, 476, 486
Williams, Emeline...486
Williams, Enoch...470
Williams, Franey...469, 477
Williams, George...67, 76, 291, 482(2)
Williams, Hannah J....483
Williams, Harbart...476
Williams, Haywood...482
Williams, Henry...476, 482
Williams, Isaac...252, 458, 482
Williams, James...85, 469
Williams, James H....400
Williams, Jane...470, 486
Williams, Jefferson...483
Williams, Jeremiah...96, 147, 154, 161(2), 214, 256, 460, 534, 562
Williams, Jerry...123, 175, 469
Williams, Jerry (B.C.)...277
Williams, John...250, 469, 476, 564
Williams, John (W.D.)...273
Williams, Joseph...194, 305, 471, 564
Williams, Josiah...301
Williams, Julia A....483
Williams, Kelly...460
Williams, Kiza...462
Williams, Laurence...470
Williams, Levi...462
Williams, Lewis...471
Williams, Lindsay...476
Williams, Lorenzo...477
Williams, Louisa...471, 482
Williams, Lydia...469, 476(2), 482
Williams, Margaret...334, 462
Williams, Marshal...462
Williams, Martha...458, 462
Williams, Martha J....460
Williams, Mary...462, 469, 470, 476, 482, 486
Williams, Mary E....486
Williams, Matthew...291, 471, 476, 486, 564
Williams, Milly...469
Williams, Missouri...482
Williams, Murdoch...486
Williams, Nancy...400, 469(2), 471(2)
Williams, Nathaniel...129
Williams, Nelly...125
Williams, Noah...460, 470, 564
Williams, Pattie...399, 486
Williams, Penelope...169
Williams, Pleasant...486
Williams, Priscilla...483
Williams, Raleigh...460
Williams, Rebecca...345, 469
Williams, Rebecca E....483
Williams, Richard M....477
Williams, Sampson...15
Williams, Sarah...399, 460
Williams, Sarah E....345
Williams, Seasor/Ceasar...144, 166
Williams, Spain...469
Williams, Steadman...469
Williams, Stephen...566
Williams, Stephen D....477
Williams, Susan...482
Williams, Susannah...460
Williams, Temperance...482, 483
Williams, Thomas...58, 161, 175, 201, 230, 325, 400, 460, 486, 566
Williams, Thomas (Little)...176
Williams, Thomas G....216, 562
Williams, Thomas Sr....283
Williams, Upshur...471
Williams, William...123, 175, 210, 462, 470, 471
Williams, William B....184
Williams, William S....345
Williams, William Sr....175
Williams, William T....477
Williams, William W....462, 562
Williams, Wyatt...462
Williamson, Alexander...461
Williamson, Allen...153, 161, 174, 216
Williamson, Allen C....474
Williamson, Andrew...461
Williamson, Asa...462
Williamson, Bailey...153, 161, 214, 460, 534, 562
Williamson, Bailey (Esq.)...269
Williamson, Bailey Jr....305
Williamson, Betsy...323
Williamson, Bradley...458
Williamson, Caroline...461
Williamson, Cornelius...461
Williamson, Cynthia...462
Williamson, David...458
Williamson, Edmond...295, 461
Williamson, Eli...458
Williamson, Eliza...458
Williamson, Elizabeth...460, 461(2)
Williamson, Henry...457
Williamson, Hiram...295, 457, 461, 562
Williamson, Isaac...461, 462, 562
Williamson, James...98, 116, 177, 248, 457, 458
Williamson, Jemima...457
Williamson, Jesse...461
Williamson, John...3, 23, 48, 59, 66, 457, 458
Williamson, John Sr....68
Williamson, Joshua...474
Williamson, Josiah...13, 28, 36
Williamson, Kearney C....461
Williamson, Kelly...461
Williamson, Kindrick...458
Williamson, Lewis...117, 177, 212, 456, 457, 562
Williamson, Lotty...458
Williamson, Madison C....461
Williamson, Mahala...265
Williamson, Margaret...456, 457, 461, 461
Williamson, Martha...460, 461, 462
Williamson, Mary...458(2), 462
Williamson, Mary E....458
Williamson, Mary H....461
Williamson, Matthew...457
Williamson, Nancy...78, 457, 461
Williamson, Noah R....461
Williamson, Rebecca...457
Williamson, Sarah...456, 474
Williamson, Sarah J....461
Williamson, Thomas...325
Williamson, Tryan Mc....462
Williamson, Wiley...458
Williamson, William...2, 15, 23, 49, 59, 65, 68, 98(2), 123, 153, 154, 161(2), 210, 248, 269, 457, 461
Williamson, William (B.)...214, 323
Williamson, William B....562
Williamson, William J....461
Williamson, William Jr....175
Williamson, William Sr....175, 285
Williamson, William W....458
Williamson, Wright W....462

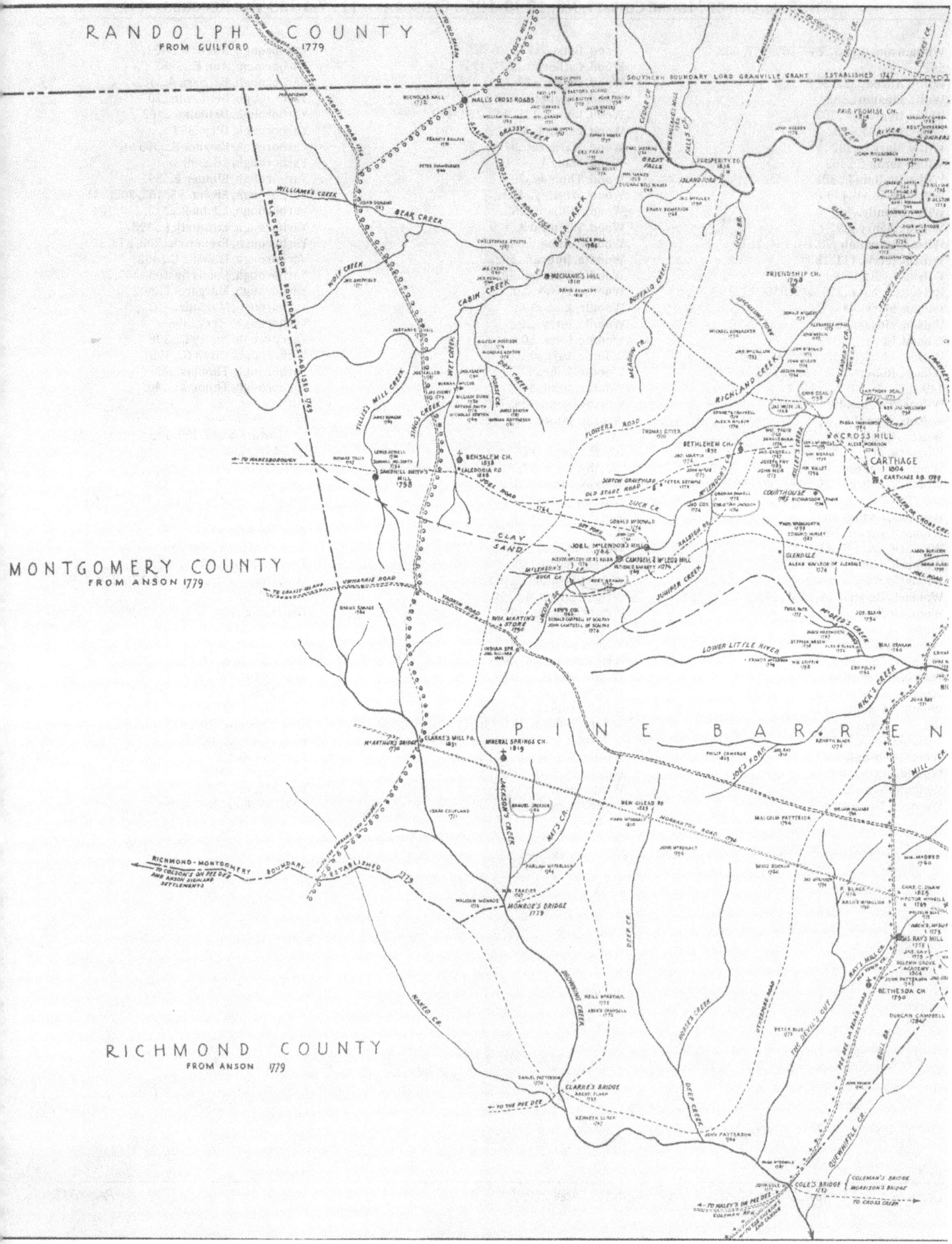
RANDOLPH COUNTY
FROM GUILFORD 1779
MONTGOMERY COUNTY
FROM ANSON 1779
RICHMOND COUNTY
FROM ANSON 1779
SOUTHERN BOUNDARY LORD GRANVILLE GRANT ESTABLISHED 1747
BLADEN ANSON BOUNDARY ESTABLISHED 1749
RICHMOND - MONTGOMERY BOUNDARY ESTABLISHED 1779
PINE BARREN
DEEP RIVER
HALL'S CROSS ROADS
NICHOLAS HALL 1772
GRASSY CREEK
SALEM CR.
CEDAR CR.
FALLS CR.
GREAT FALLS
PROSPERITY P.O. 1838
ISLAND FORD
FAIR PROMISE CH.
WILLIAMS CREEK
BEAR CREEK
WOLF CREEK
CABIN CREEK
MECHANIC'S HILL 1810
HALL'S MILL 1786
BUFFALO CREEK
MEADOW CR.
FRIENDSHIP CH. 1798
RICHLAND CREEK
TILLIS'S MILL CREEK
WET CREEK
DRY CREEK
HORSE CR.
SINGS CREEK
BENSALEM CH. 1833
CALEDONIA P.O. 1838
SANDHILL SMITH'S MILL 1758
JOEL ROAD
CLAY
SAND
FLOWERS ROAD
BETHLEHEM CH. 1832
OLD STAGE ROAD
SCOTCH GRAVEYARD
SUCK CR.
COURTHOUSE
CROSS HILL
CARTHAGE 1804
JOEL McLENDON'S MILL 1784
CAMPBELL & McLEOD MILL 1774
McLENDON'S CR.
GLENDALE
JUNIPER CREEK
UWHARRIE ROAD
YADKIN ROAD
TO GRASSY ISLAND
TO WADESBOROUGH
WM. MARTIN'S STORE 1790
McDEED'S CREEK
LOWER LITTLE RIVER
NICK'S CREEK
McARTHUR'S BRIDGE 1770
CLARKE'S MILL P.O. 1831
MINERAL SPRINGS CH. 1819
JACKSON'S CREEK
JOE'S FORK
NEW GILEAD P.O. 1823
MORGANTON ROAD 1796
MAL'S CR.
MONROE'S BRIDGE 1779
DEEP CR.
DROWNING CREEK
NAKED CR.
HORSE'S CREEK
THE DEVIL'S GUT
RAY'S MILL CR.
JAS. RAY'S MILL 1775
BETHESDA CH. 1790
BULL BR.
QUEWHIFFLE CR.
CLARKE'S BRIDGE
TO THE PEE DEE
DEEP CREEK
COLE'S BRIDGE 1752
COLEMAN'S BRIDGE
MORRISON'S BRIDGE
TO CROSS CREEK
TO HALEY'S ON PEE DEE
MILL CR.

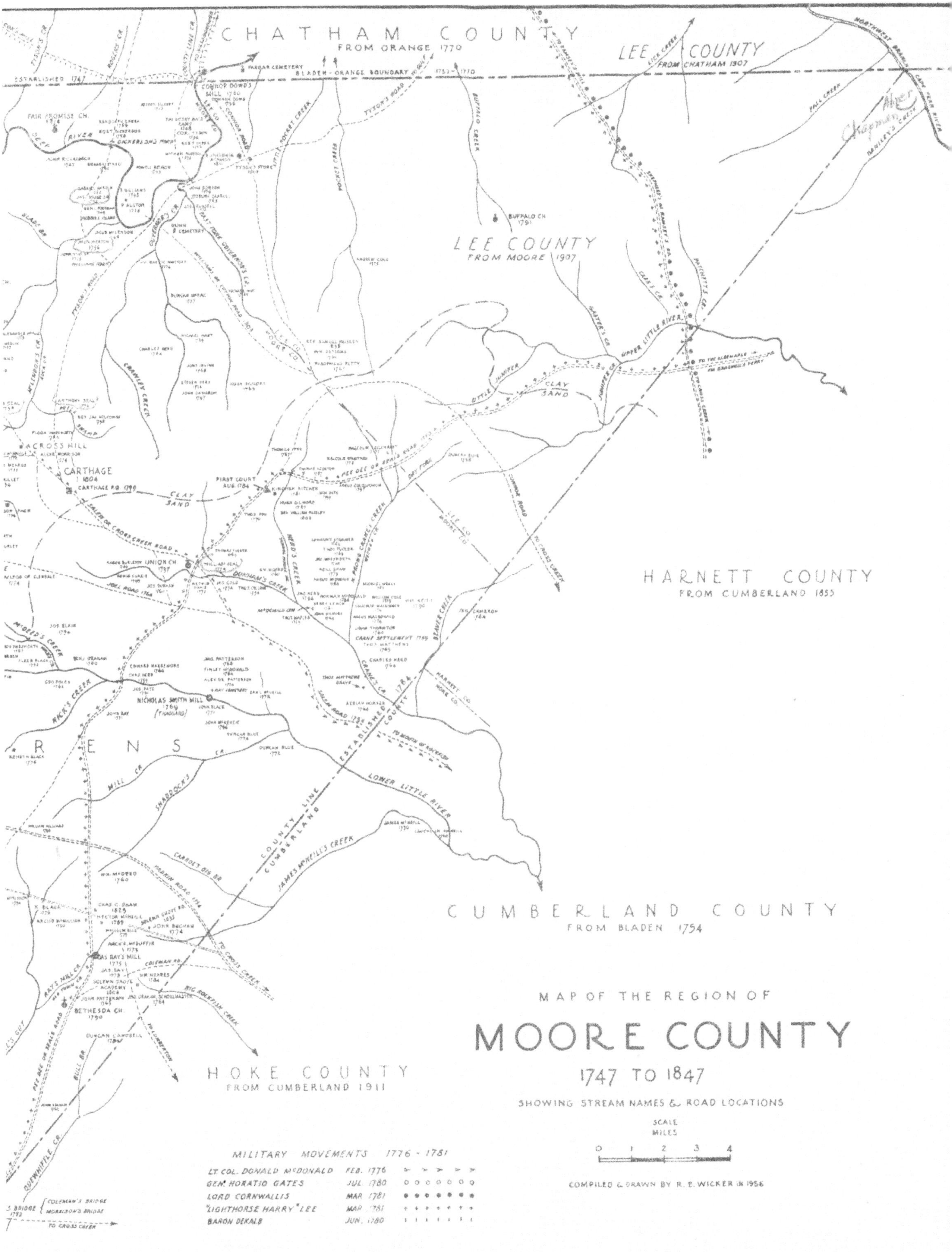

CHATHAM COUNTY
FROM ORANGE 1770
BLADEN - ORANGE BOUNDARY 1752 - 1770
ESTABLISHED 1747
LEE COUNTY
FROM CHATHAM 1907
LEE COUNTY
FROM MOORE 1907
BUFFALO CH
1791
CONNOR DOWD'S MILL 1760
FAIR PROMISE CH. 1814
DEEP RIVER
TYSON'S STORE
BUFFALO CREEK
POCKET CREEK
LITTLE POCKET CREEK
CRANE'S CR.
UPPER LITTLE RIVER
LITTLE JUNIPER
CLAY SAND
FIRST COURT AUG 1784
CROSS HILL
CARTHAGE 1804
CARTHAGE P.O. 1790
CLAY SAND
SALEM OR CROSS CREEK ROAD
UNION CH. 1797
DUNHAM'S CREEK
JOEL ROAD 1764
HARNETT COUNTY
FROM CUMBERLAND 1855
McDEED'S CREEK
NICK'S CREEK
NICHOLAS SMITH MILL 1769
BEAVER CREEK
CRANE'S CR.
ESTABLISHED COUNTY 1784
LOWER LITTLE RIVER
MILL CR
SHADDOCK'S CR.
COUNTY LINE
CUMBERLAND
JAMES McNEILL'S CREEK
YADKIN ROAD 1754
CUMBERLAND COUNTY
FROM BLADEN 1754
RAY'S MILL CR.
BETHESDA CH. 1790
BIG ROCKFISH CREEK
TO CROSS CREEK
TO LUMBERTON
HOKE COUNTY
FROM CUMBERLAND 1911
BULL BR.
QUEWHIFFLE CR.
MAP OF THE REGION OF
MOORE COUNTY
1747 TO 1847
SHOWING STREAM NAMES & ROAD LOCATIONS
SCALE
MILES
0 1 2 3 4
COMPILED & DRAWN BY R. E. WICKER IN 1956
MILITARY MOVEMENTS 1776 - 1781
LT. COL. DONALD McDONALD FEB. 1776
GEN. HORATIO GATES JUL. 1780
LORD CORNWALLIS MAR. 1781
"LIGHTHORSE HARRY" LEE MAR. 1781
BARON DEKALB JUN. 1780
COLEMAN'S BRIDGE
MORRISON'S BRIDGE
TO CROSS CREEK

www.ingramcontent.com/pod-product-compliance
Lightning Source LLC
Chambersburg PA
CBHW062020090426
42811CB00005B/907
* 9 7 8 0 5 7 8 7 0 4 5 5 5 *